Rick Steves'

ITALY

2008

D0167438

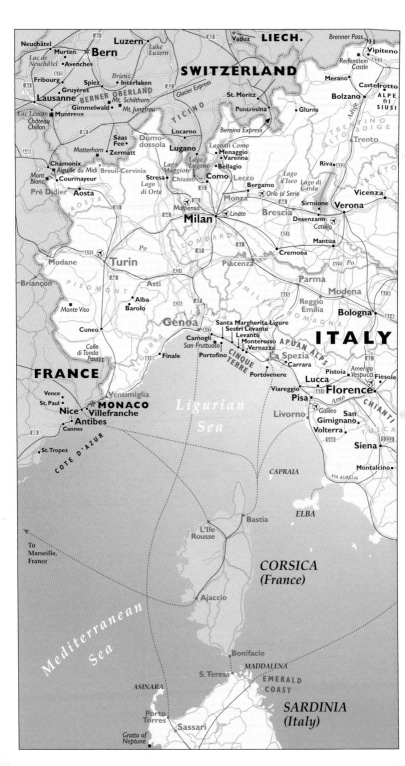

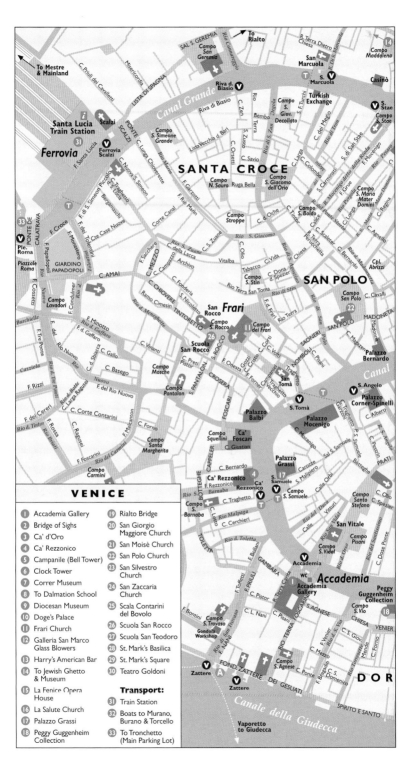

VENICE

1. Accademia Gallery
2. Bridge of Sighs
3. Ca' d'Oro
4. Ca' Rezzonico
5. Campanile (Bell Tower)
6. Clock Tower
7. Correr Museum
8. To Dalmation School
9. Diocesan Museum
10. Doge's Palace
11. Frari Church
12. Galleria San Marco Glass Blowers
13. Harry's American Bar
14. To Jewish Ghetto & Museum
15. La Fenice Opera House
16. La Salute Church
17. Palazzo Grassi
18. Peggy Guggenheim Collection
19. Rialto Bridge
20. San Giorgio Maggiore Church
21. San Moisè Church
22. San Polo Church
23. San Silvestro Church
24. San Zaccaria Church
25. Scala Contarini del Bovolo
26. Scuola San Rocco
27. Scuola San Teodoro
28. St. Mark's Basilica
29. St. Mark's Square
30. Teatro Goldoni

Transport:

31. Train Station
32. Boats to Murano, Burano & Torcello
33. To Tronchetto (Main Parking Lot)

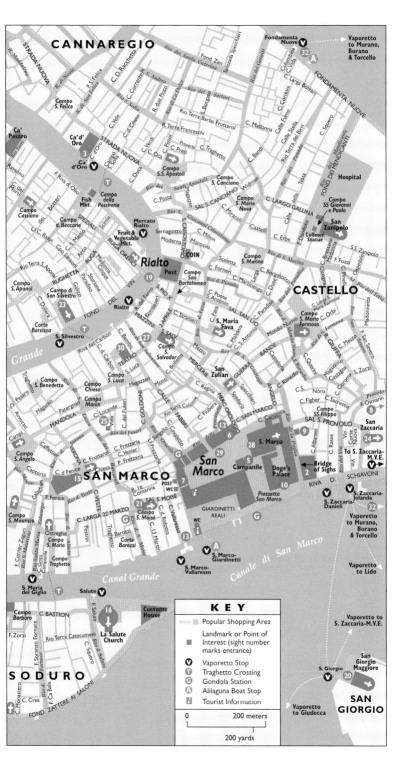

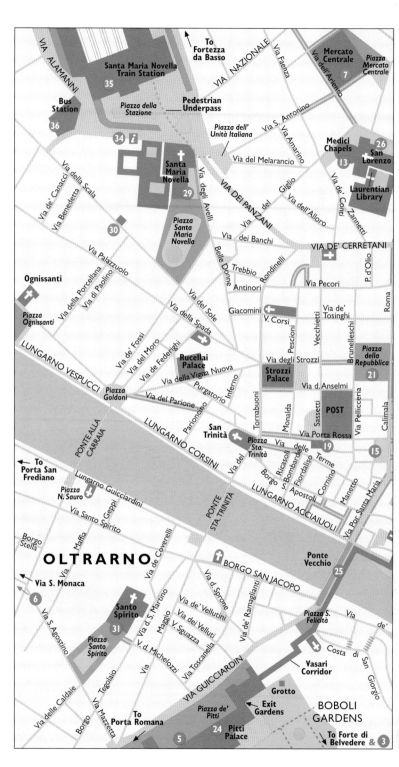

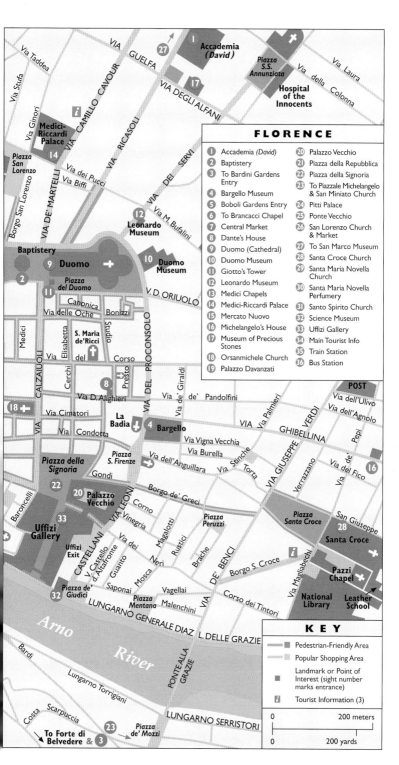

FLORENCE

1. Accademia (David)
2. Baptistery
3. To Bardini Gardens Entry
4. Bargello Museum
5. Boboli Gardens Entry
6. To Brancacci Chapel
7. Central Market
8. Dante's House
9. Duomo (Cathedral)
10. Duomo Museum
11. Giotto's Tower
12. Leonardo Museum
13. Medici Chapels
14. Medici-Riccardi Palace
15. Mercato Nuovo
16. Michelangelo's House
17. Museum of Precious Stones
18. Orsanmichele Church
19. Palazzo Davanzati
20. Palazzo Vecchio
21. Piazza della Repubblica
22. Piazza della Signoria
23. To Piazzale Michelangelo & San Miniato Church
24. Pitti Palace
25. Ponte Vecchio
26. San Lorenzo Church & Market
27. To San Marco Museum
28. Santa Croce Church
29. Santa Maria Novella Church
30. Santa Maria Novella Perfumery
31. Santo Spirito Church
32. Science Museum
33. Uffizi Gallery
34. Main Tourist Info
35. Train Station
36. Bus Station

KEY

— Pedestrian-Friendly Area
— Popular Shopping Area
■ Landmark or Point of Interest (sight number marks entrance)
i Tourist Information (3)

0   200 meters
0   200 yards

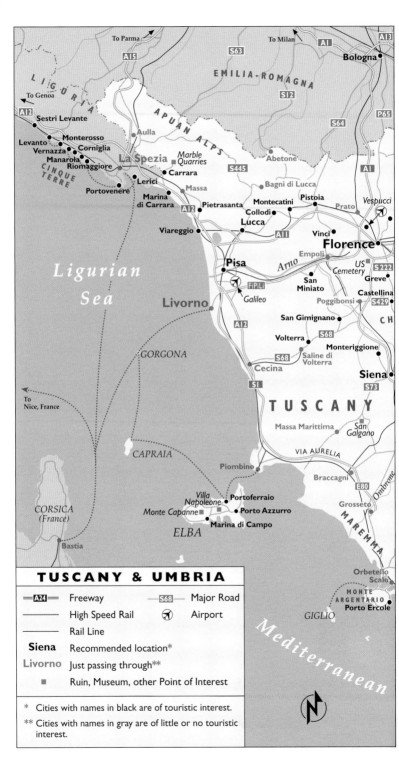

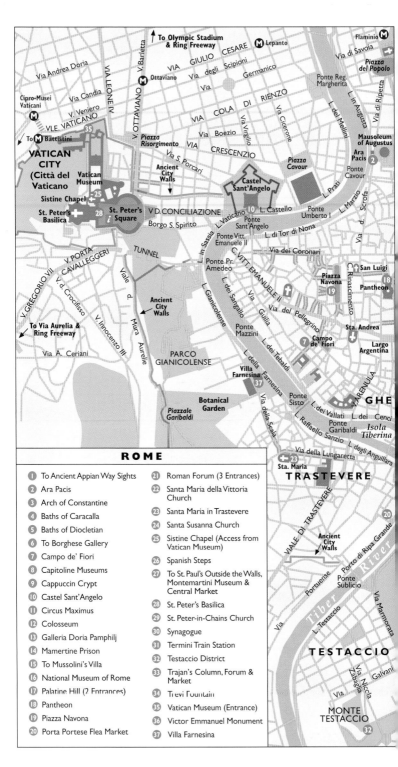

ROME

1. To Ancient Appian Way Sights
2. Ara Pacis
3. Arch of Constantine
4. Baths of Caracalla
5. Baths of Diocletian
6. To Borghese Gallery
7. Campo de' Fiori
8. Capitoline Museums
9. Cappuccin Crypt
10. Castel Sant'Angelo
11. Circus Maximus
12. Colosseum
13. Galleria Doria Pamphilj
14. Mamertine Prison
15. To Mussolini's Villa
16. National Museum of Rome
17. Palatine Hill (2 Entrances)
18. Pantheon
19. Piazza Navona
20. Porta Portese Flea Market
21. Roman Forum (3 Entrances)
22. Santa Maria della Vittoria Church
23. Santa Maria in Trastevere
24. Santa Susanna Church
25. Sistine Chapel (Access from Vatican Museum)
26. Spanish Steps
27. To St. Paul's Outside the Walls, Montemartini Museum & Central Market
28. St. Peter's Basilica
29. St. Peter-in-Chains Church
30. Synagogue
31. Termini Train Station
32. Testaccio District
33. Trajan's Column, Forum & Market
34. Trevi Fountain
35. Vatican Museum (Entrance)
36. Victor Emmanuel Monument
37. Villa Farnesina

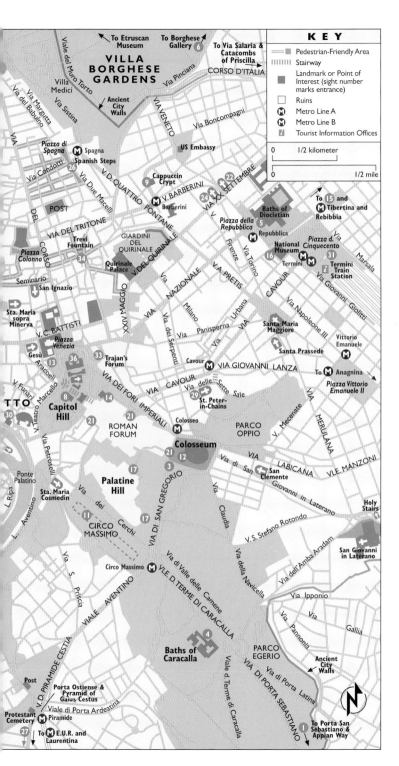

Rick Steves'

ITALY

2008

AVALON
TRAVEL

CONTENTS

Top Destinations in Italy

INTRODUCTION

Bella Italia! It has Europe's richest, craziest culture. If you take Italy on its own terms, you'll experience a cultural keelhauling that actually feels good.

Some people, often with considerable effort, manage to hate it. Italy bubbles with emotion, corruption, stray hairs, inflation, traffic jams, body odor, strikes, rallies, holidays, crowded squalor, and irate ranters shaking their fists at each other one minute and walking arm-in-arm the next. Have a talk with yourself before you cross the border. Promise yourself to relax and accept it all as a package deal.

This book will help you make the most of your trip. It breaks Italy into its top destinations—offering a comfortable mix of big cities and cozy towns, from brutal but *bella* Rome to *tranquillo*, traffic-free Riviera villages. It covers the predictable biggies and adds a healthy dose of "Back Door" intimacy. Along with marveling at Michelangelo's masterpieces, you'll enjoy a *bruschetta* snack as a village boy rubs fresh garlic on your toast. I've been selective, including only the top sights. For example, after visiting many hill towns, I recommend just the best.

You'll get all the specifics and opinions necessary to wring the

maximum value out of your limited time and money. If you plan a month or less in Italy, and you have a normal appetite for information, this book is all you need. If you're a travel-info fiend (like me), you'll find this book sorts through all the superlatives and provides a handy rack upon which to hang your supplemental information.

Italy is my favorite European country. Experiencing its culture, people, and natural wonders economically and hassle-free has been my goal for three decades of traveling, researching, and tour guiding. With this book, I pass on to you the lessons I've learned, updated for 2008.

The best is, of course, only my opinion. But after spending more than half my adult life researching Europe, I've developed a sixth sense for what travelers enjoy.

About This Book

Rick Steves' Italy is a tour guide in your pocket. Each destination covered in this book is a mini-vacation on its own, filled with exciting sights and comfortable, good-value places to stay. In the following chapters, you'll find:

Planning Your Time offers a suggested schedule with thoughts on how best to use your limited time.

Orientation includes tourist information, tips on public transportation, local tour options, helpful hints, and an easy-to-read map designed to make the text clear and your arrival smooth.

Sights provides a succinct overview of the most important sights, arranged by neighborhood, with ratings:

▲▲▲—Don't miss.

▲▲—Try hard to see.

▲—Worthwhile if you can make it.

No rating—Worth knowing about.

Sleeping and **Eating** describes my favorite hotels and restaurants, with addresses and phone numbers.

Transportation Connections has information on linking nearby destinations by train, and route tips for drivers.

The **appendix** is a traveler's tool kit, with a handy packing checklist, recommended books and films, a climate chart, detailed instructions on how to use the telephone, useful Italian phone numbers, Italian survival phrases, and lots more.

Browse through this book, choose your top destinations, and link them up. Then have a great trip! Traveling like a temporary local, you'll get the absolute most out of every mile, minute, and euro. As you travel the route that I know and love, I'm happy that you'll be meeting some of my favorite Italian people.

PLANNING

Trip Costs

Six components make up your trip cost: airfare, surface transportation, room and board, sightseeing/entertainment, shopping/miscellany, and gelato.

Airfare: A basic round-trip United States-to-Milan (or Rome) flight should cost $700–1,500, depending on where you fly from and when (cheapest in winter). Always consider saving time and money in Europe by flying "open jaw" (into one city and out of another, such as into Milan and out of Rome).

Surface Transportation: For a three-week whirlwind trip to all of my recommended destinations, allow $300 per person for public transportation (train and buses) or $800 per person (based on two people sharing a car) for a three-week car rental, including insurance, tolls, gas, and parking. Car rental is cheapest if arranged from the US. Some train passes are available only outside of Europe; you might save money by getting an Italian railpass or buying tickets as you go (see "Transportation," page 832).

Room and Board: You can easily manage in Italy on $100 a day per person for room and board (plan on $120 in the cities). This allows $10 for lunch, $5 for snacks, $20 for dinner, and $65 for lodging (based on two people splitting the cost of a $130 double room that includes breakfast). If you've got more money, I've listed great ways to spend it. And students and tightwads can enjoy Italy for as little as $50 a day ($25 for a bed, $25 for meals and snacks).

Sightseeing and Entertainment: In big cities, figure about $10–17 per major sight (museums, Colosseum), $4–8 for minor ones (climbing church towers), and $25–30 for splurge experiences (tours and concerts). An overall average of $25 a day works for most. Don't skimp here. After all, this category is the driving force behind your trip—you came to sightsee, enjoy, and experience Italy.

Shopping and Miscellany: Figure $2 per postcard, coffee, soft drink, or gelato. Shopping can vary in cost from nearly nothing to a small fortune. Good budget travelers find that this category has little to do with assembling a trip full of lifelong and wonderful memories.

Sightseeing Priorities
Depending on the length of your trip, here are my recommended priorities:

4 days:	Florence, Venice
6 days, add:	Rome
8 days, add:	Cinque Terre
10 days, add:	Civita and Siena
14 days, add:	Sorrento, Naples, Pompeii, Amalfi Coast, Paestum
18 days, add:	Milan, Lake Como, Varenna, Assisi
21 days, add:	Dolomites, Verona, Padua

(This includes everything on the "Italy's Best Three-Week Trip" map on page 5.)

Italy's Best Three-Week Trip (By Car)

Day	Plan	Sleep in
1	Arrive in Milan	Milan
2	Milan to Lake Como	Varenna
3	Lake Como	Varenna
4	To Dolomites via Verona (pick up car in Milan or Verona)	Castelrotto
5	Dolomites	Castelrotto
6	To Venice	Venice
7	Venice	Venice
8	To Florence	Florence
9	Florence	Florence
10	To Cinque Terre	Vernazza
11	Cinque Terre	Vernazza
12	To Siena via Pisa	Siena
13	Siena	Siena
14	To Assisi	Assisi
15	To Civita	Civita or Orvieto
16	To Sorrento via Pompeii	Sorrento
17	Sorrento	Sorrento
18	To Paestum via Amalfi Coast	Sorrento
19	To Rome, drop car	Rome
20	Rome	Rome
21	Rome	Rome
22	Rome, fly home	

For Train Travelers: This trip is designed to be done by car, but works fine by rail with a few modifications. An Italy Pass for Italian State Railways (four days in two months) can be convenient if you avoid trains that require reservations and pay out of pocket for short runs, such as Milan to Varenna, or the hops between villages in the Cinque Terre. In the Dolomites, consider basing yourself in Bolzano. From Venice, go directly to the

When to Go

Italy's best travel months are May, June, September, and October. November and April usually have pleasant weather with generally none of the sweat and stress of the tourist season. Off-season, expect shorter hours, more lunchtime breaks, and fewer activities.

Peak season (May–Sept) offers the longest hours and the most exciting slate of activities—but terrible crowds and, at times, suffocating heat. During peak times, many resort-area hotels maximize business by requiring that guests take half-pension, which means

Cinque Terre, then do Florence and Siena. A car is efficient in the hill towns of Tuscany and Umbria, but a headache elsewhere. Sorrento is a good home base for Naples and the Amalfi Coast. Skip Paestum unless you love Greek ruins. To save Venice for last, start in Milan and see everything but Venice on the way south, then sleep through everything you've already seen by catching the night train from Naples or Rome to Venice. This saves you a day and gives you an early arrival in Venice. (You could also consider taking a cheap flight to connect Rome and Venice—see page 843.)

buying a meal per day (usually dinner) in their restaurants. August, the local holiday month, isn't as bad as many make it out to be, but big cities tend to be quiet (with discounted hotel prices), and beach and mountain resorts are jammed (with higher hotel prices). Note that Italians generally wear shorts only at beach resort towns. If you want to blend in, wear lightweight long pants in Italy, even in summer, except at the beach.

Summer temperatures range from the 70s and 80s in Milan to the high 80s and 90s in Rome. Spring and fall can be cold, and many hotels do not turn on their heat until November 1. In the winter, it often drops to the 40s in Milan and the 50s in Rome. For weather specifics, see the climate chart in the appendix (page 848).

Travel Smart

Many people travel through Italy and think that it's a chaotic mess. They feel that any attempt at efficient travel is futile. This is dead wrong—and expensive. Italy, which seems as orderly as spilled spaghetti, actually functions quite well. Only those who understand this and travel smart can enjoy Italy on a budget.

Your trip to Italy is like a complex play—easier to follow and really appreciate on a second viewing. While no one does the same trip twice to gain that advantage, reading this book in its entirety before your trip accomplishes much the same thing.

Design an itinerary that enables you to hit the festivals and museums on the right days. As you read this book, note that Monday is a problem day, when many museums are closed. Saturdays are virtually weekdays, with earlier closing hours (though transportation connections can be less frequent than on Mon–Fri).

Sundays have the same pros and cons as they do for travelers in the US. Sightseeing attractions are generally open but have shorter hours, shops and banks are closed, and minor transportation connections are more frustrating (e.g., no bus service to or from the smaller hill towns). City traffic is light. Rowdy evenings are rare on Sundays.

Be sure to mix intense and relaxed periods in your itinerary. Every trip (and every traveler) needs at least a few slack days. Pace yourself. Assume you will return.

Reread this book as you travel, and visit local tourist information offices. Upon arrival in a new town, lay the groundwork for a smooth departure; write down the schedule for the train or bus that you'll take when you depart. Use taxis in the big cities, bring along a water bottle, and linger in the shade.

Plan ahead for laundry, picnics, and Internet stops. Get online at Internet cafés or your hotel to research transportation connections, confirm events, check the weather, and get directions to your next hotel. Buy a phone card and use it for reservations, reconfirmations, and double-checking hours.

Enjoy the friendliness of the local people. Slow down and ask questions—most locals are eager to point you in their idea of the right direction. Keep a notepad in your pocket for organizing your thoughts. Wear your money belt, and learn the local currency and how to estimate prices in dollars. Those who expect to travel smart, do.

Major Holidays and Weekends

Reserve your hotel room well in advance if you'll be in Italy over a holiday. Hotels get booked up on Easter weekend (in 2008, that's Friday, March 21 through Monday, March 24), April 25 (Liberation Day), May 1, (Labor Day), November 1 (All Saint's Day), and on Fridays and Saturdays year-round. Religious holidays and train strikes can catch you by surprise anywhere in Italy. (For more on holidays, see page 844.)

PRACTICALITIES

Red Tape: You need a passport—but no visa or shots—to travel in Italy. Pack a photocopy of your passport in your luggage in case the original is lost or stolen.

Time: In Italy—and in this book—you'll use the 24-hour clock. It's the same through 12:00 noon, then keep going: 13:00, 14:00, and so on. For anything past 12, subtract 12 and add p.m. (14:00 is 2:00 p.m.).

Italy, like most of continental Europe, is generally six/nine hours ahead of the East/West Coasts of the US. The exceptions are the beginning and end of Daylight Saving Time: Europe "springs forward" the last Sunday in March (two weeks after most of North America), and "falls back" the last Sunday in October (one week before North America). For a handy online time converter, see www.timeanddate.com/worldclock.

Business Hours: Traditionally, Italy uses the siesta plan. Nowadays, however, many businesses have adopted the government's recommended 8:00 to 14:00 workday. In tourist areas, shops are open longer. People usually work from about 8:00 to 13:00 and from 15:30 to 19:00. Stores are usually closed on Sunday, and often on Monday, as well as for a couple of weeks around August 15. Banking hours are generally Monday through Friday 8:30 to 13:30 and 15:30 to 16:30, but they can vary wildly.

Language Barrier: Many Italians in larger towns and in the tourist trade speak some English. Still, you'll get more smiles and results by using at least the Italian pleasantries. In smaller, non-touristy towns, Italian is the norm. See the "Survival Phrases" near the end of this book.

Note that Italian is pronounced much like English, with a few exceptions, such as: c followed by e or i is pronounced ch (to ask, "*Per centro*?"—To the center?—you say, pehr CHEHN-troh). In Italian, ch is pronounced like the hard c in Chianti (*chiesa*—church—is pronounced kee-AY-zah). Give it your best shot. Italians appreciate your efforts.

Know Before You Go

Your trip is more likely to go smoothly if you plan ahead.

Since **airline carry-on restrictions** are always changing, visit the Transportation Security Administration's website (www .tsa.gov/travelers) for an up-to-date list of what you can bring on the plane with you...and what you have to check. Remember to arrive with plenty of time to get through security.

Call your **debit- and credit-card companies** to let them know the countries you'll be visiting, so that they'll accept (and not deny) your international charges. Confirm what your daily withdrawal limit is; consider asking to have it raised so that you can take out more cash at each ATM stop.

Be sure that your **passport** is valid at least six months after your ticketed date of return to the US. If you need to get or renew a passport, it can take up to three months (for more on passports, see www.travel.state.gov).

Check to see if you'll be visiting during any **holidays** (such as Holy Week in Rome), when rooms can cost more and get booked up quickly (see page 844).

The popularity of Italy's top sights makes **reservations for certain museums** crucial:

In **Florence,** book ahead for the Uffizi (Renaissance paintings) and Accademia (Michelangelo's *David*) to avoid standing in long lines and to guarantee you'll get in. The Uffizi is often booked up a month in advance, while the Accademia is usually full at least a few days out. Make reservations for both as soon as you know when you'll be in town—it's easy, and explained in detail on page 382. While reservations are mandatory for both

Watt's Up? Europe's electrical system is different from North America's in two different ways: the shape of the plug (two round prongs) and the voltage of the current (220 volts instead of 110 volts). For your North American plug to work in Europe, you'll need an adapter, sold inexpensively at travel stores in the US. As for the voltage, most newer electronics or travel appliances (such as hair dryers, laptops, and battery chargers) automatically convert the voltage—if you see a range of voltages printed on the item or its plug (such as "110–220"), it'll work in Europe. Otherwise, you can buy a converter separately in the US (about $20).

News: Americans keep in touch via the *International Herald Tribune* (published almost daily via satellite throughout Europe). Every Tuesday, the European editions of *Time* and *Newsweek* hit the stands with articles of particular interest to European travelers. Sports addicts can get their daily fix online or from *USA Today*. Good websites include www.europeantimes.com and http://news.bbc.co.uk.

the Brancacci Chapel and the Medici–Riccardi Palace, spots are generally available a day or two in advance.

In **Milan,** tickets for Da Vinci's *Last Supper* can get booked more than two months in advance. Call or book online before you go (see page 265).

In **Padua,** reservations are mandatory to visit the Scrovegni Chapel (known for its frescoes by Giotto), so book well in advance (see page 125).

Rome's Borghese Gallery requires reservations—book at least a week ahead (see page 651).

The lines at the Vatican Museum are horrendous. To guarantee you'll get in, consider booking a walking tour that includes the Vatican (see page 662).

If you plan to hire a **local guide,** it's smart to reserve ahead by email. Popular guides can get booked up in peak season.

If you're taking an **overnight train** (especially between Rome and Paris), and you need a *cuccetta* (overnight bunk) or sleeper—and you *must* leave on a certain day—consider booking it in advance, even though it may cost more. Other Italian trains, like the high-speed ES trains, require a seat reservation, but it's usually possible to make arrangements in Italy just a few days ahead. (For more on train travel, see page 832.)

If you're planning on **renting a car** in Italy, you'll need an International Driver's Permit (available at your local AAA office for $15 plus the cost of two passport-type photos; see www.aaa.com).

MONEY

Banking

Throughout Europe, cash machines (ATMs) are the standard way for travelers to get local currency. Bring plastic—credit and/or debit cards—along with several hundred dollars in hard cash as an emergency backup. It's smart to bring two cards, in case one gets demagnetized or eaten by a temperamental machine. Traveler's checks are a waste of time (long waits at slow banks) and a waste of money (in fees). Avoid changing money at exchange booths; their fees can be outrageous. Use ATMs.

Cash from ATMs

To use a cash machine (called a *Bancomat* in Italy) to withdraw money from your account, you'll need a debit card (ideally with a Visa or MasterCard logo for maximum usability), plus a PIN code.

Exchange Rate

1 euro (€) = about $1.30

To convert prices in euros to dollars, add about 30 percent: €20 = about $26, €50 = about $65. Just like the dollar, one euro is broken down into 100 cents. You'll find coins ranging from €0.01 to €2, and bills ranging from €5 to €500.

Look carefully at any €2 coin you get in change. Some unscrupulous merchants are giving out similar-looking, gold-rimmed old 500-lire coins (worth $0) instead of €2 coins (worth $2.60). You are now warned!

Know your PIN code in numbers; there are only numbers—no letters—on European keypads.

Before you go, verify with your bank that your card will work overseas, and alert them that you'll be making withdrawals in Europe; otherwise, the bank may not approve transactions if it perceives unusual spending patterns.

Try to take out large sums of money to reduce your per-transaction bank fees. If the machine refuses your request, try again and select a smaller amount; some cash machines won't let you take out more than about €150 (don't take it personally). Also, be aware that some ATMs will tell you to take your cash within 30 seconds, and if you aren't fast enough, your cash may be sucked back into the machine...and you'll have a hassle trying to get it from the bank.

Italy, a land of extremes, is the most thief-ridden country you'll visit. Tourists suffer virtually no violent crime—but there is plenty of petty purse-snatching, pickpocketing, and shortchanging. Be alert! The scruffy-looking women and children who loiter around the major museums aren't there for the art. To keep your cash safe, use a money belt—a pouch with a strap that you buckle around your waist like a belt, and wear under your clothes. Thieves target tourists. A money belt provides peace of mind, allowing you to carry lots of cash safely. Don't waste time every few days tracking down a cash machine—change a week's worth of money, stuff it in your money belt, and travel!

Credit and Debit Cards

For purchases, Visa and MasterCard are more commonly accepted than American Express. Just like at home, credit or debit cards work easily at larger hotels, restaurants, and shops, but smaller businesses prefer payment in local currency (in small bills—break large bills at a bank or larger store).

Credit and debit cards—whether used for purchases or ATM

withdrawals—often come with additional, tacked-on "international transaction" fees of up to 3 percent, plus $5 per transaction. To avoid unpleasant surprises, call your credit-card company before your trip to ask about these fees.

If your cards are lost or stolen, see page 823 for advice on what to do.

SIGHTSEEING

Sightseeing can be hard work. Use these tips to make your visits to Italy's finest museums meaningful, fun, fast, and painless.

Plan Ahead

If there's a must-see sight on your list, confirm opening hours and closed days at the local TI. Or call the sight in the morning and ask: "Are you open today?" (*"Aperto oggi?"*; ah-PER-toh OH-jee) and "What time do you close?" (*"A che ora chiuso?"*; ah kay OH-rah kee-OO-zoh). I've included telephone numbers for this purpose. Don't put off visiting a must-see sight—you never know when a place will close unexpectedly for a holiday, strike, or restoration.

On holidays, expect shorter hours or closures (see list on page 844). In summer, some sights stay open late, allowing easy viewing without crowds. Many museums have shorter hours October through March.

When possible, visit key museums first thing (when your energy is best) and save other activities for the afternoon. Hit the highlights first, then go back to other things if you have the stamina and time.

Depending on the sight, there are ways to avoid crowds. This book offers tips on specific sights. Sometimes you can make reservations for an entry time (see page 8). Or you can try visiting the sight very early, at lunch, or very late. Some cities offer museum passes for admission to several museums (e.g., Roma Pass or Venice's Museum Card) that let you skip ticket-buying lines. At some popular places (Rome's Colosseum or Venice's Doge's Palace), you can waltz right in, after buying your ticket at a less-crowded sight. Booking a guided tour can also help you avoid lines at many sights.

At the Sight

Some important sights have metal detectors or conduct bag searches that will slow your entry.

Most museums require you to check daypacks and coats. They'll be kept safely. If you have something you can't bear to part with, stash it in a pocket or purse. If you don't want to check a small backpack, carry it (at least as you enter) under your arm like a purse...and hope guards don't notice.

Just the FAQs, Please

Whom do I call in case of emergency?
Dial 113 for English-speaking police help. To summon an ambulance, call 118.

What if my credit card is stolen?
Act immediately. See "Damage Control for Lost Cards," page 823, for instructions.

How do I make a phone call to, within, and from Europe?
For detailed dialing instructions, refer to page 826.

How can I get tourist information about my destination?
See page 817 for a list of tourist information offices (abbreviated **TI** in this book) located in the US. Virtually every recommended town has a TI as well.

What's the best way to pack?
Light. For a recommended packing list, see page 849.

Does Rick have other materials that will help me?
Thanks for asking. For more on my guidebooks, public television series, free audio tours, public radio show, guided tours, travel bags, accessories, and railpasses, see page 818.

Are there any updates to this guidebook?
Check www.ricksteves.com/update for changes to the most recent edition of this book.

Cameras are normally allowed, but not flashes or tripods (without special permission). Flashes damage oil paintings and distract others in the room. Even without a flash, a handheld camera will take a decent picture (or buy postcards or posters at the museum bookstore). Video cameras are usually allowed.

Some museums have special exhibits in addition to their permanent collection. Some exhibits are included in the entry price, while others come at an extra cost (which you have to pay even if you don't want to see the exhibit).

Many sights rent audioguides, which offer dry-but-useful recorded descriptions in English (about €4). For 2008, I have produced free audioguides of my tours for the major sights in this book (see page 820). If a museum lacks audioguides and the only English you encounter explains how to pay, politely ask if there are plans to include English descriptions of the art. Think of it as a service to those who follow.

Expect changes—paintings can be on tour, on loan, out sick, or shifted at the whim of the curator. To adapt, pick up any available

Can you recommend any good books or movies for my trip?
Sure. For suggestions, see pages 821–823.

Do I need to carry my passport in Italy?
Yes. Note that Italy's anti-terrorism rules require you to show your passport whenever you go online at an Internet café. Carry it in your money belt.

Do you have information on driving and train travel in Italy?
Absolutely. See page 840 for driving and page 832 for trains.

How much do I tip?
For tips on tipping, see page 824.

Will I get a student or senior discount?
Not likely. Discounts for sights are not listed in this book because they are generally limited to European residents and countries that offer reciprocal deals (the US does not).

How can I get a VAT refund on major purchases?
See the details on page 824.

How do I calculate metric amounts?
Europe uses the metric system. A liter is about a quart, four to a gallon. A kilometer is six-tenths of a mile. I figure kilometers to miles by cutting them in half and adding back 10 percent of the original (120 km: 60 + 12 = 72 miles, 300 km: 150 + 30 = 180 miles). For more metric conversions, see page 847.

free floor plans as you enter, and ask museum staff if you can't find a particular painting. Point to the photograph in this book and ask, "*Dov'è?*" (DOH-vay; it means "Where?").

Know the terms. Art historians and Italians refer to the great Florentine centuries by dropping a thousand years. The Trecento (300s), Quattrocento (400s), and Cinquecento (500s) were the 1300s, 1400s, and 1500s. Also, in Italian museums, art is dated with *sec* for *secolo* (century, often indicated with Roman numerals), A.C. (for *Avanti Cristo*, or B.C.), and D.C. (for *Dopo Cristo*, or A.D.). O.K.?

Most sights have an on-site café or cafeteria (usually a good place to rest and have a snack or light meal). The WCs at many sights are free and generally clean.

Museums have bookstores selling postcards and souvenirs. Before you leave, scan the postcards and thumb through the biggest guidebook (or skim its index) to be sure that you haven't overlooked something that you'd like to see.

Most sights stop admitting people 30–60 minutes before closing time, and some rooms close early (generally about 45 minutes before the actual closing time). Guards usher people out, so don't save the best for last.

Find Religion

Churches offer some amazing art (usually free), a cool respite from heat, and a welcome seat.

A modest dress code (no bare shoulders or shorts for anyone) is enforced at larger churches, such as Venice's St. Mark's and the Vatican's St. Peter's, but is often overlooked elsewhere. If you are caught by surprise, you can improvise, using maps to cover your shoulders and a jacket for your knees. (I wear a super-lightweight pair of long pants for my hot and muggy big-city Italian sightseeing.)

Some churches have coin-operated audioboxes that describe the art and history; just set the dial on English, put in your coins, and listen. Coin boxes near a piece of art illuminate the art (and present a better photo opportunity). Whenever possible, let there be light.

SLEEPING

For hassle-free efficiency, I favor hotels and restaurants that are handy to your sightseeing activities. Rather than list hotels scattered throughout a city, I describe two or three favorite neighborhoods and recommend the best accommodations values in each, from $20 bunks to plush $450 doubles with all the comforts.

Sleeping in Italy is expensive. Cheap big-city hotels can be depressing. Tourist information services cannot give opinions on quality of hotels. A major feature of this book is its extensive listing of good-value accommodations. I like places that are clean, small, central, quiet at night, traditional, inexpensive, and friendly, with firm beds—and not listed in other guidebooks. (In Italy, for me, six out of these nine criteria means a keeper.)

Types of Accommodations
Hotels

Double rooms listed in this book will range from about $50 (very simple, toilet and shower down the hall) to $300 (maximum plumbing and more), with most clustering at about $100 (with private bathrooms). Prices are higher in big cities and heavily touristed cities, and lower off the beaten path. Three or four people can economize by requesting larger rooms. Solo travelers find that the cost of a *camera singola* is often only 25 percent less than a *camera doppia*, and single travelers using double rooms enjoy hardly any savings at all. Most listed hotels have rooms for any party from one to five people. If there's room for an extra cot, they'll cram it in for you.

The Italian word for "hotel" is *hotel*, and in smaller, non-touristy towns, *albergo*. A few places have kept the old titles,

Sleep Code

To help you easily sort through my hotel listings, I've divided the rooms into three categories based on the price for a standard double room with bath:

$$$ **Higher Priced**
$$ **Moderately Priced**
$ **Lower Priced**

To pack maximum information into minimum space, I use this code to describe accommodations in this book. When there is a range of prices in one category, that means the price fluctuates with the season, size of room, or length of stay. Prices listed are per room, not per person.

S = Single room (or price for one person in a double).
D = Double or Twin room. "Double beds" are often two twins sheeted together and are usually big enough for nonromantic couples.
T = Triple (generally a double bed with a single).
Q = Quad (usually two double beds).
b = Private bathroom with toilet and shower or tub.
s = Private shower or tub only (the toilet is down the hall).

According to this code, a couple staying at a "Db-€85" hotel would pay a total of 85 euros (about $110) for a double room with a private bathroom. You can assume a hotel takes credit cards unless you see "cash only" in the listing. The hotel staff speaks basic English unless otherwise noted.

locanda or *pensione*, indicating that they offer budget beds.

You normally get close to what you pay for. Prices are fairly standard. Shopping around earns you a better location and more character, but rarely a cheaper price.

However, prices at nearly any hotel can get soft if you do any of the following: book direct (without using a pricey middleman like the TI or a Web booking service), volunteer to pay cash, stay at least three nights, mention this book, or visit off-season. Offer to skip breakfast for a better price. If you're on a budget, ask for a cheaper room or a discount. Always ask.

You'll save $40 if you request a room without a shower and just use the shower down the hall. Generally, rooms with a bath or shower also have a toilet and a bidet (which Italians use for quick sponge baths). The cord that dangles over the tub or shower is not a clothesline. You pull it when you've fallen and can't get up (though, oddly, they're often bundled up out of reach to keep them out of the way).

Double beds are called *matrimoniale*, even though hotels

aren't interested in your marital status. Twins are *due letti singoli*. Convents offer cheap accommodation but only *letti singoli*.

If you arrive on an overnight train, your room may not be ready. Drop your bag at the hotel and dive right into your destination.

When you check in, the receptionist will normally ask for your passport and keep it for a couple of hours. Hotels are legally required to register each guest with the local police. Relax. Americans are notorious for making this chore more difficult than it needs to be.

Assume that breakfast is included in the prices I've listed, unless otherwise noted. If breakfast is optional, you might want to skip it. While convenient, it's often a bad value—€10 for a simple continental buffet with unlimited *caffè latte*. You can sometimes request cheese or salami (about €3 extra). I enjoy taking breakfast at the corner café. It's OK to supplement what you order by bringing along a few picnic goodies.

Rooms are safe. Still, zip up camera bags and keep money out of sight. More pillows and blankets are usually in the closet or available on request. In Italy, towels and linen aren't always replaced every day. Hang your towel up to dry.

Because Europeans are generally careful with energy use, you'll find government-enforced limits on heating and air-conditioning. Many American travelers are shocked to learn that hotels aren't allowed to fire up their air conditioners except from the beginning of June through the end of September. To conserve energy, the Italian government tightly regulates when hotels can provide air-conditioning in summer and heat in winter. As Americans, the world's energy gluttons, we often have a tough time understanding the importance of these serious conservation measures enacted by far-sighted governments.

Air-conditioning—which sometimes comes with an extra per-day charge—is worth seeking out in summer. Fancier hotel rooms usually come with air-conditioning (included in the price), a little safe, and a small stocked fridge called a *frigo bar* (FREE-goh bar; pay for what you use). Many hotel rooms have a TV and phone. Conveniently, many business-class hotels drop their prices in July and August, just when the air-conditioned comfort they offer is most important.

Most hotel rooms with air conditioners come with a control stick (like a TV remote) that generally has the same symbols and features: fan icon (click to toggle through wind power, from light to gale); louver icon (choose steady airflow or waves); snowflake and sunshine icons (cold air or heat, depending on season); clock ("O" setting: run x hours before turning off; "I" setting: wait x hours to start); and the temperature control (20 or 21 degrees Celsius is comfortable).

Many hotels in resort areas will charge you for half-pension,

Calling Italy

To call Italy from the US or Canada, dial 011-39 and then the local number. If calling Italy from another European country, dial 00-39 followed by the local number. To make calls within Italy, just dial the local number. For more tips on phoning, see page 826.

called *mezza pensione,* during peak season (which can run from May through mid-October for resorts). Half-pension means that you pay for one meal per day per person (lunch or dinner, though usually dinner), whether you want to or not. Wine is rarely included. If half-pension is required, you can't opt out and pay less. Some places offer half-pension as an option; it can be worth considering. If they charge you less per meal than you've been paying for an average restaurant meal on your trip, half-pension is a fine value if the chef is good. Ask other guests about the quality or check out their restaurant yourself.

You can usually save time by paying your bill the evening before you leave instead of paying in the busy morning, when the reception desk is crowded with tourists wanting to pay up, ask questions, or check in.

Hotels near Airports: If you have an early-morning flight, I'd suggest staying in the center of town and getting to the airport via bus, train, or taxi. But if you really want a hotel near an airport for the first or last night of your trip, try www.worldairportguide.com.

Making Reservations

Given the quality of the gems I've found for this book, I'd recommend that you reserve your rooms in advance, particularly if you'll be traveling during peak season. Book several weeks ahead, or as soon as you've pinned down your travel dates. Note that some national holidays jam things up and merit your making reservations far in advance (for a list of holidays, see page 7). To make a reservation, contact hotels directly by email, phone, or fax.

Some travelers make reservations as they travel, calling hotels a few days to a week before their visit. If you prefer the flexibility of traveling without any reservations at all, you'll have greater success snaring rooms if you arrive at your destination early in the day. When you anticipate crowds, call hotels at about 9:00 on the day you plan to arrive, when the hotel clerk knows who'll be checking out and just which rooms will be available. If you encounter a language barrier, ask the fluent receptionist at your current hotel to call for you.

Most recommended hotels are accustomed to English-only travelers. Email is the clearest and most economical way to make a reservation. If phoning from the US, be mindful of time zones (see page 7). To ensure that you have all the information you need for your reservation, use the form in this book's appendix (also at www.ricksteves.com/reservation). If you don't get a reply to your email or fax, it usually means the hotel is already fully booked.

When you request a room for a certain time period, use the European style for writing dates: day/month/year. Hoteliers need to know your arrival and departure dates. For example, a two-night stay in July would be "2 nights, 16/07/08 to 18/07/08." Consider in advance how long you'll stay; don't just assume you can extend your reservation for extra days once you arrive.

If the response from the hotel gives its room availability and rates, it's not a confirmation. You must tell them that you want that room at the given rate.

The hotelier will sometimes request your credit-card number for a one-night deposit. While you can email your credit-card information (I do), it's safer to share that personal info via phone call, fax, or secure online reservation form (if the hotel has one on its website).

If you must cancel your reservation, it's courteous to do so with as much advance notice as possible (simply make a quick phone call or send an email). Hotels, which are often family-run, lose money if they turn away customers while holding a room for someone who doesn't show up. Understandably, some hotels bill no-shows for one night. Hotels in larger cities sometimes have strict cancellation policies (for example, you might lose a deposit if you cancel within two weeks of your reserved stay, or you might be billed for the entire visit if you leave early); ask about cancellation policies before you book.

Always reconfirm your room reservation a few days in advance from the road. If you'll be arriving after 17:00, let them know. Don't have the tourist office reconfirm rooms for you; they'll take a commission.

On the small chance that a hotel loses track of your reservation, bring along a hard copy of their emailed or faxed confirmation.

Private Rooms and Apartments

In small towns, there are often few hotels to choose from, but an abundance of *affitta camere*, or rental rooms. This can be anything from a set of keys and a basic bed to a cozy B&B with your own Tuscan grandmother. The local TI can give you a list of possibilities. These rooms are generally a good budget option, but since they vary in quality, shop around to find the best value. Apartment rentals, a great value for families or couples traveling together, are also listed at the TI and are very common in small towns. Apartments generally offer a couple of bedrooms, a sitting area, and a teensy *cucinetta,* usually stocked with dishes and flatware. Once you have the keys, you'll probably be on your own.

Agritourism

Agriturismo (or agricultural tourism) began in the 1980s as a way to encourage farmers to remain on their land, produce food, and offer accommodations to tourists. A peaceful home base for exploring the region, these rural Italian B&Bs are ideal for couples or families traveling by car.

As the name implies, *agriturismi* are in the countryside, although some are located within a mile of town. Most are family-run and can vary wildly in quality. Some properties are simple and rustic, while others are downright luxurious, offering amenities such as swimming pools and riding stables. The rooms are usually clean and comfortable. Breakfast is often included, and half-pension (which in this case means a home-cooked dinner) may be built into the price. Kitchenettes are often available to cook up your own feast. Make sure you know how to operate the appliances. To maximize your time, ask the owner for suggestions on local restaurants, sights, and activities.

It's wise to book several months in advance for high season (May–Sept). Weeklong stays are preferred in July and August, but shorter stays may be possible. To sleep cheaper, avoid peak season. A Tuscan farmhouse that rents for as much as $2,000 a week at peak times can go for as little as $700 in late September or October. In the winter, you might be charged extra for heat, so confirm the price ahead of time. Payment policies vary, but generally a 25 percent deposit is required (lost if you cancel), and the balance is due one month before arrival.

I've listed some *agriturismi* in this book, but there are thousands. Be aware that agricultural tourism is organized *"all'Italiana,"* which means, among other things, a lack of a single governing body. Local TIs can give you a list of farms in their area. Also visit www.agriturist.it or www.agriturismoitaly.it (among dozens of websites). For a booking agency, consider Farm Holidays in Tuscany. They book rooms and apartments at farms in Tuscany, Umbria, and elsewhere in Italy (closed Sat–Sun, tel. 0564-417-418, www.byfarmholidays.com, info@byfarmholidays.com).

EATING

The Italians are masters of the art of fine living. That means eating...long and well. Lengthy, multicourse lunches and dinners and endless hours sitting in outdoor cafés are the norm. Americans

eat on their way to an evening event and complain if the check is slow in coming. For Italians, the meal is an end in itself, and only rude waiters rush you. When you want the bill, mime-scribble on your raised palm or ask for it: *"Il conto?"* You may have to ask for it more than once. To save time, ask for the check when you receive the last item you order.

Even those of us who liked dorm food will find that the local cafés, cuisine, and wines become a highlight of our Italian adventure. Trust me: This is sightseeing for your palate, and even if the rest of you is sleeping in cheap hotels, your taste buds will relish an occasional first-class splurge. You can eat well without going broke. But be careful: You're just as likely to blow a small fortune on a disappointing meal as you are to dine wonderfully for €20.

Restaurants

When restaurant-hunting, choose places filled with locals, not the place with the big neon signs boasting, "We speak English and accept credit cards." Restaurants parked on famous squares generally serve bad food at high prices to tourists. Locals eat better at lower-rent locales. Family-run places operate without hired help and can offer cheaper meals.

The word *osteria* (traditionally a simple, local-style restaurant) stokes my appetite. For unexciting but basic values, look for a *menù*

turistico, a three- or four-course, fixed-price *menù* (also called *menù del giorno*—menu of the day, price includes service charge, no need to tip). Galloping gourmets order à la carte with the help of a menu translator. *(The Marling Italian Menu-Master* is excellent. *Rick Steves' Italian Phrase Book & Dictionary* has a menu decoder with enough phrases for intermediate eaters.) When going to an especially good restaurant with an approachable staff, my favorite strategy is to simply say, "Make me happy" (in this case, it's just fine to set a price limit).

Some restaurants have self-serve antipasti buffets, offering a variety of cooked appetizers spread out like a salad bar (pay per plate, not weight; usually costs about €6–8); a plate of antipasti combined with a pasta dish makes a healthy, affordable, interesting meal.

Eating with the Seasons

Italian cooks love to serve you fresh produce and seafood at its tastiest. If you must have porcini mushrooms outside of October and November, they'll be frozen. To get the freshest veggies at a fine restaurant, request *"Un piatto di verdure della stagioni, per favore"* ("A plate of veggies in season, please"). Here are a few examples of what's fresh when:

April–May:	Calamari, squid, green beans, aspara-gus, artichokes, and zucchini flowers
April–May and Sept–Oct:	Black truffles
May–June:	Mussels, asparagus, zucchini, canta-loupe, and strawberries
May–Aug:	Eggplant
Oct–Nov:	Mushrooms and white truffles
Fresh year-round:	Clams, meats, and cheese

A full meal consists of an appetizer (antipasto, €3–6), a first course (*primo piatto*, pasta or soup, €4–8), and a second course (*secondo piatto*, expensive meat and fish dishes, €6–12). Vegetables *(contorni, verdure)* may come with the *secondo* or cost extra (€3–4) as a side dish.

Seafood and steak are sometimes sold by weight (if you see "100 g" or "*l'etto*" by the price on the menu, you'll pay that price *per* 100 grams—about a quarter pound; sometimes also abbreviated *s.q.*, or "according to quantity"). Tourists without good language skills are commonly shell-shocked by the bill when ordering dishes sold by the weight.

Some special dishes come in large quantities meant for two people; the shorthand way of showing this on a menu is "X2" (meaning "for two people"). The price listed generally indicates the cost per person.

The euros can add up in a hurry. Light and budget eaters get a *primo piatto* each and share an antipasto. Another good option is sharing an array of antipasti—either several specific dishes or a big plate of mixed delights assembled from a buffet. Italians admit that the *secondo* is the least-interesting aspect of the local cuisine. My standard ordering procedure is to mix antipasti and *primi piatti* family-style with my dinner partners (skipping *secondi*) to keep the prices down and the experience up. When done well (e.g., under-ordering, since courses are often bigger than necessary), we eat well in better places for less than the cost of a tourist *menù* in a cheap place.

Restaurants normally pad the bill with a cover charge (*pane e coperto?*—"bread and cover charge," about €1) and a service charge (*servizio incluso,* 15 percent). These charges are listed on the menu. Italians don't tip any extra. If the charge isn't included, consider tipping 5 to 10 percent if you're pleased with the service.

Wine Bars (Enoteche)

An *enoteca* (wine bar) is a popular, fast, and inexpensive option for lunch. Surrounded by the local office crowd, you can get a fancy salad, plate of meats and cheeses, and a glass of good wine (see blackboards for the day's selection and price per glass).

Bars/Cafés

Italian "bars" are not taverns but cafés. These local hangouts serve coffee, mini-pizzas, sandwiches, and drinks from the cooler. Many dish up plates of fried cheese and vegetables from under the glass counter, ready to reheat. This budget choice is the Italian equivalent of English pub grub.

For quick meals, bars usually have trays of cheap, pre-made sandwiches (*panini* or *tramezzini*). Some kinds are delightful grilled. To save time for sightseeing and room for dinner, consider a ham-and-cheese *panino* at a bar (called "toast"), have it grilled twice (if you want it really hot) for lunch. To get food "to go," say, "*Da portar via*" (for the road). All bars have a WC *(toilette, bagno)* in the back, and customers (and the discreet public) can use it.

Bars serve great drinks—hot, cold, sweet, or alcoholic. Chilled bottled water, still *(naturale)* or carbonated *(frizzante),* is sold cheap to go.

Coffee: If you ask for "*un caffè,*" you'll get espresso. Cappuccino is served to locals before noon and to tourists any time of day. (To an Italian, cappuccino is a breakfast drink and a travesty after eating anything with tomatoes.) Italians like it only warm. To get it hot, request "*Molto caldo*" (MOHL-toh KAHL-doh; very hot) or "*Più caldo, per favore*" (pew KAHL-doh pehr fah-VOH-ray; hotter, please).

Try iced coffee in the summer. It's slightly diluted, sugared espresso, called *caffè freddo;* to get it with ice, say "*con ghiaccio*" (kohn ghee-AH-choh, with a hard g). *Cappuccino freddo* is cold cappuccino served in a tall glass.

Experiment with a few of the hot options:

• *cappuccino:* espresso with foamed milk on top
• *caffè latte:* tall glass with espresso and hot milk mixed
• *caffè hag:* instant decaf (you can order decaffeinated versions of any coffee drink—ask for it *decaffeinato:* day-kah-fey-een-AH-toh)
• *caffè macchiato* (mah-kee-AH-toh): espresso with only a little milk

• *caffè americano:* espresso diluted with water

• *caffè corretto:* espresso with a shot of liqueur

Juice: *Spremuta* means freshly squeezed as far as *succa* (fruit juice) is concerned. (Note: *Spumante* means champagne.)

Beer: Beer on tap is *alla spina*. Get it *piccola* (33 cl, 11 oz), *media* (50 cl, 17 oz), or *grande* (a liter, 34 oz).

Wine: To order a glass (*bicchiere*; bee-kee-AY-ree) of red *(rosso)* or white *(bianco)* wine, say, *"Un bicchiere di vino rosso/bianco."* *Corposo* means full-bodied. House wine *(vino della casa)* often comes in a quarter-liter carafe (8.5 oz, *un quarto*), half-liter pitcher (17 oz, *un mezzo*), or one-liter pitcher (34 oz, *un litro*). Trendy wines with small production (such as Brunello di Montalcino) are good but overpriced. For more on wine, see page 520.

Other Drinks: Some restaurants make their own after-dinner alcoholic brew (called a *digestivo*), using a secret combination of herbs to aid digestion. Popular commercial brands are Fernet Branca and Montenegro. If your tastes run sweeter, try an anise-flavored liqueur called Sambuca, served *con moscha* (with three "flies"—coffee beans).

Prices: You'll notice a two-tiered price system. Drinking a cup of coffee while standing at the bar is cheaper than drinking it at a table. If you're on a budget, check out the financial consequences before you sit down. Ask, "Same price if I sit or stand?" by saying, *"Costa uguale al tavolo o al banco?"* (KOH-stah oo-GWAH-lay ahl TAH-voh-loh oh ahl BAHN-koh?).

If the bar isn't busy, you'll often just order and then pay when you leave. Otherwise: 1) Decide what you want; 2) Find out the price by checking the price list on the wall, the prices posted near the food, or by asking the barista; 3) Pay the cashier; and 4) Give the receipt to the barista (whose clean fingers handle no dirty euros) and tell him or her what you want.

Delis, Cafeterias, Pizza Shops, and Tavola Calda ("Hot Table") Bars

Italy offers many cheap alternatives to restaurants. Stop by a *rosticceria* for great cooked deli food; a self-service cafeteria (called

"free flow" in Italian) that feeds you without the add-ons; a *tavola calda* bar for an assortment of veggies; or a Pizza Rustica shop for stand-up or take-out pizza by the slice.

Pizza is cheap and every-where. Key pizza vocabulary: *capricciosa* (generally ham, mush-rooms, olives, and artichokes),

Ordering Food at Tavola Caldas

plate of
   mixed veggies
	*piatto misto
	   di verdure*
		pee-AH-toh
		   MEES-toh
		   dee vehr-DOO-ray

"Heated, please."	*"Scaldare,
	   per favore."*
		skahl-DAH-ray,
		   pehr fah-VOH-ray

"A taste, please."	*"Un assaggio,
	   per favore."*
		oon ah-SAH-joh,
		   pehr fah-VOH-ray

artichoke	*carciofi*	kar-CHOH-fee
asparagus	*asparagi*	ah-spah-RAH-jee
beans	*fagioli*	fah-JOH-lee
breadsticks	*grissini*	gree-SEE-nee
broccoli	*broccoli*	BROH-koh-lee
cantaloupe	*melone*	may-LOH-nay
carrots	*carote*	kah-ROT-ay
green beans	*fagiolini*	fah-joh-LEE-nee
ham	*prosciutto*	proh-SHOO-toh
mushrooms	*funghi*	FOONG-ghee
potatoes	*patate*	pah-TAH-tay
rice	*riso*	REE-zoh
spinach	*spinaci*	speen-AH-chee
tomatoes	*pomodori*	poh-moh-DOH-ree
zucchini	*zucchine*	zoo-KEE-nay

(Excerpted from *Rick Steves' Italian Phrase Book & Dictionary*)

funghi (mushrooms), *marinara* (tomato sauce, oregano, garlic, no cheese), *quattro formaggi* (four different cheeses), and *quattro stagioni* (different toppings on each of the four quarters, for those who can't choose just one menu item). If you ask for *peperoni* on your pizza, you'll get green or red peppers, not sausage. Kids like the bland *margherita* (cheese with tomato sauce) or *diavola* (the closest thing in Italy to American pepperoni). At Pizza Rustica take-out shops, slices are sold by weight (100 grams, or *un etto*, is a hot and cheap snack; 200 grams, or *due etti*, makes a light meal).

For a fast, cheap, and healthy lunch, find a *tavola calda* bar with a buffet spread of meat and vegetables, and ask for a mixed plate of vegetables with a hunk of mozzarella *(piatto misto di verdure con mozzarella)*. Don't be limited by what you can see. If you'd like a salad with a slice of cantaloupe and a hunk of cheese, they'll whip that up for you in a snap. Belly up to the bar and—with a pointing finger and key words in the chart in this chapter—get a fine mixed plate of vegetables. If something's a mystery, ask for a small taste (*un assaggio;* oon ah-SAH-joh).

Beware of cheap eateries that sport big color photos of pizza and piles of different pastas. They have no kitchens and simply microwave disgusting prepackaged food. Unless you like lasagna with ice in the center, avoid these.

Picnics

In Italy, picnicking saves lots of euros and is a great way to sample local specialties. In the process of assembling your meal, you get to deal with the Italians in the market scene. On days you choose to picnic, gather supplies early. You'll probably visit several small stores or market stalls to put together a complete meal, and many close around noon. While it's fun to visit the small specialty shops, a local *alimentari* is your one-stop corner grocery store (most will slice and stuff your sandwich for you if you buy the ingredients there). A *supermercato* gives you more efficiency with less color for less cost. You'll need to take a number for deli service at busier supermarkets. (If you're buying perishables, only get what you'll eat soon; don't expect to find bags of ice for sale.) Many *alimentari* and even supermarkets will gladly make you a fresh sandwich, charging you only for the weight of what you take and the piece of bread.

Juice-lovers can get a liter (34 oz) of O.J. for the price of a Coke or coffee. Look for "100% *succo*" (juice) on the label. Hang on to the half-liter mineral-water bottles (sold everywhere for about €1). Buy juice in cheap liter boxes, then drink some and store the extra in your water bottle. Tap water—*acqua del rubinetto*—is fine to drink.

Picnics can be an adventure in high cuisine. Be daring. Try the fresh mozzarella, *presto* pesto, shriveled olives, and any UFOs the locals are excited about. Shopkeepers are happy to sell small quantities of produce. It is customary to let the merchant choose the produce for you. Say *"Per oggi"* (pehr OH-jee), or "For today," and he or she will grab you something ready to eat, weigh it, and make the sale. A typical picnic for two might be fresh rolls, 100 grams of cheese, 100 grams of meat, two tomatoes, three carrots, two apples, yogurt, and a liter box of juice. Total cost: about €10.

TRAVELING AS A TEMPORARY LOCAL

We travel all the way to Italy to enjoy differences—to become temporary locals. You'll experience frustrations. Certain truths that we find "God-given" or "self-evident," such as cold beer, ice in drinks, bottomless cups of coffee, hot showers, and bigger being better, are suddenly not so true. One of the benefits of travel is the

How Was Your Trip?

Were your travels fun, smooth, and meaningful? If you'd like to share your tips, concerns, and discoveries, please fill out the survey at www.ricksteves.com/feedback. I value your feedback. Thanks in advance—it helps a lot.

eye-opening realization that there are logical, civil, and even better alternatives. A willingness to go local ensures that you'll enjoy a full dose of Italian hospitality.

If there is a negative aspect to Italians' image of Americans (apart from our foreign policy), it's that we are big, loud, aggressive, impolite, rich, and a bit naive. Given our reluctance to work with the world on climate change issues, Europeans don't respond well to Americans complaining about being too hot or too cold. To encourage conservation, the Italian government limits when air-conditioning or central heating can be used. (Generally, heat is turned off in early April, and air-conditioning isn't allowed until June.) Bring a sweater in winter, and in summer, be prepared to sweat a little like everyone else. Also, Americans tend to be noisy in public places, such as restaurants and trains. Our raised voices

can demolish Europe's reserved and elegant ambience. Talk softly.

While Italians, flabbergasted by our Yankee excesses, say in disbelief, *"Mi sono cadute le braccia!"* ("I throw my arms down!"), they nearly always afford us individual travelers all the warmth that we deserve.

Judging from all the happy feedback I receive from travelers who have used this book, it's safe to assume you'll enjoy a great, affordable vacation—with the finesse of an independent, experienced traveler.

Thanks, and *buon viaggio!*

BACK DOOR TRAVEL PHILOSOPHY
From *Rick Steves' Europe Through the Back Door*

Travel is intensified living—maximum thrills per minute and one of the last great sources of legal adventure. Travel is freedom. It's recess, and we need it.

Experiencing the real Europe requires catching it by surprise, going casual..."Through the Back Door."

Affording travel is a matter of priorities. (Make do with the old car.) You can travel—simply, safely, and comfortably—nearly anywhere in Europe for $100 a day plus transportation costs. In many ways, spending more money only builds a thicker wall between you and what you came to see. Europe is a cultural carnival, and, time after time, you'll find that its best acts are free and the best seats are the cheap ones.

A tight budget forces you to travel close to the ground, meeting and communicating with the people, not relying on service with a purchased smile. Never sacrifice sleep, nutrition, safety, or cleanliness in the name of budget. Simply enjoy the local-style alternatives to expensive hotels and restaurants.

Extroverts have more fun. If your trip is low on magic moments, kick yourself and make things happen. If you don't enjoy a place, maybe you don't know enough about it. Seek the truth. Recognize tourist traps. Give a culture the benefit of your open mind. See things as different but not better or worse. Any culture has much to share.

Of course, travel, like the world, is a series of hills and valleys. Be fanatically positive and militantly optimistic. If something's not to your liking, change your liking. Travel is addictive. It can make you a happier American as well as a citizen of the world. Our Earth is home to six and a half billion equally important people. It's humbling to travel and find that people don't envy Americans. Europeans like us, but, with all due respect, they wouldn't trade passports.

Globe-trotting destroys ethnocentricity. It helps you understand and appreciate different cultures. Regrettably, there are forces in our society that want you dumbed down for their convenience. Don't let it happen. Thoughtful travel engages you with the world—more important than ever these days. Travel changes people. It broadens perspectives and teaches new ways to measure quality of life. Rather than fear the diversity on this planet, travelers celebrate it. Many travelers toss aside their hometown blinders. Their prized souvenirs are the strands of different cultures they decide to knit into their own character. The world is a cultural yarn shop, and Back Door travelers are weaving the ultimate tapestry. Join in!

ITALY

Italia

Italy is the cradle of European civilization, established by the Roman Empire and carried on by the Roman Catholic Church. As a traveler there, you'll see some of the world's most iconic images from this 2,000-year history: the Colosseum of Ancient Rome, the medieval Leaning Tower of Pisa, Michelangelo's *David* and Botticelli's *Venus* that signal the Renaissance, the Trevi Fountain, and the Italian city that preserves this legacy in a state of elegant decay—Venice.

Beyond these famous sights, though, Italy offers Europe's richest culture. Traditions still live within a country that is vibrant

and fully modern. Go with an eye open to both the Italy of the past and of the present.

Italy is diverse, encompassing the German-flavored Alps, Mediterranean beaches, sunbaked Sicily, romantic hill towns, the urban jungle of Naples, the businesslike city of Milan, and the art-drenched cities of Venice, Florence, and Rome. The country is small enough and laced with freeways and train lines, so you're never more than a day away from any of these. Each of the country's 20 regions has its own distinct character, whether it's scenic Tuscany, busy Lombardy, industrious Piedmont, or the place where it all mixes together—Lazio, home of the capital, Rome.

There are two Italys: The North is industrial, aggressive, and "time is money" in its outlook. The weather is temperate, and the people are more like Northern Europeans. The South is hot and sunny, crowded, poor, relaxed, farm-oriented, and traditional.

Italy Almanac

Population: 58.8 million. The population is comprised almost entirely of indigenous Italians who speak Italian (with German and French spoken in some Alpine regions) and are nominally Roman Catholic (87 percent). One in five Italians is older than 65, and nearly half use the Internet.

Area: 116,000 square miles, including the islands of Sicily, Sardinia, and others.

Latitude and Longitude: 43° N and 12° E (similar to Oregon or Maine).

Geography: Italy is shaped like a boot, 850 miles long and 150 miles wide, jutting into the central Mediterranean. (Florida is 500 miles long.) The terrain is generally mountainous or hilly, with the Alps in the north and a north–south "spine" of the Apennine Mountains.

Highs and Lows: The highest point is Mont Blanc, on the border with France. Besides the Alps, the highest point is Monte Cimone (7,100 feet). The lowest point is sea level. Italy has 5,000 miles of coastline.

Rivers: Po (the longest, 400 miles), Arno, Adige, and Tiber.

Active Volcanoes: Vesuvius, Etna, and Stromboli.

Major Cities: Rome (the capital, 2.6 million), Milan (1.3 million), and Naples (1 million).

Italian Inventions: Cologne, thermometer, barometer, pizza, wireless telegraph, espresso machine, typewriter, batteries, nitroglycerin, and the ice-cream cone.

Families here are very strong and usually live in the same house for many generations. Loyalties are to family, city, region, soccer team, and country—in that order.

Economically, Italy has had its problems, but somehow things have always worked out. Today, Italy is the world's seventh-largest industrial power and the fourth-largest in Europe. Italy is the world's second-leading wine producer, just behind France. It is sixth in cheese and wool output. Ferraris, Fiats, Maseratis, and Lamborghinis are world-renowned, though they're not really major exports. Tourism is big business—Italy is considered the world's fourth-largest tourist destination. Cronyism, which complicates my work, is an integral part of the economy. Much of Italy's business is hidden in a large "black market" unreported to government officials. Labor unions are strong, strikes are frequent, and the country today is faced with pressure to compete globally.

Italy, home of the Vatican, is overwhelmingly Catholic, but the dominant religion is life—motor scooters, soccer, fashion,

Gross Domestic Product: $1.7 trillion.

Economy: Sixty-nine percent of the economy consists of service jobs (especially tourism), 29 percent is industry (textiles, chemicals), and 2 percent is agriculture (fruit, vegetables, olives, wine, plus fishing). Pollution remains a greater problem in Italy than elsewhere in Europe. There are 10,000 miles of train lines (mostly government-run) and 4,300 miles of freeway *(autostrada)*.

Museums: 3,000.

Government: Italy is a republic, with three branches of government. The chief executive is the prime minister (currently Romano Prodi), who assumed office in May 2006 as the head of the leading vote-getting party in legislative elections. The bicameral legislature is elected by (mostly) direct voting. Since World War II, the fragmented country has had 60 national governments.

Regions: Italy is divided into 20 regions (including Tuscany, Umbria, Veneto, and Lazio). Locally, there are some 8,000 "communes," with a community council and mayor.

Flag: Three vertical bands of green, white, and red.

Average "Gio": The average Italian is 42 years old, makes $29,200 per year, and has 1.28 kids. Every day, he or she consumes two servings of pasta, a half pound of bread, and two glasses of wine, and will live to the average age of 76 years, 10 months, and 16 days.

girl-watching, boy-watching, good coffee, good wine, and *il dolce far niente* (the sweetness of doing nothing). The Italian character shows itself on the streets in the skilled maniac drivers and the classy dressers who star in the ritual evening stroll, or *passeggiata*.

Italians are outgoing, and you'll see that in trying to communicate with them. The language is fun. Be melodramatic and talk with your hands. Hear the melody; get into the flow. Italians want to communicate, and they try harder than any other Europeans. Play with them. Even in nontouristy towns, where English is rare and Italian is the norm, you can cross the language barrier with a little warmth.

Italians are more social and communal than their northern

neighbors. In small towns, everyone knows everyone. People get out of their apartments to socialize on the main square. Young women walk hand in hand, and young teenagers shove or punch each other playfully or hang all over each other.

Like most Europeans (and Americans), Italians enjoy watching TV (game shows, sitcoms, etc.), going to movies (American films are almost always dubbed, not subtitled), and listening to their homegrown pop music. Though Italy is the birthplace of opera and much classical music, it's not much more "cultured" today than America is.

And Italians love sports—though not American sports. Italian sports idols are soccer players (Francesco Totti), skiers (Giorgio Rocca), and cyclists (Paolo Savodelli). Motor racing—Formula 1/Grand Prix—is huge. And since many Italians grow up zipping through narrow streets on small Vespas, it's little wonder that motorcycle racing (*moto,* led by Valentino Rossi) is a major sport here.

Italy's undisputed number-one sport is soccer (called *il calcio*). All other sports are a distant second. On almost any given night of the year, there's yet another "absolutely crucial" soccer match in Italy. That's because the only way to feed fans' insatiable appetite for the game is to run the sport nearly year-round (roughly Sept–June), with different leagues playing their seasons concurrently.

Italy's top players play—simultaneously—for two different teams. On one night, they might suit up for their professional team (Rome, Lazio, Milan, etc.) competing to be the best in Italy. Another night, they might play for Italy's national team (La Squadra Azzura, or "The Blue Team," named for its uniforms) competing against other nations to qualify for either the Euro Cup or the World Cup, held every four years. Italy, the reigning World Cup champ, hopes to defeat the rest of Europe in the Euro Cup finals in June 2008 (held in Switzerland and Austria).

Italian soccer fans (*tifosi*) are passionate. Star players (such as Francesco Totti or Antonio Cassano) are paid millions and treated like movie stars. Little kids everywhere grow up pretending to score the winning goal just like them. On big game nights, bars are packed with men crowded around TV sets. After a loss, they drown their sorrows and call the ref a *cornuto* (cuckold). After a victory, fans celebrate by driving through the city streets honking horns and waving team flags. Many Italians place their national, regional, and personal pride on the backs of their athletes. It's a cliché that remains true: In a Europe at peace, the football field is the new battleground.

One of Italy's delights is its food. If America's specialty is fast food, Italy's is slow food: locally grown ingredients, in season, bought daily, prepared with love, and enjoyed in social circumstances with friends and family. Even in modern cities, you don't tend to find big supermarkets. Rather, people buy their bread from the baker and their meats from the butcher, enjoying a chance to catch up on gossip with  the shopkeeper. Italians buy foods in season, celebrating the arrival of porcini mushrooms in the fall or fresh artichokes in the spring. The three-hour meal is common. For many Italians, dinner is the evening's entertainment.

They eat in courses, lingering over each one. A typical meal might start with an antipasto plate of cold cuts and veggies. Next comes the pasta, then the meat dish, then a salad. No meal is complete without dessert (Italian gelato is considered the best ice cream in the world), accompanied by coffee or a dessert drink.

Complementing each course is the wine. It'd be a shame to visit Italy without sampling the specialties from each region, whether it's the famous Chianti from central Italy, a white Soave from the Veneto, Bardolinos from the north, or a Lacryma Christi from the south.

Italian "bars" are not taverns but cafés... and social watering holes. In the morning, they serve coffee, orange juice, and croissants to workers on the go. At lunch, it's sandwiches (*panini)* and mini-pizzas for university students. In the afternoon, housewives might drop in for an ice cream bar. At night, men and women enjoy a glass of wine and watch TV while the kids play the video game in the corner.

Besides food, travelers enjoy sampling Italy's other wares. While no longer a cheap country, Italy is still a hit with shoppers. Find glassware in Venice; gold, silver, leather, and prints in Florence; and high fashion in Rome and Milan.

Most of all, Italy is a mix of old and new. Appreciate the extreme changes Italian society has gone through in just 50 years: the "economic miracle" of the 1950s, the liberal reforms of the 1960s, a wave of domestic terrorism (from the left and the right) in the 1970s and 1980s, the entry into the European Union in the 1990s, and the recent turmoil over the Berlusconi government's support of the Iraq war. Today's prime minister, Romano Prodi, is known as a man of compromise and dialogue, trying to gingerly balance Italy's right- and left-wing extremes as he guides Italy into the future.

Italy is still 87 percent Catholic...but not particularly devout. Most people would never think of renouncing their faith, but they don't attend church regularly. They baptize their kids at the local church (there's one every few blocks), but they hold modern opinions on social issues, often in conflict with strict Catholic dogma. Italy is now the land of legalized abortion, the lowest birth rate in Europe, nudity on TV, socialist politics, and a society whose common language is decidedly secular.

Some traditions thrive. Italian families and communities are still more close-knit than others in the modern world. The Catholic Church maintains a measure of influence. Many Italians, especially in rural regions, still follow the traditional siesta schedule (called *reposo* in Italy). At about 13:00, shops close and people go home for a three-hour break to have lunch, socialize with friends and family, and maybe take a short nap in front of the TV. And on festival days, locals still dress up in medieval garb to paddle gondolas (Venice), race horses (Siena), battle over a bridge (Pisa), or play rugby/soccer (Florence). But these days, the traditional ways are carried on by choice. Italians are wary of the dangers of a fast-paced global lifestyle. Their history is long, and they're secure in their place in the world.

Accept Italy as Italy. Zero in on the fine points. Don't dwell on the problems. Savor your cappuccino, dangle your feet over a canal (if it smells, breathe through your mouth), and imagine what it was like centuries ago. Ramble through the rabble and rubble of Rome and mentally resurrect those ancient stones. Look into the famous sculpted eyes of Michelangelo's *David* and understand Renaissance Man's assertion of himself. Sit silently on a hilltop rooftop. Get chummy with the winds of  the past. Write a poem over a glass of local wine in a sun-splashed, wave-dashed Riviera village. If you fall off your moral horse, call it a cultural experience. Italy is for romantics.

VENICE

Venezia

Soak all day in this puddle of elegant decay. Venice is Europe's best-preserved big city. This car-free urban wonderland of a hundred islands—laced together by 400 bridges and 2,000 alleys—survives on the artificial respirator of tourism.

Born in a lagoon 1,500 years ago as a refuge from barbarians, Venice is overloaded with tourists and is slowly sinking (unrelated facts). In the Middle Ages, the Venetians became Europe's clever middlemen for East–West trade and created a great trading empire. By smuggling in the bones of St. Mark (San Marco) in A.D. 828, Venice gained religious importance as well. With the discovery of America and new trading routes to the Orient, Venetian power ebbed. But as Venice fell, her appetite for decadence grew. Through the 17th and 18th centuries, Venice partied on the wealth accumulated through earlier centuries as a trading power.

Today, Venice is home to about 62,000 people in its old city, down from a peak population of nearly 200,000. While there are about 500,000 in greater Venice (counting the mainland, not counting tourists), the old town has a small-town feel. Locals seem to know everyone. To see small-town Venice away from the touristic flak, escape the Rialto–San Marco tourist zone and savor the town early and late without the hordes of vacationers day-tripping in from cruise ships and nearby beach resorts. A 10-minute walk from the madness puts you in an idyllic Venice that few tourists see.

Planning Your Time

Venice worth at least a day on even the speediest tour. Hyper-efficient train travelers take the night train in and/or out. Sleep in

Venice Overview

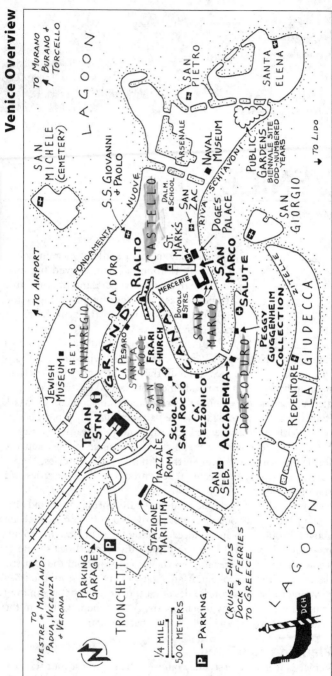

the old center to experience Venice at its best: early and late. For a one-day visit, cruise the Grand Canal, do the major sights on St. Mark's Square (the square itself, Doge's Palace, and St. Mark's Basilica), see the Frari Church for art, and wander the backstreets on a pub crawl (described in "Eating," page 100). Venice's greatest sight is the city itself. Make time to simply wander. While doable in a day, Venice is worth two. It's a medieval cookie jar, and nobody's looking.

ORIENTATION

The island city of Venice is shaped like a fish. Its major thoroughfares are canals. The Grand Canal winds through the middle of the fish, starting at the mouth where all the people and food enter, passing under the Rialto Bridge, and ending at St. Mark's Square (Piazza San Marco). Park your 21st-century perspective at the mouth and let Venice swallow you whole.

Venice is a car-less kaleidoscope of people, bridges, and odorless canals. The city has no major streets, and addresses are hopelessly confusing. There are six districts: San Marco (most touristy), Castello (behind San Marco), Cannaregio (from the train station to the Rialto), San Polo (other side of the Rialto), Santa Croce (the "eye" of the fish, east of the train station), and Dorsoduro (the belly of the fish and southernmost district of the city). Each district has about 6,000 address numbers.

To find your way, navigate by landmarks, not streets. Many street corners have a sign pointing you to *(per)* the nearest major landmark. Obedient visitors stick to the main thoroughfares as directed by these signs and miss the charm of backstreet Venice.

Tourist Information

There are TIs at the **train station** (daily 8:00–20:00, crowded and surly); at **St. Mark's Square** (daily 9:00–15:30; with your back to St. Mark's Basilica, it's at the far-left corner of the square); and near the **St. Mark's Square vaporetto stop** on the lagoon (daily 10:00–18:00, sells vaporetto tickets). Smaller offices are at **Piazzale Roma** and the **airport** (daily 9:00–20:00). For a quick question, save time by phoning 041-529-8711. The TI's official website is www.turismovenezia.it.

At any TI, confirm your sightseeing plans. Pick up the two free pamphlets that list museum hours, exhibitions, and musical events (in Italian and English), and ask for the fine brochures that outline three offbeat Venice walks.

The free monthly entertainment guide *Un Ospite di Venezia* (a listing of events, nightlife, museum hours, train and vaporetto schedules, emergency telephone numbers, and so on) is available at fancy hotel reception desks (www.aguestinvenice.com).

Maps: Of all places, you'll need a good map in Venice. Hotels give away lousy freebies, and the TI sells a simple one that isn't much better. Bookshops, newsstands, and postcard stands sell a wider range of maps; the €3 maps are pretty bad, but if you spend €5, you'll get a map that shows you everything. Invest in a good map and use it—this can be the best €5 you'll spend in Venice.

Arrival in Venice

A two-mile-long causeway (with highway and train lines) connects Venice to the mainland. Mestre, the sprawling mainland transportation hub, has fewer crowds, cheaper hotels, and plenty of cheap parking lots, but zero charm. Don't stop in Mestre unless you're parking your car or transferring trains.

By Train: Trains to Venice stop at either Venezia Mestre (on the mainland) or at the Santa Lucia station on the island of Venice itself. If your train only stops at Mestre, worry not. Shuttle trains regularly connect Mestre's station with Venice's Santa Lucia station (6/hr, 10 min).

Venice's **Santa Lucia train station** plops you right into the old town on the Grand Canal, an easy vaporetto ride or fascinating 40-minute walk to St. Mark's Square. Upon arrival, skip the station's crowded TI, because the two TIs at St. Mark's Square are better, and it's not worth a long wait for a minimal map (buy a good one from a newsstand or pick up a free one at your hotel). Confirm your departure plan (stop by train info desk or just study the *partenze*—departure—posters on walls).

Consider storing unnecessary heavy bags, although lines for **baggage check** may be very long (at head of platform 14, €8/12 hours, €11/24 hours, daily 6:00–24:00, no lockers, 45-pound weight limit on bags).

To get from the train station to downtown Venice, walk straight out of the station to the canal. On your left is the dock for **vaporetto #82** (fast boat down Grand Canal, catch from right side of dock). To your right is the dock for vaporetto #1 (slow boat down Grand Canal, catch from far right dock) and #51 (goes counterclockwise around Venice, handy for Dorsoduro hotels). See the hotel listings in the "Sleeping" section to find out which boat to catch to get to your hotel.

Buy a €6 ticket at the ticket window (a few shorter runs are only €2) and hop on a boat. You can also buy a pass for unlimited use of *vaporetti* and ACTV buses (sold in 12-hour increments— €13/12 hrs, €15/24 hrs, and so on up to €30/72 hrs). If you're taking #82 or #1, confirm that it's heading downtown (direction: Rialto or San Marco). Some boats only go as far as Rialto *(solo Rialto)*, so check with the conductor.

Arrival in Venice

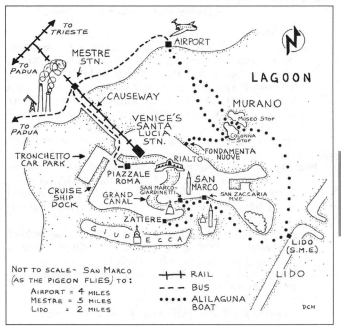

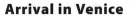

By Car: The freeway dead-ends at Venice, near several parking lots on the edge of the island. The most central lot, San Marco, is very busy and too expensive. Tronchetto (across the causeway and on the right) has a huge multistoried garage (€20/day, tel. 041-520-7555). From there, avoid the travel agencies masquerading as TIs, and head directly for the vaporetto docks for the boat connection (#82) to the town center. Don't let water taxi boatmen con you out of the relatively cheap €6 vaporetto ride.

Parking in Mestre is easy and cheap (open-air lots cost €5/day Mon—Fri, €10/day Sat—Sun, across from Mestre train station, easy shuttle-train connections to Venice's Santa Lucia Station—6/hr, 10 min). There are also huge and economical lots in Verona, Padua, and Vicenza.

By Plane: For information on Venice's airport and connections into the city, see page 112.

Passes for Venice

To help control (and confuse?) its flood of visitors, Venice offers cards and passes that cover some museums and/or transportation. For most visitors, the simple Museum Card or Museum Pass will do. Both of these passes are sold at all of the sights they cover.

Venice

Daily Reminder

Need a calendar? See the appendix.

Sunday: The Church of San Giorgio Maggiore (on an island near St. Mark's Square) hosts a Gregorian Mass at 11:00. The Church of San Polo is closed today, and these sights are open only in the afternoon: St. Mark's Basilica (14:00–16:00), Frari Church (13:00–18:00, closed Sun in Aug), and the Church of San Zaccaria (16:00–18:00). Today, the Rialto open-air market consists mainly of souvenir stalls (fish and produce sections closed). It's a bad day for a pub crawl, as most pubs are closed.

Monday: All sights are open, except for the Rialto fish market, Dalmatian School, Ca' Pesaro, and Torcello Museum (on Torcello Island). The Accademia and Ca' d'Oro close at 14:00. Don't side-trip to Verona or Vicenza today, as most sights in these towns are closed.

Tuesday: All sights are open, except for the Peggy Guggenheim Collection, Ca' Rezzonico (Museum of 18th-Century Venice), and the Lace Museum (on Burano Island).

Wednesday: All sights are open, except for the Glass Museum (on Murano Island).

Thursday/Friday: All sights are open.

Saturday: All sights are open, except for the Jewish Museum.

Notes: The Accademia is open earlier (daily at 8:15) and closes later (19:15 Tue–Sun) than most sights in Venice. Some sights close earlier off-season (such as the Doge's Palace, Correr

The **Museum Card** is really just another name for the (mandatory) combo-ticket you must buy to visit the Doge's Palace or the Correr Museum. It covers admission to both of those sights, plus the two minor museums accessed from within the Correr—the National Archaeological Museum and the Monumental Rooms of Marciana National Library (€13, called *"Museum Card per i Musei di Piazza San Marco,"* valid for 3 months; to bypass long line at Doge's Palace, purchase card at Correr Museum, then enter Doge's Palace).

The pricier **Museum Pass** includes the St. Mark's Square sights listed above, plus Ca' Rezzonico (Museum of 18th-Century Venice; see page 71), Mocenigo Palace (textiles and costumes), Casa Goldoni (home of the Italian playwright), Ca' Pesaro (modern art), and museums on the islands—Murano's Glass Museum and Burano's Lace Museum (€18, valid for 6 months). The pass pays for itself if you see the Doge's Palace, Correr Museum, and Ca' Rezzonico.

Museum, Campanile, and St. Mark's Basilica).

Churches: Modest dress is recommended at churches and required at St. Mark's Basilica—no bare shoulders, shorts, or short skirts. Some churches are closed to sightseers on Sunday morning (including St. Mark's Basilica, Frari Church, Church of San Zaccaria, and San Giorgio Maggiore), and many are closed from roughly 12:00 to 14:30 or 15:00 Monday through Saturday (this includes La Salute and San Giorgio Maggiore).

Crowd Control: Crowds can be a serious problem at the Accademia (to minimize crowds, go early or late, or call 041-520-0345 to reserve tickets in advance); St. Mark's Basilica (try going early or late, or you can skip the line if you have a bag to check—see page 61); Campanile (go early or late—it's open until 21:00 July–Aug; or skip it entirely if you're going to the similar San Giorgio Maggiore bell tower); and the Doge's Palace. For the Doge's Palace, you have three options for avoiding the ticket-sales line: Buy your Museum Card or Museum Pass at the Correr Museum (then step right up to the Doge's Palace turnstile, thus skipping the long line); visit at 17:00 (if it's April–Oct), when lines disappear; or book a Secret Itineraries Tour (see page 67). The sights that have crowd problems (St. Mark's Basilica, Doge's Palace, and Accademia) get even more crowded when it rains.

The **Chorus Pass** gives access to 16 of Venice's churches (including San Polo and the Frari, covered in this chapter) and their works of art (€8, €5 with a Venice Card—see below, or pay €2.50 per church; Chorus Family Pass costs €16 for 2 adults and kids 18 and under). You'd need to visit four churches to save money.

No cards or passes cover these top attractions: Accademia, Peggy Guggenheim Collection, Scuola San Rocco, Campanile, and the three sights within St. Mark's Basilica that charge admission.

Venice Cards: The Blue and Orange Venice Cards are transit passes (good for 1–7 days) that include the use of public toilets—not worth considering unless you have diarrhea.

"Rolling Venice" Youth Discount Pass: To those under age 30, this worthwhile pass (€4/1 day, €15/3 days) gives discounts on sights and transportation, plus information on cheap eating and sleeping. It's sold at the train station (both inside at the TI, and outside at the Vela kiosk).

Helpful Hints

Get Lost: Accept the fact that Venice was a tourist town 400 years ago. It was, is, and always will be crowded. While 80 percent of Venice is, in fact, not touristy, 80 percent of the tourists never notice. Hit the back streets. Venice is the ideal town to explore on foot. Walk and walk to the far reaches of the town. Don't worry about getting lost. In fact, get as lost as possible. Keep reminding yourself, "I'm on an island, and I can't get off." When it comes time to find your way, just follow the directional arrows on building corners or simply ask a local, *"Dov'è San Marco?"* ("Where is St. Mark's?") People in the tourist business (that's most Venetians) speak some English. If they don't, listen politely, watch where their hands point, say, *"Grazie,"* and head off in that direction. If you're lost, pop into a hotel and ask for their business card—it comes with a map and a prominent "You are here."

Be Prepared to Splurge: Venice is expensive for locals as well as tourists. The demand is huge, supply is limited, and running a business is costly. Things just cost more here; everything must be shipped in and hand-trucked to its destination. Perhaps the best way to enjoy Venice is just to succumb to its charms and blow a lot of money.

Warning: The dark, late-night streets of Venice are safe. Even so, pickpockets (often elegantly dressed) work the crowded main streets, docks, and *vaporetti* (wear your money belt and carry your day bag in front). Your biggest risk of pickpockets is actually inside St. Mark's Basilica. A service called Counter of Tourist Mediation handles complaints about local crooks, but does not give out information (tel. 041-529-8710, complaint .apt@turismovenezia.it). Immigrants selling items such as knock-off handbags on the streets are doing so illegally—if you buy goods from them, you'll risk a big fine.

Medical Help: Venice's S.S. Giovanni e Paolo hospital is a 10-minute walk from both the Rialto and San Marco neighborhoods, located on Fondamenta dei Mendicanti toward Fondamenta Nuove. Take vaporetto #41 from San Zaccaria–Jolanda to the Ospedale stop (tel. 118).

Take Breaks: Venice's endless pavement, crowds, and tight spaces are hard on the tourist. Schedule breaks in your sightseeing. Grab a cool place to sit down, relax, and recoup—meditate on a pew in an uncrowded church, or stop in a café.

Etiquette: Walk on the right and don't loiter on bridges. Picnicking is forbidden (keep a low profile). On St. Mark's Square, Venetian authorities have begun cracking down on snackers and sunbathers, who now risk being admonished by members of the "decorum patrol." The only place for a legal picnic in Venice is in Giardinetti Reali, the small park along the waterfront west of the Piazzetta near St. Mark's Square.

Dress modestly. Men should keep their shirts on. When visiting St. Mark's Basilica or other major churches, men, women, and even children must cover their shoulders and knees (or risk being turned away). Remove hats when entering a church.

Pigeon Poop: If bombed by a pigeon, resist the initial response to wipe it off immediately—it'll just smear into your hair. Wait until it dries, and it should flake off cleanly.

Public Toilets: There are handy public WCs (€1) near St. Mark's Square (one behind the Correr Museum, another at the waterfront park, Giardinetti Reali), near Rialto, and at the Accademia Bridge. You'll find public pay toilets near most major landmarks. Use free toilets—in a museum you're visiting or in a café where you're eating—when you can.

Water: Venetians pride themselves on having pure, safe, and tasty tap water piped in from the foothills of the Alps. You can actually see the mountains from Venice's bell towers on crisp, clear winter days.

Lingo: *Campo* means square, *campiello* is a small square, *calle* is street, *fondamenta* is the road running along a canal, *rio* is a small canal, *rio terra* is a street that was once a canal and has been filled in, and *ponte* is a bridge.

Services

Money: The plentiful ATMs are the easiest way to go. If you must exchange currency, be aware that bank rates vary. The American Express exchange desk is just off St. Mark's Square (see "Travel Agencies," on page 44). Non-bank exchange bureaus, such as Exacto, will charge you $10 more than a bank for a $200 exchange.

Internet Access: You'll find handy, if pricey (€5/hr), little Internet places all over town. Every hotel knows a place nearby.

Post Office: A large post office is just outside the far end of St. Mark's Square (the end farthest from the basilica; Mon–Fri 8:30–14:00, Sat 8:30–13:00, closed Sun, shorter hours off-season). The main P.O. is near the Rialto Bridge (on the St. Mark's side, Mon–Sat 8:30–18:30, closed Sun). Use post offices only as a last resort, as simple transactions can take 45 minutes if you get in the wrong line. You can buy stamps from tobacco shops and mail postcards from any of the red postboxes around town.

Bookstores: Libreria Mondadori is a gorgeous bookstore that carries a huge selection of Venice books, local guidebooks, and even my guidebooks (the tourist-oriented books are on the ground floor). This is the biggest bookstore in town, with plenty in English and three Internet terminals (daily May–Oct 10:00–23:00, Nov–April 10:00–20:00, across from American Express a block behind Piazza San Marco at 1345 Complesso del Ridotto, tel. 041-522-2193). **Libreria Studium** stocks all of the English-language guidebooks (including mine) and is located just a block behind St. Mark's Basilica (Mon–Sat 9:00–19:30, shorter hours Sun, Calle de la Canonica, tel. 041-522-2382).

Laundry: These two laundry options are near San Marco, but your hotelier can direct you to one near your hotel: A modern **self-service** *lavanderia* is on Ruga Giuffa at #4826 (wring clothes before drying, or you'll bring them home damp; June–Sept daily 8:30–20:00, shorter hours Oct–May, next to recommended Hotel al Piave—see page 90, mobile 347-870-6452, run by Massimo). **Lavanderia Gabriella** offers full service (€15/load wash and dry, Mon–Fri 8:00–12:30, closed Sat–Sun; with your back to the door of San Zulian Church, go over Ponte dei Ferali, then take first right down Calle dei Armeni, then first left on Rio Terra Colonne to #985; tel. 041-522-1758, Elisabetta).

Travel Agencies: If you need to get train tickets, make seat reservations, or arrange a *cucetta* (koo-CHET-tah—a berth on a night train), you can avoid a time-consuming trip to the crowded train station by using a downtown travel agency. They can also give advice on cheap flights. Note that you'll get a far better price if you're able to book at least a week in advance. Consider booking flights for later in your trip while you're here.

American Express books flights, sells train tickets, and makes train reservations (Mon–Fri 9:00–17:30, closed Sat–Sun, about 2 blocks off St. Mark's Square en route to Accademia at Salizada San Moisè, 1471 San Marco, tel. 041-520-0844). Avoid their €5 phone card, which only buys you about a third as many minutes as similar cards sold by corner newsstands—one more thing to erode the trust they've earned over the decades.

Oltrex, just one bridge past the Bridge of Sighs, sells train and plane tickets and happily books train reservations for a €2 fee (daily 9:00–19:00, Riva degli Schiavoni 4192, tel. 041-524-2828).

English Church Services: The **San Zulian Church** (the only church in Venice that you can actually walk around) offers a Mass in English (generally Mon–Fri at 9:30 and Sun at 11:30 May–Sept, Sun only Oct–April, 2 blocks toward Rialto off St. Mark's Square).

Haircuts: I've been getting my hair cut at **Coiffeur Benito** for 16 years. Benito has been keeping local men and women trim for 26 years. He's an artist—actually a "hair sculptor"—and a cut here is a fun diversion from the tourist grind (€20 for women, €18 for men, Tue–Fri 8:30–13:00 & 15:30–19:30, Sat 8:30–13:00 only, closed Sun–Mon, behind San Zulian Church near St. Mark's Square, Calle S. Zulian Già del Strazzariol 592a, tel. 041-528-6221).

Getting Around Venice

On Foot: Navigate by major landmarks. There are signs on street corners all over town pointing to San Marco, Accademia, Ferrovia (train station), and Piazzale Roma (the bus stop behind the train station). Determine if your destination is in the direction of a major signposted landmark, then follow the signs through the maze of squares, lanes, and bridges.

By Vaporetto: The public-transit system is a fleet of motorized bus-boats called *vaporetti*. They work like city buses, except that they never get a flat, the stops are docks, and if you get off between stops, you might drown.

For most travelers, only two lines matter: #1 is the slow boat, which takes 45 minutes to make every stop along the entire length  of the Grand Canal (leaves every 10 min); #82 is the fast boat that zips down the Grand Canal in 25 minutes (leaves every 10 min), stopping at Tronchetto (parking lot), Piazzale Roma (bus station), Ferrovia (train station), Rialto Bridge, San Tomà (Frari Church), Accademia Bridge, San Marco (west end of St. Mark's Square), San Zaccaria (east end of St. Mark's Square), and on to San Giorgio Maggiore. Some #82 boats go only as far as Rialto *(solo Rialto)*—check with the conductor before boarding.

It's a simple system, but there are a few quirks. Some stops have just one dock for boats going in both directions, so make sure the boat you get on is pointing in the direction that you want to go. Larger stops have two docks side by side (one for each direction), while some smaller stops have docks across the canal from each other (one for each direction). Check the signs to find the right dock. Electronic reader boards on busy docks display which boats are coming next and when. Signs on board indicate upcoming stops.

Some lines don't run early or late. For example, off-season the #82 fast vaporetto doesn't leave the San Marco–Vallaresso dock (at St. Mark's Square) until 9:15 (and runs only until 20:30); if you're trying to get from St. Mark's Square to the train station to catch an early train, you'd need to take a different fast boat that loops outside the Grand Canal. If there's any doubt, ask a ticket-seller or conductor. If you plan to ride a lot of *vaporetti*, consider picking up the most current ACTV timetable (free at ticket booths, in English and Italian, www.actv.it).

Standard single **tickets** are €6 each (a few shorter runs are only €2, such as the route from San Marco–Vallaresso to San Giorgio Maggiore and La Salute). Tickets are good for 60 minutes in one direction; you can hop on and off at stops during that time. Technically, you're not allowed a round-trip (though in practice, a round-trip is allowed if you can complete it within a 60-minute span). Buy tickets at the dock from ticket booths or from a conductor on board (do it before you sit down, or you risk being fined €30). Oversize luggage can cost a second ticket—but light packers have no worries.

You can also buy a **pass** for unlimited use of *vaporetti* and ACTV buses (sold in 12-hour increments—€13/12 hrs, €15/24 hrs, and so on up to €30/72 hrs). Since single tickets cost a hefty €6 a pop, these passes can pay for themselves in a hurry. And it's fun to be able to hop on and off spontaneously. On the other hand, many just walk and rarely use a boat—before buying a pass, look at a map to see how far afield your likely destinations are.

Passes must be stamped before the first use. Tickets generally come already stamped, but if for whatever reason, your ticket lacks a stamp, stick it into the time-stamping yellow machine before boarding. Riding free? There's a one-in-ten chance a conductor will fine you €30.

For vaporetto fun, take the Grand Canal Cruise (see page 50). During rush hour (about 9:00 from the Tronchetto parking lot and train station toward St. Mark's, about 17:00 in the other direction), boats are jam-packed. If you like joyriding on *vaporetti*, ride a boat around the city and out into the lagoon, then over to the Lido, and back. Ask for the circular route—*circulare* (cheer-koo-LAH-ray). It's usually the #51 or #52, leaving from the San Zaccaria–Danieli vaporetto stop (near the Doge's Palace) and from all the stops along the perimeter of Venice.

By *Traghetto*: Only three bridges cross the Grand Canal (though a fourth should be open by 2008), but *traghetti* (gondolas) shuttle locals and in-the-know tourists across the Grand Canal at

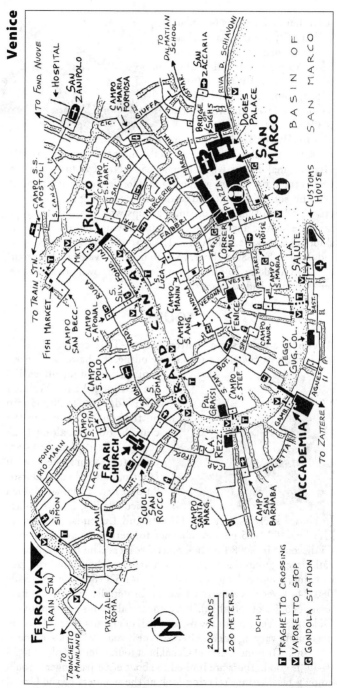

seven handy locations (see map on page 51; routes also marked on pricier maps sold in Venice). Most people stand while riding (€0.50, generally run 6:00–20:00, sometimes until 23:00, though a few run only until 14:00).

By Water Taxi: Venetian taxis, like speedboat limos, hang out at most busy points along the Grand Canal. Prices, which average €50 (about €90 to the airport, €50 to the train station, with extra fees for very early or late runs), are a bit soft. Negotiate and settle before stepping in. For travelers with lots of luggage or small groups who can split the cost, taxi rides can be a worthwhile and time-saving convenience—and skipping across the lagoon in a classic wooden motorboat is a cool indulgence. For €80 an hour, you can have a private taxi boat tour.

By Gondola: To hire a gondolier for your own private cruise, see "Gondola Rides," page 79.

TOURS

Avventure Bellissime Venice Tours—This company offers a selection of two-hour walks, including the basic St. Mark's

Square introduction called the "Original Venice Walking Tour" (daily at 11:00; 45 min on the square, 15 min in the church, 60 min along back streets). Their other walks are Cannaregio and the Jewish Ghetto; San Polo and Dorsoduro (called "Original Hidden Venice Walk"); Doge's Palace (includes secret itinerary); Ghosts and Legends; and Secret Gardens (€20–25/person, cheaper for returnees and students, €5 discount in 2008 for Rick Steves' readers who book online or call direct, group size 8–20, most tours last 2 hours and run rain or shine, English-language only, tel. 041-520-8616, mobile 340-050-2444, see www.tours-italy.com for details, info@tours-italy.com, Monica or Jonathan). The company also runs day trips to the Dolomites, Veneto hill towns, and Palladian villa tours (8-person maximum, varying prices, €10 discount if you say "Rick sent me").

Their 70-minute Grand Canal boat tour, offered daily at 16:30 (€40), is good. Tours are limited to about eight passengers. You'll enjoy a fascinating, relaxing look at the wonders of the Grand

Canal as well as the intimate back canals with a motor-mouthed (and interesting) guide. The departure is timed to give photographers the best possible light.

Classic Venice Bars Tour—Debonair local guide Alessandro Schezzini is a connoisseur of Venetian *bacari*—classic old bars serving traditional *cicchetti* (local munchies). He offers evening tours that include sampling a snack and a glass of wine at three different *bacari,* and he'll answer all of your questions about Venice (€30/person with this book in 2008, March–Nov, generally Mon, Wed, and Fri at 18:00, other evenings and off-season by request and with demand, 6–8 per group, meet at top of Rialto Bridge, call or email a day or two in advance to confirm, mobile 335-530-9024, venische@libero.it).

Venicescapes—Michael Broderick's private theme tours of Venice are intellectually demanding and beyond the attention span of most mortal tourists. Rather than a "sightseeing tour," consider your time with Michael a rolling, graduate-level lecture. Michael's objective: to help visitors gain a more solid understanding of Venice. For a description of his various itineraries, see www.venicescapes .org (book well in advance, tours last 4–6 hours: €275 for 2 people, €50/person after that, plus admissions and transportation, tel. 041-520-6361, info@venicescapes.org).

Local Guides—Licensed guides are carefully trained and love explaining Venice to visitors. The following companies and guides give excellent tours to individuals, families, and small groups. If you organize a small group from your hotel at breakfast to split the cost (€65/hr with 2-hour minimum), the fee becomes quite reasonable.

    Elisabetta Morelli is reliable, personable, and informative, giving good insight into daily life in Venice (€65/hr with this book in 2008, tours last 2–3 hours, tel. 041-526-7816, mobile 328-753-5220, bettamorelli@inwind.it).

    Venice with a Guide is a co-op of 10 equally good guides (www.venicewithaguide.com).

    Walks Inside Venice is a group of three women who are enthusiastic about teaching (€75/hr per group, 3-hour min; Cristina: mobile 348-341-5421; Roberta: mobile 347-253-0560; Sara: mobile 335-522-9714; www.walksinsidevenice.com, info @walksinsidevenice.com).

    Alessandro Schezzini isn't a licensed Italian guide (and is therefore unable to take you into actual sights), but he does a great job getting you beyond the clichés and into offbeat Venice. He offers a relaxed, two-hour, backstreet "Rick Steves-style" tour (€15/person, March–Nov, generally Mon, Wed, and Fri, meet at 16:00 at top of Rialto Bridge, call to confirm, mobile 335-530-9024, venische@libero.it). You can take this offbeat walk, and then join

Alessandro for the pub crawl immediately afterwards (see "Classic Venice Bars Tour," on previous page). Alessandro also gives private tours to groups of any size at any time (€90/2.5 hrs).

SELF-GUIDED CRUISE

▲▲▲ Welcome to Venice Grand Canal Cruise

Introduce yourself to Venice by boat. Cruise the Canal Grande all the way to San Marco, starting from Tronchetto (parking lot),

Piazzale Roma (where the airport bus stops), or Ferrovia (train station). You can ride boat #1 (slow and ideal, 45 min) or #82 (too fast to comfortably follow this tour, 25 min). When catching either boat, confirm that you're on a "San Marco via Rialto" boat (some boats finish at the Rialto Bridge, others take a non-scenic outside route). The conductor announces *"Solo Rialto!"* for boats going only as far as Rialto. You do not want boats heading for Piazzale Roma. Note that the San Marco vaporetto stop is actually called San Marco–Vallaresso.

Enjoy the best light and fewest crowds early or late. Sunset bathes the buildings in gold. After dark, chandeliers light up the building interiors. While Venice is a barrage on the senses that hardly needs a narration, these notes give the cruise a little meaning and help orient you to this great city. Some city maps (on sale at postcard racks) have a handy Grand Canal map on the back.

Overview

The Grand Canal is Venice's "Main Street." At more than two miles long, nearly 150 feet wide, and nearly 15 feet deep, it's the city's largest canal, lined with its most impressive palaces. The canal is the remnant of a river that once spilled from the mainland into the Adriatic. The sediment it carried formed barrier islands that cut Venice off from the sea, forming a lagoon. Venice was built on the marshy islands of the former delta,  sitting on pilings driven nearly 15 feet into the clay.

Venice is a city of palaces, dating from the days when Venice was the world's richest city. The most lavish palaces formed a grand chorus line along the Grand Canal. Once frescoed in reds and

Venice's Grand Canal

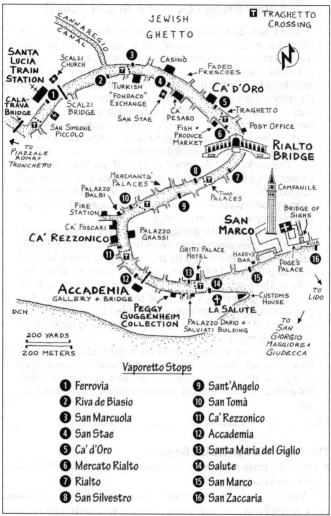

Vaporetto Stops

1. Ferrovia
2. Riva de Biasio
3. San Marcuola
4. San Stae
5. Ca' d'Oro
6. Mercato Rialto
7. Rialto
8. San Silvestro
9. Sant'Angelo
10. San Tomà
11. Ca' Rezzonico
12. Accademia
13. Santa Maria del Giglio
14. Salute
15. San Marco
16. San Zaccaria

blues, with black-and-white borders and gold-leaf trim, they made Venice a city of dazzling color. This cruise is the only way to really appreciate the palaces, approaching them at water level, where their main entrances were located. Today, strict laws prohibit any changes in these buildings, so while landowners gnash their teeth, we can enjoy Europe's best-preserved medieval city—slowly rotting. Many of the grand buildings are now vacant. Others harbor chandeliered elegance above mossy, empty (often flooded) ground floors.

A New Bridge Over the Grand Canal?

Venice's new **Calatrava Bridge,** slated for completion by 2008, is a modern structure of glass, steel, and stone. Only the fourth bridge to cross the Grand Canal, it links—or will link—the train station with Piazzale Roma. Many Venetians wonder whether it'll be done on time...if at all. Sections of the bridge are being constructed in a nearby warehouse and, once completed, will be ferried to their place and assembled. Skeptics doubt that some sections of the span of the bridge (just under 310 feet total) will be able to squeeze through Venice's narrow canals and tight corners.

The bridge was designed by Spanish architect Santiago Calatrava, whose other projects include the City of Arts and Sciences Museum in his hometown of Valencia, Spain, the twisting torso skyscraper in Malmö, Sweden, and the Olympic sports complex in Athens, Greece.

This controversial bridge draws snorts from Venetians, who have been waiting two years for its inauguration while construction was delayed by politics and finances. With an original price tag of €4 million, the cost is currently about €6.5 million. The modern design of the bridge is also a sore point for a city with such rich medieval and Renaissance architecture—but Calatrava's structure is intended to "bridge" the old traditions of the city with modern forms, using local Istrian stone to smooth the transition.

Adding fuel to the controversy is the fact that the sleek form does not allow for wheelchair access, which would clutter up the lines of the bridge. Critics also question whether it'll withstand the hordes of tourists crossing it daily. Time will tell.

The Grand Canal Cruise Begins

Start at the **train station** or **Tronchetto** parking lot. We'll orient by the vaporetto stops.

Venice's main thoroughfare is busy with all kinds of **boats:** taxis, police boats, garbage boats, ambulances, construction cranes, and even brown-and-white UPS boats. Venice's sleek, black, graceful **gondolas** are a symbol of the city. The boats run about €35,000–50,000, depending on your options (air-con, cup holders, etc). Today, with more than 400 gondoliers joyriding amid the churning *vaporetti*, there's a lot of congestion on the Grand Canal. Watch your vaporetto driver curse the better-paid gondoliers.

Ferrovia: The **Santa Lucia train station** (on the left bank of the canal), one of the few modern buildings in town, was built in 1954. It's been the gateway into Venice since 1860, when the first

station was built. "F.S." stands for "Ferrovie dello Stato," the Italian state railway system.

More than 20,000 people commute in from mainland each day, making this the busiest part of Venice during rush hour. To alleviate some of the congestion and make the commute easier, a new **bridge** (slated to be finished by 2008) will span the Grand Canal between the train station and Piazzale Roma, behind you.

Opposite the train station, atop the green dome of **San Simeone Piccolo** church, St. Simeon waves *ciao* to whomever enters or leaves the "old" city.

Riva di Biasio: About 25 yards past the Riva di Biasio stop, you'll look left down the broad **Cannaregio Canal** to see what was the **Jewish ghetto** (see page 75). The twin, pale-pink, six-story "skyscrapers"—the tallest buildings you'll see at this end of the canal—are reminders of how densely populated the world's original ghetto was. Set aside as the local Jewish quarter in 1516, this area became extremely crowded. This urban island developed into one of the most closely knit business and cultural quarters of all the Jewish communities in Italy, and gave us our word ghetto (from *geto*, the copper foundry located here). For more information, visit the Jewish Museum in this neighborhood (see page 75).

San Marcuola: The stately gray **Turkish "Fondaco" Exchange** (right side, opposite San Marcuola vaporetto stop) is one of the oldest houses in Venice. Its horseshoe arches and roofline of triangles and dingleballs are reminders of its Byzantine heritage. Turkish traders in turbans docked here, unloaded their goods into the warehouse on the bottom story, then went upstairs for a home-style meal and a place to

sleep. Venice in the 1500s was very cosmopolitan, welcoming every religion and ethnicity, so long as they carried cash. (Today, the building contains the city's Museum of Natural History—and Venice's only dinosaur.)

Venice's **Casinò** (100 yards ahead on the left) is housed in the palace where German composer Richard *(The Ring of the Nibelung)* Wagner died in 1883. See his distinct, strong-jawed profile in the white plaque on the brick wall. In the 1700s, Venice was Europe's Las Vegas, with casinos and prostitutes everywhere. *Casinòs* ("little houses") have long provided Italians with a handy escape from daily life. Today, they're run by the state to keep Mafia influence at bay. Notice the fancy front porch, rolling out the red carpet for high rollers arriving by taxi or hotel boat.

San Stae: Opposite the San Stae stop, look for the peeling plaster that once made up **frescoes** (scant remains on the lower floors). Imagine the facades of the Grand Canal at their finest. As colorful as the city is today, it's still only a sepia-toned remnant of a long-gone era, a time of lavishly decorated and brilliantly colored palaces.

Just ahead, jutting out a bit on the right, is the ornate white facade of **Ca' Pesaro.** *"Ca'"* is short for *casa* (house). Because only the house of the doge (Venetian ruler) could be called a palazzo (palace), all other Venetian palaces are technically *"Ca'."*

Look back as you pass Ca' Pesaro (which houses the International Gallery of Modern Art—see page 72). It's the only building you'll see with a fine side facade. Ahead, on the left, with its glorious triple-decker medieval arcade (just before the next stop) is Ca' d'Oro.

Ca' d'Oro: The lacy **Ca' d'Oro,** or "House of Gold" (left bank, just before the vaporetto stop), is the best example of Venetian Gothic architecture on the canal. Its three stories offer different variations on balcony design, topped with a spiny white roofline. Venetian Gothic mixes traditional Gothic (pointed arches and round medallions stamped with a four-leaf clover) with Byzantine styles (tall, narrow arches atop thin columns), filled in with Islamic frills. Like all the palaces, this was originally painted and gilded

to make it even more glorious than it is now. Today, the Ca' d'Oro is an art gallery (see page 75).

On the right is the arcade of the covered **fish market,** with the **produce market** just beyond. It bustles with people in the morning but is quiet the rest of the day. This is a great scene to wander through—even though European hygiene standards

required a remodeling job that left it cleaner...but less colorful. Find the *traghetto* gondola ferrying shoppers—standing like Washington crossing the Delaware—back and forth.

Mercato Rialto: This new stop was opened in 2007 to serve the busy market (boats stop here 8:00–20:00). Straight ahead, in the distance, rising above the huge post office, you can see the tip of the Campanile (bell tower) crowned by its golden angel at St. Mark's Square, where this tour will end. The **post office** (100 yards directly ahead, on left side, often with *servizio postale* boats moored at its blue posts, was the German Exchange, the trading center for German metal merchants, in the early 1500s.

You'll cruise by some trendy and beautifully situated wine bars on right, but look ahead as you round the corner and see the impressive Rialto Bridge come into view.

A major landmark of Venice, the **Rialto Bridge** is lined with shops and tourists. Constructed in 1588, it's the third bridge built on this spot. Until the 1850s, this was the only bridge crossing the

Grand Canal. With a span of 160 feet and foundations stretching 650 feet on either side, the Rialto was an impressive engineering feat in its day. Earlier Rialto Bridges could open to let big ships in, but not this one. When this new bridge was completed, much of the Grand Canal was closed to shipping and became a canal of palaces.

Rialto, a separate town in the early days of Venice, has always been the commercial district, while San Marco was the religious and governmental center. Today, a winding street called the Mercerie connects the two, providing travelers with human traffic jams and a mesmerizing gauntlet of shopping temptations. The restaurants that line the canal feature great views, midrange prices, and low-quality food.

Ahead 100 yards on the left, two palaces stand side by side (the city hall and the mayor's office). Their arched windows are similar and their stories are the same height, creating the effect of one long balcony.

San Silvestro: We now enter a long stretch of important

merchants' palaces, each with proud and different facades. Since ships couldn't navigate beyond the Rialto Bridge, the biggest palaces—with the major shipping needs—line this last stretch of the navigable Grand Canal.

Palaces like these were multifunctional: ground floor for the warehouse, offices and showrooms upstairs, and the living quarters above the offices on the "noble floor" (with big windows designed to allow in maximum light). Servants lived and worked on the top floors (with the smallest windows).

Sant'Angelo: Notice how many buildings have a foundation of waterproof white stone *(pietra d'Istria)* upon which the bricks sit high and dry. Many canal-level floors are abandoned as the rising water level takes its toll. The **posts**—historically painted gaily with the equivalent of family coats of arms—don't rot under water. But the wood at the waterline, where it's exposed to oxygen, does.

San Tomà: Fifty yards ahead, on the right side (with twin obelisks on the rooftop) stands the **Palazzo Balbi,** the palace of an early 17th-century captain general of the sea. These Venetian equivalents of five-star admirals were honored with twin obelisks decorating their palaces. This palace flies three flags: those of Italy (green-white-red), the European Union (blue with ring of stars), and Venice (the lion). Today, it houses the administrative headquarters of the regional government.

Look around the corner, behind the admiral's palace down a side canal. On the right of that canal, before the bridge, see the traffic light and the **fire station** (with four arches hiding fireboats parked and ready to go).

The impressive **Ca' Foscari,** with a classic Venetian facade (on the corner, across from the fire station) dominates the bend in the canal. This is the main building of the University of Venice, which has about 25,000 students. Notice the elegant lamp on the corner.

The grand, heavy, white **Ca' Rezzonico,** just before the next stop (of the same name), houses the Museum of 18th-Century Venice (see page 72). Across the canal (and a bit behind you) is the cleaner and leaner **Palazzo Grassi,** the last major palace built on the canal, erected in the late 1700s—recently purchased by a French tycoon.

Ca' Rezzonico: Up ahead, the **Accademia Bridge** leads over the Grand Canal to the **Accademia** art museum (right side), filled with the best Venetian paintings (see page 71). The bridge was put up in 1934 as a temporary one. Locals liked it, so it stayed.

Accademia: Look through the graceful bridge and way ahead to enjoy a classic view of the domed **La Salute Church** (unless it's under scaffolding in 2008; church described on page 72). This Church of Saint Mary of Good Health was built to thank God for delivering Venetians from the devastating plague of 1630 (which had killed about a third of the city's population).

The low white building among greenery (100 yards ahead, on the right, between the Accademia Bridge and the church) is the **Peggy Guggenheim Collection.** The American heiress "retired" here, sprucing up the palace that had been abandoned in mid-construction. Peggy willed the city her fine collection of modern art (described on page 72).

Santa Maria del Giglio: Back on the left stands the fancy Gritti Palace hotel (Ernest Hemingway and Woody Allen both stayed here).

Take a deep whiff of Venice. What's all this nonsense about stinky canals? All I smell is my shirt. By the way, how's your captain? Smooth dockings? To get to know him, stand up in the bow and block his view.

Salute: The huge La Salute Church, towering overhead as if squirted from a can of Catholic Cool Whip, like Venice itself, rests upon pilings. To build the foundation for the city, more than a million trees were piled together, reaching below the mud to the solid clay.

As the Grand Canal opens up into the lagoon, the last building on the right with the golden ball is the 17th-century **Customs House** (due to open to the public in 2009 as a contemporary art gallery). Its two bronze Atlases hold a statue of Fortune riding the ball. Arriving ships stopped here to pay their tolls.

San Marco: Look from left to right out over the lagoon. On the left, the green pointed tip of the Campanile marks **St. Mark's Square** (the political and religious center of Venice). A wide harborfront walk leads past the town's most elegant hotels to the green area in the distance. This is the public garden, the largest of Venice's few parks, which hosts the Biennale art show (held in odd years, next one in 2009). Farther in the distance is the **Lido,** the island with Venice's beach. It's tempting, with sand and casinos, but its car traffic intrudes on the medieval charm of Venice.

Opposite St. Mark's Square, across the water, the ghostly white church that seems to float is Andrea Palladio's **San Giorgio Maggiore.** Since your vaporetto ticket is good for an hour, consider staying on this boat for the free ride out to the church—it's worth a visit because its pointy bell tower is home to the best view in town (elevator, no lines—see listing on page 69).

Across the lagoon (to your right) is the residential island called **Giudecca,** which stretches from close to San Giorgio Maggiore past the Venice youth hostel (with a nice view, directly across) to the new Hilton Hotel (no view, far right end of island).

Cruising on, you pass (with the towering Campanile gliding behind) the bold facade of the old mint (where Venice's golden ducat, the dollar of the Venetian Republic, was made) and the library facade. Then St. Theodore and St. Mark appear, standing atop their twin columns as they have since the 15th and 16th centuries, when they welcomed VIP guests who arrived by sea to the most important square in Europe: Piazza San Marco. In the distance you can see two giant figures standing on the **Clock Tower.** They've been whacking the hour regularly since 1499. The busy domed features of **St. Mark's Basilica** are eclipsed by the lacy yet powerful facade of the **Doge's Palace.** As you cruise, look to the back side of the Doge's Palace where the **Bridge of Sighs**—leading from the palace to the prison—comes into view. The bridge in front of it is generally packed with tourists sighing at that legendary sky walk. Beyond that, to the right, begins that grand harborside promenade, the **Riva.**

San Zaccaria: Okay, you're at your last stop. Quick—muscle your way off this boat!

This boat makes three more stops before crossing the lagoon to the Lido—stay on the boat if you want to head out to San Giorgio Maggiore.

SIGHTS

San Marco District

For information on Venice's Museum Card and pricier Museum Pass, which cover most of the sights on the square, see page 40.

▲▲▲**St. Mark's Square (Piazza San Marco)**—This grand square is surrounded by splashy, historic buildings and sights (each one described in more detail below): St. Mark's Basilica, the Doge's Palace, the Campanile (bell tower), and the Correr Museum. The square is filled with music, lovers, pigeons, and tourists by day, and is your private rendezvous with the Venetian past late at night, when Europe's most magnificent dance floor is *the* romantic place to be.

With your back to the church, survey one of Europe's great urban spaces, and the only square in Venice to merit the title "Piazza." Nearly two football fields long, it's surrounded by the offices of the republic. On the right are the "old offices"

St. Mark's Square

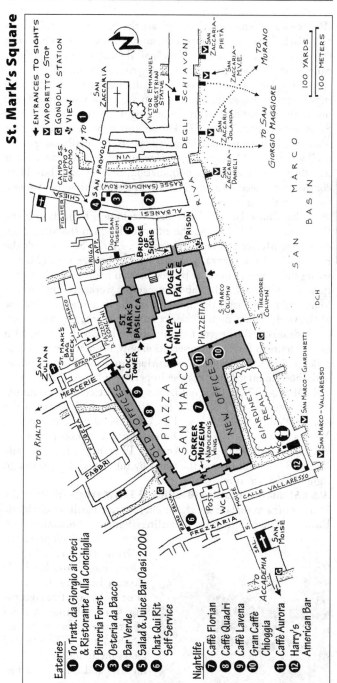

Eateries
1. To Tratt. da Giorgio ai Greci & Ristorante Alla Conchiglia
2. Birreria Forst
3. Osteria da Bacco
4. Bar Verde
5. Salad & Juice Bar Oasi 2000
6. Chat Qui Rit Self Service

Nightlife
7. Caffè Florian
8. Caffè Quadri
9. Caffè Lavena
10. Gran Caffè Chioggia
11. Caffè Aurora
12. Harry's American Bar

ENTRANCES TO SIGHTS
- Vaporetto Stop
- Gondola Station
- View

Venice

(16th-century Renaissance). At left are the "new offices" (17th-century High Renaissance). Napoleon, after enclosing the square with the more simple and austere Neoclassical wing across the far end, called this "the most beautiful drawing room in Europe."

For a slow and pricey evening thrill, invest about €15 (including the cover charge for the music) in a glass of wine or coffee at one of the elegant cafés with the dueling orchestras (see "Cafés on St. Mark's Square," page 63). For an unmatched experience that offers the best people-watching, it's worth the small splurge. But if all you have is €1, buy a bag of pigeon feed and become popular in a flurry. (To control the poopulation, the city adds bird birth control to the feed.) To get the flock to flutter airborne, toss your sweater in the air.

The **Clock Tower** (Torre dell'Orologio), built during the Renaissance in 1496, marks the entry to the main shopping drag, called the Mercerie, which connects St. Mark's Square with the Rialto. From the piazza, you can see the bronze men (Moors) swing their huge clappers at the top of each hour. In the 17th century, one of them knocked an unsuspecting worker off the top and to his death—probably the first-ever killing by a robot. Notice one of the world's first "digital" clocks on the tower facing the square (with dramatic flips every five minutes). The Clock Tower, with guided tours in English by reservation only, is not worth the headache to visit (€12, includes Correr Museum, Mon–Wed mornings and Thu-Sun afternoons; reserve in person at Correr Museum, or call 041-520-9070, or book online at www.museiciviciveneziani.it).

Venice's best **TI** is in the far-left (southwest) corner of the square (daily 9:00–15:30), and a €1 WC is 30 yards beyond St. Mark's Square (see *Albergo Diorno* sign marked on pavement, WC open daily 9:00–17:30). Another TI is on the lagoon (daily 10:00–18:00, walk toward the water by the Doge's Palace and go right, €1 WCs nearby).

▲▲▲St. Mark's Basilica (Basilica di San Marco)—Built in the 11th century to replace an earlier church, this basilica's distinctly Eastern-style architecture underlines Venice's connection with

Byzantium (which protected it from the ambition of Charlemagne and his Holy Roman Empire). It's decorated with booty from returning sea captains—a kind of architectural Venetian trophy chest. The interior glows mysteriously with gold mosaics and colored marble. Since about A.D. 830, the

saint's bones have been housed on this site.

Cost, Hours, Information: Basilica entry is free, open Mon–Sat 9:45–17:00 (until 16:30 off-season), Sun 14:00–16:00, tel. 041-522-5205. Lines can be long, the dress code is strictly enforced, and bag check is mandatory, free, and can save you time in line; for details, see below. No photos are allowed inside. Three separate exhibits inside each charge admission: the **Treasury** (€2, includes audioguide, same hours as church), the **Golden Altarpiece** (€2, same hours as church), and the **San Marco Museum** (€3, Mon–Sat 9:45–16:30, Sun 9:45–16:00).

Bag Check: While small purses are allowed inside the church, larger bags and backpacks are not. Check them for free at the nearby Ateneo San Basso, a former church (open roughly Mon–Sat 9:30–17:30, Sun 14:00–16:30; head to the left of basilica, down narrow Calle San Basso, 30 yards to the second door on your right; see map on page 62 for location).

Those with a bag to check actually get to skip the line. Here's how it works: Drop by Ateneo San Basso. Leave your bag (for up to one hour) and pick up the claim tag. Two people per tag are allowed to go to the basilica's gatekeeper, present the tag, and scoot directly in, ahead of the line. After touring the church, come back and pick up your bag.

Dress Code: To enter the church, modest dress is required even of kids (no shorts or bare shoulders). People who ignore the dress code hold up the line while they plead fruitlessly with the dress-code police.

Theft Alert: St. Mark's Basilica is the most dangerous place in Venice for pickpocketing—inside, it's always a crowded jostle.

Tours: In the atrium, see the schedule board that lists free English guided tours (schedules vary, but generally May–Oct Tue, Wed, and Thu at 11:00, 1 hour, meet guide just to the right of main doors).

Inside the Church: St. Mark's Basilica has 43,000 square feet of Byzantine mosaics, the best and oldest of which are in the atrium (turn right as you enter and stop under the last dome—this may be roped off, but dome is still visible). Facing the church, gape up (it's OK, no pigeons) and read the story of Adam and Eve that rings the bottom of the dome. Now, facing the piazza, look dome-ward for the story of Noah, the ark, and the flood (two by two, the wicked being drowned, Noah sending out the dove, a happy rainbow, and a sacrifice of thanks).

Step inside the church (the stairs on the right lead to the bronze horses in the San Marco Museum, described below—save these for later). Notice how the marble floor is richly decorated in mosaics. As in many Venetian buildings, because the best foundation pilings were made around the perimeter, the floor rolls. As

St. Mark's Basilica

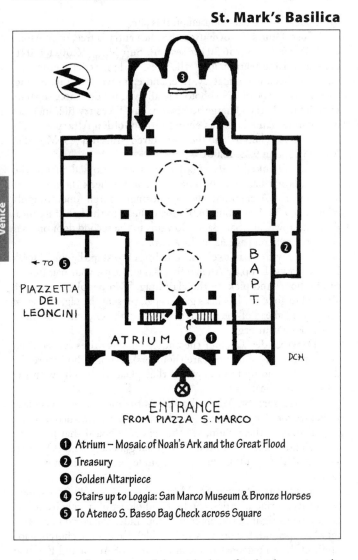

1. Atrium – Mosaic of Noah's Ark and the Great Flood
2. Treasury
3. Golden Altarpiece
4. Stairs up to Loggia: San Marco Museum & Bronze Horses
5. To Ateneo S. Basso Bag Check across Square

you shuffle under the central dome, look up for the Ascension. As you follow the one-way tourist route, consider stopping off at the Treasury and the Golden Altarpiece, described below.

Additional Sights: In the **San Marco Museum** (Museo di San Marco) upstairs, you can see an up-close mosaic exhibition, a fine view of the church interior, a view of the square from the balcony with bronze horses, and (inside, in their own room) the original horses. These well-traveled horses, made during the days of Alexander the Great (fourth century B.C.), were taken to Rome

Cafés on St. Mark's Square

Cafés line the square. All three café orchestras feature similar food, prices, and a three- or four-piece combo playing a selection of classical and pop hits, from Brahms to "Bésame Mucho." If you get just a drink, expect to pay about €15, including the cover charge. (A coffee is €3 at the bar, €6 at a table, and €12 outside when the orchestra plays.) It's perfectly acceptable to nurse a cappuccino for an hour, since you're paying for the music with the cover charge.

Caffè Florian (on the right as you face the church—see map on page 59) is the most famous Venetian café and one

 of the first places in Europe to serve coffee. It's been a popular spot for a discreet rendezvous in Venice since 1720. The orchestra plays a more classical repertoire than the other cafés. The outside tables are the main action, but do walk inside through the richly decorated, old-time rooms where Casanova, Lord Byron, Charles Dickens, and Woody Allen have all paid too much for a drink (reasonable prices at bar in back).

Caffè Quadri, exactly opposite the Florian, has an equally illustrious history of famous clientele, including the writers Stendhal and Alexandre Dumas, and composer Richard Wagner. Caffè Lavena, near the Clock Tower, is newer and less prestigious.

Gran Caffè Chioggia, on the Piazzetta facing the Doge's Palace, charges slightly less, with one or two musicians playing cocktail jazz.

Caffè Aurora, in the shadow of the Campanile, features nearly all the ambience at half the price. Enjoy coffee or gelato while listening to second-hand music from other establishments.

by Nero, to Constantinople/Istanbul by Constantine, to Venice by crusaders, to Paris by Napoleon, back "home" to Venice when Napoleon fell, and finally indoors and out of the acidic air. The staircase up to the museum is in the atrium, near the basilica's entrance, marked by a sign that says *Loggia dei Cavalli, Museo*.

San Marco's **Treasury** (ask for the included and informative audioguide when you buy ticket) and **Golden Altarpiece** give you the best chance outside of Istanbul or Ravenna to see the glories of the Byzantine Empire. Venetian crusaders looted the Christian

Venice at a Glance

▲▲▲St. Mark's Square Venice's grand main square. **Hours:** Always open.

▲▲▲St. Mark's Basilica Cathedral with mosaics, saint's bones, treasury, museum, and viewpoint of square. **Hours:** Basilica open Mon–Sat 9:45–17:00 (until 16:30 off-season), Sun 14:00–16:00; San Marco Museum open Mon–Sat 9:45–16:30, Sun 9:45–16:00.

▲▲▲Doge's Palace Art-splashed palace of former rulers, with prison accessible through Bridge of Sighs. **Hours:** Daily April–Oct 9:00–19:00, Nov–March 9:00–17:00.

▲▲▲Rialto Bridge Distinctive bridge spanning the Grand Canal, with a market nearby for locals and tourists. **Hours:** Bridge—always open; market—souvenir stalls open daily, produce market closed Sun, fish market closed Sun–Mon.

▲▲Correr Museum Venetian history and art. **Hours:** Daily April–Oct 9:00–19:00, Nov–March 9:00–17:00.

▲▲Accademia Venice's top art museum. **Hours:** Mon 8:15–14:00, Tue–Sun 8:15–19:15.

▲▲Peggy Guggenheim Collection Popular display of 20th-century art. **Hours:** Wed–Mon 10:00–18:00, closed Tue.

▲▲Frari Church Franciscan church featuring Renaissance masters. **Hours:** Mon–Sat 10:00–18:00, Sun 13:00–18:00 (closed Sun in Aug).

▲▲Scuola San Rocco "Tintoretto's Sistine Chapel." **Hours:** Daily April–Oct 9:00–17:30, Nov–March 10:00–17:00.

▲Campanile Dramatic bell tower on St. Mark's Square with elevator to top. **Hours:** Daily July–Aug 9:00–21:00, Sept–June 9:00–19:00.

▲Bridge of Sighs Famous enclosed bridge, part of Doge's Palace, near St. Mark's Square. **Hours:** Always viewable.

▲San Giorgio Maggiore Island across the lagoon, featuring church with Palladio architecture, Tintoretto paintings, and fine views back on Venice. **Hours:** Daily May–Sept 9:00–12:00 & 14:30–18:30, Oct–April 9:30–12:45 & 14:30–17:00, closed to sightseers Sun 11:00–12:00 during Mass.

Venice

▲La Salute Church Striking church dedicated to the Virgin Mary. **Hours:** Church—daily 9:00–12:15 & 14:30–17:30; sacristy—Mon–Sat 10:00–12:00 & 15:00–17:00, Sun 15:00–17:00.

▲Ca' Rezzonico Posh Grand Canal palazzo with 18th-century Venetian art. **Hours:** April–Oct Wed–Mon 10:00–18:00, Nov–March Wed–Mon 10:00–17:00, closed Tue.

▲Ca' Pesaro International modern art gallery in a canalside palazzo. **Hours:** April–Oct Tue–Sun 10:00–18:00, Nov–March Tue–Sun 10:00–17:00, closed Mon.

▲Dalmatian School Exquisite Renaissance meeting house. **Hours:** Tue–Sat 9:15–13:00 & 14:15–18:00, Sun 9:15–13:00, closed Mon.

Church of San Zaccaria Final resting place of St. Zechariah (San Zaccaria), plus a Bellini altarpiece and an eerie crypt. **Hours:** Mon–Sat 10:00–12:00 & 16:00–18:00, Sun 16:00–18:00 only.

Church of San Polo Ninth-century church with works by Tintoretto, Veronese, and Tiepolo. **Hours:** Mon–Sat 10:00–17:00, closed Sun.

Jewish Ghetto Neighborhood and Jewish Museum. **Hours:** Museum open June–Sept Sun–Fri 10:00–17:00, Oct–May Sun–Fri 10:00–16:30, closed Sat and Jewish holidays.

Ca' d'Oro Venetian Gothic palace with temporary exhibits, fronting the Grand Canal. **Hours:** Mon 8:15–14:00, Tue–Sun 8:15–19:15.

Murano Island famous for glass factories and glassmaking museum. **Hours:** Glass museum open April–Oct Thu–Tue 10:00–18:00, Nov–March Thu–Tue 10:00–17:00, closed Wed.

Burano Sleepy lacemaking island with lace museum. **Hours:** Lace museum open April–Oct Wed–Mon 10:00–17:00, Nov–March Wed–Mon 10:00–16:00, closed Tue.

Torcello Near-deserted island with old church, bell tower, and museum. **Hours:** Most sights open daily March–Oct 10:30–18:00, Nov–Feb 10:00–16:30, museum closed Mon.

Venice

city of Constantinople and brought home piles of lavish loot (perhaps the lowest point in Christian history until the advent of TV evangelism). Much of this plunder is stored in the Treasury (Tesoro) of San Marco. As you view these treasures, remember that most were made in about A.D. 500, while Western Europe was stuck in the Dark Ages. Beneath the high altar lies the body of St. Mark ("Marce") and the Golden Altarpiece (Pala d'Oro), made of 250 blue-backed enamels with religious scenes, all set in a gold frame and studded with 15 hefty rubies, 300 emeralds, 1,500 pearls, and assorted sapphires, amethysts, and topaz (c. 1100).

▲▲▲**Doge's Palace (Palazzo Ducale)**—The seat of the Venetian government and home of its ruling duke, or doge (dohzh), this was the most powerful half-acre in Europe for 400 years. The Doge's Palace was built to show off the power and wealth of the Republic. In typical Venetian Gothic style, the bottom has pointy arches and the top has an Eastern or Islamic flavor. Its columns sat on pedestals, but in the thousand years since they were erected, the palace has settled into the mud and the bases have vanished.

Enjoy the newly restored facades from the **courtyard.** Notice a grand staircase (with nearly naked Moses and Paul Newman at the top). Even the most powerful visitors climbed this to meet the doge. This was the beginning of an architectural power trip. The doge, the elected-for-life duke or leader of this "dictatorship of the aristocracy," lived with his family on the first floor near the halls of power. From his living quarters (once lavish, now sparsely furnished), you'll follow the one-way route through the public rooms of the top floor, finishing with the Bridge of Sighs and the prison. The place is wallpapered with masterpieces by Veronese and Tintoretto. Don't worry much about the great art. Enjoy the building.

In Room 12, the **Senate Hall,** the 120 senators met, debated, and passed laws. Tintoretto's large *Triumph of Venice* on the ceiling (central painting, best viewed from the top) shows the city in all its glory. Lady Venice is up in heaven with the Greek gods, while barbaric lesser nations swirl up to give her gifts and tribute. The **Armory**—a dazzling display originally assembled to intimidate potential adversaries—shows remnants of the military might that the empire employed to keep the East–West trade lines open (and the local economy booming). Squint out the window to see Palladio's Church of San Giorgio Maggiore and, to the left in the distance, the tiny green dome at Venice's Lido (beach).

The giant **Hall of the Grand Council** (175 feet by 80 feet, capacity 2,600) is where the entire nobility met to elect the senate and doge. Ringing the room are portraits of 76 doges (in chronological order). The one at the far end that's blacked out is the notorious Doge Marin Falier, who opposed the will of the

Grand Council in 1355. He was tried for treason, beheaded, and airbrushed from history.

On the wall over the doge's throne is Tintoretto's monster-piece, *Paradise,* the largest oil painting in the world. Christ and Mary are surrounded by a heavenly host of 500 saints. Its message to the electors who met here: Make wise decisions and you'll ultimately join that holy crowd.

Cross the covered **Bridge of Sighs** over the canal to the **prisons.** Circle the cells. Notice the carvings made by prisoners—from olden days up until 1930—on some of the stone windowsills of the cells, especially in the far corner of the building.

Cross back over the Bridge of Sighs, pausing to look through the marble-trellised windows at all of the tourists.

Cost: €13; this buys you the "Museum Card," which also includes admission to the Correr Museum and two other, lesser museums. For details on the Museum Card and the pricier Museum Pass, see page 40. If the line is long at the Doge's Palace, buy your ticket at the Correr Museum across the square. With that, you can go directly through the Doge's turnstile, skirting along to the right of the long ticket-buying line at the palace entrance.

Hours: Daily April–Oct 9:00–19:00, Nov–March 9:00–17:00, last entry 1 hour before closing.

Tours: The high-tech Palm Pilot **audioguide tour** is dry but informative (€5, 90 min, need ID or credit card for deposit). Pick it up after you pass through the turnstile after the ticket counter.

The fine **Secret Itineraries Tour,** which follows the doge's footsteps through rooms not included in the general admission price, must be booked in advance—it's best to book at least two days early in peak season (€16; includes admission only to the Doge's Palace, not the Correr Museum, too; in English at 9:55, 10:45 and 11:35; 75 min). Reserve online (www.museicivicivenezioni.it), by phone (041-520-9070 for advance reservations; 041-291-5911 for same day or day before), or show up at the information desk and hope for a free spot (unlikely at peak times).

▲▲**Correr Museum (Museo Civico Correr)**—This uncrowded museum gives you a good overview of Venetian history and art. In the Napoleon Wing, you'll see fine Neoclassical sculpture by Antonio Canova. Then peruse armor, banners, and paintings that re-create festive days of the Venetian republic. The upper floor lays out a good overview of Venetian art, including several paintings by the Bellini family, and just before the cafeteria is a room filled with traditional games. There are English descriptions and breathtaking views of St. Mark's Square throughout (covered by €13 Museum Card, which also includes the Doge's Palace—both are also covered by €18 Museum Pass, daily April–Oct 9:00–19:00, Nov–March 9:00–17:00, last entry 1 hour before closing, enter at far end of square directly opposite basilica, tel. 041-240-5211, www.museicivicineveneziani.it).

▲**Campanile (Campanile di San Marco)**—This dramatic bell tower replaced a shorter lighthouse, which was once part of the original fortress/palace that guarded the entry of the Grand Canal. The lighthouse crumbled into a pile of bricks in 1902, a thousand years after it was built. Ride the elevator 300 feet to the top of the reconstructed bell tower for the best view in Venice. For an ear-shattering experience, be on top when the bells ring (€6, daily July–Aug 9:00–21:00, Sept–June 9:00–19:00). The golden angel at the top always faces into the wind. Lines are longest at midday; beat the crowds and enjoy crisp morning air at 9:00, or try in the early evening (about 18:00).

La Fenice Opera House (Gran Teatro alla Fenice)—During Venice's glorious decline in the 18th century, this was one of seven opera houses in the city. A 1996 arson fire completely gutted the theater, but La Fenice ("The Phoenix") has risen from the ashes, thanks to an eight-year effort to rebuild the historic landmark. To see the results at their most glorious, attend an evening performance. If you tour the theater by day, you'll see a grand lobby and the theater itself—saccharine and bringing sadness to locals who remember the richness of the place before the fire (€7 entry fee includes 45-minute audioguide, generally open daily 10:00–16:00, can be closed for practice or performance, concert box office open daily 9:30–18:30, www.teatrolafenice.it).

Behind St. Mark's Basilica

Diocesan Museum (Museo Diocesano)—This little-known museum circles a peaceful Romanesque courtyard immediately behind the basilica (just before the Bridge of Sighs). It's filled with plunder from the Venetian Empire that never found a place in St. Mark's (€1 for cloister but the good stuff upstairs comes with an €8 fee, daily 10:00–18:00, tel. 041-522-9166).

▲**Bridge of Sighs**—Connecting two wings of the Doge's Palace high over a canal, this enclosed bridge was popularized by travelers in the Romantic 19th century. Supposedly, a condemned man would be led over this bridge on the way to the prison, take one last look at the glory of Venice, and sigh. While overhyped, the bridge is undeniably tingle-worthy—especially after dark, when the crowds have dispersed and it's just you and floodlit Venice. It's around the corner from the Doge's Palace: Walk toward the waterfront, turn left along the water, and look up the first canal on your left. You can actually cross the bridge (from the inside) by visiting the Doge's Palace.

Church of San Zaccaria—This historic church is home to a sometimes-waterlogged crypt, a Bellini altarpiece, a Tintoretto painting,

---

A Dying City?

Venice's population (62,000) is half of what it was 30 years ago, and people are leaving at a rate of a thousand a year. Of those who stay, 25 percent are 65 or older.

Sad, yes, but imagine raising a family here: Apartments are small, high up, and expensive. (A 1,000-square-foot studio can sell for up to a million dollars.) Humidity and occasional flooding make basic maintenance a pain. Home-improvement projects require navigating miles of red tape, and you must follow regulations intended to preserve the historical ambience. Everything is expensive, since it has to be shipped in from the mainland. You can easily get glass and tourist trinkets, but it's hard to find groceries or get your shoes fixed. Running basic errands involves lots of walking and stairs—imagine crossing over arched bridges while pushing a child in a stroller and carrying a day's worth of groceries.

Hosting more than 12 million visitors a year, Venetians are likely to be outnumbered by tourists on any given day. Despite government efforts to subsidize rents and build cheap housing, the city is losing its locals. The economy itself is thriving, thanks to tourist dollars and rich foreigners buying second homes. But the culture is dying. Even the most hopeful city planners worry that in a few decades, Venice will not be a city at all, but a museum, a cultural theme park, a decaying Disneyland.

---

and the final resting place of St. Zechariah, the father of John the Baptist (free, €1 to enter crypt, €0.50 coin to light up Bellini's altarpiece, Mon–Sat 10:00–12:00 & 16:00–18:00, Sun 16:00–18:00 only, two canals behind St. Mark's Basilica).

Across the Lagoon from St. Mark's Square

▲San Giorgio Maggiore—This is the dreamy island that you can see from the waterfront by St. Mark's Square. The striking church, designed by Andrea Palladio, features art by Tintoretto and good views of Venice (free entry to church, daily May–Sept 9:00–12:00 & 14:30–18:30, Oct–April 9:30–12:45 & 14:30–17:00, closed Sun 11:00–12:00 to sightseers during Mass, Gregorian Mass sung Mon–Sat at 8:00, Sun at 11:00). The church's bell tower costs €3 and is accessible by elevator until 30 minutes before the church closes. To reach the island from St. Mark's Square, take the five-minute vaporetto ride (€2, 6/hr) on #82 from the San Zaccaria–M.V.E. stop (the San Zaccaria dock farthest from the Bridge of Sighs, 50 yards past the big equestrian statue).

Floods

Venice floods about 100 times a year—but not because of tides (which are miniscule in the Mediterranean). It normally happens in March and November, when the winds blowing from the south (Egypt) combine with high barometric pressure over the southern Adriatic Sea to push water toward the sea's northern end.

Floods start in St. Mark's Square (the entry of the church is nearly the lowest spot in town). You might see stacked wooden benches in the square; during floods, the benches are placed end-to-end to create elevated sidewalks. If you think the square is crowded now, when it's flooded it turns into total gridlock, as all the people normally sharing the whole square jostle for space on these narrow wooden walkways. From a distance, it's quite a sight.

There are measuring devices at the outside base of the Campanile (near the exit, facing St. Mark's Square) that show the current sea level *(livello marea)*. Find the mark that shows the high-water level from the terrible floods of 1966 (waist-level, at Campanile exit). When the water level rises one meter above mean sea level, a warning siren sounds, and it repeats if a serious flood is imminent. Imagine being a Venetian and hearing the alarm. You rush home to remove your carpets and raise your furniture above the incoming saltwater. Many doorways have three-foot-high wooden or metal barriers to block the high water *(acqua alta)*, but the seawater still seeps in through floors and drains, rendering the barriers nearly useless. After the water recedes, you have to carefully clean everything it touched to minimize the damage caused by the corrosive seawater.

In 2006, the pavement around St. Mark's Square was taken up, and the entire height of the square was raised by adding a layer of sand, and then replacing the stones. If the columns along the ground floor of the Doge's Palace look stubby, it's because this process has been carried out many times over the centuries. Venice has been battling rising water levels since the fifth century. But today, with global warming, the water is winning.

Accademia Overview

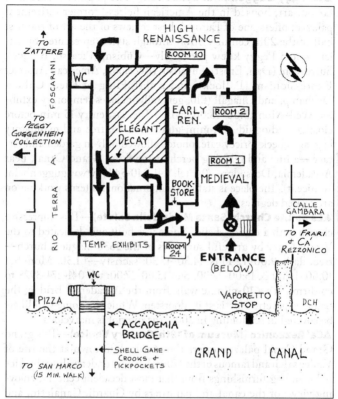

Dorsoduro District

▲▲**Accademia (Galleria dell'Accademia)**—Venice's top art museum, packed with highlights of the Venetian Renaissance, features paintings by the Bellini family, Titian, Tintoretto, Veronese, Tiepolo, Giorgione, Canaletto, and Testosterone. It's just over the wooden Accademia Bridge from the San Marco action (€6.50, Mon 8:15–14:00, Tue–Sun 8:15–19:15, last entry 30 min before closing, no photos allowed, info tel. 041-522-2247, www.gallerieaccademia .org). Expect long lines in the late morning, because they allow only 300 visitors in at a time; visit early or late to miss the crowds, or make a reservation at least a day in advance (call 041-520-0345 or visit www.gallerieaccademia.org and click *Prenotazione*). The dull audioguide costs €4 (€6 for double set or PalmPilot). One-hour guided tours in English are €5 (€7/2 people, Sat–Sun at 11:00).

At the Accademia Bridge, there's a decent canalside pizzeria (Pizzeria Accademia Foscarini—see page 105) and a public WC at the base of the bridge.

▲▲Peggy Guggenheim Collection—The popular museum of far-out art, housed in the American heiress' former retirement palazzo, offers one of Europe's best reviews of the art of the first half of the 20th century. Stroll through styles represented by artists whom Peggy knew personally—Cubism (Picasso, Braque), Surrealism (Dalí, Ernst), Futurism (Boccioni), American Abstract Expressionism (Pollock), and a sprinkling of Klee, Calder, Duchamp, and Chagall (€10, generally includes temporary exhibits, Wed–Mon 10:00–18:00, closed Tue, last entry 15 min before closing, audioguide-€7, mini-guidebook-€5, free and mandatory baggage check, pricey café, photos allowed only in garden and terrace—a fine and relaxing perch overlooking Grand Canal, near Accademia, Dorsoduro 704, tel. 041-240-5440, www.guggenheim -venice.it). The place is staffed by international interns working on art-related degrees.

▲La Salute Church (Santa Maria della Salute)—This impressive church with a crown-shaped dome was built and dedicated to the Virgin Mary by grateful survivors of the 1630 plague (church— free, daily 9:00–12:15 & 14:30–17:30; sacristy—€1.50, Mon–Sat 10:00–12:00 & 15:00–17:00, Sun 15:00–17:00; tel. 041-274-3928 to confirm). It's a 10-minute walk from the Accademia Bridge; the Salute vaporetto stop is at its doorstep. While the dome will likely be covered in scaffolding in 2008, the interior is marvelous.

▲Ca' Rezzonico (Museum of 18th-Century Venice)—This grand Grand Canal palazzo offers the best look in town at the life of Venice's rich and famous of the 1700s. Wander under ceilings by Tiepolo, among furnishings from that most decadent century, enjoying views of the canal and paintings by Guardi, Canaletto, and Longhi (€6.50, April–Oct Wed–Mon 10:00–18:00, Nov–March Wed–Mon 10:00–17:00, closed Tue, last entry 1 hour before closing, audioguide-€4 or €6/double set, free and mandatory baggage check, at Ca' Rezzonico vaporetto stop, tel. 041-241-0100).

Santa Croce District
▲▲▲Rialto Bridge—One of the world's most famous bridges, this distinctive and dramatic stone structure crosses the Grand Canal with a single confident span. The arcades along the top of the bridge help reinforce the structure...and offer some enjoyable shopping diversions, as does the **market** surrounding the bridge (souvenir stalls open daily, produce market closed Sun, fish market closed Sun–Mon).

▲Ca' Pesaro International Gallery of Modern Art—This museum features 19th- and early-20th-century art in a 17th-century canalside palazzo. The collection is strongest on Italian (especially Venetian) artists, but also presents a broad array of other well-known artists. The highlights are in one large room: Klimt's beautiful/creepy *Judith II*, with eagle-talon fingers; Kandinsky's *White Zig Zags* (plus other recognizable shapes); the colorful *Nude in the Mirror* by Bonnard that flattens the 3-D scene into a 2-D pattern of rectangles; and Chagall's surprisingly realistic portrait of his hometown rabbi, *The Rabbi of Vitebsk* (€5.50, April–Oct Tue–Sun 10:00–18:00, Nov–March Tue–Sun 10:00–17:00, closed Mon, last entry 1 hour before closing, located a 2-minute walk from the San Stae vaporetto stop, tel. 041-524-0695).

18th-Century Costume Museum—The Museo di Palazzo Mocenigo offers a walk through six rooms of a fine 17th-century mansion, filled with period furnishings, family portraits, ceilings painted (c. 1790) with family triumphs (the Mocenigos produced seven doges), Murano glass chandeliers *in situ*, and a paltry collection of costumes with sparse descriptions (€4, Tue–Sun 10:00–17:00, closed Mon, a block inland from the San Stae vaporetto stop, tel. 041-524-0695).

San Polo District

▲▲**Frari Church (Chiesa dei Frari)**—My favorite art experience in Venice is seeing art in the setting for which it was designed—as it is at the Frari Church. The Franciscan "Church of the Brothers" and the art that decorates it is warmed by the spirit of St. Francis. It features the work of three great Renaissance masters: Donatello, Giovanni Bellini, and Titian—each showing worshippers the glory of God in human terms.

In **Donatello's wood carving of St. John the Baptist** (just to the right of the high altar), the prophet of the desert—dressed in animal skins and nearly starving from his diet of bugs 'n' honey—announces the coming of the Messiah. Donatello was a Florentine working at the dawn of the Renaissance.

Bellini's *Madonna and Child with Saints and Angels* painting (in the chapel farther to the right) came later, done by a Venetian in a more Venetian style—soft focus without Donatello's harsh realism. While Renaissance humanism demanded Madonnas and saints that were accessible and human, Bellini places them in a physical setting so beautiful that it creates its own mood of serene holiness. The genius of Bellini, perhaps the greatest Venetian painter, is obvious in the pristine clarity, rich colors (notice Mary's clothing), believable depth, and reassuring calm of this three-paneled altarpiece.

Finally, glowing red and gold like a stained-glass window over the high altar, **Titian's** *The Assumption of Mary* sets the tone of exuberant beauty found in the otherwise sparse church. Titian the Venetian—a student of Bellini—painted steadily for 60 years... you'll see a lot of his art. As stunned apostles look up past the swirl of arms and legs, the complex composition of this painting draws

Frari Church

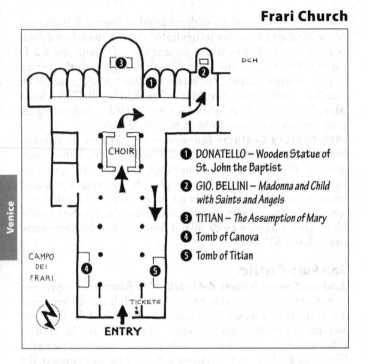

DCH

CHOIR

❶ DONATELLO – *Wooden Statue of St. John the Baptist*

❷ GIO. BELLINI – *Madonna and Child with Saints and Angels*

❸ TITIAN – *The Assumption of Mary*

❹ Tomb of Canova

❺ Tomb of Titian

CAMPO DEI FRARI

TICKETS

ENTRY

you right to the radiant face of the once-dying, now-triumphant Mary as she joins God in heaven.

Feel comfortable to discreetly freeload off passing tours. For many, these three pieces of art make a visit to the Accademia Gallery unnecessary (or they may whet your appetite for more). Before leaving, check out the Neoclassical, pyramid-shaped tomb of Canova and (opposite that) the grandiose tomb of Titian. Compare the carved marble Assumption behind Titian's tombstone portrait with the painted original above the high altar.

Cost, Hours, Information: €2.50, Mon–Sat 10:00–18:00, Sun 13:00–18:00, closed Sun in Aug (last entry 15 min before closing, audioguide-€1.60 or €2.60/double set, modest dress recommended, tel. 041-272-8618). The church often hosts evening concerts (€15, buy ticket at church; for concert details, look for fliers, call 041-272-8611, or check www.basilicadeifrari.it).

▲▲**Scuola San Rocco**—Sometimes called "Tintoretto's Sistine Chapel," this lavish meeting hall, next to the Frari Church, has some 50 large, colorful Tintoretto paintings plastered to the walls and ceilings. The best paintings are upstairs, especially the *Crucifixion* in the smaller room. View the neck-breaking splendor with one of the mirrors *(specchio)* available at the entrance (€7, includes informative audioguide, daily April–Oct 9:00–17:30,

Nov–March 10:00–17:00, last entry 30 min before closing, or see a concert here—tickets run €15–30—and arrive 30 min early to enjoy the art as an evening bonus, tel. 041-523-4864, www .scuolagrandesanrocco.it).

Church of San Polo—This nearby church, which pales in comparison to the two sights listed above, is worth a visit for art-lovers. One of Venice's oldest churches (from the ninth century), San Polo features works by Tintoretto, Veronese, and Tiepolo and son (€2.50, Mon–Sat 10:00–17:00, closed Sun, last entry 15 min before closing).

Cannaregio District

Jewish Ghetto—In 1516, Venice forced its Jews to live on an undesirable and easy-to-isolate island that was once home to the city's foundry *(geto)*, coining the word "ghetto" for a segregated neighborhood. Restricted within their tiny neighborhood (the Ghetto Nuovo, or "New Ghetto"), they expanded upward, building six-story "skyscrapers" which stand today. The main square, Campo di Ghetto Nuovo, must have been quite a scene, ringed by 70 shops and with all of Venice's Jewish commerce compressed onto this one spot. As late as the 1930s, 12,000 Jews called Venice home, but today there are only 500—and only a few dozen live in the actual Ghetto. Of the original five synagogues, only two are still active. You can spot them (with their five windows) from the square, but to visit them you have to book a tour through the Jewish Museum.

This original ghetto becomes most interesting after touring the **Jewish Museum** (Museo Ebraico). It offers two things: a museum and a synagogue. The humble two-room museum has silver menorahs, cloth covers for the Torah scrolls, various religious objects, artifacts of the old community, and scant English explanations (€3, June–Sept Sun–Fri 10:00–17:00, Oct–May Sun–Fri 10:00–16:30, closed Sat and Jewish holidays, Campo di Ghetto Nuovo, tel. 041-715-359, small café and bookstore). To see the **synagogue,** you must sign up for a half-hour English tour (€8.50, tours run hourly June–Sept Sun–Fri 10:30–17:30, Oct–May Sun–Fri 10:30–16:30, closed Sat and Jewish holidays).

Ca' d'Oro—This "House of Gold" palace, fronting the Grand Canal, is quintessential Venetian Gothic (Gothic seasoned with Byzantine and Islamic accents). Inside, there's little to see aside from special exhibitions (€5, Mon 8:15–14:00, Tue–Sun 8:15–19:15, free peek through hole in door of courtyard, Calle Ca' d'Oro 3932).

Castello District

Dalmatian School (Scuola Dalmata di San Giorgio)—This "school" (which means "meeting place") is a reminder that Venice

Water, Water Everywhere, but...

As you explore Venice, notice the wells that grace nearly every square. Well water in the middle of the sea? Venice, surrounded by water, originally had no natural source of drinking water. For centuries, locals collected water from the mainland with much effort and risk. Eventually, in the ninth century, they devised a way to collect rainwater by using town squares as catchment systems. The rain falls into the square, flows down through the slightly sloped pave-

ment, drains through the limestone grates, and filters through sand into a large clay tub under the pavement. Citizens could drop their buckets down the "well" to draw up fresh rainwater. With a safe local source of drinking water, Venice's population began to grow. Several thousand of these cisterns provided lagoon communities with drinking water right up until 1886, when an aqueduct was built (paralleling the railroad tracks across the lagoon) to bring in water from nearby mountains. Since then, the clay tubs have rotted out and the wells have been capped. Now, with a high tide, the floods show first on these limestone grates, which mark the low point of each town square.

was Europe's most cosmopolitan place in its heyday—the original melting-pot community. It was here that the Dalmatians (from the present-day country of Croatia) worshipped in their own way, held neighborhood meetings, and worked to preserve their culture. The chapel on the ground floor happens to have the most exquisite Renaissance interior in Venice, with a cycle of paintings by Carpaccio ringing the room; be sure to pick up the English descriptions to the right of the entrance (€3, Tue–Sat 9:15–13:00 & 14:15–18:00, Sun 9:15–13:00, closed Mon, last entry 30 min before closing, between St. Mark's Square and Arsenale, on Calle dei Furlani, 3 blocks southeast of Campo San Lorenzo, tel. 041-522-8828).

Santa Elena—For a pleasant peek into a completely non-touristy, residential side of Venice, walk or catch vaporetto #1 from St. Mark's Square to the neighborhood of Santa Elena (at the fish's tail). This 100-year-old suburb lives as if there were no tourism. You'll find a kid-friendly park, a few lazy restaurants, and beautiful sunsets over San Marco.

La Biennale—Every odd year (next in 2009), Venice hosts a world's fair of contemporary art in the Giardini park and the Arsenale (generally June–Oct, take vaporetto #1 or #82 to Giardini–Biennale stop, www.labiennale.org). For more information, see "Festivals" on page 80.

Venice's Lagoon

The island of Venice sits in a lagoon—a calm section of the Adriatic protected from wind and waves by the natural breakwater of the Lido. Beyond the church-topped island of San Giorgio Maggiore (directly in front of St. Mark's Square—see page 69), three interesting islands hide out in the lagoon: Murano, Burano, and Torcello.

Getting There: Murano, Burano, and Torcello are reached easily, cheaply, and slowly by **vaporetto.** Catch vaporetto #41 or #42 from the Fondamenta Nuove vaporetto stop on the north shore of Venice for the 10-minute ride to the Colonna stop on Murano (note that if you catch vaporetto #41 from the San Zaccaria–Jolanda stop on the other side of town, it takes 45 minutes to reach Murano). On Murano, leave from the Faro stop (not Colonna) for the 40-minute cruise to Burano on Line LN (or take #41 to return to Venice). Line T shuttles between Burano and Torcello in five minutes. If you plan to visit even two of these islands, get a 24-hour €15 vaporetto pass. **Speedboat tours** of these three lagoon destinations take 3–5 hours, and leave twice a day from the dock past the Doge's Palace near the shuttle dock. Look for the signs and booth (€25, April–Oct usually at 9:30 and 14:30; Nov–March 14:30 only, tel. 041-523-8835). The tours are speedy indeed—live guides race through the commentary in up to five languages, stopping for roughly 40 minutes at each island (for glassblowing and lacemaking demonstrations followed by sales pitches, leaving no time to explore the islands). Many tourists are almost kidnapped from St. Mark's Square by sales reps who bundle people onto a **free speedboat shuttle** to Murano Island, with no obligation other than to check out their factory/salesroom. It's a free and handy way to get to Murano. You must watch the 20-minute glassmaking show (and sales pitch), but then you're free to escape and see the rest of the island before finding your own way back to Venice (note that the sales-rep speedboats don't take you back to Venice).

Murano is famous for its glass factories. Upon arrival (at the Colonna vaporetto stop), wander up Via Fondamenta Vetrai (along the canal of the glassmakers), and check out the various factories (*fabricca* or *fornace*). They each offer a free 20-minute glassblowing demonstration of an artisan in action firing up something in a furnace, followed by an almost comically high-pressure sales pitch. (The spiel is brief, and there's absolutely no obligation to buy anything.)

Venice's Lagoon

The **Glass Museum** displays the very best of 700 years of Venetian glassmaking, as well as exhibits on ancient and modern glass art. While the display is pretty old-school musty, it's well-described in English (€5.50, April–Oct Thu–Tue 10:00–18:00, Nov–March Thu–Tue 10:00–17:00, closed Wed, tel. 041-739-586, www.museicivicivenezieni.it). When you're ready to go, head to the Faro vaporetto stop and take Line LN to Burano (from left side of dock) or the #41 back to Venice (right side of dock).

Burano, known for its lace and picturesque pastel houses, is a sleepy island with a sleepy community—village Venice without the glitz. Lace fans enjoy the **Lace Museum** (*Museo del Merletto di Burano,* €4, April–Oct Wed–Mon 10:00–17:00, Nov–March Wed–Mon 10:00–16:00, closed Tue, tel. 041-730-034). The main drag from the vaporetto stop into town is packed with tourists and lined with shops, some of which sell Burano's locally produced white wine. Wander to the far side of the island, and the mood shifts. Explore to the right of the leaning tower for a peaceful yet intensely pastel, small-town lagoon world. Benches lining a little promenade at the water's edge make another pretty picnic spot.

Torcello is the birthplace of Venice, where the first mainland refugees settled, escaping the barbarian hordes. Yet today, it's the least-developed island (pop. 20) and is mostly in its natural state, marshy and shrub-covered. There's little for the tourist to see except the church (a 10-min walk from the dock), which claims to be the oldest in Venice and has impressive mosaics (still, it's not worth seeing on a short visit unless you really love mosaics and can't make it to Ravenna). The complex consists of four sights: the church itself (Santa Maria Assunta), the bell tower (behind the church, climb a ramped stairway for great lagoon views), a sacristy, and a small museum (facing the church, in two separate buildings) that displays Roman sculpture and medieval sculpture and manuscripts. Tickets cost €3 for any one sight, €5.50 for any two sights, or €8 for all sights, including an audioguide (most open daily March–Oct 10:30–18:00, Nov–Feb 10:00–16:30, museum closed Mon; museum tel. 041-730-761; church/bell tower tel. 041-730-119). There's a pay WC between the museum's two buildings.

EXPERIENCES

Gondola Rides

A rip-off for some, this is a traditional must for romantics. Gondoliers charge about €75–80 for a 40-minute ride during the day; from 19:30 on, figure on €95–105 (for *musica*—singer and accordionist—it's an additional €35). You can divide the cost—and the romance—among up to six people per boat, but you'll need to save two seats for the musicians if you choose to be serenaded.

Note that only two seats (the ones in back) are next to each other. If you want to haggle, you'll find softer prices on back lanes where single gondoliers hang out, rather than at the bigger departure points. Establish the price and duration before boarding, enjoy your ride, and pay only when you're finished.

If you've hired musicians and want to hear a Venetian song *(un canto veneziano)*, try requesting *"Venezia La Luna e Tu."* Asking to hear *"O Sole Mio"* (which comes from Naples) is like asking a bartender in Cleveland to sing *"The Eyes of Texas."*

Gondolas cost lots more after 20:00 but are also more romantic and relaxing under the moon. Glide through nighttime Venice with your head on someone's shoulder. Follow the moon as it sails past otherwise unseen buildings. Silhouettes gaze down from bridges while window glitter spills onto the black water. You're anonymous in the city of masks, as the rhythmic thrust of your striped-shirted gondolier turns old crows into songbirds. This is extremely relaxing (and, I think, worth the extra cost to experience at night). Since you might get a narration plus conversation with your gondolier, talk with several and choose one you like who speaks English well. Women, beware...while gondoliers can be extremely charming, local women say that anyone who falls for one of these Romeos "has slices of ham over her eyes."

For cheap gondola thrills during the day, stick to the €0.50 one-minute ferry ride on a Grand Canal *traghetto.*

Festivals

Venice's most famous festival is **Carnevale,** the celebration Americans call Mardi Gras (Jan 25–Feb 5 in 2008, www.carnevale.venezia.it). Carnevale, which means "farewell to meat," originated centuries ago as a wild two-month-long party leading up to the austerity of Lent. In Carnevale's heyday—the 1600s and 1700s—you could do pretty much anything with anybody from any social class if you were wearing a mask. These days, it's a tamer 10-day celebration, culminating in a huge dance lit with fireworks on St. Mark's Square. Sporting masks and costumes, Venetians from kids to businessmen join in the fun. Drawing the biggest crowds of the year, Carnevale has nearly been a victim of its own success, driving away many Venetians (who skip out on the craziness to go skiing in the Dolomites).

Every odd year (next in 2009), the city hosts the **Venice Biennale International Art Exhibition,** a world-class contemporary art fair spread over the Arsenale and sprawling Castello Gardens. Artists representing 70 nations offer the latest in contemporary art forms: video, computer art, performance art, and digital photography, along with painting and sculpture (generally June–Oct, take vaporetto #1 or #82 to Giardini–Biennale stop, for details and an events calendar, see www.labienneale.org).

Other typically Venetian festival days filling the city's hotels with visitors and its canals with decked-out boats are: **Feast of the Ascension Day** (May 1 in 2008), **Feast and Regatta of the Redeemer** (third Sun in July and the preceding evening), and the **Historical Regatta** (old-time boats and pageantry, first Sat and Sun in Sept). Smaller regattas include the **Murano Regatta** (early July) and the **Burano Regatta** (mid-September).

Venice's patron saint, **St. Mark,** is commemorated every April 25. Venetian men celebrate the day by presenting roses to the women in their lives (mothers, wives, and lovers).

Every November 21 is the **Feast of Our Lady of Good Health.** On this local "Thanksgiving," a bridge is built over the Grand Canal so that the city can pile into La Salute Church and remember how Venice survived the gruesome plague of 1630. On this day, Venetians eat smoked lamb from Dalmatia (which was the cargo of the first ship admitted when the plague lifted).

Venice is always busy with special musical and artistic events. The free monthly *Un Ospite di Venezia* lists all the latest in English (free from fancy hotels, www.aguestinvenice.com). For a comprehensive list of festivals, contact the Italian tourist information office in the US (see page 817) and visit www.turismovenezia.it.

SHOPPING

Shoppers like Murano glass (described below), Burano lace (fun lace umbrellas for little girls), Carnevale masks (fine shops and artisans all over town), art reproductions (posters, postcards, and books), prints of Venetian scenes, traditional stationery (pens and marbled paper products of all kinds), calendars with Venetian scenes, silk ties, scarves, and plenty of goofy knickknacks (Titian mousepads, gondolier T-shirts, and little plastic gondola condom holders).

If you're buying a substantial amount from nearly any shop, bargain—it's accepted and almost expected. Offer less and offer to pay cash; merchants are very conscious of the bite taken by credit-card companies. Anything not made locally is pricey to bring in and therefore generally more expensive than elsewhere in Italy. The shops near St. Mark's Square charge the most.

Popular **Venetian glass** is available in many forms: vases, tea sets, decanters, glasses, jewelry, lamps, mod sculptures (such as solid-glass aquariums), and on and on. Shops will ship it home for you (snap a photo of it before it's packed up). For a cheap, packable souvenir, consider the glass-bead necklaces sold at vendors' stalls throughout Venice.

If you're serious about glass, visit the small shops on **Murano Island.** Murano's glassblowing demonstrations are fun; you'll usually see a vase and a "leetle 'orse" made from molten glass. Prices, however, are usually no better on Murano than what you'll find in Venice.

Around St. Mark's Square, various companies offer glassblowing demos for tour groups. **Galleria San Marco,** a tour-group staple, offers great demos just off St. Mark's Square every few minutes. They have agreed to let individual travelers who flash this book sneak in with tour groups to see the show (and sales pitch). And, if you buy anything, show this book and they'll take 20 percent off the listed price. The gallery faces the square behind the orchestra nearest the church; at #139, go through the shop and climb the stairs (daily 9:00–18:00, tel. 041-271-8650, manager Roberto).

Along Venice's many shopping streets, you'll notice fly-by-night street vendors selling knockoffs of famous-maker handbags (Louis Vuitton, Gucci). These vendors are willing to bargain. Buyer beware. Legitimate manufacturers are raising a stink about these street merchants, and the government is trying to rid the city of them. As authorities are frustrated in attempts to actually arrest the merchants, they have made it illegal to buy items from them. Their hope: The threat of a huge fine  will scare potential customers away from them—so unlicensed merchants will be driven out of business and off the streets.

NIGHTLIFE

You must experience Venice after dark. The city is quiet at night, as tour groups stay in the cheaper hotels of Mestre on the mainland, and the masses of day-trippers return to their beach resorts and cruise ships. **Gondolas** cost more, but are worth the extra expense (see page 79). At night, *vaporetti* are nearly empty, and it's a great time to cruise the Grand Canal on the slow boat #1.

Venice has a busy schedule of events, festivals, and entertainment. Check at the TI for listings in publications such as the free *Un Ospite di Venezia* magazine (monthly, bilingual, available at top-end hotels, www.aguestinvenice.com).

Baroque Concerts—Take your pick of traditional Vivaldi concerts in churches throughout town. Homegrown Vivaldi is as trendy here as Strauss is in Vienna and Mozart is in Salzburg. In fact, you'll find frilly young Vivaldis all over town hawking concert tickets. The TI has a list of this week's Baroque concerts (tickets from €18, shows start at 21:00 and generally last 90  min). You'll find posters in hotels all over town. There's music most nights at Scuola San Teodoro (east side of Rialto Bridge) and San Vitale Church (north end of Accademia Bridge), among others. Consider the venue carefully. The general rule of thumb: Musicians in wigs and tights offer better spectacle, musicians in black-and-white suits are better performers. For the latest on church concerts, check at any TI or visit www.turismovenezia.it.

St. Mark's Square—For tourists, St. Mark's Square is the highlight, with lantern light and live music echoing from the cafés. Just being here after dark is a thrill, as **dueling café orchestras** entertain (see "Cafés on St. Mark's Square" sidebar on page 63). Every night, enthusiastic musicians play the same songs, creating the same irresistible magic. Hang out for free behind the tables (which allows you to move easily on to the next orchestra when the musicians take a break), or spring for a seat and enjoy a fun and gorgeously set concert. If you sit a while, it can be €15 well spent (for a drink and the cover charge for music). Dancing on the square is free (and encouraged).

Streetlamp halos, live music, floodlit history, and a ceiling of stars make St. Mark's magic at midnight. You're not a tourist, you're a living part of a soft Venetian night...an alley cat with money. In the misty light, the moon has a golden hue. Shine with the old lanterns on the gondola piers, where the sloppy lagoon splashes at the Doge's Palace...reminiscing.

SLEEPING

For hassle-free efficiency and the sheer magic of being close to the action, I favor hotels that are handy to sightseeing activities. I've listed rooms in three neighborhoods: the Rialto action, St. Mark's bustle, and the quiet Dorsoduro area behind the Accademia art museum. Hotel websites are particularly valuable in Venice, because they often come with a map.

Book a room as soon as you know when you'll be in town. Hotels in Venice are usually booked up on Carnevale (Jan 25–Feb 5

Sleep Code

(€1 = about $1.30, country code: 39)
S = Single, **D** = Double/Twin, **T** = Triple, **Q** = Quad, **b** = bathroom,
s = shower only. Breakfast is included, credit cards are accepted, and English is spoken unless otherwise noted. Air-conditioning, when available, is usually only turned on in summer.

To help you easily sort through these listings, I've divided the rooms into three categories based on the price for a standard double room with bath:

$$$ Higher Priced—Most rooms €180 or more.
$$ Moderately Priced—Most rooms between €130–180.
$ Lower Priced—Most rooms €130 or less.

in 2008), Easter and Easter Monday (March 23–24), April 25 (St. Mark's Day), May 1 (Labor Day), November 1 (All Saints' Day)—and on Fridays and Saturdays year-round. Also see "Holidays and Festivals" on page 844 of the appendix. If everything's full, don't despair. Call a day or two in advance and fill in a cancellation. If you arrive on an overnight train, your room might not be ready. Leave your bag at the hotel and go sightseeing.

Venetian hoteliers are hard to pin down. They're experts at perfect price discrimination: They list a huge range of rates for the same room (e.g., €90–160) and refuse to give a firm price, enabling them to judge the demand and charge accordingly. Once they know what the market will bear, they max it out. Also, hotels are being squeezed by the very popular online-booking services (which take about a 20 percent commission). Between wanting to keep their gouging options open for high-season weekends and trying to recover these online commissions, hoteliers set their rack rates sky-high.

My listings are more likely to give a straight price. I've assured hoteliers that my readers will book direct, so they'll get 100 percent of what you pay; therefore, you'll get the fair net rate. I've listed only prices for peak season: April, May, June, September, and October. Prices will be higher during festivals, and virtually all places drop prices from November through March (except during Carnevale and Christmas) and in July and August.

If you book via a Web service, I wash my hands of your problems. Help me enforce honest business practices by reporting any hotel that charges more than the listed rates in 2008 to those who book direct. Email me at rick@ricksteves.com. Thanks.

Near St. Mark's Square

East of St. Mark's Square

Located near the Bridge of Sighs, just off the Riva degli Schiavoni waterfront promenade, these places rub drainpipes with Venice's most palatial five-star hotels. Ride the vaporetto to San Zaccaria (#51 from train station, #82 from Tronchetto parking lot).

$$$ Hotel Campiello, lacy and bright, was once part of a 19th-century convent. Ideally located 50 yards off the waterfront, on a tiny little namesake square, its 16 rooms offer a tranquil, friendly refuge for travelers who appreciate comfort and professional service (Sb-€130, Db-€200, 10 percent discount with cash and this book in 2008, strict cancellation penalties enforced, air-con, Internet access, elevator; from the waterfront street—Riva degli Schiavoni—take Calle del Vin, between pink Hotel Danieli and Hotel Savoia e Jolanda, to #4647, Castello; tel. 041-520-5764, fax 041-520-5798, www.hcampiello.it, campiello@hcampiello.it; family-run for four generations: now by Thomas and sisters Monica and Nicoletta). They also rent three modern, plush, and quiet family apartments, under rustic timbers just steps away (up to €380/night).

$$ Locanda al Leon rents 14 rooms outfitted in 18th-century Venetian style just off Campo S.S. Filippo e Giacomo (Db-€145, bigger Db-€165, these prices with cash and this book in 2008, air-con, Campo S.S. Filippo e Giacomo 4270, Castello, tel. 041-277-0393, fax 041-521-0348, www.hotelalleon.com, leon@hotelalleon.com, Giuliano and Marcella). From the San Zaccaria vaporetto stop, take Calle dei Albanesi (two streets left of pink Hotel Danieli). The hotel is at the far end of the street on the left.

$$ Locanda Correr offers five elegant rooms with silk wallpaper and gilded furniture, decorated in classic 17th-century Venetian style with all the amenities on a quiet street a few blocks from St. Mark's Square and Campo S.S. Filippo e Giacomo (Db-€145 with cash and this book in 2008, air-con, Calle Figher 4370, Castello, tel. 041-277-7847, fax 041-277-5939, www.locandacorrer.com, info@locandacorrer.com). From the San Zaccaria vaporetto stop, take the street to the right of the Bridge of Sighs to Campo S.S. Filippo e Giacomo, continue on Calle drio la Chiesa, then go left down Calle Figher, past Hotel Castello.

$$ Hotel Fontana is a two-star, family-run place with 14 rooms and lots of stairs on a touristy square two bridges behind St. Mark's Square (Sb-€110, Db-€160, family rooms, 10 percent discount with cash, quieter rooms on garden side, 2 rooms have terraces for €10 extra, air-con, Campo San Provolo 4701, Castello; tel. 041-522-0579, fax 041-523-1040, www.hotelfontana.it, info@hotelfontana.it, Diego and Gabriele). Take vaporetto #1 or #51 to San Zaccaria, then take Calle delle Rasse—to the left of pink

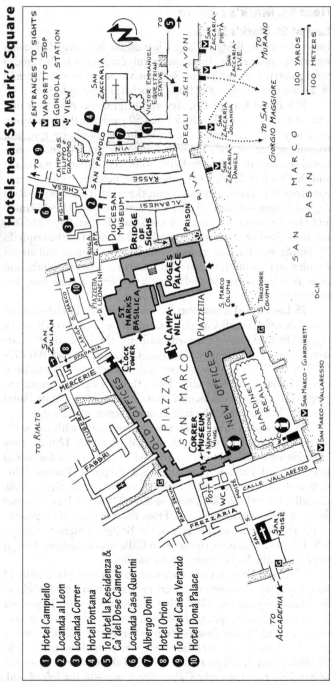

Hotels near St. Mark's Square

1. Hotel Campiello
2. Locanda al Leon
3. Locanda Correr
4. Locanda Fontana
5. To Hotel la Residenza & Ca' del Dose Camere
6. Locanda Casa Querini
7. Albergo Doni
8. Hotel Orion
9. To Hotel Casa Verardo
10. Hotel Donà Palace

ENTRANCES TO SIGHTS
Vaporetto Stop
Gondola Station
View

Hotel Danieli—turn right at the end, and continue to the first square.

$$ Hotel la Residenza is a grand old palace facing a peaceful square. Its 15 great rooms ring a huge, luxurious, and heavily frosted lounge. You'll feel like you're in the Doge's Palace after hours. This is a great value for romantics. Mention Rick Steves when you book to get the following discounted rates (Sb-€100, Db-€165, air-con, Internet access, Campo Bandiera e Moro 3608, Castello, tel. 041-528-5315, fax 041-523-8859, www.venicelaresidenza.com, info @venicelaresidenza.com, Gianni). From the Bridge of Sighs, walk east along Riva degli Schiavoni, cross three bridges, and take the first left up Calle del Dose to Campo Bandiera e Moro. Find the hotel across the square.

$$ Locanda Casa Querini rents six plush rooms on a quiet square tucked away behind St. Mark's. You can enjoy your break-fast or a sunny picnic/happy hour sitting right on the sleepy little square (Db-€150 with cash and this book through 2008, €5 more for view rooms, air-con, gazebo, halfway between San Zaccaria vaporetto stop and Campo Santa Maria Formosa at Campo San Giovanni in Oleo 4388, Castello, tel. 041-241-1294, fax 041-241-4231, www.locandaquerini.com, casaquerini@hotmail.com, Patrizia and Silvia). From the San Zaccaria vaporetto stop, take the street to the right of the Bridge of Sighs to Campo S.S. Filippo e Giacomo, continue on Calle drio la Chiesa, take the second left, and curl around to the left into the little square.

$ Albergo Doni is dark, hardwood, clean, and quiet—a bit of a time-warp—with 13 dim but classy rooms run by a likable smart aleck named Gina and her son, an Italian stallion named Nikos (D-€90, Db-€115, T-€120, Tb-€155, reserve with credit card but pay in cash for these special prices, ceiling fans, Fondamenta del Vin, 4656 Castello, tel. & fax 041-522-4267, www.albergodoni .it, albergodoni@libero.it). From the San Zaccaria vaporetto stop, cross one bridge to the right, take the first left past the pink Hotel Danieli, turn left at the little square named Ramo del Vin, jog left, and find the hotel ahead on Fondamenta del Vin.

$ Ca' del Dose Camere is a rough and funky little six-room guesthouse where high-energy Anna scrambles to keep her guests happy (Db-€100, Tb-€120, 10 percent discount with cash and this book in 2008, air-con, Castello 3801, tel. & fax 041-520-9887, www.cadeldose.com, info@cadeldose.com). It's located four bridges past the Doge's Palace, about 100 yards off the high-rent Riva degli Schiavoni on Calle del Dose, and a few steps before the wonderfully homey square called Campo Bandiera e Moro. Anna also runs the slicker Palazzo Soderini nearby (three Db-€150 rooms with breakfast, on Campo Bandiera e Moro).

North of St. Mark's Square

$$ Hotel Orion has 18 neat-as-a-pin, relaxing, and spacious rooms. Just off St. Mark's Square, it's a tranquil escape from the bustling streets (Db-€165 with this book in 2008, 5 percent discount with cash, air-con, Spadaria 700a, San Marco 30100; tel. 041-522-3053, fax 041-523-8866, www.hotelorion.it, info @hotelorion.it, cheery Massimiliano and Matteo). From St. Mark's Square, walk to the left of the basilica's facade. Turn left on Calle S. Basso (which changes to Spadari). The hotel is just before the timbered overpass.

West of St. Mark's Square

$$$ Hotel Flora sits buried in a sea of fancy designer boutiques and elegant hotels almost on the Grand Canal. It's formal, with uniformed staff and grand public spaces, yet the 43 rooms have a homey warmth and the garden oasis is a sanctuary for foot-weary guests (generally Db-€240 but check their website for deals and email Sr. Romanelli to ask about a Rick Steves discount, air-con, San Marco 2283/A, tel. 041-520-5844, fax 041-522-8217, www.hotelflora.it, info@hotelflora.it). It's at the end of Calle dei Bergamaschi, a long, skinny dead-end lane just off Calle Larga XXII Marzo on the Grand Canal side.

West of the Rialto Bridge

$$ Albergo Guerrato, above a handy and colorful produce market two minutes from the Rialto action, is run by friendly, creative, and hardworking Roberto and Piero. (Piero's the Venetian Tom Jones—a request to sing brings him great joy). Giorgio takes the afternoon shift and it's Monica in the evening. Their 800-year-old building—with 24 spacious, air-conditioned, and charming rooms—is simple, airy, and wonderfully characteristic (D-€90, Db-€130, Tb-€150, Qb-€170, Quint/b-€185, prices promised through 2008 with this book and cash, during slow times—Nov–Feb and Aug—you'll do better with their Web deals, Rick Steves readers can ask for €5 per night discount below off-season web specials, Calle drio la Scimia 240a, San Polo, tel. & fax 041-528-5927, www.pensioneguerrato.it, hguerrat@tin.it). Walk over the Rialto Bridge away from St. Mark's Square, go straight about three blocks, turn right on Calle drio la Scimia (not simply Scimia, the block before) and you'll see the hotel sign. My tour groups book this place for 50 nights each year. Sorry. The Guerrato also rents family apartments in the old center (great for groups of 4–8) for about €55 per person.

  $$ Hotel al Ponte Mocenigo is off the beaten path—a 10-minute walk northwest of the Rialto Bridge—but it's a great value. This 16th-century Venetian palazzo has a garden terrace and 10

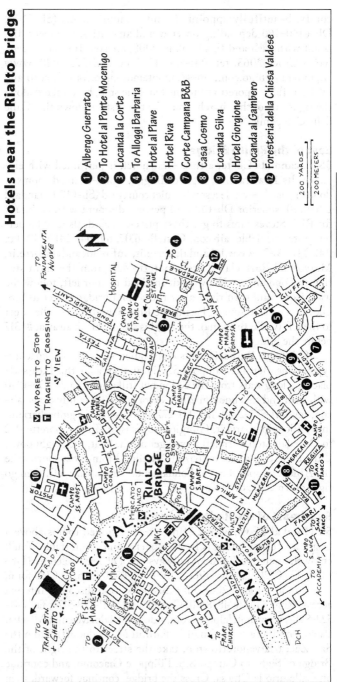

Hotels near the Rialto Bridge

1. Albergo Guerrato
2. To Hotel al Ponte Mocenigo
3. Locanda la Corte
4. To Alloggi Barbaria
5. Hotel al Piave
6. Hotel Riva
7. Corte Campana B&B
8. Casa Cosmo
9. Locanda Silva
10. Hotel Giorgione
11. Locanda al Gambero
12. Foresteria della Chiesa Valdese

200 YARDS
200 METERS

☑ VAPORETTO STOP
☐ TRAGHETTO CROSSING
☼ VIEW

Venice

comfy, beautifully appointed, and tranquil rooms (Sb-€100, Db-€140–160 depending on view and amenities, 8 percent discount with cash and this book in 2008, air-con, Internet access, Santa Croce 2063, tel. 041-524-4797, fax 041-275-9420, www.alpontemocenigo.com, info@alpontemocengio.com, Sandro and Walter). Take vaporetto #1 to the San Stae stop, head inland along the right side of the church, and take the first left down tiny Calle della Campanile.

East of the Rialto Bridge

$$ Locanda la Corte, a three-star hotel, is perfumed with elegance. Its 16 attractive, high-ceilinged, wood-beamed rooms—done in pastels—circle a small, quiet courtyard (Sb-€120, standard Db-€150, superior Db-€170, 10 percent discount with cash, ask for Rick Steves rates to get these prices, Web deals may be better, suites available, air-con, Castello 6317, tel. 041-241-1300, fax 041-241-5982, www.locandalacorte.it, info@locandalacorte.it, Marco and Raffaela). Take vaporetto #52 from the train station to Fondamenta Nuove, exit the boat to your left, follow the waterfront, and turn right after the second bridge to get to S.S. Giovanni e Paolo square. Facing the Rosa Salva bar, take the street to the left (Calle Bressana); the hotel is a short block away at #6317 before the bridge.

$ Alloggi Barbaria rents eight quiet, spacious, backpacker-type rooms. Beyond Campo S.S. Giovanni e Paolo, this Ikea-style place is a long walk from the action but still a good value (Db-€110 with cash and this book in 2008, extra bed-€30, family deals, air-con, tel. 041-522-2750, fax 041-277-5540, www.alloggibarbaria.it, info@alloggibarbaria.it, Giorgio and Fausto). Take vaporetto #52 to Ospedale stop, turn left as you get off the boat, then right down Calle de le Capucine to #6573 (Castello). From the airport, take the Alilaguna speedboat to Fondamenta Nuove, turn left, then go right down Calle de le Capucine.

Southeast of the Rialto Bridge

$$ Hotel al Piave, with 27 fine air-conditioned rooms above a bright and classy lobby, is fresh, modern, and comfortable. You'll enjoy the neighborhood and always get a cheery welcome (Db-€160, Tb-€220; family suites-€270 for 4, €300 for 5, or €330 for 6; prices good through 2008 with this book, cash discount; Internet access, Ruga Giuffa 4838/40, Castello, tel. 041-528-5174, fax 041-523-8512, www.hotelalpiave.com, info@hotelalpiave.com; Mirella, Paolo, and Ilaria speak English, faithful Molly doesn't). From the San Zaccaria vaporetto stop, take the street to the right of the Bridge of Sighs to Campo S.S. Filippo e Giacomo, and continue on Calle drio la Chiesa. Cross the bridge, continue forward, then turn left onto Ruga Giuffa until you find the Piave on your left at #4838/40.

$ Hotel Riva, with gleaming marble hallways, big exposed beams, fine antique furnishings, and bright rooms, is romantically situated on a canal along the gondola serenade route. You could actually dunk your breakfast rolls in the canal (but don't). Sandro might hold a corner *(angolo)* room if you ask, and there are also a few rooms that overlook the canal. Ten of the 32 rooms come with air-conditioning for the same price—request one when you reserve (S-€70, Sb-€90, two D with adjacent showers-€100, Db-€120, Tb-€170, €10 extra for view, reserve with credit card but pay with cash only, Ponte dell'Angelo, tel. 041-522-7034, fax 041-528-5551, www.hotelriva.it, info@hotelriva.it). Facing St. Mark's Basilica, walk behind it on the left along Calle de la Canonica, take the first left (at blue *Pauly & C* mosaic in street), continue straight, go over the bridge, and angle right to the hotel at Ponte dell'Anzolo.

$ Corte Campana B&B, run by enthusiastic and helpful Riccardo, rents three quiet and characteristic rooms just behind St. Mark's Square, plus two apartments just around the corner (Db-€125, Tb or Tb apartment-€165, Qb or Qb apartment-€190, prices are soft, cash only, 2-night minimum stay, Internet access, Calle del Remedio 4410, Castello, tel. & fax 041-523-3603, mobile 389-272-6500, www.cortecampana.com, info@cortecampana.com). Facing St. Mark's Basilica, take Calle de la Canonica (left of church) and turn left before the canal on Calle dell'Anzolo. Take the second right (onto Calle del Remedio), cross the bridge, and follow signs. Ring the bell at the black gate; the door is across the courtyard on the left wall, and the B&B is up three flights of stairs.

$ Casa Cosmo is a humble little five-room place run by Davide and his parents. While it comes with minimal services and no public spaces, it's air-conditioned, very central, inexpensive, and quiet, with a tiny terrace (Db-€110, ask for possible Rick Steves cash discount when you book, no breakfast, Calle di Mezo 4976, San Marco, tel. & fax 041-296-0710, www.casacosmo.com, info @casacosmo.com). Take vaporetto #82 to Rialto and head inland on Larga Mazzini (which becomes Merceria after passing a square and a church). Turn right onto San Salvador, then immediately left onto tiny Calle di Mezo to find the hotel ahead on your right at #4976.

$ Locanda Silva is a big, basic, beautifully located place renting 23 decent old-school rooms (S-€55, Sb-€80, D-€85, Db-€120, substantially less during slow times, Fondamenta del Remedio 4423, tel. 041-522-7643, fax 041-528-6817, www.locandasilva.it, info@locandasilva.it). From San Marco, head north toward Campo Santa Maria Formosa, go down Calle del Remedio, and turn left at the canal to Fondamenta del Remedio.

Near the Accademia Bridge

When you step over the Accademia Bridge, the commotion of touristy Venice is replaced by a sleepy village laced with canals. You'll pay a premium to sleep here but, for many, the location is worth the price. This quiet area, next to the best painting gallery in town, is a 15-minute walk from the Rialto or St. Mark's Square. The fast vaporetto #82 connects the Accademia Bridge with both the train station (15 min) and St. Mark's Square (5 min).

South of the Accademia Bridge

To reach these hotels from the train station, you can take a vaporetto to the Accademia stop (more scenic, down Grand Canal) or the Zattere stop (less scenic, around outskirts of Venice, but faster). Or, from the airport, take the Alilaguna speedboat to the Zattere stop.

$$$ Hotel Belle Arti has a grand entry and a formal, stern staff. With the ambience and comforts of a modern American hotel, it feels a bit out of place in musty Old World Venice. It has plush public areas and 65 newly renovated rooms (Sb-€130, Db-€230, Tb-€265, air-con, elevator; 100 yards behind Accademia art museum: facing museum, take left, then forced right, to Via Dorsoduro 912, Dorsoduro; tel. 041-522-6230, fax 041-528-0043, www.hotelbellearti.com, info@hotelbellearti.com).

$$$ Pensione Accademia fills the 17th-century Villa Maravege. Its 27 rooms are comfortable, elegant, and air-conditioned. You'll feel aristocratic as you glide through its grand public spaces and lounge in its wistful, breezy gardens (Sb-€140, standard Db-€220, bigger "superior" Db-€265, Qb-€340, 5 percent cash discount promised to readers during high season, 10 percent discount the rest of the year, ask for Rick Steves discount when you book; facing Accademia art museum, take first right, cross first bridge, go right to Dorsoduro 1058; tel. 041-523-7846, fax 041-523-9152, www.pensioneaccademia.it, info@pensioneaccademia.it).

$$$ Hotel agli Alboretti is a cozy, family-run, 23-room place in a quiet neighborhood a block behind the Accademia art museum. With red carpeting and wood-beamed ceilings, it feels classy (Sb-€110, Db-€200, Tb-€225, Qb-€250, air-con, elevator, 100 yards from the Accademia vaporetto stop on Rio Terra A. Foscarini at #884, Dorsoduro, tel. 041-523-0058, fax 041-521-0158, www.aglialboretti.com, info@aglialboretti.com). Facing the Accademia art museum, go left, then forced right; or from the Zattere Alilaguna stop, head inland on Rio Terra A. Foscarini 100 yards to the hotel. They run a nearby gourmet restaurant that's a local favorite.

$$ Pensione la Calcina, the home of English writer John Ruskin in 1876, maintains a 19th-century formality. It comes with

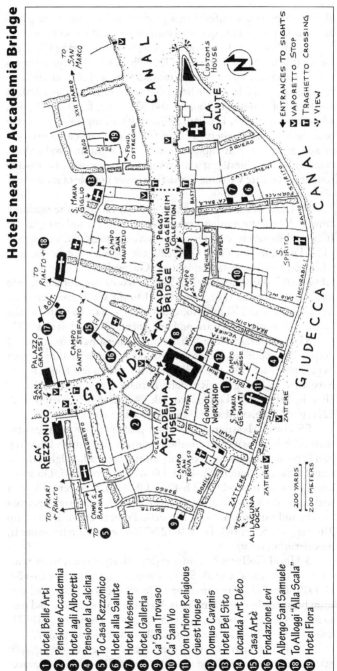

Hotels near the Accademia Bridge

1. Hotel Belle Arti
2. Pensione Accademia
3. Hotel agli Alboretti
4. Pensione la Calcina
5. To Casa Rezzonico
6. Hotel alla Salute
7. Hotel Messner
8. Hotel Galleria
9. Ca' San Trovaso
10. Ca' San Vio
11. Don Orione Religious Guest House
12. Domus Cavanis
13. Hotel Bel Sito
14. Locanda Art Déco
15. Casa Artè
16. Fondazione Levi
17. Albergo San Samuele
18. To Alloggi "Alla Scala"
19. Hotel Flora

← ENTRANCES TO SIGHTS
🚤 VAPORETTO STOP
🚢 TRAGHETTO CROSSING
✷ VIEW

all the three-star comforts in a professional yet intimate package. Its 33 rooms are squeaky clean, with good wood furniture, hardwood floors, and a peaceful canalside setting facing Giudecca Island (Sb-€100, Sb with view-€110, Db-€150–225 depending on size of room and view, air-con, rooftop terrace, killer sundeck on canal and canalside buffet-breakfast terrace, Dorsoduro 780, at south end of Rio di San Vio, tel. 041-520-6466, fax 041-522-7045, www.lacalcina.com, la.calcina@libero.it). From the Tronchetto parking lot, take vaporetto #82, or from the train station take #51 or #61, to Zattere (at vaporetto stop, exit right and walk along canal to hotel). Guests get a discounted dinner at their La Piscina restaurant and are welcome to use the terrace outside of meal times without buying anything.

$$ Casa Rezzonico is a silent getaway far from the madding crowds. Its private garden terrace has perhaps the lushest grass in Italy, and its seven spacious rooms have garden/canal views (Sb-€120, Db-€160, Tb-€180, Qb-€220, ask for Rick Steves discount when you book, air-con, Fondamenta Gherardini 2813, Dorsoduro, tel. 041-277-0653, fax 041-277-5435, www.casarezzonico.it, info @casarezzonico.it). Take vaporetto #1 to the Ca' Rezzonico stop, head up Calle del Traghetto, cross Campo San Barnaba to the canal, and continue forward on Fondamenta Gherardini to #2813.

$$ Hotel alla Salute, a basic and impersonal retreat buried deep in Dorsoduro with 50 rooms, works for those wanting a quiet Venice residence (Db-€150, cheaper with cash, a few annex rooms have air-con, facing the Rio delle Fornace Canal near La Salute church, Salute 222, Dorsoduro, tel. 041-523-5404, fax 041-522-2271, www.hotelsalute.com, info@hotelsalute.com).

$$ Hotel Messner, a sprawling place popular with groups, rents 38 bright, newly refurbished rooms (half in main building, half in nearby, simpler annex), in a peaceful canalside neighborhood near La Salute Church (Sb-€110, Db with air-con-€145, Db without air-con in annex-€115, Tb-€145, Qb-€160, 5 percent discount with cash if you book direct, peaceful garden, midway between lagoon and Grand Canal on Rio delle Fornace canal, Dorsoduro 216, tel. 041-522-7443, fax 041-522-7266, www.hotelmessner.it, messnerinfo@tin.it).

$ Hotel Galleria has nine tight, velvety rooms, most with views of the Grand Canal. Some rooms are quite narrow (S-€80, D-€110, Db-€130, big canal-view Db #8 and #10-€165, includes scant breakfast in room, fans, near Accademia art museum, and next to recommended Foscarini pizzeria, Dorsoduro 878a, tel. 041-523-2489, fax 041-520-4172, www.hotelgalleria.it, galleria@tin.it).

$ Ca' San Trovaso rents nine classy, spacious rooms split between the main hotel and a nearby annex. The location is peaceful, on a small canal (Sb-€90, Db-€115, bigger canal-view with air-con Db-€130, Tb-€145, these prices promised with cash and this book in 2008, breakfast in your room, fans, small roof terrace, Dorsoduro 1350/51, tel. 041-277-1146, fax 041-277-7190, www .casantrovaso.com, s.trovaso@tin.it, Mark and his son Alessandro). Take vaporetto #82 from the Tronchetto parking lot (or #51 from Piazzale Roma or the train station), get off at Zattere, exit left, and cross a bridge. Turn right at tiny Calle Trevisan (just past the white building with all the flags), cross another bridge, cross the adjacent bridge, take an immediate right, and then the first left.

$ Ca' San Vio is a tiny place run by the Ca' San Trovaso folks on a quiet canal with five fine air-conditioned rooms (small French bed Db-€110, bigger Db-€130, Tb-€150, cash only, breakfast in room, no public spaces, Calle delle Mende 531, Dorsoduro, tel. 041-241-3513, fax 041-241-3953, www.casanvio.com, info @casanvio.com, Roberto, Alessandro, and Marco).

$ Don Orione Religious Guest House is a big cultural center dedicated to the work of a local man who became a saint in modern times. Filling an old monastery, it feels like a modern retreat center—clean, peaceful, and strictly run, with 80 rooms. It's beautifully located, comfortable, and a fine value (Sb-€75, Db-€130, Tb-€165, profits go to mission work in the developing world, groups welcome, air-con, on the Giudecca Canal directly across from the Accademia Bridge facing Campo Sant'Agnese, Zattere 909a, Dorsoduro, tel. 041-522-4077, fax 041-528-6214, www .donorione-venezia.it, info@donorione-venezia.it).

$ Domus Cavanis, across the street from—and run by— Hotel Belle Arti (described on page 92), is a big, dim, stark place, renting 30 basic, dingy rooms for a good price (Sb-€75, Db-€120, Tb-€160, family rooms, includes breakfast at Hotel Belle Arti, air-con, hounds-of-hell bathroom fans, elevator, Dorsoduro 895, tel. 041-528-7374, fax 041-528-0043, info@hotelbellearti.com).

North of the Accademia Bridge

$$ Hotel Bel Sito offers pleasing yet well-worn Old World character, 38 rooms, a peaceful courtyard, and a picturesque location— facing a church on a small square between St. Mark's Square and the Accademia (Sb-€100, Db-€164, these special Rick Steves prices with this book in 2008, air-con, elevator; catch vaporetto #1 to Santa Maria del Giglio stop, take street inland to square, hotel is at far end to your right at Santa Maria del Giglio 2517, San Marco; tel. 041-522-3365, fax 041-520-4083, www.hotelbelsito .info, info@hotelbelsito.info, manager Rosella).

$$ Locanda Art Déco is a charming little place. While the Art Deco theme is scant, a wrought-iron staircase leads from the inviting lobby to seven thoughtfully decorated rooms (Db-€170, three-night minimum on weekends, 5 percent discount with cash, two family rooms, air-con, just north of the Accademia Bridge off Campo Santo Stefano at Calle delle Botteghe 2966, San Marco, tel. 041-277-0558, fax 041-270-2891, www.locandaartdeco.com, info@locandaartdeco.com).

$ Casa Artè has eight homey rooms with high ceilings, old-style Venetian furnishings, air-con, and thoughtful touches in a red-velvet ambience. An annex contains eight peaceful, simpler rooms (Sb-€100, Db-€140, 10 percent discount with cash, family room sleeps up to 6, just north of Accademia Bridge, 100 yards west of Campo Santo Stefano on Calle de Frutariol 2900/01, San Marco, tel. 041-520-0882, fax 041-277-8395, www.casaarte.info, info@casaarte.info, Nicole).

$ Fondazione Levi, run by a foundation that promotes research on Venetian music, offers 18 quiet, institutional, yet comfortable and spacious rooms (Sb-€64, Db-€105, Tb-€120, Qb-€140, twin beds only, elevator, San Vidal 2893, San Marco, tel. 041-786-711, fax 041-786-766, foresterialevi@libero.it). It's 80 yards from the base of the Accademia Bridge on the St. Mark's side. From the Accademia vaporetto stop, cross the Accademia Bridge and take an immediate left, crossing the bridge Ponte Giustinian and going down Calle Giustinian directly to the Fondazione. Buzz the *Foresteria* door to the right.

$ Albergo San Samuele's 12 basic budget rooms are located in a crumbling historic palazzo just a few blocks from Campo Santo Stefano (S-€60, D-€90, Db-€125, cash only, no breakfast, Salizzada San Samuele 3358, San Marco, tel. 041-522-8045, fax 041-520-5165, www.albergosansamuele.it, info@albergosansamuele.it).

$ Alloggi "Alla Scala" is a basic, grandmotherly retreat, with six homey rooms located next to the Bovolo staircase just off Campo Manin (Sb-€50, Db-€90, 6 percent cash discount, breakfast-€5, Corte Contarini del Bovolo 4306, San Marco, tel. 041-521-0629, fax 041-522-6451, www.alloggiallascala.com, info @alloggiallascala.com). At Campo Manin, ask for (or follow signs to) Corte Contarini del Bovolo—100 yards away.

Near the Train Station

I don't recommend the train station area. It's crawling with noisy, disoriented tourists with too much baggage and people whose lives' calling is to scam visitors out of their money. It's so easy just to hop a vaporetto upon arrival and get into the Venice of your dreams. Still, some like to park their bags near the station, and these places work well. The nearest self-service laundry is Speedy Wash (daily 8:00–22:00, Rio Terra S. Leonardo 5120 just east of the Guglie bridge, tel. 041-524-4188).

$$ Locanda Herion, a shiny little inn, has 17 fine rooms and a pretty little garden courtyard perfect for dinner picnics or a glass of wine (Db-€150, €10–20 discount for cash, air-con, Rio Terà San Leonardo 1704, Cannaregio, between Guglie and S. Marcuola vaporetto stops, tel. 041-275-9426, fax 041-275-6647, www.locandaherion.com, info@locandaherion.com).

$ Albergo Marin and its friendly, helpful staff offer 17 good-value, quiet, and immaculate rooms handy to the train station (Sb-€85, Db-€110, these are the maximum prices with this book in 2008, 5 percent discount with cash, fans on request, Ramo delle Chioverete #670B, Santa Croce, tel. 041-718-022, fax 041-721-485, www.albergomarin.it, info@albergomarin.it). From the station, cross the Grand Canal and turn immediately right. Take the first left, then the first right, then right again to Ramo delle Chioverete.

$ Hotel S. Lucia, just 150 yards from the station down a quiet alley, is a peaceful family-owned hotel that offers budget travelers a haven from Venice's hustle and bustle. Its 15 rooms are simple, clean, and cheery, and guests can enjoy their sunny garden terrace (S-€55, Db-€100, discounts for longer stays and cash, breakfast-€5, air-con, Calle della Misericordia 358, Cannaregio, tel. 041-715-180, fax 041-710-610, www.hotelslucia.com, info@hotelslucia.com). Exit the station toward the Grand Canal and head left, then take the second left onto Calle della Misericordia. The hotel is 100 yards ahead on the right.

$ Alloggi Henry, a homey little family-owned hotel, rents eight ramshackle rooms with dated comforters in a quiet neighborhood a five-minute walk from the train station (D-€80, Db-€90–100 with cash and this book in 2008, no breakfast, air-con, Calle Ormesini 1506e, Cannaregio, tel. 041-523-6675, fax 041-715-680, www.alloggihenry.com, info@alloggihenry.com). From the station, follow Lista di Spagna, Rio Terra San Leonardo, and Rio Terra Farsetti, then take the second left on Calle Ormesini. The hotel's at #1506.

Big, Fancy Hotels

Here are four big, plush, four-star places with greedy, sky-high rack rates (about Db-€300) that often have great discounts (as low as Db-€100) for drop-ins, off-season travelers, or online booking through their websites. If you want a sliding-glass-door, uniformed-receptionist kind of comfort and formality in the old center, these are worth considering: **$$$ Hotel Giorgione** (big, garish, shiny, near Rialto Bridge, www.hotelgiorgione.com—see map on page 89); **$$$ Hotel Casa Verardo** (elegant and quietly parked on a canal behind St. Mark's, more stately, www.casaverardo.it—see map on page 86); **$$$ Hotel Donà Palace** (sitting like Las Vegas in the touristy zone just northeast of St. Mark's, www.donapalace.it—see map on page 86); and **$$$ Locanda al**

Gambero, with 30 comfortable rooms near San Marco (www
.locandaalgambero.com—see map on page 89).

Cheap Dormitory Accommodations

$ **Foresteria della Chiesa Valdese,** warmly run by the Methodist
Church, offers 60 beds in doubles and 3- to 8-bed dorms, halfway between St. Mark's Square and the Rialto Bridge. This rundown but charming old place has elegant ceiling paintings (dorm
bed-€23, D-€60, Db-€76, includes breakfast, sheets, towels, and
lockers; must check in and out when office is open—9:00–13:00 &
18:00–20:00, Fondamenta Cavagnis 5170, Castello, tel. 041-528-
6797, fax 041-241-6238, foresteriavenezia@diaconiavaldese.org).
From Campo Santa Maria Formosa, walk past Bar all'Orologio
to the end of Calle Lunga and cross the bridge onto Fondamenta
Cavagnis.

$ **Venice's youth hostel,** on Giudecca Island with grand
views across the Bay of San Marco, is a godsend for backpackers
shell-shocked by Venetian prices (€21 beds with sheets and breakfast in 12- to 16-bed dorms, cheaper for hostel members, office
open daily 7:00–9:30 & 13:30–24:30, catch vaporetto #82 from
station to Zittele, tel. 041-523-8211, can reserve online at www
.hostelbooking.com). The budget cafeteria welcomes non-hostelers
(nightly 18:00–23:00).

EATING

While touristy restaurants are the scourge of Venice, these places
are still popular with locals and respect the tourists who happen
to come in. First trick: Walk away from triple-language menus.
Second trick: Order the daily special. Third trick: For fresh-
ness, eat fish. Most seafood dishes are the local catch-of-the-day.
Remember that seafood can be sold by weight rather than a set
price (if you see "100 g" or *"l'etto"* by a too-good-to-be-true price on
the menu, that's the cost per 100 grams—about a quarter pound).
The abbreviation *s.q.* is similar, meaning according to quantity (you
pay for the weight of the particular piece).

Near the Rialto Bridge
North of the Bridge

These restaurants are located between Campo S.S. Apostoli and
Campo S.S. Giovanni e Paolo.

Trattoria da Bepi is bright, alpine-paneled, and family run.
Owner Loris scours the market for just the best ingredients—
especially seafood—and takes good care of the hungry clientele. There's good seating inside and out (€10 pastas, €15 *secondi*,

Restaurants near the Rialto Bridge

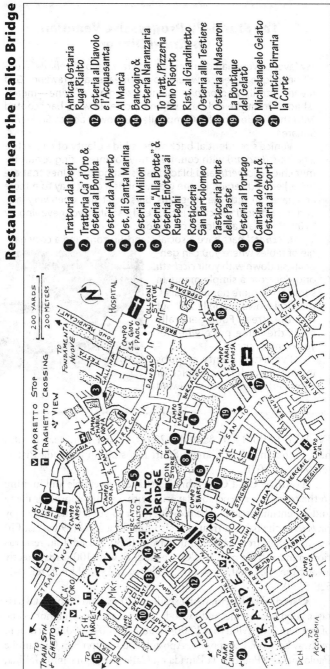

1. Trattoria da Bepi
2. Trattoria Ca' d'Oro & Osteria al Bomba
3. Osteria da Alberto
4. Ost. di Santa Marina
5. Osteria il Milion
6. Osteria "Alla Botte" & Osteria Enoteca ai Rusteghi
7. Rosticceria San Bartolomeo
8. Pasticceria Ponte delle Paste
9. Osteria al Portego
10. Cantina do Mori & Ostaria ai Storti

11. Antica Ostaria Ruga Rialto
12. Osteria al Diavolo e l'Acquasanta
13. Al Marcà
14. Bancogiro & Osteria Naranzaria
15. To Tratt./Pizzeria Nono Risorto
16. Rist. al Giardinetto
17. Osteria alle Testiere
18. Osteria al Mascaron
19. La Boutique del Gelato
20. Michelangelo Gelato
21. To Antica Birraria la Corte

Venice

The Stand-Up Progressive Venetian Pub-Crawl Dinner

My favorite Venetian dinner is a pub crawl *(giro d'ombra)*—a tradition unique to Venice, where no cars means easy crawling. (*Giro* means "stroll," and *ombra*—slang for a glass of wine—means "shade," from the old days when a portable wine bar scooted with the shadow of the Campanile bell tower across St. Mark's Square.)

Venice's residential back streets hide plenty of characteristic bars *(baccari)* with countless trays of interesting toothpick munchies *(cicchetti)* and blackboards listing the wines that are uncorked and served by the glass. This is a great way to mingle and have fun with the Venetians. Bars don't stay open very late, and the *cicchetti* selection is best early, so start your evening by 18:00. Most bars are closed on Sunday.

Cicchetti bars have a social stand-up zone and a cozy gaggle of tables where you can generally sit down with your *cicchetti* or order from a simple menu. In some of the more popular places, the local crowds happily spill out into the street. Food generally costs the same price whether you stand or sit.

I've listed plenty of pubs in walking order for a quick or extended crawl. If you've crawled

Fri–Wed 12:00–14:30 & 19:00–22:00, closed Thu, near Rialto, half a block north of Campo Santi Apostoli on Salizada Pistor, tel. 041-528-5031).

Trattoria Ca' d'Oro, while a little less accessible and inviting to the tourist, is a venerable favorite with a small, appealing menu and an enthusiastic local following. Just to sip a wine and enjoy *cicchetti* at the bar is a treat. It's also fine for a meal (€9 pastas, €10 *secondi*, lunch from 11:00, dinner from 18:30, closed Thu, reservations a must, from the Ca' d'Oro boat dock walk 100 yards directly away from the canal, cross Strada Nuova and you'll hit it, tel. 041-528-5324).

Osteria da Alberto, with excellent €20 seafood dinners, €8 pastas, a good house wine, and a woody and characteristic interior, is one of my standbys (Mon–Sat 12:00–15:00 & 19:00–23:00, closed Sun, midway between Campo S.S. Apostoli and Campo S.S. Giovanni e Paolo, next to Ponte de la Panada on Calle Larga Giacinto Gallina, tel. 041-523-8153, run by Graziano and Giovanni).

enough, most of these bars make a fine one-stop, sit-down dinner.

While you can order a plate, Venetians prefer going one by one...sipping their wine and trying this...then give me one of those...and so on. Try deep-fried mozzarella cheese, gorgonzola, calamari, artichoke hearts, and anything ugly on a toothpick. *Crostini* (small toasted bread with something on it) are popular, as are marinated seafood, olives, and prosciutto with melon. Meat and fish (*pesce;* PESH-ay) munchies can be expensive; veggies (*verdure*) are cheap, at about €3 for a meal-size plate. In many places, there's a set price per food item (e.g., €1.50). To get a plate of assorted appetizers for €8 (or more, depending on how hungry you are), ask for: *"Un piatto classico di cicchetti misti da €8"* (oon pee-AH-toh KLAH-see-koh dee cheh-KET-tee MEE-stee da OH-toh ay-OO-roh). Bread sticks (*grissini*) are free for the asking.

Bar-hopping Venetians enjoy an *aperitivo,* a before-dinner drink. Boldly order a Bellini—a *spritz con Aperol*—or a Prosecco, and draw approving looks from the locals.

Drink the house wines. A small glass of house red or white wine (*ombra rosso* or *ombra bianco*) or a small beer (*birrino*) costs about €1. The house keg wine is cheap—€1 per glass, about €4 per liter. *Vin bon,* Venetian for fine wine, may run you from €1.50–6 per little glass. There are usually several fine wines uncorked and available by the glass. A good last drink is fragolino, the local sweet wine—*bianco* or *rosso.* It often comes with a little cookie (*biscotti*) for dipping.

Cicchetti, plus Pasta: **Osteria al Bomba** is a *cicchetti* bar with a female touch. It's unusual (clean, no toothpicks, no cursing) and quite good, with lots of veggies. You can stand and eat at the bar—try a little €2 plate of polenta and cod—or oversee the construction of the house *"antipasto misto di cicchetti"* plate (€22, enough fish and vegetables for 2). Then grab a seat at the long table to complete your pub crawl with a plate of pasta (daily 18:00–23:00, near Campo S.S. Apostoli, a block off Strada Nuova on Calle dell'Oca, tel. 041-520-5175). You'll find more pubs nearby, in the side streets opposite Campo Santa Sofia, across Strada Nuova.

East of the Rialto Bridge, near Campo San Bartolomeo

Osteria di Santa Marina, on the wonderful Campo Marina, serves pricey, near-gourmet food that's made with only the best seasonal ingredients. The quality food and classy ambience make this a good splurge. Cheap eating tricks are frowned on in this elegant, border-line stuffy restaurant (enticing menu with €15 pastas and

€25 *secondi*, Sun–Mon 19:30–21:30, Tue–Sat 12:30–14:30 & 19:30–22:00, reservations smart for dinner, eat indoors or outdoors on pleasant little square, midway between Rialto Bridge and Campo Santa Maria Formosa on Campo Marina, tel. 041-528-5239).

Osteria il Milion, with bow-tied waiters and dressy, candle-lit tables indoors and out, is quietly situated next to Marco Polo's home. It's touristy but tasty (€9 pastas, €13 *secondi*, Thu–Tue 12:00–15:00 & 18:30–23:00, closed Wed; near Rialto Bridge, head north from Campo San Bartolomeo, over one bridge, take first right off San Giovanni Grisostomo before the church, walk under the sign *Corte Prima del Milion o del forno*, it's at #5841; tel. 041-522-9302).

Cicchetti: **Osteria "Alla Botte" Cicchetteria** is packed with a young, local, bohemian-jazz clientele. It's good for a *cicchetti* snack with wine at the bar, or for a light meal in the small back room—find the posted menus (Mon–Wed & Fri–Sat 10:00–15:00 & 17:30–23:00, Sun 10:00–15:00, closed Thu, two short blocks off Campo San Bartolomeo in the corner behind the statue—down Calle de la Bissa, notice the "day after" photo showing a debris-covered Venice after the notorious 1989 Pink Floyd open-air concert, tel. 041-520-9775). Just around the corner from "Alla Botte" Cicchetteria is their wine shop (eno*te*ca), which sells quality bulk wine (*vino sfuso*) for about €2 per liter. Bring an empty water bottle or pick one up there, and select among several local wines such as pinot grigio, tocai, cabernet sauvignon, or merlot to take on a picnic (Mon–Sat 10:00–13:00 & 16:00–20:00, closed Sun, Calle della Bissa 5529, San Marco, tel. 041-296-0596).

Osteria Enoteca ai Rusteghi proudly serves fine wines by the affordable glass and tasty miniature *panini* in a peaceful courtyard with alfresco tables, just a few steps from the hubbub on Campo San Bartolomeo and the Rialto Bridge (Mon–Sat 10:00–15:00 & 18:00–21:30, closed Sun, Corte del Tentor 5513, San Marco, tel. 041-523-2205). From Campo San Bartolomeo, with your back to the statue's back, head forward down the tiny alleyway on your right and turn right, then left under the overpass into the Corte del Tentor.

Rosticceria San Bartolomeo is a cheap—if confusing—self-service restaurant with a likeably surly staff. Take out, grab a table, or munch at the bar (good €6–7 pasta, great fried *mozzarella al prosciutto* for €1.30, daily 9:00–21:30, delightful fruit salad, €1 glasses of wine, prices listed on wall behind counter, no cover or service charge, tel. 041-522-3569). To find this venerable budget eatery, imagine the statue on the Campo San Bartolomeo walking backwards 20 yards, turning left, and going under a passageway—now, follow him.

If you are pub-crawling from Rosticceria San Bartolomeo, then continue over a bridge to Campo San Lio. Here, turn left, passing Hotel Canada on your right and following Calle Carminati straight about 50 yards over another bridge. On the left is the pastry shop *(pasticceria)*, and straight ahead is Osteria Al Portego (at #6015). Both are listed below.

Pasticceria Ponte delle Paste is a feminine and pastel *salon de tè*, popular for its homemade pastries and pre-dinner drinks. Italians love taking 15-minute breaks to sip a *spritz* with friends before heading home after a long day's work. Ask sprightly Monica for a *spritz al bitter* (white wine, *amaro*, and soda water, €1.80; or choose from the menu on the wall) and munch some of the free goodies at the bar at about 18:00 (daily 7:00–20:30, Ponte delle Paste).

Osteria al Portego is a friendly, local-style bar—one of the best in town. Sebastian, Ricardo, and Carlo serve great *cicchetti* (best at about 18:00, picked over by 21:00) and good meals (€10 pastas, Mon–Sat 10:30–15:00 & 18:00–21:30, closed Sun, Calle Malvasia 6015, Castello, tel. 041-522-9038). The *cicchetti* here can make a great meal, but you should also consider sitting down for an actual dinner. They have a fine menu. Prices for food and wine are posted clearly on the wall.

Cicchetterie and Light Meals West of the Rialto Bridge

All of these places (except the last one—Nono Risorto) are within 200 yards of each other, in the neighborhood around the Rialto market. This area is very crowded by day, nearly empty early in the evening, and crowded with young locals later.

Cantina do Mori has been famous with locals (since 1462) and savvy travelers (since 1982) as a classy place for fine wine and *francobolli* (a spicy selection of 20 tiny, mayo-soaked sandwiches nicknamed "stamps"). Choose from the featured wines. Go here to be abused in a fine atmosphere—the frowns are part of the shtick (Mon–Sat 12:00–20:30, closed Sun, stand-up only, arrive early before the *cicchetti* are gone, San Polo 429, tel. 041-522-5401). From Rialto Bridge, walk 200 yards down Ruga degli Orefici, away from St. Mark's Square—then turn left on Ruga Vecchia S. Giovanni, then right at Sotoportego do Mori.

Ostaria ai Storti offers lots of veggies, great prices, a homey feel, and a wonderful, fun place to congregate outdoors. Check out the photo of the market in 1909, below the bar. Prices are the same whether you stand or sit (Mon–Sat 12:00–15:00 & 18:00–22:30, closed Sun, 20 yards from Cantina do Mori on Calle do Spade 819, tel. 041-214-2255).

Antica Ostaria Ruga Rialto, a.k.a. "the Ruga," is a local fixture where Giorgio and Marco serves great bar snacks and wine to a devoted clientele. Bar or table, no problem—they are happy to make a €3, €5, or €7 mixed plate (daily 11:00–14:30 & 19:00–24:00, easy to find, just past the Chinese restaurant on Ruga Vecchia S. Giovanni 692, tel. 041-521-1243).

Osteria al Diavolo e l'Acquasanta, three blocks west of the Rialto Bridge, serves good—if pricey—Venetian-style pasta and makes a handy lunch stop for sightseers and gondola-riders. While they list *cicchetti* and wine by the glass on the wall, I'd come here for a light meal rather than for appetizers (Mon 12:00–14:30, Wed–Sun 12:00–14:30 & 19:00–21:30, closed Tue, hiding on a quiet street just off Ruga Vecchia S. Giovanni, on Calle della Madonna, tel. 041-277-0307).

Al Marcà, on Campo Cesare Battisti, is a fancy little hole-in-the-wall where young locals gather to grab drinks and little snacks. They clearly list the prices for wine and sandwiches (Mon–Sat 9:00–15:00 & 18:00–21:00, closed Sun, located on empty part of square just below courthouse).

Bancogiro (Osteria da Andrea), a simple bar behind the Rialto market, has stark outdoor seating that overlooks the Grand Canal. Peruse their wine list and menu of creative pastas and entrées at the bar, or ask for a recommendation on a few strong local cheeses to go with your wine. Order and grab a table—worth the small cover charge (Tue–Sun 10:30–24:00, closed Mon, cash only, less than 200 yards from Rialto Bridge on Campo San Giacometto, San Polo 122, tel. 041-523-2061). Consider their €15 fish and vegetable plate.

Osteria Naranzaria, which shares a prime piece of Grand Canal real estate with Bancogiro a few doors towards the Rialto Bridge, is a great stop (described on page 107, under "Romantic Canalside Settings").

Trattoria Pizzeria Nono Risorto is unpretentious, inexpensive, youthful, and famous for some of the best pizza in town. You'll sit in a gravelly garden, under a leafy canopy, surrounded by a young, enthusiastic waitstaff and Italians enjoying huge €8 salads, €9 pastas, and delicious €8 pizzas. Reserve on weekends (Thu 19:00–22:30, Fri–Tue 12:00–14:30 & 19:00–22:30, closed Wed; a 3-min walk from the Rialto fish market, find Campo San Cassiano and it's just over the bridge on Sotoportego de Siora Bettina; tel. 041-524-1169).

Near Campo Santa Maria Formosa

These eateries can be found on the map on page 99.

Ristorante al Giardinetto has white tablecloths, a formal-but-fun waitstaff, and a spacious, shady garden under a grapevine canopy. While it used to be set up for big tour groups—and still feels it—groups no longer come here, and the dining experience has improved. This is a good, solid, no-stress restaurant option (€9 pastas, €15 main courses, €2 *coperto*, closed Thu, at intersection of

Ruga Giuffa and Calle Corona, tel. 041-528-5332).

Osteria alle Testiere is my most gourmet recommendation in Venice. Hugely respected, they are passionate about quality, serving up creative, artfully presented market-fresh seafood (there's no meat on the menu) and fine wine in what the chef calls a "Venetian Nouvel" style. Reservations are required for their three daily sittings: 12:30, 19:00, and 21:15. With only 22 seats, it's tight and homey yet elegant (€15 pastas, €24 *secondi*, plan on spending €50 for dinner, closed Sun–Mon, Calle del Mondo Novo 5801, tel. 041-522-7220).

Osteria al Mascaron is where I've gone for years to watch Gigi and his food-loving band of ruffians dish up rustic-yet-sumptuous pastas with steamy seafood to salivating local foodies. The pastas, while pricey, are for two (it's okay to ask for single portions). The €16 *antipasto misto* plate—have fun pointing—and two glasses of wine make a wonderful light meal (Mon–Sat 12:00–15:00 & 19:00–22:30, closed Sun, a block past Campo Santa Maria Formosa at Calle Longa Santa Maria Formosa 5225, tel. 041-522-5995).

In Dorsoduro

Near the Accademia Bridge

For locations, see the map on page 106.

Ristorante/Pizzeria Accademia Foscarini, next to the Accademia Bridge and Galleria, offers decent €8–10 pizzas in a great canalside setting. While the food may be forgettable, this place is both scenic and practical—I grab a quick lunch here on each visit to Venice (Wed–Mon 9:00–23:00 in summer, until 20:00 in winter, closed Tue, Dorsoduro 878C, tel. 041-522-7281).

Enoteca Cantine del Vino Già Schiavi is much loved for its €1 *cicchetti*. It's also a good place for a €2 glass of wine and appetizers (Mon–Sat 8:00–20:30, closed Sun, 100 yards from Accademia art museum on San Trovaso canal; facing Accademia, take a right and then a forced left at the canal to the second bridge—S. Trovaso 992, tel. 041-523-0034). You're welcome to enjoy your wine and finger food hanging out at the bar, sitting on the bridge out front, or in the nearby square—which actually has grass. This is primarily a wine shop with great prices for bottles to go—and plastic glasses for picnickers.

Near Campo San Barnaba

A number of restaurants are worth the hike to this small square. From the Accademia, head northwest, following the curve of the Grand Canal. In five minutes, you'll spill out onto Campo San Barnaba (and the nearby Campo Santa Margherita). Follow the straight and narrow path (Calle Lunga San Barnaba) west of the square for more restaurants. With so many places within about

Restaurants near the Accademia Bridge

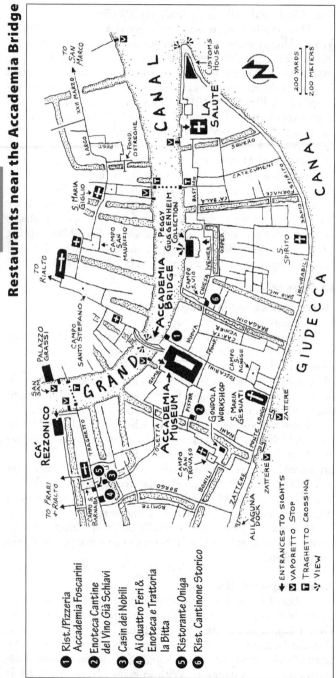

1 Rist./Pizzeria Accademia Foscarini
2 Enoteca Cantine del Vino Già Schiavi
3 Casin dei Nobili
4 Ai Quattro Feri & Enoteca e Trattoria la Bitta
5 Ristorante Oniga
6 Rist. Cantinone Storico

← ENTRANCES TO SIGHTS
V VAPORETTO STOP
T TRAGHETTO CROSSING
☆ VIEW

100 yards of each other, it would be fun to survey and choose, but reservations are often necessary.

Casin dei Nobili (Pleasure Palace of Nobles) has a diverse, reasonably priced menu in a high-energy, informal, modern setting. The patio is filled with simple tables, happy tourists, and inviting €10 daily specials (€13 pastas, €20 *secondi*, good pizzas and "fantasy salads," Tue–Sun 12:00–15:00 & 19:00–23:00, closed Mon, a half-block south of Campo San Barnaba, Calle delle Casin 2765, tel. 041-241-1841). The ambience is dark and subdued, yet family-friendly.

Ai Quattro Feri is a noisy, bustling, trattoria-style eatery, best for its catch-of-the-day seafood, especially the excellent grilled fish (€10 pastas, €12 *secondi*, Mon–Sat 12:00–15:00 & 19:00–23:00, closed Sun, just off the square on Calle Lunga San Barnaba 2754, tel. 041-520-6978, reservations required).

Enoteca e Trattoria la Bitta is dark and woody with a soft-jazz, bistro feel and a small, forgettable back patio. They serve beautifully presented, traditional Venetian food with—proudly—no fish. Their helpful waitstaff and small menu is clearly focused on quality cooking. Reservations are required (€9 pastas, €15 *secondi*, dinner only, Mon–Sat 18:30–23:00, closed Sun, cash only, next to Quattro Feri on Calle Lunga San Barnaba 2753, tel. 041-523-0531).

Ristorante Oniga, right on Campo San Barnaba, is a wine bar/restaurant serving up Italian cuisine with a modern twist (Wed–Mon 12:00–14:00 & 19:00–22:00, closed Tue, tel. 041-522-4410).

On or near Campo San Polo

Antica Birraria la Corte is an everyday eatery on the very special Campo San Polo. Enjoy a pizza or simple meal on the far side of this great, homey, family-filled square. While the interior is a sprawling beer hall, the square is a joy, where metal tables teeter on the cobbles, the wind plays with the paper mats, and children run free (daily 12:00–14:30 & 19:00–22:30, on the way to Frari Church, Campo San Polo 2168, San Polo, tel. 041-275-0570).

Romantic Canalside Settings

Of course, if you want a meal with a canal view, it generally comes with lower quality or a higher price. But if you're aiming for a canalside dining memory, these places can be great. I've listed the better-value places below, along with advice for coping with the tourist traps.

Near the Rialto Bridge: **Osteria Naranzaria** is one of two wonderful eateries on the Grand Canal between the market and the Rialto Bridge (the other is **Bancogiro,** a few doors down away from the Rialto, listed on page 104). Somehow they've taken a stretch of unbeatable but overlooked canal front property and filled it with trendy candlelit tables. Foodies appreciate Stefano Monti's Nouveau Italian cuisine. He loves sushi, and since Venice was the gateway to the Orient (remember Marco Polo), he includes sushi on his menu, along with cold cuts, inventive entrées, and fine wine. Peasants can take their glasses to the steps along the canal for bar prices, but the romantic table service doesn't cost that much extra. This is the best-value Grand Canal eatery that I have found (€10 pastas, €15 *secondi*, Tue–Sun 12:00–24:00, closed Mon, tel. 041-724-1035).

Rialto Bridge Tourist Traps: Locals are embarrassed by the lousy food and aggressive "service" at the string of joints that dominate the best romantic, Grand Canal–fringing real estate in town. Still, if you want to linger over dinner with a view of the most famous bridge and the songs of gondoliers oaring by (and don't mind eating with other tourists), this can be enjoyable. Don't trust the waiter's recommendations for special meals. The budget ideal would be to get a simple pizza or pasta and a drink for €15, and savor the ambience without getting ripped off. But few restaurants will allow you to get off that easy. To avoid a dispute over the bill, ask if there's a minimum charge—before you sit down (most places have one).

Near St. Mark's Square: At **Trattoria da Giorgio ai Greci,** a few blocks behind St. Mark's, Giorgio and sons Roberto and Davide serve homemade pastas and fresh seafood. While they have inside seating, you come here for the canalside dining—it's the best I've found anywhere in town. Call to reserve a canalside table (€17–21 fixed-price meals, daily 12:00–22:30, two canals east of St.

Mark's on Ponte dei Greci 4988, tel. 041-528-9780).

Ristorante Alla Conchiglia (Trattoria da Giorgio ai Greci's low-key neighbor) has wonderful pink tableclothed tables lining the sleepy canal. They specialize in fish and have a reasonable-for-the-romantic-setting menu. Call to reserve a canalside table (€9 pizzas, €12 big salads, €17–22 fixed-price meals, daily specials, Thu–Tue 11:30–22:15, closed Wed, Fondamenta dei Greci, tel. 041-528-9095).

Near the Accademia Bridge: **Ristorante Cantinone Storico** sits on a peaceful canal in Dorsoduro between the Accademia Bridge and the Guggenheim. It's dressy, touristy, specializes in fish and traditional Venetian dishes, has a half-dozen tables on the canal, and is worth the splurge. Reservations are smart (€15 pastas, €20 *secondi*, €3 cover, Mon–Sat 12:30–14:30 & 19:30–21:30, later in summer, closed Sun, on the canal Rio de S. Vio, tel. 041-523-9577).

On Fondamenta Nuove with a View of the Open Lagoon: **Algiubagio's** is a good opportunity to eat well while overlooking the lagoon. The name is a combination of the owners' four names—Alberto, Giulio, Barbara, and Giovanna—who strive to impress visitors with quality, creative Venetian cuisine made by using the best ingredients. Reserve a table on the lagoon facing San Michele Island or in their classy cantina dining room (€16 pastas, €25 *secondi*, €2.50 cover, Wed–Mon 12:00–15:00 & 19:00–22:30, closed Tue, to the left of the vaporetto dock as you face the water at Fondamenta Nuove 5039, Cannaregio, tel. 041-523-6084).

Eating Inexpensively Near St. Mark's Square

For locations, see the map on page 59.

"Sandwich Row" (Calle delle Rasse): This street, just steps away from the tourist intensity at St. Mark's Square, is the closest place to get a decent sandwich at a decent price with a decent place to sit down (from the Bridge of Sighs, head down the Riva and take the second lane left). The entire street is lined with sandwich bars (most open daily 7:00–24:00, €1 extra to sit). **Birreria Forst** is best, with a selection of meaty €2.50 sandwiches with tasty sauce on wheat bread, or made-to-order sandwiches for about €3 (air-con, rustic wood tables, Calle delle Rasse 4540, tel. 041-523-0557). Also good is **Osteria da Bacco,** with great *osteria*-type seating, an honest menu, and tasty wine by the glass (Calle delle Rasse 4620, tel. 041-522-2887). **Bar Verde** is a more modern sandwich bar with big €4 sandwiches and splittable €8 salads (facing Campo S. S. Filippo e Giacomo at the end of Calle delle Rasse).

At **Salad and Juice Bar Oasi 2000,** Alessandro and Giorgia serve big salads, sandwiches, a few hot pasta dishes, and fresh-squeezed juice in a small student-cantina atmosphere (daily 8:30–20:30, just behind St. Mark's Basilica off Calle San Provolo at Calle di Albanesi 4263, tel. 041-528-9937).

Chat Qui Rit Self Service is a big, fresh, modern oasis of efficiency, tucked away three blocks from the back of Piazza San Marco on Calle Frezzaria. They have a long cafeteria line of appealing dishes and reasonable prices. Sit at a table on the sidewalk, in a peaceful garden, or in an air-conditioned room behind the garden (€5 pastas, €8 *secondi,* daily 11:00–21:30; exit St. Mark's Square through middle arches, turn right, left, then right again; follow Calle Frezzaria 100 yards—it's on the right at Angolo Frezzeria, tel. 041-522-9086).

Dining Near St. Mark's Square

For the locations of these restaurants, see the "St. Mark's Square" map on page 59.

Trattoria da Remigio is well-known for high-quality, serious Venetian cuisine. Its indoors-only setting is a bit dressy, with a mix of tourists and locals, and lots of commotion (Wed–Sun lunch from 12:30, dinner from 19:30, closed Mon–Tue, just past Rio dei Greci on a tiny square at the end of Calle Madonna, tel. 041-523-0089).

The **cafés on St. Mark's Square** offer music, inflated prices, and an unbeatable setting for a drink or light meal (for a description, see page 63).

Near the Train Station

For fast, cheap food near the station, consider **Brek,** a popular self-service cafeteria (after serving breakfast, it's open daily 11:30–22:00; with back to station, facing canal, go left on Rio Terra—it becomes Lista di Spagna in two short blocks, Lista di Spagna 124, tel. 041-244-0158).

Cheap Meals

The keys to cheap eating in Venice are pizza, bars/cafés, and picnics. *Panini* and *tramezzini* (sandwiches, described on page 22) are sold fast and cheap at bars everywhere and can stave off mid-morning hunger. For speed, value, and ambience, you can get a filling plate of local appetizers at nearly any bar. For budget eating, I like small, stand-up mini-meals at *cicchetti* bars best (see page 100).

Pizzerias

Pizza is cheap and readily available. Key pizza vocabulary: *capricciosa* (generally ham, mushrooms, olives, and artichokes), *funghi* (mushrooms), *marinara* (tomato sauce, oregano, garlic, no cheese), *quattro formaggi* (four different cheeses), and *quattro stagioni* (different toppings on each of the pizza's four quarters, for those who can't choose just one menu item). If you ask for "pepperoni" on your pizza, you'll get *peperoni* (green or red peppers, not sausage). Kids like *diavola*, which is the closest thing in Italy to American pepperoni, and *margherita*—the classic mozzarella, tomato sauce, and basil pizza named for Queen Margherita in 1889.

Picnics

The **produce market** that sprawls for a few blocks just past the Rialto Bridge is a great place to assemble a picnic (best Mon–Sat 8:00–13:00, closed Sun). The adjacent fish market is wonderfully slimy (closed Sun–Mon). Side lanes in this area are speckled with fine little hole-in-the-wall munchie bars, bakeries, and cheese shops.

Gelato

La Boutique del Gelato is considered the best *gelateria* in Venice, with the most generous €1 scoops you'll find (daily 10:00–20:30,

closed Dec–Jan, located on map on page 99, two blocks off Campo Santa Maria Formosa on corner of Salizada San Lio and Calle Paradiso, next to Hotel Bruno, at #5727—just look for the crowd). *Late-Night Gelato:* At the Rialto, try **Michielangelo,** just off Campo San Bartolomeo, on the St. Mark's side of the Rialto Bridge on Salizada Pio X (daily 10:00–23:00). At St. Mark's Square, get your scoop late at **Grand Café Lavena** (daily until 24:00, first café to left of the Clock Tower, behind the first orchestra).

TRANSPORTATION CONNECTIONS

To avoid the long lines for buying train tickets and making seat and *cuccetta* reservations, many travelers use the automatic ticket machines at the station. These gray-and-yellow touch-screen **Biglietto Veloce** (Fast Ticket) machines have an English option, display train schedules, issue train tickets and reservations, and accept payment in cash or by credit/debit card. Or you could take care of these tasks at downtown **travel agencies** (see page 44). The cost is about the same (some agencies charge a small fee); it can be more convenient (if you find yourself near a travel agency while sightseeing); and the language barrier can be smaller than at the station's ticket windows.

From Venice by Train to: Padua (3/hr, 30 min), **Vicenza** (2/hr, 1 hr), **Verona** (2/hr, 1.5 hrs), **Ravenna** (hourly, 3–4 hrs, transfer in Ferrara, Faenza, or Bologna), **Florence** (roughly hourly, 3–3.5 hrs, may transfer in Bologna; often crowded so make reservations), **Dolomites** (to Bolzano about hourly, 3–4 hrs with transfer in Verona; catch bus from Bolzano into mountains), **Milan** (hourly, 3–4 hrs), **Cinque Terre/Monterosso** (8/day, 6–8 hrs, with 1–3 changes), **Cinque Terre/La Spezia** (20/day, 5–7 hrs, with 1–3 changes), **Rome** (hourly, 5–8 hrs, may transfer in Bologna, slower overnight), **Naples** (about hourly, with changes in Bologna or Rome, about 7–8 hrs), **Brindisi** (6/day, 10–12 hrs, most change in Bologna), **Bern** (6/day, change in Milan or Brig, 8 hrs), **Munich** (3–5/day, 7 hrs, may change in Verona), **Paris** (1 direct night train/day,

12.5 hrs, important to reserve ahead; 3/day, 4/night, 10–16 hrs with change in Milan), and **Vienna** (1 direct, 7 hrs; 3/day, 10–12 hrs with changes).

Marco Polo Airport

Venice's modern airport on the mainland, six miles north of the city (see map on page 39), has a sleek wood-beam-and-glass terminal, with a TI (daily, 9:00–20:00), cash machines, car-rental agencies, and a few shops and eateries (airport info tel. 041-260-9250). Check with your hotel or in Un Ospite di Venezia (the free tourist information guide at fancy hotels) for phone numbers and websites for all airlines serving Marco Polo and nearby airports.

There are four ways for you to get between the airport and downtown Venice (described in detail below): the slow but reasonable Alilaguna boat, a faster and pricier Alilaguna boat (which goes nonstop to St. Mark's Square), the fastest and priciest water taxi, and the cheap shuttle bus to the edge of Venice (with easy connections to the Grand Canal *vaporetti*). Except for the fast boat and water taxi, expect a trip between the airport terminal and St. Mark's Square (San Marco) to take up to 90 minutes. When flying out of Venice, travelers are advised to get to the airport two or more hours before departure (even for flights within Europe), but I usually arrive about 90 minutes before takeoff and manage fine.

Alilaguna Water Bus: This is the simplest transportation to and from downtown Venice. A minor drawback is that you must walk (and carry your bags) eight minutes between the airport terminal and the boat dock (follow signs, level sidewalks are fine for wheeled bags).

The Alilaguna website (www.alilaguna.it) lists times and the various lines. These are the routes for the slow boats: The Blue (BLU) Line stops at Fondamenta Nuove and Ospedale (€6, on Venice's north shore), and San Zaccaria (€12, best for hotels east of St. Mark's Square); the Red Line stops at San Marco (St. Mark's Square) and then continues west to Zattere (€12, serving Dorsoduro hotels); and the Orange (ARANCIO) Line stops at Guglie near the train station (€12). From Venice to the airport, the first boat departs from San Marco–Giardinetti at 4:00 in the morning, with the last boat leaving at 22:25. Allow roughly 70–80 minutes for the trip, depending on your stop.

The fast Alilaguna Golden (ORO) Line zips nonstop to and from San Marco–Giardinetti in 35 minutes (€25, departs from San Marco–Giardinetti for the airport about hourly from 7:40–13:30).

Buy Alilaguna tickets and get more schedule information at the airport's "Public Transport" desk (to the left as you exit baggage claim), at the airport dock, or at any other vaporetto stop in Venice that has Alilaguna service. You can also purchase tickets on board (tel. 041-523-5775).

Water Taxi: Luxury taxi speedboats zip directly between the airport and your hotel in 30 minutes, for €90 and for up to four people. This can be a smart investment—especially for small groups and those with an early departure. Arrange at the airport's water-taxi desk when you arrive, or through your hotel the day before you leave. You'll have to schlep your bags for the eight-minute walk between the dock and the airport.

Buses: Blue ATVO shuttle buses connect the airport and the Piazzale Roma vaporetto stop at the head of the Grand Canal (€3, buy from driver, 2/hr, 20 min; buses leave airport 8:20–24:00 from platform 1 directly outside arrivals terminal, leave Piazzale Roma 5:00–20:40 from far side of the lot from Hotel S. Chiara, www .atvo.it). At the Piazzale Roma vaporetto stop, the slow vaporetto #1 or faster #82 (€6 for either) head to St. Mark's Square (see "Getting Around Venice," page 45).

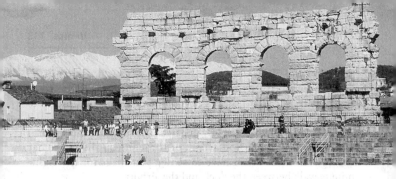

NEAR VENICE

Padua, Vicenza, Verona, and Ravenna

While Venice is just one of many towns in the Italian region of Veneto (VEN-eh-toh), few venture off the lagoon. Four important towns and possible side trips, in addition to the lakes and the Dolomites, make zipping directly from Venice to Milan (or Florence) a route strewn with temptation.

Planning Your Time

The towns of Padua, Vicenza, Verona, and Ravenna are all good stops, for various reasons. Each town gives the visitor a low-key slice of Italy that complements the urbanity of Venice, Florence, and Rome. If you can't make it to all four, pick the one that most interests you. Art-lovers will want to head to Padua to see Giotto's celebrated Scrovegni Chapel, or to Ravenna for its sumptuous Byzantine mosaics. Architecture buffs should see Palladio-designed Vicenza or the impressive Roman ruins in Verona. Verona is also the pick for star-crossed lovers retracing Romeo and Juliet's steps.

Visiting Verona, Padua, and Vicenza couldn't be easier: All are roughly 30 minutes apart on the Venice–Milan line (hourly, 3 hours). Spending a day town-hopping between Venice and Milan—with three-hour stops at Padua, Vicenza, and Verona—is exciting and efficient. Trains run frequently enough to allow flexibility and little wasted time. Of the towns included in this chapter, only Ravenna (2.5 hours from Padua or Florence) is not on the main Venice–Milan train line.

If you're Padua-bound, note that you need to reserve ahead to

Towns near Venice

see the Scrovegni Chapel (see "Booking Your Reservation," page 125). Most sights in Verona and Vicenza are closed on Monday.

Padua

Living under Venetian rule for four centuries seemed only to sharpen Padua's independent spirit. Nicknamed "the brain of Veneto," Padua (Padova is the Italian spelling) has a prestigious university (founded 1222) that hosted Galileo, Copernicus, Dante, and Petrarch. Padua's old town is elegantly arcaded, filled with students, and sprinkled with surprises. And Padua's museums and churches hold their own in Italy's artistic big leagues.

ORIENTATION

Padua's main tourist sights lie on a north–south axis through the heart of the city: from the train station to Scrovegni Chapel to the market squares (the center of town) to the Basilica of St. Anthony. It's roughly a 10-minute walk between each of these sights, or about 30 minutes from end to end.

Tourist Information

Padua has three TIs. At the train station TI, pick up a map, a list of sights, and the *Padova Today* entertainment listing (Mon–Sat 9:15–13:30 & 15:00–19:00, Sun 9:00–12:30, tel. 049-875-2077, www.turismopadova.it. Another TI is across the street from Caffè Pedrocchi (Mon–Sat 9:00–13:30 & 15:00–19:00, closed Sun, tel. 049-876-7927). You'll find a third TI at the Basilica of St. Anthony (daily April–Oct 9:00–13:30 & 15:00–18:00, closed Nov–March).

Padova Card: All the TIs sell the wonderful Padova Card (€14), which gives you 48 hours of unlimited bus travel, free parking, and entry to all the recommended sights, except the university's anatomy theater and the Basilica of St. Anthony's Oratory of St. George.

Arrival in Padua

By Train: Inside the station is the main **TI, WCs,** and **baggage deposit** (€4, daily 6:00–21:30, bring your passport, it's near track 1). An **ATM** and a **post office** (Mon–Sat 8:30–14:00, closed Sun) are outside the station, under the colonnade by the right exit. For any train business, head to a convenient travel agency, Leonardi Viaggi-Turismo, located half a block up the main drag in front of the station (Mon–Fri 8:45–19:00, Sat 9:00–13:00, closed Sun, Corso del Popolo 14, tel. 049-650-455).

By Bus: To get into town, buy a ticket (€1) for a **city bus.** These tickets are sold only from the kiosk in front of the train station, and buses leave from in front of the station. Buses #8, #12, and #18 go through town to the Basilica of St. Anthony (called "Santo" locally), departing from platform *(corsia)* #3. Get off at the end of Via Umberto I, just before Prato della Valle. If you're not sure where to get off, ask the driver, *"Santo?"* Due to pedestrian and car traffic, this relatively short distance can take 20 minutes. A taxi into town costs about €5. You'll see **hop-on, hop-off bus tours** around town. While these ubiquitous tourist transporters make sense in some towns, they're not worth it in Padua.

Long-distance buses (including buses from Venice's Marco Polo Airport) arrive at the main bus station at Piazzale Boschetti, several blocks north of the Scrovegni Chapel. From there, Via Gozzi leads into town.

Helpful Hints

Internet Access: Oddly for a college town, Padua has few Internet cafés. The TI offers free access for 15 minutes. You can also try **Internet Point** (Mon–Sat 10:00–24:00, Sun 16:00–24:00, Via Altinate 145, 5-min walk from Porta Altinate, tel. 049-659-292).

Bookstore: Feltrinelli's International Bookstore, with books in English, is near the university (Mon–Sat 9:00–13:00 & 15:30–19:30, closed Sun, Via San Francesco 1a, tel. 049-875-0792).

Laundry: Lava e Lava is about a 10-minute walk east of the Basilica of St. Anthony (daily 8:00–22:00, €12/load to wash and dry, self-service only, on the left just past the roundabout at Via San Massimo 5).

Local Guide: Charming **Cristina Pernechele** is a great teacher (€105/half-day, mobile 338-495-5453, c.pernechele@virgilio.it).

Best Gelato: Locals love the *gelateria* **Grom** for its fresh ingredients and honest flavors (on Via Roma).

Padua in Four Hours

Day-trippers can do a quick but enjoyable blitz of Padua—including a visit to the Scrovegni Chapel—in four hours. Your Scrovegni Chapel reservation will dictate the order of your sightseeing (see the booking procedure on page 125). Also, if you like markets, get an early start.

Here's one possible plan: Take the bus from the train station to the Basilica of St. Anthony at the south end of town, then walk back through the old town, sightseeing your way (using descriptions from this chapter) back to the Scrovegni Chapel, then on to the station.

Ready, set, go...

At zero hour: Arrive at the Padua train station (timing it so that you arrive three hours before your reservation for the Scrovegni Chapel). Check your bags and catch bus #3, #8, #12, or #18 to the Basilica of St. Anthony. Note that parts of the basilica close during lunch. Sightsee the basilica.

At one hour: Walk north along Via del Santo and turn left onto Via San Francesco, which leads to the huge Piazza delle Erbe and Palazzo della Ragione. The vibrant markets here start to shut down at about 13:00. Visit the town center's sights (without actually touring the university): Caffè Pedrocchi and the university's courtyard.

At 2:15 hours: Walk 10 minutes to the Scrovegni Chapel. Pick up your pre-paid and reserved ticket first, then spend 30 minutes checking out the Civic Museum and its Multimedia Room. Get in line five minutes early for the Chapel.

At three hours: Visit the Scrovegni Chapel.

Padua

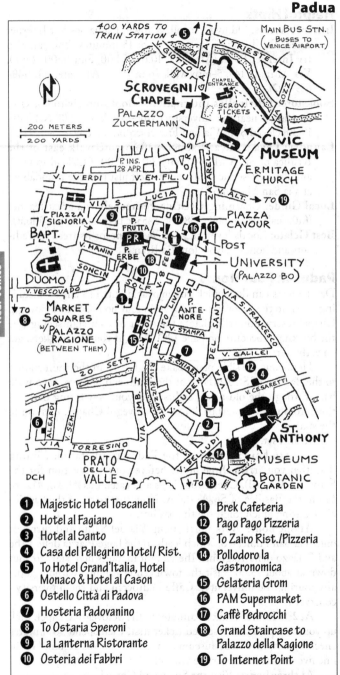

1. Majestic Hotel Toscanelli
2. Hotel al Fagiano
3. Hotel al Santo
4. Casa del Pellegrino Hotel/ Rist.
5. To Hotel Grand'Italia, Hotel Monaco & Hotel al Cason
6. Ostello Città di Padova
7. Hosteria Padovanino
8. To Ostaria Speroni
9. La Lanterna Ristorante
10. Osteria dei Fabbri
11. Brek Cafeteria
12. Pago Pago Pizzeria
13. To Zairo Rist./Pizzeria
14. Pollodoro la Gastronomica
15. Gelateria Grom
16. PAM Supermarket
17. Caffè Pedrocchi
18. Grand Staircase to Palazzo della Ragione
19. To Internet Point

At **3:30 hours:** Walk north to the train station (10–15 min) and reclaim your baggage.

At **four hours:** Catch your train. Ahhhh.

SIGHTS

▲▲Basilica of St. Anthony

Friar Anthony of Padua (1195–1231), "Christ's perfect follower and a tireless preacher of the Gospel," is buried here. For nearly

800 years, his remains and this impressive Romanesque Gothic church (building started immediately after the death of the saint in 1231) have attracted pilgrims to Padua.

Cost and Hours: The basilica is free and open daily in summer 6:30–19:45 (in winter 6:30–18:45). Note that these sights within the basilica close around lunchtime, but are open daily (in summer): Chapel of the Reliquaries (daily 8:00–12:45 & 14:30–19:30, shorter hours in winter), Sacristy (open daily), a multimedia exhibit (daily 9:00–12:30 & 14:30–18:00), the museum (daily 9:00–13:00 & 14:30–18:30, shorter hours and closed Mon in winter), and the Oratory of St. George, which costs €2.50 to enter (daily 9:00–12:30 & 14:30–19:00).

Information: In the basilica, a modest dress code is enforced. A helpful information desk with Anthony-related pamphlets is in the cloisters, located on the right side of the church (info desk open daily 8:30–13:00 & 14:00–18:30, public WC nearby). To find English versions of the pamphlets—one on the saint's life and another about the basilica—head to the Chapel of the Reliquaries and offer a donation.

There's a TI on the square facing the church (April–Oct daily 9:00–13:30 & 15:00–18:00, closed Nov–March). A 10-minute stroll north up Via del Santo takes you back into the center of town.

Exterior of Basilica

Nod to St. Anthony, who looks down from the redbrick facade and blesses us. He holds a book, a symbol of all the knowledge he accumulated as a quiet monk before starting his famous preaching career.

Guarding the church is Donatello's life-size equestrian statue of the Venetian mercenary general, Gattamelata. Though it looks like a thousand other man-on-a-horse statues, it was a landmark in Italy's budding Renaissance—the first life-size, secular, equestrian

St. Anthony of Padua
(1195–1231)

One of Christendom's most popular saints, Anthony is known as a powerful speaker, a miracle worker, and the finder of lost articles.

Born in Lisbon to a rich, well-educated family, his life changed at age 25, when he saw the mutilated bodies of some Franciscan martyrs. Their sacrifice inspired him to join the poor Franciscans and dedicate his life to Christ. He moved to Italy and lived in a cave, studying, meditating, and barely speaking to anyone.

One day, he joined his fellow monks for a service. The appointed speaker failed to show up, so Anthony was asked to say a few off-the-cuff words to the crowd. He started slowly but, filled with the Spirit, he became more confident and amazed the audience with his eloquence. Up in Assisi, St. Francis heard about Anthony and sent him on a whirlwind speaking tour.

Anthony had a strong voice, knew several languages, had encyclopedic knowledge of theology, and could speak spontaneously as the Spirit moved him. It's said he even stood on the shores of the Adriatic Sea in Rimini and enticed a school of fish to listen. Anthony also was known as a miracle worker—healing a sick horse, protecting a crowd from the rain, and making poisoned food harmless.

In 1230, Anthony retired to Padua, where he founded a monastery and initiated reforms for the poor. An illness cut his life short at age 36. Anthony once said, "Happy is the man whose words issue from the Spirit and not from himself!"

statue cast out of bronze in a thousand years. This church is technically outside of Italy—when you pass the banisters that mark its property line, you're passing into Vatican territory.

Interior

Entering the basilica, gaze down the nave, past the crowds and through the incense haze, to Donatello's glorious crucifix arising from the altar, and realize that this is one of the most important pilgrimage sites in Christendom.

Along with the crucifix, Donatello's bronze statues—Mary with Padua's six favorite saints—grace the high altar. Late in his career, the great Florentine sculptor spent a decade in Padua (1444–1455), creating the altar and Gattamelata.

St. Anthony's Tomb

Head to the left side of the nave. Here, pilgrims file slowly through a side chapel around the tomb of St. Anthony. Nine marble reliefs, Renaissance masterpieces from about 1500, show scenes and miracles from the life of the saint.

As you enter the chapel, the first relief on the left depicts St. Anthony receiving the Franciscan habit. In the next, Anthony's compassion miraculously revives a woman who has been stabbed to death by her jealous husband. Notice the etchings of familiar Paduan architecture at the top of the sculptures. In the third panel, the building with the hull-shaped roof is Palazzo della Ragione.

On the back wall of the chapel (the sixth panel), look for "the miracle of the miser's heart." Anthony dips his hand into a moneylender's side to demonstrate the absence of his heart. This relief illustrates the scriptural verse, "For where your treasure is, there your heart will be also." The heart miraculously appears in the dead man's treasure chest.

The next relief shows Anthony holding the foot of a young man who confessed to kicking his mother. Upon hearing of this act, Anthony declared that anyone so disrespectful to his mother ought to have his foot cut off. The boy took Anthony's word literally. His hysterical mother implored Anthony's help, and Anthony's prayers to God enabled him to reattach the foot.

Stand in the corner for a moment and observe the passionate devotion that pilgrims and locals alike have for Anthony. Touching his tomb or kneeling in prayer, the faithful here believe Anthony is their protector—a confidant and intercessor of the poor. And they believe he works miracles. The faithful place offerings, votives, and prayers to ask for help or to give thanks for miracles they believe he's performed. By putting their hand on his tomb while saying a silent prayer, pilgrims show devotion to Anthony and feel the saint's presence.

Popular Anthony is the patron saint of dozens of things: of travelers, amputees, donkeys, pregnant women, barren women, stewardesses, and pig farmers. Most pilgrims ask for his help in his role as the "finder of things"—from lost car keys to a life companion.

Continuing from this chapel around the corner into the next room, enter the oldest part of church—the original chapel, where Anthony was first buried in 1231. Note the fine (and impressively realistic for the 14th century) view of medieval Padua, with this church outside the wall (finished by 1300 and still looking as it looks today).

In a circa-1380 fresco, Anthony on his cloud promises that he'll watch over his town. Because people wanted to be buried near a saint, graves lie all around. If you could afford it, this was about the best piece of real estate a dead person could want. (The practice was ended with Napoleonic reforms in 1806.)

Chapel of the Reliquaries

Continue your circuit of the church by going behind the altar into the apse, to the Chapel of the Reliquaries. The most prized relic is in the glass case at center stage—Anthony's tongue. When Anthony's remains were exhumed 32 years after his death (1263), his body had decayed to dust, but his tongue was found miraculously unspoiled and red in color. How appropriate for the multilinguist who, full of the Spirit, couldn't stop talking about God.

Working clockwise around the chapel, start in front of the staircase at St. Anthony's holy, and holey, tunic *(tonaca)*. His rough-hewn wood coffin is on the left wall. His pillow—a comfy rock—is up the stairs (in first glass case). The center display case contains (top to bottom) the Saint's lower jaw *(il mento)*, his uncorrupted tongue *(lingua)*, and finally, his vocal chords (*apparato vocale*, discovered intact when his remains were examined in 1981). In the last display case, fragments of the True Cross *(la croce)* are held in a precious crucifix reliquary.

Cloisters

From the right side of the nave as you face the altar, follow signs to *chiostro;* from outside, find signs on the right side of the church. The main cloister is dominated by an exceptionally bushy magnolia tree, planted in 1810, and by the graves of the most illustrious Padovans (such as the scientists who gave their names to their discoveries: Fallopian tube and Eustachian tube).

Wander around the various cloisters. Picnic tables invite pilgrims and tourists to enjoy meals within the solitude of one of the cloisters (it's covered and suitable even when rainy, WCs in same cloister). A **multimedia exhibit** on the life of St. Anthony is presented in this cloister. Ask if they'll run the English version for you.

In the far end, a fascinating little **museum** is filled with votives and folk art recounting miracles attributed to Anthony. The abbreviation *PGR* you'll see on many votives stands for *per grazia ricevuta*—for answered prayers.

Oratory of St. George

The small but sumptuous oratory (which costs €2.50 to enter) faces the little square in front of the basilica. The oratory (*ora* means prayer) is not actually a church, though it's certainly a fine place to pray—it's filled with vivid, circa-1370 frescos and soft classical music. It's an understandably popular place for local wedding ceremonies.

Near the Basilica

Prato della Valle—The so-called "field without grass" is 150 yards southwest of the basilica (down Via Luca Belludi). Once a Roman theater and later Anthony's preaching grounds, this square claims to be the largest in Italy. It's a pleasant, 400-yard-long, oval-shaped piazza with fountains, walkways, dozens of statues of Padua's eminent citizens, and (yes) grass. It's also a **market** scene: A huge clothing, shoe, and household goods market encircles

the Prato on Saturdays (8:00–19:00). An antique market creaks into action on the third Sunday of every month (8:00–19:00).

Botanic Garden—Green thumbs appreciate this nearly five-acre botanical garden, which contains the university's vast collection of rare plants. It was founded in 1545 by the Faculty of Medicine to cultivate medicinal plants (€4, April–Oct daily 9:00–13:00 & 15:00–19:00, Nov–March Mon–Sat 9:00–13:00, closed Sun; entrance 150 yards south of Basilica of St. Anthony—with your back to the facade, take a hard left). A visitors center—in a little cottage, to the right of the garden's entrance—houses models of the garden's layout and computer programs that describe the history and composition of the garden in English (same hours as the garden).

▲▲▲Scrovegni Chapel (Cappella degli Scrovegni)

You must make reservations in advance to see this glorious, recently renovated chapel. Wallpapered with Giotto's beautifully preserved

cycle of nearly 40 frescoes, the chapel holds scenes that depict the lives of Jesus and Mary. (See "Booking Your Reservation," below.)

Painted by Giotto and his assistants from 1303 to 1305 and considered by many to be the first piece of modern art, this work makes it clear: Europe was breaking out

of the Middle Ages. A sign of the Renaissance to come, Giotto placed real people in real scenes, expressing real human emotions. These frescoes were radical for their 3-D nature, lively colors, light sources, emotion, and humanism.

The chapel was built out of guilt for white-collar crimes.

Scrovegni Chapel

1. Joachim Driven From the Temple
2. Joachim Returns to the Sheepfold*
3. Mary's Birth Announced to St. Anne
4. Birth of Jesus
5. Slaughter of the Innocents
6. Jesus Astounding the Scholars
7. Jesus Drives Out the Money Changers
8. Last Supper
9. Betrayal of Christ*
10. Jesus Beaten and Humiliated
11. Jesus Carrying the Cross
12. Lamentation (Deposition)*
13. Last Judgment*

*Described in text

Reginaldo degli Scrovegni charged sky-high interest rates at a time when that practice was forbidden by the Church. He even caught the attention of Dante, who placed him in one of the levels of hell in his *Inferno*. When Reginaldo died, the Church denied him a Christian burial. His son Enrico tried to buy forgiveness for his father's sins by building this superb chapel. After seeing Giotto's frescoes for the Franciscan monks of St. Anthony, Enrico knew he'd found the right artist to decorate the interior (and, he hoped, save his father's soul).

Cost and Hours: €12 combo-ticket with Civic Museum. The chapel is open daily 9:00–22:00 (off-season until 19:00).

The Civic Museum (and its worthwhile *pinacoteca* and Multimedia Room) are included in your entry fee. During the times the Civic Museum is closed—after 19:00 and on Mon—tickets are €8. (The Multimedia Room, which is adjacent to the Civic Museum, is always open the same hours as the chapel.)

Entry Times: Every 15 minutes (at :00, :15, :30, and :45 past the hour during the day), the chapel opens for 15-minute visits. After 19:00, the chapel opens every 20 minutes for 20-minute visits (last entry at 21:40).

Booking Your Reservation: To protect the paintings from excess humidity, only 25 people are allowed in the chapel at a time. Prepaid reservations are obligatory (booking office open Mon–Fri 9:00–19:00, Sat 9:00–13:00, closed Sun, provide your credit-card number and hotel telephone number where you can be reached the day before if necessary, call 049-201-0020—you may have to be persistent and call several times). You can also reserve faster and easier online at www.cappelladegliscrovegni.it.

Book your visit well in advance. It's sometimes possible to buy a ticket for the same day at the ticket office, but don't count on it. (A sign on the desk indicates when the next available time is.)

You'll be instructed to pick up your tickets at the ticket office at least an hour before your visit. In practice, I've found that you can arrive later, but give yourself at least 30 minutes to weather any commotion at the desk. Present your confirmation number, confirm your time, and pick up your ticket.

While you're waiting for your reserved time, blitz the museum and Multimedia Room. Read the section below before you enter, since you'll only have a short time in the chapel itself.

Be at the chapel doors (well-signed, 100 yards to the right of the ticket office as you exit) at least five minutes before your scheduled visit. The doors to the chapel are automatic, and if you're even a minute late, you'll forfeit your visit and have to rebook and repay to enter.

At your appointed time, you first enter an anteroom to watch a very instructive 15-minute video (with English subtitles) and to establish humidity levels before continuing into the chapel (no photos are allowed). Although you have only a short visit inside the chapel, it is divine. You're inside a Giotto time capsule, looking back at an artist who was ahead of his time.

Giotto's Frescoes in the Scrovegni Chapel

Giotto painted the entire chapel in 200 working days over two years, but you'll get only 15 minutes to see it.

As you enter the long, narrow chapel, look right down to the far end—the rear wall is covered with Giotto's big *Last Judgment*. Christ in a bubble is flanked by crowds of saints and by scenes of

Giotto di Bondone
(c. 1267–1337)

Though details of his life are extremely sketchy, we know that as a 12-year-old shepherd boy, Giotto was discovered painting pictures his father's sheep on rock slabs. He became the wealthiest and most famous painter of his day. His achievement is especially remarkable, since painters at that time weren't considered anything more than craftsmen and weren't expected to be innovators.

After making a name for himself by painting the life of St. Francis frescoes in Assisi, the Florentine tackled the Scrovegni Chapel (c. 1303–1305). At age 35, he was at the height of his powers. His scenes were more realistic and human than anything done for a thousand years. Giotto didn't learn technique by dissecting corpses or studying the mathematics of 3-D perspective. But he had innate talent, and his personality shines through in the humanity of his art.

The Scrovegni frescoes break ground by introducing nature—rocks, trees, animals—as a backdrop for religious scenes. Giotto's people, with their voluminous, deeply creased robes, are as sturdy and massive as Greek statues, throwbacks to the Byzantine icon art of the Middle Ages. But these figures exude stage presence. Their gestures are simple but expressive: A head tilted down says dejection, an arm flung out is grief, clasped hands are hope. Giotto created his figures not just by drawing outlines and filling them in with single colors, but as patchworks of lighter and darker shades, pioneering modern modeling techniques. Giotto's storytelling style is straightforward, and anyone with knowledge of the episodes of Jesus' life can read the chapel like a comic book.

The Scrovegni represents a turning point in European art and culture—away from scenes of heaven and toward a more down-to-earth, human-centered view.

heaven and hell. This is the final, climactic scene of the story told in the chapel's 38 panels—the three-generation history of Jesus, his mother Mary, and Mary's parents.

The story begins with Jesus' grandparents, on the long north wall (with the windows) in the upper left corner. In the first frame, a priest scolds the man who will be Mary's father (Joachim, with the halo) and kicks him out of the Temple for the sin of being

childless. In the next panel to the right, Joachim returns dejectedly to his sheep farm. Meanwhile (next panel), his wife is in the bedroom, hearing the miraculous news that their prayers have been answered—she'll give birth to Mary, the mother of Jesus.

From this humble start, the story of Mary and Jesus spirals clockwise around the chapel, from top to bottom. The top row (both north and south walls) covers Mary's birth and life.

Jesus enters the picture in the middle row of the north (windowed) wall. The first frame shows his birth in a shed-like manger. In the next frame, the Magi arrive and kneel to kiss his little toes. Then the child is presented in the tiny temple. Fearing danger, the family gets on a horse and flees to Egypt. Meanwhile, back home, all the baby boys are slaughtered to try to prevent the coming of the Messiah (Slaughter of the Innocents).

Spinning clockwise to the opposite (south) wall, you see (in a badly-damaged fresco) the child Jesus astounding the scholars with his wisdom. Next, Jesus is baptized by John the Baptist. His first miracle, at a wedding, is turning jars of water into wine. Next, he raises a mummy-like Lazarus from the dead. Riding a donkey, he enters Jerusalem triumphantly. In the Temple, he drives the wicked money changers out.

Turning again to the north wall (bottom row), we see scenes from Jesus' final days. In the first frame, he and his followers gather at a table for a Last Supper. Next, Jesus kneels humbly to wash their feet. He is betrayed with a kiss and arrested. Jesus is tried. Then he is beaten and humiliated.

Finally (south wall, bottom row), he is forced to carry his own cross, crucified, and prepared for burial, while his followers mourn (Lamentation). Then he is resurrected and ascends to heaven, leaving his disciples to carry on.

The whole story concludes on the rear wall, where Jesus reigns at the Last Judgment. The long north wall (ground level) features the Virtues that lead to heaven, while the south wall has the (always more interesting) Vices. And all this unfolds beneath the blue, starry sky overhead on the ceiling.

Some panels deserve a closer look:

Joachim Returns to the Sheepfold (north wall, upper left, second panel): Though difficult to appreciate from ground level, this oft-reproduced scene is groundbreaking. Giotto—a former shepherd himself—uses nature as a stage, setting the scene in front of a backdrop of real-life mountains, and adding down-home details like Joachim's jumping dog, frozen in mid-air.

Betrayal of Christ, a.k.a. *Il Bacio*, "The Kiss" (north wall, bottom row, center panel): Amid the crowded chaos of Jesus' arrest, Giotto focuses our eye on the central action, where Judas ensnares Jesus in his yellow robe (the color symbolizing envy), establishes meaningful eye contact, and kisses him.

Lamentation, a.k.a. *Deposition* (south wall, bottom row, middle): Jesus has been crucified, and his followers weep and wail over the lifeless body. John the Evangelist spreads his arms wide and shrieks, his cries echoed by anguished angels above. Each face is a study in grief. Giotto emphasizes these saints' human vulnerability.

Last Judgment (big west wall): Christ in the center is a glorious vision, but the action is in hell (lower right). Satan is a Minotaur-headed ogre munching on sinners. Around him, demons give sinners their just desserts in a scene right out of Dante...who was Giotto's friend and fellow Florentine. Front and center is Enrico Scrovegni in a violet robe (the color symbolizing penitence), donating the chapel to the Church in exchange for forgiveness for his father's sins.

Before you're scooted out, take a look at the actual altar. While Enrico's father's tomb is lost, Enrico Scrovegni himself is in the tomb at the altar. The three statues are by Giovanni Pisano—Mary (in the center) supports baby Jesus on her hip with a perfectly natural, maternal S-shape. She's flanked by no-name deacons.

Civic Museum (Musei Civici Eremitani)

This museum, next to the Scrovegni Chapel, was once an Augustinian hermit's monastery. Visit in order to see the *pinacoteca* and the Multimedia Room. The ground floor is a skippable archaeological museum with Roman and Etruscan artifacts and no English descriptions.

Cost, Hours, Information: €12 Scrovegni Chapel combo-ticket, €10 without the chapel. The Civic Museum is open Tue–Sun 9:00–19:00, closed Mon. The Multimedia Room is open at the same time as the Scrovegni Chapel (daily 9:00–22:00, off-season until 19:00). Another part of the museum, Palazzo Zuckermann, is open Tue–Sun 10:00–19:00, closed Mon. No photos are allowed, and there's a mandatory and free bag check (Piazza Eremitani, tel. 049-820-4551).

Pinacoteca

The museum's highlight is upstairs, in the *pinacoteca* (picture gallery). The collection has 13th- to 18th-century paintings by Titian, Tintoretto, Giorgione, Tiepolo, Veronese, Bellini, Canova, Guariento, and other Veneto artists. But I'd make a beeline for the room with the Giotto crucifix. Ask for it: *"La croce di Giotto?"*

Originally hung in the Scrovegni Chapel between the Scrovegni family's private zone and public's worshipping zone, this crucifix is painted on wood by Giotto. If you actually sit on the floor and look up, the body really pops. The adjacent "God as Jesus" painting was the only painting in the otherwise frescoed chapel. (This is hung here for preservation concerns. Its copy is the only non-original art in the chapel.) Studying these two masterpieces affirms the greatness of Giotto.

Behind the crucifix room is a collection of 14th- and 15th-century art. While the works here are exquisite—and came well after Giotto—they're clearly not as groundbreaking.

Multimedia Room

This room, dedicated to taking a closer look at the Scrovegni Chapel, is adjacent to the Civic Museum (in the same building). Rows of computer screens offer a virtual Scrovegni Chapel visit and provide cultural insights into daily life in the Middle Ages. There are explanations of the individual panels, Giotto's fresco technique, close-ups of the art, and a description of the restoration. They show a 12-minute video (English headphones available) that is similar—but not identical—to the one that precedes your chapel visit. For me, it's worth just taking some time to enjoy a second video that features a mesmerizing, slow montage of close-ups of the Giotto frescoes.

Between the museum and the chapel are the scant remains of Roman Padua. The remnants are from the wall of an arena and nicely fitting pipes that once channeled water so that the arena could be flooded (which took place during the annual celebration of a great Roman naval victory over the Greeks in 302 B.C.).

Palazzo Zuckermann

This little-visited wing of the Civic Museum, just across a busy street, is included in the same ticket as the *pinacoteca* and Multimedia Room. Its first two floors offer a commotion of applied and decorative arts from the Venetian Republic (1600s–1700s). On the top floor, the Bottacin collection takes you to the 19th century with coins and delightful (but no-name) pre-Impressionist paintings.

More Sights in the Center

Palazzo della Ragione—This grand 13th-century palazzo, commonly called *il Salone* (great hall), once held the medieval law courts. The first floor consists of a huge hall—265 feet by 90 feet—that was at one time adorned with frescoes by Giotto. A fire in 1312 destroyed those paintings, and the palazzo was redecorated with the 15th-century art that you see

today: a series of 333 frescoes depicting the signs of the zodiac, labors of the month, symbols representing characteristics of people born under each sign, and finally, figures of saints to legitimize the power of the courts in the eyes of the Church.

The hall is topped with a hull-shaped roof, which helps to support the structure without the use of columns—quite an architectural feat in its day, considering the building's dimensions. The curious stone in the right-hand corner near the entry is the "Stone of Shame," which was the seat for debtors who were punished during the Middle Ages. Instead of being sentenced to death or prison (same thing back then), debtors sat upon this stone, surrendered their possessions, and denounced themselves publicly before being exiled from the city (€4, more if there's an exhibition, Feb–Oct Tue–Sun 9:00–19:00, closed Mon, Nov–Jan closes at 18:00, enter through north end of Piazza delle Erbe, up long staircase, tel. 049-820-5006, WCs just past the exit).

▲▲Market Squares: Piazza delle Erbe and Piazza della Frutta

—The stately Palazzo della Ragione (described above) provides a dramatic backdrop for Padua's almost exotic-feeling market, filling the surrounding squares—Piazza delle Erbe and Piazza della Frutta—each morning and all day Saturday (Mon–Fri roughly 8:00–13:00, Sat 8:00–17:00, closed Sun). Second only to the produce mar-  ket in Italy's gastronomic capital of Bologna, this market has been renowned for centuries as having the freshest and greatest selection of herbs, fruits, and vegetables. And don't miss the ground floor of the Palazzo della Ragione, where you'll find various butchers, *salumerie* (delicatessens), cheese shops, bakeries, and fishmongers.

Explore this scene. Students gather here each evening, after the markets have closed, spilling out of colorful bars and cafés— drinks in hand—into the square. Pizza by the slice is dirt cheap.

The drink of choice is a *spritz*, an aperitif generally made with Campari (liquor infused with bitter herbs), white wine, and sparkling water and garnished with a blood-orange wedge. The *spritz* most popular with women (less alcohol, lighter) is made with Aperol (orange-flavored liquor), rather than Campari.

Get your *spritz* to take away *(da portar via)*, and join the young people out on the piazza. This is a classic opportunity to enjoy a real discussion with smart, English-speaking students who see tourists not as pests, but as interesting people from far away. For an instant conversation starter, ask about the current political situation in Italy, the right-wing party's policy on immigrants, or the cultural differences between Italy's North and South.

A typical snack stand selling all kinds of fresh, hot, and ready-to-eat seafood appetizers sets up in Piazza della Frutta between 17:00–20:30 (daily except Sun). Belly up to the bar with your drink and try whatever's being served.

Caffè Pedrocchi—This white-columned Neoclassical café is not just a café. A complex of meeting rooms and entertainment venues, it stirs the Italian soul (at least, patriotic Italian souls). Built in 1831 during the period of Austrian rule, the Caffè Pedrocchi was inaugurated for the fourth Italian Congress of Scientists, which convened during the mid–19th century to stir up nationalistic fervor as Italy struggled to become a united nation. As a symbol of patriotic hope, it was the target (no surprise) of a student uprising plot in 1848. You can still see a bullet hole in the wall of the Sala Bianca, where one of the insurgents was killed. Nowadays, you get more foam than fervor.

Each room is decorated and furnished in a different color: red, white, and green—representing the colors of the Italian flag. In the Sala Verde (Green Room), people are welcome to sit and enjoy the beautiful interior without ordering anything or having to pay—in fact, you can even bring your own food and eat it free. Otherwise, take a seat in the Red or White rooms and order from the menu of teahouse fare, including salads, sandwiches, and the writer Stendhal's beloved *zabaglione,* a creamy custard (June–Sept daily 9:00–24:00; Oct–May Sun–Wed 9:00–21:00, Thu–Sat 9:00–24:00; entrance is at intersection of Oberdan and VIII Febbraio, between Piazza delle Erbe and Piazza Cavour; tel. 049-878-1231).

Piano Nobile: This upper, "noble floor" is more elaborate. The rooms are all in different styles, such as Greek, Etruscan, or Egyptian, with good English descriptions throughout. These rooms were intended to evoke memories of the glory of past epochs, which a united Italy had hopes of reliving.

Museum of the Risorgimento: The Piano Nobile hosts a small museum that traces Padua's role in Italian history, from the downfall of the Venetian Republic (1797) to the founding of the Republic of Italy (1948). Exhibits, a few with English descriptions, include uniforms, medals, weaponry, old artillery, Fascist propaganda posters, and a propagandistic video (in Italian, continuous 30-min loop), which shows the town in the 1930s and, later, during WWII bombardments.

The war and propaganda posters in the last room are haunting. An old woman pleads to those who might question the Fascist-driven war effort: "Don't betray my son." Another declares, "The Germans are truly our friends." And another asks, "And you...what are you doing?" (€4, Tue–Sun 9:30–12:30 & 15:30–18:00, closed Mon, tel. 049-820-5007.) You can reach Piano Nobile by a stairway

Near Venice

to the right of the Caffè's entrance.

▲**Baptistery**—If you're an art lover, but can't get in to see the Scrovegni Chapel, Padua's Baptistery is a good alternative. Originally, it was the private chapel of Padua's ruling family. Then, in 1405, Venice took over, killing Padua's ruling family and making it a baptistery. Located next to the Duomo, the Baptistery was frescoed (c.1370, about 70 years after Giotto) by Giusto de' Menabuoi.

The complex design must have made perfect and cohesive sense to the faithful in centuries past: with almighty Christ in majesty on top; approachable Mary and the multitude of saints providing the devout with access to God; the world (as known in the 14th century) kicking off a cycle of scenes that illustrate creation; and the four evangelists (Matthew, Mark, Luke, and John) with their books and symbols in the corners. A vivid crucifixion scene faces a gorgeous annunciation (€2.50, daily 10:00–18:00).

University of Padua

The seat of this prestigious university is adjacent to Caffè Pedrocchi. Founded in 1222, it's one of the first, greatest, and most progressive universities in Europe. Back when the Church controlled university curricula, a group of professors and students broke free from the University of Bologna and created this liberal school, independent of Catholic constraints and accessible to people of alternative faiths.

A haven for free thought, the university attracted intellectuals from all over Europe, including the great astronomer Copernicus, who realized here that the universe didn't revolve around him. And Galileo—notorious for disagreeing with the Church's views on science—called his 18 years on the faculty here the best of his life.

Today, students gather in ancient courtyards, surrounded by memories of illustrious alumni, including the first woman ever to receive a university degree (in 1678).

While the tour is more involved, anyone can pop into the university's 16th-century courtyard, the school's historic core. It's littered with the coats of arms of administrators. Classrooms, which open onto the square, are still used.

The big attraction among tourists is the university's historic anatomy theater, which you can only visit on a guided tour. Try to get a ticket, but keep in mind that it's not worth any heroics to catch.

Cost, Hours, Information: While it's free to visit the university, you must sign up for a 30-minute tour (€5) to see the anatomy theater. Only 30 people may enter at a time. Tours run three times a day (Mon, Wed, and Fri at 15:15, 16:15, and 17:15; Tue, Thu, and Sat at 9:15, 10:15, and 11:15, no tours on Sun). School groups often

Graduation Antics in Padua

With 60,000 students, Padua's university graduates individuals on any given day. A constant trickle of happy grads and their friends and families celebrate the big event.

During the school year, every 20 minutes or so, a student steps into a formal room (upstairs, above the university courtyard) to formally meet with the leading professors of his or her faculty. When they're finished, the students are given a green laurel wreath. They pose for formal group photos and family snapshots. It's a sweet scene. Then, craziness takes over.

The new graduates replace their somber clothing with raunchy outfits as gangs of friends gather around them in the street in front of the university. The roast begins. The gang rolls out a giant butcher-paper poster with a generally obscene caricature of the student and a litany of *This is Your Life*–style photos and stories. The new grad, subject to various embarrassing pranks, reads the funny statements out loud. The poster is then taped to the university wall for all to see (and allowed to stay there for 24 hours).

During the roast, the friends sing the catchy but obscene local university anthem reminding their newly esteemed friend not to get too huffy: *"Dottore, dottore. Dottore del buso del cul. Vaffancul, vaffancul"* (loosely translated: "Doctor, doctor. You're just a doctor of the a-hole...go f-off, go f-off"). Once you hear this song (with its fanfare and um-pah-pah catchiness) and see all the good-natured fun, you can't stop singing it.

book the entire visit, and many of the guides speak no English.

Confirm tour times and availability by calling 049-827-3047 or stopping by the university bookstore (located inside the palace, on the right side of courtyard). If the tour isn't booked, you can buy tickets from the bookstore 15 minutes before the tour is due to start.

Anatomy Theater Tour

The first two rooms of the tour are underwhelming: One features the supposed "pulpit of Galileo" (c. 1550) and portraits of 40 famous alums. The second is the Aula Magna, a ceremonial room for festivities. Everywhere you look you see the coats of arms of important faculty and leaders of university over the ages.

The highlight is Europe's first great anatomy theater (from 1594). Despite the Church's strict ban on autopsies, more than 300 students would pack this theater to watch professors dissect human cadavers (the bodies of criminals from another town). This had to be done in a "don't ask don't tell" kind of way, because the Roman Catholic Church has only allowed the teaching of anatomy through dissection since the late 1800s.

SLEEPING

In the Center

$$$ **Majestic Hotel Toscanelli** is a central, fancy hotel with 34 pleasant, air-conditioned rooms and a touch of charm, on a relatively quiet side street (Sb-€99–115, Db-€159–175, 10 percent discount with this book in 2008, superior rooms and suites available at extra cost, includes a wonderful breakfast, about 2 blocks south of Piazza delle Erbe at Via dell'Arco 2, tel. 049-663-244, fax 049-876-0025, www.toscanelli.com, majestic@toscanelli.com). From Piazza delle Erbe, head up Via dei Fabbri and take the first left, then turn right onto Via dell'Arco.

Near the Basilica of St. Anthony

$ **Hotel al Fagiano,** located on a side street west of Piazza del Santo, has 30 bright and cheery air-conditioned rooms decorated with Rossella Fagiano's modern-art canvases (Sb-€57, Db-€80, Tb-€90, ask for special prices with this book through 2008, breakfast €3–6 extra; with your back to the Basilica of St. Anthony, take Via Belludi, then veer right onto Via Locatelli, #45 is under portico on the right; tel. & fax 049-875-3396, www.alfagiano.com, info @alfagiano.com). This hotel is all about the union of a man and a woman (quite romantic).

$ **Hotel al Santo,** run by the Tenan family, offers 15 rooms with all the comforts a few steps from the basilica (Sb-€60, Db-€90, Tb-€130, Qb-€145, double-paned windows, air-con, quieter

---

Sleep Code

(€1 = about $1.30, country code: 39)

S = Single, **D** = Double/Twin, **T** = Triple, **Q** = Quad, **b** = bathroom, **s** = shower only. Unless otherwise noted, credit cards are accepted, English is spoken, and breakfast is included in these rates.

To help you easily sort through these listings, I've divided the rooms into three categories, based on the price for a standard double room with bath:

  $$$ **Higher Priced**—Most rooms €130 or more.
   $$ **Moderately Priced**—Most rooms between €95–130.
    $ **Lower Priced**—Most rooms €95 or less.

rooms off street, some rooms have views of basilica, free Internet access, Via del Santo 147, tel. 049-875-2131, fax 049-878-8076, www.alsanto.it, alsanto@alsanto.it).

$ Casa del Pellegrino, with 160 spotless, cheap, institutional rooms, is home to the pilgrims who come to pay homage to St. Anthony in the basilica next door, but welcomes any visitor to Padua (S-€45, Sb-€58, D-€56, Db-€72, Tb-€78, Qb-€90, most rooms have air-con, ask for a room off the street, breakfast-€6, elevator, Via Cesarotti 21, tel. 049-823-9711, fax 049-823-9780, www.casadelpellegrino.com, info@casadelpellegrino.com). They have a modern wing with 30 better rooms at the same price—just request a room in the *dependenza*.

Hostel: $ Ostello Città di Padova, near Prato della Valle, is a well-run hostel with 90 beds in four-, six-, and thirteen-bed rooms (€17 beds with sheets and breakfast; 4-person family rooms-€69, with bath-€72; non-members pay €3 per night extra, laundry, bike rentals in summer and lockers, reception open 7:00–9:30 & 16:30–23:00, rooms locked during afternoon but reception staffed if you need to leave bags, 23:00 curfew; bus #3, #8, or #18 from station, get off at Prato della Valle, Via Aleardi 30; tel. 049-875-2219, www.ostellopadova.it, ostellopadova@ctgveneto.it).

Down by the Station

$$$ Hotel Grand'Italia offers four-star elegance, convenience, and prices. Housed in a palace, its 61 modern, business-class rooms are comfortable, and the breakfast room is bright and inviting (Db-generally €130 on Fri, Sat, and Sun; €165 otherwise but can be more during holidays and trade fairs, air-con, elevator, outside train station on the right side of main drag at Corso del Popolo 81, tel. 049-876-1111, fax 049-875-0850, www.hotelgranditalia.it, booking@hotelgranditalia.it).

$$ Hotel Monaco, a three-star hotel with 57 darkly decorated rooms, is a few doors away from the Grand'Italia and plain in comparison, but a heck of lot cheaper (Sb-€75, Db-€100–110, 10 percent discount with cash and this book through 2008, €5 optional breakfast, air-con, elevator, traffic noise; as you exit the station, it's to your right and across the street at Piazzale Stazione 3; tel. 049-664-344, fax 049-664-669, www.hotelmonacopadova .it, info@hotelmonacopadova.it, Adriana).

$$ Hotel al Cason, run by the Salmaso family, is a five-minute walk from the train station. It offers a good value for its 48 newly renovated and artistic rooms in a big, efficient, business-style hotel on a big, noisy, and forgettable street (Db-€98, air-con, elevator, Internet access, free parking, handy restaurant, tel. 049-662-636, fax 049-875-4217, leaving the station head to the right, Via Frà Paolo Sarpi #40, www.hotelalcason.com, info@hotelalcason.com).

EATING

The university population means cheap, good food abounds. My recommended restaurants are all centrally located in the historic core. You'd think there would be fine dining on the charming market squares, but on the piazzas, it's a take-out-pizza-and-casual-bar scene (dominated by students after dark). It's a fun place but only for drinks, rather than for a meal. (La Lanterna, at the neighboring Piazza dei Signori, is the only good, on-square dining that I've found.) The dreamily atmospheric neighborhood (just two blocks off the market squares) thrives after dark with trendy bars and a lively student *spritz* scene.

Romantic Dining in Padua

Hosteria Padovanino is very romantic, with a vanilla-candle-and-Titian-nude ambience. They serve traditional food with a creative twist and an emphasis on fish (€15 pastas, €25 *secondi*, open Mon–Sat, closed Sun, Via Santa Chiara 1, tel. 049-876-5341, reservations wise).

Ostaria Speroni offers something even more intimate than Padovanino. Foodies may appreciate the special care brought by chef Gilberto. The trick here is to talk with Gilberto and design the meal of your dreams, which is especially easy if it includes a fish dish (€12 pastas, €20 *secondi*, open nightly, Via Sperone Speroni 32, tel. 049-875-3370).

Eating near the Center

La Lanterna has a forgettable interior, but a meal here includes a rare-in-Padua chance to sit in a grand square under the stars, surrounded by great architecture. It's fine for pizza and basic meals (€8 pastas and pizzas, €14 *secondi*, Fri–Wed 12:00–15:00 & 19:00–24:00, closed Thu, Piazza dei Signori 39, tel. 049-660-770, reservations smart).

Osteria dei Fabbri, with shared rustic tables, offers just the right mix of class and accessibility, quality and price. It's a great choice for a memorable meal (Mon–Sat 12:30–14:30 & 19:30–22:30, closed Sun, Via dei Fabbri 13, tel. 049-650-336).

Brek, tucked into a corner of Piazza Cavour 20, is an easy self-service *ristorante* with healthy and affordable choices. It's big, bright, practical, and family-friendly (daily 11:30–15:30 & 18:30–22:00, tel. 049-875-3788).

If the markets are closed, stock up on picnic items at the **PAM supermarket,** in a tiny *piazzetta* east of Caffè Pedrocchi (Mon–Sat 8:00–20:30, closed Wed evenings and all day Sun, Piazzetta Garzeria 3, tel. 049-657-006).

Eating near the Basilica of St. Anthony

Pago Pago dishes up €4–8 wood-fired Neapolitan pizzas (a local favorite), a variety of big €8 salads, and daily specials. Get there early for dinner or wait (Wed–Mon 12:00–14:00 & 19:00–22:30, pizza until 24:00, closed Tue; just 2 blocks from Basilica of St. Anthony, heading north on Via del Santo take the first right onto Via Galileo Galilei to #59; tel. 049-665-558).

Casa del Pellegrino Ristorante caters to St. Anthony pilgrims with simple, basic, and hearty meals, served in a cheery dining room, just north of the basilica (€3–4 pastas, €6–12 *secondi*, pizza served only in evening, daily 12:00–14:00 & 19:30–21:30, Sun lunch by reservation only, Via Cesarotti 21, tel. 049-823-9711).

Zairo is a huge *ristorante*/pizzeria with reasonable prices, delicious and homemade pastas, Veneto specialties, snappy service, and a local clientele (Tue–Sun 11:30–15:30 & 18:30–24:00, closed Mon, east side of Prato della Valle at #51, tel. 049-663-803).

Pollodoro la Gastronomica, a take-out deli near the basilica, sells roast chicken and will make sandwiches (Wed–Sat and Mon 8:30–14:00 & 17:00–20:00, Sun 8:30–14:00, closed Tue, 100 yards from basilica at Via Belludi 34; with your back to the basilica entrance, it's under the arches on the left; tel. 049-663-718). You can picnic at the nearby cloisters of the basilica.

TRANSPORTATION CONNECTIONS

From Padua by Train to: Venice (3/hr, 30 min), **Vicenza** (2/hr, fewer on weekends, 25 min), **Milan** (1–2/hr, generally leaving at :24 and :54 past the hour, 2.5 hrs), **Verona** (2/hr, 1 hr).

By Bus to: Venice's Marco Polo Airport (€5—buy ticket from driver, hourly from 5:25–22:25, 1 hr, €1/bag, departs from Padua's bus station in Piazzale Boschetti).

Vicenza

To many architects, Vicenza (vih-CHEHN-zah) is a pilgrimage site. Entire streets look like the back of a nickel. This is the city of Andrea Palladio (1508–1580), the 16th-century Renaissance architect who gave us the Palladian style that is so influential in countless British country homes.

Palladio's real name was Andrea di Pietro della Gondola, but his genius was such that one of his patrons—responsible for the architect's liberal arts education—gave him the nickname of Palladio, an allusion to Pallas Athena, Greek goddess of wisdom and the arts.

The town's enthusiasm for its Palladian architecture is due

partly to its aggressive subjugation by Venice. While little Vicenza couldn't buck Venetian rule, it could enjoy a bit of freedom in its art. Classicism was Vicenza's revenge against Venetian Gothic and Venice's ubiquitous winged lions. But as grandiose as Vicenza's Palladian facades may feel, there is little marble here. The city lacked the wealth to build with much more than painted wood and plaster.

For the casual visitor, a quick stop to Vicenza (on any day but Mon, when major sights are closed) offers plenty of Palladio—the last great artist of the Renaissance. And 2008 promises to be a great year for Vicenza as the town celebrates Palladio's 500th birthday (see www.andreapalladio500.it).

ORIENTATION

Tourist Information

The main TI is at Piazza Matteotti 12 (daily 9:00–13:00 & 14:00–18:00, tel. 0444-320-854, www.vicenzae.org); a second office is at Piazza dei Signori 8 (daily 10:00–14:00 & 14:30–18:30). The TI sometimes offers guided tours in English (April–Sept). Architecture fans appreciate the TI's *Vicenza Città e le Ville del Palladio nel Veneto* booklet (€2.50, in English).

Arrival in Vicenza

From the train station, it's a five-minute **walk** up wide Viale Roma to the bottom of Corso Palladio. Or it's a short **bus** ride to Piazza Matteotti and the top of Corso Palladio. For a day trip, consider catching the bus #1, #2, #5, or #7 from the train station to Piazza Matteotti and doing your sightseeing on the way back (€1.10, tickets sold at *tabacchi* shop in station, stop is immediately to your left as you exit the station). Validate your ticket in the machine as you board the bus. Get off at Piazza Matteotti, a skinny, park-like square in front of a white Neoclassical building. A **taxi** to Piazza Matteotti costs about €6. Vicenza has no official baggage check, but the recommended Hotel Campo Marzio will store bags for free, even if you're not staying there.

Helpful Hints

Combo-Tickets: Most of Vicenza's sights are covered by a combo-ticket called **Card Musei** (€8/3 days, €12 Family Ticket, sold only at the Olympic Theater, which you can only enter with this card). The card also covers the Archaeological and Natural History Museum (next to the Church of Santa Corona), but doesn't cover the Palazzo Leoni Montanari or the villas outside of town. The pricier €11 combo-ticket (Biglietto

Vicenza

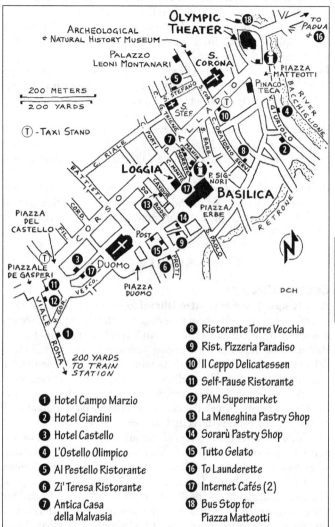

1 Hotel Campo Marzio
2 Hotel Giardini
3 Hotel Castello
4 L'Ostello Olimpico
5 Al Pestello Ristorante
6 Zi' Teresa Ristorante
7 Antica Casa della Malvasia

8 Ristorante Torre Vecchia
9 Rist. Pizzeria Paradiso
10 Il Ceppo Delicatessen
11 Self-Pause Ristorante
12 PAM Supermarket
13 La Meneghina Pastry Shop
14 Sorarù Pastry Shop
15 Tutto Gelato
16 To Launderette
17 Internet Cafés (2)
18 Bus Stop for Piazza Matteotti

Cumulativo) gets you into every sight in Vicenza except for exhibits in Basilica Palladiana.

Market Days: In the mornings (7:00–13:00), Vicenza hosts a Tuesday market on Piazza dei Signori, and a larger Thursday market on Piazza dei Signori, Piazza Duomo, Piazza del Castello, and Viale Roma.

Internet Access: Try **Vicenza.Com** (daily 10:00–13:00 & 16:00–19:30, next to TI at Piazza dei Signori 6, tel. 0444-540-430) or **Bar Michele** (Mon–Sat 7:00–19:30, closed Sun, near Piazza del Castello at Via San Francesco Vecchio 1).

Laundry: The self-service **Washing Point** is across the river, a couple of blocks from Piazza Matteotti (daily 8:00–22:00, Contrà XX Settembre 27).

Parking: Two cheap lots (Parcheggio Bassano and Parcheggio Cricoli, €2.20/day per person, not per car) are north and south of the city. At either lot, you can catch free shuttle bus #10 to the center.

Private Guide: Romina Rampazzo is a new, young guide with a command of both English and the hometown she loves (€80/half-day private tour, mobile 349-218-5656, romiramp@tin.it).

Best Gelato: Tutto Gelato is the local favorite, with natural colors and plenty of fresh and creative flavors (Tue–Sun 10:00–24:00, closed Mon, a block behind basilica at Contrà Frasche del Gambero 26).

SIGHTS

Central Vicenza

▲▲**Olympic Theater (Teatro Olimpico)**—Palladio's last work is one of his greatest. It was commissioned by the Olympic Academy, a society of Vicenzan scholars and intellectuals (including Palladio), for the purpose of staging performances and intellectual debates. Begun in 1580, shortly before Palladio died, the theater was actually completed by a fellow architect, Vincenzo Scamozzi.

Your visit includes three rooms: the first two rooms were frescoed in 1647 using Greek themes (glass cases display original 1585 oil lamps). The third is the actual theater.

Modeled after the theaters of antiquity, this theater is a wood-and-stucco festival of classical columns, statues, and an oh-wow stage bursting with perspective tricks. Behind the stage, framed by a triumphal arch, are five streets that recede at different angles. The streets, depicting an idealized city of Thebes, were created for the gala opening of *Oedipus Rex*, the first play ever performed in the theater. While designed to seat 800 people, more than 2,000 attended on that opening night in 1585. In homage to Palladio, the theater has kept the original stage set.

Sit in the middle to enjoy the perspective. Rather than marble, the theater is all bricks and plaster with reinforcing iron inside. (That's a blessing—if it had been made of precious marble, Napoleon would have carted it all back to Paris.) Perspective tricks were a real turn-on back then. The main street is only 40 feet deep. To accentuate the illusion during the theater's debut, dwarves and smaller-than-normal oil lamps appeared in the fake distance.

Many of the statues in niches on the stage are modeled after the people who funded the work—junior members are portrayed as Roman soldiers of antiquity, senior members as senators. Panels at the top show the labors of Hercules, in keeping with the classical antiquity theme that was all the rage in the 16th century. In contrast to the stunning stage, the audience's wooden benches are simple and crude (entry possible only with €8 Card Musei, which covers other Vicenza sights—no separate theater ticket available; dense 45-min audioguide-€3 or €5/two people; Tue–Sun 9:00–17:00, closed Mon, July–Aug until 19:00, last entry 30 min before closing, occasionally closed when theater is in use, entrance to the left of TI, tel. 0444-222-800). When you step back outside, look up the town's main drag—named after Palladio. It's the same main street you saw in his theater.

Performances: One of the oldest indoor theaters in Europe and considered one of the world's best, it's still used for performances from April through June (jazz and classical music) and from September through October (Greek tragedies and dramas). Shows start at 21:00 (for details, see www.vicenzae.org).

▲**Church of Santa Corona**—A block away from the Olympic Theater, this "Church of the Holy Crown" was built in the 13th century to house a thorn from the Crown of Thorns, given to the Bishop of Vicenza by the French King Louis IX (free, Mon 16:00–18:00, Tue–Sun 8:30–12:00 & 15:00–18:00). The church has two artistic highlights: the art embellishing its high altar and a fine Bellini painting.

Study the exquisite inlaid marble and mother-of-pearl work decorating the high altar (c. 1670). As Mary appears before Vicenza, you get a realistic peek at the town's skyline (at least as artists in 1670 thought the town had looked in 1426, the year Mary supposedly visited). Walk all around the altar. Find the Last Supper, the dramatic resurrection scene, Christ (in a scene as ugly as Abu Ghraib) being forced to wear the Crown of Thorns, and the King of France giving a thorn to the local bishop (the act this church was built to commemorate). Notice also the Florentine-style inlaid wood in the choir that shows off medieval Vicenza townscapes.

Giovanni Bellini's fine painting, *Baptism of Christ,* is nearby, on the left (south) side of the nave. A powerful vertical line connects the Father, Son, Holy Spirit, a cup dripping with water, and John the Baptist. Three women—clothed in radiant colors and symbolizing faith, hope, and charity—look on. It's pure Renaissance style as John realistically shifts his weight to one side. The frame is a festival of classic motifs and proportions (c. 1500, insert a €0.50 coin for light).

Archaeological and Natural History Museum—Located next door to the Church of Santa Corona, this museum's ground floor features Roman antiquities (mosaics, statues, and artifacts excavated from Rome's Baths of Caracalla, plus swords) and a barbarian warrior skeleton complete with sword and helmet. Prehistoric scraps are upstairs, and there are a few English description sheets near exhibit entryways throughout (covered by €8 Card Musei—see page 138, Tue–Sun 9:00–17:00, closed Mon, last entry 15 min before closing, tel. 0444-320-440).

Palazzo Leoni Montanari—Across the street from the Church of Santa Corona, this small museum feels overlooked. It's a palatial riot of Baroque, with cherub-cluttered ceilings jumbled like a preschool in heaven. A quick stroll shows off Venetian paintings and a floor of Russian icons (€3.50, Tue–Sun 10:00–18:00, closed Mon, Contrà Santa Corona 25).

Corso Andrea Palladio—From the Olympic Theater or Church of Santa Corona, stroll up Vicenza's main drag, Corso Andrea Palladio, and see why they call Vicenza "Venezia on terra firma." A steady string of Renaissance palaces and Palladian architecture is peopled by Vicenzans (considered by their neighbors to be as uppity as most of their colonnades) and punctuated by fancy *gelaterie*. After a few

blocks, turn left, and you'll see the basilica on Piazza dei Signori.

Piazza dei Signori—Vicenza's main square has been the center of town ever since it was the site of the ancient Roman forum. It's dominated by the commanding **Basilica Palladiana,** with its 270-foot-tall, 13th-century tower. This was not a church, but a meeting place for local big shots. It was young Palladio's proposal—to redo Vicenza's dilapidated Gothic palace of justice in the Neo-Greek style—that established him as Vicenza's favorite architect. The rest of Palladio's career was a one-man construction boom. Opposite the basilica, the brick-columned **Loggia del Capitaniato**—home of the Venetian governor and one of Palladio's last works—gives you an easy chance to compare early Palladio (the basilica) with late Palladio (the loggia).

Normally open to tourists during frequent special exhibitions, the basilica is likely to be closed throughout 2008 for restoration work (tel. 0444-322-196, see www.vicenzae.org for schedule). Even if the basilica is closed, you can climb the 15th-century stairway (unless it's blocked off for renovation). Halfway up the steps, there's a gargoyle-like lion's mouth (representing the long arm of the Venetian Republic). Centuries ago, people used to sneak notes into this mouth, anonymously reporting neighbors suspected of carrying communicable diseases that could bring on the plague.

The arcaded upper floor contains the entrance to the huge basilica. The basilica's roof, shaped like the hull of an upside-down boat, has a nautical feel, which is augmented by the porthole windows.

Outside, on Piazza dei Signori, note the two tall, **15th-century columns** topped by Jesus and the winged lion (a symbol of both St. Mark and Venice). When Venice took over Vicenza in the early 1400s, these columns were added—à la St. Mark's Square—to give the city a Venetian feel.

If you're strolling through town back to the station, finish your walk, continuing along the Corso Palladio. At Piazzale de Gasperi (where you'll find the PAM supermarket, a handy place to grab a picnic for the train ride), dip into the park called **Giardino Salvi** (for one last Palladio-style loggia, closed to visitors but viewable from outside), and then walk  five minutes down Viale Roma back to the station. Trains leave about every hour for Milan/Verona and Venice (less than an hour away).

Villas on the Outskirts of Vicenza

Vicenza is surrounded by dreamy Venetian villas. As Venice's commercial empire receded in the 1500s (when trade began to pick up along the Atlantic seaboard and dwindle in the Mediterranean), it redirected its economic agenda to terra firma—dominating the Veneto region. During the 16th century, Venice consolidated and incorporated Veneto into its economy. Rather than seagoing trade (Venice's forte), this area was busy with agribusiness—and that meant a need for lavish country villas. The region's many splendid villas were multifunctional. They provided a business headquarters, a suitable place to host VIP guests, warehouse facilities, and the family home of the farmer. The standard Palladian villa comes with three floors: kitchen and cellar in the cool basement; fancy ground-level *piano nobile*—the "noble floor"—where aristocrats lived and hosted friends among marvelous frescoes; and an upstairs, with rooms for the extended family and for storing goods. The most famous villa here, Villa la Rotonda, is an exception. It was the home not of a wealthy farmer, but of a retired church official.

The following two villas are worth a visit for architecture buffs (even with limited time). Both houses are furnished with period pieces and come with good English descriptions. Pick up the free English brochure on Palladio's villas from the TI if you plan to visit.

Villa la Rotonda—Thomas Jefferson's Monticello was inspired by Palladio's Rotonda (a.k.a. Villa Almerico Capra). Started by Palladio in 1566, it was finished by his pupil, Scamozzi. The white, gently domed building with grand colonnaded entries is built to look as if it popped out of the grassy slope. Palladio, who designed a number of country villas, had a knack for using the natural setting for dramatic effect. This private—but sometimes tourable—residence is on the edge of Vicenza (€5 to enter grounds, mid-March–mid-Oct Tue–Sun 10:00–12:00 & 15:00–18:00, closed  Mon, shorter hours off-season, confirm hours before heading out; €10 for interior—open only Wed 10:00–12:00 & 15:00–18:00; Via Rotonda 45, tel. 0444-321-793). To get to the villa from Vicenza's train station, hop a bus (#8, 2/hr, stop is to the left of the station as you're facing it on Viale Venezia—ask the driver or a local where to get off) or take a taxi. For a quick round trip any time of day, you can zip out by cab (about €8, 5-min ride from train station) to see the building sitting regally atop its hill, and then ride the same cab back.

Villa Valmarana ai Nani—The 17th-century "Villa of the Dwarves" is just up the street from Villa la Rotonda. This makes a convenient stop if you want to see a villa interior. The elegant

 Neoclassical estate features panoramic views and 18th-century murals by Tiepolo.

The villa's name comes from the local legend of an ancient manor house owned by a nobleman whose daughter was born a dwarf. Her father surrounded her with dwarf servants so she wouldn't realize she was small. One day as she was looking out the window, she saw a handsome prince ride by on his horse. Realizing she was a dwarf, she killed herself in anguish. Her servants—so saddened by her death that they turned to stone—now line the wall of the villa like petrified sentries.

The rooms in the main house include frescoes with scenes from the Trojan War, classical myths, and Italian lyrical poems. The frescoes in the guest house *(foresteria)* are nearly all by Tiepolo's son, Giandomenico, whose themes highlight 18th-century gentrified culture—the idealized tranquility of peasants, the exotic fashion and styles of the Chinese from a Western perspective, and scenes from Carnevale (€6, Tue–Sun 10:00–12:00 & 15:00–18:00, closed Mon; from Villa la Rotonda, head a few steps downhill, then up the slope on Stradella Valmarana about 200 yards; tel. 0444-321-803).

SLEEPING

Vicenza is so easy to visit from Venice or Padua that few people actually sleep here. If you do, keep in mind that several annual trade fairs cause hotel prices to skyrocket (in 2008: Jan 13–20, May 17–21, and Sept 6–10).

$$$ Hotel Campo Marzio, a four-star, American-style, pricey place, has 35 rooms with all the comforts facing a park on a busy street (Db-€169–184, pricier rooms are bigger with more amenities, air-con, elevator, free bikes, free parking, a few minutes' walk in front of train station at Viale Roma 21, tel. 0444-545-700, fax 0444-320-495, www.hotelcampomarzio.com, info @hotelcampomarzio.com).

$$ Hotel Giardini, with three stars and 17 sleek rooms, has splashy pastel colors and a refreshing feel (Sb-€83, Db-€114, air-con, elevator, on busy street but has double-paned windows, across from bus stop a block away from Piazza Matteotti/Olympic Theater on Via Giuriolo 10, tel. & fax 0444-326-458, www.hotelgiardini .com, info@hotelgiardini.com, Stefano).

$$ Hotel Castello, on Piazza del Castello, has 18 homey, artsy, quiet rooms, and lots of stairs (Sb-€90–120, Db-€120–149 depending on trade fairs, air-con, rooftop terrace, Contrà Piazza del Castello 24, tel. 0444-323-585, fax 0444-323-583, www.hotelcastelloitaly .com, info@hotelcastelloitaly.it). It's a five-minute walk from the train station (turn right after Hotel Campo Marzio, head up hill to square,

---

Sleep Code

(€1 = about $1.30, country code: 39)
S = Single, **D** = Double/Twin, **T** = Triple, **Q** = Quad, **b** = bathroom. Unless otherwise noted, credit cards are accepted, English is spoken, and breakfast is included in these rates. Prices can be higher during trade fairs.

To help you easily sort through these listings, I've divided the rooms into three categories, based on the price for a standard double room with bath.

$$$ **Higher Priced**—Most rooms €150 or more.
  $$ **Moderately Priced**—Most rooms between €110–150.
   $ **Lower Priced**—Most rooms €110 or less.

in an alley to right of Ristorante agli Schioppi).

$ *Hostel:* **L'Ostello Olimpico,** just a few years old, is wonderfully central on Piazza Matteotti, a few steps from the Olympic Theater (85 beds, 4- to 6-bed rooms-€18 per person, Db and family rooms-€23 per person, includes sheets and breakfast, non-members pay €3/night extra, closed 9:30–16:15, curfew-24:00; best to reserve several weeks in advance by fax or email, Viale Giuriolo 7/9, tel. 0444-540-222, fax 0444-547-762, www.ostellovicenza .com, ostello.vicenza@tin.it).

EATING

The local specialty is marinated cod, called *baccalà alla vicentina.*

In **Al Pestello**'s casually elegant dining room, owner Fabio patiently and lovingly describes his historic *cucina vicentina* (including *baccalà*) from a menu written in dialect. The day's offerings are created from the freshest seasonal ingredients to complement an extensive list of local and national wines (€9 pastas, €14 *secondi*, Mon 19:30–22:30, Tue–Sat 12:30–14:30 & 19:30–22:30, closed Sun, a block from Church of Santa Corona at Contrà Santo Stefano 3, tel. 0444-323-721).

Zi' Teresa is a favorite among locals for its romantic ambience and moderately priced traditional cuisine and pizzas (€6 pizzas, €7 pastas, €13 *secondi*, Thu–Tue 11:45–14:30 & 18:30–23:00, closed Wed; a couple blocks southeast of Piazza dei Signori, at intersection with Contrà Proti, Contrà S. Antonio 1; tel. 0444-321-411).

Antica Casa della Malvasia, an *osteria* since 1210, is a popular, atmospheric, cavernous joint serving up affordable regional favorites and homemade pastas (daily 12:00–15:30 & 19:00–23:30, just off Piazza dei Signori on a little alley directly across from bell tower at Contrà delle Morette 5, tel. 0444-543-704). The attached *enoteca* offers wines (€0.80–3.50/glass) and snacks (closes at 21:30 in winter).

Ristorante Torre Vecchia is an appealing, old-time bistro with Art Nouveau decor, bedecked with Gibson Girl portraits and 19th-century lovers' photos. Sample creatively prepared, reasonably priced local specialties (€6 *antipasti*, €6 pastas, €10 *secondi*) paired with great, affordable local wines (Mon–Sat 19:00–22:00, closed Sun, near the basilica at Contrà Oratorio dei Servi 19, tel. 0444-320-001).

Ristorante Pizzeria Paradiso, with indoor and outdoor seating on a narrow square, offers dozens of inexpensive options, including pasta, wood-fired pizzas, and a €5–10 seafood or veggie buffet (daily 12:00–14:30 & 19:00–23:00, closed Mon in winter, south of Piazza dei Signori and Piazza Erbe at Via Pescherie Vecchie 5, tel. 0444-322-320).

Cheap Eats: The delicatessen **Il Ceppo** makes up pasta salads, roasted meats and vegetables, lasagna, savory crepes, and sandwiches to go. To get your meal heated, request *"Riscaldare, per favore"* (Thu–Tue 8:00–13:00 & 16:00–19:30, closed Wed, Corso Palladio 196, a few steps from Piazza Matteotti, tel. 0444-544-414). Take your picnic to the nearby park (next to the Olympic Theater) or to Piazza dei Signori.

A cheap, self-service **Self-Pause Ristorante** is just off Piazza del Castello, where Corso Andrea Palladio meets Viale Roma. Expect self-service cafeteria dining for lunch; for dinner, there's a limited buffet of pizzas, pastas, salads, and dessert for €7.60 (Tue–Sat 12:00–14:30 & 19:00–22:00, Mon lunch only, Sun dinner only, Corso Andrea Palladio 10, tel. 0444-327-829).

A few steps away is the **PAM supermarket** for all your picnic needs (Mon–Tue and Thu–Sat 8:00–20:00, Wed 8:00–14:00, closed Sun, follow the curve of the road just outside the city wall).

Pastry: **La Meneghina** is an atmospheric pastry shop (Tue–Sun 8:00–24:00, closed Mon, pricey meals 12:00–16:00 & 20:00–23:00 in summer, until 22:00 in winter; on Contrà Cavour 18, a short street between Piazza dei Signori and Corso Andrea Palladio; tel. 0444-323-305).

The tiny **Sorarù** pastry shop, nearby on Piazza dei Signori, has lots of sidewalk tables within tickling distance of the Palladio statue (Thu–Tue 8:30–13:00 & 15:30–20:00, closed Wed; next to the basilica in Piazzetta Palladio, tel. 0444-320-915).

TRANSPORTATION CONNECTIONS

From Vicenza by Train to: Venice (roughly 2/hr, 1 hr), **Padua** (roughly 2/hr, 20 min), **Ravenna** (about hourly, 3–4 hours, depending on train, with changes in Padua and Ferrara or Bologna), **Verona** (2/hr, 40 min).

Verona

Romeo and Juliet made Verona a household word. Alas, a visit here has nothing to do with those two star-crossed lovers. You can pay to visit the house that falsely claims to be Juliet's (with an almost-believable balcony and a courtyard swarming with tour groups), join in the tradition of rubbing the breast of Juliet's statue to help find a lover (or pick up the sweat of someone who can't), and even make a pilgrimage to what isn't "La Tomba di Giulietta."

Despite the fiction, the town has been an important crossroads for 2,000 years and is therefore packed with genuine history. R-and-J fans will take some solace in the fact that two real feuding families, the Montecchi and the Capellos, were the models for Shakespeare's Montagues and Capulets. And, if R and J had existed and were alive today, they would recognize much of their "hometown."

Verona's main attractions are its wealth of Roman ruins; the remnants of its 13th- and 14th-century political and cultural boom; its 21st-century, quiet, pedestrian-only ambience; and a world-class opera festival each summer (www.arena.it). After Venice's festival of tourism, the Veneto's second city (in population and in artistic importance) is a cool and welcome sip of pure Italy, where dumpsters are painted by schoolchildren as class projects and public spaces are the domain of locals, not tourists. If you like Italy but don't need blockbuster sights, this town is a joy.

ORIENTATION

The vibrant and enjoyable core of Verona is along Via Mazzini between Piazza Brà (pronounced "bra") and Piazza Erbe, Verona's market square since Roman times. Head straight for Piazza Brà—and stroll. While Via Mazzini attracts mob scenes during the *passeggiata* (evening stroll), don't neglect the parallel Corso Porta Borsari. All sights of importance are located within an easy walk through the old town, which is defined by a bend in the river. For a good day trip to Verona, visit the Roman Arena and take my self-guided walk (see page 150).

Tourist Information

Verona has two TIs: at the train station (daily 8:00–19:00, tel. 045-800-0861) and at Piazza Brà (Mon–Sat 9:00–19:00, Sun 9:00–15:00; facing the large yellow-white building, the TI is across the street to your right; tel. 045-806-8680, www.tourism.verona.it, public WC on Piazza Brà). At either TI, pick up the free city map for a list of sights and opening hours, and confirm the walking-tour schedule. If you're staying the night, ask about concerts or pick up a monthly entertainment guide (either *Carnet Verona* or *Verona Live*) for about €1 at any newsstand.

Verona Card: This tourist card covers bus transportation and entrance to all the recommended Verona sights, except for the manicured garden named Giardino Giusti (€8/day or €12/3 days, sold at participating sights and at *tabacchi*—tobacco shops—in the city center). If you arrive at the train station, it makes sense to buy the card at the station TI, because it'll cover your bus ride to and from the city center and virtually all of your sightseeing for one painless price.

Arrival in Verona

By Train: Get off at Verona's Porta Nuova station. On the far left as you emerge from the passage are pay WCs, phones, an ATM, and baggage storage (€4/5 hrs, daily 7:00–23:00). From the main lobby—where the ticket windows are—a smaller hall branches off to the right, where you'll find a TI, train information desk, and another ATM.

Avoid the boring 15-minute walk from the station to Piazza Brà by catching the bus. Buses leave from directly in front of the station. To cover your trip into town, either get a Verona Card (listed above) or buy an individual ticket before boarding from a *tabacchi* shop inside the station (€1/1 hr; €3.10 valid until midnight).

Confirm the route by asking *"Per centro?"* (pehr CHEN-troh). You'll probably have a choice of bus #11, #12, or #13, leaving from Platform A (buses are orange or green-and-purple). If you have an individual ticket, validate it by stamping it in the machine in the middle of the bus. Buses stop on Piazza Brà, the square with the can't-miss-it Roman Arena. The TI is just a few steps beyond the bus stop (located along the medieval walls). Buses return to the station from the bus stop just outside the city wall (on the right), where Corso Porta Nuova hits Piazza Brà.

Taxis pick up only at taxi stands (at Piazza Brà and train station) and cost about €7 for the quick ride between the train station and Piazza Brà.

By Car: Drivers will find cheap parking at the stadium, at the long-term parking near the train station and city walls, and across the river from the Basilica of San Zeno Maggiore. There are a few free spaces across the river from the fortress/castle called Castelvecchio (on Lungoadige Cangrande). The most central lot is behind the Roman Arena on Piazza Cittadella (guarded, €1/hr). Street parking costs €1.50 per hour (buy ticket at *tabacchi* shop to put on dashboard, spaces marked with blue lines). The town center is closed to traffic, but if you're staying here, your hotel can get you permission to drive in—ask when you book. Otherwise your license plate could be photographed and you could have a €100 ticket waiting for you in the mail when you get home.

By Plane: From Verona's airport, catch a shuttle bus to the train station (€4.50, buy tickets on board, daily 6:30–23:30, 3/hr, 15 min). If going *to* the airport, catch the shuttle just to the left of the train station entrance (daily 5:40–23:10).

Helpful Hints

Sightseeing Schedules: Many sights are closed on Monday and are free on the first Sunday of every month.

Opera: In July and August, Verona's opera festival brings crowds and higher hotel prices (upper-level seats about €25, book tickets either online at www.arena.it or by calling 045-800-5151, box office open Mon–Fri 9:00–12:00 & 15:15–17:15, Sat–Sun 9:00–12:00; in opera season, it's open daily 10:00–17:45, or until 21:00 on days when there's a show).

Internet Access: Try **Internet Train** (Mon–Fri 10:00–22:00, Sat–Sun 14:00–20:00, Via Roma 17A, a couple of blocks off Piazza Brà toward Castelvecchio, tel. 045-801-3394) or **Internet Etc.** (Tue–Sat 10:30–20:00, Sun–Mon 15:30–20:00, off Via Mazzini on Via Quattro Spade 3B, tel. 045-800-0222).

Post Office: The post office is at Via Cattaneo 23E (Mon–Sat 8:30–18:30, closed Sun, near Piazza Brà).

TOURS

Walking Tours—The TI on Piazza Brà organizes 75-minute tours daily in English for €10 per person (April–Nov daily at 17:30; Sat–Mon also at 11:30; confirm schedule and meeting point at TI, call 045-810-3173 or 333-219-9645, or visit www.julietandco.com or www.venetoguide.it).

Private Guides—Two excellent and enthusiastic Verona guides enjoy giving private tours of the town and region to readers of this book (€105/half-day per group, tours tailored to your interests—villas, wine-tasting, etc.). They are Marina Menegoi (tel. 045-801-2174, mobile 328-958-1108, milanit@libero.it) and Valeria Biasi (mobile 348-9034-238, www.veronatours.com, valeria @veronatours.com).

SELF-GUIDED WALK

Welcome to Verona Town Walk

This walk covers the essential sights in the town core, starting at Piazza Brà and ending at the cathedral. Allow 90 minutes (including the tower climb and dawdling, but not the optional detours).

❶ Piazza Brà

If you're wondering where the name came from, it's a local dialect for open space. A generation ago, this piazza was noisy with cars. Now it's open and people-friendly—the community family room and natural festival grounds. The big statue is of Italy's first king, Victor Emmanuel I, and celebrates Italian unity, won back in the 1860s.

Piazza Brà is all about strolling...the *passeggiata* is a national

Verona

200 YARDS
200 METERS

☙ VIEW

ROMAN BRIDGE

CASTEL SAN PIETRO

DUOMO

ADIGE

GARIBALDI

PAVINO

PIETRA

ROMAN THEATER

SANT' ANASTASIA

VIA CAPP.

ROSA

PIGNA

VIA DUOMO

FORTI

BORSARI

SAN. FRAN

S. MARIA

SOTTORIVA

NUOVA

VITT.

S. LORENZO

CORSO CAVOUR

OBERDAN

CORSO P.

CATULLO

4 SPADE

VIA MARIO

V. ANFI

SCALA

MAZZINI

CAPELLO

END

PALAZZO RAGIONE, TORRE LAMBERTI + WC

NAVI

DOGANA

HOUSE OF JULIET

CATT.

LISTON

WC

PIAZZA BRÀ START

ARENA
(ARROW SHOWS ENTRANCE)

OLD CITY WALLS

MACELLO

CORSO PORTA NUOVA

PIAZZA CITTA-DELLA

TO TRAIN STATION

PALLONE

ALEARDI

DCH

Near Venice

❶ Piazza Brà
❷ Roman Arena
❸ Devotional Column
❹ Porta Borsari & Corso Porta Borsari
❺ Enoteca Oreste
❻ Piazza Erbe

❼ House of Juliet
❽ Piazza dei Signori
❾ Tombs of the Scaligeri Family
❿ Church of Sant'Anastasia
⓫ Ponte Pietra & River View
⓬ Duomo

sport in Italy. The broad, shiny sidewalk was named the "Liston" (ribbon) by 17th-century Venetians who made it big and wide (better for promenading socialites to see and be seen in all their finery). Just after World War II, opera singer Maria Callas lived above the Brek restaurant. As a starlet, she performed in the town's opera festival and found her husband in Verona (and likely never ate at Brek).

❷ Roman Arena

Just as modern stadiums are usually located outside of downtown districts today, Romans built this stadium outside the town walls.

With 72 aisles, this elliptical 466-by-400-foot amphitheater is the third-largest in the Roman world. Most of the stone you see is original. Dating from the first century A.D., it looks great in its pink marble. Over the centuries, crowds of up to 25,000 spectators have cheered Roman gladiator battles, medieval executions, and modern plays (including the popular opera festival, held every July and August, which takes advantage of the arena's famous acoustics). There's little to see inside except for the impressive stonework and great city views—if you climb to the top (€4, Tue–Sun 8:30–19:30, Mon 13:30–19:30, closes at 14:00 during opera season, last entry 1 hour before closing, WC near entry, tel. 045-800-3204).

❸ Devotional Column

In the Middle Ages, this column blessed a marketplace held here. Ten yards in front of it, a bronze plaque in the sidewalk shows the Roman city plan—a town of 20,000 placed strategically in the bend of the river, which provided protection on three sides. A wall enclosed the peninsula. The center of the grid was the forum, today's Piazza Erbe. (If you look down Via Mazzini, the busy main pedestrian drag, the bell tower in the distance marks Piazza Erbe).
• *From the bronze plaque, face Via Mazzini and go left (past Restaurant Rubiani) down Via Oberdan to an ancient gate, Porta Borsari.*

❹ Porta Borsari and Corso Porta Borsari

You're standing before the main entrance to Roman Verona. It functioned as a tollbooth (*borsari* means purse, referring to the collection of tolls here). Now cross into the ancient city and walk down Corso Porta Borsari, the ancient main drag, toward what was the forum. As you walk, discover bits of the town's illustrious past—chips of Roman columns, medieval reliefs, fine old facades, fossils in marble—as well as its elegant present of fancy shops in a setting that prioritizes pedestrians over cars.

• *A block before you reach Piazza Erbe, at Vicolo San Marco in Foro, detour right following the* Posso dell'Amore *sign. Twenty yards off Corso Porta Borsari, you'll find...*

❺ Enoteca Oreste

This funky wine and *grappa* bar is still run by Oreste (with his Chicagoan wife, Beverly) like a 1970s, old-style *enoteca*. Browse, munch, sample. There's no formal food, but an abundance of fun and hearty bar snacks instead. This historic *enoteca* was once the private chapel of the archbishop of Verona. Traces of the past hide between the bottles—ask Beverly to tell you the story (daily 8:00–20:00, Vicolo San Marco in Foro 7, tel. 045-803-4369). For romantics, the Posso dell'Amore (Well of Love) is in a cul-de-sac 30 yards farther along.

• *Return to Corso Porta Borsari and continue on until you hit a big square.*

❻ Piazza Erbe

This bustling market square is a photographer's delight. Its pastel buildings corral the fountains, pigeons, and people who have congregated here since Roman times, when this was a forum. Notice the Venetian lion hovering above the square, reminding locals of their conquerors since 1405. During medieval times, the stone canopy in the center held the scales where merchants measured the weight of goods they bought and sold, such as silk, wool, and wood. The fountain has bubbled here for 2,000 years. Its statue, originally Roman, had lost its head and arms. After a sculptor added a new head and arms, the statue became Verona's Madonna. She holds a small banner that reads: "I want justice and I bring peace." The city once had a San Gimignano–type skyline of noble family towers. The big families of the day erected tall towers to show off and and provide protection. Each (often feuding) local family had its own tower until the Scaligeri family (a.k.a. della Scala) took control and required its rivals to chop the tops off of their towers.

At the far end of Piazza Erbe, a market column featuring St. Zeno, the patron of Verona, oversees the action.

• *St. Zeno faces the much-appreciated House of Juliet (100 yards down Via Cappello to #23—just follow the crowds). Side-trip there now (but watch your wallet—it's a pickpocket's haven).*

❼ House of Juliet

This bogus house is Verona's touristic claim to fame. The tiny, admittedly romantic courtyard is a spectacle in itself, with tourists from all over the world posing on the balcony, Nebraskans polishing Juliet's bronze breast, and amorous graffiti everywhere. Hang

out and savor the spectacle. The information boxes offer a good history (€1 for two people: "While no documentation has been discovered to prove the truth of the legend, no documentation has disproved it either.") The "museum," which displays art inspired by the love story, plus costumes and the bed from Franco Zeffirelli's film *Romeo and Juliet*, is certainly not worth the €4 entry fee (Tue–Sun 8:30–19:30, Mon 13:30–19:30, tel. 045-803-4303).

Was there a Juliet Capulet? You just walked down the street of the cap makers (Via Cappello). Above the courtyard entry (looking out) is a coat of arms featuring a hat—representing a family that made hats and which would be named, logically, Capulet. Everyday, 10 volunteers at Verona's Juliet Club (www.julietclub .com) respond to countless letters addressed simply to Juliet, Verona, Italy.

• *Return to Piazza Erbe. From the center, head right, downhill toward the river on Via della Costa (which becomes Via Santa Maria Antica after Piazza dei Signori, below).*

The street is marked by an **arch** *with a whale's rib suspended from it. It was likely a souvenir brought home by a traveling merchant, reminding the townspeople of a big world out there. On your left is...*

❽ Piazza dei Signori

Literally the "square of the lords," this is Verona's sitting room, more quiet and harmonious than Piazza Erbe. The buildings—which span five centuries—define the square and are all linked by arches. The long portico on the left is inspired by Filippo Brunelleschi's Hospital of the Innocents (considered the first Renaissance building) in Florence.

Locals call the square Piazza Dante for the statue of the Italian poet Dante Alighieri that dominates it. Dante—always pensive, never smiling—seems to wonder why the tourists choose Juliet over him. Dante was expelled from Florence for political reasons and was granted asylum in Verona by the Scaligeri family. With the whale's rib behind you, you're facing the brick, crenellated, 13th-century Scaligeri residence. Behind Dante is the yellowish, 15th-century, Venetian Renaissance–style Portico of the Counsel. In front of Dante—and to his right (follow the white *WC* signs) is the 12th-century Romanesque **Palazzo della Ragione.**

Enter the courtyard. The impressive staircase—which goes nowhere—is the only surviving Renaissance staircase in Verona.

For a grand city view, you can climb to the top of the 13th-century **Torre dei Lamberti** (€2 for stairs, €3 for elevator, Tue–Sun 8:30–19:30, Mon 13:30–19:30, last entry 45 min before closing). The elevator saves you 245 steps—but you'll still need to climb about 45 more to get to the first viewing platform. It's not worth continuing up the endless spiral stairs to the second viewing platform.

• *Exit the courtyard the way you entered and turn right, continuing downhill. Within a block, you'll find the...*

❾ Tombs of the Scaligeri Family

These exotic and very Gothic 14th-century tombs, with their fine, original, wrought-iron protective cages, evoke the age when one family ruled Verona. The Scaligeri family was to Verona what the Medici family was to Florence. Notice the dogs' heads near the top of the tombs. On the first tomb, the dogs peer over a shield displaying a ladder. The Scaligeri family got rich making ladders, but money can't buy culture. When Marco Polo returned from Asia boasting of the wealth of Kublai Khan, the Scaligeri wanted to be associated with this powerful Khan by name. But misunderstanding Khan as *"cane"* (dog), one Scaligero changed his name to Can Grande (big dog), and another to Can Signore (lord dog).

• *Continue 20 yards to the next corner and take a left on Vicolo Cavalletto. At the first corner, turn right and walk to the big, unfinished brick facade of Verona's largest church.*

❿ Church of Sant'Anastasia

This church was built from the late 13th century through the 15th century, but the builders ran out of steam and the facade was never finished. The highlights of the interior are the grimacing hunchbacks that hold basins of holy water on their backs (near entrance at base of columns) and Pisanello's fragmented fresco of *St. George and the Princess* (above chapel to right of altar). Ask for the English  brochure, which describes the story of the church (€2.50 entry, March–Oct Mon–Sat 9:00–18:00, Sun 13:00–18:00; Nov–Feb 13:00–17:00 only).

• *Facing the church, go right and walk along its length. Take a left on Via Sottoriva. In a block, you'll reach a small riverfront park that usually has a few modern-day Romeos and Juliets gazing at each other rather than at the view. Get up on the sidewalk right next to the river.*

⓫ Ponte Pietra and a River View

The white stones of the Ponte Pietra are from the original Roman bridge that stood here. After the bridge was bombed in World War II, the Veronese fished the marble chunks out of the river to rebuild it. From here, you can see the Roman Theater, built into the hillside behind the green hedge (see sight listing, below). Way above the theater is the fortress, Castello San Pietro.

Continue up the river toward the bridge. You'll pass Gelateria Ponte Pietra (at #23) where Mirko dishes out fine gelato (try the *riso*, open Fri–Wed 14:30 until late, closed Thu). Then walk to the high point on the bridge. For some exercise, break away, cross the bridge, and visit the Roman Theater or head up to the Castello for an expansive city view (at the end of the bridge, go up the little road called Scalone Castello San Pietro at the end of the bridge, or climb the stairs to the left of the theater). Me? I'll just enjoy the view from here.

• *From the bridge, look back 200 yards at the tall spire...that's where you're heading.*

⓬ Duomo

Started in the 12th century, this church was built over a period of centuries. Its fine facade features Romanesque carvings, while its bright interior demonstrates a mishmash of styles and lack of harmony. The highlights are Titian's *Assumption* (left side of nave, Mary calmly rides a cloud—direction up—to the shock and bewilderment of the crowd below), and the ruins of an older church (last wooden door, just left of high altar). These ruins are the 10th-century foundations of the Church of St. Elena (closed Nov–Feb), turned intriguingly into a modern-day chapel. Get the English description at the entrance (April–Sept Mon–Sat 10:00–17:30, Sun 13:30–17:30, shorter hours off-season and closed Mon Nov–Feb). The peaceful Romanesque cloister is to the right as you leave the church, with mosaics from a fifth-century Christian church exposed below the walk.

SIGHTS AND ACTIVITIES

▲▲**Evening *Passeggiata***—For me, the highlight of Verona is the *passeggiata* (stroll)—especially in the evening. Make a big circle from Piazza Brà through the old town on Via Mazzini (one of Europe's many "first" pedestrian-only streets) to the colorful Piazza Erbe, and then back up Corso Porta Borsari to Piazza Brà. Consider a small town, where people know each other, all out on parade. Like peacocks, the young and nubile spread their wings. The classy shop windows are integral to the *passeggiata* as, for the ladies, shopping is a sport. Their never-finished wardrobes are considered a work in progress. This is when they gather ideas.

▲ **Castelvecchio**—Verona's powerful Scaligeri family built this castle (1343–1356) as both a residence and a fortress. Today, this 14th-century brick fantasy is a museum that shows off Verona's glory days (€4, free first Sun of month; Mon 13:30–19:30, Tue–Sun 8:30–19:30, last entry 45 min before closing, good English descriptions on sheets throughout, audioguide-€3.60 or €5.25/2 people). Locals simply appreciate the elegant and balanced design of the building. Many drop in for a stroll on the Sundays it's free. The pedestrian bridge behind the castle is a favorite for wedding-day photos.

The **ground floor** houses early Christian statues that were once vibrantly colored (notice faint traces of paint). The homier first floor held the castle's residential rooms (original wooden ceilings, traces of frescoes, religious paintings).

The **second floor** takes you out of the Middle Ages and into the Renaissance (paintings now have secular themes). Displayed on this floor are fine ancient bronze and gold artifacts and a collection of hair-raising medieval weaponry—pikes, halberds, helmets, breastplates, and enormous broadswords. On the far side of the armaments exhibit, climb the skinny stairway for a grand view from the battlements.

▲ **Basilica of San Zeno Maggiore**—This church is dedicated to the patron saint of Verona, whose remains are buried in the crypt under the main altar. In addition to being a fine example of Italian Romanesque, the basilica features Andrea Mantegna's *San Zeno Triptych* (which will probably be on the road through 2008), with its marvelous perspective, peaceful double-columned cloisters, and a set of 48 paneled 11th-century bronze doors nicknamed "the poor man's Bible." Pretend you're an illiterate medieval peasant and do some reading. Facing the altar, on the walls of the right-side aisle, you can see frescoes painted on top of other frescoes and graffiti dating from the 1300s. These were done by people who fled into the church in times of war or flooding and scratched prayers into the walls. Druidic-looking runes are actually decorated letters typical of the Gothic period, like those in illu-minated manuscripts (March–Oct Mon–Sat 8:30–18:00, Sun 13:00–18:00; Nov–Feb Sun 13:00–18:00 only).

Roman Theater (Teatro Romano)—Dating from the first century A.D., this ancient theater was discovered in the 19th century and restored. Admission includes the Roman Museum (high up in the building above the theater, reach it via elevator—start at the stage and walk up the middle set of stairs,

then continue straight on the path through the bushes).

The museum displays a model of the theater, a small Jesuit chapel, and Roman artifacts, including mosaic floors, busts and other statuary, clay and bronze votive figures, and architectural fragments. You'll find helpful English information sheets throughout (€3, free first Sun of month, Tue–Sun 8:30–19:30, Mon 13:30–19:30, last entry 45 min before closing, theater across the river near Ponte Pietra, tel. 045-800-0360). From mid-June through August, the theater stages Shakespeare plays—only a little more difficult to understand in Italian than in Elizabethan English.

Giardino Giusti—If you'd enjoy a Renaissance garden with manicured box hedges and towering cypress trees, you could find this worth the walk and fee (€5, daily 9:00–20:00, off-season 9:00 until sunset; cross river at Ponte Nuovo, continue up Via Carducci, turn left on Via Giardino Giusti).

SLEEPING

I've listed rates that you'll pay in regular season. Prices soar above these in late June, July and August (during opera season), the first week of April (during the Vinitaly wine festival), and any time of year during a trade fair or holiday. Hotel Aurora and Hotel Torcolo are my favorites for their family-run feeling.

Near Piazza Erbe

$$ Hotel Aurora, just off Piazza Erbe, has friendly family management, a terrace that overlooks the piazza, and 19 fresh, air-conditioned rooms (S-€62, Sb-€100, Db-€120, Tb-€140, Qb-€200, cheaper off-season, reserve with traveler's check or personal check for deposit, elevator, nearby church bells ring the hour early, Piazza Erbe, tel. 045-594-717, fax 045-801-0860, www.hotelaurora.biz, info@hotelaurora.biz, Rita).

$ L'Ospite, a 10-minute walk from Piazza Erbe, has six cozy, immaculate, fully equipped apartments and lots of stairs. The rooms, which sleep up to four, include air-conditioning and free use of the washing machine. Kind manager Federica Rossi, who doesn't gouge during the opera season, can also help you get opera tickets (Db-€85, Qb-€140; about €35–55/person, depending on length of stay; prefers longer stays but will take one-night stands when possible; on west side of Ponte Navi bridge, a few steps past San Paolo church on the left at Via XX Settembre 3; tel. 045-803-6994, mobile 329-426-2524, www.lospite.com, info@lospite.com).

Sleep Code

(€1 = about $1.30, country code: 39)
S = Single, **D** = Double/Twin, **T** = Triple, **Q** = Quad, **b** = bathroom,
s = shower only. Hotels accept credit cards and provide breakfast unless otherwise noted. Everyone speaks English.

To help you easily sort through these listings, I've divided the rooms into three categories, based on the price for a standard double room with bath:

$$$ **Higher Priced**—Most rooms €140 or more.
  $$ **Moderately Priced**—Most rooms between €100–140.
    $ **Lower Priced**—Most rooms €100 or less.

$ Hotel Arena is located in a peaceful courtyard off a busy street just west of Castelvecchio, and offers 17 very basic, institutional, quiet, and economical rooms (S-€42, Sb-€50, D-€65, Db-€75, cash only, no opera season gouging, no breakfast, no air-con, a few free parking spaces—request when you reserve, 100 yards from Piazza Brà at Stradone Porta Palio #2, tel. & fax 045-803-2440, www.albergoarena.it, albergoarena@yahoo.it).

Near Piazza Brà

You'll find several options in the quiet streets just off Piazza Brà, within 200 yards of the bus stop. From the square, yellow signs point you to the hotels.

$$$ Hotel Bologna, located a half block of the Roman Arena, has 30 bright, classy, and well-maintained rooms; attractive public areas; and an attached restaurant (Sb-€100, Db-€140, Tb-€175, air-con, Piazzetta Scalette Rubiani 3, tel. 045-800-6830, fax 045-801-0602, www.hotelbologna.vr.it, hotelbologna@tin.it).

$$$ Hotel Giulietta e Romeo is on a quiet side street just 50 yards behind the Roman Arena. Its 30 well-designed rooms (nine with balconies) are decorated in dark colors, but on the plus side, they have non-smoking rooms and don't take tour groups (Sb-€80–120, Db-€105–190, prices vary with season, air-con, elevator, free loaner bikes, laundry, garage-€16/day, Vicolo Tre Marchetti 3, tel. 045-800-3554, fax 045-801-0862, www.giuliettaeromeo.com, info@giuliettaeromeo.com).

$$ Hotel Europa offers sleek, modern comfort. Nearly half of its 46 rooms are non-smoking and a few rooms have little balconies that overlook the *piazzetta* below (Db-€130, off-season mention this book through 2008 when you reserve for a discount, air-con, elevator, Via Roma 8, tel. 045-594-744, fax 045-800-1852, www.veronahoteleuropa.com, hoteleuropavr@tiscali.it).

Verona Hotels and Restaurants

Near Venice

1 Bus to Station
2 Bus from Station
3 Hotel Aurora
4 To L'Ospite Apartments
5 To Hotel Arena
6 Hotel Bologna
7 Hotel Giulietta e Romeo
8 Hotel Europa
9 Hotel Torcolo
10 Locanda Catullo
11 To Villa Francescatti Hostel

12 Osteria al Duca
13 Ristorante Greppia
14 Bottega del Vin
15 Osteria le Vecete &
   Pizzeria Du de Cope
16 Enoteca Can Grande
17 Trattoria al Pompiere
18 Rist. Olivo & Brek Cafeteria
19 PAM Supermarket
20 Internet Cafés (2)

$ Hotel Torcolo offers 19 comfortable, lovingly maintained, non-smoking rooms (Sb-€65, Db-€100, €8-13 breakfast is optional except during opera season, air-con, fridge in room, elevator; standing on Piazza Brà with your back to the gardens and the Roman Arena over your right shoulder, head down the alley to the right of #16 and walk to Vicolo Listone 3; tel. 045-800-7512, fax 045-800-4058, www.hoteltorcolo.it, hoteltorcolo@virgilio.it, well-run by Silvia, Diana, and helpful Caterina).

Between Piazza Brà and Piazza Erbe

$ Locanda Catullo is an inexpensive, quiet, and quirky place deep in the old town, with 21 basic rooms up three flights of stairs. Prices are always the same. To book during the opera season—when they enforce a three-night minimum—you must prepay the entire amount by personal check or bank transfer (they'll explain the procedure). Otherwise, they generally have space and will hold a room with a phone call the day before (S-€40, D-€55, Db-€65, Q-€105, Qb-€125, cash only, no breakfast; go left off Via Mazzini onto Via Catullo, down an alley between 1D and 3A at Via Valerio Catullo 1; tel. 045-800-2786, fax 045-596-987, locandacatullo @tiscali.it, a leetle English spoken).

Hostel

$ Villa Francescatti is a good hostel (€14–16 beds with breakfast, 6-, 8-, and 10-bed rooms, some family rooms with private bathrooms, €8 dinners, launderette, rooms closed from 9:00–17:00 but reception open all day, 24:00 curfew; bus #73 from train station on weekdays or #90 at night and Sun to Piazza Isolo stop, walk over the river beyond Ponte Nuovo at Salita Fontana del Ferro 15; tel. 045-590-360, fax 045-800-9127).

EATING

Osteria al Duca is a fun, family-run place with a lively atmosphere and a winning formula. Locals line up twice a night (seatings at 19:30 and 21:30) for its affordable, two-course, €15 fixed-price meal. I much prefer their ground floor (*piano terra*—worth requesting). Reservations are a must—easier at 19:30 (closed Sun, half-block from Scaligeri family tombs at Via Arche Scaligere 2, tel. 045-594-474).

Ristorante Greppia serves typical *cucina Veronese* outside on a quiet courtyard or inside its elegant dining room (€8 pastas, €12 *secondi*, Tue–Sun 12:00–14:30 & 19:00–22:30, closed Mon, Vicolo Samaritana 3, first left off Via Mazzini if you're coming from Piazza Erbe, tel. 045-800-4577).

Bottega del Vin is pricey, venerable, and proud to have a sister

The Wines of Verona

Wine connoisseurs love the high-quality wines of this area. The hills to the east are covered with grapes to make Soave; to the north is Valpolicella country; and Bardolino comes from vineyards to the west.

Valpolicella grapes, which are used to make the fruity, red Valpolicella table wine (found everywhere), are also used to make the full-bodied red Amarone and the sweet dessert wine, Recioto. To produce Amarone, grapes are partially dried (*passito*) before fermentation, then aged for a minimum of four years in oak casks, resulting in a rich, velvety, full-bodied red. Recioto, which in local dialect means "ears," uses only the grapes from the top of the cluster (so they sort of look like the ears of a face). Since these grapes get the most sun, they mature the fastest and have the highest concentration of sugar. The grapes are dried for months until all moisture has gone out before pressing, and aged for one to three years.

Bardolino, from the vineyards near Lake Garda, is a light, fruity wine, like a French Beaujolais. It's a perfect picnic wine.

Soave, which might be Italy's best-known white wine, goes well with seafood and risotto dishes. While Soave can vary widely in quality, the best are called "Soave Classico" and come from the heart of the region, near the Soave Castle. Soave is sometimes aged in oak casks, giving it a mellow, rounded flavor.

Sample these and many others at the numerous *enoteche* (wine-tasting bars) or any restaurant around town. The first week of every April, Verona hosts Vinitaly, the most important international convention of domestic and international wines. Vintners vie for prestigious awards for the past year's vintage. Tourists are welcome to attend at the end of the week, and are shuttled to the convention hall from Piazza Brà. Hotels book up months in advance. Check with the TI for more details.

If you're visiting the area in the fall, consider a day trip to nearby Monteforte d'Alpone, east of Verona. The town hosts a fun, raucous wine festival in September—ask at the TI for more information on this and other regional wine festivals.

establishment in New York City. Under a high ceiling and walls of wine bottles, brisk black-vested waiters match traditional dishes (polenta, duck, game) with glasses of fine wine. Choose from 50 open bottles—glasses range from €1 to €14. The wait staff, ambience, and food have deep roots in local culture. I like their front room best. Reservations are a smart idea (€10 pastas, €20 *secondi*, Wed–Mon 12:00–15:00 & 19:00–24:00, closed Tue, good daily specials, take second left off Via Mazzini as you're coming from

Piazza Erbe, Via Scudo di Francia 3, tel. 045-800-4535).

Osteria le Vecete consists of just one room under open beams and walls of wine. It has an enjoyable, intimate pub setting. Choose from a dozen or so daily specials of homemade pastas and Veronese specialties—as well as simpler *bruschette* and salads—or select a few of the elaborately dressed *tartine farcite* (little open-faced *crostini* sandwiches, €1.20 each) available in the case. The blackboard lists a good selection of wine by the glass (€8 pastas, €16 *secondi*, kitchen open daily 12:30–14:30 & 18:30–22:30, drinks and snacks are served between mealtimes and until late; buried in an alley between Via Mazzini and Corso Sant'Anastasia: from Piazza Brà, go down Via Mazzini and turn left onto Via Quattro Spade, then right onto Via Pelliciai—restaurant is about a half-block down on your left at #32A; tel. 045-594-748).

Pizzeria Du de Cope buzzes with smartly attired young waiters and locals who consider the pizza to be the best in town. This high-energy, trendy place feels like the casual sidekick of a Michelin star restaurant—which it is (big €9 salads, €9 pizzas, Wed–Mon 12:00–14:30 & 18:30–23:00, closed Tue, flamboyant desserts, family-friendly, no reservations, sit inside or out, next to Osteria le Vecete at Galleria Pellicciai 10, tel. 045-595-562).

Enoteca Can Grande enjoys turning people on to great, well-matched food and wine. Their cold plates, designed for wine appreciation, make a fine main dish. I'd trust Giuliano and Corrina with a creative meal (just set a limit, such as €25 per person plus wine). A festival of *antipasti* treats, followed by a creative pasta with a sampling of top wines by the glass, can be a gourmet experience for a reasonable price (Wed–Mon 12:00–15:30 & 18:00–24:00, closed Tue, a block off Piazza Brà at Via Dietro Liston 19D—if the equestrian statue jogged slightly right, he'd head straight here, tel. 045-595-022).

Trattoria al Pompiere, which has a commitment to regional traditions, is a favorite of foodies and has earned its huge local following. Amid the bustle (contained by walls plastered with photos of local big shots), Stefano and his gang serve gourmet meats and cheeses as *antipasti*, ideal for a mixed plate to complement the huge selection of fine wines. There's not a bad table in this grand, old-style dining room. Reservations are wise (€11 pastas, €14 *secondi*, Mon–Sat 12:30–14:00 & 19:30–22:30, closed Sun, lady's menus without prices, very nice house wine, Vicolo Regina d'Ungheria 5, tel. 045-803-0537).

Eating on Piazza Brà: A cancan of nondescript restaurants line the *passeggiata* action along Piazza Brà. Of course you sacrifice service, value, and quality for the view—but the view can make it a great deal. Survey the scene and grab a table to enjoy the floodlit Roman Arena and Verona on parade. **Ristorante Olivo,** with a small menu and decent prices, is a good bet. For fast food with a superb view of Verona's main square, consider **Brek,** a modern and well-run self-service cafeteria (daily, breakfast and sandwiches from 9:30, full menu 11:30–15:00 & 18:30–22:00, indoor/outdoor seating, cheap salad plates, right on the square between historic city gate and equestrian statue at Piazza Brà 20, tel. 045-800-4561).

Eating Cheap near Piazza Brà: **PAM supermarket** is just outside the historic gate on Piazza Brà (daily 8:00–20:30, exit Piazza Brà through the gate and take the first right). The döner kebab place—just behind Hotel Europa and a few steps off Via Roma—is cheap, fast, and not Italian (great €4 meals).

TRANSPORTATION CONNECTIONS

From Verona by Train to: Venice (2/hr, 90 min), **Padua** (2/hr, 1 hr), **Florence** (about hourly with transfer in Bologna, 3 hrs, note that all Rome-bound trains stop in Florence—listed as *Firenze* on train schedules), **Bologna** (nearly hourly, 2 hrs), **Milan** (hourly, 1.5–2 hrs), **Rome** (4/day, 5–6 hrs, more with transfer in Bologna or Padua), **Bolzano** (hourly, 1.5–2 hrs; note that Brennero-bound trains stop in Bolzano).

Ravenna

Ravenna is on the tourist map for one reason: its 1,500-year-old churches, decorated with best-in-the-West Byzantine mosaics. Known in Roman times as Classe, the city was an imperial port for the large naval fleet. Briefly a capital of eastern Rome during its fall, Ravenna was taken by the barbarians. Then, in A.D. 540, the Byzantine emperor Justinian turned Ravenna into the westernmost pillar of the Byzantine Empire. A pinnacle of civilization in that age, Ravenna was a light in Europe's Dark Ages. Two hundred years later, the Lombards booted the Byzantines out, and Ravenna melted into the backwaters of medieval Italy, staying out of historical sight for a thousand years.

Today, the local economy booms with a big chemical industry, the discovery of offshore gas deposits, and the construction of a new ship canal. The bustling town center is Italy's best for bicyclists. Locals go about their business, while busloads of tourists slip quietly in and out of town for the best look at the glories of Byzantium this side of Istanbul.

Ravenna is only a 90-minute detour from the main Venice–Florence train line and worth the effort for those interested in old mosaics. While its sights don't merit an overnight stop, many find that the peaceful charm of this untouristy and classy town makes it a pleasant surprise in their Italian wandering.

ORIENTATION

Central Ravenna is quiet, with a pedestrian-friendly core and more bikes than cars. Keep to the sides of the streets; bikes take the center lane (subtly indicated by white brick paving) down the brick "pedestrian" streets. Listen for the outta-my-way bells.

On a quick visit to Ravenna, I'd see Basilica di San Vitale and its adjacent Mausoleum of Galla Placidia, Basilica di Sant'Apollinare Nuovo, the covered market, and Piazza del Popolo.

Tourist Information

The TI is a 15-minute walk (or a 5-minute pedal) from the train station (April–Sept Mon–Sat 8:30–19:00, Sun 10:00–18:00; Oct–March Mon–Sat 8:30–18:00, Sun 10:00–16:00; Via Salara 8, tel. 0544-35404, www.turismo.ravenna.it). For directions to the TI, see "Orientation Walk," below. Most sights close early in the winter months; pick up a schedule from the TI when you arrive. When you exit the station, don't be deceived by the bike-rental shop with the letter *"i"* signs on its windows: it has no tourist info.

Combo-Tickets

There are two combo-tickets for Ravenna; you'll probably want the cumulative ticket that includes the Basilica di San Vitale. Many top sights can only be seen by purchasing this €7.50 cumulative ticket (sold at the sights, good for seven days), since there are no individual admissions to these attractions. The combo-ticket includes admission to Basilica di San Vitale, Basilica di Sant'Apollinare Nuovo, and Battistero Neoniano. From March to mid-June—when school-group tours take over and space is limited—there's a €9.50 version of this combo-ticket that includes the Mausoleum of Galla Placidia; otherwise, the mausoleum is automatically included for free.

A different €6 combo-ticket covers admissions to the National Museum and the Mausoleum of Teodorico. A €8 version of this combo-ticket also includes the Church of Sant'Apollinare in Classe (either version good for three days). This ticket is only worth buying if you'll be visiting two or more of the following sights, since—unlike with the other combo-ticket mentioned above—you can buy individual admissions to these: National Museum-€4 (Tue–Sun 8:30–19:30, closed Mon, last entry 30 min before closing), Mausoleum of Teodorico-€3 (daily 8:30–19:00, last entry 30 min before closing), and Church of Sant'Apollinare in Classe-€3 (Mon–Sat 8:30–19:30, Sun 13:00–19:30, last entry 30 min before closing).

Helpful Hints

Bike Rental: The TI has 10 one-speed bikes to loan out for free on a first-come, first-served basis (must bring back by 17:30, need to bring your passport). Ask the TI for the free bike-trail map, which includes rides to the ocean, parks, and historical sites.

Coop San Vitale on Piazza Farini rents bikes (€1.10/hour, €8.50/day, Mon–Sat 7:00–20:00, closed Sun, ID required, on the left just as you exit train station, tel. 0544-37031). Many hotels have bikes as well.

Parking: There are two lots near the historic center: one accessible from the west side of Via Roma, at Via Mura di Porta Serrata (€1.50/day), or Largo Giustiniano just north of San Vitale (€2.50/day). Both lots are free overnight (20:00–8:00).

Local Guide: For a private guide, consider Claudia Frassineti (€90/half-day, mobile 335-613-2996, www.abacoguide.it, abacoguide@tiscalinet.it).

Baggage Check: Despite the baggage deposit signs in the train station, the baggage check isn't there—it's in the bike shop on your left as you exit out of the train station (€3.50 flat rate for 24 hours or less, Mon–Sat 7:00–20:00, closed Sun, Piazza Farini).

Laundry: A self-service laundromat is a five-minute walk from the train station (daily 7:00–22:00, €3.50 wash, €3.50 dry, take a left as you exit the station, then take your first left, Via Candiano 16, tel. 334-572-6354).

SIGHTS

Orientation Walk—A visit to Ravenna can be as short as a three-hour loop from the train station. From the station, walk straight down Viale Farini to **Piazza del Popolo.** This square was built in about 1500, during a 60-year period when the city was ruled by Venice. Under the Venetian architecture, the people of Ravenna gather here as they have for centuries.

Most sights are within a few minutes' walk of Piazza del Popolo. A right on Via IV Novembre takes you a block to the colorful covered market, **Mercato Coperto** (Mon–Sat 7:00–14:00,

Ravenna

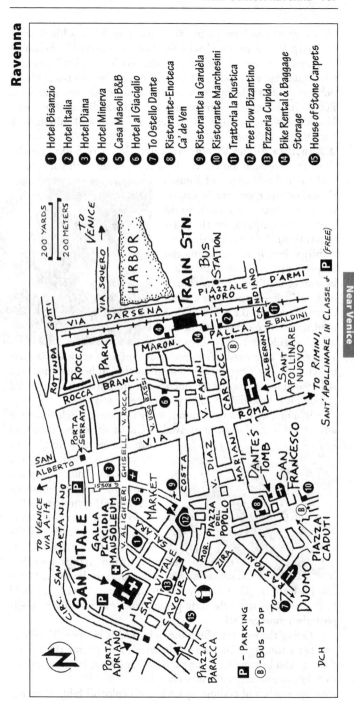

1. Hotel Bisanzio
2. Hotel Italia
3. Hotel Diana
4. Hotel Minerva
5. Casa Masoli B&B
6. Hotel al Giaciglio
7. To Ostello Dante
8. Ristorante-Enoteca Ca' de Ven
9. Ristorante la Gardela
10. Ristorante Marchesini
11. Trattoria la Rustica
12. Free Flow Bizantino
13. Pizzeria Cupido
14. Bike Rental & Baggage Storage
15. House of Stone Carpets

Near Venice

closed Sun, good for picnic fixings). The TI is a block away (head up Via Cavour and take the first right onto Via Salara 8). Ravenna's two most important sights, Basilica di San Vitale and the Mausoleum of Galla Placidia, are two blocks from Piazza del Popolo (head down San Vitale). A few blocks from Piazza del Popolo in the opposite direction is the Basilica di Sant'Apollinare Nuovo, also worth a look. From there, it's about a 10-minute walk back to the station.

▲▲**Basilica di San Vitale**—Imagine: It's A.D. 540. The city of Rome has been looted, the land is crawling with barbarians,

and the infrastructure of Rome's thousand-year empire is crumbling fast. Into this chaotic world comes the emperor of the East (Justinian), bringing order and stability, briefly reassembling the empire, and making Ravenna a beacon of civilization. His church of San Vitale—standing as a sanctuary of order in the midst of that madness—is covered with lavish mosaics: gold and glass chips the size of your fingernail. It's impressive enough to see a 1,400-year-old church. But rarer is to see one decorated in brilliant mosaics, still managing to convey the intended feeling that "this peace and stability was brought to you by your emperor and God."

In a medieval frame of mind, study the scene: High above the altar, God is in Heaven, portrayed as Christ sitting on a celestial

orb. He oversees his glorious creation, symbolized by the four rivers. And running the show on earth is Justinian (left side), sporting both a halo and a crown to indicate that he's leader of the Church and the state. Here, Justinian brings together the military leaders and the church leaders, all united by the straight line of eyes. The bald bishop of Ravenna—the only person who was actually here—is portrayed most realistically.

Facing the emperor (from the right side) is his wife, Theodora, and her entourage. Decked out in jewels and pearls, the former dancer, who became Justinian's mistress and then empress, carries a chalice to consecrate the new church.

The walls and ceilings sparkle with colorful biblical scenes told with a sixth-century exuberance. This was a time of transition, and many consider the mosaics of Ravenna to be both the last ancient Roman and the first medieval European works of art. For instance, you'll see a beardless Christ (as he was depicted by ancient Romans) next to a bearded Christ, his standard medieval portrayal.

The church's octagonal design—clearly Eastern—inspired the construction of the Hagia Sofia, the mosque-turned-museum built 10 years later in Constantinople. Charlemagne traveled here in about A.D. 800. He was so impressed that when he returned to his capital, Aix-la-Chapelle (present-day Aachen in Germany), he built a church that many consider to be the first great stone building in northern Europe, modeled after this one (included in €7.50 combo-ticket—see above, €3.50 slow-talking but thorough audioguide available in gift shop, daily 9:00–19:00 April–Sept, March and Oct until 17:30, off-season until 16:30, last entry 30 min before closing, tel. 0544-215-193).

▲▲**Mausoleum of Galla Placidia**—Just across the courtyard (and usually included in Basilica di San Vitale admission) is this tiny, humble-looking mausoleum, with the oldest—and, to many, the best—mosaics in Ravenna.

The Mausoleum of Galla Placidia (plah-CHEE-dee-ah) is reputed to be the burial place of this daughter, sister, and mother of emperors, who died in A.D. 450. The little light that sneaks through the thin alabaster panels brings a glow and a twinkle to the early Christian symbolism that fills the small room. Opposite the door is St. Lawrence martyred on a fiery grill. He's legendary for mocking his executors, reportedly saying something like "I'm done on this side, you can turn me over now." He was famous as an example of the strength of the feisty early Christians. The four Gospels clearly labeled on the bookshelf were the source of this strength as they were persecuted by the Romans.

The dome is filled with stars. Along with Mark's lion, Luke's ox, Matthew's Archangel, and John's eagle, the golden cross rises from the east bringing life to all. Doves drink from fountains, symbolic of souls finding nourishment in the word of God. Cover the light from the door with your hand to see the standard Roman portrayal of Christ—beardless and as the Good Shepherd. Jesus, dressed in gold and purple like a Roman emperor, is King of Paradise—receiving the

faithful (represented by lambs). The Eastern influence is apparent in the carpet-like decorative patterns (€9.50 for combo-ticket March–mid-June, otherwise included in €7.50 combo-ticket, daily 9:00–19:00, March and Oct until 17:30, off-season until 16:30, last entry 45 before closing, tel. 0544-215-193).

▲▲▲**Basilica di Sant'Apollinare Nuovo**—This austere sixth-century church, with a typical early-Christian-basilica floor plan, has two huge and wonderfully preserved side panels. One is a procession of haloed virgins, each bringing gifts to the Madonna and the Christ Child. Opposite, Christ is on his throne with four angels, awaiting a solemn procession of 26 martyrs. Ignoring the Baroque altar from a thousand years later, we can clearly see the rectangular Roman hall of justice or basilica plan—which was adopted by churches and used throughout the Middle Ages (included in €7.50 combo-ticket, daily April–Sept 9:00–19:00, March and Oct 9:30–17:30, Nov–Feb 10:00–17:00, last entry 15 min before closing, on Via di Roma, tel. 0544-219-518).

The **Self-Service Sant'Apollinare in Classe** is a cheap, air-conditioned, and efficient place for lunch right on the church grounds (Mon–Fri 12:00–14:45, closed Sat–Sun, tel. 0544-35679).

House of Stone Carpets—Only recently discovered, this sixth-century Byzantine *domus* (house) offers an extensive array of geometric, animal, and humanistic designs in colored stone floor mosaics (€3.50, Sun–Fri 10:00–18:30, Sat 10:00–16:30, Jun–Aug also open 21:00–23:30, off-season Mon–Sat 10:00–17:30, Sun 10:00–17:30, ask them to run English-language video, worthwhile audioguide–€1, entrance through Church of Sant'Eufemia, on Via Barbiani just off Via Cavour near Piazza Baracca, tel. 0544-32512).

▲**Church of Sant'Apollinare in Classe**—Featuring great Byzantine art, this church is a favorite among mosaic pilgrims (€3, included in upgraded €8 combo-ticket—described in "Combo-Tickets," above—with National Museum and Mausoleum of Teodorico, Mon–Sat 8:30–19:30, Sun 13:00–19:30, confirm hours Oct–March, last entry 30 min before closing, tel. 0544-473-569).

The church is two miles out of town. Catch bus #4 or #44 across the street from the train station (on the corner by the park) or from Piazza Caduti (€1, 3/hr, 15 min, reduced service Sun; with your back to the *tabacchi* shop, stop is on the corner; buy bus tickets from any *tabacchi* shop). To head back to town, walk down the same road; the stop is about 100 yards ahead on the right.

Other Sights—The **Basilica di San Francesco** is worth a look for its simple interior and flooded, mosaic-covered crypt below the main altar (daily 7:30–12:00 & 15:00–18:00, tel. 0544-33256). Nearby in Via Dante Alighieri, the **Tomb of Dante** (restored in 2007), is the true site of his remains. After being exiled from

Florence for his political beliefs, Dante lived out the rest of his life in Ravenna. The Florentines forgave Dante posthumously and wanted to bring their famous poet's bones home to rest. To protect his relics from theft by the Florentines, Ravenna hid his bones in the neighboring Basilica di San Francesco in 1519. They lay forgotten in the church for three centuries, until they were rediscovered and replaced in his tomb in 1865 (free, daily April–Sept 9:00–19:00, Oct–March 9:00–12:00 & 14:00–17:00). The Dante memorial—often mistaken for a tomb—in Florence's Santa Croce Church is empty.

Overrated Sight—The nearby beach town of Rimini is a crowded mess.

SLEEPING

$$$ Hotel Bisanzio is a business-class splurge in the city center (Sb-€98, Db-€124, larger Db-€154, air-con; from Piazza del Popolo take Via IV Novembre to the Mercato, turn left onto Via Cavour and take the first right, Via Salara 30; tel. 0544-217-111, fax 0544-32539, www.bisanziohotel.com, info@bizanziohotel .com).

$$$ Hotel Italia, located 100 yards from the train station, seems like a posh chain hotel but it's actually family-owned. Its 45 rooms provide modern comforts and lots of space (Sb-€73, Db-€120, Tb-€135, Qb-€152, Wi-Fi, free loaner bikes, free parking on first-come first-served basis, turn left out of station, Viale Pallavicini 4, tel. 0544-212-363, fax 0544-217-004, www.hitalia .it, hitalia@hitalia.it, Silvia).

$$$ Hotel Diana, with 33 bright and tasteful rooms, is a classy, peaceful haven with a restful terrace. Though a bit outside the town center, it's still an easy walk from the Basilica di San

Near Venice

Sleep Code

(€1 = about $1.30, country code: 39)
S = Single, **D** = Double/Twin, **T** = Triple, **Q** = Quad, **b** = bathroom, **s** = shower only. Unless otherwise noted, credit cards are accepted, English is spoken, and breakfast is included.

To help you easily sort through these listings, I've divided the rooms into three categories, based on the price for a standard double room with bath:

$$$ Higher Priced—Most rooms €100 or more.
$$ Moderately Priced—Most rooms between €70–100.
$ Lower Priced—Most rooms €70 or less.

Vitale (Sb-€57, Db-€110, fancier rooms available, a few balconies, air-con, free Internet access, easy parking nearby, Via G. Rossi 47, tel. 0544-39164, fax 0544-30001, www.hoteldiana.ra.it, info @hoteldiana.ra.it).

$$ Hotel Minerva, just to the right of the train station as you exit, has 18 renovated rooms (Sb-€60, Db-€90, elevator, air-con, free Internet access in rooms, Viale Maroncelli 1, tel. 0544-213-711, fax 0544-211-420, www.minerva-hotel.com, hotel.minerva @libero.it).

$$ Casa Masoli B&B's five elegantly outfitted rooms include bathrooms fit for an emperor. Grandmotherly Signora Masoli works quietly alongside her daughter Anna (Sb-€50, Db-€70, Tb-€105, peaceful garden, Via G. Rossi 22, tel. 335-609-9471, mobile 339-544-8405, www.casamasoli.it, anna@casamasoli.it).

$ Hotel al Giaciglio, near the train station, has 16 basic, tidy, budget rooms. Barbara and Moanely run it with enthusiasm and care (S-€35, D-€55, Db-€65, two guests get 3-course dinner for €15 with this book in 2008, fans, Via R. Brancaleone 42, tel. & fax 0544-39403, www.albergoalgiaciglio.com, info @albergoalgiaciglio.com).

Hostel: **$ Ostello Dante Hostel,** a 15-minute walk from the station, has Internet access, laundry service, free loaner bikes and bike rentals (€2.50/day), and a game room. There's a lockout (10:00–15:30), but you can leave your bags if you arrive by noon (110 beds, €14/bed, 4 bed rooms, Db-€36, family rooms-€16/person with bath, €3/night extra for non-Italian members, includes breakfast and sheets, towels-€1, 23:30 curfew or pay €1 for magnetic entrance key, Via Nicolodi 12, take bus #70 or tiny bus #80 from train station, tel. & fax 0544-421-164, www.hostelravenna .com, hostelravenna@hotmail.com).

EATING

The atmospheric **Ristorante-Enoteca Ca' de Ven** (House of Wine) fills a 16th-century warehouse with locals enjoying quality wine and traditional cuisine. *Piadina* (peeah-DEE-nah) dominates the menu. An unleavened bread that local kids are raised on, it's served warm with cheese and prosciutto, or as wine pourer *maestra* Rita says, "Just plain with a glass of *vino.*" Try their dessert specialty— *torta di marzipan*—made exclusively for them by a local bakery. This decadent almond-and-cocoa brownie is best with sweet red wine (Tue–Sat 11:00–14:00 & 18:00–22:30, Sun 11:00–14:30 & 17:30–22:00, closed Mon, 2-min walk from Piazza del Popolo on Via Cairoli which turns into Via C. Ricci, Via C. Ricci 24, tel. 0544-30163).

Locals like **Ristorante la Gardèla,** which offers reasonable prices and cuisine specialties from Italy's mountainous Emilia–Romagna region. These include *cappelletti in brodo*, a light, meat-stuffed pasta served in broth (Fri–Wed 12:00–14:30 & 19:00–22:00, closed Thu, from Piazza del Popolo follow Via IV Novembre past Piazza della Costa to corner of Via Ponte Marino 3, tel. 0544-217-147).

Ristorante Marchesini has a classy self-serve menu that includes some delicious salads and homemade pastas (€7 pastas, €10 *secondi*, Mon–Sat 12:00–14:30, closed Sun, 5-min walk from Piazza del Popolo, on corner of Piazza Caduti at Via Mazzini 6—ride elevator to first floor, tel. 0544-212-309).

Trattoria la Rustica is also worthwhile, featuring grilled meats and homemade pasta like *capelletti, garganelli*, and *tortelli* (about €20 for a 3-course dinner not including wine, Sat–Thu 12:00–14:30 & 19:00–22:30, closed Fri, near train station at Via Alberoni 55, tel. 0544-218-128).

Free Flow Bizantino, inside the covered market, is a self-serve cafeteria that offers lunch only (€4 pastas, €5 *secondi*, Mon–Fri 11:45–14:30, tel. 0544-32073). Or assemble a picnic at the market and enjoy your feast in the shady gardens of the **Rocca Brancaleone** fortress (May–Sept daily 8:00–21:00, Oct–April closes at sunset; 5-min walk from station, follow Via Maroncelli until you see the walls).

For a cheap and traditional lunch or snack, try a *piadina* or *crescione* (calzone-like) sandwich from **Pizzeria Cupido** just up Via Cavour, past the covered market. These tasty sandwiches (€3–4.50) come stuffed with a variety of meats, cheeses, and vegetables. Try one filled with *squacquerone*, a soft regional cream cheese, or ask to see a menu of the *pasta fresca* possibilities (daily 8:00–15:00; Tue–Wed and Sat–Sun also open from 18:00–21:00; Via Cavour 43—through the archway, tel. 0544-37529).

TRANSPORTATION CONNECTIONS

From Ravenna by Train to: Venice (hourly, 3–4 hrs, transfer in Ferrara, Faenza, or Bologna, plus possibly Venice's Mestre station), **Florence** (about hourly, 3 hrs, requires transfer in Bologna).

THE DOLOMITES

Dolomiti

Italy's dramatic rocky rooftop, the Dolomites, offers some of the best mountain thrills in Europe. Bolzano is the gateway to the Dolomites, and Castelrotto is a good home base for your exploration of Alpe di Siusi, Europe's largest alpine meadow.

The sunny Dolomites are well-developed, and the region's famous valleys and towns suffer from après-ski fever. The cost for the comfort of reliably good weather is a drained-reservoir feeling. Lovers of other parts of the Alps may miss the lushness that comes with the unpredictable weather farther north. But the bold, light, gray cliffs and spires flecked with snow, above green meadows and beneath a blue sky, offer a powerful, unique, and memorable mountain experience. Dolomite, a sedimentary rock similar to limestone, gives these mountains their distinctive shape and color. First described by the famous French geologist Dolomieu, the rock type—and the mountains in which it was identified—is named after him.

A hard-fought history has left the region bicultural, with an emphasis on the German. Locals speak German first, and some wish they were still part of Austria. In the Middle Ages, as part of the Holy Roman Empire, the region faced north. Later, it was firmly in the Austrian Hapsburg realm. By losing World War I, Austria's South Tirol became Italy's Alto Adige. Mussolini did what he could to Italianize the region, including giving each town an Italian name. But even as recently as the 1990s, local secessionist groups agitated violently for more autonomy with some success (see page 176).

The government has wooed locals with economic breaks that make it one of Italy's richest areas (as local prices attest), and today

The Dolomites

(SEE DETAIL MAP)

all signs and literature in the province of Alto Adige/Süd Tirol are in both languages. Many include a third language, Ladin—an ancient, Latin-type language still spoken in a few traditional areas. (I have listed both the Italian and German, so the confusion caused by this guidebook will match that experienced in your travels.)

In spite of all the glamorous ski resorts and busy construction cranes, the local color survives in a warm, blue-aproned, ruddy-faced, felt-hat-with-feathers way. There's yogurt and yodeling for breakfast. Culturally, as much as geographically, the area is reminiscent of Austria. The Austrian Tirol is named for a village that is now part of Italy.

Ich bin ein Italiener

Four in ten Italians living in the Dolomites region speak German. Many are fair-skinned and blue-eyed, eating strudel after their pasta, and feeling a closer bond with their ancestors in Austria than to their swarthy countrymen to the south. In the province of Alto Adige/Süd Tirol, along the Austrian border, German-speakers are the majority. Most have a passing knowledge of Italian, but they watch German-language TV, read newspapers in *Deutsch,* and live in Tirolean-looking villages. (Bolzano has both Italian and German grade schools, while in more-remote Castelrotto, the children are educated only in German.)

At the end of World War I, the region was ceded by (loser) Austria to (winner) Italy. Mussolini suppressed the Germanic elements as part of his propaganda campaign to praise all things Italian. Many German speakers hoped that Hitler would "liberate" them from Italy. But Hitler's close alliance with Mussolini prevented that from happening. Instead, in June 1939, residents were given six months to make a hard choice—move north to the Fatherland and become German citizens, or stay in their homeland *(Heimat)* under Italian rule. The vast majority (212,000, or 85 percent) made the decision to leave, but because of the outbreak of World War II, only 75,000 actually moved.

At the war's end, German-speakers were again disappointed when the Allied powers refused to grant them autonomy or repatriation (citizenship) with Austria, instead sticking with the prewar arrangement.

The region rebuilt and the two linguistic groups got along, but for the remainder of the 20th century, there was always an underlying problem: German-speakers were continually outvoted by the Italian-speaking majority in the regional government (comprising both Italian-speaking Trentino and German-speaking Alto Adige/Süd Tirol). German-speakers lobbied the national government for more control on the provincial (not regional) level, even turning to demonstrations and violence. Over the years, Rome has slowly and grudgingly granted increased local control.

Today, Alto Adige/Süd Tirol has a large measure of autonomy written into the country's 2001 constitution, though it's still officially tied to Trentino. Roads, water, electricity, communications, and schools are all under local control, including the new Free University of Bozen–Bolzano, founded in 1998.

Planning Your Time

Train travelers should side-trip into the mountains from Bolzano (90 min north of Verona). To get a feel for the alpine culture, spend at least one night in Castelrotto. With two nights in Castelrotto, you can actually get out and hike. Tenderfeet ride the bus, catch a cable car, and stroll. For serious mountain thrills, do a six-hour hike. And for a memory that won't soon fade away, spend a night in a mountain hut.

Car hikers with a day can drive the three-hour loop from Bolzano or Castelrotto (Val Gardena–Sella Pass–Val di Fassa) and ride one of the lifts to the top for a ridge walk. Connecting Bolzano and Venice by the Great Dolomite Road takes two hours longer than by the *autostrada,* but it is far more scenic (see "More Sights in the Dolomites," page 200).

Hiking season is mid-June through mid-October. The region is crowded, booming, and blooming from mid-July through mid-September. It's packed with Italian vacationers in August. Spring is usually dead, with lifts shut down, huts closed, and the most exciting trails still under snow. Many hotels and restaurants close in April and November. Ski season (Dec-Easter) is busiest of all. For more information, visit www.visitdolomites.com.

Bolzano (Bozen)

Willkommen to the Italian Tirol! If it weren't so sunny, you could be in Innsbruck. This enjoyable old town of 100,000 is the most convenient gateway to the Dolomites, especially if you're relying on public transportation. It's just the place to take a Tirolean stroll.

ORIENTATION

Tourist Information

Bolzano's TI is helpful (Mon–Fri 9:00–13:00 & 14:00–19:00, Sat 9:00–14:00, closed Sun, Piazza Walther 8, tel. 0471-307-000, www.bolzano-bozen.it). Pick up the city map and their "Historic and Cultural Route" brochure. Don't bother with the €2.50 Museum Card (offering discounts at five Bolzano museums and the skippable Runkelstein Castle), because the only sight that merits your time is the archaeological museum, with its famous Ice Man.

The excellent-for-hikers Dolomites Information Center is buried deep in the old town, on an alley between Portici/Lauben and Via Vintler Strasse at Galleria Vintler–Durchgang 16 (Mon–Fri 10:00–12:00 & 15:00–17:00, closed Sat–Sun, tel. 0471-999-955).

Arrival in Bolzano

To get to the TI and downtown from the train station, veer left up the tree-lined Viale della Stazione/Bahnhofallee, and walk past the bus station (on your left) two blocks to **Piazza Walther.** You'll see the TI on the right side of the square.

Walking through Piazza Walther, you hit the medieval heart of town. The arcaded Via dei Portici leads to **Piazza Erbe/Obstplatz,** which has an open-air produce market (see "Markets," below); the Ice Man is a couple of blocks farther beyond.

Helpful Hints

Sleepy Sundays: The city is really dead on Sunday (young locals say "and during the rest of the week, too").

Markets: Piazza Erbe/Obstplatz hosts an ancient and still-thriving open-air produce market (Mon–Fri all day, Sat morning only, closed Sun). Wash your produce in the handy drinking fountain in the middle of the market. Another market (offering more variety, not just food) is held Saturday mornings on Piazza della Vittoria.

Internet Access: Multi Kulti Internet Point is a few blocks east of Piazza Walther at Via Dottore Streitergasse 9 (daily 10:00–22:00, €2/30 min, passport required, tel. 0471-056-056).

Baggage Storage: While there's no baggage-storage service at the train station, there is a *deposito bagagli* at the bus station just a block away. It's technically for those with a bus ticket, but they don't seem to care (€3/24 hrs).

Laundry: Lava e Asciuga launderette is at Via Rosmini Strasse 81, about two blocks west of the South Tirol Museum of Archaeology (daily 7:30–22:30, last wash 21:30, €3 wash, €3 dry, mobile 340-220-2323).

Bike Rental: Rental bikes are curiously cheap here, and plenty are available for rent just off Piazza Walther on Viale della Stazione/Bahnhofallee (€1/6 hrs, €2/day, €10 refundable deposit, ID required, April–Oct Mon–Sat 7:30–18:30, closed Sun and Nov–March). The TI also has 10 bikes to rent for €5 per day (€10 refundable deposit, ID required, year-round).

Local Guide: Nancy Spinel knows her hometown and the entire Süd Tirol region very well (€112/2 hrs, mobile 333-436-8570, nancy.spinel@virgilio.it).

SELF-GUIDED WALK

Welcome to Bolzano

Everything mentioned in Bolzano is a 10-minute walk from the train station and the main square, Piazza Walther.

• *Start in...*

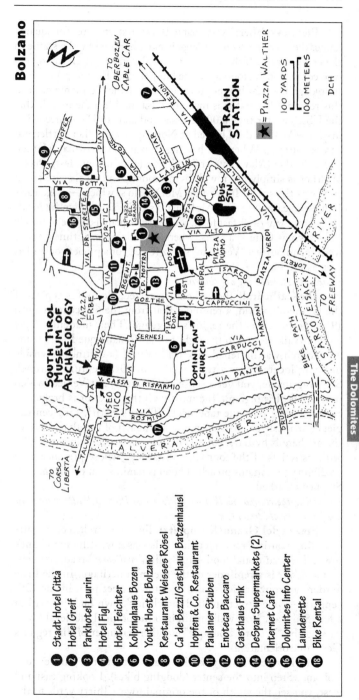

Bolzano

South Tirol Museum of Archaeology

Train Station

Bus Stn.

To Oberbozen Cable Car

Talvera River

Sarco / Eisack River

★ = Piazza Walther

100 Yards
100 Meters

DCH

1 Stadt Hotel Città
2 Hotel Greif
3 Parkhotel Laurin
4 Hotel Figl
5 Hotel Feichter
6 Kolpinghaus Bozen
7 Youth Hostel Bolzano
8 Restaurant Weisses Rössl
9 Ca' de Bezzi/Gasthaus Batzenhäusl
10 Hopfen & Co. Restaurant
11 Paulaner Stuben
12 Enoteca Baccaro
13 Gasthaus Fink
14 DeSpar Supermarkets (2)
15 Internet Café
16 Dolomites Info Center
17 Launderette
18 Bike Rental

The Dolomites

Piazza Walther: Every visit to Bolzano starts here. The square's namesake, Walther von der Vogelweide, honored by the statue in the center, was a 12th-century, politically incorrect German poet who courageously stood up to the Holy Roman Emperor. Walther's spunk against a far bigger power represents the Germanic pride of this region. (The statue is made of Lasa marble—the marble that the US chose for the 86,000 crosses and stars of David needed to mark the WWII dead buried at Normandy and other battlefields across Europe.) When not hosting Bolzano's Christmas Market, flower market (May Day), or Speck Fest (a spring ham fest), Piazza Walther is simply the town's living room. And locals care about it. It was the site of Italy's first McDonald's, which—in the early 1990s—became the first McDonald's to be shut down by locals protesting American fast food. Today, the square is home to trendy cafés such as Café Walthers, where (outside of meal times) you're welcome to nurse a "Venetian" spritz (€3.20) or a pricier cocktail as long as you like.

• *Cross the street to the big church.*

The Cathedral: The cathedral's glazed-tile roof is typical of the Germanic world, a reminder that from the 6th century until 1919, German was the region's language. Then suddenly: *Buon giorno!* Walk around to the right to the Romanesque Lion's Gate. The church was flattened in World War II (a distinct downside of being located near a train station in 20th-century Europe). Stepping inside, you get a sense of Germany, not Venice (which never took this region). The mostly Gothic interior is broken by an impressive Baroque tabernacle. There's a stiff, 15th-century pietà (obviously pre-Michelangelo) to the left of the altar. Most of the art here is by Bavarian artists. The sandstone pulpit (c. 1500), with its reliefs of the four Church fathers (whose presence gave credibility to sermons preached here) is reminiscent of Vienna's St. Stephen's Cathedral.

• *Leaving the church, walk diagonally across Piazza Walther and one block into the old town to...*

Piazza del Grano/Kornplatz: The rich architecture surrounding you is a reminder that this was a wealthy merchant's town. The traditional food stand selling *vollkorn* bread, pretzels, and *apfelsaft* is a reminder of the German heritage. In the little garden, a bronze relief shows Bolzano's street plan in the 12th century—a one-street arcaded merchants' town huddled within a fortified wall. Now walk uphill into the original medieval town, passing the "Wurstel Boutique" (another reminder of this region's Germanic orientation).

Via Portici: This was the main street in 12th-century Bolzano. Step into the center (dodging bikes). Looking east and west, you see the width of the original town. Thirty yards to the left is the old city hall—the street's only Gothic building (with frescoed pointed arches). The other buildings are all basically the same: Each had a storm cellar, cows out back, a ground-level shop, and living quarters upstairs. Bay windows were designed for maximum light—just right for clerks keeping track of accounts and for women doing their weaving. The arcades enabled merchants to exhibit their goods even in bad weather. The only balcony on the street marks the one Baroque building on the arcade—once the mercantile center (with a fine, worth-a-look courtyard), now a skippable museum.

• *Continue to the end of the arcaded Via Portici, where you'll find a lively market.*

Piazza Erbe/Obstplatz: An ancient open-air produce market bustles here (Mon–Fri all day, Sat mornings, closed Sun), that's liveliest in the morning. The historic market fountain gives Bolzano its only hint of the sea—a 17th-century statue of Neptune. Stroll around and see what's in season. The breads, strudel, and German hams all *schmecken gut.*

• *From the market, Museumstrasse (called Butcher Street until the 19th century, when a museum opened) leads straight to Frozen Fritz.*

SIGHTS

▲▲South Tirol Museum of Archaeology (Museo Archeologico dell'Alto Adige/Südtiroler Archäologiemuseum)—This excellent museum features the actual corpse of Ötzi the Ice Man. The frozen body was discovered high in the mountains on the Italian/Austrian border by some German hikers in 1991. Initially thinking the corpse was a lost hiker, officials chopped him out of the glacier, damaging his left side. But upon discovering his pre–Bronze Age

hatchet, they realized what they had found: a 5,300-year-old, nearly perfectly preserved man with clothing and gear in excellent condition for his age. With Ötzi as the centerpiece, the museum takes you on an intriguing journey through time, recounting the evolution of man—from the Paleolithic era to the Roman period and finally to the Middle Ages—in vivid detail. The exhibit offers informative displays and models, video demonstrations of Ötzi's extraction and his personal effects, a great audioguide, and interactive computers. You'll see Ötzi himself—still frozen—and glass cases that display his incredibly well-preserved and fascinating clothing and gear, including a two-color, finely-stitched coat, his loincloth, a fancy hat, shoes, a finely crafted hatchet, and fire-making gadgets (€8, daily in summer 10:00–18:00, last entry 30 min before closing, Oct–June closed Mon, essential audioguide-€2, near the river at Via Museo/Museumstrasse 43, tel. 0471-320-100, www.iceman.it).

Dominican Church (Chiesa dei Domenicani)—Drop by this 13th-century church to see its Chapel of St. John (San Giovanni; chapel is near farthest altar from the entrance and on the right), frescoed in the 14th century by the Giotto School (free, €0.50 coin lights dim interior, Mon–Sat 9:30–17:00, Sun 12:00–17:00, also see peaceful cloisters farther to right of Piazza Domenicani, entrance at #19).

Cable Car to Oberbozen—Of the three different cable cars that can whisk you out of Bolzano, the most popular is the Renon/Rittner lift to the touristy town of Oberbozen (€3.50 round-trip, daily about 7:00–19:00, 3/hr in summer, hourly and shorter opening times off-season, 12 min, operates year-round; from Bolzano train station, walk 5 blocks to the right down Via Renon to Renon/Rittner Sielbahn cable car; toll-free tel. 800-846-047 or tel. 0471-345-245 for cable-car info and trail conditions). More interesting than Oberbozen are the nearby "earth pyramids," a 20-minute walk from the cable-car station. The pyramids are Bryce Canyon–like pinnacles that rise out of the ridge. A little train runs along the ridge nearly hourly, connecting Oberbozen with other villages, including Collalbo (€3.50 round-trip). From Collalbo, you can hike another 45 minutes to more pyramids (Oberbozen TI tel. 0471-345-245, Collalbo TI tel. 0471-356-100.)

Many are tempted to wimp out on the Dolomites and see them from a distance by hiking two hours from Oberbozen to the Pemmern chairlift (€7.40 one-way including Renon/Rittner gondola, €9.20 round-trip), riding to Schwarzseespitze, and walking 45 more minutes to the Rittner Horn. You'll be atop a 7,000-foot peak with distant but often-hazy Dolomite views. It's not worth the trouble.

SLEEPING

All of the listed hotels are in the city center.

$$$ Stadt Hotel Città, a venerable old hotel with 100 modern if basic rooms, is ideally situated on Piazza Walther. The hotel's café spills out onto the piazza, offering a prime spot for people-watching (Sb-€90, Db-€130, bigger Db with view-€140, Tb-€150, air-con in some rooms, elevator, Piazza Walther 1, tel. 0471-975-221, fax 0471-976-688, www.hotelcitta.info, info@hotelcitta.info, Alessandra). This place is an especially good value if you plan to spend an afternoon in their free-for-guests Wellness Center (mid-

Sept–mid June daily 16:30–22:00, closed mid-June–mid-Sept,
Turkish bath, whirlpool, Finnish sauna, massage by appointment),
a fine way to unwind after a day of hiking in the Dolomites.

$$$ Hotel Greif is also right on Piazza Walther. When you
walk into any of their 33 rooms, which were designed by artists,
you'll feel like you're in a modern-art installation (its fine website
gives a room-by-room tour). It's not cozy, but it is striking, and a
stay here comes with perhaps the best breakfast in Italy (Sb-€140,
"comfort" Db-€178, "superior" Db-€220, claim the 10 percent Rick
Steves discount when you book online, likely to be discounted on
Fri and Sat, most rooms non-smoking, air-con, in-room Internet
access, Piazza Walther, entrance on Via della Rena/Raing, tel.
0471-318-000, fax 0471-318-148, www.greif.it, info@greif.it).
Drivers follow signs to Parking Walther (€17/day) and enter hotel
from the garage.

$$$ Parkhotel Laurin is an Old World luxury hotel, with 96
tastefully decorated rooms, marble bathrooms, classy dining room
and terrace, swimming pool, extensive garden, attentive staff, and
frescoes throughout the grand lobby depicting the legend of King
Laurin (Db-€170, parking-€13/day, Via Laurin 4, tel. 0471-311-
000, fax 0471-311-148, www.laurin.it, info@laurin.it).

$$$ Hotel Figl, warmly run by Anton and Helga Mayr, has
23 comfy, bright modern rooms and an attached café on a pedes-
trian square located a block from Piazza Walther. With rooms
better than its humble public spaces and exterior, it's a fine value
(Sb-€82, Db-€105, junior suite-€115, €5 discount with this book in
2008—ask when you reserve; breakfast extra, air-con, free Internet
access, elevator, Kornplatz 9, tel. 0471-978-412, fax 0471-978-413,
www.figl.net, info@figl.net).

$$ Hotel Feichter is a bright, cheery lodging with a characteristic alpine feel and 30 rooms—many sharing a communal

The Dolomites

terrace—overlooking the rooftops of Bolzano (Sb-€55, Db-€80, Tb-€100; leave Piazza Walther on Via Rena/Raing, then take left fork to Via Grappoli/Weintraubengasse, hotel is a few steps ahead on the right at #15; tel. 0471-978-768, fax 0471-974-803, www.hotelfeichter .it, info@hotelfeichter.it). Papà Walter, Mamma Hedwig, Hannes, and Wolfi Feichter have run this homey hotel since 1969.

$$ Kolpinghaus Bozen, modern, clean, and church-run, has 27 rooms with twin beds (placed head to toe) and all the comforts. Though institutional, it makes one feel thankful (Sb-€55, Db-€85, Tb-€128, elevator, 4 blocks from Piazza Walther near Piazza Domenicani at A. Kolping Strasse 3, tel. 0471-308-400, fax 0471-973-917, www.kolping.it/bz, kolping@tin.it). The lineup in front of the building at lunchtime consists mainly of workers waiting for the cafeteria to open (€9.50 meals, Mon–Fri 11:45–14:00 & 18:30–19:30, Sat 11:45–14:00, closed Sun).

$ Youth Hostel Bolzano, slick and new, is the most comfortable and inviting hostel that I've seen in Italy. It has 18 four-bed rooms (two bunk beds and a full bathroom each) and 10 delightful singles. The bright, clean modern rooms feel like a dorm in a fancy university. With no age limit, no need for membership, easy reservations by email, great lockers, and cheap Internet access, it is the utopian hostel (beds in quad—€20, Sb-€22, €2 extra for 1-night stays, includes breakfast, checkout time 9:00, 100 yards to right of train station as you leave it, Via Renon 23, tel. 0471-300-865, fax 0471-300-858, www.ostello.bz, bolzano@ostello.bz).

EATING

All of these recommendations are in the center of the old town. Prices are consistent (you can generally get a good plate of meat and veggies for €10). While nearly every local-style place serves a mix of Germanic Tirolean and Italian fare, I've favored the Tirolean places. My recommendation: Eat German here in Bozen.

Weisses Rössl offers affordable—mostly Tirolean—food with meat, fish, and fine vegetarian options. Located in a traditional woody setting, it's good for dining indoors among savvy locals (€10 plates, daily specials, Mon–Fri 11:00–23:00, closed Sat–Sun, 2 blocks north of Piazza Municipio at Via Bottai/Bindergasse 6, tel. 0471-973-267).

Ca' de Bezzi/Gasthaus Batzenhausl is historic. It's Bolzano's oldest inn, with a Teutonic-feeling top floor; by contrast, the patio and back room are refreshingly modern and untouristy. They make their own breads and pastas, and serve traditional Tirolean fare with a focus on fine wine—about 30 bottles are open to serve by the glass (€12 plates, daily 11:30–14:30 & 19:00–24:00, limited menu between mealtimes, a rare place open on Sun, Via Andreas

Tirolean Cuisine

During your visit to the Dolomites, take a break from Italian-style pizzas and pastas to sample some of the region's traditional cuisine...with a distinctly Austrian flavor. To reduce confusion, I've generally listed Italian names here, though local menus are in both Italian and German (and usually, English).

Wurst and sauerkraut are the Tirolean clichés. More adventurous eaters seek out *speck,* a raw (prosciutto-style) ham smoked for five months, then thinly sliced and served as an antipasto or in sandwiches. *Canederli*—large dumplings with bits of *speck,* liver, spinach, or cheese—are often served in broth, or with butter and cheese. (Never cut a dumpling with a knife—it'll destroy the chef.)

The stars of Tirolean cuisine are the hearty meat dishes—which, unlike traditional Italian main courses, are nearly always served with side dishes of doughy dumplings or vegetables and potatoes. Try *stinco di maiale* (roasted pork shank, usually garnished with potatoes) and *crauti rossi* (a sweetish sauerkraut made from red cabbage). *Carrè affumicato* is pork shank that is first smoked, then boiled. *Selvaggine,* or wild game, comes in the form of *capriolo* (fawn), *cervo* (venison), or *camoscio* (chamois/antelope). Game is eaten smoked and thinly sliced in *antipasti*; in meat sauce *(ragù)* with fresh pasta or as ravioli stuffing; or in entrees, as tender chunks grilled or roasted in a rich sauce *(spezzatino).*

For dessert, strudel is everywhere, filled with the harvest from this region's renowned apple orchards. Cakes and pies are loaded with other locally grown fruits, raisins, and nuts. *Kaiserschmarrn* is an interesting alternative: a tall, eggy crêpe prepared with raisins and topped with powdered sugar and red currant jam.

Bier (birra) is king in the Alto Adige (the best-known brand, Forst, is brewed in nearby Merano), but the wines of the area are well-matched to the local fare. *Magdalaner* is a light, dry red made from Schiava grapes. *Lagrein scuro* is a full-bodied red, dry and fruity, similar to a cabernet sauvignon or merlot. *Gewürztraminer* is a dry white wine with a spicy fruit flavor. For something stronger, try *grappa* made from Williams pears (and served with a wedge of fresh pear), or *grappa Nocino*—a darker, sweeter brew similar to Jägermeister. *Guten Appetit und Prost!*

The Dolomites

Hofer Strasse 30, tel. 0471-050-950).

Hopfen and Company fills an 800-year-old house with happy eaters, drinkers, and the beer-lover's favorite aroma—hops...or *hopfen*. A tavern since the 1600s, it's a stylish, fresh microbrewery today. This high-energy, boisterous place is packed with locals who come for its homemade beer, delicious Tirolean/Italian food, and reasonable prices (€10–15 main courses, good €7 salads, heavy, traditional beer dumplings, Mon–Sat 9:30–24:00, closed Sun, Piazza Erbe/Obstplatz 17, tel. 0471-300-788). You'll enjoy the friendly, English-speaking waitstaff.

Paulaner Stuben is a restaurant/pizzeria/*beirstube* serving good food and a favorite Bavarian beer with good outside seating and a take-me-to-Germany *stuben* or cellar downstairs (€7 pizzas, pastas, and salads, €15 dinner plates, Mon–Sat 10:00–24:00, closed Sun, Via Portici 51 and Via Argentieri 16, tel. 0471-980-407).

Enoteca Baccaro, a nondescript, hole-in-the-wall wine bar, is an intriguing spot for a glass of wine (€1–3) and bar snacks amid locals. Wines available by the glass are listed on the blackboard (Mon–Fri 9:00–21:00, closed Sat–Sun, located a half-block east of Hopfen and Company on a hidden alley off Via Argentieri/Silbergasse 17, look for *vino* sign next to fountain on south side of street, tel. 0471-971-421).

Gasthaus Fink, a busy diner, serves typical Tirolean and Italian dishes with indoor and on-the-street seating on a quiet pedestrian lane, just off Piazza Walther (€8 pastas, €12 *secondi*, Fri–Wed 10:30–14:30 & 18:00–21:30, closed Thu, Via della Mostra 9, tel. 0471-975-047).

Picnic: Assemble the ingredients at the **Piazza Erbe/Obstplatz** market and dine in the park along the Talvera River (the green area with benches past the museum). There are two **supermarkets:** One is on Piazza Erbe and the other is on Via della Rena/Raing near Piazza Walther (Mon–Fri 8:30–19:30, Sat 8:30–18:00, closed Sun; from Piazza Walther, facing TI, take street to the left for 2 blocks, supermarket is at bottom of stairs on your left).

TRANSPORTATION CONNECTIONS

From Bolzano by Train to: Milan (about hourly, 3.5 hrs, change in Verona), **Verona** (about hourly, 1.5–2 hrs), **Trento** (about hourly, 50 min), **Venice** (about hourly, 3–4 hrs, change in Verona), **Florence** (10/day, 4–6 hrs, change in Verona and/or Bologna), **Innsbruck** (every 2 hrs, usually at about half past the hour, 2 hrs), **Munich** (called "Monaco" in Italy, every 2 hrs, usually at about half past the hour, 3 hrs).

By Bus to: Castelrotto (2/hr, fewer on weekends, 50 min, generally leaves Bolzano at :10 and :40, pick up free schedule at bus station, last departure 19:10 or 19:40 on weekends, toll-free tel. 800-846-047). The bus leaves from Bolzano's bus station (1 block west of train station), stops at the train station, and then winds high into the mountains, dropping you in the center of Castelrotto. Buy a €3.50 one-way or €5 round-trip ticket at bus-station ticket window or from the driver. If you are heading directly to **Alpe di Siusi,** take the same bus, get off just past the Seiseralm Bergbahn station, and ascend on the cable car. For more on Alpe di Siusi, see page 193.

Castelrotto (Kastelruth)

The ideal home base for exploring Alpe di Siusi, Castelrotto (town population: 2,000; district population: 6,000; altitude: 3,475 feet) has more village character than any other town I know in the region. With its traffic-free center, a thousand years of history, an oversize and hyperactive bell tower, and traditionally clad locals, it seems lost in another world. Against a backdrop of mountains, Castelrotto conveys the powerful message that simple pleasures are enough. Stay two nights!

ORIENTATION

Tourist Information
The TI is on the main square, Piazza Kraus (mid-May–Oct Mon–Sat 8:30–12:30 & 14:00–18:00, Sun 9:00–12:00, shorter hours and closed Sun off-season, tel. 0471-706-333, www.kastelruth.com). If you plan to do any hiking, pick up the TI's list of suggested hikes, including estimated walking times and trail numbers.

Internet Access: You can get online at the library.

Arrival in Castelrotto
The *bushof* (bus station) is a few steps below the town's main square. The bus parking lot has a little shelter with an ATM, WC, phones, and bus schedules posted on the wall; take the stairs to the right of this building to get to the main square and TI.

Drivers can park near the bus station, and each of the recommended hotels has free parking. For Alla Torre and Hotel Cavallino d'Oro, go right through the traffic-free town center (very likely with a police escort); under the bell tower, drive through the white arch to the right of the TI, and park in the lot opposite Alla Torre. For Hotel al Lupo, park in the bus parking lot behind the hotel. The recommended private homes have free and easy parking (see "Sleeping," page 191).

SELF-GUIDED WALK

Welcome to Castelrotto

Castelrotto is tiny, with little to distract you other than the surrounding mountains and hikes. This quick walk will trace the town's history, from the ruling Krauses to yodelers who rule. Note that shops in Castelrotto close for siesta from 12:00–15:00—a good time for a long lunch, a hike in the hills...or a siesta.

• *Start in the...*

Main Square: Piazza Kraus is named for the family who ruled the town from 1550–1800. Their palace, now the City Hall and TI, overlooks the square and sports the Kraus family coat of arms.

Castelrotto uses its square well. The farmers' market takes place here Friday mornings in the summer (June–Oct) and a clothing market fills the square most Thursday mornings. While touristy, Castelrotto is not a full-blown resort; if you're on the square weekdays at 14:45, you'll see local moms gather their preschoolers, chat, then stop by the playground on Plattenstrasse. Before and after Sunday Mass, the square is crowded with villagers and farmers (who fill the church) dressed in traditional clothing. The main Mass (at 9:00 or 9:30) is in German. Another Mass takes place in Italian throughout tourist season (at 10:30) for visitors.

• *A landmark in the square is the...*

Bell Tower: At 250 feet, the free-standing bell tower domi-nates the town. It was once attached to a church, which burned in 1753. While the bell tower was quickly rebuilt, the present-day church was constructed a century later next to the gutted church (which was then torn down to make space for the square). The wire between the church and tower connects the noisy bells. The sacristan can easily ring them using an electric switch.

When you feel the pride that the locals have in their tower—which symbolizes their town—you'll better understand why Italy is called "the land of a thousand bell towers."

The bells of Castelrotto—a big part of the town experience—ring on the hour throughout the day and night. While sleepy tourists wonder why they clang through the wee hours, locals—who grew up with the chimes—find them comforting. The bells mark the hours, summon people to Mass, announce festivals, and warn when storms threaten. In the days when people used to believe that thunder was the devil approaching, the bells called everyone to pray. Townspeople thought their sound cleared the clouds. Bells ring big at 7:00, noon, and 19:00. The biggest of the eight bells

Castelrotto

① Alla Torre (Gasthof zum Turm) Hotel & Restaurant
② Hotel al Lupo (Hotel zum Wolf)
③ Hotel Cavallino d'Oro (Goldenes Rössl) Hotel & Rest.
④ Residence Garni Trocker
⑤ Haus Harderer
⑥ Haus Trocker
⑦ To Tirler Hof Farm
⑧ Stern Café
⑨ Café Doris
⑩ Silbernagl Kaufhaus Grocery
⑪ A&O Supermarket
⑫ ATM, WC & Phones
⑬ Kastelruther-Spatzen-Laden Shop
⑭ Mendel Haus

(7,500 pounds) peals only on special days. On Fridays, the bells ring at 15:00, commemorating Christ's sacrifice. The colorful poles in front of the church (yellow and white for the Vatican, red and white for Tirol) fly flags on festival days.

• *Also on the square is the...*

Church: Before entering, notice the plaque on the exterior. This commemorative inscription honors the tiny community's WWI dead—*Dorf* means from the village itself and *Fraktion* is from an outlying district. Stepping into the church, you're surrounded by harmonious art from about 1850. The church is dedicated to Sts. Peter and Paul, and the paintings that flank the high altar show how each was martyred (crucifixion and beheading). The pews (and smart matching confessionals) are carved of walnut wood.

• *Back outside, belly up to the...*

Fountain: Opposite the bell tower, Castelrotto's fountain dates from 1884. St. Florian, the protector against fires, keeps an eye on it today as he did when villagers (and their horses) first came here for a drink of water.

• *With your back to the bell tower, look a half-block down the lane to see the finely frescoed...*

Mendel Haus: This house has a traditional facade and a wood-carvers' shop. Its frescoes (from 1886) include many symbolic figures, as well as an emblem of a carpenter above the door—a relic from the days when images, rather than address numbers, identified the house. Notice St. Florian again; this time, he's pouring water on a small painting of this very house engulfed in flames. Inside Mendel Haus are fine carvings, a reminder that this region—especially nearby Val Gardena—is famous for its woodwork. You'll also see many witches, folk figures that date back to when this area was the Salem of this corner of Europe. Women who didn't fit society's mold were burned as witches, including midwives, healers, redheads, and so on.

• *Walk around behind Mendel Haus, turn left, and climb the stairs to Dolomitenstrasse. In 20 yards, on the left at the end of the street is a shop dedicated to Castelrotto's hometown heroes...*

Kastelruther–Spatzen–Laden: The ABBA of yodeling, the folk-singing group Kastelruther–Spatzen is a gang of local boys who put Castelrotto on the map. They have a huge following here, and have produced "more CDs than Michael Jackson" (or so I was proudly told). The Kastelruther–Spatzen are huge throughout the German-speaking world. Each second weekend in October, they put on a hometown concert—filling Castelrotto with fans from as far away as the Alsace, Switzerland, and the Netherlands.

Inside this shop—where you'll undoubtedly hear their inimitable music—is a yodelers' Carnaby Street. Downstairs is a folksy little museum slathered with gifts, awards, and gold records. The group has won 10 Echo Awards..."more than Robbie Williams." Watch the continuously playing video (€2 museum, refunded if you spend €5 in the shop, Mon–Fri 9:00–12:00 & 14:00–18:00, Sat 9:00–12:00, closed Sun, Via Dolomitenstrasse 21, www.kastelrutherspatzen.de).

SIGHTS

Calvario Stroll—For a scenic stroll, take a short walk around the town's hill, originally the site of the ancient Roman fortress and later the fortified home of the medieval lord. One lane circles the hill while another spirals to the top past seven little chapels, each depicting a scene from Christ's Passion and culminating in the Crucifixion. Facing the TI, take the road under the arch to the right, and then follow signs to *Kofel* (to go around the hill) or *Kalvarienberg* (to get directly to the top). This 15-minute stroll is great after dark—romantically lit and under the stars. (The lead singer of Kastelruther–Spatzen enjoyed his first kiss right here.)

Marinzen Lift—The little Marinzen cable car zips you up the mountain to the Marinzenhütte café, which has an animal park

for kids (open when the cable car runs, tel. 0471-707-158). Take the cable car back or it's a one-hour hike down (€4.50 one-way, €6.50 round-trip, runs late May–Oct daily 9:15–16:45, closed off-season and rainy mornings, tel. 0471-707-160; from town square, head down-

hill toward Wolkensteinstrasse, turn left and go another 50 yards down the road towards San Michele, find the chairlift a few steps off the road on the right).

SLEEPING

(€1 = about $1.30, country code: 39)

$$$ Alla Torre (in German, **Gasthof zum Turm**) is comfortable, clean, and alpine-traditional, with great beds and modern bathrooms (small Db-€64–96, big Db-€80–125 depending on season—price peaks in Aug, Tb-€94–165, includes breakfast, €4 extra for 1-night stays, closed April and Nov, elevator, behind TI at Kofelgasse 8, tel. 0471-706-349, fax 0471-707-268, www.zumturm .com, info@zumturm.com, Gabi and Günther).

$$ Hotel al Lupo (in German, **zum Wolf**) is pure Tirolean, with all the comforts in 23 neat-as-a-pin rooms, most with balconies (Sb-€35–50, Db-€56–85, prices vary with season and view, includes buffet breakfast, non-smoking rooms, elevator, coin-op laundry, closed April–mid-May and Nov–mid-Dec, a block below main square at Wolkensteinstrasse 5, tel. 0471-706-332, fax 0471-707-030, www.hotelwolf.it, info@hotelwolf.it, Arno).

$$ Hotel Cavallino d'Oro (in German, **Goldenes Rössl**), on the main square, has plenty of Tirolean character and plush, welcoming public rooms. Run by friendly and helpful Stefan and Susanne, the entire place is dappled with artistic woodsy touches and historic photos. If you love antiques by candlelight, this 650-year-old hotel is the best in town (Sb-€45–65, Db-€85–110 depending on season, discount for 4-night stay, no elevator, Krausplatz 1, tel. 0471-706-337, fax 0471-707-172, www.cavallino.it, cavallino @cavallino.it). Stefan converted his wine cellar into a spa and sauna (free and private for guests, great after a hike, just book an hour), complete with heated tile seats, solarium (for tanning), and tropical plants.

$$ Residence Garni Trocker is run by the Trocker family (around here, every other family is a Trocker family), who rent 10 great rooms in a place that's bomb-shelter solid yet warm-wood cozy. Their compound is beautifully laid out with a café/bar, garden, and top-notch plumbing (Sb-€40, Db-€54–86 depending on season, Fostlweg 3, tel. 0471-705-200, fax 0471-707-427, www .residencetrocker.com, garni@residencetrocker.com). Sunday is the family's day of rest; the hotel is open, but there's no service.

$ Haus Harderer, below Hotel Kastelruth (take the middle lane where it forks), rents a single plush, woody apartment for up to four (Db-€50, Tb-€60, no breakfast, cash only, 2-night minimum stay in summer, lots of stairs, view balcony, Plattenstrasse 20, tel. 0471-706-702, harderer@gmx.net, run by Oswald, Heinz, Ida, and Maunz the cat).

$ Haus Trocker, on the edge of town, is a modern home where Frau Trocker, who doesn't speak English, rents two delightful rooms that share one WC (D-€50, from the bus station, walk away from the church spire, following steps past Hotel Kastel Seiseralm to Fostlweg 6, tel. 0471-707-087). Son Roland speaks English.

$ Tirler Hof, the storybook Jaider family farm, has 40 cows, one friendly *Hund* (dog), four Old World–comfy guest rooms, and a great mountain view (D-€42, Db-€45, discount for stays longer than 1 night, includes breakfast, cash only, open year-round, most practical for drivers, it's the first farm outside of town, 100 yards past the *Leaving town* sign on the right on road to San Michele, Paniderstrasse 44; tel. & fax 0471-706-017, Paola). The ground-floor double has a private bath. The top-floor rooms share a bathroom and a great balcony. Take a stroll before breakfast.

EATING

Cavallino d'Oro Hotel Restaurant offers a variety of beautifully presented, homemade Tirolean cuisine—including wild game, *canederli* dumplings, and strudel—in a dressy but relaxed and woodsy ambience. The head waiter, Marco, is very helpful; quiz him before you order (€25 meals, daily 12:00–14:00 & 18:00–21:00). Lunch is by reservation only, unless you're staying at the hotel.

Alla Torre's Restaurant, homier and with the best terrace in town, is another fine option for traditional and international dishes (Thu–Tue 12:00–14:00 & 18:00–21:00, closed Wed, closed April and Nov).

For strudel, locals like the no-nonsense **Stern** café (Tue–Sun 7:30–19:00, closed Mon; on Plattenstrasse, facing TI, go left through arch; tel. 0471-706-382) and **Café Doris** (Wed–Mon 11:00–23:00, closed Tue, on main road at Wolkensteinstrasse 29, tel. 0471-706-340). Both have terraces.

Castelrotto has two groceries: **Silbernagl Kaufhaus** (Mon–Sat 8:00–12:00 & 15:00–19:00, closed Sun, also closed off-season on Sat afternoon, on Wolkensteinstrasse) and the smaller **A&O Supermarket,** two blocks away, also on the main drag (Mon–Sat 8:00–12:00 & 15:00–18:30, closed Sun and off-season Sat afternoons, Via Panider Strasse).

TRANSPORTATION CONNECTIONS

From Castelrotto by Bus to: Bolzano (€3.50 one-way, €5 round-trip, buy at bus-station ticket window or from driver, departures on the half-hour, fewer on weekends, 50 min, runs 6:30–19:00; in Bolzano, the bus stops at the more central Bahnhofplatz—the train station—saving you 200 yards of walking back from the bus station—the bus' last stop, toll-free tel. 800-846-047), **Canazei** (late June–mid-Sept only, 4/day, 2 hrs), and **Ortisei/St. Ulrich** and **St. Cristina** (6/day in summer, 2/day off-season, 30 min to Ortisei, 40 min to St. Cristina). Get bus schedules at the TI, call toll-free 800-846-047 or 0471-706-633, or check www.sii.bz.it. For **Alpe di Siusi** connections, see page 194.

Alpe di Siusi (Seiser Alm)

Europe's largest high-alpine meadow, Alpe di Siusi separates two of the most famous Dolomite ski-resort valleys. Eight miles wide, 20 miles long, and soaring up to 6,500 feet high, Alpe di Siusi is dotted by farm huts and wildflowers (mid-June–July), surrounded by dramatic—if distant—Dolomite peaks and cliffs, and much appreciated by hordes of walkers.

Compatsch, the modern little

tourist town at the entrance of the meadow, has a TI, food, a little strip mall, and services (described on page 196).

The Sasso Lungo mountains (Langkofel in German, Long Stone in English) at the head of the meadow provide a storybook Dolomite backdrop, while the spooky Schlern peak stands boldly staring into the haze of the peninsula. The Schlern, looking like a devilish *Winged Victory*, gave ancient peoples enough willies to spawn legends of supernatural forces. The Schlern witch, today's tourist-brochure mascot, was the cause of many a broom-riding medieval townswoman's fiery death.

Alpe di Siusi is my recommended one-stop look at the Dolomites because of Castelrotto's charm as a home base, its quintessential Dolomite mountain views, its easy accessibility for those with and without cars, and its variety of walks, hikes, and mountain-bike routes. While most hikers will enjoy the easy meadow strolls, the nearby Schlern tempts and rewards those with more energy and an adventurous spirit.

The meadow is famous for its wildflowers—a fragrant festival (best in June) blooming with flowers that grow only between 5,900 and 7,800 feet above sea level. The cows munching away in this vast meadow produce 2.5 million gallons of milk annually, much of which is sent to Bolzano to make cheese. After tourism, dairy is the leading industry here. While cows winter in Castelrotto, they summer in Alpe di Siusi. The meadow is also dotted with small, idyllic hotels and chalet restaurants. It's extremely family-friendly, with playgrounds at each stop and plenty of animals to pet. Being here on a sunny summer day comes with the ambience of a day at the beach.

ORIENTATION

Getting to Alpe di Siusi

By Car: A nature preserve, Alpe di Siusi is closed to cars during the day (9:00–17:00), unless you're staying in one of the area hotels. (Show your reservation confirmation as proof.) Parking at Compatsch (€10/day) requires that you arrive before the road closes at 9:00 in the morning, though you can drive back down at any time. Park officials encourage visitors to use the two free parking lots located at the Seiseralm Bergbahn cable-car station in Siusi/Seis (see below); park your car and take the cable car *(cabino-via)* up to Compatsch.

By Cable Car from Siusi/Seis up to Alpe di Siusi: A cable car (Seiseralm Bergbahn) runs hikers and skiers from the village of Siusi/Seis to Compatsch, the gateway to the meadow (late May–mid-Oct daily 8:00–19:00, off-season 8:00–18:00, 15-min ride to the top, €9 one-way, €12 round-trip, www.seiseralm-bergbahn

Alpe di Siusi

NOTE: THIS 3-D VIEW LOOKS SOUTHEAST & IS NOT TO SCALE. ELEVATIONS IN METERS

★ = HOTEL SEELAUS

LEGEND:
- ● TOWN
- — ROAD
- ●—● LIFT
- ······ TRAIL
- ▲ MTN. HUT (HÜTTE/ RIFUGIO)

❶ Panorama to Zallingerhütte Hike
❷ Summit Hike of Schlern
❸ "Trail of the Witches"
❹ Loop around Sasso Lungo

.com). From Compatsch, you can take a shuttle bus farther into Alpe di Siusi to Saltria (free with cable-car ticket, otherwise €2 one-way, €4 round-trip).

By Bus from Castelrotto: Buses shuttle hikers between Castelrotto's bus station *(bushof)* and the cable car (Seiseralm Bergbahn) near the village of Siusi/Seis (3/hr in season, daily 8:10–19:35, fewer midday, €3 one-way, cable-car ticket additional).

Regional buses (such as the orange SAD bus to and from Bolzano) stop at Siusi/Seis and just past the Seiseralm Bergbahn (frequent in summer, 4/day in each direction off-season, €2 one-way).

The Alpe di Siusi Express is a shuttle bus that runs from

Castelrotto all the way to Compatsch—denying you the fun experience of approaching the high meadow by cable car (6/day, 30 min, €9 one-way, €12 round-trip, see www.silbernagl.it for schedules).

For a longer stay, consider the **Combi-Card** (€28/any 3 days out of a 7-day validity period, €35/6 out of 7 days, expires 1 week after time stamp). It covers the Alpe di Siusi Express, Seiseralm Bergbahn cable car, Compatsch–Saltria shuttle bus (Almbus #11), and other shuttle buses, but not the regional orange SAD buses, such as the one to Bolzano from Castelrotto.

Getting Around Alpe di Siusi

Shuttle Buses: As the meadow is essentially car-free, the park's buses shuttle visitors to and from key points along the tiny road all the way from Compatsch—at the entry to the meadow—to the end of the line at Saltria—at the foot of the postcard-dramatic Sasso peaks (every 20 min from 9:00–18:30, 15 min, free with cable-car ticket, otherwise €2 one-way, €4 round-trip, buy from driver). At the end of the day, buses can be jam-packed.

Cable Cars and Chair Lifts: The entire meadow is served by various lifts (marked on maps). These are worth the roughly €5 per ride to get you into the higher and more scenic hiking areas—or back to the shuttle buses quickly. Keep in mind that lifts and shuttle buses stop running fairly early (often at about 17:00)—which can be a major disappointment if you're running out of steam and time, and are still high up after a long day's hike.

Compatsch

This tourist village (6,048 feet) at the entrance to the meadow is served by the Seiseralm Bergbahn cable car from the town of Siusi/Seis. You can drive to Compatsch if you are staying at a hotel in Alpe di Siusi (or if you arrive very early or leave very late, outside of park opening hours). Parking costs €10 per day.

Compatsch has a **TI** (Mon–Sat 9:00–17:00, Sun 9:00–13:00, shorter hours off-season, WCs at cable-car station, tel. 0471-727-904, www.seiseralm.it/en).

You'll also find a grocery store (open mid-June–mid-Oct), ATM, hotels, restaurants, and shops.

You can rent mountain bikes at **Sporthaus Trocker** (€8/1 hr, €18/4 hrs, mid-May–mid-Oct only, 50 yards from TI in strip mall under the Plaza Hotel, tel. 0471-727-824, www.sporthaustrocker.it). There is a world of tiny paved and gravel lanes to pedal on. Pick up their suggested routes and consider those I've described below. Rentable baby buggies are popular for those hiking with toddlers (a handy brochure lists hikes).

Trocker rents horses and provides guides (€15/1 hr, €30/2 hrs, €42/3 hrs, open June–Oct, next to Compatsch TI and near cable-car station, tel. 0471-727-807, no English spoken).

Sleeping near the Park Entrance: **$$$ Hotel Seelaus**, a 10-minute walk downhill from Compatsch, is a cozy, friendly family-run place with a Germanic feel and down comforters (Sb-€55–114, Db-€100–228, prices vary with season and type of room; includes buffet breakfast and hearty dinner, free and easy parking, and use of Wellness Center with sauna, hydro-massage, and mini-pool; Via Compatsch 8, tel. 0471-727-954, fax 0471-727-835, www .hotelseelaus.it, info@hotelseelaus.it, Roberto). There are many more chalets and huts with rooms for rent in Alpe di Siusi (which generally cost as much as a normal hotel; see TI for details).

HIKING

Easy meadow walks abound in Alpe di Siusi, giving novice hikers classic Dolomite views from baby-stroller trails. Experienced hikers should consider the tougher and more exciting treks. Before attempting a hike, call or stop by the local TI to confirm your understanding of the time and skills required. As always, when hiking in the mountains, assume weather can change quickly, and pack accordingly. Many lifts operate only mid-June through mid-October. The Panorama and Puflatsch lifts (both near Compatsch) run later into the off-season. Meadow walks, for flower-lovers and strollers, are pretty—or may be pretty boring. Chairlifts are springboards for more dramatic and demanding hikes. Trails are very well marked, and the brightly painted numbers are keyed into local maps. For simple hikes, you can basically string together three or four hut names. For anything more serious, invest in a good map, about €5 at the TI. The Kompass Bolzano map #54 covers everything in this chapter (scale 1:50,000). The Wanderkarte map of Alpe di Siusi (produced by Tabacco) offers more detail and focuses on just Alpe di Siusi (scale 1:25,000).

Walks and Hikes from Compatsch
Panorama to Zallingerhütte: The Easy Route—This is a basic four-hour, mostly level walk, giving you fine vistas from both ends of the meadow, fun stops along the way, and lifts up and down on each end. Ride the €4 lift to Panorama (6,600 feet), then hike 75 minutes to Molignonhütte (6,725 feet), and continue two hours (fairly level, follow trails #2 and then #7) to Zallingerhütte (6,725 feet). From here it's a 10-minute walk to Williamshütte (6,888 feet), where you catch the €6 Florian lift back to Saltria and the shuttle-bus stop (for Compatsch). Both Molignonhütte and Zallingerhütte have great restaurants for a drink or meal. For shorter or cheaper

The Dolomites

versions, you can ride the lift up and stroll back down.

Panorama to Plattkofelhütte: The High Route—For a more thrilling, two-hour extension of the previous hike, climb from Molignonhütte (6,725 feet) up to Plattkofelhütte (7,544 feet), follow the high trail #4 along the ridge for an hour with commanding views both left and right, and then hike steeply back down to Williamshütte (6,888 feet).

Summit Hike of Schlern (Sciliar)—For a challenging 12-mile, six-hour hike—with a possible overnight in a traditional mountain refuge (generally open mid-June–mid-Oct)—consider hiking to the summit of Schlern and spending a night in Rifugio Bolzano/Schlernhaus. This route is popular with serious hikers as the best hike in the region.

Start at the Spitzbühl chairlift (€3.50 one-way, €5 round-trip, 5,659 feet, free parking lot, first bus stop in park), which drops you at Spitzbühl (6,348 feet). Trail #5 takes you through a high meadow, down to the Saltner dairy farm (6,004 feet—you want the Saltner dairy farm at Tschapit, not the one near Zallingerhütte), across a stream, and steeply up the Schlern mountain. About three hours into your hike, you'll meet trail #1 and walk across the rocky tabletop plateau of Schlern to the mountain hotel **Rifugio Bolzano/Schlernhaus** (7,544 feet, 60 beds, Ds-€30, dorm beds-€18, includes breakfast, summer tel. 0471-612-024 or mobile 328-831-2767, call for reservation). From this dramatic setting, you can enjoy a meal and get a great view of the Rosengarten range. Hike 20 more minutes up the nearby peak (Mount Pez, 8,399 feet) where you'll find a lofty meadow, cows in the summer, and the region's ultimate 360-degree alpine panorama. From Rifugio Bolzano/Schlernhaus, you can hike back the way you came or walk farther along the Schlern (7 miles, 2 hours; past **Rifugio Alpe di Tires/Tierser Alpl**, 8,005 feet, €19 beds, €10.50 bunks, open June–mid-Oct, tel. 0471-727-958) and descend back into Alpe di Siusi, to the road where the bus or cable car will return you to your starting point or hotel.

The "Trail of the Witches"—Take a lift from Compatsch to Puflatsch (€4 one-way, €5.50 round-trip) for the two-hour loop north to Arnikahütte (with a café) and back (elevation gain about 660 feet). Walking among the legendary stone seats of witches, you'll enjoy fine views of the valley all the way down to Castelrotto.

Loop Around Sasso Lungo—Another dramatic but easy hike is the eight-hour walk around the Sasso Lungo (Langkofel) mountains, called the Federico Augusto/Friederich August trail. Ride the bus to Saltria (end of the line), take the chairlift to Williamshütte, walk past the Zallingerhütte (overnight possible, Db–€95–130, includes breakfast and dinner, open mid-May–mid-Oct, tel. 0471-727-947), and circle the Sasso Lungo group (get details and advice from the TI). On the opposite side, at Sella Pass, you ride a lift up Sasso Lungo to the Leo Demetz hut (8,790 feet), cross the saddle between Sasso Lungo and Sasso Piatto, and zigzag back into Alpe di Siusi with breathtaking views of rock climbers.

BIKING

Mountain bikes are easy to rent, welcome on the lifts, and permitted on Alpe di Siusi lanes. The Compatsch TI has a good information flier that lists the best routes (I've listed three below). Get local advice to confirm difficulty levels and your plan before starting any ride.

Mountain-Bike Rides from Compatsch

Easy High Alp Ride (2.5 Hours, Medium)—This ride stays in Alpe di Siusi and gives you the best basic look at this high meadow, with little altitude gain and easy lanes throughout.

Start from Compatsch (6,048 feet), bike or ride the lift to Panorama (6,600 feet), and take road #7, which runs generally level to Goldknopf/Punta d'Oro and then Mahlknechthütte/Molignonhütte (6,725 feet). Then follow road #8 down to Saltria (5,575 feet), and back to Compatsch (6,048 feet).

Alpe di Siusi Meadow and Val Gardena (4 Hours, Medium to Difficult)—This route covers the great views of the Alpe di Siusi meadow, gets you into Val Gardena, a classic Süd Tirol valley, to see two resort towns, and then a lift gets you easily back to your starting point.

Start at Compatsch (6,048 feet), and take the road to Saltria (5,575 feet); from the bus stop, ride the unpaved road down to Monte Pana (5,366 feet). From here, an asphalt road zigzags steeply to St. Cristina (4,592 feet on valley floor far below), then heads down the valley to St. Ulrich/Ortisei (4,264 feet), where you take the cable car to Mezdi (6,560 feet), back in the Alpe di Siusi high meadow. Complete your loop by rolling back down on a good road to Compatsch (6,048 feet).

Dramatic High Ridge Ride (4 Hours, Difficult)—This ride takes you into the dramatic rocks so characteristic of the Dolomites, with grand views and only the sound of your hardworking body and the rocks under your tires. If you get an early start, you can leave the bike at the Tierser Alpl/Alpe di Tires hut (8,006 feet) and hike to Schlernhausern/Rifugio Bolzano near the summit of the mighty Schlern—Monte Pez (2 hrs, 8,400 feet).

Start at Compatsch (6,048 feet), ride the paved road downhill for 3.5 miles to Saltria (5,575 feet), then take road #8 to the Tierser Alpl hut (8,006 feet, you could ride the lift to Williamshütte to avoid half the altitude gain). From the Tierser Alpl hut, return the way you came until just below Hotel Floralpina/Seiser Alm Haus, where you'll take the left fork and follow road #7 to Mahlknechthütte/Molignonhütte (6,725 feet) and on through Goldknopt/Punta d'Oro (6,560 feet), and back down to Compatsch (6,048 feet).

More Sights in the Dolomites

▲▲**Great Dolomite Road**—This is the definitive Dolomite drive: Belluno–Cortina–Pordoi Pass–Val di Fassa–Bolzano. Connecting Venice with Bolzano this way (the Belluno–Venice *autostrada* is slick) takes three hours longer than the direct Bolzano–Verona–Venice *autostrada*. No public transit does this trip. In spring and early summer, passes labeled "closed" are often bare, dry, and, as far as local drivers are concerned, wide-open. Call 0471-200-198 for road conditions (in Italian or German only).

▲▲**Abbreviated Dolomite Loop Drive**—See the biggies in half the miles (allow four hours, Bolzano–Castelrotto–Val Gardena–Sella Pass–Val di Fassa–Bolzano). Val Gardena (Grodner Tal) is famous for its skiing and hiking resorts, traditional Ladin culture, and wood-carvers (the wood-carving company ANRI is from the Val Gardena town of St. Cristina). It's a bit overrated, but even if its culture has been suffocated by the big bucks of hedonistic European fun-seekers, it remains a good jumping-off point for trips into the mountains. Within an hour, you'll reach Sella Pass (7,349 feet). After a series of tight, hairpin turns a half-mile or so over the pass, you'll see some benches and cars. Pull over and watch the rock climbers.

The town of Canazei, at the head of the valley and the end of the bus line, has the most ambience and altitude (4,642 feet). From there, a lift (€5.50 one-way, €9 round-trip) or gondola (€8.50 one-way, €12 round-trip, Easter–Oct daily 8:45–12:30 & 14:00–18:00, both closed Oct–Easter) takes you to Col dei Rossi Belvedere, where you can hike the Bindelweg trail past Rifugio Belvedere along an easy but breathtaking ridge to Rifugio Viel del Pan (Canazei TI for lift info: tel. 0462-609-600, infocanazei @fassa.com). This three-hour round-trip hike has views of the highest mountain in the Dolomites—the Marmolada—and the Dolo-mighty Sella range.

▲▲**Reifenstein Castle**—For one of Europe's most intimate looks at medieval castle life, let the friendly lady of Reifenstein (Frau Blanc) show you around her wonderfully preserved castle. She leads tours in Italian and German, squeezing in whatever English she can (€5, open Easter–Oct; tours Sat–Thu at 10:30, 14:00, and 15:00; mid-July–mid-Sept also at 16:00, closed Fri, picnic spot at drawbridge, tel. 0472-765-879).

To drive to the castle, exit the *autostrada* at Vipiteno (Sterzing) and follow signs toward *Bolzano*, taking three rights. The castle is just west of the freeway; park at the base of the castle's rock. Of the two castles here, Reifenstein is the one to the west. While this is easy by car, it's probably not worth the trouble by train (6/day from Bolzano, one-hour train ride followed by a one-hour hike).

▲**Glurns**—Drivers connecting the Dolomites and Lake Como by the high road via Meran and Bormio can spend the night in the amazing little town of Glurns (45 min west of touristy Meran, between Schluderns and Taufers). Glurns still lives within its square wall on the Adige River, with a church bell tower that has a thing about ringing, and real farms rather than boutiques. The town's short archways seem to cause the locals, whose families go back eons, to take on a Quasimodo-like posture. There are several small hotels in the town, but I'd stay in a private home (such as **Family Hofer,** 6 rooms, €25/person with breakfast, less for 3 nights, cash only, 100 yards from town square, near church, just outside wall on river, Via Adige 1, tel. 0473-831-597, fax 0473-835-864, www.hofer.bz.it, privatzimmer.hofer@rolmail.net).

THE LAKES

Commune with nature where Italy is welded to the Alps, in the lovely Italian lakes district. In this land of lakes, the million-euro question is: Which one? For the best mix of accessibility, scenery, and offbeat-ness, Varenna on Lake Como is my top choice, followed by Stresa on Lake Maggiore. You'll get a complete dose of Italian-lakes wonder and aristocratic-old-days romance. Bustling Milan, just an hour away from either lake, doesn't even exist. Now it's your turn to be *chiuso per restauro* (closed for restoration). If relaxation's not on your agenda, the lakes shouldn't be either. If you must choose between Lake Como and Lake Maggiore, the former is a better place to linger, while the latter makes a good day trip from Milan.

Lake Como

Planning Your Time

Lake Como (Lago di Como) is Milan's quick getaway, and the sleepy midlake village of Varenna is the gateway to the lake and the handiest base of operations. With good connections to Milan, Malpensa Airport, and midlake destinations, Varenna is my favorite home base for the lakes. Even though there are no essential activities, plan for at least two nights so that you'll have an uninterrupted day to see how slow you can get your pulse.

Lake Como—lined with elegant, 19th-century villas, crowned by snowcapped mountains, and busy with ferries, hydrofoils, and slow passenger-only boats—is a good place to take a break from the intensity and obligatory-turnstile culture of central Italy. It

The Italian Lakes

seems like half the travelers that you'll meet have tossed their itineraries into the lake and are actually relaxing.

Today, the hazy, lazy lake's only serious industry is tourism. Thousands of lakeside residents travel daily to nearby Lugano, in Switzerland, to find work. The lake's isolation and flat economy have left it pretty much the way the 19th-century Romantic poets described it.

Getting Around Lake Como

By Boat: Lake Como is well-served by boats and hydrofoils. The lake service is divided into three parts: south–north from Como

to Colico; midlake between Varenna, Bellagio, Menaggio, and Cadenabbia (Villa Carlotta); and the southeastern arm to Lecco. Unless you're going through Como, you'll probably limit your cruising to the midlake service (boat info: tel. 031-579-211). Boats go about hourly

Boat Schedule Literacy Tips

Feriali	Monday–Saturday
Festivi	Sundays and holidays
Partenze da…	Departing from…
Traghetto or *Autotraghetto*	Car ferry (walk-on passengers, too)
Aliscafo or *Servizio rapido*	Hydrofoil
Battello	Slow passenger-only boat

between Varenna, Menaggio, and Bellagio (€3.40 per hop, 15 min, daily approximately 7:00–21:00, confirm return trip when you disembark). Stopovers aren't allowed and there's no break for round-trips, so buy individual tickets for each ride. The one-day, €10 midlake pass saves you a little money if you take three rides.

The free schedule (available at TIs, hotels, and boat docks) lists prices and times. Confusingly, the schedule requires you to scan three different timetables to know all the departures:

• car ferry and passenger-only ferry (midlake "ferry-boat" or *autotraghetto* on the schedule);

• the hydrofoil (*servizio rapido*, costs a third more, enclosed, stuffy, speedy, less scenic); and the…

• all-lake slow boat *(battello)*.

This aggravation is compounded by a ferry workforce that seems to have a disdain for English. To simplify matters, I'd just consider the timetables for the two main, midlake ferry-boat services: the passenger-only ferry and the car ferry. You can ask for a ferry-only schedule that minimizes the confusion that you'll get from looking at the complete "Lago di Como" schedule. You'll see on the schedule that it's most likely that your ferry will accept cars, too. Also, be sure to note whether you are traveling on a weekday (*feriali*, Mon–Sat) or a Sunday (*festivi*). Review your possible connections (with the help of your hotelier) before you set out so you can pace your day smartly. It's a shame to miss a boat and lose out on a hike or an eagerly anticipated meal because of confusing timetables. Note that if you're traveling by hydrofoil or slow boat, you might arrive at a different dock than the ferries.

By Car: With the parking problems, constant traffic jams, and expensive car ferries, this is no place to drive if you don't have to. While you can drive around the lake, the road is narrow, congested, and lined by privacy-seeking walls, hedges, and tall fences. Parking in Bellagio is more difficult than in Varenna. Keep your car in Varenna and cruise.

You can arrange a rental car for when you leave Varenna

Central Lake Como

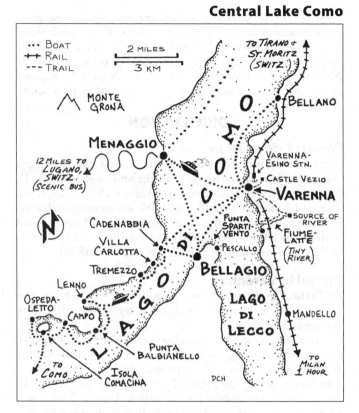

... BOAT
++ RAIL
--- TRAIL

2 MILES
3 KM

TO TIRANO &
ST. MORITZ
(SWITZ.)

MONTE
GRONA

BELLANO

MENAGGIO

12 MILES TO
LUGANO,
SWITZ.
(SCENIC BUS)

VARENNA-
ESINO STN.

CASTLE VEZIO

VARENNA

CADENABBIA

PUNTA
SPARTI-
VENTO

SOURCE OF
RIVER

FIUME-
LATTE
(TINY
RIVER)

VILLA
CARLOTTA

PESCALLO

TREMEZZO

BELLAGIO

LENNO

LAGO
DI
LECCO

OSPEDA-
LETTO

MANDELLO

CAMPO

PUNTA
BALBIANELLO

TO
MILAN
1 HOUR

TO
COMO

ISOLA
COMACINA

DCH

(contact the I Viaggi del Tivano travel agency in Varenna, listed in "Helpful Hints"), but you'll have to get to Lecco or another larger town to pick up your car. Taking your car on a ferry costs about €8 (includes driver, depends on size of car, plus €3.40 for each passenger).

Varenna

This town of 800 people offers the best of all lake worlds. Easily accessible by train, on the less-driven side of the lake, Varenna has a romantic promenade, a tiny harbor, narrow lanes, and its own villa. It's the right place to savor a lakeside cappuccino or *aperitivo*. There's

wonderfully little to do here, and it's very quiet at night, except for a few American wedding parties in summer. The *passerella* (lakeside walk, unlit but safe after dark) is adorned with caryatid lovers pressing silently against each other in the shadows. Between November and mid-March, Varenna practically shuts down; hotels close for the winter, and restaurants and shops reduce their hours.

ORIENTATION

Tourist Information

Varenna's TI (Pro Loco Varenna) is up the street from the biggest church on the main square, just past the tobacco shop on Via IV Novembre (May–Oct Tue–Sun 10:00–12:00 & 15:00–17:00, closed Mon and Nov–April, tel. 0341-830-367, www.varennaitaly.com, prolocovarenna@tin.it). A smaller, volunteer-run TI can be found at the train station (sporadic hours allegedly timed with train arrivals, daily mid-June–Sept 10:30–13:30 & 15:30–18:30).

Arrival in Varenna

By Train: Zip directly from Milan to Varenna by train. On arrival, set up, and limit your activities to the scenic midlake area (Varenna and Bellagio).

Here are the specifics: Leaving from Milan's central station, catch a train heading for Sondrio or Tirano—sometimes the departure board also says "Leccotirano." (Tirano is often confused with Torino...wrong city.) And, if you're heading for Varenna, be sure you don't accidentally catch a train to Verona. All Sondrio trains stop in Varenna, as noted in the fine print on the *Partenze* (departures) schedule posted at Milan's train station. Trains usually leave Milan about every hour or two (usually a few minutes past the hour, takes about 1 hour, approximate schedules listed in "Transportation Connections," page 218). Get a second-class ticket since first-class train cars are rare on the Sondrio–Tirano route. Stamp the ticket in the yellow box at the front of the tracks or risk a fine. Sit on the left for maximum lakeview beauty. Get off at Varenna–Esino. The name "Varenna–Esino" appears only at the train station, even though train schedules list simply "Varenna." Same place.

Know what time you're supposed to arrive in Varenna, so you can be ready to disembark with luggage in hand; the train stops just for a minute (literally). Otherwise you'll be carried on to the next town and have to backtrack. You may have to open the train door yourself, and because trains can be longer than the station, your car may actually stop before it reaches the platform (causing you to mistakenly think that you're not there yet). Look out the window. If part of the train's at the station, you'll need to get out

Varenna

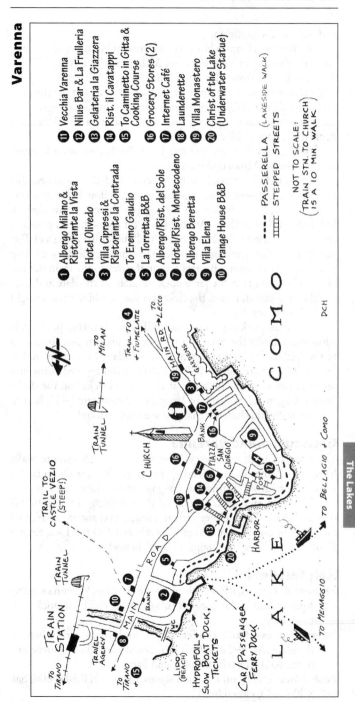

1. Albergo Milano & Ristorante la Vista
2. Hotel Olivedo
3. Villa Cipressi & Ristorante la Contrada
4. To Eremo Gaudio
5. La Torretta B&B
6. Albergo/Rist. del Sole
7. Hotel/Rist. Montecodeno
8. Albergo Beretta
9. Villa Elena
10. Orange House B&B
11. Vecchia Varenna
12. Nilus Bar & La Frulleria
13. Gelateria la Giazzera
14. Rist. il Cavatappi
15. To Caminetto in Gitta & Cooking Course
16. Grocery Stores (2)
17. Internet Café
18. Launderette
19. Villa Monastero
20. Christ of the Lake (Underwater Statue)

---- PASSERELLA (LAKESIDE WALK)
▥▥▥ STEPPED STREETS

NOT TO SCALE:
(TRAIN STN. TO CHURCH IS A 10 MIN. WALK)

TO MILAN

TRAIN TUNNEL

TRAIL TO CASTLE VEZIO (STEEP!)

TRAIN STATION

TO TRAIN

TRAVEL AGENCY

TO TRAIN + 15

TRAIN TUNNEL

LIDO (BEACH)

CHURCH

TRAIN TUNNEL

TRAIL TO + FIUMELATTE

TO → LECCO

MAIN RD.

GARDENS

COMO

BANK

BANK

MAIN ROAD

PIAZZA SAN GIORGIO

POST

WC

HYDROFOIL + SLOW BOAT DOCK, TICKETS

CAR/PASSENGER FERRY DOCK

LAKE

TO MENAGGIO

TO BELLAGIO & COMO

HARBOR

DCH

The Lakes

and walk to the platform.

By Boat via Como: For a less convenient but more scenic trip, you can also get to Varenna from Milan via the town of Como. Trains take you from Milan to Como (2/hr, 30–50-min ride). It's a 10-minute walk to the dock where you catch a boat for the one-hour (if by hydrofoil) or two-hour *battello* (slow boat—great for enjoying the scenery) ride up the lake to Varenna (€8, 3/day, last departure about 15:00).

By Taxi: A taxi can cost roughly €130–165 between Varenna and downtown Milan or Milan's airports.

By Car: In Varenna, look for the color-coded lines to decipher the parking options: white is free anytime, yellow is for residents only, and blue means you pay during peak times on weekends, holidays, and/or daily in August (look for signs, €1/hr, payment times vary—often 8:00–12:00 & 14:00–19:00, otherwise free). Buy tickets from the newsstand on the main square, the *tabacchi* shop just south of the square, Beretta Bar on the way to the train station, or Bar Cambusa near the ferry dock (scratch off the date and time you'll be parked and leave the ticket on your dashboard; overnight until 10:00 is okay).

For free parking, try: near Albergo Beretta, past Villa Monastero, along the river near the harbor, and the few spots next to the harbor. Parking is free Monday–Friday at the train station (but its €1/hr Sat–Sun 8:00–19:00, 2-hour limit—feed coins into meter at center of the lot and put the printed ticket on the dashboard). In general, parking in Varenna is complicated—it's best to confirm with your hotelier that you are safely parked.

Getting Around Varenna

Varenna is small, and everything is within a 15-minute walk (except for Hotel Eremo Gaudio). From the dock, walk up to the main road to avoid carting your luggage across the cobblestones.

If you'd prefer a taxi, you'll find them waiting at the train station and dock. From either arrival point, a taxi should charge €9 for a ride to hotels near Piazza Centrale and €10 to Hotel Eremo Gaudio (see "Taxis" in "Helpful Hints" below).

Helpful Hints

Money: A bank (with a cash machine) is near Varenna's main square; another is located inland from the boat dock (see town map).

Internet Access: Barilott offers access, fresh *panini,* and wines by the glass (Mon–Sat 7:00–20:00, closed Sun, Via IV Novembre 6, tel. 0341-815-045, Claudia and Fabrizio).

Post Office: It's just off the main square (Mon–Fri 8:30–14:00, Sat 8:30–12:30, closed Sun).

Laundry: Lavanderia Pensa Barbara can wash and dry your laundry within 24 hours. A typical load costs about €5, depending on the weight (€3.50/2 pounds, no self-service, Mon–Fri 9:00–12:30 & 15:00–19:30, Sat 9:00–12:30, closed Sun, Via Venini 31, tel. 0341-830-478).

Taxi: Reliable **Marco Barili** will meet you at the train station if you know your exact arrival time in Varenna. He can also get you to Milan and its airports, and unlike other drivers, he doesn't add surcharges for baggage or early/late departures (€130 to central Milan or Linate Airport, €140 to Malpensa Airport for up to 4 people, €195 for 5–8 passengers in a minibus, tel. 0341-815-061, taxi.varenna@tiscali.it).

Travel Agency: For bus and boat tours, consider Varenna's travel agency, **I Viaggi del Tivano,** next to Albergo Beretta, a block below the train station. They book planes, trains, and automobiles, and can offer half-day and daylong tours of the region and into Switzerland April–October; book tours by noon the day before (office open Mon–Fri 8:30–12:30 & 15:00–19:00, Sat 9:00–12:00, closed Sun, credit cards accepted but not for train tickets, can book rental cars here but pick up elsewhere, Via Esino 3, tel. 0341-814-009, www.tivanotours.com, helpful Silvia and Eleonora).

SELF-GUIDED WALK

Welcome to Varenna

Since you came here to relax, this short walk gives you just the town basics.

Bridge near Train Station: This main bridge, just below the train station, spans the tiny Esino River. The river divides two communities: Perledo (which sprawls up the hill—notice the church spire high above) and the old fishing town of Varenna (huddled around its harbor). The train station is called Varenna–Esino, named for a third community situated eight miles higher in the hills. Follow the river down to the lakeside promenade by the ferry dock. The town's public beach (or *lido*) is just over the cute pedestrian bridge (free beach, lounge chairs for rent). The inn facing the ferry dock, Hotel Olivedo, has greeted ferry travelers since the 19th century, and is named for the olive groves you can see growing halfway up the hill. Locals claim this is the farthest north where olives grow in Europe.

• *Across from Hotel Olivedo is Varenna's...*

Ferry Landing: Since the coming of the train in 1892, Varenna has been *the* convenient access point from "midlake" (the communities of Bellagio, Menaggio, and Varenna) to Milan. From this viewpoint, you can almost see how Lake Como is shaped like a man. The head is the north end (to the right, up by the Swiss Alps). Varenna is the man's left hip (to the east). Menaggio, across the lake, is the right hip (to the west). And Bellagio (hiding behind the smaller wooded hill to your left) is where the legs come together—you can see the point (Punta Spartivento—literally, "point that divides the wind"). In a more colorful description, a local poem says, "Lake Como is a man, with Colico the head, Lecco and Como the feet, and Bellagio the testicles." (In the local dialect, this rhymes—ask a local to say it for you.)

The furthest ridges high above the right hip are the border of Switzerland. The region's longtime poverty shaped the local character (much like the Great Depression shaped the outlook of a generation of Americans). Many still remember that this side of the lake was the poorest, because those on the other side (Menaggio) controlled the lucrative cigarette-smuggling business over the Swiss border. Today, the entire region is thriving—thanks to tourism.

• *Walk past the ferry dock to Varenna's elevated shoreline walk, called the...*

Passerella: A generation ago, Varenna built this elegant lakeside promenade, which connects the ferry dock with the old town center. Strolling this lane, you'll come to the tiny two-dinghy concrete breakwater of a local villa. Lake Como is lined with swanky 19th-century villas; their front doors face the lake to welcome visitors arriving by boat. At this point, the modern *passerella* cuts between this villa's water gate and its private harbor. Around the next corner, a plaque marks *Il Signore del Lago,* which means the Christ of the Lake. The local divers' association placed this crucifix (floodlit after dark) about 10 feet underwater, declaring, "We are committing ourselves to love, because this is the only certainty." (Their commitment to replacing a burnt-out light bulb, however, is not so certain.) From here, enjoy a good Varenna town view. These buildings are stringently protected by preservation laws; you can't even change the color of your villa's paint.

Just over the hump (which allows boats into a covered moorage), look up at another typical old villa—with a private *passerella,* a lovely veil of wisteria, and a prime lakeview terrace. Many of these villas are owned by the region's "impoverished nobility." They were bred and raised not to work and, therefore, are now unable to pay for the upkeep of their sprawling houses. Lately, these villas are being bought by the region's nouveau riche.

• *At the community harbor, walk to the end of the pier for a town overview, then continue under the old-time arcades to the fishermen's multi-hued homes, which face the harbor.*

Varenna Harborfront: Notice there are no streets in the old town...just characteristic stepped lanes called *contrade.* Varenna

was originally a fishing community. Even today, old-timers enjoy Lago di Como's counterpart to the Norwegian lutefisk: *missoltino*, air-dried and salted lake "sardines." They're served with the region's polenta (different from Venice's because buckwheat is mixed in with the corn).

Imagine the harbor 200 years ago—busy with coopers expertly fitting chestnut and oak staves into barrels, stoneworkers carving the local black marble that was quarried just above town, and fishing boats dragged onto the sloping beach. The little stone harbor dates from about 1600. Today, the fishing boats are just for recreation, and locals gather here with their kids to relax by the lake.

At the south end of the harbor (across from the Frulleria), belly up to the banister of the terrace for another colorful town view. Another local ditty goes, "If you love Lake Como, you know Bellagio is the pearl...but Varenna is the diamond."

• *Continue straight, leaving the harbor. A lane leads around past Hotel du Lac (its fine lakeside terrace welcomes nonresidents for a drink) to the tiny, pebbly town beach. From here, climb uphill to the town square, called...*

Piazza San Giorgio: Four churches face Varenna's town square. The main church dates from the 13th century. Romantic Varenna is an understandably popular spot for weddings—rice often litters the church's front yard. Stepping inside, you'll find a few humble but centuries-old bits of carving and frescoes. The black floor and chapels are made from the locally quarried marble. Outside, past the WWI monument, is the TI and the new Ornithology and Natural Science Museum, a small but unique collection of stuffed birds and other local wildlife (no English descriptions).

The Royal Victoria Hotel, also on the main square, recalls the 1839 visit of Queen Victoria, who registered herself as the Countess of Clare in an attempt to remain anonymous. The trees are planted to make a V for Varenna. The street plan survives from Roman times, when gutters flowed down to the lake. The little church on the lake side of the square is the baptistery. Dating from the ninth century, it's one of the oldest churches on the lake, but is rarely open for visits.

As you wander the lanes of Varenna, you'll notice plastic water bottles left out by the door. Locals believe that these keep cats from peeing on their doorstep. Something about seeing their reflection causes the cats to get self-conscious...

The Lakes

Your walk is over. From this square, you can head south to the gardens, north to go to the train station, or hike up to reach the castle.

SIGHTS AND ACTIVITIES

In Varenna

Castle—A steep and stony trail leads to Varenna's ruined hilltop castle, Castello di Vezio, located in a peaceful, traffic-free, one-chapel town. Start at the stairs to the left of Hotel Montecodeno, and figure on a 20-minute walk one-way. The castle is barren, but livened up by occasional art exhibits and a falconry-training center (€4, April–Oct daily 10:00–sunset, closed Jan and when rainy; falconry shows Sat–Sun around 16:00, Mon–Fri once daily—call in morning for times; sleepy café at entrance, mobile 335-465-186, Daniele).

Gardens—Two manicured lakeside gardens—the terraces of Villa Cipressi and the adjacent, more open grounds of the Villa Monastero—are open to the public. On weekends, the former noble residence of the Villa Monastero, filled with overly ornate furnishings from the late 1800s, is open to the public as a museum (gardens—€2.50 each, €4 combo-ticket covers both, March–Oct daily 9:00–19:00, closed Nov–March; Villa Monastero museum—€4 ticket includes garden, April–Oct Sat 13:00–17:00, Sun 10:00–13:00 & 14:00–18:00).

Swimming—There are two spots to swim in Varenna: the little free beach behind the Royal Victoria Hotel off Piazza San Giorgio, and the *lido*. The newly revamped *lido*, just west of the boat dock, is essentially a wide concrete slab with sand, and the swimming area is off an old boat ramp. It is by far better equipped, with showers, bathrooms, a bar, and lounge chairs for rent.

Near Varenna

Fiumelatte—This town, about a half mile south of Varenna, was named for its milky river. It's the shortest river in Italy (at 800 feet) and runs—like most of the local tourist industry—only from April through September. The *La Sorgente del Fiumelatte* brochure, available at Varenna's TI, lays out a walk from Varenna to the Fiumelatte to the castle and back. It's a 30-minute hike to the source *(sorgente)* of the milky river (at Varenna's monastery, take the high road, drop into peaceful and evocative cemetery, and climb steps to the wooded trail leading to the peaceful and refreshing cave from which the river sprouts). For a longer lakeside hike, ask the TI about the *Sentiero del Viandante* (hike one-way up the lake, about 90 min, much more level than the hike to the castle, return by train from Bellano, check schedule before you go).

Cooking Course—Chef Moreno picks you up in Varenna, zips you up the mountain to his restaurant 10 minutes away (experience Italian driving!), and then teaches you some basics of Italian cooking. Learn how to handcraft fresh pasta or prep regional specialties. Classes last about three hours, plus add time to *mangiare* (€30 includes trip, lesson, and lunch, Tue and Thu 10:00 pick-up from Piazza San Giorgio, reservations mandatory, tel. 0341-815-225, www.ilcaminettoonline.com, info@ilcaminettoonline.com).

SLEEPING

Reservations are tight in August, snug in July, and wide open most of the rest of the year. Many places close in winter. All places listed are family-run and have lakeview rooms. If you're expecting friendliness, especially during peak season, you'll likely be disappointed. Enjoy the view. View rooms are given (sometimes for no extra cost) to those who telephone for reservations and request a *"camera con vista."* High-season prices are listed here; prices get soft off-season (Nov–April). The TI, across from the tobacco shop down the street from the main square, has a list of *affitta camere*—houses that rent out a few rooms (tel. 0341-830-367).

$$$ Albergo Milano, located right in the old town, is graciously run by Egidio and his Swiss wife, Bettina. Fusing the best of Italy with the best of Switzerland, this well-run, romantic hotel has eight comfortable rooms with extravagant views, balconies, or big terraces (Sb-€115, Db-€150, €5 extra for view terrace, €5/day cash discount, no elevator; from the station, take main road to town and turn right at steep alley where sidewalk and guardrail break; Via XX Settembre 35; tel. 0341-830-298, fax 0341-830-061, www.varenna.net, hotelmilano@varenna.net).

The Lakes

Sleep Code

(€1 = about $1.30, country code: 39)
S = Single, **D** = Double/Twin, **T** = Triple, **Q** = Quad, **b** = bathroom, **s** = shower only. Unless otherwise noted, you can assume breakfast is included, credit cards are accepted, and English is spoken.

To help you sort easily through these listings, I've divided the rooms into three categories based on the price for a standard double room with bath:

  $$$ Higher Priced—Most rooms €150 or more.
   $$ Moderately Priced—Most rooms between €100–150.
    $ Lower Priced—Most rooms €100 or less.

This place whispers *luna di miele*—honeymoon (see website for 3-night honeymoon deal). Nearby are two equally elegant and comfortable annexes, all a great value and good for families, some with lakeside views and living rooms or kitchenettes (Db-€120–150). For €27 per person, enjoy Egidio's culinary creations for dinner; see "Eating," page 216.

$$$ Hotel Olivedo, facing the ferry dock, is a romantic, Old World hotel with antique furniture and classy parquet (Venetian *pavimento*) floors. Most of the rooms have tiny, glorious lakeview balconies. It's a fine place to practice the art of *la dolce far niente* and watch the children, boats, and sun come and go. Brusque, hardworking manager Laura doesn't smile a lot, and runs a very tight ship (prices vary with season and views: S-€65, Db-€140, half-pension required May–mid-Oct—see below, cash only, no elevator, air-con, closed mid-Nov–mid-Dec, prefers reservations by phone, tel. & fax 0341-830-115, www.olivedo.it, info@olivedo.it). Laura's excellent dinner (€22 per person, required for guests May–mid-Oct) adds €44 to the price of double room per day and doesn't include drinks.

$$ Villa Cipressi is a sprawling, centuries-old lakeside mansion with 32 warmly outfitted, modern rooms. It sits in a huge, quiet, terraced garden that non-guests pay to see (Sb-€110, non-view Db-€135, view Db-€155, extra cot-€25, these prices promised with this book in 2008, rooms without views face the street and are noisier, elevator, no air-con, Internet in lobby, Jacuzzi rental, often busy with wedding parties, garden access, mountain bike rental for guests, Via IV Novembre 18, tel. 0341-830-113, fax 0341-830-401, www.hotelvillacipressi.it, info@hotelvillacipressi.it, Davide).

$$ Eremo Gaudio stands in isolation halfway up the hill, with a commanding lake view high above Varenna. Once an orphanage, it became a hermitage run by the Catholic Church, and then—since 2000—a modern hotel accessed by a funky private funicular. Perfect for monks with champagne tastes, it's peaceful, with awe-inspiring view balconies and a breakfast terrace. Thirteen bright, plain-but-comfy rooms perch up in the main building, and 12 less-dramatic but recently updated rooms huddle below at the foot of the funicular (open March–Oct only, upper rooms: Sb-€95, Db-€110, Db with balcony-€125; lower rooms: Db-€100–115; 7 percent discount with cash and 3-night stay; all rooms have lake views, air-con, taxi from station recommended—about €10, quarter-mile south of Varenna's main square at Via Roma 11, tel. 0341-815-301, fax 0341-815-314, www.eremogaudio.it, eremogaudio@yahoo.it). Suppers are served on the upper terrace, weather permitting.

$$ La Torretta B&B, managed by Laura of Hotel Olivedo, is a restored Liberty-style villa just across from the ferry dock. It features six sunny view rooms (some with terraces), a Jane Austen lounge, and a tiny manicured garden with tables for picnics or relaxing (Db-€145 with this book in 2008, cash only, closed Nov–April, tel. & fax 0341-830-115, www.olivedo.it, info@olivedo.it, check in at Hotel Olivedo, described earlier). This would be an awesome little palace for a party of 10–12 to take over. Unlike at Hotel Olivedo, half-pension is not required here.

$$ Albergo del Sole, a no-frills hotel over a basic restaurant right on the town square without a hint of a lake view, is run by a straight-faced family who rents seven nicely renovated, comfy rooms (Sb-€85, Db-€120, €105 off-season, fans, hardwood floors, shiny bathrooms, no elevator, Piazza San Giorgio 17, tel. & fax 0341-815-218, www.albergodelsole.lc.it, albergo.sole@virgilio.it).

$ Hotel Montecodeno, with 11 decent rooms and no views, is a functional concrete box just off the main road between the train station and lake (Sb-€70, Db-€90, extra bed-€10, 15 percent discount with cash and 3-night stay, air-con, attached restaurant serves fresh fish and a €23 "Rick Steves" fixed-price meal—see "Eating," one meal included per guest with 3-night stay, Via della Croce 2, tel. 0341-830-123, fax 0341-815-227, www.hotelmontecodeno.com, ferrcas@tin.it, Marina Castelli).

$ Albergo Beretta, on the main road a block below the station, has 10 pleasant rooms, several with balconies (and street noise). Second-floor rooms are quietest. This place, above the locals' coffee shop which doubles as the reception, feels homey, lacks any lakeside glamour, and sometimes smells smoky (D-€58, Db-€68, extra bed-€12, breakfast-€6, no elevator, Via per Esino 1, tel. & fax 0341-830-132, www.hotelberetta.it, hotelberetta@iol.it, Signora Tosca doesn't speak English, but Laura and daughter Giulia do). This place reportedly tends to overbook—it's essential to reconfirm your reservation.

$ Villa Elena, a grandmotherly, low-energy place on the main square, offers the best budget beds in town. English-speaking Signora Vitali, who lives downstairs, rents her four antique-filled rooms at the same price—room #1 has a shabby bathroom and view terrace, while the others don't even have sinks. Twin beds only—not for romantics (D-€45 with or without bath, cash only, no breakfast, it's the vine-covered facade at Piazza San Giorgio 9 near Via San Giovanni, tel. 0341-830-575).

$ Orange House B&B is homey and modern, renting two rooms with a fine communal living room (April–Sept only, Sb-€39, Db-€69, extra bed-€19, includes breakfast, prices slightly higher for stays less than 3 nights, great deal for a family of 4; 2-min walk below train station, across stream from travel agency at Via Venini 156; tel. 347-918-7940, www.orangehouse.org, info@orangehouse.org, Piero speaks some English).

EATING

On the Waterfront

Ristorante la Vista, at the recommended hotel Albergo Milano, serves up a fine menu to guests and non-guests alike. Egidio's creative twist on traditional local cuisine uses seasonal produce and only the freshest lake fish. Bettina and Egidio treat you like nobility. Egi (pronounced "edgy") offers a limited selection that is great for foodies with discerning tastes. I'd go with his €27 three-course fixed-price meal (Mon and Wed–Sat 19:30–22:00, closed Sun and Tue, reservations mandatory, Via XX Settembre 35, tel. 0341-830-298).

Hotel Olivedo's restaurant, across from the ferry dock, serves candlelit meals with no-nonsense service. Depending on the weather, you may be seated under a lakefront awning (with a view) or in a classy, Old World dining hall. Laura and her capable staff serve local lake fish and simple pasta dishes—try the heavenly handmade ravioli (€25–35 dinner, daily 12:15–14:00 & 19:30–21:15, reservations recommended, tel. 0341-830-115).

Vecchia Varenna, on the harbor, is respected, pricey, and romantic. The menu features traditional cuisine and lake special-ties (€11 pastas, €15 *secondi,* Tue–Sun 12:30–14:00 & 19:30–21:30, closed Mon, also closed Tue in winter, dressy indoor seating or on harborside deck, reservations smart, tel. 0341-830-793).

The **Nilus Bar** boasts the best harborfront seating in town, and is *the* place for a light meal. The young waitstaff serves din-ner crêpes, pizzas, big mixed salads, hot sandwiches, and cock-tails with a smile (March–Nov Wed–Mon 10:00–23:00, closed Tue, hours can vary, cash only, closed Dec–Feb, tel. 0341-815-228, Fulvia and Giovanni).

Dessert: **La Frulleria** is a youthful place serving cold, sweet, and fruity treats from a fun menu. They have great harborfront seating—if you're eating dinner elsewhere without a lake view, consider skipping dessert and coming here for your finale (May–Oct Tue–Sun 12:00–24:00, closed Mon and Nov–April, 2 doors down from Nilus Bar, Samantha). To take a lakeside table, you need to order from the menu (items start at €2.50). **Gelateria la Giazzera,** also facing the harbor, is great for a cup or cone to go. Eros is the only guy in town who makes his gelato fresh every day (daily 13:00–21:00).

Off the Water, on or near Piazza San Giorgio

Ristorante del Sole, facing the town square, serves edible meals and Naples-style pizzas (€5–9). Making few concessions to the tourist crowds, this restaurant caters to locals, providing a fun atmosphere and a cozy, walled-in garden in back (daily 12:00–15:00 & 19:00–23:00, Piazza San Giorgio 21, tel. 0341-815-218).

Ristorante il Cavatappi, a five-table place on a quiet lane 100 feet off the town square, serves old-time specialties, such as *missoltino* (the air-dried lake fish that locals like more than tourists do) as an antipasto. Helpful owner-chef Mario is serious about his wine. Plan on spending €25 plus wine (Thu–Tue 12:30–14:30 & 19:00–21:45, closed Wed, tel. 0341-815-349). Reservations recommended for dinner, but mandatory at least one day in advance for Mario's special spaghetti with lobster (€25–30, depending on market price).

Ristorante la Contrada takes advantage of Villa Cipressi's elegant garden, trickling fountain, and lake view with its terrace-side location. Indoor seating glows with a warm and romantic air. Fresh daily specialties and professional service make for a worthwhile splurge (€28 meals plus wine, daily 12:30–14:00 & 19:30–21:30, closes for weddings, Via IV Novembre 18, tel. 0341-830-113).

Ristorante Montecodeno is on the main road, without a bit of lake ambience. This humble place, run by a hardworking family, serves a special "Rick Steves" fixed-price meal which gives visitors a *primo* sampler of lake cuisine at a terrific value. The €25 meal described in their menu is €23 for Rick Steves guidebook holders and includes wine or water. You get eight different fishy appetizers caught from Lake Como (including the salty run-over-by-a-car *missoltino,* described above), a *secondo* with another array of local fish, seasonal vegetables or a salad, and dessert. Other options are possible (daily 12:00–14:00 & 19:00–21:00, Via della Croce 2, tel. 0341-830-123).

Caminetto in Gitta, a homey, backwoods, mountain trattoria, requires a free, curvy 10-minute drive from Varenna. They pick you up in Piazza San Giorgio at 19:30, deliver you to their restaurant, and then dish up classic local fare at small-town prices. Interesting specialties such as risotto with porcini mushrooms and berries or old-fashioned grilled meats are made with pride by husband and wife Moreno and Rossella (€18 meals plus wine, Thu–Tue 12:30–14:00 & 19:30–21:30, closed Wed, reservations mandatory to confirm pick-up from Varenna at 19:30, Viale Progresso 4, tel. 0341-815-225).

Picnics: Varenna's two little grocery stores have all you need for a classy balcony or breakwater picnic dinner. The *salumeria* on the square is best for meats, cheese, and bread (Tue–Sun 7:30–12:30 & 15:30–19:30, Mon 7:30–12:30 only); while the market, just north of the main square, stocks fresh fruits and veggies (daily 8:00–12:30, Tue and Thu–Sat also 16:15–19:00).

TRANSPORTATION CONNECTIONS

From any destination covered in this book, you'll get to Lake Como via Milan. The quickest, easiest, and cheapest Milan connection to any point midlake (Bellagio, Menaggio, or Varenna) is via the train to Varenna. If leaving Varenna by train, purchase your ticket from the ticket machine at the train station (good luck—it rarely works), the Barilott *tabacchi* shop just off the main square, or the travel agency, I Viaggi del Tivano, next door to the Albergo Beretta. Stamp your ticket in the yellow machine at the station before boarding. If both places are closed, win the sympathy of the conductor and buy your ticket on board for an additional fee.

For a reputable taxi service between Varenna and Milan and its airports, see "Helpful Hints," page 209.

Milan to Varenna by Train: Catch a train at Milano Centrale (€4.90; likely schedule: 8:15, 9:15, 12:15, 14:15, 16:15, 17:00, 18:00, 19:05, 20:08, and 21:05; trip takes 1 hr). Confirm these times. For tips on using the train, see "Arrival in Varenna," page 206.

Varenna to Milan by Train: Trains leave Varenna for Milano Centrale (€4.90, likely schedule: 6:17, 6:47, 7:25, 8:23, 10:20, 12:21, 14:22, 16:22, 18:24, 20:20, and 21:24; trip takes 1 hour—if you take a train not listed here, it's likely a local milk-run train taking twice as long).

Malpensa Airport (Milan) to Varenna: I'd suggest taking the airport bus (see page 206) from Malpensa Airport to Milan's train station, then catching a Varenna-bound train (see "Milan to Varenna by Train" above).

Depending on demand, two buses a day (Mon–Sat at 11:00 and 20:40, no bus on Sun) go from Malpensa Airport to Como and then Varenna. They charge €24 per person but won't run unless they receive payment for four, meaning that if only two customers are on the bus, they'd have to pay €96 (2 hrs, tel. 0342-216-220, www.gianolini.it, simonaa@gianolini.it). Taxis are pricier, but more efficient.

Varenna to Malpensa Airport by Bus: Two buses a day go directly to Milan's Malpensa Airport (€24, depart Varenna at Albergo Beretta and Piazza San Giorgio at 5:36 and 16:36, 2 hrs). See "Malpensa Airport (Milan) to Varenna" above.

Varenna to Stresa by Train: Trains run about every two hours (2.75 hrs, transfer in Milan).

Varenna to St. Moritz in Switzerland by Train: From Varenna, you have fantastic access to the Bernina Express scenic train to St. Moritz. Note that this is only realistic from April through October. First, take the train to Tirano, and then transfer to St. Moritz (3/day, allow 4–5 hrs with transfer). For information on this route, stop by I Viaggi del Tivano travel agency (see above), or ask your hotelier if they have the handy tourist information book produced by the travel agency.

Bellagio

The self-proclaimed "Pearl of the Lake" is a classy combination of tidiness and Old World elegance. If you don't mind that "tramp in a palace" feeling, it's a fine place to shop for ties and umbrellas while surrounding yourself with the more adventurous posh travelers. The heavy curtains between the arcades keep the visitors and their poodles from sweating. Thriving yet still cute, Bellagio is a much more substantial town than Varenna (which has almost no shops).

ORIENTATION

Tourist Information: The TI is right downtown, at the passenger boat dock (April–Oct daily 9:00–12:30 & 13:00–18:30, Nov–March shorter hours and closed Sun and Tue, tel. 031-950-204, www.bellagiolakecomo.com, prombell@tin.it).

Arrival in Bellagio: Bellagio is best reached via ferry from Varenna or via ferry, hydrofoil, or slow boat from Como (see "Arrival in Varenna," page 206).

Parking is difficult, but you can try near the lakeside or the parking lot at the ferry dock (white lines are always free, blue lines €1/hr).

The Docks: Bellagio has two docks a few minutes' walk apart. The northern dock is for the passenger-only slow boat *(battello* or *battello navetta)* and the hydrofoil *(servizio rapido)*. The southern dock is for all "ferry-boats" *(traghetto)*: both the car ferry (cars and foot passengers) and the passenger-only ferry. To make sure you're waiting at the correct dock, check the boat schedule carefully (posted near dock and in free brochure available at kiosks at dock). Remember that if you want to know all your departure options beyond Varenna, Cadenabbia, and Menaggio, you need to study three different timetables (see "Getting Around Lake Como," page 203). Confirm your intentions at the kiosk near either dock.

Helpful Hints

Internet Access: Bellagio Point has a slick Internet café, complete with wine-tasting options (daily 10:00–22:00, Salita Plinio 8/10/12, tel. 032-950-437, www.bellagiopoint.com).

Post Office: It's on the south end of Lungo Lago Mazzini (Mon–Fri 8:30–14:00, Sat 8:30–12:30, closed Sun).

Laundry: La Lavandera is bright and new (Mon–Fri 9:00–18:30, closed Sat–Sun, €7.50 wash/dry, Salita Carlo Grandi 21—this street is also marked as Via Specula, tel. 339-410-6852).

SIGHTS AND ACTIVITIES

Villa Serbelloni Park—If you need a destination, you can visit this park, which overlooks the town, with a guide (€7, April–Oct, tours Tue–Sun at 11:00 and 15:30, no tours Mon and when rainy, 90 min, first two-thirds of walk is uphill, show up at the medieval tower in Piazza della Chiesa 15 min before tour time to buy tickets, confirm time at TI). The villa itself, owned by the Rockefeller Foundation, is not open to the public.

Strolling—Explore the steep-stepped lanes rising from the harborfront. While Johnnie Walker and jewelry sell best at lake level, the locals shop up the hill. Piazza Chiesa, near the top of town, has a worth-a-look church (art described in English-language handout).

The administrative capital of the midlake region, Bellagio is located where the two southern legs of the lake split off. For an easy break in a park with a great view, wander right on out to the crotch. Meander past the rich and famous Hotel Villa Serbelloni, and walk five minutes to Punta Spartivento ("point that divides the wind"). You'll find a Renoir atmosphere complete with an inviting bar/restaurant, a tiny harbor, and a chance to sit on a park bench and gaze north past Menaggio, Varenna, and the end of the lake to the Swiss Alps.

For another stroll, head south from the car-ferry dock down the tree-shaded promenade. Ten minutes later, you'll pass the town's concrete swimming area (closed indefinitely). The grassy, pebbly public beach is another 20 minutes farther south from there.

Villa Melzi Gardens—A 10-minute walk south from the ferry dock is this picture-perfect lakeside expanse of exotic plants, flowers, trees, and Neoclassical sculpture, assembled by the vice-president of Napoleon's Italian Republic in the early 19th century (€6,

Bellagio

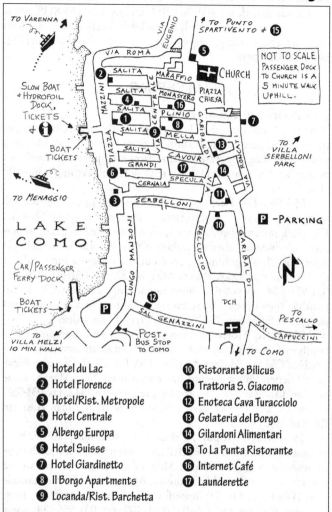

TO VARENNA

SLOW BOAT
+ HYDROFOIL
DOCK,
TICKETS

BOAT
TICKETS

TO MENAGGIO

L A K E
C O M O

CAR/PASSENGER
FERRY DOCK

BOAT
TICKETS

TO
VILLA MELZI
10 MIN. WALK

VIA ROMA

VIA EUGENIO

TO PUNTO
SPARTIVENTO

SALITA

MARAFFIO

CHURCH

SALITA

MONASTERO

PIAZZA
CHIESA

NOT TO SCALE
PASSENGER DOCK
TO CHURCH IS A
5 MINUTE WALK
UPHILL.

SALITA

PLINIO

SALITA

MELLA

SALITA

CAVOUR

GRANDI

SPECULA

CERNAIA

SERBELLONI

TO
VILLA
SERBELLONI
PARK

P –PARKING

PIAZZA MAZZINI

VIA CENTRALE

VIA GARIBALDI

VIA RONCATI

VIA GARIBALDI

LUNGO MANZONI

BELLUSIO

N

SAL. GENAZZINI

POST +
BUS STOP
TO COMO

PCH

TO COMO

TO
PESCALLO

SAL. CAPPUCCINI

1 Hotel du Lac
2 Hotel Florence
3 Hotel/Rist. Metropole
4 Hotel Centrale
5 Albergo Europa
6 Hotel Suisse
7 Hotel Giardinetto
8 Il Borgo Apartments
9 Locanda/Rist. Barchetta
10 Ristorante Bilicus
11 Trattoria S. Giacomo
12 Enoteca Cava Turacciolo
13 Gelateria del Borgo
14 Gilardoni Alimentari
15 To La Punta Ristorante
16 Internet Café
17 Launderette

March–Oct daily 9:00–18:00).

Hikes and Walks—The TI has free brochures on three well-crafted walking tours that explore the city and environs, varying from one to three hours. Sites include villas, gardens, churches, an old-fashioned dairy shop, medieval towers, and a nautical instruments museum. The TI also sells a hiking map for €3 that shows four different hikes ranging in difficulty and duration.

Outdoor Activities—**Cavalcalario Club** offers a downhill mountain-bike run; they shuttle you uphill then let you go (€25 includes bike rental, several itineraries, reservations necessary at least a day ahead; tel. 031-964-814, mobile 339-530-8138, www .bellagio-mountains.it, cavalcalarioclub@tiscalinet.it). They also offer horseback riding, paragliding, canoeing, kayaking, fishing, and sailboat rentals.

SLEEPING

(€1 = about $1.30, country code: 39)

This is a "boom or bust" lake resort, with high-season prices (those listed here) straight through from May through October, plus a brief shoulder season (with discounted prices) in April and November. Off-season (Dec–March), nearly everything is literally closed down.

$$$ Hotel du Lac, a good waterfront splurge, comes with 43 rooms, a roof terrace, and a classic ambience of comfort (Sb-€110, Db-€190, prices depend on view, plush superior Db-€220, 10 percent cash discount, air-con, parking-€8, includes access to Bellagio Sporting Club's swimming pool outside town—a long walk or shuttle-bus ride away, Piazza Mazzini 32, tel. 031-950-320, fax 031-951-624, www.bellagiohoteldulac.com, dulac@tin.it, Leoni family). They have a fine restaurant, making the €15 supplement per person for optional half-board a great dinner value.

$$$ Hotel Florence, a few doors away and 150 years old, is family-run, with 30 rooms, hardwood, bold earth tones, and a rich touch of Old World elegance (Sb-€120, Db-€200, Db suite-€250, prices depend on view and balcony, closed Nov–March, some handheld showers, fans on request, tel. 031-950-342, fax 031-951-722, www.hotelflorencebellagio.it, hotflore@tin.it, run by Austrian Ketzlar family).

$$ Hotel Metropole, a tired but grand old place with an institutional feel, dominates Bellagio's waterfront with plush public spaces and sagging floors. Most of its 42 spacious rooms are renovated but still feel bare-bones. Many have a hectic lakeside view (Db-€130, €10–20 more for view balcony or terrace, fans, stunning roof terrace, tel. 031-950-409, fax 031-951-534, www .albergometropole.it, info@albergometropole.it).

$$ Hotel Centrale, managed with pride and care by Giacomo Berelli, warmly welcomes its guests into a true-blue family operation: Signore Berelli's wife and two sons help out, his mama painted the art, and grandpa crafted much of the Art Deco–era furniture. Renovated in 2005, the 17 rooms are clean and classy and offer a great value but no lake views (Db-€100, larger rooms Db-€125, air-con, www.hc-bellagio.com, info@bellagio.com, Salita Plinio 7, tel. 031-951-940, fax 031-952-682).

$ Albergo Europa, run with low energy, is in a concrete

annex behind a restaurant, away from the waterfront. Its 10 rooms have no charm but are reasonably comfortable (Db-€90, breakfast-€8, balconies lack views but overlook quiet courtyard, no elevator, free parking, Via Roma 21, tel. & fax 031-950-471, www.hoteleuropabellagio.it, albeuropa@tiscali.it, family Marchesi).

$ Hotel Suisse, the cheapest and most neglected place on the waterfront, has 10 simple rooms, hardwood floors, dim lights, almost no service, unpredictable beds, and some great views and balconies. The only thing this place has going for it is price and location (Db-€80 through 2008 with this book, view rooms-€10 extra, breakfast-€10, no elevator, 10 percent discount in hotel restaurant with this book, Piazza Mazzini 8/10, tel. 031-950-335, fax 031-951-755, www.suissehotel.it, Guido).

$ Hotel Giardinetto, at the top of town near the church (100 steps above the waterfront), is a homey, laidback place that rents 13 cheap and spartan rooms. The rooms are stark, but the breezy, peaceful garden is a joy—and good for picnics (Sb-€42, non-view Db-€55, view Db-€60, Tb-€75, breakfast-€6, cash only, no elevator, Via Roncati 12, tel. 031-950-168, tczgnc@tiscali.it, Ticozzi family).

$ Il Borgo Apartments rents six modern *Better Homes and Gardens*–quality apartments with kitchenettes in the old center at great prices. This option is far better than a hotel room, though it lacks a 24-hour reception office. Easygoing Flavio is available for check-in daily 10:00–12:00 & 15:00–17:00, or by appointment (Db-€80, 2 bigger apartments for up to 6 people—€100, no breakfast, 2-night minimum required, 5 percent discount with this book in 2008, air-con, Salita Plinio 4, tel. 031-952-497, mobile 338-193-5559, fax 031-951-585, www.borgoresidence.it, info@borgoresidence.it).

$ Locanda Barchetta rents four breezy rooms with antique furniture and modern accents, high above the chaotic but recommended restaurant (see "Eating"). The rooms are great, with little balconies and little views, but they're an afterthought to the restaurant (Db-€80, air-con, no elevator, Salita Mella 13, tel. 031-951-030).

EATING

Ristorante Bilicus, up a steep lane from the waterfront, is a dressy place serving regional and lake cuisine with passion. While a little pricey, the restaurant is famous for value and quality cooking (€10 pastas, €12 *secondi*, April–Oct Tue–Sun 12:00–14:30 & 18:30–21:45, closed Mon and Nov–March, best to reserve for dinner, indoor/outdoor garden seating, Salita Serbelloni 30, tel. 031-950-480).

Trattoria S. Giacomo, across the street and less expensive, is respected for its traditional cuisine, such as *riso e filetto di pesce* (rice and perch fillet in butter and sage). It has daily, seasonal, inviting €15–25 fixed-price meals based on regional specialties (Mon and Wed–Thu 12:00–14:30 & 19:00–21:30, Fri–Sun open later midday and evenings, closed Tue, Salita Serbelloni 45, tel. 031-950-329).

Ristorante Barchetta, set on a bamboo-covered terrace with no lake view and bedecked with summery colors, puts a creative twist on regional specialties. The €48 tasting menu pairs three glasses of wine with a fish dish, a meat dish, and dessert. Don't confuse it with the street-level bar/trattoria—head up the stairs to the second floor. Reservations are recommended (€15 pastas, €20 *secondi*, Wed–Mon 12:00–14:30 & 19:00–22:30, closed Tue, Salita Mella 13, tel. 031-951-389).

Hotel Metropole Ristorante's terrace offers the best waterfront view. Even though the restaurant is a mediocre food value, I'd eat here to savor the lakeside setting (€10 pastas, €12 *secondi*, April–Oct daily 12:00–14:30 & 19:00–21:30, closed Nov–March, tel. 031-950-409; also see "Sleeping," earlier in the Bellagio section).

Wine Tasting: Step into the vaulted stone cellar rooms of the **Enoteca Cava Turacciolo** for a tasting of three regional wines, with a sampling of cheeses and meats (€18/person with this book, Thu–Tue 10:00–24:00, closed Wed, Salita Genazzini, tel. 031-950-975, Norberto, Piero, and Rosy).

Gelato: Locals agree that you won't find the best *gelateria* in town associated with sundaes served on the waterfront. Instead, for a particularly fluffy and light scoop of gelato heaven, head for **Gelateria del Borgo** (daily 10:00–22:30, closed Nov–March, Via Garibaldi 46, tel. 031-950-755).

Picnics: You'll find benches at the park, along the waterfront in town, and lining the promenade south of town. Pick up your picnic supplies at **Gilardoni Alimentari.** They have roast chicken, ribs, and focaccia, and are happy to make fresh sandwiches to your order (Tue–Sat 7:30–13:00 & 15:30–19:30, Sun–Mon 7:30–13:00 only, shorter hours off-season, on corner of Via Garibaldi and Salita Cavour, tel. 031-951-815).

Punto Spartivento: This dramatic park, a five-minute walk north of town (see "Strolling," page 220), is a great place for either a picnic or a meal at **La Punta Ristorante** (€9 pastas, €13 *secondi*, April–Oct daily 12:00–14:30 & 19:00–22:00, bar open 8:00–24:00 for snacks only, closed Nov–March, tel. 031-951-888).

The Lakes

Menaggio

Menaggio has more urban bulk than its neighbors. Since many visitors find Lake Como too dirty for swimming, consider spending time in Menaggio's fine public pool (look for the "Lido"). This is the starting point for a few hikes. Only a few decades ago, these trails were used by cigarette smugglers, sneaking through at night from Switzerland back into Italy with their tax-free booty. The hostel has information about mountain biking, and catching the bus to trailheads on nearby Mount Grona. (TI tel. 0344-32-924, www.menaggio.com.)

SLEEPING

(€1 = about $1.30, country code: 39)
$ La Primula Youth Hostel (Ostello la Primula) is a rare area hostel. Run by Alberto, it caters to a quiet, savor-the-lakes crowd. Located about 300 yards south of the Menaggio dock, it has a view terrace, games galore, Internet access, and a washing machine, as well as bike, canoe, and kayak rentals (€15/person in dorm bed, €16/person for 4- to 6-bed room with private bath, €3 extra for nonmembers, includes breakfast, towels extra, cash only, easy parking nearby, reception and bar open 8:00–10:00 & 16:00–24:00, rooms closed 10:30–16:00, hostel closed Nov–mid-March; hearty dinners with drinks for €12—reserve dinner by 18:00, served at 20:00; Via IV Novembre 106, tel. & fax 0344-32356, www.menaggiohostel.com, menaggiohostel@mclink.it). Show this book for a free half-hour of Internet access, and ask Alberto and Claudia for ideas about hikes and bike rides in the area.

$ La Marianna B&B is run by Ty and Paola. They rent eight rooms and run a fine restaurant in Cadenabbia, about a mile south of Menaggio on a busy road (Db with view-€90, lakeside terrace at restaurant, air-con, free Wi-Fi, tel. 0344-43095, www.la-marianna.com, inn@la-marianna.com). The hourly Como–Menaggio bus #C-10 stops here.

TRANSPORTATION CONNECTIONS

By Bus from Milan's Malpensa Airport to Menaggio: Buses run between Malpensa Airport and Como, where you change to local bus #C-10 (€3, hourly, 1-hr trip) to get to Menaggio.

From Menaggio to Milan: It's a 20-minute ferry to Varenna, where trains connect to Milan (every 2 hrs, 1-hr trip, check train schedule). More fast trains depart from Como than Varenna. From Menaggio, take local bus #C-10 to Como (see above) and catch the train (2/hr, 30 min).

From Menaggio to Switzerland: In summer the yellow Palm Express bus runs once daily to **Lugano** (1 hr) and **St. Moritz** (3 hrs). Off-season (mid-Oct–mid-June) the bus runs only on weekends (www.swisspost.ch).

MORE SIGHTS ON LAKE COMO

Villa Carlotta—If you plan to tour one of Lake Como's famed villas, this is the best. I see the lakes as a break from Italy's art, but if you're in need of a place that charges admission, Villa Carlotta offers an elegant Neoclassical interior, a famous Antonio Canova statue, and a garden that is its highlight and best in spring (€7.50, daily April–Sept 9:00–18:00, Oct 9:00–11:30 & 14:00–16:30, closed Nov–March, tel. 034-440-405, www.villacarlotta.it). Nearby Tremezzo and Cadenabbia are pleasant lakeside resorts an easy walk away. Boats serve both places (5-min walk from either dock to the villa) and are reached by *traghetto* (ferry) via Bellagio or the *battello* (slow boat) via Menaggio or Bellagio.

Isola Comacina—This remote little island (just south of Bellagio) offers peace, ancient church foundations, goats, sheep, and a lovely view of Lago di Como. It takes 30–45 minutes to walk around the island, but longer to savor it. Bring a picnic or try the snack bar at the dock. Look for trips to Isola Comacina on the Colico–Como *battello* schedule (listed in Lago di Como boat timetable, free at ticket booths at ferry docks, see page 203). The *isola* is accessible from Varenna (1 hour), Menaggio (45 min), or Bellagio (30 min). Check return times carefully (Como–Colico direction) and don't miss your boat. Usually only one trip a day each way works out for a visit. Allow about six hours, including travel time.

Como—On the southwest tip of the lake, Como has a good, traffic-free old town, an interesting Gothic/Renaissance cathedral, and a pleasant lakefront with a promenade (TI open Mon–Sat 9:00–13:00 & 14:30–18:00, closed Sun, tel. 031-269-712). It's an easy 10-minute walk from the boat dock to the train station (2/hr, 30–50 min to Milan, check schedule). Boats leave Como about hourly for midlake (ferries-€8–9, 2 hrs; hydrofoils-€11–12, 45 min, departures Mon–Sat 6:30–19:00, Sun 9:00–19:00, tel. 031-579-211).

Sleeping in Como: For a cheap overnight, try the **$ Villa Olmo Hostel** (€15, includes breakfast and sheets, €3 extra for non-members, €9–11 dinners, bike rental and laundry service available, reception open 7:00–10:00 & 16:00–22:00, lockout 10:00–16:00, 24:00 curfew, closed Dec–Feb, 20-min walk from train station or dock, Via Bellinzona 2, tel. & fax 031-573-800, www.ostellionline .org, ostellocomo@tin.it).

Lake Maggiore

Lake Maggiore is ringed by mountains, snow-capped in spring and fall, and lined with resort towns such as Stresa. While crassly touristic, the town of Stresa is a handy base from which to explore the exotic garden islands of Lake Maggiore. And many consider it a pleasant last stop before flying home from nearby Malpensa Airport.

A visit to this region is worth the trouble for two islands—each with exotic gardens and Borromeo family villas. The Borromeo family—through many generations since 1630—lovingly turned their islands into magical retreats, with elaborate villas and fragrant gardens. Isola Bella has the palace and terraced garden; Isola Madre has a villa and sprawling English-style (more casual) garden. A third island, Isola Pescatori (a.k.a. Superiore), is simply small, serene, and residential. The Borromeos, who made their money from trade and banking, enjoyed the arts—from paintings (hung in lavish abundance throughout the palace and villa) to plays (performed in an open-air theater on Isola Bella) and marionette shows (you'll see the puppets that performed here).

Tourists flock to the lakes in May and June, when flowers are in bloom, and in September. Concerts held in scenic settings draw music-lovers, particularly during the Musical Weeks in August (get details from Stresa TI). For fewer crowds, visit in April, July, and August (when Italians prefer the Mediterranean beaches), and October. In winter, the snow-covered mountains (with resorts a 90-minute drive away) attract skiers.

Planning Your Time

This region is best visited on a sunny day, when the mountains are clear, the lake is calm, and the heat of the sun brings out the scent of the blossoms. The two top islands for sightseeing are Isola Bella and Isola Madre. Isola Pescatori has no sights, but is a peaceful place for lunch.

Day Trip from Milan: Catch an early train from Milan to Stresa (take a one-hour fast train). Upon arrival in Stresa, walk 10 minutes downhill to the boat dock, and catch a boat to Isola Madre. Then work your way back to Isola Pescatori for a lazy lunch, and on to Isola Bella for the afternoon, before returning to the town of Stresa and back to Milan.

Overnight: Small, touristy Stresa makes a fine first or last stop in Italy—its connections with Milan's airport, which is located about halfway between Stresa and Milan, don't involve a transfer in big Milan (see "Transportation Connections," page 236).

Getting Around Lake Maggiore

Boats link the islands and Stresa, running about twice hourly. Allow roughly 10 minutes between stops. Since short round-trip hops add up fast (€6.40 each for Isola Bella and Isola Pescatori, €8.20 for Isola Madre), it's best to simply buy the **all-day pass:** €8.50 for two islands (Bella and Pescatori); or €11.50 for all the islands plus Pallanza (a town on the opposite shore) and Villa Taranto. A **combo-ticket** combining the villas on Isola Bella and Isola Madre with the all-day boat pass is €27.50 and saves you €1.50 (credit cards accepted).

Boats run daily April through September. The map on page 229 shows the route: Stresa, Carciano/Lido, Isola Bella, Isola Pescatori, Baveno (lakeside town), Isola Madre, Pallanza, and Villa Taranto. This route is part of a longer one. To follow the boat schedule (free, available at boat docks, TI, and maybe your hotel), look at the Arona–Locarno timetable for trips from Stresa to the islands, and the Locarno–Arona timetable for the return trip to Stresa.

Buy boat tickets directly from the dock ticket booth to the left of the TI. Don't be fooled by the private taxi-boat drivers and their little sales booth on the sidewalk in front of the public boat launch. They'll try to talk you into paying way too much (public boat info: tel. 800-551-801 or 0322-233-200).

Stresa

Stresa—which means "thin stretch"—was named for the original strip of fishermen's huts that lined the shore. Today, grand old hotels run along that same shore. The old town—basically a traffic-free touristy shopping mall—is just a few blocks deep, stretching inland from the main boat dock. A fine waterfront promenade leads past the venerable old hotels to the Lido (with the Carciano boat dock and a mountain cable car). Stresa's stately 19th-century lakeside hotels date back to the days when this town was on the "Grand Tour" circuit. In any Romantic-age resort like Stresa, hotels had names designed to appeal to Victorian aristocrats...like Palace (rather than Palazzo), Astoria, Bristol, and Victoria.

Nineteen-year-old Ernest Hemingway first came here in 1918. Wounded in Slovenia as an ambulance driver for the Italian Red Cross, he was taken to the Grand Hotel des Iles Borromees. This was the first hotel on the shore (from 1862), and it served—like its

Stresa and the Borromeo Islands

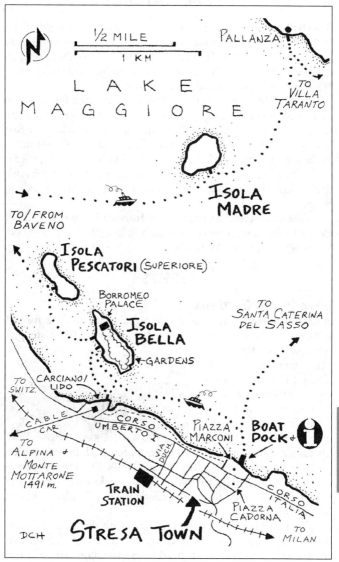

regal neighbors—as an infirmary during World War I. Hemingway returned to the same hotel in 1948, stayed in the same room (#205, now called the "Hemingway suite"—you can stay there for a couple of thousand dollars a night), and signed the guest book as "an old client." Another "old client" was Winston Churchill, who honeymooned here.

ORIENTATION

Tourist Information: The helpful TI, located to the right of the ticket window at the boat dock, gives out free maps and boat schedules (March–Oct daily 10:00–12:30 & 15:00–18:30; Nov–Feb Mon–Sat 10:00–12:30 & 15:00–18:30, closed Sun; Piazza Marconi 16, tel. 0323–30150, www.distrettolaghi.it).

Arrival in Stresa: At the train station, ask for a free city map at the newsstand (to the far right of the tracks as you exit the train). To get downtown, exit right from the station and take your first left (on Viale Duchessa di Genova). This takes you straight down to the lake (the boat dock is about four blocks to your right; ask for boat schedule at ticket window). The TI is next door on the same dock. Taxis charge a fixed rate of €8 for even the shortest ride in town.

Internet Access: The **New Data Internet Point** is a block off Piazza Cadorna in the old center (daily 9:30–12:30 & 15:30–20:00, Via de Vit 15A, tel. 0323-30323).

SIGHTS

Islands and Gardens

▲▲**Isola Bella**—This island, nearest Stresa, has the formal garden and the fanciest Baroque palace. Looking like a stepped pyramid from the water, this island was named by Charles Borromeo (spon-sor of Milan's Duomo) for his wife, Isabella. The island itself is touristy, with a gauntlet of souve-nir stands and a corral of restaurants. A few back streets provide evidence that people actually live here. While the Borromeo fam-ily now lives in Milan, they spend a few weeks each summer on Isola Bella (when their blue-and-red family flag flies from the top of the garden).

Your visit is a one-way tour, starting with the palace and fin-ishing with the garden. (There's no way to see the garden without the palace.) From the dock, head left to the huge palace, pass-ing the public WCs. In the lavishly decorated Baroque palace, stairs lead to stucco crests of Italy's top families (balls signify the Medici, bees mean the Barberini, and a unicorn symbolizes the Borromeo's motto: Humility). The next room shows a portrait of the first Borromeo. It's followed by a richly stuccoed grand hall, with an 80-foot-high dome and featuring an 18th-century model of the villa, including a grand entry that never materialized.

Next, the room with the musical instruments was the site of the 1935 Stresa Conference, in which Mussolini met with British and French diplomats in a united attempt to scare Germany out of starting World War II. This "Stresa Front" soon fizzled when Mussolini attacked Ethiopia and joined forces with Hitler. A photocopy of the treaty with Mussolini's signature is on the wall next to the exit. Napoleon's bedroom comes with an engraving that depicts his 1797 visit. (Napoleon is on a bench with his wife and sister enjoying festivities in his honor.) The last rooms display souvenirs and gifts that the Borromeo family picked up over the generations.

Downstairs, many of the famous Borromeo marionettes are on display. (A larger collection is on Isola Madre.) The 18th-century grotto, decorated from ceiling to floor with shell motifs and black-and-white stones, still serves its original function of providing a cool refuge from Italy's heat. The dreamy marble statues are by Gaetano Monti, a student of Canova. Climbing out of the basement, look up at the unique cantilevered stairs; they're from a 16th-century fortress that predates this building.

The ornate hall of 16th-century Flemish tapestries leads to the finale of this island visit: the garden, complete with Chinese white peacocks to give it all an exotic splash. Baroque—which is exactly what you see here—is all about controlling nature. The terraced gardens are crowned by the Borromeo family unicorn. Circle around the garden to the left to visit the bookshop; or head to the right to go straight to the exit. Gardeners continue on to the second exit to pass through Elisa's Greenhouse, named for Napoleon's sister and home to tropical plants.

Cost, Hours, Information: Palace and garden-€11, €16 combo-ticket includes Isola Madre, daily April–mid-Oct 9:00–18:00, last entry 30 min before closing, closed mid-Oct–March. A fine €2.50 audioguide (€4 for 2 headsets) describes the palace, which also has posted English descriptions. A WC is at the garden entrance. Tel. 0323-30556. Note that there are two docks on this island (one for each direction). Departure times are indicated by clocks at each dock. Picnicking is not allowed in the garden, but you can picnic at the point of the island (free and open to the public); take the mosaic sidewalk to the left of the palace entrance.

▲**Isola Pescatori**—This sleepy island—home to 35 families—is the smallest and most residential of the three. It has a couple of good seafood restaurants, picnic benches, views, and, blissfully, nothing to do—under arbors of wisteria. A delight for photographers and painters, the island is never really crowded, except at lunchtime.

▲▲**Isola Madre**—Don't come here unless you intend to tour the sight, because that's all there is: an interesting furnished villa and a lovely garden filled with exotic birds and plants. Visiting is a one-way affair, starting with a long stroll through the garden and finishing with the villa. Eight gardeners (with the help of water continually pumped from the lake) keep this English-style garden paradise lush and a joy even for those bored by gardens. You'll see trees from around the world, and an exotic bird menagerie with silver pheasants and Chinese peacocks. In front of the villa, a once-magnificent Himalayan cypress tree paints your world a streaky green. Knocked

down by a tornado in 2006, earnest rescue efforts are underway to save the 150-year-old tree. But with several amputated limbs and the trunk in traction, its survival is uncertain.

The 16th-century villa is the first of the Borromeo palaces. A century older than the other, it's dark, somber, and from the Renaissance. The clever angled hinges keep the doors from flapping in the lake breeze. The family's huge collection of dolls, marionettes, and exquisite 17th-century marionette theater sets—painted by a famous La Scala opera set designer—fill several rooms. A corner room is painted to take you into an 18th-century Venetian Rococo sitting room under a floral greenhouse. You'll see some of the garden's best flowers immediately after leaving the villa.

The sightseeing route is clearly signed for you, taking you through the gardens and villa, and ending at the chapel (€9, €16 combo-ticket includes Isola Bella, daily 9:00–17:30, no photos in villa, WC next to chapel, tel. 0323-30356). The €2.50 audioguide (€4 for 2 headsets) is devoted almost entirely to the garden—a good investment to properly appreciate the plantings.

While eating is best on Isola Pescatori, Isola Madre has one eatery: **La Piratera Ristorante Bar** (€22 fixed-price tourist meal, daily 8:00–18:00, sit-down meals from 12:00–15:00 and simple sandwiches to go anytime, picnic at rocky beach a minute's walk from restaurant, tel. 0323-31171).

▲**Villa Taranto Botanical Gardens**—Garden-lovers will enjoy this large landscaped park, located on the mainland a 10-minute boat ride beyond Isola Madre (across the lake from Stresa). The gardens are a Scotsman's labor of love. Starting in the 1930s, Neil MacEachern created this garden of delights—bringing in thousands of plants from all over the world—and here he stays, in the small mausoleum. The park's highlight is the terraced garden with a series of cascading pools. Villa Taranto is directly across the street from the boat dock (€8.50, April–Oct daily 8:30–19:30, ticket office closes at 18:30, closed Nov–March, tel. 0323-404-555).

Mountain Cable Car—From Stresa's Lido, a cable car takes you up—in two stages and a 20-minute ride—to the top of Mount Mottarone (about 5,000 feet). From here, you get great views of neighboring peaks and, by taking a short hike, a bird's-eye view of the small, neighboring Lake Orta (cable car runs March–Nov, €15 round-trip, €8.50 one-way, includes Alpine Gardens entry, daily 9:30–12:30 & 13:30–17:30, 2–3/hr, tel. 0323-30295).

To visit the **Alpine Gardens,** get off at the midway Alpina stop, where a 10-minute walk leads to the gardens (turn left as you leave; included in cable-car ticket, April–mid-Oct daily 9:30–18:00, closed Nov–March). The gardens come with great lake views and picnic spots, but can't compare to what you'll see on the islands.

If you plan to **hike** down, pick up the Trekking Map from the TI and allow 3.5 hours from the top of Mount Mottarone, or 1.5 hours from the Alpine Gardens.

You can rent a **bike** at the base of the cable-car lift (full-suspension mountain bike-€26/day, €21/half-day, €5.50/hr, includes helmet, tel. 338-839-5692) and bring it on the cable car with you (€10 extra). It's a treacherous ride, enjoyable only for serious bikers. While the ride is nice on top, you'll fight traffic on congested, rough, and windy roads for the rest of the trip.

Day Trips from Stresa

▲Scenic Boat and Rail Trip to Locarno and Centovalli—This enjoyable all-day excursion from Stresa involves three segments. Confirm all times, particularly the departure of the last boat from Locarno, before you embark on the trip. Take the train from Stresa to Domodossola, then catch the "Centovalli" train for a 90-minute ride that links together remote mountain villages on your way to Locarno, in the Italian-speaking Swiss canton of Ticino (bring your passport). Spend an hour or so exploring this town, on the far end of Lake Maggiore. Then take the boat past loads of small lakeside hamlets back to Italy. As a relaxing finale, you'll cruise into your home port of Stresa. The trip can also be done in reverse (with the boat trip first). A special €28 ticket covers both the train and boat tickets (you must reserve in advance; fax 0322-249-530 or email infomaggiore@navigazionelaghi.it—indicate the date you'll travel, number of passengers, and a return fax number or email address; call 800-551-801 or 0322-233-200 for info).

▲Lake Orta—Just on the other side of Mount Mottarone is the small lake of Orta. The lake's main town, Orta San Giulio, has a beautiful lakeside piazza ringed by picturesque buildings. The piazza faces the lake with a view of Isola San Giulio. Taxi boats (€3.50 round-trip) make the five-minute trip throughout the day.

The Lakes

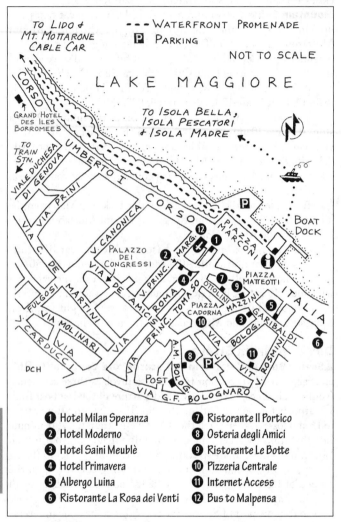

TO LIDO &
MT. MOTTARONE
CABLE CAR

- - - WATERFRONT PROMENADE
P PARKING

NOT TO SCALE

LAKE MAGGIORE

GRAND HOTEL
DES ILES
BORROMEES

TO ISOLA BELLA,
ISOLA PESCATORI
& ISOLA MADRE

TO
TRAIN
STN.

CORSO

VIALE DUCHESA DI GENOVA

VIA PRINI

VIA C. DE

UMBERTO I

V. CANONICA

CORSO

PIAZZA MARCONI

BOAT DOCK

PALAZZO
DEI
CONGRESSI

VIA DE AMICIS

V. PRINC.

V. MARG.

PIAZZA
MATTEOTTI

ITALIA

FULGOSI

VIA MARTINI

VIA MOLINARI

V. CARDUCCI

VIA

ROMA

V. PRINC. TOMASO

OTTOLINI

PIAZZA
CADORNA

MAZZINI

GARIBALDI

VIA

A.M. BOLOG.

BOLOG.

VIT.

V. ROSMINI

POST

VIA G.F. BOLOGNARO

DCH

- ① Hotel Milan Speranza
- ② Hotel Moderno
- ③ Hotel Saini Meublè
- ④ Hotel Primavera
- ⑤ Albergo Luina
- ⑥ Ristorante La Rosa dei Venti
- ⑦ Ristorante Il Portico
- ⑧ Osteria degli Amici
- ⑨ Ristorante Le Botte
- ⑩ Pizzeria Centrale
- ⑪ Internet Access
- ⑫ Bus to Malpensa

The island is worth a look for the church of San Giulio and the circular "path of silence" that takes about 10 minutes. In peak season, Orta is anything but silent, but off-season or early or late in the day, this place is full of peace and magic (**TI** tel. 0322-905-163, Wed–Sun 9:00–13:00 & 14:00–18:00, closed Mon–Tue, located on Via Panoramica next to the parking lot downhill from the train station).

The train ride from Stresa to Orta–Miasino (a short walk from the lakeside piazza) takes 1.5–2 hours and requires a change or two (4/day). Public buses from Stresa's Piazza Marconi to Orta depart from near the TI (€8 round-trip, mid-June–mid-Sept about 10:00, nearly hourly—see TI for schedule).

SLEEPING

(€1 = about $1.30, country code: 39)
Because Stresa town is just a resort, I'd day-trip from Milan. But here are good options if you'd like to stay.

$$ Hotel Milan Speranza is an impersonal, four-star, corporate-style hotel that caters mostly to tour groups, with 175 predictably comfortable rooms across from the boat dock (Db-€100–150 depending on season and view, €20–30 extra for lake views, air-con, elevator, tel. 0323-31178, fax 0323-32729, www.milansperanza.it, info@milansperanza.it).

$$ Hotel Moderno offers 54 peaceful and well-maintained pastel rooms on a pedestrian street a block from the main square (Db-€134, closed Nov–mid-March, air-con, elevator, from Piazza Matteotti, with your back to the lake, go right—up small street to Via Cavour 33, tel. 0323-933-773, fax 0323-933-775, www.hms.it, hotmoder@tin.it).

$ Hotel Saini Meublè is a cozy place with rustic stonework and warm hardwood floors, located in a pedestrian zone a couple of blocks from the boat dock in the old center. Its 14 rooms are big, modern, and quiet (Sb-€75, Db-€95, lower prices off-season, ask for 5 percent discount with this book in 2008, elevator, from Piazza Matteotti head up Via Mazzini and turn left on Via Garibaldi, Via Garibaldi 10, tel. 0323-934-519, fax 0323-31169, www.hotelsaini.it, info@hotelsaini.it). Gianni (Johnny) greets you at reception.

$ Hotel Primavera, next door to Hotel Moderno, rents 34 cheaper, decent air-conditioned rooms, most with little terraces that overlook the action in the streets below (Db-€75–100, tel. 0323-31286, fax 0323-33458, Via Cavour 39, www.stresa.it, hotelprimavera@stresa.it).

$ Albergo Luina is a clean and homey, family-run cheap sleep, with seven basic rooms above a restaurant (Sb-€30–52, Db-€50–70, some with little balconies for no extra charge, these prices for Rick Steves readers, mention this book when you reserve, breakfast-€7; Via Garibaldi 21, 2 blocks off Piazza Matteotti—with back to lake, go left up small street; tel. & fax 0323-30285, luinastresa@yahoo.it). Papa Marco cooks in the restaurant while Mamma Renata tends to the guests.

The Lakes

EATING

La Rosa dei Venti, on the main drag, caters to locals with great €7 pizzas and lakefront dining. They offer proudly homemade pastas and creative risottos for €7 (big €7 salads, €15 *secondi*, Wed–Mon 12:00–14:30 & 18:30–22:30, closed Tue, everything made to order, 2 blocks south of the boat dock at Corso Italia 50, tel. 0323-31431).

Ristorante Il Portico is a new, high-energy, friendly place. They feature several €16–26 multicourse tasting samplers and daily market specials on sidewalk tables or in their airy, fresh dining room. It's smart to reserve (piping hot €6 pizzas, €7 pastas, €9 *secondi*, Tue–Sun 12:00–15:00 & 18:30–22:00, Via Ottolini 9, tel. 0323-934-510).

Osteria degli Amici serves up tasty €9 risottos and pastas, with fast and friendly service under a canopy of grape and kiwi leaves (€7 wood-fired pizzas, daily 12:00–14:30 & 19:00–22:30, closed Wed Sept–May, deep in the old town past Piazza Cadorna at Via Bolongaro 33, tel. 0323-30453).

Le Botte offers a variety of Piedmont's regional specialties in a pub-grub casual atmosphere (€9 pastas, €13 *secondi*, daily 12:00–15:00 & 19:00–22:30 in summer, closed Thu Oct–April and all of Dec–March, Via Mazzini 6/8, tel. 0323-30462).

The main square, **Piazza Cadorna,** is a carnival of locals selling things to tourists. Still, at night it has a certain charm. It seems anyone who claims to be a musician can get a gig singing for eaters. The **Pizzeria Centrale** (on a platform in the center) is a good place to enjoy the ambience with decent pizzas, but don't order any serious food here.

TRANSPORTATION CONNECTIONS

From Stresa by Train to: Milan (about hourly, 1-hr fast train, 70–90-min slow train), **Varenna** (nearly hourly, 2.75 hrs, transfer in Milan), **Venice** (1/day direct, nearly hourly with changes in Milan, 4 hrs), **Domodossola** (near the Swiss border, hourly, 30 min).

To Malpensa Airport: For a **train/bus combination,** take the train toward Milan (hourly) and get off at Gallarate (about 40 min, 1 hour from Stresa, first train departs at 5:20, connects with first bus departure for Malpensa), where frequent, cheap shuttle buses run to Malpensa's Terminal 1 (€1.50, pay driver, about 2/hr, 10 min, from Gallarate, the bus departs from the train station and runs 6:05–19:50, from Malpensa's Terminal 1, the bus runs 5:35–19:50, tel. 0331-258-411).

Alibus Airport buses run directly between Stresa and Malpensa (€8, April–Oct, 50 min; leaves airport from bus stop 22 outside Terminal 1 at 7:30, 10:30, 14:30, 17:30, and 20:30; leaves Stresa from in front of the church next to Hotel Milan Speranza—near the ferry dock and TI—at 6:30, 9:30, 13:30, 16:30 and 19:30; confirm schedule, must reserve by 11:00 the previous day or by 11:00 Sat if booking for Sun or Mon bus, tel. 0323-552-172, www .safduemila.com).

Taxis to the airport cost €80 (1–5 people, €96 if traveling early or late: between 22:00–7:00) and take about an hour; your hotel can arrange the taxi for you, but will charge you extra for booking it. It's easy to arrange a taxi on your own at the train station's taxi stand. Salvo Taxi is reliable (mobile 335-707-8894).

MILAN

Milano

For every church in Rome, there's a bank in Milan. Italy's second city and the capital of Lombardy, Milan is a hardworking, fashion-conscious, time-is-money city of 1.3 million. It's a melting pot of people and history. Milan's industriousness may come from the Teutonic blood of its original inhabitants, the Lombards, or from the region's Austrian heritage. Milan is Italy's fashion, industrial, banking, TV, publishing, and convention capital. The economic success of modern Italy can be blamed on this city of publicists and pasta power lunches.

As if to make up for its shaggy parks, blocky fascist architecture, and bombed-out post-WWII feeling, its people are works of art. Milan is an international fashion capital with a refined taste. Window displays are gorgeous, cigarettes are chic, and even the cheese comes gift-wrapped. Yet, thankfully, Milan is no more expensive for tourists than other Italian cities.

Three hundred years before Christ, the Romans called this place Mediolanum, or "the central place." By the fourth century A.D., it was the capital of the western half of the Roman Empire. Emperor Constantine issued the Edict of Milan from here, legalizing Christianity. After some barbarian darkness, medieval Milan rose to regional prominence under the Visconti and Sforza families. By the time of the Renaissance, it was nicknamed "the New Athens," and was enough of a cultural center for Leonardo da Vinci to call home. Then came 400 years of foreign domination (Spain, Austria, France, more Austria). Milan was a center of the 1848 revolution against Austria, and helped lead Italy to unification in 1870.

Mussolini left a heavy fascist touch on the city's architecture

Greater Milan

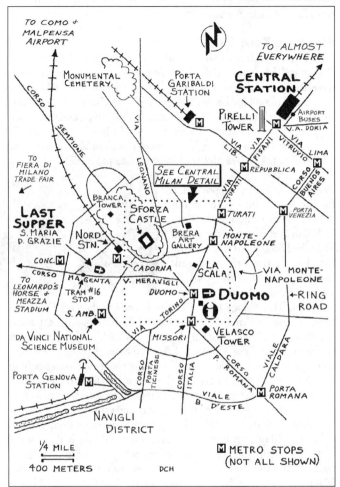

TO COMO &
MALPENSA
AIRPORT

TO ALMOST
EVERYWHERE

**CENTRAL
STATION**

MONUMENTAL
CEMETERY

PORTA
GARIBALDI
STATION

PIRELLI
TOWER

Airport
Buses
V.A. DORIA

CORSO

SEMPIONE

VIA LEGNANO

VIA L.IB.

VIA PISANI

VIA VITRUVIO

VIA LIMA

TO
FIERA DI
MILANO
TRADE FAIR

REPUBBLICA

CORSO BUENOS AIRES

SEE CENTRAL
MILAN DETAIL

VIA TURATI

**LAST
SUPPER**
S. MARIA
D. GRAZIE

BRANCA
TOWER

SFORZA
CASTLE

BRERA
ART
GALLERY

TURATI

PORTA
VENEZIA

NORD
STN.

CADORNA

LA
SCALA

MONTE-
NAPOLEONE

VIA MONTE-
NAPOLEONE

CONC.

CORSO

MAGENTA

V. MERAVIGLI

DUOMO

DUOMO

TO
LEONARDO'S
HORSE &
MEAZZA
STADIUM

TRAM #16
STOP

S. AMB.

←RING
ROAD

da VINCI NATIONAL
SCIENCE MUSEUM

VIA TORINO

MISSORI

VELASCO
TOWER

VIALE CALDARA

PORTA GENOVA
STATION

CORSO PORTA TICINESE

CORSO ITALIA

P. CORSO ROMANA

PORTA
ROMANA

VIALE B. D'ESTE

**NAVIGLI
DISTRICT**

¼ MILE

400 METERS

DCH

Ⓜ METRO STOPS
(NOT ALL SHOWN)

(such as the central train station). His excesses also led to the
WWII bombing of Milan. But Milan rose again. The 1959 Pirelli
Tower (the skinny skyscraper in front of the station) was a trend-
setter in its day. Today, Milan is people-friendly, with a great transit system and inviting pedestrian zones.

Many tourists come to Italy for the past. But Milan is today's
Italy, and no Italian trip is complete without visiting it. While it's
not big on the tourist circuit, Milan has plenty to see. And fortunately, seeing Milan—so manageable and well organized—is not
difficult.

For pleasant excursions from the city, consider visiting Lake

Como or Lake Maggiore—both are about an hour from Milan by train (see The Lakes chapter).

Planning Your Time

OK, it's a big city, so you probably won't linger. Compared to Rome and Florence, Milan's art is mediocre, but the city does have unique and noteworthy sights: the Duomo and Galleria Vittorio Emanuele, La Scala Opera House, Brera Art Gallery, Michelangelo's last *Pietà* in the Sforza Castle, and Leonardo's *Last Supper*. It's best to reserve at least two months in advance to see *The Last Supper* (see page 264); if you haven't booked ahead, your best option is to take a bus-and-walking tour (see page 247).

With two nights and a full day, you can gain an appreciation for the town and see the major sights. With 36 hours, I'd sleep in Milan and focus on the center. Tour the Duomo, hit what art you like, browse through the elegant shopping area and the Galleria Vittorio Emanuele, and try to see an opera. Technology buffs like the Leonardo da Vinci National Science and Technology Museum, while history and art buffs dig the city's early Christian churches, Brera Gallery, Pinacoteca Ambrosiana, and the Museum of Art and Science. People-watchers and pigeon-feeders could spend their entire visit never losing sight of the Duomo. And if you dig burial grounds, rattle through Milan's evocative Monumental Cemetery. To maximize your time in Milan, use the Metro and note which places stay open through the siesta.

Since Milan is a cold Italian plunge, and most flights to the US leave Milan early in the morning, you could save Milan for the end of your trip and start your journey softly by going directly by train from Milan to Lake Como (1-hour ride to Varenna), Lake Maggiore (about an hour to Stresa), or the Cinque Terre (4 hours to Vernazza). Then spend a night or two in Milan at the end of your trip before flying home.

Monday is a terrible sightseeing day, since many museums are closed (including Leonardo's *Last Supper*). August is rudely hot and muggy. Locals who can vacate, do, leaving the city pretty quiet. Those visiting in August find the nightlife sleepy; many shops, restaurants, and some hotels closed; and the hotels that are open, empty and discounted. I've indicated which recommended hotels offer air-conditioning, a splurge worth the money for a summer visit.

A Three-Hour Tour: If you're just changing trains in Milan (as, sooner or later, you will), consider this blitz tour: Check your

Rome vs. Milan: A Classic Squabble

In Italy, the North and South bicker about each other, hurling barbs, quips, and generalizations. All the classic North/South traits can be applied to Milan (the business capital) and Rome (the government capital). Although the differences have become less pronounced lately, the sniping continues.

The Milanesi say the Romans are lazy. Roman government jobs come with short hours—cut even shorter by too many coffee breaks, three-hour lunches, chats with colleagues, and phone calls to friends and relatives. Milanesi contend that *Roma ladrona* (Rome, the big thief) is a parasite that lives off the taxes of people up North. There's still a strong Milan-based movement seriously promoting secession from the South.

Romans, meanwhile, dismiss the Milanesi as uptight workaholics with nothing else to live for—gray like their foggy city. Romans do admit that in Milan, job opportunities are better and based on merit. And the Milanesi grudgingly concede the Romans have a gift for enjoying life.

While Rome is more of a family city, Milan is the place for high-powered singles on the career fast track. Milanese yuppies mix with each other...not the city's longtime residents. Milan is seen as wary of foreigners and inward-looking, and Rome as fun-loving, tolerant, and friendly. In Milan, bureaucracy (like social services) works logically and efficiently, while in Rome, accomplishing even small chores can be exasperating. Everything in Rome—from finding a babysitter to buying a car—is done through friends. While people in Milan are not as willing to discuss their personal matters, they are generous and active in charity work.

Milanesi find Romans vulgar. The Roman dialect is considered one of the coarsest in the country. Much as they try, Milanesi just can't say, "Damn your dead relatives" quite as effectively as the Romans. Still, Milanesi enjoy Roman comedians and love to imitate the accent.

The Milanesi feel that Rome is dirty and Roman traffic nerve-wracking. But despite the craziness, Rome maintains a genuine village feel. People share family news with their neighborhood grocer. Milan lacks people-friendly piazzas, and entertainment comes at a high price. But in Rome, *la dolce vita* is as close as the nearest square, and a full moon is enjoyed by all.

Milan

bag at the station, pick up a city map at the station TI, ride the subway to the Duomo (see "Arrival in Milan," page 243, for specifics), peruse the square, explore the cathedral's rooftop and interior, have a scenic coffee in the Galleria Vittorio Emanuele, spin on the floor mosaic of the bull for good luck, see a museum or two (most are within a 10-min walk of the main square), and return by subway to the station. Art fans could make time for *The Last Supper* (if they've made reservations; Metro: Cadorna or Conciliazione, or tram #16 from the Duomo, direction: San Siro), the Michelangelo *Pietà* in the Sforza Castle (no reservations necessary, Metro: Cairoli), the Brera Art Gallery (Metro: Lanza), or the Duomo Museum (may be closed the first part of 2008 for restoration, Metro: Duomo).

ORIENTATION

My coverage focuses on the old center. Most sights and hotels are within a 10-minute walk of the cathedral (Duomo), which is a straight eight-minute Metro ride from the train station.

Tourist Information

Milan's main TI is in the **central train station** (Mon–Sat 9:00–18:00, Sun 9:00–13:00 & 14:00–17:00, tel. 02-740-4318, www.milanoinfotourist.com). At track level (with your back to the tracks), look for the *APT Tourist Information* sign near the blinking orange-and-white T and black-and-white T *tabacchi* shop. The TI is down a corridor next to a Telecom telephone center (phone center open daily 10:00–19:00).

Another TI is on **Piazza del Duomo,** in a former subterranean day hotel for railworkers. It's to the left of the entrance to the Galleria; look for the staircase next to the pharmacy and head down (Mon–Sat 8:45–13:00 & 14:00–18:00, Sun 9:00–13:00 & 14:00–17:00, tel. 02-7740-4343). You can book Autostradale and Zani Viaggi city tours (see "Tours" on page 247) at the desks farthest from the entrance.

At either TI, confirm your sightseeing plans and pick up a free map. Also ask for the two free publications that list Milan's sights (including hours, prices, and directions), events, concerts, films in English, expatriate groups, and cultural insights: *Hello Milano* (monthly newspaper, www.hellomilano.it) and *Milano Mese* (less helpful, as it has scant descriptions of events in English, and events are listed by category rather than date).

While I've listed enough sights to keep you hectically busy for two days, there's much more to see in Milan. Its many thousand-year-old churches make it clear that Milan was an important beacon in the Dark Ages. The TI and local guidebooks and newspapers can point you in the right direction if you have more time.

Arrival in Milan

By Train: The huge, sternly decorated, fascist-built (in 1931) train station is a city and a sight in itself. You'll get off the train and enter the lobby at track level; another floor is downstairs at street level.

Orient from the track-level lobby with your back to the tracks. The entire station may still be under renovation, which may affect the following description. To the right and across the hall is the **baggage check** (€4/5 hours, €10/24 hours, daily 6:00–24:00, passport required, 45-pound bag limit). At your back between the two clocks facing the tracks is the **365 Travel Agency** (Mon–Fri 7:00–20:30, Sat–Sun 8:00–20:30, sells train tickets, supplements, and night-train berth reservations without a commission at the left side of the office, tel. 02-6749-3147). On your left are **cash machines** (near track 14) and the **TI** (described above). Out the side exit on the left (down the escalator), you'll find taxis (figure €8 to the Duomo) and STAM **airport shuttle buses** to Malpensa and Linate airports.

From the track level, go downstairs straight ahead to find train-ticket windows, train information and Hertz/Avis/Europcar offices (daily 7:00–21:00, validate railpasses at any window), a huge but difficult-to-find **supermarket/cafeteria** (daily 8:00–23:00; after you descend stairs from track level, go right to the far end, enter Pellini bar, and snake your way through the cafeteria to the Super Centrale market, also called Supermercato Sigma).

Also on the ground floor to the far left is a 24-hour **pharmacy** (*farmacia*, look for green neon cross), which will move upstairs to track level once construction is complete. Just outside the front of the train station is a big red *M* that marks the entrance to the Metro system (€1 to the Duomo, faster than a taxi, buy tickets downstairs at kiosk, validate in orange machines to pass through turnstiles).

Station exchange offices are a rip-off. Use an ATM in the train station (from track 14, enter the lobby—you'll find a *Bancomat* cash machine to your left.

If you need to buy train tickets, avoid the language barrier and long lines at the ticket windows by buying tickets from the user-friendly, yellow Biglietto Veloce/Fast Ticket machines on the ground floor (see page 836) or by visiting a travel agency on the track level (which may also have lines—but likely shorter than the ticket windows).

Taking the Metro to the Duomo and Back: For most quick visits, this giant city is one simple axis from the train station to the Duomo. To get to the Duomo, go straight into the Metro (look for a red *M*) and buy a €1 ticket from the underground ticket office at the Metro stop (prices listed in English overhead) or from a machine (push suitcase button). Validate (stamp) your paper ticket in the yellow or orange machines at the turnstiles. Avoid the turnstiles designated only for magnetic tickets, such as the 10-ride carnet or 24-hour passes. Follow signs for yellow line 3, direction: San Donato, and in eight minutes (four stops) you'll be facing the cathedral.

To return to the train station from the cathedral, take the yellow line 3, direction: Maciachini (new stops are currently under construction past Maciachini, so check for updates—see map on page 246). After one trip on the Metro, you'll dream up other excuses to use it.

By Car: Driving is bad enough in Milan to make the €20/day fee for a downtown garage a blessing. If you're driving, do Milan (and Lake Como) before or after you rent your car, not while you've got it. If you have a car, use the well-marked suburban *parcheggi* (parking lots), which offer affordable (€6/day) and safe parking at city-edge subway stations.

By Plane: Frequent shuttle trains and buses connect the airports and train station. See "Transportation Connections," page 278.

Helpful Hints

Theft Alert: Be on guard. Milan's thieves target tourists. At the station and around the Duomo, thieves roam dressed as beggars, sometimes in gangs of too-young-to-arrest children. Watch out for ragged people carrying newspaper and cardboard; they thrust this item at you as a distraction while they pick your pocket. If you're ripped off, fill out a report with the police—necessary if you plan to file a claim with your insurance company (Police Station, "Questura," Via Fatebenefratelli 11, Metro: Turati, open daily 24 hours, tel. 02-62261; or Piazza San Sepolcro 9 behind Pinacoteca Ambrosiana near the Duomo, daily 8:00–20:00, tel. 02-806-051). For police emergencies, call 113. For lost or stolen credit cards, see page 823.

US Consulate: It's at Via Principe Amedeo 2/10 Metro: Turati, tel. 02-290-351 for recorded info and phone tree, http://milan .usconsulate.gov).

Medical Help: A 24-hour pharmacy is in the central train station; look for the neon-green cross. Several international medical clinic/emergency care facilities are in Milan: in Galleria Strasburgo 3 (Mon–Thu 9:00–19:00, Fri 9:00–18:00, closed Sat–Sun, between Via Durini and Corso Europa, third floor, Metro: San Babila, tel. 02-763-407-20); and at Via Mercalli 11 (Mon–Fri 9:00–18:00, closed Sat–Sun, Metro: Missori or Crocetta, call for appointment, tel. 02-5831-9808). If you call any of these places after hours, an English message gives you the number for a 24-hour emergency doctor. Dial 118 for medical emergencies.

Milan

Street Markets: Milan has two very popular flea markets. **Fiera di Sinigallia** spills into a lot at Porta Genova every Saturday 8:30–17:00 (later in summer, Metro: Porta Genova). If you continue along Viale d'Annunzio to Viale Papiniano, you'll run into the **Papiniano** market (Tue morning and Sat all day). Small street markets are held every morning except Sunday in various neighborhoods; *Hello Milano* has a complete listing (free at TI). Be wary of pickpockets at any street market.

Internet Access: Two **Internet Point** shops are near Via Torino and the Duomo: at Via Valpetrosa 5 (daily 8:30–20:30, follow the street around corner to second #5, tel. 02-4547-8874) and at the FNAC superstore at the intersection of Via Torino and Via Marsilio (take escalator upstairs to purchase Internet time on second floor—€2/30 min, leftover minutes can be used later—then go to first-floor café to get online).

Bookstores: The handiest major bookstore is **Libreria Feltrinelli,** under the Galleria Vittorio Emanuele. Books in English— fiction and guidebooks—are at opposite ends of the store (Mon–Sat 10:00–23:00, Sun 10:00–20:00; store is huge but entrances are subtle—either enter at Ricordi Mediastore next to McDonald's in center of Galleria and go downstairs, or enter through Autogrill restaurant on Piazza del Duomo, store is in basement level; also sells maps; tel. 02-8699-6903). The **American Bookstore** is at Via Camperio 16, near the Sforza Castle (Mon 13:00–19:00, Tue–Sat 10:00–19:00, closed Sun, tel. 02-878-920).

Travel Agencies: You can buy train tickets and reserve an overnight berth *(cuccetta)* at the **365 Travel Agency** at the train station at no extra cost (shorter lines than ticket windows; see listing under "Arrival in Milan") or at a downtown travel agency such as **American Express,** near the Duomo (Mon–Fri 9:00–17:30, closed Sat–Sun, pay cash or use AmEx credit card, at Via Larga 4, two blocks southeast of the Duomo, tel. 02-721-041).

Getting Around Milan

By Public Transit: Use Milan's great subway system. The clean, spacious, fast, and easy three-line Metro zips you nearly anywhere you may want to go, and trams and city buses fill in the gaps. The handiest Metro line for a quick visit is the yellow line (3), which connects the train station to the Duomo. The other lines are red (1) and green (2).

A **ticket,** valid for 75 minutes, can be used for one subway, tram, or bus ride, including a transfer either within the same or another system, but not a round-trip on the same system (€1, sold at newsstands, many *tabacchi* shops, shops with ATM sticker in

Milan's Metro

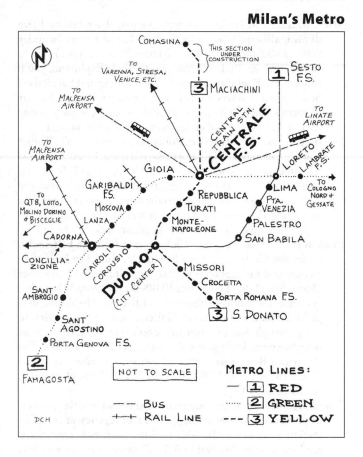

window, and at machines in subway stations—push suitcase button; note that some machines sell only the €1 ticket and offer no other options—just feed in the money).

Validate single tickets in the yellow or orange machines at the turnstiles, and keep them until you exit the Metro system. If you're asked to show your ticket and it isn't valid, you can get a €33 fine.

Other options include: a *carnet* (€9.20 for 10 rides; you get one magnetic ticket that can be validated 10 times, works in most Metro turnstiles); a **24-hour pass** (€3, worthwhile if you take four rides, can usually cover a journey the next morning since it's a 24-hour rather than a one-day pass); and a **48-hour pass** (€5.50). Once you've stamped these tickets the first time, don't stamp them anymore, and pass through the Metro gates marked *abbonati*.

If you need transit information, you'll find an underground office—called ATM Point—at the Duomo stop (near the Arengario exit, can access from square, entrance to the right of the

Duomo as you face it, Mon–Sat 7:45–19:00, closed Sun). Transit info: toll-free tel. 800-808-181, www.atm-mi.it.

I've keyed sightseeing to the subway system. While most sights are within a few blocks of each other, Milan is an exhausting city for walking. You'll rarely wait more than five minutes for a subway train. The well-marked trams can also be useful, especially to get to *The Last Supper* (tram #16) and the Monumental Cemetery (#12 or #14).

By Taxi: Small groups go cheap and fast by taxi (drop charge–€3.10, €0.70 per kilometer, additional supplements for luggage and on Sun, holidays, and at night). It's often easier to walk to a taxi stand than to flag down a cab. The handiest stands are at Piazza del Duomo and in front of the Sforza Castle.

TOURS

Bus Tours—The three-hour **Autostradale** bus-and-walking tour is a good value, has a live guide describing the city's monuments in English, and guarantees you'll see Leonardo's *Last Supper*— useful if you haven't booked ahead for this important sight. The jam-packed itinerary also includes visits to the Duomo, Galleria Vittorio Emanuele, Sforza Castle, and La Scala Opera House (€50, departs daily at 9:30). Tours depart from Piazza del Duomo, next to the taxi stand at the far end of the square from the church. There are four ways to reserve this tour: Book in advance online at www.autostradale.it; ask your hotelier to book it for you; call the TI at 02-7740-4343; or drop into the TI at Piazza del Duomo before the morning departure to see if tickets are available. To confirm details, call 02-3391-0794.

Zani Viaggi does a similar tour that includes *The Last Supper*. The guide leads a two-language tour (which always includes English), departing daily except Monday at 14:30 from their office at Foro Bonaparte 76, near the Sforza Castle (€50, 3.5 hours, tel. 02-867-131, www.zaniviaggi.it, excursions@zaniviaggi.it).

CitySightseeing Milano has hop-on, hop-off buses that do a circuit of the major sights accompanied by a recorded commentary; you can get off at a stop, tour the sight, and hop back on the bus to resume your tour (€15/24 hours, buy ticket on board, buses depart the Sforza Castle daily every 75 min from 10:00–18:45, stops at the Duomo and La Scala, tel. 02-867-131).

Private Guide—Lorenza Scorti is a hardworking young woman who knows her local history and how to teach it. She can be booked well in advance (necessary in May and Sept) or on short notice (€112/3-hr tour, €224/day, same price for individuals or groups, evenings OK, tel. 02-4801-7042, mobile 347-735-1346, lorenza .scorti@libero.it).

SIGHTS

Milan's Cathedral and Museum

To get the most out of your cathedral visit, start by visiting the adjacent Duomo Museum (see page 253; unfortunately, this may be closed the first part of 2008 for restoration), located just outside the church, around to the right, directly across from the south transept.

▲▲**Duomo (Cathedral)**—The city's centerpiece is the fourth-largest church in Europe—after the Vatican's, London's, and

Sevilla's. Back when Europe was fragmented into countless tiny kingdoms and dukedoms, the dukes of Milan wanted to impress their counterparts in Germany and France. Their goal was to earn Milan recognition and respect from both the Vatican and the kings and princes of northern Europe by building a massive, richly ornamented cathedral. Even after Renaissance-style domes were in vogue elsewhere in Italy, conservative Milan's cathedral stayed on Gothic target. The dukes—thinking northerners would relate better to Gothic—loaded it with pointed arches and spires. For good measure, the cathedral was built not of ordinary stone but of marble—pink marble of Candoglia, from top to bottom—rafted from a quarry about 60 miles away across Lake Maggiore and to a canal port at the cathedral. The lengthy restoration of the glorious facade should be finished by 2008.

Cost, Hours, Location: Free, daily 7:30–18:45, Metro: Duomo.

Audioguide: €4 for 45-min audioguide (available from kiosk located inside to right of entrance, kiosk open Mon–Sat 9:30–17:30, closed Sun, ID required).

Dress Code: Modest dress is required. Don't wear shorts or sleeveless shirts. Even kids with exposed shoulders or knees are likely to be turned away at the door.

➋ The Tour Begins: At 525 by 300 feet, the place is immense, with more than 2,000 statues inside and 52 hundred-foot-tall, sequoia-size pillars representing the weeks of the year and the liturgical calendar. If you do two laps, you've done your daily walk. It was built to hold 40,000 worshippers, the entire population of Milan when construction began.

Built from 1386 to 1810, with the final touches added in 1965, this construction project originated the Italian phrase for "never-

Central Milan

❶ Tram #16 (To *Last Supper,* Leonardo's Horse & Meazza Stadium)

❷ Tram #16 (To *Last Supper*) & Trams #12 & #14 (To Monumental Cemetery)

❸ Via Montenapoleone (High-Fashion Shops)

❹ Zani Viaggi Tours

❺ City Museum Entrance

ending": "like building a cathedral." It started out Gothic (best seen in the apse behind the altar) and was finished in the early 1800s under Napoleon (particularly the noteworthy west facade, which is wonderful late in the day, with the sun low in the sky). While the church is a good example of the Flamboyant, or "flame-like," overripe final stage of Gothic, architectural harmony is not its forte.

Walk around the entire church exterior and notice the statues, all made between the 14th and 20th centuries by sculptors from all over Europe. There are hundreds of these statues—each different

Milan at a Glance

▲▲**Duomo** Milan's showpiece cathedral, with a recently restored facade (possibly still covered during part of 2008); you can walk on its roof amid a forest of spires. **Hours:** Daily 7:30–18:45.

▲▲**Duomo Museum** Provides insight to the Duomo and a chance to see its original art. **Hours:** Normally daily 10:00–13:15 & 15:00–18:00; may be closed the first part of 2008 for restoration.

▲▲**Galleria Vittorio Emanuele** Glass-domed arcade on the main square, perfect for window-shopping and people-watching. **Hours:** Always open.

▲▲**La Scala Opera House and Museum** The world's most prestigious opera house, recently reopened after a lengthy renovation. **Hours:** Museum daily 9:00–12:00 & 13:30–17:00.

▲**Brera Art Gallery** World-class collection of Italian paintings (13th–20th centuries), including Raphael, Caravaggio, Gentile da Fabriano, Piero della Francesca, Mantegna, and the Bellini brothers. **Hours:** Tue–Sun 8:30–19:15, closed Mon.

▲*The Last Supper* Leonardo da Vinci's masterpiece, viewable only with a reservation—book at least two months in advance. **Hours:** Tue–Sun 8:15–18:45 (last visit), closed Mon.

▲**Leonardo da Vinci National Science and Technology Museum** Leonardo's designs illustrated in wooden models, plus a vast collection of historical, scientific, and technological bric-a-brac and machines. **Hours:** Tue–Fri 9:30–17:00, Sat–Sun 9:30–18:30, closed Mon.

▲**Sforza Castle** Milan's castle containing a museum whose highlight is an unfinished Michelangelo *Pietà*. **Hours:** Tue–Sun 9:00–17:30, closed Mon.

▲**Risorgimento Museum** History of Italian unification. **Hours:** Tue–Sun 9:00–13:00 closed Mon.

Milan

and quite creative. Notice the statues on the tips of the many spires...they seem so relaxed, like they're just hanging out, waiting for their big day. Functioning as drain spouts, the 96 fanciful gargoyle monsters are especially imaginative.

Interior: Enter the church. As you stand inside (at the back), notice two tiny lights: The little red one above the altar marks where a nail from the cross of Jesus is kept. This relic was brought

▲**Via Dante** Human traffic buzzes to the tune of lilting accordions on one of Europe's longest pedestrian-only boulevards. **Hours:** Always open.

▲**Monumental Cemetery** An evocative outdoor art gallery with tombs showcasing expressive art styles from 1870 to 1930. **Hours:** Tue–Sun 8:00–18:00, closed Mon.

Pinacoteca Ambrosiana Oldest museum in Milan, with works by Raphael, Leonardo, Botticelli, Titian, and Caravaggio. **Hours:** Tue–Sun 10:00–17:30, closed Mon.

Poldi Pezzoli Museum Italian paintings (15th–18th centuries), weaponry, and decorative arts. **Hours:** Tue–Sun 10:00–18:00, closed Mon.

Bagatti Valsecchi Museum 19th-century Italian Renaissance furnishings. **Hours:** Tue–Sun 13:00–17:45, closed Mon.

Church of Santa Maria presso San Satiro Pilgrim church with impressive 3-D paintings. **Hours:** Mon–Fri 7:30–12:00 & 15:30–18:30, Sat & Sun 9:30–12:30 & 15:00–17:00.

Branca Tower has 365-degree views over the city. **Hours:** Erratic—confirm at TI before heading there, roughly Tue–Sun 21:30–24:00, also Wed 10:30–12:30 and Sat–Sun 10:30–14:00, plus Fri–Sun 14:30–18:00, frequent breaks during day, closed Mon and in bad weather.

Museum of Art and Science Leonardo da Vinci's art and inventions, with hands-on exhibits on authenticating and dating various forms of art. **Hours:** Mon–Fri 10:00–18:00, Sat 10:00–14:00, closed Sun.

Leonardo's Horse Gargantuan equestrian monument built according to Leonardo's designs. **Hours:** Tue–Sun 9:00–18:00, closed Mon.

Milan

to Milan by St. Helen (Emperor Constantine's mother) in the fourth century, when Milan was the capital of the Western Roman Empire. It's on display for three days a year (in mid-Sept). Now look high to the right and find a tiny pinhole of white light. This is designed to shine a 10-inch sunbeam at noon onto the bronze line that runs across the floor, indicating where we are on the zodiac (but local guides claim they've never seen it work).

Wander deeper into the church up the right aisle. Notice the windows. Those on the right are 15th-century; these mosaics of colored glass are brilliant and expensive, bought by wealthy families seeking the Church's favor. Their purpose was to teach the illiterate masses the way to salvation through stories of the Old Testament and the life of Jesus. Many on the left date from the time of Napoleon and are dimmer, cheaper painted glass.

Belly up to the bar facing the high altar. While the church is Gothic, the area around the altar was made Baroque—the style of the Vatican in the 1570s (a Roman Catholic statement to counter the Protestant churches of the north, which were mostly Gothic). Now look to the rear up at the ceiling and see the fancy "carving" (between the ribs)—nope, that's painted. It looks expensive, but paint is more affordable than carved stone.

Notice the fine 16th-century inlaid-marble floor. The pieces around the altar are original, and you can tell that the black marble is harder than the rest—it shows (and you can feel) less wear than the other colors. A grotesque 16th-century statue of St. Bartolomeo, a martyr skinned alive by the Romans, stands in the south transept near the side (right) exit. Walk behind the poor guy wearing his skin like a robe to see his face, hands, and feet. Carved by a student of Leonardo da Vinci, this is a study in human anatomy learned by dissection, forbidden by the Church at the time.

Treasury: The treasury, or *tesoro*, to the right under the altar, thrills pilgrims. Its reliquaries contain thorns from Jesus' crown and the "Tree of Apostles," with bones, fingernails, and hair from each of the 12 apostles, with descriptions in English (€1, buy ticket at treasury ticket desk, Mon–Fri 9:30–13:30 & 14:00–18:00, Sat 9:30–13:30 & 14:00–17:00, Sun 13:30–15:30, sometimes blocked off during special Masses).

Paleo-Christian Baptistery: In the rear of the church (buy €1.50 ticket at bookshop kiosk, same hours as the Duomo), you can climb down into the church that stood here long before the present one. Milan was an important center of early Christianity. In Roman times, Mediolanum's street level was 10 feet below today's level. You'll see the scant remains of an eight-sided baptistery (where saints Augustine and Ambrose were baptized) and a little church. Back then, since you couldn't enter the church until you were baptized (which didn't happen until age 18), churches had a little "holy zone" just outside for the unbaptized. This included a Baptistery.

Cathedral Rooftop: This is the most memorable part of a Duomo visit. You'll wander through a fancy forest of spires with great views of the city, the square, and—on clear days—the crisp and jagged Italian Alps. And, 330 feet above everything, La

Madonnina overlooks it all. This
15-foot-tall gilded Virgin Mary is a
symbol of the city.

Climb the stairs for €4 (daily
mid-Feb–mid-Nov 9:00–17:20,
mid-Nov–mid-Feb 9:00–16:20),
or ride the elevator for €6 (daily
mid-Feb–mid-Nov 9:00–19:20,
mid-Nov–mid-Feb 9:00–16:20); €8
combo-ticket includes elevator and
Duomo Museum if museum is open.
The entrances to the roof are from
the outside of the church. To take the
stairs up, you'll enter on the north side across from the Rinascente
department store (tip: old European churches face roughly east).
To ascend by elevator, enter outside from either the north or south
transept—when one is closed, the other is open, and sometimes
both are open. The north elevator is near the stairs mentioned
above, but toward the back of the church; the south elevator is on
the church's opposite side, diagonal from Piazza Fontana. Once
you reach the lowest level of the roof by elevator, you may have to
climb a few more stairs.

▲▲**Duomo Museum (Museo del Duomo)**—This fine museum
may be closed the first part of 2008 for renovation. When open,
it offers an excellent opportunity to understand Milan's cathedral
and see its original art close up. While the admission is €6 (includes
treasury), their discounted €8 combo-ticket (which includes the
treasury plus the elevator to church rooftop) is an even better deal
(daily 10:00–13:15 & 15:00–18:00, in Ducal Palace next to south
side of the Duomo, Piazza del Duomo 14, Metro: Duomo, tel. 02-
860-358). Here's a tour (the renovation may shuffle things around):

Room 1: After you buy your ticket, look up. As he did pilgrims 500 years ago, greeting you is God the Father, made of
wood, wrapped in copper, and gilded. In 1425, this covered the
keystone connecting the tallest arches directly above the high altar
of the Duomo.

Room 2: Meet St. George. Among the oldest cathedral
statues, it once stood on the front spire and shows nearly 600
years of pollution and aging. Some think this is the face of Duke
Visconti—the man who started the cathedral. The museum is filled
with originals like this. On the right, finger a raw piece of *marmo
di Candoglia*—the material of the church, spires, and statues. The
duke's family gave the entire Candoglia quarry (near Stresa) to the
church for all the marble it would ever need.

Room 3: This room (which used to be the stable for the Duke's
horses) shows how Gothic was an international style. Gothic

craftsmen, engineers, and artists roamed across Europe to work on huge projects such as Milan's cathedral. The statues in this room show the national differences: Peter (near the door, showing off his big keys) is Italian. His expressive face is made even more expressive by his copper-button pupils. The smaller statues behind glass (which were models for the big ones) are German (showing inner strength) and French (more graceful). Pope Martino V, overlooking the room from his perch at the end (to the left as you enter), celebrated the first Mass in the cathedral in 1418. Study the 15th-century stained-glass windows close up. The grotesque gargoyles (originals), protruding over the door you entered, served two purposes: to scare away evil spirits and to spew rainwater away from the building. Leaving the room, you'll walk under a stylized sun—a symbol of both Jesus and the Visconti family.

Room 5: A lit panel shows how the church was built in stages from 1386 to 1774. Building resumed whenever the community had the money.

Room 6: The brick backdrop reminds us what the church would have looked like if not for the 15th-century dandy with the rolled-up contract in his hand. That's Visconti's descendant, Galeazzo Sforza, making it official—the church now owns the marble quarry (and it makes money on it to this day). A photo of the contract is opposite.

Room 7: The Byzantine-style crucifix (again, copper-sheet gilded with real gold nailed onto wood) is 900 years old. It hung in the church that stood here previously, as well as in today's cathedral. The two-sided miniature altar painting has been carried through the city on festival days for 500 years.

Room 8: These statues, from about 1500, are originals. Copies now fill their niches in the church. St. Paul the Hermit (in front of the blue curtain) got close to God by living in the desert. While wearing only a simple robe, he's filled with inner richness. The intent is for pilgrims to stare into his eyes and feel at peace (but I couldn't stop thinking of the Cowardly Lion). Check out the interactive computer that details restoration techniques and works in progress on the cathedral.

Room 9: Five hundred years ago, this sumptuous Flanders-style tapestry—woven of silk, silver, and gold—hung from the high altar. In true Flemish style, it shows fun details of everyday life woven into the theology. It tells the story of the Crucifixion by showing three scenes at once. Note the exquisite detail, down to the tears on Mary's cheeks. (A discreet **WC** hides behind the wooden door.)

Room 10: The sketchy red cartoons were designs for huge paintings (see an actual painting and photographs of others nearly opposite) that still hang between the cathedral pillars (Oct–

Christmas). Notice the 16th-century inlaid-marble floor. The black (from Lake Como) and red (from Verona) marble is harder. Go ahead, wear down the white a little more.

Room 12: Enter the long Room 12 and turn around to see the artwork that lines the wall. The terra-cotta was clay—worked in a creative frenzy and then baked. Study the quick design below the careful marble originals (flanking the doorway you entered). Notice what 300 years of acidic pigeon droppings do to marble.

The statues all around this room (c. 1600) were sculpted 100 years later than the statues in Room 8, and therefore are more expressive.

Find the painting of St. Carlo Borromeo in the black robe (high up, on your right). The 16th-century saint carries a cross showing the holy nail (the church's top relic) as he leads the plague out of Milan. In the background, see the previous 13th-century facade with today's church—before spires—behind it.

Circle the room clockwise. Crespi's monochrome painting of the *Creation of Eve (Creazione di Eva)* came first (1628). From that, the terra-cotta model was made (1629), and this served as the model for the marble statue that still stands above the center door on the church's west portal (1643). Three other sets line the wall.

Opposite *Eve,* see the swirling *Dance of Angels* and its terra-cotta model. This is the original, which decorated the ceiling over the door.

Room 20: This room (off Room 12) displays vestments on loan from the treasury. Showing off rich red robes with lavish gold brocade, it's like a priestly fashion show from the 16th through 20th centuries.

• Go back through Room 12, and at the far end, enter...

Room 13: Standing like a Picasso is the original iron frame (1772) for the statue of the Virgin Mary that still crowns the cathedral's tallest spire. In 1967, a steel replacement was made for the 33 pieces of gilded copper bolted to the frame. The carved-wood face of Mary (in the corner) is the original mold for Mary's cathedral-crowning copper face.

• Go back into Room 12 once more, and enter the nearby tunnel-like hall, into...

Room 15: Along the left wall, diagrams show competition designs proposing possible facades for the cathedral. A photo of the actual west portal is at the end of the hall.

Room 16: This huge wooden model of the cathedral was the actual model—necessary in that pre-computer age—used in the 16th century by the architects and engineers to build the church. This version of the facade wasn't actually built. Climb around the back to see the spire-filled rooftop, which you'll explore later if you like.

Room 17: The art here seems a mix of old and new, but it's all 20th-century. Notice the vibrant Pope Martin V popping out of the wall (bronze panel to the left as you enter; by artist Lucio Fontana). On the opposite wall (between the windows), Fontana's *Assumption of Mary (Maria Assunta)* is making a jump shot into heaven. Her veil looks like flowing hair, like the wings of an angel.

The last rooms are technical, showing the recent restoration work and the stabilization and reinforcement of the main pylons.

• *To exit, retrace your steps.*

Near the Duomo

▲**Piazza del Duomo**—Milan's main square is a classic European scene and a popular local gathering point. Professionals scurry, fashion-conscious kids loiter, young thieves peruse. Teens hang out near the Galleria entrance in the afternoons, waving at the balcony above in hopes of being filmed by MTV cameras located in an upper-floor studio.

Standing in the square (midway between the statue and the Galleria), you're surrounded by history. The statue is Victor Emmanuel II, first king of Italy. He's looking at the grand Galleria named for him. The words above the triumphal arch entrance read: "To Victor Emmanuel II, from the people of Milan."

Behind the statue (opposite the cathedral) is the center of medieval Milan—Piazza Mercanti. Dating from 1220, the medieval City Hall (look for its redbrick arches) marked the center of town back when the entire city stood within its immense fortified walls. The merchant's square is a strangely peaceful place today, with a fine smattering of old-time Milano architecture.

Opposite the Galleria are twin fascist buildings. Mussolini made grandiose speeches from their balconies. Study the buildings' relief panels telling—with fascist drama—the history of Milan. Between these buildings and the cathedral (set back a bit) is the historic ducal palace, Palazzo Reale. This building, now a venue for temporary art exhibits, was redone in the Neoclassical style by Maria Theresa in the late 1700s, when Milan was ruled by the Austrian Hapsburgs. For a fine view of the Duomo and the piazza, climb the steps to the balcony of the skinny, fascist-style building closest to the cathedral (can be closed for frequent *manifestazioni*—demonstrations—or any other perceived security threat). Behind the Duomo is a vibrant pedestrian shopping zone along Corso Vittorio Emanuele.

▲▲**Galleria Vittorio Emanuele**—A symbol of Milan is its great four-story, glass-domed arcade on the cathedral square. Built during the heady days of Italian unification (c. 1870), it was the first building in town to have electric lighting. Here you can turn an

expensive cup of coffee into a good value by enjoying Europe's best people-watching (or get the same view for peanuts from the strategically placed McDonald's).

The venerable **Bar Zucca** (at the entry), with a friendly staff and an Art Deco interior typical of the 1920s, is the former haunt of famous opera composer Giuseppe Verdi and conductor Arturo Toscanini, who used to stop by after their performances at La Scala. It's a fine place to enjoy a drink and people-watch (€3 for an espresso is a great deal if you relax and enjoy the view). Once called the Campari café, this is considered the birthplace of the famous Campari bitter. Now a bitter apéritif, Zucca, is their signature drink (€3.40 standing or €8.70 seated, Tue–Sun 7:30–20:00, closed Mon and Aug, tel. 02-8646-4435).

Wander around the gallery. Its art celebrates the establishment of Italy as an independent country. Around the central dome, patriotic mosaics symbolize the four major continents. The mosaic floor is also patriotic. The white cross in the center represents the king. The she-wolf with Romulus and Remus (on the south side—facing Rome) honors the city that, since 1870, has been the national capital. On the west side (facing Torino, the provisional capital of Italy from 1861–1865), you'll find that city's symbol: a *torino* (little bull). For good luck, locals step on his irresistible little testicles. Two local girls explained to me that it works better if you spin. Find the poor little bull and observe for a few minutes...it's a cute scene. With so much spinning, the mosaic is replaced every few years.

Piazza della Scala—This smart little traffic-free square, out the back between the Galleria and the opera house, is dominated by a statue of Leonardo da Vinci. The statue (from 1870) is a reminder that Leonardo spent many years in Milan working for the Sforza family (who dominated Milan as the Medici family dominated Florence). Under the great Renaissance genius stand four of his greatest "Leonardeschi." (He apprenticed a sizable group of followers.) The reliefs show his various contributions—painter, architect, and engineer. Leonardo, wearing his hydro-engineer hat, re-engineered Milan's canal system, complete with locks. (Until the 1920s, Milan was one of Italy's major ports, with canals connecting the city to the Po River and Lake Maggiore.)

▲▲**La Scala Opera House and Museum**—The statue of Leonardo behind the Galleria (described above) is looking at a plain but famous Neoclassical building, arguably the world's most prestigious opera house: Milan's Teatrale alla Scala. La Scala opened in

Milan

1778 with an opera by Antonio Salieri (of *Amadeus* fame).

At Milan's famous opera house and its adjacent museum, both recently restored, opera buffs can see the museum's extensive collection and get a glimpse of the theater.

Museum: The collection—well-described in English—features things that mean absolutely nothing to the hip-hop crowd: Verdi's top hat, Rossini's eyeglasses, Toscanini's baton, Fettuccini's pesto, original scores, diorama stage sets, costumes, busts, portraits, and death masks of great composers and musicians. The museum allows you to peek into the actual theater. The stage is as big as the seating area on the ground floor. A recent five-year renovation corrected the acoustical problems caused by WWII bombing and subsequent reconstruction. The royal box is just below your vantage point, in the center rear. Notice the massive chandelier made of Bohemian crystal (€5, daily 9:00–12:00 & 13:30–17:00, Piazza della Scala, tel. 02-8879-2473).

Opera: The show goes on at the world-famous La Scala Opera House. Schedules vary, but the opera season is nearly year-round (show time 20:00), and ballet and classical concerts are held from October through June. No performances are held in August (for information and booking call Scala Infotel Service, daily 9:00–18:00, until 20:00 on performance days, tel. 02-7200-3744—live; or tel. 02-860-775—automated booking, press 2 for English; or book online at La Scala's helpful website: www.teatroallascala .org). While tourists are usually keen on seeing an opera in La Scala, note that many of the performances are actually in a second hall, the Arcimboldi Theater, across town. On the opening night of an opera, a dress code is enforced for men (suit and tie).

Tickets generally go on sale one month before a performance. Seats sell out quickly. On performance days, 140 sky-high gallery tickets are sold at a discount only at the box office (located down the left side of the theater towards the back on Via Filodrammatici, and marked with *Biglietteria Serale* sign); check the posted announcement about when tickets will be released, then come back to get one. You can also buy tickets—but not the discounted ones—at a handy ticket office in the Duomo Metro station (daily 12:00–18:00, entrance is to right of the Duomo as you face it, underground, follow the signs to *ATM Point*), as well as on the Internet (Web sales end one hour before show time).

▲**Via Speronari**—A block off Piazza del Duomo, this is one of Milan's oldest streets, and the most charming drag in the old center. Via Speronari—named for the spurs once made and sold here—is worth a wander. Street names around here recall their medieval crafts: *speronari*—spurs, *spadari*—swords, *armorari*—armor. The weaponry made on these streets was high fashion among Europe's warrior class...like having an Armani dagger. While right in the city center, the neighborhood feels vital because it's also a residential street. Banks of doorbells indicate that families live above the shops. Start at the corner of Via Mazzini and Via Speronari, one block southwest of the Duomo. A shop on your right—*L'Ortolan Pusae Vecc de Milan*—brags in the old Milanese language that this is the oldest fruit-and-veggie store in the city. The neighboring Princi bakery is understandably popular. Its brioches are rarely more than a few minutes old. The *tavola calda*—hot table—across the street sells fresh, hearty take-out to hungry businessmen.

Where Via Speronari hits Via Torino, go 20 yards to the left to find the **Church of Santa Maria presso San Satiro** (Church of St. Mary at St. Satiro) hiding behind its Baroque facade (Mon–Fri 7:30–12:00 & 15:30–18:30, Sat–Sun 9:30–12:30 & 15:00–19:00, tel. 02-874-683). This was the scene of a temper tantrum in 1242, when a losing gambler vented his anger by hitting the baby Jesus in the Madonna-and-Child altarpiece. Blood "miraculously" spurted out, and the beautiful little church has been on the pilgrimage trail ever since. While I've never seen any blood, I'd swear I've seen a 3-D background behind the basically flat altar (a *trompe l'oeil* illusion—only about a foot deep). This church—squeezed between the earlier church of San Satiro and a street—had no room for a real apse, so, with the help of math, the Renaissance architect Donato Bramante made what looks like an apse.

In the north transept, you'll find that original ninth-century church of San Satiro (brother of St. Ambrogio, patron saint of Milan). This tiny church—with surviving bits of Byzantine fresco—predated the rest. From this chapel, look back at the main altar to see Bramante's 3-D work collapsed. On the opposite side (near entry)—with dimensions mirroring this old chapel—an eight-sided Baptistery by Bramante from the 1480s shows the mathematically based values of the Renaissance. If you have a prayer in need of an extra boost, pop a coin into the box and "light" an electric candle.

Pinacoteca Ambrosiana—This oldest museum in Milan was inaugurated in 1618 to house Cardinal Federico Borromeo's painting collection. It began as a teaching academy, which explains the many replicas, some of which you may recognize (including a painting of Leonardo's faded *Last Supper* where you buy your ticket, and some famous statues along the stairway). In this prestigious collection, look for these highlights: Leonardo da Vinci's *Portrait of a Musician* (like the *Mona Lisa*, Leonardo has you wondering, "What's he thinking?" "What's he listening to?" and "Where's his iPod?"); Leonardo's *Codex Atlanticus* (collection of his writings—originals locked up in their vault, only copies are on display); works by Botticelli and Caravaggio; and a room (#7) full of Flemish paintings—including delightful works by Jan Brueghel (study the wonderful detail in *Allegory of Fire* and *Allegory of Water*). You'll see lots of art that looks like Leonardo's but was actually done by his followers, such as Bernardino Luini. Titian was a favorite of Cardinal Borromeo, so you'll also see plenty of work by this Venetian master and his followers.

Perhaps the highlight of the collection is the Raphael cartoon (*cartone* in Italian, referring to the large sheet of paper on which the drawing is made). This is the original charcoal-on-canvas design that Raphael drew as an outline for the famous *School of Athens* fresco. If you've seen the actual painting in the Vatican Museum, you'll notice that the figure of Michelangelo (as a brooding stonecutter lounging on the steps in the foreground) is missing from the cartoon. Raphael added him to the fresco as a tribute to Michelangelo after seeing his awe-inspiring work on the ceiling of the Sistine Chapel. While the Vatican's much-adored fresco is attributed entirely to Raphael, it was actually mostly painted by his students; it's safe to say, however, that this *cartone* version was wholly sketched by the hand of Raphael. To make the fresco, they riddled this cartoon with pin pricks along the outlines of the characters, stuck it to the wall of the pope's study, and then applied a colored powder. When they removed the *cartone*, the characters' shapes would be marked on the wall, and completing the fresco was a lot like coloring figures in a coloring book (€7.50, no English descriptions but they have English maps noting major works, small English guidebook for €6.20 that covers museum's highlights nicely, Tue–Sun 10:00–17:30, last entrance 1 hour before closing, closed Mon, a couple of blocks from Piazza del Duomo at Piazza Pio XI 2, tel. 02-8069-2221, free WC behind ticket desk to the right and downstairs).

In the Brera Neighborhood

▲**Brera Art Gallery**—Milan's top collection of Italian paintings (13th–20th centuries) is world-class, but it can't top Rome's or Florence's. Established in 1809 to house Napoleon's looted art, it fills the first floor above a prestigious art college.

Enter the grand courtyard of a former monastery, where you'll be greeted by the nude *Napoleon with Tinkerbell* (by Antonio Canova). Climb the stairway (following signs to *Pinacoteca*, past all the art students), buy your ticket, and pick up an English map of the museum's masterpieces.

The gallery's highlights include works by Gentile da Fabriano, hinting at the realism of the coming Renaissance (check out the lifelike flowers and realistic, bright gold paint—he used real gold powder, Room IV). Andrea Mantegna's *The Dead Christ* is a textbook example of feet-first foreshortening (Room VI). Room XVIII hosts a permanent glass-enclosed restoration lab, allowing you to see various restoration works in progress.

In Room XXI, notice how Crivelli employs Renaissance technique (he was a contemporary of Leonardo), yet clings to the mystique of the Gothic Age (that's why I like him so much). Find eight Crivellis. Also, don't miss Raphael's *Wedding of the Madonna*, Piero della Francesca's *Madonna and Child with Four Angels* (Room XXIV), and the gritty-yet-intimate realism of Caravaggio's *Supper at Emmaus* (Room XXIX). To spice things up, look for Francesco Hayez's hot and heavy *The Kiss (Il Bacio)* in Room XXXVII.

Cost, Hours, Location: €5, more during special exhibits, open Tue–Sun 8:30–19:15, last entry 35 min before closing, closed Mon, free lockers just before the ticket counter, no photos, Via Brera 28, Metro: Lanza or Montenapoleone, tel. 02-722-631, www .brera.beniculturali.it. Since there are no English descriptions, consider the audioguide (€3.50, or €5.50 for two headsets), or pick up the fine *Guide to the Galleries* (€8.20) in the bookshop. Java junkies will seek out the great, cheap cappuccino machine: Go through Napoleon's courtyard and straight through the art school to the end of the long hall; the machine's on your left. It's fun to explore the art school on the ground floor, mill about among the many young students, and wonder if there's a 21st-century Leonardo in your midst.

▲**Risorgimento Museum**—With a quick 30-minute swing through this quiet, one-floor museum thoughtfully described in English, you'll learn the interesting story of Italy's rocky road to unity: from Napoleon (1796) to the victory in Rome (1870). It's just around the block from the Brera Art Gallery at Via Borgonuovo 23 (€2, Tue–Sun 9:00–13:00, last entry 30 min before closing, closed Mon, Metro: Montenapoleone, tel. 02-8846-4176).

Near Montenapoleone

Poldi Pezzoli Museum—This classy house of art features top Italian paintings of the 15th through 18th centuries, old weaponry, and lots of interesting decorative arts, such as a roomful of old sundials and compasses (€7, Tue–Sun 10:00–18:00, last entry 60 min before closing, closed Mon, pick up English brochure and map at ticket desk, free English audioguides, ID required, Via Manzoni 12, Metro: Montenapoleone, tel. 02-796-334).

Bagatti Valsecchi Museum—This unique 19th-century collection of Italian Renaissance furnishings was assembled by two aristocratic brothers who spent a wad turning their home into a Renaissance mansion. Museum guards pack flashlights for closer examination of fine wood carvings (€6, more if there are special exhibits, half-price on Wed, open Tue–Sun 13:00–17:45, closed Mon, good English descriptions, Via Gesù 5, Metro: Montenapoleone, tel. 02-7600-6132).

Milan

Sforza Castle and Nearby

▲**Sforza Castle (Castello Sforzesco)**—The castle of Milan tells the story of the city in brick. Built in the late 1300s as a military fortress, it guarded the gate to the city wall and defended the city from enemies "within and without." It was beefed up by the Sforza duke in 1450 in anticipation of a Venetian attack. Later, it was the Renaissance palace of the Sforza family and was even home to their in-house genius, Leonardo. During the centuries of foreign rule (16th–19th), it was a barracks for occupying Spanish, French, and Austrian soldiers. Today, it houses several museums (€3, free entry 16:30–17:00 and Fri 14:00–17:00, open Tue–Sun 9:00–17:30, last entrance 30 min before closing, closed Mon, free lockers and WCs downstairs from the ticket counter, English info fliers throughout, Metro: Cairoli, tel. 02-8846-3700).

The **gate** stands above the ditch once filled with water. A relief celebrates Umberto I, the second king of Italy. Above that, a statue of St. Ambrosius, the patron of Milan (and a local bishop in the fourth century), oversees the action. Notice the chart, just outside the gate, showing how the city was encircled first by a crude medieval wall, and then by a state-of-the-art 16th-century wall—of which this castle was a key element. It's apparent from the enormity of these walls that Milan was a strategic prize. Today, the walls are gone, giving the city two circular boulevards.

This immense, much-bombed-and-rebuilt brick fortress—exhausting at first sight—can only be described as heavy. But its courtyard has a great lawn for picnics and siestas. Its main museum, the **Museum of Ancient Art,** is fascinating, unlike the other museums in the castle. Enter the museum just past the ticket counter. It fills the old Sforza family palace with interesting medieval armor, furniture, early Lombard art, an Egyptian collection, and, most important, Michelangelo's unfinished *Pietà Rondanini* in Room XV.

This is a rare opportunity to enjoy a Michelangelo with no crowds. Michelangelo died while still working on this piece—his fourth *Pietà*. A *pietà*, by definition, is a representation of a dead Christ with a sorrowful Virgin Mary. This unfinished statue, is surrounded by a fortress-like wall to limit its viewing to a few tourists at a time, and it is unique in that it shows the genius of Michelangelo midway through a major rework—Christ's head is cut out of Mary's right shoulder, and an earlier arm is still just hanging there. But there's a certain power to this rawness. Walk around the back to see the strain in Mary's back (and Michelangelo's rough chisel work) as she struggles to support her son. The sculpture's elongated form hints at the Mannerist style that would follow. Notice the ancient Roman altar underneath the *Pietà*. This sculpture was owned by the Rondanini family until just after World War II.

At the far end of the castle's grounds is the monumental Arco della Pace, a triumphal arch. They built the arch facing Paris to welcome Napoleon's rule, because locals believed he would bring with him the ideals of the French Revolution. When they learned he was just another megalomaniac, they turned the horses around, their tails facing France.

Branca Tower—This tower, a five-minute walk from the Sforza Castle through Milan's equivalent of Central Park, offers perhaps the best view in town. For €3, a lift takes you as high as the Mary that crowns the cathedral (hours are crazy, confirm at TI before heading out there, roughly Tue–Sun 21:30–24:00, also Wed 10:30–12:30 and Sat–Sun 10:30–14:00, plus Fri–Sun 14:30–18:00, frequent breaks during day, closed Mon and in bad weather, tel. 02-331-4120).

Museum of Art and Science (Museo d'Arte e Scienza)—This hands-on museum offers an interesting look at Leonardo's works during the 20 years he spent in Milan. It includes his paintings and sketches, and inventions such as a clever drum machine and war machines in miniature. Another part of the museum describes how to tell the difference between genuine art and copies or fakes, with 10 demonstration stations (€6, Mon–Fri 10:00–18:00, Sat 10:00–14:00, closed Sun, English descriptions throughout, Via Q. Sella 4, ring bell on bank of doorbells to enter; to exit, push button to left of door; tel. 02-720-2488).

▲**Via Dante**—This grand pedestrian boulevard and popular shopping street leads from the Sforza Castle toward the town center and the Duomo. Since Via Dante was carved out of a medieval tangle of streets to celebrate Italian unification (c. 1870), all the facades lining it are relatively new. Over the vigorous complaints of merchants, the street became traffic-free in 1995. Today, they'd have it no other way. Enjoy strolling this beautiful people zone, where you'll hear the whir of bikes and the lilting melodies of accordion players, instead of traffic noise. Photo exhibits are frequently displayed here. In front of the Sforza Castle, a commanding statue of Giuseppe Garibaldi, one of the heroes of the unification movement, looks down one of Europe's longest pedestrian zones. From here you can walk to the Duomo and beyond (about 1.5 miles), nearly all traffic-free.

The Last Supper and Nearby

▲**Leonardo da Vinci's *The Last Supper* (Cenacolo)**—Reserve at least two months in advance to see this Renaissance masterpiece in the Church of Santa Maria delle Grazie.

Because of Leonardo's experimental fresco technique, deterioration began within six years of its completion. The church was bombed in World War II, but—miraculously, it seems—the wall holding *The Last Supper* remained standing. The 21-year restoration project (completed in 1999) peeled 500 years of touch-ups away, leaving a faint but vibrant masterpiece. In a big, vacant, whitewashed room, you'll see faded pastels and not a crisp edge. The feet under the table look like negatives. But the composition is dreamy—Leonardo captures the psychological drama as the Lord says, "One of you will betray me," and the apostles huddle in stressed-out groups of three, wondering, "Lord, is it I?" Some are scandalized. Others want more information. Simon (on the far right) gestures as if to ask a question that has no answer. In this agitated atmosphere, only Judas (fourth from left and the only one with his face in shadow)—clutching his 30 pieces of silver and looking pretty guilty—is not shocked.

The circle meant life and harmony to Leonardo. Deep into a study of how life emanates in circles—like ripples on a pool hit by a pebble—Leonardo positioned the 13 characters in a semicircle. Jesus is in the center, from whence the spiritual force of God emanates.

The room depicted in the painting seems like an architectural extension of the church. The disciples form an apse, with Jesus as the altar—in keeping with the Eucharist. Jesus anticipates his sacrifice—his face sad, all-knowing, and accepting. His feet even foreshadowed his death by crucifixion. Had the door, which was cut out in 1652, not been added, you'd see how Leonardo placed Jesus' feet atop each other, ready for the nail.

The room was a refectory or dining room for the Dominican friars. Traditionally, they'd gather here to eat with a Last Supper scene on one wall facing a Crucifixion scene on the opposite wall.

The perspective is mathematically correct. In fact, restorers found a tiny nail hole in Jesus' right ear, which anchored the strings Leonardo used to establish these lines. The table is cheated out to show the meal. Notice the exquisite lighting. The walls are lined with tapestries (as they would have been) and the one on the right is brighter—to fit the actual lighting in the refectory (with windows on the left). With the extremely natural effect of the light and the drama of the faces, Leonardo created an effective masterpiece.

Reservations: Reservations are mandatory. These days, because of the hype surrounding Dan Brown's blockbuster novel, *The Da Vinci Code*, spots are booked at least two months in advance—so plan ahead. To minimize the humidity problem—even though the damage has already been done—only 25 tourists are allowed in every 15 minutes for exactly 15 minutes. Prior to your appointment time, you wait in several rooms, while doors close behind you and open up slowly in front of you. The information posted on Leonardo is mainly in Italian.

It's better to book by phone than online. If you call, you'll have a greater selection of days and time slots to choose from, since their website doesn't reflect cancellations (tel. 02-8942-1146, or from the US, dial 011-39-02-8942-1146; booking office open Mon–Fri 9:00–18:00, Sat 9:00–14:00, closed Sun; the number is often busy—once you get through, dial 2 for an English-speaking operator; the process takes about two minutes and you'll hang up with an appointed entry time and a number; can pay with cash or credit card upon arrival).

If you book online, you'll see a calendar that will—ideally—show available time slots. If the days are blank, it means that all the slots for those days have been filled—or it can mean that the website (which seems user-*un*friendly) isn't functioning well. If you can't find a spot when you need it, try calling instead, because cancellations aren't registered and show up as booked slots (for booking: www.cenacolovinciano.org; general info: www.cenacolovinciano.it).

Cost: No matter how you book, the cost is €8, which includes the €1.50 reservation fee (can pay with cash or credit card if buying one or two tickets, but must pay in advance by credit card for more than two tickets, 9:30 and 15:30 visits require €3.25 extra for provided guided English tour).

Last-Minute Tickets: While "reservations are required," if spots are available (more likely on weekdays and first thing in the morning) you can book one at the desk (even if *Sold Out* sign is posted). If fewer than 25 people show up for a particular time slot, you can get lucky. But those who show up without a reservation generally kill lots of time waiting around. Only un-prepaid spots are given away if the ticket holders don't show up; prepaid no-shows are not resold. Note that the Autostradale and Zani Viaggi bus tours (see "Tours," page 247) include entry to *The Last Supper*. In a pinch, you might be able to buy tickets from Autostradale or Zani Viaggi without going on their tour. Autostradale books out the 12:00, 12:15, 17:30, and 17:45 slots, speculating that they'll fill their buses. If they don't, they release these extra tickets each morning. You can try to nab one by showing up at the Church of Santa Maria delle Grazie at 8:15.

Hours of *The Last Supper*: Tue–Sun 8:15–18:45 (last visit), closed Mon. You'll be asked to show up 20 minutes before your scheduled time. When an attendant calls your time, get up and move into the next room. Consider the fine €2.50 audioguide (€4.50 with two headsets). Its spiel fills every second of the time you're in the room—so try to start listening just before you enter. Until you're let in, you might want to listen to it in the waiting room while studying the reproduction of the actual *The Last Supper* that's there. No photos are allowed.

Getting There: Take the Metro to Cadorna or Conciliazione (plus a 5-min walk), or hop on tram #16 (catch it just off Piazza del Duomo on corner of Via Mazzini and Via Dogana), which drops you off in front of the Church of Santa Maria delle Grazie. The Science Museum (next listing) is two blocks away.

▲**Leonardo da Vinci National Science and Technology Museum (Museo Nazionale della Scienza e Tecnica "Leonardo da Vinci")**—The spirit of Leonardo lives here. Most tourists visit for the hall of Leonardo designs illustrated in wooden models, but Leonardo's mind is just as easy to appreciate by paging through a coffee-table edition of his notebooks in any bookstore. The rest of this immense collection of industrial cleverness is fascinating, with planes, trains, and automobiles, ships, radios, old musical instruments, computers, batteries, telephones, chunks of the first transatlantic cable, interactive science workshops, and on and on. Many exhibits include English descriptions. Some of the best exhibits (such as the Marconi radios) branch off the Leonardo hall. Ask for a English museum map from the ticket desk—you'll need it. Allow at least 90 minutes here (€8, Tue–Fri 9:30–17:00, Sat–Sun 9:30–18:30, last entry 30 min before closing, closed Mon, Via San Vittore 21, bus #50 or #58 from the Duomo, or Metro: Sant'Ambrogio or Cadorna, tel. 02-4855-5200).

Away from the Center

Leonardo's Horse—This largest equestrian monument in the world is a modern reconstruction of a model created in 1482 by

Leonardo da Vinci for the Sforza family. The model was destroyed in 1499 by invading French forces, who used it for target practice. In 1999, American Renaissance-art collector Charles Dent decided to build the 15-ton, 24-foot-long statue from Leonardo's design. He presented it to the Italians in appreciation for their role in the Renaissance and in homage to Leonardo's genius. The exhibit, described in English, includes statue casts and photos of the construction (free, Tue–Sun 9:30–18:00, closed Mon, WC to right of exhibit, located on outskirts near Meazza soccer stadium and San Siro racetrack; from corner of Via Mazzini and Via Dogana, take tram #16, direction: San Siro, to Stratico Palatino stop—ask conductor when to get off, then head right on Via Palatino, and left on Piazzale dello Sport to #9; or you can walk a half-mile from Metro: Lotto).

Soccer—The Milanesi claim that their soccer (football, or *calcio* in Italian) teams are the best in Europe. For a dose of Europe's soccer mania (which many believe provides a necessary testosterone vent to keep Europe out of a third big war), catch a match while you're here. A.C. Milan and Inter Milan are the ferociously competitive home teams (tickets-€7–135).

A.C. Milan tickets sold at Banca Intesa banks (one's at Via Verdi 8, Mon–Fri 8:45–13:45 & 14:45–15:45, closed Sat–Sun), online at www.acmilan.com, or at the Milan Point Shop (Tue–Sat 10:00–19:00, Piazza XXVI Maggio next to Via San Gottardo). Inter Milan tickets are sold at Banca Popolare di Milano banks (one's at Piazza Meda 4, Metro: San Babila; Mon–Fri 8:45–13:45 & 14:45–15:45, closed Sat–Sun) or online at www.inter.it.

Games are held in the 85,000-seat Meazza stadium most Sunday afternoons from September to June (Metro: Lotto, or tram #16—catch it just off Piazza del Duomo, on corner of Via Mazzini and Via Dogana, direction: San Siro; take it to last stop, where you'll find the stadium). You'll need to have your passport when you buy your ticket and bring it with you to the stadium for security reasons. For more on the Italian passion for soccer, see page 32.

▲Monumental Cemetery (Il Cimitero Monumentale)—Europe's most artistic and dreamy cemetery experience, this grand place was built just after unification to provide a suitable final resting place for the city's "famous and well-deserving men." Any cemetery is evocative, but this one—with its super-emotional portrayals of the

deceased and their heavenly escorts (in art styles c. 1870–1930)—is in a class by itself. It's a vast garden art gallery of proud busts and grim reapers, heartbroken angels and weeping widows, too-young soldiers and countless old smiles, frozen on yellowed black-and-white photos (free, Tue–Sun 8:00–18:00, last entry 30 min before closing, closed Mon, pick up map at the entrance gate, a long walk from Metro: Garibaldi FS, or catch tram #12 or #14 from the corner of Via Orefici and Via Cantu near the Duomo).

SHOPPING

World-Class Window-Shopping

The "Quadrilateral," an elegant, high-fashion shopping area around Via Montenapoleone, is fun for shoppers. This was the original Beverly Hills of Milan. In the 1920s, the top fashion shops moved in, and today it remains *the* place for designer labels. Most places close Sunday and for much of August. On Mondays, stores open only after 16:00. In this land where fur is still prized, the people-watching is as entertaining as the window-shopping. Notice also the exclusive penthouse apartments with roof gardens high above the scene. Via Montenapoleone and the pedestrianized Via Spiga are the best streets.

Whether you're gawking or shopping, here's the best route: From La Scala, walk up Via Manzoni to the Metro stop at Montenapoleone, browse down Via Montenapoleone, cut left on Via Santo Spirito (lined with grand aristocratic palazzos—peek into the courtyard at #7), turn right to window-shop down Via Spiga, turn right on Sant'Andrea and then left, back onto Montenapoleone, which leads you through a final gauntlet of temptations to Piazza San Babila. Then (for less expensive shopping thrills), walk back to the Duomo down the pedestrian-only Corso Vittorio Emanuele. From the Duomo, go down Via Dante to the Sforza Castle.

La Rinascente, next to the Duomo, is a Nordstrom-type department store with reasonable prices and a good toy selection (Mon–Sat 10:00–22:00, Sun 10:00–20:00, has a VAT refund office and recommended restaurant, faces north side of the Duomo on Piazza del Duomo).

Milan

NIGHTLIFE

For evening action, check out the artsy Brera area in the old center, with several swanky sidewalk cafés to choose from and lots of bars that stay open late. Home to Brera's Art University, this district has a sophisticated, lively people-watching scene. Another great neighborhood for nightlife is Navigli, Milan's formerly bohemian, now gentrified "Little Venice" (Metro: Porta Genova).

There are always concerts and live music playing in the city at various clubs and concert halls. Specifics change quickly, so it's best to rely on the entertainment information in periodicals from the TI.

SLEEPING

I've tried to minimize traffic-noise problems in my listings. All are within a few minutes' walk of Milan's subway system. With Milan's fine Metro, you can get anywhere in town in a flash. Anytime in March, April, September, and October, the city can be completely jammed by conventions, and hotel prices jump way up. I've listed high-season prices, but not convention-gouging prices. (For the convention schedule, see www.fieramilano.it.) Summer is usually wide-open and prices are discounted, though many hotels close in August for vacation. Hotels cater more to business travelers than to tourists, so Fridays and Saturdays are generally cheaper and available.

Near the Duomo

The Duomo area is thick with people-watching, reasonably priced eateries, and the major sightseeing attractions. From the central train station to the Duomo, it's just four stops on a direct Metro

---

Sleep Code

(€1 = about $1.30, country code: 39)
S = Single, **D** = Double/Twin, **T** = Triple, **Q** = Quad, **b** = bathroom, **s** = shower only. Unless otherwise noted, credit cards are accepted, English is spoken, and breakfast is included.

To help you sort easily through these listings, I've divided the rooms into three categories based on the price for a standard double room with bath:

  $$$ **Higher Priced**—Most rooms €150 or more.
   $$ **Moderately Priced**—Most rooms between €110–150.
    $ **Lower Priced**—Most rooms €110 or less.

line (yellow line 3, direction: San Donato) to Metro: Duomo.

$$$ Hotel Grand Duca di York, with 33 pleasant, newly refurbished rooms and lavish public spaces, is oddly stuck in the middle of banks and big-city starkness three blocks southwest of Piazza del Duomo (Sb-€128, Db-€188, Db with balconies-€218, air-con, elevator, closed Aug, near Metro stops: Cordusio or Duomo, Via Moneta 1, tel. 02-874-863, fax 02-869-0344, www .ducadiyork.com, info@ducadiyork.com).

$$$ Hotel Spadari boasts an Art Deco interior designed by the Milanese artist Giò Pomodoro ("Joe Tomato" in English). The 40 rooms have billowing drapes, big paintings, and designer doors. It's next door to the recommended Peck deli (see page 275), and two blocks from the Duomo (standard Db-€240, deluxe Db-€305, no need for the pricier suites, Via Spadari 11, tel. 02-7200-2371, fax 02-861-184, www.spadarihotel.com, reservation@spadarihotel .com).

$$ Hotel Santa Marta, a shiny little hotel on a small street, has 15 fresh, tranquil, and basic rooms (Db-€140, discounts for cash, air-con, elevator, closed Aug, Via Santa Marta 4, tel. 02-804-567, fax 02-8645-2661, www.hotel-santamarta.it, info@hotel -santamarta.it).

$$ Hotel Vecchia Milano has 27 decent, reasonably priced rooms with basic comforts and dim hallways in the heart of Milan's business district, a 10-minute walk from the Duomo (Db-€100–130, air-con, Via Borromei 4, tel. 02-875-042, fax 02-8645-4292, www.hotelvecchiamilano.it, hotelvecchiamilano@tiscali.it).

Between La Scala and the Sforza Castle

$$$ Hotel Star is a comfortable, modern 30-room place (Sb-€140, Db-€185, prices drop about €40 outside convention times, interior rooms are quieter, closed Aug, air-con, fridge, Via dei Bossi 5, tel. 02-801-501, fax 02-861-787, www.hotelstar.it, reception@hotelstar .it).

$$$ Antica Locanda dei Mercanti feels like a library in heaven, well-located and seriously quiet (no TVs, lots of books). It lacks public spaces and a breakfast area but comes with fresh flowers in each of its 14 rooms (Db-€163, Db with air-con and garden terrace-€300, optional €15 breakfast served in room, fans, elevator, no very young children, Via San Tomaso 6, Metro: Cordusio; tel. 02-805-4080, fax 02-805-4090, www.locanda.it, locanda @locanda.it).

$$$ Il Domus, a luxurious haven, offers 13 spacious, elegant, lovingly maintained rooms with down comforters, marble baths, and velvety carpets or parquet floors (Db-€175, pricier suites available, air-con, elevator, Via San Tomaso 8, tel. 02-805-1023, fax 02-805-4090, www.ildomus.it, info@ildomus.it).

Milan

Hotels and Restaurants in Central Milan

1. Hotel Grand Duca di York
2. Hotel Spadari & Peck Deli
3. Hotel Santa Marta
4. To Hotel Vecchia Milano & Hostaria Borromei
5. Hotel Star
6. Antica Locanda dei Mercanti & Il Domus
7. London Hotel
8. Trattoria Milanese
9. Ristorante Bruno
10. La Rinascente Dept. Store Restaurant
11. Latteria Cucina Veg.
12. Pastarito Pizzarito
13. Peck Italian Bar
14. Autogrill/Ciao Cafeteria
15. Ristorante Rita
16. Odeon Gelateria
17. Princi Bakeries (2)
18. Luini Panzerotti
19. Standa Superfresco Supermarket
20. Le Briciole Ristorante
21. Garbagnati Cafeteria
22. Caffè Vecchia Brera
23. To Brek Cafeterias (2)
24. McDonald's & Bar Zucca
25. Elevators to Duomo Roof (2)
26. Stairs to Duomo Roof

$$$ **London Hotel,** a simple 30-room hotel with all the amenities, is tucked away on a quiet street just off vibrant Via Dante. It's warmly run by the friendly Gambino family: mom and pop Elda and Franco don't speak English, but daughters Tanya and Licia do (S-€95, Sb-€110, D-€140, Db-€160, Tb-€200, skip their €8 breakfast and grab something on Via Dante, cheaper in July and Aug, book direct for these rates and get an additional 10 percent off with cash, air-con, elevator, near Metro: Cairoli at Via Rovello 3, on relatively quiet side street, tel. 02-7202-0166, fax 02-805-7037, www.hotellondonmilano.com, info@hotellondonmilano.com).

Near Porta Romana

$$$ **Hotel Piacenza** has 24 bright, cheery, and relaxing rooms and helpful friendly management (Sb-€100, Db-€150, air-con, Via Piacenza 4, Metro: Porta Romana, tel. 02-545-5041, fax 02-546-5269, www.hotelpiacenza.com, info@hotelpiacenza.com, Luciano takes good care of his guests).

$ **Hotel Sabotino** is a quirky, economical, grandmotherly place with 15 basic wood-paneled rooms sharing a long sunny balcony (S-€40, Sb-€75, D-€55, Db-€95, Db apartment-€95, elevator, Viale Sabotino 16, on sixth floor, Metro: Porta Romana, tel. 02-5830-8797, fax 02-5831-0400, www.hotelsabotino.com, info@hotelsabotino.com, Dea and Chiocco the poodle greet guests).

Near the Train Station

If you like to stay near the station, this is a handy, if dreary, area. In spite of its shady characters in the park and 55-year-old prostitutes after dark, the neighborhood between the train station and Corso Buenos Aires is reasonably safe. Many soulless business hotels have desperately discounted prices for those who drop in during slow times. Just walk down Via Scarlatti (with the tracks to your back, leave the station's upper hall to the left, cross the parking lot, and take the street to the left of the tallest building).

Here are some decent options:

$$$ **Hotel Florida** is a comfortable, well-maintained business-class hotel with 55 rooms on a quiet street one block from the station. Prices plummet for last-minute drop-ins outside of convention times (normally Db-€220, often more like €130, Via Lepetit 33, tel. 02-670-5921, fax 02-669-2867, www.hotelfloridamilan.com, info@hotelfloridamilan.com).

$ **"The Best" Hotel,** a five-minute walk from the station, rents 28 simple rooms and offers a peaceful garden terrace in the middle of the bustling city. The staff is hardworking and the price is great, making this a fine value (Sb-€50–60, Db-€65–85, air-con Jun–Aug only, Via B. Marcello 83, tel. 02-2940-4757, fax 02-201-966, www.thebesthotel.it, info@thebesthotel.it, helpful, friendly

Filippo and Riccardo). From Via Scarlatti (see above), turn right onto Via B. Marcello and follow it a half-block down.

$ Hotel Valley is homey, small (just 11 rooms), ordinary, and inexpensive (Ss-€35, Sb-€40, Ds-€50, Db-€60, Tb-€80, free Internet access, Via Soperga 19, tel. & fax 02-6698-7252, www .hotelvalley.it, info@hotelvalley.it, Rocco). It's three long blocks from the station: Exit station to the left, then turn left onto Via Lepetit, which becomes Via Soperga.

Hostels in Milan

For beds costing about €20, consider Milan's hostels. Most are away from the center, but I've listed one (la Cordata) closer to town.

$ Ostello la Cordata, a good choice, has some singles and doubles (€18 for beds in 6-, 8-, and 16-bed dorms; or hotel-type rooms on the second floor—Sb-€40, Db-€70, Tb-€90; reserve ahead, check in 14:00–22:00, free Internet access, Via Burigozzo 11, Metro: Missori—on the yellow line, tel. 02-583-14675, fax 02-5830-3598, www.ostellimilano.it—click on "Ostello via Burigozzo," ostello@lacordata.it).

The larger **$ AIG Piero Rotta** offers cheap, basic accommodation with a simple breakfast (€19.50 beds in 6-bed dorms, or men-only 3-bed rooms, hostel membership required, non-members pay more, near Metro: QT8—on the red line, at Viale Salmoiraghi 1, tel. 02-392-67095, fax 02-3300-0191, www.ostellomilano.it, milano@ostellionline.it).

EATING

This is a fast-food city, but fast food in a fashion capital isn't a burger and fries. Milan's bars, delis, *rosticcerìe,* and self-service cafeterias cater to people with plenty of taste and more money than time. You'll find delightful eateries all over town (but many close in Aug for vacation).

I find the price difference between basic and classy restaurants to be negligible (for example, pastas-€7–12, *secondi*-€12–20, cover-€1–3), so it's worth springing for the places that give the best experience. To eat mediocre food on a famous street with great people-watching, choose an eatery on the pedestrian-only Via Mercanti or Via Dante. To eat with students in trendy little trattorias, explore the Brera neighborhood. To eat well near the Duomo, consider the recommended places below.

Locals like to precede a lunch or dinner with an *aperitivo* (while Campari made its debut in Milan, a simple glass of *vino bianco* or *prosecco,* the Italian champagne, is just as popular). Bars fill their counters with inviting baskets of munchies, which are

Milanese Specialties

Milan's signature dishes (often served together as a *piatto unico*, or "single dish") are *risotto alla milanese* and *ossobuco*. The risotto is flavored with saffron, which gives it its intense yellow color. It's said that a 16th-century Belgian glassworker first stumbled on the use of saffron as a spice. Initially, he used saffron to tint the glass mixture for completing the stained-glass windows of the Duomo in 1574. His master joked that he'd end up adding the precious spice to his food as well. On the day of his master's daughter's wedding, the glassworker persuaded the chef to add saffron to the rice cooked for the reception. After the guests got over their initial surprise, the dish was a great success, and has been a staple on Milan's menus ever since. The subtle flavor of the saffron pairs nicely with the *ossobuco* (meaning "marrow," or literally "hole in the bone" of the veal shank). The prized marrow is extracted with special little forks and considered the best part of the meal.

served free with these drinks, at about 17:00. A cheap drink (if you're either likable or discreet) can become a light meal. For example, check out the wonderful buffet spread at Bar Brera (see page 277).

Breakfast is a bad value in hotels and fun on Via Dante or in bars. It's OK to quasi-picnic. Bring in a banana (or whatever) and order a toasted ham-and-cheese sandwich (called and pronounced *tost*) or brioche with your cappuccino.

Near the Duomo
Dining with Class
Trattoria Milanese, sophisticated and family-run, is a splurge. It has an enthusiastic and local clientele—the restaurant didn't even bother to get a phone until 1988. Expect a Milanese ambience and quality traditional local cuisine (Mon–Fri 12:00–14:45 & 19:00–22:45, closed Sat–Sun and mid-July–Aug, air-con, Via Santa Marta 11, 5-min walk from the Duomo, near Pinacoteca Ambrosiana, tel. 02-8645-1991).

Ristorante Bruno serves Tuscan cuisine with a passion for fresh fish. This place impresses with its dressy waiters, hearty food, inexpensive desserts, and a fine self-serve antipasto buffet (a plate full of Tuscan specialties for €8). You can eat inside or on the sidewalk under fascist columns (Sun–Fri 12:00–14:45 & 19:00–22:45, closed Sat and Aug, moderate prices, air-con, Via M. Gonzaga 6, reservations wise, tel. 02-804-364). Giuseppe (from Volterra) and Graziella take good care of their eaters.

Hostaria Borromei is where Milanese yuppies go for power lunches to impress clients with market-fresh, typical Lombardy dishes. Dine under an awning of vines in an elegant, mellow-yellow interior courtyard or in their cantina-chic dining rooms. Reservations are recommended (€13 pastas, €18–20 *secondi*, includes cover and service, Mon–Fri 12:30–14:45 & 19:30–22:45, Sat 19:30–22:45, closed Sun, Via Borromei 4, tel. 02-8645-3760).

Duomo Views on a Terrace: The La Rinascente department store, alongside the Duomo, has a recently renovated eighth-floor eatery with views of the cathedral's rooftop (anyone can pop up for a look at the cathedral). While you can go through the department store to take escalators to the top, it's faster to take the elevator (just inside the side entrance, on the Galleria Vittorio Emanuele side).

Eating Simply

Latteria Cucina Vegetariana is a bright hole-in-the-wall that serves a good vegetarian Italian lunch. This busy joint is overrun with tables, where local workers enjoy soup, salads, pastas, and imaginative veggie entrées at affordable prices. Try the €13 *piatto misto al forno* for a delicious assortment of soufflés, quiches, and roasted and sautéed veggies (€8–13 meals, Mon–Sat 11:45–16:30, closed Sun, just off Via Torino at Via dell'Unione 6, 2 blocks southwest of the Duomo, tel. 02-874-401). Giorgio is a hit with camera-toting eaters.

Pastarito Pizzarito is a pasta-and-pizza chain with a wonderful formula. In a bright atmosphere under literal walls of pasta, you can choose from 10 fresh big pastas and lots of sauces to create a huge dish (€5–11). Splitting is welcome. Find plenty of seating on the ground floor or upstairs. Pizzas run €4–10, large salads are €7, and the wine is reasonably priced (daily 12:00–14:30 & 19:30–23:00, air-con, 4 blocks from the Duomo, a block behind opera house at Via Verdi 6, tel. 02-862-210).

Peck Italian Bar is a hit with the sophisticated office crowd, who mob the place at lunch for its fast, excellent meals. It's owned by the same people who run the high-end Peck deli (see listing under "Picnics"), so be prepared to spend—this place's classiness alone makes it worth the money. And any time you find yourself among such a quality-conscious group of Milanesi, you know you're getting good food (€12 pastas, €18 *secondi*, Mon–Sat 11:30–20:30, closed Sun, Via Cantu 3, tel. 02-869-3017).

Ciao, a self-service cafeteria, offers a low-stress, affordable meal above a fast-food arcade on Piazza del Duomo (daily 11:30–23:00, inexpensive pasta and good salad bar, easy public WC). It's to the right of the Galleria entrance—enter through the ground floor Autogrill and go up to the second floor.

Ristorante Rita, a block behind Ciao, is a classier budget option (€4–5 pastas and *secondi*) without the Italian fast-food feel. While the downstairs has a take-out place, there's a sleek, modern restaurant upstairs with good food and cafeteria prices (Mon–Sat 12:00–15:00, closed Sun, on Via Marconi between Piazza del Duomo and Piazza Diaz, tel. 02-8699-7387).

Fast-food cheapskates enjoy the best people-watching in Milan inside the Galleria at **McDonald's** (long hours daily, salad/pasta plate and tall orange juice for €5).

Gelato: Floodlit Mary gazes down on the **Odeon Gelateria** from the top of the Duomo for good reason (next to McDonald's on Piazza del Duomo, on far side of square opposite Duomo facade, open nightly until 24:00).

Picnics

For a fun adventure, assemble an elegant dinner picnic by hitting the colorful deli, cheese, and produce shops on Via Speronari. The **Princi bakery** is mobbed with locals vying for focaccia, olive breadsticks, and luscious pastries. For most pastry items (like the brioche), pay the cashier first; for items sold by weight (such as pizza and cake), get it weighed before you pay (Mon–Sat 7:00–20:00, closed Sun, on Via Speronari, off Via Torino, a block southwest of Piazza del Duomo). At the small bar in the back, you get free, fresh munchies with your drink at about 17:00, or you can try a cheap meal (about €5 per plate, 12:00–14:00 only).

Peck is an aristocratic deli with a fancy cafè/lunchroom/pastry/gelato shop upstairs, a gourmet grocery and *rosticceria* on the main level, and an expensive *enoteca* wine cellar in the basement. Even if all you can afford is the aroma, peek in. Check out the gourmet assembly-line action in the kitchen in the back (Mon 15:30–19:30, Tue–Sat 9:15–19:30, closed Sun, Via Spadari 9, tel. 02-802-3161). The *rosticceria* serves fancy food to-go for a superb picnic dinner in your hotel. It's delectable, beautiful, sold by weight (order by the *etto*—100-gram unit, 250 grams equals about a half-pound), and pricey. Try the risotto.

Luini Panzerotti serves up piping-hot mini-calzones (*panzerotti*) stuffed with mozzarella, tomatoes, ham, or whatever you like for €3–5 (Tue–Sat 10:00–20:00, Mon 10:00–15:00, closed Sun and Aug, Via S. Radegonda 16, tel. 02-8646-1917). From the back of the Duomo, head north and look for the lines of hungry locals out front. Order from the small menus posted behind the cash registers. Traditionally, Milanesi munch their hot little meals on nearby Piazza San Fedele.

Standa Superfresco supermarket is within a few blocks of the Duomo (Mon–Sat 8:00–20:30, Sun 9:00–20:00, small deli on ground level, big supermarket in basement, on Via Torino at intersection with San Maurilio).

Near the Sforza Castle

Le Briciole, run by the Campenella family, is small and dressy, drawing a local crowd for its quality Ligurian cuisine (pesto, seafood) and friendly family feel (homemade pastas-€10, daily 12:15–14:30 & 19:15–22:30; closed Fri evening, Sat lunch, and all of Aug; Via Camperio 17, a block in front of castle, on small street at end of Via Dante, tel. 02-877-185).

Garbagnati is a tasty self-service cafeteria at Via Dante 13, near several recommended hotels and a couple of blocks in front of the castle. This is *the* place to enjoy elegant boulevard seating at self-service prices (no cover charge to sit at sidewalk tables before 15:00). For half the price of a lousy hotel breakfast, you can eat here and have a truly memorable morning meal. At lunch (daily 12:00–15:00), join the local workers on the cafeteria line (Mon–Fri 7:30–20:00, Sat–Sun 8:00–20:00, tel. 02-8646-0672).

The **Princi** bakery near the castle works the same as the one on Via Speronari (described on page 276), only it's more of a café with seating. The ground floor has cafeteria-style service; you'll pay more for full service in the basement. Or you can get your pizza, sandwiches, and pastries to-go (Mon–Sat 7:00–20:00, closed Sun, Via Ponte Vetero 10, tel. 02-7201-6067). At lunchtime, they serve up delicious homemade €5 pastas and €5–7 *secondi* courses to in-the-know locals (12:00–15:00 only).

In the Brera Neighborhood

To locate these eateries, see maps on pages 249 and 271.

The Brera neighborhood that surrounds the Church of St. Carmine is laced with narrow, inviting pedestrian streets. Make an evening of your visit by having an *aperitivo* (pre-dinner drink) with snacks at recommended Bar Brera (below) or any bar—most serve munchies with pre-dinner drinks from 17:00–21:00. Afterwards, stroll along restaurant row (Via Fiori Chiari) to survey the sidewalk cafés. The first place, **Al Treno di Mezzanotte,** is the most expensive and charming—choose between a classy, 19th-century train dining car, or elegant dining rooms and an Art Nouveau courtyard. **Ristorante Nabucco** comes recommended by locals and is a bit less expensive with the same fare, while **Trattoria dell'Angolo** offers better value with less character. Branch off onto parallel streets for other options, but less people-watching.

Obikà, on the corner of Ponte Vetero and Pontaccio, is a trendy mozzarella bar with a sleek, minimalist sushi-bar feel, featuring fresh cow, buffalo, or smoked mozzarella; big organic gourmet salads; and top-quality *salumi* (€9 pastas, daily 12:00–15:30 & 16:00–23:30, Via Ponte Vetero 28, tel. 02-8645-0568).

Bar Brera, across the street from the Brera Art Gallery, serves salads, sandwiches, and pastas to throngs of art students.

During happy hour (daily 17:00–21:00), have a seat, order a drink, and then help yourself to the buffet, which has a generous variety of antipasti from marinated veggies to prosciutto (buffet is free if you buy drinks, otherwise €6; bar open daily 6:00–2:00 in the morning, great streetside seating, Via Brera 23, tel. 02-877-091).

Caffè Vecchia Brera dishes up tempting sandwiches, €5–7 savory and sweet crêpes, and splittable €10 salads, and has full restaurant service (€7.50 pastas, €8–13 *secondi*, great €5 happy-hour buffet 17:00–21:00 that includes a drink, Mon–Sat 8:00–24:00, closed Sun, Via dell'Orso 20, tel. 02-8646-1695).

Eating Cheaply near Montenapoleone

For inexpensive, healthy food near the classy shopping street, **Brek** cafeterias are good. One Brek is near one end of Montenapoleone (daily 11:30–15:00 & 18:30–22:30; Via dell'Annunciata 2, two blocks from Montenapoleone; tel. 02-653-619), and another is near the other end, a half-block off Piazza San Babila (daily 12:00–15:00 & 18:30–22:30, Piazza Giordano 1, tel. 02-7602-3379, just off Piazza Babila; with back to "egg monument" and facing fountain, Brek is through arch in building on right).

TRANSPORTATION CONNECTIONS

From Milan by Train to: Venice (at least hourly, most departures at :05 and :55 past the hour, 3–4 hrs), **Florence** (at least hourly, high speed ES trains depart on the hour, 3 hrs, also look for trains going to Rome and Naples that stop in Florence), **Genoa** (about hourly, 2 hrs, also look for trains to La Spezia or Livorno that stop at Genoa), **Rome** (hourly, 4–7 hrs, overnight possible), **Brindisi** (4 direct/day, 9–12 hrs, more with changes), **Cinque Terre/La Spezia** (hourly, most at :10 past the hour, 3–4 hrs, may change in Genoa; trains from La Spezia to the villages go nearly hourly), **Cinque Terre/Monterosso al Mare** (hourly, most at :10 past the hour, 3–4 hrs, may change in Sestri Levante or Genoa), **Varenna** on Lake Como (small line to Lecco/Sondrio/Tirano leaves at 8:15, 9:15, 12:15, 14:15, 16:15, 18:00, 19:08, 20:08, and 21:08, confirm these times locally, 1 hr), **Stresa** on Lake Maggiore (about hourly, 1–1.5 hrs; also look for trains to Domodossola and some international destinations that stop at Stresa), **Como** (at least hourly at :25 or :45 past the hour, 1 hr, ferries go from Como to Varenna until 19:00), **Naples** (hourly, 6.5–9 hrs, longer with change in Rome).

International Destinations: Amsterdam (6/day, 14 hrs, changes required), **Barcelona** (13–20 hours, several with 2–5 changes, consider flying), **Bern** (6/day some with change in Brig, 3–4 hrs), **Frankfurt** (8/day, 9–10 hrs with changes), **London** (4/day, 12–18 hrs with changes), **Munich** (5/day, 8–10 hrs with changes), **Nice** (7/day, 4 with transfer, 5–6.5 hrs), **Paris** (5/day, 7 hrs), **Lyon** (5/day, 6 hrs with changes), **Vienna** (8/day, 11–14 hrs with changes).

Airports

To get flight information for either airport or the current phone number of your airline, call 02-74851 and wait for English options, or try 02-7485-2200.

Malpensa Airport

Most international flights land at the manageable Malpensa Airport, 28 miles northwest of Milan. Customs guards fan you through, and even the customs dog seems friendly. You'll most likely land at Terminal 1 (international flights), rather than Terminal 2 (charter flights); buses connect the two. Both have ATMs (at Terminal 1, between exit 4 and 5 at Banca Nazionale del Lavoro), banks, and exchange offices. Terminal 1 has a pharmacy, eateries, and a hotel reservation service disguised as a TI (daily 7:00–23:00; when you exit the baggage-carousel area, go right to reach services and exit; tel. 02-5858-0080). At the *tabacchi* shop, buy a phone card and confirm your hotel reservation.

You have three easy ways to get to downtown Milan: by train, shuttle bus, or taxi.

By Train: The Malpensa Express zips between Malpensa Airport and Milan's Cadorna station, which is both a Metro stop and a small train station, closer to the Duomo than the central train station (€11, 40 min, 2/hr; departing airport at :23 and :53 past the hour from 5:53–22:23, departing Cadorna at :27 and :57 past the hour from 5:57–21:27, not covered by railpasses, www .malpensaexpress.it). At the airport, as you pop out through customs, you'll see a *Treno per Malpensa* kiosk selling tickets and a big electric reader-board on the wall indicating how many minutes until the next departure. Follow signs (*Treni* and *Malpensa Express*) down the stairs to the tracks. If you're leaving Milan to go to the airport, take the Metro to the Cadorna stop, surface, and buy a ticket at the Malpensa Express office in the station. Purchase your ticket before you board, or you'll pay €2.50 extra to buy it on the train. Trains depart Cadorna from track 1. Note that there are some earlier and later departures to and from Cadorna by bus—ask when you buy your ticket. If your departure is by bus, the stop is outside the station; head left as you exit, and the stop is 50 yards to the left on Via Paleocapa.

By Bus: Two bus companies offer virtually identical, competing services between Malpensa Airport and Milan's central train station. They each charge about €5 for the 50-minute trip (buy ticket from driver) and depart from the same places: in front

Train Connections from Milan

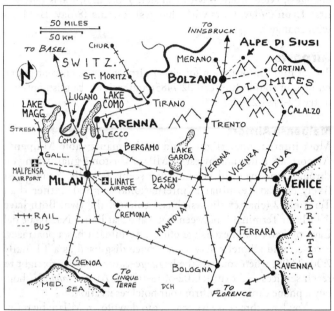

of the airport (outside exit 5, at stops 2 and 3) and from Piazza Luigi di Savoia (east side of Milan's train station). You'll generally find a bus leaving about every 15 minutes, every day, nearly all day (from downtown roughly 4:30–23:00 and from the airport roughly 5:30–24:15, tel. 02-5858-3185, www.malpensashuttle.it).

By Taxi: Taxis into Milan cost €70 (more if there's heavy traffic, insist on meter; you'll pay supplements on Sun, holidays, and early or late; avoid hustlers in airport halls, catch taxis outside exit 6). Considering how far the city is from the airport and how good the train and bus services are, Milan is the last place I'd take a taxi to the airport. To get from Milan to the airport, I taxi to the Cadorna station and then catch the Malpensa Express train.

Sleeping near Malpensa: **$ Hotel Cervo** offers 28 fresh rooms and transfers to and from the nearby airport for €3 per person (Sb-€72, Db-€103, air-con, airplane noise, restaurant open Mon–Sat 19:00–22:00, free parking, Via de Pinedo 1, Somma Lombardo, Fraz. Case Nuove, Malpensa, tel. 0331-230-821, fax 0331-230-156, www.hotelcervo.it, hotelcervo@malpensa.it).

Getting Between Malpensa and Linate: The Malpensa Shuttle company runs a bus between the airports about hourly (€9, runs 7:50–24:25, 75 min, catch bus outside Malpensa's exit 4, stops 20 and 21, buy tickets from Thomas Cook or Airport 2000 offices; coming from Linate, buses depart 4:30–21:30, bus stops at Malpensa's Terminal 1—you must request stop if you need Terminal 2; tel. 02-5858-3185, wait for English recording, www .malpensashuttle.it).

Linate Airport

Most European flights fly into Linate, five miles east of Milan. The airport has a bank (just past customs, ATM, decent rates) and a hotel-finding service disguised as a TI (daily 7:30–23:30, tel. 02-7020-0443).

You can get to downtown Milan by bus or taxi (or to Malpensa Airport by bus; see above).

By Bus: Two different buses—Starfly and ATM—take you from Linate Airport to downtown. The Starfly bus zips you to the central train station (buy €3 ticket from driver, 3/hr, 30 min, bus runs from airport 6:05–23:35, from station 5:40–21:35, leaves from east side of station at Piazza Luigi di Savoia). The cheaper ATM city bus gets you to the San Babila Metro stop (specifically to Corso Europa, just around the corner from Piazza San Babila and its Metro station; from here it's one stop to the Duomo on red line 1, direction: Molino Dorino or Bisceglie, or a 7-min walk). The bus costs €1, departs every 10 minutes, and takes 20 minutes (departures leaving city center 5:35–24:35, from airport 6:05–24:55). Either bus company works fine: Wait for the one that's handier to your hotel, or hop on the first one that shows up. From where it drops you off, take the Metro or a taxi to your hotel. Both buses leave from outside the arrival hall.

By Taxi: Taxis from Linate to the Duomo cost about €18.

THE CINQUE TERRE

The Cinque Terre (CHINK-weh TAY-reh), a remote chunk of the Italian Riviera, is the traffic-free, lowbrow, underappreciated alternative to the French Riviera. There's not a museum in sight. Just sun, sea, sand (pebbles), wine, and pure, unadulterated Italy. Enjoy the villages, swimming, hiking, and evening romance of one of God's great gifts to tourism. For a home base, choose among five *(cinque)* villages, each of which fills a ravine with a lazy hive of human activity—callused locals, sunburned travelers, and almost no Vespas. While the Cinque Terre is now discovered, I've never seen happier, more relaxed tourists.

The chunk of coast was first described in medieval times as "the five lands." In the feudal era, this land was watched over by castles. Tiny communities grew up in their protective shadows, ready to run inside at the first hint of a Turkish Saracen pirate raid. Marauding pirates from North Africa were a persistent problem until about 1400. Many locals were kidnapped and ransomed or sold into slavery, and those who remained built fires on flat-roofed watchtowers to relay warnings—alerting the entire coast to imminent attacks. The last major raid was in 1545.

As the threat of pirates faded, the villages prospered, catching fish and growing grapes. Churches were enlarged with a growing population. But until the advent of tourism in this generation, the towns remained isolated. Even today, traditions survive, and each of the five villages comes with a distinct dialect and its own proud heritage.

Sadly, a few ugly, noisy Americans are giving tourism a bad name here. Even hip, young locals are put off by loud, drunken tourists. They say—and I agree—that the Cinque Terre is an exceptional place. It deserves a special dignity. Party in Viareggio or Portofino, but be mellow in the Cinque Terre. Talk softly. Help keep it clean. In spite of the tourist crowds, it's still a real community, and we are its guests.

In this chapter, I cover the five towns in order from east to west, from Riomaggiore to Monterosso. Since I still get the names of the towns mixed up, I think of them by number: #1 Riomaggiore (a workaday town), #2 Manarola (picturesque), #3 Corniglia (on a hilltop), #4 Vernazza (the region's cover girl, the most touristy and dramatic), and #5 Monterosso al Mare (the closest thing to a beach resort of the five towns).

Arrival in the Cinque Terre

Big, fast trains from elsewhere in Italy speed past the Cinque Terre (though some stop in Monterosso). Unless you're coming from a nearby town, you'll have to change trains at least once to reach Riomaggiore, Manarola, Corniglia, or Vernazza.

Generally, if you're coming from the north, you'll be changing trains in Genoa (specifically, the Genova Piazza Principe station). If you're coming from the south or east, you'll most likely have to switch trains in La Spezia (see "Transportation Connections" on page 338). No matter where you're coming from, it's best to check in the station before you leave to see your full schedule and route options (use the computerized kiosks or ask at a ticket window). *Don't forget to validate your ticket by stamping it*—ka-CHUNK!—*in the yellow machines located on train platforms and elsewhere in the station*. See page 285 for more information on riding the train between Cinque Terre towns.

If the Cinque Terre is your first, last, or only stop on this trip, consider flying into Pisa, Genoa, or Florence, rather than Milan. These airports are less confusing than Milan's, and closer to the Cinque Terre as well.

Planning Your Time

The ideal minimum stay is two nights and a completely uninterrupted day. The Cinque Terre is served by the local train from Genoa and La Spezia. Speed demons arrive in the morning, check their bags in La Spezia, take the five-hour hike through all five towns, laze away the afternoon on the beach or rock of their choice, and zoom away on the overnight train to somewhere back in the real world. But be warned: The Cinque Terre has a strange way of messing up your momentum. (The evidence is the number of Americans who have fallen in love with both the region and/or one of its residents, and ended up staying here.) Frankly, staying fewer than two nights is a mistake that you'll likely regret.

The towns are just a few minutes apart by hourly train or boat.

There's no checklist of sights or experiences—just a hike, the towns themselves, and your fondest vacation desires. Study this chapter in advance and piece together your best day, mixing hiking, swimming, trains, and a boat ride. For the best light and coolest temperatures, start your hike early.

Market days perk up the towns from 8:00 to 13:00 on Tuesday in Vernazza, Wednesday in Levanto (covered in next chapter), Thursday in Monterosso, and Friday in La Spezia (see next chapter).

The winter is really dead—most hotels close in December and January. Easter weekend (March 21–24 in 2008) and July through August are peak of peak, the toughest time to find rooms. In spring, the towns can feel inundated with Italian school groups day-tripping on spring excursions (they can't afford to sleep in this expensive region). For more information on the region, see www.cinqueterre.it.

The Cinque Terre National Park

The creation of the Cinque Terre National Marine Park in 1999 has brought lots of money (all visitors pay a fee to hike the trails), new restrictions on land and sea to protect wildlife, and lots of concrete bolstering walkways, trails, beaches, breakwaters, and docks. Each village has a park-sponsored information center and two towns have tiny folk museums. The park is run by a powerful man—nicknamed "The Pharaoh" for his grandiose visions—who seems to double as Riomaggiore's mayor. (Powerful as he is, he can't seem to arrange a place for visitors to deposit their bags when between hotels.) For the latest, see www.parconazionale5terre.it.

Cinque Terre Cards

Visitors hiking between the towns need to pay a park entrance fee. This fee keeps the trails safe and open, and pays for viewpoints, picnic spots, WCs, and more. The popular coastal trail generates enough revenue to subsidize the development of trails and outdoor activities higher in the hills.

You have two options for covering the park fee: the Cinque Terre Card (the better deal) or the Cinque Terre Treno Card. Note that both are valid until midnight on the expiration date.

The **Cinque Terre Card,** good for one day of hiking, costs €5 (includes map, €8/2 days, €10/3 days, €20/7 days; kids under 4 free, discounts for youth, seniors, and families, see park website—listed above—for details). It covers all trails, shuttle buses, and park museums, but not trains or boats. Buy it at trailheads, at national park offices, and at most train stations (no validation required).

The **Cinque Terre Treno Card** covers what the Cinque Terre Card does, plus the use of the local trains (from Levanto to La

The Cinque Terre

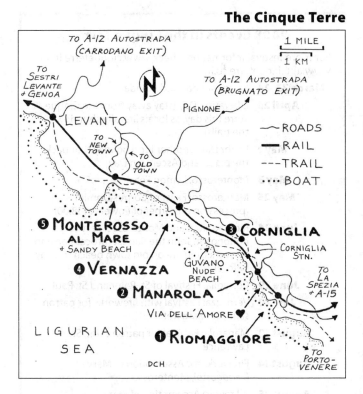

Spezia, including all Cinque Terre towns). It's sold at TIs inside train stations, but not at trailheads, and comes with a map, information brochure, and train schedule (€8/1 day, €13.50/2 days, €18.50/3 days, €34/week, kids 4–11 half-price, under 4 free; validate card at train station by punching it in the yellow machine). This card is not a good value, because you'd have to hike and take three train trips every day just to break even. Who needs the pressure?

Getting Around the Cinque Terre

Within the Cinque Terre, you'll get around the villages more cheaply by train, but more scenically by boat.

By Train

Along the coast here, trains go in only two directions: "per (to) Genova" (the Italian spelling of Genoa) or "per La Spezia." Assuming you're on vacation, accept the unpredictability of Cinque Terre trains (they're often late...unless you are, too—in which case they're on time). Relax while you wait—buy a cup of coffee at a station bar. When the train comes (know which direction to look for: La Spezia or Genova), casually walk over and hop on. This is

2008 Events in the Cinque Terre

For more festival information, check www.cinqueterre.it and www.aptcinqueterre.sp.it.

March 23–24   Easter Sunday and Monday

April 25   Liberation Day (stay away from the Cinque Terre this day, as locals literally shut down the trails)

May 1   Labor Day (another local holiday that packs the place) and Ascension Day

May 3   Monterosso: Lemon Feast

May 25   Monterosso: Feast of Corpus Domini (procession on carpet of flowers at 18:00)

June 24   Riomaggiore and Monterosso: Festival in honor of St. John the Baptist (procession and fireworks; big fire on old town beach the day before)

June 29   Corniglia: Festival of St. Peter and St. Paul

July 20   Vernazza: Festival with fireworks for patron saint, St. Margaret

August 10   Manarola: Festival for patron saint, St. Lawrence

August 14   Fireworks for Assumption of Mary (*Ferragosto*), Monterosso

August 15   All towns: Assumption of Mary

September 6   Monterosso: Salted anchovies and olive oil festival

especially easy in Monterosso, with its fine café-with-a-view on track #1 (direction: Milano/Genova).

Use the handy TV monitors in the station to make sure you're headed for the right platform. Most of the northbound trains that stop at all Cinque Terre towns and are headed toward Genova will list Sestri Levante as the *destinazione*.

By train, the five towns are just a few minutes apart. Know your stop. After the train leaves the town before your destination, go to the door and get ready to slip out before the mob packs in. Words to the wise for novice tourists, who often miss their stop: The stations are small and the trains are long, so you might have to get off deep in a tunnel. Also, the doors don't open automatically—you may have to flip open the handle of the door yourself. If a door isn't working, go quickly to the next car to leave. (When leaving a town by train, if you find the platform jammed with people, walk down the platform into the tunnel where things quiet down—though not so far that you've passed the platform.)

It's cheap to buy individual train tickets to travel between the towns. Since a one-town hop costs the same as a five-town hop (about €1) and every ticket is good for six hours with stop-overs, save money and explore the region in one direction on one ticket. Or buy a round-trip ticket from one end to the other of the region (e.g., round-trip from Monterosso to Riomaggiore and back)—it functions as a six-hour pass. Stamp the ticket at the station machine before you board. Riding without a validated ticket is very expensive (minimum €25 fine) if you meet a conductor. If you have a Eurailpass, don't spend one of your valuable flexi-days on the cheap Cinque Terre.

In general, I'd skip the train from Riomaggiore to Manarola (the trains are unreliable, and the 15-min Via dell'Amore stroll is a delight—see page 289 for more on this path).

Cinque Terre Train Schedule: Since the train is the Cinque Terre's lifeline, many shops and restaurants post the current schedule, and most hotels offer copies of it. Carry a copy of it—it'll come in handy (comes with Cinque Terre Card). Note that fast trains leaving La Spezia zip right through the Cinque Terre, and stop only in Monterosso. But the trains on the following schedule will stop at all five Cinque Terre towns. All of the below times are accurate as of 2007; most are daily and a few run Monday through Saturday, while others (not listed here) operate only on Sundays.

Trains leave La Spezia for the Cinque Terre villages at 7:12, 7:55, 10:07, 11:10, 12:00, 13:17, 14:06, 15:10, 15:25, 16:01, 17:05, 17:12, 17:25, 18:60, 19:10, 19:40, 20:18, 21:21, 23:10, and 00:50.

Going back to La Spezia, trains leave Monterosso at 6:32, 7:12, 8:13, 9:29, 10:20, 11:00, 12:06, 12:19, 13:26, 14:09, 14:20, 15:24, 15:43, 16:07, 16:17, 17:30, 18:02, 18:08, 18:20, 19:24, 20:21, 21:32, 22:24, 23:21, and 23:50 (same trains depart Vernazza about four minutes later).

Convenient TV monitors posted at several places in each station clearly show exactly what times the next trains are leaving in each direction (and if they're late, how late they are expected to be). I trust these monitors much more than my ability to read any printed schedule.

By Boat

From Easter through October, a daily boat service connects Monterosso, Vernazza, Manarola, Riomaggiore, and Portovenere. Boats provide a scenic way to get from town to town and survey what you just hiked. And boats offer the only efficient way to visit the nearby resort of Portovenere (see next chapter; the alternative is a tedious train/bus connection via La Spezia). In peaceful weather, the boats can be more reliable than the trains, but if seas are rough, they don't run at all. Because the boats nose in and tourists have to gingerly disembark onto little more than a plank, even a small chop can cancel some or all of the stops.

I see the tour boats as a syringe, injecting each town with a boost of euros. The towns are addicted, and they shoot up hourly through the summer. (Between 10:00 and 15:00—especially on weekends—masses of gawkers unload from boats, tour buses, and cruise ships, inundating the villages and changing the tenor of the region.)

Boats depart Monterosso about hourly (10:30–18:00), stopping at the Cinque Terre towns (except at Corniglia) and ending up an hour later in Portovenere. (The Portovenere–Monterosso boats run 9:00–17:00.) The ticket price depends on the length of the boat ride (e.g., Monterosso to Riomaggiore or Manarola-€11.50, Monterosso–Vernazza-€3.50, Vernazza–Manarola-€5.50, Vernazza–Riomaggiore-€6.50, Riomaggiore–Manarola-€2). Round-trip tickets are slightly cheaper than getting two one-way trips. You can buy tickets at little stands at each town's harbor (tel. 0187-732-987 and 0187-818-440). An all-day boat pass, covering the Cinque Terre towns, is about €16. Another all-day boat pass extends to Portovenere and includes a 40-minute, scenic ride around three small islands (2/day, about €20). Boats are not covered by the Cinque Terre Card. Boat schedules are posted at docks, harbor bars, Cinque Terre park offices, and hotels.

By Shuttle Bus

Shuttle buses connect each Cinque Terre town with distant parking lots and various points in the hills (for example, from Corniglia's beach and train station to its hilltop town center). Most rides cost €1.50 (and are covered by the Cinque Terre Card)—pick up bus schedules from a Cinque Terre park office or note the times posted on bus doors and at bus stops.

Hiking the Cinque Terre

All five towns are connected by good trails. You'll experience the area's best by hiking all the way from one end to the other. While you can detour to dramatic hilltop sanctuaries, I'd keep it simple by following the easy red-and-white-marked low trail between the villages. The entire seven-mile hike can be done in about four hours, but allow five for dawdling. Germans (with their task-oriented *Alpenstock* walking sticks) are notorious for marching too fast through the region (the record, however, is held by an American—my son, Andy Steves: 1 hour, 31 minutes). Take it slow...smell the cactus flowers and herbs, notice the lizards, listen to birds singing in the olive groves, and enjoy vistas on all sides.

Via dell'Amore

The Cinque Terre towns were extremely isolated until the last century. Villagers rarely married anyone from outside their

town. After the blasting of the second train line in the 1920s, a trail was made between the first two towns of the five: Riomaggiore and Manarola. A gunpowder warehouse was built along the way, safely away from the townspeople. (That building is today's Bar dell'Amore.)

Happy with the trail, the villagers asked that it be improved as a permanent connection between neighbors. But persistent landslides kept the trail closed more often than it was open. After World War II, the trail was reopened, and became established as a lovers' meeting point for boys and girls from the two towns. (After one extended closure in 1949, the trail was reopened for a Christmas marriage.) A journalist, who noticed all the amorous graffiti along the path, coined the trail's now-established name, "Via dell'Amore."

This new lane changed the social dynamics between the two villages, and made life much more fun and interesting for courting couples. Today, many tourists are put off by the cluttered graffiti that lines the trail. But it's all part of the history of the Cinque Terre's little lovers' lane.

You'll see a cluster of padlocks under the tunnel, on the Manarola side. Closing a padlock with your lover onto a cable or railing at a lovey-dovey spot—often a bridge—is the current craze in Italy, having been re-popularized by a teen novel. In case you're so inclined, the hardware store next to Bar Centrale in Riomaggiore sells these locks.

The big news a few years ago was the completion of major construction work—including the addition of tunnels—to make the trail safer and keep it open permanently. Notice how the brick-lined arcades match the train tunnel below. Rock climbers from the north ("Dolomite spiders") were imported to help with the treacherous construction work. As you hike, look up and notice the massive steel netting bolted to the cliff side. Look down at the boulders that fell before the nets were added, and be thankful for those Dolomite spiders.

Trails can be closed in bad weather or because of landslides. Remember that hikers need to pay a fee to enter the trails (see "Cinque Terre Cards," page 284). If you're hiking the entire five-town route, consider that the trails between Riomaggiore (#1), Manarola (#2), and Corniglia (#3) are easiest. The trail from Vernazza (#4) to Monterosso (#5) is the most challenging. For that hike, you might want to start in Monterosso in order to tackle the toughest section while you're fresh and to enjoy the region's most dramatic scenery as you approach Vernazza.

Maps aren't necessary for the basic coastal hikes described here. But for the expanded version of this hike (12 hours, from Portovenere to Levanto) and more serious hikes in the high country, pick up a good hiking map (about €5, sold everywhere). To leave the park cleaner than when you found it, bring a plastic bag *(sacchetto di plastica)* and pick up a little trail trash along the way. It would be great if American visitors—who get so much joy out of this region—were known for this good deed.

Riomaggiore–Manarola (20 min): Facing the front of the train station in Riomaggiore (#1), go up the stairs to the right, following signs for the Via dell'Amore. The film-gobbling promenade—wide enough for baby strollers—winds along the coast to Manarola (#2). While there's no beach here, stairs lead down to sunbathing rocks. A long tunnel and mega-nets protect hikers from mean-spirited rocks. The classy, park-run Bar & Vini A Pie de Ma wine bar—located at the Riomaggiore trailhead—offers light meals, awesome town views, and clever boat storage under the train tracks (for more info, see "Eating," page 300). There's also a scenic, peaceful cliffside bar on the Manarola end of the trail (daily in summer 9:00–24:00, until 20:00 off-season, light meals, drinks, picnic tables).

Manarola–Corniglia (45 min): The walk from Manarola (#2) to Corniglia (#3) is a little longer, more rugged, and less romantic than that from #1 to #2. To avoid the last stretch (switchback stairs leading up to the hill-capping town of Corniglia), catch the shuttle bus from Corniglia's train station (2/hr, €1.50, free with Cinque Terre Card, usually timed to meet the trains).

Corniglia–Vernazza (90 min): The hike from Corniglia (#3) to Vernazza (#4)—the wildest and greenest of the coast—is very rewarding. From the Corniglia station and beach, zigzag up to the town (via the steep stairs, the longer road, or the shuttle bus). Ten minutes past Corniglia, toward Vernazza, you'll see Guvano beach far beneath you (the region's nude beach, see page 308). The scenic trail leads past a bar and picnic tables, through lots of fragrant and flowery vegetation, into Vernazza. If you need a break before reaching Vernazza, Franco's Ristorante La Torre has a small menu but big views (between meal times only drinks are served; see listing under "Eating," page 326).

Vernazza–Monterosso (90 min): The trail from Vernazza (#4) to Monterosso (#5) is a scenic, up-and-down-a-lot trek. Trails are rough (some readers report "very dangerous") and narrow, but easy to follow. Locals frown on camping at the picnic tables located midway. The views just out of Vernazza are spectacular.

Longer Hikes: Above the trails that run between the towns, higher-elevation hikes crisscross the region. Shuttle buses make the going easier, connecting villages and trailheads in the hills. Ask locally about the more difficult six-mile inland hike to Volastra. This tiny village, perched between Manarola and Corniglia, hosts the 5-Terre wine co-op. The Cantina Sociale is a third of a mile away from Volastra, in the hamlet of Groppo. If you take this high road between Manarola and Corniglia, allow two hours one-way. In return, you'll get sweeping views and a closer look at the vineyards. Shuttle buses run about hourly to Volastra from Manarola (€2.50 or free with Cinque Terre Card, pick up schedule from park office); consider taking the bus up and hiking down.

Swimming and Kayaking

Every town has a beach or a rocky place to swim. Monterosso has the biggest and sandiest, with beach umbrellas and beach-use fees (but it's free where there are no umbrellas). Vernazza's is tiny— better for sunning than swimming. Manarola and Riomaggiore have the worst beaches (no sand), but Manarola offers the best deep-water swimming.

Wear your walking shoes and pack your swim gear. Several of the beaches have showers (no shampoo, please). Underwater sightseeing is full of fish—goggles are sold in local shops. Sea urchins can be a problem if you walk on the rocks. If you have swim shoes, this is the place to wear them.

You can rent kayaks in Riomaggiore, Vernazza, and Monterosso. (For details, see individual town listings in this chapter.) Some readers say kayaking can be dangerous—the kayaks tip easily, training is not provided, and lifejackets are not required. Mountain biking is also possible (park info booths in each town have details on rentals and maps of trails high above the coast).

Tours

Local Guides—Paola Tommarchi leads hiking, wine-tasting, and town tours throughout the Cinque Terre for individuals or groups (€110/half-day tour, €175/day, mobile 333-798-7728, paolatomma1966@libero.it). Her friend, **Andrea Bordigoni,** is also good (mobile 347-972-3317, bordigo@inwind.it).

Protect Cinque Terre—Alessandro Villa offers one-, two-, or three-day tour packages, based in his hometown of Vernazza.

Cinque Terre Cuisine 101

Local Specialties: *Acciughe* (ah-CHOO-gay) are anchovies, a local specialty—ideally served the day they're caught. If you've always hated anchovies (the harsh, cured-in-salt American kind), try them fresh here. *Tegame alla Vernazza* is the most typical main course in Vernazza: anchovies, potatoes, tomatoes, white wine, oil, and herbs. *Pansotti* are ravioli with ricotta and a mixture of greens, often served with a walnut sauce...delightful and filling. While antipasto means cheese and salami in Tuscany, here you'll get *antipasti frutti di mare,* a plate of mixed "fruits of the sea" and a fine way to start a meal. Many restaurants are particularly proud of their *antipasti frutti di mare.* Splitting one of these and a pasta dish can be plenty. Try the fun local dessert: *torta della nonna* (grandmother's cake), with a glass of *sciacchetrà* for dunking (see "Wine," below).

Pesto: This region is the birthplace of pesto. Basil, which loves the temperate Ligurian climate, is ground with cheese (half *parmigiano* cow cheese and half pecorino sheep cheese), garlic, olive oil, and pine nuts, and then poured over pasta. Try it on spaghetti, *trenette,* or *trofie* (made of flour with a bit of potato, designed specifically for pesto to cling to). Many also like pesto lasagna, always made with white sauce, never red. If you become addicted, small jars of pesto are sold in the local grocery stores and gift shops. If it's refrigerated, it's fresh; this is what you want if you're eating it today. Get the jar-on-a-shelf pesto for taking home.

Impassioned by his studies into the impact of tourism on small communities, Alessandro and his countryside friends give up-close, hands-on, in-depth contact with the area—you get to help rebuild the terraces, maintain grape vines, or learn how to cook local fare. Alessandro offers walking tours of Vernazza and boat tours, too. He's knowledgeable, but you'll need to be patient with his English (sample price: €445/person for 3-day program, 2-person minimum, includes breakfasts, dinners, accommodations, May–June and Sept–Oct only, www.protectcinqueterre.net, info @protectcinqueterre.com).

Sleeping in the Cinque Terre

If you think too many people have my book, avoid Vernazza. Monterosso is a good choice for the younger crowd (more nightlife) and rich, sun-worshipping softies (who prefer the comfort and ease of a real hotel). Hermits, anarchists, wine-lovers, and mountain goats like Corniglia. Sophisticated Italians and Germans choose Manarola. Riomaggiore is bigger than Vernazza and less resorty

Focaccia: This tasty, pillowy bread also originates from here in Liguria. Locals say the best focaccia is made between the Cinque Terre and Genoa. It's simply flatbread with olive oil and salt. The baker roughs up the dough with finger holes, then bakes it. Focaccia comes plain or with onions, sage, or olive bits, and is a local favorite for a snack on the beach. Bakeries sell it in rounds or slices by the weight (a portion is about 100 grams, or *un etto*).

Farinata: This humble fried bread snack—made from chickpea meal, water, oil, and pepper—is baked on a copper tray in a wood-burning stove. *Farinata* is sold at pizza and focaccia places.

Wine: The *vino delle Cinque Terre,* respected throughout Italy, flows cheap and easy throughout the region. It's white—great with the local seafood. *D.O.C.* is the mark of top quality. Red wine is better elsewhere. For a sweet dessert wine, the local *sciacchetrà* wine is worth the splurge (€4 per small glass, often served with a cookie). Aged *sciacchetrà* is drier, and more costly (up to €12/glass). While 10 kilos of grapes yield seven liters of local wine, *sciacchetrà* is made from near-raisins, and 10 kilos of grapes make only 1.5 liters of *sciacchetrà*. The word means "push and pull"—push in lots of grapes, pull out the best wine. If your room is up a lot of steps, be warned: *Sciacchetrà* is 18 percent alcohol, while regular wine is only 11 percent. In the cool, calm evening, sit on the Vernazza breakwater with a glass of wine and watch the phosphorescence in the waves.

than Monterosso.

While the Cinque Terre is too rugged for the mobs that ravage the Spanish and French coasts, it's popular with Italians, Germans, and in-the-know Americans. Hotels charge more and are packed on holidays, in July and August, and on Fridays and Saturdays all summer. August weekends are worst. But €65 doubles abound throughout the year. For a terrace or view, you might pay an extra €20 or more. Apartments for four can be economical for families—figure on €100–120.

Book ahead if you'll be visiting in June, July, August, on a weekend, or around a holiday (for specific dates, see "2008 Events in the Cinque Terre," page 286, and the list of Italian holidays on page 844). At other times, you can land a double room on any day by just arriving in town (ideally by noon) and asking around at bars and restaurants, or simply by approaching locals on the street. Many travelers enjoy the opportunity to shop around a bit and get the best price by bargaining. Private rooms—called *affitta camere*—are no longer an intimate stay with a family. They are generally comfortable apartments (often with small kitchens) where you get the key and come and go as you like, rarely seeing your landlord. Often landowners rent the buildings by the year to local managers, who then attempt to make a profit by filling them night after night with tourists.

For the best value, visit three private rooms and snare the best. Going direct cuts out a middleman and softens prices. Staying more than one night gives you bargaining leverage. Plan on paying cash. Private rooms are generally bigger and more comfortable than those offered by the pensions and offer the same privacy as a hotel room.

If you want the security of a reservation, make it at a hotel long in advance (smaller places generally don't take reservations that far ahead). Query by email, not fax. If you do reserve, honor your reservation (or, if you must cancel, do it as early as possible). Since people renting rooms usually don't take deposits, they lose money if you don't show up. Cutthroat room hawkers at the train stations might try to lure you away from a room that you've already reserved with offers of cheaper rates. Don't do it. You owe it to your hosts to stick with your original reservation.

Riomaggiore (Town #1)

The most substantial non-resort town of the group, Riomaggiore is a disappointment from the train station. But walk through the tunnel next to the train tracks (or ride the elevator through the hillside to the top of town), and you land in a fascinating tangle of pastel homes leaning on each other like drunken sailors.

ORIENTATION

Tourist Information

The TI and park information office are inside the train station (daily 6:30–21:00 in summer, until 20:00 in winter, tel. 0187-920-633). If the TI in the station is crowded, buy your hiking pass at the Cinque Terre park shop next door, or at the kiosk next to the stairs that lead to the Via dell'Amore trail. The park shop provides eight computers with Internet access upstairs (daily 8:00–22:00 in summer, until 20:00 in winter). A less-formal information source is friendly and helpful Ivo, who runs the Bar Centrale (see "Eating," page 301).

Arrival in Riomaggiore

The bus shuttles locals and tourists up and down Riomaggiore's steep main street and continues to the parking lot outside of town (€1.50 one-way, €2.50 round-trip, free with Cinque Terre Card, 2/hr, main stop at the fork of Via Colombo and Via Malborghetto, or flag it down as it passes). The bus heads into the hills, where you'll find the region's top high-country activities (for details, see "Hikes," page 297).

Helpful Hints

Baggage Storage: You may be able to check your bags at the park information office in 2008 (if not, complain, and see if you can store bags with Ivo at Bar Centrale, listed under "Eating," page 301). Otherwise, the nearest baggage storage is in La Spezia.

Laundry: A self-service launderette is on the main street (daily 8:00–20:00, €3.50 wash, €3.50 dry, run by Edi's Rooms next door, Via Colombo 111).

SELF-GUIDED WALK

Welcome to Riomaggiore

Here's an easy loop trip that maximizes views and minimizes uphill walking.

• *Start at the train station (if you arrive by boat, cross beneath the tracks and take a left, then hike through the tunnel along the tracks to reach the station). You'll come to some...*

Colorful Murals: These murals, with subjects modeled after real-life Riomaggiorians, glorify the nameless workers who constructed the nearly 300 million cubic feet of dry stone walls (without cement). These walls run throughout the Cinque Terre, giving the region its characteristic *muri a secco* terracing for vineyards and olive groves. The murals, done by Argentinean artist Silvio Benedetto, are well-explained in English.

• *Head to the railway tunnel entrance, and ride the elevator to the top of town (€0.50 or €1 family ticket, free with Cinque Terre Card, daily 8:00–19:45). You're at the...*

Hilltop: Here at the top of town, you're treated to spectacular sea views. To continue the view-fest, go right and follow the walkway (ignore the steps marked *Marina Seacoast* that lead to the harbor). It's a five-minute level stroll to the church. You'll pass under the city hall (flying two flags) with murals celebrating the heroic grape pickers and fishermen of the region (also by Silvio Benedetto).

• *Before reaching the church, pause to enjoy the...*

Town View: The major river of this region once ran through this valley, as implied by the name Riomaggiore (local dialect for "river" and "major"). As in the other Cinque Terre towns, the river ravine is now paved over, and the romantic arched bridges that once connected the two sides have been replaced by a practical modern road.

Notice that there are no ugly aerial antennae. In the 1980s, every residence got cable. Now, the TV tower on the hilltop behind the church steeple brings the modern world into each home. While the church was rebuilt in 1870, it was first built in 1340. It's dedicated to St. John the Baptist, the patron saint of Genoa, a maritime republic that dominated the region.

• *Continue past the church down to Riomaggiore's main street, named...*

Via Colombo: Just past the WC, you'll see flower boxes on the street, which sometimes block it. The boxes slide back electronically to let the shuttle bus past. Walk about 30 feet after the flower box, and pop into the tiny Cinque Terre Antiche museum (€0.50, free with Cinque Terre Card, daily 10:00–17:00). You can sit down for a few minutes to watch a circa-1950 video of the Cinque Terre.

Continuing down Via Colombo, you'll pass a bakery, a couple of grocery shops, and the self-service laundry. There's homemade gelato next to the Bar Centrale. When Via Colombo dead-ends (on your left), you'll find the stairs down to the Marina neighborhood, with the harbor, the boat dock, a 200-yard trail to the beach *(spiaggia)*, and an inviting little art gallery. To your right is the tunnel, running alongside the tracks, which takes you directly back to the station and the trail to the other towns. From here, you can take a train, hop a boat, or hike to your next destination.

ACTIVITIES

Beach—Riomaggiore's rugged and tiny "beach" is rocky, but it's clean and peaceful. Take a two-minute walk from the harbor: Face the harbor, then follow the path to your left. Passing the rugged boat landing, stay on the path to the beach.

Kayaks and Water Sports—The town has a diving center (scuba, snorkeling, kayaks, and small motorboats; office under the tracks on Via San Giacomo, May–Sept daily 8:00–22:00, tel. 0187-920-011, www.5terrediving.com).

Riomaggiore

VIA DELL' AMORE TO MANAROLA

⑮ MURALS

⑨ ELEVATOR TO HIGH ROAD

S. GIOVANNI CHURCH

TRAIN STATION

⑫ TO ⑲

VIA GASPERI

PED TUNNEL

VIA

VIA SIGNORINI

✚

⑧ VIA SANT.

CINQUE TERRE INFO

② ④ ⑥

⑯ ⑭ ⑰ ⑤

③ ① COLOMBO

⑩ V-TRALB

⑦ ⑬

||||— STAIRS

LIGURIAN SEA

⑪

VIA

NOT TO SCALE

⑱

TO ⑳

N

HARBOR

BOAT DOCK

BOAT TICKETS

"BEACH" SWIMMING + SHOWERS

PCH

① Edi's Rooms & Launderette
② La Dolce Vita Rooms
③ Mar Mar Rooms & Kayaks
④ Fazioli Rooms
⑤ Locanda dalla Compagnia
⑥ Locanda del Sole
⑦ Anna Michielini Apartments
⑧ Locanda Ca' dei Duxi
⑨ Rifugio Mamma Rosa
⑩ Ristorante la Lampara
⑪ La Lanterna Restaurant

⑫ Ristorante Ripa del Sole
⑬ Te La Do Io La Merenda Snack Bar
⑭ Veciu Muin Pizzeria
⑮ Bar & Vini A Pie de Ma
⑯ Bar Centrale & Gelateria
⑰ Coop Grocery
⑱ Boat Dock & Slippery Launch
⑲ To Madonna di Montenero Trail
⑳ To Torre Guardiola Botanical Pathway & WWII Bunkers

Hikes—Consider the cliff-hanging trail that leads from the beach up to old WWII bunkers and the hilltop botanical pathway of native flora and fauna with English information (free with Cinque Terre Card, daily 10:00–16:30, steep 20-minute climb, take the stairs between the boat dock and the beach, located at Torre Guardiola). Another trail climbs scenically to the 14th-century Madonna di Montenero sanctuary, high above the town (30-min, take the main road inland until you see signs). Ride the green shuttle bus from the town center to the sanctuary trail, then walk uphill five minutes (12-min trip, details at park office). The park center at the sanctuary offers bike rental.

NIGHTLIFE

With Ivo as master of ceremonies, **Bar Centrale** dominates the late-night scene in Riomaggiore. In the summer, **Bar & Vini A Pie de Ma,** at the beginning of the Via dell'Amore, has piles of charm and stays open until at least midnight (see page 301 for details on these two bars). On summer nights (after 22:00), they often have live blues or jazz, or a DJ. And the marvelous **Via dell'Amore** trail welcomes romantics after dark. The trail is free after 19:30 and is lit only with subtle ground lighting so you can see the stars (for its history, see "Via dell'Amore" on page 289).

SLEEPING

Riomaggiore has arranged its private-room rental system better than its neighbors. But with organization (and middlemen) come higher prices. Several agencies—with regular office hours, English-speaking staff, and email addresses—line up within a few yards of each other on the main drag. Each manages a corral of local rooms for rent. These offices can close unexpectedly, so it's smart to settle up the day before you leave in case they're closed when you need to depart. Expect lots of stairs. To avoid ripoffs, see my "New Ethic" in the "Sleep Code" sidebar. Private parking will run you an extra €10–20. If you don't mind the hike, the street above town has safe overnight parking (free 20:00–8:00).

Room-Finding Services

$$$ Locanda del Sole has six basic and overpriced but sparkling-clean rooms with a shared and peaceful terrace. Located at the utilitarian edge of town, it's a five-minute walk to the center. The easy parking makes it especially appealing to drivers (Db-€100 April–June and Sept–Oct, Db-€120 July–Aug, parking free with this book in 2008, Via Santuario 114, tel. & fax 0187-920-773, mobile 340-983-0090, www.locandadelsole.net, info @locandadelsole.net, Enrico).

$$ Edi's Rooms rents 20 fine rooms and apartments, most with views. Edi and her partner Luana get my best business practices award for this town (Db-€60, apartment Db-€80, apartment Qb-€150, these prices promised to readers through 2008 with this book, office open daily 8:30–20:00 in summer, winter 9:00–12:30 & 14:30–19:00, Via Colombo 111, tel. 0187-760-842, tel. & fax 0187-920-325, edi-vesigna@iol.it).

Sleep Code

(€1 = about $1.30, country code: 39)
S = Single, **D** = Double/Twin, **T** = Triple, **Q** = Quad, **b** = bathroom, **s** = shower only. Unless otherwise noted, credit cards are accepted, English is spoken, and breakfast is included (except in Vernazza).

To keep my readers from being overcharged, I've established a **"New Ethic"** *(Nuova Etica),* which means that the accommodations I recommend in the Cinque Terre will charge no more in 2008 than the prices listed in this book. Each place understands that if they exceed this agreed-upon price, my readers will let me know, and they will lose their place in next year's edition of this book. I've listed only peak-season prices—off-season can be cheaper. Please help me enforce this practice. (Email me at rick@ricksteves.com if someone overcharges you.) Hoteliers have also agreed to be honest in what they promise—for example, providing a view room if one is reserved. Honest hosts think it's a wonderful idea. The others wiggle and squirm.

To help you sort easily through these listings, I've divided the rooms into three categories based on the price for a standard double room with bath:

$$$ **Higher Priced**—Most rooms €100 or more.
 $$ **Moderately Priced**—Most rooms between €50–100.
  $ **Lower Priced**—Most rooms €50 or less.

$$ Mar Mar Rooms offers 12 rooms, 15 apartments, and a mini-hostel, with American expat Amy smoothing communications (dorm bed-€20 per person in 4- or 9-bed room, Db-€60–90 depending on view, reception open 9:00–17:00 in season, 30 yards above train tracks on main drag next to Ristorante la Lampara at Via Malborghetto 4, tel. & fax 0187-920-932, www.5terre-marmar .com, info@5terre-marmar.com).

$$ La Dolce Vita, across from Edi's, offers five rooms and eight apartments (dorm bed-€12–22, Sb-€35, Db-€40–70; open daily 9:30–19:30; if they're closed, they're full; Via Colombo 120, tel. & fax 0187-760-044, mobile 349-326-6803, www.ladolcevita5terre .com, agonatal@interfree.it, Giacomo and Simone).

$$ Luciano and Roberto Fazioli rent nine rooms of variable quality while also running a basic, 11-bed mini-hostel (dorm bed-€22, €25 Fri–Sat or for 1-night stays, D and Db-€50–80 depending on season and view, cash only, office open daily 9:00–20:00, Via Colombo 94, tel. 0187-920-904, robertofazioli@libero.it).

$$ Locanda Ca' dei Duxi rents ten good rooms—eight have air-conditioning—from an efficient little office on the main drag (Db-€70–100 depending on view and air-con, extra person-€20, 5 percent discount with this book and cash in 2008, open all year, Via Colombo 36, tel. & fax 0187-920-036, mobile 329-825-7836, www.duxi.it, info@duxi.it, Samuele).

Private Rooms and Hotels on Riomaggiore's Main Drag

$$ Locanda dalla Compagnia rents five modern rooms at the top of town, just 300 yards below the parking lot and the little church. All rooms—among the nicest in town—are on the same airy ground floor, sharing an inviting lounge. Franca runs it with Giovanna's help (Db-€80, winter Db-€50, air-con, mini-fridge, no view, Via del Santuario 232, tel. 0187-760-050, fax 0187-920-586, lacomp@libero.it).

$$ Anna Michielini rents five attractive no-seaview apartments in the center. Two apartments have kitchens and can connect to sleep up to six (Db-€60–70, Tb-€85, Qb-€100–120, cheaper Oct–mid-April and for longer stays, 2 nights minimum stay, reserve with credit card but pay cash, across from Bar Centrale at Via Colombo 143—ring bell to open door, mobile 328-131-1032, fax 0187-920-411, michielinis@yahoo.it, friendly Daniela speaks good English but her mother speaks *solo Italiano*).

Cheap Beds in Riomaggiore

To sleep cheap, head to Riomaggiore, which has better options than the other four towns. **Mar Mar Rooms** and the **Faziolis** offer dorm beds for €20 in mini-dorms (see above for both). With a little luck, you and your partner could find yourselves all alone in an eight-bed room.

Rifugio Mamma Rosa hostel is your rock-bottom option, but you get what you pay for: it's grungy (€15 per bed, she doesn't take reservations but can always find you a room, no services except for kitchen, 30 yards in front of train station, tel. 0187 760 567, www.rifugiomammarosa.com). Rosa and her husband greet arriving trains; don't let Rosa pirate you away if you already have reservations at another place.

EATING

Ristorante la Lampara, decorated like a ship, serves a *frutti di mare* pizza, *trenette al pesto*, and the aromatic *spaghetti al cartoccio*— €10 oven-cooked spaghetti with seafood in foil (daily 7:00–24:00, closed Tue in winter, doubles as a bar, just above tracks off Via Colombo at Via Malborghetto 10, tel. 0187-920-120).

La Lanterna, dressier than the Lampara, is wedged into a niche in the Marina, overlooking the harbor under the tracks (daily 12:00–22:00, Via San Giacomo 10, tel. 0187-920-589).

Ristorante Ripa del Sole is the local pick for an elegant night out, with the same prices and quality as the Lampara and Lanterna (Tue–Sun 18:30–22:00, closed Mon, closed Jan–Feb, 10-min hike above town, Via de Gasperi 282, tel. 0187-920-143).

Try **Te La Do Io La Merenda** ("I'll Give You a Snack") for a snack, pizza, or good takeout. Their counter is piled with an assortment of munchies, and they have pastas, roasted chicken, and focaccia sandwiches to go (daily 9:00–21:30, Via Colombo 161, tel. 0187-920-148).

Veciu Muin has okay pizza; you can get it to go (*d'asporto*) or take a seat (daily 12:00–14:30 & 18:30–22:00, closed Mon off-season, at Via Colombo 83, tel. 0187-920-487).

Bar & Vini A Pie de Ma, at the trailhead on the Manarola end of town, is great for a scenic light bite or quiet drink at night. Enjoying a meal at a table on its dramatically situated terrace provides an indelible Cinque Terre memory (daily 10:00–20:00, closes later in summer).

Groceries and delis on Via Colombo sell food to go, including pizza slices, for a picnic at the harbor or beach. The **Co-op grocery** is least expensive and will make sandwiches to go (Via Colombo 55).

Bar Centrale, run by sociable Ivo and his gang, is a good stop for Italian breakfast and music. Ivo lived in San Francisco and speaks good English. He fills his bar with only the best San Franciscan rock and hosts a big party on the Fourth of July. During the day, Bar Centrale is a shaded place to relax with other travelers. At night, it offers the younger set the liveliest action in town. Ivo makes "better mojitos than you can get in Cuba," plucking fresh mint leaves for your drink from a plant growing on the counter (also has €5 fast-food pastas, daily 7:30–24:00, closed Mon in winter, Via Colombo 144, tel. 0187-920-208). In you're in a jam, Ivo may store your bag for the day. For the best gelato in town, go next door.

Manarola (Town #2)

Like Riomaggiore, Manarola is attached to its station by a 200-yard-long tunnel. During WWII air raids, these tunnels provided refuge and a safe place for rattled villagers to sleep. The town itself fills a ravine, bookended by its wild little harbor to the west and a diminutive church square to the east. A delightful and gentle stroll, from the church down to the harborside park, provides the region's easiest little vineyard walk.

Cinque Terre

ORIENTATION

Arrival in Manarola

A shuttle bus runs between the low end of Manarola's main street (at the *tabacchi* shop and newsstand) and the parking lot (€1.50 one-way, €2.50 round-trip, free with Cinque Terre Card, 2/hr, just flag it down).

To get to the dock and the boats that connect Manarola with the other Cinque Terre towns, find the steps to the left of the harbor view—they lead down to the ticket kiosk. Continue around the left side of the cliff (as you're facing the water) to catch the boats.

Helpful Hints

Baggage Storage: The Cinque Terre park office is in the train station, and may have bag storage in 2008—ask (daily 7:00–20:00, €0.50/hr, tel. 0187-760-511). Otherwise, your only non-hotel option for storing bags is in La Spezia's train station.

Public WCs: They're on the opposite side of the building from the park office entrance.

SELF-GUIDED WALK

Welcome to Manarola

From the harbor, this 30-minute circular walk shows you the town and surrounding vineyards, and ends at a fantastic viewpoint.

• *Start down at the waterfront.*

The Harbor: Manarola is tiny and picturesque, a tumble of buildings bunny-hopping down its ravine to the fun-loving waterfront. Notice how the I-beam crane launches the boats. Facing the harbor, look to the right, at the hillside Punta Bonfiglio cemetery and park. (Punta Bonfiglio is where this walk ends.)

The town's swimming hole is just below. Manarola has no sand, but offers the best deep-water swimming in the area. The first "beach" has a shower, ladder, and wonderful rocks. The second has tougher access and no shower, but feels more remote and pristine (follow the paved path toward Corniglia, just around the point). For many, the tricky access makes this beach dangerous.

• *Hiking inland up the town's main drag, you'll come to the train tracks covered by Manarola's new square, called...*

Piazza Capellini: Built in 2004, this square is an all-around great idea, giving the town a safe, fun zone for kids. Locals living too near the tracks also enjoy a little less noise. Check out the

Manarola

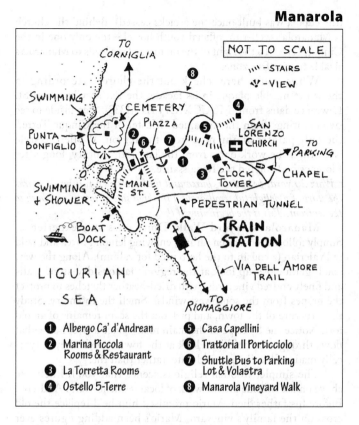

TO CORNIGLIA

NOT TO SCALE

⟋⟋ – STAIRS
☙ – VIEW

SWIMMING

CEMETERY

PIAZZA

❽

❹

PUNTA BONFIGLIO

❷

❻

❼

❺

SAN LORENZO CHURCH

TO PARKING

❶

❸

CLOCK TOWER

CHAPEL

SWIMMING + SHOWER

MAIN ST.

PEDESTRIAN TUNNEL

BOAT DOCK

TRAIN STATION

LIGURIAN

SEA

VIA DELL' AMORE TRAIL

TO RIOMAGGIORE

❶ Albergo Ca' d'Andrean
❷ Marina Piccola Rooms & Restaurant
❸ La Torretta Rooms
❹ Ostello 5-Terre
❺ Casa Capellini
❻ Trattoria Il Porticciolo
❼ Shuttle Bus to Parking Lot & Volastra
❽ Manarola Vineyard Walk

mosaic that displays the varieties of local fish in colorful enamel.

• *A few steps uphill, you'll find the...*

Sciacchetrà Museum: Run by the national park, it's hardly a museum. But pop in to its inviting room to see a tiny exhibit on the local wine industry (€0.50, free with Cinque Terre Card, daily 10:30–17:30, 15-min video in English by request, 100 yards uphill from train tracks, across from the post office).

• *Hiking farther uphill you can still hear...*

Manarola's Stream: As in Riomaggiore and Vernazza, Manarola's stream was covered over by a modern sewage system after World War II. Before that time, romantic bridges arched over its ravine. A modern waterwheel recalls the origin of the town's name—local dialect for "big wheel" (one of many possible derivations). Mills like this once powered the local olive oil industry.

• *Keep climbing until you come to the square at the...*

Top of Manarola: The square is faced by a church, an oratory—now a religious and community meeting place—and a bell tower, which served as a watch tower when pirates raided the town (the cupola was built once the attacks ceased). Behind the church is Manarola's well-run, official youth hostel—the only one in the Cinque Terre. To the right of the oratory, a lane leads to Manarola's sizable tourist-free zone.

While you're here, check out the church. According to the white marble plaque in its facade, the Parish Church of St. Lawrence dates from "MCCCXXXVIII" (1338). Step inside to see two paintings from the unnamed "Master of the Cinque Terre," the only painter of any note from the region. While the style is Gothic, the work dates from the late 15th century, long after Florence had entered the Renaissance.

• *Walk 20 yards below the church and find a wooden railing. It marks the start of a delightful stroll around the high side of town, and back to the seafront. This is the beginning of the...*

Manarola Vineyard Walk: Don't miss this experience. Simply follow the wooden railing, enjoying lemon groves and wild red valerian (a cousin to the herb used for valium). Along the way, you'll get a close-up look at the region's famous dry-stone walls and finely crafted vineyards (with dried-heather thatches to protect the grapes from the southwest winds). Smell the rosemary. Study the structure of the town, and pick out the scant remains of an old fort. Notice the S-shape of the main road—once a river bed—that flows through town. Take a look at the town's roofs; they're typically made of locally quarried slate, rather than tile.

The simple, wooden religious scenes that you'll likely see above on the hillside are the work of local resident Mario Andreoli. Before his father died, Mario promised him he'd replace the old cross on the family's vineyard. Mario's been adding figures ever since. After recovering from a rare illness, he redoubled his efforts. On religious holidays, everything's lit up: the Nativity, the Last Supper, the Crucifixion, the Resurrection, and more. Some of the scenes are left up year-round.

• *The trail ends at a T-intersection. Turn left. (A right takes you to the trail to Corniglia.) Before descending back into town, take a right, detouring into...*

The Cemetery: Ever since Napoleon—who was king of Italy in the early 1800s—decreed that cemeteries were health risks, Cinque Terre's burial spots have been located outside of town. The result? The dearly departed generally get first-class sea views. Each cemetery—with its evocative yellowed photos and finely carved Carrara marble memorial reliefs—is worth a visit. (The basic structure for all of them is the same, but Manarola's is most easily accessible.)

In cemeteries like these, there's a hierarchy of four places to park your mortal remains: a graveyard, a condo *(loculo)*, a mini bone-niche *(ossario)*, or communal ossuary. Because of the tight space (except for the big communal ossuary), there's a time limit assigned to each. Unclaimed—and therefore unfunded—bones go into the ossuary in the middle of the chapel floor after about a generation. Traditionally, locals make weekly visits to loved ones here, often bringing flowers. The rolling stepladder makes access to top-floor *loculi* easy.

• *The Manarola cemetery is on Punta Bonfiglio. Walk just below it, farther out.*

The bench at the tip of the point offers one of the most commanding views of the entire region.

SLEEPING

(€1 = about $1.30, country code: 39)

Manarola has plenty of private rooms. Ask in bars and restaurants. There's a modern, three-star place halfway up the main drag, a seaview hotel on the harbor, and a cluster of options around the church at the peaceful top of the town (a 5-min hike from the train tracks). Manarola's handy shuttle-bus service makes it easy to get to and from your car (see "Arrival in Manarola," earlier in this chapter). To ensure honest prices, see my "New Ethic" in the "Sleep Code" on page 299.

$$$ La Torretta is a trendy, upscale, 13-room place that caters to a demanding clientele. It's a peaceful refuge with all the comforts for those happy to pay, including a communal hot-tub with a view (Db-€110–120, Db suite-€150, on Piazza della Chiesa at Vico Volto 20, tel. 0187-920-327, fax 0187-760-024, www.torrettas.com, torretta@cdh.it).

$$ Albergo Ca' d'Andrean, run by Simone, is quiet, comfortable, and modern. While the welcome is formal at best, it has 10 big, sunny, air-conditioned rooms and a cool garden oasis complete with lemon trees (Sb-€70, Db-€94, breakfast-€6, cash only, send personal or traveler's check to reserve or call if you're already traveling, closed Nov–Christmas, up the hill at Via A. Discovolo 101, tel. 0187-920-040, fax 0187-920-452, www.cadandrean.it, cadandrean@libero.it).

$$ Marina Piccola offers 13 bright, slick rooms on the water—so they figure a warm welcome is unnecessary (Db-€95, €10 per person for buffet breakfast, air-con, Via Birolli 120, tel. 0187-920-103, fax 0187-920-966, www.hotelmarinapiccola.com, info@hotelmarinapiccola.com).

$ Casa Capellini rents three rooms: One has a view balcony, another a 360-degree terrace—book long in advance (Db-€46–52, €70 for the *alta camera* on the top, with a kitchen, private terrace, and knockout view; two doors down the hill from the church—with your back to the church, it's at 2 o'clock; Via Ettore Cozzani

12, tel. 0187-920-823 or 0187-736-765, www.casacapellini-5terre.it, casa.capellini@tin.it, Gianni and Franca don't speak English).

$ Ostello 5-Terre, Manarola's modern and pleasant hostel, stands like a Monopoly hotel above the church square and offers 48 beds in four- to six-bed rooms. It's smart to reserve at least a week in advance in high season. You book with your credit-card number online; if you cancel with fewer than three days' notice, you'll be charged for one night. This is not a party hostel—quiet is greatly appreciated (May–Sept dorm beds-€23, Qb-€96; off-season dorm beds-€18, Qb-€80; closed Dec–Feb, not co-ed except for couples and families, optional €4.50 breakfast and €5–6 pasta; in summer, office closed 13:00–17:00, rooms closed 10:00–17:00, 1:00 curfew; during off-season, office and rooms closed until 16:00, curfew at 24:00; open to all ages, laundry, safes, phone cards, Internet access, book exchange, elevator, great roof terrace and sunset views, Via B. Riccobaldi 21, tel. 0187-920-215, fax 0187-920-218, www .hostel5terre.com, info@hostel5terre.com, well-managed by Nicola). They rent dorm rooms as doubles for €60.

EATING

Many hardworking places line the main drag. I like the Botto family's friendly **Trattoria Il Porticciolo** (€7 pastas, Thu–Tue 12:00–15:00 & 18:00–22:30, closed Wed, just below the train tracks at Via R. Birolli 92, tel. 0187-920-083). For harborside dining, **Marina Piccola** is the winner. While less friendly and a little more expensive, the setting is memorable (Wed–Mon 11:30–16:30 & 18:30–22:00, closed Tue, tel. 0187-920-923).

Corniglia (Town #3)

This is the quiet town—the only one of the five not on the water—with a mellow main square. From the station, a footpath zigzags up nearly 400 stairs to the town. Or take the shuttle bus, generally timed to meet arriving trains (€1.50, free with Cinque Terre Card,

2/hr). Before leaving the bus, confirm departure times on the schedule posted on its door or ask at the TI in the train station (daily 6:30–19:30).

According to the (likely fanciful) local legend, the town was originally settled by a Roman farmer who named it for his mother, Cornelia (how Corniglia is pronounced). The town and its ancient residents produced a wine so famous that—some say—vases found at Pompeii touted its virtues. Regardless of the veracity of the legends, wine remains Corniglia's lifeblood today. Follow the pungent smell of ripe grapes into an alley cellar and get a local to let you dip a straw into a keg. Remote and less visited than the other Cinque Terre towns, Corniglia has fewer tourists, cooler temperatures, a few restaurants, a windy overlook on its promontory, and plenty of private rooms for rent (ask at any bar or shop, no cheaper than other towns).

SELF-GUIDED WALK

Welcome to Corniglia

We'll explore this tiny town—population 240—and end at a scenic viewpoint.

• *Begin near the bus stop, located in a...*

Town Square: The gateway to this community is "Ciappà" square, with an ATM, phone booth, old wine press, and bus stop. Now that the Cinque Terre has been designated as a national park, the change has sparked a revitalization of the town. Corniglia's young generation might now stay put, rather than migrate into big cities the way locals did in the past.

• *Stroll the spine of Corniglia, Via Fieschi. In the fall, the smell of grapes (on their way to becoming wine) wafts from busy cellars. Along the way on this main street, you'll see...*

Corniglia's Enticing Shops: The enjoyable wine bar, **Enoteca Il Pirun**—named for the odd, old-fashioned pitcher used to pour (and drink) wine—is located in a cool cantina at Via Fieschi 115 (daily, tel. 0187-812-315). Sample any of the 30 local or national wines—generally free for small tastes, or ask friendly Mario for a whole glass, and have a light appetizer or salad. Mario doesn't speak English, but he tries.

Across from Enoteca Il Pirun, Alberto and Cristina's *gelateria* is the only—and therefore best—in town. Before ordering, get a free taste of Alberto's *miele di Corniglia* (made from local honey).

In the **Butiega shop** at Via Fieschi 142, Vincenzo and Lorenzo sell organic local specialties (daily 8:00–19:30). For picnickers, they offer €2.50 made-to-order sandwiches and a fun €3.50 *antipasto misto* to go. (There are good places to picnic farther along on this walk.)

• *Following Via Fieschi, you'll end up at the...*

Main Square: On Largo Taragio, tables from two bars and a trattoria spill around a WWI memorial and the town's old well. It once piped in natural spring water from the hillside to locals living without plumbing. What looks like a church is the Oratory

Corniglia

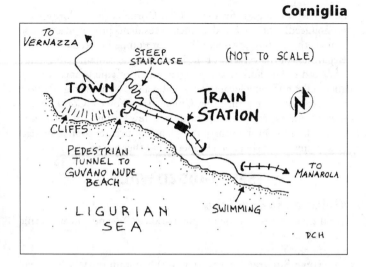

of Santa Caterina. (An oratory is a kind of a spiritual clubhouse for a service group doing social work in the name of the Catholic Church. For more information, see "Oratory of the Dead" on page 331.) Behind the oratory, you'll find a clearing that local children have made into a soccer field. The benches and viewpoint make this a peaceful place for a picnic (less crowded than the end-of-town viewpoint, below).

• *Opposite the oratory, notice how steps lead steeply down on Via alla Marina to Corniglia's non-beach. It's a five-minute paved climb to sunning rocks, a shower, and a small deck (with a treacherous entry into the water). From the square, continue down Via Fieschi to the...*

End-of-Town Viewpoint: The Santa Maria Belvedere, named for a church that once stood here, marks the scenic end of Corniglia. This is a super picnic spot. From here, look high to the west, where the village of San Bernardino straddles a ridge (a good starting point for a hike; accessible by shuttle bus or long uphill hike from Vernazza). Below is the tortuous harbor, where locals hoist their boats onto the cruel rocks.

ACTIVITIES

Beaches—This hilltop town has rocky sea access below its train station (toward Manarola). Once a beach, it's all been washed away and offers no services.

The nude Guvano (GOO-vah-noh) beach is in the opposite direction (toward Vernazza). Guvano beach was created by an 1893 landslide that cost the village a third of its farmland. The big news in modern times is its nudists. Guvano made headlines in Italy in the 1970s, as clothed locals in a makeshift armada of dinghies and fishing boats retook their town beach. But big-city nudists still work on all-over tans in this remote setting.

To reach the beach from the Corniglia train station, follow the road north, go over the tracks, and then zigzag below the tracks, following signs to the tunnel in the cliff (walk past the *proprietà privata* sign). When you buzz the intercom, the hydraulic *Get Smart*–type door is opened from the other end. After a 15-minute hike through a cool, moist, dimly lit, and unused train tunnel, you'll emerge at the Guvano beach—and get charged €5 (mid-June–mid-Sept 9:00–19:00). The beach has drinking water, but no WC. A steep (free) trail leads from the beach up to the Corniglia–Vernazza trail.

The crowd is Italian counterculture: pierced nipples, tattooed punks, hippie drummers in dreads, and exhibitionist men. The ratio of men to women is about two to one. About half the people on the pebbly beach keep their swimsuits on. With new national park standards, Guvano's future as a nudist haven is in doubt.

SLEEPING

(€1 = about $1.30, country code: 39)
Perched high above the sea on a hilltop, Corniglia has plenty of private rooms (generally Db-€60). To get to the town from the station, catch the shuttle bus or make the 15-minute uphill hike. The town is riddled with meager places that charge too much for their rooms, so it's almost never full. To keep prices under control, I've established the "New Ethic"—see the "Sleep Code" on page 299.

$$ Cristiana Ricci (not the movie star) rents four small, clean, and peaceful rooms—two with kitchens and one with a terrace and sweeping view—just inland from the bus stop (Db-€60, Qb-€90, Via Fieschi 157, check in at Bar Matteo, tel. 0187-812-541, mobile 338-937-6547, fax 0187-812-345, cri_affittacamere@virgilio.it). Her mom rents a few places in town for the same price. Cristiana, the only person I met in town who rents rooms and has good business sense, gives guests with this 2008 book a free coffee-and-brioche breakfast along with their room.

$$ Villa Cecio feels like an abandoned hotel and rents eight well-worn rooms on the outskirts of town, all with no character or warmth (Db-€60, cash preferred, great views, sagging beds, on main road 200 yards toward Vernazza, tel. 0187-812-043, fax 0187-812-138, www.cecio5terre.com, info@cecio5terre.com).

$$ Il Girasole, run by Stefano, rents five extremely humble rooms (overpriced at D-€45, Db-€60, Via Fieschi 93, tel. 0187-812-551, mobile 338-209-3565, www.corniglia.com).

EATING

Corniglia has three decent restaurants. **Cecio,** above the town, has terrace seating with a view of the sea (closed Wed). The trattoria **La Lantera,** on the main square, is most atmospheric. Neither comes with particularly charming service. At **Bar Matteo,** Cristiana and Stefano offer light meals and okay Internet access (also on the main square). Restaurant **Osteria Mananan**—between the Ciappà bus stop and the main square on Via Fieschi—serves the best food in town in its small, stony, and elegant interior (closed Tue, no outdoor seating, tel. 0187-821-166).

Vernazza (Town #4)

With the closest thing to a natural harbor—overseen by a ruined castle and a stout stone church—Vernazza is the jewel of the Cinque Terre. Only the occa-

sional noisy slurping up of the train by the mountain reminds you of the modern world.

The action is at the harbor, where you'll find outdoor restaurants, a bar hanging on the edge of the castle, a breakwater with a promenade, and a tailgate-party street market every Tuesday morning. In the summer, the beach becomes a soccer field, where teams fielded by local bars and restaurants provide late-night entertainment. In the dark, locals fish off the promontory, using glowing bobs that shine in the waves.

Proud of their Vernazzan heritage, the town's 500 residents like to brag: "Vernazza is locally owned. Portofino has sold out." Fearing the change it would bring, keep-Vernazza-small proponents stopped the construction of a major road into the town and region. Families are tight and go back centuries; several generations stay together. In the winter, the population shrinks, as many people return to more comfortable big-city apartments.

Leisure time is devoted to taking part in the *passeggiata*—strolling lazily together up and down the main street. Sit on a bench and study the passersby doing their *vasche* (laps). Explore the characteristic alleys, called *carugi*. Learn—and live—the phrase *"vita pigra di Vernazza"* (the lazy life of Vernazza).

ORIENTATION

Tourist Information

The TI/park information booth is in the train station (daily 6:30–22:00 in summer, until 19:30 in winter, tel. 0187-812-533). Public WCs are nearby in the station.

Arrival in Vernazza

A shuttle bus, generally with friendly English-speaking Beppe or Simone behind the wheel, runs from the top of Via Gavino to the non-resident parking lot about 500 yards above Vernazza (€1.50, free with Cinque Terre Card, runs 7:30–19:30, 3-4/hr).

For a cheap and scenic round-trip joyride, with a chance to chat about the region with Beppe or Simone, stay on for the entire route for the cost of a normal ticket. About once an hour, the bus also heads to two sanctuaries in the hills above town (€2.50 each way, free with Cinque Terre Card, 5/day, find schedule at park office and posted in train station). The high-country 40-minute loop—marked "panoramic tour" on the bus schedule—gives you lots of scenery without having to hike.

Helpful Hints

Money: The town has two banks and two ATMs (in center and top of town).

Internet Access: The slick **Internet Point,** run by Alberto and Isabella, is in the village center (daily 9:30–23:00 in summer, until 20:00 in winter, Wi-Fi, will burn CDs to back up your digital photos for €8, sells international phone cards, tel. 0187-812-949). The **Blue Marlin Bar,** run by Massimo and Carmen, offers Internet access as well with longer hours (Fri–Wed 7:00–24:00, closed Thu, see "Eating," page 323).

Laundry: The nearest laundromats are in Monterosso and Riomaggiore.

Parking: Driving to Vernazza is a reasonable option because of the parking lot, but it fills up quickly from May through September (€1.50/hr, €12/24 hrs, about 500 yards above town, pay first at the parking stand before getting your spot) and the hardworking shuttle service (connects the lot to the top of town every 15 min, see "Arrival in Vernazza," above). Because the shuttle buses are small and you need to manage your luggage yourself, it can make sense to drive down to the edge of town (where the shuttle will drop you off), leave your travel partner with the luggage, drive back up to park, and then shuttle down solo.

Best Views: A steep 10-minute hike in either direction from Vernazza gives you a classic village photo op (for the best light, head toward Corniglia in the morning, toward Monterosso in the evening). Franco's Ristorante La Torre, with a panoramic terrace, is at the tower on the trail toward Corniglia (listed under "Eating," page 326).

Baggage Storage: The nearest baggage storage is in La Spezia's train station.

SELF-GUIDED WALKS

Welcome to Vernazza

This tour includes Vernazza's characteristic town squares, and ends on its scenic breakwater.

• *Walk uphill until you hit the parking lot, with a bank, a post office, and a barrier that keeps out all but service vehicles. Vernazza's shuttle buses run from here to the parking lot and into the hills. Walk to the tidy, modern square called...*

Fontana Vecchia: Named after a long-gone fountain, this is where older locals remember the river filled with townswomen doing their washing. Now they enjoy checking on the baby ducks. The trail leads up to the cemetery. Imagine the entire village trudging sadly up here during funerals.

• *Glad to be here in happier times, begin your saunter downhill to the harbor. Just before the* Pensione Sorriso *sign, on your right (big brown wood doors), you'll see the...*

Ambulance Barn: A group of volunteers is always on call for a dash to the hospital, 40 minutes away in La Spezia. Opposite from the barn is a big, empty lot. Like many landowners, the owner of Pension Sorriso had plans to expand, but since the 1980s, the government said no. While some landowners are frustrated, the old character of these towns survives.

• *A few steps farther along (past the town clinic and library), you'll see a...*

World Wars Monument: Look for a marble plaque in the wall to your left, dedicated to those killed in the World Wars. Not a family in Vernazza was spared. Listed on the left are soldiers *morti in combattimento,* who died in World War I; on the right is the World War II section. Some were deported to *Germania*; others—labeled *Part* (stands for *partigiani,* or partisans)—were killed while fighting against Mussolini. Cynics considered partisans less than heroes. After 1943, Hitler called up Italian boys over 15. Rather than die on the front for Hitler, they escaped to the hills. They become "resistance fighters" in order to remain free.

The path to Corniglia leaves from here (behind and above the plaque). Behind you is a small square and playground, decorated with three millstones, once used to grind local olives into oil. From here, Vernazza's tiny river goes underground. Until the 1950s,

Vernazza

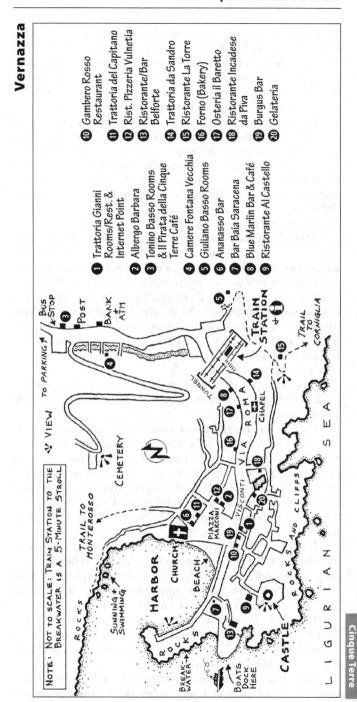

1. Trattoria Gianni Rooms/Rest. & Internet Point
2. Albergo Barbara
3. Tonino Basso Rooms & Il Pirata della Cinque Terre Café
4. Camere Fontana Vecchia
5. Giuliano Basso Rooms
6. Ananasso Bar
7. Bar Baia Saracena
8. Blue Marlin Bar & Café
9. Ristorante Al Castello
10. Gambero Rosso Restaurant
11. Trattoria del Capitano
12. Rist. Pizzeria Vulnetia
13. Ristorante/Bar Belforte
14. Trattoria da Sandro
15. Ristorante La Torre
16. Forno (Bakery)
17. Osteria il Baretto
18. Ristorante Incadese da Piva
19. Burgus Bar
20. Gelateria

NOTE: Not to scale: Train Station to the Breakwater is a 5-minute stroll.

Bus Stop

Post

Bank + ATM

VIEW to PARKING

Cemetery

TRAIL TO MONTEROSSO

HARBOR

Sunning + Swimming

CHURCH

BEACH

ROCKS

BREAKWATER

BOATS DOCK HERE

CASTLE

ROCKS AND CLIFFS

TUNNEL

VIA ROMA

CHAPEL

VIA VISCONTI

PIAZZA MARCONI

TRAIN STATION

TRAIL TO CORNIGLIA

LIGURIAN SEA

Cinque Terre

Vernazza's river ran openly through the center of town. Old-timers recall the days before the breakwater, when the river cascaded down and the surf crashed along Vernazza's main drag. Back then, the town was nicknamed "Little Venice" for the series of romantic bridges that arched over the stream, connecting the two sides of the town before the main road was built.

Before the tracks (on the left), the wall has 10 spaces, one reserved for each party's political ads during elections—a kind of local pollution control. The **map** on the right, under the railway tracks, shows the region's hiking trails. Number two is the basic favorite. The second set of tracks (nearer the harbor) was recently renovated to lessen the disruptive noise, but locals say it made no difference.

• *Follow the road downhill to the...*

Main Business Center: Here, you'll pass many locals doing their *vasche* (laps). At **Enoteca Sotto l'Arco,** Gerry and Paola sell wine—they can cork it and throw in plastic glasses—and delightful jars of local pesto which are great on bread (Wed–Mon 9:00–21:00, closed Tue, Via Roma 70). Next, you'll pass the Blue Marlin Bar (Vernazza's top night spot) and the tiny **Chapel of Santa Marta** (the small stone chapel with iron grillwork over the window), where Mass is celebrated only on special Sundays. Farther down, you'll walk by a grocery, *gelateria*, bakery, pharmacy, another grocery, and another *gelateria*.

• *On the left, in front of the second* gelateria, *an arch leads to what was a beach, where the town's stream used to hit the sea back in the 1970s. Continue down to the...*

Harbor Square and Breakwater: Vernazza, with the only natural harbor of the Cinque Terre, was established as the sole place boats could pick up the fine local wine. The two-foot-high square stone at the foot of the stairs by the Burgus Bar is marked *Sasso del Sego* (stone of tallow). Workers crushed animal flesh and fat in its basin to make tallow, which drained out of the tiny hole below. The tallow was then used to waterproof boats or wine barrels.

On the far side (behind Ristorante Pizzeria Vulnetia), peek into the tiny street with its commotion of arches. Vernazza's most characteristic side streets, called *carugi*, lead up from here. The trail (above the church, toward Monterosso) leads to the classic view of Vernazza (see "Best Views," earlier in this chapter).

Located in front of the harborside church, the tiny piazza—decorated with a river rock mosaic—is a popular hangout spot. It's where Vernazza's old ladies soak up the last bit of sun, and kids enjoy a patch of level ball field.

Vernazza's harborfront church is unusual for its strange entryway, which faces east (altar side). With relative peace and prosperity in the 16th century, the townspeople doubled the church in size, causing it to overtake a little piazza that once faced the west facade. From the square, use the "new" entry and climb the steps, keeping an eye out for the level necessary to keep the church high and dry. Inside, the lighter pillars in the back mark the 16th-century extension. Three historic portable crosses hanging on the walls are carried through town during Easter processions. They are replicas of crosses that Vernazza ships once carried on crusades to the Holy Land.

• *Finish your town tour seated out on the breakwater (and consider starting the tour directly below).*

The Burned-Out Sightseer's Visual Tour of Vernazza

• *Sit at the end of the harbor breakwater (perhaps with a glass of local white wine or something more interesting from a nearby bar—borrow the glass, they don't mind), face the town, and see...*

The Harbor: In a moderate storm, you'd be soaked, as waves routinely crash over the *molo* (breakwater, built in 1972). Waves can even wash away tourists squinting excitedly into their cameras. (I've seen it happen.) Enjoy the new waterfront piazza—carefully. The red flag proudly flying above the breakwater signifies that Vernazza is one of Italy's 130 most beautiful towns.

The train line (to your left) was constructed in 1874 to tie together a newly united Italy, and linked Turin and Genoa with Rome. A second line (hidden in a tunnel at this point) was built in the 1920s. The yellow building alongside the tracks was Vernazza's first train station. You can see the four bricked-up alcoves where people once waited for trains.

Vernazza's fishing fleet is down to just a couple of fishing boats (with the net spools). Vernazzans are still more likely to own a boat than a car. Boats are on buoys, except in winter or when the red storm flag indicates bad seas (in which case they're allowed to be pulled up onto the square—which is usually reserved for restaurant tables). In the 1970s, tiny Vernazza had one of Italy's top water polo teams, and the harbor was their "pool." Later, when the league required a real pool, Vernazza dropped out.

The Castle: On the far right, the castle, which is now a grassy park with great views (and nothing but stones), still guards the town (€1.50 donation supports the local Red Cross, daily 10:00–18:00; from harbor, take stairs by Trattoria Gianni and follow signs to Ristorante Al Castello, tower is a few steps beyond). It was the town's lookout back in pirate days. The highest umbrellas mark the recommended Ristorante Al Castello (see page 324). The squat tower on the water is great for a glass of wine or a meal. From the breakwater, you could follow the rope to the Ristorante Belforte (see page 324), and pop inside, past the submarine-strength door. A photo of a major storm showing the entire tower under a wave (not uncommon in the winter) hangs near the bar.

The Town: Vernazza has two halves. *Sciuiu* (Vernazzan dialect for "flowery") is the sunny side on the left, and *luvegu* (dank) is the shady side on the right. Houses below the castle were connected by an interior arcade—ideal for fleeing attacks. The "Ligurian pastel" colors are regulated by a commissioner of good taste in the regional government. The square before you is locally famous for some of the area's finest restaurants. The big red central house—on the site where Genoan warships were built in the 12th century—used to be a guardhouse.

Vernazza has the only natural harbor in the Cinque Terre. In the Middle Ages, there was no beach or square. The water went right up to the buildings, where boats would tie up, Venetian-style. Imagine what Vernazza looked like in those days, when it was the biggest and richest of the Cinque Terre towns. There was no pastel plaster, just fine stonework (traces of which survive above the Trattoria del Capitano). Apart from the added plaster, the general shape and size of the town has changed little in five centuries. Survey the windows and notice inhabitants quietly gazing back.

Above the Town: The small, round tower above the guardhouse—another part of the city fortifications—reminds us of Vernazza's importance in the Middle Ages, when it was a key ally of Genoa (whose archenemies were the other maritime republics, especially Pisa). Franco's Ristorante La Torre, just behind the tower, welcomes hikers who are finishing, starting, or simply contemplating the Corniglia–Vernazza hike, with great town views (between meal times, only drinks are served). Vineyards fill the mountainside beyond the town. Notice the many terraces. Someone—probably after too much of that local wine—calculated that the roughly 3,000 miles of dry stone walls built to terrace the region's vineyards have the same amount of stonework as the Great Wall of China.

Wine production is down nowadays, as the younger residents choose less physical work. But locals still maintain their tiny plots and proudly serve their family wines. The patchwork of local vineyards is atomized and complex because of inheritance traditions. Historically, families divided their land between their children. Parents wanted each child to get some good land. Because some lots were "kissed by the sun" while others were shady, the lots were split into increasingly tiny and eventually unviable pieces.

A single steel train line winds up the gully behind the tower. It is for the vintner's *trenino*, the tiny service train. Play "Where's *trenino?*" and see if you can find two trains. The vineyards once stretched as high as you can see, but since fewer people sweat in the fields these days, the most distant terraces have gone wild again.

The Church, School, and City Hall: Vernazza's Ligurian Gothic church, built with black stones quarried from Punta Mesco (the distant point behind you), dates from 1318. Note the gray stone that marks the church's 16th-century expansion. The gray-and-red house above the spire is the local elementary school (about 25 children attend). High-schoolers go to the "big city": La Spezia. The red building to the right of the schoolhouse, a former monastery, is the City Hall. Vernazza and Corniglia function as one community. Through most of the 1990s, the local government was Communist. In 1999, they elected a coalition of many parties working to rise above ideologies and simply make Vernazza a better place. Finally, on the top of the hill, with the best view of all, is the town cemetery.

ACTIVITIES

Tuesday Morning Market—Vernazza's meager business community is augmented Tuesday mornings (8:00–13:00) when a gang of cars and trucks pull into town for a tailgate market.

Beach—The harbor's sandy cove has sunning rocks and showers by the breakwater. There's also a ladder on the breakwater for deep-water access.

Boat Rental—Nord Est rents canoes, small motorboats, and jet skis from their stand on the harbor. With a rental boat, you can reach a tiny *acqua pendente* (waterfall) cove between Vernazza and Monterosso; locals call it their *laguna blu* (motorboat and jet skis-€60/4 hrs plus gas, usually about €15; canoes-€8/hr, includes snorkeling gear; June–Sept only, mobile 338-700-436, manuelamoggia @tiscali.it).

Massage—In 2000, Kate Allen moved her massage table from London to the Cinque Terre. She provides a good therapeutic rubdown for €55 an hour in the clinic across from Pensione Sorriso (call for an appointment, cash only, 100 yards above Vernazza's train tracks, tel. 0187-812-537, katarinaallen@hotmail.com).

NIGHTLIFE

Vernazza's younger generation of restaurant workers lets loose after hours. They work hard through the tourist season, travel in the winter, speak English, and enjoy connecting with international visitors.

There are just a couple of places where you're likely to find action after Vernazza's restaurants close down. (See "Eating," page 323, for details on these restaurants and bars.) The local scene starts at the **Blue Marlin Bar.** Then, everyone migrates to **Ristorante**

Belforte, which turns the old castle into a bar late in the evening (Thu–Sat only, closed in winter), with loud music and ample opportunity to dance with the locals. Then, the "after-after-hours" party moves down to the harbor.

Try the Ananasso Bar for early-evening happy-hour fun and cocktails (called "*aperitivi*") that both locals and visitors enjoy. Its harborfront tables get the last sunshine of the day. **Burgus Bar,** which is chic and hip with blasting jazzy dance music, is a popular early evening hangout as well. Sip on local wine and sample Franco and Rosita's artful, complimentary snack foods, available 18:00–20:30, at this wine bar (€8 *sciacchetrà* tasting with this book in 2008, Wed–Mon 7:00–24:00, closed Tue, Piazza Marconi 4, tel. 0187-812-556). At the top of the town, the Canoli brothers entertain their gang (of mostly tourists) at **Il Pirata delle Cinque Terre.**

For local music, hang out at **Ristorante Incadase da Piva** (tucked up the lane behind the pharmacy). When the cooking's done, Vernazza's troubadour, Piva, often gets out his guitar and sings traditional local songs as well as his own compositions.

SLEEPING

(€1 = about $1.30, country code: 39)
Vernazza, the essence of the Cinque Terre, is my top choice for a home base. There are two recommended pensions and piles of private rooms for rent.

These days, with so many rooms available, you can generally arrive without a reservation and find a place (but consider booking ahead for June–Aug, any weekend, and holidays such as Easter—for a full list of holidays, see "2008 Events in the Cinque Terre," page 286 and page 844 of the appendix). You can save money by arriving without a reservation—or gain the chance to shop around and land a place with a terrace and a view for less. Drop by any shop or bar and ask; most locals know someone who rents rooms.

Even today, pirates lurk on the Cinque Terre. People recommended here are listed for their communication skills (they speak English, have email, are reliable with bookings) and because they rent several rooms. Consequently, my recommendations charge more than comparable rooms you'll find if you just arrive and shop around. Bold travelers who drop in without a reservation and shop around will likely save €10–20 per double per night—and often get a better place and view to boot. The real Vernazza gems are stray single rooms with no interest in booking in advance or messing with email.

Anywhere you stay here requires some climbing. Night noise can be a problem if you're near the station. Rooms on the harbor come with church bells (but only from 7:00 to 22:00). Unlike in other villages, prices do not include breakfast unless otherwise noted. Only one building in Vernazza has an elevator. For details see "Sleeping in the Cinque Terre," page 292.

Be aware of—and help me enforce—my "New Ethic" system, which keeps hoteliers honest and guarantees you these prices for 2008 (see page 299).

Pensions

These pensions are listed on the map on page 313.

$$ Trattoria Gianni rents 23 small rooms and three new apartments just under the castle. The rooms are in two buildings—one funky, one modern—up a hundred tight, winding spiral stairs. The funky ones, which may or may not have private baths, are artfully decorated à la shipwreck, with tiny balconies and grand sea views *(con vista sul mare).* The new *(nuovo),* comfy rooms lack views, but have a super-scenic, cliff-hanging guests' garden. Both have modern bathrooms. Steely Marisa requires check-in before 16:00 or a phone call to explain when you're coming. Manuele

(Gianni's son, who now runs the restaurant), Simona, and the staff speak a little English (S-€43, D-€60, Db-€85, Tb-€105, 10 percent discount with cash and this book in 2008—request when you reserve, cancellations required 48 hours in advance or you'll be charged one night's deposit, closed Jan–Feb, Piazza Marconi 1, tel. & fax 0187-812-228, tel. 0187-821-003, www.giannifranzi .it, info@giannifranzi.it). Pick up your keys at Trattoria Gianni's restaurant/reception on the harbor square, and hike up scores of steps to funky old #41 or new and modern #47 at the top. If you arrive on Wednesday, when the restaurant is closed, pick up your keys at the *gelateria* by the grotto.

$$ Albergo Barbara, on the harbor square with nine simple but clean and modern rooms, is run by kindly, English-speaking Giuseppe and his Swiss wife, Patricia (D-€50, Db-€60–65, big Db with view-€100, 2-night stay preferred, fans, closed Dec–Feb, Piazza Marconi 30, tel. & fax 0187-812-398, mobile 338-793-3261, reserve online but pay cash, www.albergobarbara.it, albergobarbara@libero.it). The two big doubles on the third floor come with grand harbor views (top-floor doubles have small windows and small views).

Private Rooms (Affitta Camere)

Vernazza is honeycombed with private rooms year-round, offering the best values in town. Owners may be reluctant to reserve rooms far in advance. It's easiest to call a day or two ahead or simply show up in the morning and look around. Doubles cost €50–70, depending on the view, season, and plumbing. Most places accept only cash. Some have killer views, come with lots of stairs, and cost the same as a small dark place on a back lane over the train tracks. Little English is spoken at many of these places. If you call to let them know your arrival time (or call when you arrive, using the pay phone just below the station), they'll meet you at the train station.

Especially Well-Managed and Well-Appointed Rooms in the Inland Part of Town

These accommodations are listed on the map on page 313.

$$$ Tonino Basso rents four super, clean, modern rooms—at a steep price. Each room has its own computer for free Internet access. He's located near the post office, in the only building in Vernazza with an elevator. You get tranquility and air-conditioning, but no views. This is the only *affita camere* that takes credit cards (Sb-€60, Db-€100, Tb-€120, Qb-€150, call Tonino's mobile number upon arrival and he'll meet you, tel. 0187-821-264, mobile 335-269-436, fax 0187-812-807, toninobasso@libero.it). If you can't locate Tonino, ask his friends at Enoteca Sotto L'Arco at Via Roma 70.

$$ Camere Fontana Vecchia is a delightful place, with four bright, spacious, quiet rooms near the post office (no view). As the only place in Vernazza with almost no stairs to climb and the sound of a babbling brook outside your window, it's a great value (D-€60, Db-€75, T-€90, Tb-€110, €5 less off-season, fans and heat, open all year, Via Gavino 15, tel. & fax 0187-821-130, mobile 333-454-9371, m.annamaria@libero.it, youthful and efficient Anna speaks English).

$$ Giuliano Basso rents four pleasant rooms, crafted with care, just above town in the terraced wilds (sea views from terraces). Straddling a ravine among orange trees, it's an artfully decorated, Robinson Crusoe–chic wonderland, proudly built out of stone by Giuliano himself (Db-€70, Db-suite-€100 with air-con, apartment with private rooftop balcony-€100, fridge access, above train station—so with more train noise than others, mobile 333-341-4792, or have the Enoteca Sotto L'Arco at Via Roma 30 contact him or his American partner Michele, www.cdh.it/giuliano, giuliano@cdh.it). Call to be met at the station. To walk there, head inland from the station and hike up the Corniglia trail; 100 yards beyond Pensione Sorriso, at the second Corniglia sign, follow the lane left.

Other Reliable Places Scattered Through Town and the Harborside

$$$ **La Malà** is Vernazza's new jetsetter pad. The four pristine white rooms boast four-star-hotel-type extras, a common terrace that looks out over the rocky shore, air-conditioning, and included breakfast at a bar (Db-€140, Db-suite-€170–190, ring at Piazza Marconi 15, tel. 334-287-5718, fax 0187-812-218, www.lamala.it, Armanda).

$$$ **Monica Lercari** rents three classy rooms with modern comforts, perched on the top of town. One is a honeymooners' paradise, with a private terrace and soaring view of the ocean (D-€120 with seaview terrace and external bathroom, Db-€100 with town view; air-con, includes breakfast, next to recommended Ristorante Al Castello, tel. 0187-812-296, alcastellovernazza @yahoo.it).

$$ **Antonio and Ingrid Fenelli Camere** rent three very central, comfy, and fairly priced rooms. Friendly Antonio—a hulking man in a huge white T-shirt and bathing suit—is a fixture on the village streets (small Db-€55, Db-€65, Tb-€80, two-person apartment with terrace-€85, air-con, 10 steps above pharmacy at Via Carattino 2, tel. 0187-812-183).

$$ **Memo Rooms** offers three newly renovated, immaculate rooms overlooking the main street, in what feels like a miniature hotel. Enrica will meet you if you call upon arrival (Db-€70 maximum in 2008, Via Roma 15, tel. 0187-812-360, mobile 338-285-2385).

$$ **Martina Callo** rents four rooms overlooking the square, up plenty of steps near the silent-at-night church tower (room #1: Tb-€95 or Qb-€110 with harbor view; room #2: huge Qb family room with no view-€110; room #3: Db with grand view terrace-€75; room #4: roomy Db with no view-€55; ring bell at Piazza Marconi 26, tel. & fax 0187-812-365, mobile 329-435-5344, www .roomartina.com, roomartina@roomartina.com).

$$$ **Egi Rooms** (pronounced "edgy"), run by English-speaking Egi Verduschi, offers three good, clean, and colorful rooms, right in the center on the main drag (S-€70, D-€90, plush and designer Db-€120, Tb-€160, Qb-€180, across the street from *gelateria* just before harbor square on main drag at Via Visconti 9, mobile 338-822-3202, www.egirooms.com, egidioverduschi @libero.it).

$$ **Nicolina** rents four funky, lived-in rooms. The largest has a view; two others overlook Vernazza's main drag. Inquire at Pizzeria Vulnetia on the harbor square (viewless Db-€70, view Db-€80, Tb-€100, Qb with terrace and view-€130, Piazza Marconi 29, tel. & fax 0187-821-193, www.camerenicolina.it, camerenicolina.info @cdh.it).

$$ Rosa Vitali rents two apartments across from the pharmacy overlooking the main street. One, for up to three people, has a terrace and fridge (top floor); the other, for four, has windows and a full kitchen (Db-€75, Tb-€100, Qb-€120, €5 extra for 1-night stays, reception at Via Visconti 10 between the grotto and Piazza Marconi, tel. 0187-821-181, mobile 340-267-5009, www.rosacamere.it, rosa.vitali@libero.it).

$$ Bar Baia Saracena rents out three clean, modern rooms equipped with double-paned windows to keep out the noise of the train and main street below (Db-€60–70, located out on breakwater, mobile 349-690-9377, www.baiasaracena.com, info @baiasaracena.com).

Other Private Rooms in Vernazza

I consider many of these places overpriced but reliable. Some claim to agree to my "New Ethic" system, but I can't say for sure how committed they are—confirm these prices when reserving and let me know about violations. Consider these options only if the places above are booked up:

$$ Francamaria rents four sharp, comfortable, and creatively renovated but expensive rooms. The two rooms above Trattoria Gianni's bar offer great people-watching perches, but can be noisy until about 23:30 (Db-€75–95, Qb-€150, prices depend on view and season, Piazza Marconi 30, tel. 0187-812-002, mobile 328-711-9728, fax 0187-812-956, www.francamaria.com, francamaria @francamaria.com). Son Giovanni has three rooms of his own to rent (same prices but no views). Their reception is on the ground floor of the Albergo Barbara building.

$$ Elisabetta's Villino Azzurro has three ramshackle rooms with views. The lower room has a small window with a sea view; the two rooms upstairs come with view terraces; and the uppermost terrace has 360-degree views of the town, castle, terraced hills, and the sea—but the room is tiny. This one is not overpriced...but let me know if it's not reliable (Db-€50–62, fans, Via Carattino 62, mobile 347-451-1834, www.elisabettacarro.it, carroelisabetta @hotmail.com).

$$ Affitta Camere Alberto Basso rents two clean, modern rooms: one with a harbor view over the noisy piazza, the other quiet and behind the main street (Db-€75, check in at Internet Point in the middle of town—see map on page 313, albertobasso @hotmail.com).

$$ Tilde's cheery and clean little room has a sea view (Db-€75, up Via Mazzini 9, mobile 339-298-9323, rasocri74@alice.it).

$$ Daria Bianchi offers eight clean, spacious, and comfortable rooms near the station. Most have bright colors, worn carpeting, and either overlook the main street or the inland hills (Db-€70,

Qb-€100–120, fans, tel. 0187-812-151, mobile 338-581-4688, www .vernazzarooms.com).

$$ Affitta Camere da Annamaria offers six small basic rooms (avoid the two without views) with barnacled ambience up a series of comically tight spiral staircases (Db-€75 with town views and terrace, Db-€85 for top room with seaview terrace; at pharmacy, climb up Via Carattino to #64; tel. 0187-821-082, mobile 349-887-8150, www.camerelatorre.com).

More Options: **Eva's Rooms** (3 rooms, Db-€50–70, ask for air-con, ring at Via Roma 56, tel. 0187-821-134, www.evasrooms .it), **Armanda** (€70, no view, near castle, Piazza Marconi 15, mobile 347-306-4760, www.armanda.it, info@armanda.it), **Franca** (Db-€80, tiny terrace with big view, basic room, ring at Via Carattino 16, tel. 0187-812-274), **Manuela Moggia** (Db-€70, Qb-€120, top of town at Via Gavino 22, tel. 0187-812-397, mobile 333-413-6374, www.camere-vernazza.com, manuelanoggia@tiscali.it), **Filippo Rooms** (2 rooms, Db-€65, tel. 0187-812-244), **Patrizia** (3 rooms, all with kitchens, Db-€70, Qb-€100, on main street, next to grotto and *gelateria* at Via Visconti 30, mobile 335-653-1563, www.camere -vernazza.com, bemili@libero.it), **Villa Antonia** (2 rooms with shared bathroom, D-€60–70, on main drag, tel. 0187-821-143, mobile 333-971-5602), and **Sergio Callo Rooms** (3 spacious but dark rooms, Db-€75, Tb-€90, Via Roma 23, tel. 0187-812-284, gemmina@5terre.com).

EATING

Breakfast

Locals take breakfast about as seriously as flossing. A cappuccino and a pastry or a piece of focaccia does it. Most accommodations don't come with breakfast (when they do, I've noted so in my listings). Instead, you have several fun options.

The two harborfront bars offer the most ambience. **Ananasso Bar** feels Old World, with youthful energy and a great location (toasted *panini,* pastries). Eat a bit cheaper at the bar (you're welcome to picnic on a bench or rock) or enjoy the best-situated tables in town (Fri–Wed 8:00–late, closed Thu). **Bar Baia Saracena** has a chalkboard explaining their various fixed-price tourist meals (€5–7 for breakfast). Luca, the owner, promises a free slice of *bucellato* (the local coffee cake) for breakfast as a bonus for anyone with this 2008 book having breakfast here (opens at 7:30, closed Wed July–Aug, closed Fri Sept–June, located out on the breakwater, tel. 0187-812-113).

The **Blue Marlin Bar** (mid-town) serves a good array of clearly priced à la carte items and the only American-style eggs in town. It's run by Massimo with able help from his younger cousin,

Stefano (Fri–Wed 7:00–24:00, closed Thu, just below station, tel. 0187-821-149). If awaiting a train, the Blue Marlin's outdoor seats beat the platform.

At **Il Pirata delle Cinque Terre,** dynamic Sicilian duo Gianluca and Massimo (twins, a.k.a. the Canoli Brothers) enthusiastically offer a great assortment of handcrafted, authentic Sicilian pastries. Their fun and playful service makes up for the lack of a view. Gianluca is a pastry artist, hand-painting fanciful sculptured marzipan. Their sweet pastry breakfasts are a hit, with a stunning array of hot-out-of-the-oven treats like *panzerotto* (made of ricotta, cinnamon, and vanilla, €2) and hot meat-and-cheese pies (€2.50). Other favorites include their *granitas*—slushees made from fresh fruit (daily 6:30–24:00, simple lunches and tasty dinners, no extra charge for sitting down, by post office at top of town, Via Gavino 36, tel. 0187-812-047). While the atmosphere of the place seems like suburban Milano, it has a curious charisma among its customers—bringing Vernazza a welcome bit of Sicily.

Lunch and Dinner
If you enjoy Italian cuisine and seafood, Vernazza's restaurants are worth the splurge. All take pride in their cooking and have similar prices. Wander around at about 20:00 and compare the ambience, but don't wait too late to eat—many kitchens close at 22:00. To get an outdoor table on summer weekends, reserve ahead. Expect to spend €10 for pastas, €12 for *secondi*, and €2 for a cover charge. Harborside restaurants and bars are easygoing. You're welcome to grab a cup of coffee or glass of wine and disappear somewhere on the breakwater, returning your glass when you're done. If you dine in Vernazza but are staying in another town, be sure to check train schedules before dining, as trains run less frequently in the evening.

Harborfront View Options
Ristorante Al Castello is run by gracious and English-speaking Monica, her husband Massimo, kind Mario, and the rest of her family (you won't see mamma—she's busy personally cooking each *secondo*). Hike high above town to just below the castle for great seafood and regional specialties with commanding views (Thu–Tue 12:00–15:00 for lunch, 15:00–19:00 for drinks and snacks on cliff-hugging terrace, 19:00–22:00 for dinner, closed Wed and Nov–April, tel. 0187-812-296). Their *lasagne al pesto* and *ravioli di pesce* are time-honored family specialties and their *antipasto misto mare* is a sharable €15 treat for starters. Drop into Monica's new wine cantina and select the bottle of your choice.

Ristorante Belforte's experimental and creative cuisine includes a delicate, curry-seasoned *risotto con scampi* and the classic *antipasto del nostro chef* (€36 for six plates—plenty for two people). From the breakwater, follow either the stairs or the rope that leads up and around to the restaurant. You'll find a tangle of tables embedded in four levels of the lower part of the old castle. For the ultimate seaside perch, call and reserve one of four tables on the *terrazza con vista* (terrace with view). But skip this place if the weather's bad, since most of Belforte's seating is outdoors. Explore the delightfully translated menu. The Belforte is also a good spot, even outside of mealtimes, for a romantic drink (€13 pastas, €23 *secondi*, Wed–Mon 12:00–22:00, kitchen closed 15:30–19:00 but drinks and snacks served all day, closed Tue and Nov–March, tel. 0187-812-222, spritely Michela). For info on late-night Belforte action, see "Nightlife," page 317.

Four Harborside Winners: These places—each with fine indoor and outdoor seating—fill the harborfront with happy eaters: **Gambero Rosso,** with talented chef Claudio, is considered Vernazza's best restaurant. It feels classy and costs only a few euros more than the others (Tue–Sun 12:00–15:00 & 19:00–22:00, closed Mon and Dec–Feb, Piazza Marconi 7, tel. 0187-812-265). **Trattoria del Capitano** might serve the best food for the money, including *spaghetti chitarra* (egg-based pasta entangled with various types of seafood) and their *grigliata mista*—a mix of seasonal Mediterranean fish (Wed–Mon 12:00–15:00 & 19:00–22:00, closed Tue except in Aug, closed Dec–Jan, tel. 0187-812-201, while Paolo speaks English, grandpa Giacomo doesn't need to). **Trattoria Gianni** is an old standby for locals and tourists alike, especially for well-prepared seafood and Tonino's steady, reliable, and friendly service (Thu–Tue 12:00–15:00 & 19:30–22:00, closed Wed except July–Aug, tel. 0187-812-228). The simpler **Ristorante Pizzeria Vulnetia** serves regional specialties and €8 pizzas (Tue–Sun 12:00–15:30 & 18:30–22:00, closed Mon, Piazza Marconi 29, tel. 0187-821-193).

Inland Restaurants

Several of Vernazza's inland places manage to compete without the harbor ambience, but with slightly cheaper prices:

Trattoria da Sandro, on the main drag, mixes Genovese and Ligurian cuisine with friendly service. It can be a peaceful alternative to the harborside scene (Wed–Mon 12:00–15:00 & 19:00–22:00, closed Tue, just below train station, Via Roma 62, tel. 0187-812-223, Gabriella and Alessandro).

Antica Osteria Il Baretto is another solid bet for homey, reasonably priced, traditional cuisine, run by Simone, Zia, and family (Tue–Sat 8:00–16:00 & 18:00–24:00, closed Mon, indoor and outdoor seating, Via Roma 31).

Ristorante Incadase da Piva is a rare bit of old Vernazza.

Charismatic Piva is known for his fine *tegame alla Vernazza* (typical Vernazzan dish with anchovies, tomatoes, and potatoes baked in the oven), *risotto con frutti di mare* (seafood risotto), and love of music. The town troubadour, he often serenades his guests when the cooking's done (tucked away 20 yards off the main drag, up a lane behind the pharmacy).

Other Eating Options

Il Pirata delle Cinque Terre is popular for breakfast, lunch (only sandwiches and light fare), dinner (pastas, salads, Sicilian specialties), and its homemade desserts and drinks (at the top of town; see "Breakfast," page 323, for complete description).

Franco's Ristorante La Torre, sitting humbly above Vernazza on the trail to Corniglia, offers family-run warmth, a spectacular view, perfect peace, and especially romantic dinners at sunset. Hours can be sporadic, so confirm that he's open before hiking up the 100 steps (Wed–Mon 12:00–21:30, sometimes also open Tue, kitchen closed 15:00–19:30 but drinks are served all day, tel. 0187-821-082, mobile 338-404-1181).

Bar Baia Saracena (Saracen Bay) is a pizzeria where one waiter actually takes the pirate theme to heart, swinging around with earrings that blow in the wind. The bar has a dozen plastic tables on the breakwater and serves great pizza, but pass on the microwaved pastas (€5–7 salads, €8 pizza, €4 glasses of *sciacchetrà*—sweet dessert wine, closed Fri, also see listing under "Breakfast," page 323).

Pizzerias, Sandwiches, Groceries, Gelato: The main street creatively fills tourists' needs. Two pizzerias stay busy, and while they mostly do take-out, each will let you sit and eat for the same cheap price. One has tables on the street, and the other (**Ercole**) hides a tiny terrace and a few tables out back. The **Blue Marlin Bar** offers a good selection of *bruschetta,* salad, pizza, and sandwiches (see listing under "Breakfast," page 323).

The **Forno bakery** has good focaccia and veggie tarts, and several bars sell sandwiches and pizza by the slice. Grocery stores also make inexpensive sandwiches to order (generally Mon–Tue and Thu–Sat 8:00–13:00 & 17:00–19:30, Wed 8:00–13:00, closed Sun). Tiny jars of pesto spread give elegance to picnics. The town's three *gelaterias* are good. What looks like Gelateria Amore Mio (near the grotto, mid-town), is actually **Gelateria Stalin**—founded in 1968 by a pastry chef with that unfortunate name. His niece Sonia and nephew Francesco now run it, and are generous with free tastes (daily 8:00–24:00, 24 flavors, sit there or take it to go).

Monterosso al Mare (Town #5)

This is a resort with a few cars and lots of hotels, rentable beach umbrellas, crowds, and a thriving late-night scene. Monterosso

al Mare—the only Cinque Terre town built on flat land—has two parts: A new town (called Fegina) with a parking lot, train station, and a TI, and an old town (Centro Storico), which cradles Old World charm in its small, crooked lanes. In the old town, you'll find hole-in-the-wall shops, pastel townscapes, and a new generation of creative small-businesspeople eager to keep their visitors happy.

A pedestrian tunnel connects the old with the new. But take a small detour around the point for a nicer walk. It offers a close-up view of two sights: a 16th-century lookout tower, built after the last serious pirate raid in 1545, and a Nazi "pillbox," a small, low, concrete bunker where gunners hid. (During World War II, nearby La Spezia was an important Axis naval base, and Monterosso was bombed while the Germans were here.)

Strolling the waterfront promenade, you can pick out each of the Cinque Terre towns decorating the coast. After dark they sparkle. Monterosso is the most enjoyable of the five for young travelers wanting to connect with other young travelers and looking for a little evening action. Even so, Monterosso is not a full-blown Portofino-style resort—and locals appreciate quiet, sensitive guests.

ORIENTATION

Tourist Information

The TI Proloco is next to the train station (April–Oct daily 9:00–19:00, closed Nov–March, exit station and go left a few doors, tel. 0187-817-506, www.prolocomonterosso.it, Cristiana). The Cinque Terre has park offices on Piazza Garibaldi in the old town and in the train station in the new town (daily 8:00–22:00, until 20:00 in winter, tel. 0187-817-059, www.parconazionale5terre.it, parcoragazze @hotmail.com).

Arrival in Monterosso

By Train: Train travelers arrive in the new town, where it's a scenic, flat, 10-minute stroll to all the old-town action (leave station to the left, but for hotels in the new town, turn right out of station).

Shuttle buses run along the waterfront between the old town (Piazza Garibaldi, just beyond the tunnel), the train station, and the parking lot at the end of Via Fegina (*Campo Sportivo* stop). While the buses can be convenient, saving you a 10-minute schlepp with your bags, they only go once an hour, and are likely not worth the trouble (€1.50, free with Cinque Terre Card).

The other alternative is to take a taxi (certain vehicles have permission to drive in the old city center). They usually wait outside the train station, but you may have to call (€7 from station to Centro Storico, mobile 335-616-5842 or 335-628-0933).

By Car: Monterosso is 30 minutes off the freeway (exit: Carrodano). Parking is easy (except July, Aug, and summer weekends) in the huge beachfront guarded lot (€12/day, €24 overnight). Another lot is farther up Via Roma (€15/day, if entering Monterosso's Centro Storico from the freeway it's on the left, 10-minute downhill walk to Piazza Garibaldi). See "Driving and Parking" on page 338 for directions from Milan and tips on driving in the Cinque Terre.

Helpful Hints

Medical Help: The town's bike-riding, leather-bag-toting doctor is Dr. Vitone (mobile 338-853-0949).

Internet Access: The Net, a few steps off the main drag (Via Roma), has 10 high-speed computers. Enzo happily provides information on the Cinque Terre and can burn your photos onto a CD for €6 (daily 10:00–22:00, off-season until 19:00, Via Vittorio Emanuele 55, tel. 0187-817-288, www.monterossonet.com). There's also free Internet access for customers at the **Il Casello** restaurant/bar (see "Eating," page 337).

Laundry: A full-service launderette is at Via Mazzini 4 (13-pound wash-and-dry for €12, allow 2 hours, daily 9:00–20:00, just off Via Roma below L'Alta Marea restaurant. **Lavarapido,** in the new part of town, will return your laundry to your hotel for you, and charges the same price (Via Molinelli 17, mobile 339-4884-0940).

Massage: Giorgio Moggia, the local physiotherapist, gives good massages (€50/hr at your hotel, tel. 339-314-6127, giomogg @tin.it).

SELF-GUIDED WALK

Welcome to Monterosso

• *Hike out from the dock in the old town and climb a few rough steps to the very top of the...*

Breakwater: If you're visiting by boat, you'll start here anyway. From this point, you can survey the old town and the new town (stretching to the left, with train station and parking lot). The little fort above is a private home. The harbor now hosts more paddleboats than fishing boats. Sand erosion is a major problem. The partial breakwater is designed to save the beach from washing away. While old-timers remember a vast beach, their grandchildren truck in sand each spring to give tourists something to lie on. (The Nazis liked the Cinque Terre, too—find two of their bomb-hardened bunkers, near left and far right.)

The fancy €300-a-night, four-star Hotel Porto Roca (on the far right) marks the trail to Vernazza. High above, you see the costly road built in the 1980s to connect Cinque Terre towns with the freeway over the hills. The two capes (Punta di Montenero and Punta Mesco) define the Cinque Terre region—you can just about make out the towns from here. The closer cape, Punta Mesco, marks an important sea-life sanctuary, home to a rare sea grass that provides an ideal home for fish eggs. Buoys keep fishing boats away. The cape was once a quarry, providing employment to locals who chipped out the stones used to cobble the streets of Genoa. On the far end of the new town, you can just see the statue named *Il Gigante*. It's 45 feet tall and once held a trident. While it looks as if it was hewn from the rocky cliff, it's actually made of reinforced concrete and dates from the beginning of the 20th century, when it supported a dancing terrace for a *fin de siècle* villa. WWII bombs left the giant holding nothing but memories of Monterosso's glamorous age.

• *From the breakwater, walk to the old-town square (just past the train tracks and beyond the beach). Find the statue of a dandy holding what looks like a box cutter in...*

Piazza Garibaldi: The statue honors Giuseppe Garibaldi, the dashing firebrand revolutionary who, in 1870, helped unite the people of Italy into a modern nation. Facing Garibaldi, with your back to the sea, you'll see (from right to left) the City Hall (with the now-required European Union flag aside the Italian one), a big home and recreation center for poor and homeless elderly, and a park information center (in a building bombed in 1945 by the Allies, who were attempting to take out the train line). You'll also see the A Ca' du Sciensa pub (with historic town photos inside and upstairs, you're welcome to pop in for a look—see "Nightlife," page 333).

Monterosso al Mare

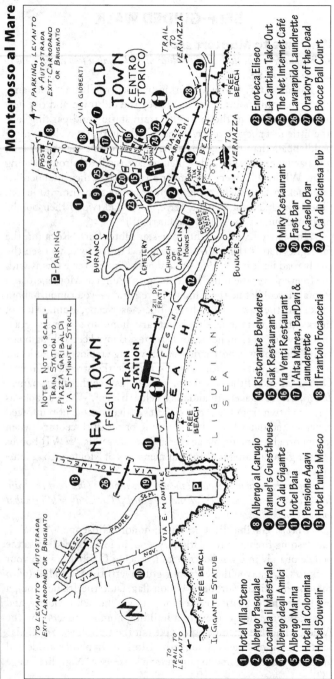

1. Hotel Villa Steno
2. Albergo Pasquale
3. Locanda il Maestrale
4. Albergo degli Amici
5. Albergo Marina
6. Hotel la Colonnina
7. Hotel Souvenir
8. Albergo al Carugio
9. Manuel's Guesthouse
10. A Cà du Gigante
11. Hotel Baia
12. Pensione Agavi
13. Hotel Punta Mesco
14. Ristorante Belvedere
15. Ciak Restaurant
16. Via Venti Restaurant
17. L'Alta Marea, BarDavi & Launderette
18. Il Frantoio Focacceria
19. Miky Restaurant
20. Fast Bar
21. Il Casello Bar
22. A Ca' du Sciensa Pub
23. Enoteca Eliseo
24. La Cantina Take-Out
25. The Net Internet Café
26. Lavarapido Launderette
27. Oratory of the Dead
28. Bocce Ball Court

Cinque Terre

Just under the bell tower (with back to the sea, it's on your left) a set of covered arcades facing the sea is where the old-timers hang out (they see all and know all). The crenellated bell tower marks the church.

• *Go to church (the entrance is on the inland side).*

Church of St. John the Baptist: This black-and-white church, with marble from Carrara, is typical of this region's Romanesque style. Note the lacy stone rose window above the entrance. The church dates from 1307—the proud inscription on the middle column inside reads "MilleCCCVII." Outside the church, on the side facing the main street, find the high-water mark from a November 1966 flood (the same month as the flood that devastated Florence).

• *Leaving the church, turn left immediately and go to church again.*

Oratory of the Dead: During the Counter-Reformation, the Catholic Church offset the rising influence of the Lutherans by creating brotherhoods of good works. These religious Rotary clubs were called "confraternities." Monterosso had two, nicknamed White and Black. This building is the oratory of the Black group, whose mission—as the macabre decor indicates was to arrange for funerals and take care of widows, orphans, the shipwrecked, and the souls of those who ignore the request for a €1 donation. It dates from the 16th century, and membership has passed from father to son for generations. Notice the fine 17th-century carved choir stalls just inside the door. Look up on the ceiling to find the symbol of the confraternity: a skull, crossbones, and an hourglass... death awaits us all.

• *Return to the beach and find the brick steps that lead up to the hill-capping convent (starting between the train tracks and the pedestrian tunnel).*

The Switchbacks of the Monks: Follow the yellow brick road (OK, it's orange...but I couldn't help singing as I skipped skyward). Go constantly uphill until you reach a convent church, then a cemetery, in a ruined castle at the summit. The lane *(Salita dei Cappuccini)* is nicknamed *Zii di Frati* (switchbacks of the monks). Midway up the switchbacks, you'll see a statue of St. Francis and a wolf enjoying a grand view.

• *From here, backtrack 20 yards and continue uphill. When you reach a gate marked Convento e Chiesa Cappuccini, you have arrived. Enter the church.*

Church of the Cappuccin Monks: The former convent (until recently a hotel) is now accommodating monks. Before stepping inside, notice the church's striped Romanesque facade. It's all fake. Tap it—no marble, just cheap 18th-century stucco. Sit in the rear pew. The high altarpiece painting of St. Francis can be rolled up on special days to reveal a statue of Mary, which stands behind it. Look at the statue of St. Anthony to the right and smile (you're on convent camera). Wave at the security camera—they're nervous about the precious painting to your left.

This fine painting of the Crucifixion is attributed to Antony Van Dyck, the Flemish master who lived and worked for years in nearby Genoa (though art historians suspect that, at best, it was painted by someone in the artist's workshop). When Jesus died, the earth went dark. Notice the eclipsed sun in the painting, just to the right of the cross. Do the electric candles work? Pick one up, pray for peace, and plug it in. (Leave €0.50, or unplug it and put it back.)

• *Leave and turn left to hike uphill to the cemetery that fills the remains of the castle, capping the hill. Look out from the gate and enjoy the view.*

Cemetery and Ruined Castle: In the Dark Ages, the village huddled within this castle. Slowly it expanded. Notice the town view from here—no sea. You're looking at the oldest part of Monterosso, huddled behind the hill, out of view of 13th-century pirates. Explore the cemetery, but remember that cemeteries are sacred and treasured places (as is clear by the abundance of fresh flowers). Ponder the black-and-white photos of grandparents past. *Q.R.P.* is *Qui Riposa in Pace* (a.k.a. R.I.P.). Rich families had their own little tomb buildings. See if you can find the Odoardo family tomb—look to the wall on the left (apparently, February 30 happened in Monterosso). Climb to the very summit—the castle's keep, or place of last refuge. Priests are buried in a line of graves closest to the sea, but facing inland—the town's holy sanctuary high on the hillside (above the road, hiding behind trees). Each Cinque Terre town has a lofty sanctuary, dedicated to Mary and dear to the village hearts.

• *From here, your tour is over—any trail leads you back into town.*

ACTIVITIES

Beaches—Monterosso's beaches, immediately in front of the train station, are easily the Cinque Terre's best and most crowded. This town is a sandy resort with rentable beach extras: Figure €15 to rent two chairs and an umbrella for the day. Light lunches are served by beach cafés to sunbathers at their lounge chairs. It's often worth the euros to enjoy a private beach. Beaches are free (and marked on the map on page 330) only where you see no umbrellas. The local hidden beach, which is free and generally less crowded, is tucked away under Il Casello restaurant at the east end of town, near the trailhead to Vernazza. The bocce ball court (next to Il Casello) is busy with the old boys enjoying their favorite pastime.

Kayaks—Kayak rental is available on the beach in front of the train station (€6/hr for 1-person kayak, €10/hr for 2-person kayak, mobile 328-288-6827 or 339-681-0265, Maurizio). The paddle to Vernazza is a favorite.

Shuttle Buses for High-Country Hikes—Monterosso's bus service (described in "Arrival in Monterosso," page 328) continues beyond the town limits but check the schedules—only one or two departures a day head upward. A route goes to Colle di Gritta, where you can hike back down to Monterosso via the Sanctuary of Soviore (1 hour, easy) or to Levanto via Punta Mesco (2.5 hours, strenuous). Rides cost €1.50 (free with Cinque Terre Card, pick up schedule from park office). For hiking details, ask at either park info booth (at the train station or Piazza Garibaldi).

Boat Rides—From the old-town harbor, boats run nearly hourly (10:30–17:00) to Vernazza, Manarola, Riomaggiore, and Portovenere. Schedules are posted in Cinque Terre park offices (for details, see page 284). A smaller, privately operated boat connects Vernazza and Monterosso more frequently (2/hr).

NIGHTLIFE

Wander over to **Il Casello** for nightlife with a sea view. Enthusiastically run by Bacco, it's the best on-the-beach drinking spot—inexpensive and hip—with a creative and fun drink list. Built in about 1870 as the town's first train station, Il Casello overlooks the beach on the road toward Vernazza, with outdoor tables on a rocky outcrop sandwiched between old-town beaches. It's also a great place for a salad or sandwich during the day (daily 10:30–24:00, closed Oct–March, shorter hours outside June–Aug, tel. 0187-818-330).

A Ca' du Sciensa has nothing to do with science—it's the last name of the town moneybags who owned this old mansion. The antique dumbwaiter is still in use—a remnant from the days when servants toiled downstairs while the big shots wined and dined up top. This classy-yet-laid-back pub offers breezy square seating, bar action on the ground level, an intimate lounge upstairs, and discreet balconies overlooking the square to share with your best travel buddy. It's a good place for light meals (until 23:00) and plenty of drinks. Luca and Andrea encourage you to wander around the place and enjoy the old Cinque Terre photo collection (daily 11:00–24:00 and often later, serves late-night sandwiches and pasta, closed Wed Nov–March, Piazza Garibaldi 17, tel. 0187-818-233).

Enoteca Eliseo, the first wine bar in town, comes with operatic ambience. Eliseo and his wife, Mary, love music and wine. You can select a fine bottle from their shop shelf, and for €6 extra, enjoy it and the village action from their cozy tables. They serve complimentary light snacks. Wines sold by the glass *(bicchiere)* are posted (daily 9:00–24:00, closed Tue Nov–Feb, Piazza Matteotti

3, a few blocks inland behind church, tel. 0187-817-308).

BarDavi showcases owners Daniele's and Valeria's stylish knack for delicious entertainment. Each day after 17:00, they offer a "cocktails *con tapas*" deal: Buy a €6 drink or glass of wine and get a light meal's worth of good, local appetizers for free (daily 7:30–22:00, closed Tue Sept–June, under the arch on main drag, Via Roma 34, tel. 0187-817-019).

Fast Bar, where young travelers and night owls gather, is located on Via Roma in the old town. Customers mix travel tales with big, cold beers, and the crowd gets noisier as the night rolls on (sandwiches and snacks served until midnight, open nightly until 2:00, closed Thu Nov–March).

SLEEPING

(€1 = about $1.30, country code: 39)

Monterosso, the most beach-resort of the five Cinque Terre towns, offers maximum comfort and ease. The TI Proloco just outside the train station can give you a list of €30–35 per-person double rooms. To locate the hotels, see the map on page 330.

In the Old Town

$$$ Hotel Villa Steno is lovingly managed and features great view balconies, private gardens off some rooms, air-conditioning, and the friendly help of English-speaking Matteo and his wife, Carla. Of their 16 rooms, 12 have view balconies (Sb-€95, Db-€105, Tb-€175, Qb-€200, includes hearty buffet breakfast, €10 per night discount with cash and this book in 2008, Internet access, full-service laundry for guests, Via Roma 109, tel. 0187-817-028 or 0187-818-336, fax 0187-817-354, www.pasini.com, steno@pasini.com). It's a 10-minute hike (or €7 taxi ride) from the train station to the top of the old town. Readers get a free Cinque Terre info packet and a glass of the local sweet wine, *sciacchetrà,* when they check in—ask for it. The Steno has a tiny parking lot (free, but call to reserve a spot).

$$$ Albergo Pasquale is a modern, comfortable place, run by the same family as the Hotel Villa Steno (previous listing). It's just a few steps from the beach, boat dock, tunnel entrance to the new town, and train tracks. Noise is not a problem (same prices and welcome drink as Villa Steno; air-con, all rooms with sea view, elevator, Via Fegina 8, tel. 0187-817-550 or 0187-817-477, fax 0187-817-056, www.pasini.com, pasquale@pasini.com, Felicita and Marco).

$$$ Locanda il Maestrale rents six small, stylish rooms in a sophisticated and peaceful little inn. While renovated with all the modern comforts, it retains centuries-old character under frescoed ceilings. Its peaceful sun terrace overlooks the old town and Via Roma action (small Db-€110, Db-€130, suite-€170, less off-season, includes breakfast, Via Roma 37, tel. 0187-817-013, mobile 338-4530-531, fax 0187-817-084, www.locandamaestrale.net, maestrale@monterossonet.com).

$$$ Albergo Marina, run by an enthusiastic husband-and-wife team, has 25 decent rooms and a garden with lemon trees (Db-€100–130, 10 percent discount with cash and this book, elevator, air-con, free bikes, kayak and snorkel equipment, Via Buranco 40, tel. & fax 0187-817-242 or 0187-817-613, www.hotelmarinacinqueterre.it, marina@cinqueterre.it).

The not-as-nice **$$$ Albergo degli Amici,** located just next door, has 43 basic rooms (Db-€93–128, Db with optional half-pension-€185–213, breakfast-€8, no views from rooms, elevator, peaceful above-it-all view garden with lawn chairs, next door to Albergo Marina at Via Buranco 36, tel. 0187-817-544, fax 0187-817-424, www.hotelamici.it, amici@cinqueterre.it).

$$$ Hotel la Colonnina, a comfy, modern place with 19 big rooms, is buried in the town's fragrant and sleepy back streets (Db-€130, Tb-€160, Qb-€195, €15 more for bigger rooms with view-less terrace, cash only, air-con, elevator, barren rooftop terrace, garden, Via Zuecca 6, tel. 0187-817-439, fax 0187-817-788, www.lacolonninacinqueterre.it, info@lacolonninacinqueterre.it, Paola and Ilaria). The hotel is in the old town by the train tracks, directly behind the statue of Garibaldi (take street to left of A Ca' du Sciensa one block up, hotel is to the right).

$$ Hotel Souvenir is Monterosso's cash-only backpacker's hotel. It has two buildings, each utilitarian but comfortable (one more stark than the other). The first is for students (S-€30, Sb-€35, D-€50, Db-€60, T-€75); the other is nicer and pricier, with a lounge and pleasant, leafy courtyard (Sb-€40, Db-€80, Tb-€120, breakfast-€5). Walk three blocks inland from the main old-town square to Via Gioberti 24 (tel. 0187-817-822, tel. & fax 0187-817-595, www.souvenirhotel.eu, hotel_souvenir@yahoo.com).

$$ Albergo al Carugio is a simple, practical 10-room place in a big apartment-style building at the top of the old town. It's quiet, comfy-yet-forgettable, and run in a crooked-painting-on-the-wall way (Db-€80 July–Aug, Db-€70 otherwise, Via Roma 100, tel. 0187-817-453).

$$ Manuel's Guesthouse is a ramshackle place run by a ramshackle artist and his nephew with five big, basic rooms and a grand view (Db-€60, Tb-€75, prices good with this book in 2008, cash only, Manuel has an honor-system beer and wine bar, €5/liter; in old town, up about 100 steps, behind church at top of town, mobile 328-842-6885 or 333-439-0809, Via San Martino 39, www.manuelsguesthouse.com, info@manuelsguesthouse.com).

In the New Town

Of these four, the first and last offer by far the best value for what you get—but they don't have a view. The middle two are tired, impersonal, and overpriced, cashing in on their seaside location, with varying levels of comfort.

$$$ A Cà du Gigante, despite its name, is a tiny yet classy refuge. About 100 yards from the beach (and surrounded by blocky apartments on a modern street), the interior is done with taste and modern comfort in mind (Db-€160, Db-suite €170, includes parking, air-con, 10 percent discount with 3-night stay and this book in 2008, Via IV Novembre 11, tel. 0187-817-401, fax 0187-817-375, www.ilgigantecinqueterre.it, gigante@ilgigantecinqueterre.it).

$$$ Hotel Baia (by-yah), overlooking the beach near the station, has clean, high-ceilinged, dimly lit rooms, dark hallways, and impersonal staff. Of the hotel's 28 rooms, half have views. The best little two-chair view balconies are on top floors. Request a view room, since it's the same price (Db-€150, elevator only for baggage and the disabled, minimum 3-night stay May–Sept, Via Fegina 88, tel. 0187-817-512, fax 0187-818-322, www.baiahotel.it, info@baiahotel.it).

$$$ Hotel Punta Mesco has 17 quiet, modern rooms without views, but 10 have little terraces (Db-€121, 5 percent discount with cash, air-con, free bike loan, free parking, exit right from station and take first right to Via Molinelli 35, tel. & fax 0187-817-495, www.hotelpuntamesco.it, info@hotelpuntamesco.it). For the price, it's the best comfort in town.

$$ Pensione Agavi has 10 bright, airy, tranquil, and quiet rooms, about half overlooking the beach near the big rock. This is not a place to party—it feels like an old hospital with narrow hallways (S-€40, Sb-€60, D-€80, Db-€100, no breakfast, cash only, refrigerators, turn left out of station to Fegina 30, tel. 0187-817-171, mobile 333-697-4071, fax 0187-818-264, hotel.agavi@libero.it, spunky Hillary).

EATING

Ristorante Belvedere is *the* place for a good-value meal indoors or outdoors on the harborfront. Their *amfora belvedere*—mixed seafood stew—is huge, and can easily be shared by up to four (€45). Share with your group and add pasta for a fine meal. It's energetically run by Federico and Roberto (Wed–Mon 12:00–14:30 & 19:00–22:00, usually closed Tue, on the harbor in the old town, tel. 0187-817-033).

L'Alta Marea offers special fish ravioli, the catch of the day, and huge crocks of fresh, steamed mussels. Young chef Marco cooks with charisma, while his wife, Anna, takes good care of the guests. This place is quieter, buried in the old town two blocks off the beach, and has covered tables out front for people-watching (Thu–Tue 12:00–15:00 & 18:30–22:00, open later in summer, closed Wed, Via Roma 54, tel. 0187-817-170).

Ciak—a cut above its neighbors in elegance and also a little higher in price—is known for their three huge sizzling terra-cotta crocks for two, crammed with the day's catch and either accompanied by risotto or spaghetti, or swimming in a soup *(zuppa)*. Another popular choice is the seafood *antipasto* Lampara. Stroll a couple of paces past the outdoor tables up Via Roma to see what Ciak's got on the stove (Thu–Tue 12:00–15:00 & 19:00–22:30, closed Wed, tel. 0187-817-014).

Via Venti is a fun little trattoria, buried in an alley deep in the heart of the old town, where Papa Ettore creates imaginative seafood dishes using the day's catch and freshly-made pasta. Son Michele and Ilaria serve up delicate and savory gnocchi (tiny potato dumplings) with crab sauce, tender ravioli stuffed with fresh fish in a swordfish sauce, and unusual vegetarian items such as *risotto alle fragole* (strawberry risotto). There's nothing pretentious here...just good cooking, service, and prices. From the bottom of Via Roma, with your back to the sea and the church to your left, head to the right to head down Via XX Settembre and follow it to the end to #32 (€11 pastas, €15 *secondi*, Fri–Wed 12:00–15:30 & 18:00–22:00, closed Thu, tel. 0187-818-347).

Miky is packed with well-dressed locals who know their seafood and want to eat it in a classy environment, but don't want to spend a fortune. For elegantly presented, top-quality food, this could be the best value in the entire Cinque Terre. It's clearly a family operation: Miky (dad), Simonetta (mom), and charming Sara (daughter) all work hard. All their pasta is "pizza pasta"—cooked normally but finished in a bowl that's encased in a thin pizza crust. They cook the concoction in a wood-fire oven to keep in the aroma. Miky's has the best wine list in the area, with most available by the glass if you ask (€12 pastas, €22 *secondi*, €6 sweets, Wed–Mon 12:00–15:00 & 19:00–23:00, closed Tue, reservations wise in summer, in the new town, 100 yards north of train station at Via Fegina 104, tel. 0187-817-608).

Light Meals, Take-Out Food, and Breakfast

Lots of shops and bakeries sell pizza and focaccia for an easy picnic at the beach or on the trail. At **Il Frantoio,** Simone makes tasty pizza to-go or to munch perched on a stool (daily 9:00–14:00 & 16:00–19:30, just off Via Roma at Via Gioberti 1, tel. 0187-818-333).

Il Casello is the only place for a fun, light meal on a terrace overlooking the old town beach. With outdoor tables on a rocky outcrop—located between the old-town beaches—it's a good bet for a salad or sandwich (June–Aug daily 10:30–24:00, shorter hours May and Sept, closed Oct–April, tel. 0187-818-330).

BarDavi serves the best breakfast in town with a €12 buffet available 7:00–12:00. They also make a €5 picnic box to go—ideal for the beach or for a hike (Via Roma 34; see page 334).

La Cantina, a hole-in-the-wall behind Via Roma, dishes up made-on-the-spot regional specialties, such as *lasagne al pesto* or freshly fried anchovies, in take-away containers (€5 portions, daily 9:00–19:00 June–Sept, Oct–March until 14:00, Via XX Settembre 24, tel. 328-174-9054, sisters Stefania and Chiara).

TRANSPORTATION CONNECTIONS

Trains

The five towns of the Cinque Terre are on a pokey, milk-run train line (described in "Getting Around the Cinque Terre," page 285). Erratically timed, but roughly hourly trains connect each town with the others, La Spezia, and Genoa. While a few of these local trains go to more distant points (Milan or Pisa), it's much faster to change in La Spezia or Monterosso to a bigger train (local train info tel. 0187-817-458).

From La Spezia by Train to: Rome (9/day, 4 hrs), **Pisa** (hourly, 1 hr, direction: Livorno, Rome, Salerno, Naples, etc.), **Viareggio** (3–4/hr, 30–60 min), **Florence** (3/day direct, otherwise nearly hourly, 2.5 hrs), **Milan** (hourly, 3 hrs direct or 4 hrs with change in Genoa), **Venice** (20/day, 5–7 hrs, 1–3 changes).

From Monterosso by Train to: Venice (8/day, 6–8 hrs, 1–3 changes), **Milan** (11/day, 3 hrs, change in Genoa), **Genoa** (hourly, 1.2–2 hrs), **Turin** (8/day, 3–4 hrs), **Pisa** (8/day, 35–60 min), **Sestri Levante** (hourly, 20–40 min, most trains to Genoa stop here), **La Spezia** (nearly hourly, 20 min), **Levanto** (nearly hourly, 6 min), **Santa Margherita Ligure** (hourly, 1 hr), **Rome** (10/day, 4–5 hrs). For destinations in **France,** change trains in Genoa.

Driving and Parking

Milan to the Cinque Terre (130 miles): Drivers speed south on *autostrada* A7 from Milan, skirt Genoa, and drive a little bit of Italy's curviest and narrowest freeways toward the port of La Spezia (A12). Another option is to take the slightly straighter A1 via the city of Parma, followed by the A15 to La Spezia. This route takes the same amount of time (about 2.5 hours), even though it covers more miles.

Coming from either direction, and for either Monterosso or Vernazza, exit the *autostrada* at *uscita* Carrodano, west of La Spezia. Monterosso is 30 minutes from the *autostrada*. Note that about three miles above Monterosso, a fork directs you to *Centro*

Storico (old part of town—parking lot with a few spots, and parking for Villa Steno guests) or Fegina (the new town and beachfront parking, most likely where you want to go). You have to choose which area, because you can't drive directly from the new town to the old center, which is closed to cars without special permits.

Vernazza is 45 minutes from the *autostrada*. The drive down to Vernazza is scenic, narrow, and scary, and you'll probably lose time looking for parking.

Within the Cinque Terre: On busy weekends, holidays, and in July and August, both Vernazza and Monterosso fill up, and police at the top of town will deny entry to anyone without a hotel reservation. It's smart to have a confirmation in hand. If you don't, insist (politely) that they allow you to enter—but only if you actually have a room reserved (the police might call your hotel to check your story). To drive to Riomaggiore, Corniglia, or Manarola, leave the freeway at La Spezia.

Each Cinque Terre town has a parking lot and a once-an-hour shuttle bus to get you into town (except Corniglia). In Corniglia, only residents can park on the main road between Villa Cecio and the point where the steep switchback staircase meets the road. Beyond that area, parking is €1.50/hr. Monterosso's guarded beachfront lot fills up only in August and on weekends (€12/day until midnight, then pay another €12). Parking is theoretically available in Vernazza, but it's hard to get a spot.

If you plan to find parking in any of the Cinque Terre towns, try to arrive between 10:00 and 11:00, when people are usually departing.

You can park your car in La Spezia or Levanto (see next chapter). Confirm that parking is OK and leave nothing inside to steal.

RIVIERA TOWNS
near the CINQUE TERRE

The Cinque Terre is tops, but several towns to the north have a breezy beauty and more beaches. Towns to the south offer a mix of marble, trains, and yachts.

Levanto, the northern gateway to the Cinque Terre, has a long beach and a scenic, strenuous 2.5-hour trail to Monterosso al Mare. Sestri Levante, on a narrow peninsula flanked by two beaches, is for sun-seekers. Santa Margherita Ligure is more of a real town, with actual sights, beaches, and easy connections with Portofino by trail, bus, or boat. All three towns are a straight shot to the Cinque Terre by train.

South of the Cinque Terre, you'll likely pass through (don't stay unless you're desperate) the workaday town of La Spezia, the southern gateway to the Cinque Terre. Carrara is a quickie for marble-lovers who are driving between Pisa and La Spezia. The picturesque village of Portovenere, near La Spezia, has scenic boat connections with Cinque Terre towns.

Public transportation is the best way to get around this region. All of the places in this chapter are well connected by train and/or boat.

North of the Cinque Terre

Levanto

Graced with a long, sandy beach, Levanto is packed in summer. The rest of the year, it's just a small, sleepy town, with less colorful charm and fewer tourists than the Cinque Terre. With quick con-

Riviera Towns near the Cinque Terre

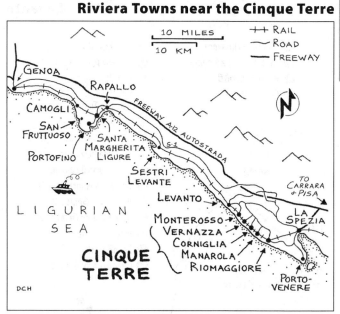

nections to Monterosso (4 min by train), Levanto makes a decent home base if you can't snare a room in the Cinque Terre.

Levanto has a new section (with a regular grid street plan) and a twisty old town (bisected by a modern street), plus a few pedestrian streets and a castle (not tourable). From Levanto, you can take a no-wimps-allowed hike to Monterosso (2.5 hours) or hop a boat to the Cinque Terre towns and beyond.

ORIENTATION

Tourist Information

The TI is on Piazza Mazzini (Mon–Sat 9:00–13:00 & 15:00–19:00, Sun 9:00–13:00, shorter hours in winter, tel. 0187-808-125, www .comune.levanto.sp.it).

Arrival in Levanto

By Train: It's a 10-minute walk from the Levanto train station to the TI in town (head down stairs in front of station, turn right, cross bridge, then follow Corso Roma to Piazza Mazzini).

By Car: Drivers can use the cheap day parking in lots on either side of the train station (€6/day, note that you have to pay each day—at the machines—so long-term parking is difficult). Another option is the lot near the hospital on the way into town, or north of the church on Via del Mercato (can be free during

Levanto

1 Albergo Primavera
2 Rist. la Loggia Rooms
3 Villa Clelia B&B
4 Garden Hotel
5 Villa Margherita B&B
6 To Erba Persa Agriturismo
7 Ostello Ospitalia del Mare
8 Osteria Tumelin
9 Da Rino Trattoria
10 Taverna Garibaldi
11 La Picea Pizzeria
12 Focacceria il Falcone
13 Crai Supermarkets (2)
14 Il Pinguino Gelateria
15 Il Porticciolo Gelateria
16 Internet Café
17 Launderette
18 Canoe & Kayak Rental

TO MONTEROSSO & AUTOSTRADA A-12 (CARRODANO EXIT)

TRAIN STATION

MARKET

P - PARKING

VIA DOM.

VIA MARTIRI DELLA LIBERTÀ

VIA VIVIANI

GHIARARO RIVER

VIA TRENTO TRIESTE

VIA GARIBALDI

ROMA

CORSO

VIA ROMA

SCALINATA DELL' OROLOGICO

V. S. NICOLO

MATT. VINZ.

CONCIA

VAREGO

V. JAC.

LEV.

DANTE ALI.

V. GUA

RIMEMB.

PARODI

III

ZOPPI

POST TOWN

NEW TOWN

CAIROLI

PZA. STAG.

PZA. POPOLO

FIN.

OLD TOWN

S. ANDREA

CORSO ITALIA

MAZZINI

ELEVATED ROAD

POM GRILL

DON ARE

BOG

GAETANO

S. SEMENZA

PIAZZA MAZZINI

BEACH

POOL

TRAIL TO MONTE-ROSSO

FREE BEACH

FREE BEACH

FREE BEACH

LIGURIAN SEA

BOATS TO CINQUE TERRE

DCH

high season, except Wed before 14:00). For long-term parking, try the lots at Piazza Mazzini and to the west of the TI; in high season these charge more than double the cost of the train station parking lot, but are inexpensive off-season (Nov–April). Parking is always in flux, so confirm rates and availability with your hotelier or the TI.

Helpful Hints

Markets: Levanto's modern, covered *mercato,* which sells produce and fish, is on Via del Mercato, between the TI and train station (Mon–Sat 8:00–13:00, closed Sun). On Wednesday morning, an **open-air market** with clothes, shoes, and housewares fills the street in front of the *mercato.*

Internet Access: Try Internet Buffet (€3/30 min, Mon–Sat 10:30–20:00, closed Sun, Via Garibaldi 68, tel. 0187-804-025).

Baggage Storage: None is available at the station. The nearest baggage storage is in Santa Margherita Ligure (see page 350).

Laundry: A self-service launderette is at Piazza Staglieno 38 (open 24 hours daily, €5 wash, €5 dry, includes soap, mobile 335-653-5964).

SIGHTS

Beach—The beach is just two blocks away from the TI. As you face the harbor, the boat dock is to your far left and the diving center is to your far right (rental boats available at either place in summer). You can also rent a kayak or canoe on the beach, just below the east end of the Piazza Mazzini parking lot.

During the summer, three parts of the beach are free: both sides of the boathouse, and to the right of Casinò Lido swimming pool. The rest of the beach is broken up into private sections that charge admission. You can always stroll along the beach, even through the private sections—just don't sit down. Off-season, roughly October through May, the entire beach is free, and you can lay your towel anywhere you like.

Old Town and Trailhead—The old town, several blocks from the TI and beach, clusters around Piazza del Popolo. Until 15 years ago, the town's open-air market was held at the 13th-century *loggia* (covered set of archways) in the square. Explore the back streets.

To reach the trailhead to Monterosso: From Piazza del Popolo, head uphill to the striped church, Chiesa di Sant'Andrea (with your back to the *loggia,* go straight ahead—across the square and up Via Don Emanuele Toso to the church). From the church courtyard, follow the sign to the *castello* (a private residence), go under the stone arch, and continue uphill. Or, if you're coming from the seaside promenade (Via Gaetano Semenza), head under the arches and up the stairs, and follow the signs to the *castello*. Either route leads you to a sign that points you toward Punta Mesco, the rugged tip of the peninsula. From here, you can hike up to Monterosso (2.5 hours).

SLEEPING

In this popular beach town, many hotels want you to take half-pension (lunch or dinner) in summer, especially in July and August. The high number of four-person rooms in Levanto make it particularly welcoming to families who want to explore the Cinque Terre. Many hotels rent out large apartments with kitchenettes (without a half-pension requirement), and parking is free or very reasonable.

$$$ Albergo Primavera is family-run, with 17 vibrantly colored rooms—10 with balconies but no views—just a half-block from the beach. Owner Carlo is a good cook. Try dining here once during your visit (€25 fixed-price meal); let him know a couple of hours in advance if you'd like dinner (Db-€95–115, includes hearty breakfast buffet, air-con, parking-€5/day June–Sept, free off-season, request a quiet room off the street, Via Cairoli 5, tel. 0187-808-023, fax 0187-801-588, www.primaverahotel.com, info @primaverahotel.com). Friendly Carlo and Daniela speak a little English, and daughters Gloria and Giuditta do their homework in the dining room.

$$$ Villa Margherita B&B is 300 yards out of town, but the shady gardens, 11 characteristic, tiled rooms (some with little terraces), and tranquility are worth the walk (Db-€85–130, Tb-€85–150, elevator, free Internet access and Wi-Fi, free parking, 10-min walk to town, 5-min walk to train station, free shuttle service from station if you tell them when you'll arrive, Via Trento e Trieste 31, tel. & fax 0187-807-212, mobile 328-842-6934, www .villamargherita.net, info@villamargherita.net). They also have apartments for two to six people (some are central, 3-night minimum stay).

$$ Ristorante la Loggia has four pleasant, summery rooms perched above the old *loggia* on Piazza del Popolo (Db-€50–70, air-con, request balcony, quieter rooms in back, two side-by-side apartments great for families of 4–8, Piazza del Popolo 7, tel. & fax 0187-808-107, mobile 335-641-7701, www.tigulliovino.it /ristorantelaloggia.htm).

$$ Villa Clelia B&B has six peaceful, air-conditioned rooms (named for the winds—*scirocco*, *maestrale*, and so on) with mini-fridges and terraces in a garden courtyard just 50 yards from the sea (Db-€75–85, minimal in-room breakfast, free parking, with *loggia* on your left it's straight ahead at Piazza da Passano 1, tel.

Sleep Code

(€1 = about $1.30, country code: 39)
S = Single, **D** = Double/Twin, **T** = Triple, **Q** = Quad, **b** = bathroom,
s = shower only. Unless otherwise noted, credit cards are
accepted, English is spoken, and breakfast is included.

To help you sort easily through these listings, I've divided
the rooms into three categories based on the price for a standard double room with bath:

$$$ **Higher Priced**—Most rooms €100 or more.
  $$ **Moderately Priced**—Most rooms between €50–100.
    $ **Lower Priced**—Most rooms €50 or less.

0187-808-195, mobile 328-797-6403, www.villaclelia.it, info
@villaclelia.it). They also have five central apartments that economically sleep up to four (Qb-€90, 3-night minimum stay). B&B
rooms are cleaned daily; you're on your own at the apartments.

$$ Garden Hotel offers 17 tidy, bright, and modern rooms,
all with balconies (but no real views due to the seawall), a block
from the beach on busy Corso Italia (Db-€80–100, new third-floor
rooms with views and terraces go for Db-€95–125, closed mid-
Nov–mid-March, air-con, elevator for some floors, free Internet
access and Wi-Fi, free parking but not on-site—can unload bags
and then park near the station, Corso Italia 6, tel. 0187-808-173,
fax 0187-803-652, www.nuovogarden.com, info@nuovogarden
.com, Davide).

$$ Erba Persa Agriturismo, a rustic farmhouse run by sunny
Grazia Lizza and her gardener husband Claudio, hosts cats, dogs,
pet rabbits, and donkeys among their plots of organic fruits and
vegetables. It's a 10-minute walk from the train station and about a
20-minute walk from town (D or Db with balcony and view-€70,
free parking, free Internet access, free loaner bikes, free mosquitoes, Via N. S. della Guardia 21, mobile 339-400-8587, fax 0187-
801-376, www.erbapersa.it, erbapersa@alice.it).

Hostel: **$ Ostello Ospitalia del Mare** has 70 beds, airy rooms,
Internet access, an elevator, and a terrace in a well-renovated medieval palazzo a few steps from the old town (beds-€18–30 in 4-,
6-, and 8-bed rooms with private bath, Db-€60, includes breakfast and sheets, non-members welcome, co-ed unless you strenu-
ously object, no curfew, no lockout, office open daily April–Oct
8:00–13:00 & 16:00–20:00, later weekend nights, Nov–March
10:00–12:00 & 16:00–18:00, Via San Nicolò 1, tel. 0187-802-562,
fax 0187-803-696, www.ospitaliadelmare.it, ospitalia@libero.it).

EATING

Osteria Tumelin, a local favorite, is more expensive than other options, but has great ambience and fresh seafood (daily 12:00–14:30 & 19:00–23:30, closed Thu in winter, reservations recommended in summer, Via d. Grillo 32, across street from *loggia,* tel. 0187-808-379).

Da Rino, a small trattoria on a quiet pedestrian street, dishes up reasonably priced, fresh seafood and homemade Ligurian specialties prepared with care. Consider the grilled *totani* (squid), *pansotti con salsa di noci* (cheese ravioli with walnut sauce), and *trofie al pesto* (local pasta with pesto sauce). Dine indoors, or at one of the few outdoor tables (€8 pastas, €13 *secondi,* daily mid-March–Oct 19:00–22:00, closed Nov–mid-March, Via Garibaldi 10, mobile 328-3890-350).

Ristorante la Loggia (also recommended under "Sleeping"), next to the old *loggia,* makes fine gnocchi with saffron sauce, *gattafini* (Levanto-style fritters filled with herbs and cheese), and daily fish specials served in a homey, wood-paneled dining room or on a little terrace overlooking the square (€10 pastas, €16 *secondi,* daily 12:30–14:00 & 19:30–22:00, closed Nov–Dec, Piazza del Popolo 7, tel. 0187-808-107).

Taverna Garibaldi is a good-value, cozy place on the most characteristic street in Levanto, serving focaccia with various toppings, made-to-order *farinata* (savory chickpea crêpe), pizzas, and salads (€7 light meals, daily in summer 19:30–23:00, closed Tue Sept–June, Via Garibaldi 57, tel. 0187-808-098).

La Picea serves up wood-fired pizzas to go, or dine at one of the few small tables (Tue–Sun 16:30–22:00, closed Mon, just off the corner near Via Varego at Via della Concia 18, tel. 0187-802-063).

A Picnic or Bite on the Go: Focaccerie, rosticcerie, and delis with take-out pasta abound on Via Dante Alighieri. **Focacceria il Falcone** has a great selection of focaccia with different toppings (daily 9:30–20:00, until 22:00 May–Sept, Via Cairoli 19, tel. 0187-807-370). For more picnic options, try the *mercato* (mornings except Sun; see "Helpful Hints," page 343). There are two **Crai supermarkets,** one just off Via Jacopo da Levanto at Via del Municipio 5 (Mon–Sat 8:00–13:00 & 17:00–20:00, Sun 8:30–13:00); the other is nearby on Piazza Staglieno. Piazza C. Colombo, with its benches and sea view, makes an excellent picnic spot. For a shadier setting, lay out your spread on a bench in the grassy park at Piazza Staglieno.

And for Dessert: Compare **Il Pinguino Gelateria** on Piazza Staglieno 2 (daily until late) with **Il Porticciolo Gelateria,** at the end of Via Cairoli at Piazzetta Marina (daily in summer, closed Mon Sept–May, mobile 392-982-5474).

TRANSPORTATION CONNECTIONS

From Levanto: To get to the Cinque Terre, take the **train** (nearly hourly, 4 min to Monterosso) or the **boat,** which stops at every Cinque Terre town—except Corniglia—before heading to Portovenere (roughly 2/day Easter–Oct, more in summer, none Nov–Easter; €6 one-way to Monterosso, €10.50 round-trip, or €16 for half-day pass to Portovenere—departing Levanto at about 14:30, with 1-hour stop before return to Levanto; as much as €23 for all-day weekend pass to Portovenere; 1 return boat each day from Portovenere departs at about 17:00; pick up boat schedule and price sheet from TI or boat dock, or call 0187-732-987 or 0187-777-727).

Sestri Levante

This peninsular town is squeezed as skinny as a hot dog between its two beaches. The pedestrian-friendly Corso Colombo, which runs down the middle of the peninsula, is lined with shops that sell take-away pizza, pastries, and beach paraphernalia.

Hans Christian Andersen enjoyed his visit here in the mid-1800s, writing, "What a fabulous evening I spent in Sestri Levante!" One of the bays—Baia delle Favole—is named in his honor (*favole* means "fairy tale"). During the last week of May, the town holds a street festival, culminating in a ceremony for locals who write the best fairy tales (four prizes for four age groups, from pre-kindergarten to adult). The "Oscar" awards are little mermaids. The small mermaid curled on the edge of the fountain (behind the TI) is another nod to the beloved Danish storyteller.

ORIENTATION

Tourist Information: From the train station, it's a five-minute walk to the TI, where you can pick up a map (May–Sept Mon–Sat 9:30–12:30 & 15:00–19:30, Sun 9:30–12:30 & 16:30–19:30, Oct–April closes at 17:30 and on Sun; go straight out of station on Via Roma, turn left at fountain in park, TI at next square—Piazza Sant'Antonio 10; tel. 0185-457-011).

Baggage Storage: None is available at the station. The nearest baggage storage is in Santa Margherita Ligure (see page 350).

Market Day: Saturday at Piazza Aldo Moro (8:00–13:00).

ACTIVITIES

Stroll the Town—From the TI, take Corso Colombo (to the left of Bermuda Bar, eventually turns into Via XXV Aprile), which runs up the peninsula. Follow this street—lively with shops and eateries—for about five minutes. Just before you get to the large white church at the end, turn off for either beach (free Silenzio beach is on your left). Or take the street on the left of the church to head uphill. You'll pass the evocative arches of a ruined chapel (bombed during World War II, and left as a memorial). Continue a few minutes farther to the Hotel Castelli and consider a drink at their view café (so-so view, reasonably priced drinks, daily 10:00–24:00, café entrance is at end of parking lot). The rocky, forested bluff at the end of the town's peninsula is actually the huge, private backyard of this fancy hotel.

Beaches—These are named after the bays *(baia)* that they border. The bigger beach, Baia delle Favole, is divided up much of the year (May–Sept) into sections that you must pay to enter. The fees, which can soar up to €28 per day in August (no hourly rate), generally include chairs, umbrellas, and fewer crowds. There are several small free sections: at the ends and in the middle (look for *libere* signs, and ask "*Gratis?*" to make sure that it's free). For less-expensive sections of beach (where you can rent less than the works), ask for *spiaggia libera attrezzata* (spee-AH-jah LEE-behr-ah ah-treh-ZAHT-tah). The usual beach-town activities are clustered along this *baia:* boat rentals, sailing lessons, and bocce courts—ask if you can get in on a game.

The town's other beach, Baia del Silenzio, is narrow, virtually all free, and packed, providing a good chance to see Italian families at play. There isn't much more to do here than unroll a beach towel and join in. At the far end of Baia del Silenzio is Citto Beach bar, which offers front-row seats of bay views (daily June–Aug 10:00–24:00, May and Sept–Oct until 20:00, closed Nov–April).

SLEEPING

(€1 = about $1.30, country code: 39)
Prices listed here are the maximum during high season (April–Sept) and should be 15–20 percent lower in the off-season. Some hotels are closed off-season, so call ahead.

$$$ Hotel Due Mari, located in an old Genoese palazzo, has three stars, 65 fine rooms, and a rooftop terrace with a super view of both beaches. Ideally, reserve well in advance (Db-€100–165 depending on view and type of room, half-pension required July–Aug for €27 per person, closed mid-Oct–Dec, air-con, elevator, garden, outdoor and heated indoor seawater swimming pools, wet sauna, small gym, parking-€10/day, take Corso Colombo to the end, hotel is behind church in Piazza Matteotti—take either alleyway flanking church, Vico del Coro 18, tel. 0185-42695, fax 0185-42698, www.duemarihotel.it, info@duemarihotel.it).

$$$ Hotel Helvetia, overlooking Baia del Silenzio, is another good three-star bet, with 21 bright rooms, a large sun terrace, and a peaceful garden atmosphere (Db-€150–170 depending on view/balcony, closed Nov–March, air-con, elevator, off-site parking-€10/day with free shuttle, from Corso Colombo turn left on Via Palestro and angle left at the small square to Via Cappuccini 43, tel. 0185-41175, fax 0185-457-216, www.hotelhelvetia.it, helvetia @hotelhelvetia.it).

$$$ Hotel Genova, run by the Bertoni family, is a shipshape hotel with 24 shiny-clean, modern, and cheery rooms, a rooftop sundeck, free loaner bikes, and a good location just two blocks from Baia delle Favole (Sb-€70, Db-€102, Tb-€155, ask for quieter room in back, air-con, elevator, parking-€5/day; from the train station, walk straight ahead, turn right at the T-intersection and find the white building with flags ahead on the right, Viale Mazzini 126; tel. 0185-41057, fax 0185-457-213, www.hotelristorantegenova .it, info@hotelristorantegenova.it).

$$ Hotel Elisabetta, less central, has 38 stark rooms on a busy street at the end of Baia delle Favole, a block from the beach. Some rooms have a tiny view that peaks between the cement buildings out front (D-€90, Db-€100, half-pension available but not required; air-con, elevator, double-paned windows, free parking, walk straight out of station, then turn right at park, 12-min walk to Viale Mazzini 276; tel. 0185-41128, fax 0185-487-206, albergoelisabetta@libero.it, a leetle English spoken).

$$ Villa Jolanda is a homey, kid-friendly, basic *pensione* with 17 simple rooms, five with little balconies but no views, and a garden courtyard—perfect for families on a budget (Db-€70, Qb-€110, 3-night minimum stay, €6.50 breakfast isn't worth it but owner Mario's €23 home-cooked dinners are, new bathrooms, free parking, located near Baia del Silenzio—take alley just to the right of the church on Piazza Matteotti, Via Pozzetto 15, tel. & fax 0185-41354, www.villaiolanda.com, info@villaiolanda.com).

EATING

Everything I've listed is on classic Via XXV Aprile, which also abounds with *focaccerie*, take-out pizza by the slice, and little grocery shops. Assemble a picnic or try one of the places below.

At **L'Osteria Mattana,** where everyone shares long tables in two dining rooms (the second one is in the back, past the wood oven and brazier), you can mix with locals while enjoying traditional cuisine, listed on the chalkboard menus (Tue–Thu 19:30–23:30, Fri–Sun 12:30–14:30 & 19:30–22:30, closed Mon except in Aug, follow Corso Colombo from TI as it turns into Via XXV Aprile, restaurant on right at #36, tel. 0185-457-633).

Polpo Mario is classier but affordable, with a fun people-watching location on the main drag (€35 fixed-price meal, Tue–Sun 12:15–14:30 & 19:30–22:30, closed Mon, Via XXV Aprile 163, tel. 0185-480-203).

Osteria Mainolla offers big salads, focaccia sandwiches, and reasonably priced pastas near Baia del Silenzio (daily in summer 12:00–15:00 & 19:00–22:00, bar service open later, closed Tue off-season, Via XXV Aprile 187, tel. 0185-42556).

Gelato: Locals flock to **Ice Cream's Angels** at the intersection of Via XXV Aprile and Via della Chiusa. Riccardo and Elena artfully load up your cone with intermingling flavors, and top it with a dollop of Nutella chocolate hazelnut cream (open daily until late in summer, closed Tue off-season, mobile 348-402-1604).

Crema e Cioccolato *gelateria* has lots of flavors to choose from (open daily until late in summer, closed Mon off-season, Via XXV Aprile 126).

Supermarket: You can stock up on picnic supplies at the **Co-op supermarket,** just to the left of the train station (Mon–Sat 8:15–13:00 & 15:30–19:30, closed Sun).

TRANSPORTATION CONNECTIONS

Sestri Levante is just 20 to 30 minutes away from Monterosso by **train** (hourly connections with Monterosso, nearly hourly with other Cinque Terre towns).

Boats depart to the Cinque Terre, Portofino, and San Fruttuoso from the dock *(molo)* on the peninsula. Pick up a schedule of departures and excursion options from the TI or ask at your hotel (boats run Easter–Oct; to get to the dock: facing the church in Piazza Matteotti, take the road on the right with the sea on your right, about halfway down Via P. Queirolo; tel. 0185-284-670, www.traghettiportofino.it).

Santa Margherita Ligure

If you need the movie star's Riviera, park your yacht at Portofino. Or you can settle down in the nearby and more personable Santa Margherita Ligure (15 min by bus from Portofino and 1 hour by train from the Cinque Terre). While Portofino's velour allure is tarnished by snobby residents and a nonstop traffic jam in peak season, Santa Margherita tumbles easily downhill from its train

station. The town has a fun resort character and a breezy harborfront.

On a quick day trip from Milan or the Cinque Terre, walk the beach promenade and see the small old town of Santa Margherita Ligure before catching the bus (or boat) to Portofino to see what all the fuss is about. With more time, Santa Margherita makes a fine overnight stop.

ORIENTATION

Tourist Information

Pick up a map at the harborside info kiosk (daily 9:00–13:00 & 15:00–19:00 April–Oct, closed Nov–March) or at the TI (April–Oct Mon–Sat 9:30–12:30 & 15:00–19:30, shorter hours on Sun; Nov–March Mon–Sat 9:30–12:30 & 14:30–17:30, closed Sun; Via XXV Aprile 2B, tel. 0185-287-485, www.apttigullio.liguria.it).

Arrival by Train

To get to the city center from the station, take the stairs marked *Mare* (sea) down to the harbor. The harborfront promenade is as wide as the skimpy beach. (The real beaches, which are pebbly, are a 10-min walk farther on, past the port.)

To reach the pedestrian-friendly old town and the TI, take a right at Piazza Veneto (with the roundabout, flags, and park) onto Largo Antonio Giusti. For the TI, angle left on Via XXV Aprile. For the old town (a block off Piazza Veneto), head toward the TI, but turn left on Via Torino, which opens almost immediately onto Piazza Caprera, a square with a church and morning fruit vendors in the midst of pedestrian streets.

Helpful Hints

Internet Access: Internet Point gives readers with this book a free additional 30 minutes in 2008 (€3 for the first 30 min, Mon–Sat 9:30–13:00 & 15:00–20:00, closed Sun, off Piazza Mazzini at Via Guincheto 39, tel. 0185-293-092, run by owners of recommended Hotel Fasce).

Post Office: It's just under the train station (Mon–Fri 8:00–18:30, Sat 8:00–12:30, Via Roma 36).

Baggage Storage: Day-trippers arriving by train can stash their bags at the station's café/bar (€2.50/day per piece, daily 5:00–20:00).

Bike Rental: GM Rent has two locations; the more convenient is at Via XXV Aprile 11, right across from the TI (€10/5 hours, €20/24 hours, also rents scooters and Smart Cars, daily 10:00–13:00 & 16:00–20:00, other location at Via Favale 37b, tel. 0185-284-420, mobile 329-406-6274, www.gmrent.it).

Parking: Hotel Mediterraneo offers free parking to its guests and a few hotels have limited spots for a fee. Otherwise, try a private lot (about €6/half-day, €15/24 hours, Via Roma 38, next to post office).

Local Guide: Roberta De Beni knows the Ligurian Coast, its history, and its art very well (€100/half-day, €165/day, mobile 349-530-4778, diodebe@inwind.it).

SELF-GUIDED WALK

Welcome to Santa Margherita Ligure

Explore Santa Margherita Ligure on the following self-guided stroll.

• *Begin at Piazza della Libertà. Walk out to the tip of the boat dock and turn around to survey the...*

Town View: From here you can take in all of Santa Margherita Ligure, from the villas dotting the hills and the castle built in the 16th century (closed except for special exhibitions), to the exclusive hotels. Sharing the dock with you is a statue of "Santa Margherita Virgin Martyr."

• *Wander along the harborfront (down Corso Marconi) past the castle and to the...*

Marina: What's left of the town's fishing fleet ties up here. The fishing industry survives, drag-netting octopus, shrimp, and miscellaneous "blue fish"—plus mountains of anchovies attracted to midnight lamps. The fish market (inside the rust-colored building with arches and columns) wiggles daily at about, oh, maybe 17:00–20:00 or so. Residents complain that it's easier to buy their locally-caught fresh fish in Milan than here.

• *Behind the fish market stands the...*

Oratory of Sant'Erasmo: This small church is named for St. Erasmus, the protector of the fishermen. Notice the fine and typically local black-and-white pebble mosaic *(riseu)* in front of the church (with maritime themes). The church is actually an "oratory," where a brotherhood of faithful men who did anonymous good deeds congregated and worshipped. It's decorated with ships and paintings of storms that—thanks to St. Erasmus—the local sailors survived. The huge crosses are carried through town on special religious holidays (church supposedly only open during Mass, but often open at other times, too).

• *Next, double-back to climb the looooong stairway (Via Tre Novembre) overlooking the bay to reach the...*

Santa Margherita Ligure

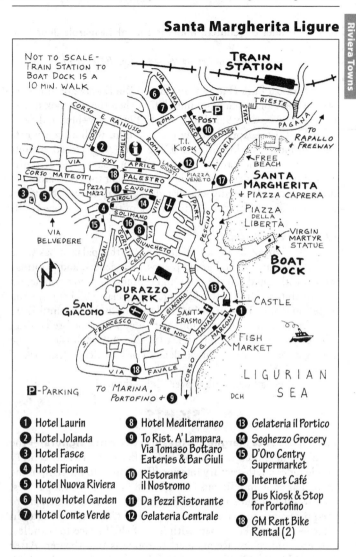

NOT TO SCALE—
TRAIN STATION TO
BOAT DOCK IS A
10 MIN. WALK

TRAIN STATION

TO RAPALLO & FREEWAY

FREE BEACH

SANTA MARGHERITA + PIAZZA CAPRERA

PIAZZA DELLA LIBERTA

VIRGIN MARTYR STATUE

BOAT DOCK

CASTLE

FISH MARKET

LIGURIAN SEA

VILLA DURAZZO PARK

SAN GIACOMO →

SANT' ERASMO

VIA BELVEDERE

P — PARKING

TO MARINA, PORTOFINO →

DCH

- ❶ Hotel Laurin
- ❷ Hotel Jolanda
- ❸ Hotel Fasce
- ❹ Hotel Fiorina
- ❺ Hotel Nuova Riviera
- ❻ Nuovo Hotel Garden
- ❼ Hotel Conte Verde
- ❽ Hotel Mediterraneo
- ❾ To Rist. A' Lampara, Via Tomaso Bottaro Eateries & Bar Giuli
- ❿ Ristorante il Nostromo
- ⓫ Da Pezzi Ristorante
- ⓬ Gelateria Centrale
- ⓭ Gelateria il Portico
- ⓮ Seghezzo Grocery
- ⓯ D'Oro Centry Supermarket
- ⓰ Internet Café
- ⓱ Bus Kiosk & Stop for Portofino
- ⓲ GM Rent Bike Rental (2)

Church of San Giacomo: Even though this is a secondary church in a secondary town, it's impressively lavish (daily 8:30–12:00 & 15:00–18:00). The region's aristocrats amassed wealth from trade in the 11th to 15th centuries. When Constantinople fell to the Turks, free trade in the Mediterranean stopped and Genovese traders became bankers—making even more money. A popular saying of the day was, "Silver is born in America, lives in Spain, and dies in Genoa." Bankers here served Spain's 17th-century royalty and aristocracy, and the accrued wealth paid for a Golden Age of art. Wander the church, noticing the inlaid-marble floors and chapels.

• *Step out of the church and enjoy the sea view. Then turn left and step into...*

Durazzo Park (Parco Comunale Villa Durazzo): This park was an abandoned shambles until 1973, when the city took it over (free, July–Aug daily 9:00–20:00, until 19:00 May–June and Sept, until 17:30 Oct–April). Today it's a delight, with a breezy café enjoyed mostly by locals (closed Tue May–Aug, closed entirely Oct–March). The garden has two distinct parts: the carefully coiffed Italian garden (designed to complement the villa's architecture) and the calculatedly wild "English garden" below. The Italian garden is famous for its collection of palm trees—each one is different.

• *In the park, you'll see...*

Villa Durazzo: Typical of the region, this palazzo has some period furniture, several grand pianos, chandeliers, and paintings strewn with cupids on the walls and ceilings. For most people, it's not worth the entry fee (€5.50, more for special exhibits, July–Aug Tue–Sun 9:30–20:00, until 19:00 May–June and Sept, until 17:00 Oct–April, always closed Mon, last entry 1 hour before closing, WC opposite entry on left, tel. 0185-205-449). Classical music concerts are held here in July (ask at TI or villa ticket desk, or call 0185-293-135).

Your self-guided walk is over. Enjoy the park.

SIGHTS

Church of Santa Margherita (Basilica di Nostra Signora)—The town's main church is textbook Italian Baroque. Its 18th-century facade hides a 17th-century interior. The chapels to the right of the high altar contain religious "floats" used in local festival parades. The wooden groups in the niches higher up used to be part of the processions too. The altar is typical of 17th-century Ligurian altars—shaped like a boat, with lots of shelf space for candles, flowers, and relics. Remember, Baroque is like theater. After Vatican II in the 1960s, priests faced their flock, turning their back on the old altars rather than the people. For this reason, all over the Catholic world, modern tables serving as post–Vatican II altars stand in front of earlier altars that are no longer the center of attention during the Mass (daily 7:30–12:00 & 15:00–19:00).

Via Palestro—This promenade (a.k.a. *caruggio*—"the big street" in local dialect) is *the* strolling street for window-shopping, people-watching, and studying the characteristic Art Nouveau house painting from about 1900. Before 1900, people distinguished their buildings with pastel paint and distinctive door and window

Rise of a Resort: The History of Santa Margherita Ligure

This town, like the entire region (from the border of France to La Spezia), was once ruled by the Republic of Genoa. In the 16th century, when Arab pirates from North Africa plagued the entire coastal area, Genoa built castles in the towns and look-out towers in the neighboring hills.

At the time, Santa Margherita was actually two bickering towns—each with its own bay. In 1800, Napoleon came along, took over the Republic of Genoa, and made it one city—naming it Porto Napoleone. When Napoleon fell in 1815, the town stayed united and took the name of the patron saint of its leading church, Santa Margherita.

In 1850, residents set to work creating a Riviera resort. They imported palm trees from North Africa and paved a fine beach promenade. Santa Margherita and the area around it was studded with fancy villas built by the aristocracy of Genoa (which was controlled by just 35 families). English, Russian, and German aristocrats also discovered the town in the 19th century. Mass tourism only hit in the last generation. Even with the increased crowds, the town decided to stay chic and kept huge developments out. Its neighbor, Rapallo, chose the extreme opposite—giving Italian its word for uncontrolled growth ruining a once-cute town: *rapallizzazione*.

frames. Then they decided to get fancy and paint entire exteriors with false balconies, weapons, saints, beautiful women, and 3-D Gothic concentrate.

As you wander from the Church of Santa Margherita inland, pop into the fanciest grocer/deli in town—**Seghezzo** (immediately to the right of the church on Via Cavour, closed Wed). Locals know that this venerable institution has whatever odd ingredient the toughest recipe calls for.

Farther up Via Palestro, you might drop into the traditional old **Panificio** (bakery, open daily) for a slice of fresh focaccia. Saying *"Vorrei un etto di focaccia"* will get you a Ligurian olive-oily, 100-gram, €1 hunk of every kid's favorite beach munchie. Locals claim the best focaccia in Italy is made along this coast.

Markets—From about 17:00 to 20:00 on weekdays, fishing boats unload their catch, which is then sold to waiting customers at

Mercato del Pesce. Find it in the rust-colored building with arches and columns on Corso Marconi, on the harbor, just past the castle. The open-air market, a commotion of clothes and produce, is held every Friday morning along Corso Matteotti, inland from Piazza Mazzini (8:00–13:00). Piazza Caprera (facing the main church) daily hosts a few farmers selling their produce from stalls.

Beaches—The handiest, free Santa Margherita beaches are just below the train station toward the boat dock. But the best beaches are on the south side of town. Among these, I like "Gio and Rino beach" (just before Covo di Nord Est)—not too expensive, with fun, creative management and a young crowd. Also nice is the beach on the south side of Hotel Miramare, which offers a more relaxing, sun-worshipping experience. Both beaches have free entry and rentable chairs and umbrellas. They're a 20-minute walk from downtown, or take the bus from either the train station or Piazza Veneto (€0.80 each way, buy tickets from kiosk, news-stands, or *tabacchi* shops).

Paraggi beach, which is halfway to Portofino (with an easy bus connection, see "Portofino" below), is better than any Santa Margherita beach, but it's *very* expensive. One Paraggi beach operator, Bosetti, offers a reasonable rate (€25/day, no hourly rates, includes umbrella, lounge chair, and towel) while rates at other beaches may soar up to €50/day in July and August. In high sea-son, the Paraggi beach may be all booked up by big shots from Portofino, which has no beach—only rocks. A skinny patch of sand smack-dab in the middle of Paraggi beach is free.

SLEEPING

In the Center
(€1 = about $1.30, country code: 39)
To locate these hotels, see the map on page 353. Prices listed here peak in high season (May–Sept) and run at least 15 percent lower the rest of the year.

$$$ Hotel Jolanda is a solid, professionally-run hotel with 50 rooms, a revolving door, and a friendly staff. With the lavish pub-lic spaces and regal colors, you'll feel like nobility here (Db-€134, superior Db-€148, 10 percent discount in 2008 with this book if you mention it when you reserve, air-con, elevator, Internet access, free use of small weight room, wet sauna extra, 2 blocks from TI at Via Luisito Costa 6, tel. 0185-287-512, fax 0185-284-763, www .hoteljolanda.it, info@hoteljolanda.it). They have 10 free loaner bikes parked at the front door.

$$$ Hotel Fiorina has 44 airy rooms decorated in a light-and-dark color scheme, some with views. On a busy square with quieter rooms in the back, it's family-run with pride and care (Db-

€130, fans in every room, some rooms with balconies, sun terrace, 2 blocks inland from pedestrian Piazza Caprera at Piazza Mazzini 26, tel. 0185-287-517, fax 0185-281-855, www.hotelfiorina.com, fiorinasml@libero.it).

$$$ Hotel Mediterraneo, run by the Melegatti family, offers 30 spacious rooms (a few with balconies or sun terraces) in a family-friendly, comfy-cozy palazzo a five-minute walk from Piazza Veneto (Sb-€105, Db-€150, Tb-€160, closed Jan–March, free laundry service, park-like sun garden with lounge chairs and lots of semi-private space, free parking, free loaner bikes, take street immediately to the right of Church of Santa Margherita and find hotel straight ahead at Via della Vittoria 18A, tel. 0185-286-881, fax 0185-286-882, www.sml-mediterraneo.it, info@sml-mediterraneo.it).

$$$ Hotel Laurin is a slick, air-conditioned, modern, American-style place fixated on its harborfront views. All of its 43 rooms face the sea, most have terraces, and there's a small pool on the sundeck, as well as a gym and wet sauna. As it's a Best Western, it feels corporate (Sb-€145, Db-€205, bigger with view terrace Db-€276, 10 percent discount with this book in 2008 if you mention it when you reserve, double-paned windows, elevator, 15-yard walk past the castle, or €13 taxi ride from station, Corso Marconi 3, tel. 0185-289-971, fax 0185-285-709, www.laurinhotel .it, info@laurinhotel.it).

$$$ Hotel Fasce is a hardworking 16-room hotel surrounded by flowers and greenery, and run enthusiastically by intense Englishwoman Jane Fasce and her husband, Aristide. Jane gets mixed reviews from my readers—some find her helpful, while others find her rules too strict...my advice is to toe the line (Sb-€90, Db-€108, Tb-€135, Qb-€156, see website for deals, two rooms have private bathroom located across the hall, no elevator, free happy-hour welcome drink, free round-trip train tickets to Cinque Terre for 3-night stays if you book room through their website, no-nonsense 21-day cancellation policy, free loaner bikes, English newspapers, rooftop garden, laundry service-€16, parking-€18/ day, 10-min walk or €13 cab ride from station at Via Bozzo 3, tel. 0185-286-435, fax 0185-283-580, www.hotelfasce.it, hotelfasce @hotelfasce.it).

$$$ Hotel Nuova Riviera is a stately old villa surrounded by a peaceful garden. The Sabini family rent nine non-smoking rooms (Db-€102, Tb-€130, Qb-€160, these prices good with this book in 2008 if you mention it when you reserve, additional 5 percent discount with cash, fans, some balconies, Internet access, no elevator, no breakfast, limited free parking, 10-min walk or €10 taxi ride from station; walking or driving, follow signs to hospital, then watch for hotel signs on Piazza Mazzini, it's at Via Belvedere 10; tel.

& fax 0185-287-403, www.nuovariviera.com, info@nuovariviera
.com). They also run a nearby annex where four rooms share two
bathrooms (D-€82, T-€100, Q-€120, cash only).

By the Train Station

Expect a little train noise at these places, both a few blocks from
the station.

$$$ **Nuovo Hotel Garden** is tucked away down a side street.
Though its 31 squeaky-clean rooms are decorated in a style that's
a strange conglomeration of past decades, this hotel is well-
maintained (Sb-€90, Db-€140, Qb-€200, prices depend on season
and size of room, air-con, double-paned windows on train side, ter-
race, bar, free loaner bikes, limited parking-€7/day; it's a block from
train station—instead of taking the stairs down to harbor, face stairs
and go right to Via Zara 13; tel. 0185-285-398, fax 0185-290-439,
www.nuovohotelgarden.com, info@nuovohotelgarden.com).

$$$ **Hotel Conte Verde,** on the same street as Nuovo Hotel
Garden and with decor equally trapped in time, rents 31 rooms
of varying quality and price. Ask if a room with a big terrace is
available (Sb-€75, D-€65, Db-€110, price higher in July–Aug and
for bigger rooms, no air-con, fans available but shaded rooms stay
cool, elevator, exercise room, garden patio for picnics, free loaner
bikes, big public areas, parking-€10–15/day, Via Zara 1, see directions for above hotel, tel. 0185-287-139, fax 0185-284-211, www
.hotelconteverde.it, info@hotelconteverde.it).

EATING

For information on some of the regional specialties, see page 292.

Ristorante "A' Lampara" is the locals' favorite for *casalinga*
(home-cooked) Genovese cuisine, prepared by the endearing
Barbieri family—Mamma Maria Luisa oversees the dining room,
son Mario cooks, and daughter Natalina serves. Try their specialties, such as *ravioli di pesce* (homemade fish ravioli with tomato
sauce) or *pansotti con salsa di noce*—cheese ravioli with walnut sauce
(Fri–Wed 12:30–14:00 & 19:30–22:00, closed Thu, veggie options,
follow Corso Marconi 4 blocks past the fish market, turn right
onto Via Maragliano and find #33 a block and a half ahead on left,
tel. 0185-288-926).

Ristorante il Nostromo, more central, also specializes in
seafood, such as grilled scampi or local shrimp. Owners Jane
and Umberto offer a €20 fixed-price meal plus à la carte options
(Wed–Sun 12:30–14:30 & 19:00–22:00, Mon–Tue 19:00–22:00, a
block off Piazza Veneto, take Via Gramsci and turn inland on Via
dell'Arco to #6, tel. 0185-281-390).

Da Pezzi, with a cheap, cafeteria-style atmosphere, is packed with locals at midday and at night, munching *farinata* (crêpe made from chickpeas, available Nov–May) at the bar and enjoying pesto and fresh fish in the dining room. Consider their deli counter for picnic ingredients (Sun–Fri 12:00–14:00 & 18:00–21:00, closed Sat, Via Cavour 21, tel. 0185-285-303).

Waterfront Dining: All along Via Tomaso Bottaro, you'll find restaurants, pizzerias, and bars serving food with a harbor view. **Gennaro Pizzeria,** in Piazza della Libertà by the boat dock, makes popular Neapolitan-style pizzas. **Bar Giuli,** the only place actually on the harbor, serves forgettable salads and sandwiches for a reasonable price (about 150 yards south of the fish market).

Gelato: The best *gelateria* I found in town (with chocolate-truffle *tartufato*) is **Il Portico** (closed Mon off-season, under the castle, closest to the water at Piazza della Libertà 48). **Gelateria Centrale,** just off Piazza Veneto near the cinema, serves up their specialty—*pinguino* (penguin), a cone with your choice of gelato dipped in chocolate (closed Wed Sept–May).

Groceries: **Seghezzo** is classiest (open daily June–Aug, closed Wed Sept–May, immediately to the right of the church on Via Cavour). The **D'Oro Centry** supermarket, just off Piazza Mazzini, has better prices (Mon–Thu 8:00–13:00 & 15:30–19:30, Fri–Sat 8:00–19:30, Sun 8:30–13:00, across from Hotel Fiorina at Piazza Mazzini 38, tel. 0185-286-470).

TRANSPORTATION CONNECTIONS

From Santa Margherita Ligure by Train to: Sestri Levante (hourly, 30 min), **Monterosso** (hourly, 1 hr), **La Spezia** (hourly, 1–1.5 hrs), **Pisa** (about hourly, 2–2.5 hrs, more with transfer in La Spezia), **Genoa** (2/hr, 45–60 min), **Milan** (10/day, 2–2.5 hrs, more with transfer in Genoa), **Ventimiglia**/French border (1/day, 4 hrs, hourly with change at Genova Piazza Principe station), **Venice** (8/day, 6–7 hrs with 1–3 changes). For **Florence,** transfer in Pisa (5/day, allow 3.5–4 hrs). The schedule for the **Cinque Terre** is confusing. It's a 60-minute trip, with hourly departures, but beware—some trains are much slower, while the fastest trains stop only at Monterosso and Riomaggiore, and most trains run late. Look for the schedule on the train station wall that specifically lists Cinque Terre trains. Most hoteliers have a current Cinque Terre train schedule handy.

From Santa Margherita Ligure by Boat to the Cinque Terre: Day-trip cruises from Santa Margherita to the Cinque Terre depart at 9:00, with lengthy stops in three Cinque Terre towns (Wed and Sat only July–Sept, €18 one-way, €29 round-trip). Some all-day trips include the Cinque Terre and Portovenere (depart at 9:00 Sun May–Sept and Tue and Thu late July–Sept, €18 one-way,

€29 round-trip). And there are half-day boat trips to the Cinque Terre (depart at 13:30 Mon and Fri July–Sept, €15 one-way, €22 round-trip, tel. 0185-284-670, www.traghettiportofino.it).

Portofino

Santa Margherita Ligure, with its aristocratic architecture, hints at old money, whereas nearby Portofino, with its sleek shops, reeks of new money. Fortunately, a few pizzerias, *focaccerie*, bars, and grocery shops are mixed in with Portofino's jewelry shops, art galleries, and *haute couture* boutiques, making the town affordable. The *piccolo* harbor, classic Italian architecture, and wooded peninsula can even turn glitzy Portofino into an appealing package. It makes a fun day trip from Santa Margherita Ligure.

Ever since the Romans founded Portofino for its safe harbor, it has had a strategic value (appreciated by everyone, from Napoleon to the Nazis). In the 1950s, *National Geographic* did a beautiful exposé on the idyllic port, and locals claim that's when the Hollywood elite took note. Liz Taylor and Richard Burton came here annually (as did Liz Taylor and Eddie Fisher). During one famous party, Rex Harrison dropped his Oscar into the bay (it was recovered). Ava Gardner came down from her villa each evening for a drink—sporting her famous fur coat. Greta Garbo loved to swim naked in the harbor, not knowing that half the town was watching. Truman Capote also called Portofino home. But VIPs were here a century earlier. In one of his books, Friedrich Nietzsche wrote about philosophizing with mythical prophet Zarathustra on the path between Portofino and Santa Margherita.

My favorite Portofino plan: Visit for the evening. Leave Santa Margherita on the bus at about 16:30, hike the last 20 minutes from Paraggi beach, explore Portofino, splurge for a drink on the harborfront, and return by bus to Santa Margherita for dinner (confirm late departures). Portofino does offer fancy harborside dining, but the quality doesn't match the high prices.

Getting to Portofino

Portofino makes an easy day trip from Santa Margherita by bus, boat, bike, or foot.

By Bus: Catch bus #82 or #882 from Santa Margherita's train station or at bus stops along the harbor (2–3/hr, 15 min, €0.80 to Paraggi, €1 to Portofino). Buy tickets at the bar next to the station, at Piazza Veneto's bus kiosk (daily 6:55–19:25), from the blue machine in front of the kiosk, or at any newsstand, *tabacchi,* or shop that displays a *Biglietti Bus* sign.

In Portofino, get tickets at the newsstand or from the blue

Portofino Area

machine next to the bus stop (go uphill and you'll come to Piazza Martiri della Libertà, machine and bus stop on right side, directions in English).

By Boat: The boat makes the trip with more class and without the traffic jams (€4.50 one-way, €7 round-trip, €0.50 more on Sun and holidays; May–Sept departs nearly hourly daily 10:15–16:15, Oct–April daily at 10:15 and 14:15 only; dock is a 2-min walk from Piazza Veneto off Piazza Martiri della Libertà, call to confirm or pick up schedule from TI, tel. 0185-284-670, check at www .traghettiportofino.it). These boats also run to the Cinque Terre (see page 287).

The boats run between Rapallo and the San Fruttuoso Abbey, stopping in between at Santa Margherita Ligure and Portofino. (Another boat line runs from Recco, Camogli, and Punta Chiappa to the abbey.)

By Bike: The 25-minute bike ride from Santa Margherita to Portofino is a popular option. Many of my recommended hotels provide free loaner bikes (though they may not be in the best condition); you can also rent your own wheels (see "Helpful Hints," page 351). Biking along the narrow road isn't too dangerous, as traffic is slow in summer, and there are no steep hills to struggle up.

On Foot: To hike the entire distance from Santa Margherita

Ligure to Portofino, you have two options: You can follow the sidewalk along (and sometimes hanging over) the sea (1 hour, 2.5 miles)—although traffic can be noisy. Or, if you're hardy and ambitious, you can take a quieter two-hour hike by leaving Santa Margherita at Via Maragliano, then follow the Ligurian-symbol trail markers (look for red-and-white stripes—they're not always obvious, sometimes numbered according to the path you're on, usually painted on rocks or walls, especially at junctions). This hike takes you high into the hills. Keep left after Cappelletta delle Gave. Several blocks past a castle, you'll drop down into the Paraggi beach, where you'll take the Portofino trail the rest of the way.

Bus and Hike Option: For a shorter hike (20 min) into Portofino, ride bus #82 or #882 only as far as the ritzy Paraggi beach. At the far end of the beach, cross the street and follow the paved trail marked *Pedonali per Portofino* high above the road. Twenty minutes later, you'll enter Portofino at a yellow-and-gray-striped church labeled *Divo Martino*—which I figure means "the divine Martin" and has something to do with Dean Martin giving us all "Volare" (which I couldn't get out of my head for the rest of the day).

ORIENTATION

Tourist Information

Portofino's snooty TI—downhill from the bus stop, on your right under the portico—reluctantly gives out information (Easter–Sept daily 10:30–13:30 & 14:30–19:30; Oct–Easter Tue–Sun 10:00–13:00 & 13:30–16:30, closed Mon; Via Roma 35, tel. 0185-269-024). Pick up a free town map and a rudimentary hiking map.

SIGHTS AND ACTIVITIES

In Portofino

Museo del Parco—For an artsy break, stroll around a park littered with contemporary sculpture, just above the harbor (€5, June–Sept Wed–Mon 10:00–13:30 & 15:00–20:00, closed Tue, closed Oct–May and in bad weather, mobile 337-333-737).

Hikes—One option is the paved stone path that winds up and down to the lighthouse *(faro)* at a scenic point with a bar (bar open May–Sept, hedges block views until the end, 25-min walk). Consider popping into **Castello Brown,** a medieval castle, on the way. It features lush gardens and a black-and-white portrait gallery of stars and famous personages who once frequented Portofino, including Clark Gable, Sophia Loren, Kim Novak, Grace Kelly, John Wayne, Ernest Hemingway, Humphrey Bogart, and Lauren

Bacall. Original decorations and photos are explained in English (€4, daily 10:00–19:00, shorter hours in winter, tel. 0185-267-101).

Or you could stroll the pedestrian promenade from Portofino to Paraggi beach, and, if you're lucky, see a wild boar en route (20 min, path starts to the right of yellow-and-gray-striped Divo Martino church—look for clock tower, parallels main road, ends at ritzy beach where it's easy to catch bus back to Santa Margherita Ligure).

Or you can hike out to San Fruttuoso Abbey (see below, 2.5 hours, steep at beginning and end, trail starts on the inland-most point of town in Santa Margherita past Piazza della Libertà; from Portofino, pick up the trailhead at the top of town, past the *carabinieri* station).

Near Portofino

San Fruttuoso Abbey—This 11th-century abbey, accessible only by foot or boat (from Portofino or Santa Margherita), isn't the main attraction (€4.50, more for special exhibits; May–Sept daily 10:00–18:00; March–April and Oct Tue–Sun 10:00–16:00, closed Mon; Nov–Feb open Sun only; tel. 0185-772-703). The more intriguing draw is 60 feet underwater offshore from the abbey: the statue *Christ of the Abyss (Cristo degli Abissi)*. A rowboat will take you from the dock below the Portofino boat dock to the statue, where you can look down through a lens to just barely see the arms of Jesus—outstretched, reaching upward. Some people bring goggles and dive in for a better view (€3 for the 20-min round-trip, these rowboats run only during boat arrival hours from Portofino—generally daily June–Sept 9:00–17:00; rowboats don't run in rough seas, so call the abbey before making the trip—tel. 0185-772-703). From Easter through September, boats continue north from San Fruttuoso Abbey to Punta Chiappa, Camogli, and Recco (€5–7 one-way, can return to Santa Margherita by train or buy round-trip boat tickets, call 0185-772-091 or inquire at Portofino or Santa Margherita TI for information).

South of the Cinque Terre

La Spezia

While just a quick train ride away from the fanciful Cinque Terre (20–30 min), the working town of La Spezia feels like reality Italy. Primarily a jumping-off point for travelers, the town is slim on sights, and has no beaches. The pedestrian zone on Via del Prione to the gardens along the harbor makes a pleasant stroll. The nearly deserted **Museo Amedeo Lia** displays Italian paintings from the

13th to 18th centuries, including minor works by Venetian masters Titian, Tintoretto, and Canaletto (€6, Tue–Sun 10:00–18:00, closed Mon, last entry 30 min before closing, English descriptions on laminated sheets in most rooms, audioguide-€3, WCs down the hall from ticket desk, no photos allowed, 10-min walk from station at Via del Prione 234, tel. 0187-731-100, www.castagna.it/mal).

To grab a meal while you wait for a train, see "Eating," page 367. Stay on the Cinque Terre if you can, but if you're in a bind I've listed several La Spezia accommodations later in this section.

ORIENTATION

Tourist Information

A TI and a Cinque Terre National Park office are located at the far end of the station, past the McDonald's (TI open April–Sept Mon–Sat 9:00–19:00, Sun 9:30–12:30; Oct–March closes at 16:00 Mon–Sat).

A second TI is near the waterfront (Mon–Sat 9:00–13:00 & 14:00–17:00, Sun 9:30–12:30, shorter hours in winter, Viale Italia 5 at Via del Prione, tel. 0187-770-900). Across the way is another Cinque Terre National Park branch (daily 8:00–19:00, Internet access-€1/hr).

Arrival in La Spezia

By Train: You can check your bags in the train station (see "Helpful Hints," below). Most of the hotels listed here are an easy walk from here.

By Car: Drivers will find free parking at Piazza d'Armi; from there it's a 20-minute walk to the train station, or take the €1 shuttle service to Piazza Brin, a five-minute walk from the station (3/hr). To reach Piazza d'Armi from the highway, follow the La Spezia *autostrada* as it becomes Viale Carducci and ends at Viale Italia, then turn left and follow the road as it bends right, following signs for parking.

A guarded parking garage is on Via Crispi, just after the Galleria (tunnel) Spallanzani on the right. Look for the AciPark sign (€16/day for 1–3 days, €13/day for longer stays, Mon–Fri 7:00–20:30, Sat 7:00–13:30, closed Sun, reserve in advance only if you'll be arriving when they're closed, tel. 0187-510-545, acipark @libero.it).

Helpful Hints

Market Days: A colorful covered market sets up in Piazza Cavour (Mon–Sat 8:00–13:00). On Fridays, a huge, all-day open-air market sprawls along Viale Garibaldi, about six blocks from the station.

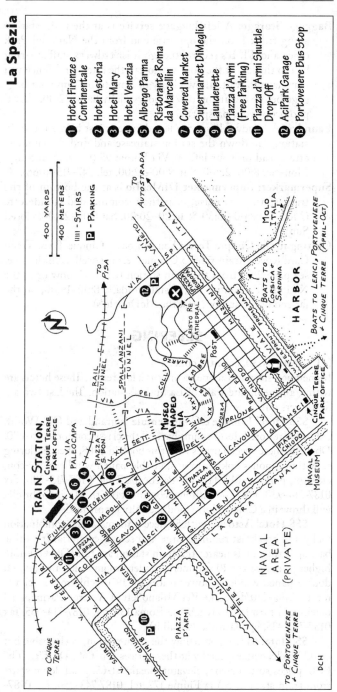

La Spezia

1. Hotel Firenze e Continentale
2. Hotel Astoria
3. Hotel Mary
4. Hotel Venezia
5. Albergo Parma
6. Ristorante Roma da Marcellin
7. Covered Market
8. Supermarket DiMeglio
9. Launderette
10. Piazza d'Armi (Free Parking)
11. Piazza d'Armi Shuttle Drop-Off
12. AcIPark Garage
13. Portovenere Bus Stop

Baggage Storage: A left-luggage service is at the train station along track 1, on the opposite end from the National Park office and TI. It's secure, though it isn't always staffed—ring bell to the left of the doorway to call the attendant. Since you may have to wait, allow plenty of time to pick up your baggage before departing (€3/12 hours, daily 8:00–22:00, they'll photocopy your passport).

Laundry: A handy self-service launderette is just below the train station. Go down the station staircase and find the launderette ahead on your left, at Via Fiume 95 (€7 wash and dry, Mon–Sat 8:00–22:00, Sun 9:00–22:00, tel. 347-915-4066).

Supermarket: Supermarket DiMeglio is at the bottom of the train-station staircase, near the recommended launderette (Mon–Fri 8:00–13:30 & 16:00–20:00, Sat 8:00–20:00, closed Sun).

Getting to the Cinque Terre: You can buy a Cinque Terre Treno Card (covers train ride to Cinque Terre as well as hiking fee; see page 284) from the train station ticket window or at the National Park office in the station (daily 8:00–19:00, on the far end of the station, past the McDonald's).

SLEEPING

(€1 = about $1.30, country code: 39)

Remember, sleep in La Spezia only as a last resort. These hotels are within a five-minute walk of La Spezia's station. The last two are for drivers only.

$$$ Hotel Firenze e Continentale is grand and Old World, but newly restored. Its 67 rooms have all the classy comforts (Sb-€80, Db-€118, these special prices with this book in 2008, cheaper during slow times, non-smoking rooms, double-paned windows, air-con, elevator, parking-€13/day, Via Paleocapa 7, tel. 0187-713-200, fax 0187-714-930, www.hotelfirenzecontinentale.it). Maria Gabriella will throw in a Cinque Terre food specialty for my readers.

$$$ Hotel Astoria, with 56 decent rooms, has a combination lobby and breakfast room as large as a school cafeteria. It's a fine backup if the hotels nearer the train station are full (Db-€80–130, higher prices for the 10 summery, modern rooms with air-con and double-paned windows, lower prices for 1970s-chic rooms, elevator, parking-€10/day, take Via Milano left of Albergo Parma, go 3 blocks and turn left to reach Via Roma 139, tel. 0187-714-655, fax 0187-714-425, hotelastoria@tiscali.it).

$$ Hotel Mary, just below the train station, is sleepable but could be cleaner...especially at these prices (Sb-€60, Db-€95, Tb-€110, prices soft, air-con, elevator, breakfast-€5, head down stairs from train station to Via Fiume 177, tel. 0187-743-254, fax 0187-

743-375, www.hotelmary.it, info@hotelmary.it).

$$ Hotel Venezia, across the street from Hotel Firenze e Continentale, is run with low energy, but its 19 rooms are pleasantly modern (Sb-€55, Db-€90, elevator, Via Paleocapa 10, tel. & fax 0187-733-465, hotelvenezia@telematicaitalia.it).

$$ Albergo Parma, with 36 rooms, is a little worn around the edges but is a cheap option (D-€50, Db-€60, these prices promised through 2008 with this book, breakfast-€4, no fans, double-paned windows, just below train station and down the stairs at Via Fiume 143, tel. 0187-743-010, fax 0187-743-240, albergoparma@libero.it, some English spoken).

$$ Il Gelsomino, for drivers only, is a homey B&B in the hills above La Spezia overlooking the Gulf of Poets. It has three tranquil rooms: one with a bayview terrace, one with hillside views, and a third that lacks views and a terrace (D-€70, Db-€80, Tb-€90, Q-€110, confirm arrival time in advance, large breakfast, Via dei Viseggi 9, tel. & fax 0187-704-201, www.ilgelsomino.biz, ilgelsomino@inwind.it, gracious Carla and Walter Massi).

$ Santa Maria del Mare Monastery, a last resort for drivers, rents 15 comfortable rooms high above La Spezia in a scenic but institutional setting (for Db and dorm beds, €30/person donation requested; Via Montalbano 135B, tel. 0187-711-332, fax 0187-708-490, monaster22@monasterosantamariadelmare.191.it).

EATING

Ristorante Roma da Marcellin has better food than you'll find at the station and is reasonably priced, with a cool, leafy terrace that's ideal for relaxing while you await your train (daily 12:00–15:00 & 19:00–23:00, just a few steps downhill—not downstairs—from the station, turn right as you exit station, across from Hotel Firenze e Continentale at Via Paleocapa 18, tel. 0187-715-921).

TRANSPORTATION CONNECTIONS

From La Spezia by Train to: Rome (10/day, 4 hrs), **Pisa** (hourly, 1 hr, direction: Livorno, Rome, Salerno, Naples, etc.), **Viareggio** (3–4/hr, 30–60 min), **Florence** (nearly hourly, 2.5 hrs, change in Pisa), **Milan** (hourly, 3 hrs direct or change in Genoa), **Venice** (4/day, 6 hrs, with change in Pisa and Florence or in Milan; or 1 direct/day, in summer only), **Monterosso** (hourly, 20–30 min).

By Bus to Portovenere: City buses depart from Viale Garibaldi (3/hr, 30 min, €1.45 each way, buy tickets at *tabacchi* shops or newsstands, bus stop 11P—just past Corso Cavour). From the La Spezia train station, exit left, and head downhill, following the street to the first square (S. Bon). Continue down Via Fiume to Piazza Garibaldi, then turn right at the fountain in the square onto Viale Garibaldi; the bus stop for Portovenere-bound buses is after the first stoplight on the right side of the street.

Carrara

Perhaps the world's most famous marble quarries are just east of La Spezia in Carrara. Michelangelo himself traveled to these valleys to pick out the marble that he would work into his masterpieces. The towns of the region are dominated by marble. The quarries higher up are vast digs that dwarf their hardworking trucks and machinery. The Carrara museum allows visitors to trace the story of marble-cutting here from pre-Roman times until today.

For a guided visit, **Sara Paolini** is excellent (€80/half-day tour, mobile 347-888-3833, sarapaolini@hotmail.com). She is accustomed to meeting drivers at the Carrara freeway exit, or she can pick you up at the train station.

Portovenere

While the gritty port of La Spezia offers little in the way of redeeming touristic value, the nearby resort of Portovenere is enchanting. This Cinque Terre–esque village clings to a rocky promontory that juts into the sea and protects the harbor from the crashing waves. On the harbor, next to colorful bobbing boats, a row of restaurants—perfect for *al fresco* dining—feature local specialties such as *trenette* pasta with pesto and *spaghetti frutti di mare*.

Local boats take you on a 40-minute excursion around three nearby islands or over to Lerici, the town across the bay. Lord Byron swam to Lerici (not recommended). Hardy hikers enjoy the five-hour (or more) hike to Riomaggiore, the nearest Cinque Terre town.

Portovenere—not to be confused with Portofino—is an easy day trip from the Cinque Terre by boat (Easter–Oct 4–6/day 9:00–17:00, 45 min, €4 one-way, €6.50 round-trip), or take the bus from La Spezia (30 min, buy tickets at *tabacchi* shops or newsstands, for directions to the bus stop in La Spezia, see "Transportation Connections," page 367).

Parking is a nightmare here from May through September. In peak season, buses shuttle drivers from the parking lot just outside Portovenere to the harborside square. Otherwise, test your luck with the spots on the seaside (€1.50/hr).

The TI is easy to find in the main piazza (June–mid-Oct Thu–Tue 10:00–12:00 & 16:00–19:00, closed Wed; mid-Oct–May

Thu–Tue 10:00–12:00 & 15:00–18:00, closed Wed; Piazza Bastreri 7, tel. 0187-790-691).

Sleeping in Portovenere: If you forgot your yacht, try **$$$ Albergo Il Genio,** in the building where the main street hits the piazza (Db-€90–120, breakfast-€6, parking-€5/day, no elevator, Piazza Bastreri 8, tel. & fax 0187-790-611, www .hotelgenioportovenere.com). If your *vita* is feeling *dolce,* consider **$$$ Grand Hotel Portovenere,** which has striking sea views (from €117 for a viewless double off-season to €224 for a view suite in summer, optional half-pension €32 per person, tel. 0187-792-610, fax 0187-790-661, Via Garibaldi 5, www.portovenerehotel .it, ghp@village.it).

FLORENCE

Firenze

Florence, the home of the Renaissance and birthplace of our modern world, is a "supermarket sweep," and the groceries are the best Renaissance art in Europe.

Get your bearings with a Renaissance walk. Florentine art goes beyond paintings and statues—there's food, fashion, and handicrafts. You can lick Italy's best gelato while enjoying some of Europe's best people-watching.

Planning Your Time

If you're in Italy for three weeks, Florence deserves at least a well-organized day. Make reservations at least a month in advance for the Uffizi Gallery (best Italian paintings anywhere) and a few days in advance for the Accademia (Michelangelo's *David*). Some hoteliers will make these reservations for you—request this service when booking your room (see page 382 for details).

For a day in Florence, see the Accademia, tour the Uffizi Gallery, visit the underrated Bargello (best statues), and do the Renaissance ramble (explained on page 386).

Art-lovers will want to chisel out another day of their itinerary for the many other Florentine cultural treasures. Shoppers and ice cream–lovers may need to do the same.

Plan your sightseeing carefully: Opening hours can be erratic, and crowds can cause long lines. Before heading into Florence, carefully check all the opening and closing times of your must-see museums at the TI, by phone, or online. This is especially true if you'll be in town for only a day or two during the crowded summer months.

The major sights—the Uffizi Gallery and the Accademia—are

closed on Monday. While many travelers spend several hours a day in lines at the Uffizi and Accademia, you can easily avoid this by making reservations. A couple of Florence's popular sights—the Bargello and the Museum of San Marco—close at 13:50 (though the latter is open later on weekends). Other museums close early only on certain days (e.g., the first Sunday of the month, second and fourth Monday, etc.). In general, Sundays and Mondays are bad, with many museums either closed or with shorter hours.

Connoisseurs of smaller towns should consider taking the bus to Siena for a day or evening trip (75-min one-way, confirm when last bus returns). Siena is magic after dark. For more information, see the Siena chapter.

ORIENTATION

The best of Florence lies mostly on the north bank of the Arno River. The main historical sights cluster around the red-brick dome of the cathedral (Duomo). Everything is within a 20-minute walk of the train station, cathedral, or Ponte Vecchio (Old Bridge). The less impressive but more characteristic Oltrarno area (south bank) is just over the bridge. Though small, Florence is intense. Prepare for scorching summer heat, kamikaze motor scooters, slick pickpockets, few WCs, steep prices, and long lines.

Tourist Information

There are three TIs in Florence: across from the train station, near Santa Croce Church, and on Via Cavour.

The TI across the square from the train station is most crowded—expect long lines (Mon–Sat 8:30–19:00, Sun 8:30–14:00; with your back to tracks, exit the station—it's 100 yards away, across the square in wall near corner of church at Piazza Stazione 4; tel. 055-212-245, www.firenzeturismo.it). In the train station, avoid the Hotel Reservations "Tourist Information" window (marked *Informazioni Turistiche Alberghiere*) near the McDonald's; it's not a real TI, but a hotel-reservation business instead.

The TI near Santa Croce Church is pleasant, helpful, and uncrowded (Mon–Sat 9:00–19:00, Sun 9:00–14:00, shorter hours off-season, Borgo Santa Croce 29 red, tel. 055-234-0444).

Another winner is the TI three blocks north of the Duomo (Mon–Sat 8:30–18:30, Sun 8:30–13:30, closed Sun in winter, Via Cavour 1 red, tel. 055-290-832, international bookstore across street).

At any TI, pick up these handy resources:

• a free map (ask for the "APT" map, which has bus routes of interest to tourists on the back),

• a current museum-hours listing (extremely important, since

Greater Florence

no guidebook—including this one—has ever been able to accurately predict the hours of Florence's sights for the coming year), and any information on entertainment, including the TI's monthly *Florence News* (good for events and entertainment listings); the free (and ad-driven) monthly *Florence Concierge Information* magazine (which lists museums, plus concerts, markets, sporting events, church services, shopping ideas, bus and train connections, and an entire similar section on Siena); and *The Florentine* newspaper (published every other Thu in English, for expats and tourists, with great articles giving cultural insights; download latest issue at www.theflorentine.net). These English freebies are available at TIs and hotels all over town.

Arrival in Florence

By Train: Florence's main station is Santa Maria Novella (*Firenze S.M.N.* on schedules and signs). The city has two suburban stations (Firenze Rifredi and Firenze Campo di Marte), and some trains don't stop at the main station. Before boarding, confirm that you're heading for S.M.N. or you may overshoot the city. (If this happens, don't panic; you're a short taxi ride from the center.)

Minimize time in the station—doing business here is generally intense, crowded, and overpriced. The banks of user-friendly, grayish-blue-and-yellow machines are handy. They take euros and credit cards, display schedules, issue tickets, and even make reservations for railpass-holders. Still, it can be quicker to get tickets and train info from travel agencies in town (such as American Express, page 378).

With your back to the tracks, look left to see a 24-hour pharmacy (*Farmacia Comunale,* near McDonald's), the fake "Tourist Information" office (funded by hotels), city buses, bus ticket booth, the taxi stand (fast-moving line, except on holidays), and the entrance to the underground mall/passage that goes across the square to the Church of Santa Maria Novella. (Note: Pickpockets frequent this tunnel, especially the surface point near the church.) Baggage check is near track 16 (€8/12 hrs, daily 6:00–24:00, passport required, maximum 35 pounds, no explosives—sorry). The real TI is across the square, 100 yards in front of the station (see page 371).

By Car: The *autostrada* has several exits for Florence. Get off at the Nord, Sud, or Certosa exits and follow signs toward—but not into—the *Centro.*

Don't even attempt driving into the city center. Florence has a traffic-reduction system that's complicated and confusing even to locals. Every car passing the city perimeter is photographed; those that haven't jumped through bureaucratic hoops to get a permit are fined in the mail about €70 per infraction; if you get lost and cross the line several times...you get several fines. The no-go zone (defined basically by the old medieval wall, now a boulevard circling the historic center of town) is roughly the area between the river, main train station, Piazza della Libertà, Piazza Donatello, and Piazza Beccaria. Look out for *Zona Traffico Limitato* signs (see page 842).

Fortunately, the city center is ringed with big, efficient parking lots (signposted with the standard big *P*), each with taxi and bus service into the center. I just head for "Parcheggio Parterre," just beyond Piazza della Libertà (€1.50/hr, €18/day, €65/week, open 24 hours daily, 600 spots, automated, pay with cash or credit card, never fills up completely, tel. 055-650-5295). From the freeway, follow the signs to *Centro,* then *Stadio,* then *P;* at the elevator exit, you'll see a taxi stand and the bus stop for the #7, which heads to

Florence Overview

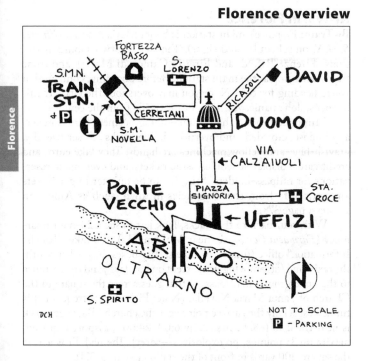

Piazza San Marco, the Duomo, and the train station.

You can park for free along any suburban curb near a bus stop that feels safe, and take the bus into the city center from there. Check for signs indicating parking restrictions—for example, a circle with a slash through it and *dispari giovedì, 0,00–06,00* means don't park on Thursdays between midnight and 6 in the morning. If you park in the wrong place on a street-cleaning day, you'll get towed.

Free parking is easy up at Piazzale Michelangelo (see page 402), but don't park where the buses drop people off; park on the side of the piazza farthest from the view. To get from Piazzale Michelangelo to the center of town, take bus #12 or #13 (see "Getting Around Florence," page 378).

If you're picking up a rental car upon departure, don't struggle with driving into the center. Taxi with your luggage to the car-rental office, and head out from there.

By Plane: Florence has its own airport and Pisa's is nearby. See "Transportation Connections" on page 423 for details.

Helpful Hints

Theft Alert: Florence has particularly hardworking thief gangs. They specialize in tourists and hang out where you do: near the train station, the station's underpass (especially where the tunnel surfaces), and major sights. Also be on guard at two squares frequented by drug pushers (Santa Maria Novella and Santo Spirito). American tourists—especially older ones—are considered easy targets. Bus #7 (to Fiesole) is a favorite with tourists and, therefore, with thieves.

Medical Help: There's no shortage of English-speaking medical help in Florence. To reach a doctor who speaks English, call 055-475-411 (they answer 24/7, reasonable house calls to your hotel—arriving within an hour for €130, only €50 if you go to the clinic at Via L. Magnifico 59, near Piazza della Libertà when the doctor is in: Mon–Fri 11:00–12:00 & 17:00–18:00, Sat 11:00–12:00, house calls only on Sun, no appointment necessary).

Dr. Stephen Kerr is an English doctor who specializes in helping sick tourists. His clinic is a block off Piazza della Signoria, with a 24-hour pharmacy nearby (clinic open for drop-ins Mon–Fri 15:00–17:00, other times by appointment, €80 per visit, Via Porta Rossa 1, tel. 055-288-055, mobile 335-83-1682). The TI has a list of other English-speaking doctors.

There are 24-hour pharmacies at the train station and on Borgo San Lorenzo (near the Duomo).

Churches: Many churches now operate like museums, charging an admission fee to see their art treasures. Modest dress for men, women, and even children is required in some churches, and recommended for all of them—no bare shoulders, short shorts, or short skirts. Be respectful of worshippers and the paintings; don't use a flash. Churches usually close from 12:00 or 12:30 to 15:00 or 16:00.

Addresses: Street addresses list businesses in red and residences in black (color-coded on the actual street number and indicated by a letter following the number in printed addresses: r = red, no indication = black). *Pensioni* are usually black but can be either. The red and black numbers each appear in roughly consecutive order on streets but bear no apparent connection with each other. I'm lazy and don't concern myself with the distinction (if one number's wrong, I look for the other) and can easily find my way around.

Internet Access: In bustling, tourist-filled Florence, you'll see small Internet cafés on virtually every street (remember to bring your passport, which you're required to show to go online).

Internet Train is the dominant chain, with bright and cheery rooms, speedy computers, and long hours (€3.50/hr, reusable card good for any other Internet Train location, daily 9:30–24:00, www.internettrain.it). Find branches at the train

Daily Reminder

Sunday: The Duomo's dome, Museum of Precious Stones, and the Mercato Centrale are closed. These sights close early: Duomo Museum (at 13:40) and the Baptistery's interior (at 14:00). A few sights are open only in the afternoon: Duomo (13:30–16:45), Santa Croce Church (13:00–17:30), Church of San Lorenzo (13:30–17:00), and Brancacci Chapel and Church of Santa Maria Novella (both 13:00–17:00). Both the Bargello and the Museum of San Marco are closed on the first, third, and fifth Sundays of the month (but on the second and fourth, San Marco stays open until 19:00). The Medici Chapels and Palazzo Davanzati close on the second and fourth Sundays. The Science Museum is generally closed (but open Oct–May on the second Sunday of the month). Santo Spirito Church is open for worshippers, but closed to sightseers. Need a calendar? Look in the appendix.

It's not possible to reserve tickets by phone on Sunday for the major sights (Accademia, Uffizi Gallery) because the telephone-reservation office for both is closed; try other options instead (see page 382 for details).

Monday: The biggies are closed, including the Accademia *(David)* and the Uffizi Gallery, as well as the Orsanmichele Church and the Pitti Palace's Palatine Gallery and Modern Art Gallery.

The Medici Chapels close on the first, third, and fifth Mondays of the month. The Museum of San Marco and the Bargello close on the second and fourth Mondays. At the Pitti Palace, the Grand Ducal Treasures and the Boboli and Bardini gardens close on the first and last Mondays. Palazzo Davanzati closes on the first, third, and fifth Mondays. The San Lorenzo Market is closed Monday in winter.

Target these sights on Mondays: Duomo, Duomo Museum, Giotto's Tower, Baptistery, Medici–Riccardi Palace, Brancacci Chapel, Mercato Nuovo, Michelangelo's House, Science Museum, Palazzo Vecchio, and churches (including

station (downstairs), near Piazza della Repubblica (Via Porta Rossa 38 red), behind the Duomo (Via dell'Oriolo 40), Piazza Santa Croce (Via de Benci 36 red), near David and recommended hotels (Via Guelfa 54 red), and near Ponte Vecchio (Borgo San Jacopo 30 red). Internet Train offers phone cards, disc burning, and other related services.

Bookstores: Local guidebooks (sold at kiosks) are cheap and give you a map and a decent commentary on the sights. For brand-name guidebooks in English, try **Feltrinelli International** (Mon–Sat 9:00–19:30, closed Sun, a few blocks north of the

Santa Croce). Or take a walking tour.

Tuesday: All sights are open except for Michelangelo's House and the Brancacci Chapel. The Science Museum closes early (13:00).

Wednesday: All sights are open except for the Medici–Riccardi Palace. The Santo Spirito Church is open only in the morning (10:00–12:00).

Thursday: All sights are open. These sights close early: Duomo (16:00) and Palazzo Vecchio (14:00).

Friday: All sights are open. The Church of Santa Maria Novella opens only in the afternoon (13:00–17:00).

Saturday: All sights are open, but the Science Museum closes at 13:00 June–Sept. The Duomo's dome closes early (17:40), and it closes especially early (16:00) on the first Saturday of the month, as does the Duomo's interior (15:30).

Early-Closing Warning: Some of Florence's sights close surprisingly early every day (or nearly so), most notably the Bargello, which closes at 13:50 daily. The Museum of Precious Stones closes at 14:00 (Mon–Wed and Fri–Sat), as does the Mercato Centrale (open Mon–Sat, closed Sun).

Late-Hours Relief: The Accademia, Uffizi, and Palatine Gallery in the Pitti Palace are open Tue–Sun until 18:50. Many other sights are open until 19:00: Museum of San Marco (Sat–Sun), Museum of Precious Stones (Thu), San Lorenzo Market (daily), Medici–Riccardi Palace (Thu–Tue), the Duomo's dome (Mon–Fri), Baptistery (Mon–Sat), Mercato Nuovo (daily), and Palazzo Vecchio (Fri–Wed). These sights are open until 19:30: Duomo Museum (Mon–Sat), Giotto's Tower (daily), Boboli and Bardini Gardens in the Pitti Palace (daily, June–Aug only), and San Miniato Church (daily). The Leonardo Museum is open until 20:30 (daily). Sometimes in summer, the Uffizi and Accademia are open until 22:00 one night a week; ask at the TI.

Duomo and across the street from the TI and the Medici–Riccardi Palace at Via Cavour 20 red, tel. 055-219-524), **Edison Bookstore** (Mon–Sat 9:00–24:00, Sun 10:00–24:00, sells CDs and novels on Renaissance and a lot more on its four floors, facing Piazza della Repubblica, tel. 055-213-110), or **Paperback Exchange** (cheaper, all books in English, bring in your used book for a discount on a new one, Mon–Fri 9:00–19:30, Sat 10:00–19:30, closed Sun, just south of the Duomo on Via delle Oche 4 red, tel. 055-293-460).

Laundry: The **Wash & Dry Lavarapido** chain offers long hours and efficient, self-service launderettes at several locations (about €7 for wash and dry, daily 8:00–22:00, tel. 055-580-480). These are close to recommended hotels: Via dei Servi 105 (and a rival launderette at Via Guelfa 55, off Via Cavour; both near Accademia and *David*), Via del Sole 29 red and Via della Scala 52 red (between train station and river), Via Ghibellina 143 red (Palazzo Vecchio), Via Faenza 26 (near station), and Via dei Serragli 87 red (across the river in Oltrarno neighborhood).

Travel Agency: Get train tickets, reservations, and supplements at travel agencies rather than at the congested train station. The cost is often the same, though sometimes there's a minimal charge. Ask your hotel for the nearest travel agency, or try American Express.

American Express offers all the normal services, but is most helpful as an easy place to get your train tickets, reservations, supplements (all the same price as at the station), or just information on trains (Mon–Fri 9:00–17:30, closed Sat–Sun, 3 short blocks north of Palazzo Vecchio at Via Dante Alighieri 22 red, tel. 055-50-981).

Chill Out: Schedule several cool breaks into your sightseeing where you can sit, pause, and refresh yourself with a sandwich, gelato, or coffee.

Getting Around Florence

I organize my sightseeing geographically and do it all on foot.

I think of Florence as a Renaissance treadmill—it requires a lot of walking. Its **buses** don't really cover the old center well.

Of the many bus lines, I found these of most value for sightseeing: Lines #7, #31, and #32, which connect the train station, the Duomo, and Piazza San Marco. Bus #7 continues on to the Parterre parking lot at Piazza della Libertà and then on to Fiesole. Lines #12 and #13 go from the train station to Porta Romana, up to San Miniato Church and Piazzale Michelangelo, and on to Santa Croce.

Fun little *elettrico* **minibuses** wind through the tangled old center of town and up and down the river—just €1.20 gets you a 70-minute joyride. *Elettrico* A winds around the congested old center from the train station to Piazza Beccaria. *Elettrico* B goes up and down the Arno River from Ognissanti to Santa Croce Church. *Elettrico* D goes from the train station to Ponte Vecchio, cruising through Oltrarno and finishing at Ponte San Niccolo. You'll likely be sitting with eccentric local seniors. The free TI map comes with a handy inset that shows all these bus routes.

Buy tickets in *tabacchi* shops, newsstands, or at the train station bus stop, as tickets bought on board are a little pricier (€2) and

Florence

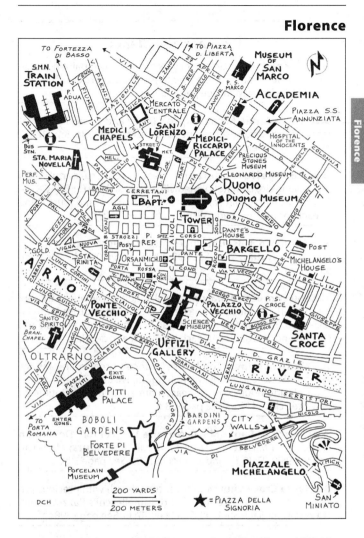

require exact change (€1.20/70 min, €4.50/4 tickets, €5/24 hrs, €12/3 days, validate in machine on the bus, route map available at TI, tel. 800-424-500). Follow general bus etiquette: Board at the front or rear doors, exit out the center.

Hop-on, hop-off bus tours stop at the major sights (see the next section, "Tours").

The minimum cost for a **taxi** ride is €4, or €6 after 22:00 and on Sundays (rides in the center of town should be charged as tariff #1). A taxi ride from the train station to Ponte Vecchio costs about €8.50. Taxi fares and supplements (e.g., €2 extra if you call a cab rather than hail one) are clearly explained on signs in each taxi.

Florence at a Glance

▲▲▲**Uffizi Gallery** Greatest collection of Italian paintings anywhere. Reserve at least one month in advance. **Hours:** Tue–Sun 8:15–18:50, closed Mon. See page 394.

▲▲▲**Accademia** Michelangelo's *David* and powerful (unfinished) *Prisoners*. Reserve ahead. **Hours:** Tue–Sun 8:15–18:50, closed Mon. See page 385.

▲▲▲**Bargello** Underappreciated sculpture museum (Michelangelo, Donatello, Medici treasures). **Hours:** Daily 8:15–13:50; closed first, third, and fifth Sun and second and fourth Mon of each month. See page 391.

▲▲▲**Duomo Museum** Underrated cathedral museum with sculptures. **Hours:** Mon–Sat 9:00–19:30, Sun 9:00–13:40. See page 391.

▲▲▲**Museum of San Marco** Best collection anywhere of artwork by the early Renaissance master Fra Angelico. **Hours:** Mon–Fri 8:15–13:50, Sat–Sun 8:15–19:00; closed first, third, and fifth Sun and second and fourth Mon of each month. See page 385.

▲▲**Medici Chapels** Tombs of Florence's great ruling family, designed and carved by Michelangelo. **Hours:** Tue–Sun 8:15–17:00; closing hours vary off-season but are generally until 14:00 in winter, closed Mon. See page 388.

▲▲**Church of Santa Maria Novella** 13th-century Dominican church with Masaccio's famous 3-D painting. **Hours:** Mon–Thu and Sat 9:00–17:00, Fri and Sun 13:00–17:00. See page 399.

▲▲**Santa Croce Church** 14th-century church with precious art, tombs of famous Florentines, and Brunelleschi's Pazzi Chapel. **Hours:** Mon–Sat 9:30–17:30, Sun 13:00–17:30. See page 398.

▲▲**Science Museum** Fascinating collection of old clocks, telescopes, maps, and Galileo's finger. **Hours:** June–Sept Mon and Wed–Fri 9:30–17:00, Tue and Sat 9:30–13:00, closed Sun; Oct–May Mon and Wed–Sat 9:30–17:00, Tue 9:30–13:00, generally closed Sun but open second Sun of month 10:00–13:00. See page 397.

▲▲**Pitti Palace** Three museums in lavish palace: Palatine Gallery (Raphael art), Modern Art Gallery, Grand Ducal Treasures (Medici treasure chest), plus sprawling Boboli and Bardini gardens. **Hours:** Palatine Gallery and Modern Art Gallery: Tue–Sun

8:15–18:50, closed Mon. Grand Ducal Treasures, plus Boboli and Bardini gardens: Daily 8:15–18:30, until 19:30 June–Aug, closed first and last Mon of the month. See page 400.

▲▲**Brancacci Chapel** Works of Masaccio, early Renaissance master who reinvented perspective. **Hours:** Mon and Wed–Sat 10:00–17:00, Sun 13:00–17:00, closed Tue. Reservations required. See page 401.

▲▲**Duomo (Santa Maria del Fiore)** Gothic cathedral with colorful facade, and the first dome built since ancient times. **Hours:** Mon–Wed and Fri–Sat 10:00–17:00 except first Sat of month 10:00–15:30, Thu 10:00–16:00, Sun 13:30–16:45. See page 389.

▲**Climbing the Duomo's Dome** Grand view into the cathedral, close-up of dome architecture, and after 463 steps, a glorious Florence vista. **Hours:** Mon–Fri 8:30–19:00, Sat 8:30–17:40 except first Sat of month 8:30–16:00, closed Sun. Long and slow lines, go early, no reservations accepted. See page 390.

▲**Giotto's Tower** Has views equaling Duomo's, 50 fewer steps, and fewer lines. **Hours:** Daily 8:30–19:30. See page 390.

▲**Baptistery** Bronze doors fit to be the gates of paradise. **Hours:** Doors always viewable; Baptistery open Mon–Sat 12:15–19:00, Sun 8:30–14:00. See page 391.

▲**Medici-Riccardi Palace** Lorenzo the Magnificent's home, with fine art, frescoed ceilings, and a lovely Chapel of the Magi. **Hours:** Thu–Tue 9:00–19:00, closed Wed. See page 389.

▲**Palazzo Vecchio** Fortified palace once the home of the Medici family, wallpapered with history and Renaissance themes. **Hours:** Fri–Wed 9:00–19:00, Thu 9:00–14:00. See page 396.

▲**Ponte Vecchio** Famous bridge lined with gold and silver shops. **Hours:** Bridge always open (shops closed at night). See page 397.

▲**Michelangelo's House** Museum featuring early, lesser-known works of the master. **Hours:** Wed–Mon 9:30–20:30, closed Tue. See page 399.

▲**Piazzale Michelangelo** Hilltop square with stunning view of Duomo and Florence. **Hours:** Always open. See page 402.

Make Reservations to Avoid Lines

Florence has a reservation system for its top five sights—Uffizi, Accademia, Bargello, Medici Chapels, and Pitti Palace. I highly recommend getting reservations for the Accademia (Michelangelo's *David*) and the Uffizi (Renaissance paintings). While you can generally get an entry time for the Accademia within a few days, the Uffizi is often booked up a month in advance (though it's easier in the off-season). Your best strategy is to get reservations for both as soon as you know when you'll be in town. After learning how easy this is and seeing hundreds of bored, sweaty tourists waiting in lines without the reservation, it's hard not to be amazed at their cluelessness.

There are several ways to make a reservation: Have your hotelier arrange it, call the reservation number directly, use an online booking service (for a fee), or go in person in advance to one of the museums.

Most hoteliers are accustomed to offering this service either for free or for a fee (€3–5) when clients make a room reservation. Just request it with your hotel booking. For most people, this is easiest.

If you want to make the booking(s) yourself, dial 055-294-

TOURS

Tour companies big and small offer plenty of tours out to smaller towns in the Tuscan countryside (the most popular day trips: Siena, San Gimignano, Pisa, and into Chianti country for wine tasting). They also do city tours, but for most people, the city is really best on foot (and the book you're holding provides as much information as you'll get with a generic bus tour).

For extra insight with a personal touch, consider the tour companies and individual Florentine guides listed here. They are hardworking, creative, and offer a worthwhile array of organized sightseeing activities. Study their websites for details. If you're taking a city tour, remember that individuals save money with a scheduled public tour (such as those offered daily by Walking Tours of Florence). If you're traveling as a family or small group, however, you're likely to save money by booking a private guide (since rates are based on roughly €55/hour for any size of group).

Walking Tours of Florence—This company offers a variety of tours (up to 12/day year-round) featuring downtown Florence, Uffizi highlights, and Tuscany day trips. Their guides are native

883 within Italy (Mon–Fri 8:30–18:30, Sat 8:30–12:30, closed Sun). From the US, call 011-39-055-294-833. Unfortunately, the reservation line is often busy, and even if you get through, you may be disconnected while on hold. Try again. And again.

When you do get through, an English-speaking operator walks you through the process, and two minutes later you say *grazie,* with appointments (15-min entry window) and six-digit confirmation numbers for each of the top museums and galleries.

Some booking agencies offer reservations online for a hefty fee (minimum €5/ticket, such as tickitaly.com or www .weekendafirenze.com).

The "Original Florence in One Day" tour run by Walking Tours of Florence includes admission to the Uffizi and the Accademia (see below for more info).

Besides these main attractions, the only other places you should book in advance are the Brancacci Chapel (reservations are mandatory to see the Masaccio frescoes) and the Medici–Riccardi Palace (for quick entry into the sumptuous Chapel of the Magi, reservations are recommended). You do this direct (phone numbers are included in the sight listings), and spots are generally available a day in advance.

Ticket phone numbers are often busy; be persistent. The best time to call is at about 14:00–15:00 or just before closing.

English-speakers. The three-hour "Original Florence" walk hits the main sights but gets offbeat to weave a picture of Florentine life in medieval and Renaissance times. Tours go rain or shine with as few as two participants (€25 for 3-hour Original Florence walk daily at 9:15, get the student rate of €20 with this book—just ask when you make your reservation, office open Mon–Sat 8:00–18:00, Sun 8:30–13:30 but off-season closed on Sun and for lunch, booking necessary for all tours, near Piazza della Repubblica at Via dei Sassetti 1, second floor, above Odeon Cinema, tel. 055-264-5033 during day or mobile 329-613-2730 18:00–20:00, www.italy .artviva.com, staff@artviva.com). For schedule details, pick up their extensive brochure in your hotel lobby.

Florentia—Top-notch, private walking tours—geared for thoughtful, well-heeled travelers with longer than average attention spans—are led by local scholars. The tours range from introductory city walks and museum visits to in-depth thematic walks such as the Golden Age of Florence, the Medici Dynasty, and side-trips into Tuscany (tour prices start at €150 for 2 hours, groups range from 2 to 6 people, reserve in advance, tel. 338-890-8625, US tel. 510/759-5059, www.florentia.org, info@florentia.org).

Context Florence—This group of graduate students and professors lead "walking seminars" as scholarly as Florentia's (above). Their tours include a three-hour Michelangelo seminar, an in-depth study of the artist's work and influence (€80/person, including Accademia admission) and a two-hour evening orientation stroll (€35/person, tel. 06-482-0911, US tel. 888-467-1986, www .contextflorence.com, info@contextflorence.com). For all the latest on their innovative offerings (lecture series, food walks, kids' tours, and programs in Venice, Rome, and Paris), see their website.

Local Guides—Good guides include Paola Barubiani and her partners at Walks Inside Florence (tel. 335-526-6496, www .walksinsideflorence.it, barubiani.paola@walksinsideflorence.it) and Alessandra Marchetti (mobile 347-386-9839, aleoberm@tin .it). Cynthia Black Nesti, an American married to a Florentine, enjoys leading visitors around her adopted town (€55/hr per group, tel. 055-641-625, nesti12@interfree.it).

Tuscany Tours—Paola Migliorini and her partners offer museum tours, city walking tours, and Tuscan excursions by van (you can tailor tours as you like). Go anywhere in the center of Florence by van and enjoy the city nearly sweat-free (€55/hr, €65/hr in an 8-seat van, Via San Gallo 120, tel. 055-472-448, mobile 347-657-2611, www.florencetour.com, info@florencetour.com).

Hop-on, Hop-off Bus Tours—Around town, you'll see big double-decker sightseeing buses double-parking near major sights. Tourists on the top deck can listen to brief recorded descriptions of the sights, snap photos, and enjoy an effortless drive-by look at the major landmarks. Tickets cost €20 (good for 24 hours, first bus at 9:30, last bus at 18:00, pay as you board, tickets include two bus lines—Blue is 1 hour with a trip up to Piazzale Michelangelo, Green is 2 hours with a side-trip to Fiesole, www.firenze.city -sightseeing.it). As the name implies, you can hop off when you want and catch the next bus (usually every 30 min, depending on the season). Hop-on stops include the train station, Duomo, and Pitti Palace. As most sights are buried in the old center where big buses can't go, Florence doesn't really lend itself to this kind of tour bus. Look at the route map before committing yourself to this tour.

Accidental Tourist—This tour company picks you up in a van for a day of cooking classes, hiking, biking, or wine-tasting, then drops you off back in Florence (prices vary, e.g., €85 for cooking class, 9:30–17:00, book online in advance, allow 4 days for reply to emails, US tel. 348/659-0040, www.accidentaltourist.com, info @accidentaltourist.com).

SIGHTS

▲▲▲ Accademia (Galleria dell'Accademia)

This museum houses Michelangelo's *David* and powerful (unfinished) *Prisoners*. Eavesdrop as tour guides explain these masterpieces. *David* gazes ahead with the newfound self-awareness and optimism of the Renaissance. This was a radical break with the past. Hello, humanism. Man was now a confident individual, no longer a plaything of the supernatural. And life was now more than just a preparation for what happened after you died.

The Renaissance was the merging of art, science, and humanism. In a humanist vein, *David* is looking at the crude giant of medieval darkness and thinking, "I can take this guy." (David was an apt mascot for a town surrounded by big bully city-states.) Back on a religious track, notice *David*'s large and overdeveloped right hand. This is symbolic of the hand of God that powered David to slay the giant...and enabled Florence to rise above its crude neighboring city-states.

Beyond the magic marble are two floors of mildly interesting pre-Renaissance and Renaissance paintings, including a couple of lighter-than-air Botticellis.

Cost, Hours, Location: €6.50, plus €3 fee for recommended reservation, Tue–Sun 8:15–18:50, closed Mon (last entry 30 min before closing, Via Ricasoli 60, tel. 055-238-8609). To avoid waiting in line, reserve ahead; see page 382 for details.

Nearby: Piazza S.S. Annunziata, behind the Accademia, displays lovely Renaissance harmony. Facing the square are two fine buildings: the 15th-century Santissima Annunziata church (worth a peek) and Brunelleschi's Hospital of the Innocents (Spedale degli Innocenti, not worth going inside), with terra-cotta medallions by Luca della Robbia. Built in the 1420s, the hospital is considered the first Renaissance building.

Near the Accademia

▲▲ Museum of San Marco (Museo di San Marco)—Located one block north of the Accademia, this 15th-century monastery houses

A Renaissance Walk Through Florence

During the Dark Ages, it was especially obvious to the people of Italy—sitting on the rubble of Rome—that there had to be a brighter age before them. The long-awaited rebirth, or Renaissance, began in Florence for good reason. Wealthy because of its cloth industry, trade, and banking; powered by a fierce city-state pride (locals would pee into the Arno with gusto, knowing rival city-state Pisa was downstream); and fertile with more than its share of artistic genius (imagine guys like Michelangelo and Leonardo attending the same high school)—Florence was a natural home for this cultural explosion.

Take a two-hour walk through the core of Renaissance Florence by starting at the Accademia (home of Michelangelo's *David*) and cutting through the heart of the city to the Ponte Vecchio on the Arno River.

At the Accademia, you'll look into the eyes of Renaissance man—humanism at its confident peak. Then walk to the cathedral (Duomo) to see the dome that kicked off the architectural Renaissance. Step inside the Baptistery to view a ceiling covered with preachy, flat, 2-D, medieval mosaic art. Then, to learn what happened when art met math, check out the realistic 3-D reliefs on the doors. The painter, Giotto, also designed the bell tower—an early example of a Renaissance genius who could excel in many areas. Continue toward the river on Florence's great pedestrian mall, Via de' Calzaiuoli (or "Via Calz")—part of the original grid plan given to the city by the ancient Romans. Stop by any gelato shop for some cool refreshment. Down a few blocks, compare medieval and Renaissance statues on the exterior of the Orsanmichele Church. Via Calz connects the cathedral with the central square (Piazza della Signoria), the city palace (Palazzo Vecchio), and the Uffizi Gallery, which contains the greatest collection of Italian Renaissance paintings in captivity. Finally, walk through the Uffizi courtyard—a statuary think tank of Renaissance greats—to the Arno River and the Ponte Vecchio.

the greatest collection anywhere of frescoes and paintings by the early Renaissance master Fra Angelico. The ground floor features the monk's paintings, along with some works by Fra Bartolomeo. Upstairs are 43 cells decorated by Fra Angelico and his assistants. While the monk/painter was trained in the medieval religious style, he also learned and adopted Renaissance techniques and sensibilities, producing works that blended Christian symbols and Renaissance realism. Don't miss the cell of Savonarola, the charismatic monk who rode in from the Christian right, threw out the

Renaissance Walk

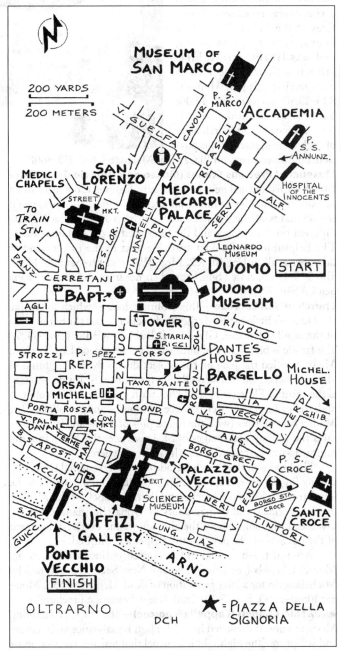

Florence

MUSEUM OF SAN MARCO

ACCADEMIA

200 YARDS
200 METERS

P. S. MARCO

V. L.

GUELFA

CAVOUR

RICASOLI

P. S. S. ANNUNZ.

MEDICI CHAPELS

SAN LORENZO

MEDICI-RICCARDI PALACE

HOSPITAL OF THE INNOCENTS

TO TRAIN STN.

STREET

MKT.

B. S. LOR.

VIA MARTELLI

VIA

PUCCI

SERVI

V. ALF.

LEONARDO MUSEUM

DUOMO START

PANZ.

CERRETANI

DUOMO MUSEUM

BAPT.

ORIUOLO

AGLI

TOWER

S. MARIA RICCI

DANTE'S HOUSE

BARGELLO

MICHEL. HOUSE

STROZZI

P. SPEZ.

REP.

CORSO

TAVO. DANTE

ORSAN-MICHELE

PORTA ROSSA

V. PAL. DAVAN.

COV. MKT.

COND.

VIA V. G. VECCHIA

VERGHIB.

TERME

S. MARIA

ANG.

BORGO GRECI

P. S. CROCE

B. S. APOST.

L. ACCIAIUOLI

EXIT

SCIENCE MUSEUM

PALAZZO VECCHIO

V. NERI

BENCI

BORGO STA. CROCE

SANTA CROCE

S. JAC.

GUICC.

UFFIZI GALLERY

LUNG. DIAZ

TINTORI

PONTE VECCHIO FINISH

ARNO

OLTRARNO

DCH

★ = PIAZZA DELLA SIGNORIA

Medicis, turned Florence into a theocracy, sponsored "bon-fires of the vanities" (burning books, paintings, and so on), and was finally burned himself when Florence decided to change channels (€4, Mon–Fri 8:15–13:50, Sat–Sun 8:15–19:00; but closed first, third, and fifth Sun and second and fourth Mon of each month; reservations pos-

sible but unnecessary, on Piazza San Marco, tel. 055-238-8608).

Museum of Precious Stones (Museo dell'Opificio delle Pietre Dure)—This unusual gem of a museum features room after room of exquisite mosaics of inlaid marble and stones. Upstairs, you'll see remnants of the Medici workshop from 1588, including 500 different precious stones and the tools used to cut and inlay them. The helpful loaner booklet available next to the ticket window describes it all in English (€2, Mon–Wed and Fri–Sat 8:15–14:00, Thu 8:15–19:00, closed Sun, around corner from Accademia at Via degli Alfani 78, tel. 055-26-511).

Church of San Lorenzo—This redbrick dome—which looks like the Duomo's little sister—is the Medici church and the burial place of the family's founder, Giovanni di Bicci de' Medici (1360–1429). The facade is big, ugly, and unfinished because Pope Leo X (also a Medici) pulled the plug on the project due to dwindling funds—after Michelangelo had labored on it for four years. Inside, though, is the spirit of Florence in the 1420s, with gray-and-white columns and arches in perfect Renaissance symmetry and simplicity. The Medici coat of arms (with the round pills of these "medics") decorates the ceiling, and images of St. Lawrence, the Medici patron saint who was martyred on a grill, are everywhere.

Highlights of the church include two finely sculpted Donatello pulpits (in the nave), Filippo Lippi's glowing *Annunciation* (in the left transept), Filippo Brunelleschi's burial chapel for the Medicis (far left corner), and bronze doors by Donatello (flanking altar). Overhead, the dome above the altar shows the exact arrangement of the heavens on the day that the chapel was finished.

Around the back end of the church is the entrance to the Medici Chapels (see below) and the New Sacristy, designed by Michelangelo for a later generation of dead Medicis (€2.50, Mon–Sat 10:00–17:00, Sun 13:30–17:00, free information brochure).

▲▲**Medici Chapels (Cappelle Medicee)**—The chapel, containing Medici tombs, is drenched in lavish High Renaissance architecture and sculpture. The highlight is a chapel that features interior decoration by Michelangelo, including the brooding *Night, Day, Dawn,*

and *Dusk* statues (€6, Tue–Sun 8:15–17:00; closing hours vary off-season but are generally until 14:00 in winter, closed Mon; reservations possible but unnecessary, tel. 055-238-8602).

Nearby: Behind the chapels on Piazza Madonna degli Aldobrandini is the lively **San Lorenzo Market,** with a scene that I find just as interesting. Take a stroll through the huge double-decker **Mercato Centrale** (central food market) one block north.

▲**Medici–Riccardi Palace (Palazzo Medici–Riccardi)**—Lorenzo the Magnificent's home is worth a look for its art. The tiny Chapel of the Magi contains colorful Renaissance gems like the *Procession of the Magi* frescoes by Benozzo Gozzoli. The Multimedia Room helps you navigate through details of Gozzoli's Magi frescoes, shown on a large video screen. The former library has a Baroque ceiling fresco by Luca Giordano, a prolific artist from Naples known as Fast Luke *(Luca fa presto)* for his ambidextrous

painting abilities. While the Medicis originally occupied this 1444 house, in the 1700s it became home to the Riccardi family, who added the Baroque flourishes. As only eight people are allowed into the Chapel of the Magi every seven minutes, it's smart to call for a reservation if you want to avoid a wait (€5, Thu–Tue 9:00–19:00, closed Wed, kitty-corner from Church of San Lorenzo, one long block north of Baptistery, ticket entrance is north of the main gated entrance, Via Cavour 3, tel. 055-276-0340).

Leonardo Museum—This small, entrepreneurial venture is overpriced but fun for anyone who wants to crank the shaft and spin the ball bearings of Leonardo's genius inventions. While this exhibit has no actual historic artifacts, it shows about 30 of Leonardo's inventions made into models, each described in English. What makes this exhibit special is that you're encouraged to touch and play with the models—it's great for kids (€6, daily 9:30–20:30, Via dei Servi 66 red).

Duomo and Nearby

▲▲**Duomo (Santa Maria del Fiore)**—Florence's Gothic cathedral (built 1300–1435) has the third-longest nave in Christendom.

The noisy neo-Gothic facade (added later, from the 1870s) is covered with pink, green, and white Tuscan marble. Since nearly all of its great art is stored in the Duomo Museum (behind the church), the best thing about the interior is the shade. The inside of the dome is decorated by one of the largest paintings of the Renaissance, a huge *Last Judgment* by Giorgio Vasari and Federico Zuccari.

Think of the confidence of the age: The Duomo was built with a hole awaiting a dome in its roof. This was before the technology to span it with a dome was available. No matter. They knew that someone soon could handle the challenge... and the local architect Filippo Brunelleschi did. The cathedral's claim to artistic fame is Brunelleschi's magnificent dome—the first Renaissance dome and the model for domes to follow.

Cost and Hours: Free entry to church (there's a cost to climb dome—see below), Mon–Wed and Fri–Sat 10:00–17:00 except first Sat of month 10:00–15:30, Thu 10:00–16:00, Sun 13:30–16:45, modest dress code enforced, tel. 055-230-2885. Note: The massive crowds that overwhelm the entrance in the morning clear out by afternoon.

▲**Climbing the Duomo's Dome**—For a grand view into the cathedral from the base of the dome, a peek at some of the tools used in the dome's construction, a chance to see Brunelleschi's "dome-within-a-dome" construction, a glorious Florence view from the top, and the equivalent of 463 plunges on a Stairmaster, climb the dome. When planning St. Peter's in Rome, Michelangelo rhymed (not in English), "I can build its sister—bigger, but not more beautiful" than the dome of Florence.

To avoid the long, dreadfully slow-moving line, arrive by 8:30 or drop by very late (€6, Mon–Fri 8:30–19:00, Sat 8:30–17:40 except first Sat of month 8:30–16:00, closed Sun, enter from outside church on south side, tel. 055-230-2885).

▲**Giotto's Tower (Campanile)**—The 270-foot bell tower has 50 fewer steps than the Duomo's dome (but that's still 414 steps—no elevator), offers a faster, less-crowded climb, and has a view of the Duomo to boot, but the cage-like top makes taking good photographs difficult (€6, daily 8:30–19:30, last entry 40 min before closing).

▲Baptistery—Michelangelo said its bronze doors were fit to be the gates of paradise. Check out the gleaming copies of Lorenzo Ghiberti's bronze doors that face the Duomo. Making a breakthrough in perspective, Ghiberti used mathematical laws to create the illusion of receding distance on a basically flat surface.

The doors on the north side of the building were designed by Ghiberti when he was young; he'd won the honor and opportunity by beating Brunelleschi in a competition (the rivals' original entries are in the Duomo Museum).

Inside, sit and savor the medieval mosaic ceiling, where it's always Judgment Day and Jesus is giving the ultimate thumbs-up and thumbs-down (€3, interior open Mon–Sat 12:15–19:00, Sun 8:30–14:00, last entry 30 min before closing; bronze doors are on the outside, so always "open"; original panels are in the Bargello).

▲▲▲Duomo Museum (Museo dell'Opera del Duomo)—The underrated cathedral museum, behind the church (at Via del

Proconsolo 9), is great if you like sculpture. It has masterpieces by Donatello (a gruesome wood carving of Mary Magdalene clothed in her matted hair, and the *cantoria*, a delightful choir loft bursting with happy children) and by Luca della Robbia (another choir loft, lined with the dreamy faces of musicians praising the Lord). Look for a late Michelangelo *Pietà* (Nicodemus, on top, is a self-portrait), Brunelleschi's models for his dome, and the original restored panels of Ghiberti's doors to the Baptistery (€6, Mon–Sat 9:00–19:30, Sun 9:00–13:40, last entry 40 min before closing, one of the few museums in Florence open on Mon, tel. 055-230-2885).

If you find all this church art intriguing, look through the open doorway of the Duomo art studio, which has been making and restoring church art since the days of Brunelleschi (a block toward the river from the Duomo at Via dello Studio 23a).

Between the Duomo and Piazza della Signoria

▲▲▲Bargello (Museo Nazionale)—This underappreciated sculpture museum is in a former police station-turned-prison that looks like a mini–Palazzo Vecchio. It has Donatello's painfully beautiful *David* (the very influential first male nude to be sculpted in a thousand years), works by Michelangelo, and rooms of Medici treasures cruelly explained in Italian only (politely suggest to the staff that English descriptions would be wonderful). Moody Donatello, who embraced realism with his lifelike

statues, set the personal and artistic style for many Renaissance artists to follow. The best works are in the ground-floor room at the foot of the outdoor staircase and in the room directly above (€4, but mandatory special exhibitions often increase the price to €7; daily 8:15–13:50 but closed first, third, and fifth Sun and second and fourth Mon of each month, last entry 40 min before closing; reservations possible but unnecessary, Via del Proconsolo 4, tel. 055-238-8606).

Dante's House (Casa di Dante)—Dante Alighieri (1265–1321), the poet who gave us *The Divine Comedy*, is the Shakespeare of Italy, the father of the modern Italian language, and the face on the country's €2 coin. Dante fans can trace his interesting life

and works through photos and artifacts, and novices can learn a little about the man and the city he lived in. On the first two floors, be on the lookout for a map of Dante's Florence (it was a walled city of many towers, housing feuding clans), a picture of his muse Beatrice, the *Book of the Nail* forever condemning him to exile (for political reasons), and photos of his tomb in Ravenna. The top floor displays copies of paintings by famous artists and a video of scenes from *The Divine Comedy*, which demonstrate just how much Dante inspired the imagination of later artists. Some call him the father of the Renaissance (€4, Tue–Sat 10:00–17:00, open sporadic hours on Sun, closed Mon, near Bargello at Via Santa Margherita 1, tel. 055-219-416).

▲Orsanmichele Church—In the ninth century, this *loggia* (covered courtyard) was a market used for selling grain (stored upstairs). Later, it was closed in to make a church.

Outside are dynamic, statue-filled niches, some with accompanying symbols from the guilds that sponsored the art. Donatello's *St. Mark* and *St. George* (on the northeast and northwest corners) step out boldly in the new Renaissance style.

The interior has a glorious Gothic tabernacle (1359) that houses the painted wooden panel depicting *Madonna delle Grazie* (1346). The iron bars spanning the vaults were the Italian Gothic answer to the French Gothic external buttresses. Look for the rectangular holes in the piers—these were once wheat chutes that connected to the upper floors (church is free, Tue–Sun 10:00–17:00, closed

Mon, niche sculptures always viewable from the outside). You can give the *Madonna della Grazie* a special thanks if you're in town when an evening concert is held inside the Orsanmichele (tickets sold on day of concert from door facing Via de' Calzaiuoli).

The museum upstairs, currently closed, holds many of the church's precious originals. Someday, tourists might be able to enjoy the fine statues by Ghiberti, Donatello, and company.

A block away, you'll find the...

▲**Mercato Nuovo (a.k.a. the Straw Market)**—This market *loggia* is how Orsanmichele looked before it became a church. Originally a silk and straw market, Mercato Nuovo still functions as a rustic yet touristy market today (at the intersection of Via Calimala and Via Porta Rossa). Prices are soft, but the San Lorenzo Market is much better for haggling. Notice the circled X in the center, which marks the spot where people hit after being hoisted up to the top and dropped as punishment for bankruptcy. You'll also find *Porcellino* (a statue of a wild boar nicknamed "little pig"), which people rub and give coins to in order to ensure their return to Florence. This new copy, while only a few years old, already has a polished snout. At the back corner, a wagon sells tripe (cow innards) sandwiches—a local favorite (daily 9:30–19:00).

▲**Piazza della Repubblica and Nearby**—This large square sits on the site of Florence's original Roman Forum. The lone column—nicknamed "the belly button of Florence"—once marked the intersection of the two main Roman roads. All that survives of Roman Florence is its grid street plan and this column. Look at the map (by the benches—where the old boys hang out to talk sports and politics) to see the ghost of Rome in its streets. Roman Florence was a garrison town—a rectangular fort with this square marking the intersection of the two main roads (Via Corso and Via Roma).

Today's piazza, framed by a triumphal arch, is a nationalistic statement that celebrates the unification of Italy. Florence, the capital of the country (1865–1870) until Rome was "liberated" (from the Vatican), lacked a square worthy of this grand new country. So the neighborhood here—once the Jewish quarter—was razed to open up an imposing, modern forum surrounded by stately circa-1890 buildings.

Venerable cafés and stores line the square. The fancy La Rinascente department store, facing Piazza della Repubblica, is one of the city's finest (WC on fourth floor, go up the stairs for the pricey bar with an impressive view terrace).

▲**Palazzo Davanzati**—This five-story, late-medieval tower house offers a rare look at a noble dwelling built in the 14th century. It hopes to be the museum of medieval Florence. Like other buildings of the age, the exterior is festooned with 14th-century horse-tethering rings made out of iron, torch holders, and poles upon which to hang laundry and fly flags. Inside, while the furnishings are pretty sparse, you'll see richly painted walls, a long chute that functioned as a well, plenty of fireplaces, and even toilets (€5, daily 8:15–13:30; closed first, third and fifth Mon and second and fourth Sun; Via Porta Rossa 13, tel. 055-238-8610).

▲▲▲Uffizi Gallery

This greatest collection of Italian paintings anywhere features works by Giotto, Leonardo, Raphael, Caravaggio, Rubens, Titian, and Michelangelo, and a roomful of Botticellis, including his *Birth of Venus.*

The museum is nowhere near as big as it is great. Few tourists spend more than two hours inside. The paintings are displayed on one comfortable, U-shaped floor in chronological order, from the 13th through 17th centuries. After entering the building, either take the elevator or climb four long flights of stairs to reach the art. The left wing—starring the Florentine Middle Ages to the Renaissance—is the best. The connecting corridor contains sculpture, and the right wing focuses on High Renaissance and Baroque.

Essential stops are (in this order): Gothic altarpieces (narrative, pre-Realism, no real concern for believable depth) including

Giotto's altarpiece, which progressed beyond "totem-pole angels"; Paolo Uccello's *Battle of San Romano,* an early study in perspective (with a few obvious flubs); Fra Filippo Lippi's cuddly Madonnas; the Botticelli room, filled with masterpieces, including a pantheon of classical fleshiness and the small *La Calunnia,* showing the glasnost of Renaissance free-thinking being clubbed back into the darker age of Savonarola; two minor works by Leonardo da Vinci; the octagonal classical sculpture room with an early painting of Bob Hope and a copy of Praxiteles' *Venus de' Medici*—considered the epitome of beauty in Elizabethan Europe; a view of the Ponte Vecchio through the window—dreamy at sunset; Michelangelo's only surviving easel painting, the round *Holy Family;* Raphael's noble *Madonna of the Goldfinch* (which may be

Uffizi Gallery

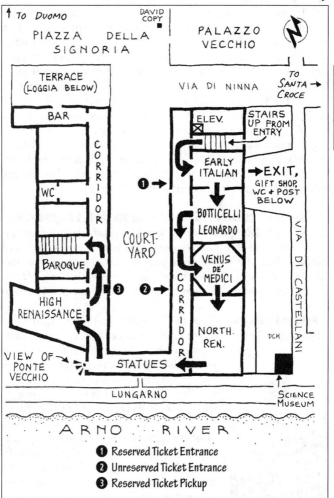

1 Reserved Ticket Entrance
2 Unreserved Ticket Entrance
3 Reserved Ticket Pickup

under restoration in 2008); Titian's voluptuous *Venus of Urbino;* and Duomo views from the café terrace (WC near café).

Cost, Hours, Reservations: €9.50, plus €3 for recommended reservation, cash required to pick up reserved tickets, Tue–Sun 8:15–18:50, closed Mon, last entry 45 min before closing.

As only 600 visitors are allowed into the museum at a time, there are infamously long lines to get in. Avoid the three-hour peak-season wait by getting a reservation. Reserved spots can fill up more than a month in advance, especially for Sat, Sun, and Tue. If you plan to book ahead, you have several options for beating the line—all of which are explained on page 382.

If you don't have a reservation, there's a small chance you may be able to get a same-day ticket for the Uffizi, depending on luck and availability. Try booking directly at the Uffizi's ticket office (enter the left side of door #2, pay cash for a ticket up front, same hours as museum). Sometimes, by the end of the day (an hour before closing), there are no lines and you can just walk right in.

In the Uffizi's Courtyard: Enjoy the courtyard (free), full of artists and souvenir stalls. (Swing by after dinner when it's completely empty.) The surrounding statues honor earthshaking Florentines: artists (Michelangelo), philosophers (Niccolò Machiavelli), scientists (Galileo), writers (Dante), explorers (Amerigo Vespucci), and the great patron of so much Renaissance thinking, Lorenzo "the Magnificent" de' Medici.

Other Sights on and near Piazza della Signoria

The square fronting the Palazzo Vecchio, Piazza della Signoria, is a tourist's world with pigeons, postcards, horse buggies, and tired hubbies. And, if it would make your tired hubby happy, the ritzy Rivoire café—with the best view seats in town—is famous for its fine desserts and pudding-thick hot chocolate (expensive, closed Sun).

▲**Palazzo Vecchio**—With its distinctive castle turret, this fortified palace—the Town Hall, officially called the Palazzo della

Signoria—is a Florentine landmark. But if you're visiting only one palace interior in town, the Pitti Palace (see page 400) is better. The Palazzo Vecchio interior is worthwhile only if you're a real fan of coffered and gilded ceilings, of Florentine history, or of the artist Giorgio Vasari, who wallpapered the place with mediocre magnificence. The museum's most famous statues are Michelangelo's *Victory* and Donatello's bronze statue of *Judith and Holerfernes* (€6, €8 combo-ticket with Brancacci Chapel, Fri–Wed 9:00–19:00, Thu 9:00–14:00, ticket office closes one hour earlier, tel. 055-276-8224 or 055-276-8558). A metal-detector checkpoint can create long lines.

Even if you don't go to the museum, do step into the **free courtyard** behind the fake *David* just to feel the essence of the Medicis (you'll have to go through metal detectors but you don't have to pay). Until 1873, Michelangelo's *David* stood at the entrance, where the copy is today. While the huge statues in the square are important only as the whipping boys of art critics and as rest stops for pigeons, the nearby **Loggia dei Lanzi** has several important statues. Look for Benvenuto Cellini's bronze statue of Perseus holding the head of Medusa. The plaque on the pavement in front of the fountain marks the spot where the monk Savonarola was burned in MCDXCVIII, or 1498.

Children's Museum: The Museo dei Ragazzi in the Palazzo Vecchio offers activities for children (for age 4 to teens) on a reservation-only basis. The kids can take a guided English tour with a historically costumed character, or make their own fresco on a souvenir tile (€6 plus €2/activity, family rates, no reservation fee, call center to reserve, daily 9:00–18:00, tel. 055-276-8224 or 055-276-8558).

▲▲Science Museum (Museo di Storia della Scienza)—When we think of the Florentine Renaissance, we think of visual arts:

painting, mosaics, architecture, and sculpture. But when the visual arts declined in the 1600s (abused and co-opted by political powers), music and science flourished in Florence. The first opera was written here. And Florence hosted many scientific breakthroughs, as you'll see in this fascinating collection of Renaissance and later clocks, telescopes, maps, and ingenious gadgets. Trace the technical innovations as modern science emerges from 1000 to 1900. One of the most talked-about bottles in Florence is the one here that contains Galileo's finger. The first floor features various tools for gauging the world, from a compass and thermometer to Galileo's telescopes. The second floor delves into clocks, pumps, medicine (which some find macabre), and chemistry. Loaner English guidebooklets are available. It's friendly, comfortably cool, never crowded, and just a block east of the Uffizi on the Arno River (€6.50, June–Sept Mon and Wed–Fri 9:30–17:00, Tue and Sat 9:30–13:00, closed Sun; Oct–May Mon and Wed–Sat 9:30–17:00, Tue 9:30–13:00, generally closed Sun but open second Sun of month 10:00–13:00; Piazza de' Giudici 1, tel. 055-265-311, www.imss.fi.it).

▲Ponte Vecchio—Florence's most famous bridge is lined with shops that have traditionally sold gold and silver. A statue of Cellini, the master goldsmith of the Renaissance, stands in the center, ignored by the flood of tacky tourism. This is a very romantic spot late at night (when lovers gather,

and a top-notch street musician performs).

Notice the "prince's passageway" above the bridge. In less secure times, the city leaders had a fortified passageway connecting the Palazzo Vecchio and Uffizi with the mighty Pitti Palace, to which they could flee in times of attack. This passageway, called the **Vasari Corridor,** is technically open to the public, but a visit is almost impossible to arrange, and if you do manage it, it's usually a disappointment (open sporadically, check at the Uffizi to see if it's open or try a private tour company such as www.weekendafirenze .com).

▲▲**Santa Croce Church**—This 14th-century Franciscan church, decorated with centuries of precious art, holds the tombs of great Florentines.

The loud 19th-century Victorian Gothic facade faces a huge square ringed with tempting shops and littered with tired tourists. Escape into the church and admire its sheer height and spaciousness. On the left wall (as you face the altar) is the **tomb of Galileo Galilei** (1564–1642), the Pisan who lived his last years under house arrest near Florence. Having defied the Church by saying that the Earth revolved around the sun, his heretical remains were only allowed in the church long after his death. (For more on Galileo, see his relics in the Science Museum—page 397.) Directly opposite (on the right wall) is the **tomb of Michelangelo Buonarroti** (1475–1564).

The first chapel to the right of the main altar features the famous fresco by Giotto of the *Death of Saint Francis.* With simple but eloquent gestures, Francis' brothers bid him a sad farewell. One folds his hands and stares longingly at Francis' serene face. Another bends to kiss Francis' hand, while others raise their arms in grief. It's one of the first expressions of human emotion in modern painting. It's also one of the first to create a real three-dimensional grouping of figures.

At the end of the right transept, a left turn at the first door leads into the sacristy, where you'll find a rumpled bit of St. Francis' tunic *(Parte di Tunica)* and old sheets of music. In the bookshop, notice the photos of the devastating flood of 1966 high on the wall. Beyond that is the "leather school," the first shop of what is now a popular leather district. Wander through the former dorms for monks, watch the leatherworking in action, and browse the finished products—for sale, of course.

Exit between the Rossini and Machiavelli tombs into the

cloister (open-air courtyard). On the left, enter Brunelleschi's Pazzi Chapel, considered one of the finest pieces of Florentine Renaissance architecture.

Cost, Hours, and Dress Code: €5 ticket includes the Pazzi Chapel and a small museum, Mon–Sat 9:30–17:30, Sun 13:00–17:30, €4 slow-talking audioguide, modest dress code is enforced, tel. 055-246-6105. The leather school is free, with its own entry around back (daily 9:30–18:00).

▲**Michelangelo's House (Casa Buonarroti)**—Fans enjoy a house that stands on property once owned by Michelangelo. The house was built by the artist's grand-nephew, who turned it into a little museum honoring his famous relative. You'll see some of Michelangelo's early, less-than-monumental statues and a few sketches. Be warned: Michelangelo's descendants attributed everything they could to their famous relative, but very little here (beyond two marble relief panels and a couple of sketches) is actually by Michelangelo (€6.50, Wed–Mon 9:30–14:00, closed Tue, English descriptions, Via Ghibellina 70, tel. 055-241-752).

Near the Train Station

▲▲**Church of Santa Maria Novella**—This 13th-century Dominican church, just south of the train station, is rich in art.

Along with crucifixes by Giotto and Brunelleschi, there's every textbook's example of the early Renaissance mastery of perspective: *The Holy Trinity* by Masaccio; it's opposite the side entrance. The exquisite chapels trace art in Florence from medieval times to early Baroque. The outside of the church features a dash of Romanesque (horizontal stripes), Gothic (pointed arches), Renaissance (geometric shapes), and Baroque (scrolls). Step in and look down the 330-foot nave for a 14th-century optical illusion (€2.50, Mon–Thu and Sat 9:00–17:00, Fri and Sun 13:00–17:00).

Nearby: A palatial **perfumery** (Farmacia di Santa Maria Novella) is around the corner, 100 yards down Via della Scala at #16 (free but shopping encouraged, Mon–Sat 9:30–19:30, Sun 10:30–18:30, tel. 055-216-276). Thick with the lingering aroma of centuries of spritzes, it started as the herb garden of the Santa Maria Novella monks. Well-known even today for its top-quality products, it is extremely Florentine. Pick up the history sheet at the desk, and wander deep into the shop. From the back room, you can peek at one of Santa Maria Novella's cloisters with its dreamy frescoes and imagine a time before Vespas and tourists.

You can get a closer look inside the **Museum and Cloisters,** adjacent to the church, but they're definitely lesser sights (€2.70, entry to the left of the church's facade; Mon–Thu and Sat 9:00–17:00, closed Fri and Sun).

South of the Arno River

To locate these sights, see map on page 412.

▲▲**Pitti Palace**—The imposing Pitti Palace, several blocks southwest of Ponte Vecchio, has three separate museums and two gardens. The main reason to visit is to see the Palatine Gallery, but if you want to see all of the Pitti Palace, you'll need to buy two tickets: one for the Palatine Gallery (which also covers the Modern Art Gallery) and one for the Grand Ducal Treasures and palace gardens.

The second-best collection of paintings in town, the **Palatine Gallery** also happens to be in the most sumptuous palace you can tour in Florence. The building itself is mammoth, holding several different museums. Stick primarily to the gallery, forget about everything else, and the palace becomes a little less exhausting (€8.50, covers Modern Art Gallery, Tue–Sun 8:15–18:50, closed Mon, tel. 055-294-883). If there's a long line, bypass it (and the line at the metal detector) by going to the quick reservations window, asking to enter immediately, and buying a ticket with the €3 reservation fee.

You'll walk through one palatial, chandeliered room after another, walls sagging with masterpieces by 16th- and 17th-century masters, including Rubens, Titian, and Rembrandt. Its Raphael collection is the second biggest anywhere—the Vatican beats them by one. The paintings are hung according to "courtly taste" (meaning: everywhere). Each room and its paintings are well-described in English. The collection is all on one floor with a one-way system (so you can't get lost). Before you exit, consider taking a detour down a straight line of about six palatial rooms—preserved as royal apartments, with period furnishings—where you get a feel for the splendor of the dukes' world: 200 years of Medicis, 100 years of Hapsburgs, and a short time under the Savoy family, Italy's first royal family.

The Rest of the Pitti Palace: If you've got the energy, it'd be a Pitti to miss the palace's other offerings.

The **Modern Art Gallery** (included in the Palatine Gallery ticket, same hours) features Romantic, Neoclassical, and Impressionist works by 19th- and 20th-century Tuscan painters.

The **Grand Ducal Treasures (Museo degli Argenti)** is the Medici treasure chest, with jeweled crucifixes, exotic porcelain, gilded ostrich eggs, and so on, made to entertain fans of applied arts (€6; ticket includes the mildly interesting Costume Museum, Porcelain Museum, and Boboli and Bardini gardens; daily 8:15–18:30, open 1 hour later June–Aug).

The **Boboli Gardens and Bardini Gardens,** located behind the palace, offer a sprawling, shady, landscaped refuge from the city heat (€6 ticket covers both gardens and Grand Ducal Treasures listed above, same hours as Treasures). Enter the Boboli Gardens from the Pitti Palace courtyard. The Bardini Gardens are a 10-minute walk beyond the Boboli Gardens.

▲▲**Brancacci Chapel**—For the best look at Masaccio's works (he's the early Renaissance master who reinvented perspective),

see his restored frescoes here. Instead of medieval religious symbols, Masaccio's paintings feature simple, strong human figures with facial expressions that reflect their emotions. The accompanying works of Masolino and Filippino Lippi provide illuminating contrasts.

Get reservations in advance (see below). For €2 (in addition to the entrance fee), you can see a 45-minute English film on the church, the frescoes, and Florence. It starts promptly at the top of the hour. Computer animation brings the paintings to life—making them appear to move and giving them 3-D depth—while narration describes the events depicted in the panels. Yes, it's a long time commitment, and the film takes liberties with the art. But it's visually interesting and your best way to see the frescoes close up.

Cost, Reservations, Hours, Location: €4, or €8 combo-ticket with Palazzo Vecchio. Free reservations required—it's very easy...just call (dial 055-276-8224 or 055-276-8558; it's frequently busy, but keep trying—the best time to call is about 14:00–15:00). Reservation times begin every 15 minutes, with a maximum of 30 visitors per time slot. You have 15 minutes in the actual chapel. Open Mon and Wed–Sat 10:00–17:00, Sun 13:00–17:00, closed Tue, ticket office closes at 16:30. Cross Ponte Vecchio and turn right on Borgo San Jacopo, walk 10 min, then turn left into Piazza del Carmine; tel. 055-276-8224 or 055-276-8558.

The neighborhoods around the church are considered the last surviving bits of old Florence.

Santo Spirito Church—This church has a classic Brunelleschi interior and a painted, carved wooden crucifix attributed to Michelangelo. The sculptor donated this early work to the monastery in appreciation for allowing him to dissect and learn about bodies. Pop in to see a delightful Renaissance space and a chance to marvel at a Michelangelo all alone (free, Thu–Sat and Mon–Tue 10:00–12:00 & 16:00–17:30, Wed 10:00–12:00, closed Sun to sightseers, Piazza Santo Spirito, tel. 055-210-030).

▲Piazzale Michelangelo—Overlooking the city from across the river (look for the huge statue of *David*), this square is worth the 30-minute hike, drive (free parking), or bus ride (either #12 or #13 from the train station) for the view of Florence and the stunning dome of the Duomo. It makes sense to take a taxi or ride the bus up, and then enjoy the easy downhill walk back into town. Off the west side of the piazza is a somewhat hidden terrace, an excellent place to retreat from the mobs. After dark, the square is packed with local school kids licking ice cream and each other. About 200 yards beyond all the tour groups and teenagers is the stark, beautiful, crowd-free, Romanesque San Miniato Church.

▲San Miniato Church—The martyred St. Minias, this church's namesake, died on this hill and is buried here in the crypt. The  church's green-and-white marble facade is classic Florentine Romanesque. The church has wonderful 3-D paintings, a plush ceiling of glazed terracotta panels by Luca della Robbia, and a sumptuous Renaissance chapel (located front and center). For me, though, the highlight is the brilliantly preserved art in the sacristy (behind altar in the room on right) showing scenes from the life of St. Benedict (c. 1350) by a follower of Giotto. Drop a euro into the box to light the room for five minutes (church is free, daily 8:00–19:30, Gregorian chants April–Sept daily at the 17:30 Mass—17:00 in winter, 200 yards above Piazzale Michelangelo, take bus #12 or #13 from train station, tel. 055-234-2731).

EXPERIENCES

Gelato

Gelato is an edible art form. Italy's best ice cream is in Florence—one souvenir that can't break and won't clutter your luggage. But beware of scams at touristy joints on busy streets that turn a simple request for a cone into a €10 "tourist special" rip-off.

A key to gelato appreciation is sampling liberally and choosing flavors that go well together. Ask, as the locals do, for *"Un assaggio, per favore?"* (A taste, please?; oon ah-SAH-joh pehr fah-VOH-ray) and *"Che si sposano bene?"* (What marries well?; kay see spoh-ZAH-noh BEN-ay).

Artiginale, nostra produzione, and *produzione propia* mean gelato is made on the premises, and gelato displayed in covered metal tins (rather than white plastic) is more likely to be homemade. Gelato aficionados avoid colors that don't appear in nature—for less chemicals and real flavor, go for mellow hues (bright colors attract children). These places are open daily for long hours.

Near the Duomo: The new favorite in town, **Grom** uses organic ingredients and seasonal fresh fruit. Their traditional approach and quality give locals déjà vu, reminding them of the good old days and the ice cream of their childhood. Marco, who really cares, describes his "gelato as cuisine" approach to ice cream, and posts special notes on his various flavors on the wall in English (Via delle Oche 24a).

Near Ponte Vecchio: Try **Gelateria Carrozze,** a longtime local favorite (on riverfront 30 yards from Ponte Vecchio toward the Uffizi at Piazza del Pesce 3).

Near the Accademia: A Sicilian choice on a tourist thoroughfare, **Gelateria Carabè** is particularly famous for its luscious *granite*—Italian ices made with fresh fruit. Antonio, whose family has made ice cream the Sicilian way for more than 100 years, can tell you why that's important (from the Accademia, a block towards the Duomo, Via Ricasoli 60 red).

Near Orsanmichele Church: For gelato served in a brash, neon environment, stop by **Festival del Gelato** or **Perchè No!,** located just off the busy main pedestrian drag (Via de' Calzaiuoli). They serve a stunning array of brightly colored, kid-pleasing flavors (Festival del Gelato is at Via del Corso 75; Perchè No! is at Via dei Tavolini 19).

Near the Church of Santa Croce: The venerable favorite, **Vivoli's** still serves great gelato—but it's more expensive and stingy in its servings (closed Mon, Aug, and Jan; opposite the Church of Santa Croce, go down Via Torta a block and turn right on Via Stinche). Before ordering, try a free sample of their rice flavor—*riso.*

Across the River: If you want an excuse to check out the little village-like neighborhood across the river from Santa Croce, enjoy a gelato at the tiny no-name *(senza nome) gelateria* at Via San Miniato 5 red (just before Porta San Miniato).

SHOPPING

Florence is a great shopping town—known for its sense of style since the Medici days. Busy street scenes and markets abound, especially near San Lorenzo, near Santa Croce, on Ponte Vecchio, and at Mercato Nuovo (a covered market square 3 blocks north of Ponte Vecchio, listed on page 397). Leather (often better quality for less than the US price), gold, silver, art prints, and tacky plaster mini-*David*s are most popular.

Shops usually have promotional stalls in the market squares. Prices are soft in the markets—go ahead and bargain. Many people spend entire days shopping.

For ritzy Italian fashions, browse along Via de' Tornabuoni, Via della Vigna Nuova, and Via Strozzi. Typical chain department stores are **Coin,** the local equivalent of Macy's (Mon–Sat 10:00–20:00, Sun 10:30–20:00, on Via de' Calzaiuoli, near Orsanmichele Church); the similar, upscale **La Rinascente** (Mon–Sat 9:00–21:00, Sun 10:30–20:00, on Piazza della Repubblica, expensive café and view terrace on fifth floor); and **Oviesse,** the local version of JCPenney, a discount clothing chain (Mon–Sat 9:00–19:30, Sun 10:00–19:30, near train station at intersection of Via Panzani and Via del Giglio).

For shopping ideas, ads, and a list of markets, see *The Florentine* newspaper or *Florence Concierge Information* magazine (free from TI and many hotels).

SLEEPING

Nearly all of my recommended accommodations are located in Florence's downtown core, within minutes of the great sights.

The accommodations scene varies wildly with the season. Spring and fall are very tight and expensive, while mid-July through August is wide open and discounted. November through February is also generally empty. I've listed prices for peak season: April, May, June, September, and October.

With good information and an email or phone call beforehand, you can find a stark, clean, and comfortable double with breakfast and a private bath for about €100 (less at the smaller places, such as the *soggiorni*). You get elegance in peak season for €160.

Sleep Code

(€1 = about $1.30, country code: 39)
S = Single, **D** = Double/Twin, **T** = Triple, **Q** = Quad, **b** = bathroom,
s = shower only. Unless otherwise noted, credit cards are accepted, English is spoken, and breakfast is included in these rates.

To help you easily sort through these listings, I've divided the rooms into three categories based on the price for a standard double room with bath during high season:

$$$ **Higher Priced**—Most rooms €165 or more.
$$ **Moderately Priced**—Most rooms between €110–165.
$ **Lower Priced**—Most rooms €110 or less.

Museum-goers take note: When you book your room, you can usually ask your hotelier to book entry times for you to visit the popular Uffizi Gallery and the Accademia (Michelangelo's *David*). This service is fast, easy, and offered free or at a minimal charge at most hotels—the only requirement is advance notice. Ask them to make appointments for you any time the day after your arrival for the Uffizi and the Accademia. For details, see page 382.

Between the Station and Duomo

$$ Hotel Accademia is an elegant place with marble stairs, parquet floors, attractive public areas, 21 pleasant rooms, and a floor plan that defies logic (Db-€145, Tb-€175, prices promised through 2008 with this book, 5 percent additional discount with cash, air-con, tiny courtyard, Via Faenza 7, tel. 055-293-451, fax 055-219-771, www.hotelaccademiafirenze.com, info@hotelaccademiafirenze.com, Enrico).

$$ Residenza dei Pucci, a block north of the Duomo, has 12 tastefully decorated rooms—in soothing earth tones—with aristocratic furniture. It's fresh and bright (Sb-€135, Db-€150, Tb-€170, Db suite with grand Duomo view-€207, Qb-€233, 10 percent discount through 2008 with cash and this book, air-con, Via dei Pucci 9, additional suites available across the Arno, tel. 055-281-886, fax 055-264-314, www.residenzadeipucci.com, residenzadeipucci@residenzadeipucci.com, Mirella).

$$ Hotel Centrale, with 20 spacious and recently renovated rooms, is indeed central (Db-€140, Tb-€172, 5 percent discount with this book and cash through 2008, air-con, elevator, free Internet access, Via dei Conti 3, tel. 055-215-761, fax 055-215-216, www.hotelcentralefirenze.it, info@hotelcentralefirenze.it, Christina).

Florence Hotels

★ = PIAZZA DELLA SIGNORIA

1. Hotel Accademia
2. Residenza dei Pucci
3. Hotel Centrale
4. Galileo Hotel
5. Hotel Enza
6. Casa Rabatti
7. Affittacamere Lucia Freda
8. Soggiorno Magliani
9. Hotel Loggiato dei Serviti
10. Hotel Morandi alla Crocetta
11. Palazzo Niccolini al Duomo
12. Residenza il Villino
13. Albergo Chiazza & Oblate Sisters of the Assumption
14. Hotel Dalí
15. Hotel Pendini
16. Hotel Maxim
17. Soggiorno Battistero
18. Albergo Firenze
19. Hotel Torre Guelfa & Hotel Alessandra
20. In Piazza della Signoria B&B
21. Hotel Davanzati
22. Hotel Pensione Elite
23. Bellevue House
24. Hotel Sole
25. Hotel il Bargellino

$$ Galileo Hotel, a classy business hotel of 31 rooms, is run with familial warmth (Sb-€80, Db-€120, Tb-€150, ask for a 10 percent Rick Steves discount if you book direct through 2008, quadruple-pane windows effectively shut out street noise, free Internet access, Via Nazionale 22a, tel. 055-496-645, fax 055-496-447, www.galileohotel.it, info@galileohotel.it, Nicolas and Patricia).

$ Hotel Enza rents 19 decent rooms for a fine value (Sb-€50, Db-€80, prices promised through 2008 with this book and cash, extra bed-€20, breakfast-€5, air-con, Via San Zanobi 45, tel. 055-490-990, fax 055-473-672, www.hotelenza.it, info@hotelenza.it, Katia).

$ Casa Rabatti is the ultimate if you always wanted to be a part of a Florentine family. Its four simple, clean rooms are run with motherly warmth by Marcella, who speaks minimal English. Seeing 15 years of my family Christmas cards on their walls, I'm reminded how long she has been keeping budget travelers happy (D-€50, Db-€60, €25 extra per bed in shared quad or quint, prices good with this book through 2008, cash only but secure reservation with credit card, no breakfast, fans available, 5 blocks from station at Via San Zanobi 48 black, tel. 055-212-393, casarabatti @inwind.it).

If she's booked up, Marcella will put you up in her daughter's place nearby, at Via Nazionale 20 (five big, airy rooms with fans, no breakfast, closer to the station). While daughter Patricia works, her mom runs the B&Bs. Getting bumped to Patricia's gives you slightly more comfort and slightly less personality...certainly not a net negative.

$ Affittacamere Lucia Freda is basic, clean, and super-cheap. Unlike Rabatti (listed above) and Magliani (below), there's no hint of a family here—just quiet, street-level rooms. While it may seem a bit dreary at first, it soon becomes homey. Its four rooms share two bathrooms, a kitchenette, and a leafy garden terrace (S-€45, D-€50, T-€70, cash only, no breakfast, Via San Zanobi 76 but ring at #31, tel. 055-487-533, mobile 380-546-2386, luciafreda@libero .it, run by kind Lucia and son Claudio).

$ Soggiorno Magliani is central and humble, with seven rooms that feel and smell like a great-grandmother's home (S-€39, D-€49, T-€65, cash only but secure reservation with credit card, no breakfast, a little traffic noise but has double-paned windows, near Via Guelfa at Via Santa Reparata 1, tel. 055-287-378, hotel -magliani@libero.it, run by the friendly duo Vincenza and her English-speaking daughter, Cristina).

East of the Duomo

$$$ Hotel Loggiato dei Serviti, at the most prestigious address in Florence on the most Renaissance square in town, gives you

Old World romance with hair dryers. Stone stairways lead you under open-beam ceilings through this 16th-century monastery's classy public rooms—it's so artful, you'll be snapping photos everywhere. The 33 cells—with air-conditioning, TVs, mini-bars, and telephones—wouldn't be recognized by their original inhabitants. The hotel staff is both professional and

warm (Sb-€120, Db-€180 promised with this book through 2008, family suites from €263, elevator, Piazza S.S. Annunziata 3, tel. 055-289-592, fax 055-289-595, www.loggiatodeiservitihotel.it, info @loggiatodeiservitihotel.it, Cinzia, Fabio, Chiara, and Simonetta). To avoid piazza night noise, reserve a room in the back. When they're full, they rent five spacious and elegant rooms in a 17th-century annex a block away. While it lacks the monastic mystique, the rooms are bigger, gorgeous, and cost the same.

$$$ Hotel Morandi alla Crocetta, another former convent, envelops you in a 16th-century cocoon. Located on a quiet street with 10 rooms, period furnishings, parquet floors, and wood-beamed ceilings, it takes you back a few centuries (Sb-€100, Db-€177, breakfast not worth €11, a block off Piazza S.S. Annunziata at Via Laura 50, tel. 055-234-4747, fax 055-248-0954, www .hotelmorandi.it, welcome@hotelmorandi.it). The hotel is well run by Maurizio, Rolando, Paolo, Mirko, and Frank.

$$$ Palazzo Niccolini al Duomo, one of five elite Historic Residence Hotels in Florence, is run by Sra. Niccolini da Camugliano. The lounge is palatial, and the 10 rooms are big and splendid, with original 16th-century frescoes. If you have the money and want a Florentine palace to call home, this is a very good bet, located just one block from the Duomo (Db-€300, prices vary based on the luxuriousness of the room, check online to choose a room and consider last-minute deals, Via dei Servi 2, tel. 055-282-412, fax 055-290-979, www.niccolinidomepalace.com, info@niccolinidomepalace.com).

$$ Residenza il Villino, popular and friendly, aspires to offer a Florentine home. It has 10 rooms and a pleasant, peaceful little courtyard (small Db-€110, Db-€130, Qb apartment-€160, 5 percent discount through 2008 with cash and this book, air-con, free Internet access, just north of Via degli Alfani at Via della Pergola 53, tel. 055-200-1116, fax 055-200-1101, www.ilvillino.it, info @ilvillino.it, Sergio, Elisabetta, and son Lorenzo).

$ Albergo Chiazza is a homey, old-school throwback, where Mauro and family rent 14 rooms mostly overlooking a quiet courtyard. If you don't mind the blistered wallpaper, it's a fine value (Db-€70–95, request a quiet room when you book, air-con, Borgo Pinti 5, tel. 055-248-0363, fax 055-234-6888, www.chiazzahotel .com, hotel.chiazza@tin.it).

$ Hotel Dalí (listed in all the guidebooks) has 10 decent, basic rooms in a nice location for a great price (S-€40, D-€65, Db-€80, extra bed-€25, no breakfast, has fans, request quiet room when you book, free parking, 2 blocks behind the Duomo at Via dell'Oriuolo 17, tel. & fax 055-234-0706, hoteldali@tin.it, Marco).

$ Oblate Sisters of the Assumption run an institutional 30-room hotel in a Renaissance building with a dreamy garden, great public spaces, appropriately simple rooms, and a quiet, prayerful ambience. The staff doesn't speak English; it's best to reserve by fax, using basic English that God only knows how they translate (S-€40, Db-€80, Tb-€120, Qb-€160, cash only, single beds only, breakfast-€3, air-con, elevator, Borgo Pinti 15, tel. 055-248-0582, fax 055-234-6291, sroblateborgopinti@virgilio.it, sisters are likely to speak French, Sister Theresa is very helpful).

Near Piazza della Repubblica

These are the most central of my accommodations recommendations (and therefore a little overpriced). While worth the extra cost for many, given Florence's walkable core, nearly every hotel can be considered central.

$$ Hotel Pendini, a venerable three-star hotel overlooking Piazza della Repubblica, has 42 rooms with Old World tiles and chandeliers (Sb-€70–110, Db-€90–155, reserve a quiet room on the courtyard when you book, air-con, elevator, free Internet access, fine lounge and breakfast room, Via Strozzi 2, tel. 055-211-170, fax 055-281-807, www.hotelpendini.net, pendini@florenceitaly.net, Barbara).

$ Hotel Maxim, right on Via de' Calzaiuoli, is a big and institutional-feeling place warmly run by a family team: father Paolo, son Nicola, and daughter Chiara. Its halls are narrow, but the 26 basic rooms are comfortable and well-maintained (Sb-€80, Db-€108, Tb-€138, Qb-€155, 5 percent discount with cash and this book through 2008, air-con, elevator, free Internet access, Via de' Calzaiuoli 11, tel. 055-217-474, fax 055-283-729, www .hotelmaximfirenze.it, hotmaxim@tin.it).

$ Soggiorno Battistero rents seven simple, airy rooms, most with great views, literally overlooking the Baptistery and the Duomo square. Request a great view or a larger, quieter room in the back when you book by email. It's a pristine, fresh, and minimalist little place run by Italian Luca and his American wife Kelly, who makes the place particularly welcoming (Sb-€75, Db-€98, Tb-€135, Qb-€145, prices good through 2008 with this book,

5 percent cash discount, breakfast served in room, air-con, no elevator, double-paned windows, Piazza San Giovanni 1, third floor, tel. 055-295-143, fax 055-268-189, www.soggiornobattistero .it, info@soggiornobattistero.it).

$ Albergo Firenze, a big, efficient place, offers 58 modern, basic rooms in a central locale two blocks behind the Duomo (Sb-€68–82, Db-€78–103, Tb-€108–138, Qb-€135–168, air-con, elevator, noisy, at Piazza Donati 4 across from Via del Corso 8, tel. 055-214-203, fax 055-212-370, www.albergofirenze.org, info @albergofirenze.org, Giuseppe).

Near Piazza della Signoria and Ponte Vecchio

$$$ Hotel Torre Guelfa is topped by a fun medieval tower with a panoramic rooftop terrace and a huge living room. Its 24 pricey rooms vary wildly in size. Room 15, with a private terrace (€240), is worth reserving several months in advance (standard Db-€190, Db junior suite-€235, family deals, 5 percent discount with cash through 2008, air-con, elevator, a couple blocks northwest of Ponte Vecchio, Borgo S.S. Apostoli 8, tel. 055-239-6338, fax 055-239-8577, www.hoteltorreguelfa.com, info@hoteltorreguelfa.com, Sabina, Giancarlo, and Sandro).

$$$ In Piazza della Signoria B&B, overlooking Piazza della Signoria, is peaceful, refined, and homey at the same time. Fit for a honeymoon, the 10 rooms here come with all the special touches and little extras you'd expect in a top-end American B&B. Of all my listings, this is the only place where you'll be served fresh-squeezed orange juice (viewless Db-€200, view Db-€260, Tb-€280, ask for a 10 percent discount when you go direct with this book through 2008, family apartments, lavish bathrooms, air-con, tiny elevator, free Internet access, Via dei Magazzini 2, tel. 055-239-9546, mobile 348-321-0565, fax 055-267-6616, www.inpiazzadellasignoria.com, info@inpiazzadellasignoria.com, Sonia and Alessandro).

$$$ Hotel Davanzati, bright and shiny with artistic touches, has 33 cheery rooms with all the comforts. The place is a family affair, thoughtfully run by friendly Tommaso and father Fabrizio, who offer drinks and snacks each evening at their candlelit happy hour (Sb-€110, Db-€170, Tb-€225, prices good through 2008 with this book, 5 percent discount for payment in cash, PlayStation 2 and DVD player in every room, air-con, elevator, free Internet access, Via Porta Rossa 5, tel. 055-286-666, fax 055-265-8252, www.hoteldavanzati.it, info@hoteldavanzati.it).

$$ Hotel Alessandra is 16th-century, tranquil, and sprawling, with 27 big, elegant rooms. It offers budget prices—rare in this locale (S-€67, Sb-€110, D-€110, Db-€150, T-€145, Tb-€195, Q-€165, Qb-€215, 5 percent discount with cash, air-con, Borgo S.S. Apostoli 17, tel. 055-283-438, fax 055-210-619, www.hotelalessandra.com, info@hotelalessandra.com, Anna and son Andrea).

Near the Train Station

As with any big Italian city, the area around the train station is a magnet for hardworking pickpockets on the alert for lost, vulnerable tourists with bulging money belts hanging out of their khakis.

$ Hotel Pensione Elite is run with warmth by sunny Nadia. You'll find 10 comfortable if plainly furnished rooms (Ss-€60, Sb-€80, Ds-€75, Db-€90, Tb-€110, Qb-€130, air-con, Via della Scala 12, second floor, tel. & fax 055-215-395, hotelelitefi@libero.it).

$ Bellevue House is a fourth-floor (no elevator) oasis of tranquility, with six spacious rooms flanking a long, mellow-yellow lobby. It's a peaceful time warp thoughtfully run by Rosanna and Antonio di Grazia (Db-€95 in April–June, Sept, and Oct; Db-€75 off-season, family deals, prices promised through 2008 with this book, 5 percent cash discount, includes breakfast in a street-level bar, Via della Scala 21, tel. 055-260-8932, mobile 333-612-5973, fax 055-265-5315, www.bellevuchousc.it, info@bcllcvuchousc.it).

$ Hotel Sole is a clean, minimal, non-English-speaking, family-run place renting eight bright, modern rooms (Sb-€50, Db-€80, Tb-€110, 5 percent cash discount, no breakfast, air-con, elevator, 1:00 curfew, a block toward river from Piazza Santa Maria Novella at Via del Sole 8, tel. & fax 055-239-6094, htlsole@tiscali.it).

$ Hotel Il Bargellino, run by Bostonian Carmel and her Italian husband Pino, has 10 summery rooms decorated with funky antique furniture and Pino's modern paintings. It's located just a few blocks north of the train station. Guests enjoy relaxing with Carmel on her big, breezy, momentum-slowing terrace (S-€45, D-€75, Db-€85, extra bed-€25, air-con-€10, no breakfast, Via Guelfa 87, tel. 055-238-2658, www.ilbargellino.com, carmel@ilbargellino.com).

Oltrarno, South of the River

Across the river in the Oltrarno area, between the Pitti Palace and Ponte Vecchio, you'll still find small, traditional crafts shops, neighborly piazzas, and family eateries. The following places are an easy walk from Ponte Vecchio. Only the first one is a real hotel—the rest are a ragtag gang of budget alternatives.

$$ Hotel Silla, a classic three-star hotel with 35 cheery, spacious, pastel, and modern rooms, is a good value. It faces the river and overlooks a park opposite the Santa Croce Church (Db-€110–170, Tb-€210, discount through 2008 with this book, air-con, Via dei Renai 5, tel. 055-234-2888, fax 055-234-1437, www.hotelsilla.it, hotelsilla@hotelsilla.it, Laura, Chiara, and Stefano).

$ Istituto Gould is a Protestant Church–run place with 41 clean and spartan rooms with twin beds and modern facilities

Oltrarno Hotels

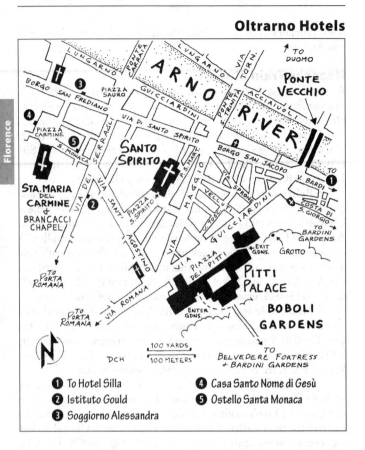

1. To Hotel Silla
2. Istituto Gould
3. Soggiorno Alessandra
4. Casa Santo Nome di Gesù
5. Ostello Santa Monica

(S-€36, Sb-€43, D-€52, Db-€58, Tb-€75, Qb-€92, no breakfast, quieter rooms in back, Via dei Serragli 49, tel. 055-212-576, fax 055-280-274, www.istitutogould.it, gould.reception@dada.it). You must arrive when the office is open (Mon–Fri 8:45–13:00 & 15:00–19:30, Sat 9:00–13:00 & 14:30–18:00, no check-in Sun or holidays).

$ Soggiorno Alessandra has five bright, comfy, and smallish rooms. Because of its double-paned windows, you'll hardly notice the traffic noise (D-€72, Db-€77, Tb-€97, Qb-€127, air-con-€8, just past the Carraia Bridge at Via Borgo San Frediano 6, tel. 055-290-424, fax 055-218-464, www.soggiornoalessandra.it, info @soggiornoalessandra.it, Alessandra).

$ Casa Santo Nome di Gesù is a grand, 29-room convent whose sisters—Franciscan Missionaries of Mary—are thankful to rent rooms to tourists. Staying in this 15th-century palace, you'll be immersed in the tranquil atmosphere created by a huge, peaceful garden, generous and prayerful public spaces, and smiling nuns (D-€70, Db-€85, twin beds only, memorably convent-ual breakfast room, 23:00 curfew, Piazza del Carmine 21, tel. 055-213-856, fax 055-281-835, www.fmmfirenze.it, info@fmmfirenze.it).

Hostels

$ Ostello Santa Monaca, a cheap, well-run hostel, is a long block south of the Brancacci Chapel in the Oltrarno area. It attracts a young backpacking crowd (€17 beds with sheets, 4- to 20-bed rooms, 2:00 curfew, Via Santa Monaca 6, tel. 055-268-338, fax 055-280-185, www.ostello.it, info@ostello.it).

$ Villa Camerata, classy for an IYHF hostel, is in a pretty villa three miles northeast of the train station, on the outskirts of Florence (€18.50 per bed with breakfast, 4- to 12-bed rooms, must have hostel membership card, take bus #17 to Salviatino stop, Via Righi 2, tel. 055-601-451, fax 055-610-300, www.hihostels.com, firenze@ostellionline.org).

EATING

To save money and time for sights, you can keep lunches fast and simple, eating in one of countless self-service places and pizzerias or just picnicking (try juice, yogurt, cheese, and a roll for €5). For good sit-down meals, consider the following. Remember, restaurants like to serve what's fresh. If you're into flavor, go for the seasonal best bets—featured in the *piatti del giorno* ("special of the day") sections of the menus.

North of the River

Restaurants near Piazza Santa Maria Novella and the Train Station

Trattoria al Trebbio serves traditional food with simple Florentine elegance at fair prices in its candlelit interior. Tables spill out onto a romantic little square—an oasis of Roman Trastevere-like charm (daily 12:00–15:00 & 19:15–23:00, reserve for outdoor seating, half a block off of Piazza Santa Maria Novella at Via delle Belle Donne 47, tel. 055-287-089).

Osteria Belle Donne makes you feel like you're eating dinner in a crowded terrarium piled high with decorative knickknacks. Old-fashioned Tuscan food is served on tight tables—a few tables hunker on the street. They take no reservations and tend to steamroll tourists; arrive early or wait (€12 pastas, €12 *secondi*, daily 12:00–15:00 & 19:00–23:00, Via delle Belle Donne 16 red, tel. 055-238-2609, run by sprightly Giacinto).

Trattoria Marione serves sincerely home-cooked-style meals to a mixed group of tourists and locals in a happy, crowded, food-loving, and steamy ambience (€8 pastas, €10 *secondi*, daily 12:00–15:00 & 19:00–22:30, Via della Spada 27 red, tel. 055-214-756).

Florence Restaurants

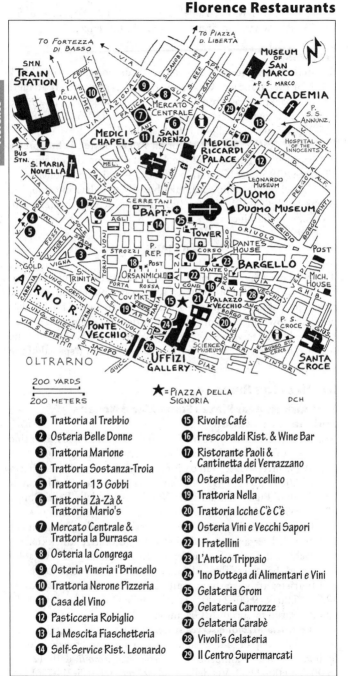

Florence

★ = PIAZZA DELLA SIGNORIA

200 YARDS
200 METERS

DCH

1. Trattoria al Trebbio
2. Osteria Belle Donne
3. Trattoria Marione
4. Trattoria Sostanza-Troia
5. Trattoria 13 Gobbi
6. Trattoria Zà-Zà & Trattoria Mario's
7. Mercato Centrale & Trattoria la Burrasca
8. Osteria la Congrega
9. Osteria Vineria i'Brincello
10. Trattoria Nerone Pizzeria
11. Casa del Vino
12. Pasticceria Robiglio
13. La Mescita Fiaschetteria
14. Self-Service Rist. Leonardo
15. Rivoire Café
16. Frescobaldi Rist. & Wine Bar
17. Ristorante Paoli & Cantinetta dei Verrazzano
18. Osteria del Porcellino
19. Trattoria Nella
20. Trattoria Icche C'è C'è
21. Osteria Vini e Vecchi Sapori
22. I Fratellini
23. L'Antico Trippaio
24. 'Ino Bottega di Alimentari e Vini
25. Gelateria Grom
26. Gelateria Carrozze
27. Gelateria Carabè
28. Vivoli's Gelateria
29. Il Centro Supermarcati

Trattoria Sostanza-Troia, characteristic and well-established, is famous for its beef. Hearty steaks and pastas are splittable. Whirling ceiling fans and walls strewn with old photos evoke earlier times, while the artichoke pies remind locals of grandma's cooking. Crowded, shared tables with paper tablecloths give this place a bistro feel. They offer two dinner seatings, at 19:30 and 21:00, which require reservations (dinners for about €30 plus wine, lunch Mon–Sat 12:30–14:00, closed Sun, closed Sat in off-season, Via del Porcellana 25 red, tel. 055-212-691).

Trattoria 13 Gobbi ("13 Hunchbacks") is a trendy favorite, glowing with candles around a tiny garden. Romantic in front and family-friendly in back, it serves beautifully presented, surprisingly reasonable Tuscan food on big, fancy plates to a mostly tourist crowd (€8 pastas, €14 *secondi*, daily 12:15–15:00 & 19:30–23:00, Via del Porcellana 9 red, tel. 055-284-015).

Restaurants near Mercato Centrale and San Lorenzo Market

Each of the following market neighborhood eateries is distinct and within a hundred yards of each other. Scout around and choose your favorite.

Trattoria Zà-Zà is a fun, old, characteristic, high-energy place facing the Mercato Centrale. It's a family-friendly festival of food. Locals lament the invasion of tourists, but everyone's happy, and the food is still great. *Ribollita*, a Tuscan soup, is their specialty. They serve big splittable salads and T-bone steaks (*bistecca alla fiorentina*). Arrive early or make a reservation, especially for the wonderful outdoor piazza seating. Even though it's confusing, don't mistake their outside seating with the neighboring restaurant (daily 11:30–23:00, Piazza del Mercato Centrale 26 red, tel. 055-215-411).

Trattoria la Burrasca is *Flintstones*-chic, family-run, and ideal for Tuscan home cooking. It's small—10 tables—and often filled with our readers. Anna and Antonio Genzano have cooked and served here with passion since 1982. If Archie Bunker were Italian, he'd eat at this *trattoria* for special nights out. Everything is homemade except the desserts, and if you want good wine cheap, this is the place (€4 pastas, €6 *secondi*, Fri–Wed 12:00–15:00 & 19:00–22:30, closed Thu, north corner of Mercato Centrale at Via Panicale 6, tel. 055-215-827, very little English spoken).

Osteria la Congrega brags that it's "a Tuscan wine bar designed to help you lose track of time." In a fresh, romantic, two-level setting, chef/owner Mahyar takes pride in his fun, easy menu, which features modern Tuscan cuisine, top-notch meat, and seasonal produce. He offers quality vegetarian dishes, creative salads, and an inexpensive but excellent house wine. With just 10 uncramped tables, reservations are required for dinner (€8 pastas,

€12 nightly specials, daily 12:00–15:00 & 19:00–23:00, a block from Mercato Centrale, Via Panicale 43 red, tel. 055-264-5027). Mahyar offers fine wines by the glass (see list on blackboard) and occasional live jazz. Between meals, he teaches cooking classes here.

Osteria Vineria i'Brincello is a bright, happy, no-frills diner with lots of spirit, friendly service, and few tourists during lunchtime. Notice the Tuscan daily specials on the blackboard hanging from the ceiling (daily 12:00–15:00 & 18:30–22:30, corner of Via Nazionale and Via Chiara at Via Nazionale 110 red, tel. 055-282-645, Gabriel and Max).

Trattoria Nerone Pizzeria serves up cheap, hearty Tuscan dishes and decent pizzas. The lively, flamboyantly outfitted space (once the garden courtyard of a convent) feels like a good but kitschy American Italian chain restaurant (€7 pizzas, €5 pastas, €10 *secondi*, daily 11:30–23:00, just north of Via Nazionale at Via Faenza 95–97 red, tel. 055-291-217).

Lunching Cheap and Simple near Mercato Centrale and San Lorenzo Market

For piles of picnic produce, people-watching, or just a rustic sandwich, **ad-lib lunch in the Mercato Centrale,** grazing through the huge marketplace (Mon–Sat 7:00–14:00, closed Sun, a block north of San Lorenzo street market). The cheap eateries within the market can be more colorful than sanitary. Buy a picnic of fresh mozzarella cheese, olives, fruit, and crunchy bread to munch on the steps of the nearby Church of San Lorenzo, overlooking the bustling street market.

Trattoria Mario's, next to Trattoria Zà-Zà (listed above), has been serving hearty lunches to market-goers since 1953 (Fabio and Romeo are the latest generation). Their simple formula: bustling service, old-fashioned good value, a lunch-only fixed-price meal, and shared tables. It's *cucina casalinga*—home cooking *con brio*. This place is extremely popular, so go early. If there's a line, put your name on the list (€4 pastas, €7 *secondi*, Mon–Sat 12:00–15:30, closed Sun, cash only, no reservations, Via Rosina 2, tel. 055-218-550).

Casa del Vino, Florence's oldest operating wine shop, offers glasses of wine from among 25 open bottles. Owner Gianni, whose family has owned the Casa for 70 years, also serves interesting *panini* (Mon–Fri 9:30–17:30, closed Sat–Sun, hidden behind stalls of the San Lorenzo Market at Via dell'Ariento 16 red). Gianni's *carta dei panini* lists the many €3 sandwiches, and the *carta dei vini* lists the wines available by the glass. During meals, it's a mob scene. You'll eat standing outside, with local workers on a quick lunch break.

Budget Lunches near the Accademia and Museum of San Marco

Pasticceria Robiglio, a classy little café, opens up its stately dining area and sets out a few tables on the sidewalk for lunch on workdays. They have a small menu of daily pasta and *secondi* specials, and they seem determined to do things like they did in the elegant, pre-tourism days (generous €8 plates, a great "fantasy salad," pretty pastries, good wines by the glass, smiling service, Mon–Sat 12:00–15:00, longer hours as a café, closed Sun, a block towards the Duomo off Piazza S.S. Annunziata at Via dei Servi 112 red, tel. 055-212-784). Before you leave, be tempted by their pastries—famous among Florentines.

La Mescita Fiaschetteria is a characteristic hole-in-the-wall just around the corner from *David*—but a world away from all the tourism. It's where locals and students enjoy daily pasta specials and hearty sandwiches with good house wine. You can trust Mirco; just point to what looks good and eat lunch quickly, well, and inexpensively. The place can either be mobbed by local students or in a peaceful time warp, depending upon when you stop by (Mon–Sat 12:00–16:00, closed Sun, Via degli Alfani 70 red, mobile 347-795-1604).

Picnic on the Ultimate Renaissance Square: There's a handy supermarket across from the Accademia *(David)* which happily makes sandwiches to your specs (Il Centro Supermarcati, Mon–Sat 8:00–20:00, Sun 10:00–19:00, Via Ricasoli 109). Choose your fresh bread and tasty meat and cheese (assembled and sold by the weight); embellish with some veggies, milk, yogurt, or juice; and hike around the block to Piazza S.S. Annunziata, the first Renaissance square in Florence. There's a fountain for washing fruit on the square. Grab a stony seat anywhere you like, and savor one of my favorite cheap Florence eating experiences. (Or, drop by either of the two places listed above for a sandwich and juice to go.)

Eating Fast and Cheap near the Duomo

Self-Service Ristorante Leonardo is inexpensive, air-conditioned, quick, and handy. It's just a block from the Duomo, southwest of the Baptistery (tasty €3.50 pastas, €5 main courses, Sun–Fri 11:45–14:45 & 18:45–21:45, closed Sat, upstairs at Via Pecori 11, tel. 055-284-446). Luciano (like Pavarotti) runs the place with enthusiasm.

Dining near Palazzo Vecchio

Great-View, Bad-Value Dining on Piazza della Signoria: The square facing the Palazzo Vecchio is ringed by beautifully situated yet touristy eateries serving overpriced, probably microwaved food. Still, the food won't make you sick, and the view is really tasty.

If determined to eat on the square, I'd have pizza at Ristorante il Cavallino or bar food from the Irish pub next door. Piazza della Signoria's saving grace is dessert at the famous **Rivoire** café, with its fancy desserts and thick hot chocolate. While obscenely expensive, it has the best view tables on the square (Mon–Sat 7:40–24:00, closed Sun).

For better values off the square, consider the following places:

Frescobaldi Ristorante and Wine Bar, the showcase of Italy's aristocratic wine family, is a wonderful restaurant. Candlelight reflects on glasses, and high-vaulted ceilings complement the elegantly presented dishes and fine wines. This is *the* place for a formal dinner in Florence. You can have a hearty plate of mixed meats and cheeses, or enjoy the modern, creative cuisine. Get as dressy as you can, and make a reservation for dinner (€10 appetizers and pastas, €17 *secondi*, Mon–Sat 12:15–15:30 & 19:00–24:00, closed Sun, lunch salads, air-con, half a block north of the Palazzo Vecchio—past the racks of bikes—at Via dei Magazzini 2–4 red, tel. 055-284-724). To show off their wines, they offer an extensive tasting menu of single glasses or fun little three-glass tasting sets (€12 Sangiovese tasting, €24 Super Tuscans).

Ristorante Paoli serves wonderful local cuisine to loads of cheerful eaters being served by jolly little old men under a richly frescoed Gothic vault. Because of its fame and central location, it's filled mostly with tourists, but for a classy, traditional Tuscan splurge meal, this is a decent choice (€10 pastas, €14 *secondi*, Wed–Mon 12:00–14:30 & 19:00–22:30, closed Tue, reserve for dinner, €21 tourist fixed-price meal, à la carte is pricier, midway between Piazza della Signoria and the Duomo at Via dei Tavolini 12 red, tel. 055-216-215). Salads are dramatically cut and mixed from a trolley right at your table. The walls are sweaty with memories that go back to 1824, and the service is flamboyant and fun-loving (but don't get taken—confirm prices). Woodrow Wilson slurped spaghetti here (his bust looks down on you as you eat).

Osteria del Porcellino offers a romantic setting and a seasonal fixed-price meal of Tuscan classics with a creative flair. This dark, dense, candlelit place is packed with a mix of locals and tourists and run with style and enthusiasm by friendly chef Enzo and his sister Maria. In summer, they also have inviting outdoor seating in a secretive setting out back (€9 pastas, €20 *secondi,* €12 lunch specials, daily 12:00–15:00 & 19:00–24:00, reserve for dinner, Via Val di Lamona 7 red, half a block behind Mercato Nuovo, tel. 055-264-148).

Trattoria Nella serves good, typical Tuscan cuisine at affordable prices. Save room for the *panna cotta* cooked cream dessert (€9 pastas, €13 *secondi*, Mon–Sat 12:00–15:00 & 19:00–22:00, closed Sun, reserve for dinner, 3 blocks northwest of Ponte Vecchio, Via delle Terme 19 red, tel. 055-218-925). Twin brothers Federico and Lorenzo carry on their dad's tradition of keeping their clientele well-fed and happy.

Trattoria Icche C'è C'è (EE-kay chay chay; dialect for "whatever there is, there is") is a small, family-style eatery where fun-loving Gino and his wife Mara serve quality, traditional food, including a €13 three-course, fixed-price meal (€6 pastas, €10 *secondi*, Tue–Sun 12:30–14:00 & 19:30–22:00, closed Mon, midway between Bargello and river at Via Magalotti 11 red, tel. 055-216-589).

Eating Cheap and Simple near the Palazzo Vecchio and Uffizi Gallery

Cantinetta dei Verrazzano is a long-established bakery/café/wine bar serving delightful sandwich plates in an elegant, old-time setting. You can grab a hot focaccia sandwich to go. Their *specialità Verrazzano* is a fine plate of four little crostini (like mini-bruschetta) proudly featuring different breads, cheeses, and meats from the Chianti region (€7.50). The *tagliere di focacce* (confirm the €6.50 per person price), a sampler plate of mini-focaccia sandwiches, is also fun. Add a glass of Chianti to either of these dishes to make a fine, light meal. Office workers pop in for a quick lunch, and it's traditional to share tables (Mon–Sat 8:00–21:00, closed Sun, just off Via de' Calzaiuoli on a side street across from Orsanmichele Church at Via dei Tavolini 18, tel. 055-268-590). They also have benches and tiny tables for eating at take-out prices. Simply step to the back and point to the *focacce* sandwich (€2.50) you'd like, order a drink at the bar, and take away your food or sit with locals and watch the action while you munch.

Osteria Vini e Vecchi Sapori, half a block north of Palazzo Vecchio, is a colorful 16-seat hole-in-the-wall serving traditional food, including plates of mixed crostini (€1 each—step right up and choose at the bar) and €10 daily specials (Tue–Sat 12:30–15:00 & 19:30–22:00, Sun 12:30–15:00, closed Mon; facing the bronze equestrian statue in Piazza della Signoria, go behind its tail into the corner and to your left; Via dei Magazzini 3 red, run by Mario while his wife Rosanna cooks and his son Thomas serves).

I Fratellini is a rustic little eatery where the "little brothers" have served peasants 29 different kinds of sandwiches and cheap glasses of Chianti wine (see list on wall) since 1875. Join the local crowd to order, then sit on a nearby curb or windowsill to munch, placing your glass on the wall rack before you leave (€4 for sandwich and wine, Mon–Sat 9:00–20:00, closed Sun, 20 yards in front of Orsanmichele Church on Via dei Cimatori). Be adventurous with the menu (easy to order by number). Consider *finocchiona* (the special local salami), *lardo di Colonnata* (lard aged in Carrara marble), and *cinghiale piccante* (spicy wild boar) sandwiches. Order the most expensive wine they're selling by the glass (Brunello for €4; bottles are labeled).

L'Antico Trippaio is an antique tripe stand that's a fixture in the town center (next to American Express on Via Dante Alighieri). Cheap and authentic as can be, this is where locals come daily for specialties like *panino con trippa alla fiorentina* (tripe sandwiches), *lampredotto* (cow's stomach), and a list of more appetizing sandwiches. The best place to munch your sandwich is three blocks away, on Piazza della Signoria.

'Ino Bottega di Alimentari e Vini is a stylish little shop filled with gifty edibles. Serena and Alessandro love to serve sandwiches and wine—you'll get your €5–6 sandwich on a napkin with a free glass of wine as you perch on a tiny stool. They can also make a fine *piatto misto* of cheeses and meats; just say how much you'd like to spend (daily 10:00–20:00, immediately behind Uffizi Gallery on Ponte Vecchio side, Via dei Georgofili 3 red, tel. 055-219-208).

Oltrarno, South of the River
Dining with a Ponte Vecchio View
Golden View Open Bar is a lively, trendy place, good for a romantic meal or just a salad, pizza, or pasta with fine wine and a fine view of the Ponte Vecchio and the Arno River. Reservations for window tables are essential (reasonable prices, €10 pizzas and big salads, daily 11:30–24:00, pizza and wine served even later, impressive wine bar, 50 yards upstream from Ponte Vecchio at Via dei Bardi 58, tel. 055-214-502, run by Francesco, Antonio, Marco, and Tomaso). They have three areas (with the same menu and prices) for whatever mood you're in: a riverside pizza place, a classier restaurant, and a jazzy lounge with a wine bar. Mixing their fine wine, river views, and live jazz (Sat, Sun, Mon, and Wed at 21:00) makes for a wonderful evening.

Restaurants on Via di Santo Spirito and Borgo San Jacopo
Several good and colorful restaurants line this multinamed street a block off the river in Oltrarno. Reservations are smart in the evening.

Olio & Convivium Gastronomia Restaurant started as an elegant deli whose refined oil-tasting room morphed into a romantic, aristocratic restaurant. Their three intimate rooms are surrounded by fine *prosciutti*, cheeses, and wine shelves. It's an intimidating place that foodies would appreciate—quiet atmosphere, a list of €15 *gastronomia* plates offering an array of taste treats, and fine wines by the glass (€12 pastas, €15 *secondi,* Mon 10:00–15:00, Tue–Sat 10:00–15:00 & 17:30–22:30, closed Sun, elegant €15 lunches, strong

Oltrarno Restaurants

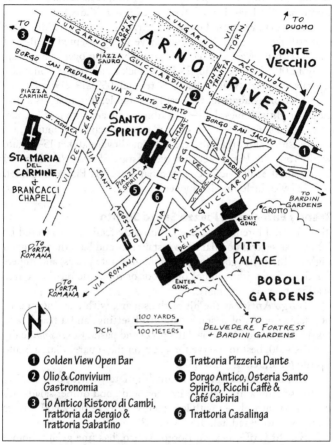

- **1** Golden View Open Bar
- **2** Olio & Convivium Gastronomia
- **3** To Antico Ristoro di Cambi, Trattoria da Sergio & Trattoria Sabatino
- **4** Trattoria Pizzeria Dante
- **5** Borgo Antico, Osteria Santo Spirito, Ricchi Caffè & Café Cabiria
- **6** Trattoria Casalinga

air-con, Via di Santo Spirito 4, tel. 055-265-8198).

Antico Ristoro Di Cambi is a meat-lover's dream, thick with Tuscan traditions, rustic elegance, and T-bone steaks. As you walk in, you'll pass a glass case filled with red chunks of Chianina beef. These cost €40 each, and can be split by two or even more—the perfect chance to enjoy the famous *bistecca alla fiorentina*. You can enjoy the convivial woody interior, or sit outside on a square (€6 pastas, €8 *secondi*, Mon–Sat 12:00–14:30 & 19:30–22:30, closed Sun, reserve on weekends and to sit outside, Via Sant'Onofrio 1 red, tel. 055-217-134, run by Stefana and Fabio, the Cambi cousins).

Trattoria da Sergio, a tiny eatery about a block before Porta San Frediano, has homey charm and a strong local following. The food is on the gourmet side of home-cooking and therefore a bit more expensive, but it's worth the little splurge (€9 pastas, €14 *secondi*, Tue–Sun 19:30–23:00, closed Mon, reservations a must, Borgo San Frediano 145 red, tel. 055-223-449, Marco).

Trattoria Pizzeria Dante is a thriving family-friendly place that still feels a little classy. They serve well-presented meals and thick or thin pizzas cooked in a wood-burning oven (€8 pizzas, daily 12:00–15:00 & 18:30–23:30, a block south of the Ponte alla Carraia at Piazza Nazario Sauro 12 red, tel. 055-219-219).

Trattoria Sabatino, farthest away and least touristy, is a spacious, brightly lit mess hall—disturbingly cheap, with family character and a simple menu. A super place to watch locals munch, it's just outside the Porta San Frediano (medieval gate), a 15-minute walk from the Ponte Vecchio (€3 pastas, €5 *secondi*, Mon–Fri 12:00–14:30 & 19:15–22:00, closed Sat–Sun, Via Pisana 2 red, tel. 055-225-955, little English spoken).

Trendy Eateries on Piazza Santo Spirito
This classic Florentine square (a bit seedy-feeling but favored by locals) has several popular little restaurants and bars that are open nightly. They offer good local cuisine, moderate prices, and impersonal service, with a choice of indoor or romantic on-the-square seating (reservations smart).

Borgo Antico is the hit of the square, with enticing pizzas, big deluxe plates of pasta, a delightful setting, and a trendy and boisterous young local crowd (€9 pizza and pasta, €18 *secondi*, daily 12:00–24:00, best to reserve for a seat on the square, Piazza Santo Spirito 6 red, tel. 055-210-437).

Osteria Santo Spirito is much quieter, with good seating on the square, a hip, eclectic interior, and good dinner salads. It's mod and youthful, but with low energy (daily 12:00–23:00, Piazza Santo Spirito 16 red, tel. 055-238-2383).

Ricchi Caffè, next to Borgo Antico, has fine gelato, homemade desserts, shaded outdoor tables, and €4.50 pasta dishes at lunch (Mon–Sat 7:00–24:00, closed Sun). After noting the plain facade of the Brunelleschi church facing the square, step inside the café and pick your favorite picture of the many ways it might be finished.

Café Cabiria, on the other side of Borgo Antico, is a trendy local hangout with good, light meals, noisy 21st-century music, and a cozy Florentine-funky room in back (Wed–Mon 10:30–1:30, closed Tue, tel. 055-215-732).

Trattoria Casalinga, an inexpensive standby, comes with aproned women bustling around the kitchen. It's probably been too popular for too long, as the service has gone a bit surly and it feels like every student group, backpacker, and Florentine artisan ends up here. Still, locals and tourists alike pack the place and leave full and happy, with euros to spare for gelato (€5 pastas, €6 *secondi*,

Mon–Sat 12:00–14:30 & 19:00–21:30, after 20:00 reserve or wait, closed Sun and Aug, just off Piazza Santo Spirito, near the church at Via dei Michelozzi 9 red, tel. 055-218-624).

TRANSPORTATION CONNECTIONS

From Florence by Train to: Pisa (3/hr, 1.25 hrs, €5), **Lucca** (roughly 3/hr, 1.5 hrs), **Siena** (2/hr, 1.5 hrs, €5.60, half require transfer in Empoli; bus is better), **Livorno**—port of call for many cruise ships (15/day, 1.5 hours), **La Spezia** (for the Cinque Terre, at least hourly, 2.5 hrs, most involve change in Pisa), **Milan** (at least hourly, 2–3 hrs), **Venice** (roughly hourly, 3–3.5 hrs), **Assisi** (10/day, 2.5 hrs, more frequent with transfers, direction: Foligno), **Orvieto** (hourly, 2 hrs, some with change in Campo di Marte station), **Rome** (2/hr, 1.5–2.5 hrs, most connections require seat reservations), **Naples** (hourly, 3.5–5 hrs), **Brindisi** (3/day, 8–11 hrs with change in Bologna), **Frankfurt** (4/day, 12–13 hrs, 1–3 changes), **Paris** (6/day, 12–13 hrs, 1–2 changes, important to reserve overnight train ahead), **Vienna** (4/day, 10–15 hrs).

Buses: The SITA bus station (100 yards west of the Florence train station on Via Santa Caterina da Siena) is traveler-friendly—a big, old-school lot with numbered stalls and all the services you'd expect. Schedules for regional trips are posted everywhere, and TV monitors show imminent departures. Bus service drops dramatically on Sunday. You'll find buses to: **San Gimignano** (hourly, 1.25–2 hrs, €6, change in Poggibonsi), **Siena** (2/hr, 75-min *corse rapide* buses are faster than the train, avoid the 2-hr *diretta* scenic but slow buses, €6.50), **Volterra** (5/day, 2 hrs, €7), and the **airport** (2/hr, 20 min, €4). Buy tickets in the station if possible, as you'll pay 30 percent more if you buy tickets on the bus. Bus info: tel. 800-373-760 (Mon–Fri 8:30–18:30, Sat–Sun 8:30–12:30); some schedules are listed in the *Florence Concierge Information* magazine.

Taxi: For small groups with more money than time, zipping to nearby towns by taxi can be a good value (e.g., €120 from your Florence hotel to your Siena hotel).

Arrival by Cruise Ship: Cruise ships dock in the coastal town of **Livorno,** located about 60 miles west of the city. Livorno and Florence are most easily connected by train (see above). Most cruise ships offer a shuttle to the train station; you can also take a taxi between the port and station for about €10.

Airports

Florence's Amerigo Vespucci Airport is several miles northwest of Florence (TI, cash machines, and car-rental agencies, airport info tel. 055-306-1300, flight info tel. 055-306-1700—domestic only, www.aeroporto.firenze.it). Shuttle buses connect the airport with

Florence's SITA bus station, 100 yards west of the train station (2/hr, 30 min, daily 5:30–23:30, €4). Allow about €25 for a taxi.

Pisa's Galileo Galilei Airport handles more and more international and domestic flights (TI open daily 11:00–23:00, tel. 050-503-700, cash machine, car-rental agencies, limited-hours baggage deposit, self-service cafeteria, flight info tel. 050-849-300, www.pisa-airport.com).

Livorno Cruise Ship Port

If you're coming to Florence by cruise ship, you'll be getting off the boat in the coastal town of Livorno, Florence's official port and cruise ship dock, located about 60 miles west of the city.

A branch TI is open at the port in summer (tel. 0586-895-320). The main TI is located in the town center on Piazza Municipio (tel. 0586-204-611, www.costadeglietruschi.it). Livorno and Florence are most easily connected by train (15/day, 1.5 hrs, stops in Pisa, Lucca connection possible). Most cruise ships offer a shuttle to the train station; you can also take a taxi between the port and station for about €10.

Near Florence: Fiesole

Perched on a hill overlooking the Arno valley, Fiesole gives weary travelers a break in the action and—during the heat of summer—a breezy location from which to admire the city below. It's a small town with a main square, a few restaurants and shops, a few minor sights, and a great view. The ancient Etruscans knew a good spot when they saw one, and chose to settle here, establishing Fiesole about 400 years before the Romans founded

Florence. Wealthy Renaissance families in pre-air-conditioning days also chose Fiesole (fee-AY-zoh-lay) as a preferred vacation spot, building villas in the surrounding hillsides. Later, 19th-century Romantics spent part of the Grand Tour admiring the vistas, much like the hordes of tourists do today. Most come here for the view—the actual sights pale in comparison to those in Florence.

ORIENTATION

Getting to Fiesole: From the Florence train station, take bus #7—enjoying a peek at gardens, vineyards, orchards, and villas—to the last stop, Piazza Mino (4/hr, fewer after 20:00, 30 min, €1.20;

departs Florence from the line of bus stops, just out of the east exit of train station and also from south side of Piazza San Marco; wear your money belt—thieves frequent this bus). Taxis from Florence cost about €20 (ride to highest point you want to visit—La Reggia Ristorante for view terrace or Church of San Francesco—then explore downhill).

Tourist Information: The TI is immediately to the right of the Roman Archaeological Park (listed below), at Via Portigiani 3 (Mon–Sat 9:00–18:00, Sun 10:00–13:00 & 14:00–18:00, tel. 055-598-720).

Market Day: A modest selection of food and household items fills Piazza Garibaldi on Saturdays (8:00–13:00).

SIGHTS

Fiesole's main sights are either free or covered under one €7 combo-ticket, available at the Roman Theater (see below).

▲▲**Terrace with a View**—Catch the sunset (and your breath) from the view terrace just below La Reggia Ristorante. It's a steep seven-minute hike from the Fiesole bus stop: Face the bell tower and take Via San Francesco, on the left. (For similar views and a peek at residential Fiesole, climb up the opposite side of the square, along the road hugging the ridgeline.)

Church of San Francesco—For even more hill-climbing, continue up from the view terrace to this charming little church. The small scale of this church and several colorful altar paintings make this church more enjoyable than Fiesole's Duomo (free, daily 9:30–12:00 & 15:00–18:00, Via San Francesco 13).

Ethnographic Missionary Museum—This eclectic little collection, hidden beneath the church of San Francesco, includes an Egyptian mummy, ancient coins, Chinese Buddhas, and the *in situ* ruins of a third-century Etruscan wall (donation suggested, Tue–Fri 10:00–12:00 & 15:00–17:00, Sat–Sun open afternoon only, closed Mon, unmarked door inside church leads to cloisters and museum).

Duomo—While this church has a drab, 19th-century exterior, the interior is worth a look, if only for the blue-and-white glazed Giovanni della Robbia statue of St. Romulus over the entry door (free, daily 7:30–12:00 & 15:00–18:00, across Piazza Mino from the bus stop).

Roman Theater and Archaeological Park—Occasionally used today for plays, this well-preserved theater held up to 2,000 people. The site's other ruins are, well, ruined, and lacking in explanation. But the valley view and peaceful setting are lovely (€7 combo-ticket also covers Civic and Bandini museums, daily 9:30–19:00; from the bus stop, cross Piazza Mino, heading toward the back of the Duomo). Warning: They have a greedy habit of forcing visitors to pay more for special exhibits (often totaling about €13)—more than this sight is worth.

Civic Museum—Located within the Archaeological Park, the museum imparts insight into Fiesole's Etruscan and Roman roots with well-displayed artifacts, with a few English description sheets in the corners (covered by €7 combo-ticket, daily 9:30–19:00).

Bandini Museum—This petite museum displays the wooden panels of lesser-known Gothic and Renaissance painters as well as the glazed terra-cotta figures of Andrea della Robbia (covered by €7 combo-ticket, daily 9:30–19:00, behind Duomo at Via Dupre 1).

SLEEPING

(€1 = about $1.30, country code: 39)
For the Sleep Code, see page 405.

$ Hotel Villa Bonelli in Fiesole has three stars, 20 dim, outdated rooms, an abandoned ambience, and a good price (Sb-€60, Db-€90, Tb-€100, air-con; 250 yards from bus stop up Via Gramsci, right on Via Poeti to #1; tel. 055-59-513, fax 055-598-942, www.hotelvillabonelli.com, info@hotelvillabonelli.com).

EATING

These two restaurants are on Piazza Mino, where the bus stops from Florence.

Ristorante Perseus, a local favorite, serves authentic Tuscan dishes at a fair price in a rambling interior. They also have seating at a few sidewalk tables or on a shady garden terrace in fair weather (daily 12:00–15:00 & 19:00–23:30, tel. 055-59-143, friendly Giorgio speaks English).

Ristorante Aurora is an upscale alternative with a view terrace overlooking the city of Florence (daily 12:00–14:30 & 19:00–22:30, tel. 055-59-363).

Picnics: Fiesole is made to order for a scenic and breezy picnic. Grab a pastry at Fiesole's best *pasticceria*, **Alcedo** (head up the main drag from the bus stop to Via Gramsci 27). Round out your goodies at the **Co-op** supermarket on Via Gramsci before walking up to the panoramic terrace. Or, for more convenience and less view, picnic at the shaded park on the way to the view terrace (walk up Via San Francesco about halfway to the terrace, and climb the stairs to the right).

PISA AND LUCCA

Florence is within easy striking distance of a number of great cities—as their fortifications attest. Along with Siena (which merits solo coverage in another chapter), Pisa and Lucca show that Florence wasn't the only power and cultural star of the late Middle Ages and Renaissance.

Pisa is touristy, but worth visiting for its Field of Miracles (Leaning Tower, Cathedral, and Baptistery). Lucca, contained within its fine Renaissance wall, has a charm that causes many connoisseurs of Italy to claim it as a favorite stop. While Pisa is best as a short stopover, to really enjoy Lucca it's best to spend the night. Thirty minutes from each other, each is a 90-minute train ride from Florence and well-served by the excellent *autostrada*.

Pisa

In A.D. 1200, Pisa's power peaked. For nearly three centuries (1000–1300), Pisa rivaled Venice and Genoa as a sea-trading power, exchanging European goods for luxury items in Muslim lands. As a port near the mouth of the Arno River (six miles from the coast), the city enjoyed easy access to the Mediterranean, plus the protection of sitting a bit upstream. ("Pisa" is an ancient word meaning "delta.") The Romans had made it a navy base, and by medieval times, it was a major player.

Pisa's 150-foot galleys cruised the Mediterranean, gaining control of the islands of Corsica, Sardinia, and Sicily, and trading with Europeans, Muslims, and Byzantine Christians as far south as North Africa and as far east as Syria. European Crusaders hired

Pisa and Lucca

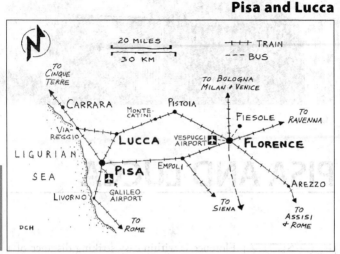

Pisan boats to carry them and their supplies as they headed off to conquer the Muslim-held Holy Land. The Pisan "Republic" prided itself on its independence from both popes and emperors. The city used its sea-trading wealth to build the grand monuments of the Field of Miracles, including the now-famous Tower.

But the Pisan fleet was routed in battle by Genoa (1284, at Meloria, off Livorno), their overseas outposts were taken away, the port silted up, and Pisa was left high and dry, with only its Field of Miracles and its university keeping it on the map.

Pisa's three important sights—the Duomo, Baptistery, and bell tower—float regally on the best lawn in Italy. The style throughout is Pisa's very own "Pisan Romanesque." Even as the church was being built, the Piazza del Duomo was nicknamed the "Campo dei Miracoli," or Field of Miracles, for the grandness of the undertaking.

The Tower has reopened after a decade of restoration and topple-prevention. To ascend, you'll have to make a reservation when you buy your €15 ticket (for details, see "Climbing the Tower," page 435).

Planning Your Time

Pisa is a touristy quickie. Seeing the Tower, visiting the square, and wandering through the church are 90 percent of the Pisan thrill. By car, it's a headache, and a 45-minute detour off the freeway. By train, it's a joy, and train travelers may need to change trains in Pisa anyway. From the Pisa train station, hop on the bus to go see the Tower (a 15-min ride each way).

If you want to climb the Tower, go straight to the ticket office to snag an appointment—usually for a couple of hours later. For an extra €2, you can book a time online at www.opapisa.it (must book at least two weeks in advance). Sophisticated sightseers stop more for the Pisano carvings in the Duomo and Baptistery than for a look at the tipsy Tower. There's nothing wrong with Pisa, but I'd stop only to see the Field of Miracles and get out of town.

ORIENTATION

Tourist Information

One TI is about 200 yards from the train station—exit and walk straight up the left side of the street to the big, circular Piazza Vittorio Emanuele II. The TI is on the left, around the corner from #16 (Mon–Fri 9:00–19:00, Sat 9:00–13:30, closed Sun, tel. 050-42-291, www.pisa.turismo.toscana.it). Another, less-enthusiastic TI is east of the Tower, in the Duomo Museum (daily 10:00–17:00, tel. 050-560-464). There's also a TI at the airport (daily 11:00–14:00 & 16:00–23:00, tel. 050-503-700).

Arrival in Pisa

By Train: If you want to check your baggage upon arrival, look for *deposito bagagli*—as you get off the train, it's to the right at the far end of platform 1, past the police office (€3/bag per 12 hrs, daily 6:00–21:00, they photocopy your passport to check ID, ignore nonfunctional lockers).

To get to the Field of Miracles from the station, you can **walk** (45 min, get free map from TI and they'll mark the best route, or follow the walk below), take a **taxi** (€6, tel. 050-541-600, taxi stand at station) or go by **bus.** Take bus LAM Rossa (4/hr, after 20:00 3/hr), which stops across the street from the train station, in front of Jolly Hotel Cavaliere. Buy a €0.90 bus ticket from the *tabacchi*/magazine kiosk in the train station's main hall or at any *tabacchi* shop (€1.50 if you buy it on board, good for 1 hour, round-trip permitted). Before getting on the bus, confirm that your bus is indeed going to "Campo dei Miracoli" (ask driver, a local, or TI) or risk taking a long tour of Pisa's suburbs. The correct buses let you off at Piazza Manin, in front of the gate to the Field of Miracles; drivers make sure that tourists don't miss it.

To return to the train station from the Leaning Tower, catch the bus in front of the BNL bank, across the street from where you got off (again, confirm the destination). You'll also find a taxi stand 30 yards from the Tower (just in front of the Bar Duomo).

By Car: To get to the Tower, follow signs for the *Duomo* or *Campo dei Miracoli*, located on the north edge of town. If you're coming from the Pisa Nord *autostrada* exit, you won't have to mess with the city center, but you will likely have to endure some terrible

Pisa

1/4 MILE
400 METERS

DCH

P – PARKING
T – TAXI STAND
B – BUS STOP

① Hotel Alessandro della Spina
② Hotel Villa Kinzica
③ Hotel Milano
④ La Lupa Ghiotta Tavola Calda
⑤ Pizzeria/Trattoria La Buca

⑥ Ristorante Galileo
⑦ Paninoteca il Canguro
⑧ Produce Market & Via delle Colonne Restaurants
⑨ Bus To/From Train Station (2)

Pisa and Lucca

traffic. There's free parking just outside the town wall a block from the Tower at Parcheggio Pietrasantina.

By Plane: From Pisa's airport, take bus LAM Rossa (€0.90, 4/hr, after 20:00 3/hr, 15 min) or a taxi (€6) into town.

Helpful Hints

Markets: An open-air produce market attracts picnickers to Piazza della Vettovaglie, one block north of the Arno River near Ponte di Mezzo (Mon–Sat 8:00–18:00, closed Sun). A street market bustles on Wednesday and Saturday mornings between Via del Brennero and Via Paparrelle (just outside of wall, about 6 blocks east of the Tower).

Festivals: The month of June has many events, culminating in a celebration for Pisa's patron saint (June 16–17).

SELF-GUIDED WALK

Welcome to Pisa:
From the Train Station to the Tower

A leisurely 45-minute stroll from the station to the Leaning Tower is a good way to get acquainted with the more subtle virtues of this Renaissance city. It's also a more pleasant alternative to the tourist-mobbed buses. You'll find Pisa to be a student-filled, classy, Old World town with an Arno-scape much like its rival upstream.

• *Exit straight out of the station, walking north up Viale Gramsci to circular Piazza Vittorio Emanuele II (where the TI is). Continue straight north, up the pedestrian-only shopping street Corso Italia, and cross the Arno River at the modern...*

Bridge: The Ponte di Mezzo, constructed on the same site where the Romans built a bridge, is the center of Pisa and the heart of local festivals. Continue north up the elegantly arcaded Borgo Stretto, Pisa's main shopping street.

The first left, Via delle Colonne, is a worthwhile one-block detour, leading to Piazza Vettovaglie, a couple of atmospheric restaurants, and the small but lively open-air produce market just beyond (Mon–Sat 7:00–18:00, closed Sun).

• *Continue north on Borgo Stretto another 100 yards or so. Take the second left on nondescript Via Ulisse Dini; it's not obvious—turn left immediately after the arcade's end just before the pharmacy to pass through Pisa's...*

Historic Core: On Piazza dei Cavalieri, see the ancient clock, colorfully decorated palace, and statue of Cosimo I de' Medici (the Florentine who ruled Pisa in the 16th century). The frescoes on the exterior of the square's buildings, though damaged by salty sea air and years of neglect, reflect the fading glory of Pisa under the Medicis.

The palace and the compound behind the gates to the right (Scuola Normale) house Pisa's famous university. The university is one of Europe's oldest, with roots in a law school dating as far back as the 11th century. In the mid-16th century, it was a hotbed of controversy, as spacey professors like Galileo Galilei studied the solar system—with results that challenged the Church's powerful doctrine.

• *From here, take Via Corsica (to the left of the clock). Ahead on the left, duck into the side entrance of the humble...*

Church of San Sisto: Take a quick peek at this church. With simple bricks, assorted reused columns, heavy walls, and few windows, it is the typical "Romanesque" style compared to the more lavish "Pisan Romanesque" of the Field of Miracles structures.

• *Follow Via Corsica as it turns into Via dei Mille, and then turn right on Via Santa Maria, which leads you north, through increasingly touristy claptrap, directly to the Tower.*

SIGHTS

▲▲**Leaning Tower**—Pisa's bell tower is nearly 200 feet tall and 55 feet wide, weighing 14,000 tons and leaning at a 5-degree angle (15 feet off the vertical axis). It started to lean almost immediately after construction began. There are eight stories—a simple base, six stories of columns (forming arcades), and a belfry on top. The inner, structural core is a hollow cylinder built of limestone bricks, faced with white marble barged here from San Giuliano, northeast of the city. The thin columns of the open-air arcades make the heavy Tower seem light and graceful.

The Tower was built over two centuries by at least three different architects. You can see how each successive architect tried

to correct the leaning problem—once halfway up (after the fourth story), once at the belfry on the top.

The first stones were laid in 1173, probably under the direction of the architect Bonanno Pisano (who also designed the Duomo's bronze back door). Five years later, just as they'd finished the base and the first arcade, someone said, "Is it just me, or does that look crooked?" The heavy Tower—resting on a very shallow 13-foot foundation—was obviously sinking on the south side into the marshy, multilayered, unstable soil. (Actually, all the Campo's buildings tilt somewhat.)

Pisa's Field of Miracles

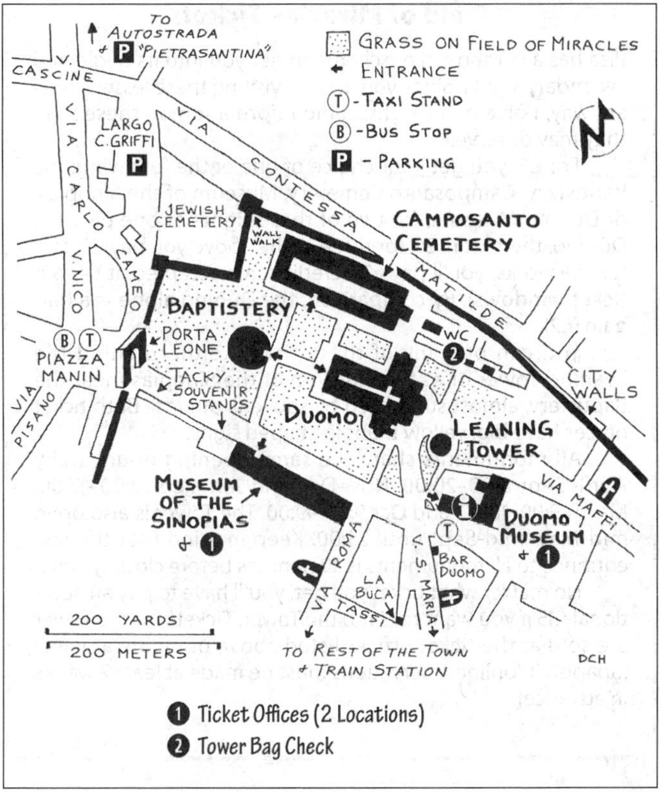
TO AUTOSTRADA + P "PIETRASANTINA"
GRASS ON FIELD OF MIRACLES
ENTRANCE
T - TAXI STAND
B - BUS STOP
P - PARKING
V. CASCINE
VIA CARLO
LARGO C. GRIFFI
VIA CONTESSA MATILDE
JEWISH CEMETERY
WALL WALK
CAMPOSANTO CEMETERY
V. NICO
CAMEO
BAPTISTERY
PORTA LEONE
PIAZZA MANIN
WC
CITY WALLS
TACKY SOUVENIR STANDS
VIA PISANO
DUOMO
LEANING TOWER
MUSEUM OF THE SINOPIAS + 1
VIA MAFFI
DUOMO MUSEUM + 1
VIA ROMA
V. S. MARIA
BAR DUOMO
LA BUCA
VIA TASSI
200 YARDS
200 METERS
TO REST OF THE TOWN + TRAIN STATION
DCH
1 Ticket Offices (2 Locations)
2 Tower Bag Check

They carried on anyway, until they'd finished four stories (the base plus three arcade floors). Then, construction was suddenly halted—no one knows why—and for a century, the Tower sat half-finished and visibly leaning.

In about 1272, the next architect continued, trying to correct the problem by angling the next three stories backward, in the opposite direction of the lean. The project then again sat mysteriously idle for nearly another century. Finally, Tommaso Pisano put the belfry on the top (c. 1350–1372), also kinking it backward.

Man Versus Gravity: After the Tower's completion, several attempts were made to stop its slow-motion fall. The architect/artist/writer Giorgio Vasari reinforced the base (1550), and it actually worked. But in 1838, well-intentioned engineers pumped out groundwater, destabilizing the Tower, and causing it to increase its lean at a rate of a millimeter a year.

It got so bad that in 1990 the Tower was closed for repairs, and $30 million were spent trying to stabilize it. Engineers dried the

Field of Miracles Tickets

Pisa has a combo-ticket scheme to get you into its neglected secondary sights. Since you may be visiting these lesser sights anyway, I give more sightseeing information on these than they may deserve.

For €5, you get your choice of one of the following: the Baptistery, Camposanto Cemetery, Museum of the Sinopias, or Duomo Museum; for two of these sights or one plus the Duomo, the cost is €6; for three of the above you pay €8; and for the works, you'll pay €10 (credit cards accepted at certain ticket windows). By comparison, the Duomo alone is a bargain (€2).

You can buy any of these tickets either behind the Leaning Tower or at the Museum of the Sinopias (near the Baptistery, almost suffocated by souvenir stands). Both ticket offices have big, yellow triangle-shaped signs.

All monuments share the same opening hours: Daily April–Sept 8:00–20:00, Nov–Dec and Jan–Feb 10:00–17:00, March 9:00–18:00, and Oct 9:00–19:00. The Tower is also open mid-May–mid-Sept until 23:00. Keep in mind that the last entrance to all monuments is 30 minutes before closing time.

No matter what ticket you get, you'll have to pay an additional €15 if you want to climb the Tower. Tickets for the Tower are sold at the ticket offices listed above or online at www.opapisa.it (online reservations must be made at least 2 weeks in advance).

---

soil with steam pipes, anchored the Tower to the ground with steel cables, and buried 600 tons of lead on the north side as a counterweight (not visible)—all with little success. The breakthrough came when they drilled 15-foot holes in the ground on the north side and sucked out sixty tons of soil, allowing the Tower to sink on the north side and straighten out its lean by about six inches.

As well as gravity, erosion threatens the Tower. Since its construction, 135 of the Tower's 180 marble columns have had to be replaced. Stone decay, deposits of lime and calcium phosphate, accumulations of dirt and moss, cracking from the stress of the lean—all of these are factors in its decline.

Thanks to the Tower's lean, there are special trouble spots. The lower south side (which is protected from cleansing rain and wind) is black from dirty airborne particles, while the stone on the upper areas, though clean, has more decay (from eroding rain and wind).

The Tower, now stabilized, is getting cleaned. Cracks are filled, and accumulations removed, using atomized water sprays and poultices of various solvents.

All the work to shore up, straighten, and clean the Tower has probably turned the clock back 200 years on the still-leaning—and probably still-falling—Tower.

Climbing the Tower: Every 30 to 40 minutes, 30 people can clamber up the 294 tilting stairs to the top (€15, kids under 8 not allowed, April–Sept daily 8:00–20:00, until 23:00 mid-May–mid-Sept, shorter hours off-season, reservations required, ticket office opens 30 min early).

To reserve in person, go to the ticket office behind the Tower, on the left in the yellow building, or to the Museum of the Sinopias ticket office hidden behind the souvenir stalls. You choose a 35-minute time slot for your visit. If you visit in summer, it will likely be a couple of hours before you're able to go up (see the rest of the monuments and grab lunch while waiting). The wait is usually much shorter if you arrive at the beginning or end of the day. You must pick up your ticket(s) at least an hour before your time slot, and show up 10 minutes before your appointment at the meeting point outside the ticket office.

For an extra €2, you can book a time at www.opapisa.it. Online bookings are accepted no more than 45 days—and no fewer than 14 days—in advance.

You can't take any bags up the Tower, but daybag-size lockers are available at the ticket office—show your Tower ticket to check your bag. Even though it's technically a "guided" visit, that only means you're accompanied by a museum guard who makes sure you don't stay up past your scheduled appointment time. For your 35-minute time slot, figure about 10 minutes to climb and 10 to descend, leaving about 15 minutes for vertigo at the top.

Caution: There are skinny railings, the steps are slanted, and rain makes the marble slippery. Anyone with balance issues of any sort should think twice before ascending.

▲▲**Field of Miracles (Campo dei Miracoli)**—Scattered across a golf-course-green lawn are four large white buildings that make up Pisa's religious center—the cathedral (or Duomo), its bell tower (the Leaning Tower), the Baptistery, and the Camposanto Cemetery. The four buildings share similar building materials—bright white marble—and comparable decoration. Each has a simple ground floor and rows of delicate columns and arches that form open-air arcades, giving the Campo a pleasant visual unity.

The style is dubbed Pisan Romanesque. Where traditional Romanesque has a heavy fortress feel—thick walls, barrel arches, few windows—Pisan Romanesque is light and elegant. At ground level, most of the structures have simple half-columns and arches. On the upper levels, you'll see a little of everything—tight rows of thin columns; pointed Gothic gables and prickly spires; Byzantine mosaics and horseshoe arches; and geometric designs (such as diamonds) and striped colored marbles inspired by mosques in Muslim lands.

Architecturally, the Campo is unique and exotic. Theologically, the Campo's buildings mark the main events of every Pisan's life: christened in the Baptistery, married in the Duomo, honored in ceremonies at the Tower, and buried in the Camposanto Cemetery.

Lining this field of artistic pearls is a gauntlet of Europe's tackiest souvenir stands, as well as dozens of amateur mimes "propping up" the Leaning Tower while tourists take photos.

▲▲**Duomo (Cathedral)**—The huge Pisan Romanesque cathedral, with its carved pulpit by Giovanni Pisano, is artistically more important than its more famous bell tower (€2, daily April–Sept 8:00–20:00, shorter hours off-season, last entry 30 min before closing). Shorts are OK as long as they're not too short, and shoulders should be covered (although it's not really enforced). Big backpacks are not allowed, nor is storage provided. If you have a daybag, carry it.

Begun in 1063, the Duomo is the centerpiece of the Field of Miracles' complex of religious buildings. The architect Buschetto created the style of Pisan Romanesque that set the tone for the Baptistery and Tower.

The **bronze back doors** (Porta San Ranieri) at the Tower end were designed by Bonnano Pisano (c. 1186). The doors have 24 different panels that show Christ's story using the same simple, skinny figures found in Byzantine icons. (The doors are actually copies; the originals are housed—but not always on display—in the Duomo Museum). Cast using the lost-wax technique, these doors were an inspiration for Lorenzo Ghiberti's bronze doors in Florence.

Go inside. The 320-foot **nave** was the longest in Christendom when it was built. The striped marble and arches-on-columns give it an exotic, almost mosque-like feel. Dim light filters in from the small upper windows of the galleries, where the women worshipped. The gilded coffered ceiling has shields of Florence's Medicis, including the round symbols (pills). This powerful family—who began as medics, later became cloth merchants, and finally bankers—took over Pisa after its glory days.

In the apse (behind the altar) is a **mosaic** (c. 1300, partly done by Cimabue) showing Christ as the Ruler of All (Pantocrator) between Mary and John the Evangelist. Looking up into the **dome,** the heavens open, and rings of saints and angels spiral up to a hazy God. Beneath the dome is an inlaid-marble, Cosmati-style mosaic floor.

The 15-foot-tall, octagonal **pulpit** by Giovanni Pisano is the last, biggest, and most complex of the four pulpits by the Pisano father-and-son team. Christ's life unfolds in a series of panels crammed with figures. Giovanni left no stone uncarved in his pursuit of beauty. Originally, this and the other pulpits were frosted with paint, gilding, and colored pastes.

The bronze **incense burner** that hangs from the ceiling (near the pulpit) is a replica of the one that supposedly caught teenage Galileo's attention when a gust of wind set the lamp swinging. He timed the swings and realized that the burner swung back and forth in the same amount of time regardless of how wide the arc. (This pendulum motion was a constant that allowed Galileo to measure our ever-changing universe.) Legend says the Pisa-born Galileo also threw objects off the Tower to time their falls, fascinated by gravity.

Pause at the **tomb of Holy Roman Emperor Henry VII,** the German king (c. 1275–1313) who invaded Italy and was welcomed by Pisans as a leader of unity and peace. Unfortunately, Henry took ill and died young, leaving Ghibelline Pisa at the mercy of its Guelph rivals such as rising Florence. Pisa never recovered.

In a glass-lined casket on the altar, Pisa's patron saint—**St. Ranieri**—lies mummified, encased in silver at his head and feet, with his hair shirt covering his body. The son of a rich sea-trader, Ranieri (1117–1161) was a hard-partying, touring musician who was later inspired to give away his money, join a monastery, and give spirited sermons from the Duomo pulpit.

▲**Baptistery**—The Baptistery, the biggest in Italy, is interesting for its pulpit and interior ambience, and especially for its great acoustics (daily April–Sept 8:00–20:00, shorter hours off-season, last entry 30 min before closing, located in front of the Duomo's facade).

The building is 180 feet tall—John the Baptist on top looks eye-to-eye with the tourists atop the nearly 200-foot Leaning Tower. Notice that the Baptistery leans nearly six feet to the north (the Tower leans 15 feet to the south). The building (begun 1153) is modeled on the circular domed Church of the Holy Sepulchre in Jerusalem, seen by Pisan Crusaders who occupied Jerusalem in 1099.

Inside, it's simple, spacious, and baptized with light. Tall arches encircle just a few pieces of religious furniture. In the center sits the **octagonal font** (1246, topped with a statue of the first baptist... John), which contains plenty of space for baptizing adults by immersion (the medieval custom), plus four wells for dunking babies.

Nicola Pisano's **pulpit** is arguably the world's first Renaissance sculpture. It's the first authenticated (signed) work by the "Giotto of sculpture," working in what came to be called the "Renaissance" style. The pulpit is a freestanding sculpture with classical columns, realistic people and animals, and 3-D effects in the carved panels.

The speaker's platform stands on columns that rest on the backs of animals, representing Christianity's triumph over paganism. The

relief panels, with scenes from the life of Christ, are more readable than the Duomo pulpit. Read left to right, starting from the back: Nativity, Adoration of the Magi, Presentation in the Temple, Crucifixion, Last Judgment.

The remarkable **acoustics** of the building—a medieval form of digital delay—are due to the 250-foot-wide dome. Make a sound in here and it echoes for a good 10 seconds (a 10-second "decay"). A priest standing at the baptismal font (or a security guard today) can sing three tones within the 10 seconds—"Ave Maria"—and make a chord, singing haunting harmonies with himself. Recent computer analysis suggests that the 15th-century architects who built the dome intended this building to be not just a Baptistery but also a musical instrument. A security guard sings every half hour, starting at 10:00.

Camposanto Cemetery—This site, bordering the Field of Miracles on the north, has been a cemetery since ancient times. Lined with faint frescoes, the ancient cemetery is famous for its Holy Land dirt, said to reduce a body into a skeleton within a day (April–Sept daily 8:00–20:00, shorter hours off-season).

Highlights are the building's cloistered interior courtyard (with intricately carved arches surrounding grass growing in Holy

Dirt); some ancient Roman and Greek sarcophagi; and the 1,000-square-foot, 14th-century fresco, *The Triumph of Death*. The fresco captures Pisa's mood in the wake of the bubonic plague (1348), which killed one in three Pisans. Grim stuff, but appropriate for the Camposanto's permanent residents.

Museum of the Sinopias (Museo delle Sinopie)—Across from the Baptistery, housed in a 13th-century hospital, this museum displays some of the original sketches used to make the frescoes in the Camposanto Cemetery. If you loved *The Triumph of Death* and others in the Camposanto, or if you're interested in fresco technique, this museum is worthwhile. If not, you'll wonder why you're here (April–Sept daily 8:00–20:00, shorter hours off-season).

Sinopias are sketches in red paint painted directly on the wall just before the final colored version. The master always did the sinopia himself; if he liked the results, his assistants copied or traced the sinopia onto paper, called a cartoon. Then the wall was covered with plaster (completely covering up the sinopia), and the assistants redrew the outlines, using the cartoon as a guide. While the plaster was still wet, the master quickly filled in the color and details, producing the final frescoes (now on display at the Camposanto). These sinopias—never meant to be seen—were uncovered by the bombing and restoration of the Camposanto and brought here.

Duomo Museum (Museo dell'Opera del Duomo)—The museum behind the Leaning Tower is big on Pisan art, displaying treasures of the cathedral, paintings, silverware, and sculptures (from the 12th–14th centuries, particularly by the Pisano dynasty), as well as ancient Egyptian, Etruscan, and Roman artifacts. It houses many of the original statues that once adorned the Campo's buildings (where copies stand today), notably the statues by Nicola and Giovanni Pisano. You can stand face-to-face with the Pisanos' very human busts that ring the outside of the Baptistery. You'll see a mythical sculpted hippogriff (a medieval jackalope) and other oddities brought back from the Holy Land by Pisan Crusaders. The museum also has several large-scale wooden models of the Duomo and Baptistery (April–Sept daily 8:00–20:00, shorter hours off-season, Piazza Arcivescovado 18).

Panoramic Walk on the Wall—This much-advertised, often-closed walk, which includes just a small section of the 12th-century wall, isn't worth your time or €2 (sporadically open June–Aug daily 11:00–14:00 & 15:00–18:00, entrance near the Baptistery at Porta Leone).

Museo Nazionale di San Matteo—On the river and in a former convent, this art museum displays 12th- to 15th-century sculptures, illuminated manuscripts, and paintings by Martini, Ghirlandaio, Masaccio, and others (€4, Tue–Sat 8:30–19:00, Sun 8:30–13:00,

Sleep Code

(€1 = about $1.30, country code: 39)
S = Single, **D** = Double/Twin, **T** = Triple, **Q** = Quad, **b** = bathroom, **s** = shower only. Unless otherwise noted, credit cards are accepted and breakfast is included, and English is generally spoken.

To help you sort easily through these listings, I've divided the rooms into three categories based on the price for a standard double room with bath:

$$$ **Higher Priced**—Most rooms €120 or more.
$$ **Moderately Priced**—Most rooms between €80–120.
$ **Lower Priced**—Most rooms €80 or less.

closed Mon, near Piazza San Paolo at Lungarno Mediceo, tel. 050-541-865).

SLEEPING

To locate these hotels, see the map on page 430.

$$$ Hotel Alessandro della Spina, in a nondescript neighborhood near the train station, has 16 elegant and colorful rooms, each named after a flower (Sb-€110, Db-€130, discounts off-season and for drop-ins, air-con, free parking; head straight out of train station, turn right on Viale F. Bonaini, take the third right on Via Alessandro della Spina, and the hotel is on your left at #7; tel. 050-502-777, fax 050-20-583, www.hoteldellaspina.it, info @hoteldellaspina.it).

$$ Hotel Villa Kinzica, with 33 decent rooms, is just steps away from the Field of Miracles—ask for a room with a view of the Tower (Sb-€78, Db-€108, Tb-€124, Qb-€135, air-con, elevator, attached restaurant, Piazza Arcivescovado 2, tel. 050-560-419, fax 050-551-204, www.hotelvillakinzica.it, info@hotelvillakinzica.it).

$ Hotel Milano, near the train station, offers 10 spacious, tidy rooms; ask for a room off the street when you book (D-€55, Db-€78, breakfast extra, air-con, Via Mascagni 14, tel. 050-23-162, fax 050-44-237, www.hotelmilano.pisa.it, info@hotelmilano .pisa.it).

EATING

For a quick lunch or dinner, the pizzeria/trattoria **La Buca,** just a block from the Tower, is adequate and convenient (Sat–Thu 12:00–15:00 & 18:30–22:30, closed Fri, at Via Santa Maria 171 and Via

Pisa and Lucca

A. G. Tassi, tel. 050-560-660).

Ristorante Galileo, south of the Arno, has excellent pizza (dinner only) and pasta (€5–8, Wed–Mon 12:30–15:30 & 19:30–23:30, closed Sun at lunch and all day Tue, Via Silvestri 12, tel. 050-28-287).

At **Paninoteca il Canguro,** friendly Fabio makes warm, hearty sandwiches to order. Try their popular primavera sandwich (Mon–Fri 10:00–24:00, Sat 10:30–21:00, closed Sun, Via Santa Maria 151, tel. 050-561-942).

Drop by cheery **La Lupa Ghiotta Tavola Calda** for a cheap, fast, and tasty meal a few steps from the train station. It's got everything you'd want from a *ristorante* at half the price with faster service (build your own salad—5 ingredients for €4.50; Mon and Wed–Sat 12:15–15:00 & 19:15–24:00, Tue 12:15–15:00 only, closed Sun, Viale F. Bonaini 113, tel. 050-21-018).

The street that houses the daily market, **Via delle Colonne** (a block north of the Arno, west of Borgo Stretto), has a few atmospheric, mid-price restaurants and several fun, greasy take-out options.

TRANSPORTATION CONNECTIONS

From Pisa by Train to: Florence (3/hr, 1.25 hrs, €5), **Rome** (at least hourly, 3–4 hrs), **La Spezia,** gateway to Cinque Terre (hourly, 1 hr), **Siena** (change at Empoli: Pisa–Empoli, roughly 2/hr, 45 min; Empoli–Siena, hourly, 1 hr, €6.60), **Lucca** (roughly 2/hr, 2/day Sun, 30 min). Even the fastest trains stop in Pisa, so you might change trains here whether you plan to stop or not.

By Car: The drive between Pisa and Florence is that rare case where the non-*autostrada* highway (free, more direct, and at least as fast) is a better deal than the *autostrada*.

Pisa's Airport: For information on Pisa's Galileo Galilei Airport, see page 424.

Lucca

Surrounded by well-preserved ramparts, layered with history, alternately quaint and urbane, Lucca charms its visitors. Romanesque churches seem to be around every corner, as do fun-loving and shady piazzas filled with soccer-playing children. Despite Lucca's appeal, few tourists seem to put it on their maps, and it remains a city for the Lucchesi (loo-KAY-zee).

ORIENTATION

Tourist Information

The main TI is just inside the Porta Santa Maria, on Piazza Santa Maria (daily April–Oct 9:00–20:00, Nov–March 9:00–12:30 & 15:00–18:30, Internet access, WCs, can book walking tours, Piazza Santa Maria 35, tel. 0583-919-931, fax 0583-469-964, www.luccatourist.it, info@luccaturismo.it).

Another TI, on Piazzale Verdi, offers information, a room-booking service, Internet access, walking tours, and baggage check (daily 9:00–19:00, off-season 9:00–17:30, bike rental, 80-min city-walk audioguide-€9, additional audioguide-€3 more; bag storage-€1.50/hr per bag or €5 for up to 5 hrs, they need to photocopy your passport; futuristic WC, tel. 0583-583-150).

A third TI, at Piazza Curtatone, has the handiest baggage-check near the train station (daily 10:00–18:00, bag storage-€1.50/day per bag, exit the station, cross the square in front and head right, it's just ahead on right, tel. 0583-495-730).

Arrival in Lucca

To reach the city center from the **train** station, walk toward the walls and head left, to the entry at Porta San Pietro. Taxis are sparse at midday, but try calling 0583-492-691 or 0583-494-190. There is no baggage check at the train station, but you can check your bag at the TI in nearby Piazza Curtatone (see "Tourist Information," above).

Drivers: Lucca has a serious lack of public parking places. Try parking lots at Porta Santa Maria and Porta Sant'Anna (€1/hour), or consider parking outside of the gates near the train station or on the boulevard surrounding the city. Lucca's TIs have maps that show the location of free parking lots just outside the walls.

Helpful Hints

Combo-Tickets: A €6 combo-ticket includes visits to the Ilaria del Carretto tomb in San Martino Cathedral (€2), the Cathedral Museum (€4), and San Giovanni Church (€2.50). A different €6 ticket combines the Guinigi Tower (€4) and the Clock Tower (€4). Yet another combo-ticket covers Palazzo Mansi and Villa Guinigi for €6.50 and is valid three days (€4 each if purchased separately).

Tours: The TI at Piazzale Verdi books interesting city walking tours in English on Lucca's history, architecture, and culture with a live guide (€10, 1 hour—can go longer if also translated into another language, offered Easter–Oct on Mon, Thu, and Sat at 15:00, Nov–Easter only on Sat at 15:00, purchase ticket at TI or just show up, groups average 8–10 people, meet under loggia of Palazzo Pretorio in Piazza San Michele, tel. 0583-342-404, www.turislucca.com).

Shops and Museums Alert: Shops close most of Sunday and Monday mornings. Many museums are closed on Monday as well.

Markets: Lucca's atmospheric markets are worth visiting. Every third Saturday and Sunday of the month, one of the largest **antiques markets** in Italy unfurls in the blocks from Piazza Antelminelli to Piazza San Giovanni (8:00–19:00). The last weekend of the month, local artisans sell **arts and crafts** throughout the town (also 8:00–19:00). At the **general market,** held Wednesdays and Saturdays, you'll find produce and household goods (8:00–13:00, outside of the walls, a few blocks north of Porta Elisa around the stadium—may move to a lot outside Porta San Donato; check with TI or your hotel).

Concerts: San Giovanni Church hosts several musical concerts each week throughout the year, featuring highlights from hometown composer Giacomo Puccini (usually starts at 19:00; get schedule at church, TI, or your hotel, or check www .puccinielasualucca.com; tickets €16.50 in advance, €15 at the door). You can buy tickets online, right before the concert, or when the church is open (Mon–Fri 9:30–17:45, Sat 9:30–18:45; Sun between Masses: 9:30–10:45 & 12:00–17:45).

Festival: On September 13 and 14, the city celebrates Volto Santo ("Holy Face"), with a procession of the treasured local crucifix and a fair in Piazza Antelminelli.

Internet Access: You can get online at two of the TIs (see "Tourist Information," above) or at **Mondo Chiocciola** (April–Oct Mon–Sat 15:30–20:00, closed Sun, shorter hours Nov–March, one block behind Piazza del Anfiteatro at Via Santa Zita 4, tel. 0583-440-510).

Laundry: Lavanderia Self-Service Niagara is just off Piazza Santa Maria at Via Rosi 26 (daily 8:00–22:00).

Bike Rental: Several places with identical prices cluster around Piazza Santa Maria (€2.50/hr, €12.50/day, tandem bikes available, open daily, last rental at about sunset). These easygoing shops rent good bikes: **Antonio Poli** (Piazza Santa Maria 42, tel. & fax 0583-493-787, enthusiastic Cristiana) and **Cicli Bizzarri** (Piazza Santa Maria 32, tel. 0583-496-031, Australian Dely). A one-hour rental gives you two leisurely loops around the ramparts.

SIGHTS AND ACTIVITIES

▲▲**Bike the Ramparts**—Lucca's most remarkable feature, its Renaissance wall, is also its most enjoyable attraction—especially when circled on a rental bike. Stretching for 2.5 miles, this is an ideal place to come for an overview of the city by foot or bike.

Lucca has had a protective wall for 2,000 years. You can read three walls into today's map: the first rectangular Roman wall, the later medieval wall (nearly the size of today's), and the 16th-century Renaissance wall.

With the advent of cannons, thin medieval walls were suddenly vulnerable. A new design—the same one that stands today—was state-of-the-art when it was built (1550–1650). Much of the old medieval wall (look for the old stones) was incorporated into the Renaissance wall (with uniform bricks). The new wall was squat: a 100-foot-wide mound of dirt faced with bricks, engineered to absorb a cannonball pummeling. The townspeople cleared a wide no-man's-land around the town, exposing any attackers from a distance. Ten heart-shaped bastions  (inviting picnic areas today) were designed to minimize exposure to cannonballs and maximize defense capabilities. The ramparts were armed with 130 cannons.

The town invested a third of its income for more than a century to construct the wall, and—since it kept away the Florentines and nasty Pisans—it was considered a fine investment. In fact, nobody ever bothered to try to attack the wall. Locals say the only time it actually defended the city was during an 1812 flood, when the gates were sandbagged and its ramparts kept the high water out.

Today, the ramparts seem made-to-order for a leisurely bike ride (20-min pedal, wonderfully smooth). You can rent bikes cheap and easy from one of several bike-rental places in town (see "Helpful Hints," on previous page).

Roman Amphitheater—Just off the main shopping street, the architectural ghost of a Roman amphitheater can be felt in the delightful Piazza Anfiteatro. With the fall of Rome, the theater (which seated 10,000) was gradually cannibalized for its stones and inhabited by a mishmash of huts. The huts were cleared away at the end of the 19th century to better appreciate the town's illustrious past. Today, the square is a circle of touristy shops and mediocre restaurants that becomes a lively bar-and-café scene after dark.

Lucca

1 La Romea B&B
2 To Hotel San Marco
3 La Locanda Sant'Agostino
4 Hotella Luna
5 La Bohème B&B
6 Alla Dolce Vita Guest House
7 Le Violette B&B
8 La Magnolia B&B
9 To Sogni d'Oro Guest House
10 Ostello San Frediano
11 Puccini Ristorante
12 Ristorante Canuleia
13 Vecchia Trattoria Buralli
14 Trattoria da Leo
15 Osteria Baralla
16 Bella 'Mbriana
17 Trattoria Gigi
18 Pizzeria da Felice
19 Bike Rental

Today's street level is nine feet above the original arena floor. The only bits of surviving Roman stonework are a few arches on the northern exterior (at Via Fillungo 42 and on Via Anfiteatro).

Via Fillungo—This main pedestrian drag is southwest of the Roman amphitheater. *The* street to stroll, Via Fillungo takes you from the amphitheater almost all the way to the cathedral. Along the way, you'll get a taste of Lucca's rich past, including several elegant, century-old storefronts. Many of the original storefront paintings, reliefs, or mosaics survive—even if today's shopkeeper sells something entirely different.

At #97 is a classic old **jewelry store** with a rare storefront that has kept its T-shaped arrangement (when closed, you see a wooden T, and during open hours it unfolds with a fine old-time display). This design dates from a time when the merchant sold his goods in front, did his work in the back, and lived upstairs.

Di Simo Caffè at #58 has long been the hangout of Lucca's artistic and intellectual elite. Composer and hometown boy Giacomo Puccini tapped his foot while sipping coffee here. Pop in to check out the 1880s ambience.

A surviving five-story **tower house** is at #67. Remember, there was a time when each corner sported its own tower. The stubby stones that still stick out once supported wooden staircases (there were no interior connections up or down). So many towers cast shadows over this part of town that the street just before it is called Via Buia (Dark Street). Step into Via Buia and look back toward Via Fillungo for a peek at the town's tallest tower, Guinigi, with its characteristic oak trees sprouting from the top.

At #45 and #43, you'll see two more good examples of tower houses. Across the street, the **Clock Tower** (Torre delle Ore) has a hand-wound Swiss clock that has clanged four times an hour since 1754 (€4 to climb up and see the mechanism flip into action on the

quarter hour, €6 combo-ticket includes Guinigi Tower, April–Oct daily 10:00–19:00, shorter hours off-season, corner of Via Fillungo and Via del'Arancio).

The intersection of Via Fillungo and Via Roma/Via Santa Croce marks the center of town (where the two

The History of Lucca

Lucca began as a Roman settlement. In fact, the grid layout of the streets (and the shadow of an amphitheater) survives from Roman times. Trace the rectangular Roman wall—indicated by today's streets—on the map. As in typical Roman towns, two main roads quartered the fortified town, crossing at what was the forum (main market and religious/political center)—today's Piazza San Michele.

Christianity came here early: It's said that the first bishop of Lucca was a disciple of St. Peter. While churches were built here as early as the fourth century, the majority of Lucca's elegant Romanesque churches date from about the 12th century.

Feisty Lucca, though never a real power, enjoyed a long period of independence (maintained by clever diplomacy). Aside from 30 years of being ruled from Pisa in the 14th century, Lucca was basically an independent city-state (until Napoleon came to town).

In the Middle Ages, wealthy Lucca's economy was built on the silk industry, dominated by the Guinigi (gwee-NEE-gee) family. Without silk, Lucca would have been just another sleepy Italian town. In 1500, the town had 3,000 silk looms employing 25,000 workers. Banking was also big. Many pilgrims stopped here on their way to the Holy Land, deposited their money for safety...and never returned to pick it up.

In its heyday, Lucca packed 160 towers—one on nearly every corner—and 70 churches within its walls. Each tower was the home of a wealthy merchant family. Towers were many stories tall, with single rooms stacked atop each other: ground-floor shop, upstairs living room, and top-floor fire-safe kitchen, all connected by exterior wooden staircases. The rooftop was generally a vegetable garden with trees that provided shade. Later, the wealthy city folk moved into the countryside, trading away life in their city palazzos to establish farm estates, complete with fancy villas. (You can visit some of these villas today—the TI has a brochure—but they're convenient only for drivers and are generally not worth the cost of admission.)

In 1799, Napoleon stormed into Italy and took a liking to Lucca. He liked it so much that he gave it to his sister as a gift. It was later passed on to Napoleon's widow, Marie Louise. With a feminine sensitivity, Marie Louise was partially responsible for turning the city's imposing (but no longer particularly useful) fortified wall into a fine city park that is much enjoyed today.

original Roman roads crossed). As you go right down Via Roma, you'll pass a Leonardo exhibit (€5 to see a room full of "don't touch" modern models of his sketches...not worth the money, daily 9:30–19:30) before reaching **Piazza San Michele** (once the Roman Forum). Towering above the church's fancy Pisan Romanesque facade, the archangel Michael stands ready to flap his wings—which he actually did on special occasions. (See the stairs behind the facade, which church officials would climb to pull some strings and wow their gullible flock.) Piazza San Michele is as fun a people center today as it has been since Roman times.

▲**San Martino Cathedral**—This church, begun in the 11th century, is an entertaining mix of architectural and artistic styles. Its elaborate Pisan Romanesque **facade**—featuring biblical scenes, animals, and candy-cane-striped columns—dominates the piazza. The central figure of the facade is St. Martin, a Roman military officer from Hungary who, by offering his cloak to a beggar, more fully understood the beauty of Christian compassion. (The impressive original, a fine example of Romanesque sculpture, is just inside, hiding from the pollution.) Each of the columns on the facade is unique. Notice how the facade is asymmetrical: The clock tower was already in place when the cathedral was built, so the builders cheated on the right side to make it fit the space. Over the right portal, the architect Guideo from Como holds a document declaring that he finished the facade in 1204. On the right (at eye level), a labyrinth set into the wall relates the struggle and challenge our souls face in finding salvation. The Latin plaque just left of the main door is where moneychangers and spice traders met to seal deals (on the doorstep of the church—to underscore the reliability of their promises). Notice the date: *An Dni MCXI* (A.D. 1111).

The **interior** features Gothic arches, Renaissance paintings, and stained glass from the 19th century. On the left side of the nave, a small, elaborate temple displays the wooden crucifix called Volto Santo (Holy Face). It's said to have been sculpted by Nicodemus in Jerusalem and set afloat in an unmanned boat that landed on the coast of Tuscany, from where wild oxen miraculously carried it to Lucca in 782. The sculpture (which is actually 12th-century Byzantine-style) has quite a jewelry collection, which you can see in the Cathedral Museum (see next listing).

On the right side of the nave, the sacristy houses the enchantingly beautiful **memorial tomb of Ilaria del Carretto** by Jacopo della Quercia (1407). Pick up a handy English description to the right of the door as you enter the sacristy. This young bride of silk baron Paolo Guinigi is decked out in the latest, most expensive fashions, with the requisite little dog curled up at her feet in eternal sleep. She's so realistic that the statue was nicknamed "Sleeping Beauty." Her nose is partially worn off because of a long-standing tradition of lonely young ladies rubbing it for luck in finding a boyfriend (free entry to cathedral, Ilaria tomb-€2, Mon–Fri 9:30–17:45, Sat 9:30–18:45; Sun open sporadically between Masses: 9:30–10:45 & 12:00–17:45; Piazza San Martino).

Cathedral Museum (Museo della Cattedrale)—This beautifully presented museum houses original paintings, sculptures, and vestments from the cathedral and other Lucca churches. The first room displays jewelry made to dress up the Volto Santo crucifix, including gigantic gilded silver shoes. Upstairs, notice the fine red brocaded silk—a reminder that this precious fabric is what brought riches and power to the city. The exhibits in this museum have very brief descriptions and are meaningful only with the €1 audioguide—if you're not in the mood to listen, skip the place altogether (€4, April–Oct daily 10:00–18:00; Nov–March Mon–Fri 10:00–14:00, Sat–Sun 10:00–17:00; next to cathedral on Piazza Antelminelli).

San Giovanni Church—This first cathedral of Lucca is interesting only for its archaeological finds. The entire floor of the 12th-century church has been excavated (1969–1992), revealing layers of Roman houses, ancient hot tubs dating back to the time of Christ, early churches, and theological graffiti. Eager students can request an English translation of the floor plans from the ticket office to know what's what. As you climb under the church's present-day floor and wander the lanes of Roman Lucca, remember that the entire city sits on similar ruins (€2.50, peak season daily 10:00–18:00; off-season Sat–Sun 10:00–17:00, closed Mon–Fri; kitty-corner from cathedral at Piazza San Giovanni).

Palazzo Mansi—Minor paintings by Tintoretto, Pontormo, Veronese, and others vie for attention, but the palazzo itself, a sumptuously furnished and decorated 17th-century confection, steals the show. This is your chance to appreciate the wealth of Lucca's silk merchants (€4, Tue–Sat 8:30–19:30, Sun 8:30–13:30, closed Mon, last entry 30 min before closing, no photos, request English booklet at ticket desk, Via Galli Tassi 43, tel. 0583-55-570). All visitors must be accompanied by a museum custodian, so there may be a bit of a wait during high season.

Guinigi Tower (Torre Guinigi)—Many Tuscan towns have towers, but none quite like the Guinigi family's. Up 227 steps is a small garden with fragrant trees surrounded by fantastic views (€5, €6 combo-ticket includes Clock Tower, daily July–Aug 9:00–24:00, Sept–Oct 9:30–18:00, Nov–March

9:30–16:30, April–June 9:00–21:00, late hours can vary—confirm with TI, Via Sant'Andrea, tel. 336-203-221).

Puccini's House—Opera enthusiasts (but nobody else) will want to visit the home where Giacomo Puccini (1858–1924) grew up, but—tragedy—it's closed. A pitched battle is going on between Puccini's grandniece—who actually owns the house and wants to renovate the museum—and the city of Lucca, which wants to preserve the house unchanged. Until one or the other relents, the museum will remain closed. Call 0583-584-028 or check with the TI to see if it's reopened (Corte San Lorenzo 9).

Villa Guinigi—Built by Paolo Guinigi in 1418, the family villa is now a stark, abandoned-feeling museum displaying artifacts, sculptures, and paintings. Monumental paintings by multitalented Giorgio Vasari are the best reason to visit (€4, Tue–Sat 8:30–19:30, Sun 8:30–13:30, closed Mon, last entry 30 min before closing, may have to wait in high season for a museum custodian to accompany you, Via della Quarquonia, tel. 0583-496-033).

SLEEPING

(€1=about $1.30, country code: 39)

$$$ La Romea B&B, in an air-conditioned, restored 14th-century palazzo near Guinigi Tower, feels like a royal splurge. Its four posh rooms and one suite are lavishly decorated in handsome colors, with stately parquet floors (Db-€130–160 depending on room size, Qb suite-€176, 3 percent cheaper with cash; from Via Fillungo, take Via Sant'Andrea to the Church of Sant'Andrea and turn right on Vicolo delle Ventaglie to #2; tel. 0583-464-175, fax 0583-471-280, www.laromea.com, info@laromea.com, Giulio and wife Gaia).

$$$ Hotel San Marco, a seven-minute walk outside the Porta Santa Maria, is a postmodern place decorated à la Stanley Kubrick. Its 42 rooms are sleek, with all the comforts (Sb-€87, Db-€126, includes nice breakfast spread, air-con, elevator, pool, free parking, taxi from station-€6, Via San Marco 368, tel. 0583-495-010, fax 0583-490-513, www.hotelsanmarcolucca.it, info@hotelsanmarcolucca.com).

$$$ La Locanda Sant'Agostino, run by gracious Sarah, has three tastefully decorated, romantic, spacious rooms. The vine-draped terrace and quaint views invite you to relax (Db-€160, extra bed-€25, 5 percent discount with cash and this book in 2008, air-con, free Internet access, from Via Fillungo take Via San Giorgio to Piazza Sant'Agostino 3, best to reserve by email, tel. & fax 0583-467-884, www.locandasantagostino.it, info@locandasantagostino.it).

$$ La Bohème B&B has a cozy yet elegant ambience, offering five large, charming, chandeliered rooms, each painted with a different rich color scheme (Db-€110, less off-season, 5 percent discount with cash and this book in 2008, air-con, Via del Moro 2, tel. & fax 0583-462-404, www.boheme.it, info@boheme.it, run by kindly Ranieri).

$$ Hotel la Luna has 29 classy, spotless rooms in the heart of the city. Updated rooms are split between two adjacent buildings right off of the main shopping street. Frescoed top-floor suites are a palatial, romantic splurge (Sb-€83, Db-€115, suite-€175, rates promised through 2008 for Rick Steves readers, overpriced breakfast-€12, air-con, elevator, parking-€15/day, Via Fillungo at Corte Compagni 12, tel. 0583-493-634, fax 0583-490-021, www .hotellaluna.com, info@hotellaluna.com, lovely Lulu greets you at reception).

$ Alla Dolce Vita Guest House is a good value, with four big, clean, comfortable rooms in a handy location right next to the medieval gate at the end of Via Fillungo (Db-€67, Tb-€77, €5/person discount with cash, communal kitchen, free shuttle to and from station with advance notice; follow Via Fillungo to the medieval gate, turn left and head to the small piazza on the right to #232—right of the bar; Via Fillungo 232, tel. 0583-467-768, mobile 329-582-5062, fax 0583-957-612, www.luccabed.com, info@luccabed.com, run by helpful Davide).

$ At Le Violette B&B, friendly Anna (who's still learning English—her granddaughter Sara speaks English) will settle you into one of her six homey, tidy, quiet rooms just a couple of blocks away from the train station inside Porta San Pietro (D-€60, Db-€75, extra bed-€15, communal kitchen, €5 to use washer and dryer, Via della Polveriera 6, tel. 0583-493-594, mobile 349-823-4645, fax 0583-429-305, www.leviolette.it, leviolette@virgilio.it). Once inside Porta San Pietro, head inward on Via G. Saladini and turn left onto Via F. Carrara, then right onto Via Girolamo, then right again onto Via della Polveriera.

$ La Magnolia offers five clean, quiet rooms with an intimate atmosphere and relaxing garden in a central location (Sb-€50–65 Db-€70–85, includes breakfast at nearby bar, 5 percent discount with cash and this book in 2008, 1 block behind Roman amphitheater at Via Mordini 63, tel. 0583-467-111, www.lamagnolia .com, info@lamagnolia.com, Andrea and Laura).

$ Sogni d'Oro Guest House ("Sleep like Gold"), run by Davide from Alla Dolce Vita (listed above), is a handy budget option for drivers, with five basic rooms and a cheery communal kitchen (grocery store next door). It's a 10-minute walk from the train station and a five-minute walk from the city walls (D-€50, Db-€65, €5/person discount with cash; free shuttle to and from station with advance notice; from the station, head straight out to main boulevard Viale Regina Margherita and turn right, following the street as it turns into Viale della Curtatone, then taking a right onto Via A. Cantore to #169; tel. 0583-467-768, mobile 333-498-3045, fax 0583-957-612, www.bbsognidoro.com, info@bbsognidoro.com).

$ Ostello San Frediano, in a central, sprawling ex-convent with a peaceful garden, is a cut above the average hostel. The rooms are bright and modern, and some have fun lofts (Db-€48, Qb-€95, €19 beds in 6- to 8-person dorms, €3 extra for non-members, cash only, lockout 11:00–15:30, no curfew, Internet access, cheap restaurant, free parking, Via della Cavallerizza 12, tel. 0583-469-957, fax 0583-461-007, www.ostellolucca.it, info@ostellolucca.it).

EATING

Puccini Ristorante is the place to splurge for a fancy €50 dinner. Fish and meat are featured here, as well as homemade bread, pasta, and desserts, with gourmet preparation and elegant presentation. Skip the basic sidewalk seats for the classy, modern art–strewn dining room (€45–55 3-course fixed-price meals, Wed 19:30–22:30, Thu–Mon 12:30–14:30 & 19:30–22:30, closed Tue, reserve on weekends, across the street from Puccini's House, Corte San Lorenzo 1, tel. 0583-316-116).

Ristorante Canuleia makes everything fresh in their small kitchen. While the portions aren't huge, the food is tasty. You can eat in their tiny dining room or garden courtyard. Reserve ahead for dinner (Mon–Sat 12:30–14:00 & 19:30–21:30, closed Sun, Via Canuleia 14, tel. 0583-467-470).

Vecchia Trattoria Buralli, on quiet Piazza Sant'Agostino, is a good bet for traditional cooking and juicy steaks, with fine indoor and piazza seating, though the service can be uneven (€20–40 dinner, Thu–Tue 12:00–14:45 & 19:15–22:30, closed Wed, Piazza Sant'Agostino 10, tel. 0583-950-611).

Osteria Baralla, a few steps from the Roman amphitheater, is popular with locals for its quality mid-price meals. They have a breezy, spacious dining room under medieval vaults or a few quiet tables on the pedestrian street (Mon–Sat 12:30–14:30 & 19:30–22:30, closed Sun, reservations smart for dinner, Via Anfiteatro 7/9, tel. 0583-440-240).

Trattoria da Leo, a cousin of Vecchia Trattoria Buralli above, packs in chatty locals for typical, cheap home-cooking in a hash-slingin' Mel's diner atmosphere. Arrive early or reserve in advance (daily 12:00–14:30 & 19:30–22:30, cash only, exit Piazza San Salvatore on Via Asili and take the first left, Via Tegrimi 1, tel. 0583-492-236).

Specialties in Lucca

Lucca has some tasty specialties worth seeking out. *Ceci* (CHEH-chee), also called *cecina* (cheh-CHEE-nah), makes an ideal cheap snack any time of day. This garbanzo-bean crêpe is sold in pizza shops and is best accompanied by a nip of red wine.

Farro, a grain (spelt) dating back to ancient Roman cuisine, shows up in restaurants in soups or as a creamy rice-like dish *(risotto di farro)*.

Tordelli, the Lucchesi version of *tortelli,* is homemade ravioli. It's traditionally stuffed with meat and served with more meat sauce, but chefs creatively pair cheeses and vegetables, too.

Meat, not fish, is the star at most restaurants, especially steak, which is listed on menus as *filetto di manzo* (filet), *tagliata di manzo* (thin slices of grilled tenderloin), or the king of steaks, *bistecca alla fiorentina*. Order *al sangue* (rare), *medio* (medium rare), *cotto* (medium) or *ben cotto* (well). Anything more than *al sangue* is considered a travesty for steak connoisseurs.

Note that steaks (as well as fish) are often sold by weight, noted on menus as *s.q.* (according to quantity ordered) or *l'etto* (cost per 100 grams—250 grams is about an 8-ounce steak). *Buon appetito!*

Trattoria Gigi offers fine traditional Lucchese cuisine, including homemade pastas (try the *tordelli*) and roasted meat, served with creative flair on an inviting square or in their cheery dining room (Mon 12:00–15:00 only, Tue–Sun 12:00–15:00 & 19:30–23:00, Piazza del Carmine, tel. 0583-467-266,).

Bella 'Mbriana focuses on doing one thing very well: turning out piping hot, wood-fired pizzas to happy locals in a welcoming wood-paneled dining room. Order at the counter, and they bring your pizza to you. Consider take-out to munch on the nearby walls. Prices range from €3.50 for your basic *napolitano* to €12 for their specialty, with buffalo mozzarella and other gourmet ingredients (Wed–Mon 12:30–14:30 & 18:30–23:30, closed Tue, to the right as you face San Frediano Church, Via della Cavalerizza 29, tel. 0583-495-565).

Pizzeria da Felice is a little mom-and-pop hole-in-the-wall serving *cecina* (chickpea crêpes) and slices of freshly baked pizza to throngs of snackers. Grab a *cecina* and a short glass of wine for €2 (Via Buia 12, tel. 0583-494-986).

TRANSPORTATION CONNECTIONS

From Lucca by Train to: Florence (roughly 3/hr, 1.5 hrs), **Pisa** (roughly 2/hr, 2/day Sun, 30 min), **Milan** (nearly hourly except Sun, 4–5 hrs, transfer in Florence or Prato), **Rome** (hourly except Sun, 3 hrs, change in Florence or Pisa).

SIENA

Siena was medieval Florence's archrival. And while Florence ultimately won the battle for political and economic superiority, Siena still competes for the tourists. Sure, Florence has the heavyweight sights, but Siena seems to be every Italy connoisseur's favorite pet town. In my office, whenever Siena is mentioned, someone moans, "Siena? I looove Siena!"

Once upon a time (from about 1260–1348), Siena was a major banking and trade center, and a military power in a class with Florence, Venice, and Genoa. With a population of 60,000, it was even bigger than Paris. Situated on the north–south road to Rome (the Via Francigena), Siena traded with all of Europe. Then, in 1348, the Black Death (bubonic plague) that swept through Europe hit Siena and cut the population by more than a third. Siena never recovered. In the 1550s, Florence, with the help of Philip II's Spanish army, conquered the flailing city-state, forever rendering Siena a nonthreatening backwater. Siena's loss became our sightseeing gain, as its political and economic irrelevance pickled the city in a purely medieval brine. Today, Siena's population is still 60,000, compared to Florence's 420,000.

Siena's thriving historic center, with redbrick lanes cascading every which way, offers Italy's best medieval city experience. Most people do Siena, just 35 miles south of Florence, as a day trip, but it's best experienced at twilight. While Florence has the blockbuster museums, Siena has an easy-to-enjoy soul: Courtyards sport flower-decked wells, alleys dead-end at rooftop views, and the sky is a rich blue dome.

For those who dream of a Fiat-free Italy, pedestrians rule in the old center of Siena. Sit at a café on the redbrick main square. Wander narrow streets lined with colorful flags and iron rings for tethering horses. Take time to savor the first European city to eliminate automobile traffic from its main square (1966) and then, just to be silly, wonder what would happen if they did it in your home town.

Planning Your Time

On a quick trip, consider spending two nights in Siena (or three nights with a whole-day side trip into Florence). Whatever you do, enjoy a sleepy medieval evening in Siena. The next morning, you can see the city's major sights in half a day.

ORIENTATION

Siena lounges atop a hill, stretching its three legs out from Il Campo. This main square, the historic meeting point of Siena's neighborhoods, is pedestrian-only. And most of those pedestrians are students from the local university.

Everything I mention is within a 15-minute walk of the square. Navigate by three major landmarks (Il Campo, Duomo, and Church of San Domenico), following the excellent system of street-corner signs. The typical visitor sticks to the San Domenico–Il Campo axis. Make a point to stray from the current of this main artery.

Siena itself is one big sight. Its individual sights come in two little clusters: the square (Civic Museum and City Tower) and the cathedral (Baptistery and Duomo Museum with its surprise viewpoint). Check these sights off, and you're free to wander.

Tourist Information

The TI office can be an exasperating place but they do offer some good handouts and a free map (daily 9:00–19:00, located on Il Campo at #56, tel. 0577-280-551, www.terresiena.it, incoming @terresiena.it). The helpful booklet *Terre di Siena* lists current hours and prices for sights in Siena and outlying towns. The little TI across the street from the Church of San Domenico, while primarily for hotel promotion, sells a €0.50 Siena map and organizes walking tours of the old town (€15, daily April–Sept) and of San Gimignano.

Arrival in Siena

By Train: The small train station, located on the edge of town, has a bar and bus office (no baggage check or lockers). To get from the station to the city center, hike 20 minutes uphill, or catch a city

Greater Siena

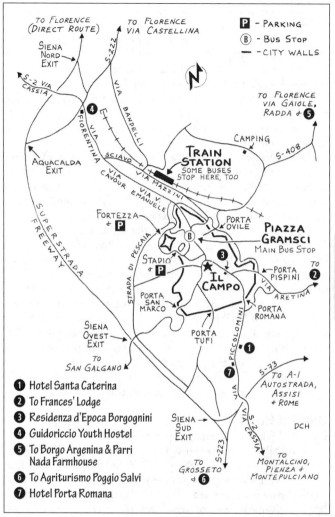

TO FLORENCE
(DIRECT ROUTE)

TO FLORENCE
VIA CASTELLINA

P – PARKING
B – BUS STOP
— – CITY WALLS

SIENA
NORD
EXIT

S-222

VIA BANDELLI

N

TO FLORENCE
VIA GAIOLE,
RADDA & **5**

S-2 VIA
CASSIA

4

VIA FIORENTINA

VIA SCIAVO

CAMPING

S-408

AQUACALDA
EXIT

VIA CAVOUR
EMANUELE
VIA V.

VIA MAZZINI

**TRAIN
STATION**
SOME BUSES
STOP HERE, TOO

SUPERSTRADA FREEWAY

FORTEZZA
P

STRADA DI PESCAIA

STADIO
P

B

PORTA
OVILE

**PIAZZA
GRAMSCI**
MAIN BUS STOP

TO
2

3

PORTA
PISPINI

VIA ARETINA

IL
CAMPO

PORTA
SAN
MARCO

PORTA
ROMANA

SIENA
OVEST
EXIT

VIA PICCOLOMINI

PORTA
TUFI

1

TO
SAN GALGANO

7

S-73
TO A-1
AUTOSTRADA,
ASSISI
& ROME

SIENA
SUD
EXIT

S-223

VIA S-2 CASSIA

DCH

TO
GROSSETO
& **6**

TO
MONTALCINO,
PIENZA &
MONTEPULCIANO

1 Hotel Santa Caterina
2 To Frances' Lodge
3 Residenza d'Epoca Borgognini
4 Guidoriccio Youth Hostel
5 To Borgo Argenina & Parri
Nada Farmhouse
6 To Agriturismo Poggio Salvi
7 Hotel Porta Romana

Siena

bus or taxi. The **taxi stand** but the city is chronically short on cabs and getting a taxi here can take forever (about €9 to Il Campo, taxi tel. 0577-49-222).

To get from the station into town by **city bus,** buy a €1 ticket from the newsstand or information window in the station lobby (daily 6:00–20:00), or from the blue machine in the lobby (touch screen for English and select "urban" for type of ticket). Then walk to the bus stop—a covered shelter under the umbrella pines 100 yards to your left as you exit the station—by crossing the parking lot and the wide roundabout in front of the station. Buses pick up travelers only at this covered stop (not at the station). Buses run about every 10 minutes (fewer on Sun and after 22:00).

Every orange bus goes from here to the town center. (Caution: Blue ones go to other cities.) Confirm by asking *"Centro?"* and then punch your ticket in the machine on the bus to validate it; ride to the last stop, Piazza Gramsci (or nearby Piazza del Sale).

To leave Siena by train, catch a city bus from Piazza Gramsci to the station. Confirm with the driver that the bus is going to the *stazione* (stat-zee-OH-nay). Remember to purchase your ticket in advance from a *tabacchi* shop.

By Intercity Bus: Buses arrive in Siena at Piazza Gramsci (a few blocks from city center). The main bus companies are Sena and the confusingly named Tra-In (TRAH-in). Day-trippers can store baggage underneath Piazza Gramsci in Sottopassaggio la Lizza (€3.50, daily 7:00–19:45, no overnight storage).

By Car: Drivers coming from the *autostrada* take the *Siena Ovest* exit and follow signs for *Centro*, then *Stadio* (stadium, soccer ball). The soccer-ball signs take you to the stadium lot (Parcheggio Stadio, €1.60/hr, pay when you leave) near the huge, bare-brick Church of San Domenico. The Fortezza lot nearby charges the same amount. Technically, hotel customers are allowed to drop bags off at their hotel before finding a place to park overnight, but getting permission to do so isn't worth the trouble. On parking spots, blue stripes mean "pay and display"; white stripes mean "free parking." You can park free in the lot west of the Fortezza, in white-striped spots behind Hotel Villa Liberty, behind the Fortezza, and overnight in most city lots from 20:00–8:00.

Helpful Hints

Combo-Tickets: A deranged person cobbled together a pile of illogically paired combo-tickets to give some travelers a small savings. Nothing covers everything, and most are conflicting. The meager savings are just not worth the brain power it takes to figure out the system. The only worthwhile combo-ticket is "My Name is Duccio," which covers the Duomo and Duomo Museum (buy at museum, skip line at Duomo).

Wednesday Morning Market: The weekly market (clothes, knick-knacks, and food) sprawls between the Fortezza and Piazza Gramsci along Viale Cesare Maccari and the adjacent Viale XXV Aprile.

Internet Access: In this university town, there are lots of places to get plugged in. **Internet Point** is just off Piazza Matteotti, at Via Paradiso 10 (just downhill from McDonald's, Mon–Fri 9:00–13:00 & 15:00–20:00, closed Sat–Sun). **Internet Train,** near Il Campo at Via di Città 121 is part of a chain; buying a

Siena at a Glance

▲▲▲**Il Campo** Best square in Italy. **Hours:** Always open.

▲▲▲**Duomo** Art-packed cathedral with mosaic floors and statues by Michelangelo and Bernini. **Hours:** March–Oct Mon–Sat 10:30–19:00, Sun 13:30–17:30, Nov–Feb Mon–Sat 10:30–17:00, Sun 13:30–16:30.

▲▲**Duomo Museum** Displays cathedral art (including Duccio's *Maestà*) and offers sweeping Tuscan view. **Hours:** Daily March–Oct 9:30–19:00, Nov–Feb 9:30–17:00.

▲**Palio al Cinema** Short film runs away with horse-racing history. **Hours:** May–mid-June and mid-Sept–Oct Mon–Sat 9:30–15:30, mid-June–mid-Sept Mon–Sat 9:30–17:30, closed Sun; no film Nov–April.

▲**Civic Museum** City museum in City Hall with Sienese frescoes of Good and Bad Government. **Hours:** Daily March–Oct 10:00–19:00, Nov–Feb 10:00–17:30. May be open late summer evenings.

▲**City Tower** 330-foot tower climb. **Hours:** Daily March–Oct 10:00–19:00, Nov–Feb 10:00–16:00.

▲**Pinacoteca** Fine Sienese paintings. **Hours:** Sun–Mon 8:30–13:15, Tue–Sat 8:15–19:15.

▲**Baptistery** Cave-like building has baptismal font decorated by Ghiberti and Donatello. **Hours:** Daily March–Oct 9:30–19:00, Nov–Feb 9:30–17:00.

▲**Santa Maria della Scala** Museum with vibrant ceiling and wall frescoes depicting day-to-day life in a medieval hospital, much of the original *Fountain of Joy*, and an Etruscan artifact exhibit. **Hours:** Daily mid-March–Oct 10:30–18:30, Nov–mid-March 10:30–16:30.

Church of San Domenico Huge brick church with St. Catherine's head and thumb. **Hours:** Daily March–Oct 7:00–18:30, Nov–Feb 9:00–18:00.

Sanctuary of St. Catherine Home of St. Catherine. **Hours:** Daily 9:30–18:00.

card here gives you access to places all over Italy (Mon–Sat 10:00–20:00, Sun 12:00–20:00, tel. 0577-226-366).

Books: The Book Shop sells books in English with an emphasis on Italian-related topics. Lisa, the American who runs the shop, stocks Rick Steves guidebooks, too (Mon–Sat 10:00–19:30, closed Sun, off Via di Città just before the Pinacoteca at Galleria S. Pietro 19). The **Feltrinelli** bookstore closer to the Campo also sells books and magazines in English (daily 9:00–19:30, Banchi di Sopra 52).

Laundry: Two modern, self-service launderettes are **Lavarapido Wash and Dry** (Via di Pantaneto 38, near Logge del Papa) and **Onda Blu** (Via del Casato di Sotto 17, 50 yards from Il Campo). Both are open daily 8:00–22:00, with last loads at 21:00.

Travel Agency: Palio Viaggi, on Piazza Gramsci, sells train and plane tickets but no bus tickets (Mon–Fri 9:00–13:00 & 15:00–19:00, Sat 9:00–13:30, closed Sun, La Lizza 12, tel. 0577-280-828, info@palioviaggi.it).

Local Guides: Roberto Bechi, a hardworking Sienese guide, specializes in off-the-beaten-path tours of the surrounding countryside by minibus (up to eight passengers, convenient pick-up at hotel). Married to an American (Patti) and having run restaurants in Siena and the US, Roberto communicates well with Americans. His passions are Sienese culture, Tuscan history, and local cuisine. Ideally, you should book well in advance, but you might be able to schedule a tour if you call the day before (seven different tours: full-day tours €70–90/person, half-day tours €25–75/person, entry fees are extra, mobile 328-727-3186 or 328-425-5648, www.toursbyroberto.com, info@toursbyroberto.com). If he's booked, Roberto can recommend other good guides.

    Federica Olla is a smart young guide with a knack for creative teaching (mobile 338-133-9525, olla.siena@tin.it). **Maria Torchio** is also good (mariaelenatorchio-siena@virgilio.it). The standard fee for local guides is €55 per hour.

    Il Casato Viaggi runs half-day bus tours from Siena into Chianti country—with winery visits and tastings—and the Tuscan countryside (€35, 10 percent discount with this book, four different 5-hour tours, live guides, leave from Piazza Gramsci, office at Via Il Casato di Sotto 12, tel. 057-746-091, www.terresiena.it).

SIGHTS

▲▲▲ Il Campo: Siena's Main Square

Il Campo is the heart—geographically and metaphorically—of Siena. The square fans out from the City Hall (Palazzo Pubblico) to create an amphitheater, where the citizens are the stars.

Originally, this area was just a field *(campo)* located outside the former city walls. You can still see some of the old tufa-stone blocks incorporated into today's redbrick Caffè Fonte Gaia (along the right side of the square as you face City Hall).

As the city expanded, Il Campo eventually became the historic junction of Siena's various competing districts, or *contrade,* and the old marketplace. The brick surface is divided into nine sections, representing the council of nine merchants and city bigwigs who ruled medieval Siena. The square and its buildings are the color of the soil upon which they stand...a color known to artists and Crayola-users as "Burnt Sienna."

The City Hall and its 330-foot tower dominate the square. In medieval Siena, this secular building was the center of the city, and the whole focus of the Campo flows down to it.

The City Hall's 330-foot-tall **City Tower** (Torre del Mangia), Italy's tallest secular tower, was named after a hedonistic watchman who consumed his earnings like a glutton consumes food—his chewed-up statue is in the courtyard, to the left as you enter. (Tower admission details below.)

The chapel located at the base of the tower was built in 1348 as thanks to God for ending the Black Death (after it killed more than a third of the population). It should also be used to thank God that the tower—just plunked onto the building with no extra foundation—still stands. These days, the chapel is used only to bless the Palio contestants, and the tower's bell only rings for the race.

The *Fountain of Joy (Fonte Gaia)* by Jacopo della Quercia marks the square's high point. Find the snake-handler woman, the two naked guys about to be tossed in, and the pigeons politely waiting their turn to tightrope gingerly down slippery spouts to slurp a drink from wolves' snouts. The relief panel on the left

Siena

- View
- Parking

1 Sottopassaggio la Lizza (Underground Bus Depot, Bag Storage & Bus Tickets)
2 Palio al Cinema
3 Il Casato Viaggi Tours
4 Palio Viaggi Travel Agency

(as you face the fountain) shows God creating Adam by helping him to his feet. It's said that this reclining Adam influenced Michelangelo when he painted his Sistine Chapel ceiling. This fountain is a copy—you can see most of the original fountain in an interesting exhibit at Siena's Santa Maria della Scala, described on page 470.

To say that Siena and Florence have always been competitive

is an understatement. In medieval times, a statue of Venus stood on Il Campo. After the plague hit Siena, the monks blamed the pagan statue. The people cut it to pieces and buried it along the walls of Florence.

Picture Il Campo during the famous Palio horse races (every year on July 2 and Aug 16). Ten snorting horses and their nervous riders (selected from 17 *contrade,* or neighborhoods) line up near the Antica Siena shop (right side of square) to await the starting signal. Then they race like crazy three times around the perimeter (the gray pavement), which is covered with dirt. Mattresses pad the sharpest turns. Spectators waving the banners of their neighborhoods cram (for free) into the center of the square or watch from temporary bleachers or, if they have the money, from the balconies. Every possible vantage point and perch is packed with people straining to see the action. The winner crosses the line, and 1/17th of Siena goes berserk for the next 365 days.

▲**Civic Museum (Museo Civico)**—At the base of the City Tower is Siena's City Hall (Palazzo Pubblico), the spot where secular government got its start in early Renaissance Europe. There, you'll find city government still at work, along with a sampling of local art.

In the following order, you'll see: the Sala Risorgimento, with dramatic scenes of Victor Emmanuel I's unification of Italy (surrounded by statues that don't seem to care); the chapel, with impressive inlaid-wood chairs in the choir; and the Sala del Mappamondo, with Siena's first fresco, Simone Martini's *Maestà* (*Enthroned Virgin*—a groundbreaking, down-to-earth Madonna), facing the faded *Guidoriccio da Folignano* (a mercenary providing a more concrete form of protection).

Next is the Sala della Pace—where the city's fat cats met. Looking down on the oligarchy during their meetings were two interesting frescoes, *Effects of Good and Bad Government.* Notice the whistle-while-you-work happiness of the utopian community ruled by the utopian government (in the better-preserved fresco) and the fate of a community ruled by politicians with more typical values (in a terrible state of repair). The message: Without justice, there can be no prosperity.

Siena's Palio

In the Palio, the feisty spirit of Siena's 17 *contrade* (neighborhoods) lives on. Each *contrada* has its own parish church, well, or fountain,

and even a historical museum. Each is represented by a mascot (porcupine, unicorn, wolf, and so on) and unique colors worn proudly by residents.

Contrada pride is evident year-round in Florence's parades and colorful banners, lamps, and wall plaques. (If you hear the thunder of distant drumming, run to it for some medieval action, often featuring flag-throwers.) You are welcome to participate in these lively neighborhood festivals. Buy a scarf in *contrada* colors, grab a glass of Chianti, munch on some *panforte*, and join in the merriment.

Contrada passion is most visible twice a year—on July 2 and August 16—when the city erupts during its world-famous horse race, the Palio di Siena. Ten of the 17 neighborhoods compete (chosen by rotation and lot), hurling themselves with medieval abandon into several days of trial races and traditional revelry. Jockeys—usually from out of town—are considered hired guns... paid mercenaries. Bets are placed on which *contrada* will win... and lose. Despite the shady behind-the-scenes dealing, on the big day, the horses are taken into their *contrada's* church to be blessed. ("Go and return victorious," says the priest.) It's considered a sign of luck if a horse leaves droppings in the church.

On the evening of the race, Il Campo is stuffed to the brim with locals and tourists. Dirt is brought in and packed down to create the track's surface, while mattresses pad the walls of surrounding buildings. The most treacherous spots are the sharp corners, where many a rider bites the dust. One lap around the course is about a third of a mile (350 meters); three laps make a full circuit. In this literally no-holds-barred race—which lasts

Take a moment to savor one of those to-sigh-for rural panoramas out the window of the Sala della Pace. The view is essentially the same as that from the top of the big stairs.

Cost and Hours: €7.50, €12 combo-ticket with City Tower. Daily March–Oct 10:00–19:00, Nov–Feb 10:00–17:30, last entry 45 min before closing; may be open late on summer evenings. Tel. 0577-292-232.

▲**City Tower (Torre del Mangia)**—Siena gathers around its City Hall more than its church. Medieval Siena was a proud republic,

just more than a minute—a horse can win even without its rider (jockeys perch precariously without saddles on the sweaty horses' backs, and often fall off).

The winning neighborhood is the scene of grand celebrations afterward. Winners receive a *palio* (banner), typically painted by a local artist and always featuring the Virgin Mary. But the true prize is proving your *contrada* is *numero uno,* and mocking your losing rival.

All over town, sketches and posters depict the Palio. This is not some folkloristic event. It's a real medieval moment. If you're packed onto the square with 15,000 people, all hungry for victory, you won't see much, but you'll feel it. Bleacher and balcony seats are expensive, but it's free to join the masses in the square. Be sure to go with an empty bladder as there are no WCs, and be prepared to surrender any sense of personal space.

While the actual Palio packs the city, you could side-trip in from Florence to see the horse-racing trials—called *prove*—each of the three days before the main event (usually at 9:00 and about 19:30, free seats in bleachers). For more information, visit www .ilpalio.org.

▲**Palio al Cinema**—This 20-minute film, *Siena, the Palio, and its History,* helps recreate the craziness. See it at the air-conditioned Cinema Moderno in Piazza Tolomei, two blocks from Il Campo (€5.25, with this book pay €4.25/person or €8/two, get the DVD for €10, film shows May–Oct only; May–mid-June and mid-Sept– Oct Mon–Sat 9:30–15:30, mid-June–mid-Sept Mon–Sat 9:30–17:30, closed Sun; English showings generally hourly at half past the hour—schedule posted on door, tel. 0577-289-201). Call or drop by to confirm when the next English showing is scheduled—there are usually nine a day.

and this tall tower is the exclamation point of its "declaration of independence." Its 300 steps get pretty skinny at the top, but the reward is one of Italy's best views (€6, €12 combo-ticket includes Civic Museum, daily March–Oct 10:00–19:00, Nov–Feb 10:00–16:00, last

entry 45 min before closing, closed in rain, sometimes long lines, avoid midday crowd, limit of 30 tourists at a time, often sold out, mandatory and free bag check).

▲**Pinacoteca**—If you're into medieval art, you'll likely find this quiet, uncrowded, colorful museum delightful. The museum takes you on a walk through Siena's art chronologically from the 12th through the 16th century, when a revolution in realism was percolating in Tuscany. For the casual sightseer, the Sienese art in the Civic and Duomo Museums is adequate. But art fans enjoy this opportunity to trace the evolution of Siena's delicate and elegant works, from stiff, gold-backed icon-like Madonnas to curvy, graceful Madonnas to Italian Renaissance. Concentrate on pieces by Duccio (artist of the *Maestà* in the Duomo Museum), Simone Martini (who did the *Maestà* in the Civic Museum), the brothers Ambrogio and Pietro Lorenzetti (Ambrogio did the *Effects of Good and Bad Government* in the Civic Museum), Pinturicchio (who did the Piccolomini Library in the Duomo), and Domenico Beccafumi (who inlaid pavement in the Duomo).

Cost, Hours, Location: €4, Sun–Mon 8:30–13:15, Tue–Sat 8:15–19:15, last entry 30 min before closing, free and mandatory bag check, tel. 0577-46-052). To reach the museum from Il Campo, walk out Via di Città and go left on Via San Pietro.

Siena's Cathedral Area

▲▲▲**Duomo**—If the Campo is the heart of Siena, the Duomo (or cathedral) is its soul. The white and dark-green striped church,

sitting on an artificial platform atop Siena's highest point, is visible for miles around. The current structure dates from 1215, with the major decoration done during Siena's heyday from 1250–1350. This ornate but surprisingly secular shrine to the Virgin Mary is stacked with colorful art inside and out, from the inlaid-marble floors to the stained-glass windows. The interior is a Renaissance riot of striped columns, intricate marble inlays, Michelangelo statues, and Bernini sculptures. In the Piccolomini Library, a series of captivating frescoes by the Umbrian painter Pinturicchio tell the story of Aeneas Piccolomini, Siena's consummate Renaissance Man who became Pope Pius II.

Cost and Hours: €3 includes cathedral and Piccolomini Library, €6 "My Name is Duccio" combo-ticket includes Duomo Museum (sold 100 yards away at the museum, allows you to skip the line at the Duomo). There's a €3.50 audioguide for the church and the library; add the Duomo Museum and it's €4.50

(ID required for deposit). The Duomo and Library are both open March–Oct Mon–Sat 10:30–19:00, Sun 13:30–17:30, Nov–Feb Mon–Sat 10:30–17:00, Sun 13:30–16:30, last entry 30 min before closing. Modest dress is required to enter, but paper ponchos are provided if needed.

Audioguides: Audioguide for church and library-€3.50; add the Duomo Museum-€4.50 (ID required for deposit). Two headphones are available at a price break.

➲ Self-Guided Tour: In the **nave**, the heads of 172 popes—who reigned from St. Peter to the 12th century—peer down from above, looking over the fine inlaid art on the floor. With a forest of striped columns, a coffered dome, a large stained-glass window at the far end (it's a copy—the original is viewable close-up in the nearby Duomo Museum), and a museum's worth of early Renaissance art, this is one busy interior. Looking closer at the popes, you see the same four faces repeated over and over.

For almost two centuries (1373–1547), 40 artists paved the marble floor with scenes from the Old Testament, allegories, and intricate patterns. The earliest are simple black-and-white, with engraved details, but the later ones use inlay technique with many colored marbles. The series starts with historical allegories near the entrance. The larger, more elaborate scenes surrounding the altar are mostly stories from the Old Testament. Many of the floor panels may be protected with sheet flooring.

Grab a seat under the **dome**. It sits on a 12-sided base but its "coffered" ceiling is actually a painted illusion. Get oriented to the vast church's array of sights by thinking of the floor as a big 12-hour clock. You're the middle, and the altar is high noon: You'll find the *Slaughter of the Innocents* pavement panel roped off on the floor at 10:00, Pisano's pulpit between two pillars at 11:00, Duccio's round stained-glass window at high noon, Bernini's chapel at 3:00, the Piccolomini Altar with a Michelangelo statue (next to doorway leading to a shop, snacks, and WC) at 7:00, the Piccolomini Library at 8:00, and a Donatello statue at 9:00.

Nicola Pisano's octagonal Carrara marble **pulpit** (1268) rests on the backs of lions—symbols of Christianity triumphant. Like the lions, the Church eats its catch (devouring paganism) and nurses its cubs. The seven relief panels tell the life of Christ in rich detail. (Buy light from the coin-op machine.)

Above is Duccio's stained-glass **Rose Window.** This is a copy of the original window, which was moved to the Duomo Museum a few years ago. The famous rose window was created in 1288 and dedicated to the Virgin Mary. For more information, read the complete description on page 469.

Look for the *Slaughter of the Innocents* inlaid pavement panel. Herod (left), sitting enthroned amid Renaissance arches, orders the massacre of all babies, to prevent the coming of the promised Messiah. It's a chaotic scene of angry soldiers, grieving mothers, and dead babies, reminding locals that a republic ruled by a tyrant will experience misery.

Donatello's rugged *St. John the Baptist* in his famous rags stands in a chapel to the right of the library. To understand why Giovanni Lorenzo Bernini is considered the greatest Baroque sculptor, step into the sumptuous **Bernini Chapel.** This last work in the cathedral, from 1659, is enough to make even a Lutheran light a candle. Move up to the altar and look back at the two Bernini statues: Mary Magdalene in a state of spiritual ecstasy and St. Jerome playing the crucifix like a violinist lost in beautiful music.

Over the altar is the *Madonna del Voto,* a Madonna and Child painted by Duccio and adorned with a real crown of gold and jewels. Tilting her head, she looks out sympathetically. This is the Mary that the Palio is dedicated to, special in the hearts of the Sienese. The faithful's prayers to Mary are accompanied by offerings, found outside the chapel, hanging on the wall to the left, as you exit.

The **Piccolomini Altar** (left wall, marble altarpiece decorated with statues), was designed for the tomb of the Sienese-born Pope Pius III. It's most interesting for Michelangelo's statue of Paul (lower right, who is clearly more interesting than the bland, bored popes above him). Paul has the look of Michelangelo's *Moses,* the broken-nosed self-portrait of the sculptor himself, and the dangling hand of his *David.* It was the chance to sculpt *David* in Florence that enticed Michelangelo to abandon the Siena project.

The brilliantly frescoed **Piccolomini Library** captures the exuberant, optimistic spirit of the 1400s, when humanism and the Renaissance were born. The frescoes, never restored, look nearly as vivid today as the day they were finished 550 years ago. The painter Pinturicchio (c. 1454–1513) was hired to celebrate the life of one of Siena's hometown boys. Start from the window and work clockwise, following 10 scenes in the life of the man many call "the first humanist," Aeneas Piccolomini (1405–1464), who became Pope Pius II.

The library also contains intricately decorated, illuminated music scores, and a statue (a Roman copy of a Greek original) of the Three Graces.

Exit the Duomo, and make a U-turn to the left, walking alongside the church to Piazza Jacopo della Quercia. Worshippers

would have entered the church from the far end of the piazza through the unfinished wall. (Look way up at the highest part of the unfinished church wall. That's the viewpoint accessible from inside the Duomo Museum.) The nave of the Duomo was supposed to be where the piazza is today.

When rival republic Florence began its grand cathedral, proud Siena decided to build the biggest church in all Christendom. The existing cathedral would be used as a transept. Some of the nave's green-and-white-striped columns were built, but are now filled in with a brick wall. The wall, connecting the Duomo with the museum of the cathedral, was as far as Siena got before a plague killed the city's ability to finish the project. Round white stones in the pavement mark the place where columns would have stood. Look through the unfinished entrance facade, seeing blue sky where the stained-glass windows might have been, and ponder the struggles, triumphs, and failures of the human spirit.

▲▲**Duomo Museum (Museo dell'Opera e Panorama)**—On the Il Campo side of the church (look for the yellow signs), Siena's most enjoyable museum was built to house the

cathedral's art. The ground floor is filled with the cathedral's original Gothic sculpture by Giovanni Pisano (who spent 10 years in the late 1200s carving and orchestrating the decoration of the cathedral) and a fine Donatello *Madonna and Child*. A slender, tender Mary gazes down at her chubby-cheeked baby, and her sad eyes say she knows the eventual fate of her son.

On the opposite side of the room is Duccio's stained-glass Rose Window. Until a couple of years ago, this original window was located above and behind the Duomo's altar. Now the church has a copy, and art-lovers can enjoy a close-up look at this masterpiece. The rose window—20 feet across, made in 1288—is dedicated (like the church and the city itself) to the Virgin Mary and combines elements from rigid Byzantine icons with a budding sense of 3-D realism.

Upstairs to the left awaits a private audience with Duccio's *Maestà* (*Enthroned Virgin*, 1311). Grab a seat and study one of the great pieces of medieval art. The flip side of the *Maestà* (displayed on the opposite wall) features 26 smaller panels—the medieval equivalent of pages—showing colorful scenes from the Passion of Christ.

Climb onto the "Panorama del Facciatone." For a surprise view of Siena, leave the landing just before the top floor, walk through the rooms on the right—a stairwell is through the small doorway. Climb down the steps and then up the claustrophobic spiral staircase to the viewpoint. Look back over the Duomo and consider this: If the grandiose plan for the church had been completed, you'd be looking straight down the nave.

Cost and Hours: €6 "My Name is Duccio" combo-ticket includes the Duomo; worthwhile 40-min audioguide-€3, audioguide with Duomo-€4.50, ID required for deposit; daily March–Oct 9:30–19:00, Nov–Feb 9:30–17:00, tel. 0577-283-048.

▲**Baptistery**—Siena is so hilly that there wasn't enough flat ground on which to build a big church. What to do? Build a big church and prop up the overhanging edge with the Baptistery. This dark and quietly tucked-away cave of art is worth a look for its cool tranquility and the bronze panels and angels—by Ghiberti, Donatello, and others—adorning the pedestal of the baptismal font (€3, daily March–Oct 9:30–19:00, Nov–Feb 9:30–17:00, confirm with TI).

The nearby "crypt" of the cathedral is important archaeologically, but expensive and of little interest to the average tourist.

▲**Santa Maria della Scala**—This museum (opposite the Duomo entrance) was used as a hospital until the 1980s. Its labyrinthine 12th-century cellars—carved out of tufa and finished with brick—go down several floors, and once stored supplies for the hospital upstairs during medieval times. Today, the hospital and its cellars are filled with museum exhibits, including these main attractions: the fancy frescoed hall (Pellegrinaio Hall, ground floor), most of the original *Fountain of Joy*, St. Catherine's Oratory chapel (first basement), and the Etruscan collection in the Archaeological Museum (second basement).

Pellegrinaio Hall: Sumptuously frescoed, this hall shows medieval Siena's innovative health care and social welfare system in action (c. 1442, wonderfully described in English). Starting in the 11th century, the hospital nursed the sick and cared for abandoned children, as is vividly portrayed in these frescoes. The good works paid off, as bequests and donations poured in, creating the wealth that's evident throughout this building.

Fountain of Joy **Exhibit:** Downstairs you'll find an engaging exhibit on Jacopo della Quercia's early 15th-century *Fountain of Joy (Fonte Gaia)*—and the disassembled pieces of the original fountain itself. In the 19th century, after serious deterioration, the ornate fountain was dismantled and plaster casts were made. (From these casts, they made the replica that graces Il Campo today.) Here you'll see the eroded original panels paired with their restored casts, along with the original statues that used to stand on the edges of the fountain.

On the same floor, pop into the small chapel or oratory where St. Catherine prayed and received visions. A holy nail thought to be from Jesus' cross is on the altar.

Archaeological Museum: Descend into the cavernous second basement under groin vaults to be alone with piles of ancient Etruscan stuff excavated from tombs centuries before Christ (displayed in a labyrinthine exhibit). Remember, the Etruscans dominated this part of Italy before the Roman Empire swept through—even Rome originated as an Etruscan town.

Cost and Hours: €6, €10 combo-ticket with Civic Museum, daily mid-March–Oct 10:30–18:30, Nov–mid-March 10:30–16:30, last entry 30 min before closing. The chapel just inside the door to your left is free (English description inside chapel entrance on left).

Siena's San Domenico Area

Church of San Domenico—This huge brick church is worth a quick look. The spacious, plain interior (except for the colorful flags

of the city's 17 *contrade*, or neighborhoods) fits the austere philosophy of the Dominicans and invites meditation on the thoughts and deeds of St. Catherine. Walk up the steps in the rear to see paintings from the life of St. Catherine, patron saint of Siena. Halfway up the church on the right, find a metal bust of St. Catherine, a small case that contains her thumb (sometimes loaned out to other churches), and a reliquary on the lowest shelf that contains the chain she used to scourge herself. In the chapel (15 feet to the left), surrounded by candles, you'll see Catherine's actual head atop the altar (free, daily March–Oct 7:00–18:30, Nov–Feb 9:00–18:00; WC for €0.50 at far end of parking lot—facing church entrance, it's to your right).

Sanctuary of St. Catherine—Step into Catherine's cool and peaceful home. Siena remembers its favorite hometown gal, a simple, unschooled, but mystically devout soul who, in the

St. Catherine of Siena
(1347–1380)

The youngest of 25 children born to a Sienese cloth dyer, Catherine began experiencing heavenly visions as a child. At 16, she became a Dominican nun, locking herself away for three years in a room in her family's house. She lived the life of an ascetic, which culminated in a vision wherein she married Christ. Catherine emerged from solitude to join her Dominican sisters, sharing her experiences, caring for the sick, and gathering both disciples and enemies. At age 23, she lapsed into a spiritual coma, waking with the heavenly command to spread her message to the world. She wrote essays and letters to kings, dukes, bishops, and popes, imploring them to find peace for a war-ravaged Italy. While visiting Pisa during Lent of 1375, she had a vision in which she received the stigmata, the wounds of Christ.

Still in her twenties, Catherine was invited to Avignon, France, where the pope had taken up residence. With her charm, sincerity, and reputation for holiness, she helped convince Pope Gregory XI to return the papacy to the city of Rome. Catherine also went to Rome, where she died young. She was canonized in the next generation (by a Sienese pope) and her relics were distributed to churches around Italy.

mid-1300s, helped convince the pope to return to Rome from France. This schism split the Continent in the 14th century, but because of her intervention, Catherine is honored today as Europe's patron saint. Pilgrims have visited her home since 1464, and architects and artists have greatly embellished what was probably once a humble home (her family worked as wool-dyers). Enter through the courtyard, and walk down the stairs at the far end. The church on your right contains the wooden crucifix upon which Catherine was meditating when she received the stigmata. The chapel on your left was originally the kitchen. Go down the stairs to the left of the kitchen to reach the saint's room. Catherine's bare cell is behind see-through doors. Much of the art throughout the sanctuary depicts scenes from her life (free, daily 9:30–18:00, Via Tiratoio). It's a few downhill blocks toward the center from San Domenico (follow signs to *Santuario di Santa Caterina*).

SHOPPING

The main drag, Via Banchi di Sopra, is a can-can of fancy shops. The big local department store is **Upim** (Mon–Sat 8:30–20:00, Sun 9:00–20:00, Piazza Matteotti).

For easy-to-pack souvenirs, get some of the large, colorful scarves/flags that depict the symbols of Siena's 17 different neighborhoods (such as the wolf, the turtle, and the snail). Pick up a few extra to decorate your home (€7 each for large size, sold at souvenir stands).

Local Sweets: All over town, **Prodotti Tipici** shops sell Sienese specialties. Siena's claim to caloric fame is its *panforte*, a rich, chewy concoction of nuts, honey, and candied fruits that impresses even fruitcake-haters. There are a few varieties: *margherita*, dusted in powdered sugar, is more fruity; *panpepato* has a spicy, peppery crust. Locals prefer a chewy, white macaroon-and-almond cookie called *ricciarelli*.

NIGHTLIFE

Join the evening *passeggiata* (peak strolling time is 19:00) along Via Banchi di Sopra with gelato in hand.

The **Enoteca Italiana** is a good wine bar in a cellar in the Fortezza (sample glasses in three different price ranges: €2, €3, €5.50; Mon 12:00–20:00, Tue–Sat 12:00–24:00, closed Sun; bottles and snacks available; cross bridge and enter fortress, go left down ramp, not to be confused with Enoteca Toscana—same location but not as nice, tel. 0577-288-497).

SLEEPING

Finding a room in Siena is tough during Easter (March 23 in 2008) or the Palio (July 2 and August 16). Call ahead any time of year, as all the guidebooks list Siena's few budget places. While day-tripping tour groups turn the town into a Gothic amusement park in midsummer, Siena is basically yours in the evenings and off-season.

Most of the listed hotels lie between Il Campo and the Church of San Domenico. Part of Siena's charm is its lively, festive character—this means that all hotels can be plagued with noise, even (and sometimes especially) the hotels in the pedestrian-only zone. If tranquility is important for your sanity, ask for a room that's off the street, or consider staying at the recommended places outside the center.

Simple Places Near Il Campo

Each of these listings is forgettable but inexpensive, and just a horse wreck away from one of Italy's most wonderful civic spaces.

$$ Palazzo Masi is a modern B&B run by husband-and-wife team Alizzardo and Daniela. Just steps away from Il Campo, it has six pleasant, quiet rooms and shared common areas on the second

Sleep Code

(€1 = about $1.30, country code: 39)
S = Single, **D** = Double/Twin, **T** = Triple, **Q** = Quad, **b** = bathroom,
s = shower only.

Breakfast is not included unless noted. If your hotel doesn't provide it, have breakfast on Il Campo or in a nearby bar. Credit cards are generally accepted, but I note if they aren't. (If you need cash, there are ATMs all over town.) Hotel staff generally speak English unless noted otherwise.

To help you sort easily through these listings, I've divided the rooms into three categories based on the price for a standard double room with bath:

$$$ **Higher Priced**—Most rooms €120 or more.
$$ **Moderately Priced**—Most rooms between €90–120.
$ **Lower Priced**—Most rooms €90 or less.

and third floors of a renovated medieval 14th-century townhouse (D-€80, Db-€120, these rates promised to readers through 2008 if you book direct, cash only; take the road to the far right of the City Hall as you're facing it and head down Casato di Sotto for about 50 yards to Via Casato di Sotto 29; tel. 0577-378-150, mobile 349-600-9155, fax 0577-288-928, www.palazzomasi.it, info@palazzomasi.it).

$$ Palazzo Bruchi B&B offers seven tranquil rooms in a 17th-century palazzo that overlooks the Tuscan countryside. There's one fancy, spacious room *(luxe)* that features Old World, heavy walnut furnishings and period paintings. The six other rooms are smaller, named for flowers, have a bright cheery decor, and overlook a quiet interior courtyard. Mariacristina and her daughter Camilla take good care of their guests (Sb-€75–90, Db-€85–100, *luxe* Db/Tb-€150, Tb-€120–175, 4 percent cash discount, elevator; take Banchi di Sotto until it turns into Via Pantaneto, located on left, just before the Church of San Giorgio at Via Pantaneto 105; tel. & fax 0577-287-342, www.palazzobruchi.it, masignani@hotmail.com).

$ Albergo Tre Donzelle is a fine budget value with 20 plain, institutional, and well-worn rooms. Don't hang out here...think of Il Campo, a block away, as your terrace (S-€38, D-€49, Db-€60, T-€70, Tb-€85; with your back to the tower, leave Il Campo to the right at 2:00, Via Donzelle 5; tel. 0577-280-358, fax 0577-223-933, tredonzelle@hotmail.it).

$ Piccolo Hotel Etruria has 20 decent air-conditioned rooms but not much soul. The hotel is a bit overpriced though well-located and sleepable (S-€48, Sb-€53, Db-€86, Tb-€114, Qb-€142,

Siena Hotels

1. Palazzo Masi & Onda Blu Launderette
2. To Palazzo Bruchi B&B, Hotel Santa Caterina, Hotel Porta Romana & Res. d'Epoca Borgognini
3. Albergo Tre Donzelle
4. Piccolo Hotel Etruria
5. Locanda Garibaldi
6. Hotel Cannon d'Oro
7. Casa di Antonella B&B
8. To Hotel Duomo & Pensione Palazzo Ravizza
9. Hotel Chiusarelli
10. To Hotel Villa Elda & Hotel Villa Liberty
11. Alma Domus
12. Albergo Bernini
13. To Guidoriccio Youth Hostel
14. Lavarapido Launderette

optional breakfast-€5, curfew at 1:00, next to Albergo Tre Donzelle at Via Donzelle 1–3, tel. 0577-288-088, fax 0577-288-461, www .hoteletruria.com, info@hoteletruria.com, Fattorini family).

$ Locanda Garibaldi is a modest, very Sienese place. Gentle Marcello rents seven pleasant rooms up a funky, artsy staircase (Db-€78, Tb-€100, family deals, cash only, takes reservations only a week in advance, half a block downhill off the square at Via Giovanni Dupre 18, tel. 0577-284-204, Marcello and Sonia speak very little English).

$ Hotel Cannon d'Oro, a few blocks up Via Banchi di Sopra, has 30 spacious and comfortable rooms, but is a bit noisy and group-friendly (Sb-€71, Db-€90, Tb-€115, Qb-€136, these discounted prices good with this book through 2008, family deals, includes breakfast, Via Montanini 28, tel. 0577-44-321, fax 0577-280-868, www.cannondoro.com, info@cannondoro.com, Maurizio). This is just a couple of blocks from the bus station.

$ Casa di Antonella B&B, in the heart of town, is neat-as-a-pin, relaxing, and a decent value. Antonella's five rooms have views of the Duomo, San Domenico, or the rooftops of Siena, and share a communal kitchen and dining room. Four rooms share two baths, and one room has a private bath (D-€65, includes buffet breakfast, no elevator, 3 floors up, located between Piazza Matteotti and Piazza Indipendenza on Via delle Terme 72, tel. & fax 0577-48-436, mobile 339-300-4883, anto.landi@libero.it). They also rent three €65 doubles in their annex.

Sleeping Fancy, Southwest of Il Campo

These two classy and well-run places are a 10-minute walk from Il Campo.

$$$ Hotel Duomo has 25 spacious rooms and a bizarre floor plan (Sb-€104, Db-€130, Tb-€171, Qb-€186, suite-€200, includes breakfast, air-con, elevator, picnic-friendly roof terrace, free parking; follow Via di Città—which becomes Via Stalloreggi—to Via Stalloreggi 38; tel. 0577-289-088, fax 0577-43-043, www .hotelduomo.it, booking@hotelduomo.it, Luca and Stefania). If you arrive by train, take a taxi (€8) or bus #3 to the Due Porte stop just a few steps from the hotel; if you drive, go to Porta San Marco, turn right and follow the signs to the hotel, drop off your bags, and then park in the nearby "Il Campo" lot.

$$$ Pensione Palazzo Ravizza is elegant and friendly, with an aristocratic feel and a peaceful garden (Sb-€140, small loft Db-€145, standard Db-€180, superior Db-€210—see website for room differences, Tb-€260, suites available, includes breakfast, back rooms face open country, air-con, elevator, good restaurant, free parking, Via Piano dei Mantellini 34, tel. 0577-280-462, fax 0577-221-597, www.palazzoravizza.it, bureau@palazzoravizza.it).

Near San Domenico Church

These hotels are within a 10-minute walk northeast of Il Campo. Albergo Bernini and Alma Domus, which enjoy views of the old town and cathedral, are about the best values in town.

$$$ Hotel Chiusarelli, with 49 rooms in a beautiful building, has a handy location but on a very busy street, making it a last resort. Expect traffic noise at night—ask for a quieter room in the back (can be guaranteed with reservation). Readers report that the staff is indifferent (S-€66, Sb-€85, Db-€125, Tb-€168, ask for Rick Steves discount when you book, air-con, rental bikes-€4/half-day, across from San Domenico at Viale Curtatone 15, tel. 0577-280-562, fax 0577-271-177, www.chiusarelli.com, info @chiusarelli.com).

$$ Hotel Villa Elda rents 11 bright and light rooms in a newly renovated villa. Classy and stately, it's in a fine neighborhood just a few minutes' walk past the Church of San Domenico (Db-€120, extra person €15; 10 percent discount promised by Sr. Polzinetti if you have this book, request when you reserve, and stay two nights or more; includes breakfast, air-con, Viale Ventiquattro Maggio 10, tel. 0577-247-927, www.villaeldasiena.it, info@villaeldasiena.it).

$$ Hotel Villa Liberty, a bit farther out, is a former private mansion with 18 big, bright, comfortable rooms and lots of street noise (Sb-€70, Db-€110–120, air-con, elevator, bar, courtyard, free and easy street parking, facing fortress at Viale V. Veneto 11, tel. 0577-44-966, fax 0577-44-770, www.villaliberty.it, info @villaliberty.it).

$ Alma Domus is ideal—unless nuns make you nervous, you need a double bed, or you plan on staying out past the 23:30 curfew (no mercy given). This hotel (it's not a convent) is run with firm but angelic smiles by non-English-speaking sisters who offer 43 clean, quiet, little rooms for a steal and save the best views for foreigners. Bright lamps, quaint balconies, fine views, grand public rooms, top security, and a pleasant atmosphere make this a great value. The checkout time is strictly 10:00, but they will store your luggage in their secure courtyard (Sb-€42, Db-€65, Tb-€80, Qb-€95, cash only, ask for view room *(con vista)*, central air-con, elevator; from San Domenico, walk downhill with the church on your right toward the view, turn left down Via Camporegio, make a U-turn at the little chapel down the brick steps to Via Camporegio 37; tel. 0577-44-177, fax 0577-47-601).

$ Albergo Bernini makes you part of a Sienese family in a modest, clean home with nine fine rooms. Friendly Nadia and Mauro and son Alessandro (who speaks English) welcome you to their spectacular view terrace for breakfast and picnic lunches and dinners (Sb-€78, D-€62, Db-€82, less in winter, breakfast-€7, cash only, non-smoking, midnight curfew, on the main Il Campo–San

Domenico drag at Via Sapienza 15, tel. & fax 0577-289-047, www
.albergobernini.com, hbernin@tin.it). When booked up, they recommend their charming, bigger, but more expensive apartments
(Db-€100, non-smoking, no curfew, located just a few steps downhill from Albergo).

Southeast of Il Campo, Farther from the Center

The first two places are near each other, just outside the Porta
Romana city gate. To get to and from downtown Siena (Piazza del
Mercato, just below Il Campo), catch shuttle bus #A (4/hr, €1). To
connect with the bus and train stations, take bus #2 (2/hr). For the
location of the hotels, see the map on page 475.

$$$ **Hotel Santa Caterina** is a three-star, 18th-century place.
Professionally run with real attention to quality, most of the
hotel's 22 comfortable rooms were recently renovated, and there's a
delightful garden outside (Sb-€105, small Db-€105, Db-€145, Tb-
€195, prices promised with this book through 2008, includes buf-
fet breakfast, fridge in room, elevator; garden side is quieter, but
street side—with multipaned windows—isn't bad; parking-€15/
day—request when you reserve, 100 yards outside Porta Romana at
Via E.S. Piccolomini 7, tel. 0577-221-105, fax 0577-271-087, www
.hscsiena.it, info@hscsiena.it, Lorenza and Andrea).

$$ **Hotel Porta Romana** is at the edge of town off a busy
road. Twelve rooms face the open countryside and breakfast is
served in the garden (Sb-€90, Db-€110, extra person-€20, 10 percent Rick Steves discount if you book direct and pay cash, family rooms, free parking, 50 yards from convenient bus to center,
Via E.S. Piccolomini 35, tel. 0577-42299, www.hotelportaromana
.com, info@hotelportaromana.com, Anna).

$$ **Residenza d'Epoca Borgognini** is a grand old palazzo
with seven cool, solid, and tastefully decorated rooms. You'll find
high ceilings, lots of stairs, and a warm welcome from Maria
Antonietta (D-€80, Db-€90, Tb-€120–150, 10 percent discount
with this book and cash in 2008, save even more with three-night
stay, includes breakfast at nearby bar, Via Pantaneto 160, tel. &
fax 0577-44-055, mobile 338-764-0933, www.hotelborgognini.it,
hotelborgognini@yahoo.it).

$ **Guidoriccio Youth Hostel** has 100 cheap beds and wel-
comes anyone, but is outside the center (€14 beds in doubles,
triples, and dorms with sheets, D-€28, cash only, €2 breakfast,
lock-out 9:30–14:00, bus #10 or #77 from train station or bus #10
or #15 from Piazza Gramsci—about 20 min, Via Fiorentina 89
in Stellino neighborhood, tel. 0577-52-212, fax 0577-50-277, siena
@ostellionline.org).

Outside of Siena

The following accommodations, best for drivers, are in the lush, peaceful countryside surrounding Siena. To locate these places, see the map on page 457.

$$$ Frances' Lodge is a small farmhouse B&B a mile out of Siena. Franca and Franco rent four modern rooms and two apartment-suites in a rustic yet elegant old place with an inviting living room, swimming pool, peaceful garden, eight acres of olive trees and vineyards, and great Siena views (small Db-€160, Db-€190, Db suite-€250, Tb-€210–220, Tb suite-€250, Qb suite-€280, these prices promised to Rick Steves readers through 2008, includes great breakfast, air-con-€10, easy parking, €10 taxi into town, Strada di Valdipugna 2, tel. & fax 0577-281-061, www.franceslodge.it). Consider a view picnic dinner in their garden.

$$$ Borgo Argenina is a well-maintained, pricey splurge of a B&B, located a 20-minute drive north of Siena in the Chianti region. It's run by helpful Elena Nappa (Db-€180, beautiful gardens, tel. 0577-747-117, fax 0577-747-228, www.borgoargenina.it, info@borgoargenina.it).

$ Agriturismo Poggio Salvi has three pleasant, spacious apartments—rentable only by the week—set in a grassy field near the tiny burg of Poggio Salvi, 15 minutes southwest of Siena. Dwellings are separate with modern conveniences (rentals from Sat–Sat, €620/2 people and €970/4 people during high season, Loc. Poggio Salvi 249, 53010 San Rocco a Pilli, tel. & fax 0577-349-443, mobile 333-290-7890, fax 0577-347-686, www.poggiosalvi.net, info@poggiosalvi.net).

$ Parri Nada Farmhouse, a good choice for families, is tucked away in the vineyards in the hills of Chianti 12 miles northeast of Siena. Luca and Elena Masti rent two rooms in their comfortable home (D-€75, T-€90, Q-whole apartment-€110, one-night rentals OK, kitchen, pool, private yard, Località Santa Chiara 4, tel. & fax 0577-359-072, mobile 333-840-8448 or 338-868-3810, www.farm-house.it, info@farm-house.it).

EATING

Sienese restaurants are reasonable by Florentine and Venetian standards. You can enjoy ordering high on the menu here without going broke.

Dining in the Old Town

Antica Osteria Da Divo is *the* place for a dressy and candlelit €45 meal. The kitchen is creative, the ambience is candlelit, and the food is fresh and top-notch. While the cuisine is flamboyant and almost over-the-top, they serve up my favorite splurge dinner in

Siena Restaurants

1. Antica Osteria da Divo
2. To Ristorante il Capriccio & Osteria Nonna Gina
3. Nello la Taverna
4. Ristorante Guidoriccio
5. Trattoria la Torre, Key Largo Bar, Ciao Cafeteria & Spizzico Pizza
6. To Taverna San Giuseppe
7. Osteria la Chiacchera
8. Osteria Trombicce
9. Spadaforte
10. Bar il Palio
11. Il Bandierino
12. Gelateria la Costarella
13. Bar Paninoteca San Paolo
14. Antica Pizzicheria al Palazzo della Chigiana
15. Consorzio Agrario Siena Grocery

town. Chef Pino is fanatic about fresh ingredients, enjoys giving traditional dishes his creative spin, and is understandably proud of his desserts (daily 12:00–14:30 & 19:00–22:30, closed summer Sun and winter Tue, reservations smart; facing baptistery door, take the far right and walk one long curving block to Via Franciosa 29; tel. 0577-286-054). Those dining here with this book can finish with a complimentary biscotti and *vin santo* or coffee (upon request).

Ristorante Il Capriccio serves traditional Sienese dishes with a presentation that matches the restaurant's classic, understated elegance. With a soundtrack of softly playing music, the dressy setting is made cozy by head waiter Ariol. On balmy evenings the best tables are in the peaceful garden out back (€8 pastas, €15 *secondi*, Slow Food movement, sensitivity to organic production, handmade pasta, Tue–Mon 19:30–22:00, closed Wed, next to and run by recommended Pensione Palazzo Ravizza at Pian dei Mantellini 32, tel. 0577-281757). Reservations are smart because they only serve about 50 dinners a night.

Nello la Taverna, an artsy and romantic restaurant with a minimalist dining room, is run by English-speaking Mauro and his wife Simonetta with a stylish flair. The vision is for clients to dine on a cloud, lose track of time, and enjoy the jazz in a Nello-world of less is more. Their menu features whatever is in season paired with homemade pasta, creative vegetarian options, and well-presented hot desserts (€9 pastas, €12 *secondi*, Mon–Sat 12:00–15:00 & 19:00–22:30, closed Sun, a few steps off Il Campo on Via Porrione 28, to the left of the City Tower as you're facing it, tel. 0577-289-043).

Eating Traditional and Rustic in the Old Town

Ristorante Guidoriccio, just a few steps below Il Campo, feels warm, classy, and welcoming, with smiling service by Ercole and Elisabetta and prices good for the locale (€7 pastas, €13 *secondi*, Mon–Sat 12:30–14:30 & 19:00–22:30, closed Sun, air-con, Via G. Dupre 2, tel. 0577-44-350).

Trattoria la Torre is a thriving *casalinga* (home-cooking) eatery, popular for its homemade pasta, tables of which entice eaters as they enter. The sound of its busy open kitchen adds to the conviviality. Ten tables are packed under one medieval brick arch (Fri–Wed 12:00–15:00 & 19:00–21:30, closed Thu, just steps below Il Campo at Via Salicotto 7, tel. 0577-287-548, Alberto Boccini).

Taverna San Giuseppe, a local favorite, offers modern Tuscan cuisine in a dressy grotto atmosphere. Check the posters tacked around the entry for daily specials. Reserve or arrive early to get a table (€8 pastas, €10 *secondi*, Mon–Sat 12:00–14:30 & 19:00–22:00, closed Sun, can be hot and stuffy, 7-min climb up street to the right of City Hall, Via Giovanni Dupre 132, tel. 0577-42-286).

Osteria Nonna Gina wins praise from locals for its good-quality, rustic cuisine and reasonable prices (€8 pastas, €10 *secondi*, Tue–Sun 12:30–14:30 & 19:30–22:30, closed Mon, 10-min walk from Il Campo, two blocks beyond Hotel Duomo, Piano dei Mantellini 2, tel. 0577-287-247). While the front room is charming, I'd avoid the basement.

Osteria la Chiacchera is a youthful hole-in-the-brick-wall that plays hip music and serves "peasant food" at peasant prices on simple tables and paper place mats. It's an eat-it-and-beat-it, pasta-slinging place, with rickety outside tables clinging to the steep, stepped lane (€5 pastas, €6 *secondi*, daily 12:00–15:30 & 19:00–24:00, great cakes, skip the *trippa*—tripe, down the street to the left of Pension Bernini at Costa di San Antonio 4, tel. 0577-280-631).

Osteria Trombicce is cheap and small, with tight indoor seating and two tiny outdoor tables from which to watch the street scene. They serve fast, hearty food to a young crowd (€5 *ribollita*—bean-and-vegetable soup, closed Sun, Via delle Terme 66, tel. 0577-288-089).

Eating on Il Campo

If you choose to eat (or drink) on perhaps the finest town square in Italy, you'll pay a premium, meet waiters who don't need to hustle, and get mediocre food. And yet I recommend it. The clamshell-shaped square is lined with venerable cafés, bars, restaurants, and pizzerias. **Caffè Fonte Gaia,** which was long the classic place to see and be seen, is now a bit tired. For location, I'd choose **Spadaforte** (my favorite views) or **Bar il Palio** (best for drinks, straight prices, no cover, decent waiters, great perch). For value, everyone agrees: it's **Il Bandierino,** with the square's best food but worst view (€8 pizza or pasta, no cover, tel. 0577-282-217). For a trendy vibe popular with young people, pick the dynamic little **Osteria Liberamente** (fine wine by the glass, cocktails with good tapas, breakfasts, noisy music inside but great outdoor tables, tel. 0577-274-733). If your hotel doesn't serve breakfast or if you'd like something more memorable, consider breakfast on Il Campo—there are plenty of options.

Drinks or Snacks From Balconies Overlooking Il Campo

Three places have skinny balconies with benches overlooking the main square for their customers. Sipping a coffee or nibbling a pastry here while marveling at the Il Campo scene is one of my favorite things to do in Europe. And it's very cheap. Survey these three places from Il Campo (from the base of the tower, using an imaginary 12-hour clock, they are at 10:00, high noon, and 3:00, respectively).

Gelateria la Costarella has good ice cream, drinks, and light snacks such as cute little €1 sandwiches (Fri–Wed 8:00–late, closes 22:00 off-season, closed Thu, Via di Città 33).

Bar Paninoteca San Paolo, with a youthful pub ambience, has a row of stools overlooking the square and serves big salads and 50 kinds of sandwiches (hot and cold, €3.50 each, €0.50 extra if you sit outside, food served daily 12:00–2:00, on Vicolo di S. Paolo on the stairs leading down to the top of Il Campo).

Key Largo Bar has two benches in the corner offering a great secret perch (daily 7:00–22:00 or until midnight, on Via Rinaldini). Buy your drink or snack at the bar (no extra charge to sit), climb upstairs, and slide the ancient bar to open the door. Suddenly you're imagining Palio ponies zipping wildly around your corner.

Eating Cheaply in the Center

Antica Pizzicheria al Palazzo della Chigiana may be the official name, but I imagine locals just call it Antonio's. For most of his life, frenzied Antonio has carved salami and cheese for the neighborhood. For most of the day, a hungry line spills into the street as locals wait for their sandwiches: meat and cheese sold by the weight, and a plastic glass of good Chianti (€3). Antonio and his boys offer a big cheese-and-meat plate (€15, 30 minutes of eating) and pull out a tiny tabletop in the corner so that you can munch or sip while standing and watch the hamhocky scene (daily 8:00–20:00, Via di Città 93, tel. 0577-289-164). Even if you don't get a sandwich, pop in to inhale the commotion or peruse Antonio's gifty traditional edibles.

Ciao Cafeteria, at the bottom of Il Campo, offers easy self-service lunches, no ambience, and no views (daily 12:00–15:00). The crowded **Spizzico,** a pizza counter in the front half of Ciao, serves huge, inexpensive quarter-pizzas; on sunny days, people take the pizza—trays and all—out on Il Campo for a picnic (daily 11:00–22:00, to left of City Tower as you face it).

Budget eaters look for *pizza al taglio* shops, scattered throughout Siena, selling pizza by the slice. Of all the grocery shops, the biggest is **Consorzio Agrario Siena** (Mon–Sat 8:00–19:30, closed Sun, a block off Piazza Matteotti, toward Il Campo at Via Pianigiani 5).

TRANSPORTATION CONNECTIONS

Siena has sparse train connections, but is a great hub for buses to the hill towns, though frequency drops on Sundays and holidays. For most, Florence is the gateway to Siena. Even if you are a rail-pass user, I'd connect these two cities by bus—it's faster.

From Siena by Train to: Florence (2/hr, 1.75 hrs, €5.60, half require transfer in Empoli), **Pisa** (change at Empoli: Pisa–Empoli, roughly 2/hr, 45 min; Empoli–Siena, hourly, 1 hr, €6.60), **Rome** (every 2 hrs, 2.75–4 hrs, transfer in Florence or Chiusi, about €17; more frequent if you go on Eurostar via Florence), **Assisi** (10/day, 4 hrs, most involve 2 transfers, bus is more efficient). For more information, visit www.trenitalia.com.

By Bus to: Florence (2/hr, 75-min *corse rapide* buses are faster than the train, avoid the 2-hr *diretta* slow buses unless you have time to enjoy the beautiful scenery en route, €6.50, can buy tickets at *tabacchi* shops if bus ticket office is closed, Florence buses depart from in front of Jolly Hotel on Piazza Gramsci), **San Gimignano** (5/day, 75 min, €5.20, by Tra-In bus, more frequent with transfer in Poggibonsi, tickets also available at *tabacchi* shops), **Assisi** (2/day, 2 hrs, €10, by Sena bus; the morning bus goes direct to Assisi, though the afternoon bus might terminate 3 miles below Assisi at Santa Maria degli Angeli where a city bus finishes the ride, Assisi-only buses depart from the train station), **Rome** (10/day, 3 hrs, €17.50, by Sena bus, arrives at Rome's Tiburtina station on Metro line B with easy connections to the central Termini train station), **Milan** (4/day, 4.5 hrs, €25).

Unless otherwise noted, buses depart Siena from Piazza Gramsci; confirm when you purchase your ticket. You can get tickets for Tra-In buses or Sena buses at the train station: Tra-In buses at the newsstand (Mon–Sat 6:00–20:00, Sun 6:00–16:00), and Sena buses at the window to the left of the train ticket office (Mon–Sat 7:40–12:40 & 14:30–18:30, closed Sun). You can also get tickets under Piazza Gramsci at **Sottopassaggio la Lizza**—look for stairwells to this underground passageway in front of the Jolly Hotel (Tra-In bus office: Mon–Sat 5:50–20:00, Sun 6:00–19:30, tel. 0577-204-246, toll-free tel. 800-570-530, www.trainspa.it; Sena bus office: Mon–Sat 7:45–19:45, closed Sun, if Sena bus ticket office is closed, buy Sena tickets next door at Tra-In office, tel. 800-930-960, www.senabus.it).

Sottopassaggio la Lizza, the passageway under Piazza Gramsci, also has a cash machine (neither bus office accepts credit cards), luggage storage (€5.50/day, daily 7:00–19:45, no overnight storage), posted bus schedules, TV monitors (listing all the imminent departures for several bus companies), an elevator, and expensive WCs (€0.50). On schedules, the fastest buses are marked *rapide*—I'd stick with these. Note that if a schedule lists your departure point as either Via Tozzi or Piazza la Lizza, you actually catch the bus at Piazza Gramsci (Via Tozzi is the street that runs alongside Piazza Gramsci, and Piazza la Lizza is the name of the bus-hub square). Confusing? Absolutely.

ASSISI

Assisi is famous for its hometown boy, St. Francis, who made very good. While Francis the saint is interesting, Francesco Bernardone the man is even more so, and mementos of his days in Assisi are everywhere—where he was baptized, a shirt he wore, a hill he prayed on, and a church where a vision changed his life.

About the year 1200, this simple friar from Assisi countered the decadence of Church government and society in general with a powerful message of nonmaterialism and a "slow down and smell God's roses" lifestyle. Like Jesus, Francis taught by example, living without worldly goods and aiming to love all creation. A huge monastic order grew out of his teachings, which were gradually embraced (some would say co-opted) by the Church. Christianity's most popular saint and purest example of simplicity is now glorified in beautiful churches, along with his female counterpart, St. Clare. In 1939, Italy made Francis one of its patron saints; Clare was made a saint in 1958.

Francis' message of love, simplicity, and sensitivity to the environment has a broad and timeless appeal. But every pilgrimage site inevitably gets commercialized, and Francis' legacy is now Assisi's basic industry. In summer, this Umbrian town bursts with flash-in-the-pan Francis fans and Franciscan knickknacks. Those able to see past the glow-in-the-dark rosaries and bobblehead friars can actually have a "travel on purpose" experience. On my last research visit, I asked a local friend who runs a recommended hotel if my readers were missing anything. He said, "Faith."

Assisi Area

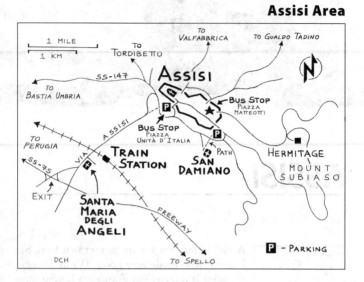

Planning Your Time

Assisi is worth a day and a night. Its old town has a half day of sightseeing and another half day of wonder. The essential sight is the Basilica of St. Francis. For a good visit, take my self-guided "Welcome to Assisi" walk (page 488), ending at the Basilica of St. Francis. Schedule time to linger on the main square, Piazza del Comune.

Most visitors are day-trippers. While the town's a zoo by day, it's a delight at night. Assisi after dark is closer to a place Francis could call home.

ORIENTATION

Crowned by a ruined castle, Assisi spills downhill to its famous Basilica of St. Francis. The town is beautifully preserved and rich in history. A 5.5-magnitude earthquake in 1997 did more damage to the tourist industry than to the local buildings. Fortunately, tourists—whether art-lovers, pilgrims, or both—have returned, drawn by Assisi's special allure.

The city sprawls across a ridge that rises from a flat plain. The Basilica of St. Francis sits at the low end of town, Piazza Matteotti is at the high end (bus station and car parking), and the main square, Piazza del Comune, lies in between. Via San Francesco runs from Piazza del Comune to the basilica. Capping the hill above the town is a ruined castle called the Rocca Maggiore, and rising above that is Mt. Subasio. The town is small, and slopes uphill from west to east. Walking from the basilica to Piazza

Matteotti (uphill) takes 30 minutes, while the downhill journey takes about 15 minutes. Some Francis sights lie outside the city walls, both in the valley beneath the ridge, and in the hills above.

Tourist Information

The TI is in the center of town on Piazza del Comune (Mon–Sat 8:00–14:00 & 15:00–18:00, Sun 10:00–13:00, tel. 075-812-534).

A **combo-ticket** (*biglietto cumulativo*, €4.50/1 day, includes audioguide) covers three minor sights: Rocca Maggiore (castle), Pinacoteca (paintings), and the Roman Forum.

Arrival in Assisi

By Train and Bus: City buses connect Assisi's train station with the old town of Assisi on the hilltop (2/hr, 15 min, €1), stopping at Piazza Unità d'Italia (near Basilica of St. Francis), then Largo Properzio (near Basilica of St. Clare), and finally Piazza Matteotti (top of old town). Buses usually leave from the train station at :16 and :46 past the hour.

Going from the old town to the train station, buses usually run from Piazza Matteotti at :10 and :40 past the hour (stopping in Piazza Unità d'Italia a few minutes later).

At Piazza Unità d'Italia (the big parking lot for cars and buses below the Basilica of St. Francis), there are two bus stops *(fermata bus):* one sign reads *per f.s. S.M. Angeli* (to the train station), and the other reads *per P. Matteotti* (to the top of the old town, departures at :22 and :52 past the hour). Hop on a bus if you're exhausted after your basilica visit and need a sweat-free, five-minute return to Piazza Matteotti (near where many of my recommended hotels are).

Taxis from the train station to the old town cost about €12. There are legitimate extra charges for luggage, night service, and for additional people (four is customary, more pay extra), but beware: Many taxis rip off tourists by using tariff #2 (Sun and holiday fare); the meter should be set on tariff #1 (€2.85 drop). You can check bags at the train station (€2.60/12 hrs, daily 6:30–19:30), but not in the old town.

When departing the old town of Assisi, you'll find taxi stands at Piazza Unità d'Italia, the Basilica of St. Clare, and Piazza del Comune (or have your hotel call for you, tel. 075-813-100).

By Car: Drivers just coming in for the day should follow the signs to Piazza Matteotti's wonderful underground parking garage at the top of the town (which comes with bits of ancient Rome in the walls; €1/hr, €15.75/24 hrs, daily 7:00–21:00, until 23:00 in summer; pick up your car first, then pay, then exit). Another big lot, Parking San Pietro, is just below the Basilica of St. Francis (€1/hr).

Helpful Hints

Minibuses in Old Town: Cute electrical minibuses connect the top of the town with the bottom. While it's only a 15-minute stroll downhill from top to bottom, the climb back up can have you looking for a lift. Before boarding, confirm the destination (Basilica of St. Francis, Piazza del Comune, or Piazza Matteotti). You can buy a bus ticket (good on any city bus) at a newsstand or kiosk for €1, or get a ticket from the driver for €1.50.

Travel Agency: You can purchase train tickets and most bus tickets (but not for Siena) at **Agenzia Viaggi Stoppini,** between Piazza del Comune and the Basilica of St. Clare (Mon–Fri 9:00–12:30 & 15:30–18:30, Sat 9:00–12:00, closed Sun, Corso Mazzini 31, tel. 075-812-597). Fabrizio, who runs the agency, is patient with tourists' needs and charges exactly what you'd pay at the train station for tickets. Bus tickets for Siena are sold only at **Agenzia Viaggi Maritur** (Via Frate Elia 1b, near Basilica of St. Francis, or pay more to purchase tickets on the bus; see "Transportation Connections," page 516).

Internet Access: Facing the Cathedral of San Rufino, **Caffè Duomo** offers free Internet access to anyone ordering even just a drink (otherwise €2.50/hr, snacks, Piazza San Rufino 5, tel. 075-815-398).

Local Guide: **Giuseppe Karabotis** is a good, licensed local guide (€110/2 hours for up to 15 people, mobile 328-867-0567, iokarabot@tele2.it); if he's busy, he can recommend other guides. **Anne Robichaud,** an American who has lived here since 1975, is a bundle of entrepreneurial energy and gives tours of Umbrian hill towns and the surrounding countryside and runs cooking classes (see www.annesitaly.com for specifics).

Best Shopping: Tacky knickknacks line the streets leading to the Basilica of St. Francis. The best variety of better shops (with local handicrafts) are on Via San Rufino and Corso Mazzini (both just off Piazza del Comune). A Saturday morning market fills Piazza Matteotti (which has a good parking garage).

SELF-GUIDED WALK

▲▲ Welcome to Assisi

There's much more to Assisi than St. Francis and what the blitz tour groups see. This walk covers the town from Piazza Matteotti at the top, down to the Basilica of St. Francis at the bottom. To get to Piazza Matteotti, ride the bus from the train station (or from Piazza Unità d'Italia) to the last stop; drive there (underground parking with Roman ruins); or hike five minutes uphill from Piazza del Comune.

Assisi

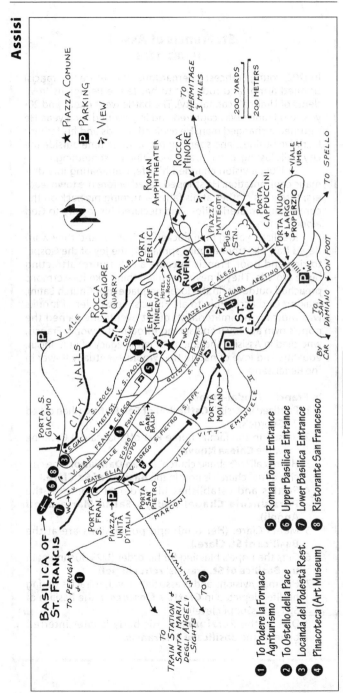

★ PIAZZA COMUNE
P PARKING
⅄ VIEW

200 YARDS
200 METERS

1 To Podere la Fornace Agriturismo
2 To Ostello della Pace
3 Locanda del Podestà Rest.
4 Pinacoteca (Art Museum)
5 Roman Forum Entrance
6 Upper Basilica Entrance
7 Lower Basilica Entrance
8 Ristorante San Francesco

St. Francis of Assisi
(1181/82–1226)

In 1202, young Francesco Bernardone (the future St. Francis) donned armor and rode out to battle the Perugians (residents of Umbria's capital city). The battle went badly, and 20-year-old Francis was captured and imprisoned for a year. He returned a changed man. He avoided friends and his father's lucrative business and spent more and more time outside the city walls fasting, praying, and searching for something.

In 1206, a vision changed his life, culminating in a dramatic confrontation. He stripped naked before the town leaders, threw his clothes at his father—turning his back on the comfortable material life—and declared his loyalty to God alone.

Idealistic young men flocked to Francis, and they wandered Italy like troubadours, spreading the joy of the Gospel to rich and poor. Francis became a cult figure, attracting huge crowds. They'd never seen anything like it—sermons preached outdoors, in the local language (not Church Latin), making God accessible to all. Francis' new order of monks was radically nonmaterialist, but it eventually gained the pope's own approval and spread through the world. Francis, who died in Assisi at the age of 45, left a legacy of humanism, equality, and love of nature that would eventually flower in the Renaissance.

In Francis' Sandal-Steps
1. Baptized in Assisi's **Cathedral of San Rufino** (then called St. George's).
2. Raised in the family home just off Piazza del Comune (now the **Chiesa Nuova**).
3. Heard call to "rebuild church" in **San Damiano.** (The crucifix of the church is now in the **Basilica of St. Clare.**)
4. Settles and establishes his order of monks at the **Porziuncola Chapel** (today's **Santa Maria degli Angeli**).
5. Meets Clare. (Her tomb and possessions are at the **Basilica of St. Clare.**)
6. Gets the pope's blessing for his order (1223 document in the **Basilica of St. Francis' relic chapel**).
7. Has many visions and is associated with miracles during his life (depicted in **Giotto's frescoes** in the Basilica of St. Francis' upper level).
8. Dies at the **Porziuncola.** His body is later interred beneath the **Basilica of St. Francis.**

• *Start 50 yards beyond Piazza Matteotti (away from city center—see map).*

❶ The Roman Amphitheater

A lane named Via Anfiteatro Romano leads to a cozy circular neighborhood built around a Roman amphitheater—a reminder that Assisi was once an important Roman town. Circle the amphitheater counterclockwise. Imagine how colorful the town laundry (on the right) must have been in the last generation when the women of Assisi gathered here to do their wash. Adjacent to the laundry is a small rectangular pool filled with water; above it are the coats of arms of Assisi's leading families. A few steps farther, hike up the stairs to the top of the hill for an aerial view of the oval amphitheater. The Roman stones have long been absorbed into the medieval architecture. It was Roman tradition to locate the amphitheater outside of town...which this used to be. While the amphitheater dates from the first century A.D., the buildings filling it today were built in the 13th and 14th centuries.

• *Continue on, enjoying the grand view of the fortress in the distance. The lane leads down to a city gate and an...*

❷ Umbrian View

Step outside of Assisi at the Porta Perlici for a commanding view. Umbria, called the "green heart of Italy," is the country's geographical center and only landlocked state. Enjoy the greens: silver green on the valley floor (olives), emerald green (grapevines), and deep green on the hillsides (evergreen oak trees). Also notice Rocca Maggiore ("big fortress"), which provided townsfolk a refuge in times of attack, and, behind you atop the nearer hill, Rocca Minore ("little fortress"). The quarry (under the Rocca Maggiore) provided a handy source for Assisi's characteristic pink limestone.

• *Go back through the gate and follow Via Porta Perlici downhill—it's immediately on your right into town (towards Hotel La Rocca). Enjoy the higgledy-piggledy architecture (this neighborhood has perhaps the most photogenic back lanes in town). At Hotel La Rocca (after about 200 yards), turn left, passing under two medieval gates, and follow Via Porta Perlici downhill until you hit a fine square facing a big church. (Caffè Duomo, facing Piazza San Rufino, is a nice place for a drink or snack; it also has free Internet access for customers.)*

❸ Cathedral of San Rufino

While Francis is one of Italy's patron saints, Rufino (the town's first bishop, martyred and buried here in the third century) is Assisi's. The cathedral (seat of the local bishop) is 12th-century Romanesque with a Neoclassical interior. While the facade is considered one of the best and purest Romanesque facades in all of Umbria, the big

Welcome to Assisi Walk

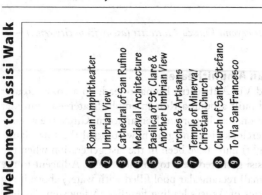

1. Roman Amphitheater
2. Umbrian View
3. Cathedral of San Rufino
4. Medieval Architecture
5. Basilica of St. Clare & Another Umbrian View
6. Arches & Artisans
7. Temple of Minerva/ Christian Church
8. Church of Santo Stefano
9. To Via San Francesco

P Parking

🔭 View

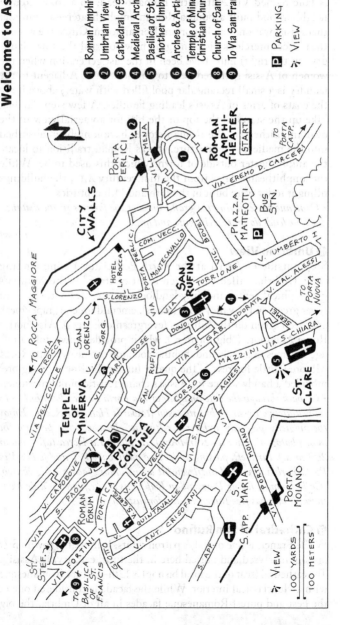

triangular top of it (just a decorative wall) was added in Gothic times. Enter the church (daily 7:00–12:30 & 14:30–19:00). To your right (in the back corner of the church with the black iron grate) is an old baptism font. About the year 1182, a baby boy was baptized in this font. His parents were upwardly mobile Francophiles who called him Francesco ("Frenchy"). In 1194, a nobleman baptized his daughter Clare here. Eighteen years later, Clare's and Francis' paths crossed in this same church, when Clare attended a class and became mesmerized by the teacher—Francis. Traditionally, the children of Assisi are still baptized here.

The striking glass panels in the church floor reveal foundations preserved from the ninth-century church that once stood here. You're walking on history. After the 1997 earthquake, the church was checked from ceiling to floor by structural inspectors. When they looked under the paving stones, they discovered graves (it used to be a common practice to bury people in churches, until Napoleon decreed otherwise), and underneath, Roman foundations and some animal bones (suggesting the possibility of animal sacrifice). There might have been a Roman temple here; churches were often built upon temple ruins. Standing at the back of the church (facing the altar), look left to the Roman cistern (inside the great stone archway). If you take the three steps down, an automatic light should go on. Marvel at the fine stonework and Roman engineering. In the Middle Ages, this was the town's emergency water source when under attack.

Underneath the church, incorporated into the Roman ruins, are the foundations of an earlier Church of San Rufino, now the crypt. When it's open, you can go below to see the saint's sarcophagus and the small museum (€3, mid-March–mid-Oct Thu–Tue 10:00–13:00 & 15:00–18:00, in winter closes at 17:30, closed Wed).
• *Leaving the church, take a sharp left (on Via Dono Doni), following the sign for Santa Chiara. After 20 yards, take a right and down the stairway to see some...*

❹ Medieval Architecture

At the bottom of the stairs, notice the pink limestone pavement, part of the surviving medieval town. The arches built over doorways indicate that the buildings date from the 12th through the 14th centuries, when Assisi was booming. Italian cities such as Assisi—thriving on the north–south trade between northern Europe and Rome—were in the process of inventing capitalism, dabbling in democratic self-rule, and creating the modern urban lifestyle. The vaults you see that turn lanes into tunnels are reminders of medieval urban expansion (mostly 15th century). While the population grew, people wanted to live within its protective walls. Medieval Assisi had several times the population density of today's Assisi.

Notice the flowering balconies; Assisi holds a competition each June. Continue steeply downhill. When you arrive at a street, turn left, going slightly uphill for a block, take the low road at the Y, and head down Via Sermei. Pause at #6b (on your left) to check out Signore Silvano Giombolini's display of mechanized figures petting sheep, sawing wood, and drawing well water. Look for the nativity scene, featuring an adored baby Jesus captioned with scriptures and Franciscan-style admonitions to love one another and appreciate life's simple pleasures (free but donations appreciated).

• *Continue ahead, following the* S. Chiara *sign downhill to the big church.*

➎ Basilica of St. Clare (Basilica di Santa Chiara)

Dedicated to the founder of the order of the Poor Clares, this Umbrian Gothic church is simple, in keeping with the Poor Clares' dedication to a life of contemplation. In Clare's lifetime, the order was located in the humble Church of San Damiano, in the valley below, but after Clare's death, they needed a bigger and more glorious building. The church was built in 1265, and the huge buttresses were added in the next century. The interior's fine frescoes were whitewashed in Baroque times.

The Chapel of the Crucifix of San Damiano, on the right, has the wooden crucifix that changed Francis' life. In 1206, an emaciated, soul-searching, stark-raving Francis knelt before this crucifix (then located in the Church of San Damiano) and asked for guidance. The crucifix spoke: "Go and rebuild my Church, which you can see has fallen into ruin." And Francis followed the call.

Stairs lead from the nave down to the tomb of St. Clare. Her tomb is at the far end (the image is wax, her bones lie underneath). As you circulate with the crowd of pilgrims, notice the paintings on the walls depicting spiritual lessons from Clare's life and death (see sidebar). At the opposite end of the crypt (back between the stairs, in a large glassed-in area) are important relics: the saint's robes, hair (in a silver box), and an enormous tunic she made—along with relics of St. Francis (including a shoe that he was wearing when he received the stigmata). The attached cloistered community of the Poor Clares has flourished for 700 years (church open daily 6:30–12:00 & 14:00–19:00, until 18:00 in winter).

• *Leave the church and belly up to the viewpoint at the edge of the square for...*

Another Umbrian View

On the left is the convent of St. Clare (global headquarters of all the Poor Clares). Below you lies the olive grove of the Poor Clares since the 13th century. In the distance is a grand Umbrian view.

St. Clare
(1194–1253)

The 18-year-old rich girl of Assisi fell in love with 30-year-old Francis' message, and made secret arrangements to meet him. The night of Palm Sunday, 1212, she slipped out of her father's mansion in town and escaped to the valley below. A procession of friars with torches met her and took her to (today's) Santa Maria degli Angeli. There, Francis cut her hair, clothed her in a simple brown tunic, and welcomed her into a life of voluntary poverty. Clare's father begged, ordered, and physically threatened her to return, but she would not budge.

Clare was joined by other women who banded together as the Poor Clares. She spent the next 40 years of her life within the confines of the convent of San Damiano: barefoot, vegetarian, and largely silent. Her regimen of prayer, meditation, and simple manual labor—especially knitting—impressed commoners and popes, leading to her canonization almost immediately after her death. St. Clare is often depicted carrying a monstrance (a little temple holding the Eucharist wafer), because according to legend, she saved the convent from attack by holding up a monstrance.

Assisi overlooks the richest and biggest valley in otherwise hilly and mountainous Umbria. The municipality of Assisi has a population of 25,000, but only 3,500 people live in the old town. The lower town grew up with the coming of the railway in the 19th century. In the haze, the blue-domed church is St. Mary of the Angels (Santa Maria degli Angeli, see page 509), the cradle of the Franciscan order, marking the place St. Francis lived and worked and a popular pilgrimage sight today.

Spanish-speaking Franciscans settled in California. Three of their missions grew into major cities: Los Angeles (named after this church), San Francisco (named after St. Francis), and Santa Clara (named after St. Clare).

• *From the church square, step out into Via Santa Chiara. You can see gates in both directions.*

❻ Arches and Artisans

The gate over the road behind the church dates from 1265. (Beyond it, you can just see the crenellations of the 1316 Porta Nuova, which marks the final expansion of Assisi.) Toward the city center (on Via Santa Chiara, the high road), an arch marks the site of the Roman wall. These three gates mark the town's three walls, illustrating how much the city has grown since ancient times.

Walk uphill along Via Santa Chiara (which becomes Corso

Mazzini) to the city's main square. The street is lined with interesting shops selling traditional embroidery, religious souvenirs, and gifty local edibles. About 20 yards before the arch, at #1b, a plaque over the door explains that the old printing press (a national monument now, just inside the door) was used to make fake documents for Jews escaping the Nazis in 1943 and 1944.

Ahead, at Corso Mazzini 14d, the small shop (Poiesis) sells olive-wood carvings. It's said that St. Francis made the first nativity scene to help humanize and, therefore, teach the Christmas message. That's why you'll see so many crèches in Assisi. Even today, nearby villages are enthusiastic about their "living" manger scenes, and Italians everywhere enjoy setting up elaborate crèches in churches for Christmas.

You're walking up what was, in ancient times, the main drag into town. Ahead of you, the six fluted Corinthian columns of the Temple of Minerva marked the forum (today's Piazza del Comune). Sit at the fountain on the piazza for a few minutes of people-watching—don't you love Italy? Within a few hundred yards of this square, on either side, were the medieval walls. Imagine a commotion of 5,000 people confined within these walls. No wonder St. Francis needed an escape for some peace and quiet.

• *Now, head over to the temple on the square.*

❼ Temple of Minerva/Christian Church

Assisi has always been a spiritual center. The Romans went to great lengths to make this first-century B.C. Temple of Minerva a centerpiece of their city. Notice the columns that cut into the stairway. It was a tight fit here on the hilltop. In ancient times, the stairs went down—about twice as far as they do now—to the main drag, which has gradually been filled in over time. The Church of Santa Maria sopra (over) Minerva was added in the ninth century. The bell tower is from the 13th century. Pop inside the temple/church (Mon–Sat 7:15–19:30, Sun 8:00–19:30, closes at sunset and midday in winter).

Today's interior is 17th-century Baroque. Flanking the altar are the original Roman temple floor stones. You can even see the drains for the bloody sacrifices that took place here. Behind the statues of Peter and Paul, the original Roman embankment peeks through.

Across the square at #11, step into the 16th-century frescoed vaults from the old market. Notice the Italian flair for design. Even this smelly market was once finely decorated. The art style was "grotesque"—literally, a painting in a grotto. This was painted after 1492. How do art historians know? Because turkeys—first seen in Europe after Columbus returned with his bag of exotic souvenirs—are featured. The turkeys painted here may have been that bird's European debut.

• *From the main square, hike past the temple up the high road, Via San Paolo. After 200 yards, a sign directs you down a lane to the...*

❽ Church of Santo Stefano

Surrounded by cypress, fig, and walnut trees, Santo Stefano—which used to be outside the town walls in the days of St. Francis—is a delightful bit of offbeat Assisi. Legend has it that Santo Stefano's bells miraculously rang on October 3, 1226, the day St. Francis died. Step inside. This is the typical rural Italian Romanesque church—no architect, just built by simple stonemasons who put together the most basic design (daily 8:30–21:30, until 18:30 in winter).

• *The lane zigzags down to Via San Francesco. Turn right and walk under the arch toward the Basilica of St. Francis.*

❾ Via San Francesco

This was the main drag that led from the town to the basilica holding the body of St. Francis. Francis was a big deal even in his own day. He died in 1226 and was made a saint in 1228—the same year that the basilica's foundations were laid—and his body was moved in by 1230. Assisi was a big-time pilgrimage center, and this street was its booming main drag. The arch marks the end of what was Assisi in St. Francis' day. Notice the fine medieval balcony just below the arch. A few yards farther down (on the left), cool yourself at the fountain. The hospice next door was built in 1237 to house pilgrims. Notice the three surviving faces of its fresco: Jesus, Francis, and Clare.

Continuing on, you'll eventually reach Assisi's main sight, the Basilica of St. Francis.

SELF-GUIDED TOUR

▲▲▲ Basilica of St. Francis

The Basilica di San Francesco is one of the artistic and religious highlights of Europe. In 1226, St. Francis was buried (with the outcasts he had stood by) outside of his town on the "Hill of the Damned"—now called the "Hill of Paradise." The basilica is frescoed from top to bottom by the leading artists of the day: Cimabue, Giotto, Simone Martini, and Pietro Lorenzetti. A 13th-century historian wrote, "No more exquisite monument to the Lord has

been built."

From a distance, you see the huge arcades "supporting" the basilica. These were 15th-century quarters for the monks. The arcades lining the square leading to the church housed medieval pilgrims.

Cost, Hours, Information: Free entry; lower basilica daily 6:30–18:45, until 18:00 in winter; relic chapel in lower basilica supposedly 9:00–18:00 but often closed; upper basilica daily 8:30–18:50, until 17:50 in winter (tel. 075-819-100, www .sanfrancescoassisi.org). Modest dress is required to enter the church—no sleeveless tops or shorts for men, women, or children. The church courtyard at the entrance of the lower basilica has an info office (ask about €4 audioguide, 75 min) and a bookshop, which sells the excellent guidebook, *The Basilica of Saint Francis— A Spiritual Pilgrimage* (€2.50, by Goulet, McInally, and Wood; I used it as a source for my self-guided tour—see below). To worship in the basilica, consider joining the Franciscan brothers in the lower basilica in the early morning (sung morning prayers at 6:25, Mass at 7:00).

Overview

The Basilica of St. Francis, a theological work of genius, can be difficult for the 21st-century tourist/pilgrim to appreciate. Since the basilica is the reason that most people visit Assisi, and the message of St. Francis has even the least-devout blessing the town Vespas, I've designed this self-guided tour with an emphasis on the place's theology (rather than art history).

A disclaimer before we start: Just as Francis used many Bible legends to help teach the Christian message, legends from the life of Francis were used in later ages to teach the same message. Are they true? Generally probably not. Are they in keeping with Francis' message? Yes. Do I share legends here as if they are historic? Sure.

The church has three parts: the upper basilica, the lower basilica, and the saint's tomb (below the lower basilica). In the 1997 earthquake, the lower basilica—with walls nearly nine feet thick—was unscathed. The upper basilica, with bigger windows and walls only three feet thick, was damaged. Following a restoration, the entire church was reopened to visitors in late 1999.

To get oriented, stand at the lower entrance in the courtyard. Opposite the entry to the lower basilica is the information center. (There are two different WCs within a half-block—up the road in a squat building, and halfway down the big piazza on the left.)

Enter through the grand doorway of the lower basilica. Just inside, decorating the top of the first arch, look up and see St. Francis, who greets you with a Latin inscription. Sounding a bit

The Franciscan Message

Francis' message caused a stir. Not only did he follow Christ's teachings, he adopted his lifestyle, living as a poor, wandering preacher. He traded a life of power and riches for one of obedience, poverty, and chastity. He was never ordained a priest, but his influence on Christianity was monumental.

The Franciscan existence (Brother Sun, Sister Moon, and so on) is a space where God, man, and the natural world frolic harmoniously. Francis treated every creature—animal, peasant, pope—with equal respect. He and his "brothers" (*fratelli,* or friars) slept in fields, begged for food, and exuded the joy of nonmaterialism. Franciscan friars were known as the "Jugglers of God," modeling themselves on French troubadours (*jongleurs,* or jugglers) who roved the countryside singing, telling stories, and cracking jokes.

In an Italy torn by conflict between towns and families, Francis promoted peace and the restoration of order. (He set an example by reconstructing the crumbled San Damiano chapel.) While the Church was waging bloody Crusades, Francis pushed ecumenism and understanding. Even today the leaders of the world's great religions meet here for summits.

This richly decorated basilica seems to contradict the teachings of the poor monk it honors, but it was built as an act of religious and civic pride to remember the hometown saint. It was also designed—and still functions—as a pilgrimage center and a splendid classroom. Monks in robes are not my idea of easy-to-approach people, but the Franciscans of today are still God's jugglers (and most of them speak English).

Here is Francis' message, in his own words:

The Canticle of the Sun

Good Lord, all your creations bring praise to you!
Praise for Brother Sun, who brings the day. His radiance reminds us of you!
Praise for Sister Moon and the stars, precious and beautiful.
Praise for Brother Wind, and for clouds and storms and rain that sustain us.
Praise for Sister Water. She is useful and humble, precious and pure.
Praise for Brother Fire who cheers us at night.
Praise for our sister, Mother Earth, who feeds us and rules us.
Praise for all those who forgive because you have forgiven them.
Praise for our sister, Bodily Death, from whose embrace none can escape.
Praise and bless the Lord, and give thanks, and, with humility, serve him.

like John Wayne, he says the equivalent of "Slow down and be joy-ful, pilgrim. You've reached the Hill of Paradise, and this church will knock your spiritual socks off."

• *Start with the tomb (enter the nave and turn left; midway down the nave to your right, follow signs and go downstairs to the tomb).*

The Tomb

The saint's remains are above the altar in the stone box with the iron ties. In medieval times, pilgrims came to Assisi because St. Francis was buried here. Holy relics were the "ruby slippers" of medieval Europe. Relics gave you power—they answered your prayers and won your wars—and ultimately helped you get back to your eternal Kansas. Assisi made no bones about promoting the saint's relics, but hid his tomb for obvious reasons of security. His body was buried secretly while the basilica was under construc-tion, and over the next 600 years, the exact location was forgotten. When the tomb was to be opened to the public in 1818, it took a month and a half to find his actual remains.

Francis' four closest friends and first followers are memorial-ized in the corners of the room. Opposite the altar, up four steps in between the entrance and exit, notice the small copper box behind the metal grill. This contains the remains of Francis' rich Roman patron, Jacopa dei Settesoli. She traveled to see him on his death-bed, but was turned away because she was female. Francis waived the rule and welcomed "Brother Jacopa" to his side.

The candles you see are the only real candles in the church (others are electric). Pilgrims pay a coin, pick up a candle, and place it at the tomb. Franciscans will light it later.

• *Climb back to the lower nave.*

Nave of Lower Basilica

Appropriately Franciscan—subdued and Romanesque—this nave was frescoed with parallel scenes from the lives of Christ (right) and Francis (left), connected by a ceiling of stars. Unfortunately, after the church was built and decorated, side chapels needed to be built to provide mausoleums for the rich families that patronized the work of the order. Huge arches were cut out of some scenes, but others survive. In the fresco directly above the entry to the tomb, Christ is being taken down from the cross (just the bottom half of his body can be seen, to the left), and it looks like the story is over. Defeat. But in the opposite fresco (above the tomb's exit), we see Francis preaching to the birds, reminding the faithful that the message of the Gospel survives.

These stories directed the attention of the medieval pilgrim to the altar, where he could meet God through the sacraments. The church was thought of as a community of believers sailing toward

Basilica of St. Francis—Lower Level

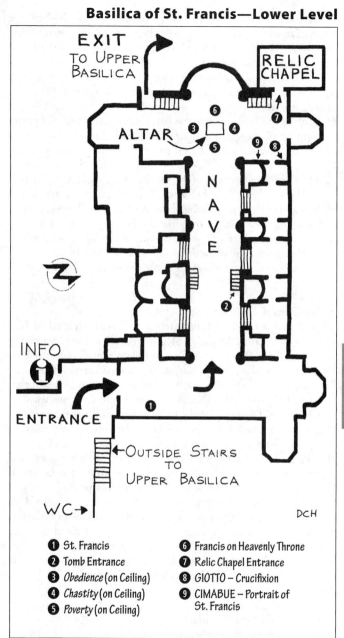

EXIT
TO UPPER BASILICA

RELIC CHAPEL

ALTAR

NAVE

INFO

ENTRANCE

←OUTSIDE STAIRS TO UPPER BASILICA

WC→

DCH

❶ St. Francis
❷ Tomb Entrance
❸ *Obedience* (on Ceiling)
❹ *Chastity* (on Ceiling)
❺ *Poverty* (on Ceiling)
❻ Francis on Heavenly Throne
❼ Relic Chapel Entrance
❽ GIOTTO – Crucifixion
❾ CIMABUE – Portrait of St. Francis

Assisi

God. The prayers coming out of the nave (*navis*, or ship) fill the triangular sections of the ceiling—called *vele*, or sails—with spiritual wind. With a priest for a navigator and the altar for a helm, faith propels the ship.

Stand behind the altar (toes to the bottom step) and look up. The three scenes in front of you are: to the right, *Obedience* (Francis appears twice: wearing a rope harness and kneeling in front of Lady Obedience); to the left, *Chastity* (in a tower of purity held up by two angels); and straight ahead, *Poverty*. Here Jesus blesses the marriage as Francis slips a ring on Lady Poverty. In the foreground, two "self-sufficient" yet pint-size merchants (the new rich of a thriving northern Italy) are throwing sticks and stones at the bride. But Poverty, in her patched wedding dress, is fertile and strong, and even those brambles blossom into a rosebush crown.

Putting your heels to the altar and bending back like a drum major, look up at Francis on a heavenly throne in a rich, golden robe. He traded a life of earthly simplicity for glory in heaven.

• *Now, turn to the right and march to the corner, where steps lead down into the...*

Relic Chapel

This chapel is filled with fascinating relics (which a €0.50 flier explains in detailed English). Step in and circle the room clockwise. You'll see the silver chalice and plate that Francis used for the bread and wine of the Eucharist (in small, dark, windowed case set into wall, marked *Calice e Patena*). Francis believed that his personal possessions should be simple, but the items used for worship should be made of the finest materials. In the corner display case is a small section of the itchy haircloth *(cilizio)* worn by Francis as penitence. In the next corner are the tunic and slippers that Francis wore during his last days. Next, find a prayer (in a fancy silver stand) that St. Francis wrote for Brother Leo, signed with his tau cross. The last letter in the Hebrew alphabet, tav ("tau" in Greek) is symbolic of faithfulness to the end. Francis signed his name with this simple capital-T-shaped character. Next is a papal document (1223) legitimizing the Franciscan order and assuring his followers that they were not risking a (deadly) heresy charge. Finally, see the tunic that was lovingly patched and stitched by followers of the five-foot, four-inch-tall St. Francis.

• *Return up the stairs to the...*

Transept of Lower Basilica

This church brought together the greatest Sienese (Lorenzetti and Simone Martini) and Florentine (Cimabue and Giotto) artists of the day. Look around at the painted scenes. In 1300, this was radical art—believable homespun scenes, landscapes, trees, real people. Study Giotto's painting of the Crucifixion, with the eight sparrow-like angels. For the first time, holy people are expressing emotion: One angel turns her head sadly at the sight of Jesus, and another scratches her hands down her cheeks, drawing blood. Mary (lower left), previously in control, has fainted in despair. The Franciscans, with their goal of bringing God to the people, found a natural partner in Europe's first modern (and therefore naturalist) painter, Giotto.

To grasp Giotto's Renaissance leap, compare his work with the painting to the right, by Cimabue. It's Gothic, without the 3-D architecture, natural backdrop, and slice-of-life reality of Giotto's work. Cimabue's St. Francis (far right) shows the saint with the stigmata—Christ's marks of the Crucifixion. Contemporaries described Francis as being short, with a graceful build, dark hair, and sparse beard. (This is considered the most accurate portrait of Francis—done according to the description of one who knew him.) The sunroof haircut (tonsure) was standard for monks of the day. According to legend, the brown robe and rope belt was an invention of necessity. When Francis stripped naked and ran away from Assisi, he grabbed the first clothes he could, a rough wool peasant's tunic and a piece of rope, which became the uniform of the Franciscan order. To the left, at eye level (under the sparrow-like angels), enjoy Simone Martini's saints and their exquisite halos.

Francis' friend, "Sister Bodily Death," was really not all that terrible. In fact, Francis would like to introduce you to her now (above and to the right of the door leading into the relic chapel). Go ahead, block the light and meet her. Before his death, Francis added a line to *The Canticle of the Sun*: "Praise for our sister, Bodily Death, from whose embrace none can escape."

• *Now cross the transept to the other side of the altar (enjoying some of the oldest surviving bits of the inlaid local-limestone flooring—c. 13th-century) for the staircase going up. Immediately above the stairs is Pietro Lorenzetti's* Francis Receiving the Stigmata. *(Francis is considered the first person ever to earn the marks of the cross through his great faith and love of the church.) Make your way to the...*

Courtyard

The treasury to the left of the bookstore is free (donation requested) and features ornately decorated chalices, reliquaries, vestments, and altarpieces. There's a clean WC two-thirds of the way down the great hall on your right.

• *From the courtyard, climb the stairs (next to the bookshop) to the...*

Basilica of St. Francis—Upper Level

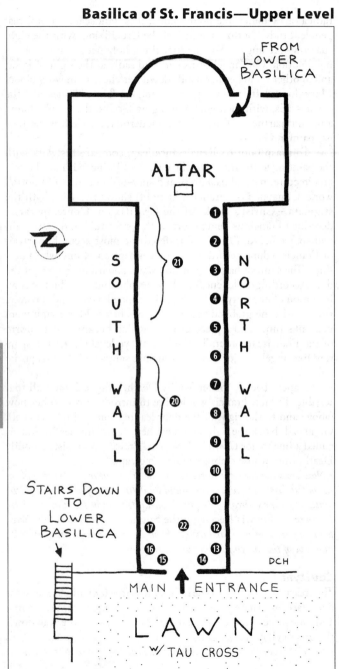

1 A Common Man Spreads his Cape Before Francis

2 Francis Offers his Cape to a Needy Stranger

3 Francis is Visited by the Lord in a Dream

4 Francis Prays to the Crucifix

5 Francis Relinquishes his Possessions

6 The Pope has a Dream

7 The Pope Confirms the Franciscan Order

8 A Vision of the Flaming Chariot

9 A Vision of Thrones

10 Exorcism of Demons in Arezzo

11 St. Francis Before the Sultan

12 Ecstasy of St. Francis

13 The Crèche at Greccio

14 Miracle of the Spring

15 Sermon to the Birds

16 The Knight of Celano Invites Francis to his Deathbed

17 Preaching for Pope Honorius III

18 The Apparition at Arles

19 Francis Receives the Stigmata

20 Francis' Death, Funeral, Burial, and Canonization

21 Three "Post Mortem Miracles" Associated with St. Francis

22 Tan Patches on Ceiling (1997 Earthquake Damage)

Upper Basilica

Built later than its counterpart below, the upper basilica is brighter, Gothic (the first Gothic church in Italy, 1228), and was practi-

cally wallpapered by Giotto and his assistants in about 1297–1300 (or perhaps subcontracted to other artists—scholars debate it). For more on Giotto, see page 125 of the Near Venice chapter. The gallery of frescoes shows 28 scenes from the life of St. Francis. The events are a mix of documented history and folk legend.

• *Get oriented by facing the basilica's main altar. Working clockwise, start on the right-hand (north) wall. Note that the subtitles in the black strip below the frescoes describe each scene in clear Latin—and affirm my interpretation.*

1 **A common man spreads his cape before Francis** in front of the Temple of Minerva on Piazza del Comune. Before his conversion, young Francis was the model of Assisian manhood—handsome, intelligent, and well-dressed, befitting the son of a wealthy cloth dealer. Above all, he was liked by everyone, a natural charmer who led his fellow teens in nights of wine, women, and song. Medieval pilgrims understood a deeper meaning in this scene: The "eye" of God (symbolized by the rose window in the Temple of Minerva) looks over 20-year-old Francis, a dandy "imprisoned" in his own selfishness (the Temple—with barred windows—was once a prison).

❷ **Francis offers his cape to a needy stranger** (next panel). Francis was always generous of spirit. He became more so after he'd been captured in battle, held for a year as a prisoner of war, and suffered illness. Charity was a Franciscan forte.

❸ **Francis is visited by the Lord in a dream.** Still unsure of his calling, Francis rode off to the Crusades. One night, he dreams of a palace filled with armor marked with crosses. Christ tells him to leave the army and go home to wait for a nonmilitary assignment in a new kind of knighthood. He returned to Assisi and, while reviled as a coward, would fight for spiritual wealth, not earthy power and riches.

❹ **Francis prays to the crucifix** in the Church of San Damiano. After months of living in a cave, fasting, and meditating, Francis kneels in the rundown church and prays. The crucifix speaks, telling him: "Go and rebuild my Church, which you can see has fallen into ruin." Francis hurried home and sold his father's cloth to pay for God's work. His furious father dragged him before the bishop.

❺ **Francis relinquishes his possessions.** In front of the bishop and the whole town, Francis strips naked, gives his dad his clothes, credit cards, and time-share on Capri. Francis raises his hand and says, "Until now, I called you father. From now on, my only father is my Father in Heaven." He then ran off into the hills, naked and singing. In this version, Francis is covered by the bishop, symbolizing his transition from a man of the world to a man of the Church. Notice the disbelief and concern on the bishop's advisors' faces; subtle expressions like these wouldn't have made it into other medieval frescoes of the day.

❻ **The pope has a dream.** Francis headed to Rome, seeking the pope's blessing on his fledgling movement. Initially rebuffing Francis, the pope then dreams of a simple man propping up his teetering Church, and then...

❼ **The pope confirms the Franciscan order,** handing Francis the document now displayed in the relic chapel.

Francis' life was surrounded by visions and miracles, shown in three panels in a row: (❽) **A vision of the flaming chariot,** (❾) **A vision of thrones,** and (❿) **Exorcism of demons in Arezzo.** Next see...

⓫ **St. Francis before the sultan.** Francis' wandering ministry took him to Egypt during the Crusades (1219). He walked unarmed into the Muslim army camp. They captured him, but the sultan was impressed with Francis' manner and let him go. Depicted here, the sultan on his throne gestures—he reportedly whispered, "I'd convert to your faith, but they'd kill us both."

⓬ **Ecstasy of St. Francis.** This oft-painted scene shows the mystic communing with God.

⓭ **The Crèche at Greccio.** A creative teacher, Francis invents the tradition of manger scenes in 1223.

• *Around the corner, see the...*

⓮ **Miracle of the spring.** Shown here getting water out of a rock to quench a stranger's thirst, Francis felt closest to God when in the hills around Assisi, seeing the Creator in the creation.

⓯ **Sermon to the birds.** The most well-known miracle is when Francis was surrounded by birds who listened to him teach. Francis embraces all levels of creation. One interpretation of this scene is that the birds, which are of different species, represent the diverse flock of humanity and nature, all created and beloved by God and worthy of each other's love.

• *Continue to the south wall for the rest of the panels.*

Despite the hierarchical society of his day, Francis was welcomed by all classes, shown in these three panels: (⓰) **The knight of Celano invites Francis to his deathbed;** (⓱) **Preaching for Pope Honorius III,** who listens carefully; and (⓲) **The apparition at Arles,** which illustrated how Francis could be in two places at once (something only Jesus and saints can pull off). The proponents of Francis, who believed he was destined for sainthood, show him performing the necessary miracles.

⓳ **Francis receives the stigmata.** It's September 17, 1224, and Francis is fasting and praying on  nearby Mt. Alverna when a six-winged angel (called a seraph) appears with holy, laser-like powers to burn in the marks. For the strength of his faith, Francis is given the marks of his master, the "battle scars of love"...the stigmata. These five wounds Christ suffered during crucifixion (nails in palms and feet, lance in side) marked Francis' body for the rest of his life.

The next panels (⓴) deal with **Francis' death, funeral, and canonization.** The last panels (㉑) show **miracles** associated with the saint after his death, proving that he's in heaven and bolstering his eligibility for sainthood.

Before you leave, look up at the ceiling above the rose window at the front entrance to see large **tan patches** (㉒). In 1997, when a 5.5-magnitude quake hit Assisi, it shattered the upper basilica's frescoes into 300,000 fragments that had to be meticulously picked up and pieced back together. Shortly after the quake, two monks and two art scholars were standing here when an aftershock shook the ceiling frescoes down, killing them.

Outside, on the lawn, are the Latin *pax* (peace) and the Franciscan tau cross. For more *pax,* take the high lane back to town, up to the castle, or into the countryside.

SIGHTS

In Assisi

Roman Forum (Foro Romano)—For a look at Assisi's Roman roots, tour the Roman Forum, which is actually under Piazza del

Comune. The floor plan is sparse, and there are odd bits and obscure pieces, but it's well-explained in English (a 10-page booklet is loaned to you when you enter). During your visit, you'll actually walk on an ancient Roman road. For a better understanding of the original setting of the Forum and temple, check out the poster for sale at the entry (€3.50 entry, included in €4.50 combo-ticket, daily 10:00–13:00 & 14:30–18:00, closes at 17:00 in winter; from Piazza del Comune, go one-half block down Via San Francesco—it's on your right; tel. 075-813-053).

Pinacoteca—This small museum attractively displays its 13th- to 17th-century art (mainly frescoes), with general English information in nearly every room. There's a damaged Giotto Madonna and a rare secular fresco (to the right of Giotto art), but it's mainly a peaceful walk through a pastel world—best for art-lovers (€3.50, included in €4.50 combo-ticket, daily 10:00–13:00 & 14:30–18:00, Via San Francesco, no building number, look for banner above entryway, on main drag between Piazza del Comune and Basilica of St. Francis, tel. 075-812-033).

▲Rocca Maggiore—The "big castle" offers a good look at a 14th-century fortification and a fine view of Assisi and the Umbrian countryside (€2, included in €4.50 combo-ticket, daily from 10:00 until an hour before sunset). If you're pinching your euros, the view is just as good from outside the castle, and the interior is pretty bare.

Commune with Nature—For a picnic with the same birdsong and views that inspired St. Francis, leave the tourists behind and hike to the Rocca Minore (small private castle, not tourable) above Piazza Matteotti.

In Santa Maria degli Angeli

This modern part of Assisi, in the flat valley below the hill town, has two sights: The basilica that marks the spot where Francis lived, worked, and died; as well as the church where the crucifix spoke to him.

▲▲St. Mary of the Angels Basilica (Basilica di Santa Maria degli Angeli)—This huge basilica, towering above the buildings below Assisi, was built in the 18th century around the tiny but

historic Porziuncola Chapel (now directly under the dome). After Francis' conversion, some local monks gave him this *porziuncola,* or "small portion"—a little land with a fixer-upper chapel. Francis lived here after he founded the Franciscan Order in 1208, and this was where he consecrated St. Clare as a Bride of Christ. What would humble Francis think of the huge church—Christianity's seventh largest—that was built over his tiny chapel?

Behind the chapel on the right, find the Cappella del Transito, which marks the site of Francis' death. Francis died as he'd lived—simply, in a small hut located here. On his last night on earth, he invited some friars to join him in a Last Supper–style breaking of bread. Then he undressed, lay down on the bare ground, and began to recite Psalm 141, "Lord, I cry unto thee." He spoke the last line, "Let the wicked fall into their own traps, while I escape"...and he passed on (Oct 3, 1226).

Follow *Roseta* signs to the rose garden. Francis, fighting a temptation that he never named, threw himself onto roses. As the story goes, the thorns immediately dropped off. Ever since, thornless roses have grown here.

When you reach the statue of Francis petting a sheep, look to the right, through the window at the rose garden. The Rose Chapel (Cappella delle Rose) is built over the place where Francis lived.

In the autumn, a room in the next hallway displays a giant, animated nativity scene. The bookshop has some books in English and the free *museo* has a few monastic cells interesting to pilgrims (donation requested, museum open Mon–Fri 9:00–12:30 & 15:00–18:00).

Hours: The basilica is open daily 7:00–13:00 & 14:30–19:30. There's a little TI across the street in the arcaded building (daily 10:00–12:30 & 16:00–18:30, tel. 075-804-4554). Facing the church, the WC is on your left, behind the hedge.

Getting There: To get to St. Mary of the Angels Basilica from Assisi's train station, it's a five-minute walk (exit station left, take first left at McDonald's—you'll see the dome in the distance). When you leave the basilica, you can catch a bus directly to the station and on to Assisi's old town (leaving church, stop is on your right). The orange city buses run twice hourly (buses to the old town depart the basilica at :10 and :40 after the hour; tickets cost €0.90 if you buy at *tabacchi* or newsstand, €1.50 if you buy from driver; 20-min ride up to old town).

It's efficient to visit this basilica either on your way to the old town of Assisi or when you leave. You can easily walk to the basilica from the station (baggage check available, daily 6:30–19:00, €2.60/12 hrs).

Church of San Damiano—Located in the valley beneath the Basilica of St. Clare, this church and convent was where Francis received his call and where Clare spent her days as Mother Superior of the Poor Clares. Today, there's not much to see, but it's a peaceful escape from touristy Assisi. Drivers can zip right there, while walkers descend pleasantly from Assisi for 15 minutes through an olive grove (start at Porta Nuova parking lot at the south end of town; see map on page 489).

In 1206, Francis was inside the church when he heard the wooden crucifix order him to rebuild the church. (The crucifix in San Damiano is a copy; the original is now displayed in the Basilica of St. Clare.) Francis initially interpreted these miraculous words as a call to rebuild crumbling San Damiano. He sold his father's cloth for stones and physically rebuilt it himself. (The church we see today, however, was rebuilt later by others.) Eventually, Francis realized the call was to revitalize the Christian Church at large.

Approaching the end of his life, Francis came to San Damiano to visit his old friend Clare. She set him up in a simple reed hut in the olive grove where, in September, 1225, he was inspired to write his poem, "The Canticle of the Sun" (see page 499).

Outside of Assisi

Hermitage (Eremo delle Carcere)—If you want to follow further in St. Francis' footsteps, take a trip up the rugged slopes of nearby Mt. Subasio to the humble hermitage Francis and his followers retreated to for solitude. The highlight is a look at the tiny dank cave he retired to for prayer (daily 7:00–19:00, until 18:00 off-season, tel. 075-812-301). There is no public transportation; either take a taxi or walk up. Starting from Assisi's Porta Cappuccini gate, it's a stiff three-mile, 90-minute hike with an elevation gain of 800 feet. Wear sturdy shoes and bring water.

SLEEPING

Assisi accommodates large numbers of pilgrims on religious holidays (see list on page 844). Finding a room at any other time should be easy. Few hotels are air-conditioned. Locals suggest that you keep your windows closed in the middle of the day so that your room can be as cool as possible in the evening.

Hotels and Rooms

$$$ Hotel Umbra, a quiet villa in the middle of town, has 25 rooms with great views and fine accommodations (Sb-€75, Db-€123, Tb-€155, 10 percent cash discount for two or more nights with this book in 2008, air-con, peaceful garden and view sun terrace, most rooms have views, good restaurant, dinner only, closed Nov–mid-March, just off Piazza del Comune under the arch at Via degli Archi 6, tel. 075-812-240, fax 075-813-653, www .hotelumbra.it, info@hotelumbra.it, family Laudenzi).

$$$ Hotel Ideale, on the top edge of town overlooking the valley, offers 12 airy, modern rooms (all with view, 10 with balconies), a tranquil garden setting, and free parking (Sb-€60, Db-€95, prices good with this book through 2008, may be cheaper off-season, air-con, confirm your arrival time especially if arriving after 17:00, Piazza Matteotti 1, tel. 075-813-570, fax 075-813-020, www.hotelideale.it, info@hotelideale.it, friendly sisters Lara and Ilaria). This hotel, close to the bus stop (and parking lot) at Piazza Matteotti at the top end of town, is easy to reach by public transportation.

$$ Hotel Belvedere, a great value, is a modern building with 16 big, spacious rooms—nine come with sweeping views (Sb-€45, Db-€65, breakfast-€5, elevator, large communal view terrace, 2 blocks past Basilica of St. Clare at Via Borgo Aretino 13, tel.

Assisi

Sleep Code

(€1 = about $1.30, country code: 39)

S = Single, **D** = Double/Twin, **T** = Triple, **Q** = Quad, **b** = bathroom, **s** = shower only. Unless otherwise noted, credit cards are accepted, English is spoken, and breakfast is included.

To help you sort easily through these listings, I've divided the rooms into three categories based on the price for a standard double room with bath:

$$$ Higher Priced—Most rooms €90 or more.

$$ Moderately Priced—Most rooms between €55–90.

$ Lower Priced—Most rooms €55 or less.

075-812-460, fax 075-816-812, www.assisihotelbelvedere.it, info @assisihotelbelvedere.it, run by Enrico and Mary from New Jersey).

$$ La Pallotta, a recommended restaurant (see below), offers seven clean, bright rooms and a communal view room on the top floor (Sb-€40, Db-€65, free Internet access; a block off Piazza del Comune at Via San Rufino 6—go up a short flight of stairs outside building, above the arch, to reach entrance; tel. & fax 075-812-307, www.pallottaassisi.it, pallotta@pallottaassisi.it, Stefano and family).

$$ Hotel Sole, well-located with 35 rooms in a 15th-century building, is tired and forgettable but works in a pinch (Sb-€45, Db-€65, Tb-€85, breakfast-€5, easy parking, Corso Mazzini 35, 100 yards before Basilica of St. Clare, tel. 075-812-373, fax 075-813-706, www.assisihotelsole.com, info@assisihotelsole.com). Half of its rooms are in a newer annex across the street (elevator in annex).

$ Hotel La Rocca, on the peaceful top end of town, has 35 solid and modern rooms in a medieval shell (Sb-€40, Db-€50, Tb-€70, breakfast-€5, parking-€6, sunny rooftop terrace, a 3-min walk from Piazza Matteotti at Via Porta Perlici 27, tel. & fax 075-812-284, www.hotelarocca.it, info@hotelarocca.it).

$ Hotel San Rufino offers a great locale, solid stone quality, and 11 comfortable rooms (Sb-€46, Db-€55, Tb-€68, breakfast-€5; from Cathedral of San Rufino, follow sign to Via Porta Perlici 7; tel. & fax 075-812-803, www.hotelsanrufino.it, info@hotelsanrufino.it). Their nine-room annex, Albergo Il Duomo (listed below), saves you about €10 a night with no loss in comfort.

$ Albergo Il Duomo is tidy and *tranquillo,* with nine rooms on a stair-stepped lane one block up from San Rufino. Check in at Hotel San Rufino (Sb-€35, Db-€46, breakfast-€5, Vicolo San Lorenzo 2, tel. & fax 075-812-742, www.hotelsanrufino.it, info @hotelsanrufino.it).

$ Camere Annalisa Martini is a cheery home swimming in vines, roses, and cats in the town's medieval core. Annalisa enthusiastically accommodates her guests with a picnic garden, a washing machine (€7 per small load, including drying and ironing), a communal refrigerator, and six homey rooms (S-€25, Sb-€28, D-€38, Db-€42, Tb-€58, Qb-€68, cash only, 3 rooms share 2 bathrooms, no breakfast; 1 block from Piazza del Comune, go downhill toward basilica, turn left on Via San Gregorio to #6; tel. & fax 075-813-536, cameremartini@libero.it, Mama Martini doesn't speak English, but Annalisa does).

$ *Hostel:* Francis probably would have bunked with the peasants in Assisi's **Ostello della Pace** (€15 beds in 4- to 8-bed rooms, dinner-€9.50, laundry service, lockout 9:30–16:00, 23:30 curfew; get off bus at Piazza Unità d'Italia, then take 10-min walk to Via

Central Assisi Hotels and Restaurants

1. Hotel Umbra
2. Hotel Ideale
3. To Hotel Belvedere
4. La Pallotta Rooms
5. Hotel Sole
6. Hotel La Rocca
7. Hotel San Rufino
8. Albergo Il Duomo
9. Camere Annalisa Martini
10. St. Anthony's Guest House
11. Ristorante Medioevo
12. La Pallotta Restaurant
13. Trattoria da Erminio
14. Taverna dei Consoli
15. Caffè Duomo
16. La Bottega dei Sapori

P Parking

🏛 View

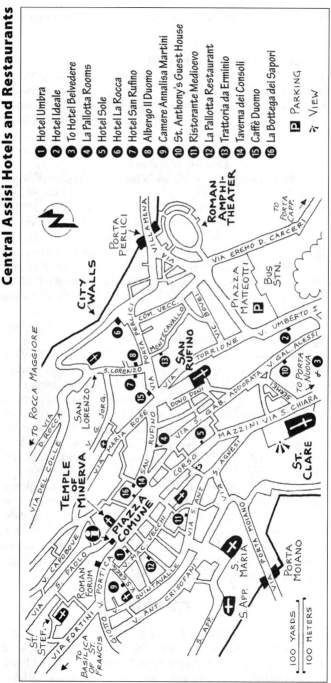

Assisi

di Valecchie 177; tel. & fax 075-816-767, www.assisihostel.com, assisi.hostel@tiscalinet.it).

Sweet Dreams in a Convent

Assisi is filled with convents, most of which rent rooms to pilgrims and travelers. While you don't need to be a pilgrim or even a Christian to be welcome, it's just common sense to stay in a convent *only* if you're approaching Assisi with a contemplative mindset. Convents feel institutional; house many groups; are not particularly inexpensive; and come with all the facilities you might need to enjoy a spirit-filled visit to Assisi.

$ St. Anthony's Guest House is where the Franciscan Sisters of the Atonement (including several Americans and Canadians) offer a very warm and tranquil welcome. Their oasis of peace is just above the Basilica of St. Clare. With only 35 beds in 20 rooms at a great price, they book literally months in advance (Sb-€35, Db-€55, Tb-€75, 2-night minimum, cash only, no problem if couples want to share a bed, 23:00 curfew, closed mid-Nov–March, library, views, picnic garden, parking, just below Piazza Matteotti at Via Galeazzo Alessi 10, tel. 075-812-542, fax 075-813-723, atoneassisi @tiscali.it).

Agriturismi near Assisi

$$ Podere la Fornace is a renovated farmhouse in the tiny village of Tordibetto, just a few miles outside Assisi. The five apartments (with 1–3 bedrooms) have full kitchens and a living room that can sleep an extra person. Local wine, olive oil, and pasta are available on-site (Db-€80, apartment-€100–180 depending on size and season, less in off-season, 2-night minimum, games for children, swimming pool, bikes, Via Ombrosa 3, tel. 075-801-9537, mobile 338-990-2903, fax 075-801-9630, www.lafornace.com, info @lafornace.com).

$$ Alla Madonna del Piatto is a six-room *agriturismo* located about five miles outside of Assisi. The Dutch–Italian owners have taken a centuries-old farm into the modern age, making pesticide-free olive oil on the premises and offering cooking classes (Db-€80–95, non-smoking, in the village of Pieve San Nicolò at Via Petrata 37, tel. 075-819-9050, mobile 328-702-5297, www.incampagna .com, letizia.mattiacci@libero.it).

EATING

I've listed decent, central, good-value restaurants. Assisi's food is heavy and rustic. Locals brag about their sausage and love to grate truffles on pasta. To bump up any meal, consider a glass or bottle of the favorite homegrown red wine, Sagrantino de Montefalco.

Umbria's answer to Brunello (although locals here would say it's Brunello that has to measure up to Sagrantino), it stirs dancing girls and flames.

Dining

Ristorante Medioevo is my vote for your best splurge. With heavy-feeling but spacious cellar vaults, this restaurant is an elegant yet accessible playground. William Ventura will guide you to the best of Umbrian cuisine. He features traditional cuisine with a modern twist, dictated by what's in season. While his first passion is cooking, his second is music—mellow jazz and bossa nova give a twinkle to the medieval ambience. Dishes are well-presented, knives are sharpened at your table, beef is a specialty, and the wonderful Sagrantino wine is served by the glass (not listed on the menu, you have to ask). With €10 pastas and €14 *secondi* courses, it's a fine value (Tue–Sun 12:30–15:00 & 19:30–22:45, closed Mon; from the fountain on the Piazza del Comune, hike downhill two blocks to Via Arco dei Priori 4; tel. 075-813-068).

La **Pallotta,** a local favorite run by a friendly and hardworking family, offers delicious, well-presented regional specialties, such as *piccione* (squab, a.k.a. pigeon) and *coniglio* (rabbit). Reservations are smart (€6 pastas, €10 *secondi*, interesting €25 fixed-price sampler, Wed–Mon 12:15–14:30 & 19:15–21:30, closed Tue, vegetarian options, a few steps off Piazza del Comune across from temple/church at Vicolo della Volta Pinta 2, tel. 075-812-649).

Ristorante San Francesco, a small dining hall that overlooks the basilica, is good—if you don't mind paying for the view. Come here for an elegant and dressy meal after a visit to the basilica. They offer a €25 traditional Umbrian fixed-price meal along with Mediterranean cuisine (Thu–Tue serving from 12:00 and from 19:30, closed Wed, Via San Francesco 52, tel. 075-812-329). Their more casual café/bar is nice for a drink or an after-basilica snack.

Casual Eateries

Trattoria da Erminio is a charming place with 10 tables under a big, medieval, brick vault. Run by Federico and his family for three generations, it specializes in local meat cooked on an open-fire grill. They have good Umbrian wines—before you order, ask Federico for a taste of the Petranera wine (€13 tourist fixed-price meal, Fri–Wed 12:00–14:30 & 19:00–21:00, closed Thu, also seating on a quiet little square; from Piazza San Rufino, go a block up Via Porta Perlici and turn right to Via Montacavallo 19; tel. 075-812-506).

At **Locanda del Podestà,** chef Selvio serves up tasty grilled Umbrian sausages, *gnocchi alla locanda*, and all manner of truffles, while Romina graciously serves happy diners. Try the tasty *scottaditto* ("scorch your fingers") lamb chops (€6 pastas, €12 *secondi*, Thu–Tue 12:00–15:00 & 19:00–22:00, closed Wed and Jan, 5-min walk uphill from basilica, San Giacomo 6c, tel. 075-813-034).

Taverna dei Consoli has a fine Assisian perch, snappy service, and a sampling of regional cooking. In the summer, relax on its terrace, which overlooks Piazza del Comune (Thu–Tue 12:00–14:30 & 19:00–21:30, closed Wed and Jan, tel. 075-812-516). Friendly third-generation owner Moreno, who speaks a leetle English, recommends the bruschetta, *filet al tartufo, cinghiale* (boar), and *stringozzi* (noodles named for the cords that poor people used to strangle priests who extorted sky-high tithes).

Caffè Duomo, which faces the Cathedral of San Rufino, has good indoor and great outdoor seating. It's run by enthusiastic young stallions, has a nice jazz ambience, and offers free Internet access to anyone ordering even just a drink (otherwise €2.50/hr). They also sell sandwiches and ice cream (Piazza San Rufino 5, tel. 075-815-398). Across the street, you can get pizza by the slice.

Picnic on the Main Square

There are many little grocery stores *(alimentari)* nearby.

Try **La Bottega dei Sapori** for a picnic of Umbrian treats: good prosciutto sandwiches and specialty items, including truffle paste and olive oil. Friendly Fabrizio may give you a taste (daily 9:00–20:00, closed Jan–Feb, Piazza del Comune 34, tel. 075-812-294).

TRANSPORTATION CONNECTIONS

From Assisi by Train to: Rome (12/day, 2–3 hrs), **Florence** (10/day, 2–2.5 hrs, half involve change), **Orvieto** (15/day, 2–2.5 hrs, 1 or 2 transfers), **Siena** (10/day, 3–4 hrs, most involve 2 transfers; bus is more efficient), **Cortona** (hourly, 2 hrs, change in Terontola). Train station tel. 075-804-0272.

By Bus: Several different bus companies offer service to: **Rome** (2–4/day, 3 hrs, €16.50, pay driver, departs Assisi's Piazza Unità d'Italia, arrives at Rome's Tiburtina station), **Siena** (2/day at about 7:00 and 16:00, 2 hrs, €13 if you buy from driver, sold for €10 at Assisi's Agenzia Viaggi Maritur at Via Frate Elia 1b, open Mon–Fri 9:00–13:00 & 15:00–18:00, Sat 9:30–13:00 only, closed Sun, tel. 075-812-377, departs from Porta S. Pietro below the basilica). The bus occasionally departs from Santa Maria degli Angeli (stopping immediately at the side of the church).

Don't take the bus to **Florence;** the train is better. From mid-June to mid-October, buses make day-trip runs to the nearby hill towns of **Gubbio, Spello, Perugia, Todi, Lake Trasimeno,** and more. Pick up a schedule from the TI or call 075-812-534.

HILL TOWNS
of CENTRAL ITALY

The sun-soaked hill towns of central Italy offer what to many is the quintessential Italian experience: sun-dried tomatoes, homemade pasta, wispy cypress-lined driveways following desolate ridges to fortified 16th-century farmhouses, and dusty old-timers warming the same bench day after day while soccer balls buzz around them like innocuous flies.

Italy's hill towns retain their medieval charm, and are best enjoyed by adapting to the pace of the countryside. So...slow...down...and enjoy the delights that these villages offer. Spend the night if you can, as many hill towns are mobbed by day-trippers.

Planning Your Time

How in Dante's name does a traveler choose from Italy's hundreds of hill towns? I've listed some of my favorites in this chapter. The one(s) you visit will depend on your time, interests, and mode of transportation. There's no hard-and-fast best plan. Go where you want and stay as long as you want.

Multitowered San Gimignano is a classic, but because it's such an easy hill town to visit (75-min bus ride from Florence), peak-season crowds can overwhelm the town's charms. For rustic vitality not trampled by tourist crowds, out-of-the-way Volterra is the clear winner. Wine aficionados head for Montalcino and Montepulciano—each a happy gauntlet of wine shops and art galleries (the latter being my favorite). Fans of architecture and urban design appreciate Pienza's well-planned streets and squares. Art-lovers and those enamored by Frances Mayes' memoir *(Under the Tuscan Sun)* make the pilgrimage to Cortona. Urbino, well off the tourist track and quite remote, is known for its huge Ducal

Hill Towns of Central Italy

Palace. The grand, classic town of Orvieto is famous for its wine, ceramics, and colorful cathedral. But my longtime favorite is the tiny, obscure, and—to be honest—dying hill town of Civita di Bagnoregio (pictured on previous page).

For a relaxing break from big-city Italy, settle down in an *agriturismo*—a farmhouse that rents out rooms to travelers (usually for a minimum of a week in high season). These rural B&Bs—almost by definition in the middle of nowhere—provide a good home base from which to find the magic of Italy's hill towns. I've listed several

good options throughout this chapter (for more information, see "Agritourism" in the Introduction, page 19).

Hill Towns: Public Transportation

A - VOLTERRA
B - SAN GIMIGNANO
C - MONTALCINO
D - PIENZA
E - MONTEPULCIANO

---BUS
— RAIL

NOT TO
SCALE

Getting Around the Hill Towns

Bigger destinations (such as Cortona and Orvieto) are doable by public transportation. Most hill towns are easier and more efficient to visit by car.

By Bus or Train: Traveling by public transportation is cheap and connects you with the locals. While trains link some of the towns, hill towns—being on hills—don't quite fit the railroad plan. Stations are likely to be in the valley a couple of miles from the town center, usually connected by a local bus.

Buses are often the only public-transportation choice to get between small Tuscan towns. You can usually get anywhere you want to by bus, as long as you're not in a hurry, and plan ahead using bus schedules (pick up at local TIs). If you're pinched for time, it makes sense to narrow your focus to one or two hill towns, or rent a car to see more.

Buy bus tickets at newsstands or *tabacchi* shops (with the big *T* signs). Confirm the departure point *("Dov'è la fermata?")*—some piazzas have more than one bus stop, so double-check that the

Hill Towns

Wines in Tuscany

Tuscany produces some of the most famous and tastiest wines in Italy. The characteristics of the soil, temperature, and exposure make each wine unique to its area. Even if you don't often drink wine, try some in Tuscany.

Choosing a wine can be intimidating, but the Italian government tries to help you choose something decent, even if you're clueless. In general, wines are designated to one of four categories:

Vino da Tavola (table wine) is the lowest grade—drink this one with pizza. While inexpensive *vino della casa*, or "house wines," fall into this category, they can be decent. Many restaurants, even modest ones, take pride in their house wine, bottling their own or working with local wineries.

Denominazione di Origine Controllata (DOC), a cut above table wine, is usually cheap, but can be surprisingly good. More than 700 wines have earned the DOC designation. You'll see plenty of DOC wines in Tuscany, since many come from the Chianti region, located between Florence and Siena.

Denominazione di Origine Controllata e Guarantita (DOCG) is the highest grade, and can be identified by the pink or green label on the neck and the scary price tag on the shelf. Only

posted schedule lists your destination and departure time. In general, orange buses are local city buses, and blue buses are for long distances.

Once the bus arrives, confirm the destination with the driver. You are expected to stow big backpacks underneath the bus (open the luggage compartment yourself if it's closed).

Sundays and holidays are problematic; even from cities such as Siena, schedules are sparse, departing buses are jam-packed, and ticket offices are often closed. Plan ahead and buy your ticket in advance. Most agencies book bus and train tickets with little or no commission.

By Car: Exploring small-town Tuscany by car can be a great experience. But since a car is an expensive, worthless headache in big cities (such as Florence and Siena), wait to pick up your car until the last big city you visit (or pick it up at the nearest airport to avoid big-city traffic). Then use the car for lacing together the hill towns and exploring the countryside.

21 wines in Italy can be called DOCG. They're generally a good bet if you want a quality wine, but you don't know anything else about the winemaker.

A recently created category called **Indicazione Geographica Tipica** (IGT) is a broad group of wines that range from basic to some of Italy's best. It includes the "Super Tuscans"—wines that don't follow the strict "recipe" required for DOC or DOCG status, but that give local vintners more opportunity to be creative. Super Tuscans are made from a mix of international grapes (such as cabernet sauvignon) grown in Tuscany and aged in small oak barrels for only two years. The result is a lively full-bodied wine that dances all over your head...and is worth the steep price.

Visit a Tuscan *enoteca* (wine bar) and sample some of these wines side-by-side to figure out what you like—and what suits your pocketbook.

Words to Live By, or...How to Describe Wine in Italian

dry	**secco**	SAY-koh
sweet	**dolce**	DOHL-chay
earthy	**terroso**	tay-ROH-zoh
fruity	**fruttoso**	froo-TOH-zoh
full-bodied	**corposo**	kor-POH-zoh
elegant	**elegante**	ay-lay-GAHN-tay

Be warned that Italian drivers can be aggressive. They tailgate as if it was required. They pass where Americans are taught not to—on blind corners and just before tunnels. Roads have narrow shoulders or none at all. Fortunately, driving in the Tuscan countryside is less stressful than driving through Italy's urban areas, but you'll need to be on alert nonetheless.

Buy a big, detailed Tuscany road map (at a newsstand or gas station). Although roads are numbered on maps, actual road signs don't list any route numbers. Instead, roads are indicated by blue signs with a city name on them (for example, if you want to take the road heading west out of Montepulciano—marked route #146 on your map—you'd follow signs to Pienza, the next town along this route). The signs are inconsistent—they may direct you to the nearest big city or simply the next town along the route. If you end up on a truckers' route, you might see provocatively dressed woman standing by the side of the road; they're not having car trouble.

Parking throughout Tuscany can be challenging. Some towns

don't allow nonresidents to park in the city center, so you'll need to leave your car outside the walls and walk into town. If you drive in restricted zones, your car license may be photographed and you can receive a hefty fine (mailed to your home address); for specifics, see "Driving" on page 841 of the appendix. Parking lots, indicated by big blue *P* signs, are usually free and plentiful outside city walls. I prefer to use guarded lots, which are worth the expense to reduce the threat of theft (no guarantees, though). In some towns, you can park on the street; nearby kiosks sell "pay and display" tickets. If you're staying overnight, ask your hotelier for parking suggestions. Wherever you park, keep your valuables out of sight, and ideally, out of the car (they're safer with you or in your room).

For two particularly scenic drives, from Siena to Montalcino, and from Montalcino to Montepulciano, see "Crete Senese Drives" on page 561.

By Tour: Il Casato Viaggi runs bus tours from Siena to the Tuscan countryside, with plenty of wine-tasting opportunities (see "Tours" on page 460, Via Il Casato di Sotto 12 in Siena, tel. 057-746-091, fax 057-727-9863, www.sienaholiday.com).

San Gimignano

The epitome of a Tuscan hill town, with 14 medieval towers still standing (out of an original 60 or so), San Gimignano (sahn jee-meen-YAH-noh) is a perfectly preserved tourist trap. The locals seem corrupted by the easy money of tourism, and most of the rustic is faux. But San Gimignano is so easy to visit and visually so beautiful that it remains a good stop.

In the 13th century, back in the days of Romeo and Juliet, feuding noble families ran the towns. They'd periodically battle things out from the protection of their respective family towers. Pointy skylines, like San Gimignano's, were the norm in medieval Tuscany.

San Gimignano's cuisine is mostly what you might find in Siena—typical Tuscan home cooking. *Cinghiale* (cheeng-GAH-lay, wild boar) is served in almost every way: stews, soups, cutlets and, even better, as salami. Most shops will give you a sample before you commit to buying. The city is well known for having some of the best saffron in Italy; look for it on menus at finer restaurants (it's fairly expensive). Although Tuscany is normally a red-wine region, the most famous Tuscan white wine comes from here: the

San Gimignano

1. Hotel la Cisterna
2. Palazzo al Torrione
3. To Ponte a Nappo Rooms
4. Arco di Goro Rooms
5. Santa Fina Rooms
6. Tortoli Rooms

7. Locanda il Pino & Rist. il Pino
8. Trattoria Chiribiri
9. La Mangiatoia
10. La Grotta Ghiotta
11. Locanda di Sant'Agostino
12. Co-op Supermarket

Hill Towns

inexpensive, light and fruity Vernaccia di San Gimignano. Look for the green "DOCG" label around the neck for the best quality (see "Wines in Tuscany" page 520).

ORIENTATION

While the basic three-star sight here is the town of San Gimignano itself, there are a few worthwhile stops. From the town gate, head straight up the traffic-free town's cobbled main drag to Piazza della Cisterna (with its 13th-century well). The town sights cluster around the adjoining Piazza del Duomo.

Tourist Information: The helpful TI is in the old center on Piazza del Duomo (daily March–Oct 9:00–13:00 & 15:00–19:00, Nov–Feb 9:00–13:00 & 14:00–18:00, free maps, sells bus tickets, books rooms, tel. 0577-940-008, www.sangimignano.com, prolocsg@tin.it). You can drop your bag at the TI. The TI rents **audioguides** (€5 for 2-hour tour, exteriors only).

The town offers a two-hour **guided walk** in English and Italian at 15:00 daily except Sunday (runs March–Oct, €15, pay and meet at small TI—actually a hotel booking office—at Porta San Giovanni).

Arrival in San Gimignano: The bus stops at the main town gate, Porta San Giovanni. You can't drive within the walled town. There are three pay lots a short walk outside the walls; the handiest is Parcheggio Montemaggio, just outside Porta San Giovanni.

Helpful Hints: Thursday is market day on Piazza del Duomo, but for local merchants, every day is a sales frenzy. While the town has no formal baggage-check service, the TI will let you park your bags there for free. A public WC is just off Piazza della Cisterna (€0.50), and another is around the corner from Porta San Giovanni. A little electric shuttle bus does its laps all day from Porta San Giovanni to Piazza della Cisterna to Porta San Matteo (€0.50, 2/hr, buy ticket from TI or *tabacchi* shop).

SELF-GUIDED WALK

Welcome to San Gimignano

This quick walking tour will take you from the bus stop at Porta San Giovanni through the town's main squares to the Duomo and Sant'Agostino Church.

• *Start, as most tourists do, at the Porta San Giovanni gate at the bottom end of town.*

Porta San Giovanni: San Gimignano lies about 25 miles from both Siena and Florence, a good stop for pilgrims en route to those cities, and on a naturally fortified hilltop that encouraged settlement. The town's walls were built in the 13th century, with gates that helped regulate who came and went. Today, modern posts keep out all but service and emergency vehicles. The small square just outside the gate features a memorial to the town's WWII dead. Follow the pilgrims' route (and the flood of modern tourists) through the gate and up the main drag.

About 100 yards up, on the right, is a pilgrims' shelter (12th-century, Pisan Romanesque). The Maltese cross indicates that this was built by the Knights of Malta. It was one of 11 such shelters in town. Today, only this shelter's wall remains.

• *Carry on, up to the town's central Piazza della Cisterna. Sit on the steps of the well.*

Piazza della Cisterna is named for the cistern that is served by the old well standing in the center of this square. A clever system of pipes drained rainwater from the nearby rooftops into the underground cistern. This square has been the center of the town since the ninth century. Each Thursday, it fills with a weekly market—as it has for more than a thousand years.

• *Notice San Gimignano's famous towers.*

The Towers: Of the original 60 or so towers, only 14 survive. Before effective walls were developed, rich people fortified their own homes with these towers: They provided a handy refuge when ruffians and rival city-states were sacking the town. These towers became a standard part of medieval skylines. Even after town walls were built, the towers continued to rise—now to fortify noble families feuding within a town (Montague and Capulet style).

In the 14th century, San Gimignano's good times turned very bad. In the year 1300, about 13,000 people lived within the walls. Then in 1348, a six-month plague decimated the population, leaving the once-mighty town with barely 4,000 alive. Once fiercely independent, now crushed and demoralized, San Gimignano came under Florence's control, and was forced to tear down its towers. (The Banca Toscana building is the remains of one such toppled tower.) And, to add injury to injury, Florence redirected the vital trade route away from San Gimignano. The town never recovered, and poverty left it in a 14th-century architectural time warp. That well-preserved cityscape, ironically, is responsible for the town's prosperity today.

• *From the well, walk 30 yards uphill to the adjoining square with the cathedral.*

Piazza del Duomo faces the former cathedral. The twin towers to the right are 10th-century, among the first in town. The stubby tower opposite the church is typical of a merchant's tower: main door on ground floor, warehouse upstairs, holes to hold beams that once supported wooden balconies and exterior staircases, heavy stone on the first floor, cheaper and lighter brick for upper stories.

Hill Towns

• *On the piazza are the Civic Museum and Torre Grossa, worth checking out (see "Sights," below). You'll also see the...*

Duomo (or Collegiata): Walk inside San Gimignano's Romanesque cathedral. Sienese Gothic art (14th-century) lines the nave with parallel themes, Old Testament on the left and New Testament on the right. (For example: the suffering of Job opposite the suffering of Jesus, Creation facing the Annunciation, and the birth of Adam facing the Nativity.) This is a classic example of using art to teach. Study the fine Creation series (top left). Many scenes are portrayed with a local 14th-century "slice of life" setting, to help lay townspeople relate to Jesus—in the same way that many white Christians are more comfortable thinking of Jesus as Caucasian (€3.50, €5.50 combo-ticket includes mediocre Religious Art Museum, Mon–Fri 9:30–19:30, Sat 9:30–17:00, Sun 12:30–17:30).

From the church, hike uphill (passing the church on your left) following signs to *Rocca e Parco di Montestaffoli*. You'll enter a peaceful hilltop park and olive grove within the shell of a 14th-century fortress. A few steps take you to the top of a little tower (free) for the best views of San Gimignano's skyline; the far end of town and the Sant'Agostino Church (where this walk ends); and a commanding 360-degree view of the Tuscan countryside. San Gimignano is surrounded by olives, grapes, cypress trees and—in the Middle Ages—lots of wild dangers. Back then, farmers lived inside the walls and were thankful for the protection.

• *Return to the bottom of Piazza del Duomo, turn left, and continue your walk across town, cutting under the double arch (from the town's first wall) and into the new section where a line of fine noble palaces— now a happy can-can of wine shops and galleries—cheers you down Via San Matteo to...*

Sant'Agostino Church: This tranquil church, at the opposite end of town, has fewer crowds and more soul. Behind the altar, a lovely fresco cycle by Benozzo Gozzoli (who painted the exquisite Chapel of the Magi in the Medici–Riccardi Palace in Florence— see page 389) tells of the life of St. Augustine, a North African monk who preached simplicity. The kind, English-speaking friars (from Britain and the US) are happy to tell you about their church and way of life, and also have Mass in English on Sundays at 11:00. Pace the tranquil cloister before heading back into the tourist mobs (free, but €0.50 lights the frescoes, daily 7:00–12:00 & 15:00–19:00).

SIGHTS

Civic Museum (Museo Civico)—This small, fun museum is inside City Hall (Palazzo Comunale). Enter the room called Sala di Consiglio (a.k.a. Danti Hall). It's *molto* medieval and covered in festive frescoes, including the *Maestà* by Lippo Memmi. This virtual copy of Simone Martini's *Maestà* in Siena proves that Memmi doesn't have quite the same talent as his famous brother-in-law. Upstairs, the Pinacoteca displays a classy little painting collection, with a 1422 altarpiece by Taddeo di Bartolo honoring St. Gimignano. You can see the saint, with the town in his hands, surrounded by events from his life. As you exit, be sure to stop by the Camera del Podesta to check out the medieval dating scene (€5, includes Torre Grossa, audioguide-€2, daily March–Oct 9:30–19:00, Nov–Feb 10:00–17:00, Piazza del Duomo).

Torre Grossa—The city's tallest tower, at 200 feet, can be climbed (€5, includes Civic Museum, same hours as museum, Piazza del Duomo).

SLEEPING

Although a zoo during the daytime, when evening comes, locals outnumber tourists, and San Gimignano becomes peaceful and enjoyable.

$$ Hotel la Cisterna, right on Piazza della Cisterna, offers 49 overpriced, predictable rooms, some with panoramic view terraces (Sb-€72, Db-€100, Db with view-€110, Db with view terrace-€124, 8 percent discount in 2008 with this book, buffet breakfast, elevator, good restaurant with great view, closed Jan–Feb, Piazza della Cisterna 23, tel. 0577-940-328, fax 0577-942-080, www.hotelcisterna.it, info@hotelcisterna.it, Alessio).

$$ Palazzo al Torrione, just inside Porta San Giovanni, is quiet and handy. They have 10 modern rooms, generally better than most hotels and at two-thirds the price, though they don't have a full-time reception (Db-€75–120, Tb-€95–150, Qb/family

Hill Towns

Sleep Code

(€1 = about $1.30, country code: 39)
S = Single, **D** = Double/Twin, **T** = Triple, **Q** = Quad, **b** = bathroom, **s** = shower only. Unless otherwise noted, credit cards are accepted and breakfast is included (but usually optional). English is generally spoken, but I've noted exceptions.

To help you sort easily through these listings, I've divided the rooms into three categories based on the price for a standard double room with bath:

$$$ **Higher Priced**—Most rooms €100 or more.

$$ **Moderately Priced**—Most rooms between €70–100.

$ **Lower Priced**—Most rooms €70 or less.

suite-€110–180, breakfast-€7, cheap parking, inside and left of gate at Via Berignano 76; operated from *tabacchi* shop 2 blocks away, on the main drag at Via San Giovanni 59; tel. 0577-940-480, mobile 338-938-1656, fax 0577-955-605, www.palazzoaltorrione.com, palazzoaltorrione@palazzoaltorrione.com, Francesco).

$$ Ponte a Nappo, run by enterprising Carla Rossi (who doesn't speak English) and her son Francesco (who does), has comfortable rooms and apartments in a farmhouse just outside San Gimignano (Db-€85, apartments for 2–6 people €110–180 with this book in 2008, air-con, parking, pool, 15-min walk or 5-min drive from Porta San Giovanni, tel. 0577-955-041, mobile 349-882-1565, fax 0577-941-268, www.accommodation-sangimignano .it, info@rossicarla.it). A picnic dinner—lounging on their comfy garden furniture as the sun sets—is good Tuscan living. About 100 yards below the monument square at Porta San Giovanni, find Via Vecchia (not left or right, but down a tiny road toward several listed accommodations).

$ In-Town Rossi Apartments, also owned by the Rossi family, are in the town center (rooms are named Arco di Goro, Santa Fina, and Tortoli, Db-€60–90 with this book in 2008, apartments-€80–130, same contact info as Ponte a Nappo farm, above). See their website for details on their confusing array of good-quality rooms for rent.

$ Locanda il Pino is tiny (five rooms), dank but super-clean, and quiet, run by a family above their elegant restaurant just inside Porta San Matteo (Db-€55, no breakfast, easy parking just outside the gate, Via Cellolese 4, tel. 0577-940-415, laurabeconcini @supereva.it). While far from the bus stop, this is a great value for those with a car.

EATING

Trattoria Chiribiri, just inside Porta San Giovanni, serves homemade pastas and desserts at a remarkably fair price (daily 11:00–23:00, Piazza della Madonna 1, tel. 0577-941-948).

La Mangiatoia is a good local splurge, especially if you like wild game and candlelight (€10 pastas, €16 *secondi*, Wed–Mon 12:30–14:30 & 19:30–21:30, closed Tue, good outdoor seating, near Porta San Matteo at Via Mainardi 5, tel. 0577-941-528).

Ristorante il Pino, run by the same family since 1929, is subdued, pricey, and dressy. It's *the* place for "dainty game" on pink tablecloths under medieval arches (Fri–Wed 12:30–14:00 & 19:30–22:00, closed Thu, seafood as well as game, Via Cellolese 8, tel. 0577-940-415).

La Grotta Ghiotta sells local specialties and makes good soup and sandwiches that can be packed up *da portar via*—to go (daily

12:30–19:30, Via Santo Stefano 10, tel. 0577-942-074).

Locanda di Sant'Agostino spills out onto the peaceful square, facing Sant'Agostino Church. It's cheap and cheery, serving lunch and dinner daily. Dripping with onions and atmosphere on the inside, there's shady on-the-square seating outside (daily 9:30–23:30, closed Jan, Piazza Sant'Agostino 15, tel. 0577-943-141).

Picnics: The big, modern **Co-op supermarket** sells all you need for a nice spread (Mon–Sat 8:30–20:00, closed Sun, at parking lot below Porta San Giovanni). Or browse the little shops guarded by wild boar heads within the town walls; they sell boar meat (*cinghiale*). Pick up 100 grams (about a quarter pound) of boar, cheese, bread, and wine and enjoy a picnic in the garden at the Rocca or the park outside Porta San Giovanni.

TRANSPORTATION CONNECTIONS

Bus tickets are sold at the bar just inside the town gate or at the TI.

From San Gimignano by Bus to: Florence (hourly, 1.25–2 hrs, change in Poggibonsi), **Siena** (5/day, 75 min, more with change in Poggibonsi), **Volterra** (4/day, 2 hrs, change in Colle di Val d'Elsa). Sunday buses are few, far between, and crowded.

By Car from Florence: San Gimignano is an easy 45-minute drive from Florence (take the A1 exit marked *Firenze Certosa*, then a right past tollbooth following *Siena per 4 corsie* sign; exit the freeway at Poggibonsi).

Volterra

Encircled by impressive walls and topped with a grand fortress, Volterra sits high above the rich farmland. More than 2,000 years ago, Volterra was one of the most important Etruscan cities, a city much larger than the one we see today. Greek-trained Etruscan artists worked here, leaving a significant stash of art, particularly funerary urns. Eventually absorbed into the Roman Empire, the city bitterly fought against the Florentines in the Middle Ages, but like many Tuscan towns, it lost in the end and was given a fortress atop the city to "protect" its citizens. For more information on the Etruscans, see "Under the Etruscan Sun" on page 806.

Unlike other famous towns in Tuscany, Volterra feels not cutesy or touristy...but real, vibrant, and almost oblivious to the allure of the tourist dollar. A refreshing break from its more commercial neighbors, it's my favorite small town in Tuscany.

ORIENTATION

Compact and walkable, the city stretches out from the pleasant Piazza dei Priori to the old city gates.

Tourist Information: The helpful TI is on the main square, at Piazza dei Priori 20 (daily 9:00–13:00 & 14:00–19:00, €5 audio-guides discounted 20 percent with this book, tel. 0588-87257).

Arrival in Volterra: Buses stop at Piazza Martiri della Libertà in the town center. Drivers will find the town ringed with easy parking lots. The most central lots are the pay lots at Porta Fiorentina and underground at Piazza Martiri della Libertà (€1.50/hr or €11/24 hrs).

Helpful Hints: Market day is Saturday near the Roman Theater.

Local Guide: American Annie Adair married into the local community, organizes American marriages in Tuscany, and is an excellent private guide (€100/half-day, €200/day, mobile 347-143-5004, tel. & fax 0588-87774, www.tuscantour.com, info @tuscantour.com).

SIGHTS

▲**Porta all'Arco**—Volterra's most famous sight is its Etruscan Gate, built of massive, volcanic tuff *(tufa)* stones in the fourth century B.C. Volterra's original wall was four miles around—twice the size of the wall that encircles it today. With 25,000 people, Volterra was a key Etruscan trade center—one of 12 leading towns that made up the Etruscan Dodecapolis (a league of Etruscan cities). The three seriously eroded heads, dating from the first cen-

tury B.C., show what happens when you leave something outside for 2,000 years. The newer stones are part of the 13th-century city wall, which incorporated parts of the much older Etruscan wall.

A plaque just outside remembers June 30, 1944. Near that time, Nazi forces were planning to blow up the arch to slow the Allied advance. To save their treasured landmark, Volterrans ripped up the stones that pave Via Porta all'Arco and plugged the gate, managing to convince the Nazi commander that there was no need to blow up the arch. Today, all the stones are back in their places, and, like silent heroes, they welcome you through the oldest-standing Etruscan gate into Volterra.

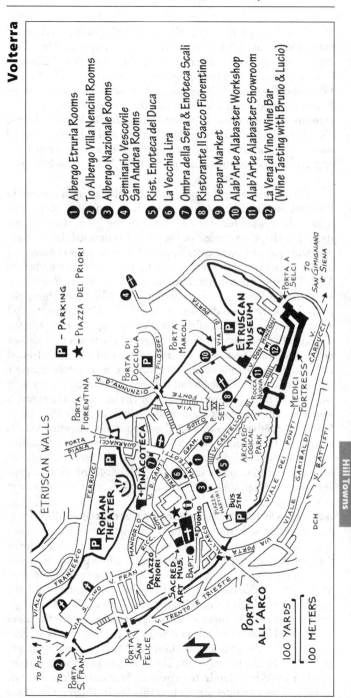

Volterra

1 Albergo Etruria Rooms
2 To Albergo Villa Nencini Rooms
3 Albergo Nazionale Rooms
4 Seminario Vescovile San Andrea Rooms
5 Rist. Enoteca del Duca
6 La Vecchia Lira
7 Ombra della Sera & Enoteca Scali
8 Ristorante Il Sacco Fiorentino
9 Despar Market
10 Alab'Arte Alabaster Workshop
11 Alab'Arte Alabaster Showroom
12 La Vena di Vino Wine Bar (Wine Tasting with Bruno & Lucio)

Hill Towns

Pass through the arch. Wander up Via Porta all'Arco 50 yards, then climb left up Via Laberinti to a viewpoint. (On a clear day, you can see the Mediterranean and the mountains of Corsica.) Continue uphill, pondering the town's nickname, "The City of Wind and Rock," until Vicolo degli Abbandonati deposits you on Piazza San Giovanni, where you face the cathedral.

Duomo—A common arrangement in the Middle Ages was for the church to face the baptistery (you couldn't enter the church until you were baptized)...and for the hospital to face the cemetery. All of these overlooked the same square. That's how it is in Pisa, as it is here.

This 12th-century church is not as elaborate as its cousin in Pisa, but the simple facade and central nave flanked by monolithic stone columns are beautiful examples of the Pisan Romanesque style. The chapel to the left of the entry has unusual, large dioramas with painted terra-cotta figures. The interior was decorated mostly in the late 16th century, during Florentine rule under the Medici family (and much restored in the 19th century). You'll see a lot of the Medici coat of arms (with the six pills, representing the family's first trade—as doctors, or *medici*). The 12th-century pulpit is beautifully carved. All of the apostles are together except Judas, who's under the table with the evil dragon (his name is the only one not carved onto the relief). The dreamy painted-and-gilded-wood Deposition (Jesus being taken down from the cross, 13th-century) is restored true to its original form, showing emotion and motion way ahead of its time. Recorded Gregorian chants add to the church's wonderful ambience (free, daily 8:00–12:30 & 15:00–17:00).

Sacred Art Museum—This humble three-room museum collects sacred art from deconsecrated churches and small, unguarded churches from nearby villages (€8 combo-ticket includes Etruscan Museum and Pinacoteca, daily 9:00–13:00 & 15:00–18:00, morning only in winter, well-explained in English, next to the Duomo at Via Roma 1).

▲Etruscan Museum (Museo Etrusco Guarnacci)—Filled top to bottom with rare Etruscan artifacts, this museum—even with few English explanations—makes it easy to appreciate how advanced this pre-Roman culture was. The exhibit, while pretty dusty and old-school, is considered the third-best Etruscan museum anywhere, after the Vatican and the British Museum. It starts with the pre-Etruscan Villanovian artifacts (c. 1500 B.C.). The seemingly endless collection of funerary urns (designed to contain the ashes of cremated loved ones) all show the subject lounging, as if kicking back with the gods at some heavenly banquet, popping grapes and just enjoying the moment. They indicate that the Etruscans believed you'd have fun in the afterlife. Artifacts such as mirrors, coins, and jewelry offer a peek into this fascinating culture. Fans of Alberto Giacometti will be amazed at how the tall, skinny figure called *The Shadow of Night (L'Ombra della Sera)* looks just like the modern Swiss sculptor's work—only 2,500 years older (€8, includes—like it or not—the Pinacoteca and Sacred Art Museum, daily 9:00–19:00, Nov–March closes at 13:45, mildly interesting English pamphlet available, audioguide-€3, Via Don Minzoni 15, tel. 0588-86-347). An alabaster workshop and a recommended wine bar are across the street; see listings below.

Pinacoteca—This museum fills a 14th-century palace with fine paintings that feel more Florentine than Sienese—a reminder of whose domain this town was in. Its highlights are Luca Signorelli's beautifully lit *Annunciation,* an example of classic High Renaissance (from the town cathedral), and (to the right) *Deposition from the Cross,* the ground-breaking Mannerist work by Rosso Fiorentino (note the elongated bodies and harsh emotional lighting and colors). Notice also Domenico Ghirlandaio's *Christ in Glory.* The two devout-looking, kneeling women are actually pagan, pre-Christian Etruscan demigoddesses, Attinea and Greciniana, but the church identified them as obscure saints to make the painting acceptable (€8 combo-ticket includes Etruscan and Sacred Art museums, daily April–Oct 9:00–19:00, Nov–March closes at 13:45, Via dei Sarti 1, tel. 0588-87-580).

Roman Theater—Built in about 10 B.C., this well-preserved theater is considered to have some of the best acoustics of its kind. Because of the fine aerial view you get from the city-wall promenade, you may find it unnecessary to pay admission to enter. Belly up to the 13th-century wall and look down. The wall you're standing on divided the theater from the town center...so, naturally, the theater became the town dump. Over time, the theater was forgotten—covered in the garbage of Volterra. Luckily, it was rediscovered in the 1950s.

The stage wall was standard Roman design—with three levels from which actors would appear: one for humans, one for heroes, and the top one for gods. Parts of two levels still stand. Gods leaped out onto the third level for the last time in the fourth century A.D., when the town decided to abandon the theater and to use its stones to build fancy baths instead. You can see the remains of the baths behind the theater, including the round sauna with brick supports to raise the heated floor (€2, but you can view the theater free from Via Lungo le Mure, April–Oct daily 10:30–17:30, Nov–March Sat–Sun only 10:00–16:00).

From the vantage point on the city-wall promenade, you can trace Volterra's vast Etruscan wall. Find the church in the distance, on the left, and notice the stones just below. They are from the Etruscan wall that followed the ridge into the valley and defined Volterra five centuries before Christ.

Hill Towns

Palazzo dei Priori—Volterra's City Hall (c. 1209) claims to be the oldest of any Tuscan city-state. It clearly inspired the more famous Palazzo Vecchio in Florence. Town halls like this were emblematic of an era when city-states were powerful. They were architectural exclamation points declaring that, around here, no pope or emperor called the shots. Towns such as Volterra were truly city-states—proudly independent and relatively democratic. They had their own armies, taxes, and even weights and measures. Notice the horizontal "cane" cut into the City Hall wall. For a thousand years, this square hosted a market and the "cane" was the local yardstick. When not in use for meetings, the city council chambers—lavishly painted and lit with fun dragon lamps—are open to visitors (€1, daily April–Oct 10:30–17:30, Nov–March Sat–Sun only 10:00–17:00).

▲**Via Matteotti**—The town's main drag, named after the popular socialist leader killed by the Fascists in 1924, provides a good cultural scavenger hunt and guided walk. Start your walk just 30 yards from the Palazzo dei Priori (City Hall) at the start of Via Matteotti. At #1 there's a typical Italian bank security door. (Step in and say, "Beam me up, Scotty.") Look up and all around. Find the medieval griffin torch holder—symbol of Volterra—and imagine the town torch lit. The pharmacy sports the symbol of its medieval guild. As you head down Via Matteotti, notice how the doors show centuries of refitting work—be careful. There's a wild boar, which is a local delicacy, at #10.

At #12, notice how the typical palace, once the home of a single rich family, is now occupied by many middle-class families (judging from the line of doorbells). After the social revolution in the 18th century and the rise of the middle class, former palaces were condominium-ized. Even so, like in *Dr. Zhivago*, the original family still lives here. Apartment #1 is the home of Count Guidi.

At #19, La Vecchia Lira is a lively cafeteria (see page 537). The Bar L'Incontro across the street is a favorite for homemade gelato and pastries. Until recently, #20 was the headquarters of the local Communist party. Americans get all Khrushchev-nervous when confronted with euro-communism, but in Western Europe it's actually a mild form of socialism that remains pretty strong today. Bologna is famously Red, as is Tuscany in general. In the 1970s, 60 percent of Tuscany voted Communist. The strength of the local Communist party has its roots in WWII anti-fascism.

Across the street, up Vicolo delle Prigioni, is a fun bakery (*panificio*). They're happy to sell small quantities if you want to try the local *cantuccini* (almond biscotti) or munch a cannoli.

At #27, look up and imagine heavy beams cantilevered out, supporting extra wooden rooms, and balconies crowding out over the street. Throughout Tuscany, today's stark and stony old building fronts once supported a tangle of wooden extensions. Doors that once led to these extra rooms are now half-bricked up to make windows. Imagine the density in the 14th century, before the plague thinned out the population.

At #30, pop into an alabaster showroom. Alabaster, quarried nearby, has long been a big industry here. Volterra alabaster—softer and more porous than marble—was sliced thin to serve as windows for Italy's medieval churches. At #51, a bit of Etruscan wall is artfully used to display more alabaster art. And #56B is the surreal alabaster art gallery of Paolo Sabatini.

Locals gather early each evening at #57 for the best cocktails in town—served with free munchies. The cinema is across the street. Movies in Italy are rarely in *versione originale*. Italians are used to getting their movies dubbed into Italian.

At #66, the end of the street is marked by another Tuscan tower. This noble house has a ground floor with no interior access to the safe upper floors. Rope ladders were used to get upstairs. The tiny door was wide enough to let in your skinny friends...but definitely no one wearing armor and carrying big weapons.

Alabaster Workshop—Alab'Arte offers a fun peek into the art of alabaster. Their showroom is across from the Etruscan Museum. A block downhill is their powdery workshop, where you can watch Roberto Chiti and Giorgio Finazzo at work. Lighting shows off the translucent quality of the stone and the expertise of these artists (Mon–Sat 10:00–13:00 & 15:00–19:00, closed Sun, showroom at Via Don Minzoni 18, workshop at Via Orti Sant'Agostino 28, tel. 0588-85-506). If you want to see more artisans in action, ask the TI for their list of the town's many workshops open to the public.

Wine Tasting with Bruno and Lucio—La Vena di Vino, also just across from the Etruscan Museum, is a fun *enoteca* where two guys have devoted themselves to the wonders of wine and share it with a fun-loving passion. Each day, Bruno and Lucio open six or eight bottles, serve your choice by the glass, pair it with characteristic munchies, and offer fine music (guitars available for patrons) and an unusual decor (the place is strewn with bras). Here is your chance to try the latest phenom in the wine world, the Super Tuscan—a creative mix of international grapes grown in Tuscany. According to Bruno, "While the Brunello (€6 a glass) is just right for wild boar, the Super Tuscan (also €6) is just right for meditation" (Wed–Mon 12:00–1:00 in the morning, closed Tue, Via Don Minzoni 30, tel. 0588-81-491).

Medici Fortress and Archaeological Park—The Parco Archeologico marks what was the acropolis of Volterra from 1500 B.C. until A.D. 1472, when Florence conquered the pesky city and burned its political and historic center, turning it into a grassy commons (today's park) and building the adjacent Medici Fortezza.

Hill Towns

The old fortress—a symbol of Florentine dominance—now keeps people in rather than out. It's a maximum-security prison housing only 60-or-so special prisoners. (Note that when you're driving from San Gimignano to Volterra, you pass another big, modern prison—almost surreal in the midst of all the Tuscan wonder.) Authorities prefer to keep organized-crime figures locked up far away from their family ties in Sicily.

SLEEPING

(€1 = about $1.30, country code: 39)

$$ Albergo Etruria, on Volterra's main drag, rents 21 fresh, modern, and spacious rooms within an ancient stone structure. They have a welcoming TV lounge and a great roof garden (Sb-€70, Db-€90, Tb-€110, 10 percent discount with cash and this book in 2008, Via Matteotti 32, tel. 0588-87377, fax 0588-92784, www.albergoetruria.it, info@albergoetruria.it). Lisa and Giuseppina take very good care of their guests.

$$ Albergo Villa Nencini, just outside of town, is big, modern, and professional, with 36 fine rooms, a large pool, and free parking (Sb-€62, Db-€83, Tb-€112, 10 percent discount with cash and this book in 2008, Borgo San Stefano 55, a 15-minute uphill walk to main square, tel. 0588-86386, fax 0588-80601, www.villanencini.it, info@villanencini.it, run by Nencini family).

$$ Albergo Nazionale, with 38 big rooms, is simple, a little musty but clean, popular with school groups, and steps from the bus stop (Sb-€56, Db-€81, Tb-€112, less off-season, Via dei Marchesi 11, tel. 0588-86284, fax 0588-84097, www.hotelnazionale-volterra.com, info@hotelnazionale-volterra.com).

$ Seminario Vescovile Sant'Andrea has been training priests for 500 years. Today, the remaining eight priests still train students, and their 30 rooms—separated by vast and holy halls—are rented very cheap to travelers (S-€14, Sb-€18, D-€28, Db-€36, T-€42, Tb-€54, breakfast-€3, closes at 24:00, groups welcome, free parking, easy 7-minute walk from Etruscan Museum, Viale Vittorio Veneto 2, tel. 0588-86028, seminaristi@diocesivolterra.it).

EATING

Menus feature a Volterran take on regional dishes. *Zuppa alla Volterra* is a fresh vegetable-and-bread soup, similar to *ribollita* (except that it isn't made from leftovers). *Torta di ceci*, also known as *cecina*, is a savory cake-like dish made with garbanzo beans. Those with more adventurous palates dive into *trippa* (tripe), the traditional breakfast of the alabaster carvers. Although it might be hard to find on restaurant menus, a cocoa sauce called *dolce forte* is popular with home cooks, who use it in meat dishes, like a Tuscan mole sauce. As the city is close to the sea, fans of fish dishes will have plenty to choose from.

Ristorante Enoteca del Duca, with a locally respected chef, serves refined Tuscan cuisine. You can dine under a medieval arch, with walls lined with wine bottles, or on a nice little patio out back (€47 food-sampler fixed-price meal, €10 pastas, €17 *secondi,* a good place for truffles, fine wine list, friendly staff, closed Tue, near City Hall at Via di Castello 2, tel. 0588-81510).

La Vecchia Lira is a classy self-serve eatery that's a hit with locals as a quick and cheap lunch spot by day, and a fancier fish restaurant at night (Fri–Wed 12:00–15:00 & 19:30–22:30, closed Thu, Via Matteotti 19, tel. 0588-86180).

Ombra della Sera serves the best pizza in town and more (Tue–Sun 12:00–15:00 & 19:00–22:00, closed Mon, Via Guarnacci 16, tel. 0588-85274). The Ristorante Ombra della Sera, on Via Gramsci, is a pricier place.

Ristorante Il Sacco Fiorentino is a local favorite for traditional cuisine (Thu–Tue 12:00–14:45 & 19:00–21:45, closed Wed, Piazza XX Settembre 18, tel. 0588-88537).

For fresh sandwiches and wine, try friendly **Enoteca Scali** (daily 9:00–22:00, Via Guarnacci 3, tel. 0588-81170).

Picnics: You can assemble a picnic at the few *alimentari* (grocery) shops around town (try Despar Market at Via Gramsci 12) and eat in the breezy Archaeological Park.

TRANSPORTATION CONNECTIONS

The nearest train station is in **Saline di Volterra,** a 30-minute bus ride away (8/day). In Volterra, buses come and go from Piazza Martiri della Libertà (buy tickets at any *tabacchi* shop). There is virtually no bus service in or out of town on Sundays or holidays.

From Volterra by Bus to: Florence (4/day, 2 hrs, change in Colle Val d'Elsa), **Siena** (4/day, 2 hrs, change in Colle di Val d'Elsa), **San Gimignano** (4/day, 2 hrs, change in Colle di Val d'Elsa), **Pisa** (9/day, 2 hrs, change in Pontedera). For Siena, Florence, and San Gimignano, Tra-In bus tickets only get you as far as Colle di Val d'Elsa; you must then buy another ticket (from another bus company) at the newsstand near the bus stop.

Montalcino

On a hill overlooking vineyards and valleys, Montalcino—famous for its delicious and pricey Brunello di Montalcino red wines—is a must-sip for wine lovers.

In the Middle Ages, Montalcino (mohn-tahl-CHEE-noh) was considered Siena's biggest ally. Originally allied with Florence, the town switched sides after the Sienese beat up Florence in the battle of Montaperti in 1260. The Sienese persuaded the Montalcini to join their side by forcing them to sleep one night in the bloody Florentine-strewn battlefield.

Montalcino prospered under Siena, but like its ally, it waned after the Medici family took control of the region. The village regained fame when, in the late 19th century, the Biondi Santi family created a fine, dark red wine, calling it Brunello—"the brunette."

Non–wine-lovers may find Montalcino a bit too focused on *vino*, but one sip of Brunello makes even wine skeptics believe that Bacchus was on to something. Note that Rosso di Montalcino (a younger version of Brunello) is also very good, at half the price. Those with sweet tooths will enjoy munching *ossi di morta* ("bones of the dead"), a crunchy cookie with almonds.

ORIENTATION

Sitting atop a hill amidst a sea of vineyards, Montalcino is surrounded by walls and dominated by the Fortezza (a.k.a. "La Rocca"). From here, roads lead down into the two main squares: Piazza Garibaldi and Piazza del Popolo.

Tourist Information: The TI, just off Piazza Garibaldi in the City Hall, can find you a room (Db-€50–60) for no fee (daily 10:00–13:00 & 14:00–17:50, closed Mon in winter, tel. & fax 0577-849-331, www.prolocomontalcino.it).

Arrival in Montalcino: The bus station is on Piazza Cavour, about 300 yards from the town center. Drivers coming in for a short visit should drive right through the old gate under the fortress (it looks almost forbidden) and grab a spot in the pay lot at the fortress (€1.50/hr, free 20:00–8:00). Otherwise, park for free a short walk away.

Helpful Hints: Market day is Friday (7:00–13:00) on Viale della Libertà. Day-trippers be warned: Montalcino has no baggage-check service. In a jam, try the TI.

SIGHTS

Fortezza—This 14th-century fort, built under the rule of Siena, is now little more than an empty shell. People visit for its *enoteca* (wine bar)—see below. Climb the ramparts to enjoy a panoramic view of the Asso and Orcia valleys, or enjoy a picnic in the park surrounding the fort (€3.50 for rampart walk, €6 combo-ticket includes Civic Museum, daily 9:00–20:00, closed Mon off-season).

Montalcino

MADONNA DEL SOCCORSO

PORTA BURELLI

PIAZZA CAVOUR

VIALE ROMA

V. DEL PINO

VIA SPAGNI

VIALE DELLA

C. SPAGNI

V. CIALDINI

VIA MAZZINI

BUS STN.

S. FRAN.

V. MOGLIO

V. MISTERO

V. CAST.

PORTA CASTEL-LANA

V. S. LUCIA

DUOMO

V. SPAGNI

SANT' AGO.

VIA SCUOLE

PIAZZA DEL POPOLO

CITY HALL, & TOWER

LIBERTÀ

FREE

VIALE STROZZI

CIVIC MUSEUM

PIAZZA GARIBALDI

VIA MA

VIA DONNOLI

CITY WALLS

BOLD.

PAN.

VIA SALONI

VIA CASERME

SALONI LANDI

C. GATTOLI

PORTA AL CASSERO

P. FORTEZZA

PORTA GATTOLI

VIA A. MORO

FORTEZZA & ENOTECA

PORTA CERBAIA

P –PARKING

100 YARDS

100 METERS

TO SANT'ANTIMO

TO VIA CASSIA, SIENA, PIENZA & MONTEPULCIANO

DCH

❶ Palazzina Cesira B&B
❷ Hotel il Giglio
❸ Ristorante il Moro Rooms
❹ Affittacamere Mariuccia
❺ Caffè Fiaschetteria Italiana
❻ Taverna il Grappolo Blu
❼ Trattoria l'Angolo
❽ Osteria al Giardino
❾ Co-op Supermarket

Hill Towns

Civic Museum (Museo Civico)—Gothic art is the star of this museum, with works from Montalcino's heyday, the 13th to 16th centuries. Wooden sculptures and religious objects round out the collection. In 2008, a new archaeology section is scheduled to open (€4.50, Tue–Sun 10:00–13:00 & 14:00–17:50, closed Mon, Via Ricasoli, tel. 0577-846-014).

Bell Tower (Il Campanone)—Newly restored, the town's medieval bell tower affords a grand view over the surrounding rooftops and countryside (price and hours not yet set, check with TI or Civic Museum, Piazza del Popolo).

Wineries—While there are plenty of *enoteche,* there are no real wineries inside the city. The nearby countryside, however, is littered with them, and most wineries will give tastings. While some require an appointment, many also are happy to serve a potential buyer a glass and show them around. Banfi, the most touristy, produces well-respected wines (daily 10:00–17:00, tours Mon–Fri at 16:00, reserve in advance, 10-minute drive south of Montalcino in Sant'Angelo Scalo, tel. 0577-840-111, www.castellobanfi.com, reservations@banfi.it).

The Montalcino TI can give you the list of more than 150 regional wineries. Or check with the vintners' consortium (tel. 0577-848-246, www.consorziobrunellodimontalcino.it, info @consorziobrunellodimontalcino.it).

SLEEPING

$$ Palazzina Cesira, right in the heart of the old town, rents five spacious and tastefully decorated rooms in a fine 13th-century residence with a palatial lounge. You'll enjoy a refined and tranquil ambience, a nice breakfast, and the chance to get to know Lucilla and her American husband Roberto (Db-€85, suites-€100–110, cash only, 2-night minimum, Via Soccorso Saloni 2, tel. & fax 0577-846-055, www.montalcinoitaly.com, cesira@mail.montalcinoitaly.com).

$$ Hotel il Giglio, although lacking in warmth, has 12 comfortable rooms, some with vaulted ceilings. Ask for a room with a view (Sb-€58, Db-€90–100, Tb-€110, 10 percent discount with this book and cash in 2008, breakfast-€6.50, Via Soccorso Saloni 5, tel. & fax 0577-848-167, www.gigliohotel.com, info@gigliohotel.com).

$ Ristorante il Moro rents four pleasant, modern rooms around the corner from their restaurant. The two upper rooms have views, the lower rooms have terraces, and they all share a cozy common room with a kitchen (Db-€55, no breakfast, 100 yards from bus station at Via Mazzini 44, tel. 0577-849-384, Alessandro and Julia).

$ Affittacamere Mariuccia has three basic, Ikea-chic rooms on the main drag over a heaven-scented bakery (Db-€44, no breakfast, check-in at Enoteca Pierangioli, Piazza del Popolo 16, rooms across the street at #28, tel. & fax 0577-849-113, www .enotecapierangioli.com, enotecapierangioli@hotmail.com, Stefania doesn't speak English).

EATING

Taverna il Grappolo Blu is unpretentious and friendly, serving local specialties and vegetarian options to an enthusiastic crowd (€7 pastas, €12 *secondi,* daily 12:00–15:00 & 19:00–22:00, reservations smart, near the main square, a few steps off Via Mazzini at Scale di Via Moglio 1, tel. 0577-847-150).

Trattoria l'Angolo, a family-run hole-in-the-wall, has nine small tables and homemade desserts (€7 pastas, €8 meat dishes, Wed–Mon 12:00–14:30 & 19:00–21:30, closed Tue, Via Ricasoli 9, tel. 0577-848-017).

Osteria al Giardino serves near-gourmet local cuisine at the bus station end of town. Owner and chef Giovanni Luca makes everything fresh, from the bread to the desserts (€7 pastas, €12 *secondi*, Thu–Tue 12:30–15:00 & 19:30–22:00, closed Wed, Piazza Cavour 1, tel. 0577-849-076).

Gather ingredients for a picnic at the **Co-op supermarket** on Via Sant'Agostino, just off Via Ricasoli in front of the Sant'Agostino Church, then enjoy your feast in front of the Fortezza.

Wine Tasting

While wine snobs turn up their noses, the medieval setting inside Montalcino's fort at **Enoteca la Fortezza** is a hit for most visitors. Spoil yourself with Brunello in the cozy *enoteca* or at outdoor tables (3 tastes-€12, snacks for 2 people-€9, daily 9:00–20:00, closes at 18:00 in off-season, inside the Fortezza, tel. 0577-849-211, www .enotecalafortezza.it).

Caffè Fiaschetteria Italiana was founded by Ferruccio Biondi Santi, who created the famous Brunello wine. The wine library in the back of the café boasts many local wine choices, including a prized bottle from 1955, a vintage year. A meeting place since 1888, this grand café also serves light lunches and espresso to tourists and locals alike (€15 for a glass of Brunello and plate of snacks, daily 7:30–23:00, Piazza del Popolo 6, tel. 0577-849-043).

TRANSPORTATION CONNECTIONS

The nearest train station is a 20-minute bus ride away in Buonconvento. Montalcino's bus station is on Piazza Cavour, within the town walls. Bus tickets are sold at the bar on Piazza Cavour or at *tabacchi* shops, but not on board. Check schedules at

Hill Towns

the TI or the bus station.

From Montalcino by Bus to: Siena (6/day, 90 min, €3.20), **Montepulciano/Pienza** (8/day, change to line #114 in Torrieneri, one hour plus changing time). Anyone going to Florence changes in Siena.

Pienza

Set on a crest, surrounded by green, rolling hills, the small town of Pienza packs a lot of Renaissance punch. In the 1400s, locally born Pope Pius II of the Piccolomini family decided to remodel his birthplace in the style that was all the rage—Renaissance. Propelled by papal clout, the town of Corsignano was transformed—in only five years' time—into a jewel of Renaissance architecture. It  was renamed Pienza, after Pope Pius. The plan was to remodel the entire town, but work ended in 1564 when both the pope and his architect, Bernardo Rossellino, died. The architectural focal point is the square Piazza Pio II, surrounded by the Duomo and the pope's family residence, Palazzo Piccolomini. While Piazza Pio II is Pienza's pride and joy, the entire town—a mix of old stonework, potted plants, and grand views—is fun to explore, especially with a camera or sketchpad in hand. You can walk each lane in the tiny town in a few minutes.

Nearly every shop sells the town's specialty—Pecorino cheese. This pungent sheep's cheese is available fresh *(fresco)* or aged *(secco)*, and sometimes contains other ingredients, such as truffles or peppers. Look on menus for warm *(al forno* or *alla griglia)* Pecorino, often topped with honey or pears and served with bread. Along with a glass of local wine, this just might lead you to a new understanding of *la dolce vita.*

Tourist Information: The TI is 10 yards up the street from Piazza Pio II, inside the Diocesan Museum (Mon–Sat 10:00–13:00 & 15:00–19:00, closed Sun, tel. & fax 0578-749-905).

Arrival in Pienza: Free street parking is available—if you can find it. Otherwise you can park at the large lot near Largo Roma (€1.50/hr).

Helpful Hints: Market day is Friday. A public WC is just outside the town gate on Piazza Dante Alighieri.

SIGHTS

▲**Piazza Pio II**—One of Italy's classic piazzas, this square is famous for its elegance and artistic unity. The square and the surrounding buildings were all designed by Rossellino to form an "outdoor room." Spinning around, you'll see the City Hall (13th-century bell tower with a Renaissance facade and a fine loggia), the Bishop's Palace (now an art museum), the Piccolomini family palace (well worth touring—see below), and the Duomo. Just to the left of the church, a lane leads to the best viewpoint in town.

Duomo—Its classic, symmetrical Renaissance facade—with the Piccolomini family coat of arms (modestly) front and center—dominates Piazza Pio II. The interior is charming, with several Gothic altarpieces and painted arches. Windows feature the crest of Pius II, with five half-moons advertising the number of crusades that his family funded.

▲▲**Palazzo Piccolomini**—The home of Pius II (see page 468) and the Piccolomini family (until 1962) can be visited with a guided tour. While the 30-minute tour (in English and Italian) visits only six rooms and the loggia, it offers a fascinating slice of 15th-century aristocratic life and is the sightseeing highlight of the town. In fact, it's the most impressive small-town palace experience that I've found in Tuscany. Don't miss this one. Check out the well-preserved painted courtyard for free. In Renaissance times, most buildings were covered with elaborate paintings like these (€7, Tue–Sun 10:00–12:30 & 15:00–18:00, closed Mon and in winter, tel. 0578-748-392).

Diocesan Museum (Museo Diocesano)—This collection of religious paintings from local churches fills the cardinal's Renaissance palace. The art is provincial Sienese, displayed in chronological order from the 12th through 17th centuries, conveniently all on one floor (€4.10, Wed–Mon 10:00–13:00 & 15:00–19:00, closed Tue, in winter open Sat–Sun only, Corso il Rossellino 30).

View Terrace—Facing the church, a lane leads left to the panoramic promenade. Views from the terrace include the Tuscan countryside and Monte Amiata, the largest mountain in southern Tuscany, in the distance.

SLEEPING

(€1 = about $1.30, country code: 39)

$ Oliviera Camere, which has six simple rooms in the town center, is run by soft-spoken Nello, who doesn't speak English (Db-€50, breakfast in room, cash only, Via Condotti 4, tel. 0578-748-205, mobile 338-952-0459).

Hill Towns

$ Il Giardino Segreto Camere rents six humble rooms with a lush, peaceful garden (Db-€62, apartment Db-€67, Via Condotti 13, tel. 0578-748-539, mobile 338-899-5879, www.ilgiardinosegreto .toscana.nu, muccirossi@bcc.tin.it).

Agriturismi: **$$ Agriturismo Terrapille** sits just below Pienza, on a little grassy bluff surrounded by 360 degrees of dreamy Tuscan scenery. It's private and rustic, yet cozy and romantic. Four country rooms and two apartments come with modern comforts (Db-€103, Qb-€160, breakfast-€8.50, pool, about a mile out of town, take road #18 in direction of Monticchiello, tel. & fax 0578-749-146 at farm, www.terrapille.it, terrapille@bccmp.com). Lucia, who runs the place, lives in Pienza (home tel. 0578-748-434, mobile 338-920-4470).

$ Agriturismo Cretaiole is warmly run by Isabella and her husband Carlo. This family-friendly farm welcomes visitors for weeklong stays in six comfortable apartments overlooking Pienza and convenient to several classic Tuscan hill towns. The hosts are eager to share their local culture, cooking demonstrations, hands-on truffle hunting, grape and olive harvesting, and gardening or whatever's in season with guests (Db-€700/week, prices soft off-season, Via S. Gregorio 14, tel. & fax 0578-748-378, Isabella's mobile 338-740-9245, www.cretaiole.it, info@cretaiole.it).

EATING

Latte di Luna, lively with great indoor and outdoor seating, is a good, quality choice (Wed–Mon 12:30–14:30 & 19:30–21:30, closed Tue, at Porta al Giglio, Via San Carlo 2, tel. 0578-748-606).

La Taverna di Re Artu serves *bruschetta* and a variety of wines (daily 11:00–20:30, Via della Rosa 4).

Ristorante dal Falco, just outside the town wall, is touristy but offers a decent value (€7 pastas, €12 *secondi*, Sat–Thu 12:00–15:00 & 19:00–22:00, closed Fri, Piazza Dante Alighieri 3, tel. 0578-748-551).

Assemble a picnic at any of the numerous cheese and wine shops, and dine with a fantastic view along the walls of the view terrace.

TRANSPORTATION CONNECTIONS

Bus tickets are sold at the bar just inside Pienza's town gate.

From Pienza by Bus to: Siena (6/day, 90 min), **Montepulciano** (8/day, 30 min).

Montepulciano

Curving its way along a ridge, Montepulciano (mohn-tay-pull-chee-AH-noh) delights visitors with *vino* and views. Alternately under Sienese and Florentine rule, the city still retains its medieval

contrade districts, each with a mascot and flag. The neighborhoods compete the last Sunday of August in the Bravio delle Botti, where teams of men push large wine casks uphill from Piazza Marzocco to Piazza Grande, all hoping to win a banner and bragging rights.

The city is a collage of architectural styles, but the elegant San Biagio Church, at the base of the hill, is its most impressive Renaissance building. Most ignore the architecture and focus more on the city's other creative accomplishment, the tasty Vino Nobile di Montepulciano red wine.

ORIENTATION

The action in Montepulciano centers on two streets, the steep Via di Gracciano nel Corso (nicknamed Corso) and Via Ricci, but the quiet back streets are well worth a visit.

Tourist Information: The TI is near the bus station, just below Piazza Don Minzoni. It books hotels and wine tours, sells train tickets, and can book taxis (Mon–Sat 9:30–12:30 & 15:00–20:00, Sun 9:30–12:30, tel. 0578-757-341, www.prolocomontepulciano .it).

Note that there's a more central office that looks like a TI, but it's a privately run "Strada del Vino" (Wine Road) agency. It doesn't have city info, but provides wine-road maps and organizes **wine tours** in the city, and minibus winery tours farther afield (Piazza Grande, tel. 0578-717-484, www.stradavinonobile.it).

Arrival in Montepulciano: Most visits begin at the fortified Porta al Prato gate, near the bus station. From the gate, it's a 15-minute walk uphill along the Corso, the bustling main drag (note the Etruscan reliefs on the foundation of Palazzo Bucelli—see photo above) to the main square, Piazza Grande. If you arrive at the bus station, ask about a shuttle bus that will bring you closer to Piazza Grande; it's a good strategy to take the bus up and walk back down.

Drivers arriving by car should park outside the walls (it isn't wise to tackle the tiny roads inside the city), either at the bus station or the numerous lots on the edge of town. For a free spot near the top of the hill, follow signs for lot #8.

Helpful Hints: Market day is Thursday. There's no official baggage check in town, but the TI might let you leave bags with them if they have space. Public WCs are located at the TI, next to Palazzo Comunale, and at the Church of St. Augustine.

SIGHTS

Piazza Grande—This pleasant, lively piazza is surrounded by a grab bag of architectural sights. The medieval Palazzo Comunale

may remind you of Palazzo Vecchio in Florence—that's because Florence dominated this town in the 15th and 16th centuries. The crenellations along the roof were never intended to hide soldiers—they're there just to symbolize power. Climbing the **clock tower** rewards you with a windy but beautiful view from the terrace below the clock. Go into the Palazzo Comunale and head up the stairs (€1.60, daily 10:00–18:00, closed in winter). The Palazzo de' Nobili–Tarugi is a Renaissance arcaded confection; meanwhile, the unfinished **Duomo** looks glumly on, wishing the city hadn't run out of money for its facade. Many such churches were built until they had a functional interior, and then, for various practical reasons, the facades were left unfinished. You can see the rough stonework just waiting for the final marble veneer. Step inside the Duomo, and you are rewarded with a beautiful Andrea della Robbia *Altar of the Lilies* behind the baptismal font (on the left as your enter) and a luminous, early-Renaissance Assumption triptych by Taddeo di Bartolo, an artist from Siena (daily 9:00–13:00 & 15:00–19:00). The Contucci Palace (left of the church) is lucky enough to have a 16th-century Renaissance facade. The Contucci family still lives in their palace, producing and selling their own wine. The town is fortunate to be graced with so many bold and noble palazzos—Florentine nobility favored Montepulciano as a breezy and relaxed place for a secondary residence.

▲▲Contucci Cantina—Montepulciano's most popular attraction isn't made of stone...it's the famous wine, Vino Nobile. This robust red can be tasted in any of the cantinas lining Via Ricci and Via di Gracciano nel Corso, but the cantina in the basement of the Contucci Palace is the most fun. While the palace has a formal wine-tasting showroom facing the square, head down the lane on the right to the actual cellars, where you'll meet lively Adamo, who has been making wine since 1953 and welcomes tourists into his

Montepulciano

1 Mueble il Riccio Rooms
2 Camere Bellavista Rooms
3 Ai Quattro Venti
4 Osteria dell'Aquacheta

TO SIENA &
A-1 AUTOSTRADA
FREEWAY

TO
CHIUSI

SANT'
AGNESE

PIAZZA
MARZOCCO

PIAZZA
DON
MINZONI

POGGIO-
FANTI
GARDENS

VIA E. BERNABEI

VIA DELLE LETTERE

PORTA AL
PRATO

WC

PALAZZO
BUCELLI

VIALE 1 MAGGIO

VIA DEL MAGGIO

ST.
AUGUSTINE

WC

BUS
STATION

S.
LUCIA

NEL CORSO

PIANA

Post

ARCHI

POGGIOLO

VIA GRACCIANO

SAN
FRAN.

VIA DI ORIOLO

★ = PIAZZA GRANDE

P = PARKING

TO
SAN
BIAGIO

VIA DI
SAN BIAGIO

VIA RICCI

TALOSA

CIVIC
MUSEUM

VOLT.

GESÙ

CIRCONVALLAZIONE

PALAZZO
COMUNALE

WC

★

1

CONTUCCI
CANTINA

3

DUOMO

FIOR VECCHIA

4

OPIO CORSO

VIA SAN PIETRO

P

VIA COLLAZZI

DONATO

TEATRO

VIA DEL OPIO CORSO

PORTA DI FARINE

FORTEZZA

BUS
STOP

100 YARDS

V. POLIZIANO

VIA DI
FILOSOFI

100 METERS

S. MARIA

TO PIENZA & MONTALCINO

Hill Towns

cellar. Adamo usually has a dozen bottles open (tasting is free, no food, daily 8:30–12:30 & 14:30–18:30, Piazza Grande 7, tel. 0578-757-006). Groups are welcome with a reservation.

After sipping a little wine with Adamo, explore the 13th-century vaults of the palace basement, now filled with huge barrels of wine. Countless barrels of Croatian, Italian, and French oak (1,000 to 2,500 liters each) cradle the wine through a two-year in-the-barrel aging process, while the wine picks up the personality of the wood. After about 35 years, an exhausted barrel has

nothing left to offer its wine, and it's retired. Adamo explains that the French oak gives the wine "pure elegance," the Croatian is more masculine, and the Italian oak is a marriage of the two. Each barrel is labeled with the size in liters, the year the wine was barreled, and the percentage of alcohol (determined by how much sun shone in that year). "Nobile"-grade wine needs a minimum of 13 percent alcohol.

Civic Museum (Museo Civico)—Small and eclectic, the highlight of this well-presented museum is its colorful della Robbia ceramic altarpieces and Etruscan artifacts (€4.10, Tue–Sat 10:00–13:00 & 15:00–18:00, Sun 10:00–18:00, closed Mon, Via Ricci 10, tel. 0578-757-341).

San Biagio Church—Down a picturesque driveway lined with cypress, this church—designed by Antonio da Sangallo—is Renaissance perfection. The proportions of the Greek cross plan give the building a pleasing rhythmic quality. The lone tower was supposed to have a twin, but it was never built. The soaring interior, with a high dome and lantern, creates a fine Renaissance space (daily 9:00–13:00 & 15:00–19:00). The street Via di San Biagio, leading from the church up into town, makes for an enjoyable, if challenging, walk.

SLEEPING

(€1 = about $1.30, country code: 39)

$$ Mueble il Riccio ("hedgehog" in Italian) is medieval-elegant, with six modern rooms, an awesome roof terrace, and friendly owners (Sb-€75, Db-€85, Tb-€101, breakfast-€8, air-con, parking, a block below the main square at Via Talosa 21, tel. & fax 0578-757-713, www.ilriccio.net, info@ilriccio.net, Gio and Ivana speak English). Gio (or his son) gives country tours (€25/hr) in one of their classic Italian cars; for tour details, see their website.

$ Camere Bellavista has 10 simple rooms, some with better views than others. Room 6 has a view terrace worth reserving (Db-€60, nicer Db-€70, breakfast-€2.50, cash only, no elevator, Via Ricci 25, no reception—call before arriving, mobile 347-823-2314, fax 0578-716-341, bellavista@bccmp.com, little English spoken).

EATING

Ai Quattro Venti is fresh, flavorful, fun, and right on Piazza Grande, offering good indoor and outdoor seating (€7 pastas, Fri–Wed 12:30–14:00 & 19:30–22:30, closed Thu, next to City Hall on Piazza Grande, tel. 0578-717-231).

Osteria dell'Aquacheta serves pastas and salads at reasonable prices, with a mix of locals and tourists (€6 pastas and salads, Wed–Mon 12:30–15:00 & 19:30–22:30, closed Tue, Via del Teatro 22, tel. 0578-717-086).

TRANSPORTATION CONNECTIONS

All buses leave from Piazza Pietro Nenni. Check for schedules at www.sienamobilita.it.

From Montepulciano by Bus to: Siena (4/day, 75 min, none on Sun), **Pienza** (8/day, 30 min). There are hourly bus connections to **Chiusi**, a town on the main Florence–Rome rail line; Chiusi is a much better bet than the distant Montepulciano station (5 miles away), which is served only by milk-run trains.

To Montalcino: This connection is problematic by public transportation—consider asking at the TI for a taxi. Although expensive (about €50), a taxi could make sense for two or more people. **Drivers** find route #146 to Montalcino particularly scenic (see "Crete Senese Drives," page 561).

Cortona

Cortona blankets a 1,700-foot hill surrounded by dramatic Tuscan and Umbrian views. Frances Mayes' books, such as *Under the Tuscan Sun,* have placed this town in the touristic limelight, just as Peter Mayle's books popularized the Luberon region in France. But long before Mayes ever published a book, Cortona was popular with Romantics and considered one of the classic Tuscan hill towns. Unlike San Gimignano, Cortona maintains a rustic and gritty personality—even with its long history of foreigners who, enamored with its Tuscan charm, made this their adopted home.

The city began as one of the largest Etruscan settlements, the remains of which can be seen at the base of the city walls, as

well as in the nearby tombs. (Also see "Under the Etruscan Sun" on page 806.) It grew to its present size in the 13th to 16th centuries, when it was a colorful and crowded city, eventually allied with Florence. The farmland that fills almost every view from the city was marshy and uninhabitable until about 200 years ago, when it was drained and turned into some of Tuscany's most fertile land.

Art-lovers know Cortona as the home of Renaissance painter Luca Signorelli, Baroque master Pietro da Cortona (Berretini), and the 20th-century Futurist artist Gino Severini. The city's museums and churches reveal many of the works of these native sons.

ORIENTATION

Most of the main sights, shops, and restaurants cluster around the level streets on the Piazza Garibaldi–Piazza del Duomo axis, but Cortona will have you huffing and puffing up some steep hills.

Tourist Information: The helpful TI is on the main drag at Via Nazionale 42 (April–Oct daily 9:00–13:00 & 15:00–19:00, shorter hours and closed Sun off-season, sells train and bus tickets, tel. 0575-630-352, www.apt.arezzo.it, www.cortona-musei.it for museums).

Private Guide: Giovanni Adreani exudes energy and a love of his city and Tuscan high culture. He is great at bringing the fine points of the city to life and can take visitors around in his car for no extra price. As this region is speckled with under-appreciated charms, having Giovanni for a day as your driver/guide promises to be a fascinating experience (€110/half-day, €180/day, tel. 0575-630-665, mobile 347-176-2830, www.adreanigiovanni.com, adreanigiovanni@libero.it).

Arrival in Cortona: Buses stop at Piazza Garibaldi. From here, it's a level five-minute walk down bustling, shop-lined Via Nazionale (stop by the TI) to Piazza della Repubblica, the heart of the town, dominated by City Hall (Palazzo della Comune). From this square, it's a two-minute stroll past the interesting Etruscan Museum and theater to Piazza del Duomo, where you'll find the recommended Diocesan Museum. Steep streets, many of them stepped, lead from Piazza della Repubblica up to the San Niccolò and Santa Margherita churches and the Medici Fortress (a 30-minute climb from Piazza della Repubblica).

Drivers will find several free lots right outside the walls. Viale

Cortona

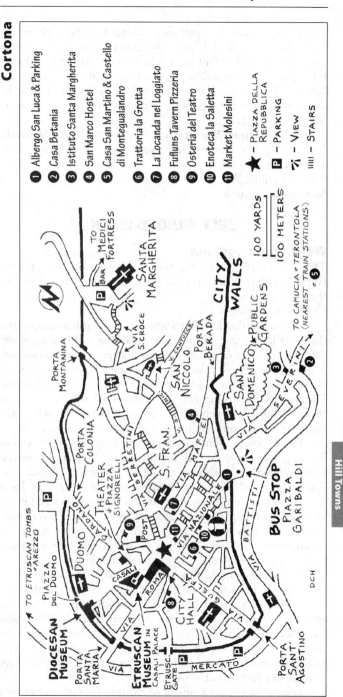

1. Albergo San Luca & Parking
2. Casa Betania
3. Istituto Santa Margherita
4. San Marco Hostel
5. Casa San Martino & Castello di Montegualandro
6. Trattoria la Grotta
7. La Locanda nel Loggiato
8. Fufluns Tavern Pizzeria
9. Osteria del Teatro
10. Enoteca la Saletta
11. Market Molesini

★ – Piazza della Repubblica
P – Parking
🎯 – View
||||| – Stairs

Hill Towns

Battisti may be your best bet; after parking, take the escalator into town. Piazza Garibaldi is perfectly central (where the buses stop, a two-minute walk from Piazza della Repubblica) and has a handful of pay spots (marked by blue lines, pay & display, cheap, free 20:00–8:00). The small town is actually very long, and it can be smart to drive to the top for sightseeing there (parking at Santa Margherita Basilica).

Helpful Hints: Market day is Saturday on Piazza Signorelli (early–14:00). The town has no baggage check, so try asking nicely at a hotel or museum if you'd like to like to store your bag there. The best public WC is located in Piazza del Duomo, under St. Margherita's statue.

SELF-GUIDED WALK

Welcome to Cortona

This introductory walking tour will take you from Piazza Garibaldi, up the main strip, to the town center, its piazzas, and the Duomo.

• *Start at the bus stop in...*

Piazza Garibaldi: Many visits start and finish in this square, thanks to its bus stop. While the piazza, bulging like a big turret out from the town fortifications, looks like part of an old rampart, it's really a souvenir of those early French and English Romantics—the ones who first created the notion of a dreamy, idyllic Tuscany. During the Napoleonic age, the French built this balcony (and the scenic little park behind the adjacent San Domenico Church) simply to enjoy a commanding view of the Tuscan countryside.

With Umbria about a mile away, Cortona marks the end of Tuscany. This is a major cultural divide, as Cortona was the last town in Charlemagne's empire and the last under Medici rule. Umbria, just to the south, was papal territory for centuries. These deep-seated cultural disparities were a great challenge for the visionaries who unified the fractured region to create the modern nation of Italy during the 1860s. A statue in the center of this square honors one of the heroes of the struggle for Italian unification—the brilliant revolutionary general, Giuseppe Garibaldi.

Enjoy the commanding view from here. Assisi is just over the ridge on the left. Lake Trasimeno peeks from behind the hill, looking quite normal today. But, according to legend, it was blood-red after Hannibal defeated the Romans here in 217 B.C. and 15,000 died in the battle. The only sizable town you can see, on the right, is Montepulciano. Cortona is still defined by its Etruscan walls—remnants of these walls, with stones laid 2,500 years ago, stretch from here in both directions.

Frances Mayes put Cortona on the map for many Americans

with her book and the movie, *Under the Tuscan Sun*. Her book describes her real-life experience buying, fixing up, and living in a rundown villa in Cortona with her husband Ed. The movie romanticized the story, turning Frances into a single, recently divorced writer who restores the villa and her peace of mind. Frances' villa isn't "under the Tuscan sun" very often; it's named "Bramasole"—literally, "craving sun." On the wrong side of the hill, it's in the shade after 15:00. She and her husband still live there part of each year and are respected members of their adopted community (outside the walls, behind the hill on the left).

• *From this square, head into town along...*

Via Nazionale: The only level road in town, locals have nicknamed Via Nazionale the *ruga piana* (flat wrinkle). This is the main commercial street in this town of 2,500, and it's been that way for a long time. Every shop seems to have a medieval cellar or an Etruscan well. Notice the crumbling sandstone door frames. The entire town is constructed out of this grainy, eroding rock.

• *Via Nazionale leads to...*

Piazza della Repubblica: The City Hall faces Cortona's main square, where three flags fly: Europe, Italy, and peace (Tuscany is famously left-wing and likes peace). Note how the City Hall is a clever hodgepodge of twin medieval towers, with a bell tower added to connect them, and a grand staircase to lend some gravitas. Notice also the fine wood balconies on the left. In the Middle Ages, wooden extensions such as balconies were common features on the region's stone buildings. These balconies (not original, but rebuilt in the 19th century) would have fit right in the medieval cityscape. These days, you usually see only the holes that once supported the long-gone wooden beams.

This square has been the town center since Etruscan times. Four centuries before Christ, an important street led from here up to the hill-capping temple. Later, the square became the Roman forum. Opposite the City Hall is a handy grocery store for good, cheap sandwiches (see "Eating," page 557). Above that is the loggia—once a fish market, now a recommended restaurant.

• *The second half of the square, to the right of the City Hall, is...*

Piazza Signorelli: Dominated by Casali Palace, this square was the headquarters of the Florentine captains who used to control the city. Peek into the palace entrance for a look at the coats of arms. Every six months, Florence would send a new captain to Cortona, who would help establish his rule by inserting his family coat of arms into the palace's wall. These date from the 15th to the 17th century, and were once painted with bright colors. Cortona's fine Etruscan Museum (listed in "Sights," next page) is in the Casali Palace courtyard, which is lined with many more of these family coats of arms. The inviting Caffè del Teatro fills the loggia of the theater that is named for the town's most famous artist, Luca Signorelli.

• *Head down the street just to the right of the museum to...*

Piazza del Duomo: Here you'll find the Diocesan Museum (see "Sights," below), cathedral, and a statue of St. Margherita. If the cathedral seems a little underwhelming and tucked away, that's because it is. Cortona loves its patron saint, Margherita, and put the energy it would normally invest in its cathedral into the Santa Margherita Basilica, at the top of the hill. Margherita was a 13th-century rich girl who took good care of the poor and was an early follower of St. Francis and St. Clare. Many locals believe that Margherita protected Cortona from WWII bombs. (Many also thank her for the best public toilets in town—clean and free, just under her statue.)

The Piazza del Duomo terrace comes with a commanding view of the Tuscan countryside. Find the town cemetery in the distance. If you were standing here before the time of Napoleon, you'd be surrounded by tombstones. But Cortona's graveyards—as with other urban graveyards throughout Napoleon's realm—were cleaned out in the early 1800s to reclaim land and improve hygiene.

• *Next, enter the...*

Duomo: The Cortona cathedral is not—strictly speaking—a cathedral, because it no longer has a bishop. The white-and-gray Florentine Renaissance–style interior is mucked up with lots of Baroque chapels filling once-spacious side niches. In the rear (on the right) is an altar cluttered with relics. Technically any Catholic altar, in order to be consecrated, needs a relic embedded in it. Go ahead—gently lift up the tablecloth. The priest here doesn't mind. You'll see a little marble patch that holds a bit of a saint (daily 7:30–12:30 & 15:00–19:00).

• *From here, you can visit the nearby Diocesan Museum or head back to Piazza della Repubblica to visit the Etruscan Museum (see "Sights," below, for both), or to get a bite to eat (see "Eating" on page 557).*

SIGHTS

▲**Etruscan Museum (Museo dell'Accademia Etrusca)**— Established in 1727, this was one of the first galleries dedicated to artifacts from the Etruscan civilization. Along with lots of gold and jewelry, you'll find a seventh-century B.C. grater (for some really old Parmesan cheese) and a magnificent fourth-century B.C. bronze oil lamp with 16 spouts, set in a small, four-pillared temple. Don't miss the library of the Etruscan Academy upstairs. The academy was founded in 1727 to promote an understanding of the city through the study of archaeology. This eclectic museum also has an Egyptian section, fine Roman mosaics, and a room dedicated to modern works by Severini (€7, April–Oct Tue–Sun 10:00–19:00, Nov–March Tue–Sun 10:00–17:00, closed Mon, Casali Palace on Piazza Signorelli, tel. 0575-637-235).

▲**Diocesan Museum (Museo Diocesano)**—This collection of art from the town's many churches has works by Fra Angelico and Pietro Lorenzetti, and masterpieces by hometown hero and Renaissance master Luca Signorelli.

Don't miss Fra Angelico's sumptuous *Annunciation*. In this scene, Mary says, "Yes," consenting to bear God's son. Notice how the house sits on a pillow of flowers...the new Eden. The old Eden, featuring the expulsion of Adam and Eve from Paradise, is in the upper left. The painting comes with comic-like narration: The angel's lines are top and bottom, Mary's answer is upside-down (logically, since it's directed to God, who would be reading from heaven).

Another highlight is Luca Signorelli's *Mourning of the Dead Christ (Compianto sul Cristo Morto)*. Signorelli was a generation ahead of Michelangelo and, with his passion for painting ideas, was an inspiration for the young artist. Everything in his painting has a meaning: The skull of Adam sits under the sacrifice of Jesus; the hammer represents the Passion (the Crucifixion leading to the Resurrection); the lake is blood; and so on. I don't understand all of the medieval symbolism, but it's intense (€5, helpful audioguide-€3, daily April–Oct 10:00–19:00; Nov–March Tue–Sun 10:00–17:00, closed Mon; Piazza del Duomo 1, tel. 0575-62-830). For more on Signorelli, see page 576.

Church of San Francesco—Established by St. Francis' best friend, Brother Elias, this church dates from the 13th century. Francis fans visit for its precious Franciscan relics. In the sacristy, you'll find his tunic, the little Gospel that he always carried, and his pillow. If the church is closed, you can ring the bell from the cloister of the adjacent Franciscan Monastery and ask to be let in.

San Niccolò Church—Signorelli enthusiasts will want to make the pilgrimage up to this tiny church. Ring the bell, and the caretaker might give you a short tour in Italian (€1 donation, daily in summer 9:00–12:00 & 15:00–19:00, daily off-season 9:00–12:00 & 15:00–17:00). The highlight of this humble church is an altarpiece painted on both sides by Signorelli. The caretaker activates a tricky arm mechanism that moves the picture away from the wall to reveal the painting behind it.

Santa Margherita Basilica—From San Niccolò Church, a steep path leads uphill 10 minutes to this basilica, which houses the remains of the town's favorite saint. St. Margherita, an unwed mother from Montepulciano, found her calling with the Franciscans in Cortona, tending to the sick and poor. Her son eventually became a Franciscan monk.

Hill Towns

Still need more altitude? Head uphill five more minutes to the Medici Fortezza (usually open daily 9:00–12:00 & 15:00–19:00). The views are stunning, stretching all the way to distant Lake Trasimeno.

Etruscan Tombs near Cortona—Guided tours to nearby "Il Sodo" tombs (called *melone* for their melon-like shape) are complicated to arrange. But the excavation site and bits of the ruins are easy to visit and can be seen from outside the fence in the morning. It's just a couple miles outside of Cortona on the Arezzo road (#71), at the edge of Camucia at the foot of the Cortona hill; ask anyone for "Il Sodo."

SLEEPING

(€1 = about $1.30, country code: 39)

In Cortona

$$$ Albergo San Luca, perched on a cliff side, has 57 modern, business-class, impersonal rooms, half with stunning views of Lago Trasimeno. It's friendly, well-run, and conveniently located right at the bus stop (Sb-€85, Db-€120, Tb-€160, request a view room when you reserve, popular with Americans and groups, Piazza Garibaldi 1, tel. 0575-630-460, fax 0575-630-105, www.sanlucacortona.com, info@sanlucacortona.com). If driving, there's a small public parking lot at the hotel where you might find a spot (cheap and easy meters).

$ Casa Betania, a big wistful convent with a large, inviting view terrace, rents 35 fine rooms (only twin beds) for the best price in town. While it's primarily for "thoughtful travelers," anyone looking for a peaceful place to call home will feel welcome in this pilgrims' resort (S-€32, Sb-€38, D-€44, Db-€48, breakfast-€4, about a third of a mile outside of town, parking, a few minutes' walk below Piazza Garibaldi at Via Gino Severini 50, tel. & fax 0575-630-423, www.casaperferiebetania.com, info@casaperferiebetania.com).

$ Istituto Santa Margherita, run by the Serve di Maria Riparatrici sisters, rents 60 cheap and simple beds in a smaller and more institutional-feeling convent across the street (Sb-€32, Db-€46, breakfast-€3, Viale Cesare Battisti 15, tel. 0575-630-336, fax 0575-630-549, comunitacortona@smr.it).

$ San Marco Hostel, at the top of town, is housed in a remodeled 13th-century palace (bed in dorm-€13.50, in 2-bed and 4-bed rooms-€16, includes breakfast, coed bathrooms, lockout 10:00–15:30, Via Maffei 57, tel. & fax 0575-601-392).

Near Cortona

$$$ Casa San Martino, a 30-minute drive east of Cortona near the isolated village of Lisciano Niccone, is a 250-year-old country-side farmhouse run as a B&B by American Italophile Lois Martin. While Lois reserves the summer (June–Aug) for people staying at least one week, she'll take guests staying a minimum of three nights for the rest of the year (Db-€140, 10 percent discount for my readers in 2008—mention this book when you reserve, pool, Casa San Martino 19, Lisciano Niccone, tel. 075-844-288, fax 075-844-422, www.tuscanyvacation.com, csm@tuscanyvacation.com). Lois' neighbors, Ernestine and Gisbert Schwanke, run the tidy **La Villetta di San Martino B&B** (Db-€100, 2-night minimum, cash only, common kitchen and sitting room, San Martino 36, tel. & fax 075-844-309, www.tuscanyvacation.com, erni@netemedia.net).

$$$ Residence la Ferriera, on the Ciuffenna River, has 19 two- or three-room apartments and offers a variety of options: fishing, a pool, tennis, cooking classes, wine tours, and more (Db-€95–170 depending on season, bigger apartments also available, breakfast-€6, one hour northwest of Cortona—and 50 minutes southwest of Florence—at Via la Ferriera 4 in Loro Ciuffenna, tel. 055-917-4006, fax 055-917-1921, www.laferriera.it, info@residencelaferriera.it).

$$ Castello di Montegualandro is a well-preserved castle on a hill opposite Cortona, overlooking the lake and countryside. The Marti family rent four charming medieval apartments, formerly peasants' quarters, inside the peaceful castle walls. Each one is unique and named for its former use—the Fornaci's sunken living room used to be a kiln. The castle's chapel is a popular spot for weddings (apartments range from €460–570 for 3-night minimum stay, €700–800/week, cash only; for a 5-night stay, mention this book for a 7 percent discount in 2008, 10 percent discount for longer stays; 10 min southeast of Cortona in Tuoro sul Trasimeno, tel. & fax 075-823-0267, mobile 347-237-2070, www.montegualandro.com, info@montegualandro.com).

EATING

Trattoria la Grotta, just off Piazza della Repubblica, is a traditional, cave-like place with daily specials and an enthusiastic following (€7 pastas, €8 meat dishes, Wed–Mon 12:00–14:30 & 19:00–22:00, closed Tue, Piazza Baldelli 3, tel. 0575-630-271).

La Locanda nel Loggiato serves up big portions of Tuscan cuisine on the loggia overlooking Piazza della Repubblica. While they have fine indoor seating, I'd eat here only for the chance to gaze at the square over a meal (€7 pastas, €7–15 meat dishes, Thu–Tue 12:15–15:00 & 19:15–23:00, closed Wed, Piazza Pescheria 3, tel. 0575-630-575).

Hill Towns

Fufluns Tavern Pizzeria (that's the Etruscan name for Dionysus) is easy-going, friendly, and remarkably unpretentious for its location in the town center. It's popular with locals for its good, inexpensive Tuscan cooking and friendly staff (cheap, lots of pizza plus more, good house wine, Wed–Mon 12:15–14:30 & 19:15–22:30, closed Tue, a block below Piazza della Repubblica at Via Ghibellina 3, tel. 057-560-4140).

Osteria del Teatro tries very hard to create an Old World atmosphere and does it well. It serves nicely presented and tasty Tuscan standards amid feminine, nostalgic elegance (closed Wed, 2 blocks uphill from the main square at Via Maffei 2, tel. 0575-630-556).

Enoteca la Saletta, dark and classy, is good for some fine wine and a light meal. You can sit inside surrounded by wine bottles or outside to people-watch on the town's main drag (daily 7:30–24:00, Via Nazionale 26, tel. 057-560-3366).

Picnics: On the main square, the chic little **Market Molesini** makes tasty sandwiches (see list on counter and order by number) and sells whatever you might want for a picnic (daily including Sun morning, Piazza della Repubblica 23). Munch your picnic across the square on the steps of City Hall, or just past Piazza Garibaldi in the public gardens behind San Domenico Church.

TRANSPORTATION CONNECTIONS

Cortona connects with the rest of Italy by train. To get from Cortona down to the town's train station, at the foot of the hill, take a taxi or bus (€1, 2/hr between Piazza Garibaldi and station, buy tickets at newsstand or *tabacchi* shop).

From Cortona by Train to: Rome (10/day, 2–2.5 hrs), **Florence** (hourly, 90 min), **Assisi** (hourly, 2 hrs, change in Terontola), **Montepulciano** (10/day, 60–75 min, change in Chiusi). Most trains stop at Cortona's Camucia train station, but fast trains to/from Rome and Florence stop at Terontola, 10 miles away (bus to/from Cortona runs hourly, €1.70, tel. 0575-670-034).

More Sights in Tuscany

Chianti Sculpture Park

This unique, outdoor, contemporary sculpture park lies within a peaceful 35-acre forest in northern Tuscany, and features large works by renowned artists from five continents. Most pieces were designed for a specific site within the park and are gracefully integrated with their natural surroundings (€7.50, April–Oct daily 10:00–sunset, Nov–March by reservation only, gift shop sells sculptures, located roughly between Florence and Siena, La Fornace 48/49, tel. 0577-357-151, fax 0577-357-149, www.chiantisculpturepark.it).

▲ Galgano Monastery

Of southern Tuscany's several evocative monasteries, San Galgano is the best. Set in a forested area called the Montagnolo (medium-size mountains), the isolated abbey and chapel are postcard-perfect.

St. Galgano was a 12th-century saint who renounced his past as a knight to become a hermit. Lacking a cross to display, he created his own by miraculously burying his sword up to its hilt into a stone, à la King Arthur, but in reverse. After his death, a large Cistercian monastery complex grew. Today, all you'll see is the roofless, ruined abbey and, on a nearby hill, the Chapel of San Galgano with its fascinating dome and sword in the stone.

Getting There: Although a bus reportedly comes here from Siena, this sight is realistically accessible only for drivers. It's just outside of Monticiano (not Montalcino), about an hour south of Siena. A warning to the queasy: These roads are curvy.

The Abbey: This picturesque, Cistercian abbey was once a powerful institution in Tuscany. Known for their skill as builders, the Cistercians oversaw the construction of Siena's cathedral. But the abbey, after losing most of its population in the plague of 1348, never really recovered and was eventually deconsecrated.

The Cistercian order was centered in France, and the architecture of the abbey shows a heavy French influence. Notice the large, high windows and the pointy, delicate arches. This is pure

French Gothic, a style that never fully caught on in Italy. (Compare it with the chunky, elaborately decorated cathedral in Siena, built about the same time.)

As you enter the church, notice the small section of the cloister wall to the left. This used to surround the garden, and was the only place that the monks were allowed to talk, for one hour each day. From inside the church, the empty windows frame the view of the chapel up on the hill.

The Chapel: A path from the abbey leads up the hill to the Chapel of San Galgano. The unique, beehive-like interior houses San Galgano's sword and stone, recently confirmed to date back to the 12th century. Don't try and pull the sword from the stone—the small chapel to the left displays the severed arms of the last guy who tried. The chapel also contains some deteriorated frescoes and more interesting *sinopie* (fresco sketches). The adjacent gift shop sells a little bit of everything, from wine to postcards to herbs, some of it monk-made (free, daily 8:00–sunset in summer, 8:00–12:00 & 14:00–sunset off-season). For a quick snack, a small, touristy bar at the end of the driveway is your only option.

Other, more accessible Tuscan monasteries worth visiting include Sant'Antimo (6 miles south of Montalcino) and Monte Oliveto Maggiore (15 miles south of Siena, mentioned in "Crete Senese Drives," on facing page.

▲Chiusi

This small hill town (rated ▲▲ for Etruscan fans) was once one of the most important Etruscan cities. Today, it's a key train junction and a pleasant, workaday Italian village with an enjoyable historic center and few tourists.

The region's trains (to Florence, Siena, Orvieto, and Assisi) go through or change at this hub, making Chiusi an easy day trip. Buses link the train station with the town center two miles away (depart every 40 min, tickets at *tabacchi* shop). Easy and free parking lots are a five-minute walk from the center.

The **TI** is on the main square (Mon–Fri 10:00–13:00 & 15:00–18:00, Sat 10:00–13:00, closed Sun, www.comune.chiusi .siena.it).

The **Archaeological Museum,** just off the main square, thoughtfully presents a high-quality collection with plenty of explanations in English. The collection of funerary urns, some in painted terra-cotta and some in *pietra fetida* ("stinky stone"), are remarkably intact (€4, daily 9:00–20:00, Via Porsenna 93, tel. 05782-0177). The museum also arranges tours to visit tombs outside of town. One of the tombs is multichambered, with several sarcophagi. Another, the **Tomba della Scimmia** (Tomb of the Monkey), has some well-preserved frescoes. Visiting the tombs requires a guide, a car, and an advance reservation (€2, 2/day Tue, Thu, and Sat; 25 visitors per tour).

Troglodyte alert! The **Cathedral Museum** on the main square has a dark, underground labyrinth of Etruscan tunnels. The mandatory guided tour of the tunnels ends in a large Roman cistern from which you can climb the church bell tower for an expansive view of the countryside (museum–€2, labyrinth–€3, combo-ticket–€4, daily 9:30–12:45 & 16:00–19:00, tunnel tours every 40 min during museum hours, Piazza Duomo 1, tel. 0578-226-490).

Craving more underground fun? The **Museo Civico** provides hourly tours of the Etruscan water system, which includes an underground lake (€3, Tue–Sun 10:00–13:00 & 15:00–18:00, closed Mon, Via II Ciminia 1, mobile 349-554-4729).

▲US Cemetery

The compelling sight of endless rows of white marble crosses and Stars of David recalls the heroism of the young Americans who fought so valiantly to free Italy (and ultimately Europe) from the grips of fascism. This particular cemetery is the final resting place of more than 4,000 Americans who died in the liberation of Italy during World War II. Climb the hill past the perfectly manicured lawn, lined with grave markers, to the memorial, where maps and a history of the Italian campaign detail the Allied advance (daily mid-April–Sept 9:00–18:00, Oct–mid-April 9:00–17:00, 7 miles south of Florence, off Via Cassia, which parallels the *superstrada* between Florence and Siena, 2 miles south of Florence Certosa exit on A-1 *autostrada*). Buses from Florence stop just outside the cemetery.

▲▲Crete Senese Drives

South of Siena, the hilly area known as the "Sienese Crests" is full of colorful fields and curvy, scenic roads. You'll see an endless parade of classic Tuscan scenes, rolling hills topped with medieval towns, olive groves, rustic stone farmhouses, and a skyline punctuated with cypress trees. You won't find many wineries here, since the clay soil is better for wheat and sunflowers, but you will find the pristine, panoramic Tuscan countryside that you find on calendars and postcards.

During the spring, the fields are painted in yellow and green with fava beans and broom, dotted by red poppies on the fringes. Sunflowers decorate the area during July and August, and expanses of windblown grass fill the landscape almost all year.

Most roads to the southeast of Siena will give you a taste of this area, but one of the most scenic stretches is the Laurentina road (Siena–Asciano–San Giovanni d'Asso, #438 on road maps; you can also take #2, Via Cassia, toward Rome and turn off at *Asciano* sign; either way allows you to easily continue to Montalcino). You'll come across plenty of turnouts for panoramic photo opportunities on this road, as well as a few roadside picnic areas.

For a break from the winding road, about 15 miles from Siena, you'll find the quaint and non-touristy village of **Asciano.** With a medieval town center and several interesting churches and museums, this town offers a rare look at everyday Tuscan living—and a great place for lunch (TI at Corso Matteotti 78, tel. 0577-718-811). If you're in town on Saturday, gather a picnic at the outdoor market (Via Amendola, 8:00–13:00).

Five miles south of Asciano, the **Abbey of Monte Oliveto Maggiore** houses a famous fresco cycle of the life of St. Benedict, painted by Renaissance masters Il Sodoma and Luca Signorelli (free, daily April–Oct 10:30–13:00 & 15:00–18:00, Nov–March closes at 17:00, Gregorian chanting Sun at 11:00 and Mon–Fri at

18:15, call to confirm, tel. 0577-707-262). Once you reach the town of **San Giovanni d'Asso**, it's only another 12 miles southwest to Montalcino.

Another scenic drive is the lovely stretch between Montalcino and Montepulciano (#146 on road maps). This route alternates between the grassy hills of the Crete Senese and sun-bathed vineyards of the Orcia River valley. Stop by Pienza en route.

Sleeping in the Crete Senese: **Agriturismo il Molinello** rents four apartments, two built over a medieval mill. Hardworking Alessandro and Elisa share their organic produce and sometimes offer wine-tastings. With children, friendly dogs, toys, and a swimming pool, this is ideal for families (Qb-€70–100, apartment for up to 8 people-€130, optional breakfast-€8, 1-week stay required in summer, discounts and 2-night minimum off-season, mountain-bike rentals, near Asciano, 30 min southeast of Siena, tel. 0577-704-791, mobile 335-692-5720, fax 0577-705-605, www.molinello.com, info@molinello.com).

Urbino

Urbino is famous as the hometown of the artist Raphael and architect Donato Bramante, yet the town owes much of its fame to the Duke of Montefeltro.

This mercenary general turned Urbino into an important Renaissance center, attracting artists such as Piero della Francesca, Paolo Uccello, and Raphael's *papà*, Giovanni Santi.

Today, Urbino is a small remote town of 24,000—the majority of whom are students studying at the local university. Its primary economy is in serving the students, rather than tourists, and in spite of its historic and artistic importance, it feels far from the Italian mainstream. Since this was Vatican territory for more than 200 years, you'll see lots of churches.

A classic hill town (550 yards above sea level), Urbino has a medieval wall with four gates. Two main roads crisscross at the town's main square, Piazza della Repubblica. Called simply "the Piazza," this is café central—a great place to nurse an *aperitivo* or coffee and feel the town's pulse. There's barely a level road, with ridged lanes fading into steep stairways, giving hardy locals traction as they clamber about the village. While everything's a steep hike, it's a small town and the climbs are short.

ORIENTATION

Apart from the ambience, Urbino can be "seen" in half a day. Ninety percent of the tourist thrills are in the Ducal Palace. The only other must-sees are the Oratory of St. John and the town view from the fortress.

Tourist Information: The tiny TI is just across from the Ducal Palace (Tue–Fri 9:00–13:00 & 15:00–18:00, Mon and Sat 9:00–13:00 only, closed Sun, Piazza Duca Federico 35, tel. 0722-2613, www.urbinoculturaturismo.it).

Arrival in Urbino: The big entry square (Piazza Mercatale) holds an underground garage where buses stop and cars park (€1/hr). The old town looms above you. While it's a short hike through the old gate up Via Mazzini to Piazza della Repubblica at the center of town, it's very steep. Fortunately, there's an elevator to lift you up fast and easy to Corso Garibaldi (€0.50, Mon–Sat 8:00–20:00, doesn't operate Sun). From here, it's a short, level walk to Piazza della Repubblica.

Helpful Hints

Public WC: It's just below the main square on Via Mazzini and near the Ducal Palace.

Laundry: A self-service launderette is on Via C. Battisti.

Local Guide: Claudia Taglianetti is a good private guide (€80/3 hrs for 1–5 people, €105/3 hrs for 6 or more people, tel. 0722-350-070, claudiataglianetti@libero.it).

Best Gelato: Urbino has two places—each a few steps off Piazza della Repubblica—where gelato is made on the premises: One is on Via Vittorio Veneto and the other is across from the Church of San Francesco.

SIGHTS

▲▲Ducal Palace (Palazzo Ducale)—Built in the mid-1400s, the Ducal Palace is a sprawling and fascinating place. While the rooms are fairly bare, the palace holds a few very special paintings, as well as exquisite inlaid-wood decorations. It's a monument to how one man—the Duke of Montefeltro—brought the Renaissance to his small town, about 50 years after it started in Florence (€4, but sometimes shoots up to €8 for special exhibits, Tue–Sun 8:30–19:15, Mon 8:30–14:00, last entry 1 hour before closing, tel. 0722-322-625).

Your visit is simple: the library and basement (off the main courtyard) and the first floor. The second floor was added a century after the rest of the building; it's filled with porcelain and Mannerist paintings—you can skip it. Precious little is explained

Urbino

1 Albergo Italia
2 Albergo San Domenico

3 Hotel Raffaello
4 Taverna degli Artisti

5 Il Coppiere Ristorante
6 Ristorante/Pizzeria Tre Piante
7 Enoteca (Wine Bar)

in English. Buy a book or follow this basic self-guided tour:

Courtyard: Just past the ticket desk, you'll enter the courtyard, exuberantly Renaissance in its flavor. Architect Luciano Laurana patterned it after the trendsetting Medici palace in Florence, with the same graceful arches atop Corinthian columns. Their light color contrasts pleasantly with the darker colored brick. In the upper story (added later), windows and half-columns match perfectly with the arches and columns beneath them. Notice how the courtyard bows up in good Renaissance style—it collected rainwater, helping power the palace's fancy plumbing system.

Library (Biblioteca del Duca): When the Pope took over Urbino in 1657, he also removed the duke's collection of more than

Federico da Montefeltro
(1422–1482)

The Duke of Montefeltro is *the* man in Urbino history. The bastard son of a small-town noble, he became Duke by killing the rightful heir, his half-brother. Federico went on to get rich as a soldier-for-hire with his own private army, fighting other peoples' wars—for example, fighting for Florence against the pope, then the pope against Florence. In the process, the Duke lost an eye and a hunk of his nose in action, and consequently is portrayed only in profile—with his (relatively) good side showing. He expanded his Duchy into an Italian power, amassed a fortune, then settled down to life as a scholar and gentleman. He studied Latin, collected manuscripts, and renovated the palace. Portraits of the Duke often show his dual personality—holding the helmet of a warrior while reading a manuscript like a scholar. Federico aimed to make the Ducal Palace the "dwelling place of the Muses," attracting the big names of his day to this remote cradle of humanism high on a hill in the Marche region. One visitor, Baldassare Castiglione, wrote a book about life here under Federico's son that became a classic profile of the enlightened Renaissance ruler—*The Courtier.*

2,000 manuscripts—Duke Federico had preferred manuscripts to newfangled books—transporting them back to the Vatican. Today, the library displays the travertine (soft marble) reliefs that used to decorate the palace exterior with scenes of work and war. The duke's eagle-in-the-sun emblem on the ceiling symbolizes how he brought enlightenment to his realm.

Basement (Sotterranei): Wandering through the basement, look for bits of exposed plumbing, a huge cistern-like refrigerator (where snow was packed each winter), and a giant stable with a clever horse-pie disposal system. The palace is so big—with five levels and several hundred rooms—it was called "a city in the shape of a palace."

First Floor: Your route is a one-way system with numbered rooms and meager English descriptions. The first section—the guest rooms—is now filled with the Galleria Nazionale delle Marche, the most important collection of paintings in the Marche region. At one time, this palace held many of the highlights of Florence's Uffizi collection (such as Titian's *Venus of Urbino*). As the Vatican army was about to take the city, the last duchess fled to Florence and later married a Medici. She took with her as many of her family's art treasures as possible—quite a dowry.

Room 1: The fireplace—with an orgy of Greek-style decoration—is typical of the Renaissance, celebrating the rebirth of the cultural greatness that Europe hadn't seen since the glory days of ancient Greece and Rome. Piero della Francesca's *Flagellation* is worth a close look. Pontius Pilate, dressed as a Turk, watches Jesus being whipped—an allegory of the Turks threatening Christendom. The three men on the right seem to discuss

how Europe will handle this threat from the east. Notice how, in true Renaissance fashion, Jesus stands under a column capped with a classical statue. Together, Jesus and the pre-Christian god seem to illuminate the ceiling. To a Renaissance thinker, there was no contradiction in celebrating Christian and pre-Christian ideals simultaneously.

The Duke's Study: The duke's richly-paneled study is the highlight of the palace. Take time to really look at the exquisite inlaid images. Note the mastery of perspective (for example, the latticed cupboard doors appear perfectly open). Let the duke share his passions: art, culture, religion, war, love, music, and caged birds. The period instruments include a delightful lute with a broken string. The duke considered himself an intellectual, inspired by the many great scholars he portrayed on the walls higher up.

Room 20: In the duke's bedroom, the inlaid door shows a medieval fortress facing a Renaissance palazzo—a clear allegory of how war brings darkness, while the new enlightened thought leads to a wide-open sea (in the background), a symbol of good and cultured living. The mercenary warlord put his initials—*FEDVX* (Federico Duke)—over the palazzo rather than the old-school fortress.

Room 21: This is called the "Angels' Room" for the fun-loving angels—with golden penises—decorating the fireplace mantle. The whole idea in these humanistic times was that life is good—angels can party, and people are invited, too. It's *dolce vita* time! Note the painting of the ideal city by Luciano Laurana—the primary architect of this complex and marvelous palace (see facing page).

While Laurana's city was never built, it shows the "divine proportions" of the day—emphasizing balance, harmony, and light. The church is round, like a classical temple. Uninhabited, with black windows, it has a metaphysical feeling. A utopian city...is it possible? The only hint of real life: two tiny birds. Nearby, the long,

skinny panel by Uccello tells the sad story of a Christian woman who pawns some communion bread to a Jewish moneylender. He toasts it and it overflows with blood. She is executed, and so is the Jew (with his entire family—children and all, burned at the stake). Because she asked for forgiveness, angels at the woman's death-bed wait to catch her soul the moment it vacates the body (normal exit path: through the mouth). The devils at her feet don't stand a chance.

Room 23: This room features the early-Renaissance paintings of Giovanni Santi, Raphael's father.

Room 25: You'll find the actual Raphaels here. The prize of the collection is Raphael's *Portrait of a Gentlewoman* (a.k.a. *La Muta*), a divinely beautiful portrait of a young woman. (Some think this artwork is a hidden self-portrait of Raphael.) Her hands are perfectly realistic. One possible interpretation of the scene is that the woman has accepted an offer of marriage: Her necklace is knotted (her heart is tied up); she holds a letter (which told of the offer); and the portrait was sent to the nobleman who asked for her hand. Her melancholy but determined face seems to say, "This is a serious commitment that I am ready to undertake." Raphael painted this (as Leonardo painted the *Mona Lisa*) with oil on wood. Mussolini, thinking it only right that at least one great Raphael should reside in the hometown of the master, had this piece moved from Florence to Urbino. The tiny altar wing (to the right) was purchased from the Marcos estate in the Philippines.

Room 28: Look out the window for a good view of the lower town—the palace is built right on the edge of a cliff. The cluster of houses below you was the Jewish ghetto (synagogue on lower left, with the two semicircular windows). The fortress on the hilltop guarded the town. Today, it offers a postcard view of Urbino— worth the climb (see "Fortress View," below).

Leaving the Palace: Locals consider the adjacent cathe-dral an eyesore for its towering Neoclassical facade. In a town of fine Renaissance facades, this church (built after an earthquake destroyed the original in about 1800) sticks out like a sore thumb.

Next to the cathedral is the bishop's residence, and across the street from that is the City Hall with its three flags: Europe, Italy, and UNESCO (the town is proud of its World Heritage Site status).

▲**Oratory of St. John**—The Oratory of St. John (San Giovanni), the only other important interior in town, is worth a look for its remarkable frescoes. It was built by a brotherhood dedicated to St. John the Baptist. They were committed to performing random acts of kindness while wearing masks, in order to be humble about their Christian charity. The interior tells the story of the life of St. John the Baptist, from the events leading up to his birth to his beheading at the request of Herod's dancing daughter Salomé (the scene where Herod presents his head to the *femme fatale* is missing).

Study the exuberant scene engulfing the Crucifixion. The two thieves crucified alongside Jesus meet their eternal fates—the soul of the man who repented is grabbed by an angel, the other by the devil. The mischievous devil was given mirrors for eyes—sure to freak out the faithful 600 years ago. Above it all, a pelican pecks flesh from its own breast to feed its children—symbolic of the amazing power of Christian love.

This fresco was painted in 1400, before the Renaissance arrived in Urbino. It's a good example of the last stage of Gothic—called "International Gothic"—characterized by lots of color, jam-packed with detail and decor, and featuring a post-plague "we survived, let's enjoy life" outlook. Take a peek at Urbino circa 1400 in the people and slice-of-life corners of this art.

Before you leave, check out the view of the Duke's Palace and the ghetto from the little room adjacent to the chapel (€2, Mon–Sat 10:00–12:30 & 15:00–17:30, Sun 10:00–12:30, 5-min walk from main square—follow signs, Piazza Baricci 31; if no one's there, find attendant at the Oratory of San Giuseppe a few steps away, tel. 347-671-1181).

Fortress View—For the ultimate Urbino view, complete with its hilly countryside, climb up to the fortress (closed but surrounded by a grassy park). The Franciscan church spire, on the left, marks the main square. The hill behind that is the site of a huge kite festival (first Sun of Sept). In the distance, on a ridge to the right, is the duke's mausoleum, with the cypress trees next to it marking the community cemetery. The city gathers around the immense Ducal Palace. To the right of the palace, you can see today's parking lot, once the parade ground for the duke's army. The long front of its once-immense horse stables leads to a round tower, which provided a spiral ramp for horses to romp right up to the palace. While the fortress behind you is empty, the nearby bar is inviting.

SLEEPING

(€1 = about $1.30, country code: 39)

In Urbino

The TI has a line on lots of local families who rent out rooms. Otherwise, Urbino's accommodations scene is limited to a few comfortable, expensive hotels.

$$$ **Albergo San Domenico** is a four-star former monastery and convent across from the Ducal Palace, with 31 spacious, air-conditioned rooms. It offers all the modern comforts, but none of the traditional character (Db-€110–194, breakfast-€11, convenient parking-€8/day, Piazza Rinascimento 3, tel. 0722-2626, fax 0722-2727, www.viphotels.it, sandomenico@viphotels.it).

$$$ **Hotel Raffaello** is a more humble place tucked away in the back streets, a two-minute walk from the main square, with 14 newly renovated rooms (Db-€115 with breakfast, air-con, Vicolino Santa Margherita 40, tel. 0722-4784, fax 0722-328-540, www.albergoraffaello.com, info@albergoraffaello.com).

$$ **Albergo Italia** has 43 modern, business-class rooms in the old town (Db-€90, air-con, ride elevator from town entry and walk 100 yards down Corso Garibaldi arcade to Corso Garibaldi 38; after 20:00, when the elevator shuts down, walk through Porta Valbona, up Via Mazzini, and take a right on Corso Garibaldi; tel. 0722-2701, fax 0722-322-664, www.albergo-italia-urbino.it, info@albergo-italia-urbino.it).

Near Urbino

At $$$ **Locanda della Valle Nuova,** a 185-acre organic farm eight miles outside Urbino, they raise cattle, pigs, and poultry; grow grapes for their wine; and harvest wheat for their homemade bread and pasta. The six rooms are tranquil and cozy (Db-€104 includes buffet breakfast, Db-€156 also includes 5-course evening meal, 3-night minimum, reserve at least 1 day in advance, two apartments with kitchenettes available, closed early Nov–May, ceiling fans, swimming pool, horseback riding, 2 miles south of Fermingnano at La Cappella 14 in Sagrata di Fermingnano, tel. & fax 0722-330-303, www.vallenuova.it, info@vallenuova.it).

EATING

Taverna degli Artisti is a friendly place with a breezy terrace and good traditional cuisine (daily 12:30–14:30 & 19:30–22:30, sometimes closed Tue, great pizzas, Via Bramante 52, tel. 0722-2676).

At **Il Coppiere,** your entire meal, including the post-dinner *grappa*, can involve truffles (daily 12:00–14:30 & 19:00–22:30, Via

Santa Margherita 1, tel. 0722-322-326).

Ristorante/Pizzeria Tre Piante serves great food with a smile on a delightful terrace overlooking the Marche hills (Tue–Sun 12:00–14:30 & 19:00–23:30, closed Mon, Via Voltaccia della Vecchia 1, tel. 0722-4863). The *enoteca* at the top of Via Raphael (at #54)—which sells good locals wines by the glass—is a fun place to drop by.

TRANSPORTATION CONNECTIONS

Buses connect Urbino with Pesaro, on the Ravenna–Pescara train line (buses run hourly, 60-min trip). From Venice, Florence, or Rome, trains leave for Pesaro almost hourly and take 3–5 hours. The Pesaro bus stop is 100 yards from its train station in Piazza Matteotti. In Urbino, buses come and go from the Piazza Mercatale parking lot below the town, where an elevator lifts you up to the base of the Ducal Palace (or take a 5-min steep walk up Via Mazzini to Piazza della Repubblica).

Orvieto

Just off the freeway and the main train line, Umbria's grand hill town entices those heading to and from Rome. While no secret, it's well worth a visit. The town sits majestically a thousand feet above the valley floor on a big chunk of tufa, a very easy-to-dig volcanic rock. While a regional power in the  Middle Ages, it was also one of the major dozen Etruscan cities centuries before Christ. Some historians believe Orvieto may have been a kind of Etruscan Mecca (locals are looking for archaeological proof—the town and surrounding countryside are dotted with Etruscan ruins).

Orvieto, which has three popular claims to fame (cathedral, Classico wine, and ceramics), is loaded with tourists by day and quiet by night. Drinking a shot of the local white wine in a ceramic cup as you gaze up at the cathedral lets you experience Orvieto's three C's all at once. (Is the cathedral best in the afternoon, when the facade basks in golden light, or early in the morning, when it rises above the hilltop mist? You decide.) And a visit to Orvieto comes with a wonderful bonus: an easy bus connection with my favorite hill town, Civita di Bagnoregio (covered on page 586).

Hill Towns

Orvieto

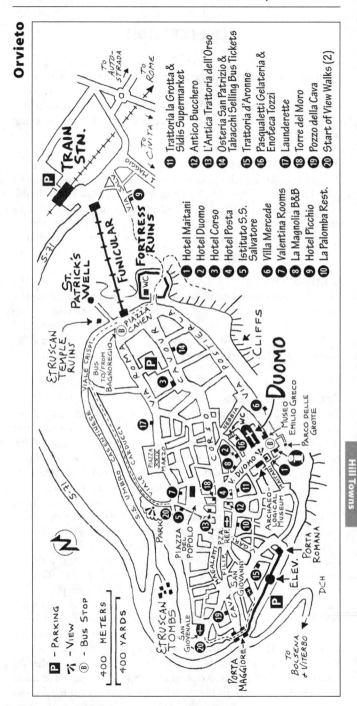

1. Hotel Maitani
2. Hotel Duomo
3. Hotel Corso
4. Hotel Posta
5. Istituto S.S. Salvatore
6. Villa Mercede
7. Valentina Rooms
8. La Magnolia B&B
9. Hotel Picchio
10. La Palomba Rest.
11. Trattoria la Grotta & Sidis Supermarket
12. Antico Bucchero
13. L'Antica Trattoria dell'Orso
14. Osteria San Patrizio & Tabacchi Selling Bus Tickets
15. Trattoria d'Aronne
16. Pasqualetti Gelateria & Enoteca Tozzi
17. Launderette
18. Torre del Moro
19. Pozzo della Cava
20. Start of View Walks (2)

P – PARKING
ⵎ – VIEW
Ⓑ – BUS STOP

400 METERS
400 YARDS

Hill Towns

ORIENTATION

Orvieto has two distinct parts: the old-town hilltop and the new town below. Whether coming by train or car, you first arrive in the forgettable, modern lower part of town. From there you can drive or take the funicular up to the medieval upper town, an atmospheric labyrinth of streets and squares where all the sightseeing action is.

Tourist Information

The TI is at Piazza Duomo 24 on the cathedral square (Mon–Fri 8:15–13:50 & 16:00–19:00, Sat–Sun 10:00–13:00 & 15:00–18:00, tel. 0763-341-772). Pick up the free city map and ask about train and bus schedules. The ticket office (next to the TI) sells combo-tickets (see below) and books reservations for the underground tours.

Combo-Ticket

The €18 **Carta Unica** combo-ticket covers entrance to the 10 top city sights (virtually every sight recommended here, including Underground Orvieto Tours, but not Museo Emilio Greco) and includes either five hours of parking (at *parcheggio* Campo della Fiera) or a full day of public transportation (bus and funicular; www.cartaunica.it).

Arrival in Orvieto

By Train: The train station is at the foot of the hill town; from the station a funicular carries you to the top. Buy your ticket at the entrance to the *funiculare*; look for the *biglietteria* sign (€0.90, good for 70 min, includes minibus from Piazza Cahen to Piazza Duomo, Mon–Sat 7:20–20:30, every 10 min; Sun 8:00–20:30). If you arrive outside the funicular's operating hours, you can take a bus or taxi to the upper town. Note that there's no baggage check at the train station (the nearest place for day-trippers to store bags is the recommended Hotel Picchio); €4/bag.

As you exit the funicular at the top, you're in Piazza Cahen, located at the east end of the upper town. To your left is a ruined fortress with a garden, WC, and a commanding view. To your right, down a steep road, is St. Patrick's Well (see page 579). Farther to the right is a park with Etruscan ruins and another sweeping view. Just in front of you is the orange shuttle bus, waiting to take you to Piazza del Duomo. The bus fills up fast, but the views from the ruined fortress are worth pausing for—if you miss the bus, you can wait for the next one, or just walk to the cathedral (head uphill on Corso Cavour; after about 10 minutes take a left onto Via del Duomo). In Piazza del Duomo you're near the TI and within easy walking distance of most of my recommended sights. If you forgot to check at the station for the train schedule to your next destination, no problem. The train schedule is posted at the top of the funicular and is also available at the TI.

By Car: You can park for free at the base of the hill at the huge lot behind the train station (5 min off the *autostrada*, follow the *P funiculare* signs), in Piazza Cahen (north half, with white lines), or on Via Roma; otherwise go to the pay lot to the right of Orvieto's cathedral (€1.50 for first hour, €1/hr thereafter). Generally, white lines indicate free parking, blue lines require that you get a "pay and display" slip from a nearby machine.

By Taxi: Taxis line up in front of the station; a ride to the cathedral costs about €12.

Helpful Hints

Market Days: On Thursday and Saturday mornings, Piazza del Popolo becomes a busy farmers market.

Laundry: A self-service launderette is at Via Arnolfo di Cambio 33 (Mon–Fri 10:00–19:30, closed Sat–Sun, €3 wash, €3 dry, Alex speaks English and is ready to help).

Internet Access: It's expensive to get online in Orvieto. Try Caffè Montanucci (€3.10/30 min, 4 terminals, Corso Cavour 21, daily 6:30–24:00).

Driver: For a private car hire, consider Giuliotaxi, enthusiastically run by charming and English-speaking Giulio and his sister Maria Serena. They charge €35 for a ride to Bagnoregio, and provide a good way to explore the region (mobile 360-433-057, www.umbria-transfer.com).

Local Guide: Manuela Del Turco is a good local guide (€100/2.5-hour tour, manueladel@virgilio.it).

After Dark: In the evening, there's little going on other than strolling and eating. The big *passegiatta* scene is down Via del Duomo and Corso Cavour. Il Vincaffè is *the* place for the classy young crowd late at night, with lots of good wines by the glass (Via Filippeschi 39).

SELF-GUIDED WALK

Welcome to Orvieto

A quickie L-shaped walk takes you through Orvieto's historic center. Each evening, this route is the scene of the local *passegiatta*. Facing the cathedral, head left. Stroll under the clock tower (first put here in 1347 for the workers building the cathedral), which marks the start of Via del Duomo, lined with shops selling ceramics. Via dei Magoni (first left) has several artisan shops and the crazy little Il Mago di Oz ("Wizard of Oz") shop, a wondrous toyland created by eccentric Giuseppe Rosella (Via dei Magoni 4, tel. 0763-342063). Have Giuseppe push a few buttons, and you're far from Kansas.

Via del Duomo continues to Orvieto's main intersection (where it meets Corso Cavour and the tall, stark tower). The Torre del Moro marks the center of town, serves as a handy orientation tool, and is decorated by the coats of arms of past governors. The elevator leaves you with 173 steps still to go to earn a commanding view (€3, daily 10:00–19:00).

This crossroads divides the town into four quarters (notice the *Quartiere* signs on the corners). Residents of these four districts compete in a lively equestrian competition on Piazza del Popolo during the annual Corpus Christi celebration. Historically, the four streets led from here to the market, City Hall, the Duomo, and the well.

Head left down Corso Cavour past classic storefronts to Piazza della Repubblica and the City Hall. The original vision— though it never came to fruition—was for City Hall to have five arches flanking the main central arch (marked by the flags today). Check out the Church of Sant'Andrea (left of City Hall), which sits atop an Etruscan temple that was likely the birthplace of the city centuries before Christ. Inside is an interesting architectural progression: Romanesque (with scant frescos remaining), Gothic, and a Renaissance barrel vault in the apse (behind the altar)—all lit by fine alabaster windows.

From City Hall, you can continue to the far end of town (to the Church of San Giovenale), from where you can take a left and walk the cliffside ramparts (see "View Walks," page 580).

SIGHTS

▲▲Duomo

The cathedral has Italy's liveliest facade (from 1330, by Lorenzo Maitani and others). This colorful, prickly Gothic facade, divided by four pillars, has been compared to a medieval altarpiece. Grab a gelato (buy it to the left of the church) and study this gleaming mass of mosaics, stained glass, and sculpture.

At the base of the cathedral, the four broad marble pillars carved with biblical scenes tell the story of the world from left to right in four acts (Genesis, Old Testament, New Testament, Revelation). The relief on the far left shows the Creation (see God performing surgery as he extracts Adam's rib, and the snake tempting Eve). Next is the Tree of Jesse (Jesus' family tree—with Mary, then Jesus on top) flanked by Old Testament stories, then the New Testament (look for the unique manger scene and other famous scenes from the life of Christ). On the far right is the Last

Orvieto's Duomo

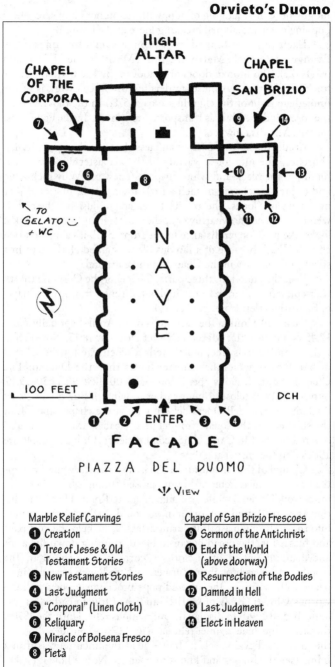

CHAPEL OF THE CORPORAL

CHAPEL OF SAN BRIZIO

HIGH ALTAR

❼

❺

❻

❽

← TO GELATO ☺ & WC

❾

❿ ←

⓭ ←

⓫

⓬

⓮

N A V E

100 FEET

DCH

❶ ❷ ENTER ❸ ❹

F A C A D E

PIAZZA DEL DUOMO

↙ VIEW

Hill Towns

Marble Relief Carvings
❶ Creation
❷ Tree of Jesse & Old Testament Stories
❸ New Testament Stories
❹ Last Judgment
❺ "Corporal" (Linen Cloth)
❻ Reliquary
❼ Miracle of Bolsena Fresco
❽ Pietà

Chapel of San Brizio Frescoes
❾ Sermon of the Antichrist
❿ End of the World (above doorway)
⓫ Resurrection of the Bodies
⓬ Damned in Hell
⓭ Last Judgment
⓮ Elect in Heaven

Judgment (Christ judging on top, with a commotion of sarcophagi popping open and all hell breaking loose at the bottom).

Each pillar is topped by a bronze symbol of one of the Evangelists: angel (Matthew), lion (Mark), eagle (John), and ox (Luke). The bronze doors are modern, by the Sicilian sculptor Emilio Greco. (A museum devoted to Greco's work is to the immediate right of the church; see page 578.) In the mosaic below the rose window, Mary is transported to heaven. In the uppermost mosaic, Mary is crowned.

Inside, the nave is spacious and less cluttered than most Italian churches. The interior is warmly lit (by alabaster windows) that highlight the black-and-white striped stonework. Why such a big and impressive church in such a little town? Well, first of all, it's not as big as it looks. The architect created an illusion—the nave is wider at the back and narrower at the altar so that from the back it looks like it's a longer distance to the front. Still, it's a big and rich church. That's because of a famous blood-stained cloth, kept in a silver-gilt reliquary in the Chapel of the Corporal.

Visit the church in three parts: Chapel of the Corporal (north transept, left of altar, in front), high altar (center front), and Chapel of San Brizio (left front, paid entry).

Cost and Hours: The Duomo is open April–Sept daily 7:30–12:45 & 14:30–19:15, March and Oct closes at 18:15, Nov–Feb at 17:15. Admission is free, but there is a €5 charge for the Chapel of San Brizio, which has shorter hours than the Duomo. The Chapel of San Brizio is open Mon–Sat 9:00–12:45 & 14:30–19:15, Sun 14:30–18:45 (closes 1 hour earlier in winter). Buy the €5 ticket (includes Museo dell'Opera del Duomo) at the chapel, the TI, or the shop across the square from church façade. Admission is also covered by the €18 Carta Unica combo-ticket. Only 25 people are allowed in the chapel at a time.

Chapel of the Corporal: In 1263, or so the story goes, a skeptical priest named Peter of Prague passed through Bolsena (a few miles from Orvieto) while on a pilgrimage to Rome. He had doubts that the bread used in Communion could really be transformed into the body of Christ. But during Mass, as he held the host aloft and blessed it, the bread began to bleed, running down his arms and dripping onto a linen cloth (a "corporal") on the altar. The bloody cloth was brought to Orvieto, where Pope Urban IV happened to be visiting. The amazed pope proclaimed a new holiday, Corpus Christi (Body of Christ), and the Orvieto cathedral was built (begun 1290) to display the miraculous relic. Until the 1970s, the silver-and-blue enamel reliquary (c. 1358)—considered one of the finest medieval jewels in Italy—held the linen relic as if in a frame (see the hinges and knobs to open it). Notice how it evokes the facade of this cathedral. For centuries, the precious linen was paraded through the streets of Orvieto in this ornate frame.

The room was frescoed in the 14th century with scenes attesting to Christ's presence in the communion wafer (e.g., it bleeds if you cook it). You can see the Miracle of Bolsena depicted in the fresco on the chapel's right wall (light it with a coin in the box).

The new cathedral put Orvieto (then known as "Urbs Vetus") on the map, and with lots of pilgrims came lots of wealth. Two future popes used the town as a refuge when their enemies forced them to flee Rome.

The High Altar: The brilliant stained glass from the 14th century is original and painstakingly restored. The fine organ has more than 5,000 pipes. The *pietà* (statue of Mary holding Jesus' just-crucified body) was carved from one piece of marble in 1579 by local artist Ippolito Scalza. Notice the alabaster rose window. Also note from here how the architect's trick, making the church look bigger from the rear, works in reverse from here. If you look to the back, the church feels stubbier than it actually is.

Chapel of San Brizio: This chapel, to the right of the altar, is Orvieto's one must-see artistic sight. It features Luca Signorelli's brilliantly lit frescoes of the Apocalypse (painted 1499–1504). Step into the chapel and you're surrounded by vivid scenes crammed with figures. The frescoes depict events at the end of the world, but they also reflect the turbulent political and religious atmosphere of late-15th-century Italy.

The chapel is decorated in one big and cohesive story. Follow the plot (counterclockwise): Antichrist, end of world, resurrection, hell, Judgment Day (Fra Angelico's Jesus above the window), and finally heaven.

In the Sermon of the Antichrist (left wall), a crowd gathers around a man preaching from a pedestal. It's the Antichrist, who comes posing as Jesus to mislead the faithful. This befuddled Antichrist forgets his lines mid-speech, but the Devil is on hand to whisper what to say next. His words sow wickedness through the world, including executions (upper right). The worried woman in red and white (foreground, left of pedestal) gets money from a man for something she's not proud of (perhaps receiving funds from a Jewish moneylender—notice the Stars of David on his purse).

Most likely, the Antichrist himself is a veiled reference to Savonarola (1452–1498), the charismatic Florentine monk who defied the pope, drove the Medici from power, and riled the populace with apocalyptic sermons. Many Italians—including the painter Signorelli—viewed Savonarola as a tyrant and heretic, the Antichrist who was ushering in the Last Days.

In the upper left, notice the hardworking angel. He looks as if he's at batting practice, hitting followers of the Antichrist back to earth as they try to get through the pearly gates. In the bottom left corner of the scene is a self-portrait of the artist, Luca Signorelli (c. 1450–1523), well-dressed in black with long golden hair. Signorelli, from nearby Cortona, was at the peak of his powers, and this chapel was his masterpiece. He looks out proudly as if to say, "I did all this in just five years, on time and on budget," confirming his reputation as a speedy, businesslike painter. Next to him is the artist Fra Angelico, who started the chapel decoration five decades earlier, but completed only a small part of it.

Around the arch, opposite the windows, are signs of the end of the world: eclipse, tsunami, falling stars, earthquakes, violence in the streets, and a laser-wielding gray angel.

On the right wall (opposite the Antichrist) is the Resurrection of the Bodies. Trumpeting angels blow a wake-up call, and the dead climb dreamily out of the earth to be clothed with new bodies. On the same wall (below the action, at eye level) is a gripping *pietà*.

The altar wall (with the windows) features the Last Judgment. To the left of the altar (and continuing on the left wall) are the Elect in Heaven. They spend eternity posing like bodybuilders while listening to celestial Muzak. To the right (and continuing on the right wall) are the Damned in Hell, in the scariest mosh pit ever. Devils torment sinners in graphic detail, while winged demons control the airspace overhead. In the center, one lusty demon turns to tell the frightened woman on his back exactly what he's got planned for their date. (According to legend, this was Signorelli's lover, who betrayed him...and ended up here. You'll see this couple all over town.) Signorelli's ability to tell a story through human actions and gestures, rather than symbols, inspired his younger contemporary, Michelangelo, who meticulously studied the elder artist's nudes.

Below everything are Greek and Latin philosophers, plus Dante, struggling to reconcile Classic truth with Church doctrine. You can see the intellectual challenge on their faces as they ponder this puzzle. They're immersed in fine Grotesque decor (the frilly, fanciful "wallpaper pattern" popular in the Renaissance).

During the Counter-Reformation, the male figures in Signorelli's frescoes were given penis-covering sashes. During a 1982 restoration most—but not all—of the sashes were removed. While during the Renaissance nakedness symbolized purity, attitudes changed during the Counter-Reformation. A little of that prudishness survives today, as those in heaven were left with their sashes.

After leaving the cathedral, if you want to visit a viewpoint park, exit left and pass the small parking lot. The nearest WCs are in the opposite direction, down the stairs from the left transept.

Near the Duomo

Archaeological Museum (Museo Claudio Faina e Museo Civico)—Across from the entrance to the cathedral is a former palace holding a fine Etruscan collection (for background on the Etruscans, see page 806). The highlights of the first floor are the Roman coins (push the brass buttons and they dance). A first-floor balcony affords a grand view of the cathedral. The best of the Etruscan vases and bronzes are on the top floor, where you'll also find a WC and free coffee (€4.50, April–Sept daily 9:30–18:00; Oct–March Tue–Sun 10:00–17:00, closed Mon; free info booklet in English at ticket counter, tel. 0763-341-511).

National Archaeological Museum of Orvieto—Immediately behind the cathedral, in the ground floor of the papal palace, is a small four-room collection showing off a trove of Etruscan bronze and ceramics with colors surviving from 500 B.C. Golini's Tombs show scenes from an afterlife banquet (€3, daily 8:30–19:30).

Museo dell'Opera del Duomo—This museum, behind the cathedral in Piazza Duomo, shows off the art treasures (statues and paintings) of the Duomo—with two Madonnas by Simone Martini (€5, includes Chapel of San Brizio, daily 9:30–19:00, shorter hours off-season, location and times may change—confirm at TI).

▲**Museo Emilio Greco**—Emilio Greco (1913–1995) was a Sicilian artist who designed the modern doors of Orvieto's cathedral. His sketches and bronze statues show his absorption with gently twisting and turning nudes. Greco's sketchy outlines of women are simply beautiful. The artful installation of his work in this palazzo, with walkways and even a spiral staircase up to the ceiling, allows you to view his sculptures from different angles (€2.50, €5.50 includes St. Patrick's Well, daily 10:30–13:00 & 15:30–17:00, shorter hours and closed Mon off-season, next to cathedral, marked *Museo*, tel. 0763-344-605).

Underground Orvieto

If you're short on time and have to choose one means of going underground in Orvieto, I'd recommend Pozzo della Cava or St. Patrick's Well over Underground Orvieto Tours.

▲**St. Patrick's Well (Pozzo di San Patrizio)**—Modern engineers are impressed by this deep well—175 feet deep and 45 feet wide—designed in the 16th century with a double-helix pattern. The two spiral stairways allow an efficient one-way traffic flow: intriguing now, but critical then. Imagine if donkeys and people, balancing jugs of water, had to go up and down the same stairway. At the bottom is a bridge that people could walk on to scoop up water.

The well was built because a pope got nervous. After Rome was sacked in 1527 by renegade troops of the Holy Roman Empire, the pope fled to Orvieto. He feared that even this little town (with no water source on top) would be besieged. He commissioned a well, which was started in 1527 and finished 10 years later. It was a huge project. (As it turns out, the town was never besieged, but supporters believe that the well was worth the cost and labor because of its deterrence value—attackers would think twice about besieging a town with a water source.) Even today, when a local is faced with a difficult task, people say, "It's like digging St. Patrick's Well." It's a total of 496 steps up and down—lots of exercise and not much to see other than some amazing 16th-century engineering (€4.50, €5.50 includes Museo Emilio Greco, April–Sept daily 9:00–18:45, shorter hours in winter, the well is to your right as you exit the funicular). Bring a sweater if you plan to descend to the chilly depths.

Pozzo della Cava—While renovating its trattoria, a local family discovered a vast underground network of Etruscan-era caves, wells, and tunnels. The excavation started in 1984 and continues to this day. It's well-explained in English and makes for a fun subterranean hike (€3, Tue–Sun 9:00–20:00, closed Mon, Via della Cava 28, tel. 0763-342-373).

Underground Orvieto Tours (Parco delle Grotte)—Guides weave a good archaeological history into an hour-long look at about 100 yards of Etruscan and medieval caves. You'll see the remains of an old olive press, two impressive 130-foot-deep Etruscan well shafts, and the remains of a primitive cement quarry (€5.50; 1-hour English tours depart from TI at 11:00, with more scheduled according to demand; book tour at ticket office adjacent to TI, confirm times at TI or by calling 0763-340-688, www.orvietounderground.it).

▲View Walks

Thanks to its dramatic hilltop setting, several fine little walks wind around the edges of Orvieto. The best (especially after dark, when it's lamplit and very romantic) is along the ramparts of the far west end of town. Start at the Church of San Giovenale. With your back to the church, go a block to the right to the end of town, and follow Vicolo Volsinia to the Church of San Giovanni.

For another good walk, stroll along Viale Carducci and leave town through the ruined fortress at Piazza Cahen, then follow the small lane below the cliffs along the south side of town.

Near Orvieto

Wine Tasting—Orvieto Classico white wine is justly famous. For a short tour of a local winery with Etruscan cellars, visit Tenuta Le Velette, where English-speaking Corrado and Cecilia (cheh-CHEEL-yah) Bottai will welcome you—if you've called ahead to set up an appointment (€8–18 for tour and tasting, price varies depending on wines, Mon–Fri 8:30–12:00 & 14:00–17:00, Sat 8:30–12:00, closed Sun, also have accommodations—see listing below, tel. 076-329-090, mobile 348-300-2002, www.levelette.it). From their sign (5-min drive past Orvieto at top of switchbacks just before Canale, on road to Bagnoregio), cruise down a long, tree-lined drive, then park at the striped gate (must call ahead; no drop-ins).

SLEEPING

(€1 = about $1.30, country code: 39)

In Orvieto

All of my recommended hotels are in the old town, except Hotel Picchio, which is in a more modern neighborhood near the station.

$$$ Hotel Maitani is the best splurge in town. Its grand public spaces and 39 rooms—each elegant and individual, and most with an attached sitting room—fill a venerable centuries-old building half a block from the Duomo. Giuseppi and Norma keep the Morino family tradition of hospitality alive in this four-star hotel (Sb-€77, Db-€126, Db-suite €150 and €170, claim your 8 percent Rick Steves discount if you book direct, breakfast-€10, air-con, 20 yards from the bus stop behind the TI at Via Lorenzo Maitani 5, tel. & fax 0763-342-011, www.hotelmaitani.com, direzione @hotelmaitani.com).

$$$ Hotel Duomo, centrally located, is modern, with splashy art and 17 sleek rooms (Sb-€80, Db-€120, Db suite-€140, Tb-€160, 10 percent cash discount with this book in 2008, buffet breakfast, air-con, elevator, Internet access, sunny terrace, a block from Duomo behind *gelateria* at Via di Maurizio 7, tel. 0763-341-887, fax 0763-394-973, www.orvietohotelduomo.com, hotelduomo @tiscalinet.it, Gianni and Maura Massaccesi don't speak English). The nearby church bells cost some guests a little sleep.

$$ Hotel Corso is friendly, with 18 comfy, modern rooms—some with balconies and views. Everyone can enjoy their sunlit little terrace (Sb-€62, Db-€87, Tb-€115, 10 percent discount with this book in 2008, buffet breakfast-€6.50, air-con, elevator, free Internet access, free parking nearby, on main street up from funicular toward Duomo at Via Cavour 339, tel. & fax 0763-342-020, www.hotelcorso.net, info@hotelcorso.net, Carla).

$ Hotel Posta is a short walk from the cathedral into the medieval core. It's a big, old, formerly elegant palazzo with a breezy garden, an elevator, and a grand old lobby. Twenty spacious, clean, well-worn, and quirky rooms hold vintage rickety furniture (S-€31, Sb-€37, D-€44, Db-€56, breakfast-€6, cash only, Via Luca Signorelli 18, tel. & fax 0763-341-909, hotelposta@orvietohotels.it, little English spoken).

$ The sometimes-surly sisters of the **Istituto S.S. Salvatore** rent 15 spotless twin rooms in their convent with a peaceful terrace (Db-€55 May–Oct, Db-€45 Nov–April, cash only, elevator, parking, just off Piazza del Popolo at Via del Popolo 1, tel. & fax 0763-342-910, istitutosansalvatore@tiscalinet.it, no English spoken). **Villa Mercede** is a similar religious institution renting cheap and simple twin-bed rooms (Db-€60, Tb-€70, a half-block from Duomo at Via Soliana 2, tel. 0763-341-766, fax 0763-340-119, www.argoweb.it/casareligiosa_villamercede, villamercede @orvienet.it).

$ Valentina rents six clean, airy, well-appointed rooms and two apartments, all with big beds and antique furniture. Her place is located in the heart of Orvieto, behind the grand staircase near Piazza del Popolo (Db-€57, Tb-€71, studio with kitchen-€80, apartment for up to 5 people-€150, special cash-only prices in 2008 with this book, discount for longer stays, breakfast-€2, air-con, Via Vivaria 7, tel. 0763-341-607, mobile 393-9705-868, valentina.z @tiscalinet.it). She also rents three rooms across the square that share a kitchen (Db-€50, no air-con).

$ La Magnolia B&B has lots of fancy terra-cotta tiles, frescoed ceilings, terraces, and other welcoming touches. Its seven rooms, some like mini-apartments with kitchens, are *tranquillo* despite being on the town's main drag (Sb-€30–35, Db-€65, plush Db apartment-€70, extra person-€15–20, book direct and stay at least 2 nights to get a 10 percent Rick Steves discount, cash only, no elevator, use of washing machine-€3, Via Duomo 29, tel. 0763-342-808, mobile 338-902-7400, www.bblamagnolia.it, info @bblamagnolia.it, Serena).

$ Hotel Picchio is a hardworking little family-run place with 27 decent rooms stuck back in the modern world, in a forgettable zone 300 yards from the train station at the base of the hill (Sb-€37, Db-€58–65, Tb-€63, 10 percent discount with this book in 2008, air-con-€6, free parking, Via G. Salvatori 17, tel. & fax 0763-301-144, hotelpicchio@tin.it, Alessandra and the Picchio family). A trail leads from here up to the old town.

Near Orvieto

$$$ Agriturismo Fattoria di Vibio produces olive oil and honey, sells organic products, and offers classes and spa services. In

August, its 14 rooms rent at peak prices, and you're required to stay a week, arriving and departing on a Saturday (Db-€180–220, includes breakfast and dinner; Db-€1,260–1,540 for weekly rental in Aug, otherwise €980–1,400; located 20 miles northeast of Orvieto, tel. 075-874-9607, fax 075-878-0014, www.fattoriadivibio.com, info@fattoriadivibio.com).

$$$ Agriturismo La Rocca Orvieto, run by Emiliano and Sabrin, is a fancy, spa-type place, located 15 minutes north of Orvieto by car. They produce their own olive oil and wine and have 10 double rooms and nine apartments—all with air conditioning (Db-€90–130, half-board-€140–180, 10 percent discount with this book—mention when you make reservation, pool, "wellness center" with Jacuzzi and steam room, gym, mountain bikes, a bocce court, hiking paths, tel. 0763-344-210, mobile 348-640-0845, fax 0763-395-155, www.laroccaorvieto.com, info@laroccaorvieto.com).

At **$$$ Agriturismo Locanda Rosati,** you'll be greeted by gracious hosts Paolo and Giampiero Rosati, who rent 10 tastefully decorated rooms in a pleasant, homey atmosphere (Db/Tb-€120, full traditional dinners €30 on request, 5 miles from Orvieto on the road to Viterbo, tel. 0763-217-314, www.locandarosati.it, info@locandarosati.orvieto.tr.it).

$$ Le Velette Wine Estate is a sprawling family-run farmhouse. Cecilia and Corrado Bottai rent six fully furnished apartments and villas housing two to 14 people in perfect Umbrian rural peace and tranquility (Db apartment-€70–90, see website for details on various villas, 3-night minimum, 20 percent discount for weekly stay, cash only, pool, bocce ball, 5 min from Orvieto—drive toward Bagnoregio–Canale and follow signs to Tenuta le Velette, mobile 348-300-2002, fax 0763-29114, www.levelette.it, cecilialevelette@libero.it). They also offer wine tastings, listed above in "Near Orvieto."

$ Agriturismo Pomonte Umbria, seven miles east of Orvieto, offers home-cooked meals, lovely vistas, and seven comfortable rooms in a recently built guest house (Db-€56, includes breakfast, €90-half-pension, €110-full pension, Loc. Canino di Orvieto 1, Corbara, tel. 076-330-4041, fax 076-330-4080, www.pomonte.it, info@pomonte.it).

EATING

Trattoria la Grotta, pricey and classy, prides itself on serving only the freshest food and good wine. The decor is Signorelli mod and the ambience is quiet, with courteous service. Owner/chef Franco—who's been at it for 40 years—plays his wall of wine like a pipe organ. Franco promises diners a free coffee, *grappa, limoncello,* or *vin santo* with this book in 2008 (Wed–Mon opens at 12:00 for lunch and at 19:00 for dinner, closed Tue, Via Luca Signorelli 5, tel. 0763-341-348).

La Palomba features game and truffle specialties in a wood-paneled dining room. Gianpiero, Enrica, and the Cinti family take care of their local regulars and visiting travelers alike, offering both a fine value and a classy conviviality. As firm believers in the Slow Food movement, their food is organic and locally produced (€6 pastas, €10 *secondi*, Thu–Tue 12:30–14:15 & 19:30–22:00, closed Wed, reservations smart, just off Piazza della Repubblica at Via Cipriano Manente 16, tel. 0763-343-395).

Antico Bucchero makes a nice splurge with its classy candlelit ambience and good food (€8 pastas, €12 *secondi*, Mon–Sat 12:00–15:00 & 19:00–23:00, closed Sun, indoor/outdoor seating, a half-block south of Corso Cavour, between Torre del Moro and Piazza della Repubblica at Via de Cartari 4, tel. 0763-341-725).

L'Antica Trattoria dell'Orso offers well-prepared Umbrian cuisine paired with fine wines in a homey and peaceful atmosphere. Ciro and chef Gabriele will steer you toward the freshest seasonal plates (Wed–Sun 12:00–14:00 & 19:30–22:00, closed Mon–Tue, just off Piazza della Repubblica at Via della Misericordia 18/20, tel. 0763-341-642).

Osteria San Patrizio, near the funicular, presents memorable and creative versions of traditional Umbrian specialties. It requires a hike almost back to the funicular, but expats consider chef Ernesto's cooking (especially the risotto) about the best dining experience in town, and well worth the walk. The atmosphere is elegant yet relaxed and the service is attentive. Corinne patiently explains the seasonal specials to guests. In this landlocked region, this is a rare place that takes fish seriously. For a near-gourmet extravaganza, consider their €35 *menù degustazione* sampler meal. Reservations are smart (Tue–Sat 12:00–15:00 & 19:00–23:00, Sun 12:00–15:00, closed Mon, Corso Cavour 312, tel. 0763-341-245).

Trattoria d'Aronne, buried in the distant...bowels is not quite the right word...of the old town, is bright and casual with indoor/outdoor seating and an ever-changing variety of moderately priced Umbrian dishes, wood-fired pizzas, and oven-baked pastas. Christian and his mother Rolanda will give you recommendations while his aunt does the cooking (€7 pastas, €11 *secondi*, Fri–Wed 12:00–16:00 & 19:00–23:30, closed Thu, 10 percent discount with this book in 2008, Piazza Ranieri 1A–2, tel. 076-334-4456).

Enoteca Tozzi, to the left of the Duomo, serves up rustic *panini*—try the roast suckling pig (*porchetta*, por-KET-tah) if it's available (daily 8:30–21:00, 9:00–20:00 in winter, Piazza Duomo 13, tel. 0763-344-393).

Sidis supermarket, tucked away two minutes from the Duomo,

Orvieto and Civita Area

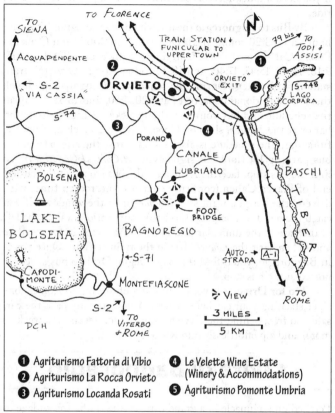

TO FLORENCE

N

TO SIENA

ACQUAPENDENTE

TRAIN STATION & FUNICULAR TO UPPER TOWN

79 bis TO TODI & ASSISI

❷

ORVIETO

"ORVIETO" EXIT

❺

S-2 "VIA CASSIA"

S-448

LAGO CORBARA

S-74

❸

PORANO

❹

CANALE

LUBRIANO

BASCHI

BOLSENA

CIVITA

FOOT BRIDGE

TIBER

LAKE BOLSENA

BAGNOREGIO

←S-71

AUTO-STRADA

A-1

CAPODI-MONTE

MONTEFIASCONE

VIEW

TO ROME

S-2

TO VITERBO & ROME

DCH

3 MILES

5 KM

❶ Agriturismo Fattoria di Vibio

❷ Agriturismo La Rocca Orvieto

❸ Agriturismo Locanda Rosati

❹ Le Velette Wine Estate (Winery & Accommodations)

❺ Agriturismo Pomonte Umbria

has what you need to put together a functional picnic or stock your hotel room pantry (daily 8:00–13:00 & 17:00–20:00, next to recommended Trattoria la Grotta at Via Luca Signorelli 23).

Gelato: For dessert, try the deservedly popular *gelateria* **Pasqualetti** (daily 12:30–24:00, closed in winter, next to left transept of church, Piazza Duomo 14; another branch is at Corso Cavour 56, open until 20:30 in winter).

TRANSPORTATION CONNECTIONS

From Orvieto by Train to: Rome (hourly, 1–1.5 hrs, consider leaving your car at the large parking lot behind Orvieto station), **Florence** (hourly, 2.25 hrs, use Firenze S.M.N. station—see page 423), **Siena** (8/day, 2–3 hrs, change in Chiusi, all Florence-bound trains stop in Chiusi), **Assisi** (roughly hourly, 2–3 hrs, 1 or 2 transfers). The train station's Buffet della Stazione is surprisingly good if you need a quick focaccia sandwich or pizza picnic for the train ride.

By Bus to Bagnoregio (near Civita di Bagnoregio): It's a one-hour trip (€3.20 round-trip). Departures in 2007 from Orvieto's Piazza Cahen on the blue Cotral bus, daily except Sunday: 6:15, 9:10, 12:45, 15:45, 17:40, and 18:20 (buses stop at Orvieto's train station 5 min later). During the school year (roughly Sept–June), there are additional departures at 7:20, 7:50, and 13:55. Confirm the schedule and buy your round-trip ticket at the train-station bar or at the *tabacchi* shop on Corso Cavour, a block up from the funicular. The schedule is also posted across the street from the bus parking lot (look for sign saying *A.Co.Tral Capolinea*). To find the bus stop, face the funicular. The bus stop is at the far left end of Piazza Cahen (confirm departure and return times with driver—the bus you want says *Bagnoregio* in the window). If you catch the bus down below at Orvieto's train station, wait at the left of the base of the funicular station (as you're facing it, for schedule and tickets visit the *tabacchi*/bar in the train station). Once you're in Bagnoregio, you'll find the Bagnoregio–Orvieto bus schedule posted at the bus stop.

Tip for Drivers: If you're thinking of driving to Rome, consider stashing your car here instead. You can easily park the car, safe and free, behind the Orvieto train station (even for a week or more), and zip effortlessly into Rome by train (75 min).

Civita di Bagnoregio

Perched on a pinnacle in a grand canyon, the traffic-free village of Civita di Bagnoregio is Italy's ultimate hill town. Civita (chee-VEE-tah) is terminally ill. Only a handful of residents—mostly in their 80s—remain as, bit by bit, the town is being purchased by rich big-city Italians who come here to escape on vacation. Civita is connected to the world and the town of Bagnoregio by a long pedestrian bridge—and a website (run by B&B owner Franco; see "Sleeping" page 591).

Civita's history goes back to Etruscan and ancient Roman times. In the early Middle Ages, Bagnoregio was a suburb of Civita, which had a population of about 4,000. Later, Bagnoregio surpassed Civita in size. (You'll notice Bagnoregio is dominated by Renaissance-style buildings while, architecturally, Civita remains stuck in the Middle Ages.)

While Bagnoregio lacks the pinnacle-town romance of Civita, it's actually a healthy, vibrant community (unlike Civita, the suburb now nicknamed "the dead city"). In Bagnoregio, get a haircut, sip a coffee on the square, and walk down to the old laundry (ask, *"Dov'è la lavanderia vecchia?"*). Off-season, when Civita and Bagnoregio are deadly quiet—and cold—I'd side-trip in quickly from Orvieto or skip the area altogether.

ORIENTATION

Arrival in Bagnoregio, near Civita

If you're taking the bus from Orvieto, you'll get off at the bus stop in Bagnoregio. Look at the posted bus schedule and write down the return times to Orvieto. (Drivers, see "Transportation Connections" on page 593.)

From Bagnoregio to Civita: Civita sits at the opposite end of Bagnoregio, about a mile away. From Bagnoregio, you can walk (20 min) or take a little orange shuttle bus to the base of the bridge to Civita. From here, you have to walk the rest of the way (a 10-min hike up a pedestrian bridge).

The little yellow shuttle **bus** runs from Bagnoregio (catch bus across from gas station) to the base of the bridge (hourly, 10-min ride, €1, pay driver, first bus runs Mon–Sat at about 7:30, Sun at 8:50, last at 18:45, spotty service off-season). If you want to return to Bagnoregio by bus, check the schedule posted near the bridge (at edge of parking lot, where bus let you off) before heading up to Civita.

To **walk** from the Bagnoregio bus stop to the base of Civita's bridge (about 20 min, fairly level), take the road going uphill (overlooking the big parking lot). Once on the road, take the first right and an immediate left onto the main drag, Via Roma. Follow this straight out to the belvedere for a superb viewpoint. From the viewpoint, backtrack a few steps (staircase at end of viewpoint is a dead end) and take the stairs down to the road leading to the bridge.

Drivers can avoid a long walk by driving through Bagnoregio, and parking under the bridge at the base of Civita (for more information, see "Transportation Connections" below).

Helpful Hints

Market Day: A lively market fills the Bagnoregio bus station parking lot each Monday.

Baggage Storage: While there's no official baggage-check service in Bagnoregio, I've arranged with Mauro Laurenti, who runs the Bar/Enoteca/Caffè Gianfu and Cinema Alberto Sordi, to let you leave your bags there (€1/bag, daily 7:00–13:00 &

13:30–24:00, closed Thu Oct–March). As you get off the bus, go back 50 yards or so in the direction that the Orvieto bus just came from, and go right around corner).

Food near Bagnoregio Bus Stop: About 100 yards from the bus stop, within a few steps of the Porta Albana (old gate to the town), you'll find both a small grocery store and a great little bakery (L'Arte del Pane—with fresh pizza by the slice, Via Matteotti 5).

SELF-GUIDED WALK

Welcome to Civita

Civita was once connected to Bagnoregio, before the saddle between the separate towns eroded away. Photographs around town show the old donkey path, the original bridge. It was bombed in World War II and replaced in 1966 with the new footbridge that you're climbing today. The town's hearty old folks hang on to the bridge's hand railing when fierce winter weather rolls through.

• *Entering the town, you'll pass through a cut in the rock and a 12th-century Romanesque...*

Arch: This was the main Etruscan road leading to the Tiber Valley and Rome. The stone passageway was cut by the Etruscans 2,500 years ago.

• *Inside the town gate, to the left, is an unmarked WC. It faces the town's old laundry, which dates from just after World War II, when water was brought to the town. Until recently, this was a lively village gossip center. Nearby, across from Ivana's wine shop, are the remains of a...*

Renaissance Palace: The wooden door and windows (above the door) lead only to thin air. They were part of the facade of one of five palaces that once graced Civita. Much of the palace fell into the valley, riding a chunk of the ever-eroding rock pinnacle. Today, the door leads to a remaining section of the palace—complete with Civita's first hot tub—owned by the "Marchesa," a countess who married into Italy's biggest industrialist family.

Peek into the small **Pina's Pizzeria** (daily 9:30–18:00). Pina's homemade cookies—*biscotti de Civita*—are hard to resist. Check out the canyon viewpoint a few steps to your left as you exit Pina's. Just beyond that is the site of the long-gone home of Civita's one famous son, St. Bonaventure, known as the "second founder of the Franciscans" (look for the small plaque on the wall to your right).

• *Now wander to the main square and Civita's church.*

Piazza: Here in the town square are Civita's only public

Civita di Bagnoregio

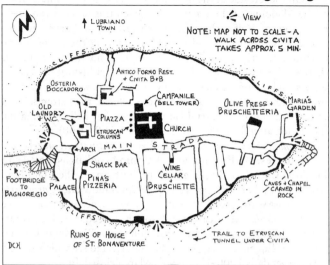

↑ LUBRIANO TOWN

VIEW

NOTE: MAP NOT TO SCALE – A WALK ACROSS CIVITA TAKES APPROX. 5 MIN.

CLIFFS

CLIFFS

Antico Forno Rest. + Civita B+B

Osteria Boccadoro

CAMPANILE (BELL TOWER)

OLIVE PRESS + BRUSCHETTERIA

MARIA'S GARDEN

OLD LAUNDRY + W.C.

PIAZZA

ETRUSCAN COLUMNS

CHURCH

ARCH   MAIN   STRADA

SNACK BAR

FOOTBRIDGE TO BAGNOREGIO

PINA'S PIZZERIA

PALACE

WINE CELLAR + BRUSCHETTE

CAVES + CHAPEL CARVED IN ROCK

CLIFFS

RUINS OF HOUSE OF ST. BONAVENTURE

TRAIL TO ETRUSCAN TUNNEL UNDER CIVITA

DCH

phone, Pepponi's Bar (if it's chilly, go inside for the inviting fire), two restaurants—and wild donkey races on the first Sunday of June and the second Sunday of September. The pillars that stand like giants' bar stools are ancient Etruscan. The church with its *campanile* (bell tower) marks the spot where an Etruscan temple, and then a Roman temple, once stood.

• *Go into the church.*

Church: A cathedral until 1699, the church houses records of about 60 bishops that date back to the seventh century. Inside you'll

see frescoes and statues from "the school of Donatello." The central altar is built upon the relics of the Roman martyr St. Victoria, who once was the patron saint of the town. St. Marlonbrando served as a bishop here in the ninth century; an altar dedicated to him is on the right.

The fine crucifix, carved out of pear wood in the 15th century, is from the school of Donatello. It's remarkably expressive and greatly venerated by locals. Jesus' gaze is almost haunting. Some say his appearance changes based on what angle you view him from: looking alive from the front, in agony from the left, and dead from the right. Regardless, his eyes follow you from side to side. On Good Friday, this crucifix goes out and is the focus of the midnight procession.

Hill Towns

On the left side of the nave above an altar is an intimate fresco of the Madonna of the Earthquake, given this name because—in the shake of 1695—the whitewash fell off and revealed this tender fresco of Mary and her child. (During the Baroque era, a white-and-bright interior was in vogue, and churches such as these—which were covered with precious and historic frescoes—were simply whitewashed over.) On the same wall—toward the front—find a faded portrait of Santa Apolonia, the patron saint of your teeth; notice the scary-looking pincers. Say hello to Annarita, the church attendant (daily 9:30–13:00 & 15:00–18:00).

• *Just around the corner from the church, on the main street, are several...*

Eateries: At Rossana and Antonio's cool **Bruschette con Prodotti Locali,** pull up a chair and let them or their children, Arianna and Antonella, serve you *panini* (sandwiches), *bruschetta* (garlic toast with optional tomato topping), wine, and a local cake called *ciambella.* After eating, ask to see the cellar with its traditional wine-making gear and provisions for rolling huge kegs up the stairs. Tap on the kegs in the bottom level to see which are full (April–Oct daily 11:00–17:00, Nov–March closed Thu).

The rock below Civita is honeycombed with ancient cellars like this (for keeping wine at the same temperature all year) and cisterns (for collecting rainwater, since there was no well in town). Many date from Etruscan times.

Farther down on the left, you'll find **Antico Frantoio Bruschetteria,** a rustic place for a bite to eat. Vittoria's sons, Sandro, and Felice, and her grandsons Maurizio and Fabrizio (with his American wife, Heather) toast delicious *bruschetta* (roughly 10:00–20:00 in summer, tel. 0761-948-429). Peruse the menu, choose your topping (chopped tomato is super), and get a glass of wine for a fun, affordable snack.

While waiting for your *bruschetta,* take a look around to see Vittoria's mill *(mulino),* an atmospheric collection of old olive presses. The huge **olive press** in the entry is about 1,500 years old. Until the 1960s, blindfolded donkeys trudged in the circle here, crushing olives, and creating paste that filled the circular filters and was put into a second press. Notice the 2,500-year-old sarcophagus niche. The hole in the floor (with the glass top) was a garbage hole. In ancient times, residents would toss their jewels down when under attack; excavations uncovered a windfall of treasures (if you're not eating here, a €1 donation is requested).

• *On the left 20 yards farther down is...*

Maria's Garden (Maria's Giardino): Maria shares her garden's grand views (€1 donation) with a helping of historical misinformation (she says Civita and Lubriano were once connected). Maria's husband, Peppone, used to carry goods on a donkey back and forth 40 times a day on the path between the old town and

Bagnoregio. These two are the last of the native Civita residents (aged 82 and 90). As you view the canyon in which Civita is stranded, imagine the work the two rivers did—in the same style as the Colorado River—to carve all this. Listen to the roosters and voices from distant farms.

• *At the end of town, the main drag winds downhill. On your right are small...*

Etruscan Caves: The first two caves were used as stables until a few years ago. The third cave is an unusual chapel, cut deep into the rock, with a barred door; this is the **Chapel of the Incarcerated** (Cappella del Carcere). In Etruscan times, the chapel—with a painted tile depicting the Madonna and child—may have originally been a tomb, and in medieval times, it was used as a jail. When Civita's few residents have a religious procession, they come here in honor of the Madonna of the Incarcerated.

• *After the chapel, the paving-stone path peters out into a dirt trail leading down and around to the right to an...*

Etruscan Tunnel: Now barred to entry, this tunnel dates from the Etruscan era. Tall enough for a woman with a jug on her head to pass through, it may have served as a shortcut to the river below. It was widened in the 1930s so that farmers could get between their scattered fields more easily. Think of the scared villagers who huddled here for refuge during WWII bombing raids.

• *Backtrack to return to the...*

Piazza: Evenings on Civita's town square are a bite of Italy. The same people sit on the same church steps under the same moon, night after night, year after year. I love my cool, late evenings in Civita. If you visit in the morning, have cappuccino and rolls at the small café on the town square.

Whenever you visit, stop halfway up the donkey path and listen to the sounds of rural Italy. Reach out and touch one of the Monopoly houses. If you know how to turn the volume up on the crickets, do so.

SLEEPING

(€1 = about $1.30, country code: 39)
There are only eight rooms up for grabs here, in two B&Bs (Franco's B&B in Civita—wonderful yet less conveniently located, and Pucci's B&B—more practical, in Bagnoregio). Bagnoregio's two sizable hotels (hotels Fidanza and Al Boschetto) are derelict—there are hopes that they'll be reopened if proper owners

turn up. Outside the town are plenty of *agriturismi*; otherwise, there's always Orvieto.

$ Civita B&B, run by Franco Sala (who also owns Trattoria Antico Forno and the only dog in Civita—Birillo), has three fine little rooms, each overlooking Civita's main square (D-€62, Db-€68, T-€78, includes continental breakfast, €17 more per person for optional half-pension, Piazza del Duomo Vecchio, tel. 0761-760-016, mobile 347-611-5426, www.civitadibagnoregio.it, fsala @pelagus.it).

$$ Romantica Pucci B&B is a haven for city-weary travelers. Its five spacious rooms are indeed romantic, with canopied beds and flowing veils. Both homey and elegant, it's like sleeping at Katharine Hepburn's place. Pucci and Lamberto take special care of their guests (Db-€80, includes breakfast; free parking, attached restaurant is popular with guests—go for the "Trust Pucci" €15–20 special family-style dinner, Piazza Cavour 1, tel. 0761-792-121, www.hotelromanticapucci.it, hotelromanticapucci@libero.it). It's just above the parking lot you see when you arrive in Bagnoregio—look for a sign marking its private parking place—and it's half a block before the town's main square, facing the main drag.

EATING

In and near Civita

While the food's nothing special in Civita, the ambience is hard to beat. **Trattoria Antico Forno** serves up pasta at affordable prices. Franco and his able assistants Anna and Nina serve a "Bring it all on, Franco!" meal for €17, which includes lots of courses, wine, and an after-dinner drink (€7 pastas, €8 *secondi,* daily for lunch 12:30–15:30 and sporadically for dinner 19:30–22:00, on main square, also rents rooms—see Civita B&B listing above, tel. 0761-760-016). This place used to be called "Trattoria Al Forno," but Franco got tired of being called "Al."

Osteria Boccadoro serves visitors on its covered patio just off Civita's main square (maybe daily 12:30–17:00 & 19:00–23:00 but can close at owner's whim, tel. 0761-780-775). **Pina's Pizzeria** cooks up good pizza and homemade sweets to eat there or to go (daily 12:00–22:00, near entry into town).

Hostaria del Ponte is *the* place for serious cooking. It offers light, creative, and traditional cuisine with a great view terrace at the parking lot at the base of the bridge to Civita. Big space-heaters make it comfortable to enjoy the wonderful view as you dine from their rooftop terrace, even in spring and fall (€6.50 pastas, €10 *secondi*, reservations smart, Tue–Sun 12:30–14:30 & 19:30–21:30, closed Mon, Nov–April closed Sun, tel. 0761-793-565, Lorena).

TRANSPORTATION CONNECTIONS

From Bagnoregio to Orvieto: Public buses (6/day, 1 hr, €3.20 round-trip) connect Bagnoregio to the rest of the world via Orvieto. Departures in 2007 from Bagnoregio, daily except Sunday: 5:30, 9:55, 10:10, 13:00, 14:25, and 17:25. During the school year (roughly Sept–June), buses also run at 6:35, 6:50, 13:35, and 16:40 (for info on coming from Orvieto, see "Transportation Connections" for Orvieto, page 585).

Driving from Orvieto to Bagnoregio: Orvieto overlooks the *autostrada* (and has its own exit). The shortest way to Civita from the freeway exit is to turn left (below Orvieto) and then simply follow the signs to Lubriano and Bagnoregio.

The more winding and scenic route takes 20 minutes longer: From the freeway, pass under hill-capping Orvieto (on your right, signs to Lago di Bolsena, on Viale I Maggio), then take the first left (direction: Bagnoregio), winding up past great Orvieto views through Canale, and through farms and fields of giant shredded wheat to Bagnoregio.

Either way, just before Bagnoregio, follow the signs left to Lubriano and pull into the first little square by the church on your right for a breathtaking view of Civita. You'll find an even better view farther inside the town, from the tiny square at the next church (San Giovanni Battista). Then return to the Bagnoregio road.

Drive through the town of Bagnoregio (following yellow *Civita* signs) to the lot at the base of the steep pedestrian bridge. In summer or on some weekends you'll need to pay €1 for your visit (not per hour) at the restaurant or shop opposite (same family). If no one's there, just park and don't worry. The bridge at this parking lot leads up to the traffic-free, 2,500-year-old, canyon-swamped pinnacle town of Civita di Bagnoregio.

More Hill Towns

If you haven't gotten your fill of hill towns, here are more to check out.

▲Gubbio

This handsome town climbs Monte Ingino in northeast Umbria. Tuesday is market day, when Piazza 40 Martiri (named for 40 local martyrs shot by Nazis) bustles. Nearby, the ruins of the Roman amphitheater are perfect for a picnic. Head up Via della Repubblica to the main square with the imposing Palazzo dei Consoli. Farther up, Via San Gerolamo leads to the funky lift that will carry you up the hill, in two-person "baskets," for a stunning view from the top, where the Basilica of San Ubaldo is worth a look. The **TI** is at Via della Repubblica 15 (April–Sept Mon–Fri 8:00–13:45 & 15:30–18:30, Sat 9:00–13:00 & 15:30–18:30, Sun 9:30–12:30 & 15:30–18:30, Oct–March closes at 18:00 daily; tel. 075-922-0693, www.gubbio-altochiascio.umbria2000.it). Buses from Gubbio run to Perugia, Rome, and Florence.

▲Bevagna

This sleeper of a town south of Assisi has Roman ruins, interesting churches, and more. Locals offer their guiding services for free (usually Italian-speaking only) and are excited to show visitors their town. Get a map at the **TI** at Piazza Silvestri 1 (daily 9:30–13:00 & 15:00–19:00, tel. 0742-361-667) and wander. Highlights are the Roman mosaics, remains of the arena that now houses a paper-making workshop, the Romanesque Church of San Silvestro, and a gem of a 19th-century theater. Bevagna has all the elements of a hill town except one—a hill. You can see the main sights easily in a couple of hours. For an overnight stay, consider the fancy **$$ Hotel Palazzo Brunamonti** (Sb-€47–88, Db-€70–110, Tb-€80–155, air-con, Corso Giacomo Matteotti 79, tel. 0742-361-932, fax 0742-361-948, www.brunamonti.com, hotel@brunamonti .com). Buses connect Bevagna with Foligno (except on Sun).

▲Spello

Umbrian hill town aficionados always include Spello on their list. Just six miles south of Assisi, this town is much less touristy than its neighbor to the north. Spello will give your legs a workout. Via Consolare goes up, up, up to the top of town. Views from the terrace of the Il Trombone restaurant will have you singing a tune. The **TI** is on Piazza Giacomo Matteotti 3 (summer hours 9:30–12:30 & 16:30–18:30, shorter hours in winter, tel. 0742-301-009). Spello is on the Perugia–Assisi–Foligno train line. Buses run to Assisi.

ROME

Roma

Rome is magnificent and brutal at the same time. It's a showcase of Western civilization, with astonishingly ancient sights and a modern vibrancy. But if you're careless, you'll be run down or pickpocketed. And with the wrong attitude, you'll be frustrated by the kind of chaos that only an Italian can understand. On my last visit, a cabbie struggling with the traffic said, *"Roma chaos."* I responded, *"Bella chaos."* He agreed.

While Paris is an urban garden, Rome is a magnificent tangled forest. If your hotel provides a comfortable refuge; if you pace yourself; if you accept—and even partake in—the siesta plan; if you're well-organized for sightseeing; and if you protect yourself and your valuables with extra caution and discretion, you'll love it. (And Rome is much easier to live with if you avoid the midsummer heat.)

For me, Rome is in a three-way tie with Paris and London as Europe's greatest city. Two thousand years ago, the word "Rome" meant civilization itself. Everything was either civilized (part of the Roman Empire, Latin- or Greek-speaking) or barbarian. Today, Rome is Italy's political capital, the capital of Catholicism, and the center of the ancient world, littered with evocative remains. As you peel through its fascinating and jumbled layers, you'll find Rome's buildings, cats, laundry, traffic, and 2.6 million people endlessly entertaining. And then, of course, there are its stupendous sights.

Tour St. Peter's, the greatest church on earth, and scale Michelangelo's 328-foot-tall dome, the world's largest. Learn something about eternity by touring the huge Vatican Museum. You'll find the story of Creation—bright as the day it was painted—in the restored Sistine Chapel. Do the "Caesar Shuffle" through ancient Rome's Forum and Colosseum. Savor Europe's most sumptuous building, the Borghese Gallery, and take an early evening "Dolce Vita Stroll" down the Via del Corso with Rome's beautiful people. Enjoy an after-dark walk from Campo de' Fiori to the Spanish Steps, lacing together Rome's Baroque and bubbly nightspots. Dine well at least once.

Planning Your Time

Rome is wonderful, but it's huge (pop. 2.6 million) and exhausting. On a first-time visit, many travelers find that Rome is best done quickly—Italy is more charming elsewhere. But whether you're here for a day or a week, you won't be able to see all of Rome's attractions, so don't try—you'll keep coming back to Rome. After several dozen visits, I still have a healthy list of excuses to return.

Rome in a Day: Some people actually try to "do" Rome in a day. Crazy as that sounds, if all you have is a day, it's one of the most exciting days that Europe has to offer. See the Vatican City (two hours in the Vatican Museum and Sistine Chapel—if the line's not too long—then one hour in St. Peter's), taxi over the river to the Pantheon (picnic on its steps), then hike over Capitol Hill, through the Forum, and to the Colosseum. Have dinner on Campo de' Fiori and dessert on Piazza Navona. (With typical crowds, you'll likely have to skip the Vatican Museum. But the rest is entirely doable.) Note: If you only want a day in Rome, consider side-tripping in from Orvieto or Florence, and maybe before the night train to Venice.

Rome in Two to Three Days: On the first day, do the "Caesar Shuffle" from the Colosseum to the Forum, then over Capitol Hill to the Pantheon. After a siesta, join the locals strolling from Piazza del Popolo to the Spanish Steps (see my recommended "Dolce Vita Stroll," page 621). On the second day, see Vatican City (St. Peter's, climb the dome, tour the Vatican Museum). Have dinner on the atmospheric Campo de' Fiori, then walk to the Trevi Fountain and Spanish Steps (see my recommended "Night Walk Across Rome," page 623). With a third day, add the Borghese Gallery (reservations required) and the National Museum of Rome.

ORIENTATION

Sprawling Rome actually feels manageable once you get to know it. Containing most of the tourist sights, the old core sits in a diamond formed by the Termini train station (in the east), the Vatican (west), Villa Borghese Gardens (north), and the Colosseum (south). The Tiber River runs through the diamond from north to south. In the center of the diamond sits Piazza Venezia, a busy square and traffic hub. It takes about an hour to walk from the Termini train

Rome's Neighborhoods

station to the Vatican.

Think of Rome as a series of neighborhoods, huddling around major landmarks:

Ancient Rome: In ancient times, this was home for the grandest buildings of a city of a million people. Today, the best of the classical sights stand in a line from the Colosseum to the Forum to the Pantheon. (See "Ancient Rome" map, page 636.)

Pantheon Neighborhood (The Heart of Rome): The Pantheon anchors the neighborhood I like to call the "Heart of Rome." It stretches eastward from the Tiber River through Campo de' Fiori and Piazza Navona, past the Pantheon to the Trevi Fountain. (See "Pantheon Neighborhood" map, page 645.)

North Rome: With the Spanish Steps, Villa Borghese Gardens, and trendy shopping streets (Via Veneto and the "shopping triangle"), this is a more modern, classy area. (See "North Rome" map, page 651.)

Vatican City: Located west of the Tiber, it's a compact world of its own, with two great, huge sights: St. Peter's Basilica and the Vatican Museum. (See "Vatican City" map, page 661.)

Trastevere: This seedy, colorful, wrong-side-of-the-river neighborhood is village Rome. It's the city at its crustiest—and

Rome

perhaps most "Roman." (See "Trastevere" map, page 670.)

Termini: Though light on sightseeing highlights, this train-station neighborhood has many recommended hotels and public-transportation connections. (See "Near Termini Train Station" map, page 647.)

Pilgrim's Rome: Several prominent churches dot the area south of Termini train station. (See "Pilgrim's Rome" map, page 650.)

South Rome: South of the city center, you'll find the gritty/colorful Testaccio neighborhood, the 1930s suburb of E.U.R., and the Appian Way, home of the catacombs. (See "South of Testaccio" map, page 676.)

Within each of these neighborhoods, you'll find elements from the many layers of Rome's 2,000-year history: the marble ruins of ancient times; tangled streets of the medieval world; early Christian churches; grand Renaissance buildings and statues; Baroque fountains and church facades; 19th-century apartments; and 20th-century boulevards choked with traffic.

Because no one is allowed to build taller than St. Peter's dome, and because virtually no buildings have been constructed in the city center since Mussolini got distracted in 1938, Rome has no modern skyline. The Tiber River is basically ignored—after the last floods (1870), the banks were built up very high, and Rome turned its back on its naughty river.

Tourist Information

While Rome has several tourist information offices, the dozen or so TI kiosks scattered around the town at major tourist centers are handy and just as helpful. If all you need is a map, forget the TI and get one at your hotel or at a newsstand kiosk.

Rome has a helpful TI call center that is answered by English-speakers: 06-8205-9127 (daily 9:00–19:00, press 2 for English). Many travelers find this to be Rome's single best source of tourist information.

If you want to visit a TI in person, you'll find one in the airport at Terminal C (daily 8:00–19:00) and two at the Termini train station (both open daily 8:00–21:00; one is near a travel agency and baggage check alongside track 24; the other branch is outside the station in a big glass building near the bus parking lot).

Smaller TIs (daily 9:00–18:00) include kiosks near the Forum (on Piazza del Tempio della Pace), at Via del Corso (on Largo Goldoni), in Trastevere (on Piazza Sonnino), on Via Nazionale (at Palazzo delle Esposizioni), at Castel Sant'Angelo (at Piazza Pia), at Santa Maria Maggiore Church, at Piazza Navona (at Piazza delle Cinque Lune), and near the Trevi Fountain (at Via del Corso and Via Minghetti).

At any TI, ask for a city map, a listing of sights and hours (in the free *Museums of Rome* booklet), and *Passepartout*, the free seasonal entertainment guide for evening events and fun. Don't book rooms through a TI; you'll save money by booking direct.

Roma c'è is a cheap little weekly entertainment guide with a useful English section (in the back) on musical events (€1.20, new edition every Thu, sold at newsstands, www.romace.it).

Websites on Rome: Check out www.whatsoninrome.com (events and news), www.romaturismo.com (music, exhibitions, and events), www.wantedinrome.com (job openings and real estate, but also festivals and exhibitions), and www.vatican.va (the pope's website).

Arrival in Rome

By Train at Termini Station: Rome's main train station, called **Termini**, is a buffet of tourist services: TI (daily 8:00–21:00, poorly marked, 100 yards down track 24 near baggage deposit), train info office (daily 7:00–21:00), ATMs, late-hours banks, 24-hour thievery, cafés, and two good self-service cafeterias (Ciao is upstairs, with fine views and seating; Food Village Chef Express is on the track level, daily 11:00–22:30). Borri Books, near the front of the station, sells books in English, including popular fiction, Italian history and culture, and kids' books, plus maps upstairs (daily 7:00–23:00). In the modern mall downstairs, you'll find a grocery (daily 7:00–22:00). There are two pharmacies (both open daily 7:30–22:00, at track 1 and downstairs below track 24). Baggage deposit is along track 24 downstairs (€4 for up to 5 hours, €0.60/hr thereafter, daily 6:00–24:00). The "Leonardo Express" train to Fiumicino Airport runs from track 24 (see "Rome's Airports," near the end of this chapter).

Termini is also a local transportation hub. The city's two Metro lines intersect at the Termini Metro station (downstairs). Buses (including Rome's hop-on, hop-off bus tours—see page 613) leave from the square directly in front of the main station hall. Taxis queue in front; avoid con men hawking "express taxi" services in unmarked cars (only use ones marked with the word *taxi* and a phone number). To avoid the long taxi line, simply hike out past the buses to the main street and hail one. The station has some sleazy sharks with official-looking business cards; avoid anybody selling anything unless they're in a legitimate shop at the station.

From Termini train station, most of my accommodation listings are easily accessible by foot (for hotels near the Termini train station) or by Metro (for hotels in the Colosseum and Vatican neighborhoods).

By Train or Bus at Tiburtina Station: Some slower trains use Rome's Tiburtina station, which is also the city's main bus hub

Rome

Greater Rome

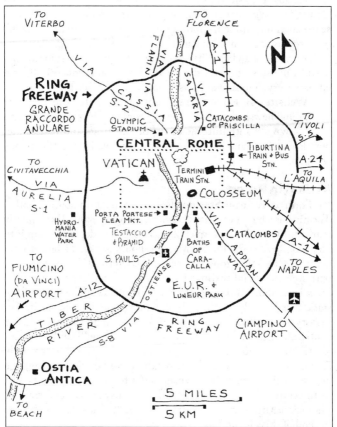

for destinations all across Italy. Buses depart from the piazza in front of the station. Ticket offices are located in the piazza and around the corner on Circonvallazione Nomentana. Within the train station are a currency-exchange office and a 24-hour grocery. Tiburtina station is on Metro line B, with easy connections to Termini train station (a straight shot, four stops away) and the entire Metro system. Or take bus #492 from Tiburtina to various city-center stops (such as Piazza Barberini, Piazza Venezia, and Piazza Cavour) and the Vatican neighborhood.

By Plane: For information on Rome's airports and connections into the city, see "Rome's Airports" at the end of this chapter.

Helpful Hints

Internet Access: If your hotel doesn't offer free or cheap Internet access, your hotelier can point you to the nearest Internet café.

Soccer: The National Obsession

One of Rome's most local "sights" is a soccer match. Winston Churchill said that Italians lose wars like soccer matches and soccer matches like wars; soccer, or *calcio,* is the national

obsession. Everyone, regardless of age or social class, is an expert, quick with an opinion on a coach's lousy decision or a referee's unprofessional conduct. Fans love to insult officials: a favorite is *"arbitro cornuto!""*—the referee is a cuckold (i.e., his wife sleeps around). The country's obsession turned into jubilation on July 9, 2006, when

Italy won the World Cup, and Rome—along with every other city, town, and village in Italy—went crazy with joy. For more on soccer leagues throughout Italy, see page 32).

Rome has a special passion for soccer. It has two teams, Roma (representing the city) and Lazio (the region), and the rivalry is fanatic. When Romans are introduced, they ask each other, *"Laziale o romanista?"* The answer can compromise a relationship. Both Roma (jersey: yellow and red; symbol: she-wolf) and Lazio (jersey: light blue and white; symbol: imperial eagle) claim to be truly Roman. Lazio is older (founded in 1900), but Roma has more supporters. Lazio is supposed to be more upper-class and Roma more popular, but the social division is blurred. When Lazio was implicated in the match-fixing scandal that swept through Italy's professional soccer league in the summer of 2006, Roma fans watched gleefully (Lazio escaped with a slap on the wrist).

The most eagerly awaited sporting event of the year is the derby, when the two teams fight it out at the Olympic Stadium. All of Italy acknowledges that team spirit is most fervent in Rome. Fans prepare months in advance, and on the day of the match they fill the entire stadium with team colors, flags, banners, and smoke candles.

Witty slogans on banners work like dialogues: A Roma banner proclaimed, "Roma: Only the sky is higher than you." The Lazio banner replied, "In fact, the sky is blue and white" (like its team colors). The exchange revealed that there had been a Lazio informer on the Roma side, which traumatized Roma fans for weeks. Tourists go to a match more for the action in the stands than the action on the field—it's one of the most Roman of all experiences.

Both teams call the Stadio Olimpico home, so you can catch a game most weekends from September to May (Metro Line A to Flaminio, then catch tram #225 to the end of the line, Piazza Mancini, and cross the bridge to the stadium).

Tips on Sightseeing in Rome

Sightseeing Passes: Rome offers two passes to help you save money on your sightseeing. For most visitors, the Roma Pass is the clear winner.

The **Roma Pass** costs €20 and is valid for three days, covering public transportation and free or discounted entry to Roman sights. You get free admission to your first two sights (where you also get to skip the ticket line), and then a discount on the rest within the three-day window. Sights covered (or discounted) by the pass include the following: Colosseum/Palatine Hill, Borghese Gallery (though you still must make a reservation and pay the €2 booking fee), Capitoline Museums, all four branches of the National Museum of Rome (considered as a single "sight"), Castel Sant'Angelo, Montemartini Museum, Ara Pacis, Museum of Roman Civilization, Etruscan Museum, Baths of Caracalla, Trajan's Market, and some of the Appian Way sights.

If you'll be visiting any two of the major sights in a three-day period, this money- and time-saver is a no-brainer. The pass is sold at participating sights, and at the TIs at the airport and Termini train station (includes map and brochure listing additional discounts, www.romapass.it).

Validate your Roma Pass by writing your name and validation date on the card. Then simply insert it directly into the turnstile at your first two (free) sights. At other sights, show it at the ticket office to get your reduced (ridotto) price—usually a discount of about one-third.

To get the most of your pass, visit the two most expensive sights first—for example, the Colosseum (€11) and the National Museum (€10). Definitely use it to bypass the long ticket line at the Colosseum. For sights that normally sell a combo-ticket (such as the Colosseum–Palatine or the four National Museum branches), visiting the combined sight counts only as a single entrance.

The Roma Pass also includes a three-day transit pass. Write your name and birth date on the transit pass, validate it in the machine on your first bus or Metro ride, and you can take

Remember to bring your passport, which you may be asked for before getting online.

Bookstores: These stores (all open daily) sell travel guidebooks—**Borri Books** (at the Termini train station), two handy locations of **Feltrinelli International** (one at Largo Argentina and the other just off Piazza della Repubblica at Via Vittorio Emanuele Orlando 84, tel. 06-482-7878), **Almost Corner Bookshop** in Trastevere (Via del Moro 45, tel. 06-583-6942), and the **Anglo American Bookshop** (a few blocks south of the Spanish Steps at Via della Vite 102, tel. 06-679-5222).

unlimited rides until midnight of the third day.

Those visiting several ancient sights should also consider the **Archeologia Card.** It costs €22, is valid for seven days, and covers many of the biggies: the Colosseum, Palatine Hill, Baths of Caracalla, Tomb of Cecilia Metella (on Appian Way), Villa of the Quintilli (barren Roman villa on the outskirts of Rome), and all four branches of the National Museum of Rome: Palazzo Massimo (the main branch), Museum of the Bath at the Baths of Diocletian (Roman inscriptions), Crypta Balbi (medieval art), and Palazzo Altemps (so-so sculpture collection). This combo-ticket saves you money if you plan to visit at least three of the major sights, such as the Colosseum, National Museum of Rome, and the Baths of Caracalla (sold at participating sights).

If buying both a Roma Pass and an Archeologia Card, use your free Roma Pass entries for sights *not* covered by the Archeologia Card (such as the Borghese Gallery and Capitoline Museums).

Museums: Plan ahead. The marvelous Borghese Gallery requires **reservations** well in advance (see page 651). You can also make reservations for the often-crowded Colosseum (see page 632), or reserve a tour with a tour company to avoid the long lines at the Vatican Museum (see page 656). Nero's Golden House also requires advance booking (see page 636).

Churches: Churches generally open early (about 7:00–7:30), close for lunch (roughly 12:00–15:00), and close late (about 19:00). Kamikaze tourists maximize their sightseeing hours by visiting churches before 9:00 and seeing the major sights that stay open during the siesta (St. Peter's, Colosseum, Forum, Capitol Hill Museum, and National Museum of Rome), while Romans are taking it cool and easy.

Many churches have "modest dress" requirements, which means no bare shoulders, miniskirts, or shorts—for men, women, or children. However, this dress code is strictly enforced only at St. Peter's Basilica and St. Paul's Outside the Walls.

Laundry: Your hotelier can direct you to the nearest launderette. The **Bolle Blu** launderette chain comes with Internet access (about €7 to wash and dry a 15-pound load, usually open daily 8:00–22:00, near Termini train station at Via Palestro 59 and at Via Principe Amedeo 116, tel. 06-446-5804).

Travel Agencies: You can get train tickets and railpass-related reservations and supplements at travel agencies, to avoid a trip to a train station. The cost is often the same, though sometimes there's a minimal charge. Your hotelier will know of a convenient agency nearby. The **American Express** office near

Rome

the Spanish Steps sells train tickets and makes reservations for no extra fee (Mon–Fri 9:00–17:30, closed Sat–Sun, Piazza di Spagna 38, tel. 06-67641).

Dealing with (and Avoiding) Problems

Theft Alert: With sweet-talking con artists meeting you at the station, well-dressed pickpockets on buses, and thieving gangs of children at the ancient sites, Rome is a gauntlet of rip-offs. While it's nowhere near as bad as it was a few years ago, and there's no great physical risk, green or sloppy tourists will be scammed. Thieves strike when you're distracted. Don't trust kind strangers. Keep nothing important in your pockets. Be most on guard while boarding and leaving buses and subways. Thieves crowd the door, then stop and turn while others crowd and push from behind. The sneakiest thieves are well-dressed businessmen (generally with something in their hands); lately many are posing as tourists with fanny packs, cameras, and even Rick Steves guidebooks. Scams abound: Don't give your wallet to self-proclaimed "police" who stop you on the street, warn you about counterfeit (or drug) money, and ask to see your cash. If a bank machine eats your ATM card, see if there's a thin plastic insert with a tongue hanging out that thieves use to extract it.

If you know what to look out for, the gangs of children picking the pockets and handbags of naive tourists are no threat, but an interesting—albeit sad—spectacle. Gangs of city-stained children (just 8–10 years old—too young to be prosecuted, but old enough to rip you off) troll through the tourist crowds around the Colosseum, Forum, Piazza della Repubblica, and train and Metro stations. Watch them target tourists who are overloaded with bags or distracted with a video camera. The kids look like beggars and hold up newspapers or cardboard signs to confuse their victims. They scram like stray cats if you're on to them. A fast-fingered mother with a baby is often nearby. The terrace above the bus stop near the Colosseo Metro stop is a fine place to watch the action...and maybe even pick up a few moves of your own.

Reporting Losses: To report lost or stolen passports and documents, or to make an insurance claim, you must file a police report (at Termini train station, with Polizia at track 1 or with Carabinieri at track 20; offices are also at Piazza Venezia). To replace a passport, file the police report, then go to your embassy (see page 828). To report lost or stolen credit cards, see page 823.

Emergency Numbers: Police—tel. 113. Ambulance—tel. 118.

Hit and Run: Walk with extreme caution. Scooters don't need to stop at red lights, and even cars exercise what drivers call the "logical option" of not stopping if they see no oncoming traffic. As noisy gasoline-powered scooters are replaced by electric ones, they'll be quieter (hooray) but more dangerous for pedestrians. Follow locals like a shadow when you cross a street (or spend a good part of your visit stranded on curbs). When you do cross alone, don't be a deer in the headlights. Find a gap in the traffic and walk with confidence while making eye contact with approaching drivers—they won't hit you if they can tell where you intend to go.

Staying/Getting Healthy: The siesta is a key to survival in summertime Rome. Lie down and contemplate the extraordinary power of gravity in the Eternal City. I drink lots of cold, refreshing water from Rome's many drinking fountains (the Forum has three). There's a pharmacy (marked by a green cross) in every neighborhood. Pharmacies stay open late in the Termini train station (daily 7:30–22:00, downstairs below track 24) and at Piazza dei Cinquecento 51 (open 24 hours daily, next to Termini train station on Via Cavour, tel. 06-488-0019). Embassies can recommend English-speaking doctors. Consider MEDline, a 24-hour home-medical service (tel. 06-808-0995, doctors speak English). Anyone is entitled to free emergency treatment at public hospitals. The hospital closest to Termini train station is Policlinico Umberto 1 (entrance for emergency treatment on Via Lancisi, translators available, Metro: Policlinico). The American Hospital, a private hospital on the edge of town, is accustomed to helping Yankees (Via Emilio Longoni 69, tel. 06-225-571).

Getting Around Rome

Sightsee on foot, by city bus, by Metro, or by taxi. I've grouped your sightseeing into walkable neighborhoods. Make it a point to visit sights in a logical order. Needless backtracking wastes precious time.

Public transportation is efficient, cheap, and part of your Roman experience. It starts running at about 5:30 and stops at about 23:30, sometimes earlier. After midnight, there are a few very crowded night buses, and taxis become more expensive and hard to get. Don't try to hail one—go to a taxi stand.

You can use the same ticket on the bus or the Metro (€1, valid for one Metro ride—including transfers underground—plus unlimited buses during a 75-minute period); you can also buy an all-day bus/Metro pass (€4, good until midnight), a three-day pass (€11), or a one-week pass (€16—about the same cost of two taxi rides).

You can buy tickets and passes at some newsstands, tobacco shops (*tabacchi*, marked by a black-and-white *T* sign), and major Metro stations and bus stops, but not on board. It's smart to stock up on tickets early, or to buy an all-day pass or a Roma Pass (which includes a three-day transit pass—see page 602). That way, you don't have to run around searching for an open *tabacchi* when you spot your bus approaching. Metro stations rarely have human ticket-sellers, and the machines are often either broken or require exact change (it helps to insert your smallest coin first).

Validate your ticket by sticking it in the Metro turnstile (brown stripe down) or in the machine when you board the bus—watch others and imitate. If the validation machine won't work, you can ride with your ticket unstamped, but you must write the date, time, and bus number on it. For more information, visit www.atac.roma.it or call 800-431-784.

Buses (especially the touristy #64) and the Metro are havens for thieves and pickpockets. Assume that any commotion is a thief-created distraction. If one bus is packed, there's likely a second one on its tail with far fewer crowds and thieves. Once you know the bus system, it's easier than searching for a cab.

By Metro

The Roman subway system (Metropolitana, or "Metro") is simple, with two clean, cheap, fast lines—A and B—that intersect at Termini train station. You'll notice lots of big holes in the city, as a new line is being built. (Line C, from the Colosseum to Largo Argentina, will likely be done in 2020.) The subway's first and last compartments are generally the least crowded.

While much of Rome is not served by its skimpy subway, the following stops are helpful.

Termini (intersection of lines A and B): Termini train station, National Museum of Rome, and recommended hotels

Repubblica (line A): Baths of Diocletian/Octagonal Hall, Via Nazionale, and recommended hotels

Barberini (line A): Cappuccin Crypt and Trevi Fountain

Spagna (line A): Spanish Steps, Villa Borghese, and classy shopping area

Flaminio (line A): Piazza del Popolo, start of recommended "Dolce Vita Stroll" down Via del Corso

Ottaviano (line A): St. Peter's and Vatican City

Cipro–Musei Vaticani (line A): Vatican Museum and recommended hotels

Tiburtina (line B): Tiburtina train and bus station

Colosseo (line B): Colosseum, Roman Forum, bike rental, and recommended hotels

Rome's Metro

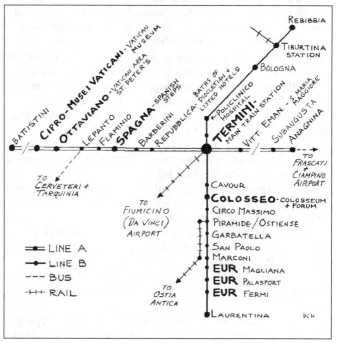

REBIBBIA
TIBURTINA STATION
BOLOGNA
BATTISTINI
CIPRO - MUSEI VATICANI - VATICAN MUSEUM
OTTAVIANO - VATICAN AREA ST. PETER'S
LEPANTO
FLAMINIO
SPAGNA - SPANISH STEPS
BARBERINI
REPUBBLICA - BATHS OF DIOCLETIAN + LISTED HOTELS
POLICLINICO HOSPITAL
TERMINI - MAIN TRAIN STATION
VITT. EMAN.
S. MARIA MAGGIORE
SUBAUGUSTA
ANAGNINA
TO FRASCATI + CIAMPINO AIRPORT
TO CERVETERI + TARQUINIA
CAVOUR
COLOSSEO - COLOSSEUM + FORUM
TO FIUMICINO (DA VINCI) AIRPORT
CIRCO MASSIMO
PIRAMIDE / OSTIENSE
GARBATELLA
SAN PAOLO
MARCONI
EUR MAGLIANA
EUR PALASPORT
EUR FERMI
TO OSTIA ANTICA
LAURENTINA
DCH

LINE A
LINE B
BUS
RAIL

Piramide (line B): Protestant Cemetery and trains to Ostia Antica

E.U.R. (line B): Mussolini's futuristic suburb

By Bus

Bus routes are clearly listed at the stops. Ask the TI for a bus map (bus info: tel. 06-4695-2027). Think of Largo Argentina as a hub. Tickets have a bar code and must be stamped on the bus in the yellow box with the digital readout (be sure to retrieve your ticket). Punch your ticket as you board (magnetic stripe down), or you are cheating. While relatively safe, riding without a stamped ticket on the bus is stressful. Inspectors fine even innocent-looking tourists €52. General bus etiquette (not always followed) is to board at the front or rear doors and exit out the middle.

Here are a few buses worth knowing about:

Rome

#64: Termini train station, Piazza della Repubblica (sights), Via Nazionale (recommended hotels), Piazza Venezia (near Forum), Largo Argentina (near Pantheon), and St. Peter's Basilica (get off just past the tunnel). Ride it for a city overview and to watch pickpockets in action (can get horribly crowded, awkward for female travelers uncomfortably close to male strangers).

#40: This express bus following the #64 route is especially helpful—fewer stops, crowds, and pickpockets.

#8: This tram connects Largo Argentina with Trastevere (get off at Piazza Belli, just after crossing the Tiber River).

#62: Largo Argentina to St. Peter's Square.

#81: San Giovanni in Laterano, Colosseum, Largo Argentina, and Piazza Risorgimento (Vatican).

#H: Express connecting Termini train station and Trastevere, with a few stops on Via Nazionale (for Trastevere, get off at Piazza Belli, just after crossing the river).

#492: Stazione Tiburtina (train and bus stations), Piazza Barberini, Piazza Venezia, Piazza Cavour (Castel Sant'Angelo), and Piazza Risorgimento (Vatican).

#714: Termini train station, Santa Maria Maggiore, San Giovanni in Laterano, Terme di Caracalla (Baths of Caracalla), and on to E.U.R.

#23 and #280: Links Vatican with Trastevere, stopping at Porta Portese (Sunday flea market), Trastevere (Piazza Belli), Castel Sant'Angelo, and Vatican Museum (nearest stop is Via Leone IV).

Rome has cute *elettrico* minibuses that wind through the narrow streets of old and interesting neighborhoods (daily, fewer on Sun). These are handy for sightseeing and fun for simply joy-riding:

Elettrico **#116:** Through the medieval core of Rome: Ponte Vittorio Emanuele II (near Castel Sant'Angelo) to Campo de' Fiori, then to Piazza Barberini via the Pantheon, and finally through the scenic Villa Borghese Gardens.

Elettrico **#117:** San Giovanni in Laterano, Colosseo, Via dei Serpenti, Trevi Fountain, Piazza di Spagna, and Piazza del Popolo.

By Taxi

I use taxis in Rome more often than in other cities. They're reasonable and useful for efficient sightseeing in this big, hot metropolis. Taxis start at about €2.50, then charge about €1 per kilometer (surcharges: €1 on Sun, €2.75 for nighttime hours of 22:00–7:00, €1 for luggage, tip by rounding up to the nearest euro). Sample fares: Termini train station to Vatican-€9; Termini train station to Colosseum-€6; Colosseum to Trastevere-€7. From the airport

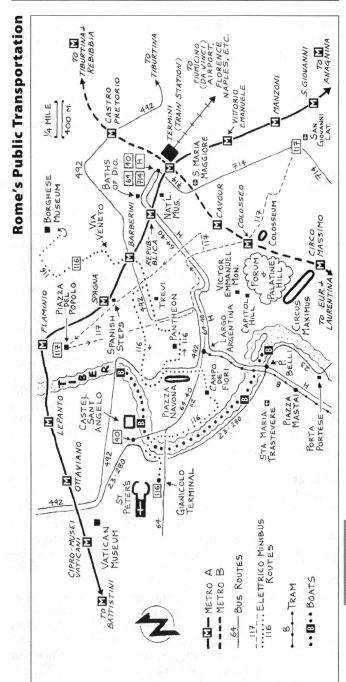

Rome's Public Transportation

to anywhere in central Rome is a strictly fixed €40 rate (up to four people and their bags). Three or four companions with more money than time should taxi almost everywhere. It's tough to wave down a taxi in Rome. Find the nearest taxi stand by asking a passerby or a clerk in a shop, *"Dov'è una fermata dei taxi?"* (doh-VEH OO-nah fehr-MAH-tah DEHee TAHK-see). Some taxi stands are listed on my maps. To save time and energy, have your hotel or restaurant call a taxi for you; the meter starts when the call is received (generally adding a euro or two to the bill). To call a cab on your own, dial 06-3570, 06-4994, or 06-88177. It's routine for Romans to ask the waiter in a restaurant to call a taxi when they ask for the bill. The waiter will tell you how many minutes you have to enjoy your coffee.

Beware of corrupt taxis. If hailing a cab on the street, be sure the meter is restarted when you get in (should be about €2.50; it may be higher if you called for the taxi). Many meters show both the fare and the time elapsed during the ride—and some tourists pay €8.30 for an eight-and-a-half-minute trip (more than the fair meter rate). When you arrive at the train station or airport, beware of hustlers conning naive visitors into unmarked rip-off "express taxis." Only use official taxis, with a *taxi* sign and phone number marked on the door. By law, they must display a multilingual official price chart. If you have any problems with a taxi, point to the chart and ask the cabbie to explain it to you. Making a show of writing down the taxi number (to file a complaint) can motivate a driver to quickly settle the matter. Tired travelers arriving at the airport might find it less stressful to take the airport shuttle to their hotel or catch the train to the Termini train station and take the Metro or a cheaper taxi from there (see page 709 for details on the shuttle and train).

By Boat

Tourist-laden boats slowly float their way down the Tiber (€1 per ride, schedules posted at stops). While this is a valiant attempt by Rome to re-energize its neglected river, the boat rides are unreliable, inconvenient, and not that interesting. I wouldn't bother with Tiber boats (either tours or those offering "public transport").

By Bike

Cool Rent, near the Colosseo Metro stop, is well located for renting a bike for a trip out to the Appian Way (€3/hr, €10/day, daily 9:00–20:00, €100 cash or driver's license for deposit, 20 yards to the right as you exit the Metro). A second outlet is just off Via del Corso (on Largo di Lombardi, near corner of Via del Corso and Via della Croce). You can also rent a bike at the Appian Way (see page 679)

By Car with Driver

You can hire your own private car with driver through **Autoservizi Monti Concezio,** run by gentle, capable, and English-speaking Ezio (car-€35/hr, minibus-€40/hr, 3-hour minimum, mobile 335-636-5907 or 349-674-5643, www.montitours.com, concemon @tin.it).

TOURS

Rome has many good, highly competitive tour companies. I've listed my favorites here, but without a lot of details on their offerings. Before your trip, spend some time on their websites to get to know your options, as each company has a particular teaching and guiding personality. Some are highbrow, and others are less scholarly. It's sometimes required, and always smart, to book a spot in advance (easy online). The following companies all offer Vatican tours—a convenient way to skirt that museum's exasperating lines. While it may seem like a splurge to have a local or an American expat show you around, it's a treat that makes brutal Rome suddenly your friend.

Context Rome—Americans Paul Bennett and Lani Bevacqua offer walking tours for travelers with longer-than-average attention spans. Their orientation walks lace together lesser-known sights from antiquity to the present. Tours vary in length from two to four hours and range in price from €25 to €60. Try to book in advance, since their groups are limited to six and fill up fast (tel. 06-482-0911, US tel. 888-467-1986, www .contextrome.com). They also offer orientation chats in your hotel that can be well worth the price (€50/1 hr). Similar Context programs are offered in Venice, Florence, and Paris. See their website for other creative Context teaching initiatives.

If you're interested in weeklong classes on Rome, look into the **American Institute for Roman Culture**—an innovative, educational organization run by Tom Rankin and his colleague, archaeologist Darius Arya (www.romanculture.org).

Enjoy Rome—This English-speaking information service offers five different walking tours (€24 plus entry fees, 3 hours, groups limited to 25, reserve by phone or online). It also provides a free, useful city guide and an informative website (Mon–Fri 8:30–19:00, Sat 8:30–14:00, closed Sun, 3 blocks north of Termini train station, Via Marghera 8a, tel. 06/445-1843, fax 06/445-0734, www .enjoyrome.com, info@enjoyrome.com).

Daily Reminder

Sunday: These sights are closed—the Vatican Museum (except for the last Sunday of the month, when it's free and even more crowded), Villa Farnesina, Nero's Golden House, Santa Maria della Vittoria Protestant Cemetery in Testaccio, and the Catacombs of San Sebastian.

Monday: Many sights are closed, including the National Museum of Rome, Borghese Gallery, Capitoline Museums, Catacombs of Priscilla, Octagonal Hall and Museum of the Bath (both at Baths of Diocletian), Castel Sant'Angelo, Ara Pacis, Montemartini Museum, E.U.R.'s Museum of Roman Civilization, Trajan's Market, Nero's Golden House, Etruscan Museum, and Ostia Antica. All of the ancient sights (e.g., Colosseum and Forum) and the Vatican Museum, among others, are open. The Baths of Caracalla close early in the afternoon.

Tuesday: All sights are open in Rome.

Wednesday: All sights are open, except for the Catacombs of San Callisto. St. Peter's Basilica may be closed in the morning for a papal audience.

Thursday: All sights are open, except for Galleria Doria Pamphilj.

Friday: All sights are open in Rome.

Saturday: All major sights are open in Rome. The Vatican Museum closes early (10:00–14:45, until 13:45 in winter). The Synagogue and Jewish Museum are closed, as is Nero's Golden House.

Rome Walks—The licensed guides give tours in fluent English to small groups (2–10 people). Sample tours include Colosseum/Forum/Palatine Walk (€51, includes admission to Colosseum, 3 hours), Scandal Tour (€40, 3 hours to dig up the dirt on Roman emperors, royalty, and popes), Vatican City Walk (€58, includes admission to Vatican Museum, 4 hours), Twilight Rome Evening Walk (€25, all the famous squares that offer lively people scenes, 2 hours), and a Jewish Ghetto and Trastevere walk (€40, explore the back streets of Rome, 3 hours). They also do pricier, private tours to more far-flung places such as Orvieto (for wine and olives), Ostia Antica, the Appian Way, and the Catacombs (mobile 347-795-5175, www.romewalks.com, info@romewalks.com, Annie Frances Gray).

Roman Odyssey—This expat-led tour company offers various two- to three-hour, €25–50 walks led by native English speakers who are licensed guides (15 percent discount for readers of this book in 2008, tel. 06-580-9902, mobile 328-912-3720, www.romanodyssey.com, Rahul).

Through Eternity—This company offers several walking tours, all led by native English speakers who strive to bring the history to life. The tours, which run nearly daily and are limited to groups of 20, do not include entry fees to museums or sights. Tours include St. Peter's and the Vatican Museum (€46, 5 hours); the Colosseum and Roman Forum (€30, 3 hours); and Rome at Twilight (€30, nightly). The company offers a 10 percent Rick Steves discount if you book by phone or online (tel. 06-700-9336, mobile 347-336-5298, www.througheternity.com, info@througheternity.com, Rob Allyn).

Angel Tours—This gang of hardworking Irish Italophiles mix light narrative with their charming gift of gab. They generally do a free 19:00 Pantheon tour, hoping the charm and quality of the guide will encourage people to take the rest of that evening walk or book another tour. Their website lists tours and departure times (€25 plus entry fees, 2.5 hours, English only, groups limited to 15, tel. 06-772-03048, mobile 348-7341-850, www.romanrain.com, Sean).

Private Guides—Consider a personal tour. Any of the tour companies I list can provide a guide (about €55/hr). I work with Francesca Caruso, a licensed Italian guide who speaks excellent English, loves to teach and share her appreciation of her city, and has contributed generously to this book. She has a broad range of expertise and can tailor a walk to your interests, and enjoys working with readers of this book (€45/hr, chris.fra@mclink.it).

Hop-on, Hop-off Tours—Several different agencies, including the ATAC public bus company, run hop-on, hop-off tours around Rome. These tours are constantly evolving and offer varying combinations of sights. While you can grab one (and pay as you board) at any stop, Termini train station and Piazza Venezia are handy hubs. Although the city is perfectly walkable and traffic jams can make the bus dreadfully slow, these open-top bus tours remain popular. Several tour companies offer essentially the same deal. Trambus Open 110 (below) seems to be the best.

Trambus Open 110, operated by the ATAC city bus lines, offers an orientation tour on big red double-decker buses with an open-air upper deck. In less than two hours, you'll have 80 sights pointed out to you (with a recorded narration). While you can hop on and off, the service can be erratic (mobbed midday, not ideal in bad weather). It's best to think of this as an efficient, two-hour quickie orientation with scant information and lots of images. The 11 stops include Via Veneto, Via Tritone, Ara Pacis, Piazza Cavour, St. Peter's Square, Corso Vittorio Emanuele (for Piazza Navona), Piazza Venezia, Colosseum, and Via Nazionale. Bus #110 departs every 10 minutes (runs daily 8:40–20:30, tel. 06-684-0901, www.trambusopen.com). Buy the €13 ticket as you board (or at platform

E in front of Termini train station).

Archeobus is an open-top bus that runs hourly from Termini train station out to the Appian Way (with stops at the Colosseum, Baths of Caracalla, San Callisto, San Sebastian, the Tomb of Cecilia Metella, and the Aqueduct Park). This is a handy way to see the sights down this ancient Roman road, but it can be frustrating (sparse narration, sporadic service, not ideal for hopping on and off; €8, daily 9:30–16:00, hourly departures from Termini train station and Piazza Venezia, tel. 06-684-0901). A similar bus laces together all the Christian sights.

SELF-GUIDED WALKS

Here are three walks that give you a moving picture of Rome, an ancient yet modern city. You'll walk through history ("Roman Forum Walk"), take a refreshing early-evening stroll ("The Dolce Vita Stroll"), and enjoy the thriving night scene ("Night Walk Across Rome").

Roman Forum Walk

The Forum was the political, religious, and commercial center of the city. Rome's most important temples and halls of justice were here. This was the place for religious processions, political demonstrations, elections, important speeches, and parades by conquering generals. As Rome's empire expanded, these few acres of land became the center of the civilized world.

Cost, Hours, Location: Free, daily 8:30–19:00, until 17:00 in winter, last entry 1 hour before closing. Metro: Colosseo, tel. 06-3996-7700. Get basic info from two kiosks: one near the Via dei Fori Imperiali entrance (near Basilica Aemilia), and another near the Arch of Titus, at the foot of Palatine Hill. A €4 unexciting yet informative audioguide helps decipher the rubble (rent at kiosk near the Arch of Titus). Guided tours in English (€3.50) depart from the Arch of Titus kiosk nearly hourly in summer (in winter, once daily at about 12:15). Street vendors at several ancient sites sell small *Rome: Past and Present* books with plastic overlays that restore the ruins (marked €11, offer less).

• *Walk through the entrance nearest the Colosseum, hiking up the ramp marked* Via Sacra. *Stand next to the triumphal...*

❶ **Arch of Titus (Arco di Tito):** This arch commemorated the Roman victory over the province of Judaea (Israel) in A.D. 70. The Romans had a reputation as benevolent conquerors who tolerated the local customs and rulers. All they required was allegiance to the empire, shown by worshipping the emperor as a god. No problem for most conquered people, who already had half a dozen gods on their prayer lists anyway. But Israelites believed in only

---

Rome—Republic and Empire
(500 B.C.–A.D. 500)

Ancient Rome spanned about a thousand years, from 500 B.C. to A.D. 500. During that time, Rome expanded from a small tribe of barbarians to a vast empire, then dwindled slowly to city size again. For the first 500 years, when Rome's armies made her ruler of the Italian peninsula and beyond, Rome was a republic governed by elected senators. Over the next 500 years, a time of world conquest and eventual decline, Rome was an empire ruled by a military-backed dictator.

Julius Caesar bridged the gap between republic and empire. This ambitious general and politician, popular with the people because of his military victories and charisma, suspended the Roman constitution and assumed dictatorial powers in about 50 B.C., and in a few years was assassinated by a conspiracy of senators. His adopted son, Augustus, succeeded him, and soon "Caesar" was not just a name but a title.

Emperor Augustus ushered in the Pax Romana, or Roman peace (from A.D. 1–200), a time when Rome reached her peak and controlled an empire that stretched even beyond Eurail—from Scotland to Egypt, and from Turkey to Morocco.

---

one god, and it wasn't the emperor. Israel revolted. After a short but bitter war, the Romans defeated the rebels, took Jerusalem, sacked their temple, and brought home 50,000 Jewish slaves...who were forced to build this arch (and the Colosseum).

• *Start down the Via Sacra into the Forum. After about 50 yards, turn right and follow a path uphill to the three huge arches of the...*

❷ **Basilica of Constantine (a.k.a. Basilica Maxentius):** Yes, these are big arches. But they represent only one-third of the original Basilica of Constantine, a mammoth hall of justice. The arches were matched by a similar set along the Via Sacra side (only a few squat brick piers remain). Between them ran the central hall, which was spanned by a roof 130 feet high—about 55 feet higher than the side arches you see. (The stub of brick you see sticking up began an arch that once spanned the central hall.) The hall itself was as long as a football field, lavishly furnished with colorful inlaid marble, a gilded bronze ceiling, and statues, and filled with strolling Romans. At the far (west) end was an enormous marble statue of Emperor Constantine on a throne. (Pieces of this statue, including a man-size hand, are on display in Rome's Capitoline Museums.)

The basilica was begun by the emperor Maxentius, but after he was trounced in battle (see page 635), the victor—Constantine—

Roman Forum Walk

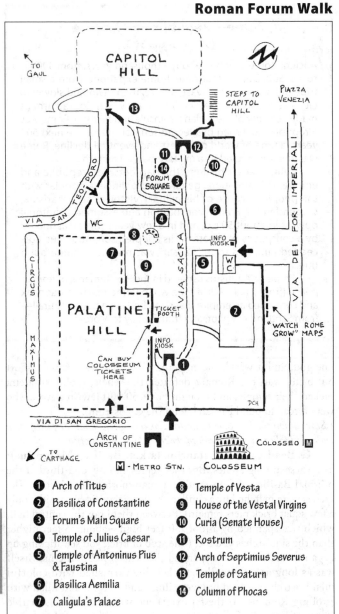

1. Arch of Titus
2. Basilica of Constantine
3. Forum's Main Square
4. Temple of Julius Caesar
5. Temple of Antoninus Pius & Faustina
6. Basilica Aemilia
7. Caligula's Palace
8. Temple of Vesta
9. House of the Vestal Virgins
10. Curia (Senate House)
11. Rostrum
12. Arch of Septimius Severus
13. Temple of Saturn
14. Column of Phocas

completed the massive building. No doubt about it, the Romans built monuments on a more epic scale than any previous Europeans, wowing their "barbarian" neighbors.

• *Now stroll deeper into the Forum, downhill along the Via Sacra, through the trees. Many of the large basalt stones under your feet were walked on by Caesar Augustus 2,000 years ago. Pass by the only original bronze door still swinging on its ancient hinges (green, on right) and continue between ruined buildings until the Via Sacra opens up to a flat, grassy area.*

❸ **The Forum's Main Square:** The original Forum, or main square, was this flat patch about the size of a football field, stretching to the foot of Capitol Hill. Surrounding it were temples, law courts, government buildings, and triumphal arches.

Rome was born right here. According to legend, twin brothers Romulus (Rome) and Remus were orphaned in infancy and raised by a she-wolf on top of Palatine Hill. Growing up, they found it hard to get dates. So they and their cohorts attacked the nearby Sabine tribe and kidnapped their women. After they made peace, this marshy valley became the meeting place and then the trading center for the scattered tribes on the surrounding hillsides.

• *At the near (east) end of the main square (the Colosseum is to the east) are the foundations of a temple now capped with a peaked wood-and-metal roof.*

❹ **The Temple of Julius Caesar (Tempio del Divo Giulio, or "Ara di Cesare"):** Julius Caesar's body was burned on this spot (under the metal roof) after his assassination. Peek behind the wall into the small apse area, where a mound of dirt usually has fresh flowers—given to remember the man who, more than any other, personified the greatness of Rome.

Caesar (100–44 B.C.) changed Rome—and the Forum—dramatically. He cleared out many of the wooden market stalls and began to ring the square with even grander buildings. Caesar's house was located behind the temple, near that clump of trees. He walked right by here on the day he was assassinated ("Beware the Ides of March!" warned a street-corner Etruscan preacher).

Though he was popular with the masses, not everyone liked Caesar's urban design or his politics. When he assumed dictatorial powers, he was ambushed and stabbed to death by a conspiracy of senators, including his adopted son, Brutus *("Et tu, Brute?")*.

The funeral was held here, facing the main square. The citizens gathered, and speeches were made. Mark Antony stood up to say (in Shakespeare's words), "Friends, Romans, countrymen, lend me your ears. I come to bury Caesar, not to praise him." When Caesar's body was burned, the citizens who still loved him threw anything at hand on the fire, requiring the fire department to come put it out. Later, Emperor Augustus dedicated this temple in his

name, making Caesar the first Roman to become a god.
• *Behind and to the left of the Temple of Julius Caesar are the 10 tall columns of the...*

❺ **Temple of Antoninus Pius and Faustina:** The Senate built this temple to honor Emperor Antoninus Pius (A.D. 138–161) and his deified wife, Faustina. The 50-foot-tall Corinthian (leafy) columns must have been awe-inspiring to out-of-towners who grew up in thatched huts. Although the temple has been inhabited by a church, you can still see the basic layout—a staircase led to a shaded porch (the columns), which admitted you to the main building (now a church), where the statue of the god sat. Originally, these columns supported a triangular pediment decorated with sculptures.

Picture these columns, with gilded capitals, supporting brightly painted statues in the pediment, and the whole building capped with a gleaming bronze roof. The stately gray rubble of today's Forum is a faded black-and-white photograph of a 3-D Technicolor era. (Also picture the Forum covered with dirt as high as the green door—as it was until excavated in the 1800s.)
• *There's a ramp next to the Temple of A. and F. Walk halfway up it and look to the left to view the...*

❻ **Basilica Aemilia:** A basilica was a covered public forum, often serving as a Roman hall of justice. In a society that was as legal-minded as America is today, you needed a lot of lawyers—and a big place to put them. Citizens came here to work out matters such as inheritances and building permits, or to sue somebody.

Notice the layout. It was a long, rectangular building. The stubby columns all in a row form one long, central hall flanked by two side aisles. Medieval Christians required a larger meeting hall for their worship services than Roman temples provided, so they used the spacious Roman basilica as the model for their churches. Cathedrals from France to Spain to England, from Romanesque to Gothic to Renaissance, all have the same basic floor plan as a Roman basilica.
• *Return again to the Temple of Julius Caesar. To the right of the temple are the three tall Corinthian columns of the Temple of Castor and Pollux. Beyond that is Palatine Hill—the corner of which may have been...*

❼ **Caligula's Palace (a.k.a. the Palace of Tiberius):** Emperor Caligula (ruled A.D. 37–41) had a huge palace on Palatine Hill overlooking the Forum. It actually sprawled down the hill into the Forum (some supporting arches remain in the hillside).

Caligula was not a nice person. He tortured enemies, stole senators' wives, and parked his chariot in disabled spaces. But Rome's luxury-loving emperors only added to the glory of the Forum, with each one trying to make his mark on history.
• *To the left of the Temple of Castor and Pollux, find the remains of a*

small, white, circular temple.

❽ **The Temple of Vesta:** This is perhaps Rome's most sacred spot. Rome considered itself one big family, and this temple represented a circular hut, like the kind that Rome's first families lived in. Inside, a fire burned, just as in a Roman home. And back in the days before lighters and butane, you never wanted your fire to go out. As long as the sacred flame burned, Rome would stand. The flame was tended by priestesses known as Vestal Virgins.

• *Around the back of the Temple of Vesta, you'll find two rectangular brick pools. These stood in the courtyard of the...*

❾ **House of the Vestal Virgins:** The Vestal Virgins lived in a two-story building surrounding a long central courtyard with these two pools at one end. Rows of statues depicting important Vestal Virgins flanked the courtyard. This place was the model—both architecturally and sexually—for medieval convents and monasteries.

Chosen from noble families before they reached the age of 10, the six Vestal Virgins served a 30-year term. Honored and revered by the Romans, the Vestals even had their own box opposite the emperor in the Colosseum.

As the name implies, a Vestal took a vow of chastity. If she served her term faithfully—abstaining for 30 years—she was given a huge dowry and allowed to marry. But if they found any Virgin who wasn't a virgin, she was strapped to a funeral car, paraded through the streets of the Forum, taken to a crypt, given a loaf of bread and a lamp...and buried alive. Many women suffered the latter fate.

• *Return to the Temple of Julius Caesar and head to the Forum's west end (opposite the Colosseum). As you pass alongside the big open space of the Forum's main square, consider how the piazza is still a standard part of any Italian town. It has reflected and accommodated the gregarious and outgoing nature of the Italian people since Roman times.*

Stop at the big, well-preserved brick building (on right) with the triangular roof and look in.

❿ **The Curia (Senate House):** The Curia was the most important political building in the Forum. While the present building dates from A.D. 283, this was the site of Rome's official center of government since the birth of the republic. Three hundred senators, elected by the citizens of Rome, met here to debate and create the laws of the land. Their wooden seats once circled the building in three tiers; the Senate president's podium sat at the far end. The marble floor is from ancient times. Listen to the echoes in this vast room—the acoustics are great.

Rome prided itself on being a republic. Early in the city's history, its people threw out the king and established rule by elected representatives. Each Roman citizen was free to speak his mind

Rome Falls

Remember that Rome lasted 1,000 years—500 years of growth, 200 years of peak power, and 300 years of gradual decay. The fall had many causes, among them the barbarians who pecked away at Rome's borders. Christians blamed the fall on moral decay. Pagans blamed it on Christians. Socialists blamed it on a shallow economy based on the spoils of war. (Republicans blamed it on Democrats.) Whatever the reasons, the far-flung empire could no longer keep its grip on conquered lands, and it pulled back. Barbarian tribes from Germany and Asia attacked the Italian peninsula and even looted Rome itself in A.D. 410, leveling many of the buildings in the Forum. In 476, when the last emperor checked out and switched off the lights, Europe plunged into centuries of ignorance, poverty, and weak government—the Dark Ages.

But Rome lived on in the Catholic Church. Christianity was the state religion of Rome's last generations. Emperors became popes (both called themselves "Pontifex Maximus"), senators became bishops, orators became priests, and basilicas became churches. The glory of Rome remains eternal.

and have a say in public policy. Even when emperors became the supreme authority, the Senate was a power to be reckoned with. The Curia building (A.D. 280) is well-preserved, having been used as a church since early Christian times. In the 1930s, it was restored and opened to the public as a historic site. (Note: Although Julius Caesar was assassinated in "the Senate," it wasn't here—the Senate was temporarily meeting across town.)

A statue and two reliefs inside the Curia help build our mental image of the Forum. The statue, made of porphyry marble in about A.D. 100 (with its head, arms, and feet now missing), was a tribute to an emperor, probably Hadrian or Trajan. The two relief panels may have decorated the Rostrum. Those on the left show people (with big stone tablets) standing in line to burn their debt records following a government amnesty. The other shows the distribution of grain (Rome's welfare system), some buildings in the background, and the latest fashion in togas.

• Go back down the Senate steps and find the 10-foot-high wall at the base of Capitol Hill, marked...

⓫ **Rostrum (Rostra):** Nowhere was Roman freedom more apparent than at this "Speaker's Corner." The Rostrum was a raised platform, 10 feet high and 80 feet long, decorated with statues, columns, and the prows of ships *(rostra)*.

On a stage like this, Rome's orators, great and small, tried to draw a crowd and sway public opinion. Mark Antony rose to offer

Caesar the laurel-leaf crown of kingship, which Caesar publicly (and hypocritically) refused while privately becoming a dictator. Men such as Cicero railed against the corruption and decadence that came with the city's newfound wealth. In later years, daring citizens even spoke out against the emperors, reminding them that Rome was once free. Picture the backdrop that these speakers would have had—a mountain of marble buildings piling up on Capitol Hill.

• *The big arch to the right of the Rostrum is the...*

⑫ Arch of Septimius Severus: In imperial times, the Rostrum's voices of democracy would have been dwarfed by images of empire such as the huge, six-story-high Arch of Septimius Severus (A.D. 203). The reliefs commemorate the African-born emperor's battles in Mesopotamia. Near ground level, see soldiers marching captured barbarians back to Rome for the victory parade. Despite Severus' efficient rule, Rome's empire was crumbling under the weight of its own corruption, disease, decaying infrastructure, and the constant attacks by foreign "barbarians."

• *Pass underneath the Arch of Septimius Severus and turn left. On the slope of Capitol Hill are the eight remaining columns of the...*

⑬ Temple of Saturn: These columns framed the entrance to the Forum's oldest temple (497 B.C.). Inside was a humble, very old wooden statue of the god Saturn. But the statue's pedestal held the gold bars, coins, and jewels of Rome's state treasury, the booty collected by conquering generals.

• *Standing here, at one of the Forum's first buildings, look east at the lone, tall...*

⑭ Column of Phocas: This is the Forum's last monument (A.D. 608), a gift from the powerful Byzantine Empire to a fallen empire—Rome. Given to commemorate the pagan Pantheon's becoming a Christian church, it's like a symbolic last nail in ancient Rome's coffin. After Rome's 1,000-year reign, the city was looted by Vandals, the population of a million-plus shrank to about 10,000, and the once-grand city center—the Forum—was abandoned, slowly covered up by centuries of silt and dirt. In the 1700s, an English historian named Edward Gibbon overlooked this spot from Capitol Hill. Hearing Christian monks singing at these pagan ruins, he looked out at the few columns poking up from the ground, pondered the "Decline and Fall of the Roman Empire," and thought, "Hmm, that's a catchy title...."

The Dolce Vita Stroll

This is the city's chic stroll, from Piazza del Popolo (Metro: Flaminio) down a wonderfully traffic-free section of Via del Corso, and up Via Condotti to the Spanish Steps each evening at about 18:00 (Sat and Sun are best). Shoppers, people-watchers,

The Dolce Vita Stroll

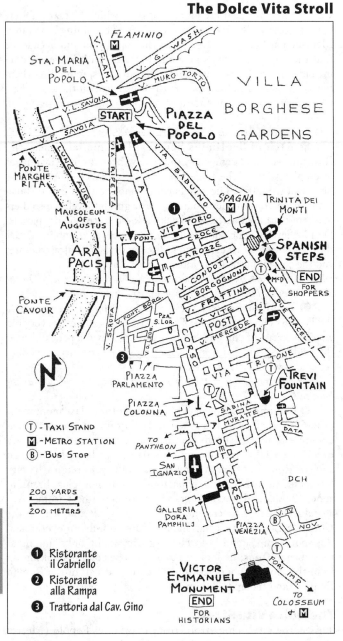

and flirts on the prowl fill this neighborhood of some of Rome's most fashionable stores (open after siesta 16:30–19:30). While both the crowds and the shops along Via del Corso have gone downhill recently, elegance survives in the grid of streets between this street and the Spanish Steps.

Start on **Piazza del Popolo.** The delightfully car-free square is marked by an obelisk that was brought to Rome by Augustus after he conquered Egypt. (It used to stand in the Circus Maximus.) In medieval times, this area was just inside Rome's main entry.

The Baroque church of **Santa Maria del Popolo,** on the square, contains Raphael's Chigi Chapel (KEE-gee, third chapel on left) and two paintings by Caravaggio (the side paintings in chapel left of altar). The church is open daily (Mon–Sat 7:00–12:00 & 16:00–19:00, Sun 8:00–13:30 & 16:30–19:30, next to gate in the old wall, on far side of Piazza del Popolo, to the right as you face gate).

From Piazza del Popolo, shop your way down **Via del Corso.** If you need a rest or a viewpoint, join the locals sitting on the steps of various churches along the street.

At Via Pontefici, historians turn right and walk a block past lots of fascist architecture to see the massive, rotting, round-brick **Mausoleum of Augustus,** topped with overgrown cypress trees. Beyond it, next to the river, is Augustus' **Ara Pacis** ("Altar of Peace"), now enclosed within a protective glass-walled museum (see page 654).

From the mausoleum, return to Via del Corso and the 21st century, continuing straight until **Via Condotti.** Shoppers should take a left to join the parade to the **Spanish Steps.** The streets that parallel Via Condotti to the south (Borgognona and Frattini) are more elegant. You can catch a taxi home at the taxi stand a block south of the Spanish Steps (at Piazza Mignonelli).

Historians: Ignore Via Condotti and forget the Spanish Steps. Stay on Via del Corso, which has been straight since Roman times, a half-mile down to the Victor Emmanuel Monument. Climb Michelangelo's stairway to his glorious (especially when floodlit) square atop Capitol Hill. From the balconies at either side of the mayor's palace, catch the lovely views of the Forum as the horizon reddens and cats prowl the unclaimed rubble of ancient Rome.

Night Walk Across Rome: Campo de' Fiori to the Spanish Steps

Rome can be grueling. But a fine way to mix romance into all the history, enjoy the cool of the evening, and enliven everything with some of Europe's best people-watching is to take an after-dark walk. My favorite nighttime stroll laces together Rome's floodlit nightspots and fine urban spaces with real-life theater vignettes.

Rome

Night Walk Across Rome

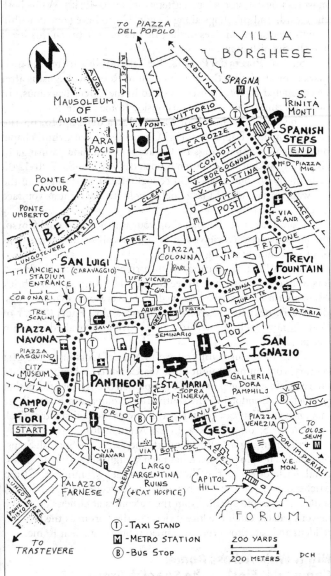

Sitting so close to a Bernini fountain that traffic noises evaporate; jostling with local teenagers to see all the gelato flavors; observing lovers straddling more than the bench; jaywalking past *polizia* in flak-proof vests; and marveling at the ramshackle elegance that softens this brutal city for those who were born here and can imagine living nowhere else—these are the flavors of Rome best tasted after dark.

Start this mile-long walk at the **Campo de' Fiori** ("Field of Flowers"), my favorite outdoor dining room after dark (see "Eating," page 698). The statue of Giordano Bruno, an intellectual heretic who was burned on this spot in 1600, marks the center of this great and colorful square. Bruno overlooks a busy produce market in the morning and strollers after sundown. This neighborhood is still known for its free spirit and occasional demonstrations. When the statue of Bruno was erected in 1889, local riots overcame Vatican protests against honoring a heretic. Bruno faces his nemesis, the Vatican Chancellery (the big white building in the corner a bit to his right), while his pedestal reads, "And the flames rose up." Check out the reliefs on the pedestal for scenes from Bruno's trial and execution.

At the east end of the square (behind Bruno), the ramshackle apartments are built right into the old outer wall of ancient Rome's mammoth Theater of Pompey. This entertainment complex covered several city blocks, stretching from here to Largo Argentina. Julius Caesar was assassinated in the Theater of Pompey, where the Senate was renting space.

The square is lined with and surrounded by fun eateries. Bruno faces **Ristorante la Carbonara,** the only real restaurant on the square. The **Forno,** next door to the left (daily 7:30–20:00), is a popular place for hot and tasty take-out *pizza bianco.* Step in and at least observe the frenzy as pizza is sold hot out of the oven. You can order an *etto* (100 grams) by pointing, then take your snack to the counter to pay. The many bars lining the square are fine for drinks and people-watching. Late at night on weekends, the place is packed with beer-drinking kids, turning what was once a charming medieval square into one vast Roman street party.

If Bruno did a hop, step, and jump forward, then turned right on Via dei Baullari and marched 200 yards, he'd cross the busy Corso Vittorio Emanuele; then, continuing another 150 yards on Via Cuccagna, he'd find **Piazza Navona.** Rome's most interesting night scene features street music, artists, fire-eaters, local Casanovas, ice cream, fountains by Bernini, and outdoor cafés (worthy of a splurge if you've got time to sit and enjoy Italy's human river).

This oblong square retains the shape of the original racetrack that was built by the emperor Domitian. (To see the ruins of the

Rome at a Glance

▲▲▲**Colosseum** Huge stadium where gladiators fought. **Hours:** Daily from 9:00 until one hour before sunset: April–Aug until 19:00, Sept until 18:30, Oct until 18:00, Nov–Feb until 16:00, March until 16:30. See page 632.

▲▲▲**Roman Forum** Ancient Rome's main square, with ruins and grand arches. **Hours:** Daily 8:30–19:00, until 17:00 in winter. See page 637.

▲▲▲**Palatine Hill** Ruins of emperors' palaces, Circus Maximus view, and museum. **Hours:** Daily 8:30–19:00, museum closes at 18:30, until 17:00 in winter. See page 637.

▲▲▲**Pantheon** The defining domed temple. **Hours:** Mon–Sat 8:30–19:30, Sun 9:00–18:00, holidays 9:00–13:00, closed for Mass Sat at 17:00 and Sun at 10:30. See page 644.

▲▲▲**National Museum of Rome** Greatest collection of Roman sculpture anywhere. **Hours:** Tue–Sun 9:00–19:45, closed Mon. See page 646.

▲▲▲**Borghese Gallery** Bernini sculptures and paintings by Caravaggio, Raphael, and Titian in a Baroque palazzo. Reservations mandatory. **Hours:** Tue–Sun 9:00–19:00, closed Mon. See page 650.

▲▲▲**Vatican Museum** Four miles of the art of Western civilization, culminating in the Sistine Chapel. **Hours:** March–Oct Mon–Fri 10:00–16:45, Sat 10:00–14:45 (sometimes until 16:45); Nov–Feb Mon–Sat 10:00–13:45; closed on religious holidays and Sun, except last Sun of the month (when it's open 9:00–13:45). See page 656.

▲▲▲**St. Peter's Basilica** Most impressive church on earth, with Michelangelo's *Pietà* and dome. **Hours:** Church—daily April–Sept 7:00–19:00, Oct–March 7:00–18:00, often closed Wed mornings; dome—daily April–Sept 8:00–17:45, Oct–March 8:00–16:45. See page 663.

▲▲**Capitoline Museums** Ancient statues, mosaics, and expansive view of Forum. **Hours:** Tue–Sun 9:00–20:00, closed Mon. See page 641.

▲▲**Ara Pacis** Shrine marking the beginning of Rome's Golden Age. **Hours:** Tue–Sun 9:00–19:00, closed Mon. See page 654.

Rome

▲▲Catacombs Layers of tunnels with tombs, mainly Christian, outside the city. **Hours:** Open 8:30–12:00 & 14:30–17:30, until 17:00 in winter (San Callisto closed Wed and Feb, San Sebastiano closed Sun and Nov, Priscilla closes at 17:00 year-round and all day Mon). See page 655.

▲Arch of Constantine Honors the emperor who legalized Christianity. **Hours:** Always viewable. See page 635.

▲St. Peter-in-Chains Church with Michelangelo's *Moses*. **Hours:** Daily 8:00–12:30 & 15:00–19:00, until 18:00 in winter. See page 635.

▲Trajan's Column Tall column with narrative relief, on Piazza Venezia. **Hours:** Always viewable. See page 638.

▲Capitol Hill Square Hilltop piazza designed by Michelangelo with a museum, grand stairway, and Forum overlooks. **Hours:** Always open. See page 639.

▲Galleria Doria Pamphilj Fancy palace packed with art. **Hours:** Fri–Wed 10:00–17:00, closed Thu. See page 645.

▲Trevi Fountain Baroque hotspot into which tourists throw coins to ensure a return trip to Rome. **Hours:** Always flowing. See page 646.

▲Baths of Diocletian Once ancient Rome's immense public baths, now a Michelangelo church—Santa Maria degli Angeli— and the Octagonal Hall, a room with minor ancient Roman sculptures. **Hours:** Church—Mon–Sat 7:00–18:30, Sun 7:00–19:30; Octagonal Hall—Tue–Sat 9:00–14:00, Sun 9:00–13:00, closed Mon. See page 647.

▲Santa Maria della Vittoria Church with Bernini's swooning *St. Teresa in Ecstasy*. **Hours:** Mon–Sat 8:30–12:00 & 15:30–18:00, closed Sun. See page 648.

▲Cappuccin Crypt Decorated with the bones of 4,000 monks. **Hours:** Daily 9:00–12:00 & 15:00–18:00. See page 654.

▲Castel Sant'Angelo Hadrian's Tomb turned castle, prison, papal refuge, now museum. **Hours:** Tue–Sun 9:00–18:00, closed Mon. See page 667.

Rome

original entrance, exit the square at the far—or north—end, then take an immediate left, and look down to the left 25 feet below the current street level.) Since ancient times, the square has been a center of Roman life. In the 1800s, the city would flood the square to cool off the neighborhood.

The **Four Rivers Fountain** in the center is the most famous fountain by the man who remade Rome in Baroque style, Gian Lorenzo Bernini. Four burly river gods (representing the four continents that were known in 1650) support an Egyptian obelisk that once stood on the ancient Appian Way. The water of the world gushes everywhere. The Nile has his head covered, since the headwaters were unknown then. The Ganges holds an oar. The Danube turns to admire the obelisk, which Bernini had moved here from a stadium on the Appian Way. And the Rio de la Plata from Uruguay tumbles backward in shock, wondering how he ever made the top four. Bernini enlivens the fountain with horses plunging through the rocks and exotic flora and fauna from these newly discovered lands. Homesick Texans may want to find the armadillo. (It's the big, weird armor-plated creature behind the Plata river statue.)

The Plata river god is gazing upward at the church of St. Agnes, worked on by Bernini's former-student-turned-rival, Francesco Borromini. Borromini's concave facade helps reveal the dome and epitomizes the curved symmetry of Baroque. Tour guides say that Bernini designed his river god to look horrified at Borromini's work. Or maybe he's shielding his eyes from St. Agnes' nakedness, as she was stripped before being martyred. But either explanation is unlikely, since the fountain was completed two years before Borromini even started work on the church.

At the **Tre Scalini** bar (near the fountain), sample some *tartufo* "death by chocolate" ice cream, world-famous among connoisseurs of ice cream and chocolate alike (€4 to-go, €8 at a table, open daily). Seriously admire a painting by a struggling artist. Listen to the white noise of gushing water and exuberant café-goers.

Leave Piazza Navona directly across from the Tre Scalini bar, go east past rose peddlers and palm readers, jog left around the guarded building, and follow the brown sign to the Pantheon. The Pantheon is straight down Via del Salvatore. (There's a cheap pizza place on the left a few yards before you reach the piazza, and a WC at the McDonald's.)

Sit for a while under the floodlit and moonlit portico of the **Pantheon.** The 40-foot, single-piece granite columns of the Pantheon's entrance show the scale that the ancient Romans built on. The columns support a triangular, Greek-style roof with an inscription that says "M. Agrippa" built it. In fact, it was built *(fecit)* by Emperor Hadrian (A.D. 120), who gave credit to the builder of an earlier structure. This impressive entranceway gives no clue that the greatest wonder of the building is inside—a domed room that inspired later domes, including Michelangelo's St. Peter's and Filippo Brunelleschi's Duomo (in Florence).

With your back to the Pantheon, veer to the right down Via Orfani, toward the Albergo Abruzzi. On the right, you'll see signs for **Tazza d'Oro Casa del Caffè,** one of Rome's top coffee shops, which dates back to the days when this area was licensed to roast coffee beans. Locals come here for its fine *granita di caffè con panna* (coffee slush with cream). Look back at the fine view of the Pantheon from here. Then take Via Orfani uphill to Piazza Capranica.

Piazza Capranica is home to the big, plain, Florentine Renaissance–style Palazzo Capranica (directly opposite as you enter the square). Big shots, like the Capranica family, built towers on their palaces—not for any military use, but just to show off. Leave the piazza to the right of the palace, between the palace and the church. The street Via Aquiro leads to a sixth-century B.C. **Egyptian obelisk** (taken as a trophy by Augustus after his victory in Egypt over Mark Antony and Cleopatra). The obelisk was set up as a sundial. Walk the zodiac markings to the front door of the guarded parliament building.

To your right is Piazza Colonna, where we're heading next—unless you like gelato...

A short detour to the left (past Albergo National) brings you to Rome's most famous *gelateria*. **Giolitti** is cheap for take-out or elegant and splurge-worthy for a sit among classy locals (open daily until very late, Via Uffici del Vicario 40); get your gelato in a cone *(cono)* or cup *(coppetta)*.

Piazza Colonna features a huge second-century column that honors Marcus Aurelius. The big, important-looking palace houses the headquarters for the deputies (or cabinet) of the prime minister. The **Via del Corso** is named for the Berber horse races—without riders—that took place here during Carnevale until the 1800s, when a horse trampled a man to death in front of a horrified queen. Historically the street was filled with meat shops. When it became Rome's first gaslit street in the 1800s, these butcher shops were banned and replaced by classier boutiques, jewelers, and antique dealers. Nowadays most of Via del Corso is closed to traffic every evening and becomes a wonderful parade of Romans out for a stroll (see "Dolce Vita Stroll" on page 621).

Cross **Via del Corso,** Rome's noisy main drag. Continue through the Y-shaped Galleria del Sordi shopping gallery, forking to the right (but if you're out past 20:00, walk to the right past the gallery and take the first left), and head down Via dei Sabini to the roar of the water, light, and people of the Trevi Fountain.

The **Trevi Fountain** shows how Rome took full advantage of the abundance of water brought into the city by its great aqueducts. This watery Baroque avalanche was completed in 1762 by Nicola Salvi, hired by a pope who was celebrating the reopening of the ancient aqueduct that powers it. Salvi used the palace behind the fountain as a theatrical backdrop for the figure of "Ocean," who represents water in every form. The statue surfs through his wet kingdom—with water gushing from 24 spouts and tumbling over 30 different kinds of plants—while Triton blows his conch shell. (From here, the water goes underground, then bubbles up again at Bernini's Four Rivers Fountain in Piazza Navona.)

The magic of the square is enhanced by the fact that no streets directly approach it. You can hear the excitement as you approach, and then—*bam!*—you're there. The scene is always lively, with lucky Romeos clutching dates while unlucky ones clutch beers. Romantics toss a coin over their shoulder, thinking it will give them a wish and assure their return to Rome. That may sound silly, but every year I go through this tourist ritual...and it actually seems to work.

Take some time to people-watch (whisper a few breathy *bello*s or *bella*s) before leaving. There's a peaceful zone at water level on the far right.

Face the fountain, then go past it on the right down Via delle Stamperia to Via del Triton. Cross the busy street and continue 100 yards. Veer right at Via S. Andrea, a street that changes its name to Via Propaganda before ending at the Spanish Steps.

The **Piazza di Spagna,** with the very popular Spanish Steps, is named for the Spanish Embassy to the Vatican, which has been here for 300 years. It's been the hangout of many Romantics over the years (Keats, Wagner, Openshaw, Goethe, and others). The British poet John Keats pondered his mortality, then died in the pink building on the right side of the steps. Fellow Romantic Lord Byron lived across the square at #66.

The Sinking Boat Fountain at the foot of the steps, built by Bernini or his father, Pietro, is powered by an aqueduct. All of Rome's fountains are aqueduct-powered; their spurts are determined by the water pressure provided by the various aqueducts. This one, for instance, is much weaker than Trevi's gush.

The piazza is a thriving night scene. Window-shop along Via Condotti, which stretches away from the steps. This is where Gucci and other big names cater to the trendsetting jet set.

Facing the Spanish Steps, you can walk right, about a block, to tour one of the world's biggest and most lavish McDonald's (salad bar, WC). There's a taxi stand in the courtyard outside McDonald's; or, if you'd prefer, the Spagna Metro stop (usually open until 23:30, but can close as early as 21:00) is just to the left of the Spanish Steps, ready to zip you home.

Rome

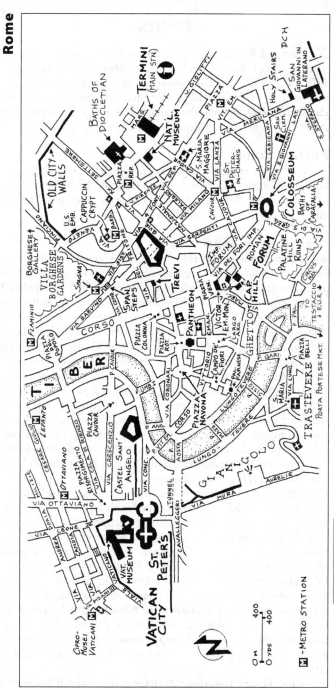

VATICAN CITY
ST. PETERS

TRASTEVERE

PANTHEON

Termini (Main Stn)

COLOSSEUM

FORUM

VILLA BORGHESE GARDENS

SPANISH STEPS

TREVI

Castel Sant'Angelo

PIAZZA NAVONA

Baths of Diocletian

Nat'l Museum

0 m   400
0 yds 400

M – METRO STATION

SIGHTS

I've clustered Rome's sights into walkable neighborhoods, some quite close together (see the "Rome Neighborhoods" map on page 597). For example, the Colosseum and the Forum are a few minutes' walk from Capitol Hill; a 10-minute walk beyond that is the Pantheon. I like to group these sights into one great day, starting at the Colosseum and ending at the Pantheon.

Ancient Rome

The core of the ancient city, where the grandest monuments were built, is between the Colosseum and Capitol Hill. To the north, this ancient area flows into the Renaissance at Capitol Hill, then into the modern era at Piazza Venezia.

The Colosseum and Nearby

▲▲▲**Colosseum (Colosseo)**—This 2,000-year-old building is *the* great example of Roman engineering. The Romans pioneered the use of concrete and the rounded arch, which enabled them to build on this tremendous scale. While the essential structure is Roman, the four-story facade is decorated with the three types of Greek columns—Doric (ground level), Ionic (second story), Corinthian, and, on the top, half-columns with a mix of all three. Built when the Roman Empire was at its peak in A.D. 80, the Colosseum represents Rome at its grandest. The Flavian Amphitheater (its real name) was an arena for gladiator contests and public spectacles. When killing became a spectator sport, the Romans wanted to share the fun with as many people as possible, so they stuck two theaters together to create a freestanding amphitheater. The outside (where slender cypress trees stand today) was decorated with a 100-foot-tall bronze statue of Nero that gleamed in the sunlight. The final structure was colossal—a "coloss-eum," the wonder of its age. It could accommodate 50,000 roaring fans (100,000 thumbs). The whole thing was topped with an enormous canvas awning that could be hoisted across by armies of sailors to provide shade for the spectators—the first domed stadium. This was where ancient Romans—whose taste for violence was the equal of modern America's—enjoyed their *Dirty Harry* and *Terminator*. Gladiators, criminals, and wild animals fought to the death in every conceivable scenario. The floor of the Colosseum is missing, exposing underground passages. Animals were kept in cages beneath the arena floor, then lifted up in elevators. Released at floor level, the animals would pop out from behind blinds into the arena—the gladiator didn't know where, when, or by what he'd be attacked.

Cost, Hours, Location: €11 ticket also includes Palatine Hill

Colosseum

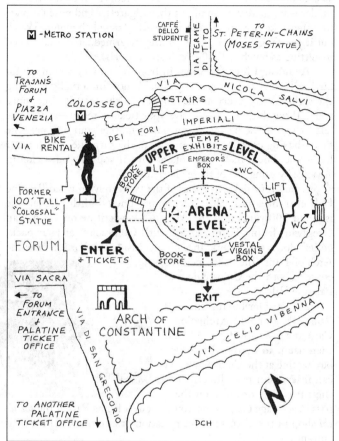

and special exhibits (ticket valid all day, or—if purchased after 13:30—for 24 hours). It's open daily from 9:00 until one hour before sunset: April–Aug until 19:00, Sept until 18:30, Oct until 18:00, Nov–Feb until 16:00, March until 16:30. A dry but fact-filled audioguide is available just past the turnstiles (€4.50 for 2 hours of use). Guided one-hour tours in English depart several times per day between the hours of 9:45 and 17:15 (€3.50). Taking this tour allows you to skip the ticket line. Metro: Colosseo. Information tel. 06-3996-7700.

Like at the Forum, vendors outside the entrance of the Colosseum sell handy little *Rome: Past and Present* books with plastic overlays to un-ruin the ruins (marked €11, price soft, offer less). Tiny, crowded WCs are inside; the better, bigger, and cleaner WC is behind the Colosseum (facing ticket entrance, go right;

WC is under stairway). Caution: For a fee, the incredibly crude modern-day gladiators snuff out their cigarettes and pose for photos. They take easy-to-swindle tourists for too much money. Watch out if you tangle with these guys (they're armed...and accustomed to getting as much as €100 from naive tourists).

Avoiding Lines: The lines in front of the Colosseum are for buying tickets and for security checks, not for actually entering the sight. While everyone has to wait in the security line, once you're through that—if you have your ticket already—stay to the left (which is the passage for groups), muscle your way past the ticket-buying crowd, and go directly to the turnstile, which never has a line. You'll likely save lots of time if you get your ticket in advance by using one of these alternatives:

1. Buy your ticket at either of the two rarely crowded Palatine Hill entrances near the Colosseum. The (slightly) closer one is about 200 yards past the Arch of Constantine on Via di San Gregorio (facing Forum entry, with Colosseum at your back, go left down the street). The other is inside the Forum, near the Arch of Titus. The ticket includes entry to both the Colosseum and Palatine Hill.

2. Consider buying the €20 Roma Pass or €22 Archeologia Card at a less-crowded sight, and then use it to bypass the ticket-buying line at the Colosseum; you can insert your pass directly into the turnstile (for more on these passes, see page 602). Note: You can buy a Roma Pass at the *tabacchi* shop in the Colosseo Metro station or at either Palatine Hill entrance.

3. Book a tour with a guide. Tickets for official tours, offered by the Colosseum's guides, are purchased inside the Colosseum near the ticket counter (described above). Tell the guard that you want to purchase a guided tour, and he will usher you toward the ticket booth.

Walking-tour guides (or their American assistants) may approach you, offering tours that include the admission fee and allow you to skip the line. This will cost you a few extra euros (€20 for two-hour tours of the Colosseum and Forum, including the €11 Colosseum ticket), but can save time. But beware: It can be hard to instantly judge the length of the ticket line, because it's tucked into the Colosseum arcade—and besides, there's often a line just to get through the metal detector. Guides might tell you that there's a long line, when there is none at all. Also note that you may buy a tour ticket, only to get stuck waiting for them to sell enough tickets to assemble a group.

4. You can reserve ahead online, choosing a specific entrance time and paying a €5 booking fee (try www.tickitaly.com). But, considering how easy it is to get a ticket at the Palatine Hill entrance, I wouldn't bother with this option.

▲**Arch of Constantine**—The arch, next to the Colosseum, marks one of the great turning points in history—the military coup that made Christianity mainstream. In A.D. 312, Emperor Constantine defeated his rival Maxentius in the crucial Battle of the Milvian Bridge. The night before, he had seen a vision of a cross in the sky. Constantine—whose mother and sister were Christians—became sole emperor and legalized Christianity. With this one battle, a once-obscure Jewish sect with a handful of followers was now the state religion of the entire Western world. In A.D. 300, you could be killed for being a Christian; later, you could be killed for not being one. Church enrollment boomed.

This newly restored arch is like an ancient museum. By decorating it with exquisite carvings of high Roman art—works that glorified previous emperors—Constantine put himself in their league. Fourth-century Rome may have been in decline, but Constantine clung to its glorious past.

▲**St. Peter-in-Chains Church (San Pietro in Vincoli)**—Built in the fifth century to house the chains that held St. Peter, this church is most famous for its Michelangelo statue. Check out the much-venerated chains under the high altar, then focus on mighty *Moses* (free, daily 8:00–12:30 & 15:00–19:00, until 18:00 in winter, modest dress required; the church is a 15-minute, uphill, zigzag walk from the Colosseum, or a shorter, simpler walk from the Cavour Metro stop—exiting the Metro stop, go up the steep flight of steps, take a right at the top, and walk a block to the church). Note that this isn't the famous St. Peter's Basilica, which is at Vatican City.

Pope Julius II commissioned Michelangelo to build a massive tomb, with 48 huge statues, crowned by a grand statue of this ego-maniacal pope. The pope had planned to have his tomb placed in the center of St. Peter's Basilica. When Julius died, the work had barely been started, and no one had the money or necessary commitment to Julius to finish the project. Michelangelo finished one statue—*Moses*—and left a few unfinished statues: Leah and Rachel flanking Moses in this church, the *Prisoners* (now in Florence's Accademia), and the *Slaves* (now in Paris' Louvre).

This powerful statue of Moses—mature Michelangelo—is worth studying. The artist worked on it in fits and starts for 30 years. Moses has received the Ten Commandments. As he holds the stone tablets, his eyes show a man determined to stop his tribe from worshipping the golden calf and idols...a man determined to win salvation for the people of Israel. Why the horns? Centuries

Ancient Rome

ago, the Hebrew word for "rays" was mistranslated as "horns."

▲**Nero's Golden House (Domus Aurea)**—The sparse underground remains of Emperor Nero's "Golden House" are a faint shadow of their ancient grandeur. In its heyday, the gold-leaf-encrusted residence was huge, with its original entrance all the way over at the Arch of Titus in the Forum. Nero's massive estate once sprawled across the valley (where the Colosseum now stands) and up the hill—the part you tour today. Unfortunately, the Golden House is in a sad state of ruin, more historically significant than interesting—unless you're an archaeologist. Nero (ruled A.D. 54–68) was Rome's most notorious emperor. He killed his own mother, kicked his pregnant wife to death, and crucified St. Peter. When Rome burned in A.D. 64, Nero was accused of torching it to clear land for his domestic building needs. The Romans rebelled, the Senate declared him a public enemy, and his only noble option was suicide. With the help of a slave, Nero stabbed himself in the neck, crying, "What an artist dies in me!" (€5 plus €1 booking fee, Tue–Fri 10:00–16:00, closed Sat–Mon; advance booking required—reserve at www.pierreci.it or call 06-3996-7700).

The Roman Forum and Nearby

▲▲▲**Roman Forum (Foro Romano)**—This is ancient Rome's birthplace and civic center, and the common ground between

Rome's famous seven hills. As just about anything important that happened in ancient Rome happened here, it's arguably the most important piece of real estate in Western civilization. While only a few fragments of that glorious past remain, history-seekers find plenty to ignite their imaginations amid the half-broken columns and arches (free, daily 8:30–19:00, until 17:00 in winter, last entry 1 hour before closing, Metro: Colosseo, tel. 06-3996-7700). See my self-guided walk on page 614.

▲▲▲**Palatine Hill (Monte Palatino)**—The hill above the Forum contains scant remains of the imperial palaces and the foundations of Rome, from Iron Age huts to the legendary house of Romulus (under corrugated tin roof in far corner). We get our word "palace" from this hill, where the emperors chose to live. The Palatine Hill was once so filled with palaces that later emperors had to build out. (Looking up at it from the Forum, you see the substructure that supported these long-gone palaces.) The Palatine museum has sculptures and fresco fragments but is nothing special. From the pleasant garden, you'll get an overview of the Forum. On the far side, look down into an emperor's private stadium and then beyond at the dusty Circus Maximus, once a chariot course. Imagine the cheers, jeers, and furious betting.

While many tourists consider Palatine Hill just extra credit after the Forum, it offers an insight into the greatness of Rome that's well worth the effort. (And, if you're visiting the Colosseum, you've got a ticket whether you like it or not.)

Cost, Hours, Location: €11 ticket also includes Colosseum. If you purchase the ticket after 13:30, you may use it the next day to see the Colosseum (but not to return to Palatine Hill). It's open daily 8:30–19:00 (museum closes at 18:30, until 17:00 in winter, last site entry 1 hour before closing). The main entrance and ticket office—which also sells Colosseum tickets, enabling smart sightseers to avoid that long line—is near the Arch of Titus and Colosseum. Another Palatine entrance is on Via di San Gregorio.

Audioguides cost €4 (must leave ID). Guided tours in English are offered once daily (€3.50); ask for information at the ticket booth or at the kiosk near the Arch of Titus.

▲**Mamertine Prison**—This 2,500-year-old, cistern-like prison, which once held the bodies of Sts. Peter and Paul, is worth a look.

When you step into the room, ignore the modern floor and look up at the hole in the ceiling, from which prisoners were lowered. Then take the stairs down to the level of the actual prison floor. Downstairs, you'll see the column to which Peter was chained. It's said that a miraculous fountain sprang up in this room so that Peter could convert and baptize his jailers, who were also subsequently martyred. The upside-down cross commemorates Peter's upside-down crucifixion (donation requested, daily 9:00–19:00, at the foot of Capitol Hill, near Forum's Arch of Septimius Severus).

Imagine humans, amid fat rats and rotting corpses, awaiting slow deaths. On the walls near the entry are lists of notable prisoners (Christian and non-Christian) and the ways they were executed: *strangolati*, *decapitato*, *morto per fame* (died of hunger). The sign by the Christian names reads, "Here suffered, victorious for the triumph of Christ, these martyred saints."

▲**Trajan's Column, Market, and Forum (Colonna, Foro, e Mercati de Traiano)**—This offers the grandest column and best example of "continuous narration" from antiquity. More than 2,500 figures scroll around the 140-foot-high column, telling of Trajan's victorious Dacian campaign (circa A.D. 103, in present-day Romania), from the assembling of the army at the bottom to the victory sacrifice at the top. The ashes of Trajan and his wife were once held in the base while the sun once glinted off a polished bronze statue of Trajan at the top. (Today, St. Peter is on top.) Study the propaganda that winds up the column like a scroll, trumpeting Trajan's wonderful military exploits. You can see this close up for free (always open and viewable, just off Piazza Venezia, across the street from the Victor Emmanuel Monument). Viewing balconies once stood on either side, but it seems likely that Trajan fans came away only with a feeling that the greatness of their emperor and empire was beyond comprehension (for a rolled-out version of the column's story, visit the E.U.R.'s Museum of Roman Civilization). This column marked "Trajan's Forum," which was built to handle the shopping needs of a wealthy city of more than a million people. Commercial, political, religious, and social activities all mixed in the forum.

For a fee, you can wander around the **Trajan's Forum**, but going upstairs inside **Trajan's Market** is possible only with a visit to the new Museum of the Imperial Forums, which may open in 2008 (€6.20, Tue–Sun 9:00–14:00, last entry 1 hour before closing, closed Mon, entrance is uphill from the column on Via IV Novembre, tel. 06-679-0048).

Trajan's Column is just a few steps off Piazza Venezia, on Via dei Fori Imperiali, across the street from the Victor Emmanuel Monument. Trajan's Forum stretches southeast of the column toward the Colosseo Metro stop and the Colosseum itself.

Time Elevator Roma—This cheesy and overpriced show is really just for kids. It starts with a stand-up, Italian-only, 15-minute intro, followed by a 30-minute, multiscreen show with seats jolting through the centuries. Equipped with headphones, you get nauseous in a comfortable, air-conditioned theater as the history of Rome unfolds before you—from the founding of the city, through its rise and fall, to its Renaissance rebound, and up to the present (€11, daily 10:30–19:30, shows at the bottom of each hour, no kids under 39 inches, just off Via del Corso, a 3-minute walk from Piazza Venezia at Via dei S.S. Apostoli 20, tel. 06-9774-6243, www.time-elevator.it).

Capitol Hill Area

There are several ways to get to the top of Capitol Hill. (While I call it "Capitol Hill" for simplicity, it's correctly called "Capitoline Hill," and the piazza on top is called the Campidoglio). If you're coming from the north (from Piazza Venezia), take Michelangelo's impressive stairway to the right of the big, white Victor Emmanuel Monument. Coming from the southeast (the Forum), take the steep staircase near the Arch of Septimius Severus. From near Trajan's Forum along Via dei Fori Imperiali, take the winding road. All three converge at the top, in the square called Campidoglio (kahm-pee-DOHL-yoh).

▲**Capitol Hill Square (Campidoglio)**—This hill, once the religious and political center of ancient Rome, is still the home of the city's government. Michelangelo redesigned the hilltop's main square (Campidoglio) in Renaissance times. The square's centerpiece is a copy of the famous equestrian statue of Marcus Aurelius (the original is in the adjacent museum). The twin buildings on either side are the Capitoline Museums. Behind the statue is the mayoral palace (Palazzo Senatorio).

Michelangelo intended that people approach the square from his grand stairway off Piazza Venezia. From the top of the stairway, you see the new Renaissance face of Rome, with its back to the Forum. Michelangelo gave the buildings the "giant order"—huge pilasters make the existing two-story buildings feel one-storied and more harmonious with the new square. Notice how the statues atop these buildings welcome you and then draw you in.

The terraces just downhill (past either side of the mayor's palace) offer grand views of the Forum. To the left of the mayor's

Capitol Hill and Piazza Venezia

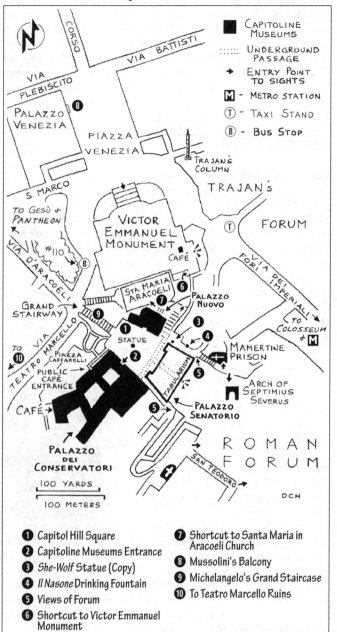

Legend:
- ■ CAPITOLINE MUSEUMS
- :::::: UNDERGROUND PASSAGE
- ➜ ENTRY POINT TO SIGHTS
- Ⓜ - METRO STATION
- Ⓣ - TAXI STAND
- Ⓑ - BUS STOP

Map labels:
CORSO
VIA BATTISTI
VIA PLEBISCITO
Ⓑ
PALAZZO VENEZIA
PIAZZA VENEZIA
TRAJAN'S COLUMN
S. MARCO
TO GESÙ & PANTHEON
TRAJAN'S
VICTOR EMMANUEL MONUMENT
FORUM
VIA D'ARACOELI
#110
Ⓑ
CAFÉ
Ⓣ
VIA DEI FORI IMPERIALI
STA. MARIA ARACOELI
GRAND STAIRWAY
PALAZZO NUOVO
TO COLOSSEUM & Ⓜ
VIA TEATRO MARCELLO
STATUE
MAMERTINE PRISON
TO TEATRO MARCELLO
PIAZZA CAFFARELLI
PUBLIC CAFÉ ENTRANCE
TABULARIUM
ARCH OF SEPTIMIUS SEVERUS
CAFÉ
PALAZZO SENATORIO
PALAZZO DEI CONSERVATORI
ROMAN FORUM
SAN TEODORO
100 YARDS
100 METERS
DCH

Numbered list:
1. Capitol Hill Square
2. Capitoline Museums Entrance
3. *She-Wolf* Statue (Copy)
4. *Il Nasone* Drinking Fountain
5. Views of Forum
6. Shortcut to Victor Emmanuel Monument
7. Shortcut to Santa Maria in Aracoeli Church
8. Mussolini's Balcony
9. Michelangelo's Grand Staircase
10. To Teatro Marcello Ruins

Rome

palace is a copy of the famous *She-Wolf* statue on a column. Farther down is *il nasone* ("the big nose"), a refreshing water fountain. Block the spout with your fingers, and water spurts up for drinking. Romans joke that a cheap Roman boy takes his date out for a drink at *il nasone*. Near the *She-Wolf* statue is the staircase that leads to a shortcut to the Victor Emmanuel Monument.

Shortcut to Victor Emmanuel Monument: A clever little "back door" gives you access from the top of Capitol Hill directly to the top of the Victor Emmanuel Monument, saving lots of uphill stair-climbing. Near the *She-Wolf* statue (to the left of the mayoral palace), climb the wide set of stairs (the highest set of stairs you see), pass through the iron gate at the top of the steps, and enter the small unmarked door at #13 on the right. You'll soon emerge on a café terrace at the top of the monument with vast views and the entrance to the Museum of the Risorgimento (see "Victor Emmanuel Monument" listing, page 643). This shortcut also gives you easy access to Santa Maria in Aracoeli (described below).

Santa Maria in Aracoeli—This church is built on the site where Emperor Augustus (supposedly) had a premonition of the coming of Mary and Christ standing on an "altar in the sky" *(Ara Coeli)*. The church is Rome in a nutshell, where you can time-travel across 2000 years by standing in one spot (daily 9:00–12:00 & 14:30–17:30). It's atop Capitol Hill, squeezed between the Victor Emmanuel Monument and the square called Campidoglio. While dedicated pilgrims climb up the long, steep staircase from street level (the right side of Victor Emmanuel monument, as you face it), casual sightseers prefer to enter through the "back door," on the shortcut between the Capitoline Museums and Victor Emmanuel monument (described above): As you climb the stairs from Campidoglio to the shortcut, look for a sign that points left to *Santa Maria in Aracoeli*.

▲▲**Capitoline Museums (Musei Capitolini)**—This museum encompasses two buildings (Palazzo dei Conservatori and Palazzo Nuovo) and the underground vacant Tabularium, which has a panoramic overlook of the Forum (€8, €10 combo-ticket includes Montemartini Museum, Tue–Sun 9:00–20:00, closed Mon, last entry 1 hour before closing, good €5 audioguide, tel. 06-8205-9127, www.museicapitolini.org).

To identify the museum's two buildings, face the equestrian statue (with your back to the grand stairway). The Palazzo Nuovo is on your left, the Palazzo dei Conservatori (where you buy your ticket and start your self-guided tour) is on your right, closer to the river. Ahead is the Palazzo Senatorio (mayoral palace, not open to public); below it—and out of sight—is the Tabularium.

Buy your ticket and consider renting the good €5 audioguide at the Palazzo dei Conservatori entrance.

The **Palazzo dei Conservatori** is one of the world's oldest museums, at 500 years old. In the courtyard, enjoy the massive chunks of Constantine: his head, hand, and foot. When intact, this giant held the place of honor in the Basilica of Constantine in the Forum. The museum is worthwhile, with lavish rooms and several great statues. You'll see the original (500 B.C.) Etruscan *Capitoline Wolf* (the little statues of Romulus and Remus were added in the Renaissance). Don't miss the *Boy Extracting a Thorn* and the enchanting *Commodus as Hercules*. Behind Commodus is a statue of his dad, Marcus Aurelius, on a horse. The greatest surviving equestrian statue of antiquity, this was the original centerpiece of the square (where a copy stands today). While most such pagan statues were destroyed by Dark Age Christians, Marcus was mistaken for Constantine (the first Christian emperor) and therefore spared.

The second-floor painting gallery—except for two Caravaggios—is forgettable. The adjacent café, Caffè Capitolino, with a splendid patio offering city views, is lovely at sunset (public entrance for non-museum-goers off Piazza Caffarelli).

Walk across the square to **Palazzo Nuovo,** which houses mostly portrait busts of forgotten emperors. But it has two must-see statues: the *Dying Gaul* and the *Capitoline Venus* (both on the first floor up).

Head downstairs to the **Tabularium.** Built in the first century B.C., this once held the archives of ancient Rome. The word *Tabularium* comes from "tablet," on which the Romans wrote their laws. You won't see any tablets, but you will see a superb head-on view of the Forum from the windows.

Piazza Venezia

Dominated by the big, white Victor Emmanuel Monument, this vast square is a major transportation hub and the focal point of modern Rome. Stand with your back to the monument and look down the Via del Corso, the city's axis, surrounded by Rome's classiest shopping district. In the 1930s, Benito Mussolini whipped up Italy's nationalistic fervor here from a balcony above the square (with your back to Victor Emmanuel Monument, it's the less-grand balcony on the left). Fascist masses filled the square screaming, "Four more years!"—or something like that. Mussolini lied to his people, mixing fear and patriotism to push his country to the right and embroil the Italians in expensive and regrettable wars. In 1945, they shot and hung Mussolini from a meat hook in Milan.

Circling around the right side of the Victor Emmanuel Monument, look down into the ditch on your left to see the ruins of an ancient apartment building from the first century A.D.; part of it was transformed into a tiny church (faded frescoes and bell tower). Rome was built in layers—almost everywhere you go, there's an earlier version beneath your feet. (The hop-on, hop-off Trambus Open 110 stops just across the busy intersection from here.)

Continuing on, you reach two staircases that lead up Capitol Hill. One is Michelangelo's grand staircase up to the Campidoglio. The longer of the two leads to the Santa Maria in Aracoeli church, a good example of the earliest style of Christian churches (described above). The contrast between this climb-on-your-knees ramp to God's house and Michelangelo's elegant stairs illustrates the changes that Renaissance humanism brought to civilization.

From the bottom of Michelangelo's stairs, look right several blocks down the street to see a condominium actually built upon the surviving ancient pillars and arches of Teatro Marcello.

Victor Emmanuel Monument—Built to celebrate the 50th anniversary of the country's unification in 1870, this oversize monument to Italy's first king was part of Italy's push to overcome the new country's strong regionalism and

to create a national identity. The scale of the monument is over-the-top—a person could fit into the equestrian statue's hoof. Open to the public, the structure offers a grand view of the Eternal City (free, 242 punishing steps to the top—unless you take the shortcut from Capitol Hill, described on page 641).

Romans think of the 200-foot-high, 500-foot-wide monument not as an altar of the fatherland, but as "the wedding cake," "the typewriter," or "the dentures." It wouldn't be so bad if it weren't sitting on a priceless acre of ancient Rome and if they had chosen better marble (this is in-your-face white and picks up the pollution horribly). Soldiers guard Italy's Tomb of the Unknown Soldier as the eternal flame flickers.

The Victor Emmanuel Monument houses a little-visited **Museum of the Risorgimento,** which explains the movement and war that led to the unification of Italy in 1870 (free, daily 9:00–19:00, café).

Pantheon Neighborhood: The Heart of Rome

I call the area around the Pantheon the "Heart of Rome." This neighborhood stretches eastward from the Tiber River through Campo de' Fiori and Piazza Navona, past the Pantheon to the

Trevi Fountain. Besides the neighborhood's ancient sights and historic churches, it's also the place that gives Rome its urban-village feel. Wander narrow streets, sample the many shops and eateries, and gather with the locals in squares marked by a bubbling fountain. Exploring is especially good in the evening, when the restaurants bustle and streets are jammed with foot-traffic. For more on nocturnal sightseeing, see the "Night Walk Across Rome" on page 623.

Getting There: To reach the Pantheon neighborhood, you can walk (it's a 20-minute walk from Capitol Hill), take a taxi, or catch a bus. Buses #64 and #40 carry tourists and pickpockets frequently between the Termini train station and Vatican City, stopping at a chaotic square called Largo Argentina, located a few blocks south of the Pantheon. (Take either Via dei Cestari or Via Torre Argentina north to the Pantheon.) The *elettrico* minibus #116 runs between Campo de' Fiori and Piazza Barberini via the Pantheon. The most dramatic approach is on foot, coming from Piazza Navona along Via Giustiniani, which spills directly into Piazza della Rotunda, offering the classic Pantheon view.

▲▲▲**Pantheon**—For the greatest look at the splendor of Rome, antiquity's best-preserved interior is a must (free, Mon–Sat 8:30–19:30, Sun 9:00–18:00, holidays 9:00–13:00, closed for Mass Sat at 17:00 and Sun at 10:30, tel. 06-6830-0230). Because the Pantheon became a church dedicated to the martyrs just after the fall of Rome, the barbarians left it alone, and the locals didn't use it as a quarry. The portico is called "Rome's umbrella"—a fun local gathering in a rainstorm. Walk past its one-piece granite columns (biggest in Italy, shipped from Egypt) and through the original bronze doors. Sit inside under the glorious skylight and enjoy classical architecture at its best.

The dome, 142 feet high and wide, was Europe's biggest until the Renaissance. Michelangelo's dome at St. Peter's, while much higher, is about three feet narrower. The brilliance of this dome's construction astounded architects through the ages. During the Renaissance, Brunelleschi was given permission to cut into the dome (see the little square hole above and to the right of the entrance) to analyze the material. The concrete dome gets thinner and lighter with height—the highest part is volcanic pumice.

This wonderfully harmonious architecture greatly inspired Raphael and other artists of the Renaissance. Raphael, along with Italy's first two kings, chose to be buried here.

As you walk around the outside of the Pantheon, notice the "rise of Rome"—about 15 feet since it was built. The nearest WCs are at bars and downstairs in the McDonald's on the square. Several reasonable eateries are a block or two north, up Via del Pantheon. Some of Rome's best gelato and coffee are nearby. For

Pantheon Neighborhood

ANCIENT STADIUM ENTRANCE · CORONARI · TRE SCALINI · PIAZZA NAVONA · PIAZZA PASQUINO · CITY MUSEUM · CAMPO DE' FIORI · PALAZZO FARNESE · TO TRASTEVERE · PONTE SISTO · LUNGOTEVERE · TIBER · PONTE UMBERTO · LUNGOTEVERE MARZIO · SAN LUIGI (CARAVAGGIO) · UFF. VICARIO · COPPELLE · SALV. · GIUST. · PIAZZA ROTUNDA · SEMINARIO · PANTHEON · STA MARIA SOPRA MINERVA · VITTORIO EMANUELE · CESTARI · ARACOELI · VIA BOTT. OSC. · LARGO ARGENTINA RUINS (& CAT HOSPICE) · CAPITOL HILL · FORUM · TO PIAZZA DEL POPOLO · PIAZZA COLONNA · PARL. · AQUIRO · PIAZZA PIETRA · SABINA · MURATTE · DATAR. · TO SPANISH STEPS · VIA · TRITONE · TREVI · SAN IGNAZIO · GALLERIA DORA PAMPHILJ · PIAZZA VENEZIA · IV NOV. · FORI IMP. · V.E. MON. · TO COLOSSEUM · TO BARB. · VIA DEL CORSO

T - TAXI STAND
M - METRO STATION
B - BUS STOP

200 YARDS
200 METERS

DCH

eating suggestions, see page 701.

▲▲**Churches near the Pantheon**—The **Church of San Luigi dei Francesi** has a magnificent chapel painted by Caravaggio (free, Fri–Wed 7:30–12:30 & 15:30–19:00, Thu 8:00–12:30, sightseers should avoid Mass at 7:30 and 19:00). The only Gothic church in Rome is **Santa Maria sopra Minerva,** with a little-known Michelangelo statue, *Christ Bearing the Cross* (free, Mon–Sat 7:00–19:00, Sun 8:00–19:00, on a little square behind Pantheon, to the east). The **Church of St. Ignazio,** several blocks east of the Pantheon, is a riot of Baroque illusions, including a painted false dome on its ceiling (free, daily 7:30–12:30 & 15:00–19:15). A few blocks away, across Corso Vittorio Emanuele, is the rich and Baroque **Gesù Church,** headquarters of the Jesuits in Rome (free, daily 6:30–12:45 & 16:00–19:15). Modest dress is recommended at all churches.

▲**Galleria Doria Pamphilj**—This underappreciated gallery, tucked away in the heart of the old city, fills a palace on Piazza del Collegio Romano. It offers a rare chance to wander through a noble family's lavish rooms with the prince who calls this downtown mansion home. Well, almost. Through an audioguide, the prince lovingly narrates his family's story, including how the Doria Pamphilj (pahm-FEEL-yee) family's cozy relationship with the pope inspired the word "nepotism." Highlights include paintings by Caravaggio, Titian, and Raphael, and portraits of Pope Innocent X by Diego Velázquez (on canvas) and Gian Lorenzo Bernini (in marble). The fancy rooms of the palace are interesting, with a mini-Versailles-like hall of mirrors and paintings that line the walls to the ceiling in the style typical of 18th-century galleries (€8, includes worthwhile audioguide, Fri–Wed 10:00–17:00, closed Thu, from Piazza Venezia walk 2 blocks up Via del Corso and take a left, Piazza del Collegio Romano 2, tel. 06-679-7323, www.doriapamphilj.it).

Piazza di Pietra (Piazza of Stone)—This square was actually a quarry set up to chew away at the abandoned Roman building. You can still see the holes that hungry medieval scavengers chipped into the columns to steal the metal pins that held the slabs together (two blocks toward Via del Corso from Pantheon).

▲Trevi Fountain—This bubbly Baroque fountain, worth ▲ by day and ▲▲ by night, is a minor sight to art scholars...but a major nighttime gathering spot for teens on the make and tourists tossing coins. (For more information, see page 630.)

Near Termini Train Station

These sights are within a 10-minute walk of the train station. By Metro, use the Termini stop for the National Museum and the Piazza della Repubblica stop for the rest.

▲▲▲National Museum of Rome (Museo Nazionale Romano Palazzo Massimo alle Terme)—This museum houses the greatest collection of ancient Roman art anywhere. It's a historic yearbook of Roman marble statues with some rare Greek originals. On the ground floor alone, you can look eye-to-eye with Julius and Augustus Caesar, Alexander the Great, and Socrates.

On the second floor, along with statues and busts showing such emperors as Trajan and Hadrian, you'll see the best-preserved Roman copy of the Greek *Discus Thrower*. Statues of athletes like this commonly stood in the baths, where Romans cultivated healthy bodies, minds, and social skills. Other statues on this floor once stood in the pleasure gardens of the Roman rich—surrounded by greenery, with the splashing sound of fountains, the statues all painted in bright, lifelike colors. Though executed by Romans, the themes are mostly Greek, with godlike humans and human-looking gods.

The second floor features a collection of frescoes and mosaics

Near Termini Train Station

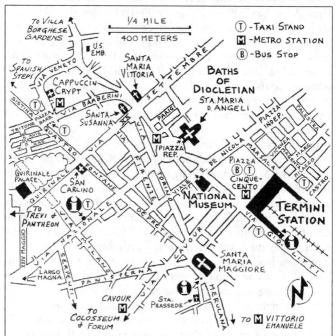

that once decorated Roman villas. The frescoes—in black, red, yellow, and blue—show a few scenes of people and animals, but are mostly architectural designs, with fake columns and "windows" that "look out" on landscape scenes.

Finally, descend into the basement to see fine gold jewelry, dice, an abacus, and vault doors leading into the best coin collection in Europe, with fancy magnifying glasses maneuvering you through cases of coins from ancient Rome to modern times.

Cost and Hours: €10 (includes entry to the other three branches of the National Museum—below—and the Montemartini Museum). Open Tue–Sun 9:00–19:45, closed Mon, last entry 45 min before closing. An audioguide costs €4 (rent at ticket counter). The museum is about 100 yards from the Termini train station (Metro: Termini). As you leave the station, it's the sandstone-brick building on your left. Enter at the far end, at Largo di Villa Peretti (tel. 06-3996-7700).

▲**Baths of Diocletian (Terme di Diocleziano)**— About A.D. 300, Emperor Diocletian built the largest baths in Rome. This sprawling meeting place—with baths and schmoozing spaces to accommodate 3,000 bathers at a time—was a big deal in ancient times. While much of it is still closed, three sections are open: the **Church of**

Rome

Santa Maria degli Angeli, once the great central hall of the baths (free, Mon–Sat 7:00–18:30, Sun 7:00–19:30, closed to sightseers during Mass, faces Piazza Repubblica); the **Octagonal Hall,** once a gymnasium, now a gallery of Roman bronze and marble statues (free, open sporadically Tue–Sat 9:00–14:00, Sun 9:00–13:00, closed Mon, faces Piazza della Repubblica); and the skippable **Museum of the Bath,** which displays ancient Roman inscriptions on tons of tombs and tablets—but, despite its name, has nothing on the baths themselves (€9, includes entry to three other National museums within three days, Tue–Sun 9:00–19:45, closed Mon, last entry 45 min before closing, audioguide-€4, Viale E. de Nicola 79, entrance faces Termini train station, tel. 06-4782-6152).

Santa Maria degli Angeli: From noisy Piazza della Repubblica, step through the curved brick wall of the ancient baths and into the vast and cool church built upon the remains of a vast and steamy Roman bath complex. The church we see today was (at least partly) designed by Michelangelo (1561), who used the baths' main hall as the nave. Later, when Piazza Repubblica became an important Roman intersection, another architect renovated the church. To allow people to enter from the grand new piazza, he spun it 90 degrees, turning Michelangelo's nave into a long transept. The eight red granite columns in the transept are original, from ancient Rome—stand next to one and feel its five-foot girth. (The others are made of plastered-over brick.) In Roman times, this hall was covered with mosaics, marble, and gold, and lined with statues.

Octagonal Hall: This octagonal building, capped by a dome with a hole in the top, may have served as a cool room *(frigidarium),* with small pools of cold water for plunging into. Or, because of its many doors, it may simply have been a large intersection, connecting other parts of the baths. Either way, it's one of Rome's best-preserved ancient rooms. Originally, the floor was 25 feet lower—as you can see through the glass-covered hole in the floor. The graceful iron grid overhead supported the canopy of a 1928 planetarium. Today, the hall is a free gallery showing off fine bronze and marble statues, some of which once decorated the Baths of Caracalla. The statues are mostly Roman copies of Greek originals—athletes, gods, Hercules, satyrs, and portraits.

▲**Santa Maria della Vittoria**—This church houses Bernini's statue of a swooning *St. Teresa in Ecstasy* (free, Mon–Sat 8:30–12:00 & 15:30–18:00, closed Sun, about 5 blocks northwest of Termini train station on Largo Susanna, Metro: Repubblica).

Once inside the church, you'll find St. Teresa to the left of the altar. Teresa has just been stabbed with God's arrow of fire. Now, the angel pulls it out and watches her reaction. Teresa swoons, her eyes roll up, her hand goes limp, she parts her lips...and moans. The

smiling, cherubic angel understands
just how she feels. Teresa, a 16th-
century Spanish nun, later talked of
the "sweetness" of "this intense pain,"
describing her oneness with God in
ecstatic, even erotic, terms.

Bernini, the master of multimedia, pulls out all the stops to make
this mystical vision real. Actual
sunlight pours through the alabaster
windows, bronze sunbeams shine on a
marble angel holding a golden arrow.
Teresa leans back on a cloud and
her robe ripples from within, charged with her spiritual arousal.
Bernini has created a little stage-setting of heaven. And watching
from the "theater boxes" on either side are members of the family
that commissioned the work.

Santa Susanna Church—The home of the American Catholic
Church in Rome, Santa Susanna holds Mass in English daily at 18:00
and on Sunday at 9:00 and 10:30. Their website, www.santasusanna
.org, contains tips for travelers and a long list of convents that rent out
rooms. They give out free tickets for the Wednesday general papal
audience (see page 661) and have a library that includes my Venice,
Florence, and Rome guidebooks (Mon–Fri 9:00–12:00 & 16:00–
19:00, closed Sat–Sun, Via XX Settembre 15, near recommended Via
Firenze hotels, Metro: Repubblica, tel. 06-4201-4554).

Pilgrim's Rome

East of the Colosseum (and south of Termini train station) are
several venerable churches that Catholic pilgrims make a point of
visiting.

Church of San Giovanni in Laterano—Built by Constantine, the
first Christian emperor, this was Rome's most important church
through medieval times. A building alongside the church houses
the Holy Stairs said to have been walked up by Jesus, which today
are ascended by pilgrims on their knees (free, daily 7:00–18:30,
Piazza San Giovanni in Laterano, Metro: San Giovanni, tel. 06-
0669-8643).

Church of Santa Maria Maggiore—Some of Rome's best-
surviving mosaics line the nave of this church, which was built as
Rome was falling. The nearby church of Santa Prassede has still
more early mosaics (free, daily 7:00–19:00, Piazza Santa Maria
Maggiore, Metro: Termini or Vittorio Emanuele, tel. 06-48-3058).

▲**Church of San Clemente**—Besides the church itself, with
frescoes by Masolino, you can also descend into the ruins of an
earlier church. Descend yet one more level and enter the eerie

Pilgrim's Rome

remains of a pagan temple to Mithras (upper church—free, lower church—€5, both open Mon–Sat 9:00–12:30 & 15:00–18:00, Sun 10:00–18:00, Via di San Giovanni in Laterano, Metro: Colosseo, tel. 06-7045-1018.

North Rome

Borghese Gardens and Via Veneto

▲ **Villa Borghese Gardens**—Rome's scruffy, three-square-mile "Central Park" is great for its shade and people-watching (plenty of modern-day Romeos and Juliets). The best entrance is at the head of Via Veneto (Metro: Barberini and 10-minute walk up Via Veneto). There you'll find a cluster of buildings with a café, a kiddie arcade, a cinema center, and bike rental (€5/4 hrs). Rent a bike and follow signs to discover the park's cafés, fountains, statues, museums (including the Borghese Gallery and Etruscan Museum—listed below), lake, and prime picnic spots.

North Rome

A map of North Rome showing landmarks including the Etruscan Museum, Modern Art Museum, Zoo, Borghese Gallery, Villa Borghese Gardens, Flaminio, S. Maria, Piazza del Popolo, Pincio, Galoppatoio Track, Bike Rental, Ancient City Walls, Porta Pinciana, Via Veneto, Ara Pacis, Via Spagna, Trinità del Monti, Cappuccin Crypt, Spanish Steps, Mausoleum of Augustus, Trevi Fountain, Barberini, Via Tritone, Piazza Venezia, Termini Station, and Tiber River.

Legend:
"Shopping Triangle"
Ⓜ Metro Station
Ⓣ Taxi Stand

1/4 mile
.5 KM
DCH

▲▲▲**Borghese Gallery (Galleria Borghese)**—This plush museum, filling a cardinal's mansion in the park, was recently restored and offers one of Europe's most sumptuous art experiences. You'll enjoy a collection of world-class Baroque sculpture, including Bernini's *David* and his excited statue of Apollo chasing Daphne, as well as paintings by Caravaggio, Raphael, Titian, and Rubens. The museum's slick mandatory reservation system keeps the crowds at a manageable size.

The essence of the collection is the connection of the Renaissance with the classical world. As you enter, notice the second-century Roman reliefs with Michelangelo-designed panels

Borghese Gallery—Ground Floor

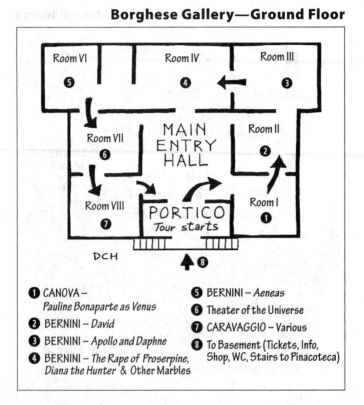

Room VI — **5**
Room IV — **4**
Room III — **3**
Room VII — **6**
MAIN ENTRY HALL
Room II — **2**
Room VIII — **7**
PORTICO
Tour starts
Room I — **1**
DCH
8

1 CANOVA – *Pauline Bonaparte as Venus*
2 BERNINI – *David*
3 BERNINI – *Apollo and Daphne*
4 BERNINI – *The Rape of Proserpine, Diana the Hunter* & Other Marbles
5 BERNINI – *Aeneas*
6 Theater of the Universe
7 CARAVAGGIO – Various
8 To Basement (Tickets, Info, Shop, WC, Stairs to Pinacoteca)

above either end of the portico. The villa was built in the early 17th century by the great art collector Cardinal Scipione Borghese, who wanted to prove that the glories of ancient Rome were matched by the Renaissance.

In the main entry hall, opposite the door, notice the thrilling relief of the horse falling (first century A.D., Greek). Pietro Bernini, father of the famous Gian Lorenzo Bernini, completed the scene by adding the Renaissance-era rider.

Each room seems to feature a Baroque masterpiece. The best of all is in Room III: Bernini's *Apollo and Daphne*. It's the perfect Baroque subject—capturing a thrilling, action-filled moment. In the mythological story, Apollo races after Daphne. Just as he's about to reach her, she turns into a tree. As her toes turn to roots and branches spring from her fingers, Apollo is in for one rude surprise. Walk slowly around. It's more air than stone.

Cost and Hours: €8.50, includes €2 reservation fee, Tue–Sun 9:00–19:00, closed Mon. No photos allowed.

Reservations: Reservations are mandatory and easy to get in English by booking online (www.ticketeria.it) or calling 06-328-101 (if you get an Italian recording, press 2 for English; office hours: Mon–Fri 9:00–18:00, Sat 9:00–13:00, office closed Sat in Aug and Sun year-round). Every two hours, 360 people are allowed to enter the museum. Entry times are 9:00, 11:00, 13:00, 15:00, and 17:00. Reserve a *minimum* of several days in advance for a weekday visit, at least a week ahead for weekends. Reservations are tightest at 11:00 and on weekends. On off-season weekdays, you may be able to get a same-day reservation if you're flexible about the entry time (but not on weekends).

When you reserve, request a day and time, and you'll get a claim number. While you'll be advised to come 30 minutes before your appointed time, I was told that you can arrive 10 minutes beforehand. After that, you become a no-show, and your ticket is sold to stand-bys.

If you don't have a reservation, try calling to see if there are any openings, or just show up and hope for a cancellation. No-shows are released a few minutes after the top of the hour. Generally, out of 360 reservations, a few will fail to show (but more than a few may be waiting to grab them). You're most likely to land a stand-by ticket at 13:00. Visits are strictly limited to two hours. Budget most of your time for the more interesting ground floor, but set aside 30 minutes for the paintings of the Pinacoteca upstairs (highlights are marked by the audioguide icons). You may avoid some of the crowds by seeing the Pinacoteca first. The fine bookshop and cafeteria are best visited outside your two-hour entry window.

Tours: Guided English tours are offered at 9:10 and 11:10 for €5; reserve with entry reservation (or consider the excellent audioguide tour for €5 or a "videoguide" for €7).

Getting There: The museum is in the vast Villa Borghese Gardens. To avoid missing your appointment, allow yourself plenty of time to find the place. A taxi drops you 100 yards from the museum (tell the cabbie your destination: gah-leh-REE-ah bor-GAY-zay). Getting to the museum by public transportation can be confusing, and requires a walk in the park. From the Spagna Metro stop (or the Spanish Steps), it's a 20-minute walk: From inside the station, follow signs to *Villa Borghese*, which take you on an underground labyrinth of escalators and moving sidewalks to the top of Via Veneto. From there, cross the street, enter the park, turn right, and follow the signs.

Etruscan Museum (Villa Giulia Museo Nazionale Etrusco)— The fascinating Etruscan civilization thrived in this part of Italy in about 600 B.C., when Rome was an Etruscan town. The Villa Giulia (a fine Renaissance palace) hosts a museum that tells the story. While I prefer the Vatican Museum's Etruscan section for a first look at this civilization, aficionados of all things Etruscan come here for the famous "husband and wife sarcophagus" (a dead couple seeming to enjoy an everlasting banquet from atop their tomb—sixth century B.C. from Cerveteri); the *Apollo from*

Veii statue (of textbook fame); and an impressive room filled with gold sheets of Etruscan printing and temple statuary from the Sanctuary of Pyrgi (€4, Tue–Sun 9:00–19:30, closed Mon, closes earlier off-season, Piazzale di Villa Giulia 9, tel. 06-322-6571).

Via Veneto—In the 1960s, movie stars from around the world paraded down curvy Via Veneto, one of Rome's glitziest night-spots. Today, it's still lined with the city's poshest hotels and the American Embassy, but any hint of local color has faded to bland.

▲**Cappuccin Crypt**—If you want to see artistically arranged bones, this is the place. The crypt is below the church of Santa Maria della Immacolata Concezione on Via Veneto, just up from

Piazza Barberini. The bones of more than 4,000 monks who died between 1528 and 1870 are in the base-ment, all lined up for the delight—or disgust—of the always-wide-eyed visitor. The soil in the crypt was brought from Jerusalem 400 years ago, and the monastic message on the wall explains that this is more than just a maca-bre exercise: "We were what you are...you will become what we are now. *Buon giorno*." Pick up a few of Rome's most interesting postcards (donation requested, daily 9:00–12:00 & 15:00–18:00, Metro: Barberini, tel. 06-487-1185). Just up the street, you'll find the American Embassy, Federal Express, Hard Rock Café, and fancy Via Veneto cafés filled with the poor and envious looking for the rich and famous.

Spanish Steps Area
▲**Spanish Steps**—The wide, curving staircase, culminating with an obelisk between two Baroque church towers, makes for one of Rome's iconic sights. Beyond that, it's a people-gathering place. By day, the area hosts shoppers looking for high-end fashions; on warm evenings, it attracts young people in love with the city.

"Shopping Triangle"—Draw a triangle on your map from the Spanish Steps, to Piazza Venezia, then up the Via del Corso to Piazza del Popolo. This area has Rome's the highest concentration of upscale boutiques and fashion stores.

▲▲ **Ara Pacis (Altar of Peace)**—On January 30, 9 B.C., soon-to-be-emperor Augustus led a procession of priests up the steps and into this newly-built "Altar of Peace." They sacrificed an animal on the altar and poured an offering of wine, thanking the gods for helping Augustus pacify barbarians abroad and rivals at home. This marked the dawn of the Pax Romana (c. A.D. 1–200), a Golden Age

of good living, stability, dominance, and peace *(pax)*. The Ara Pacis hosted annual sacrifices by the emperor until the area was flooded by the river Tiber. Buried under silt, it was abandoned and forgotten until the 16th century, when various parts were discovered and excavated. Mussolini gathered the altar's scattered parts and reconstructed them here in 1938. In 2006, the Altar of Peace reopened to the public in a striking modern building. As the first new building allowed to be built in the old center since 1938, it was controversial, but its quiet, air-conditioned interior may signal the dawn of another new age in Rome.

The Altar of Peace was originally located east of here, along today's Via del Corso. A model shows where it stood in relation to the Mausoleum of Augustus (now next door) and the Pantheon. Approach the Ara Pacis and look through the doorway to see the raised altar. This simple structure has just the basics of a Roman temple: an altar for sacrifices surrounded by cubicle-like walls that enclose a consecrated space. Its well-preserved reliefs celebrate Rome's success.

The reliefs on the north and south sides probably depict the parade of dignitaries who consecrated the altar, while reliefs on the west side (near the altar's back door) celebrate the two things Augustus brought to Rome: peace (goddess Roma as a conquering Amazon, right side) and prosperity (fertility goddess). Imagine the altar as it once was, standing in an open field, painted in bright colors—a mingling of myth, man, and nature.

Cost, Hours, Location: €6.50, tightwads can look in through huge windows for free; Tue–Sun 9:00–19:00, closed Mon, last entry 1 hour before closing; audioguide (€3.50/€5 double) also available as free podcast on the Web at www.arapacis.it, good WC downstairs. The Ara Pacis is a long block west of Via del Corso on Via di Ara Pacis, on the east bank of the Tiber near Ponte Cavour, Metro: Spagna; a 10-minute walk down Via dei Condotti. Tel. 06-8205-9127.

Catacombs of Priscilla (Catacombe di Priscilla)—For the most intimate catacombs experience, many prefer this smaller, more obscure option to the crowded catacombs on the Appian Way (San Callisto and San Sebastiano, both described on page 682). The Catacombs of Priscilla, once situated under the house of a Roman noble family, were used for some of the most important burials during antiquity. Best of all, because they're on the opposite side of town from the most popular catacombs, you'll have them mostly to yourself. You'll actually be in the care of a nun with a flashlight as you walk through the evocative chambers that are claimed to show the first depiction of Mary with Jesus (€5, Tue–Sun 8:30–12:00 & 14:30–17:00, closed Mon, two miles northeast of Villa Borghese Gardens, near Piazza Crati at Via Salaria 430, bus #63 from Largo Argentina or €10 taxi ride, tel. 06-862-06272, http://web.tiscali.it/catacombe_priscilla/. For more on catacombs, see "Catacombs," page 680.

Vatican City

Vatican City, a tiny independent country, contains the Vatican Museum (with Michelangelo's Sistine Chapel) and St. Peter's Basilica (with Michelangelo's exquisite *Pietà*). A helpful **TI** is just to the left of St. Peter's Basilica as you're facing it (Mon–Sat 8:30–19:00, closed Sun, tel. 06-6988-1662, Vatican switchboard tel. 06-6982, www.vatican.va). The entrances to St. Peter's and to the Vatican Museum are a 15-minute walk apart (follow the outside of the Vatican wall, which links the two sights). The nearest Metro stops involve a 10-minute walk to either sight: for St. Peter's, the closest stop is Ottaviano; for the Vatican Museum, it's Cipro–Musei Vaticani.

▲▲▲**Vatican Museum (Musei Vaticani)**—The four miles of displays in this immense museum—from ancient statues to Christian frescoes to modern paintings—are topped by the Raphael Rooms and Michelangelo's glorious Sistine Chapel. (If you have binoculars, bring them.) This is one of Europe's top three or four houses of art. It can be exhausting, so plan your visit carefully, focusing on a few themes. Allow two hours for a quick visit, three or four for the time to enjoy it. Be warned: You risk waiting in a very long line, and then having the door shut just as you reach it (see "Avoiding Lines," page 659).

Start, as civilization did, in **Egypt and Mesopotamia.** Next, the Pio Clementino collection features **Greek and Roman statues.** Decorating its courtyard are some of the best Greek and Roman statues in captivity, including the *Laocoön* group (first century B.C., Hellenistic) and the *Apollo Belvedere* (a second-century Roman copy of a Greek original). The centerpiece of the next hall is the *Belvedere Torso* (just a 2,000-year-old torso, but one that had a great impact on the art of Michelangelo). Finishing off the classical statuary are two fine fourth-century porphyry sarcophagi. These royal purple tombs were made (though not used) for the Roman emperor Constantine's mother and daughter. They were Christians—and therefore outlaws—until Constantine made Christianity legal (A.D. 312). Both sarcophagi were quarried and worked in Egypt. The technique for working this extremely hard stone (a special tempering of metal was required) was lost after

Vatican Museum Overview

- 1 Main Entrance & Exit
- 2 Egyptian Rooms
- 3 Cortile della Pigna
- 4 Octagonal Courtyard
- 5 Tapestries
- 6 Map Gallery & View of Vatican City
- 7 Raphael Rooms
- 8 Sistine Chapel & Exit to St. Peter's
- 9 Pinacoteca
- 10 Café

this, and porphyry was not chiseled again until Renaissance times in Florence.

After long halls of tapestries, old maps, broken penises, and fig leaves, you'll come to what most people are looking for: The Raphael Rooms (or *stanza*) and Michelangelo's Sistine Chapel.

These outstanding works are frescoes. A fresco (meaning "fresh" in Italian) is technically not a painting. The color is mixed into wet plaster, and, when the plaster dries, the painting is actually part of the wall. This is a durable but difficult medium, requiring speed and accuracy, as the work is built one patch at a time.

After fancy rooms illustrating the "Immaculate Conception of Mary" (in the 19th century, the Vatican codified this hard-to-sell doctrine, making it a formal part of the Catholic faith) and the triumph of Constantine (with divine guidance, which led to his conversion to Christianity), you enter rooms frescoed by **Raphael** and his assistants. The highlight is the newly restored *School of Athens*. This is remarkable for its blatant pre-Christian classical orientation, especially since it originally wallpapered the apartments of Pope Julius II. Raphael honors the great pre-Christian thinkers—Aristotle, Plato, and company—who are portrayed as the leading artists of Raphael's day. The bearded figure of Plato is Leonardo da Vinci. Diogenes, history's first hippie, sprawls alone in bright blue on the stairs, while Michelangelo broods in the foreground—supposedly added later. Apparently, Raphael snuck a peek at the Sistine Chapel and decided that his arch-competitor was so good that he had to put their personal differences aside and include him in this tribute to the artists of his generation. Today's St. Peter's was under construction as Raphael was working. In the *School of Athens*, he gives us a sneak preview of the unfinished church.

Next is the brilliantly restored **Sistine Chapel.** This is the pope's personal chapel and also the place where, upon the death of the ruling pope, a new pope is elected (as in April of 2005).

The Sistine Chapel is famous for Michelangelo's pictorial culmination of the Renaissance, showing the story of creation, with a powerful God weaving in and out of each scene through that busy first week. This is an optimistic and positive expression of the High Renaissance and a stirring example of the artistic and theological maturity of the 33-year-old Michelangelo, who spent four years on this work.

Later, after the Reformation wars had begun and after the Catholic army of Spain had sacked the Vatican, the reeling Church began to fight back. As part of its Counter-Reformation, a much older Michelangelo was commissioned to paint the *Last Judgment* (behind the altar). Brilliantly restored, the message is as clear as the day Michelangelo finished it: Christ is returning, some will go to hell and some to heaven, and some will be saved by the power of the rosary.

In the recent and controversial restoration project, no paint was added. Centuries of dust, soot (from candles used for lighting and Mass), and glue (added to make the art shine) were removed, revealing the bright original colors of Michelangelo. Photos are allowed (without a flash) elsewhere in the museum, but as part of the deal with the company who did the restoration, no photos are allowed in the Sistine Chapel.

For a shortcut, a small door at the far-right corner of the Sistine Chapel allows groups and individuals (without an audioguide) to escape directly to St. Peter's Basilica. If you exit here, you're done with the museum. The Pinacoteca is the only important part left. Consider doing it at the start. Otherwise it's a 15-minute heel-to-toe slalom through tourists from the Sistine Chapel to the entry/exit.

After this long march, you'll find the **Pinacoteca** (the Vatican's small but fine collection of paintings, with Raphael's *Transfiguration*, Leonardo's unfinished *St. Jerome,* and Caravaggio's *Deposition*), a cafeteria (long lines, uninspired food), and the underrated early-Christian art section, before you exit via the souvenir shop.

Cost, Hours, Information: €13, March–Oct Mon–Fri 10:00–16:45, Sat 10:00–14:45 (sometimes until 16:45); Nov–Feb Mon–Sat 10:00–13:45; closed on religious holidays and Sun except last Sun of the month (when it's free, more crowded, and open 9:00–13:45). Last entry is 75 minutes before closing. Hours are subject to constant change and frequent holidays; check www .vatican.va for current times. Tel. 06-6988-3860 or 06-6988-1662.

The museum is closed on many holidays (mainly religious ones) including, for 2008: Jan 1 (New Year's), Jan 6 (Epiphany), Feb 11 (Vatican City established), March 19 (St. Joseph), March 23–24 (Easter Sunday and Monday), May 1 (Labor Day and Ascension Thursday), May 22 (Corpus Christi), June 29 (Sts. Peter and Paul), Aug 15 plus either Aug 14 or 16—it varies year to year (Assumption of the Virgin), Nov 1 (All Saints' Day), Dec 8 (Immaculate Conception), and Dec 25–26 (Christmas). Other holidays and changes in opening hours may pop up—again, remember to check the hours and 2008 calendar at www.vatican.va.

The Sistine Chapel closes before the museum. Individual rooms may close at odd hours, especially after 13:00. TV screens inside the entrance list closures. The rooms described here are usually open.

Avoiding Lines: The museum is generally hot and crowded. The most crowded days are Saturday, the last Sunday of the month, Monday, rainy days, and any day before or after a holiday closure. Afternoons or Wednesday mornings before 11:00 are best.

Vatican City

This tiny independent country of little more than 100 acres, contained entirely within Rome, has its own postal system, armed guards, helipad, mini-train station, and radio station (KPOP). Politically powerful, the Vatican is the religious capital of 1.1 billion Roman Catholics. If you're not a Catholic, become one for your visit.

The pope is both the religious and secular leader of Vatican City. For centuries, locals referred to him as "King Pope." Italy and the Vatican didn't always have good relations. In fact, after unification (in 1870), when Rome's modern grid plan was built around the miniscule Vatican, it seemed as if the new buildings were designed to be just high enough so no one could see the dome of St. Peter's from street level. Modern Italy was created in 1870, but the Holy See didn't recognize it as a country until 1929, when the pope and Mussolini signed the Lateran Pact, giving sovereignty to the Vatican and a few nearby churches.

Like every European country, Vatican City has its own versions of the euro coin (with a portrait of Pope Benedict XVI, and before him, of Pope John Paul II). You're unlikely to find one in your pocket, though, as they are snatched up by collectors before falling into actual circulation.

Small as it is, Vatican City has two huge sights: St. Peter's Basilica (with Michelangelo's *Pietà*) and the Vatican Museum (with the Sistine Chapel). The Vatican **post office,** with offices on St. Peter's Square (next to TI) and in the Vatican Museum, is more reliable than Italy's mail service (Mon–Sat 8:30–19:00, closed Sun). The stamps are a collectible bonus. Vatican stamps are good throughout Rome, but to use the Vatican's mail service, you need to mail your cards from the Vatican; write your postcards ahead of time. (Note that the Vatican won't mail cards with Italian stamps.)

Seeing the Pope: Your best chances for a sighting are on Sunday and Wednesday. The pope usually gives a blessing at noon on Sunday from his apartment on St. Peter's Square (except in July and August, when he speaks at his summer residence at Castel Gandolfo, 25 miles from Rome; train leaves Rome's Termini station). St. Peter's is easiest (just show up) and, for most, enough of a "visit." Those interested in a more formal appearance (but not more intimate) can get a ticket for the Wednesday general audience (at 10:30) when the pope, arriving in his bulletproof Popemobile, greets and blesses the crowds at St. Peter's from a balcony or canopied platform on the square (except in winter, when he speaks at 10:30 in the 7,000-seat Aula Paolo VI Auditorium, next to St. Peter's Basilica). If you only want to see the Vatican—but not the pope—minimize crowd problems by avoiding these times.

For the Wednesday general audience: While anyone can

Vatican City Overview

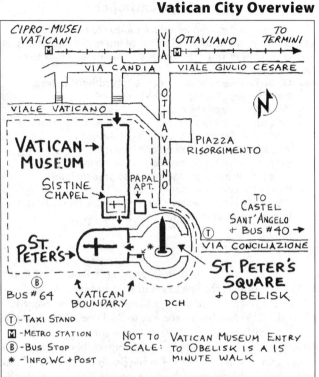

CIPRO - MUSEI VATICANI Ⓜ ⊢+—+—+— VIA OTTAVIANO Ⓜ +—+—+— OTTAVIANO · TO TERMINI

VIA CANDIA · VIALE GIULIO CESARE

VIALE VATICANO

Ⓝ

VATICAN → MUSEUM

PIAZZA RISORGIMENTO

SISTINE CHAPEL →

PAPAL APT. ↓

TO CASTEL SANT'ANGELO + BUS #40 →

Ⓣ

VIA CONCILIAZIONE

ST. PETER'S →

*

ST. PETER'S SQUARE + OBELISK

Ⓑ
BUS #64 · VATICAN BOUNDARY · DCH

Ⓣ - TAXI STAND
Ⓜ - METRO STATION
Ⓑ - BUS STOP
* - INFO, WC + POST

NOT TO SCALE:

VATICAN MUSEUM ENTRY TO OBELISK IS A 15 MINUTE WALK

observe from a distance, you need a ticket to actually get close to the papal action. To find out the pope's schedule, call 06-6988-4631. Tickets are free and easy to get, but must be picked up on Tuesday for the Wednesday service. You can get tickets from Santa Susanna Church or the papal guard (at the Vatican).

Santa Susanna Church hands out tickets Tuesdays between 17:00 and 18:45 (Via XX Settembre 15, near recommended Via Firenze hotels, Metro: Repubblica, tel. 06-4201-4554, www .santasusanna.org). While they have lots of tickets, the sure way to have a ticket held for you is to email your request to tickets @santasusanna.org. Their hours are timed in the hopes that you'll stay for the English-language Mass at 18:00.

Probably less convenient is picking up a ticket directly from the Vatican guard at St. Peter's Basilica. They hand out tickets from their station at the bronze doors (just to the right of the basilica) Tuesdays from 12:00 to 19:30 (just join the long line).

While many visitors come hoping for a more intimate audience, private audiences ended with the death of Pope John Paul II. Pope Benedict doesn't do them.

Is the Pope Catholic?

Rome's tour guides, who introduce tourists to the city's great art and Christian history, field a lot of interesting questions and comments from their groups. Here are a few of their favorites:

- Oh, to be here in Rome...where our Lord Jesus walked.
- Is this where Christ fought the lions?
- Who's the guy on the cross?
- This guy who made so many nice things, Rene Sance, who is he? (Say it fast, and you'll get the gist.)
- Was John Paul II the son of John Paul I?
- What's the Sistine Chapel worth in US dollars?
- How did Michelangelo get Moses to pose for him?
- What's Michelangelo doing now?
- (Upon seeing the arrow-pierced St. Sebastian) Oh, you Italians had problems with the Indians, too.

On days the museum closes at 16:45, arriving at about 13:00 works well. Most mornings, the line to get in stretches around the block. (Stuck in the line? Figure about a 10-minute wait for every 100 yards. If the line stretches all the way to St. Peter's Square, count on waiting nearly two hours.) There's little advantage to arriving early in the morning, as the place is already mobbed with early-bird tour groups when it opens—so the line moves slowly. If you do arrive before the museum opens, be sure to line up against the Vatican City wall (to the left of the entrance); the other line is for guided tours. After 9:45, there is only one line. To skip the long line for individuals (and just wait in the shorter line for groups), consider taking a guided tour—see "Tours," below.

Unfortunately for the tourist, the Vatican insists on ridiculously short hours, claiming "not enough staff"—but in reality, it's for private showings and big shots. For us mere mortals, the only alternative to the long lines is to skip the museum altogether, remembering that the Capitoline Museums and the National Museum at the Palazzo Massimo have equally great ancient art with far fewer crowds...and more reasonable hours (but unfortunately, no Raphael Rooms or Sistine Chapel).

Modest dress (no short shorts or bare shoulders) is appropriate and often required.

Tours: Both **private tour companies** and **private guides** offer guided tours of the museum, allowing you to skip the long ticket-buying line. If going with a tour, look for the tour entrance (to the right of the individual entrance), which sometimes has a (shorter) line. For a listing of several companies, see page 611. These tours can be expensive—shop around for the best deal.

There are also English tours with a **Vatican guide,** but these are extremely difficult to join—they can book up as much as a year in advance (for details, see www.vatican.va). If you don't hear back—which you probably won't—it means that they're full.

If you rent a €6 **audioguide** (available at the top of the ramp/escalator), you lose the option of taking the shortcut from the Sistine Chapel to St. Peter's (audioguides must be returned at museum entrance).

▲▲▲**St. Peter's Basilica**—There is no doubt: This is the richest and most impressive church on earth. To call it vast is like calling God smart. Marks on the floor show where the next-largest churches would fit if they were put inside. The ornamental cherubs would dwarf a large man. Birds roost inside, and thousands of people wander about, heads craned heavenward, hardly noticing each other. Don't miss Michelangelo's *Pietà* (behind bulletproof glass) to the right of the entrance. Bernini's altar work and seven-story-tall bronze canopy are brilliant.

For a quick walk through the basilica, follow these points (see map on page 664):

❶ The atrium is larger than most churches. The huge white columns on the portico date from the first church (fourth century). Notice the historic doors (the Holy Door, on the right, won't be opened until the next Jubilee Year, in 2025).

❷ The purple, circular porphyry stone marks the site of Charlemagne's coronation in A.D. 800 (in the first St. Peter's church that stood on this site). From here, get a sense of the immensity of the church, which can accommodate 60,000 worshippers standing on its six acres.

❸ Michelangelo planned a Greek-cross floor plan, rather than the Latin-cross standard in medieval churches. A Greek cross, symbolizing the perfection of God, and by association the goodness of man, was important to the humanist Michelangelo. But accommodating large crowds was important to the Church in the fancy Baroque age, which followed Michelangelo, so the original nave length was doubled. Stand halfway up the nave and imagine the stubbier design that Michelangelo had in mind.

❹ View the magnificent dome from the statue of St. Andrew. See the vision of heaven above the windows: Jesus, Mary, a ring of saints, rings of angels, and, on the very top, God the Father.

❺ The main altar sits directly over St. Peter's tomb and under Bernini's seven-story bronze canopy.

❻ The stairs lead down to the crypt to the foundation, chapels, and tombs of popes (including the simple tomb of John Paul II).

❼ The statue of St. Peter, with an irresistibly kissable toe, is one of the few pieces of art that predate this church. It adorned the

St. Peter's Basilica

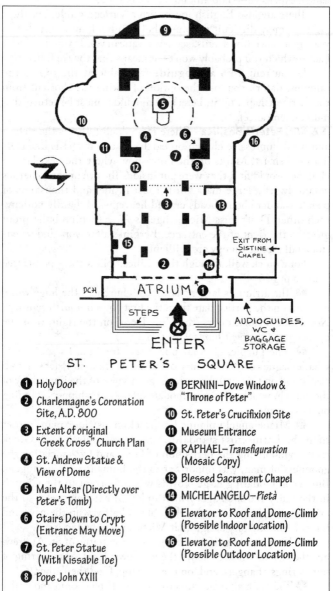

1 Holy Door

2 Charlemagne's Coronation Site, A.D. 800

3 Extent of original "Greek Cross" Church Plan

4 St. Andrew Statue & View of Dome

5 Main Altar (Directly over Peter's Tomb)

6 Stairs Down to Crypt (Entrance May Move)

7 St. Peter Statue (With Kissable Toe)

8 Pope John XXIII

9 BERNINI—Dove Window & "Throne of Peter"

10 St. Peter's Crucifixion Site

11 Museum Entrance

12 RAPHAEL—*Transfiguration* (Mosaic Copy)

13 Blessed Sacrament Chapel

14 MICHELANGELO—*Pietà*

15 Elevator to Roof and Dome-Climb (Possible Indoor Location)

16 Elevator to Roof and Dome-Climb (Possible Outdoor Location)

first St. Peter's church.

❽ The tomb of Pope John XXIII (1958–1963), who oversaw major reforms in the Vatican II conference.

❾ St. Peter's throne and Bernini's starburst dove window is the site of a daily Mass (Mon–Sat at 17:00, Sun at 17:30).

❿ St. Peter was crucified here when this location was simply "the Vatican Hill." The obelisk now standing in the center of St. Peter's square marked the center of a Roman racecourse long before a church stood here.

⓫ For most, the museum (in the sacristy) is not worth the admission.

⓬ The church is filled with mosaics, not paintings. Notice the mosaic version of Raphael's *Transfiguration*.

⓭ Blessed Sacrament Chapel.

⓮ Michelangelo sculpted his *Pietà* when he was 24 years old. (A pietà is a work that represents Mary with the body of Christ taken down from the cross.) Michelangelo's mastery of the body is obvious in this powerfully beautiful masterpiece. Jesus is believably dead, and Mary, the eternally youthful "handmaiden" of the Lord, accepts God's will...even if it means giving up her son.

The Holy Door (to the right of the *Pietà*, covered in gray concrete with a gold cross) won't be reopened until Christmas Eve, 2024, the dawn of the next Jubilee Year. Every 25 years, the Church celebrates an especially festive year derived from the Old Testament idea of the Jubilee Year (originally every 50 years), which encourages new beginnings and the forgiveness of sins and debts. In Jubilee Year 2000, Pope John Paul II tirelessly—and with significant success—promoted debt relief for the world's poorest countries.

⓯ An elevator leads to the roof and the stairway up the dome (€6, allow an hour to go up and down). The dome, Michelangelo's last work, is (you guessed it) the biggest anywhere. Taller than a football field is long, it's well worth the sweaty climb for a great view of Rome, the Vatican grounds, and the inside of the basilica—particularly heavenly while there is singing. Look around— Rome has no modern skyline. No building is allowed to exceed the height of St. Peter's. The elevator takes you to the rooftop of the nave. From there, a few steps take you to a balcony at the base of the dome looking down into the church interior. After that, the one-way, 323-step climb (for some people, it's claustrophobic) to the cupola begins. The rooftop level (below the dome) has a gift shop, WC, drinking fountain, and a commanding view.

Dress Code: No shorts or bare shoulders (applies to men, women, and children), and no miniskirts. This dress code is strictly enforced.

Hours of Church: Daily April–Sept 7:00–19:00, Oct–March 7:00–18:00. Mass is held daily (Mon–Sat at 8:30, 10:00, 11:00,

Pope Benedict XVI

When Josef Ratzinger became the 265th pope, he introduced himself as "a simple, humble worker in the vineyard of the Lord."

But the man has a complex history, a reputation for intellectual brilliance, a flair for the piano, and a penchant for controversy, thanks to his unbending devotion to traditional Catholic doctrine.

Born in small-town Bavaria in 1927, he lived life under Nazi rule as many Germans did—outwardly obeying leaders while inwardly conflicted. Like all 14-year-old boys, he joined the Hitler Youth and, like most German men, was drafted into the Army. During World War II, he trained to spray flak from anti-aircraft guns, saw Jews transported to death camps, and, like many Germans in the final days of the war, he deserted his post.

After the war, he completed his studies in theology and became a rising voice of liberal Catholicism, serving as an advisor at the Second Vatican Council (1962–1965). But after the May 1968 student revolts rocked Europe's Establishment, he became increasingly convinced that Church tradition was needed to offset the growing chaos of the world.

12:00, and 17:00; Sun and holidays at 9:00, 10:30, 11:30, 12:10, 13:00, 16:00, and 17:30; confirm schedule locally). The church closes on Wednesday mornings during papal audiences. The best time to visit the church is early or late; I like to be here at 17:00, when the church is fairly empty, sunbeams can work their magic, and the late-afternoon Mass fills the place with spiritual music.

Tours: The Vatican TI conducts free 90-minute tours of St. Peter's (depart daily from TI at 14:15, confirm schedule at TI, tel. 06-6988-1662). Audioguides can be rented near the checkroom (€5).

Tours are the only way to see the Vatican Gardens. Book at least two weeks in advance by faxing 06-6988-5100 or emailing visiteguidate.musei@scv.va; no response means they're full (€12; Tue, Thu, and Sat at 10:00; tours start at Vatican Museum tour desk and finish on St. Peter's Square).

Excellent Vatican guides take groups of 12 to the excavations in the well-lit pagan Necropolis and the saint's tomb (€10, 2 hours, ages 15 and older only, book well in advance by emailing scavi @fsp.va, fax to 06-6987-3017, or ask directly at the Excavations

Pope John Paul II appointed him to several positions, and Ratzinger became John Paul II's closest advisor and good friend. Every Friday afternoon for two decades, they met for lunch, intellectual sparring, and friendly conversation.

Under John Paul II, Ratzinger served as the Church's "enforcer" of doctrine, earning the nickname "God's Rottweiler." He spoke out against ordaining women, chastised Latin American priests for fomenting class warfare (Liberation theology), reassigned bishops who were soft on homosexuality, reaffirmed opposition to birth control, and wrote thoughtful papers challenging the secular world's moral relativism. He also punished pedophile priests, though critics charged him with glossing over the issue to preserve the Church's image.

Ratzinger chose the name of "Benedict" to recall both Pope Benedict XV (who tried to bring Europeans together after World War I) and the original St. Benedict (c. 480–543), the monk who symbolizes Europe's Christian roots. A true pan-European who speaks many languages, Ratzinger heads a Church that thrives everywhere except Europe, which is becoming increasingly secular and Muslim. In 2006, Benedict stirred controversy among many Muslims with some unguarded remarks. Generally, Benedict XVI has continued John Paul II's two priorities: defending Catholic doctrine in a changing world and building bridges with fellow Christians.

Office—Mon–Sat 9:00–17:00, closed Sun and holidays). Follow the detailed instructions at www.vatican.va to submit a request. No response to your fax or email means that they're booked up. The Crypt is open for free to the public, but this tour gets you closer to St. Peter's tomb.

Cost and Hours of Dome: The view from the dome is worth the climb (€6 elevator plus 323-step climb, allow an hour to go up and down, daily April–Sept 8:00–17:45, Oct–March 8:00–16:45).

▲**Castel Sant'Angelo**—Built as a tomb for the emperor; used through the Middle Ages as a castle, prison, and place of last refuge for popes under attack; and today, visited as a museum, this giant pile of ancient bricks is packed with history.

Ancient Rome allowed no tombs within its walls—not even the emperor's. So Emperor Hadrian grabbed the most commanding position just outside the walls and across the river and built a towering tomb (c. A.D. 139) well within view of the city. His mausoleum was a huge cylinder (210 by 70 feet) topped by a cypress grove and crowned by a huge statue of Hadrian himself riding a chariot. For nearly a hundred years, Roman emperors (from Hadrian to Caracalla, in A.D. 217) were buried here.

In the year 590, the Archangel Michael appeared above the mausoleum to Pope Gregory the Great. Sheathing his sword, the angel signaled the end of a plague. The fortress that was Hadrian's mausoleum eventually became a fortified palace, renamed for the "holy angel."

Castel Sant'Angelo spent centuries of the Dark Ages as a fortress and prison, but was eventually connected to the Vatican via an elevated corridor at the pope's request (1277). Since Rome was repeatedly plundered by invaders, Castel Sant'Angelo was a handy place of last refuge for threatened popes.

Touring the place is a stair-stepping workout. After you walk around the entire base of the castle, take the small staircase down to the original Roman floor (following the route of Hadrian's funeral procession). In the atrium, study the model of the mausoleum as it was in Roman times. From here, a ramp leads to the right, spiraling 400 feet. At the end of the ramp, a bridge crosses over the room where the ashes of the emperors were kept. From here, the stairs continue out of the ancient section and into the medieval structure (built atop the mausoleum) that housed the papal apartments. Don't miss the Sala del Tesoro (Treasury), where the wealth of the Vatican was locked up in a huge chest. (*Do* miss the 58 rooms of the military museum.) From the pope's piggy bank, a narrow flight of stairs leads to the rooftop and perhaps the finest Rome view anywhere—pick out landmarks as you stroll around.

Cost, Hours, Location: €5, Tue–Sun 9:00–18:00, closed Mon, audioguide-€4, near Vatican City, Metro: Lepanto or bus #64, tel. 06-3996-7600.

Ponte Sant'Angelo—The bridge leading to Castel Sant'Angelo was built by Hadrian for quick and regal access from downtown to his tomb. The three middle arches are actually Roman originals, and a fine example of the empire's engineering expertise. The statues of angels (each bearing a symbol of the Passion of Christ—nail, sponge, shroud, and so on) are

Bernini-designed and textbook Baroque. In the Middle Ages, this was the only bridge in the area that connected St. Peter's and the Vatican with downtown Rome. Nearly all pilgrims passed this bridge to and from the church. Its shoulder-high banisters recall a tragedy: During a Jubilee Year festival in 1450, the crowd got so huge that the mob pushed out the original banisters, causing nearly 200 to fall to their deaths.

Trastevere

Trastevere (trahs-TAY-veh-ray) is the colorful neighborhood across *(tras)* the Tiber *(Tevere)* River and offers the best look at medieval-village Rome. The action unwinds to the chime of the church bells. Go there and wander. Wonder. Be a poet. This is Rome's Left Bank.

This proud neighborhood was long a working-class area. Now that it's becoming trendy, high rents are driving out the source of so much color. Still, it's a great people scene, especially at night. Stroll the back streets (for restaurant recommendations, see page 697).

To reach Trastevere by foot from Capitol Hill, cross the Tiber on Ponte Cestio (over Isola Tiberina). You can also take tram #8 from Largo Argentina, or bus #H from Termini train station and Via Nazionale (get off at Piazza Belli). From the Vatican (Piazza Risorgimento), it's bus #23 or #271.

Linking Trastevere with the "Night Walk Across Rome": You can walk from Trastevere to Campo de' Fiori to link up with the beginning of the "Night Walk Across Rome" (page 623): From Trastevere's church square (Piazza di Santa Maria), take Via del Moro to the river and cross at Ponte Sisto, a pedestrian bridge that has a good view of St. Peter's dome. Continue straight ahead for one block. Take the first left, which leads down Via di Capo di Ferro through the scary and narrow darkness to Piazza Farnese, with the imposing Palazzo Farnese. Michelangelo contributed to the facade of this palace, now the French Embassy. The fountains on the square feature huge, one-piece granite hot tubs from the ancient Roman Baths of Caracalla. One block from there (opposite the palace) is the atmospheric square of Campo de' Fiori.

▲**Santa Maria in Trastevere Church**—One of Rome's oldest churches, this was made a basilica in the fourth century, when Christianity was legalized (free, daily 7:00–21:00). It was the first church dedicated to the Virgin Mary. The portico (covered area just outside the door) is decorated with fascinating ancient fragments filled with early Christian symbolism. Most of what you see dates from about the 12th century, but the granite columns are from ancient Roman buildings (notice the mismatched capitals, some with tiny pagan heads of Egyptian gods), and the ancient basilica floor plan (and ambience) survives. The intricate coffered ceiling

Rome

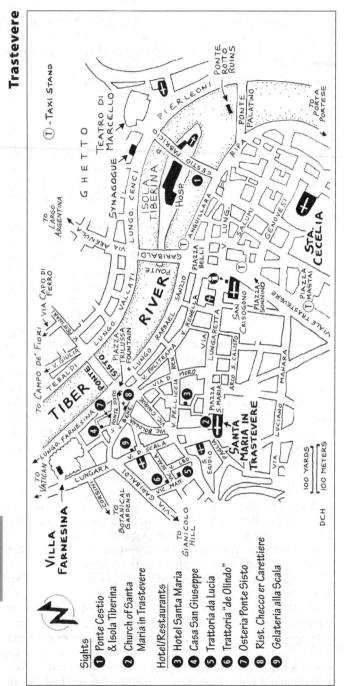

Trastevere

(T) - TAXI STAND

N

VILLA FARNESINA

Sights
1 Ponte Cestio & Isola Tiberina
2 Church of Santa Maria in Trastevere

Hotel/Restaurants
3 Hotel Santa Maria
4 Casa San Giuseppe
5 Trattoria da Lucia
6 Trattoria "de Olindo"
7 Osteria Ponte Sisto
8 Rist. Checco er Carettiere
9 Gelateria alla Scala

100 YARDS
100 METERS

DCH

has an unusual image of Mary painted on copper at the center. The striking 12th-century mosaics behind the altar are notable for their portrayal of Mary—which local tour guides claim is the first to show her at the throne with Jesus in Heaven. Below, the scenes from the life of Mary (mosaics by Cavallini, 1300s) predate the Renaissance by a hundred years.

The church is on Piazza di Santa Maria. While today's fountain is from the 17th century, there has been a fountain here since Roman times.

▲**Villa Farnesina**—Here's a unique opportunity to see a sumptuous Renaissance villa in Rome decorated with Raphael paintings. It was built in the early 1500s for the richest man in Renaissance Europe, Siennese banker Agostino Chigi. Architect Baldassare Peruzzi's design—a U-shaped building with wings that enfold what used to be a vast garden—successfully blended architecture and nature in a way that both ancient and Renaissance Romans loved. Orchards and flowerbeds flowed down in terraces from the palace to the river banks. Later construction of modern embankments and avenues robbed the garden of its grandeur, leaving it with a more melancholy charm.

In the **Loggia of Galatea,** find Raphael's painting of the nymph Galatea (on the wall by the entrance door). Galatea is considered Raphael's vision of female perfection—not a portrait of an individual woman, but a composite of his many lovers in an idealized vision. Raphael and his assistants also painted the subtly erotic **Loggia of Psyche.**

Cost, Hours, Location: €5; April–June and mid-Sept–Oct Mon–Fri 9:00–13:00, Sat 9:00–16:00, closed Sun; July–mid-Sept and Nov–March Mon–Sat 9:00–13:00, closed Sun; across the river from Campo de' Fiori, a short walk from Ponte Sisto on Via della Lungara, tel. 06-6802-7268.

Gianicolo Hill Viewpoint—From this park atop a hill, the city views are superb, and the walk to the top holds a treat for architecture buffs. Start at Trastevere's Piazza di San Cosimato, and follow Via Luciano Manara to Via Garibaldi, at the base of the hill. Via Garibaldi winds its way up the side of the hill to the church of San Pietro in Montorio. To the right of the church, in a small courtyard, is the **Tempietto** by Donato Bramante. This tiny church, built to commemorate the martyrdom of St. Peter, is considered a jewel of Italian Renaissance architecture. Continuing up the hill, Via Garibaldi connects to Passeggiata del Gianicolo. From here, you'll find a pleasant park with panoramic city views. Ponder the many Victorian-era statues, including that of baby-carrying, gun-wielding, horse-riding Anita Garibaldi. She was the Brazilian wife of the revolutionary General Giuseppe Garibaldi, who helped forge a united Italy in the late 19th century.

Near Trastevere: Jewish Quarter

From the 16th through the 19th centuries, Rome's Jewish population was forced to live in a cramped ghetto at an often-flooded bend of the Tiber River. While the medieval Jewish ghetto is long gone, this area—just across the river and towards Capitol Hill from Trastevere—is still home to Rome's synagogue and fragments of its Jewish heritage.

Synagogue (Sinagoga) and Jewish Museum (Museo Ebraico)— Rome's modern synagogue stands proudly on the spot where the medieval Jewish community lived in squalor for more than 300 years. The site of a historic visit by Pope John Paul II, this synagogue features a fine interior and a museum filled with artifacts of Rome's Jewish community (€7.50, includes synagogue and museum; May–Sept Sun–Thu 10:00–19:00, Fri 9:00–16:00, closed Sat; Oct–April Sun–Thu 10:00–17:00, Fri 9:00–14:00, closed Sat; on the riverbank road called Lungotevere dei Cenci near the bridge crossing Isola Tiberina, tel. 06-6840-0661, www.museoebraico .roma.it).

South Rome

Testaccio

In the gritty Testaccio neighborhood, four fascinating but lesser sights cluster at the Piramide Metro stop between the Colosseum and E.U.R. (This is a quick and easy stop as you return from E.U.R., or when changing trains en route to Ostia Antica.)

Working-class since ancient times, the Testaccio neighborhood has recently gone trendy-bohemian. Visitors wander through an awkward mix of yuppie and proletarian worlds, not noticing—but perhaps sensing—the "Keep Testaccio for the Testaccians" graffiti. This has long been the neighborhood of slaughterhouses, and its restaurants are renowned for their ability to cook up the least palatable part of the animals...the "fifth quarter." For a meal you won't forget, try **Trattoria "Da Oio" a Casa Mia** (at Via Galvani 43; see page 708 in Eating). High-end shoe and clothing boutiques are moving into the neighborhood, and this is now one of the best areas in Rome to have shoes custom-made. The Testaccio market in the center is hands-down the best, most authentic outdoor food market in Rome—this is where Romans shop while tourists flock to Campo de' Fiori. (It's on Piazza Testaccio, two blocks west of Via Marmorata.)

Testaccio

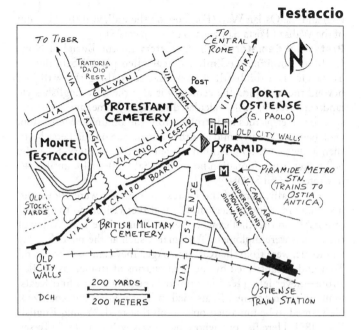

To Tiber • To Central Rome • Via Galvani • Trattoria "Da Oio" Rest. • Via Marm. • Post • Via Pira. • Porta Ostiense (S. Paolo) • Protestant Cemetery • Via Zabaglia • Via Cestio • Via Caio • Old City Walls • Monte Testaccio • Pyramid • Piramide Metro Stn. (Trains to Ostia Antica) • V. Cave Ard. • Campo Boario • Via Ostiense • Underground Moving Sidewalk • M • Old Stock Yards • Viale • British Military Cemetery • Old City Walls • Via Ostiense • 200 Yards • 200 Meters • DCH • Ostiense Train Station • N

Pyramid of Gaius Cestius—The Mark Antony/Cleopatra scandal
(c. 30 B.C.) brought exotic Egyptian
styles into vogue. A rich Roman magis-
trate, Gaius Cestius, had this pyramid
built as his tomb. Made of brick and
covered in marble, it was completed
in just 330 days (as stated in its Latin
inscription). While much smaller than
actual Egyptian pyramids, its proportions are correct. It was later incorporated into the Aurelian Wall, and it
now stands as a marker to the entrance
of Testaccio (next to the Piramide
Metro stop).

Porta Ostiense and Museo della via Ostiense—This formidable
gate (also next to the Piramide Metro stop; tiny museum free, Tue–
Sun 9:00–13:30, closed Mon) is from the Aurelian Wall, begun
in the third century under Emperor Aurelian. The wall, which
encircled the city, was 12 miles long and averaged about 26 feet
high, with 14 main gates and 380 72-foot-tall towers. Most of what
you'll see today is circa A.D. 400, but the barbarians reconstructed
the gate later, in the sixth century. If you climb up (enter nearest
the pyramid), you can enjoy a free ramble along the ramparts and
exhibits and models of Ostia Antica (Rome's ancient port; see page

682) and the Ostian Way. (For more on the wall, visit the Museum of the Walls at Porta San Sebastian; see page 681.)

Protestant Cemetery—The Cemetery for the Burial of Non-Catholic Foreigners (Cimitero Acattolico per gli Stranieri al Testaccio) is a tomb-filled park that runs along the wall just beyond the pyramid. The cemetery is also the only English-style landscape (rolling hills, calculated vistas) in Rome, and a favorite spot for quiet picnics and strolls. From the Piramide Metro stop, walk between the pyramid and the Roman gate on Via Persichetti, then go left on Caio Cestio to the gate of the cemetery. Ring the bell to get inside (donation box, Mon–Sat 9:00–16:40, until 15:40 in winter, closed Sun).

Originally, none of the Protestant epitaphs were allowed to make any mention of heaven. Signs direct visitors to the graves of notable non-Catholics who died in Rome since 1738. Many of the buried were diplomats. And many, such as the poets Shelley and Keats, were from the Romantic Age. They came on the Grand Tour and—"captivated by the fatal charms of Rome," as Shelley wrote—never left. Head left toward the pyramid to find Keats' tomb, in the far corner. Keats died in his twenties, unrecognized. He wanted to be unnamed on a tomb that read, "Young English Poet, 1821. Here lies one whose name was writ in water." (To see Keats' tomb if the cemetery is closed, look through the tiny peep-hole on Via Caio Cestio, 10 yards off Via Marmarata.)

From inside the cemetery (nearest the pyramid), look down on Matilde Talli's cat hospice (flier at gate of cat zone, near pyramid). Volunteers use donations to care for these "Guardians of the Departed" who "provide loyal companionship to these dead."

Notice the beige travertine post office from 1932 (across the big street from the cemetery). This is textbook Mussolini-era fascist architecture. The huge X design on the stairwells celebrates the 10th anniversary of the dictator's reign.

Monte Testaccio—Just behind the Protestant Cemetery (as you leave, turn left and continue two blocks down Caio Cestio) is a 115-foot-tall ancient trash pile. It's made of broken *testae*—earthenware jars mostly used to haul oil 2,000 years ago, when this was a gritty port warehouse district. For 500 years, rancid oil vessels were discarded here. Slowly, Rome's lowly eighth hill was built. Because the caves dug into the hill stay cool, trendy bars, clubs, and restaurants compete with gritty car-repair places for a spot. The neighborhood was once known for a huge slaughterhouse and a Roma (Gypsy) camp that squatted inside an old military base. Now it's home to the Testaccio Village, a site for concerts and techno-raves. To do the full monty, arrive after 21:00, when the restaurant-and-club scene is youthful and lively (Metro: Piramide).

South of Testaccio

▲Montemartini Museum (Musei Capitolini Centrale Monte-martini)—This museum houses a dreamy collection of 400 ancient statues, set evocatively in a classic 1932 electric power plant, among generators and *Metropolis*-type cast-iron machinery. While the art is not as famous as the collections that you'll see downtown, the effect is fun and memorable—and you'll encounter absolutely no tourists (€4.20, €10 combo-ticket includes Capitoline Museums and National Museum of Rome, Tue–Sun 9:00–20:00, closed Mon, last entry 1 hour before closing, Via Ostiense 106, a short walk from Metro: Garbatella, tel. 06-3996-7800, www.museicapitolini.org). If tackling Rome with kids, this museum is ideal (cool, immersed in an old power plant, with no crowds, and art placed at kid level).

▲St. Paul's Outside the Walls (Basilica San Paolo Fuori le Mura)—This was the last major construction project of Imperial Rome (c. 380) and the largest

church in Christendom until St. Peter's. After a tragic 19th-century fire, St. Paul's was rebuilt in the same general style and size as the original. Step inside and feel as close as you'll get in the 21st century to experiencing a monumental Roman basilica. Marvel at the ceiling, and imagine building it with those massive wood beams in A.D. 380.

It feels sterile, but in a good way—like you're already in heaven. Along with St. Peter's Basilica, San Giovanni in Laterano, and Santa Maria Maggiore, this church is part of the Vatican rather than Italy. The church is built upon the supposed grave of St. Paul, whose body is buried under the altar. (Paul was decapitated two miles from this spot, and his head is at San Giovanni in Laterano.)

Alabaster windows light the vast interior, and fifth-century mosaics decorate the triumphal arch leading to the altar. Mosaic portraits of 264 popes, from St. Peter to the present, ring the place—with blank spots ready to depict future popes. Pope #265—

Benedict XVI—should show up here any day now; the portraits are put up near the start of a pope's reign. Find John Paul II (to the right of the high altar: *Jo Paulus II*) and John Paul I (to his right, with a reign of only one month and three days). Wander the ornate yet

South of Testaccio

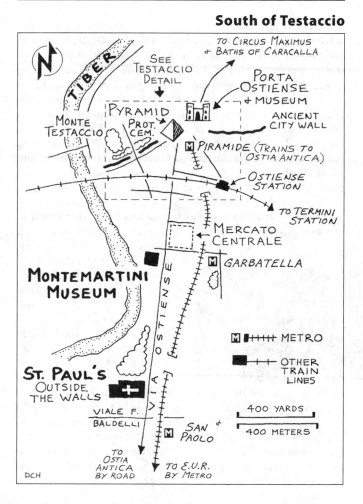

peaceful cloister—decorated with fragments from early Christian tombs and sarcophagi of people who wanted to be buried close to Paul (cloister closed 13:00–15:00).

The courtyard leading up to the church is typical of early Christian churches—even the first St. Peter's had this kind of welcoming zone (free, daily 7:00–18:00, modest dress code enforced, Via Ostiense 186, Metro: San Paolo).

E.U.R.

In the late 1930s, Italy's dictator, Benito Mussolini, planned an international exhibition to show off the wonders of his fascist society. But these wonders brought us World War II, and Il Duce's celebration never happened. The unfinished mega-project was

E.U.R.

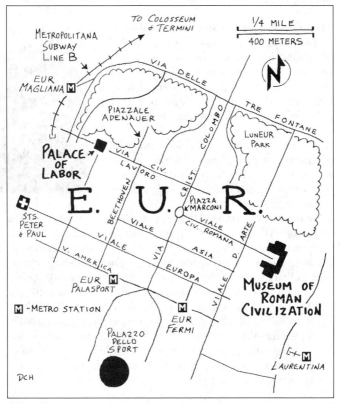

completed in the 1950s, and today it houses government offices and big, obscure museums filled with important, rarely visited relics.

If Hitler and Mussolini had won the war, our world might look like E.U.R. (AY-oor). Hike down E.U.R.'s wide, pedestrian-unfriendly boulevards. Patriotic murals, aren't-you-proud-to-be-an-extreme-right-winger pillars, and stern squares decorate the soulless planned grid and stark office blocks. Boulevards named for Astronomy, Electronics, Social Security, and Beethoven are more exhausting than inspirational. Today, E.U.R. is worth a trip for its Museum of Roman Civilization (described later in this section). And because a few landmark buildings of Italian modernism are located here and there, E.U.R. has become an important destination for architecture buffs.

The Metro skirts E.U.R. with three stops (10 min from the Colosseum). Use E.U.R. Magliana for the "Square Colosseum" and E.U.R. Fermi for the Museum of Roman Civilization. Consider walking 30 minutes from the palace to the museum through the center of E.U.R.

Palace of the Civilization of Labor (Palazzo della Città del Lavoro)—From the E.U.R. Magliana Metro stop, stairs lead uphill to this epitome of fascist architecture. With its giant, no-questions-asked patriotic statues and its black-and-white simplicity, this is E.U.R.'s tallest building and key landmark. It's understandably nicknamed the "Square Colosseum." Around the corner, Café Palombini is still decorated in a 1930s style and is quite popular with young Romans (daily 7:00–22:00; good gelato, pastries, and snacks; Piazzale Adenauer 12, tel. 06-591-1700).

▲**Museum of Roman Civilization (Museo della Città Romana)**—With 59 rooms of plaster casts and models illustrating the greatness of classical Rome, this vast and heavy museum gives a strangely lifeless, close-up look at Rome. Each room has a theme, from military tricks to musical instruments. One long hall is filled with casts of the reliefs of Trajan's Column. The highlight is the 1:250-scale model of Constantine's Rome, circa A.D. 300 (€6.20, Tue–Sun 9:00–14:00, last entry 1 hour before closing, closed Mon, Piazza G. Agnelli; leave the E.U.R. Fermi Metro station on Via America, turn right, and walk past McDonald's, then at T-intersection turn left and go uphill three blocks to Via dell'Arte, you'll see its colonnade on the right; tel. 06-592-6041).

Southeast Rome

Baths of Caracalla (Terme di Caracalla)—Inaugurated by Emperor Caracalla in A.D. 216, this massive bath complex could accommodate 1,600 visitors at a time. Today, it's just a shell—a huge shell—with all of its sculptures and most of its mosaics moved to museums. You'll see a two-story, roofless brick building surrounded by a garden, bordered by ruined walls. The two large rooms at either end of the building were used for exercise. In between the exercise rooms was a pool flanked by two small mosaic-floored dressing rooms. Niches in the walls once held statues.

In its day, this was a remarkable place to hang out. For ancient Romans, bathing was a social experience. The Baths of Caracalla functioned until Goths severed the aqueducts in the sixth century. In modern times, grand operas are performed here (€5, Mon 9:00–14:00, Tue–Sun 9:00–19:30, last entry 1 hour before closing, audioguide-€4, good €8 guidebook can be read in shaded garden while sitting on a chunk of column, Metro: Circus Maximus, plus a 5-minute walk south along Via delle Terme di Caracalla, tel.

The Appian Way

TO SAN SEBASTIANO GATE,
MUSEUM OF THE WALLS
& DOWNTOWN ROME

¼ MILE

.5 KM

N

DOMINE
QUO VADIS
CHURCH

B

C

VIA ARDEATINA

VIA APPIA

PEDESTRIAN WALKWAY

COLUMBARIUM

SECOND MILESTONE

**CATACOMBS
OF SAN
CALLISTO**

TO
FOSSE
ARDEANTINE

VIA D. SETTE CHIESE

C

B

VILLA
OF
MAXENTIUS

CIRCUS
OF
MAXENTIUS

**CATACOMBS
OF
SAN SEBASTIANO**

C

B

APPIA ANTICA

VIA PLATONIA

VIA DI SAN SEB.

TOMB OF
CECILIA
METELLA

VIA CECILIA METELLA

C

THIRD
MILESTONE

A

TO
AQUEDUCT
PARK

**CASA DELL'APPIA
ANTICA**
CAFÉ +
BIKE RENTAL

VIA CAPO DI BOVE

SCENIC
SECTION

A Bus #660 Stop
B Bus #118 Stops
C Archeobus Stops

DCH

TO 4TH THROUGH 11TH
MILESTONES + BRINDISI

06-3996-7700). The baths' statues are displayed elsewhere: Several are in Rome's Octagonal Hall, and the immense *Toro Farnese* (a marble sculpture of a bull surrounded by people) snorts in Naples' Archaeological Museum (see page 718).

▲**The Appian Way**—For a taste of the countryside around Rome and more wonders of Roman engineering, take the four-mile trip from the Colosseum out past the wall to a stretch of the ancient Appian Way, where the original pavement stones are lined by several interesting sights. Ancient Rome's first and greatest highway, the Appian Way once ran from Rome to the Adriatic port

Catacombs

The catacombs are burial places for (mostly) Christians who died in ancient Roman times. By law, no one was allowed to be buried within the walls of Rome. While pagan Romans were into cremation, Christians preferred to be buried (so that they could be resurrected when the time came). But land was expensive, and most Christians were poor. A few wealthy, landowning Christians allowed their property to be used as burial places.

The 40 or so known catacombs are scattered outside the ancient walls of Rome. From the first through the fifth centuries, Christians dug an estimated 375 miles of tomb-lined tunnels, with networks of galleries as many as five layers deep. The volcanic tufa stone that Rome sits atop—soft and easy to cut, but which hardens when exposed to air—was perfect for the job. The Christians burrowed many layers deep for two reasons: to get more mileage out of the donated land, and to be near martyrs and saints already buried there. Bodies were wrapped in linen (like Christ's). Since they figured the Second Coming was imminent, there was no interest in embalming the body.

When Emperor Constantine legalized Christianity in A.D. 313, Christians had a new, interesting problem: There would be no more recently persecuted martyrs to bind them together and inspire them. Instead, the early martyrs and popes assumed more importance, and Christians began making pilgrimages to their burial places in the catacombs.

In the 800s, when barbarian invaders started ransacking the tombs, Christians moved the relics of saints and martyrs to the safety of churches in the city center. For a thousand years, the catacombs were forgotten. In early modern times, they were

of Brindisi, the gateway to Greece. Today, you can walk (or bike) some stretches of the road, rattling over original paving stones, past crumbling monuments that once lined the sides.

The wonder of its day, the Appian Way (named after Appius Claudius Caecus, a Roman official) was the largest, widest, fastest road ever, called the "Queen of Roads." Built in 312 B.C., it connected Rome with Capua (near Naples), running in a straight line for much of the way, ignoring the natural contour of the land. Just as Hitler built the Autobahn system in anticipation of empire maintenance, the expansion-minded Roman government realized the military and political value of a good road system.

Today, the road and the landscape around it are preserved as a cultural park. For the tourist, the ancient Appian Way means three things: the road itself with its ruined monuments, the best two Christian catacombs open to visitors (described below), and the

excavated and became part of the Romantic Age's Grand Tour of Europe.

When abandoned plates and utensils from ritual meals were found, 18th- and 19th-century Romantics guessed that persecuted Christians hid out in these candlelit galleries. The popularity of this legend grew—even though it was untrue. By the second century, more than a million people lived in Rome, and the 10,000 early Christians no longer had to camp out in the catacombs. They hid in plain view, melting into obscurity within the city itself.

The underground tunnels, while empty of bones, are rich in early Christian symbolism, which functioned as a secret lan-

guage. The dove represented the soul. You'll see it quenching its thirst (worshipping), with an olive branch (at rest), or happily perched (in paradise). Peacocks, known for their purportedly "incorruptible flesh," embodied immortality. The shepherd with a lamb on his shoulders was the "good shepherd," the first portrayal of Christ as a kindly leader of his flock. The fish was used because the first letters of these words—"Jesus Christ, Son of God, Savior"—spelled "fish" in Greek. And the anchor is a cross in disguise. A second-century bishop had written on his tomb, "All who understand these things, pray for me." You'll see pictures of people praying with their hands raised up—the custom at the time.

peaceful atmosphere, which provides a respite from the city (especially when you take the pedestrian path). Be aware that the road today is busy with traffic—and actually quite treacherous in spots.

The road starts at the massive **San Sebastiano Gate and Museum of the Walls,** about two miles south of the Colosseum (€2.60, Tue–Sun 9:00–14:00, closed Mon, tel. 06-8205-9127). The stretch that's of most interest to tourists starts another two miles south of the gate.

Getting There: You can Ride the **Archeobus** from Termini train station (see "Tours," page 614). This stops at all the key attractions—you can hop off, tour the sights, and pick up a later bus (runs every 40 min).

For a Metro/bus option, consider **bus #118.** In Rome, take the Metro to the Circo Massimo Metro stop, then catch the #118 heading south; it'll stop at the San Sebastiano Gate, Quo Vadis

Church, Catacombs of San Callisto, and Catacombs of San Sebastiano. Another Metro/bus alternative is **bus #660** (take the Metro to the Colli Albani stop, then catch the bus), which takes you to the far end of the interesting section of the Appian Way (get off at the Tomb of Cecilia Metella); you can walk back along the Appian Way, tour the catacombs, and then catch bus #118 to return to Rome.

▲▲**Catacombs of San Sebastiano**—A guide leads you underground through the tunnels where early Christians were buried. You'll see faded frescoes and graffiti by early-Christian tag artists. Besides the catacombs themselves, there's a historic fourth-century basilica with holy relics (€5, includes 25-min tour, 2/hr, Mon–Sat 8:30–12:00 & 14:30–17:30, closed Sun and Nov, closes at 17:00 in winter, Via Appia Antica 136, tel. 06-785-0350).

▲▲**Catacombs of San Callisto**—The larger of the two Christian catacombs, San Callisto also is more prestigious, having been the burial site for several early popes. Of the two main catacombs, which is the best to visit? All in all, they're both quite similar, and either one will fit the bill (€5, includes tour, Thu–Tue 8:30–12:00 & 14:30–17:30, closed Wed and Feb, closes at 17:00 in winter, Via Appia Antica 110, tel. 06-5130-1580).

Near Rome

▲▲▲**Ostia Antica**—For an exciting day trip, pop down to the Roman port of Ostia, which is similar to Pompeii but a lot closer and, in some ways, more interesting. Because Ostia was a working port town, it shows a more complete and gritty look at Roman life than wealthy Pompeii. Wandering around today, you'll see the remains of the docks, warehouses, apartment flats, mansions, shopping arcades, and baths that served a once-thriving port of 60,000 people. Later, Ostia became a ghost town, and it's now excavated. Start at the 2,000-year-old theater, buy a map, explore the town, and finish with its fine little museum.

Getting There: Getting to Ostia Antica from downtown Rome is a snap—it's a 45-minute combination Metro/train ride. It'll cost you just one Metro ticket each way (your €1 Metro ticket also covers the train—so just €2 total round-trip). From Rome, take Metro line B to the Piramide stop (which really *is* next to a pyramid, and several other interesting sights—it's worth a quick stop, see page 673). At Piramide, the train tracks are just a few steps from the Metro tracks—follow signs to *Lido*. All trains depart in the direction *Lido*, leave every 15 minutes, and stop at Ostia Antica along the way. Hop on a train, ride for about 30 minutes (keep your Metro ticket handy), and get off at the Ostia Antica stop. Leaving the train station in Ostia Antica, cross the road via the blue sky-bridge and walk straight down Via della Stazione di Ostia

Antica, continuing straight until you reach the parking lot. The entrance is to your left.

Cost and Hours: €4, site—summer Tue–Sun 8:30–19:00, winter Tue–Sun 8:30–17:00, last entry 1 hour before closing, museum—Tue–Sat 9:00–13:30 & 14:15–18:30, Sun 9:30–13:30, closes 30 minutes before site in winter, both site and museum are closed on Mon, tel. 06-5635-8099, www.ostiaantica.net. A map of the site with suggested itineraries is available for €2 from the ticket office. Audioguides, when available, cost €5.

SLEEPING

The absolute cheapest beds in Rome are €20 in small, backpacker-filled hostels. A nicer hotel (about €140 with a bathroom and air-con) provides an oasis and refuge, making it easier to enjoy this intense and grinding city. If you're going door to door, prices are soft—so bargain. Built into a hotel's official price list is a kickback for a room-finding service or agency; if you're coming direct, they pay no kickback and may lower the price for you. Many hotels have high-season (mid-March–June, Sept–Oct) and low-season prices. If traveling outside of peak times, ask about a discount. Room rates are lowest in sweltering August. Easter, September, and Christmas are the most crowded and expensive (see list of holidays on page 844). Particularly on Easter (March 23 in 2008) and Saint Peter and Paul's Day (June 29), the entire city gets booked up.

Traffic in Rome roars. With the recent arrival of double-paned windows and air-conditioning, night noise is not the problem it once was. Even so, light sleepers who ask for a *tranquillo* room will likely get a room on the back...and sleep better.

Sleep Code

(€1 = about $1.30, country code: 39)
S = Single, **D** = Double/Twin, **T** = Triple, **Q** = Quad, **b** = bathroom, **s** = shower only. Breakfast is included in all but the cheapest places. Unless I note otherwise, the staff speaks English. You can assume a hotel takes credit cards unless you see "cash only" in the listing.

To help you sort easily through these listings, I've divided the rooms into three categories based on the price for a standard double room with bath:

$$$ **Higher Priced**—Most rooms €180 or more.
$$ **Moderately Priced**—Most rooms between €120–180.
$ **Lower Priced**—Most rooms €120 or less.

As you look over the listings, you'll notice that many hotels promise special prices to my readers who book direct (without using a room-finding service or hotel-booking website, which takes a commission). To get these rates, mention this book when you reserve, then show the book upon arrival. During slow times, rooms might be offered for even less than listed. To get the best price, first ask the price, then request the discount with the book. Many places prefer hard cash. "Rack rates" (the highest rates a hotel charges, usually to travel agencies and Web-booking services) are much higher.

Most hotels are eager to connect you with a shuttle service to the airport. It's reasonable and easy for departure, but upon arrival, I just catch a cab or the train into the city.

Almost no hotels have parking, but nearly all have a line on spots in a nearby garage (about €24/day).

Although I list only five, Rome has many convents that rent out rooms. See the Church of Santa Susanna's website for a long list (www.santasusanna.org, select "Coming to Rome"). At convents, the beds are twins and English is often in short supply, but the price is right.

Consider these nun-run places, all listed in this chapter: the expensive but divine **Casa di Santa Brigida** (near Campo de' Fiori), the **Suore di Santa Elisabetta** (near Santa Maria Maggiore), the **Istituto Il Rosario** (near Piazza Venezia), and the most user-friendly of all, **Casa per Ferie Santa Maria alle Fornaci dei Padri Trinitari** (near the Vatican).

Near Termini Train Station

While not as atmospheric as other areas of Rome, the hotels near Termini train station are less expensive, restaurants are plentiful, and the many public-transportation options link it easily with the entire city. The city's two Metro lines intersect at the station, and most buses leave from here. Piazza Venezia is a 20-minute walk down Via Nazionale.

Via Firenze

Via Firenze is safe, handy, central, and relatively quiet. It's a 10-minute walk from Termini train station and the airport shuttle, and two blocks beyond Piazza della Repubblica and the TI. The Defense Ministry is nearby, so you've got heavily armed guards watching over you all night.

The neighborhood is well-connected by public transportation (with the Repubblica Metro stop nearby). Virtually all the city buses that rumble down Via Nazionale (#64, #70, #115, #640, and the #40 express) take you to Piazza Venezia (Forum) and Largo Argentina (Pantheon). From Largo Argentina, the #64 bus

Hotels near Termini Train Station

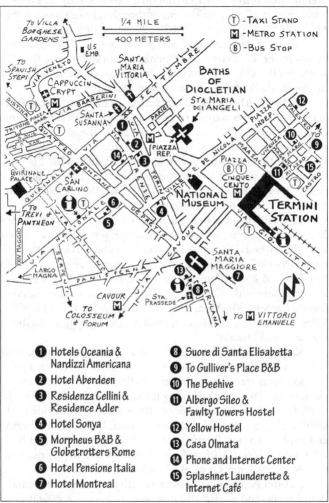

- ① Hotels Oceania & Nardizzi Americana
- ② Hotel Aberdeen
- ③ Residenza Cellini & Residence Adler
- ④ Hotel Sonya
- ⑤ Morpheus B&B & Globetrotters Rome
- ⑥ Hotel Pensione Italia
- ⑦ Hotel Montreal
- ⑧ Suore di Santa Elisabetta
- ⑨ To Gulliver's Place B&B
- ⑩ The Beehive
- ⑪ Albergo Sileo & Fawlty Towers Hostel
- ⑫ Yellow Hostel
- ⑬ Casa Olmata
- ⑭ Phone and Internet Center
- ⑮ Splashnet Launderette & Internet Café

(jammed with people and thieves) and the #40 express bus both continue to the Vatican. Or, at Largo Argentina, you can transfer to electric trolley #8 to Trastevere (get off at first stop after crossing the river).

A 24-hour **pharmacy** near the recommended hotels is Farmacia Piram (Via Nazionale 228, tel. 06-488-4437).

$$ Hotel Oceania is a peaceful slice of air-conditioned heaven. This 15-room, manor house–type hotel is spacious and quiet, with spotless, tastefully decorated rooms, run by a pleasant father-and-son team. While Armando (the dad) serves world-famous coffee,

Stefano (the son) works to maintain a caring family atmosphere with a fine staff and provides lots of thoughtful extra touches (Sb-€125, Db-€158, Tb-€190, Qb-€212, 20 percent less in Aug, 35 percent less in winter, large roof terrace, family suite, Internet access, videos in the TV lounge, Via Firenze 38, third floor, tel. 06-482-4696, fax 06-488-5586, www.hoteloceania.it, info@hoteloceania.it; Anna, Radu, and Enrico round out the staff).

$$ Hotel Aberdeen, which perfectly combines high quality and friendliness, is warmly run by Annamaria, with support from cousins Sabrina and Cinzia and sister Laura. The 37 comfy, modern, air-conditioned, and smoke-free rooms are a terrific value. Enjoy the frescoed breakfast room (Sb-€92, Db-€150, Tb-€165, Qb-€190, 30 percent less in Aug and winter, check website for deals, Via Firenze 48, tel. 06-482-3920, fax 06-482-1092, www.travel.it/roma/aberdeen, hotel.aberdeen@travel.it).

$$ Residenza Cellini is a gorgeous 11-room place that feels like the guest wing of a Neoclassical palace. It offers "ortho/anti-allergy beds" and four-star comforts and service (Db-€175, larger Db-€195, Tb-€200–220, spacious family apartment, extra bed-€25, €35 less in Aug and mid-Nov–mid-March, prices good through 2008 with this book and cash, air-con, terrace, elevator, Internet access, Via Modena 5, tel. 06-4782-5204, fax 06-4788-1806, www.residenzacellini.it, residenzacellini@tin.it; Barbara, Gaetano, and Donato).

$$ Residence Adler offers breakfast on a garden patio, wide halls, and eight quiet, simple, air-conditioned rooms in a good location (plus more rooms in their Bellesuite wing). It's run the old-fashioned way by a charming family (Db-€130, Tb-€170, Qb-€190, Quint/b-€220, these prices through 2008 with this book, additional 5 percent off if you pay with cash, 15 percent less in Aug and winter, elevator, Internet access, Via Modena 5, second floor, tel. 06-484-466, fax 06-488-0940, www.hoteladler-roma.com, info@hoteladler-roma.com, Alessandro).

$ Hotel Nardizzi Americana, with 33 pleasant, air-conditioned rooms and a delightful rooftop terrace, is an excellent value (Sb-€95, Db-€120, Tb-€150, Qb-€170, email them for instructions on getting these special Rick Steves rates in 2008, 15 percent discounts for off-season and long stays, additional 10 percent off any time with cash, elevator, Internet access, Via Firenze 38, fourth floor, tel. 06-488-0035, fax 06-488-0368, www.hotelnardizzi.it, info@hotelnardizzi.it, Mario).

Between Via Nazionale and Santa Maria Maggiore

$$ Hotel Sonya is small and family-run but impersonal, with 23 well-equipped rooms, a central location, and decent prices (Sb-€90, Db-€130, Tb-€150, Qb-€170, Quint/b-€185, 5 percent less if you pay cash, 30 percent less off-season, air-con, elevator, faces the opera at Via Viminale 58, Metro: Repubblica or Termini, tel. 06-481-9911, fax 06-488-5678, www.hotelsonya.it, info@hotelsonya .it, Francesca and Litu).

$$ Morpheus B&B is a cozy, quiet, and minimal place renting 10 rooms and serving breakfast in your room (Sb-€90, Db-€130, Tb-€160, Qb-€180, 15 percent Rick Steves discount in 2008 if you book direct and ask for discount when you reserve, elevator, Via Palermo 36, fourth floor, tel. 06-4890-5582, fax 06-474-1679, www.morpheusbb.it, info@morpheusbb.it, Katty).

$ Hotel Pensione Italia, in a busy, interesting, and handy locale, is placed safely on a quiet street next to the Ministry of the Interior. Thoughtfully run by Andrea, Sabrina, Nadine, and Gabriel, it has 31 comfortable, clean, and bright rooms (Sb-€80, Db-€120, Tb-€160, Qb-€180, all rooms 30 percent less mid-July–Aug and Nov–mid-March, air-con-€10 extra per day, elevator, Internet access, Via Venezia 18, just off Via Nazionale, Metro: Repubblica or Termini, tel. 06-482-8355, fax 06-474-5550, www .hotelitaliaroma.com, info@hotelitaliaroma.com). While you need to secure your reservation with a credit card, they accept cash only for payment. They also have eight decent annex rooms across the street.

$ Hotel Montreal, run with care, is a bright, solid, business-class place with 27 rooms on a big street a block southeast of Santa Maria Maggiore (special Rick Steves rates for 2008: Sb-€95, Db-€120, Tb-€150; in July–Aug and Jan–Feb rates drop to Db-€95, Tb-€130; air-con, elevator, Internet access, good security, Via Carlo Alberto 4, 1 block from Metro: Vittorio Emanuele, 3 blocks west of Termini train station, tel. 06-445-7797, fax 06-446-5522, www.hotelmontrealroma.com, info@hotelmontrealroma.com, Pasquale).

$ Suore di Santa Elisabetta is a heavenly Polish-run convent with a peaceful garden and tidy twin-bedded (only) rooms. Often booked long in advance, with such tranquility, it's a super value (S-€40, Sb-€48, D-€64, Db-€83, Tb-€106, Qb-€128, Quint/b-€142, elevator, fine view roof terrace and breakfast hall, 23:00 curfew, a block southwest of Santa Maria Maggiore at Via dell'Olmata 9, Metro: Termini or Vittorio Emanuele, tel. 06-488-8271, fax 06-488-4066, ist.it.s.elisabetta@libero.it, Anna).

$ Gulliver's Place B&B has five fun, nicely decorated rooms in a large, secure building next to a university (D-€85, Db-€95, Tb-€125, less off-season, air-con, elevator, east of Termini train station, 100 yards from Metro: Castro Pretorio at Viale Castro Pretorio 25, tel. 06-4470-4012, mobile 393-917-3040, www .gulliversplace.com, stay@gulliversplace.com, Simon and Sara). They run another B&B on Via Cavour (Db-€110).

Sleeping Cheaply, Northeast of the Train Station

The cheapest beds in town are northeast of the Termini train station (Metro: Termini). Some travelers feel this area is weird and spooky after dark, but these hotels feel plenty safe. With your back to the train tracks, turn right and walk two blocks out of the station. **Splashnet** launderette/Internet café is handy if you're staying in this area (just off Via Milazzo at Via Varese 33, €6 self-serve wash and dry, Internet access-€1.50/hr, €2 luggage storage per day—or free if you wash and go online, daily 8:30–24:00, mobile 3906-4938-0450).

$ **The Beehive** gives vagabonds—old and young—a cheap, clean, and comfy home in Rome, thoughtfully and creatively run by a friendly young American couple, Steve and Linda. They offer six great-value, artsy-mod double rooms (D-€75) and an eight-bed dorm (€22 bunks, Internet access, private garden terrace, cheery café, 2 blocks north of Termini train station at Via Marghera 8, tel. 06-4470-4553, www.the-beehive.com, info@the-beehive.com). Steve and Linda also run a B&B-booking service (private rooms and apartments in the old center of Rome, Florence, and Venice; rates start at €30 per person, check out your options at www.cross -pollinate.com).

$ **Albergo Sileo,** with shiny chandeliers, has a contract to house train conductors who work the night shift—so its 10 simple, pleasant rooms are usually rentable from 19:00 to 9:00 only (though sometimes you can get one for the full day). If you can handle this, it's a wonderful value. During the day, they store your luggage, and though you won't have access to a room, you're welcome to shower or hang out in the homey lobby or bar (D-€55, Db-€65, Tb-€75, Db for 24 hours-€70 when available, cash only, elevator, Via Magenta 39, fourth floor, tel. & fax 06-445-0246, www .hotelsileo.com, info@hotelsileo.com; friendly Alessandro and Maria Savioli don't speak English, but their daughter Anna does).

Hostels and Backpacker Dorm Beds near the Station

$ **Yellow Hostel** rents 130 beds mostly in 4- and 6-bed co-ed dorms ranging from about €24 to €34 per bed, depending on plumbing, size, and season. It's well-run with fine facilities, including lockers and free Internet access (6 blocks from the station, just past Via Vicenze at Via Palestro 44, tel. 06-493-82682, www.the-yellow .com).

$ **Casa Olmata** is a ramshackle, laid-back backpackers' place a block southwest of Santa Maria Maggiore, midway between Termini train station and the Colosseum (50 beds, dorm beds-€22, S-€38, D-€57, Qb-€100, rooftop terrace with views and twice-weekly spaghetti parties, communal kitchen, Via dell'Olmata 36, third floor, Metro: Vittorio Emanuele, tel. 06-483-019, fax 06-486-819, www.casaolmata.com, info@casaolmata.com, Mirella and Marco).

$ Globetrotters Rome is a fun little hostel in a safe and handy location. Its 22 beds in cramped quarters work fine for backpackers (€24 per bunk in 8-bed dorm, €28 per bunk in 6-bed dorm, includes breakfast, small kitchen, closed 12:00–16:00, 1:00 curfew, Via Palermo 36, tel. 06-481-7680, www.globetrottersrome .net, info@globetrottersrome.net). For similar backpacker dives, see www.backpackers.it.

$ Fawlty Towers Hostel is well-run and ideal for backpackers arriving by train. It offers 50 beds and lots of fun, games, and extras (4-bed dorms-€23 per person, S-€55, D-€65, Db-€80, Q-€90, includes sheets, from station walk a block down Via Marghera and turn right to Via Magenta 39, tel. & fax 06-445-0374, www .fawltytowers.org, info@fawltytowers.org). Their nearby annex, **Bubbles,** offers similar beds and rates and shares the same reception desk.

Near Ancient Rome

Stretching from the Colosseum to Piazza Venezia along the barren boulevard called Via dei Fori Imperiali, this area is central. Sightseers are a short walk from the Colosseum, Roman Forum, and Trajan's Column. Busy Piazza Venezia—the geographical center of the city—is a major hub for city buses.

Near the Colosseum

$$ Hotel Paba has seven rooms, chocolate-box-tidy and lovingly cared for by Alberta Castelli. Though it overlooks busy Via Cavour just two blocks from the Colosseum, it's quiet enough (Db-€135, extra bed-€40, 5 percent discount if you pay cash, huge beds, breakfast served in room, air-con, elevator, Via Cavour 266, Metro: Cavour, tel. 06-4782-4902, fax 06-4788-1225, www .hotelpaba.com, info@hotelpaba.com).

$$ Hotel Lancelot is a homey yet elegant refuge—a 60-room hotel with the ambience of a B&B. It's quiet and safe, with a shady courtyard, restaurant, bar, and communal sixth-floor terrace. Some rooms have private terraces big enough to host friends. Well-run by Faris and Lubna Khan, it's popular with returning guests (Sb-€115, Db-€175, Tb-€198, Qb-€235, €10 extra for first-floor terrace room, €15 extra for sixth floor, air-con, elevator, wheelchair-accessible, parking-€10/day, 10-min walk behind Colosseum near San Clemente Church at Via Capo d'Africa 47, tel. 06-7045-0615, fax 06-7045-0640, www.lancelothotel.com, info@lancelothotel .com, Lubna speaks the Queen's English).

$ Hotel Ferraro is a tiny and minimal place with 10 fine rooms run by Pina and her daughter Manuela from an office 30 yards down the street (prices for Db vary wildly from €80–120—email

Hotels near Ancient Rome

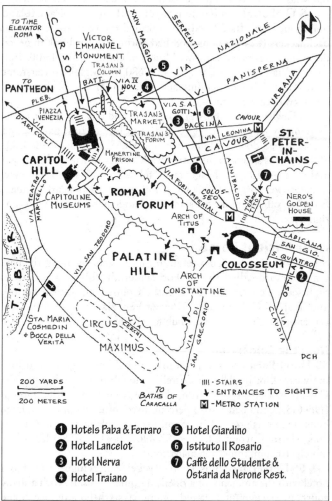

● Hotels Paba & Ferraro
● Hotel Lancelot
● Hotel Nerva
● Hotel Traiano
● Hotel Giardino
● Istituto Il Rosario
● Caffè dello Studente & Ostaria da Nerone Rest.

for a quote, 6 rooms are on peaceful back side, 4 are on the busy street, Via Cavour 266, office at Via Cavour 286, tel. 06-4890-6292, fax 06-474-3683, www.hotelferraro.com, info@hotelferraro .com).

Near Piazza Venezia

To locate these hotels, see the map above.

$$$ Hotel Nerva is a three-star slice of tranquility on a surprisingly quiet back street just steps away from the Roman Forum. Its 19 rooms come with elegant touches, including exposed-beam ceilings and balconies or floor-to-ceiling windows. It's run by brothers Umberto and Amelio, with the help of daughter Anna (Sb-€150, Db-€180, Qb with loft-€350, extra bed-€45, ask for Rick Steves discount, rates very soft—especially off-season, they also have three rooms in a nearby apartment for the same prices, big breakfast, air-con, elevator, Via Tor de' Conti 3, tel. 06-678-1835, fax 06-6992-2204, www.hotelnerva.com, info@hotelnerva.com).

$$ Hotel Traiano is a grand old four-star hotel across a busy street from Trajan's Forum, with plush and generous public spaces, an ornate breakfast hall, and 40 comfy rooms—a good value considering the amenities offered and killer location (Db-€160 most of the year, €240 during festivals, €110 off-season, 26 rooms on the street, 14 on the quiet back side—worth requesting, Via IV Novembre, tel. 06-678-3862, fax 06-678-3674, www.hoteltraiano .it, htraiano@tin.it).

$$ Hotel Giardino, thoughtfully run by Englishwoman Kate (and Sergio), offers 11 pleasant rooms in a central location three blocks northeast of Piazza Venezia. With a tiny central lobby and a small breakfast room, it suits travelers who prize location over big-hotel amenities (March–mid-July and Sept–mid-Nov: Sb-€85, Db-€130; mid-July–Aug and mid-Nov–Feb: Sb-€60, Db-€90, one smaller Db for 15 percent less; these prices promised through 2008 with this book and cash, check website for specials, air-con, effective double-paned windows, on a busy street off Piazza di Quirinale at Via XXIV Maggio 51, tel. 06-679-4584, fax 06-679-5155, www .hotel-giardino-roma.com, info@hotel-giardino-roma.com).

$ Istituto Il Rosario is a peaceful, well-run Dominican convent renting 40 rooms to both pilgrims and tourists in a good neighborhood (S-€40, Sb-€50, Db-€86, Tb-€117, roof terrace, 23:00 curfew, midway between the Quirinale and Colosseum near bottom of Via Nazionale at Via Sant'Agata dei Goti 10, bus #40 or #170 from Termini, tel. 06-679-2346, fax 06-6994-1106, irodopre@tin.it).

In the Pantheon Neighborhood (The Heart of Rome)

Winding, narrow lanes filled with foot traffic and lined with boutique shops and tiny trattorias...this is village Rome at its best. You'll pay for the atmosphere, but this is where you want to be—especially at night, when Romans and tourists gather in the floodlit piazzas for the evening stroll, the *passeggiata*.

Near Campo de' Fiori

You'll pay a premium (and endure a little extra night noise) to stay in the old center. But each of these places is romantically set deep in the tangled back streets near the idyllic Campo de' Fiori and, for

Hotels in the Heart of Rome

❶	Casa di Santa Brigida	❹	Hotel Nazionale
❷	Hotel Smeraldo	❺	Albergo Santa Chiara
❸	Dipendenza Smeraldo	❻	Hotel Due Torri

many, worth the extra money.

$$$ Casa di Santa Brigida overlooks the elegant Piazza Farnese. With soft-spoken sisters gliding down polished hall-ways and pearly gates instead of doors, this lavish 20-room con-vent makes exhaust-stained Roman tourists feel like they've died and gone to heaven. If you don't need a double bed, this is worth the splurge (Sb-€110, twin Db-€190, 3 percent extra if you pay with credit card, air-con, tasty €20 dinners, roof garden, plush library, Monserrato 54, tel. 06-6889-2596, fax 06-6889-1573, hesselblad@tiscalinet.it, many of the sisters are from India and speak English). If you get no response to your fax or email within three days, consider that a "no."

$$ Hotel Smeraldo, with 50 rooms, is well-run, clean, and a great deal (Sb-€100, Db-€130, Tb-€150, 25 percent less off-season, buffet breakfast-€7, centrally controlled air-con, elevator, flowery roof terrace, midway between Campo de' Fiori and Largo Argentina at Vicolo dei Chiodaroli 9, tel. 06-687-5929, fax 06-6880-5495, www.smeraldoroma.com, albergosmeraldoroma@tin.it, Massimo).

$ Dipendenza Smeraldo, run by Hotel Smeraldo, offers 16 modern, high-ceilinged rooms in an adjacent building. It offers similar comforts for a little less money (Sb-€100, Db-€120, ask for Rick Steves discount, €25 less off-season, breakfast-€7 extra, air-con, elevator, roof terrace, Via dei Chiavari 32, same contact info as Hotel Smeraldo, above).

In the Jewish Ghetto
To locate this hotel, see map on page 670.

$$ Hotel Arenula, with 50 decent rooms, is the only hotel in Rome's old Jewish ghetto. While it has the ambience of a gym and attracts lots of students, it's a fine value in the thick of old Rome (Sb-€95, Db-€128, Tb-€149, 5 percent off with this book in high season of 2008, about 25 percent less off-season, extra bed-€21, air-con, just off Via Arenula at Via Santa Maria de' Calderari 47, tel. 06-687-9454, fax 06-689-6188, www.hotelarenula.com, hotel.arenula@flashnet.it, Rosanna).

Near the Pantheon
These places are buried in the pedestrian-friendly heart of ancient Rome, each within a four-minute walk of the Pantheon. You'll pay more here—but you'll save time and money by being exactly where you want to be for your early and late wandering.

$$$ Hotel Nazionale, a four-star landmark, is a 16th-century palace that shares a well-policed square with the Parliament building. Its 92 rooms are accentuated by lush public spaces, fancy bars, a uniformed staff, and a marble-floored restaurant. It's a big, stuffy hotel with a revolving front door, but it's a worthy splurge if you want security, comfort, and ancient Rome at your doorstep (Sb-€223, Db-€340, giant deluxe Db-€470, extra person-€67, ask for 10 percent Rick Steves discount in 2008; cheaper in Aug, winter, and when slow—check online for summer and weekend discounts; air-con, elevator, Piazza Montecitorio 131, tel. 06-695-001, fax 06-678-6677, www.nazionaleroma.it, hotel@nazionaleroma.it).

$$$ Albergo Santa Chiara is big, solid, and hotelesque. Flavia, Silvio, and their fine staff offer marbled elegance (but basic furniture) and all the hotel services in the old center. Its ample public lounges are dressy and professional, and its 100 rooms are quiet and spacious (Sb-€138, Db-€215, Tb-€260, book online direct and request these special Rick Steves rates, check website for better slow-time deals, elevator, behind Pantheon at Via di Santa Chiara 21, tel. 06-687-2979, fax 06-687-3144, www.albergosantachiara .com, info@albergosantachiara.com).

$$$ Hotel Due Torri, hiding out on a tiny, quiet street, is a little overpriced but beautifully located. It feels professional yet homey, with an accommodating staff, generous public spaces, and 26 comfortable rooms scattered by a higgledy-piggledy floor plan (Sb-€120, Db-€195, family apartment-€250 for 3 and €275 for 4, air-con, a block off Via della Scrofa at Vicolo del Leonetto 23, tel. 06-6880-6956, fax 06-686-5442, www.hotelduetorriroma.com, hotelduetorri@mclink.it).

In Trastevere

Colorful and genuine in a gritty sort of way, Trastevere is a treat for travelers looking for a less touristy and more bohemian atmosphere. Choices are few here, but by trekking across the Tiber, you can have the experience of being comfortably immersed in old Rome. To locate the following two places, see the map on page 670.

$$$ Hotel Santa Maria sits like a lazy hacienda in the midst of Trastevere. Surrounded by a medieval skyline, you'll feel as if you're on some romantic stage set. Its 19 small but well-equipped, air-conditioned rooms—former cells in a cloister—are all on the ground floor, as are a few suites for up to six people. The rooms circle a gravelly courtyard of orange trees and stay-awhile patio furniture (Db-€180, Tb-€220, you must pay cash and stay at least three nights to get these 20–25 percent discounted rates, which are promised through 2008 with this book; bigger discounts off-season, family rooms, free loaner bikes and Internet access; face church on Piazza Maria Trastevere and go right down Via della Fonte d'Olio 50 yards to Vicolo del Piede 2; tel. 06-589-4626, fax 06-589-4815, www.htlsantamaria.com, hotelsantamaria@libero.it, Stefano).

$$ Casa San Giuseppe is down a characteristic, laundry-strewn lane with views of Aurelian walls. While convent-owned, it's a secular place renting 29 plain but peaceful, spacious, and spotless rooms (Sb-€110, Db-€150, Tb-€180, Qb-€210, garden-facing rooms are quiet, air-con, elevator, parking-€15, just north of Piazza Trilussa at Vicolo Moroni 22, tel. 06-5833-3490, fax 06-5833-5754, casasangiuseppe@fastwebnet.it, Germano).

Near Vatican City

Sleeping near the Vatican is expensive, but some enjoy calling this neighborhood home. Even though it's handy to the Vatican (when the rapture hits, you're right there), everything else is a long way away. The first two hotels listed here offer free airport transfers for guests, though you must reserve when you book your room and wait for a scheduled shuttle (every two hours).

Hotels and Restaurants near Vatican City

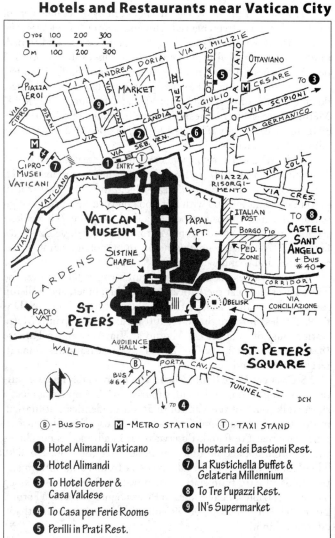

Oyds 100 200 300
Om 100 200 300

(B) – BUS STOP   M – METRO STATION   (T) – TAXI STAND

1 Hotel Alimandi Vaticano
2 Hotel Alimandi
3 To Hotel Gerber & Casa Valdese
4 To Casa per Ferie Rooms
5 Perilli in Prati Rest.

6 Hostaria dei Bastioni Rest.
7 La Rustichella Buffet & Gelateria Millennium
8 To Tre Pupazzi Rest.
9 IN's Supermarket

$$$ Hotel Alimandi Vaticano, facing the Vatican Museum, is beautifully designed. Run by the Alimandi family (Enrico, Irene, Germano), it features four stars, 24 spacious rooms, and all the modern comforts you can imagine (Sb-€170, standard Db-€200, big Db with 2 double beds-€230, Tb-€260, 5 percent discount if you pay cash, air-con, elevator, Viale Vaticano 99, Metro: Cipro–Musei Vaticani, tel. 06-397-45562, fax 06-397-30132, www.alimandi.it, alimandi@hotelalimandie.191.it).

$$ Hotel Alimandi is a good value, run by other members of the friendly and entrepreneurial Alimandi family—Paolo, Grazia, Luigi, Marta, and Barbara. Their 35 rooms are air-conditioned, modern, and marbled in white (Sb-€90, Db-€160, Tb-€190, 5 percent discount if you pay cash, elevator, grand buffet breakfast served in great roof garden, small gym, pool table, piano lounge, down the stairs directly in front of Vatican Museum, Via Tunisi 8, Metro: Cipro–Musei Vaticani, reserve by phone at tel. 06-3972-3941, toll-free in Italy tel. 800-122-121, fax 06-3972-3943, www .alimandi.it, alimandi@tin.it).

$$ Hotel Gerber, set in a quiet residential area, is modern and air-conditioned, with 27 well-polished, businesslike rooms (two S without air-con-€60, Sb-€105, Db-€145, Tb-€165, Qb-€185; 10 percent discount in 2008 with this book on their best price in high season, 15 percent in low season; Via degli Scipioni 241, at inter-section with Ezio, a block from Metro: Lepanto, tel. 06-321-6485, fax 06-321-7048, www.hotelgerber.it, info@hotelgerber.it; Peter, Simonetta, and friendly dog Kira).

$ Casa Valdese is an efficient church-run hotel just over the Tiber River and near the Vatican, with 35 big, quiet, and well-run rooms. It feels safe if a bit institutional (two external Sb-€49, Db-€119, €10 less for 3-night stays, 100 yards from Lepanto Metro station, just off Via Piazza Magno at Via Alessandro Farnese 18, tel. 06-321-5362, fax 06-321-1843, www.casavaldeseroma.it, reception@casavaldeseroma.it).

$ Casa per Ferie Santa Maria alle Fornaci dei Padri Trini-tari houses pilgrims and secular tourists with simple class just a short walk south of the Vatican in 54 stark, identical, utilitarian, mostly twin-bedded rooms. This is the most user-friendly convent-type place that I've found. Reserve as far in advance as possible—they're often booked up to a year in advance (Sb-€60, Db-€90, Tb-€125, air-con, elevator; take bus #64 from Termini train sta-tion to San Pietro train station, then walk 100 yards north along Via della Stazione di San Pietro to Piazza Santa Maria alle Fornaci 27; tel. 06-393-67632, fax 06-393-66795, www.trinitaridematha.it, cffornaci@tin.it).

EATING

Romans spend their evenings eating rather than drinking, and the preferred activity is simply to enjoy a fine, slow meal, buried deep in the old city. Rome's a fun and cheap place to eat, with countless little eateries that serve memorable €20 meals.

Although I've listed a number of restaurants, I recommend that you just head for a scenic area and explore. Piazza Navona, the Pantheon area, Campo de' Fiori, and Trastevere are neighborhoods packed with characteristic eateries. Sitting with tourists on a famous square and enjoying the scene works fine. (As my Roman friend explained: "When you're in a bad restaurant, the best way to survive is bread, olive oil, and salt.") But for more of a local flavor, consider my recommendations. In general, I'm impressed by how small the price difference is from a mediocre restaurant to a fine one. You can pay about 20 percent more for double the quality.

Trastevere

Colorful Trastevere is now pretty touristy. Still, Romans join the tourists to eat on the rustic side of the Tiber River. Start at the central square (Piazza Santa Maria). Then choose: Eat with tourists enjoying the ambience of the famous square, or wander the back streets in search of a mom-and-pop place with barely a menu. My recommendations are within a few minutes' walk of each other (between Piazza Santa Maria Trastevere and Ponte Sisto; see map on page 670).

Trattoria da Lucia lets you enjoy simple, traditional food at a good price in a great scene. It offers the quintessential, rustic, 100 percent Roman Trastevere dining experience and has been family-run since World War II. You'll meet Renato, his uncle Ennio, and Ennio's mom—pictured on the menu in the 1950s. The family specialty is *spaghetti alla Gricia,* with pancetta bacon (inexpensive, Tue–Sun 12:30–15:30 & 19:30–24:00, closed Mon, cash only, homey indoor or evocative outdoor seating, Vicolo del Mattonato 2, tel. 06-580-3601, some English spoken).

Trattoria "da Olindo" takes homey to extremes. You really feel like you dropped in on a family that cooks for the neighborhood to supplement their income (cheap, Mon–Sat dinner from 20:00 until late, closed Sun, cash only, indoor and funky cobbled outdoor seating, on the corner of Vicolo della Scala and Via del Mattonato at #8, tel. 06-581-8835).

Osteria Ponte Sisto, small and Mediterranean, specializes in Neapolitan cuisine with a menu that changes daily. Just outside the tourist zone, it caters mostly to Romans and offers beautiful desserts and a fine value (daily 12:30–15:30 & 19:30–24:00, Via Ponte Sisto 80, tel. 06-588-3411). It's easy to find: Crossing Ponte Sisto (pedestrian bridge) toward Trastevere, continue across the little square (Piazza Trilussa) and you'll see it on the right.

Ristorante Checco er Carettiere is a big, classic, family-run place that's been a Trastevere fixture for four generations. With white tablecloths, well-presented food, and dressy local diners, this is *the* place for a special meal in Trastevere. While it's a bit pricey, you'll eat well amidst lots of fun commotion (€13 pastas, €16 *secondi,* daily 12:30–15:00 & 19:30–23:30, reservations smart, Via Benedetta 10/13, tel. 06-580-0985).

Gelato: **Gelateria alla Scala** is a terrific little ice-cream shop that dishes up delightful cinnamon *(cannella)* and oh-wow pistachio (daily 12:00–24:00, Piazza della Scala 51, across from the church on Piazza della Scala). Seek this place out.

In the Heart of Rome

On and near Campo de' Fiori

While it is touristy, Campo de' Fiori offers a sublimely romantic setting. And, since it's so close to the collective heart of Rome, it remains popular with locals. For greater atmosphere than food value, circle the square, considering your choices. The square is lined with popular and interesting bars, pizzerias, and small restaurants—all great for people-watching over a glass of wine.

Ristorante la Carbonara is a venerable standby with the ultimate Campo de' Fiori outdoor setting and dressy waiters. While the service gets mixed reviews, the food and Italian ambience are wonderful. Meals on small surrounding streets may be a better value, but they lack that Campo de' Fiori magic. While La Carbonara's on-square dining is classic, the big room upstairs is good too (€10 pastas, €15 *secondi*, Wed–Mon 9:00–15:30 & 16:30–24:00, closed Tue, Campo de' Fiori 23, tel. 06-686-4783).

Osteria da Giovanni ar Galletto is nearby, on the more elegant and peaceful Piazza Farnese. Angelo entertains an upscale local crowd and offers magical outdoor seating. Regrettably, service can be horrible and single diners aren't treated very well. Still, if you're in no hurry and ready to savor my favorite *al fresco* setting in Rome (while humoring the waiters), this is a good bet (Mon–Sat 12:15–15:00 & 19:30–23:00, closed Sun, tucked in corner of Piazza Farnese at #102, tel. 06-686-1714).

Osteria Enoteca al Bric is a mod bistro-type place run by Maurizio, a man who loves to cook, serve good wine, and listen to jazz. With only the finest ingredients, and an ambience elegant in its simplicity, he's created the perfect package for a romantic night out. Wine-case lids decorate the wall like happy memories. With candlelit grace and few tourists, it's perfect for the wine snob in the mood for pasta and fine cheese. Aficionados choose their bottle from the huge selection lining the walls near the entrance. Beginners order fine wine by the glass with help from the waiter when they order their meal (daily 12:30–15:00 & from 19:30 for dinner, closed Mon June–Sept, reserve after 20:30, 100 yards off Campo de' Fiori at Via del Pellegrino 51, tel. 06-687-9533). Al Bric offers my readers a special "Taste of Italy for Two" deal (fine plate of mixed cheeses and meats with two glasses of full-bodied red wine and a pitcher of water) for €22 from 19:30, but you may need to finish by 20:30. This could be a light meal if you're kicking off an evening stroll, a substantial appetizer, or a way to check this place

Restaurants in the Heart of Rome

- ❶ Ristorante la Carbonara
- ❷ Ostaria da Giovanni ar Galletto
- ❸ Osteria Enoteca al Bric
- ❹ Filetti de Baccala
- ❺ Trattoria der Pallaro
- ❻ Hostaria Costanza
- ❼ Cul de Sac & L'Insalata Ricca
- ❽ L'Antica Birreria Peroni
- ❾ Rist. Pizzeria Sacro e Profano
- ❿ Gelateria San Crispino

out for a serious meal later. While Al Bric can be pricey, feel free to establish a price limit (e.g., €40 per person) and trust Maurizio to feed you well.

Filetti de Baccala, a tradition for many Romans, is basically a fish bar with paper tablecloths and cheap prices. Its grease-stained, harried waiters serve old-time favorites—€4 fried cod fillets, a strange bitter *puntarelle* salad, and their antipasto (anchovies with butter on Wonder bread)—to nostalgic locals. Study what others are eating and order by pointing. Nothing is expensive (see the menu on the wall). Urchins can get a cod stick to go and sit on the barnacle church doorsteps just outside. Say *ciao* to Marcello, who runs the place like a swim coach (Mon–Sat 17:00–22:30, closed Sun, cash only, a block east of Campo de' Fiori, tumbling onto long tables in a tiny and atmospheric square, Largo dei Librari 88, tel. 06-686-4018).

Trattoria der Pallaro, which has no menu, has a slogan: "Here, you'll eat what we want to feed you." Paola Fazi—with a towel wrapped around her head turban-style—and her family serve up a five-course meal of typically Roman food for €22, including wine, coffee, and a tasty mandarin-juice finale. Make like Oliver Twist asking for more soup and get seconds on the juice. As many locals return every day, each evening features a different menu (daily 12:00–15:00 & 19:00–24:00, indoor/outdoor seating on quiet square, a block south of Corso Vittorio Emanuele, down Largo del Chiavari to Largo del Pallaro 15, tel. 06-6880-1488).

Hostaria Costanza has crisp-vested waiters, a local following, and lots of energy. You'll eat traditional Roman cuisine on a ramshackle patio or inside under arches from the ancient Pompeo Theater (Mon–Sat 12:30–15:00 & 19:30–23:30, closed Sun, Piazza Paradiso 63, tel. 06-686-1717).

Piazza Pasquino

Located just a block off Piazza Navona (toward Campo de' Fiori) on Piazza Pasquino, these bustling places have low prices and a happy clientele. As they are neighbors and each is completely different, check both before choosing.

Cul de Sac is packed with enthusiastic locals cobbling together fun meals from an Italian dim sum–type menu of traditional dishes (daily 12:00–16:00 & 18:00–24:00).

L'Insalata Ricca is a popular chain that specializes in hearty and healthy €7 salads and much less healthy pizzas (daily 12:00–15:45 & 18:45–24:00, tel. 06-6830-7881).

Near the Trevi Fountain

L'Antica Birreria Peroni is Rome's answer to a German beer hall. Serving hearty mugs of the local Peroni beer and lots of just plain fun beer-hall food, the place is a hit with locals for a cheap night out (Mon–Sat 12:00–24:00, closed Sun, midway between Trevi Fountain and Capitol Hill, a block off Via del Corso at Via di San Marcello 19, tel. 06-679-5310).

Ristorante Pizzeria Sacro e Profano fills an old church with spicy south Italian (Calabrian) cuisine; some pricey, exotic dishes; and satisfied tourists. Run with enthusiasm and passion by Pasquale and friends, this is just far enough away from the Trevi mobs. Their hearty €15 *antipasti* plate offers a delightful montage of Calabrian taste treats—plenty of food for a light, memorable meal (daily 12:00–15:00 & 18:00–24:00, a block off Via del Tritone at Via dei Maroniti 29, tel. 06-679-1836). And for dessert...

Gelato: Around the corner, **Gelateria San Crispino,** well-respected by locals, serves particularly tasty gourmet gelato using creative ingredients. Because of their commitment to natural ingredients, the colors are muted and they serve cups, but no cones (Wed–Mon 12:00–24:00, closed Tue, Via della Panetteria 42, tel. 06-679-3924).

Near the Pantheon

Eating on the square facing the Pantheon is a temptation (there's even a McDonald's that offers some of the best outdoor seating in town), and I'd consider it just to relax and enjoy the Roman scene. But if you walk a block or two away, you'll get less view and better value. Here are some suggestions:

Ristorante da Fortunato is an Italian classic, with fresh flowers on the tables and white-coated, black-tie waiters politely serving good meat and fish to local politicians, foreign dignitaries, and tourists with good taste. Don't leave without perusing the photos of their famous visitors—everyone from former Iraqi Foreign Minister Tariq Aziz to Bill Clinton seems to have eaten here. All are pictured with the boss, Fortunato, who, since 1975, has been a master of simple edible elegance. The outdoor seating is fine for watching the river of Roman street life flow by, but the atmosphere is inside. For a dressy night out, this is a reliable and surprisingly reasonable choice—but be sure to reserve ahead (plan to spend €45 per person, Mon–Sat 12:30–15:00 & 19:30–23:30, closed Sun, a block in front of the Pantheon at Via del Pantheon 55, tel. 06-679-2788).

Ristorante Enoteca Corsi is a wine shop that grew into a thriving lunch-only restaurant. The Paiella family serves straightforward, traditional cuisine at great prices to an appreciative crowd of office workers. Check the blackboard for daily specials (gnocchi on Thursday, fish on Friday, and so on). Friendly Juliana, Claudia, and Manuela welcome diners to step into their wine shop and pick out a bottle. For the cheap take-away price, plus €2, they'll uncork it at your table. With €6 pastas, €9.50 main dishes, and fine wine at a third of the price you'd pay in normal restaurants, this can be a superb value (Mon–Sat 12:00–15:00, closed Sun, a block toward the Pantheon from the Gesù Church at Via del Gesù 87, no reservations possible, tel. 06-679-0821).

Miscellanea is run by much-loved Mikki, who's on a mission to keep foreign students well-fed. You'll find cheap pasta, hearty and fresh €3 sandwiches, and a long list of €6 salads. Mikki often tosses in a fun little extra, including—if you have this book on the table—a free glass of Mikki's "sexy wine" (homemade from *fragoline*—strawberries). This place is popular with American students on foreign study programs (daily 11:00–24:00, indoor/outdoor

Rome

Restaurants near the Pantheon

100 YARDS
100 METERS

(T) - TAXI STAND
(M) - METRO STATION
(B) - BUS STOP

1. Ristorante da Fortunato
2. Ristorante Enoteca Corsi
3. Miscellanea Restaurant
4. Osteria da Mario & Restaurant Coco
5. Le Coppelle Taverna
6. To Trattoria dal Cav. Gino
7. Antica Salumeria
8. L'Antica Bottega della Pizza
9. Gelateria Giolitti
10. Crèmeria Monteforte

seating, a block toward Via del Corso from the Pantheon at Via delle Paste 110).

Osteria da Mario, a homey little mom-and-pop joint with a no-stress menu, serves traditional favorites in a fun dining room or on tables spilling out onto a picturesque old Roman square (€7 pastas, €10 *secondi*, Mon–Sat 13:00–15:30 & 19:00–23:00, closed Sun, from the Pantheon walk 2 blocks up Via Pantheon, go left on Via delle Coppelle, take first right to Piazza delle Coppelle 51, tel. 06-6880-6349, Marco).

Restaurant Coco is good for a quick and atmospheric €10 buffet lunch on weekdays. After assembling your plate, sit on the square next to a produce market, and watch local politicians stroll in and out of their dining hall across the way (Mon–Fri 12:30–15:30, closed Sat–Sun, classy indoor and rustic outdoor seating, Piazza delle Coppelle 54, tel. 06-6813-6545).

Le Coppelle Taverna is simple, good, and inexpensive—especially for pizza—with a checkered-tablecloth ambience (daily 12:30–15:00 & 19:30–23:30, Via delle Coppelle 39, tel. 06-6880-6557, Alfonso).

Trattoria dal Cav. Gino, tucked away on a tiny street behind the parliament, has been a local favorite since 1963. Grandpa Gino shuffles around grating the parmesan cheese while his sister and son (Fabrizio, who speaks English) serve up traditional Roman favorites and make sure things run smoothly. Reserve ahead, even for lunch (€7 pastas, €10 *secondi*, fish on Friday, cash only, Mon–Sat 13:00–14:45 & 20:00–22:30, closed Sun, behind Piazza del Parlamento and just off Via di Campo Marzio at Vicolo Rosini 4, tel. 06-687-3434).

Picnic on the Pantheon Porch

Antica Salumeria is an old-time *alimentari* (grocery) store on the Pantheon square. Eduardo speaks English and will help you assemble your picnic: artichokes, mixed olives, bread, cheese, meat (they're proud of their Norcia prosciutto), and wine (with plastic glasses). Their pastries are fresh from their own bakery. While you can create your own (sold by the weight, more fun, and cheaper), they also sell quality ready-made sandwiches. Now take your peasant's feast over for a temple-porch picnic. Enjoy the shade at the base of a column and munch your meal (daily 8:00–21:00, mobile 334-340-9014).

L'Antica Bottega della Pizza, a handy little fast-food joint, sells pizza by the gram (200 grams, or 2 *etti*, makes a light meal and costs about €3) and offers a cafeteria line of hot plates. You can get your pizza in a box to go (dine on the Pantheon porch, as described above) or take advantage of the seating on the square (no extra charge to sit there if you buy a drink, too). The place is great for a quick bite in the old center (open long hours daily, midway between Largo Argentina and the Pantheon at Via dei Cestari 38, air-con, mobile 340-5279-127).

Super Market Di per Di is a convenient place for groceries in the old center (daily 8:00–21:00, 50 yards off Via del Plebiscito at Via del Gesù 59).

Gelato near the Pantheon

Two fine *gelateria*s are within a two-minute walk of the Pantheon. Rome's most famous and venerable ice-cream joint is **Gelateria**

Caffè Pasticceria Giolitti, with cheap take-away prices and elegant Old World seating (just off Piazza Colonna and Piazza Monte Citorio at Via Uffici del Vicario 40, tel. 06-699-1243). For mellow hues (gelato purists consider bright colors a sign of unnatural chemicals used to attract children) and traditional quality, try **Crèmeria Monteforte,** facing the right side of the Pantheon (Tue–Sun 10:00–24:00, closed Mon, Via della Rotonda 22).

In North Rome: Near the Spanish Steps

Many simple and lively places line Via della Croce. To locate these restaurants, see the "Dolce Vita Stroll" map on page 622.

Ristorante il Gabriello is inviting and small—modern under medieval arches—and offers a peaceful and local-feeling respite from all the top-end fashion shops in the area. Claudio serves with charisma, while his brother Gabriello cooks creative Roman cuisine using fresh, organic products from his wife's farm. Italians normally just trust the waiter and say, "Bring it on." Tourists are understandably more cautious, but you can be trusting here. Simply close your eyes and point to anything on the menu. Or invest €40 in "Claudio's Extravaganza" (not including wine), and he'll shower you with edible kindness. Specify whether you'd prefer fish, meat, or both. When finished, I stand up, hold my belly, and say, *"La vita è bella"* (€9 pastas, €12 *secondi*, dinner only, Mon–Sat 19:00–23:30, closed Sun, reservations smart, air-con, dress respectfully—no shorts please, 3 blocks from Spanish Steps at Via Vittoria 51, tel. 06-6994-0810).

Ristorante alla Rampa, just around the corner from the touristy crush of the Spanish Steps, offers Roman cooking, indoor/outdoor ambience at a moderate price, piles of tourists, and impersonal service. They take no reservations, so arrive by 19:30, or be prepared to wait. For a simple meal, go with the €10 *piatto misto all'ortolana*—a self-service trip to their antipasti spread with meat, fish, and veggies. Even though you get just one trip to the buffet (and fried items are generally cold), this can be a meal in itself (Mon–Sat 12:00–15:00 & 18:00–23:00, closed Sun, 100 yards east of Spanish Steps at Piazza Mignanelli 18, tel. 06-678-2621).

In Ancient Rome: Eating Cheaply near the Colosseum

You'll find good views but poor value at the restaurants directly behind the Colosseum. To get your money's worth, eat at least a block away. Here are two handy eateries at the top of Terme di Tito. They're a long block uphill from the Colosseum, near St. Peter-in-Chains church—of Michelangelo's *Moses* fame. For directions, see page 635, or see the map on page 690).

Caffè dello Studente is a lively spot popular with local engineering students attending the nearby University of Rome. Pina, Mauro, and their perky daughter Simona (speaks English, but you can teach her some more) give my readers a royal welcome and serve typical *bar gastronomia* fare: toasted sandwiches and simple pastas and pizzas. You can get your food to go *(da portare via)*; stand up and eat at the crowded bar; sit at an outdoor table and wait for a menu; or—if it's not busy—show this book when you order at the bar and sit without paying extra at a table (Mon–Sat 7:30–21:00, Sun 9:00–18:00, tel. 06-488-3240).

Osteria da Nerone, next door, is a more formal restaurant. Their €8 *antipasti* plate is a good value for a quick lunch (Mon–Sat 12:00–15:00 & 19:00–23:00, closed Sun, indoor/outdoor seating, Via delle Terme di Tito 96, tel. 06-481-7952, run by Teo).

Near Termini Train Station

You have several eating options near my recommended hotels on Via Firenze.

Ristorante del Giglio is a circa-1900 place with a long family tradition of serving traditional Roman dishes (though the quality can be uneven). You'll eat in a big hall of about 20 tables with dressy locals and tourists following the recommendations of nearby hotels (€8 pastas, €15 *secondi,* Mon–Sat 12:00–15:00 & 19:00–23:00, closed Sun, Via Torino 137, tel. 06-488-1606).

Restaurant Target serves decent pizza and pasta in a modern and casual setting. Run by an enthusiastic, friendly (and good-looking) gang of men, it generates lots of happy feedback from my readers (Mon–Sat 12:00–15:30 & 19:00–24:00, Sun 19:00–24:00, indoor/outdoor seating, Via Torino 33, tel. 06-474-0066).

Cafeteria Nazionale, with woody elegance, offers light lunches—including salads—at fair prices. It's noisy with local office workers being served by frantic red-vested wait staff (Mon–Sat 7:00–20:00, closed Sun, Via Nazionale 26–27, at intersection with Via Agostino de Pretis, tel. 06-4899-1716). Their lunch buffet is a delight but gets picked over early (€7.50 for a small dish, Mon–Sat 12:00–15:00).

The **McDonald's** restaurants on Piazza della Repubblica (free piazza seating outside), Piazza Barberini, and Via Firenze offer air-conditioned interiors and salad bars.

Flann O'Brien Irish Pub is an entertaining place for a light meal (of pasta...or something *other* than pasta, such as grilled beef, served early and late, when other places are closed), fine Irish beer, live sporting events on TV, and perhaps the most Italian crowd of all. Walk way back before choosing a table (daily 7:30–24:00, Via Nazionale 17, at intersection with Via Napoli, tel. 06-488-0418).

Rome

Restaurants near Termini Train Station

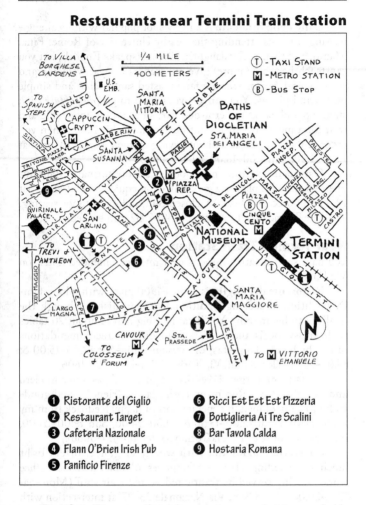

① Ristorante del Giglio

② Restaurant Target

③ Cafeteria Nazionale

④ Flann O'Brien Irish Pub

⑤ Panificio Firenze

⑥ Ricci Est Est Est Pizzeria

⑦ Bottiglieria Ai Tre Scalini

⑧ Bar Tavola Calda

⑨ Hostaria Romana

Panificio Firenze offers take-out pizza, sandwiches, and old-fashioned *alimentari* (grocery) with everything you'd need for a picnic. It's such a favorite with locals that it doesn't even need a sign (Mon–Fri 7:00–19:00, Sat until 14:00, closed Sun, Via Firenze 51–52, tel. 06-488-5035).

Ricci Est Est Est Pizzeria, a venerable old pizzeria, has plenty of historical ambience and good €7 pizzas (Tue–Sun 19:00–24:00, closed Mon, Via Genova 32, tel. 06-488-1107).

Bottiglieria Ai Tre Scalini is a relaxed and characteristic little wine bar popular with young neighborhood regulars, who pop in to sip a glass of fine wine and munch some light Roman pub grub to jazz or blues music. It's nothing earth-shaking—just a serviceable wine bar with wines by the glass listed on the blackboard (nightly until late, 100 yards off Via Nazionale at Via Panisperna 251, tel. 06-4890-7495).

Bar Tavola Calda is a local workers' favorite for a quick, cheap lunch. They have good, fresh, hot dishes ready to go for a fine price (lunch only Mon–Sat, closed Sun, Via Torino 40).

Hostaria Romana is a busy bistro with a hustling and fun-loving gang of waiters and noisy walls graffitied by happy eaters. While they specialize in fish and traditional Roman dishes, their *antipasti* plate can make a good meal in itself (Mon–Sat 19:15–23:00, closed Sun, a block up the lane just past the entrance to the big tunnel near the Trevi Fountain at Via de Boccaccio 1, tel. 06-474-5284).

Near Vatican City

Avoid the restaurant-pushers handing out fliers near the Vatican: bad food and expensive menu tricks. Try any of these instead (see map on page 695).

Perilli in Prati is bright, modern, and just far enough away from the tourist hordes. While friendly Lucia and Massimo specialize in pizza, fish, and grilled meats, the highlight is their excellent €8 lunch buffet (Mon–Fri 12:30–15:00 & 19:30–23:30, Sat 19:30–23:30, closed Sun, one block from Ottaviano Metro stop, Via Otranto 9, tel. 06-370-0156).

Hostaria dei Bastioni, run by Emilio, is conveniently located midway on your hike from St. Peter's to the Vatican Museum, with noisy streetside seating and a quiet interior (€6 pastas, €8–12 *secondi*, no cover charge, Mon–Sat 12:00–15:30 & 19:00–23:00, closed Sun, Via Leone IV 29, at corner of Vatican wall, tel. 06-3972-3034). The *gelateria* three doors away is good.

La Rustichella serves a famous and sprawling *antipasti* buffet (€7 for a single meal–size plate). Arrive when it opens at 19:30 to avoid a line and have the pristine buffet to yourself (Tue–Sun 12:30–15:00 & 19:30–23:00, closed Mon, near Metro: Cipro–Musei Vaticani, opposite church at end of Via Candia, Via Angelo Emo 1, tel. 06-3972-0649). Consider the fun and fruity **Gelateria Millennium** next door.

Viale Giulio Cesare: This street is lined with cheap Pizza Rustica shops, self-serve places, and inviting eateries. Restaurants such as **Tre Pupazzi** (Mon–Sat 12:00–15:00 & 19:00–23:00, closed Sun, tel. 06-686-8371), which line the pedestrians-only Borgo Pio—a block from Piazza San Pietro—are worth a look.

Picnic Supplies: Turn your nose loose in the wonderful **Via Andrea Doria** open-air market, three blocks north of the Vatican Museum (Mon–Sat roughly 7:00–13:30, until 16:30 Tue and Fri except summer, corner of Via Tunisi and Via Andrea Doria). If the market is closed, try the nearby **IN's supermarket** (Mon–Sat

8:30–13:30 & 16:00–20:00, closed Thu eve and Sun, a half-block straight out from Via Tunisi entrance of open-air market, Via Francesco Caracciolo 18).

In South Rome's Testaccio Neighborhood

To locate this restaurant, see the map on page 673.

Trattoria "Da Oio" A Casa Mia serves good-quality, traditional cuisine to a local crowd. It's an upbeat little eatery where you understand the Testaccio passion for the "fifth quarter." (Testaccio, dominated for centuries by its slaughterhouses, is noted for restaurants that are experts at preparing undesirable bits of the animals.) The menu is a minefield of soft meats. Anything that comes with their *pajata* (baby veal intestines) sauce will give you the edible tripe of a lifetime. While having just a pasta for lunch is fine, at dinner they expect diners to order two courses (€10 pastas, €12 *secondi*, Mon–Sat 12:30–15:00 & 19:30–23:30, closed Sun, Via Galvani 43, tel. 06-578-2680).

TRANSPORTATION CONNECTIONS

Termini is the central station (see "Arrival in Rome" on page 599; Metro: Termini). Tiburtina is the train and bus station (on Metro line B, four Metro stops away from train station; Metro: Tiburtina).

From Rome's Termini Train Station by Train to: Venice (roughly hourly, 5–8 hrs, may transfer in Bologna, slower overnight possible), **Florence** (2/hr, 1.5–2 hrs, most connections require seat reservation), **Orvieto** (hourly, 1–1.5 hrs), **Assisi** (12/day, 2–3 hrs), **Pisa** (at least hourly, 3–4 hrs), **La Spezia** (10/day, 4 hrs, overnight option), **Milan** (hourly, 4.5–6 hrs, overnight possible), **Naples** (at least hourly, 1.5–3 hrs), **Civitavecchia** cruise-ship port (2/hr, 1.25 hrs), **Brindisi** (6/day, 6–9 hrs, overnight possible), **Amsterdam** (7/day, 20 hrs, overnight unavoidable), **Bern** (6/day, 9 hrs, plus several overnight options), **Frankfurt** (7/day, 14 hrs, plus several overnight options), **Munich** (4/day, 11 hrs, plus several overnight options), **Nice** (6/day, 10 hrs, overnight possible), **Paris** (3/day, 13–16 hrs, plus several overnight options, important to reserve ahead), **Vienna** (3/day, 13–15 hrs, plus several overnight options).

From Rome by Bus to: Assisi (2–4/day, 3 hrs), **Siena** (10/day, 3 hrs), **Sorrento** (1–2/day, 4 hrs; this is the quickest and easiest way to go straight to Sorrento).

Rome's Airports

Rome's two airports—Fiumicino (a.k.a. Leonardo da Vinci) and the small Ciampino—share the same website (www.adr.it).

Fiumicino Airport

Rome's major airport has a TI (daily 8:00–19:00, tel. 06-8205-9127, press 2 for English), ATMs, banks, luggage storage, shops, and bars.

A slick, direct **"Leonardo Express" train** connects the airport and Rome's central Termini train station in 30 minutes for €11. Trains run twice hourly in both directions from roughly 6:00 to 23:00 (leaving the airport on the half-hour, double-check train times if you have a late-night or early-morning flight to catch). From the airport's arrival gate, follow signs to *Stazione/Railway Station*. Buy your ticket from a machine or the Biglietteria office. Make sure the train you board is going to the central "Roma Termini" station, not "Roma Orte" or others.

Going from the Termini train station to the airport, trains depart at about :22 and :52 past the hour, from track 24. Check the departure boards for "Fiumicino Aeroporto"—the local name for the airport—and confirm with an official or a local on the platform that the train is indeed going to the airport (€11, buy ticket from computerized ticket machines or any *tabacchi* shop in the station). Read your ticket: If it requires validation, stamp it in the yellow machine near the platform before boarding. Know whether your plane departs from terminal A, B, or C.

Shuttle van services run to and from the airport. Consider Rome Airport Shuttle (€28 for one or two people, extra people €6 each, 30 percent more during late night or early morning, tel. 06-4201-4507 or 06-4201-3469, www.airportshuttle.it).

Rome's **taxis** now have a fixed rate to and from the airport (€40 for up to four people with bags). Your hotel can arrange a taxi to the airport at any hour. To get from the airport into town cheaply by taxi, try teaming up with any tourist also just arriving (most are heading for hotels near yours in the center). Be sure to wait at the taxi stand. Avoid unmarked, unmetered taxis; these guys will try to tempt you away from the taxi stand line-up by offering an immediate (rip-off) ride.

For **airport information,** call 06-65951. To inquire about flights, call 06-6595-3640 (Alitalia: tel. 06-2222, British Airways: tel. 06-5249-2800, SAS: tel. 06-6501-0771, Continental: tel. 06-6605-3030, Delta: toll-free tel. 800-477-999, KLM/Northwest: tel. 199-414-199, Swiss International: tel. 848-868-120, United: tel. 848-800-692).

Ciampino Airport

Rome's smaller airport (tel. 06-6595-9515) handles budget airlines, such as easyJet or Ryanair, and charter flights. To get to downtown Rome from the airport, you can take the LILA/Cotral bus (2/hr, 40 min) to the Anagnina Metro stop, where you can connect by

Metro to the stop nearest your hotel. Rome Airport Shuttle (listed above) also offers service to and from Ciampino. The Terravision Express Shuttle connects Ciampino and Termini, leaving every 20 minutes (€7 one-way, €11.50 round-trip, www.terravision.it).

Driving in Rome

The Grande Raccordo Anulare circles greater Rome. This ring road has spokes that lead you into the center. Entering from the north, leave the *autostrada* at the Settebagni exit. Following the ancient Via Salaria (and the black-and-white *Centro* signs), work your way doggedly into the Roman thick of things. This will take you along the Villa Borghese Gardens and dump you right on Via Veneto in downtown Rome. Avoid rush hour and drive defensively: Roman cars stay in their lanes like rocks in an avalanche.

Parking in Rome is dangerous. Park near a police station or get advice at your hotel. The Villa Borghese underground garage is handy (Metro: Spagna). Garages charge about €24 per day.

Consider this: Your car is a worthless headache in Rome. Avoid a pile of stress and save money by parking at the huge, easy, and relatively safe lot behind the train station in the hill town of Orvieto (follow *P* signs from *autostrada*) and catching the train to Rome (every 2 hours, 75 min).

Civitavecchia Cruise Ship Port

Hundreds of cruise chips—including Carnival, Royal Caribbean, Princess, and Celebrity lines—dock each year at the Port of Civitavecchia, about 45 miles northwest of Rome. Port facilities include a waiting room, ATMs, bag storage, and snack bar (tel. 0766-366-201, www.port-of-rome.org). A **TI** is located between the port and train station at 42 Viale Garibaldi (tel. 0766-23078 or 0766-25348). Limited tourist information is available at www .civitavecchia.com; see also the Civitavecchia section of www .portoframe.it.

Getting Between Civitavecchia and Downtown Rome

Twice-hourly **trains** connect Civitavecchia and Rome's Termini station in 75 minutes (€12). To reach the Civitavecchia train station from the ship, take the free shuttle bus to the port entrance, and walk about 10–15 minutes straight along the seaside road. Some shuttle buses may take you all the way to the station—ask. To reach the port from the station, turn right after you exit. Local taxis also run between the port and the train station (tel. 0766-26121 or 0766-24251).

The road traffic between Civitavecchia and Rome is terrible, making trains faster and more economical than any of your other options. **Taxis** can run €200–400 between Civitavecchia and

Rome. A slightly less expensive option is to hire a **private limousine** (figure €150 for up to three people).

Getting Between Civitavecchia and Fiumicino Airport

Two **trains** are required between Civitavecchia and Fiumicino Airport: one between the airport and Rome's Termini station, and another between Termini and Civitavecchia. See "Rome's Airports," page 708.

Shuttle van services run between the port and Rome's Fiumicino Airport (see page 709). Try **Rome Airport Shuttle** (€125 for one to two people, €165 for up to six people, 30 percent more during late night or early morning, tel. 06-4201-4507 or 06-4201-3469, www.airportshuttle.it).

Day Trips to Rome from Civitavecchia

Do-it-yourselfers will find it easy to visit Rome for a day by using the **train** (see details above). Your round-trip train ticket covers Rome's Metro and bus system for 24 hours. Consider disembarking the train at Rome's San Pietro station instead of the more-central Termini station, in order to start your sightseeing with St. Peter's Basilica and the Vatican. Then take the Metro to the Spanish Steps to explore Rome's other sights. If you return to the port from Rome's Termini station, note that Civitavecchia trains generally leave from tracks 27–30, a 10-minute walk from the station entrance.

If your cruise ship stops in Civitavecchia for the day, you may be offered a **shore excursion** to Rome. Many of Civitavecchia's private limousine companies and the Rome Airport Shuttle also offer Rome **tours.** Look for a tour that is a minimum eight hours in length: six hours for sightseeing and two-plus hours of travel time. On shorter tours, you'll see most of Rome from the bus window. Plan to spend about €200 per person.

Rome

NAPLES

Napoli

If you like Italy as far south as Rome, go farther south. It gets better. If Italy is getting on your nerves, don't go farther. Italy intensifies as you plunge deeper. Naples is Italy in the extreme—its best (birthplace of pizza and Sophia Loren) and its worst (home of the Camorra, Naples' "family" of organized crime). Just beyond Naples are three of the best ancient Rome sights anywhere: the impressive ruins of Pompeii and Herculaneum...and the brooding volcano that did them both in, Mount Vesuvius.

Twenty-five-hundred years ago, Neapolis ("new city") was a thriving Greek commercial center. Today, it remains southern Italy's leading city, offering a fascinating collection of museums, churches, and eclectic architecture.

Naples—Italy's third-largest city, with more than 2 million people—has almost no open spaces or parks, which makes its position as Europe's most densely populated city plenty evident. Watching the police try to enforce traffic sanity is almost comical in Italy's grittiest, most polluted, and most crime-ridden city. But Naples surprises the observant traveler with its impressive knack

for living, eating, and raising children in the streets with good humor and decency.

Overcome your fear of being run down or ripped off long enough to talk with people. Enjoy a few smiles and jokes with the man running the neighborhood tripe shop and the woman taking her day-care class on a walk

Naples

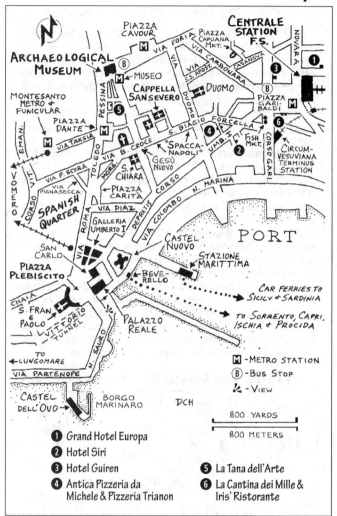

Naples map legend:

- M – METRO STATION
- B – BUS STOP
- ↗ – VIEW

800 YARDS
800 METERS

1. Grand Hotel Europa
2. Hotel Siri
3. Hotel Guiren
4. Antica Pizzeria da Michele & Pizzeria Trianon
5. La Tana dell'Arte
6. La Cantina dei Mille & Iris' Ristorante

through the traffic. (For a conversation starter, ask a local about the New Year's Eve tradition of tossing chipped dinner plates off of balconies into the streets.)

The pulse of Italy throbs in Naples. Like Cairo or Bombay, it's appalling and captivating at the same time, the closest thing to "reality travel" that you'll find in Western Europe. But this tangled mess still somehow manages to breathe, laugh, and sing—with a captivating Italian accent.

Naples

Planning Your Time in the Region

On a quick trip, give the entire area—including Sorrento and Naples—a minimum of three days. With Sorrento as your sunny springboard (see next chapter), spend a day in Naples, a day exploring the Amalfi Coast, and a day split between Pompeii and the town of Sorrento. While Paestum (Greek temples), Mount Vesuvius, Herculaneum (an ancient Roman site like Pompeii), and the island of Capri are decent options, they are worthwhile only if you give the area more time. All sights mentioned are covered in this book.

Regional Pass: If you're planning serious time in the area, consider getting the **Campania ArteCard.** This €25 three-day pass offers free entry to two sights of your choice in this area (Pompeii and Herculaneum are the most expensive, so choose those as your freebies) and 50 percent off on all other sights covered by the card, including Naples' Archaeological Museum and Royal Palace, Paestum, and many more. The card also covers Naples' Metro, buses, funiculars, and airport bus, as well as the regional Circumvesuviana trains and the train to Paestum. The three-day card pays for itself if you visit Pompeii and Naples' Archaeological Museum, taking the train in between (seven-day version costs €28 and covers all sights but no transportation). For details, visit www.campaniartecard.it. ArteCards are sold at participating sights, Naples' Metro and train stations (including a kiosk in Naples' Centrale station), travel agencies, and Naples' airport.

Naples, the Amalfi Coast, and Paestum

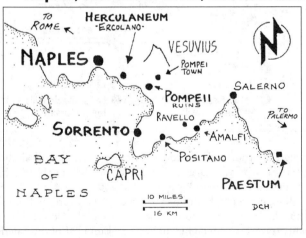

Planning Your Time

Naples makes an ideal day trip either from Rome or the comfortable home base of Sorrento, located an hour south (see next chapter), although I've listed a few accommodations for those who want to stay overnight here.

On a quick visit, start with the Archaeological Museum (see page 718), do "A Slice of Neapolitan Life Walk" (see page 722), and celebrate your survival with pizza. Of course, Naples is huge. But even with limited time, if you stick to the described route and grab a cab when you're lost or tired, it's fun. Treat yourself well in Naples; the city is cheap by Italian standards.

For a blitz tour from Rome, you could have breakfast on the early Rome–Naples express train (about 7:00–9:00), do Naples and Pompeii in a day, and be back in Rome in time for *Letterman*. That's exhausting, but more memorable than a fourth day in Rome.

Remember that in the afternoon, Naples' street life slows and many sights close as the temperature soars. The city comes back to life in the early evening.

ORIENTATION

Tourist Information

The TI is in the Centrale train station (Mon–Sat 9:30–20:00, closed Sun; with your back to the tracks, the TI is in the lobby to your left, look for *Ente Provinciale Turismo* sign; tel. 081-268-779, www.inaples.it). Pick up a map and—even though the odds are against you—ask for the *Qui Napoli* booklet. When they say they're "finished," ask for an old one. Be persistent. Another TI is at Piazza Reale 1, across from the entrance to the Royal Palace (same hours as above).

Arrival in Naples

By Train: There are several Naples train stations, but all trains coming into town stop at either Napoli Centrale or Garibaldi—essentially the same stop, one on top of the other.

Centrale is the busiest, facing Naples' main square, Piazza Garibaldi. You'll find all the administrative facilities in Centrale, including the TI, the Circumvesuviana stop for commuter trains to Sorrento and Pompeii, and a baggage check (€3.80/5 hours, €0.60/hr after, daily 7:00–23:00, clearly marked *deposito bagagli*).

Garibaldi (a.k.a. Napoli Collegamento F.S.) is a subway station used by trains that just make a quick stop as they barrel through. The two stations are connected by escalators.

By Boat: Naples is a ferry hub with great boat connections to Sorrento, Capri, and other nearby ports. If you're arriving at Naples' Port Beverello, it's a short walk (past the gigantic Castel

Nuovo) to Piazza del Plebiscito and the old city center for sight-seeing (see map). From the port, there are easy taxi, bus, and tram connections to the Napoli Centrale train station. The taxi stand is at the end of the port; figure on €10 to get to the train station, plus supplements for baggage, on Sundays, holidays, and late evenings. Buses #152 and #R2 and tram #1 all head to Piazza Garibaldi and the train station (6/hr, 15 min, buy €1 ticket at *tabacchi*, validate ticket in yellow box on the bus as you board).

Helpful Hints

Theft Alert: Err on the side of caution. Don't venture into neigh-borhoods that make you uncomfortable. Walk with con-fidence, as if you know where you're going and what you're doing. Assume able-bodied beggars are thieves. Tighten your money belt and keep it completely hidden.

Stick to busy streets and beware of gangs of hoodlums. A third of the city is unemployed, and past local governments have set an example that the Mafia would be proud of. Assume con artists are cleverer than you. Any jostle or commotion is probably a thief-team smokescreen. Any bags are probably kept safest when checked at the Centrale train station.

Perhaps your biggest risk of theft is while catching or riding the Circumvesuviana commuter train. Remember, if you're connecting from a major train, you'll be stepping from a relatively secure compartment into a crowded Naples subway that's filled with thieves hunting disoriented American tour-ists with luggage. While I ride the Circumvesuviana comfort-ably and safely, each year I hear of many who get ripped off on this ride. You won't be mugged—just conned or pickpocketed. Especially late at night, the Circumvesuviana train is plagued by intimidating ruffians. For maximum safety and peace of mind, sit in the front car, where the driver will double as your protector.

Con artists may say you need to "transfer" by taxi to catch the Circumvesuviana; you don't. Anyone offering to help you with your bags is likely a thief, despite displayed credentials. There are no porters at the Centrale station or in the base-ment where the Circumvesuviana station is located. Wear your money belt, hang on to your bag, and don't display any valuables.

Traffic: In Naples, red lights are discretionary, and pedestrians need to be wary, particularly of motor scooters. Smart tourists jaywalk in the shadow of bold and confident locals, who gen-erally ignore crosswalks. Wait for a break in traffic, cross with confidence, and make eye contact with approaching drivers. The traffic will stop.

Naples

Naples Transportation

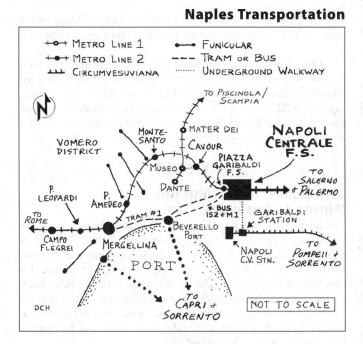

Local Guides: Roberta Mazzarella, who sorts through the wonders of Naples as only a local can, is excellent for a city walk (about €50/hr depending on itinerary, mobile 339-135-7619, robertamazzarella@yahoo.it). Roberta also gives tours of Capri and Pompeii.

Pina Esposito specializes in art and archaeology, and does fine tours of Naples' great but often hard-to-appreciate Archaeological Museum, as well as tours of Pompeii and Herculaneum (€100/2 hrs, €150/half-day, mobile 338-763-4224, annamariaesposito1@virgilio.it). She generally works at the Archaeological Museum; you can call any time.

Getting Around Naples

By Subway: Naples' subway, the Servizio Metropolitana, has two lines. Line 2, the main line, runs from the Centrale station through the center of town (direction: Pozzuoli), stopping at Piazza Cavour (a 5-min walk from the Archaeological Museum) and Montesanto (top of Spanish Quarter and Spaccanapoli street). Line 1 runs from Piscinola/Scampia (suburbs) into the city center, stopping at the Museo station, near the Archaeological Museum (connects to Line 2's Piazza Cavour station). Tickets cost €1 and are good for 90 minutes. All-day tickets cost €3.

By Taxi: If you can afford a taxi, don't mess with the buses. A short taxi ride costs about €5 (insist on the meter, €2 supplement after 22:00, €1.50 supplement on Sun, extra for baggage and holidays).

On a Hop-on Hop-off Bus Tour: The "Sightseeing Napoli" hop-on hop-off tour bus makes three loops through the city, allowing ticket holders to stop and go as they lace the city's sights together (€20, tickets good for 24 hours, buy from driver or from kiosk in front of Castel Nuovo near the port, scant tape-recorded narration, for details, see the brochure at hotels and TI).

SIGHTS

▲▲▲Archaeological Museum (Museo Archeologico)

For lovers of antiquity, this museum makes Naples a worthwhile stop. Considering the importance of its collection and its popularity, it's remarkable how ramshackle, unkempt, and dumpy its displays are. Still, if you can overlook the dust bunnies, this museum offers the best possible peek into the artistic jewelry boxes of Pompeii and Herculaneum. When Pompeii was excavated (early 1800s), Naples' Bourbon king bellowed, "Bring me the best of what you find!" The actual excavation sights are impressive but barren; the finest art and artifacts ended up here.

Cost and Hours: €6.50, covered by Campania ArteCard (see page 714), more when there's a mandatory charge for a temporary exhibit, Wed–Mon 9:00–19:30, closed Tue. To visit the Secret Room (Gabinetto Segreto), which contains erotic art from Pompeii, you have to make an appointment at the information counter, which is immediately on your right as you enter (included in admission, you get a 30-min window; room described later in this chapter).

Getting There: From the Centrale train station, follow signs to the Metro, called *Servizio Metropolitano* (downstairs). Buy tickets from the yellow kiosk and ask which track—"*Binario?*"—to Piazza Cavour. It's usually track 4, *quattro* (direction: Pozzuoli). Go through a *solo metropolitano* turnstile and ride the subway one stop. As you leave the Metro, you can exit and hike uphill, or follow *Museo* signs through a long series of underground moving sidewalks to a new stop (on a different line) right by the museum. Either way, the museum is a grand old red building located up a flight of stairs at the top of the block.

Information: If you want a **guided tour,** look for Pina Esposito (see "Helpful Hints," above; €100/2-hr tour, help her assemble a group to split this cost with up to 10 others). **Audioguides** cost €4 (at ticket desk, rentable for 3 hours). Photos are allowed without a flash. The shop sells a worthwhile green *National Archeological*

Museum of Naples guidebook for €7.50. Bag check is obligatory and free.

The entire museum is in flux—everything is being moved around and renovated. Try to get an up-to-date floor plan as you enter (or buy one for €0.50 at the bookstore). If you can't find a particular work, ask a museum custodian, *"Dov'è?"* (DOH-vay, which means "Where?"), followed by the item's name.

Self-Guided Tour: Overview

Entering the museum, stand at the base of the grand staircase. To your right, on the ground floor, are larger-than-life statues from the Farnese Collection, starring the *Toro Farnese*. Up the stairs
on the mezzanine level (turn left at
the lion) are mosaics and frescoes
from Pompeii, including the *Battle
of Alexander* and the Secret Room
of erotic art. On the top floor is a
scale model of Pompeii and bronze
statues from Herculaneum (a
nearby town destroyed in the same
eruption that devastated Pompeii).
You'll find WCs by circling behind
the staircase.

• *From the base of the grand staircase, turn right and head to the far end.*

Ground Floor: The Farnese Collection

The museum's ground floor alone has enough Greek and Roman art to put any museum on the map. Its highlight is the Farnese Collection, a grand hall of huge, bright, and wonderfully restored statues excavated from Rome's Baths of Caracalla.

The ***Toro Farnese***—a tangled group with a woman being tied to a bull—is the largest intact statue from antiquity. At 13 feet,

it's the tallest ancient marble group ever
found. A third-century A.D. copy of a lost
bronze Hellenistic original, it was carved
out of one piece of marble. Michelangelo
and others "restored" it at the pope's
request—meaning that they integrated
surviving bits into a new work. Panels on
the wall show which pieces are actually
carved by Michelangelo (in blue on the
chart): the head of the woman in back, the
torso of the aunt under the bull, and the
dog. (Imagine how the statue would stand

out if it was thoughtfully lit and not surrounded by white walls.)

Here's the story behind the statue: Once upon an ancient Greek time, King Lycus was bewitched by Dirce. He abandoned his pregnant wife, Antiope (standing regally in the background). The single mom gave birth to twin boys (shown here), who grew up to kill their deadbeat dad and tie Dirce to the horns of a bull to be bashed against a mountain. Captured in marble, the action is thrilling: cape flailing, dog snarling, hooves in the air. You can almost hear the bull snorting. And in the back, Antiope oversees this harsh ancient justice with satisfaction.

At the far end of the hall stands **Hercules** with his club. In a small room behind Hercules is a glass case with the sumptuous **Farnese Cup** *(Tazza Farnese,* second century B.C., from Egypt*).* This large, ancient cameo made of agates looks less like a cup than a cereal bowl. Its decorations are both Egyptian (the Nile toting a lush cornucopia) and, on the flip side, Greek (Medusa's head).

• *Now head up to the mezzanine level.*

Mezzanine: Pompeiian Mosaics and the Secret Room

Most of these mosaics—of animals, musicians, and geometric designs—were taken from Pompeii's House of the Faun (see page 744). The house's delightful centerpiece is a 20-inch-high statue of the *Dancing Faun.* This rare surviving Greek bronze statue (from the fourth century B.C.) is surrounded by some of the best mosaics from the age.

A highlight is the grand *Battle of Alexander,* a second-century B.C. copy of the original Greek fresco, done a century earlier. It decorated a floor in the House of the Faun. It was found intact; the damage you see occurred as this treasure was moved from Pompeii to the king's collection here. The painting (on left, made before it was moved) shows how it once looked. Alexander (left side of the scene, with curly hair and sideburns) is  about to defeat the Persians under Darius (central figure, in chariot with turban and beard). This pivotal victory allowed Alexander to quickly overrun much of Asia (331 B.C.). Alexander is the only one without a helmet...a confident master of the battlefield while everyone else is fighting for their lives, eyes bulging with fear. Notice the shading and perspective, which Renaissance artists later worked so hard to accomplish. (A modern reproduction of the mosaic is now back in the House of the Faun; see page 744.)

The **Secret Room (Gabinetto Segreto),** contains a sizable assortment of erotic frescoes, well-hung pottery, and perky statues that once decorated bedrooms, meeting rooms, brothels, and even shops at Pompeii and Herculaneum. You'll have to make an appointment to view the room (see "Cost and Hours," above), and at those times, you might also be escorted by a local guide (offering a 20-minute tour primarily in Italian but, if you ask nicely, likely in English). Even without a guide, the art speaks for itself (and comes with good printed descriptions in English).

The first room contains big stone penises that once projected over Pompeii's doorways. A massive phallus was not necessarily a sexual symbol, but a magical amulet used against the "evil eye." It symbolized fertility, happiness, good luck, riches, straight As, and general well-being.

The next room is furnished and decorated as an ancient brothel might have been. The 10 frescoes on the wall functioned as both a menu of services offered and as a kind of *Kama Sutra* of sex positions.

These bawdy statues and frescoes—often found in Pompeii's grandest houses—were entertainment for guests. (By the time they made it to this museum, in 1819, the frescoes could only be viewed with permission from the king—see the letters in the glass case just outside the door.) The Roman nobles commissioned the wildest scenes imaginable. Think of them as ancient dirty jokes: Find the horny pygmies from Africa in action. In a nearby fresco, a faun playfully pulls the sheet off a beautiful woman, only to be grossed out by the plumbing of a hermaphrodite. (Perhaps the original *"Mamma mia!"*) Venus, the patron goddess of Pompeii, was a favorite pin-up girl. In a particularly high-quality statue, a goat and a satyr illustrate the act of sodomy.

• *So, now that your travel buddy is finally showing a little interest in art...let's finish the visit on the top floor.*

Top Floor: Statues, Artifacts, and a Model of Pompeii

Climb the stairs to the top floor and enter a grand, empty hall. This was the great hall of the university (17th and 18th centuries) until the building became the royal museum in 1777. The sundial (from 1791) still works. At noon, a sunray strikes the spot, indicating today's date...if you know your zodiac.

To your right are rooms containing **bronze statues** from Herculaneum—of racers, dancers, and fauns (first-century B.C. copies of fourth-century B.C. originals). They once decorated the holiday home (Villa dei Papyri in Herculaneum) of Julius Caesar's father-in-law. Look into the life-like blue eyes of the intense *atleta*

(athletes)—bent on doing their best. The *Five Dancers*, with their inlaid-ivory eyes and graceful poses, decorated a portico. *Resting Hermes* (with his tired little heel wings) is taking a break. The *Drunken Faun* (singing and snapping his fingers to the beat, with a wineskin at his side) is clearly living for today—true to the *carpe diem* preaching of the Epicurean philosophy. Caesar's father-in-law was an Epicurean philosopher, and his library—with 2,000 papyrus scrolls—supported his outlook.

Return to the grand hall and continue to the other side, passing through several rooms of vases, statuettes, spoons, glassware, and other objects found at Pompeii. Keep going to the far end, where you'll find a **scale model** of the archaeological site of Pompeii, circa 1879 *(plastico di Pompeii)*. Belly up to the railing and find the Porta Marina entrance and the large rectangle of the town's forum. Another model on the wall shows the site in 2004, after more excavations.

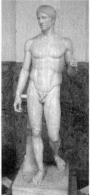

For extra credit, visit **Doriforo**. (Ask a guard, *"Dov'è il Doriforo?"* He was last spotted on the ground floor, in the hall to the left, as you face the staircase.) This seven-foot-tall "spear-carrier" (the literal translation of *doriforo*) just stands there, holding a missing spear. What's the big deal about this statue, which looks like so many others? It's a marble copy made by the Romans of one of the most-copied statues of antiquity, a fifth-century B.C. bronze Greek original by Polycletus. This copy once stood in a Pompeii gym, where it inspired ancient athletes with the ideal proportions of Greek beauty. Centuries later, the *Doriforo*—so full of motion, and so realistic in its *contrapposto* pose (weight on one foot)—inspired Donatello and Michelangelo, triggering the Renaissance. And so the glories of ancient Pompeii, once buried and forgotten, live on today.

SELF-GUIDED WALK

▲▲▲A Slice of Neapolitan Life Walk

Walk from the Archaeological Museum through the heart of town and back to the Centrale train station. Allow at least three hours, plus pizza and sightseeing stops. If you have limited time, do a shorter, hour-long version of this walk by walking briskly and skipping the sights south of Spaccanapoli (including the Royal Palace, Teatro di San Carlo, and Galleria Umberto I).

Naples, a living medieval city, is its own best sight. Couples artfully make love on Vespas surrounded by more fights and smiles

"A Slice of Neapolitan Life" Walk

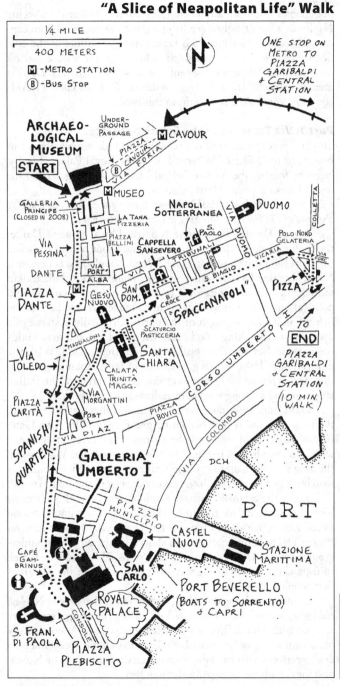

¼ MILE
400 METERS
Ⓜ – METRO STATION
Ⓑ – BUS STOP

ONE STOP ON METRO TO PIAZZA GARIBALDI & CENTRAL STATION

ARCHAEO-LOGICAL MUSEUM
START
GALLERIA PRINCIPE (CLOSED IN 2008)
VIA PESSINA
DANTE
PIAZZA DANTE
VIA TOLEDO →
PIAZZA CARITÀ
SPANISH QUARTER

UNDER-GROUND PASSAGE
Ⓜ CAVOUR
PIAZZA CAVOUR
Ⓑ A FORIA
Ⓜ MUSEO
LA TANA PIZZERIA
PIAZZA BELLINI
VIA PORT' ALBA
VIA
GESÙ NUOVO
SAN DOM.
MADDALONI
CALATA TRINITÀ MAGG.
VIA MORGANTINI
POST
VIA DIAZ

NAPOLI SOTTERRANEA
S. PAOLO
CAPPELLA SANSEVERO
TRIBUNALI
S. BIAGIO
B. CROCE
SCATURCIO PASTICCERIA
SANTA CHIARA
PIAZZA BOVIO

VIA DUOMO
DUOMO
POLO NORD GELATERIA
VIA FORC.
VICARIA
PIZZA
SPACCANAPOLI
S. CROCE

COLLETTA

I
TO
END
PIAZZA GARIBALDI & CENTRAL STATION
(10 MIN. WALK)

CORSO UMBERTO
VIA COLOMBO
DCH

GALLERIA UMBERTO I
PIAZZA MUNICIPIO

PORT

CAFÉ GAM-BRINUS
ⓘ
ⓘ
SAN CARLO
ROYAL PALACE
S. FRAN. DI PAOLA
CONSOLE
PIAZZA PLEBISCITO

CASTEL NUOVO
PORT BEVERELLO (BOATS TO SORRENTO) & CAPRI

STAZIONE MARITTIMA

Naples

per cobblestone than anywhere else in Italy. Rather than seeing Naples as a list of sights, see its one great museum and then capture its essence by taking this walk through the core of the city. Should you become overwhelmed or lost, step into a store and ask for directions: "Where is the central station?" in Italian is *"Dov'è la stazione centrale?"* (DOH-vay lah staht-zee-OH-nay chen-TRAH-lay?). Or point to the next sight in this book.

Part 1: Via Toledo and the Spanish Quarter

The first part of this walk is a straight one-mile ramble down this boulevard to Galleria Umberto I, near the Royal Palace. Ideally, begin by touring the Archaeological Museum (see page 718; at the top of Piazza Cavour, Metro: Cavour).

• *Leaving the Archaeological Museum, turn right and go one block, to the head of Via Pessina. This busy street leads downhill to...*

Piazza Dante: This square is marked by a statue of Dante, the medieval poet. Here you can feel Italy...but many locals feel the repression of the central state. When Napoleon was defeated, Naples became its own independent kingdom. But with Italian unification in 1861, Naples went from being a thriving cultural and political capital to a provincial town, its money used to help establish the industrial strength of the north. Originally, a statue of a Spanish Bourbon king stood here. The grand red-and-gray building is typical of Bourbon buildings from that period. With the unification of Italy, the king, symbolic of Italy's colonial subjugation, was replaced by Dante—considered the father of the Italian language and a strong symbol of Italian nationalism.

Old Dante looks out over an urban area that was once grand, then chaotic, and is now becoming grand again. The Alba Gate, part of Naples' old wall and the entrance to a small street lined with book vendors, is behind Dante's right shoulder. Via Pessina, the long straight road that you're walking, originated as a military road built by Spain in the 16th century. It skirted the old town wall to connect the Spanish military headquarters (now the museum) with the Royal Palace (down by the bay). A new subway station called Dante (with a modern-art flair) was recently built here on Piazza Dante. Construction was slowed by the city's rich underground history: 13 feet down—Roman ruins; 23 feet down—Greek ruins; and every inch of the way—big headaches for the construction people.

Continue walking downhill, remembering that here in Naples, red lights are considered "decorations." When crossing a street, try to cross with a local. The people here are survivors: A long history of corrupt and greedy colonial overlords has taught Neapolitans to deal creatively with authority—many credit this aspect of Naples' past for the advent of organized crime here.

Naples

Via Pessina becomes Via Toledo (another reminder of Spanish rule), Naples' principal shopping street. In 1860, from the white marble balcony (on the Neoclassical building) overlooking Piazza Sette Settembre, the famous revolutionary Giuseppe Garibaldi declared Italy united and Victor Emmanuel II its first king. Not until 1870, when Rome fell to the unification forces, was the dream of Italian unity actually realized.

• *Continue straight on Via Toledo (even though the arterial jogs left). At the next left (Via Maddaloni), about three blocks below Piazza Dante (and a block past Piazza Sette Settembre), you'll come to the long straight street called...*

Spaccanapoli: Before crossing the street—whose name literally translates as "split Naples"—look left. Look right. Since ancient times, this thin street (which changes names several times: Maddaloni, Via B. Croce, Via S. Biagio dei Librai, Forcella, and Vicaria) has bisected the city. We'll return to this intersection later. (If you want to abbreviate this walk, turn left here and skip ahead to "Part 2," page 727.)

• *Stay on Via Toledo, and it runs through...*

Piazza Carità: Surrounded by fascist architecture from 1938, this square is full of stern, straight, obedient lines. (For the best fascist architecture in town, side-trip from here—with your back to Via Toledo, leave Piazza Carità downhill on the right-hand corner and walk a block to the Poste e Telegrafi building. There you'll see several government buildings with stirring reliefs singing the praises of a totalitarian society.)

• *From Piazza Carità, wander south down Via Toledo for a few blocks, looking (on the left) for more examples of...*

Fascist Architecture (Banks): Notice the two banks. Try robbing the second one (Banco di Napoli, Via Toledo 178). Step across the street and notice the Banco di Napoli's architecture: typical fascist arches and reliefs, built to celebrate the bank's 400th anniversary (est. 1539—how old is your bank?).

On the next corner, another bank (Banca Commerciale Italiana) fills an older palace and has a Caravaggio painting on its second floor. (You're welcome to drop in and ask, *"Posso vedere il Caravaggio?"* and hope that it's back from its world tour.)

• *From the Banco di Napoli, side-trip uphill three blocks into the...*

Spanish Quarter: This is a classic world of *basso* (low) living. In such tight quarters, families generally do it in the road. This is *the* cliché of life in Naples, as shown in so many movies. The

Spanish Quarter is Naples at its rawest, poorest, and most characteristic. The only things predictable about this Neapolitan tide pool are the ancient grid plan of its streets (which survives from Greek times), the friendliness of its shopkeepers, and the boldness of its mopeds. Concerned locals will tug on their lower eyelids, warning you to be wary. Pop into a grocery shop and ask the man to make you his best ham and mozzarella sandwich. The price should be about €3.

• *Return to Via Toledo (clogged with more people than cars) and work your way down to the immense...*

Piazza del Plebiscito: This square celebrates the 1861 vote (*plebiscito:* plebiscite), when Naples chose to join Italy. Walk to the middle of the square. From here, you'll see the Church of San Francesco di Paola, with its Pantheon-inspired dome and broad, arcing colonnades.

• *Opposite is the...*

Royal Palace (Palazzo Reale): Having housed Spanish, French, and even Italian royalty, this building displays them all—look for eight kings in the niches, each from a different dynasty (left to right: Norman, German, French, Spanish, Spanish, Spanish, French—the brother-in-law of Napoleon—and, finally, Italian: Victor Emmanuel II, King of Savoy). The statues were done at the request of V. E. II's son, so his dad is the most dashing of the group. This huge, lavish palace welcomes the public (€7.50, Thu–Tue 9:00–19:00, closed Wed, shorter hours off-season, last entry 1 hour before closing, audioguide-€4/1 person, €5/2 people, tel. 081-400-547).

The palace's grand Neoclassical staircase leads up to a floor with 30 plush rooms. You'll follow a one-way route (with some English descriptions) featuring paintings by "the Caravaggio Imitators," Neapolitan tapestries, fine inlaid-stone tabletops, and more. Don't miss the huge Hercules room and the chapel with a fantastic Nativity scene (a commotion of 18th-century ceramic figurines).

• *Continue 50 yards past the Royal Palace to enjoy a...*

Fine Harbor View: While boats busily serve Capri and Sorrento, Mount Vesuvius smolders ominously in the distance. Look back to see the vast "Bourbon red" palace—its color inspired by Pompeii. On the hilltop above the Piazza del Plebiscito is Naples' Carthusian Monastery and the Castle of St. Elmo. This street continues to Naples' romantic harborfront—the fishermen's quarters or Borgo Marinaro—a fortified island connected to the mainland by a stout causeway, with its fanciful Castel dell'Ovo (castle of the egg) and trendy harborside restaurants. Farther along the harborfront stretches the Lungomare promenade and Santa Lucia district. (The long harborfront promenade, Via Francesco

Caracciolo, is a delightful people scene on balmy nights; see "Lungomare *Passeggiata*," page 732.)

The **Gran Caffè Gambrinus,** facing Piazza del Plebiscito, takes you back to the elegance of 1860. It's a classic place to sample a unique Neapolitan pastry called *sfogliatella* (crispy, scallop shell–shaped pastry filled with sweet ricotta cheese). Or you might prefer the mushroom-shaped, rum-soaked bread-like cakes called *babà*, which come in a huge variety. Stand at the bar, pay double to sit, or just wander around and try to imagine the café buzzing with the ritzy intellectuals, journalists, and artsy bohemian types who would have munched on *babà* during Naples' 19th-century heyday (Mon–Sun 7:00–24:00, Piazza del Plebiscito 1, tel. 081-417-582).

• *Now walk away from the piazza to go behind the palace, where you can peek inside the Neoclassical...*

Teatro di San Carlo: Europe's oldest opera house—from 1737, built 41 years before Milan's La Scala—is Italy's second-most-respected (after La Scala). The theater burned down in 1816, and was rebuilt within the year. Guided visits basically just show you the fine auditorium with its 184 boxes—each with a big mirror to reflect the candle lighting (daily 9:00–17:30, tel. 081-664-545, www.teatrosancarlo.it).

Beyond Teatro di San Carlo, the huge Castel Nuovo on the harborfront just beyond the palace houses government bureaucrats and the Civic Museum, featuring 14th- to 16th-century art (€5, Mon–Sat 9:00–19:00, closed Sun, tel. 081-795-5877).

Across the street from Teatro di San Carlo, go through the tall yellow arch into the Victorian iron and glass of the 100-year-old shopping mall, **Galleria Umberto I.** Gawk up.

• *For Part 2 of this walk, double back up Via Toledo to Piazza Carità, veering right on Via Morgantini to Via Maddaloni (or avoid the backtracking and uphill walk by catching a €6 taxi to the church of Gesù Nuovo; JAY-zoo noo-OH-voh).*

Part 2: Spaccanapoli Back to the Station

You're back at the straight-as-a-Greek-arrow Spaccanapoli, formerly the main thoroughfare of the Greek city of Neapolis.

• *Stop at...*

Piazza Gesù Nuovo: Visit the two bulky old churches (both churches free, daily 7:00–13:00 & 16:00–19:00). The square is marked by a towering 18th-century Baroque monument to the Counter-Reformation. Although the Jesuit order was powerful in

Naples due to its Spanish heritage, locals never attacked Protestants here with the full fury of the Spanish Inquisition.

• *Check out the austere, fortress-like, 17th-century...*

Church of Gesù Nuovo: The unique pyramid-grill facade survives from a fortified 15th-century noble palace. Step inside for a brilliant Neapolitan Baroque interior. The second chapel on the right features a much-adored statue of Giuseppe Moscati, a Christian doctor famous for helping the poor. Moscati was fast-tracked to sainthood in 1987 (only six years after he died).

• *Continue on to the third chapel and enter the...*

Sale Moscati: Enter a huge room filled with "Ex Votos"—tiny red-and-silver plaques of thanksgiving for prayers answered with the help of St. Moscati (each has a symbol of the ailment cured). Naples' practice of using Ex Votos, while incorporated into its Catholic rituals, goes back to its pagan Greek roots. Rooms from Moscati's nearby apartment are on display, and a glass case shows possessions and photos of the great doctor. As you leave the Sale Moscati, notice the big bomb casing that hangs in the left corner. It fell through the church's dome in 1943, but caused almost no damage...yet another miracle.

• *Head across the street, to the simpler...*

Church of Santa Chiara: Dating from the 14th century, this church is from a period of French royal rule under the Angevin dynasty. Consider the stark contrast between this church (Gothic) and the Gesù Nuovo (Baroque). Notice the huge, inlaid-marble, Angevin coat of arms on the floor. The faded Trinity (on back wall, the dove representing the Holy Spirit is between the head of God the Father and Christ, c. 1414, left of entry) is an example of the fine frescoes that once covered the walls. Most were stuccoed-over during Baroque times or destroyed in 1943 by WWII bombs. The altar is adorned with four finely carved Gothic tombs of Angevin kings. A chapel stacked with Bourbon royalty is just to the right.

• *Leaving the church, take a right and head to the back of the church. Continue through the archway straight ahead, and pass all the parked cars to reach the farthest door on the right. Here you'll find the bright, ornate, majolica-tiled...*

Cloistered Courtyard of Santa Chiara: Note the sprawling nativity scene immediately on your right as you enter—a cartoon-ish 3-D snapshot of Old World Napoli. Stop in at its museum (€4, Mon–Fri 9:30–17:30, Sun 9:30–14:00). There's a recommended little lunch spot, Trattoria da Titina e Gennaro, just across the street.

• *Now return to the main drag, turn right, and continue straight down traffic-free Via B. Croce.*

Since this is a university district, you'll see lots of students and bookstores. This neighborhood is also extremely superstitious.

Look for incense-burning women with carts of good-luck charms for sale. At Via Santa Chiara, a detour to the left leads to shops of antique musical instruments.

• *Farther down Spaccanapoli, you'll see the next square...*

Piazza San Domenico Maggiore: This square is marked by an ornate 17th-century plague monument (built to thank God for ending the plague). But more important is the well-loved **Scaturchio Pasticceria,** another good place to try *sfogliatella* (€1.30 to go, costs double at a table in the square, daily 7:20–20:40, tel. 081-551-6944).

• *From this square, detour left along the right side of the castle-like church, then follow yellow signs, taking the first right and walking one block to...*

Cappella Sansevero: Be warned that no photos are allowed in the chapel (but postcards are for sale in the gift shop).

This small chapel is a Baroque explosion mourning the body of Christ, who lies on a soft pillow under an incredibly realistic veil. It's also the personal chapel of Raimondo de Sangro, an eccentric Freemason. The monuments to his relatives have a second purpose: to share the Freemason philosophy of freedom through enlightenment.

Study the incredible *Veiled Christ* in the center. Carved out of marble, it's like no other statue I've seen (by Giuseppe "Howdee-doodat" Sammartino, 1753). The Christian message (Jesus died for our salvation) is accompanied by a Freemason message (the veil represents how the body and ego are an obstacle to real spiritual freedom). As you walk from Christ's feet to his head, notice how the expression of Jesus' face goes from suffering to peace.

Raimondo de Sangro lies buried at the far (altar) end. An inventor, he created the deep-green pigment used on the ceiling fresco. The inlaid M.C. Escher–esque maze on the floor around de Sangro's tomb is another Freemason reminder of how the quest for knowledge gets you out of the maze of life.

To the right of the altar, the statue of *Despair* struggles with a marble rope net (carved out of a single piece of stone), symbolic of a troubled mind. The Freemason symbolism shows how knowledge—in the guise of an angel—frees the human mind. On the opposite side of the altar from *Despair*, a veiled woman fingers a broken plaque, symbolizing...something.

Your Sansevero finale is downstairs: two mysterious...skeletons. Perhaps another of the mad inventor's fancies: Inject a corpse with a fluid to fossilize the veins so that they'll survive the body's decomposition. While that's the legend, it was most likely constructed to illustrate how the circulation system works (€6, Mon and Wed–Sat 10:00–18:00, Sun 10:00–13:30, closed Tue, Via de Sanctis 19).

• *Return to Via B. Croce (a.k.a. Spaccanapoli), turn left, and continue your cultural scavenger hunt. At the intersection of Via Nilo, find the...*

Statue of the Nile (on the left): A reminder of the multi-ethnic make-up of Greek Neapolis, this statue is in what was the Egyptian quarter. Locals like to call this statue *The Body of Naples,* with the overflowing cornucopia symbolizing the abundance of their fine city. (I once asked a Neapolitan man to describe the local women, who are famous for their beauty, in one word. He replied simply, "Abundant.") This intersection is considered the center of old Naples.

• *Five yards farther down (on the right) is the tiny...*

"Chapel of Maradona": Look for a niche on the wall dedi-

cated to Diego Maradona, a soccer star who played for Naples in the 1980s. Locals consider soccer almost a religion (see page 732)...and this guy was practically a deity. You can even see a "hair of Diego" and a teardrop from the city when he went to another team for more money. Unfortunately, his reputation has been sullied with organized crime, drugs, and police problems.

A few blocks farther, at the tiny square, Via San Gregorio Armeno leads left into a colorful district (and also to the underground Napoli Sotterranea archaeological site—see page 731). You'll see many shops that sell tiny components of fantastic manger scenes (including figurines caricaturing local politicians and celebrities—if you want to add the local Dick Cheney to your nativity set).

• *As Via B. Croce becomes Via S. Biagio dei Librai, notice the...*

Gold and Silver Shops: Some say stolen jewelry ends up here, is melted down immediately, and appears in a saleable form as soon as it cools. The inimitable Sr. Grassi runs the Ospedale delle Bambole (doll hospital) at #81.

• *Cross busy Via Duomo.*

Here, the street and side-street scenes along Via Vicaria intensify. This is known as a center of the Camorra (organized crime).

Paint a picture with these thoughts: Naples has the most intact street plan of any ancient Roman city. Imagine this city during those times (and retain these images as you visit Pompeii), with streetside shop fronts that close up after dark to form private homes. Today, it's just one more page in a 2,000-year-old story of a city: all kinds of meetings, beatings, and cheatings; kisses, near misses, and little-boy pisses.

You name it, it occurs right on the streets today, as it has since

ancient times. People ooze from crusty corners. Black-and-white death announcements add to the clutter on the walls. Widows sell cigarettes from buckets. For a peek behind the scenes in the shade of wet laundry, venture down a few side streets. Buy two carrots as a gift for the woman on the fifth floor if she'll lower her bucket to pick them up. The neighborhood action seems best at about 18:00.

At the tiny fenced-in triangle of greenery, hang out for a few minutes and just observe the crazy motorbike action.

• *From here, veer right onto Via Forcella (which leads to the busy boulevard that takes you to the Centrale train station). A tiny, round traffic island protects a chunk of the ancient Greek wall of Neapolis (fourth century B.C.). But first, turn right on busy Via Pietro Colletta, walk 50 yards and step into the North Pole, at the...*

Polo Nord Gelateria: The oldest *gelateria* in Naples has had four generations of family working here since 1931. Sample a few flavors—all are made fresh daily (Mon–Sat 10:00–24:00, Sun 10:00–14:00 & 17:00–24:00, sample their *bacio* or "kiss" flavor before ordering, Via Pietro Colletta 41, tel. 081-205-431). Via Pietro Colletta leads past Napoli's two most competitive **pizzerias** (see "Eating," page 734) to Corso Umberto I.

• *Turn left on the grand-boulevard-like Corso Umberto I. From here to the Centrale train station, it's at least a 10-minute walk (if you're tired, hop on a bus; they all go to the station). To finish the walk, continue on Corso Umberto I—past a gauntlet of purse/CD/sunglasses salesmen and shady characters hawking stolen camcorders—to the vast, ugly Piazza Garibaldi. On the far side is the station. You made it.*

More Sights and Activities

▲▲**Napoli Sotterranea**—This archaeological site, an underground man-made maze of passageways and ruins from Greek and Roman times, is tourable only with a guide. Visits in English are at set times (€9.30; includes 90-min tour daily at 12:00, 14:00, and 16:00; plus 10:00 and 18:00 Sat–Sun, tel. 081-296-944, mobile 368-354-0585). Descend 121 steps under the modern city to explore; bring a light sweater. First stop is the old Greek tufa-stone quarry used to build the city of Neopolis, and later converted into an immense aqueduct by the Romans. Next is an excavated portion of the Greco-Roman theater. The tour involves a lot of stairs, as well as a long, narrow (20-inch-wide) walkway that uses an ancient water channel (an obese person could not comfortably fit through this). Although there's not much to actually see, the experience is fascinating, and includes a little WWII history.

The site is just off Via Duomo, a 10-minute walk from the Archaeological Museum, at Piazza Gaetano 68 (look for signs). From Spaccanapoli, it's just a couple blocks uphill from the Statue of the Nile (ask for Piazza Gaetano, and look for the *Sotterranea* signs).

Open-Air Fish Market—Naples' fish market squirts and stinks as it has for centuries under the Nolana Port (gate in the city wall) just four blocks from the Centrale train station. Of the town's many boisterous outdoor markets, this will net you the most photos and memories. From Piazza Nolana, wander under the medieval gate and take your first left down Vico Sopramuro, enjoying this wild and entirely edible cultural scavenger hunt (Tue–Sun 8:00–14:00, closed Mon).

Two other markets with more clothing and less fish are at Piazza Capuana (several blocks northwest of the Centrale train station and tumbling down Via Sant'Antonio Abate, Mon–Sat 8:00–18:00, Sun 9:00–13:00) and a similar cobbled shopping zone along Via Pignasecca (just off Via Toledo, west of Piazza Carità).

Grand View from Certosa San Martino—This ultimate view—overlooking Naples, its bay, and a volcano—comes with a €6 price tag. The monastery, founded in 1325 and dissolved in the early 1800s, is popular today for its museum, church, and dramatic view gardens (Thu–Tue 8:30–18:30, closed Wed, a 10-min well-posted walk from top of Montesanto funicular at Largo San Martino 5, tel. 081-558-5942).

Lungomare *Passeggiata*—Each evening, relaxed and romantic Neapolitans in the mood for a scenic harborside stroll do their *vasca* (laps) along the inviting Lungomare promenade. To join in this elegant people-watching scene (best on evenings after 19:00), stroll about 15 minutes from Piazza del Plebiscito along Via Nazario Sauro (in Santa Lucia district).

Detour out along the fortified causeway to poke around Borgo Marinaro ("fishermen's quarters"—a trendy restaurant scene where you can dine amidst yachts with a view of Vesuvius), with its striking Castel dell'Ovo. This is also known as the Santa Lucia district because this is where the song "Santa Lucia" was first sung. (The song is probably so famous in America because immigrants from

Naples sang it to remember the old country.) Beyond that stretches Naples' Lungomare. This long harborfront promenade, along Via Francesco Caracciolo, is a delightful people scene on balmy evenings. Taxi home or retrace your steps back to the old center.

SLEEPING

With Sorrento just an hour away (see next chapter), I can't imagine why you'd sleep in Naples. But, if needed, here are several places. The first and last hotels are within a few blocks of the train station. The area can feel unnerving, especially after dark.

$$ Grand Hotel Europa, a gem set in the seedy neighborhood around the train station, has 84 modern rooms decorated with not-quite-right reproductions of famous paintings (Sb-€78, Db-€90, Tb-€104, air-con, cheery breakfast room, elegant restaurant, turn right out of station onto Corso Novara and take the first right—on Corso Meridionale—to #14, tel. 081-267-511, www .grandhoteleuropa.com, info@grandhoteleuropa.com).

$$ Hotel Siri, a 10-minute walk from the train station, offers 16 spacious, bare-bones rooms (Sb-€40–50, Db-€70–80, Tb-€90–100, skip meager breakfast, air-con, Via Mignogna 15, tel. 081-554-3122, fax 081-554-3098, info@hotelsiri.it). Leaving the train station, walk along the left side of Piazza Garibaldi, turn left on Corso Umberto I, and take the second left onto Via Mignogna; the hotel is ahead on the left.

$$ Hotel Guiren has 37 polished, quiet rooms two blocks from the station (Sb-€65, Db-€85, Tb-€110, air-con, Via Bologna 114, tel. 081-202-897, fax 081-200-893, www.hotelguiren2.it, info@hotelguiren.it). Exit the station by the McDonald's, go along the right side of the square for two blocks, and turn right onto Via Bologna.

Sleep Code

(€1 = about $1.30, country code: 39)
S = Single, **D** = Double/Twin, **T** = Triple, **Q** = Quad, **b** = bathroom, **s** = shower only. Unless otherwise noted, credit cards are accepted, English is spoken, and breakfast is included.

To help you sort easily through these listings, I've divided the rooms into three categories based on the price for a standard double room with bath:

  $$$ **Higher Priced**—Most rooms €110 or more.
  $$ **Moderately Priced**—Most rooms between €75–110.
  $ **Lower Priced**—Most rooms €75 or less.

EATING

Drop by one of the two most traditional pizzerias (both at the end of the walking tour described earlier in this chapter). Naples—whose pizzerias bake just the right combination of fresh dough, mozzarella, and tomatoes in traditional wood-burning ovens—is the birthplace of pizza. For something other than pizza, consider the last two listings.

Antica Pizzeria da Michele, a few blocks from the train station, is for pizza purists. Filled with locals, it serves two kinds of pizza: *margherita* (tomato sauce and mozzarella) or *marinara* (tomato sauce, oregano, and garlic, no cheese). Come early to sit and watch the pizza artists in action. A pizza with beer costs €5 (Mon–Sat 10:00–24:00, closed Sun, tel. 081-553-9204). With the train station at your back, turn off Piazza Garibaldi at 11 o'clock—using an imaginary clock for a compass—onto Corso Umberto I, then turn right on Via Pietro Colletta, and look for the vertical red *Antica Pizzeria* sign at the intersection of Via Pietro Colletta and Via Cesare Sersale (at #1).

Pizzeria Trianon, across the street, has been da Michele's archrival since 1923. It offers more choices, slightly higher prices (€3.80–7.50), air-conditioning, and a cozier atmosphere. For less chaos, head upstairs. Waiting for your meal, you can survey the evolution of a humble wad of dough into a smoldering bubbly feast in their entryway pizza kitchen (daily 11:00–15:30 & 18:30–23:00, Via Pietro Colletta 42, tel. 081-553-9426).

La Tana dell'Arte, a handy pizzeria with outdoor seating on a quiet pedestrian square, is located just past Galleria Principe, near the Archaeological Museum. The fresh homemade pastas are a unique find among the menu of flash-fired Neapolitan pizzas (daily 12:00–17:00 & 19:00–24:00, Via Bellini 29, tel. 081-549-1844).

La Cantina dei Mille, a block in front of the train station, is a traditional family-style place serving good basic food to good basic people indoors and out. It's about the only charming place I found on Piazza Garibaldi (€4 pizza and pasta, Tue–Sun 9:00–16:00 & 17:00–24:00, closed Mon; with your back to the station, it's about halfway up the left side of Piazza Garibaldi at #126; tel. 081-283-448).

Next door, **Iris'** cadre of bow-tied waiters sling good, reasonably priced seafood, pastas, and pizzas in a comfortable *ristorante* with an outdoor patio (Sun–Fri 12:00–16:00 & 17:00–24:00, closed Sat, Piazza Garibaldi 121–125, tel. 081-269-988).

TRANSPORTATION CONNECTIONS

From Naples by Boat to: Sorrento (7/day, 40 min, €10), **Capri** (2/hr, 40 min, €15), **Amalfi** (mid-May–mid-Oct only, 4/day, 90 min, €12). For a map showing boat connections, see page 735.

By Train to: Rome (at least hourly, usually 2–3 hrs but the new Eurostar Italia AV takes 90 min—your ticket gets you into plush station lounges), **Florence** (hourly, 3.5–5 hrs), **Salerno** (3/hr, 60–90-min trip, avoid slow *diretto* train), **Brindisi** (8/day, 5–8 hrs, overnight possible; from Brindisi, ferries sail to Greece), **Milan** (hourly, 6.5–9 hrs, overnight possible, longer with change in Rome), **Venice** (almost hourly, with changes in Bologna or Rome, about 7–8 hrs), **Palermo** (5/day, 10 hrs), **Nice** (2/day, 12 hrs with change in Genoa), **Paris** (3/day, 14–18 hrs with change in Rome or Milan).

By Circumvesuviana Train: See "Getting Around the Region" sidebar on page 736 for information on getting to Herculaneum, Pompeii, and Sorrento.

Naples Airport: Naples International Airport (Capodichino) is located four miles northeast of the city center (tel. 081-789-6111 for operator, tel. 848-888-777 for info, www.gesac.it). Orange buses marked *anm* and Alibus shuttle buses make the 10-minute run between the airport and Napoli Centrale train station/Piazza Garibaldi (€3, daily 6:30–23:30). You can also catch a Curreri bus from the airport direct to Sorrento (€6, pay driver, 6/day, runs 9:00–19:30 in each direction, 75 min, www.curreriviaggi.it). It's tough to get a taxi to use the meter from the airport.

Pompeii, Herculaneum, and Vesuvius

Stopped in their tracks by the eruption of Mount Vesuvius in A.D. 79, Pompeii and Herculaneum offer the best look anywhere at

what life in Rome must have been like 2,000 years ago. These two cities of well-preserved ruins are yours to explore. Of the two sites, Pompeii is grander, while Herculaneum is smaller and more intimate. Vesuvius, still smoldering ominously, rises up on the horizon. It last erupted in 1944, and while still an active volcano, it's considered safe to visit. Shuttle buses drop you a short hike from the summit.

Naples

Getting Around the Region

To connect Naples, Sorrento, and the Amalfi Coast, you can travel on land by train, bus, and taxi. Whenever possible, consider taking a boat—it's faster, scenic, cooler, and you can take photos of the coastline that you can't get from the bus or train. For specific travel times and costs, check the "Transportation Connections" sections of the Naples, Sorrento, and Amalfi Coast chapters.

By Circumvesuviana Train: This useful commuter train—popular with commuters, tourists, and pickpockets—links Naples, Herculaneum, Pompeii, and Sorrento. At Naples' Centrale Station, signs direct you downstairs to the Circumvesuviana. In the long corridor in the basement, the ticket windows—marked *Circumvesuviana*—are on your left. Schedules are posted on the wall just to the right of window 5. When you buy your ticket, ask which track your train will depart from (*"Quale binario?"*; KWAH-lay bee-NAH-ree-oh). Don't go through the turnstiles opposite the ticket windows—instead, follow *Circumvesuviana* signs down the corridor and jog right when it does, down another long corridor that has turnstiles at the end (where you insert your ticket). The train platforms are just beyond.

The Circumvesuviana also has its own terminal (one Metro stop or a 10-minute walk beyond the Centrale station), but there's no reason to use it unless you're headed in that direction. Two trains per hour, marked *Sorrento*, take you to Herculaneum (Ercolano) in about 25 minutes, Pompeii in about 35 minutes, and Sorrento, the end of the line, in 70 minutes (€3.20 one-way, not covered by railpass but covered by Campania ArteCard—see page 714). Not all of the trains go as far as Sorrento; check the schedule carefully or confirm with a local before boarding to make sure the train goes to where you want. Express trains marked *DD* (12/day) will get you to Sorrento 20 minutes sooner. When returning to the Napoli Centrale station on the Circumvesuviana, get off at the second-to-the-last station, at the Collegamento FS or Garibaldi stop (Centrale station is just up the escalator). Bonus: When returning from Sorrento, your Circumvesuviana ticket includes a ride anywhere on the Naples Metro system within 180 minutes of validation.

While I have not had a problem, many readers report being ripped off on this train (see "Theft Alert," page 716).

By Bus: SITA buses (often blue or green-and-white) connect the towns. Buses that travel along the highly touristed Amalfi Coast can be crowded—for tips, see "The Amalfi Coast by Bus" on page 778.

By Taxi: Some people prefer paying the price for door-to-door transport. For €80–100, you can take a taxi from Naples 30 miles directly to your Sorrento hotel; agree on a set price without the meter and pay upon arrival. You can hire a cab on Capri for

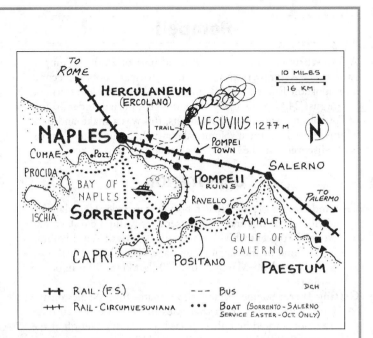

about €60/hr. Taxis in the Amalfi Coast are generally expensive, and more than willing to overcharge you, but they can be convenient, especially with a larger group. See "The Amalfi Coast by Taxi" on page 780.

By Boat: Four primary ferry companies service the Naples, Sorrento, and Amalfi Coast areas: Caremar, SNAV, Metro del Mare, and one company that goes by three names—LMS, LMP, or Alilauro. Each company has different destinations and prices; some compete for the same trips. The quicker the trip, the higher the price. A hydrofoil skims between Naples and Sorrento—it's faster, safer from pickpockets, and more scenic than the Circumvesuviana train (7/day, departs every 2 hours, 40 min, €10). Taking a taxi from Naples' Centrale train station to the port costs about €10 (extra charge for bags, Sundays, holidays, and evenings after 22:00).

Check schedules at any TI or at the Port Beverello boat dock (near Piazza del Plebescito). Ticket windows clearly display the next available departure. The number of boats that run per day depends on the season (with a few more boats per day in July–Aug). Trips are canceled in bad weather. Most boats charge an extra fee for luggage (about €2).

If you plan to arrive and leave a destination by boat, make note upon your arrival of the return times, since the last boat usually leaves before 19:00.

Pompeii

A once-thriving thriving commercial port of 20,000, Pompeii (worth ▲▲▲) grew from Greek and Etruscan roots to become an important Roman city. Then, at one o'clock in the afternoon on August 24, A.D. 79, everything stopped, buried under 30 feet of hot volcanic ash. For archaeologists, this was a shake-and-bake windfall, teaching them volumes about daily Roman life. Pompeii was rediscovered in the 1600s; excavations began in 1748.

ORIENTATION

Cost and Hours: €11, or €20 combo-ticket includes Herculaneum (called Ercolano) and three lesser sites (valid 3 days), can be free or 50 percent off with Campania ArteCard (see "Planning Your Time in the Region" on page 714). Open April–Oct 8:30–19:30, Nov–March 8:30–17:00 (last entry 90 min before closing).

Getting There: Pompeii is about 35 minutes from Naples on the Circumvesuviana train that goes to Sorrento (€3.20 one-way, not covered by railpasses, at least hourly). Get off at the *Pompei Scavi, Villa dei Misteri* stop. Although you can check your bag at the train station's bar for a small fee (€1.50, pick up by 19:00, off-season 18:00), it's free to check it at the Pompeii site. From the Pompei Scavi train station, turn right and walk down the road about a block to the entrance (first left turn). The TI is farther down the street, but it's not a necessary stop for your visit.

Information: A good map and information booklet are included with your admission, but you must pick them up yourself at the TI window (to the left of the WCs). Tel. 081-857-5347, www.pompeiisites.org.

The bookshop sells the small Pompeii and Herculaneum *Past and Present* book. Its helpful text and plastic overlays allow you to re-create the ruins—with the "present" actually being 1964 (€12 in bookstores; if you buy from a street vendor, pay no more than €12).

In 2008, the Baths of the Forum and the House of the Vetti may still be closed for renovation.

Tours: Live guides (about €115/2 hrs) cluster near the ticket booth. If you gather 10 people, the price is reasonable when you split the cost. Knowledgeable, energetic **Gaetano Manfredi** can breeze you through the highlights in two hours, bringing the dusty ruins to life. Avoid Gaetano impersonators. Find the real one only at the Porta Marina entrance; he'll be wearing his official badge that bears his name and the number seven (mobile 338-725-5620, tel. 081-863-9816, 3387255620@tim.it).

Audioguide Tours: They're available from a kiosk near the ticket booth at the Porta Marina entrance (€6.50, €10 for 2, ID required); they offer basically the same info as your free booklet.

Length of This Tour: Allow three hours.

Baggage Check: A free baggage check is near the turnstiles at the site entrance (retrieve bags by 19:20).

Connecting to Vesuvius: If you want to visit Mount Vesuvius, you can catch a bus from Pompeii at Piazza Esedra and Piazza Anfiteatro (8/day, every half hour from 9:30–10:30, hourly beginning at 11:25, 1-hour trip, €8.60 round-trip; see "Vesuvius" on page 750).

Cuisine Art: Inside the site, there's a decent-value cafeteria that offers three options: basic sandwiches, a self-service cafeteria line, and a fancier restaurant in a more elegant, ancient gymnasium setting. A few mediocre restaurants cluster between the entrance and the train station.

Starring: Roofless (collapsed) but otherwise intact Roman buildings, plaster casts of hapless victims, a few erotic frescoes, and the dawning realization that these ancient people were no different from us.

Background

Pompeii was a booming Roman trading city. Not rich, not poor,

it was middle class, making it a perfect example of typical Roman life. Most streets would have been lined with stalls and jammed with customers from sunup to sundown. Chariots vied with shoppers for street space. Two thousand years ago, Rome controlled the entire Mediterranean—making it a kind of free-trade zone—and Pompeii was a central and bustling port.

There were no posh neighborhoods in Pompeii. Rich and poor mixed it up as elegant houses existed side by side with simple homes. While nearby Herculaneum would have been a classier place to live (traffic-free streets, fancier houses, far better drainage), Pompeii was the place for action and shopping. It served an estimated 20,000 residents with more than 40 bakeries, 30 brothels, and 130 bars, restaurants, and hotels. With most buildings covered by brilliant, white, ground-marble stucco, Pompeii in A.D. 79 was an impressive town.

Pompeii

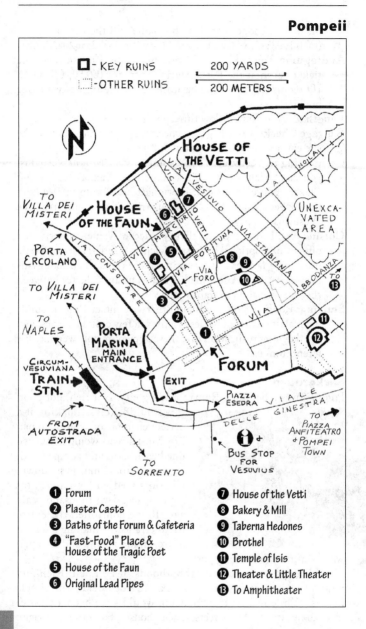

- ☐ – KEY RUINS
- ⬚ – OTHER RUINS

200 YARDS
200 METERS

1 Forum
2 Plaster Casts
3 Baths of the Forum & Cafeteria
4 "Fast-Food" Place & House of the Tragic Poet
5 House of the Faun
6 Original Lead Pipes

7 House of the Vetti
8 Bakery & Mill
9 Taberna Hedones
10 Brothel
11 Temple of Isis
12 Theater & Little Theater
13 To Amphitheater

Naples

As you tour Pompeii, remember that its best art is in the Archaeological Museum in Naples (described on page 718).

SELF-GUIDED TOUR

• *Just past the ticket-taker, start your approach up to the...*

Porta Marina

This was the original town gate. Before Vesuvius blew, the sea came nearly to here. Look down to the left to see the rings that

were used to tie ships to the dock. Also notice the two openings in the gate. Both were left open by day to admit major traffic. At night, they would close the larger one for better security.

• *Pass through the Porta Marina and continue up the street, pausing at the three large stepping stones in the middle.*

Pompeii's Streets

Every day, Pompeiians flooded the streets with gushing water to clean them, and the stones let pedestrians cross. These three

stones tell us that this street was a major thoroughfare. Chariots (all with standard-size axles) could straddle the stones traveling in either direction. One stone in a road means it was a one-way-street, two stones an ordinary two-way, and three a major arterial like this.

• *Continue up the street a few steps, where it opens up into...*

❶ The Forum (Foro)

Pompeii's commercial, religious, and political center stands at the

intersection of the city's two main streets. While it's the most ruined part of Pompeii, it's grand nonetheless. Picture the piazza surrounded by two-story buildings on all sides (some building ruins remain). The pedestals that line the square once held statues, now in the

The Eruption of Vesuvius

At noon on August 24, A.D. 79, Mount Vesuvius blew, sending a mushroom cloud of ash, dust, cinders, and rocks 12 miles into the air. It spewed for 18 hours straight, as winds blew the cloud southward. The white-gray ash settled like snow on Pompeii, collapsing roofs and floors, but leaving the walls intact. Two thousand of the town's 20,000 residents were entombed under eight feet of fine powder.

The next morning, Vesuvius' column of ejected material collapsed, picking up speed as it fell to earth, creating a cloud of ash, pumice, and gas. The red-hot avalanche (a "pyroclastic flow") sped down the side of the mountain at nearly 100 mph. Four minutes later, it engulfed the city of Herculaneum four miles away, burying it in nearly 60 feet of hot mud. The mud cooled into stone, freezing the moment in time.

museum in Naples.

At this (closest to you) end of the square are the squat remains of the **city hall** *(curia)*, built with brick and mortar, but originally faced with marble. Note that while Pompeii was destroyed by the eruption of A.D. 79, it was also devastated by an earthquake in A.D. 62. It's safe to assume that any brick you see dates from between A.D. 62 and A.D. 79—restoration work done by Pompeiians after the quake.

The forum was dominated by the **Temple of Jupiter,** at the far end. You can still see remains of the grand staircase and a few tall columns.

Facing the Temple of Jupiter, with your back to the city hall, look to the building on your left, the **basilica.** Step inside and see the layout of the column stumps. This ancient law court has the same floor plan as many Christian churches (which are also called basilicas). Two narrower aisles flank a central nave, or hallway. The columns are made of bricks in a flower-petal pattern, originally covered with a plaster made of marble dust. Along the side walls are traces of original marble.

Cross to the opposite side of the forum to look down Pompeii's **main street.** Lined with shops, bars, and restaurants, it was a lively place and a pedestrian-only zone (notice the traffic barriers that kept chariots out). Many of Pompeii's streets were off-limits to chariots during shopping hours, and were marked with street signs showing pictures of men carrying vases—pedestrians only. On this busy street, to keep rowdy late-night crowds from getting out of hand, a gate at the head of the street dropped down to seal off the forum (see the remains).

Looking north beyond the Temple of Jupiter, five miles away looms the ominous back story to this site: **Mount Vesuvius.** Mentally draw a triangle up from the two remaining peaks to reconstruct the mountain before the eruption. When it blew, Pompeiians had no idea that they were living under a volcano, since Vesuvius hadn't erupted for 1,200 years. (Still active, Vesuvius last blew in 1944.) Imagine the wonder—then the horror—as the column of smoke roared upward, and then began to fall like hail, rain, and snow, collapsing roofs and burying everything in a blanket of ash.

• *Walk toward the far end of the forum along the left side, passing alongside some sheds containing...*

❷ Plaster Casts of Victims

Two thousand Pompeii citizens suffocated under the ash, and these eerie casts capture them in their last moments. Archaeologists made these casts when, while excavating, they detected hollows underfoot—left by decomposed bodies. They'd pour liquid plaster into the cavities (which acted as molds), let it dry, and dig up the casts. The sheds also display many *amphorae*—the tall clay jars Romans used to transport food, wine, and olive oil. Pompeii, a seaport trading town, had thousands of these.

Just past the sheds, turn left into an **ancient public WC** that once served the forum. Notice the ditch that led to the sewer (marked by an arch in the corner). The stone supports once held wooden benches with the appropriate holes.

• *From the toilets, backtrack a while, then turn left on Via del Foro, passing a convenient 21st-century cafeteria. Just past the cafeteria, on the left-hand side, are the...*

❸ Baths of the Forum (Terme del Foro)

This may be closed for renovation. But if it's open, you'll enter through the gymnasium. After working out, clients would find four rooms: a waiting room, warm bath *(tepidarium)*, hot bath *(caldarium)*, and cold-plunge bath *(frigidarium)*.

The *tepidarium* is ringed by mini-statues or *telamones* (male caryatids, figures used as supporting pillars), which divided the lockers. Clients would undress and warm up here, perhaps stretching out on one of the benches near the bronze heater for a massage. Notice the ceiling: half crushed by the eruption and half surviving, with its fine blue-and-white stucco work.

Next, in the *caldarium*, you'd get hot. Notice the engineering. The double floor was heated from below—so nice with bare feet (look into the grate to see the brick support towers). The double walls with brown terra-cotta tiles held the heat. Romans soaked in the big tub, which was filled with hot water. To keep condensation from dripping annoyingly from the ceiling, the fluting (ribbing) was added to carry the drips down the walls.

Next came the cold plunge in the *frigidarium*—a circular marble basin with the spout spewing frigid water, opposite the entry.

• *At the intersection past the baths (near the triumphal arch), turn left. After a few steps, you'll find...*

❹ Wheel Grooves, Fast Food, and Barking Dogs

In the pavement, notice the **oxcart-wheel grooves,** dug in by centuries of use. There are also more stepping stones for pedestrians to cross the flooded streets.

Along the right side of the street are rectangular marble counters. This shop was a **fast-food place.** The holes in the counters held the pots for the food. Most ancient Romans did not cook for themselves in their tiny apartments, and to-go places like this can be found on many of Pompeii's streets. Notice the groove in the shop's front doorstep. Shops had sliding doors (or, more precisely, folding accordion doors) that fit into these grooves. Holes out on the curb likely were for cords that stretched awnings over the sidewalk to shield the clientele.

Just up the street a few steps (also on the right) is the **House of the Tragic Poet** (Casa de Poeta Tragico), with its famous "Beware of Dog" *(Cave Canem)* mosaic in the entryway.

• *Facing the House of the Tragic Poet, turn right and walk downhill two blocks. On your left, at #1, you'll find the...*

❺ House of the Faun (Casa del Fauno)

The small bronze statue of the *Dancing Faun* (the original is in Naples' Archaeological Museum—see page 718) welcomes you to Pompeii's largest home. With 40 rooms and 27,000 square feet, the House of the Faun covers an entire city block. Wander past the welcome mosaic (*HAVE* or "hail to you") and through its courtyards. The next floor mosaic, with an intricate diamond-like design, decorates the homeowner's office. Beyond that is the famous floor mosaic of the *Battle of Alexander* (the original is in Naples' Archaeological Museum—see page 718). This reproduction was only recently placed here in its original location. The restoration team first traced a photo of the original and laid the tracing on wet clay to make an impression. Then they painstakingly filled in the outlines with 1.5 million tiny pieces of tile and rock to recreate the 18-foot-by-9-foot mosaic. The house's back courtyard leads to the exit in the far right corner. It's lined with pillars rebuilt after the A.D. 62 earthquake. Take a close look at the brick, mortar, and fake marble stucco veneer. (If this exit is closed, return to the entrance and make a U-turn left, around to the back of the house.)

• *Exit the House of the Faun at the back end and turn right. Along the right-hand side of the street are metal cages protecting...*

❻ Original Lead Pipes

These 2,000-year-old pipes (made of lead imported from Britannia) were part of the city's elaborate water system. A huge water tank—fed by an aqueduct—stood at the high end of town. Three independent pipe systems supplied water to the city from here: one for baths, one for private homes, and one for public water fountains. If there was a water shortage, democratic priorities prevailed: First the baths were cut, then the private homes. The last water to be cut was that which fed the public fountains, the place where everyone could get their water for drinking and cooking.

• *Take your first left (on Vicolo dei Vetti) and find the entrance (on the left) to the...*

❼ House of the Vetti (Casa dei Vetti)

If it's not closed for renovation, enter Pompeii's best-preserved home. The House of the Vetti, which has retained its mosaics and frescoes, was the bachelor pad of two wealthy merchant brothers. In the entryway, see if you can spot the erection. This is not pornography. There's a meaning here: The penis and the sack of money balance each other on the goldsmith scale above a fine bowl of fruit. The meaning: Only with a balance of fertility and

money can you have abundance.

Step into the atrium, with its ceiling open to the sky to collect light and rainwater. The pool, while decorative, was a functional water-supply tank. It's flanked by large money boxes anchored to the floor. The brothers were certainly successful merchants, and possibly moneylenders, too.

Exit on the right, passing the tight servant quarters, and go into the kitchen, with its bronze cooking pots (and a touchable lead pipe on the back wall). The passage dead-ends in the little Venus Room, with its erotic frescoes behind glass.

Return to the atrium and pass into the big colonnaded garden. It was planted according to the plan indicated by traces of roots excavated in the volcanic ash. Richly frescoed entertainment rooms ring this courtyard. Circle counterclockwise. The dining room is finely decorated in "Pompeiian red" (from iron rust) and black. Study the detail. Notice the lead humidity seal between the wall and the floor, designed to keep the moisture-sensitive frescoes dry. (Had Leonardo da Vinci taken this clever step, his *Last Supper* in Milan might be in better shape today.) Continuing around, notice the square white stones inlaid in the floor. Imagine them reflecting like cats' eyes as the brothers and their friends wandered around by oil lamp late at night. Frescoes in the Yellow Room (near the exit) show off the ancient mastery of perspective, which was not matched elsewhere in Europe for nearly 1,500 years.

• *After visiting the House of the Vetti (or just looking in the door, if the house is under renovation), get oriented from the entrance to the house.*

Facing the entrance to the House of the Vetti, turn left and walk one long block (along Vicolo dei Vetti) to a T-intersection (Via della Fortuna), marked by a stone fountain with a bull's head for a spout. Intersections like this were busy neighborhood centers, where the rent was highest and people gathered. Turn left, then immediately right, walking along a gently curving road. On the left side of the street, at #22, find four big stone cylinders.

❽ The Bakery and Mill (Forno e Mulini)

The brick oven looks like a modern-day pizza oven. And the stubby stone towers are flour grinders. Grain was poured into the top, and donkeys pushed wooden bars that turned the stones. The powdered grain dropped out of the bottom as flour—flavored with tiny bits of rock.

• *Continue to the next intersection (Via degli Augustali, where there's another fast-food joint) and turn left. About 50 yards down this (obviously one-way) street, on the left at #44 you'll find the...*

❾ Taberna Hedones

This bar must have been a happy, hedonistic place. The cute welcome mosaic reads *HAVE* ("hail to you"), with the bear licking his wounds. The place still has its original floor and, deeper in, the mosaic arch of a grotto fountain.

• *Just past the tavern, turn right and walk downhill to #18, on the right.*

❿ The Brothel *(Lupanare)*

Prostitutes were nicknamed *lupe* (she-wolves). Wander into the brothel, a simple place with stone beds and pillows. The ancient graffiti includes tallies and exotic names of the women, indicating they came from all corners of the Mediterranean. The faded frescoes above the cells may have served as a kind of menu for services offered. Note the idealized portrayal of women (white, considered beautiful) and men (dark, considered horny).

• *Leaving the brothel, continue going downhill two blocks to the intersection with Pompeii's main drag, Via dell'Abbondanza. (The forum—and exit—are to the right, for those that may wish to opt out from here. The huge amphitheater—which is certainly skippable—is 10 min to your left.) But we'll go straight ahead, down Via dei Teatri, then left before the columns, downhill to the...*

⓫ Temple of Isis

This Egyptian temple served Pompeii's Egyptian community. The little shrine with the plastic roof housed holy water from the Nile. Pompeii must have had a synagogue, but it has yet to be excavated.

• *Exit the temple where you entered, and take an immediate right down an alleyway to our last stop, the...*

⓬ Theater and Little Theater

Originally a Greek theater (Greeks built theirs with the help of a hillside), this marks the spot of the birthplace of the Greek port here in 470 B.C. During Roman times, the theater sat 5,000 in three price ranges: the five marble terraces up close (filled with romantic wooden seats for two), the main section, and the cheap nosebleed section (surviving only on the right). The square stones above the cheap seats once supported a canvas rooftop. Notice the high-profile boxes, flanking the stage, for guests of honor. From this perch, you can see the gladiator barracks—the colonnaded courtyard beyond the theater. They lived in tiny rooms, trained in the courtyard, and fought in the nearby amphitheater. Just next door, the **Little Theater** (Teatro Piccolo) is a more intimate space that seated 1,000.

• *You've seen Pompeii's highlights. When you're ready to leave, backtrack to the main road and turn left, going uphill to the forum, where you'll find the main entrance/exit.*

Or consider taking a look at the...

ⓑ Amphitheater

There's much more to see—75 percent of Pompeii's 164 acres has been excavated, and our tour has only covered about one-third of the site. After the theaters—if you still have energy to see more—go back to the main road, and take a right toward the eastern part of the site, where the crowds thin out. A 10-minute walk leads to the **amphitheater.** Climb to the upper level and—with Vesuvius looming in the background—mentally replace the tourists below with gladiators and wild animals locked in combat.

Walk along the top of the amphitheater and look down into the grassy rectangular area surrounded by columns. This is the **Palaestra,** an area once used for athletic training. Facing the other way, look for the bell tower that tops the roofline of the modern city of Pompei, where locals go about their daily lives in the shadow of the volcano, just as their ancestors did 2,000 years ago.

• *The exit near the amphitheater deposits you in Piazza Anfiteatro. To get back to the main Pompeii entrance, take a right down Via Plinio and walk for 15 minutes.*

HAVE!

Herculaneum (Ercolano)

Smaller, less ruined, and less crowded than its famous big sister, Herculaneum (worth ▲▲) offers a closer, more intimate peek into ancient Roman life but lacks the grandeur of Pompeii (there's barely a colonnade).

ORIENTATION

Cost, Hours, Information: €11, €20 combo-ticket includes Pompeii and three lesser sites (valid 3 days), can be free or 50 percent off with Campania ArteCard (see "Planning Your

Time in the Region" on page 714). Open daily April–Oct 8:30–19:30, Nov–March 8:30–17:00, ticket office closes 90 min earlier (tel. 081-77-7008, www.pompeiisites.org). Be sure to pick up a free detailed map of the site when you purchase your ticket. The info office across from the ticket window gives out a free, excellent booklet, with numbered explanations of each building. The informative and interesting **audioguide** sheds light on the ruins and life in Herculaneum in the first century A.D. (€6.50, €10 for 2, ID required, turn in 30 min before closing). The WCs are to the left of the audioguide kiosk.

Getting to Herculaneum: Herculaneum (Ercolano) is about 25 minutes from Naples and roughly 45 minutes from Sorrento on the same Circumvesuviana train that goes to Pompeii (see page 767 for information). Get off at the train stop called "Ercolano Scavi." To walk to the ruins, leave the Ercolano station and turn right, then left, following the brown signs; go eight blocks straight downhill from the station to the end of the road. The ticket office and baggage check (pick up bags 30 min prior to site closing) are beneath the grand arch.

SELF-GUIDED TOUR

Caked and baked by the same A.D. 79 eruption that pummeled Pompeii, Herculaneum is a small community of intact buildings with plenty of surviving detail. While Pompeii was initially smothered in ash and pumice, Herculaneum was buried under nearly 60 feet of boiling mud, which hardened into baked tufa *(tufo)*, perfectly preserving the city until excavations began in 1738.

After leaving the ticket window, walk the long path around the site to the entrance. From here, you can get a sense of just how much lava piled up. The present-day city of Ercolano looms just above, and the modern buildings don't look much different than their ancient counterparts.

After crossing into the excavation site, stroll straight to the end of the street and find the **Seat of the Augustali** (Sede degli Augustali). Decorated with frescoes of Hercules (for whom this city was named), it was a forum for freed slaves climbing their way up the ladder of Roman society.

Leave the building and go to the right, down a lane. The adjacent *thermopolium* was the Roman equivalent to fast food, with giant tubs for wine, oil, and snacks. Most of the buildings along here were shops, with apartments above. Look around doorways for ancient bits of lava-charred wood. Most buildings were made of stone, but the floors and beams were wood (which doesn't survive at any other ancient sight).

The **Bottega ad Cucumas** wine shop still has charred remains of beams and its drink list frescoed on the wall.

Down the street to the right, **The House of Neptune and Amphitrite** (Casa di Nettuno e Anfitrite) has colorful mosaics and an intact shell frame.

At the far end of the site is the don't-miss-it **gymnasium** *(palestra)* complex with its Hydra of Lerna. This sculpted bronze fountain features the seven-headed monster defeated by Hercules as one of his 12 labors. Find the Hydra by walking through the triangular-shaped entrances carved in the tufa wall. To light up this cavernous space, go to the second doorway on the left wall and press the switch. Just outside, take a close look at the "marble" columns. While important buildings in Rome had solid marble columns, these are typical of ordinary buildings. They're made of rounded bricks covered with a thick layer of plaster, shaped to look like carved marble.

The House of the Deer (Casa dei Cervi) is also worth seeking out. It's named for the statues of deer being attacked by dogs in the garden courtyard (these are copies; the originals are in the Archaeological Museum in Naples).

The **baths** (possibly closed for restoration through 2008) illustrate the city's devastation. After you descend into the baths, look back at the steps. You'll see the original wood charred in the disaster, protected by the wooden planks you just walked on. At the bottom of the stairs, in the waiting room to the right, notice where the floor collapsed under the sheer weight of the volcanic mud. (The sunken pavement reveals the baths' heating system; hot air generated by wood-burning furnaces circulated between the different levels of the floor.) A doorway in the room in front of the stairs is still filled with solidified mud. Despite the damage, elements of refinement remain intact, such as the delicate stuccoes in the *caldarium* (hot bath).

Make your way to the arches. As you descend, you're walking across what was formerly Herculaneum's beach. The **arches** that you see were boat storage areas. During excavations in 1981, hundreds of bodies were found here—between the wall of volcanic stone behind you and the city in front of you. Some of Herculaneum's 4,000 citizens had a little more time than the people of Pompeii to flee the eruption. They tried to escape to the sea, but never made it out of Herculaneum.

Vesuvius

The 4,000-foot-high Vesuvius, mainland Europe's only active volcano, has been sleeping restlessly since 1944.

Getting to Vesuvius: The summit is accessible year-round

by car (just drive to the end of the road, where you pay €2.50 to park), taxi (€80 round-trip from Naples), or by the usually blue or gray Vesuviana Mobilità bus (weather permitting in winter). The bus runs from **Herculaneum** (daily at 9:00 and 12:45, €7.60 round-trip), and more predictably and frequently from **Pompeii** (8/day, every half hour from 9:30–10:30, hourly beginning at 11:25, 1-hour trip, departs from Piazza Anfiteatro and Piazza Esedra in front of TI, €8.60 round-trip). Check with driver upon arrival at the summit regarding schedule for return trips. The bus may make a bathroom stop at a tourist shack along the way (for an annoyingly long time, up to 30 min, in hope that you'll buy things).

At Vesuvius: Admission, with a mandatory guide, costs €6.50 (daily 9:00–15:00, tel. 081-771-0911, www.vesuviopark.it). From the parking lot, it's a steep 30-minute hike to the top for a sweeping view of the Bay of Naples (often cold and windy, bring a coat, especially Oct–April). Up here, it's desolate and lunar-like, and the rocks are newly minted. Walk the entire crater lip for the most interesting views; the far end overlooks Pompeii. Be still and alone to hear the wind and occasional cascades of rocks tumbling into the crater. Any steam? Closed when erupting.

SORRENTO AND CAPRI

Without a hint of big-city Naples and just an hour to the south, serene Sorrento makes an ideal home base for exploring all the fascinating sights in the region, from Naples to the Amalfi Coast to Paestum. And the jet-setting island of Capri is just a short cruise from Sorrento, offering more charm and fun (outside of the crowded months of July and August) than its glitzy reputation would lead you to believe.

Sorrento

Wedged on a ledge under the mountains and over the Mediterranean, spritzed by lemon and olive groves, Sorrento is an attractive resort of 20,000 residents and—in the summer—as many tourists. It's as well-located for regional sightseeing as it is a fine place to stay and stroll. The Sorrentines have gone out of their way to create a completely safe and relaxed place for tourists to come and spend money. Everyone seems to speak fluent English and work for the Chamber of Commerce. This gateway to the Amalfi Coast has an unspoiled old quarter, a lively main shopping street, and a spectacular cliffside setting. Locals are proud of the many world-class romantics who've vacationed here, such as the famed tenor Enrico Caruso, who chose Sorrento as the place to spend his last weeks in 1921.

Planning Your Time

With Sorrento as your home base, spend a minimum of three days and nights in the region. On your way to or from Sorrento, visit Naples as a day-trip. After settling in Sorrento, spend a day touring the Amalfi Coast by bus, and another day split between Sorrento and Pompeii (accessible by Circumvesuviana train—see page 767). With more time, catch a quick boat ride to the nearby island of Capri or linger on the Amalfi Coast (see next chapter), getting as far south as Paestum's Greek temples.

ORIENTATION

Sorrento is long and narrow. The main drag, Corso Italia (50 yards in front of the Circumvesuviana train station), runs parallel to the sea from the station through the town center and out to the cape, where it's renamed Via Capo. The town's center is the square called Piazza Tasso. Everything mentioned here (except the hotels on Via Capo) is within a 10-minute walk of the train station. Sorrento hibernates in January and February, when many places close down.

Tourist Information

The TI (labeled *Soggiorno e Turismo*)—located inside the Foreigners' Club—hands out a free monthly *Surrentum* magazine with a great city map and schedules of boats, buses, concerts, and festivals (Mon–Sat 8:45–18:15, closed Sun, shorter hours off-season, tel. 081-807-4033, www.sorrentotourism.com, info@sorrentotourism .com). To reach the TI from the train station, go left on Corso Italia and walk five minutes to Piazza Tasso, turn right at the end of the square, head down Via L. de Maio through Piazza Sant'Antonino, and continue about 30 yards downhill to the Foreigners' Club mansion at #35. If you arrive after the TI closes, look for the useful TI handouts in the lobby of the Foreigners' Club (open until midnight).

If you need only quick advice, the fake tourist office—located in a green caboose just outside the train station—can be of help. While they're a private business and hope you'll purchase one of their overpriced excursions, they're willing to give basic information on directions, buses, and ferries.

Arrival in Sorrento

By Train: Those arriving by train (the last stop of the Circumvesuviana) find taxis waiting to overcharge them (generally €12 to most hotels) and an Amalfi bus stop. All recommended hotels—except those on Via Capo—are within a 10-minute walk.

Sorrento

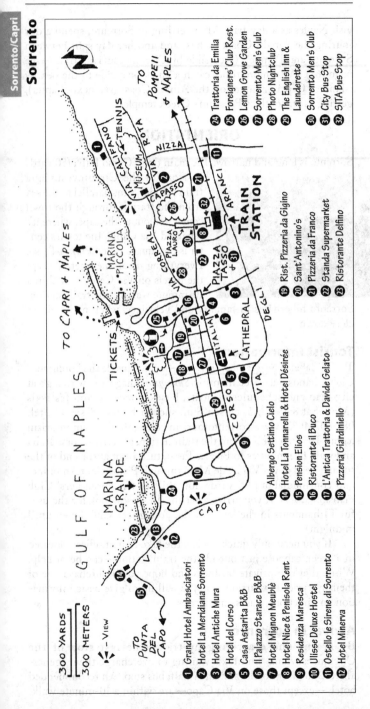

1. Grand Hotel Ambasciatori
2. Hotel La Meridiana Sorrento
3. Hotel Antiche Mura
4. Hotel del Corso
5. Casa Astarita B&B
6. Il Palazzo Starace B&B
7. Hotel Mignon Meublé
8. Hotel Nice & Penisola Rent
9. Residenza Maresca
10. Ulisse Deluxe Hostel
11. Ostello le Sirene di Sorrento
12. Hotel Minerva
13. Albergo Settimo Cielo
14. Hotel La Tonnarella & Hotel Désirée
15. Pension Elios
16. Ristorante il Buco
17. L'Antica Trattoria & Davide Gelato
18. Pizzeria Giardiniello
19. Rist. Pizzeria da Gigino
20. Sant'Antonino's
21. Pizzeria da Franco
22. Standa Supermarket
23. Ristorante Delfino
24. Trattoria da Emilia
25. Foreigners' Club Rest.
26. Lemon Grove Garden
27. Sorrento Men's Club
28. Photo Nightclub
29. The English Inn & Launderette
30. Sorrento Men's Club
31. City Bus Stop
32. SITA Bus Stop

While either blue or green-and-white SITA buses head from here to Via Capo hotels (direction: Sant'Agata via Massa, departing every 40 min), many more buses leave from Piazza Tasso in the city center, a five-minute walk from the train station (go down a block and turn left on Corso Italia).

By Boat: Those arriving by boat dock at Marina Piccola, Sorrento's little harbor. To get to Piazza Tasso, it's a 15-minute uphill hike or a short bus ride (3/hr, any orange bus, tickets at adjacent Metro del Mar kiosk). All buses stop at Piazza Tasso.

Helpful Hints

Laundry: A handy laundry is at Corso Italia 30. Enter through the alley (daily 8:00–20:00, full-service—11 pounds for €13, self-service—€9/load, bring coins, includes soap, tel. 081-078-1185).

Where It's At: The **Foreigners' Club** provides reasonably priced snacks and drinks, music, dancing, magnificent views from its cliffside terrace, and a handy place for visitors to meet locals (March–Oct daily 9:30–24:00, behind TI, public WC, tel. 081-877-3263); see "Nightlife" and "Eating" later in this chapter. Drop in for the view overlooking the harbor and the Bay of Naples.

Getting Around Sorrento

By Bus: Orange and orange-and-blue city buses all stop in the main square (Piazza Tasso, only one stop—under flags closest to the sea). Bus #A runs to Meta beach and the hotels on Via Capo, Buses #B and #C go to the port (Marina Piccola), and Bus #D heads to the fishing village (Marina Grande). Tickets cost €1 within the city limits (buy at *tabacchi* shops and newsstands, purchase before boarding, and stamp upon entering). You can buy a ticket from the driver, but you'll pay €0.50 extra.

By Rental Wheels: Many places rent motor scooters for about €40 per day, such as Sorrento Rent-A-Car (daily 9:00–13:00 & 16:00–21:00, Corso Italia 210, tel. 081-878-1386, info@sorrento.it) and Penisola Rent, a half-block away (daily 8:30–21:00, located in Hotel Nice, tel. 081-877-4664, www.penisolarent.com). Don't rent a car in summer unless you enjoy traffic jams.

By Taxi: Taxis are expensive, charging at least €12 for the short ride from the station to hotels. Because of heavy traffic and the complex one-way road system, you can often walk faster than you can ride. If you do use a taxi, even if you agree to a set price, be sure it has a meter. All official taxis have one.

SELF-GUIDED WALK

Welcome to Sorrento

Get to know Sorrento with this lazy self-guided town stroll.

• *Begin on the main square. Stand under the flags with your back to the sea, and face...*

Piazza Tasso: As in any southern Italian town, this "piazza" is Sorrento's living room. It may be noisy and congested, but locals want to be where the action is...and be part of the scene. The most expensive apartments and top cafés are on or near this square. Buses stop here on their way to Marina Piccola (where boats depart for Naples and Capri, at the harbor, a 10-minute hike below you), to the train station (left), and to Via Capo (right).

This square spans a gorge that divided the town until the 19th century. The old town (on your right) still has some surviving ancient Greek streets. The new town (to your left) was farm country just two centuries ago. If you walk a block inland, belly up to the green railing, and look down, you'll see steps from the fifth century B.C.

Sorrento's name came from the Greek word for "siren," the legendary half-bird, half-woman who sang an intoxicating lullaby. No one had ever sailed by the sirens without succumbing to their incredible musical charms...and to death. But Ulysses was determined to hear the song. He put wax in his oarsmen's ears and had himself lashed to the mast of his ship. Oh, it was nice. The sirens, thinking they had lost their powers, threw themselves into the sea, and the place became safe to inhabit. Ulysses' odyssey was all about the westward expansion of Greek culture, and to the ancient Greeks, places like Sorrento were the wild, wild west.

• *With your back still to the sea, head to the far-right corner of the square, behind the statue of Signor Tasso, the square's namesake. (He was a 16th-century Renaissance poet who was born here.) Pop into the flower shop (#18, big courtyard, behind the statue in the right corner) for the feeling of an 18th-century aristocratic palace's courtyard, lined with characteristic tiles. Then, as you're leaving the courtyard, on your immediate left you'll see the narrow...*

Via Santa Maria della Pietà: Here, just a few yards off the noisy main drag, is a street that goes back centuries before Christ. About 100 yards down the lane at #24, find a 13th-century palace (no balconies back then...for security reasons). Continuing on for 10 yards, you'll find a tiny shrine across the street. It's typical of southern Italy, where the faithful pray to their saint, who contacts Mary, who contacts Jesus, who contacts God. This shrine is a bit more direct—it starts right with Mary.

• *Continue down the lane, which ends at the...*

Cathedral: This is the seat of the local bishop. Pop in for a cool stroll around the ambulatory, checking out the impressive *intarcio* (inlaid-wood) doors and the 14 Stations of the Cross, which describe Jesus' last hours.

• *Backtrack 10 yards down Via Santa Maria della Pietà, turn left, cross busy Corso Italia, and go straight on Via Padre R. Giuliani, following the...*

Old Greek Street Plan: Notice here how streets are laid out: east–west for the most sunlight and north–south for the prevailing and cooling breeze. While the gust is welcome in the summer, even in ancient times, documents reported locals complaining about the cold winter wind making them sick.

• *One block ahead is a fine old covered portico, the...*

Sorrento Men's Club: Once the meeting place of the town's nobles, this club has been a retreat for retired working-class men for generations. Strictly no women—and no phones.

Italian men venerate their mothers. (Italians joke that Jesus must have been a southern Italian, because his mother believed her son was God, he believed his mom was a virgin, and he lived at home with her until he was 30.) But Italian men have also built into their culture ways to be on their own. Here, men play cards and gossip under an historic emblem of the city and a finely frescoed 16th-century dome.

• *At the Men's Club, turn right, onto...*

Via San Cesareo: This touristy, pedestrians-only shopping street leads four or five blocks back to Piazza Tasso. All along the way, you can peruse (and sample) lemon products in the very competitive shops. Notice the huge ancient doorways with their tiny doors—to carefully let in people during a dangerous age.

• *At the noisy street on the edge of Piazza Tasso, turn left and fight the traffic downhill to the next square, with a...*

Statue of St. Anthony (Antonino): Sorrento's patron saint humbly looms among the palms, facing the basilica where his reliquary lies. From here, you can quit the walk and stay in the city center, or continue to the village-like waterfront (if it's before 20:00, you can catch a bus to get back). Exit the square diagonally to the left and gradually wind your way downhill to Marina Grande.

• *After a block or so, on the right you'll see a...*

Cliffside Square: This fine public square overlooks the harbor. From here, an elevator takes people down to Marina Piccola, where lounge chairs filled by vacationers working on tans line the sundeck. Enjoy the view of the little harbor and the Bay of Naples. The Franciscan church fronting this square comes with a great little cloister (pop in to see Sicilian Gothic—a 13th-century mix of Norman, Gothic, and Arabic styles).

• *Continue downhill, as the road turns into stairs that zigzag down to the Marina Grande—Sorrento's big harbor. Just before reaching the harbor, you pass under an...*

Ancient Greek Gate: This gate is a reminder that Marina Grande is a separate town from Sorrento, with its own proud residents. It's said that even their cats look different. Sorrentines—who believe that Marina Grande dwellers come from Saracen (Turkish pirate) stock—still scare their children by saying, "Behave—or the Turks will take you away."

Marina Grande's economy is still based on its fishing fleet. People respect old traditions. Women wear black when a relative dies (one year for an uncle, three for a husband). Men get off easy, just wearing a black button if their wife dies. There are two recommended restaurants on the harbor. **Trattoria da Emilia** has an old newspaper clipping about Sophia Loren's filming here tacked near the door. On the far side of the harbor, **Ristorante Delfino** boasts a sundeck for a lazy drink before or after lunch. (See "Eating," page 766, for more details on these places.)

From here, buses return to the center every hour (usually at :25 past the hour, note schedule, buy €1.50 ticket from driver or use €1 ticket purchased from *tabacchi* shop).

SIGHTS AND ACTIVITIES

▲**Strolling**—Take time to explore the surprisingly pleasant old city between Corso Italia and the sea. Views from the public park next to Imperial Hotel Tramontano are worth the detour. The evening *passeggiata* (along Corso Italia and Via San Cesareo) peaks at about 22:00.

▲**Lemon Products Galore**—Via San Cesareo is lined with hardworking, competitive shops selling a mind-boggling array of lemon products and offering samples of lots of sour goodies. Poke around for a pungent experience.

▲**Lemon Grove Garden (L'Agruminato)**—This small park consists of an inviting lemon and orange grove lined with paths. The owners of the grove are seasoned green thumbs, working the orchard through many generations. You'll see that they've even grafted orange-tree branches onto a lemon tree, so that both fruits now grow on the same tree. The garden is dotted with benches, tables, and an inviting little tasting (and buying) stand. They offer free samples of chilled *limoncello* (see sidebar) and various other homemade liqueurs made from basil, mandarins, or fennel (free, daily April–Sept 10:00–21:00, Oct–March 10:00–16:00). The shop selling their organic homemade products is outside the Corso Italia entrance. Enter the garden on Corso Italia (100 yards north of the train station across from Corso Italia #275—where painted tiles show lemon fantasies), or at the intersection of Via Capasso and Via Rota (next to the Hotel La Meridiana Sorrento).

Lemons

Around here, *limoni* are ubiquitous: screaming yellow painted on ceramics, dainty bottles of *limoncello*, and lemons the  size of softballs at the fruit stand. The area of the Amalfi Coast and Sorrento produces several different kinds of lemons.

The gigantic, bumpy lemons are actually citrons, called *cedri*, and are more for show—they're pulpier, rather than juicier, and make a good marmalade. The juicy *sfusato sorrentino*, grown only in Sorrento, is shaped like an American football, while the *sfusato amalfitano*, with knobby points on both ends, is less juicy but equally aromatic. These two kinds of luscious lemons are used in sweets such as *granita* (shaved ice doused in lemonade), *limoncello* (a local candy-like liqueur with a big kick, called *limoncino* on the Cinque Terre), *delizia* (a dome of fluffy cake filled and slathered with a thick, whipped lemon cream), *spremuta di limone* (fresh-squeezed lemon juice), and of course, gelato or *sorbetto alla limone*.

▲**Swimming near Sorrento**—If you require immediate tanning, you can rent a chair on the pier by the port. There are no great beaches in Sorrento—the gravelly, jam-packed private beaches of **Marina Piccola** are more for partying than pampering—there's just a tiny spot for public use.

A sandy beach is two miles away at **Meta.** While the Meta Circumvesuviana stop is a very long walk from the beach (or a €25 cab ride), the orange or orange-and-blue bus #A goes directly from Piazza Tasso to the beach (last stop, schedule posted for hourly returns). At Meta, you'll find pizzerias, snack bars, and a little free section of beach—but it's mostly dominated by several sprawling private-beach complexes. If you go, pay for a spot in one of these. Lido Metamare seems best, and the manager, Aldo, offers readers of this book 30 percent off on everything—including the entry fee (€2.50 entry; also available—and discounted—are lockable changing cabins, lounge chairs, etc.). It's a very Italian scene, with light lunches, a playground, a manicured beach, loud pop music...and no international tourists.

Tarzan might take Jane to the wild and stony beach at **Punta del Capo,** a 15-minute bus ride from Piazza Tasso (2/hr, get off at last stop in front of the American Bar, then walk 10 minutes past ruined Roman Villa di Pollio). From the American Bar bus stop, you can also walk to **Marina di Poulo,** a tiny fishing town popular in the summer for its sandy beach, surfside restaurants, and beach-front disco (15-min walk, follow signs).

Tennis—The Sorrento Sport Snack Bar has fine courts open to the public (daily 9:30–23:00, until 20:00 in winter, €15/hr including rackets and balls for 2 people, call for reservation, across from recommended Ambasciatori Hotel at Via Califano 5, tel. 081-807-1616).

Scuba Diving—To escape the shops, dive deep into the Mediterranean. First, boat out for one hour to the protected marine zone that lies between Sorrento and Capri. There, you can try the beginners' dive (€90, includes instruction and complete supervision, 14:00 daily year-round), or the dives for experienced certified divers (1 dive-€55, 2 dives-€95, April–Oct 9:00 and 14:00). The whole experience takes about three hours, and the prices include all equipment, transportation, and the dive itself, which lasts about 40 minutes for both novices and experts (20 yards east of port at Via Marina Piccola 63, tel. 081-877-4812, mobile 335-130-9363, www.sorrentodivingcenter.it, info@sorrentodivingcenter.it).

NIGHTLIFE

English vacationers come here in droves. Many have holidayed here annually for decades. The town is filled with pubs that try to help British guests feel right at home.

The **English Inn** offers a rough-feeling pub or a more refined-feeling garden out back (daily, open 24 hours, closed Dec; serves baked beans on toast, fish and chips, draft beer; fun music, Internet access, Corso Italia 53, tel. 081-807-4357).

Photo has a modern scene, light food, and DJ music. It's fun for a drink—and people-watching—among stylish Italians on vacation (daily 12:00–3:00 in the morning, Via Correale 19, just off Piazza Tasso, tel. 081-877-3686).

The **Foreigners' Club** offers live Neapolitan songs, Sinatra-style classics, and jazzy elevator-type music nightly at 21:00 throughout the summer. It's just right for old-timers feeling frisky (in the center, see "Tourist Information," page 753). Two places offer touristy folkloric "Tarantella" shows nearly nightly at 21:00 (ask at TI for specifics).

SLEEPING

Sorrento offers the whole range of rooms. Hotels often charge the same for a room whether it has a view, balcony, or neither. At hotels that offer sea views, ask for a room *"con balcone, con vista sul*

Sleep Code

(€1 = about $1.30, country code: 39)
S = Single, **D** = Double/Twin, **T** = Triple, **Q** = Quad, **b** = bathroom,
s = shower only. Unless otherwise noted, credit cards are
accepted, English is spoken, and breakfast is included.

To help you sort easily through these listings, I've divided
the rooms into three categories based on the price for a standard double room with bath:

$$$ **Higher Priced**—Most rooms €140 or more.
$$ **Moderately Priced**—Most rooms between €80–140.
$ **Lower Priced**—Most rooms €80 or less.

---

mare" (with a balcony, with a sea view). *"Tranquillo"* is taken as a
request for a quieter room off the street. Hotels listed are either
near the train station and city center or along the way to Punta del
Capo, a 20-minute walk (or short bus ride) from the station. While
many hotels close for the winter, you should have no trouble finding a room any time outside of August, when the place is jammed
and many hotel prices go way up. Outside of summer, prices can
be soft—it doesn't hurt to ask for a discount (always show this
book). Splurge for a hotel with air-conditioning if you wilt in the
heat, but be aware that it often costs extra. Note: The spindly, more
exotic, and more tranquil Amalfi Coast town of Positano (see next
chapter) is also a good place to spend the night.

East of the Center

To reach these hotels, head a block in front of the train station,
turn right onto Corso Italia, then left down Via Capasso, which
winds right and becomes Via Califano.

$$$ Grand Hotel Ambasciatori is a sumptuous four-star
hotel with 100 rooms, a cliffside setting, a sprawling garden, and
a pool. This is Humphrey Bogart land, with plush public spaces, a
relaxing stay-a-while ambience, and a free elevator to its "private
beach"—actually a sundeck built out over the water (viewless Db-
€230, seaview Db-€330, closed Jan–March, air-con, balconies,
parking, Via Califano 18, tel. 081-878-2025, fax 081-807-1021,
www.ambasciatorisorrento.com, ambasciatori@manniellohotels
.com).

$$$ Hotel La Meridiana Sorrento, a fine three-star place
with everything but character, offers business-class public spaces
and 45 soulless rooms (Db-€140, Tb-€190, required Aug half-
pension at Db-€200 and Tb-€280, prices soft when slow, big rooftop terrace with grand views, next door to public Lemon Grove

Garden, Via Rota 1, tel. 081-807-3535, fax 081-807-3484, www
.lameridianasorrento.com, info@lameridianasorrento.com).

In the Town Center

$$$ **Hotel Antiche Mura** is a 50-room, four-star place—sophisti-
cated, elegant, and plush, with all the amenities you could need in
a hotel. Surrounded by lemon trees, the pool and sun deck are an
oasis. Just a block off the main square, it's cheaper and quieter than
other hotels nearby because it faces a ravine (high-windowed Db-
€150, Db-€180, balcony Db-€250, Michele promises 15 percent off
in 2008 with this book and cash—claim discount when you book,
about a third less Nov–March, a block inland from Piazza Tasso
at Via Fuorimura 7, tel. 081-807-3523, fax 081-807-1323, www
.hotelantichemura.com, info@hotelantichemura.com).

$$ **Hotel del Corso,** a funky, Old World, three-star hotel, has
26 decent rooms. While it's central, family-run, and comfortable,
the staff can be curt (Db-€130, Tb-€160, Qb-€180, ask for €10/day
Rick Steves discount and for room off busy street when you book,
bottom-floor rooms are like new, air-con, rooftop sun terrace, near
Piazza Tasso at Corso Italia 134, tel. 081-807-1016, tel. & fax 081-
807-3157, www.hoteldelcorso.com, info@hoteldelcorso.com).

$$ **Casa Astarita B&B** is a shining gem in the middle of
town, with a crazy-quilt tiled entryway. You'll find six bright,
tranquil, air-conditioned rooms (three with little balconies) and
a fully stocked communal fridge and sideboard for help-yourself
breakfasts (Db-€95–105, Tb-€130, prices promised with this book
in 2008, double-paned windows, elevator, Internet in rustic-yet-
elegant common room, just past Ristorante Parrucchiano as you're
coming from the station on Corso Italia at #67, tel. 081-877-4906,
fax 081-807-1146, www.casastarita.com, info@casastarita.com).
While there's no reception, it's easy to arrange a check-in meeting
with Annamaria or Rita.

$$ **Il Palazzo Starace B&B,** a lesser value than hotels in
this price range, offers seven tidy rooms in a little alley off Corso
Italia (opposite Hotel del Corso, listed above), one block from
Piazza Tasso (Db-€95 June–Sept, otherwise €85, 10 percent off
with cash and this book in 2008, includes small breakfast at a bar
around the corner, no elevator but a luggage dumbwaiter, air-con,
ring bell at Via Santa Maria della Pietà 9 then climb 3 floors, tel.
081-878-4031, fax 081-532-9344, www.palazzostarace.com, info
@palazzostarace.com).

$$ **Hotel Mignon Meublè** rents 24 elegant, soothing, blue
rooms in a central location a block off Corso Italia (Sb-€90,
Db-€105, Tb-€130, air-con, Internet access, roof-top sundeck,
double-paned windows on first floor, some balconies but no
views; from station, turn left on Corso Italia and it's a 10-min

walk to Via Sersale 9; tel. 081-807-3824, fax 081-877-4348, www .sorrentohotelmignon.com, info@sorrentohotelmignon.com, friendly and warm Anna).

$$ Hotel Nice rents 29 simple, cramped rooms with high ceilings 100 yards in front of the train station on the noisy main drag. Alfonso guarantees that you can have a quiet room—critical at this busy location—if you request it with your booking email (Db-€85, Tb-€100, Qb-€120, 10 percent discount with cash and this book in 2008, air-con, elevator, rooftop terrace, Corso Italia 257, tel. 081-878-1650, fax 081-878-3086, www.hotelnice.it, info @hotelnice.it).

$ Residenza Maresca is a humble two-building, 12-room sideline for the recommended Pizzeria Giardiniello, which serves food at the reception (see "Eating," page 765). Eight of the 12 large, modern rooms are at the end of Corso Italia (at #5). Witty owner Franco may struggle with his English and be tardy when he meets you for check-in, but the price can't be beat (Db-€65, Tb-€90, cash only, air-con, mini-fridge, Via Accademia 7–9, tel. 081-878-4616, casamarescaresidence@libero.it).

$ Ulisse Deluxe Hostel, more of an elegant four-star hotel than a hostel, has 56 new, marble-tiled rooms with huge private bathrooms. Reserve a room here before the management regains their sanity (€18–35 per person in 2- to 4-bed rooms, cash only, spa and pool use extra, membership not required, near Marina Grande at Via del Mare 22, tel. 081-877-4753, fax 081-877-4093, www .ulissedeluxe.com, info@ulissedeluxe.com).

$ Ostello le Sirene di Sorrento, a tiny hostel four blocks from the train station, offers 50 of the cheapest beds in town (€18 for a bunk in 8- to 10-bed dorms with bath, Db-€60, includes breakfast, cash only, membership not required, Internet in lobby, open year-round, Via degli Aranci 160, tel. & fax 081-877-1371, www.hostel .it, info@hostellesirene.com).

With a View on Via Capo

These hotels are outside of town, near the cape (straight out Corso Italia, which turns into Via Capo; from the city center, it's a 15-minute walk, a €15 taxi ride, or a cheap bus ride). The bus situation is goofy because there are two competing companies. To get from the train station to Via Capo, you can catch a SITA bus (usually blue or green-and-white, any bus except those heading for Positano/Amalfi) or an orange or orange-and-blue Circumvesuviana bus (#A). Tickets for both (€1) are sold at the station newsstand and tobacco shops (€0.50 more if you buy from the driver). The orange buses run more frequently (3/hr). The first two hotels are my favorite Sorrento splurges, and the last two hotels are clearly the best budget bets. If you're in Sorrento to stay put and luxuriate, these accommodations are perfect (although I'd rather luxuriate in Positano—see page 784). When you're returning to downtown Sorrento, catch any bus heading downhill from Hotel Belair.

$$$ Hotel Minerva is like a sun-worshipper's temple. Catch the elevator at Via Capo 32. Getting off on the fifth floor, you'll step into a spectacular terrace with outrageous Mediterranean views and a small, cliff-hanging swimming pool and a cold-water Jacuzzi *con vista* complementing 60 large, tiled *limoncello* rooms (Db-€160, Tb-€185, Qb-€210, plus €10 for a balcony, these prices—discounted about €30—are promised with this book through 2008 only if claimed at time of inquiry, no summer half-pension requirement, air-con, parking-€10/day, Via Capo 30–32, tel. 081-878-1011, fax 081-878-1949, www.minervasorrento.com, minerva@acampora.it).

$$$ Albergo Settimo Cielo, the aptly named "Seventh Heaven," offers all the views and lazy resort trappings you could want, run by a family that really hustles to provide a fine value. At this old-fashioned cliff-hanger, the reception is just off the road, and the elevator takes you down through four floors with 50 rooms—all with grand views, and many with balconies (Sb-€120, Db-€140, Tb-€180, Qb-€210, 5 percent discount in 2008 if you mention this book when reserving and show it at reception desk, air-con June–Sept, free parking, inviting pool and sun terrace, Via Capo 27, tel. 081-878-1012, fax 081-807-3290, www.hotelsettimocielo.com, info@hotelsettimocielo.com). It's 300 steps above Marina Grande.

$$$ Hotel La Tonnarella is a freshly renovated Sorrentine villa with several terraces, stylish tiles, a dreamy, chandeliered dining room, and disinterested owners. Eighteen of its 24 rooms have views of the sea (non-view Db-€155, seaview Db-€160, Db with view balcony-€165, Db with view terrace-€170, exotic view suite with terrace-€270, €25/person half-pension available in Aug, rooms near kitchen come with clanging pots and pans, air-con, free Internet access, small beach with elevator access, Via Capo 31, tel. 081-878-1153, fax 081-878-2169, www.latonnarella.it, info@latonnarella.it).

$$ Hotel Désirée, run by friendly Corinna and staff, is a drab affair, with humbler vistas but no traffic noise. Half of the 22 slightly scruffy rooms have high, cliff-facing views, balconies, or both (all same price). Most rooms have fans, and there's a fine rooftop sunning terrace, lovable cats, and no half-pension requirements (maximum prices: Sb-€67, small Db-€85, Db-€97, Tb-€115, Qb-€133, cash only, laundry-€8, rooms on bottom floor in better condition, shares driveway and free beach access with La Tonnarella, Via Capo 31, tel. & fax 081-878-1563, www.desireehotelsorrento.com). Corinna is hugely helpful with tips on exploring the peninsula.

$ The humble **Pension Elios,** warmly run by Maria and daughter Gianna, is much like a Sorrentine *nonna*'s house. It offers 14 simple but spacious rooms—most with balconies and views—and a panoramic sun terrace (Db-€75, Tb-€90, family rooms, cheaper off-season but closed Dec–March, cash only, free parking, Via Capo 33, tel. 081-878-1812, www.hotelelios.it, info@hotelelios .it, a little English spoken).

EATING

Downtown Splurges

In a town proud to have no McDonald's, consider eating well for a few extra bucks. Both of these places are worthwhile splurges in the old center.

Ristorante il Buco, once the cellar of an old monastery, is now a small dressy restaurant that serves delightfully presented, top-quality food under a grand, rustic arch. The dashing team of cooks build their sophisticated dishes in a state-of-the-art kitchen, while a plasma-screen TV shows all the action to diners. They showcase good wine (especially from Campania) and offer snappy service. The owner, Peppe, designs his menu around whatever's fresh, and travels in the winter to assemble a wine list sure to offer connoisseurs something new and memorable. He enjoys explaining each of the many courses of his €75 tasting *menù* (€16 pastas, €22 *secondi*, always a good vegetarian selection, dinners run about €50 plus wine, Thu–Tue 12:00–15:00 & 19:00–23:00, closed Wed and Jan, just off Piazza Sant'Antonino; facing the basilica, go under the grand arch on the left and immediately enter the restaurant at II Rampa Marina Piccola 5; tel. 081-878-2354). Reservations are generally necessary to sit inside under their elegant vault. For outside dining, I'd go elsewhere.

L'Antica Trattoria serves more traditional cuisine from an inviting menu in a *romantico* candlelit ambience. It has intimate nooks ideal for small groups. Aldo and sons will take good care of you in a place busy with enthusiastic eaters and professional but contagiously fun waiters (€20 pastas, €30 *secondi*; fixed-price meals from €35; always vegetarian options). Its wine list is more predictable, featuring well-known wines from the region. Walk around the labyrinthine interior before you select a place to sit (daily 12:00–15:00 & 19:00–23:30, closed Mon Nov–Feb, air-con, shaded verdant terrace, non-smoking sections, reservations smart, Via Padre R. Giuliani 33, tel. 081-807-1082).

Eating Well and Cheaply Downtown

Pizzeria Giardiniello is a family show, offering good food, friendly smiles, and a peaceful tropical garden setting (€5 pizzas and pastas, daily 12:00–24:00, Via Accademia 7, tel. 081-878-4616). Like an old sailor checking the lines, Franco makes sure you're well-fed. Franco's son, Luigi, runs a wine-and-tapas bar downstairs (nightly 18:00 until past midnight).

Ristorante Pizzeria da Gigino, lively and small, makes huge, tasty, Neapolitan-style pizzas in their wood-burning oven (Wed–Mon 12:00–15:00 & 17:00–24:00, closed Tue but daily July–Aug; just off Piazza Sant'Antonino, take first road to the left of Sant'Antonino as you face him, pass under archway and take first left to Via degli Archi 15; tel. 081-878-1927).

Sant'Antonino's nearby offers friendly service, red-checkered tablecloths, an outdoor patio spotted with lemon trees, an open kitchen, decent prices, and edible food (€7 pastas and pizzas, daily 12:00–16:00 & 18:30–24:00, closed Wed Dec–March, just off Piazza Sant'Antonino on Santa Maria delle Grazie 6, tel. 081-877-1200).

Pizzeria da Franco seems to be the local favorite for basic, casual pizza in a fun, untouristy atmosphere. There's nothing fancy about this place—just hot sandwiches and great pizzas served on waxed paper in a square tin. It's packed to the rafters with a youthful crowd that doesn't mind the plastic cups (€7 pizzas, daily 10:00–2:00, just across from Lemon Grove Garden on busy Corso Italia at #265, tel. 081-877-2066).

Picnics: You'll find many markets and take-out pizzerias in the old town. If you fancy a picnic dinner on your balcony, on the hotel terrace, or in the Lemon Grove Garden, get a pizza to go at Pizzeria da Franco (listed above) or groceries at the **Standa supermarket** (Mon–Sat 8:30–13:20 & 16:30–20:25, closed Sun, Corso Italia 223).

Gelato: A few doors downhill from L'Antica Trattoria, **Davide Gelato** has many repeat customers (so many flavors, so little time). Walk the most enticing chorus line in Italy before ordering. Sample *Profumi di Sorrento* (an explosive sorbet of mixed local fruits) and lemon mousse (mid-June–mid-Sept daily 9:30–24:00, otherwise closed Mon, 2 blocks off Corso Italia at Via Padre R. Giuliani 39).

Dinner with Sea Views

For a decent dinner *con vista,* the following places come with great view terraces.

Ristorante Delfino gets their seafood right off the fishermen's boats at Marina Grande, and serves it up in big portions to hungry locals in a quiet and bright pier restaurant. It's lovingly run by effervescent Luisa, her brothers Andrea and Roberto, and her husband Antonio. They take good care of their guests, play Dean Martin, and give travelers who carry this book a little glass of *limoncello* to cap the experience (daily 11:30–15:30 & 18:30–23:00, closed Nov–March; at Marina Grande, facing the water, go all the way to the left and follow signs; tel. 081-878-2038). If you're here for lunch, there's a great sundeck and lounge chairs.

Trattoria da Emilia, on the tranquil Marina Grande waterfront, is inexpensive and good for straightforward, typical Sorrentine home-cooking, including *maccheroni, gnocchi di mamma,* and fresh fish (daily 12:00–15:00 & 19:30–22:30, no reservations, indoor and outdoor seating, cash only, tel. 081-807-2720).

The **Foreigners' Club Restaurant** is a place where the English Patient could recuperate. It has the best sea views in town (under breezy palms), live music nightly at 21:00 (April–Oct, no cover), and passable meals. It's a good spot for dessert or an after-dinner *limoncello* (March–Oct daily, bar opens at 9:30, snacks served 11:30–15:30, dinner 19:00–23:00, closed in winter, Via L. De Maio 35, tel. 081-877-3263).

Hotel Restaurant La Tonnarella takes pride in its kitchen and service. While its dining hall is elegant, its incredible view terrace is where you'll want to be on balmy evenings. This is a good bet for those staying on Via Capo, since it's 100 yards from those recommended hotels (€8 pastas, €15 *secondi,* fine *antipasto misto* buffet and good wine list, open daily, Via Capo 31, tel. 081-878-1153).

TRANSPORTATION CONNECTIONS

It's impressively fast to zip by boat from Sorrento to most coastal towns and islands during the summer, when there are many more departures. In fact, locals routinely get around quicker by fast boat than by car or train (see "Boats," below, and the map on page 771).

From Sorrento to Naples, Pompeii, and Herculaneum by Circumvesuviana Train: This commuter train runs about every 30 minutes between Naples and Sorrento. From Sorrento, it's 30 minutes to Pompeii, 45 minutes to Herculaneum (€1.80 one-way for either trip), and 70 minutes to Naples (€3.20 one-way). The trip is covered by the Campania ArteCard—see page 714. The schedule is printed in the free *Surrentum* magazine (available at TI). See Naples' "Transportation Connections," page 736, for more information on the Circumvesuviana and theft precautions. Note that the risk of theft is mostly limited to suburban Naples, but can be a problem anywhere. Going between Sorrento and Pompeii or Herculaneum is generally safer.

From Sorrento to the Naples Airport: Six Curreri buses run daily to and from the airport; confirm the schedule at the TI (€6, pay driver, runs 9:00–19:30 in each direction, 75 min, depart Piazza Stazione, look for bus with *Curreri* written high on windshield, www.curreriviaggi.it).

To the Amalfi Coast: See page 778.

To Rome: Most people ride the Circumvesuviana 70 minutes to Naples, then catch the express train to Rome. However, the direct Sorrento–Rome bus can actually be more convenient. Marozzi buses (colors vary) leave Sorrento's Piazza Tasso daily for Rome's Tibertina station (€16, 4 hrs, leaves at 6:00 and 17:00 daily, buy tickets by phone, at some travel agencies, or on board for a €4 surcharge, tel. 0805-790-111, www.marozzivt.it).

Boats

The number of boats that run per day varies according to the season. The frequency indicated here is for roughly mid-May through September, with two to four more boats per day in July and August. All schedules should be checked with the TI. The Caremar line, a subsidized state-run ferry company, is slower—but about 50 percent cheaper—than the other lines (for example, trips to Capri cost about €9 rather than €13; fewer departures).

From Sorrento by Boat to: Capri (at least hourly; infrequent ferry: 25 min, €8.80; fastest and priciest jet boat: 20 min, €12.50; 8:25 boat is best—buy ticket at 8:00, depart by 9:30 at the latest—these early boats can be jammed, but it's worth it to avoid crowds on Capri), **Naples** (7/day, 40 min, €10; for more info, see page 734), **Positano** (3/day daily mid-May–mid-Oct only, 50 min for €10; 90 min for €8), **Amalfi** (4/day daily mid-June–mid-Oct, Easter–mid-June weekends only, no boats off-season, 50 min, €7, www.metrodelmare.com). For a slightly less touristy alternative to Capri, consider the nearby island of **Ischia** (1/day, Easter–Nov only, departure usually around 9:30, otherwise from Naples, 55 min, €15).

Getting to Sorrento's Port: To get from Sorrento's Piazza Tasso to Marina Piccola (the port), walk down the stairs near the statue's left side or take orange shuttle bus #B or #C (3/hr). Boat tickets are sold only at the port. Various lines go to different destinations.

Capri

Capri was made famous as the vacation hideaway of Roman emperors Augustus and Tiberius. In the 19th century, it was the haunt of Romantic Age aristocrats on their Grand Tour of Europe. But these days, the island is a world-class tourist trap, packed with gawky, name-tag-wearing visitors searching for the rich and famous, and finding only their prices.

The "Island of Dreams" is a zoo in July and August—overrun with tacky, low-grade group tourism at its worst. Other times of year, however, it provides a relaxing and scenic break from the cultural gauntlet of Italy.

Planning Your Time

This is the best day-trip plan from Sorrento: Take an early jet boat to Capri (buy ticket at 8:00, boat leaves at 8:25 and arrives at 9:00—smart). Go directly to  the Blue Grotto, then catch a bus from the Grotto to Anacapri and ride the chairlift to Monte Solare. From the summit, hike down (or return by chairlift). Stroll out from the base of the chairlift to Villa San Michele for the view, then catch a bus to Capri for the rest of your stay. At the end of the day, ride the funicular down to Marina Grande to catch the boat back to Sorrento. For an efficient way to connect destinations, many travelers coming from Sorrento check their bag at the harbor, see Capri, and sail from here directly to Naples.

Note that two companies handle the Sorrento–Capri crossings: LMP and Caremar. Their ferries and hydrofoils vary in price, frequency, and trip duration (check schedules, best deal is the infrequent 25-minute fast ferry with Caremar for €8.80).

If you buy a one-way ticket to Capri (there's no round-trip discount), you'll have maximum schedule flexibility and can take either company's boat back. (Check times for the last return crossing upon arrival; at Capri get a schedule from the TI or check at boat-ticket kiosk.) During July and August, however, it's wise to get a round-trip boat ticket with a late return (improving your odds of getting a spot on a boat when they're most crowded; available from LMP line)—and you can use the ticket to return earlier if you like. Be 20 minutes early or you can be bumped.

Day-trippers come down from Rome, creating a daily rush hour in each direction. The trip to the Blue Grotto is just a 20-minute boat ride (€10) away from the arrival dock, but the commotion there can amount to a two-hour delay (see page 774). If you're heading to Capri specifically to see the Blue Grotto, be sure to check that the tide isn't too high or the water too rough—ask the TI or your hotelier before heading over.

ORIENTATION

First thing—pronounce it right: KAH-pree, not kah-PREE like the song or the pants. The island is small—just four miles by two miles—and is separated from the Sorrento Peninsula by a narrow strait. There are only two towns to speak of (Capri and Anacapri). The island also has some scant Roman ruins and a few interesting churches and villas. But its chief attraction is its famous Blue

Grotto, and its best activity is a chairlift up the island's Monte Solaro, followed by a scenic hike down.

Arrival in Capri

Get oriented on the boat before you dock. As you near the harbor, Capri spreads out before you: The dock is **Marina Grande** (TI, boats to **Blue Grotto,** buses to anywhere, funicular to the town of Capri). **Capri town** fills the ridge high above the harbor. Emperor Tiberius' palace ruins, **Villa Jovis,** cap the peak on the left. The dramatic *"Mamma mia!"* road arcs around the highest mountain on the island **(Monte Solare)** on the right, leading up to **Anacapri** (the island's second town, just out of sight). Notice the zigzag steps that date from ancient times below that road. The white house on the ridge above the zigzags is **Villa San Michele** (where you'll go later for a grand view of boats like the one you're on now).

Upon arrival, get your bearings. Boats dock in two places: On the long pier or directly by the main street. If your boat arrived on the main street, take a right to get to the long pier. Stand with your back to the pier: The **funicular** is across the street. The fourth little shop to the right of the funicular (no sign, sells clothes and souvenirs) provides **baggage storage** in the back of the store (€3/day per bag, daily 9:00–18:00). The kiosk that sells **bus and funicular tickets** is around the end of the pier to your right. Kiosks that sell return **boat tickets** (for the two competing companies) are behind that; across the street from all this are the **public WCs**.

The **TI** is behind you on the dock (April–Oct daily 8:30–20:30; Nov–March Mon–Sat 9:00–13:00 & 15:30–18:30, closed Sun; pick up €1 map only if you'll be venturing to the outskirts of Capri town or Anacapri, tel. 081-837-0634).

From the port, you have three transit options: boat to the Blue Grotto (best early—ideally upon arrival), bus to Anacapri, or ride the funicular up to Capri town (4/hr, 5 min; if funicular isn't running, use bus—departs from station 50 yards uphill to right).

Helpful Hints

Money-Saving Tips: A cheap day trip to Capri is tough. If you're on a budget, bring a picnic lunch packed in from Sorrento (for info on where to buy supplies, see page 766).

From Sorrento to Capri by boat is about €9–12.50 each way, and Blue Grotto tickets (plus transportation and tip) come to €21. That's about €40–46 per person. Consider skipping the boat to the Blue Grotto and taking the bus instead (see below, saves about €7 per person). And remember, after 18:00, anyone can see the Blue Grotto for free...if you're willing to swim in.

Capri

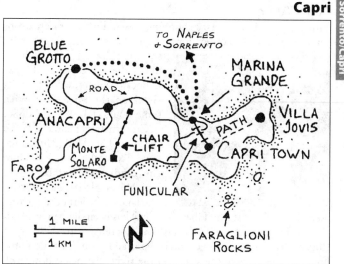

Local Guide: Roberta Mazzarella is good (about €50/hr but depends on itinerary, mobile 339-135-7619, robertamazzarella @yahoo.it).

Getting Around Capri

The buses and funicular are covered by the same ticket options: €1.30 per ride (two single tickets are the best option if going straight to Blue Grotto by public bus), €2.10 for 60 minutes of unlimited use, or €6.70 for an all-day pass (return the pass at the end of the day to get €1 deposit back). Schedules are clearly posted at all bus stations. You can hire a taxi for about €60 per hour—negotiate.

Buses from the Port at Marina Grande: Buses pick up just uphill from where you bought your ticket. Get in line under the appropriate sign: either under *S. Costanzo* for going up to the town of **Capri** (4/hr), where you could then transfer to Anacapri (4/hr, 7 min, there's routinely a long queue for this Capri–Anacapri bus); or direct to **Anacapri** (2/hr).

Buses from Anacapri: Buses go to **Capri town** (at least 4/ hr, can be packed; guarantee a seat by catching the bus before the Anacapri stop, at the end-of-the-line stop called "Caprile"—a 10-min walk down main road, ask for directions). Buses also run to the **Blue Grotto** (from a different end-of-the-line stop called "Piazza del Cimitero," which is a 5-min walk on the main road from Anacapri's main square). If you're coming from the town of Capri and want to transfer to the Blue Grotto buses, don't get off when the driver announces "Anacapri." Instead, ride one more stop, then transfer to the well-signed Grotta Azzurra (Blue Grotto) buses.

Capri Town

This is a cute but touristy shopping town. The *funiculare* drops you just around the corner from Piazza Umberto, the town's main

square. The **TI** fills a closet under the bell tower on Piazza Umberto (less crowded than its sister on the port—and with same hours, tel. 081-837-0686, WC downstairs behind TI). To the left of City Hall (Municipio, lowest corner), a lane leads into the medieval part of town, which has plenty of eateries. The lane to the left of the many-domed church (past Bar Tiberio, on left) has been dubbed by locals "Rodeo Drive" because it's the fashion shopping strip. Walk down Rodeo Drive to Quisisana Hotel, the island's top old-time hotel. For great views, take the street on the right that heads downhill. At the "T" in the road, you can go left to the 14th-century Certosa Monastery (free, Tue–Sat 9:00–14:00, Sun 9:00–13:00, closed Mon), or right to the lovely public garden, Giardini Augusto (free, daily 9:00–17:00).

Emperor Tiberius' now-ruined villa, **Villa Jovis,** is a scenic 45-minute hike from Capri town. Tiberius ruled Rome from here for a decade (c. A.D. 30). There are no statues and no mosaics. You go for evocative stones and a lovely view (€2, €1 English flier, daily from 9:00 until an hour before sunset, tel. 081-837-4549).

SLEEPING

(€1 = about $1.30, country code: 39)
$$$ Casa per Ferie Villa Helios, a church-run former convent with charming dignity, rents 24 spacious, simple, and pleasant rooms to raise money for the adjacent seniors' home. It's located at the top of Capri town, a 10-minute walk away from the tourist intensity (Db-€140 mid-May–mid-Sept, Db-€110 off-season, extra bed-€30, family rooms, some with air-con, view terrace, leave main square following *Villa Jovis* signs, Via Croce 4, tel. & fax 081-837-0240, www.villahelios.it, info@villahelios.it).

EATING

Bar Columbus, in the same building as the chairlift to Monte Solaro (in Anacapri), is a handy though pricey place for a quick bite. Only the downstairs is a bar—upstairs you'll find a peaceful place to enjoy lunch without any tour groups, which they discourage (open daily, good antipasti dishes, Via Caposcuro 8, tel. 081-837-1441).

Anacapri

Capri's second town has no sea views but some fun and interesting activities. From the busy Piazza Vittoria, where the bus drops you, head down the pedestrian street to reach the TI (Mon–Sat 9:00–15:00, closed Sun, often closed Nov–Easter, Via Orlandi 59, tel. 081-837-1524).

For a sweeping island view, go to the top of the stairs in Piazza Vittoria, take the pedestrian path that heads left, past the deluxe Capri Palace Hotel (venture in if you can get past the treacherous swimming pool windows), and below the Villa San Michele. (The view is even better from the villa—see below.)

SIGHTS AND ACTIVITIES

Villa San Michele—The 19th-century mansion of Capri's grand personality, Avel Munthe, offers an insight into the scene here when this was the only comfortable refuge for Europe's artsy gay community. Oscar Wilde, D.H. Lawrence, and company hung out here back when being gay could land you in jail...or worse. Munthe, a Swedish doctor who lived here until 1949, left this impressive mansion littered with Roman statues, the Olivetum (museum of local birds and bugs), and a delightful garden. From the sphinx, you'll enjoy one of Capri's best views (€5, daily 9:00–17:00).

▲**St. Michael's Church**—This church has a remarkable majolica floor showing paradise on Earth in a classic 18th-century Neapolitan style. The entire floor is ornately tiled, featuring an angel (with flaming sword) driving Adam and Eve from paradise. The devil is wrapped around the trunk of a beautiful tree. The animals—happily ignoring this momentous event—all have human expressions (€1, daily 9:00–16:45, in town center, 100 yards after the TI take a right to the church).

Faro—The lighthouse is a favorite place to enjoy the sunset, with a private beach, pool, small restaurants, and a few fishermen. Reach it by bus from Anacapri (2/hr, cemetery stop, Piazza del Cimitero).

▲▲**Chairlift up to Monte Solaro**—From Anacapri, ride the chairlift to the 1,900-foot summit of Monte Solaro for a commanding view of the Bay of Naples. Work on your tan as you float over hazelnut, walnut, chestnut, apricot, peach, kiwi, and fig trees and past a montage of tourists (mostly cruise-ship types; when the Grotto is closed—as it often is—they bring passengers here instead). As you ascend, consider how real estate has been priced out of reach of locals. The ride takes 15 minutes each way, and you'll want at least 30 minutes on top.

At the summit, you'll enjoy the best panorama possible: lush cliffs busy with seagulls enjoying the ideal nesting spot. The Faraglioni Rocks are an icon of the island—with tour boats squeezing through every few minutes. The pink building nearest the rocks was an American R&R base during World War II. Eisenhower and Churchill met here. On the peak closest to Cape Sorrento, you can see the distant ruins of the Emperor Tiberius' palace, Villa Jovis. Pipes from the Sorrento Peninsula bring water to Capri, which long ago exceeded the supply of its three natural springs. The Galli Islands mark the Amalfi Coast in the distance. Cross the bar terrace for views of Mount Vesuvius and Naples (€7 round-trip, €5.50 one-way, daily in summer 9:30–17:00, last run down at 17:30, Nov–March last run 15:30).

A highlight for many visitors is the pleasant 40-minute downhill hike from the top of Monte Solaro, through lush vegetation and ever-changing views, past the 14th-century Chapel of Santa Maria Cetrella, and back into Anacapri.

▲▲ Blue Grotto

Three thousand tourists a day pay about €20 and spend a couple of hours visiting Capri's Blue Grotto (Grotto Azzurra). I did—early, without the frustration of crowds, and with choppy waves nearly

making entrance impossible...and it was great.

The actual cave experience isn't much: a five-minute dinghy ride through a three-foot-high entry hole to reach a 60-yard-long cave, where the sun reflects brilliantly blue on its limestone bottom. But the experience—getting there, getting in, and getting back—is a scenic hoot. You get a fast ride on a 30-foot boat partway around the gorgeous island, seeing bird life and dramatic limestone cliffs with scant narration. You'll understand why Roman emperors appreciated the invulnerability of the island—it's surrounded by cliffs, with only one access point, and therefore easy to defend. Then, at the grotto's "distribution center," you pile in with mostly Japanese tourists into awaiting eight-foot dinghies, where ruffian rowers elbow their way to the tiny hole and pull fast and hard on the cable at the low point of the swells to squeeze you into the grotto. Then your man rows you around, spouting off a few descriptive lines and singing "O Sole Mio." Depending upon the strength of the sunshine that day, the blue light inside is brilliant. Typically, they extort an extra tip (about €2) out of you before taking you back outside to your big boat.

Cost and Logistics: The round-trip boat from Marina Grande costs €10 (daily 9:00 until an hour before sunset, boats don't run in stormy weather or during high tides—check this out *before* you purchase boat ticket). Once you reach the grotto, you pay €5 for a rowboat to take you in for the five-minute row around the inside of the grotto (after your rower jockeys for position for at least 20 minutes), plus €4 to cover the admission to the grotto (total €19, but your rower will expect a tip at the end—€2 is enough, though don't tip if rower did poorly). Anyone can dive in for free after 18:00, when the boats stop running—a magical experience and a favorite among locals.

If the waves or high tide make entering dangerous, the boats don't go in—the grotto can close with no notice, sending tourists (flush with anticipation) home without a chance to squeeze through the little hole. (If this happens to you, consider a one-hour, €13 boat ride along the spectacular coastline to the Faraglioni Rocks.)

You can take the boat back, or be dropped off on a small dock next to the grotto by request and return by bus to Anacapri (no discount on round-trip boat ticket, stairs lead to bus stop, schedule posted at the stop, generally 3/hr, buy ticket from driver). By taking the bus from Anacapri directly to the grotto, you save about €7, and see a beautiful, calmer side of the island (every 20 min from Piazza del Cimitero, a 5-min walk on the main road beyond Piazza Vittoria in Anacapri; your 60-min ticket is enough time to visit the grotto and take the bus back to town).

If you're coming from Capri's port, allow one to three hours for the entire visit, depending on the chaos at the caves (early trips often come with the boatmen in their dinghies who hitch a ride behind your boat, resulting in less chaos at the entry point).

TRANSPORTATION CONNECTIONS

From Capri by Boat to: Positano (mid-May–Sept only; 6/day fast boat: 40 min, €15; 1/day slow boat: 50 min, €13.50), **Amalfi** (mid-May–Sept only; 2/day hydrofoil: 1 hr, €14; 2/day slow boat: 75 min, €11.50), **Sorrento** (at least hourly; fast ferry: 25 min, €8.80; fastest and priciest jet boat: 20 min, €12.50), **Naples** (2/hr, 40 min, €15). Confirm the schedule carefully—last boats usually leave between 18:00 and 20:10.

AMALFI COAST AND PAESTUM

With its stunning scenery, hill- and harbor-hugging towns, and historic ruins, Amalfi is Italy's coast with the most. The bus trip from Sorrento to Salerno along the breathtaking Amalfi Coast is one of the world's great bus rides. It will leave your mouth open and your film exposed. You'll gain respect for the Italian engineers who built the roads in the 1800s—and even more respect for the bus drivers who drive it today. Cantilevered garages, hotels, and villas cling to the vertical terrain, and beautiful sandy coves tease from far below and out of reach. As you hyperventilate, notice how the Mediterranean, a sheer 500-foot drop below, really twinkles. All this beautiful scenery apparently inspires local Romeos and Juliets, with the evidence of late-night romantic encounters littering the roadside turnouts. Over the centuries, the spectacular scenery and climate have been a siren call for the rich and famous, luring Roman emperor Tiberius, Richard Wagner, Sophia Loren, Gore Vidal, and others to the Amalfi Coast's special brand of *la dolce vita*.

Planning Your Time

On a quick trip, use Sorrento as your home base and do the Amalfi Coast as a day trip. But for a small-town vacation from your vacation, spend a few more days on the coast, perhaps sleeping in Positano or Amalfi town.

Trying to decide between staying in Sorrento, Positano, or Amalfi? Sorrento is the largest and most touristy of the three, with the best transportation connections. Positano is the most chic and picturesque, with a decent beach. The town of Amalfi has the most actual sights and the best hiking opportunities.

Getting Around the Amalfi Coast

Amalfi Coast towns are pretty but are generally touristy, congested, overpriced, and a long hike above tiny, pebbly beaches. Most beaches are private, and access to those is generally expensive. Check and understand your bills in this greedy region. The real thrill here is the scenic Amalfi drive. This is treacherous stuff—even if you have a car, you may want to take the bus or hire a taxi. Some enjoy seeing the coast by scooter or motorbike (rent in Sorrento, be sure to get a helmet). The most logical springboard for this trip is Sorrento (see previous chapter), but Positano and Amalfi work, too.

Many travelers do the Amalfi Coast as a round-trip by bus, but a good strategy is go one way by bus and return by boat. For example, instead of busing from Sorrento to Salerno (end of the line) and back, consider taking the bus to Salerno, then catching the ferry back to Amalfi or Positano, and from either town, hop a ferry to Sorrento.

Perhaps the simplest option is to take the bus to Positano and boat from there back to Sorrento (or vice-versa). Note that ferry service for this trip decreases off-season to only weekends (mid-Oct–early June), and that boats don't run in stormy weather.

Looking for exercise? Consider an Amalfi Coast hike (see "Hikes," page 792). Numerous trails connect the main towns along the coast with villages on the hills. Get a good map and/or book before you venture out.

The Amalfi Coast by Bus

From Sorrento: Blue or green-and-white SITA buses depart from Sorrento's train station nearly hourly (in peak season, 20/day, marked *Amalfi via Positano*) and stop at all Amalfi Coast towns (Positano in 40 min, €1.30; Amalfi in another 50 min, €2.40, tickets valid for 2 hours, no savings on round-trip tickets), ending up in Salerno at the far end of the coast in just less than three hours (one easy transfer in Amalfi; return trips might also transfer in

Positano). While the all-day ticket (€4.70) saves some money, it's good only after 10:00, when buses are considerably more crowded. It can be worth it to spend a bit more and get an earlier start. Buses start running as early as 6:30 and run as late as 20:00 (22:00 in summer). Buy tickets at the tobacco shop nearest any bus stop before boarding. (There's a *tabacchi*/newsstand at street level in the Sorrento station.)

Getting Around the Amalfi Coast

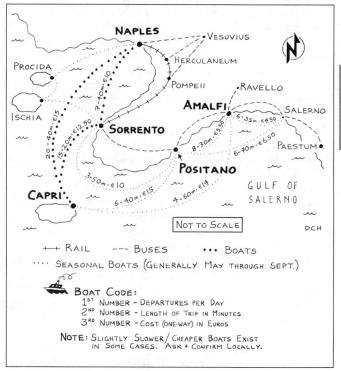

Line up under the *Riservato SITA* sign (where a schedule is posted on the wall) in front of the station (10 steps down). Carefully note the lettered codes that differentiate daily buses from weekend-only buses. *Giornaliero* means daily; *Feriale* notes Monday–Saturday departures; and *Festivo* is for Sundays and holidays.

Leaving Sorrento, grab a seat on the right for the best views. If you return by bus, it's fun to sit directly behind the driver for a box seat with a view over the twisting hairpin action. Sitting towards the front will also minimize carsickness.

Avoiding Crowds on the Bus: Buses are routinely unable to handle the demand during summer months and holidays. Occasionally, an extra bus is added to handle the overflow. Generally, if you don't get on, you're well-positioned to catch the next bus (bring a book). In the morning, arrive early. Buses start running as early as 6:30 and, starting at 8:25, depart about every 30 minutes. Departures between 9:00 and 11:00 are crowded and frustrating. Count the line: Buses pull in empty and seat 48 (plus 25 standing).

Returning to Sorrento: The congestion can be so bad in the summer, during July and August in particular, that return buses don't even stop in Positano (because they were filled in Amalfi). Those trying to get back to Sorrento are stuck with taking an extortionist taxi (except for Carmello Monetti—the local cabbie recommended below) or, if in Positano, hopping a boat...if one's running. If touring the coast by bus, do Positano first and come home from Amalfi to avoid the problem of packed buses.

The Amalfi Coast by Boat

Several companies compete for passengers, and often claim to know nothing about their rivals' services. It's wise any time of year to check posted schedules, pick up ferry schedules from the TI, and confirm times to figure out the best plan. The boats servicing Sorrento, Positano, and Amalfi start operating on weekends after Easter, then run daily from mid-June through mid-October (4/day in peak season, 50 min, €7, buy ticket on dock, pick up schedule at TI, www.metrodelmare.com). No boats run off-season.

From Salerno, ferries run from June through September from Piazza Concordia to Amalfi (6/day, 35 min, €4.50) continuing to Positano (6/day, 70 min total, €6.50, tickets and info at TravelMar, Piazza Concordia, tel. 089-872-950). Salerno's dock is conveniently located at the Amalfi Coast bus stop.

The Amalfi Coast by Taxi

Given the hairy driving, impossible parking, congested buses, and potential fun, you might consider splurging to hire your own car and driver for the Amalfi day. (Don't bother for Pompeii, as the Circumvesuviana serves it conveniently and only licensed guides can take you into the site.)

Fun-loving **Carmello Monetti** (a jolly, singing, in-love-with-life, grandfatherly type who speaks non-stop "inventive English"), his son Raffaele (much better English, fewer smiles, more information), and brother-in-law Tony (similar to Raffaele) have long taken excellent care of my readers' transportation needs from Sorrento.

Sample trips and rates for their taxi: Amalfi Coast Day (Positano–Amalfi–lunch in Ravello), seven hours, €220; Amalfi Coast and Paestum, 10 hours, €300; transfer to Naples airport or train station, one hour, €110. To get these special prices, promised for up to four people through 2008, mention this book.

The Monettis can take six passengers—at a higher rate schedule—in their air-conditioned minivan. Payment is by cash only. Their reservation system is simple, easygoing, and reliable (Raffaele's mobile 335-602-9158, Carmello's mobile 338-946-2860, "office" run by Raffaele's English-speaking wife, Susanna, fax 081-807-4531, www.monettitaxi17.it, monettitaxi17@libero.it).

Be careful: Many cabbies claim to be the Monettis. The Monettis drive Mercedes station wagon taxi #17, usually found at Sorrento's Piazza Tasso. Carmello's specialty is helping Italian Americans find their families in southern Italy. Email him in advance if you want to find your long-lost relatives, and he can put together a meeting and transportation package. If in any kind of a jam, call Raffaele's mobile phone for information.

Umberto and Giovanni Benvenuto offer transport and narrated excursions throughout the Amalfi Coast, as well as to Rome, Naples, Pompeii, and more. While just as friendly, they are more upmarket and formal, with rates explained on their website (Via Roma 54, tel. 089-874-024, mobile 334-307-8342 or 330-353-294, www.benvenutolimos.com, info@benvenutolimos.com).

Rides Only: If you're hiring a cabbie off the street for a ride and not a tour, here are sample fares from Sorrento to Positano: up to four people one-way for about €65 in a car, or up to six people for €75 in a minibus. Figure on paying 50 percent more to Amalfi. While taxis must use a meter within a city, a fixed rate is OK otherwise. Negotiate—ask about a round-trip.

SELF-GUIDED TOUR

Hugging the Amalfi Coast

The trip from Sorrento to Salerno is one of the all-time great white-knuckle rides. Gasp from the right side of the bus as you go out and from the left as you return to Sorrento. (Those on the

wrong side really miss out.) Traffic is so heavy that private tour buses are only allowed to go in one direction (southbound from Sorrento)—summer traffic is infuriating. Policemen are actually posted at tough bends at peak hours to help fold in side-view mirrors.

Here's a loosely guided tour of what you're seeing, from west to east:

Leaving Sorrento, the road winds up into the hills past lemon groves and hidden houses. Traveling the coast, you'll see several Saracen (Turkish pirate) watchtowers placed within sight of each

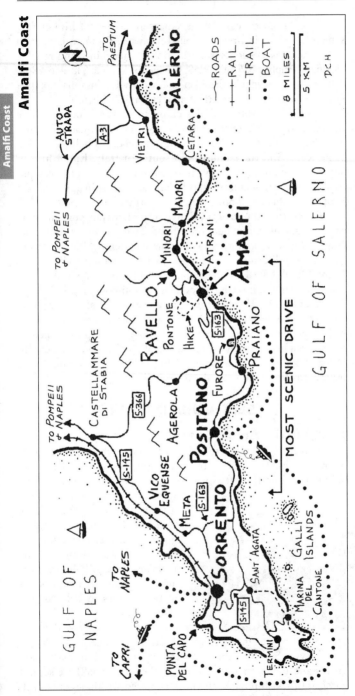

other, so that a relay of rooftop bonfires could spread word of an attack. The gray-green trees are olives. Dark, green-leafed trees planted in dense groves are the source of the region's lemons—many destined to become *limoncello* liqueur. The black nets over the orange and lemon groves create a greenhouse effect, trapping warmth and humidity for maximum tastiness.

Atop the ridge outside of Sorrento, look to your right: the two small islands after Sorrento are the **Galli Islands;** the bigger one (on the left) is Ulysses Island (see page 756 for the ancient connection). These islands, once owned by the famed ballet dancer Rudolf Nureyev, mark the boundary between the Bay of Naples and the Bay of Salerno. Technically, the Amalfi Coast drive begins here.

The limestone cliffs, plunging into the sea, were traversed by an ancient trail that became a modern road in the mid-19th century. Fruit stands sell produce from farms and orchards just over the hill. Limestone absorbs the heat, making this south-facing coastline a suntrap, with temperatures as much as 10 degrees higher than in nearby Sorrento. Bougainvillea and geraniums grow like weeds in the summer.

Views of Positano, the main stop along the coast, are dramatic on either side of town. Just south of Positano, **St. Peter's Hotel** (camouflaged below the tiny St. Peter's church) is about the most posh stop on the coast. Notice the elevator to the beach and dock. Bring your credit card.

Praiano is notable for its cathedral, with the characteristic majolica-tiled roof and dome—a reminder of this region's respected ceramics industry. Just past the tunnel stands a Saracen watchtower.

Marina di Praiano is a tiny and unique fishing hamlet wedged into a tight ravine with a couple of good restaurants and a small hotel.

The next Saracen tower guarded the harbor of the Amalfi navy until the fleet was destroyed by a tidal wave in 1343.

The most striking stretch of coastline ends at **Amalfi** and **Atrani** (both described below). As you leave Amalfi, look up to the left. The white house that clings to a cliff (Villa Rondinaia) was home for many years to the writer Gore Vidal. Atop the cliff is the town of **Ravello** (see page 794). From here, the western half of the Amalfi Coast is mostly wild and unpopulated until you hit Salerno.

Positano

P – PARKING
—— ROADS FOR CARS
- - – PEDESTRIAN STREETS

200 YARDS
200 METERS

SS-163
VIA MARCONI SS-163
VIALE CRISTOFORO
TO SORRENTO
VIA MARCONI SS-163
CHIESA BUS STOP
VIA COLOMBO
VIALE PASITEA
VIA MULINI
VIA FORNILLO
VIA T. GENOINO
VIA POSITANESI
CHURCH
SPIAGGIA GRANDE
SPONDA BUS STOP
TO AMALFI
FORNILLO BEACH
MEDITERRANEAN SEA
TO CAPRI, SORRENTO & NAPLES
TO AMALFI & SALERNO

❶ Hotel Marincanto
❷ Albergo California
❸ Residence la Tavolozza
❹ Hotel Savoia
❺ Villa Maria Antonietta
❻ Hotel Bougainville
❼ Brikette Hostel
❽ Bar Mulino Verde

Amalfi Coast

Positano

According to legend, the Greek god Poseidon created Positano for Pasitea, a nymph he lusted after. History says the town was founded when ancient Greeks at Paestum decided to move out of the swamp (and escape malaria). Specializing in scenery and sand, Positano hangs halfway between Sorrento and Amalfi town on the most spectacular stretch of the coast.

The village, a ▲▲▲ sight from a distance, is a pleasant gathering of cafés and expensive women's clothing stores, with a good but pebbly beach. Positano is famous for its fashions—90 percent of its shops

are fashion boutiques.

Squished into a ravine, with narrow alleys that cascade down to the harbor, Positano requires you to stroll, whether you're going up or heading down. The center of town has no main square (unless you count the beach). There's little to do here but eat, window-shop, and enjoy the beach and views (hence the town's popularity).

Consider seeing Positano as a day trip from Sorrento: Take the bus out and the afternoon ferry home, but be sure to check the boat schedules when you arrive—the last ferry often leaves before 18:00.

The "skyline" looks like it did a century ago. Notice the town's characteristic Saracen-inspired rooftop domes. Filled with sand, these provide insulation—cool in summer and hot in winter. It's been practically impossible to get a building permit in Positano for 25 years now, and landowners making renovations can make no external changes. The steep stairs are a way of life for the 4,000 hardy locals. Only one street in Positano allows motorized traffic—the rest are steep pedestrian lanes. Because hotels don't take large groups (bus access is too difficult), the town—unlike Sorrento—has been spared the ravages of big-bus tourism.

Spend the night to enjoy the magic of Positano. The town has a local flavor at night, when the grown-ups stroll and the kids play soccer on the church porch.

ORIENTATION

Tourist Information

The TI is a half-block from the beach, in a small building at the bottom of the church steps (April–Sept Mon–Sat 8:00–20:00, closed Sun, Oct–March normally 8:00–14:00 only, tel. 089-875-067).

Arrival in Positano

The main coast highway winds above the town. Regional SITA buses (blue or green-and-white) stop at two scheduled bus stops located at either end of town: Chiesa (at Bar Internazionale, nearer Sorrento) and Sponda (nearer Amalfi town). From either stop, roads lead downhill through the town to the beach. To minimize your descent, use the Sponda stop (the second Positano stop, if you're coming from Sorrento). It's a 20-minute stroll/shop/munch from here to the beach (and TI).

If you're catching the SITA bus back to Sorrento, remember that it may leave from the Sponda stop five minutes before the printed departure. There's no room for the bus to wait, so in case the driver is early, you should be, too (€1.30, departures about hourly, daily 7:00–22:00, until 20:00 off-season, €1.30, buy tickets from Bar Mulino Verde or Positour Agency—both are on Via

Colombo, about 300 yards below the stop). If the walk up to the stop is too tough, take the dizzy little local orange bus (marked *Interno Positano*), which constantly loops through Positano, connecting the lower town with the highway's two bus stops (2/hr, €1, buy tickets on board, from convenient stop at the corner of Via Colombo and Via dei Mulini, heads up to Sponda). Bar Mulino Verde (as close as cars, taxis, and the shuttle bus can get to the beach) is located just across from the stop for the little orange bus, with a fine, breezy terrace you can enjoy if you're waiting.

Drivers must go with the one-way flow, entering the town only at the Chiesa bus stop (closest to Sorrento) and exiting at Sponda. Driving is a headache here. Parking is worse.

ACTIVITIES

Beach—Positano's pebbly and sandy primary beach, called Spiaggia Grande, is colorful with umbrellas as it stretches wide around the cove. It's mostly private (€10–15/person, April–Oct, cost includes use of sun beds and umbrellas) with a free section near the middle, close to where the boats take off. The nearest WC is behind the waterfront Bucca di Bacco bar.

Boat Trips—At the west side of the beach (right as you face the sea), you'll see a series of booths selling boat tickets. Some little boats make the three-minute journey to Fornillo Beach—a quieter beach just around the bend. The ride is free if you agree to eat at a certain restaurant (if they try to charge you, say "*ristorante...no pay*"), or rent a beach lounge and umbrella (usually cheaper than at Spiaggia Grande). Fornillo is an easy 10-min walk from Spiaggia Grande (take trail near ticket booths).

Consider renting a rowboat or taking various boat tours to a nearby cave (La Grotta dello Smeraldo—Emerald Cave), fishing village (Nerano), or small islands. Ferries run to Amalfi, Capri, and Sorrento; see "Transportation Connections," page 788.

SLEEPING

These hotels (but not the hostel) are all on Via Colombo, which leads from the Sponda SITA bus stop down into the village. Prices given are for the highest season (June–Sept)—at other times, they should be at least €10 less per day. Expect to pay more than €20 a day to park.

$$$ Hotel Marincanto is a newly restored four-star hotel with a bright breakfast terrace practically teetering on a cliff. Suites seem to be designed for a *luna di miele*—honeymoon (Db-€215, superior Db-€245, suites with seaview balconies-€300–350, large sundeck, private stairs to beach, parking, 50 yards below the

Sleep Code

(€1 = about $1.30, country code: 39)
S = Single, **D** = Double/Twin, **T** = Triple, **Q** = Quad, **b** = bathroom,
s = shower only. Unless otherwise noted, credit cards are
accepted, English is spoken, and breakfast is included.

To help you sort easily through these listings, I've divided
the rooms into three categories based on the price for a standard double room with bath:

$$$ **Higher Priced**—Most rooms €150 or more.
 $$ **Moderately Priced**—Most rooms between €100–150.
  $ **Lower Priced**—Most rooms €100 or less.

Sponda bus stop at Via Colombo 50, tel. 089-875-130, fax 089-
875-595, www.marincanto.it, info@marincanto.it).

$$$ Hotel Savoia is family-run and has 39 sizeable, breezy,
bright, air-conditioned rooms (viewless Db-€140, Db with view-
€210, deluxe Db-€230, at least €10/day off with this book in
2008, Via Colombo 73, tel. 089-875-003, fax 089-811-844, www
.savoiapositano.it, info@savoiapositano.it).

$$$ Albergo California has lofty views, spacious rooms (15
of 20 with sea views), and a grand terrace draped with vines (Db-
€160 June–Sept, €150 May and Oct, windowless Db-€100 all year,
prices promised with this book through 2008, air-con, free parking, Via Colombo 141, tel. 089-875-382, fax 089-812-154, www
.hotelcaliforniapositano.it, info@hotelcaliforniapositano.it, Maria,
Frank, and Antonio).

$$ Hotel Bougainville rents 14 comfortable rooms (viewless
Db-€108, Db with sea view-€140, 5 percent discount only with this
book in 2008, air-con, some traffic noise and fumes, Via Colombo
25, tel. 089-875-047, www.bougainville.it, info@bougainville.it,
Simon and Marella).

$ Residence la Tavolozza is an attractive eight-room hotel,
warmly run by Celeste (cheh-LEHS-tay), her sisters, and daugh-
ter. Flawlessly restored, each room comes with a view, a balcony,
fine tile, and silence (Db-€87 promised through 2008 with this
book, families can ask for "Royal Apartment," cash only, must
call to confirm if arriving late, lavish breakfast extra, air-con,
closed Dec–Feb, Via Colombo 10, tel. & fax 089-875-040, celeste
.dileva@tiscali.it, Francesca).

$ Villa Maria Antonietta is a humble family place with
seven decent rooms, all with a view of the back alley and the ocean
beyond. Head down a grungy lane off the elegant main drag and
then up a few big flights of stairs (Db-€90, more in Aug, cash only;

follow signs from Via Colombo 41; tel. 089-875-071, Maria).

$ Brikette Hostel offers your best cheap, dorm-bed option in this otherwise ritzy town. Renting 50 beds and offering a great sun and breakfast terrace, it's bright and clean with the normal hostel rules: 11:00–14:30 lockout, cushy 2:00 curfew, and checkout by 11:00 (dorm bed-€22, Db-€75, breakfast extra but cheap, dinner available, closed Nov–March, Via G. Marconi 358, leave bus at Chiesa/Bar Internazionale stop and backtrack uphill 500 feet, tel. & fax 089-875-857, www.brikette.com, info@brikette.com, Cristiana is full of energy). She also rents four hotel-style rooms on top (D-€65, one big suite Db-€90, family deals).

EATING

The pizzerias and restaurants facing the beach, while overpriced, are pleasant and convenient. At the waterfront, I like **Cambuso,** but the neighboring places also leave people fat and happy. The unassuming **Restaurant Bruno** is a better-than-average value for Positano, near the top of Via Colombo—handy if you don't want to hike down into the town center for dinner.

If a picnic dinner on your balcony or the beach sounds good, sunny Emilia at **Delikatessen** can supply the ingredients (*antipasto misto* to go at €1.40/100 grams, sandwiches made and sold by weight; daily March–Oct 7:00–22:00, Nov–Feb 7:00–20:00, just below car park at Via del Mulini 5, tel. 089-875-489). **Vini e Panini,** another small grocery, is a block from the beach a few steps above the TI (daily 8:00–14:00 & 16:00–22:00, tel. 089-875-175, just off church steps).

TRANSPORTATION CONNECTIONS

Always check boat schedules, since the last boats often leave Positano before 18:00. The schedule varies drastically according to time of year—be sure to check it with the TI.

From Positano by Boat to: Amalfi (8/day, 30 min, Easter–Oct only, €5.50), **Capri** (mid-May–Sept only; 6/day fast boat: 40 min, €15; 1/day slow boat: 50 min, €13.50), **Sorrento** (3/day daily mid-May–mid-Oct only, otherwise only weekends, 50 min for €10; 90 min for €8). Direct boats to **Naples** are unlikely, but check with the TI; you can also change boats in Sorrento or Capri.

Amalfi Town

The Amalfi Coast is named for this town. It was founded (according to legend) when the girlfriend of Hercules was buried here. After Rome fell, Amalfi was one of the first cities to trade goods—coffee, carpets, and paper—between Europe and points east. Its heyday was the 10th and 11th centuries, when it was a powerful maritime republic—a trading power with a fleet that controlled this region and rivaled Genoa and Venice. The Republic of Amalfi founded a hospital in Jerusalem and claims to have founded the Knights of Malta order—even giving them the Amalfi cross, which became the famous Maltese cross. Amalfi minted its own coins and established "rules of the sea"—the basics of which survive today. Paper has been a vital industry here since the glory days in the Middle Ages. They'd pound rags into pulp in a big vat, pull it up using a screen, and air-dry it to create paper (the same technique used to make paper still sold in Amalfi shops). For a demonstration of this ancient technique, check out the Paper Museum (see "Sights," page 792).

In 1343, this little powerhouse was destroyed by a freak tidal wave caused by an undersea earthquake. That disaster, compounded by devastating plagues, left Amalfi a humble backwater. Today, its 7,000 residents live off tourism (and paper).

ORIENTATION

The waterfront of this town is dominated by a bus station, a parking lot, two gas stations, a statue of local boy Flavio Gioia—the inventor of the compass (see sidebar)—and a TI.

Amalfi, the most big-bus accessible of the towns along the coast, is a classic tourist trap. It's packed during the day with big-bus tours (whose drivers pay €50 an hour to park while their groups shop for *limoncello* and ceramics).

Before you enter the town, notice the colorful tile above the Porta della Marina gateway, showing off the domain of the maritime Republic of Amalfi. Just to the left, along the busy road, are a series of arches that indicate the long, narrow, vaulted halls of its arsenal—where ships were built in the 11th century.

Venture into the town, and you find its once rich and formidable medieval shell is filled with trendy shops, a main square sporting a springwater-spewing statue of St. Andrew, and a cathedral—the town's most important sight.

The further you get away from the water, the more local Amalfi gets. The Paper Museum (see page 792) is a 10-minute walk up Via Lorenzo d'Amalfi, the main drag. From here, the road narrows

Flavio Gioia

You'll see a statue of Flavio Gioia towering above the chaos of cars and buses on the seaside piazza. Amalfi residents credit this hometown boy with the invention of the magnetic compass back in 1302, but historians can't verify that he actually existed. While an improvement to the compass did occur in Amalfi during that time period, the Chinese and Arabs had been using rudimentary compasses for years. In Gioia's time, seamen used a needle bobbing around in water as a kind of medieval GPS. If Gioia existed at all, he probably just figured out how to secure that needle inside a little box. Locals, however, have no doubts that Flavio Gioia is an inventor extraordinaire.

and you can turn off onto a path leading to the shaded Valle dei Mulini; it's full of paper-mill ruins that recall this once proud and prosperous industry. The ruined castle clinging to the rocky ridge above Amalfi is Torre dello Ziro, a good lookout point for intrepid hikers (see "Activities," page 792). Amalfi is not as picturesque as Positano or as well-connected as Sorrento, but take some time to explore the town. Amalfi's charms will reveal themselves, especially early and late in the day when tourist crowds dissipate.

Tourist Information

The TI is on Corso della Repubbliche Marinare 27 (Mon–Fri 8:30–13:00 & 15:00–17:00, maybe until 20:00 June–Aug, Sat 8:30–13:00, closed Sun, tel. 089-871-107, www.amalfitouristoffice .it). It's about 100 yards south of the center, next to the post office, facing the sea.

Helpful Hints

Don't Get Stranded: Be warned, the last bus back to Sorrento leaves at 20:00 (at 22:00 in summer) and can be full. Without a public bus, your only option is a €100 taxi ride.

Internet Access: L'Altra Costiera, on the main drag, looks more like a travel agency but has Internet service (daily 9:00–21:00, Via Lorenzo d'Amalfi 34, tel. 089-873-6082).

Hiking Guidebook: The best book on hiking is *Sorrento Amalfi Capri Car Tours and Walks*, on sale at many local bookstores. It has useful, color-coded maps and info on public transportation to the trailheads.

Laundry: The full-service laundry offers same-day service (Mon–Sat 8:00–13:00 & 16:00–20:30, closed Sun, drop off before 10:00 and pick up same day after 19:00). It's a one-minute walk west from the main square: Across from the cathedral steps, walk through the set-back archway with a sign for *Piazza dei Dogi*. In this little piazza, the laundry is in the far left corner.

Speedboat Charters: For ferry transport from Amalfi, to join a boat tour, or to hire your own boat for a tour of the coastline from Amalfi (or to Capri), consider **Charter La Dolce Vita** (www.ladolcevitataxicharter.com, mobile 329-460-3771, Paolo Corsaro).

SIGHTS

Cathedral—This church is "Amalfi Romanesque" (a mix of Moorish and Byzantine flavor, built c. 1000–1300) with a fanciful neo-Byzantine facade from the 19th century. The 1,000-year-old bronze door was given to Amalfi by a wealthy local merchant who had it made in Constantinople. Climb the imposing stairway—which functions as a handy outdoor theater for town events—and go inside (€2.50, daily in summer 9:00–19:00, winter 10:00–17:00, closed Jan–Feb, pick up English flier, tel. 089-871-324).

Visitors are directed on a oneway circuit through the cathedral complex with these four stops:

"Cloister of Paradise": This courtyard of 120 graceful columns was the cemetery of the nobles (note their stone sarcophagi). Don't miss the fine view of the bell tower and its majolica tiles.

Basilica of the Crucifix: The original ninth-century church is now a museum filled with the art treasures of the cathedral. The Angevin Mitre, with a "pavement of tiny pearls" setting off its gold and gems, has been worn by bishops since the 14th century. On the far wall is a plank from a Saracen pirate ship that wrecked just outside of town in 1544 during another freak storm. This storm was caused by a saint, rather than an earthquake—and saved the town, rather than destroyed it. The plank still reminds locals how St. Andrew (see below) rescued the town from certain Turkish pillage and plunder.

Crypt of St. Andrew: As Venice needed Mark to get on the pilgrimage map, Amalfi got St. Andrew—one of the apostles who left his nets to become the original "fishers of men." What are believed to be his remains (under the huge bronze statue) were brought here from Constantinople in 1206 during the Crusades— an indication of the wealth and importance of Amalfi back then.

Cathedral: The interior is notable for its fine 13th-century wooden crucifix. The painting behind it shows St. Andrew martyred on an X-shaped cross flanked by two Egyptian granite columns supporting a triumphal arch. Before leaving, check out the delicate mother-of-pearl crucifix (right of door in back).

▲**Paper Museum**—At this cavernous, cool 13th-century paper-mill-turned-museum, a multilingual guide collects groups at the entrance (no particular times) for a 45-minute tour that recounts the history and process of paper making, a long-time industry for the town of Amalfi (€3.50, March–Oct daily 10:00–18:30, sporadic hours Nov–Feb, a 10-min walk up the main street from the cathedral, tel. 089-830-4561, www.museodellacarta.it).

ACTIVITIES

Hikes—Amalfi is the starting point for several fine hikes (see hiking guidebook listed under "Helpful Hints," above). Here are two:

Hike #1: This loop trail leads up the valley past paper-mill ruins, ending in the tiny town of **Pontone;** you can get lunch there, and head back down to the town of Amalfi (allow three hours total). Bring a good map, since it's easy to veer off the main route. Start your hike by following the main road (Via Lorenzo d'Amalfi) away from the sea.

After the Paper Museum, jog right, then left to join the trail, leading through the shaded woods along a babbling stream. Heed the signs to stay away from the ruins of paper mills (no matter how tempting), since many are ready to collapse on unwary hikers. Continue up to Pontone, where Trattoria l'Antico Borgo offers wonderful cuisine and a great view (Via Noce 4, tel. 089-871-469). After lunch, return to Amalfi via a steep stairway.

If you're feeling ambitious, before you head back to Amalfi, add a one-hour detour (30 min each way) to visit the ridge-hugging **Torre dello Ziro** (ask a local how to find the trail to this tower). You'll be rewarded with a spectacular view.

Hike #2: For an easier hike—more of a stroll—head to the nearby town of **Atrani.** This village, just a 15-minute stroll beyond Amalfi town, is a world apart; its 1,500 residents consider themselves definitely *not* from Amalfi. Leave Amalfi via the main road, and stay on the water side until the sidewalk ends. Cross the street and head up the stairs; the paved route takes you over the hill, and drops you into Atrani in about 15 minutes. Piazza Umberto is the core of town, with cafés and a little grocery store that makes sandwiches. Amazingly, Atrani has none of the trendy resort feel of Amalfi, with relatively few tourists, a delightful town square, and a free, sandy beach (pay for parking at harbor).

From Atrani, you can continue up to **Ravello** (see below). But be warned: Unless you're part mountain goat, you'll probably prefer catching the bus to Ravello from the town of Amalfi instead.

SLEEPING

(€1 = about $1.30, country code: 39)

Sleeps are better in Positano, but if you're marooned in Amalfi, here are some options. High season on the Amalfi Coast (especially July–Sept) demands the highest prices; prices listed here are peak-season rates (roughly April–Oct).

$$ Hotel Amalfi, with 40 rooms and a garden, is lacking in warmth, but is a fine choice (Db-€75–150 depending on the time of year, peaking in Aug; €10 extra for air-con, roof-terrace breakfast, no sea views, 50 yards from cathedral, head up the pedestrian street and take staircase to the left before underpass, Via dei Pastai 3, tel. 089-872-440, fax 089-872-250, www.hamalfi.it, hamalfi @starnet.it).

$$ Residenze del Duca is a fancy little seven-room boutique B&B taking advantage of its wonderful location in the heart of this touristy enclave (Db-€70–160, air-con, glimpses of ocean through the rooftops; up a lot of stairs just 25 yards uphill from Piazza Duomo, take a left at Via Mastalo II Duca 3; tel. 089-873-6365, www.residencedelduca.it, info@residencedelduca.it, friendly Daniella).

$$ Hotel Bussola, a five-minute walk north along the harbor, rises above the ocean with its 60 adequate, sunny rooms, most boasting terraces with a breezy ocean view (Db-€126, €10 extra for air-con, parking, Lungomare dei Cavalieri 16, tel. 089-871-533, www.labussolahotel.it, info@labussolahotel.it).

In Atrani: Accommodation options are limited in Atrani, a small-town Amalfi hideaway without the glitz and hill-climbing of Positano (see "Hikes," earlier in chapter).

$ A'Scalinatella is a dingy, informal backpackers' hostel, with a honeycomb of cramped three- to 10-bed dorms, way-overpriced private rooms, and a communal kitchen. It's run by English-speaking owners, Filippo and Gabriele (€22 per bed in dorms, D-€60, Db-€83, prices very soft, cash only, no membership required, 100 yards up from main square at Scalinatella Piazza Umberto I 5, tel. 089-871-492, www.hostelscalinatella.com, info@hostelscalinatella .com).

$ L'Argine Fiorito B&B, which stands like a little castle overlooking a ravine at the top of town, rents five tidy and tiled rooms (Db-€95 July–Sept, €85 April–June and Oct, €75 off-season, tel. 089-873-6309, www.larginefiorito.it, Alfonso).

Ravello

Ravello sits atop a lofty perch 1,000 feet above the sea and offers an interesting church, two villas, and a chance to catch a glimpse of celebrities. American author Gore Vidal, who lived here for decades, is one of a sizable group of rich and famous artists—including Richard Wagner, D.H. Lawrence, William Longfellow, and Greta Garbo—who have succumbed to Ravello's charms.

To see the sights listed below, start at the bus stop and walk through the tunnel to the main square, where you'll find the church on the right, Villa Rufolo on the left, and the **TI** (9:00–20:00 daily, 100 yards from the square—follow the signs to Via Roma 18, tel. 089-857-096, pick up the color-coded trail map called *Passeggiata/Walks*). A 10-minute walk through the town (follow the signs) leads to Villa Cimbrone.

SIGHTS AND ACTIVITIES

Duomo—You can't miss Ravello's cathedral, located right on the main square. The two main features of this church are the bronze doors, with 54 scenes of the life of Christ, the carved marble pulpit supported by six lions, and a chance to climb behind the altar for a close-up look at the relic of holy blood. The geometric designs show Arabic influence. The humble cathedral museum (€2) is two rooms of well-described carved marble evoking the historical importance of the town (church open daily 8:00–13:00 & 16:30–19:00, museum open daily 9:00–19:00; you can generally get into the church all day long via the museum).

Villa Rufolo—The villa, built in the 13th century, is only a barren ruin today. It has pleasant Arabic/Norman gardens which provide a delightful frame for the commanding coastline view (you can enjoy the same view, without the entry fee, from the bus parking lot just below the villa). During the concert season (March–Oct), locals build a bandstand to perch on the edge of the cliff, giving concert attendees the combination of wonderful music and a dizzying view. Wagner visited here and was impressed enough to set the second act of his opera *Parsifal* in the villa's magical gardens. A concert on the cliff is a sublime experience (villa entry-€5, daily June–Sept 9:00–20:00, Oct–May 9:00–18:00, tel. 089-857-657, concert information tel. 089-858-149, www.ravelloarts.org, ask at

TI about Ravello's annual arts festival held here).

Villa Cimbrone—This villa, located at the other end of Ravello, was built in the 20th century by Englishman William Beckett. It offers extensive gardens and a killer film-devouring view from the "Terrace of Infinity." Consider buying a picnic in town and munching it here discreetly with magnificent Italian panoramas at your feet. A wander through the gardens will reveal reproductions of famous sculptures and lots of great views (€5, daily 9:00–sunset).

Hike to Amalfi Town from Villa Cimbrone—To walk downhill from Ravello's Villa Cimbrone to the town of Amalfi (a path for hardy hikers only—follow the TI's *Passeggiata/Walks* brochure), retrace your steps back toward town. Take the first left that turns into a stepped path winding its way below the cliff. Pause here to look back up at the rock with a big white mansion—Villa La Rondinaia, where Gore Vidal lived for many years. Continue down the fairly steep path about 40 minutes to the town of Atrani, where several bars on the main square offer well-deserved refreshment. From here, it's about a 15-minute walk back to Amalfi (see "Hikes," page 792).

EATING

Ravello is full of overpriced eateries with views—avoid them.

Try family-run **Cumpa Cosimo** instead, where they serve up a fun *piatto misto*, a plate full of five different pastas. Mamma Annetta will make sure you finish (daily 12:00–15:30 & 19:00–22:00, Via Roma 44, tel. 089-857-156).

TRANSPORTATION CONNECTIONS

Ravello and the town of Amalfi are connected by a winding road and a bus. Coming from Amalfi town, buy your ticket at the bar on the waterfront, and ask where the bus stop is; buses usually stop to the left as you face the water, near the statue of Flavio Gioia on the waterfront Piazza Flavio Gioia. Line up early, since the buses are often crowded (hourly, 25 min, €1, buy ticket in *tabacchi;* catch bus 100 yards off main square, just past tunnel).

Paestum

Paestum (PASTE-oom) has one of the best collections of Greek temples anywhere—and certainly the most accessible to Western Europe. Serenely situated, it's surrounded by fields and wildflowers, and has a sandy beach and only a modest commercial strip.

This town was founded as Poseidonia by Greeks in the sixth century B.C., and became a key stop on an important trade route. In the fifth century B.C., the Lucans, a barbarous inland tribe, conquered Poseidonia, changed its name to Paistom, and tried to adopt the cultured ways of the

Greeks. The Romans, who took over in the third century B.C., gave Paestum the name it bears today. The final conquerors of Paestum, malaria-carrying mosquitoes, kept the site wonderfully deserted for nearly a thousand years. Rediscovered in the 18th century, Paestum today offers the only well-preserved Greek ruins north of Sicily.

ORIENTATION

Tourist Information: At the TI, next to Paestum's museum, pick up a free info booklet of the site (July–Aug Mon–Sat 9:00–19:00, Sun 9:00–13:00, hours vary off-season, tel. 082-881-1016, www .infopaestum.it).

Arrival at Paestum: Buses from Salerno (see "Transportation Connections," page 800) stop near a corner of the ruins (at a little bar/café). Or, if you're arriving by train, exit the station and walk through the old city gate; the ruins are an eight-minute walk straight ahead.

Cost, Hours, Information: €4 for the museum, €4 for the site, €6.50 for a combo-ticket. The site is free (or 50 percent off) with the Campania ArteCard (see page 714).

Both the museum and site open daily at 9:00 (except the first and third Mon of each month, when museum is closed though the site is open). Year-round, the museum closes at 19:00 (last ticket sold at 18:30). The site closes one hour before sunset (as late as 19:30 June–Aug, as early as 15:30 in winter, last ticket sold 1 hour before closing). Several mediocre guidebooks are offered at the museum's bookshop, including a €13 past-and-present guide. Dull €4 audioguides are available to rent at the site entrance and cover both museum and site (ID required). There's little English information at the site itself. The site and museum have separate entrances. The museum, just outside the ruins, is in a cluster with the TI and a small paleo-Christian basilica.

Planning Your Time: Allow two hours, including the museum. Depending on your interest and the heat of the day, start with either the museum or the site.

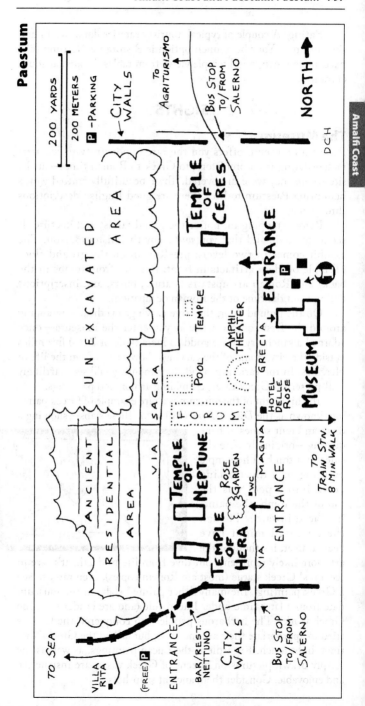

Eating: A couple of typical, touristy eateries flank the TI and site entrance. Your best lunch option is Ristorante Nettuno (€12 fixed-price lunch, good temple views from tables, located at south entrance).

SIGHTS

The Museum

Paestum's museum offers you the rare opportunity to see artifacts—dating from prehistoric to Greek to Roman times—at the site where they were discovered. These beautifully crafted works help bring Paestum to life. There are good English descriptions throughout.

Before stepping in, notice the proud fascist architecture. It seems to command that you *will* enjoy this history lesson. The exhibit comes in two levels: pre-Roman on the ground floor (Temple of Hera artifacts in front, frescoes from tombs in the back) and Roman art upstairs (statues, busts, and inscriptions dating from the time of the Roman occupation).

On the ground floor, the large carvings overhead—wrapping around the first room you see as you enter the museum—once adorned a sanctuary of the goddess Hera (wife of Zeus) five miles outside the city. Some of the carvings show scenes from the life of Hercules. In the various ground-floor rooms, you'll see startlingly well-preserved Greek vases, crumbling armor, and paintings.

The highlight of the museum is a rare example of Greek painting, known as the *Diver's Tomb* (480 B.C.). These slabs—showing a

diver and four scenes of banqueting—originally were the sides of a tomb. The simple painting of a diver arcing down into a pool was the top of the tomb (the painting faced inward). Though the deceased might have been a diver, it's thought the art more likely represents our dive from life to death. It's rare to see a real Greek statue (most are Roman copies), even rarer to see a Greek painting. The many other painted slabs in the museum date from a later time under Lucan rule (and are cruder than the Greek work). The barbarous people who conquered the Greeks tried to appropriate their art and style, but lacked the Greeks' distinct, light touch. Regardless, the Lucan paintings, as well as the crisply drawn pictures on dozens of Greek vases, are instructive and enjoyable. Consider them ancient snapshots.

The Site

The key ruins are the impossible-to-miss Temples of Neptune, Hera, and Ceres, but the scattered village ruins are also interesting. Lonely Ceres, in an evocative setting, is about a 10-minute walk from Neptune and Hera, which stand together. The two main entrances to the site are in front of the Temple of Ceres and on the south side near the Temple of Hera. If you already have a ticket, you can enter at the Temple of Neptune.

The Temple of Neptune is simply overwhelming. Constructed in 450 B.C., it's a textbook example of the Doric style. Archaeologists are not sure which deity the misnamed temple was dedicated to, but Apollo, Zeus, and Hera are the top contenders. Better preserved than the Parthenon in Athens, this huge structure is a tribute to Greek engineering and aesthetics. Contemplate the word "renaissance"—the rebirth of this grand Greek style of architecture. Notice how the columns angle out and the base bows up (scan the short ends of the temple). This was a trick ancient architects used to create the illusion of a perfectly straight building. All important Greek buildings were built using this technique. Now imagine it richly and colorfully decorated with marble and statues.

Adjacent to the Temple of Neptune is the almost-delicate Temple of Hera, dedicated to the Greek goddess of marriage in 550 B.C.

SLEEPING

(€1 = about $1.30, country code: 39)
Paestum at night, with views of the floodlit ruins, is magic.

In Paestum

$ Hotel delle Rose, with 10 small, basic rooms and a respectable restaurant, is near the Neptune entrance, on the street bordering the ruins (Db-€65 June–Aug, Db-€55 Sept–May, Luigi promises these prices with this book in 2008, Via Magna Grecia 193, tel. 082-881-1070, www.hotelristorantedellerose.com, info @hotelristorantedellerose.com, no English spoken).

$ Hotel Villa Rita is a tidy, quiet country hotel set on two acres within walking distance of the beach and the temples. It has 19 bright, modern, air-conditioned rooms, a kid-friendly swimming pool, and free parking (Db-€86 mid-June–mid-Sept, €76 rest of year, Luigi promises a 10 percent discount with this book, Via Principe di Piemonte—a.k.a. Via Nettuno—9; tel. 0828-811-081, fax 0828-722-555, www.hotelvillarita.it, info@hotelvillarita.it). The hotel is a 10-minute walk west of the Hera entrance and public bus stop, and a 15-minute walk from the train station.

Nearby

$$ Agriturismo Seliano offers 14 spacious, spotless rooms on a peaceful, ramshackle, once-elegant farm estate with a pool (Db-€115 in Aug, €90 in July, €75 Sept–June, air-con, serves a fine €20 lunch or dinner with produce fresh from the garden, 1 mile north of ruins on main road, sign directs you down long dirt driveway, best for drivers, tel. 082-872-3634, www.agriturismoseliano.it, seliano @agriturismoseliano.it, run by an English-speaking baroness).

TRANSPORTATION CONNECTIONS

Salerno and Paestum

Salerno, the big city just north of Paestum, is the nearest transportation hub. From Naples or Sorrento, you'll change buses or trains in Salerno to get to Paestum. Salerno's TI has bus, ferry, and train schedules (Mon–Sat 9:00–14:00 & 15:30–20:00, closed Sun, shorter hours off-season, on Piazza Veneto, just outside train station, tel. 089-231-432, toll-free 800-213-289).

Salerno to Paestum by Bus: Four companies (CSTP, SCAT, Giuliano, and Lettieri) offer a Salerno–Paestum bus service, all conveniently leaving from the same stop at Piazza della Concordia on the waterfront (2–3/hr, 70 min, schedules extremely sparse on Sun). Buy the €3 round-trip ticket on the bus, except on CSTP buses (buy these from the nearby *tabacchi*). No clear schedule is posted at the Salerno stop. Simply ask a local or a bus representative at the stop for the next bus to Paestum; otherwise, get a schedule at the TI (more impartial, since they don't represent a particular company and their schedule shows all companies and times). Note that orange city buses use the same stop; ignore these.

When leaving Paestum, catch a northbound bus from either of the intersections that flank the ruins (see map on page 801). Flag down any bus, ask "Salerno?" and buy the ticket on board (except for CSTP buses—buy ticket at bar closest to stop).

Salerno to Paestum by Train: The train from Salerno to Paestum (hourly, 40 min, direction: Paola or Sapri) runs far less frequently than the buses, though it's a quicker ride because it's immune to traffic jams; check schedules at Salerno's TI or train station. Paestum's train station is an eight-minute walk from the ruins (from station, go through old city wall, ruins are straight ahead). If you plan to leave Paestum by train, buy your train ticket at the bar/café near the TI, because the station is not staffed (train schedules at TI). Leaving Paestum, trains bound for Salerno (direction: Battipaglia) usually continue to Naples.

Naples to Salerno by Train: 3/hr, 60–90-min trip (don't board the extra-slow *diretto* train; note that some trains stop at Pompeii).

Salerno Connections

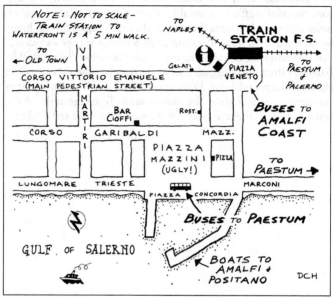

NOTE: Not to scale — TRAIN STATION TO WATERFRONT IS A 5 MIN. WALK.

TO NAPLES

TRAIN STATION F.S.

TO ← OLD TOWN

GELATI.

PIAZZA VENETO

TO PAESTUM & PALERMO

CORSO VITTORIO EMANUELE (MAIN PEDESTRIAN STREET)

VIA MARTIRI

BAR CIOFFI

ROST.

BUSES TO AMALFI COAST

CORSO

GARIBALDI

MAZZ.

PIAZZA MAZZINI (UGLY!)

PIZZA

TO PAESTUM →

LUNGOMARE

TRIESTE

PIAZZA CONCORDIA

MARCONI

BUSES TO PAESTUM

GULF OF SALERNO

BOATS TO AMALFI & POSITANO

DCH

Amalfi Coast

Sorrento to Salerno by Bus: The scenic three-hour Amalfi Coast drive (blue or green-and-white SITA bus, 12/day, 3 hrs, easy transfer in Amalfi) drops you at the Salerno train station, where the TI is located, or you can get off earlier at the seaside Piazza della Concordia, if you want to catch the bus to Paestum.

If you plan to take a bus from Salerno to Sorrento (or points in between), you'll find the bus stop directly in front of Salerno's train station exit, on the median strip under the *Fermata SITA* sign. Buy your bus ticket at the newsstand inside the train station and tell the vendor your destination (prices vary). If it's closed, try the ticket windows in the train station or walk two blocks to Bar Cioffi (CHOH-fee), across the square from Piazza della Concordia (see map above). Ticket vendors change periodically; if Bar Cioffi no longer sells tickets, ask anyone or a clerk at a *tabacchi* or magazine shop, "Who sells bus tickets to _____?" by saying, *"Chi vende i biglietti dell'autobus per _____?"* (kee VEHN-dee ee beel-YET-tee del-OW-toh-boos pehr _____).

Sorrento to Salerno by Train: Ride the Circumvesuviana to Naples' Centrale station (2/hr, 70 min) and catch the Salerno train (2/hr, 45 min).

Salerno to Amalfi Towns by Ferry to: Amalfi (6/day, 35 min, €4.50), **Positano** (6/day, 70 min, €6.50). Most ferries depart from Salerno's Piazza della Concordia, see map above (tickets and info at TravelMar, Piazza della Concordia, tel. 089-872-950).

Drivers: While the Amalfi Coast is a thrill to drive off-season, summer traffic is miserable. From Sorrento, Paestum is 60 miles and three hours via the coast and a much smoother two hours by *autostrada*. To reach Paestum from Sorrento via the *autostrada*, drive toward Naples, catch the *autostrada* (direction: Salerno), skirt Salerno (direction: Reggio), exit at Battipaglia, and drive straight through the roundabout. During your ride, you'll see many signs for *mozzarella di bufala*, the cheese made from the milk of the water buffalo that graze here. Try it here—it can't be any fresher.

ITALIAN HISTORY

Italy has a lot of history, so let's get started.

Origins

A she-wolf breastfed two human babies, Romulus and Remus, who grew to build the city of Rome in 753 B.C.—you buy that? Closer to fact, farmers and shepherds of the Latin tribe settled near the mouth of the Tiber River, a convenient trading location. The crude settlement was sandwiched between two sophisticated civilizations—Greek colonists to the south (Magna Grecia, or greater Greece), and the Etruscans of Tuscany, whose origins and language are still a mystery to historians. Baby Rome was both dominated and nourished by these societies.

When an Etruscan king raped a Roman woman (509 B.C.), her husband led a revolt, driving out the Etruscan kings and replacing them with elected Roman senators and (eventually) a code of law ("Laws of the Twelve Tables," 450 B.C.). The Roman Republic was born.

The Roman Republic Expands (c. 500 B.C.–A.D. 1)

Located in the center of the peninsula, Rome was perfectly situated for trading salt and wine. Roman businessmen, backed by a disciplined army, expanded through the Italian peninsula, establishing a Roman infrastructure as they went. Rome soon swallowed up its northern Etruscan neighbors, conquering them by force and absorbing their culture.

Next came Magna Grecia, with Rome's legions defeating the Greek general Pyrrhus after several costly, "Pyrrhic" victories (c. 275 B.C.). Rome now ruled a united federation stretching from Tuscany to the toe, with a standard currency, a system of roads (including the Via Appia), and a standing army of a half million soldiers ready for the next challenge—Carthage.

Carthage (modern-day Tunisia) and Rome fought the three bitter Punic Wars for control of the Mediterranean (264–201 b.c. and 146 b.c.). The balance of power hung precariously in the Second Punic War (218–201 b.c.), when Hannibal of Carthage crossed the sea to Spain with a huge army of men and elephants. He marched 1,200 miles overland, crossed the Alps, and forcefully penetrated Italy from the rear. Almost at the gates of the city of Rome, he was finally turned back. The Romans prevailed and, in the mismatched Third Punic War, they burned the city of Carthage to the ground (146 b.c.).

The well-tuned Roman legions easily subdued sophisticated Greece in three Macedonian Wars (215–146 b.c.). Though Rome conquered Greece, Greek culture dominated the Romans. From hairstyles to statues to temples to the evening's entertainment, Rome was forever "Hellenized," becoming the curators of Greek culture, passing it down to future generations.

By the first century b.c., Rome was master of the Mediterranean. Booty, cheap grain, and thousands of captured slaves poured in, transforming the economic model from small farmers to unemployed city dwellers living off tribute from conquered lands. The Republic had changed.

Civil Wars and the Transition to Empire (First Century b.c.)

With easy money streaming in and traditional roles obsolete, Romans bickered among themselves over their slice of the pie. Wealthy landowners (patricians, the ruling Senate) wrangled with the middle and working classes (plebeians) and with the growing population of slaves, who demanded greater say-so in government. In 73 b.c., Spartacus—a Greek-born soldier-turned-Roman-slave who'd been forced to fight as a gladiator—escaped to the slopes of Mount Vesuvius, where he amassed an army of 70,000 angry slaves. After two years of fierce fighting across Italy, the Roman legions crushed the revolt and crucified 6,000 rebels along the Via Appia as a warning.

Amid the chaos of class war and civil war, charismatic generals who could provide wealth and security became dictators—men such as Sulla, Crassus, Pompey...and Caesar. Julius Caesar (100–44 b.c.) was a cunning politician, riveting speaker, conqueror of Gaul, author of *The Gallic Wars*, and lover of Cleopatra, Queen of Egypt. In his four-year reign, he reformed and centralized the government around himself. Disgruntled Republicans feared that he would make himself king. At his peak of power, they surrounded Caesar in the Senate on the "Ides of March" (March 15, 44 b.c.) and stabbed him to death.

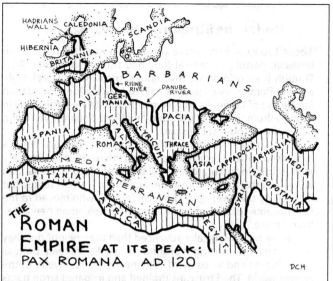

Julius Caesar died, but the concept of one-man rule lived on in his adopted son. Named Octavian at birth, he defeated rival Mark Antony (another lover of Cleopatra, 31 B.C.) and was proclaimed Emperor Augustus (27 B.C.). Augustus outwardly followed the traditions of the Republic, while in practice he acted as a dictator with the backing of Rome's legions and the rubber-stamp approval of the Senate. He established his family to succeed him (making the family name "Caesar" a title), and set the pattern of rule by emperors for the next 500 years.

The Roman Empire (c. A.D. 1–500)

In his 40-year reign, Augustus ended Rome's civil wars and ushered in 200 years of prosperity and relative peace called the Pax Romana. Rome ruled an empire of 54 million people, stretching from Scotland to Africa, from Spain to the Cradle of Civilization (modern-day Iraq). Conquered peoples were welcomed into the fold of prosperity, linked by roads, common laws, common gods, education, and the Latin language. The city of Rome, with more than a million inhabitants, was decorated with Greek-style statues and monumental structures faced with marble. It was the marvel of the known world.

The empire prospered on a (false) economy of booty, slaves, and cheap imports. On the Italian peninsula, traditional small farms were swallowed up by large farming and herding estates. In this "global economy," the Italian peninsula became just one province of many in a worldwide, Latin-speaking empire, ruled

Under the Etruscan Sun (c. 900 B.C.–A.D. 1)

About 550 B.C.—just before the Golden Age of Greece—the Etruscan people of central Italy had their own Golden Age. Though their origins are mysterious, their mix of Greek-style art with Roman-style customs helped lay a civilized foundation for the rise of Rome. As you travel through Italy—particularly in Tuscany (from "Etruscan"), Umbria, and North Latium—you'll find traces of the long-lost Etruscans.

The Etruscans first appeared in the ninth century, when a number of cities sprouted up in sparsely-populated Tuscany and Umbria, including today's hill towns of Cortona, Chiusi, and Volterra. Perhaps they were immigrants from Western Turkey, but more likely they were just the local farmers who moved to the city, became traders and craftsmen, and welcomed new ideas from Greece.

More technologically advanced than their neighbors, they mined metal, exporting it around the Mediterranean, both as crude ingots and as some of the finest-crafted jewelry in the known world. The Etruscans drained and irrigated large tracts of land, creating the fertile farmland of central Italy's breadbasket. With their disciplined army, warships, merchant vessels, and (from the Greek perspective) pirate galleys, they ruled central Italy and the major ports along the Tyrrhenian Sea. For nearly two centuries (c. 700–500 B.C.), much of Italy lived a golden age of peace and prosperity under the Etruscan sun.

Judging from the many luxury items that have survived, the Etruscans enjoyed the good life. Frescoes show men and women looking remarkably like how the Greeks and Romans described them: healthy, vibrant, and well-dressed, playing flutes, dancing with birds, or playing party games. Etruscan artists celebrated individual people, showing their wrinkles, crooked noses, silly smiles, and funny haircuts.

Thousands upon thousands of surviving ceramic plates, cups, and vases attest to the importance of food. Hosting a banquet was a symbol that you'd arrived. Men and women ate together, propped on their elbows on dining couches, surrounded by colorful frescoes and terra-cotta tiles. According to contemporary accounts, the Etruscans were Europe's best-dressed people, even their slaves. They ate off dinnerware either imported from Greece or made in the Greek style—red and black ceramics, decorated with warriors, nymphs, sphinxes, and gods. The banqueters were entertained with music and dancing and served by elegant and well-treated slaves.

Scholars today have deciphered the Etruscans' Greek-style alphabet and some individual words, but they've yet to fully master the grammar or crack the code. Virtually no long-enough Etruscan documents survive.

Much of what we know of the Etruscans comes from their

The Etruscan Empire

tombs, often clustered in a necropolis. The tomb was your home in the hereafter, fully furnished for the after-life, complete with all your belongings. The sarcopha-gus might have a statue on the lid of the deceased at a banquet—lying across a dining couch, spooning with his wife, smiles on their faces, living the good life for all eternity.

Seven decades of wars with Greeks (545–474 B.C.) disrupted the trade routes and drained the League, just as a new Mediterranean power was emerging...Rome. In 509 B.C., the Romans overthrew their Etruscan king, and Rome expanded, capturing Etruscan cit-ies one by one (the last in 264 B.C.). Etruscan resisters were killed, the survivors intermarried with Romans, their kids grew up speak-ing Latin, and the culture became Romanized. By Julius Caesar's time, the only remnants of Etruscan culture were Etruscan priests, who became Rome's professional soothsayers. The shape a flock of birds made, the bend in a lightning flash, or a scar on a goat's liver could tell a priest how a client's business might fare next year. Interestingly, the Etruscan prophets had foreseen their own demise, having predicted that Etruscan civilization would last 10 centuries.

But Etruscan culture lived on in Roman religion (pantheon of gods, household gods, and divination rituals), art (realism), life-style (the banquet), and in a taste for Greek styles—the mix that became our "Western civilization."

Etruscan Sights in Italy
Here are some of the more important and more accessible Etruscan sights (all are mentioned in this book):

Rome: Traces of original Etruscan engineering projects (e.g., Circus Maximus), Vatican Museum artifacts, and Villa Giulia Museum, with the famous "husband and wife sarcophagus."

Orvieto: Archaeological Museum (coins, dinnerware, and a sar-cophagus), necropolis, and underground tunnels and caves.

Volterra: Etruscan gate (Porta dell'Arco, from fourth century B.C.) and Etruscan Museum (funerary urns).

Chiusi: Museum, tombs, and tunnels.

Cortona: Museum and dome-shaped tombs.

Italian History

by an emperor who was likely born elsewhere. The empire even survived the often turbulent and naughty behavior of emperors such as Caligula (r. 37–41) and Nero (r. 54–68).

Decline and Fall (A.D. 200–500)

Rome peaked in the second century A.D. under the capable emperors Trajan (r. 98–117), Hadrian (r. 117–138), and Marcus Aurelius (r. 161–180). For the next three centuries, the Roman Empire declined, shrinking in size and wealth, a victim of corruption, disease, an overextended army, its false economy, and the constant pressure of "barbarian" tribes pecking away at the borders. By the third century, the army had become the real power, handpicking figurehead emperors to do its bidding—in a 40-year span, 15 emperors were saluted then assassinated by fickle generals.

Trying to stall the disintegration, Emperor Diocletian (r. 284–305) split the empire into two administrative halves under two equal emperors. Constantine (r. 306–337) solidified the divide by moving the capital of the empire from decaying Rome to the new city of Constantinople (330, present-day Istanbul). Almost instantly, the once-great city of Rome became a minor player in imperial affairs. (The eastern "Byzantine" half of the empire would thrive and live on for another thousand years.) Constantine also legalized Christianity (313), and the once-persecuted cult soon became virtually the state religion, the backbone of Rome's fading hierarchy.

By 410, "Rome" had shrunk to the city itself, surrounded by a protective wall. Barbarian tribes from the north and east poured in to loot and plunder. The city was sacked by Visigoths (410), vandalized by Vandals (455), and the pope had to plead with Attila the Hun for mercy (451). The peninsula's population fell to six million, trade and agriculture were disrupted, schools closed, and the infrastructure collapsed. Peasants huddled near powerful lords for protection from bandits, planting the seeds of medieval feudalism.

In 476, the last emperor sold his title for a comfy pension, and Rome fell like a huge column, kicking up dust that would plunge Europe into a thousand years of darkness. For the next 13 centuries, there would be no "Italy," just a patchwork of rural dukedoms and towns, victimized by foreign powers. Italy lay helpless.

Invasions (A.D. 500–1000)

In 500 years, Italy suffered through a full paragraph of invasions: Lombards (568) and Byzantines (under Justinian, 536) occupied the north. In the south, Muslim Saracens (827) and Normans (1061) established thriving kingdoms. Charlemagne, King of the Franks (a Germanic tribe), defeated the Lombards, and on Christmas Day A.D. 800, he knelt before the pope in St. Peter's in Rome to be crowned "Holy Roman Emperor." For the next thousand years, Italians would pledge nominal allegiance to weak, distant German kings as their "Holy Roman Emperor," an empty title meant to resurrect the glory of ancient Rome united with medieval Christianity.

Through all of the invasions and chaos, the glory of ancient Rome was preserved in the pomp, knowledge, hierarchy, and wealth of the Christian Church. Strong popes (Leo I, 440–461; and Gregory the Great, 590–604) ruled like small-time emperors, governing territories in central Italy called the Papal States.

Prosperity and Politics (A.D. 1000–1300)

Italy survived Y1K, and the economy picked up. Sea-trading cities like Venice, Genoa, Pisa, Naples, and Amalfi grew wealthy as middlemen between Europe and the Orient. During the Crusades (e.g. First Crusade 1097–1130), Italian ships ferried Europe's Christian soldiers eastward, then returned laden with spices and highly marked-up luxury goods from the Orient. Trade spawned banking, and Italians became capitalists, loaning money at interest to Europe's royalty. Italy pioneered a new phenomenon in Europe—cities *(comuni)* that were self-governing commercial centers. The medieval prosperity of the cities laid the foundation of the future Renaissance.

Politically, the Italian peninsula was dominated by two rulers—the pope in Rome and the German "Holy Roman Emperor" (with holdings in the north). It split Italy into two warring political parties: supporters of the popes (called Guelphs, centered in urban areas) and those of the emperors (Ghibellines, popular with the rural nobility).

The Unlucky 1300s

In 1309, the pope—enticed by Europe's fast-rising power, France—moved from Rome to Avignon, France. At one point, two rival popes reigned, one in Avignon and the other in Rome, and they excommunicated each other. The papacy eventually returned to Rome (1377), but the schism had created a breakdown in central authority that was exacerbated by an outbreak of bubonic plague (Black Death, 1347–1348) that killed a third of Italians.

In the power vacuum, new powers emerged in the independent cities. Venice, Florence, Milan, and Naples were under the protection and leadership of local noble families *(signoria)* such as the Medici in Florence. Florence thrived in the wool and dyeing trade, which led to international banking, with branches in all of Europe's capitals. A positive side effect of the terrible Black Death was that the smaller population got a bigger share of the land, jobs, and infrastructure. By century's end, Italy was poised to enter its most glorious era since antiquity.

Top 10 Italians

Romulus: Breastfed on wolf milk, this legendary orphan grew to found the city of Rome (traditionally in 753 B.C.). Over the next seven centuries, his descendants dominated the Italian peninsula, ruling from Rome as a Republic.

Julius Caesar (100–44 B.C.): After conquering Gaul (France), subduing Egypt, and winning Cleopatra's heart, Caesar ruled Rome with king-like powers. In an attempt to preserve the Republic, senators stabbed him to death, but the concept of one-man rule lived on.

Augustus (born Octavian, 63 B.C.–A.D. 14): Julius's adopted son became the first of the Caesars that ruled Rome during its 500 years as a Europe-wide power. He set the tone for emperors both good (Trajan, Hadrian, Marcus Aurelius) and bad (Caligula, Nero, and dozens of others).

Constantine (c. 280–337 A.D.): Raised in a Christian home, this emperor legalized Christianity, almost instantly turning a persecuted sect into a Europe-wide religion. With the Fall of Rome, the Church was directed by strong popes and so guided Italians through the next 1,000 years of invasions, plagues, political decentralization, and darkness.

Lorenzo the Magnificent (1449–1492): Soldier, poet, lover, and ruler of Florence in the 1400s, this Renaissance Man embodied the "rebirth" of ancient enlightenment. Lorenzo's wealthy Medici family funded Florentine artists who pioneered a realistic 3-D style.

Michelangelo Buonarroti (1475–1564): His statue of *David*—slaying an ignorant brute—stands as a monumental symbol of Italian enlightenment. Along with fellow geniuses Leonardo da Vinci and Raphael, Michelangelo spread the Italian Renaissance (painting, sculpture, architecture, literature, and ideas) to a worldwide audience.

The Renaissance (1400s)

The Renaissance *(Rinascimento)*—the "rebirth" of ancient Greek and Roman art styles, knowledge, and humanism—began in Italy (c. 1400), and spread through Europe over the next two centuries. Many of Europe's most famous painters, sculptors, and thinkers—Michelangelo, Leonardo, Raphael, etc.—were Italian.

It was a cultural boom that changed people's thinking about every aspect of life. In politics, it meant democracy. In religion, it meant a move away from Church dominance and toward the assertion of man (humanism) and a more personal faith. Science and

Giovanni Lorenzo Bernini (1598–1680): The "Michelangelo of Baroque" kept Italy a major exporter of sophisticated trends. Bernini's ornate statues and architecture decorated palaces of the rising power France, even as Italy was reverting to an economically stagnant patchwork of foreign-ruled states.

Victor Emmanuel II (1820–1878): As the only Italian-born ruler on the peninsula, this King of Sardinia became the rallying point for Italian unification. Aided by the general Garibaldi, writer Mazzini, and politician Cavour (with a soundtrack by Verdi), he became the first ruler of a united, democratic Italy in September 1870. (The preceding proper nouns have since come to adorn streets and piazzas throughout Italy.)

Benito Mussolini (1883–1945): A kinder, gentler Hitler, he derailed Italy's fledgling democracy, becoming dictator of a fascist state, leading the country into defeat in World War II. No public places honor Mussolini, but many streets and piazzas throughout Italy bear the name of Giacomo Matteotti (1885–1924), a politician whose outspoken opposition to Mussolini got him killed by Fascists.

Federico Fellini (1920–1993): Fellini's films (La Strada, La Dolce Vita, 8 ½) chronicle Italy's postwar years in gritty black and white—the poverty, destruction, and disillusionment of the war followed by the optimism, decadence, and materialism of the economic boom. He captured the surreal chaos of Italy's abrupt social change from traditional Catholic to a secular, urban world presided over by Mafia bosses and weak government.

Top Italian Number 11 (?): Has Italy produced another recent citizen who's dominant enough to make his or her mark on the world? Could it be former Prime Minister Silvio Berlusconi, Italy's richest man? Opera singer Luciano Pavarotti? Or big-pec'd model "Fabio" Lanzoni, named "Sexiest Man on Earth" by *Cosmopolitan* magazine? The world awaits.

Italian History

secular learning were revived after centuries of superstition and ignorance. In architecture, it was a return to the balanced columns and domes of Greece and Rome. In painting, the Renaissance meant 3-D realism.

Italians dotted their cities with publicly financed art—Greek gods, Roman-style domed buildings. They preached Greek-style democracy and explored the natural world. The cultural boom was financed by booming trade and lucrative banking. In the Renaissance, the peninsula once again became the trendsetting cultural center of Europe.

End of the Renaissance, France and Spain Invade (1500s)

In May 1498, Vasco da Gama of Portugal landed in India, having found a sea route around Africa. Italy's monopoly on trade with the East was broken. Portugal, France, Spain, England, and Holland—nation-states under strong central rule—began to overtake decentralized Italy. Italy's once-great maritime cities now traded in an economic backwater, just as Italy's bankers (such as the Medici in Florence) were going bankrupt. While the Italian Renaissance was all the rage throughout Europe, it declined in its birthplace. Italy—culturally sophisticated but weak and decentralized—was ripe for the picking by Europe's rising powers.

France and Spain invaded (1494 and 1495)—initially invited by Italian lords to attack their rivals—and began divvying up territory for their noble families. Italy also became a battleground in religious conflicts between Catholics and the new Protestant movement. In the chaos, the city of Rome was brutally sacked by foreign mercenary warriors (1527).

Foreign Rule (1600–1800)

For the next two centuries, most of Italy's states were ruled by foreign nobles, serving as prizes for the winners of Europe's dynastic wars. Italy ceased to be a major player in Europe, politically or economically. Italian intellectual life was often cropped short by a conservative Catholic Church trying to fight Protestantism. Galileo, for example, was forced by the Inquisition to renounce his belief that the earth orbited the sun (1633). But Italy did export Baroque art (Giovanni Lorenzo Bernini) and the budding new medium of opera.

The War of the Spanish Succession (1713)—a war in which Italy did not participate—gave much of northern Italy to Austria's ruling family, the Hapsburgs (who now wore the crown of "Holy Roman Emperor"). In the south, Spain's Bourbon family ruled the Kingdom of Naples (known after 1816 as the Kingdom of the Two Sicilies), making it a culturally sophisticated but economically backward area, preserving a medieval, feudal caste system.

In 1720, a minor war (the War of Austrian Succession) created a new state at the foot of the Alps, called the Kingdom of Sardinia (a.k.a. the Kingdom of Piedmont, or Savoy). Ruled by the Savoy family, this was the only major state on the peninsula that was actually ruled by Italians. It proved to be a toehold to the future.

Italy Unites—The Risorgimento (1800s)

In 1796, Napoleon Bonaparte swept through Italy and changed everything. He ousted Austrian and Spanish dukes, confiscated Church lands, united scattered states, and crowned himself "King

Italian Unification

Note: Dates indicate the year of annexation to the Kingdom of Sardinia. After 1861, this became the Kingdom of Italy.

of Italy" (1805). After his defeat (1815), Italy's old ruling order (namely, Austria and Spain) was restored. But Napoleon had planted a seed: What if Italians could unite and rule themselves like Europe's other modern nations?

For the next 50 years, a movement to unite Italy slowly grew. Called the Risorgimento—a word that means "rising again"—the movement promised a revival of Italy's glory. It started as a revolutionary, liberal movement—taking part was punishable by death. Members of a secret society called the Carbonari (led by a professional revolutionary named Giuseppe Mazzini) exchanged secret handshakes, printed fliers, planted bombs, and assassinated conservative rulers. Their small revolutions (1820–1821, 1831, 1848) were easily and brutally slapped down, but the cause wouldn't die.

Gradually, Italians of all stripes warmed to the idea of unification. Whether it was a united dictatorship, a united papal state, a united kingdom, or a united democracy, most Italians could agree that it was time for Spain, Austria, and France to leave.

The movement coalesced around the Italian-ruled Kingdom of Sardinia and its king, Victor Emmanuel II. In 1859, Sardinia's prime minister, Camillo Cavour, cleverly persuaded France to drive Austria out of northern Italy, leaving the region in Italian hands. A plebiscite (vote) was held, and several central Italian states (including some of the pope's) rejected their feudal lords and chose to join the growing Kingdom of Sardinia.

After victory in the north, Italy's most renowned Carbonari general, Giuseppe Garibaldi (1807–1882), steamed south with a thousand of his best soldiers *(I Mille)* and marched on the Spanish-ruled city of Naples (1860). The old order simply collapsed. In two short months, Garibaldi had achieved a seemingly impossible victory against a far superior army. Garibaldi sent a one-word telegram to the king of Sardinia: *"Obbedisco"* (I obey). The following year, an assembly of deputies from throughout Italy met in Turin and crowned Victor Emmanuel II "King of Italy." Only the pope in Rome held out, protected by French troops. When the city finally fell easily to the unification forces on September 20, 1870, the Risorgimento was complete. Italy went ape.

The Risorgimento was largely the work of four men: Garibaldi (the sword), Mazzini (the spark), Cavour (the diplomat), and Victor Emmanuel II (the rallying point). Today, street signs throughout Italy honor them and the dates of their great victories.

Mussolini and War (1900–1950)

Italy—now an actual nation-state, not just a linguistic region—entered the 20th century with a progressive government (a constitutional monarchy), a collection of colonies, and a flourishing northern half of the country. In the economically backward south (the Mezzogiorno), millions of poor peasants emigrated to the Americas. World War I (1915–1918) left 650,000 Italians dead, but being on the winning Allied side, survivors were granted possession of the alpine regions. In the postwar cynicism and anarchy, many radical political parties rose up—Communist, Socialist, Popular, and Fascist.

Benito Mussolini (1883–1945), a popular writer for socialist and labor-union newspapers, led the Fascists. ("Fascism" comes from Latin *fasci,* the bundles of rods that symbolized unity in ancient Rome.) Though only a minority (6 percent of the parliament in 1921), they intimidated the disorganized majority with organized violence by black-shirted Fascist gangs. In 1922, Mussolini seized the government (see sidebar) and began his rule as dictator for the next two decades.

Mussolini solidified his reign among Catholics by striking an agreement with the pope (Concordato, 1929), giving Vatican City to the pope, while Mussolini ruled Italy with the implied blessing

---

The March on Rome

In October 1922, Benito Mussolini, head of the newly formed Fascist Party, boldly proposed a coup d'état, saying: "Either the government will be given to us, or we will take it by marching on Rome." Throughout Italy, black-shirted Fascists occupied government buildings in their hometowns. Others grabbed guns, farming hoes, and kitchen knives and set off to converge on the outskirts of Rome. (Estimates of the size of the Fascist band range from 300 to the 300,000 of Fascist legend.) Mussolini sent the government an ultimatum to surrender. Though the Fascists were easily outmanned and outgunned by government forces, the show of force intimidated the king, Victor Emmanuel III, into avoiding a nasty confrontation. He invited Mussolini to Rome. Mussolini arrived the next day (by first-class train), was made prime minister, then marched his black-shirted troops triumphantly through the streets of Rome.

---

of the Catholic Church. Italy responded to the great worldwide Depression (1930s) with big public works projects (including Rome's subway), government investment in industry, and an expanded army.

Mussolini allied his country with Hitler's Nazi regime, drawing an unprepared Italy into World War II (1940). Italy's lame army was never a factor in the war, and when Allied forces landed in Sicily (1943), Italians welcomed them as liberators. The Italians toppled Mussolini's government and surrendered to the Allies, but Nazi Germany sent troops to rescue Mussolini. The war raged on as Allied troops inched their way north against German resistance. Italians were reduced to dire poverty. In the last days of the war (April 1945), Mussolini was captured by the Italian resistance. They shot him and his girlfriend and hung their bodies upside down in a public square in Milan.

Postwar Italy

At war's end, Italy was physically ruined and extremely poor. The nation rebuilt in the 1950s and 1960s (the "economic miracle") with Marshall Plan aid from America. Many Italian men moved to northern Europe to find work; many others left the farm and flocked to cities. Italy regained its standing among nations, joining the United Nations, NATO, and, eventually, the European Union.

However, the government remained weak, changing on average once a year, shifting from right to left to centrist coalitions (it's had 60 governments since World War II). All Italians acknowledged that the real power lay in the hands of backroom politicians and organized crime—a phenomenon called *Tangentopoli*, or "Bribe City." The country remained strongly divided between the rich, industrial north and the poor, rural south.

Italian society changed greatly in the 1960s and 1970s, spurred by the liberal reforms of the Catholic Church at the Vatican II conference (1962–1965). The once-conservative Catholic country legalized divorce and contraception, and the birth rate plummeted. In the 1970s, the economy slowed thanks to inflation, strikes, and the worldwide energy crisis. Italy suffered a wave of violence from left- and right-wing domestic terrorists and organized crime, punctuated by the assassination of the prime minister Aldo Moro (1978). A series of coalition governments in the 1980s brought some stability to the economy.

In the early 1990s, the judiciary launched a campaign to rid politics of corruption and Mafia ties. Though still ongoing, the investigation sent a message that Italy would no longer tolerate evils that were considered necessary just a generation earlier. In 2001, billionaire Silvio Berlusconi, the owner of many of Italy's media outlets and Italy's richest person, won 30 percent of the popular vote, and became prime minister, heading a center-right coalition. In 2003, Berlusconi backed the US invasion of Iraq, a policy that polarized Italy. But three years later, he lost a close election to former Prime Minister Romano Prodi, who has taken a strong stance against the Iraq war.

As you travel through Italy today, you'll encounter a thriving country with a rich history and a per capita income that rivals its neighbors to the north. Italy is enthusiastically part of Europe...yet it's as wonderfully Italian as ever.

APPENDIX

CONTENTS

RESOURCES

Tourist Offices

In the US

Before you go, you can contact the nearest Italian tourist office (abbreviated **TI** in this book) in the US to briefly describe your trip and request information. You'll get the general packet and, if you ask for specifics (city map, calendar of festivals, etc.), an impressive amount of help. If you have a specific problem, they're a good source of sympathy.

Their offices are...

In New York: Tel. 212/245-5618, brochure hotline tel. 212/245-4822, fax 212/586-9249, enitny@italiantourism.com; 630 Fifth Ave. #1565, New York, NY 10111.

In Illinois: Tel. 312/644-0996, fax 312/644-3019, enitch @italiantourism.com; 500 N. Michigan Ave. #2240, Chicago, IL 60611.

In California: Tel. 310/820-1898, fax 310/820-6357, enitla @italiantourism.com; 12400 Wilshire Blvd. #550, Los Angeles, CA 90025.

Websites on Italy: Visit www.italiantourism.com (Italian Tourist Board in the US), www.museionline.it (museums in Italy), and www.trenitalia.com (train info and schedules).

In Italy

During your trip, your first stop in each town should be the tourist information office (marked *i, turismo,* and *APT* in Italy). While Italian TIs are about half as helpful as those in other countries, their information is twice as important. Prepare. Have a list of questions and a proposed plan to double-check. If you're arriving late, telephone ahead (and try to get a map for your next destination from a TI in the town you're departing from). Since Italy is ever-changing, ask the local TI for a current list of the city's sights, hours, and prices.

Be wary of the travel agencies or special information services that masquerade as TIs but serve fancy hotels and tour companies. They're in the business of selling things you don't need.

While the TI is eager to book you a room, use its room-finding service only as a last resort. They are unable to give hard opinions on the relative value of one place over another. The accommodations stakes are too high to go potluck through the TI. You'll do better going direct with the listings in this book.

Guidebooks and Online Updates

This book is updated every year in person—but once you pin Italy down, it wiggles. For the latest, visit www.ricksteves.com/update. Also at my website, you'll find a valuable list of reports and experiences—good and bad—from fellow travelers (www.ricksteves .com/feedback).

This book is one of more than 30 titles in my series on European

travel, which includes country guidebooks, city guidebooks (Venice, Rome, Paris, etc.), and my budget-travel skills handbook, *Rick Steves' Europe Through the Back Door.* My phrase books—for Italian, French, German, Spanish, and Portuguese—are practical and budget-oriented. My other books are *Europe 101* (a crash course on art and history, newly expanded and in full color), *European Christmas* (on traditional and modern-day celebrations), and *Postcards from Europe* (a fun memoir of my travels

Begin Your Trip at www.ricksteves.com

At our travel website, you'll find a wealth of free information on European destinations, including fresh monthly news and helpful tips from thousands of fellow travelers.

Our **online Travel Store** offers travel bags and accessories specially designed by Rick Steves to help you travel smarter and lighter. These include Rick's popular carry-on bags (wheeled and rucksack versions), money belts, totes, toiletries kits, adapters, other accessories, and a wide selection of guidebooks, planning maps, and DVDs.

Choosing the right **railpass** for your trip—amidst hundreds of options—can drive you nutty. We'll help you choose the best pass for your needs, plus give you a bunch of free extras.

Rick Steves' Europe Through the Back Door travel company offers **tours** with more than two dozen itineraries and 450 departures reaching the best destinations in this book... and beyond. Our Italy tours include "the best of" in 17 days, Village Italy in 14 days, South Italy in 13 days, Sicily in 12 days, Venice–Florence–Rome in 10 days, and weeklong city tours (one for Rome and one for Florence). You'll enjoy great guides, a fun bunch of travel partners (with small groups of generally about 25), and plenty of room to spread out in a big, comfy bus. You'll find European adventures to fit every vacation length. For all the details, and to get our Tour Catalog and a free Rick Steves Tour Experience DVD (filmed on location during an actual tour), visit www.ricksteves.com or call us at 425-608-4217.

over 25 years, offering an insight into Florentine culture that you won't find in guidebooks). For a complete list of my books, see the inside of the last page of this book.

Public Television and Radio Shows

My TV series, *Rick Steves' Europe*, covers European destinations in 70 shows, with 13 episodes on Italy. My weekly public radio show, *Travel with Rick Steves*, features interviews with travel experts from around the world, including several hours on Italy and Italian culture. All the TV scripts and radio shows (which are easy and free to download to an MP3 player) are at www.ricksteves.com.

Free Audio Tours of Italy

Rick Steves and Gene Openshaw (the co-authors of seven books in the Rick Steves series) have produced free, self-guided audiotours of Florence, Rome, and Venice for users of iPods and other MP3 players.

The tours allow you to focus on what you're seeing rather than on what you're reading. Additional tours of Paris are available, covering that city's greatest sights.

These free tours are available through iTunes and at www.ricksteves.com after January 2008. Simply download them onto your computer and transfer them to your iPod or MP3 player. (Remember to bring a Y-jack and extra set of ear buds for your travel partner.)

Maps

The maps in this book are drawn by Dave Hoerlein, who is well-traveled in Italy. Dave's maps help you locate recommended places and get to the tourist information offices, where you can pick up a more in-depth map (usually free) of the city or region. More detailed maps, such as the Michelin series, are sold—more cheaply than in the US—at newsstands, bookstores, and gas stations. Look before you buy to be sure the map has the level of detail you want. For drivers, I'd recommend a 1:200,000- or 1:300,000-scale map.

Other Guidebooks

Especially if you'll be traveling beyond my recommended destinations, you may want some supplemental information. When you consider the improvements they'll make in your $3,000 vacation, $30 for extra maps and books is money well spent. Particularly for several people traveling by car, the weight and expense are negligible. One budget tip can save the price of an extra guidebook. Note that none of the following series is updated annually; check the publication date before you buy.

Lonely Planet's *Italy* is thorough, well researched, and packed with travel information, maps, and hotel recommendations for various budgets. The similar *Rough Guide to Italy* is also good and more insightful, updated by British researchers. The highly opinionated *Let's Go: Italy*, researched by Harvard students, is great for students and vagabonds. If you're a low-budget train traveler interested in hosteling and the youth and nightlife scene (which I have largely ignored), get *Let's Go: Italy*. The Italy section in the bigger *Let's Go: Europe* is sparse.

Cultural and Sightseeing Guides: The colorful Eyewitness series, which focuses mainly on sights, has editions on Italy, its various regions, and the major cities. They're fun for their great graphics and photos, but they're relatively skimpy on content and weigh a ton. You can buy them in Italy (no more expensive than in the US) or simply borrow a book for a minute from other travelers at certain sights to make sure that you're aware of that place's highlights. The tall, green Michelin guides to Italy and Rome have minimal information on room and board, but include great maps for drivers and lots of solid, encyclopedic coverage of sights, customs, and culture (sold in English in Italy). The Cadogan guides to various parts of Italy offer a thoughtful look at the rich and confusing local culture, as does *Culture Shock: Italy*.

Recommended Books and Movies

To get the feel of Italy past and present, consider reading some of these books or seeing these films:

Non-Fiction

For the classics of Italian history, look to Machiavelli's *The Prince* and *Florentine Histories*. Written in the 18th century, Edward Gibbon's *Decline and Fall of the Roman Empire* is the landmark history of ancient Rome.

Travelers' Tales Italy (Calcagno) is an excellent compilation of travel writing. Susan Cahill collected travelogues by female authors in *Desiring Italy*. In *Italian Days*, Barbara Grizzuti Harrison crafts travel essays on destinations ranging from Milan to Naples.

Italian Neighbors (Parks) describes life as an Englishman in a small Italian town, while *The Italians* (Barzini), written by an Italian, sheds light on the national character of this fascinating country.

Florence history buffs would enjoy reading the story of the Renaissance city's first family, *The House of Medici* (Hibbert). *Brunelleschi's Dome* (King) describes the trials involved with building Florence's magnificent Duomo. *Under the Tuscan Sun* was a bestseller for Frances Mayes (and is better than the movie of the same name).

Out of Paul Hofmann's multiple books about Italy, *The Seasons of Rome* is the favorite among readers. Elizabeth Gilbert's eloquent *Eat Pray Love* describes her time in Rome (in the "Eat" section). David Macaulay's illustrated books about the Eternal City—*Rome Antics* and *City: A Story of Roman Planning and Construction*—please both kids and adults.

For a solid overview of Venice, try *A History of Venice* (Norwich). Mary McCarthy's *Venice Observed* is a well-written memoir. In *The City of Falling Angels*, John Berendt tells the real-life mystery of the La Fenice Opera House fire.

For a true story about the Sicilian Mafia, consider *Excellent Cadavers* (Stille). *Midnight in Sicily* (Robb) offers a good general history of the Mob. In the memoir, *Christ Stopped at Eboli: The Story of a Year,* Carlo Levi describes his banishment to southern Italy.

Pomp And Sustenance: Twenty-Five Centuries Of Sicilian Food (Simeti) is both a cookbook and an historical overview. Gourmets also like *The Marling Menu-Master for Italy.*

Fiction

Fans of classical literature will want to read Dante's *Divine Comedy* and Boccaccio's *Decameron.* Among the Shakespeare plays set in Italy are *Romeo and Juliet* (Verona), *The Merchant of Venice, Much Ado About Nothing* (Sicily), *The Two Gentlemen of Verona,* and *The Taming of the Shrew* (Padua).

In his 18th-century collection of writings titled *Italian Journey,* Goethe describes his travels to Rome, Sicily, and Naples. Henry James often wrote stories with an Italian theme, and three recommended books—*The Wings of the Dove, Italian Hours,* and *The Aspern Papers and Other Stories*—use Venice as their backdrop. Another classic tale is Thomas Mann's *Death in Venice.*

For historical fiction that brings ancient Rome to life, try *The First Man in Rome* (McCullough) and *I, Claudius* (Graves). *Pompeii* (Harris), set in the ancient doomed city, tells of a young man's rescue attempt.

In the 19th and early 20th centuries, great European writers fell in love with Florence. Two great books from this time are George Eliot's *Romola* and E.M. Forster's *A Room with a View.* Modern novels with Florence as the setting include *The Passion of Artemisia* (Vreeland), *The Sixteen Pleasures* (Hellenga), *Birth of Venus* (Dunant), and *Galileo's Daughter* (Sobel).

If Venice is on your itinerary, consider reading *Invisible Cities* (Calvino), set in the city during Marco Polo's time; the complex tale of love, *The Passion* (Winterson); and *In the Company of the Courtesan* (Dunant), a novel that chronicles the romantic intrigues of Renaissance Venice.

Regarded as one of the most important works of Italian literature, *The Leopard* (di Lampedusa) describes Sicilian life during the Risorgimento. *A Bell for Adano,* set in Sicily, won John Hersey the Pulitzer Prize in 1945. *A Soldier of the Great War* (Helprin)—which takes place partially in the Italian Alps and partially in Sicily—is a brutal tale set in World War I.

One of the best (and bestselling) murder mysteries is Umberto Eco's *The Name of the Rose,* set in a 14th-century Italian monastery. Mystery fans should also consider the books by Michael Dibdin, including *Ratking* (set in Umbria) and *Cabal* (Rome), *A Full Rich Death* (Florence), and *Dead Lagoon* (Dibdin). Dan Brown, the author of the *Da Vinci Code,* used Rome as the backdrop for his earlier murder mystery, *Angels and Demons.* Two Florentine-based mysteries are *The Dante Game* (Langton) and *Bella Donna* (Cherne). Donna Leon's detective stories often take place in Venice; *Death at La Fenice* is one of her most popular.

Films

Roberto Rossellini's *Open City* (1945) and Vittorio de Sica's *Bicycle Thieves* (1949), both classics of Italian Neorealism, continue to inspire audiences today.

In *Roman Holiday* (1953) Audrey Hepburn and Gregory Peck sightsee the city on his scooter. Two campy, big-budget Hollywood flicks bring ancient Rome to life: *Ben-Hur (1959)* and *Spartacus* (1960). In *La Dolce Vita* (1961), Fellini captures the Roman character, while *Gladiator* (2000) was a crowd-pleaser and an Academy Award winner.

1900 (1977) is Bernardo Bertolucci's epic tale of life under fascism; it stars Robert De Niro and Gérard Depardieu.

A Room with a View (1986), a close adaptation of the classic novel, captures Florence's appeal to turn-of-the-century English travelers. Oscar-winning *Life Is Beautiful* (1997) has sections set in a Tuscan town.

In *Bread and Tulips* (2000), a harassed Italian housewife discovers beauty, love, and her true self in Venice. For an adrenaline-laced chase scene through Venice's canals, rent the 2003 version of *The Italian Job*.

Cinema Paradiso (1990), about a film projectionist and a little boy in post-WWII Sicily, won the Oscar for Best Foreign Picture. In *Enchanted April* (1991), filmed in Portofino, an all-star British cast fall in love, discuss relationships, eat well, and take naps in the sun. *Ciao, Professore!* (1994) shows the influence of a grade-school teacher in Southern Italy. In *Il Postino* (1995), poet Pablo Neruda befriends his Italian postman. *Nuovomondo* (2006, also called *The Golden Door*) tells the story of Sicilian immigrants leaving home for Ellis Island.

MONEY MATTERS

Damage Control for Lost Cards

If you lose your credit, debit, or ATM card, you can stop people from using your card by reporting the loss immediately to the respective global customer-assistance centers. Call these 24-hour US numbers collect: Visa (410/581-9994), MasterCard (636/722-7111), and American Express (623/492-8427).

At a minimum, you'll need to know the name of the financial institution that issued you the card, along with the type of card (classic, platinum, or whatever). Providing the following information will allow for a quicker cancellation of your missing

Appendix

card: full card number, whether you are the primary or secondary cardholder, the cardholder's name exactly as printed on the card, billing address, home phone number, circumstances of the loss or theft, and identification verification (your birth date, your mother's maiden name, or your Social Security number—memorize this, don't carry a copy). If you are the secondary cardholder, you'll also need to provide the primary cardholder's identification-verification details. You can generally receive a temporary card within two or three business days in Europe.

If you promptly report your card lost or stolen, you typically won't be responsible for any unauthorized transactions on your account, although many banks charge a liability fee of $50.

Tipping

Tipping in Italy isn't as automatic and generous as it is in the US, but for special service, tips are appreciated, if not expected. As in the US, the proper amount depends on your resources, tipping philosophy, and the circumstances, but some general guidelines apply.

Restaurants: Check the menu to see if the service is included (*servizio incluso*—generally 15 percent); if not, you could tip 5 to 10 percent for good service, though be advised that Italians rarely tip.

Taxis: To tip the cabbie, round up. For a typical ride, round up to the next euro on the fare (to pay a €4.50 fare, give €5). If the cabbie hauls your bags and zips you to the airport to help you catch your flight, you might want to toss in a little more. But if you feel like you're being driven in circles or otherwise ripped off, skip the tip.

Special Services: It's thoughtful to tip a couple of euros to someone who shows you a special sight and who is paid in no other way. Tour guides at public sites sometimes hold out their hands for tips after they give their spiel; if I've already paid for the tour, I don't tip extra, though some tourists do give a euro or two, particularly for a job well done. I don't tip at hotels, but if you do, give the porter a euro for carrying bags and leave a couple of euros in your room at the end of your stay for the maid if the room was kept clean. In general, if someone in the service industry does a super job for you, a tip of a couple of euros is appropriate...but not required.

When in doubt, ask. If you're not sure whether (or how much) to tip for a service, ask your hotelier or the tourist information office; they'll fill you in on how it's done on their turf.

Getting a VAT Refund

As is the case throughout the European Union, wrapped into the purchase price of your Italian souvenirs is a Value Added Tax

(VAT) of about 20 percent. If you purchase more than €155 (about $200) worth of goods at a store that participates in the VAT-refund scheme, you're entitled to get most of that tax back. Getting your refund is usually straightforward and, if you buy a substantial amount of souvenirs, well worth the hassle. If you're lucky, the merchant will subtract the tax when you make your purchase. (This is more likely to occur if the store ships the goods to your home.) Otherwise, you'll need to:

Get the paperwork. Have the merchant completely fill out the necessary refund document, called a "cheque." You'll have to present your passport.

Get your stamp at the border or airport. Process your cheque(s) at your last stop in the EU with the customs agent who deals with VAT refunds. It's best to keep your purchases in your carry-on for viewing, but if they're too large or dangerous (such as knives) to carry on, track down the proper customs agent to inspect them before you check your bag. You're not supposed to use your purchased goods before you leave. If you show up at customs wearing your new leather shoes, officials might look the other way—or deny you a refund.

Collect your refund. You'll need to return your stamped document to the retailer or its representative. Many merchants work with a service, such as Global Refund (www.globalrefund.com) or Premier Tax Free (www.premiertaxfree.com), which have offices at major airports, ports, or border crossings. These services, which extract a 4 percent fee, can refund your money immediately in your currency of choice or credit your card (within two billing cycles). If the retailer handles VAT refunds directly, it's up to you to contact the merchant for your refund. You can mail the documents from home, or quicker, from your point of departure (using a stamped, addressed envelope you've prepared or one that's been provided by the merchant)—and then wait. It could take months.

Customs for American Shoppers

You are allowed to take home $800 worth of items per person duty-free, once every 30 days. The next $1,000 is taxed at a flat 3 percent. After that, you pay the individual item's duty rate. You can also bring in duty-free a liter of alcohol (slightly more than a standard-size bottle of wine, pack carefully in checked bag; you must be at least 21), 200 cigarettes, and up to 100 non-Cuban cigars. Cans or sealed jars of food are okay (if no meat is included). Some, but not all, types of cheese are allowed but fresh fruits and vegetables are not. To check customs rules and duty rates before you go, visit www.cbp.gov, and click on "Travel," then "Know Before You Go."

TELEPHONES, EMAIL, AND MAIL

Telephones

Smart travelers learn the phone system and use it daily to reserve or reconfirm rooms, get tourist information, reserve restaurants, confirm tour times, or phone home.

Types of Phones

You'll encounter various kinds of phones on your trip:

Card-operated phones—where you insert a locally bought phone card into a public pay phone—are common in Europe.

Coin-operated phones, the original kind of pay phone, require you to have enough change to complete your call.

Hotel-room phones are sometimes cheap for local calls (confirm at the front desk first), but can be a rip-off for long-distance calls unless you use an international phone card (described below). But incoming calls are free, making this a cheap way for friends and family to stay in touch, provided they have a good long-distance plan for calls to Europe.

American mobile phones work in Europe if they're GSM-enabled, tri-band or quad-band, and on a calling plan that includes international calls. They're convenient, but pricey. For example, with a T-Mobile phone, you'll pay $1 per minute for calls.

European mobile phones run about $75 (for the most basic models) and come without con-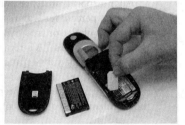tracts. If you don't speak Italian, the mechanics of using these phones is almost impossible, but any young Italian can bail you out in a snap. These phones are loaded with prepaid calling time that you can recharge as you use up the minutes. As long as you're not "roaming" outside the phone's home country, incoming calls are free. If you're traveling to multiple countries within Europe, make sure the phone is electronically "unlocked," so that you can swap out its SIM card (a fingernail-size chip that holds the phone's information) for a new one in other countries.

Using Phone Cards

Get a phone card for your calls. Prepaid phone cards come in two types: international and insertable (both described below). Neither type of card works outside of Italy. While traveling, you can share either type of card with your companions (and, in the case of an international phone card, your buddy doesn't even need the actual card—just the numbers on it). If you have time left on a card when you leave the country (as you likely will), simply give it to another traveler—anyone can use it.

You'll get the best deal with an **international phone card.** It enables you to make calls to the US for as little as two cents per minute, and also works for local calls. You can use these cards from any phone, including the one in your hotel room (check to make sure your phone is set on tone instead of pulse, and ask the hotel about hidden fees on toll-free calls). You can buy the cards at small newsstand kiosks, *tabacchi* (tobacco) shops, Internet cafés, hostels, and hole-in-the-wall long-distance phone shops. Because there are so many brand names, simply ask for an international phone card (*carta telefonica prepagata internazionale,* KAR-tah teh-leh-FOHN-ee-kah pray-pah-GAH-tah in-ter-naht-zee-oh-NAH-lay). Tell the vendor where you'll be making most calls (*"per Stati Uniti"*—to America), and he'll select the brand with the best deal. Buy a lower denomination in case the card is a dud. I've had good luck with the Europa card, which offers 220 minutes from Italy to the US for €5.

To use an international phone card, dial the toll-free number listed on the card; you'll reach an automated operator. When prompted, dial in a scratch-to-reveal code number. Then dial your number (start with 001 for calls to the US).

Generally you'll get more minutes—sometimes up to five times as many—if you do two things: use your international phone card from your hotel room, rather than from a pay phone; and use the local access number (if you're in that city), rather than the toll-free number (which uses up the card more quickly).

An **insertable phone card** can only be used at a pay phone. These Telecom cards, considered "official" since they're sold by Italy's phone company, give you the best deal for calls within Italy and are reasonable for international calls.

You can buy Telecom cards (in denominations of €5 or €10) at *tabacchi* shops, post offices, and machines near phone booths (many phone booths have signs indicating where the nearest phone-card sales outlet is located).

Rip off the perforated corner to "activate" the card, and then physically insert it into a slot in the pay phone. It displays how much money you have remaining on the card. Then just dial away. The price of the call is automatically deducted while you talk.

Using Hotel-Room Phones, Metered Phones, VoIP, or US Calling Cards

The phone in your **hotel room** is convenient...but expensive. While incoming calls (made by folks back home) can be the cheapest way to keep in touch, charges for *outgoing* calls can be a very unpleasant surprise. Make sure you understand all the charges and fees

Important Phone Numbers

Consulates and Embassies

US Consulates: Milan—tel. 02-290-351 (Via Principe Amedeo 2/10, http://milan.usconsulate.gov), Rome—tel. 06-46741 (Via Vittorio Veneto 119/A, http://rome.usconsulate.gov/english), Florence—tel. 055-266-951 (Lungarno Vespucci 38, http://florence.usconsulate.gov), Naples—tel. 081-5838-111 (Piazza della Repubblica, http://naples.usconsulate.gov).

Canadian Embassies: Rome—automatic tel. 06-854-443-937, emergency tel. 06-854-441 (Via Zara 30), Naples—tel. 081-401-338 (29 Via Carducci), Padua—tel. 049-876-4833 (Riviera Ruzzante 25). The website for all locations is www.canada.it.

Emergency

English-speaking police: 113
Military police: 112
Ambulance: 118
Road Service: 116

Assistance

Telephone Help (in English; free directory assistance): 170
Directory Assistance (for €0.50, an Italian-speaking robot gives the number twice, very clearly): 12

associated with outgoing calls before you pick up that receiver.

Dialing direct from your hotel room—without using an international phone card (described above)—is usually quite expensive for international calls. Always ask first how much you'll be charged, even for local and (supposedly) toll-free calls.

If your family has an inexpensive way to call Europe, either through a long-distance plan or prepaid calling card, have them call you in your hotel room. Give them a list of your hotels' phone numbers before you go. Then, as you travel, send them an email or make a quick pay-phone call to set up a time for them to give you a ring.

Metered phones are sometimes available in bigger post offices. You can talk all you want, then pay the bill when you leave—but be sure you know the rates before you have a lengthy conversation.

If you're traveling with a laptop, consider trying **VoIP (Voice over Internet Protocol).** With VoIP, two computers act as the phones, allowing for a free Internet-based call. The major providers are Skype (www.skype.com) and Google Talk (www.google.com/talk).

US Calling Cards (such as the ones offered by AT&T, MCI, or Sprint) are the worst option. You'll nearly always save a lot of money by paying with a phone card (see above).

How to Dial

Calling from the US to Europe, or vice versa, is simple—once you break the code. The European calling chart on page 830 will walk you through it.

Dialing Within Italy

Italy has a direct-dial phone system (no area codes). To call anywhere within Italy, just dial the number. For example, the number of one of my recommended Florence hotels is 055-289-592. That's the number you dial whether you're calling it from Florence's train station or from Rome. Keep in mind that Italian phone numbers vary in length; a hotel can have, say, an eight-digit phone number and a nine-digit fax number.

Italy's toll-free numbers start with 800 (like US 800 numbers, though in Italy you don't dial a 1 first). In Italy, these 800 numbers—called *freephone* or *numero verde* (green number)—can be dialed free from any phone without using a phone card or coins. Note that you can't call Italy's toll-free numbers from America, nor can you count on reaching America's toll-free numbers from Italy.

Dialing Internationally

If you want to make an international call, follow these three steps:

1) Dial the international access code (00 if you're calling from Europe, 011 from the US or Canada). If you see a phone number that begins with +, you have to replace the + with the international access code.

2) Dial the country code of the country you're calling (39 for Italy, or 1 for the US or Canada).

3) Dial the local number. Note that in most European countries, you have to drop the zero at the beginning of the local number—but in Italy, you dial it.

So, to call the Florence hotel from the US, dial 011 (the US international access code), 39 (Italy's country code), then 055-289-592. To call my office in Edmonds, Washington, from Italy, I dial 00 (Europe's international access code), 1 (the US country code), 425 (Edmonds' area code), and 771-8303.

Email and Mail

Email: Many travelers set up a free email account with Yahoo, Microsoft (Hotmail), or Google (Gmail). Email use among European hoteliers is quite common. Internet cafés and little hole-in-the-wall Internet-access shops (offering a few computers, no food, and cheap prices) are popular in most cities. More and more hotels now offer Internet access in their lobbies for guests, and some even have wireless connections (Wi-Fi) for travelers with laptop computers. Ask if your hotel has access. If it doesn't, your

European Calling Chart

Just smile and dial, using this key:
AC = Area Code, LN = Local Number.

European Country	Calling long distance within ...	Calling from the US or Canada to ...	Calling from a European country to ...
Austria	AC + LN	011 + 43 + AC (without the initial zero) + LN	00 + 43 + AC (without the initial zero) + LN
Belgium	LN	011 + 32 + LN (without initial zero)	00 + 32 + LN (without initial zero)
Bosnia-Herzegovina	AC + LN	011 + 387 + AC (without initial zero) + LN	00 + 387 + AC (without initial zero) + LN
Britain	AC + LN	011 + 44 + AC (without initial zero) + LN	00 + 44 + AC (without initial zero) + LN
Croatia	AC + LN	011 + 385 + AC (without initial zero) + LN	00 + 385 + AC (without initial zero) + LN
Czech Republic	LN	011 + 420 + LN	00 + 420 + LN
Denmark	LN	011 + 45 + LN	00 + 45 + LN
Estonia	LN	011 + 372 + LN	00 + 372 + LN
Finland	AC + LN	011 + 358 + AC (without initial zero) + LN	999 + 358 + AC (without initial zero) + LN
France	LN	011 + 33 + LN (without initial zero)	00 + 33 + LN (without initial zero)
Germany	AC + LN	011 + 49 + AC (without initial zero) + LN	00 + 49 + AC (without initial zero) + LN
Greece	LN	011 + 30 + LN	00 + 30 + LN
Hungary	06 + AC + LN	011 + 36 + AC + LN	00 + 36 + AC + LN
Ireland	AC + LN	011 + 353 + AC (without initial zero) + LN	00 + 353 + AC (without initial zero) + LN

European Country	Calling long distance within...	Calling from the US or Canada to...	Calling from a European country to...
Italy	LN	011 + 39 + LN	00 + 39 + LN
Montenegro	AC + LN	011 + 382 + AC (without initial zero) + LN	00 + 382 + AC (without initial zero) + LN
Netherlands	AC + LN	011 + 31 + AC (without initial zero) + LN	00 + 31 + AC (without initial zero) + LN
Norway	LN	011 + 47 + LN	00 + 47 + LN
Poland	LN	011 + 48 + LN (without initial zero)	00 + 48 + LN (without initial zero)
Portugal	LN	011 + 351 + LN	00 + 351 + LN
Slovakia	AC + LN	011 + 421 + AC (without initial zero) + LN	00 + 421 + AC (without initial zero) + LN
Slovenia	AC + LN	011 + 386 + AC (without initial zero) + LN	00 + 386 + AC (without initial zero) + LN
Spain	LN	011 + 34 + LN	00 + 34 + LN
Sweden	AC + LN	011 + 46 + AC (without initial zero) + LN	00 + 46 + AC (without initial zero) + LN
Switzerland	LN	011 + 41 + LN (without initial zero)	00 + 41 + LN (without initial zero)
Turkey	AC (if no initial zero is included, add one) + LN	011 + 90 + AC (without initial zero) + LN	00 + 90 + AC (without initial zero) + LN

- The instructions above apply whether you're calling a land line or mobile phone.
- The international access codes (the first numbers you dial when making an international call) are 011 if you're calling from the US or Canada, or 00 if you're calling from virtually anywhere in Europe (except Finland, where it's 999).
- To call the US or Canada from Europe, dial 00, then 1 (the country code for the US and Canada), then the area code and number. In short, 00 + 1 + AC + LN = Hi, Mom!

hotelier will direct you to the nearest place to get online.

Because of a recent anti-terrorism law in Italy, you may be asked to show your passport (carry it in your money belt) when using a public Internet terminal at an Internet café or in a hotel lobby. The proprietor will likely make a copy of your passport.

Mail: While you can arrange for mail delivery to your hotel (allow 10 days for a letter to arrive), phoning and emailing are so easy that I've dispensed with mail stops altogether.

Mail service in Italy has improved over the last few years, but even so, mail nothing precious from Italy. Federal Express makes pricey two-day deliveries.

TRANSPORTATION

By Car or Train?

Each has pros and cons. Public transportation is one of the few bargains in Italy. Trains and buses are inexpensive and good. City-to-city travel is faster, easier, and cheaper by train than by car. Trains give you the convenience and economy of doing long stretches overnight. By train, I arrive relaxed and well-rested—not so by car.

Parking, gas (about $6/gallon), and freeway tolls (about $6/hr) are expensive in Italy. But drivers enjoy more control, especially in the countryside. Cars carry your luggage for you, generally from door to door—especially important for heavy packers (such as chronic shoppers and families traveling with children). And groups know that the more people you pack into a car or minibus, the cheaper it gets per person.

Considering how handy and affordable Italy's trains and buses are (and that you're likely to go both broke and crazy driving in Italian cities), I'd do most of Italy by public transportation. If you want to drive, consider doing the big, intense stuff (Rome, Naples area, Milan, Florence, and Venice) by train or bus and renting a car for the hill towns of Tuscany and Umbria and for the Dolomites. A car is a worthless headache on the Riviera and in the Lake Como area.

Trains

To travel by train cheaply in Italy, you can simply buy tickets as you go. Though train station lines can be long, ticket machines work well and are easy to use (see "Buying Tickets," later in this section). Pay all ticket costs in the station before you board or pay a nasty penalty on the train.

Most people traveling within Italy find that the Italy Pass for Italian State Railways saves neither time nor hassle (see "Railpasses," page 838). Use the price map on page 835 to add up

Italy's Public Transportation

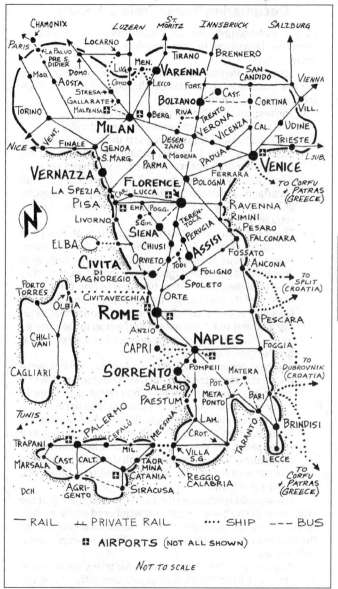

RAIL ⊥ PRIVATE RAIL •••• SHIP --- BUS

✈ AIRPORTS (NOT ALL SHOWN)

NOT TO SCALE

Deciphering Italian Train Schedules

At the station, look for the big yellow posters labeled *Partenze*—Departures (ignore the white posters, which show arrivals).

Schedules are listed chronologically, hour by hour, showing the trains leaving the station throughout the day. Each schedule has columns:

- The first column *(Ora)* lists the time of departure.
- The next column *(Treno)* shows the type of train.
- The third column *(Classi Servizi)* lists the services available (first- and second-class cars, dining car, *cuccetta* berths, etc.) and, more important, whether you need reservations (usually denoted by an *R* in a box). Note that all Eurostar (ES) and InterCityPlus (ICP) trains, many InterCity (IC) and EuroCity (EC) trains, and most international trains require reservations.
- The next column lists the destination of the train *(Principali Fermate Destinazioni)*, often showing intermediate stops, followed by the final destination, with arrival times listed throughout in parentheses. Note that *your* final destination may be listed in fine print as an intermediate destination. If you're going from Milan to Florence, scan the schedule and you'll notice that virtually all trains that terminate in Rome stop in Florence en route. Travelers who read the fine print end up with a far greater choice of trains.
- The next column *(Servizi Diretti e Annotazioni)* has pertinent notes about the train, such as "also stops in..." *(ferma anche a...)*, "doesn't stop in..." *(non ferma a...)*, "stops in every station" *(ferma in tutte le stazioni)*, and so on.
- The last column lists the track *(Binario)* the train departs from. Confirm the *binario* with an additional source: a ticket seller, the electronic board that lists immediate departures, TV monitors on the platform, or the railway officials who are usually standing by the train unless you really need them.

For any odd symbols on the poster, look at the key at the end. Some of the phrasing can be deciphered easily, such as *servizio periodico* (periodic service—doesn't always run). For the trickier ones, ask a local or railway official, or simply take a different train.

You can also check schedules—for trains anywhere in Italy, not just from the station you're currently in—at the handy gray-and-yellow ticket machines. Enter the date and time of your departure (to or from any Italian station), and you can view all your options.

Italy by Train

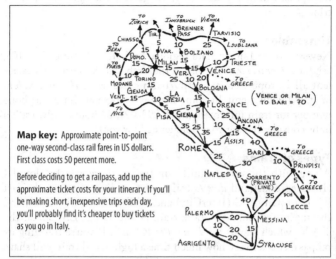

Map key: Approximate point-to-point one-way second-class rail fares in US dollars. First class costs 50 percent more.

Before deciding to get a railpass, add up the approximate ticket costs for your itinerary. If you'll be making short, inexpensive trips each day, you'll probably find it's cheaper to buy tickets as you go in Italy.

your ticket costs. Although the pass covers the full cost of getting you from A to B on many trains in Italy, it doesn't cover the cost of seat reservations or overnight berths. Reservations are optional for many trains, but are required for the fastest trains between major Italian cities (see "Types of Trains," later in this section). While the pass does save you from having to buy each train ticket as you go, if you'll be taking a few fast trains, you'll still have to spend time in line—essentially eliminating the point of buying this pass.

Multi-Country Railpasses
For travel exclusively in Italy, an 18-country **Eurailpass** is a bad value. If you're branching out beyond Italy, the **Eurail Selectpass** allows you to tailor a pass to your trip, provided you're traveling in three, four, or five adjacent countries directly connected by rail or ferry. For instance, with a three-country pass allowing 10 days of train travel within a two-month period ($648 in 2007), you could choose France–Italy–Greece or Germany–Austria–Italy. A **France and Italy Pass** combines just those two countries and covers night trains to and from Paris via Switzerland (but if your route crosses Switzerland by day, you'll pay extra—so the Selectpass is a better choice if you want to see the Alps). Before you buy a Selectpass or France and Italy Pass, think carefully how many travel days you'll really need. Use the pass only for travel days that involve long hauls or several trips. Pay out of pocket for tickets on days you're taking only short, cheap rides.

For a summary of railpass deals, check my Guide to Eurail Passes at www.ricksteves.com/rail. If you decide to get a railpass, this guide will help you know you're getting the right one for your trip.

Timetables

Newsstands sell up-to-date regional and all-Italy timetables (€5, ask for the *orario ferroviaro*). On the Web, check Germany's excellent all-Europe website, http://bahn.hafas.de/bin/query.exe/en, or Italy's www.trenitalia.com. There is a single all-Italy telephone number for train information (tel. 892-021, 24 hours daily, Italian only, consider having your hotelier call for you).

Types of Trains

Along with the various milk-run trains, there are the slow IR (Interregional) and *diretto* trains, the medium *espresso*, the fast EC (EuroCity), IC (InterCity) and IC Plus (InterCity Plus), and the space-age Eurostar Italia train (abbreviated "ES," a.k.a. the T.A.V., which stands for *Treno Alta Velocità*). If you're traveling by railpass, check to see how much time a high-speed train will shave off before plunking down an extra €15 for your Eurostar Italia reservation. If you're buying tickets as you go, fast trains are affordable (e.g., a second-class Rome–Venice Eurostar ticket costs about €50, including the reservation, at any ticket window or machine, only €8 more than the IC train).

Tickets

Avoid big-city train station ticket lines whenever possible by using automated ticket machines (in train stations) or going to local travel agencies. You'll be able to easily purchase tickets, make seat reservations, and even book a *cuccetta* (koo-CHEHT-tah; overnight berth).

Automated ticket machines are user-friendly and found in all but the tiniest stations in Italy. You can pay by cash (they give change) or by debit or credit card. Select English, then wade through a menu of destinations. If you don't see the city you're traveling to, keep keying in the spelling until it's listed. You can choose from first- and second-class seats, request tickets for more than one traveler, and (on the high-speed Eurostar trains) choose an aisle or window seat. When the machine prompts you—"Fidelity Card?"—choose no. Americans will need to select full-price tickets, since we're not eligible for any EU or resident discounts. You can even validate your ticket in the same machine if you're boarding your train right away.

At **local travel agencies,** such as CIT or American Express, you'll pay either the same or a little bit more (about €2) than at the train station, and encounter shorter lines and less of a language barrier.

Anatomy of an Italian Train Ticket

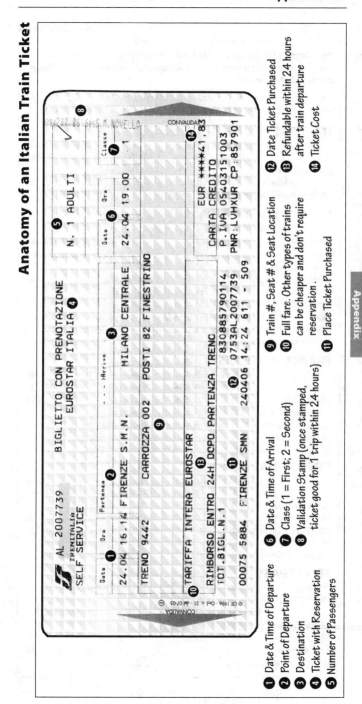

1. Date & Time of Departure
2. Point of Departure
3. Destination
4. Ticket with Reservation
5. Number of Passengers
6. Date & Time of Arrival
7. Class (1 = First; 2 = Second)
8. Validation Stamp (once stamped, ticket good for 1 trip within 24 hours)
9. Train #, Seat # & Seat Location
10. Full fare. Other types of trains can be cheaper and don't require reservation.
11. Place Ticket Purchased
12. Date Ticket Purchased
13. Refundable within 24 hours after train departure
14. Ticket Cost

Railpasses

Prices listed are for 2007 and are subject to change. For the latest prices, details, and train schedules (and easy online ordering), see my comprehensive *Guide to Eurail Passes* at www.ricksteves.com/rail.

"Saver" prices are per person for two or more people traveling together. "Youth" means under age 26. The fare for children 4–11 is half the adult individual fare or Saver fare. Kids under age 4 travel free.

ITALY PASS

	Individual 1st Class	Individual 2nd Class	Saver 1st Class	Saver 2nd Class	Youth 2nd Class
3 days in 2 months	$245	$196	$209	$168	$165
Extra rail days (max 7)	30	25	27	20	20

Italy passes may also be sold in Italy at major train stations.

ITALY RAIL & DRIVE PASS

Any 3 rail days and 2 car days in 2 months.

Car Category	1st Class	2nd Class	Extra Car Day
Economy	$334	$277	$54
Compact	352	295	72
Intermediate	361	305	82
Small Automatic	384	327	104
Extra rail days (max 7)	34	29	

Prices are per person, two traveling together. Solo travelers pay about 20 percent more. To order a Rail & Drive pass, call your travel agent or Rail Europe at 800-438-7245. *This pass is not sold by Europe Through the Back Door.*

FRANCE–ITALY PASS

	Individual 1st Class	Individual 2nd Class	Saver 1st Class	Saver 2nd Class	Youth 2nd Class
4 days in 2 months	$352	$306	$306	$271	$230
Extra rail days (max 6)	40	35	35	30	27

Be aware of your route. Many daytime connections from Paris to Italy pass through Switzerland (an additional $50 if not covered by your pass). Routes via Nice, Torino, or Modane will bypass Switzerland. Paris–Italy night trains are covered by the pass, regardless of their route.

GREECE–ITALY PASS

	Individual 1st Class	Individual 2nd Class	Saver 1st Class	Saver 2nd Class	Youth 2nd Class
4 days in 2 months	$343	$274	$294	$235	$233
Extra rail days (max 6)	35	28	28	23	22

Covers deck passage on overnight Superfast Ferries between Patras, Greece and Bari or Ancona, Italy (starts use of one travel day). Or 50 percent discount on Hellenic Mediterranean Line ferry with basic cabin Patras-Corfu-Brindisi (does not use a travel day). Does not cover travel to or on Greek islands.

SELECTPASS

This pass covers travel in three adjacent countries. Please visit **www.ricksteves.com/rail** for four- and five-country options.

	Individual 1st Class	Saver 1st Class	Youth 2nd Class
5 days in 2 months	$429	$365	$279
6 days in 2 months	471	402	309
8 days in 2 months	562	478	365
10 days in 2 months	648	550	420

You can buy tickets **online** through www.trenitalia.com if you're Web-savvy, patient, prepared (you have only a 15-minute window of time to place your order), and certain of your needs (don't expect to make changes to your ticket afterwards). You usually won't save money booking online, but you'll be able to nail your major trips down well in advance and have e-tickets that won't require validation at the station.

First-class tickets cost 50 percent more than **second-class.** While second-class cars go as fast as their first-class neighbors, Italy is one country where I would consider the splurge of first class. The easiest way to "upgrade" a second-class ticket once on board a crowded train is to nurse a drink in the snack car.

Before boarding the train, you must **validate** (stamp) your train documents in the yellow box near the platform. This includes whatever you need to take a particular trip, which can be as simple as a single ticket, but can also involve a supplement, seat reservation, or *cuccetta* reservation on an overnight train. If you forget to stamp your ticket, go right away to the train conductor—before he comes to you—or you'll pay a fine. Note that you don't need to stamp a railpass or e-ticket.

Reservations

Trains can fill up, even in first class. If you're on a tight schedule, you'll want to reserve a few days ahead for fast trains (€4 for most trains, or €10–15 for railpass holders on the Eurostar Italia). If you don't have a reservation, and if your train originates at your departure point (e.g., you're catching the Milan–Venice train in Milan), arriving at least 15 minutes before the departure time will help you snare a seat.

Some major stations have train composition posters on the platforms showing where first- and second-class cars are located when the trains arrive (letters on the poster are supposed to correspond to letters posted over the platform—but they don't always). Since most trains now allow you to make reservations up to the time of departure, conductors are no longer marking reserved seats with a card—instead, they simply post a list of the reservable and non-reservable seat rows (sometimes in English) in each train car's vestibule. This means that if you board a crowded train and get one of the last seats, you may be ousted when the reservation holder comes along.

Baggage Storage, Theft Concerns, and Strikes

Many stations have *deposito bagagli* where you can safely leave your bag for €3 per 12-hour period (payable when you pick up the bag, double-check closing hours). Since the terrorist attacks of September 11, 2001, no Italian stations have lockers.

Italian trains are famous for their thieves. Never leave a bag unattended. I've noticed that police now ride the trains, and things seem more controlled. Still, for an overnight trip, I'd feel safe only in a *cuccetta* (a bunk in a special sleeping car with an attendant who keeps track of who comes and goes while you sleep—approximately €20 in a 6-bed compartment, €25 in a less-cramped four-bed compartment).

Strikes, which are common, generally last a day. Train employees will simply explain, "*Sciopero*" (strike). But in actuality, sporadic trains, following no particular schedule, lumber down the tracks during most strikes. When a strike is pending, travel agencies (and Web-savvy hoteliers) can check the Web for you to see when the strike goes into effect and which trains will continue to run.

Renting a Car

To drive in Italy, you'll need an International Driver's Permit (available at your local AAA office for $15, plus the cost of two passport-type photos; see www.aaa.com).

To rent a car here, you must be at least 18 years old and have held your license for one year. Drivers under the age of 25 may incur a young-driver surcharge, and some rental companies do not rent to anyone 75 and over. If you're considered too young or old, look into leasing, which has less-stringent age restrictions.

Research car rentals before you go. It's cheaper to arrange car rentals from the US, either with your travel agent or directly with the company you choose. Two reputable companies among many are Auto Europe (www.autoeurope.com) and Europe by Car (www.europebycar.com). Rent by the week with unlimited mileage. I normally rent the smallest, least-expensive model with a stick shift (cheaper than an automatic). For a three-week rental, allow $800 per person (based on two people sharing a car), including insurance, tolls, gas, and parking. If you'll be renting for three weeks or more, consider leasing; you'll save money on insurance and taxes. Compare pick-up costs (downtown can be cheaper than the airport) and explore drop-off options (south of Rome can be a problem).

If you want a car for only a couple of days, a rail-and-drive pass (such as a EurailDrive, Selectpass Drive, or Italy Rail and Drive) can be put to thoughtful use. Certain areas are great by car, such as the Dolomites and the hill towns of Tuscany and Umbria, while most of Italy (including the Cinque Terre) is best by train. The basic Italy Rail and Drive Pass, which includes theft insurance and CDW (described below), comes with two days of car rental and three days of rail in two months. While rail-and-drive passes are convenient, they're also pricey, particularly for solo travelers.

Car Insurance Options

When you rent a car, you are liable for a very high deductible, sometimes equal to the entire value of the car. There are various ways you can limit your financial risk in case of an accident. For Italy, you have two options: buy Collision Damage Waiver (CDW) coverage from the car-rental company (figure roughly 25 percent extra), or get coverage through your credit card (free, if your card automatically includes zero-deductible coverage).

CDW includes a very high deductible (typically $1,000–1,500). When you pick up the car, you'll be offered the chance to "buy down" the deductible to zero (for $10–30/day; this is often called "super CDW").

If you opt for **credit-card coverage,** there's a catch. You'll technically have to decline all coverage offered by the car-rental company, which means they can place a hold on your card for the full deductible amount. In case of damage, it can be time-consuming to resolve the charges with your credit-card company. Before you decide on this option, quiz your credit-card company about how it works and ask them to explain the worst-case scenario.

Buying CDW insurance (plus "super CDW") is the easier but pricier option. Using the coverage that comes with your credit card saves money, but can involve more hassle. For trips of at least three weeks, leasing—which includes taxes and insurance—is the best way to go.

Note that **theft insurance** (separate from CDW insurance) is mandatory in Italy. The insurance usually costs about $10–15 a day, payable when you pick up the car.

For all the fine print about car-rental insurance, see www.ricksteves.com /cdw.

Driving

Driving in Italy can be scary—a video game for keeps, and you only get one quarter. Seatbelts are mandatory.

Autostrada: Italy's freeway system is as good as our interstate system, but you'll pay about a dollar for every 10 minutes of use.

STOP AND LEARN THESE ROAD SIGNS

Speed Limit (km/hr) — Yield — No Passing — End of No Passing Zone

One Way — Intersection — Main Road — Freeway

Danger — No Entry — No Entry for Cars — All Vehicles Prohibited

Parking — No Parking — Customs — Peace

Driving in Italy: Distance and Time

SWITZERLAND

Brenner Pass

AUSTRIA

Villach

Dolo-
mites

70m • 2h

260m • 5h

175m • 3h

Mt.
Blanc
Tunnel

Lake
Como

SLOVENIA

155m • 2.5h

95m • 1.75h

Trieste

145m • 2.5h

30m • .75h

100m • 2.25h

255m • 4.5h

170m • 3h

CROATIA

Milan

200m • 4h

185m • 3.25h

Venice

175m • 2.75h

135m • 2.5h

225m • 4h

85m • 2.5h

160m • 2.75h

90m • 1.75h

230m • 3.5h

155m • 3h

Ravenna

FRA.

Cinque
Terre
(La Spezia)

50m • 1h

70m • 1.5h

115m • 2h

Florence

125m • 2.5h

Ventimiglia

Pisa

45m
1h

100m • 2h

Assisi

Siena

80m
2h

100m • 2h

210m • 4h

75m • 1.5h

75m • 1.75h

55m
1.5h

115m • 2.25h

35m • 1h

Orvieto

75m • 1.5h

Rome

N

Note: Your times
may vary based on
traffic, construction,
and road conditions.

m = miles
h = hours

155m • 2.5h

30m • .5h

Naples

Salerno

30m • .75h

Sorrento

30m
1h

60m • 3h

Paestum

(I paid €20 for the four-hour drive from Bolzano to Pisa.) While I
favor the freeways because I feel they're safer, cheaper (saving time
and gas), and less nerve-racking than smaller roads, savvy local
drivers know which toll-free *superstradas* are actually faster and
more direct than the *autostrada* (e.g., Florence to Pisa). For more
information, visit www.autostrade.it.

Gas: Most cars take unleaded gas (*senza piombo*, from green
pumps, available everywhere). *Autostrada* rest stops are self-service
stations open daily without a siesta
break. Small-town stations are usually cheaper and offer full service but
shorter hours. Many 24-hour-a-day
stations are entirely automated, with
machines that trade gas for paper
money.

Restricted Traffic Zones: Car
traffic is restricted in many of Italy's
city centers, including Rome, Florence,
Milan, Lucca, Siena, San Gimignano,

ZONA
TRAFFICO LIMITATO

red

Orvieto, and Verona. Don't drive or park in any area that has a sign reading *Zona Traffico Limitato* (*ZTL*, often shown above a red circle, see previous page). If you do, your license plate can be photographed and a hefty (€100-plus) ticket mailed to your home. If your hotel is within a restricted area, ask your hotelier to register your car as an authorized vehicle or to direct you to parking outside the restricted zone.

Parking: White lines generally mean parking is free. Blue lines mean you'll have to pay—usually €1 per hour (use machine, leave time-stamped receipt on dashboard). If there's no meter, there's probably a roving attendant who will take your money. Study the signs. Often the free zones have a 30- or 60-minute time limit. Signs showing a street cleaner and a day of the week indicate which day the street is cleaned; there's a €100 tow-fee incentive to learn the days of the week in Italian.

Zona disco has nothing to do with dancing. Italian cars have a time disk (a cardboard clock), which you set at your arrival time and lay on the dashboard so the attendant knows how long you've been parked. This is a fine system that all drivers should take advantage of. (If your rental car doesn't come with a *zona disco*, pick one up at a tobacco shop or just write your arrival time on a piece of paper and place it on the dashboard.)

Garages are safe, save time, and help you avoid the stress of parking tickets. Take the parking voucher with you to pay the cashier before you leave.

Theft: Cars are routinely vandalized and stolen. Try to make your car look locally owned by hiding the "tourist-owned" rental-company decals and putting a local newspaper in your back window. Be sure all of your valuables are out of sight and locked in the trunk, or even better, with you or in your room.

Cheap Flights

If you're visiting one or more Italian cities on a longer European trip—or linking up far-flung Italian cities (e.g., Venice and Rome)—you might want to look into the affordable intra-European airlines. While trains are still the best way to connect places that are close together, a flight can save both time and money on long journeys.

One of the best Web sites for comparing inexpensive flights is www.skyscanner.net. Other comparison search engines include www.kayak.com, www.mobissimo.com, www.sidestep.com, and www.wegolo.com.

Well-known cheapo airlines include easyJet (www.easyjet.com) and Ryanair (www.ryanair.com). Other budget airlines that touch down in Italy include Belle Air (www.belleair.it), Flybaboo (www.flybaboo.com), and Sterling (www.sterlingticket.com).

Appendix

Italy-based discount airlines that you may see include AlpiEagles (www.alpieagles.com) and Air One (www.flyairone.it).

Be aware of the potential drawbacks of flying on the cheap: nonrefundable and nonchangeable tickets, rigid baggage restrictions (and fees if you have more than what's officially allowed), use of airports far outside town, tight schedules that can mean more delays, little in the way of customer assistance if problems arise, and, of course, no frills. To avoid unpleasant surprises, read the small print—especially baggage policies—before you book.

HOLIDAYS AND FESTIVALS

Italy celebrates many holidays, which close sights and bring crowds. Each town has a local festival honoring its patron saint. Italy shuts down on these national holidays: January 1, January 6 (Epiphany), Easter Sunday and Monday (March 23–24 in 2008), April 25 (Liberation Day), May 1 (Labor Day), Ascension Day (May 1 in 2008), June 2 (Anniversary of the Republic), August 15 (Assumption of Mary), November 1 (All Saints' Day), December 8 (Immaculate Conception of Mary), and December 25 and 26 (Christmas). This isn't a complete list. Holidays strike without warning.

Your best source for general information is the tourist information office in each town. You can also check with Italy's national tourist offices (listed at the beginning of the appendix). Be warned that the Vatican closes for many lesser-known Catholic holidays—confirm their schedule at www.vatican.va.

Italian Holidays in 2008

Jan 1:	New Year's Day
Jan 6:	Epiphany Fair (religious festival), Rome
Jan 9–12:	Fashion convention, Florence (hotel prices increase)
Jan 25–Feb 5:	Carnevale (Mardi Gras, www.carnevale.venezia.it), Venice
March 23:	Easter Sunday (and *Scoppio del Carro* fireworks in Florence)
March 24:	Easter Monday
First week of April:	Vinitaly (wine festival), Verona
April/May:	Italy's Cultural Heritage Week (check www.beniculturali.it for 2008 dates)
April 21:	City Birthday, Rome
April 25:	Liberation Day, St. Mark's Day, Venice
May 1:	Labor Day, Ascension Day
May 4:	Annual Cricket Festival, Florence (music, entertainment, food, crickets sold in cages)

2 0 0 8

JANUARY

S	M	T	W	T	F	S
		1	2	3	4	5
6	7	8	9	10	11	12
13	14	15	16	17	18	19
20	21	22	23	24	25	26
27	28	29	30	31		

FEBRUARY

S	M	T	W	T	F	S
					1	2
3	4	5	6	7	8	9
10	11	12	13	14	15	16
17	18	19	20	21	22	23
24	25	26	27	28	29	

MARCH

S	M	T	W	T	F	S
						1
2	3	4	5	6	7	8
9	10	11	12	13	14	15
16	17	18	19	20	21	22
23/30	24/31	25	26	27	28	29

APRIL

S	M	T	W	T	F	S
		1	2	3	4	5
6	7	8	9	10	11	12
13	14	15	16	17	18	19
20	21	22	23	24	25	26
27	28	29	30			

MAY

S	M	T	W	T	F	S
				1	2	3
4	5	6	7	8	9	10
11	12	13	14	15	16	17
18	19	20	21	22	23	24
25	26	27	28	29	30	31

JUNE

S	M	T	W	T	F	S
1	2	3	4	5	6	7
8	9	10	11	12	13	14
15	16	17	18	19	20	21
22	23	24	25	26	27	28
29	30					

JULY

S	M	T	W	T	F	S
		1	2	3	4	5
6	7	8	9	10	11	12
13	14	15	16	17	18	19
20	21	22	23	24	25	26
27	28	29	30	31		

AUGUST

S	M	T	W	T	F	S
					1	2
3	4	5	6	7	8	9
10	11	12	13	14	15	16
17	18	19	20	21	22	23
24/31	25	26	27	28	29	30

SEPTEMBER

S	M	T	W	T	F	S
	1	2	3	4	5	6
7	8	9	10	11	12	13
14	15	16	17	18	19	20
21	22	23	24	25	26	27
28	29	30				

OCTOBER

S	M	T	W	T	F	S
			1	2	3	4
5	6	7	8	9	10	11
12	13	14	15	16	17	18
19	20	21	22	23	24	25
26	27	28	29	30	31	

NOVEMBER

S	M	T	W	T	F	S
						1
2	3	4	5	6	7	8
9	10	11	12	13	14	15
16	17	18	19	20	21	22
23/30	24	25	26	27	28	29

DECEMBER

S	M	T	W	T	F	S
	1	2	3	4	5	6
7	8	9	10	11	12	13
14	15	16	17	18	19	20
21	22	23	24	25	26	27
28	29	30	31			

Appendix

June 1–30: Annual Flower Display, Florence (carpet of flowers on the main square, Piazza della Signoria)

June 2: Anniversary of the Republic

June 17: Festival of St. Ranieri, Pisa

June 18–21: Fashion convention, Florence (hotel prices increase)

June 24: St. John the Baptist Day, Rome; Festival of St. John in Florence (parades, dances, boat races); and Calcio Fiorentino (costumed soccer game on Florence's Piazza Santa Croce)

June 29: Sts. Peter and Paul Day, most fervently celebrated in Rome

Late June– Early Sept: Florence's annual outdoor cinema season (contemporary films)

July–Aug:	Annual Florence Dance Festival, Verona Opera season
July 2:	Palio horse race, Siena
Mid-July:	Feast of the Redeemer (third Sun in July and the preceding evening—parade, fireworks), Venice
Aug:	Musical Weeks, Lake Maggiore
Aug 10:	St. Lawrence Day, Rome
Aug 15:	Assumption of Mary
Aug 16:	Palio horse race, Siena
Sept:	Chestnut Festivals (festivals, chestnut roasts), most towns, mainly north of Rome
Sept, first week:	Festa della Rificolona, Florence (children's procession with lanterns, street performances, parade)
Sept:	Historical Regatta boat parade (first Sat and Sun in Sept), Venice; Festival of San Gennaro (religious festival), Naples
Sept 13–14:	Volto Santo, Lucca
Nov 1:	All Saints' Day
Nov 21:	Feast of Our Lady of Good Health, Venice
Dec:	Christmas Market, Rome, Piazza Navona, and crèches in churches throughout Italy
Dec 8:	Feast of the Immaculate Conception
Dec 25:	Christmas
Dec 26:	St. Stephen's Day

Appendix

CONVERSIONS AND CLIMATE

Numbers and Stumblers

- Europeans write a few of their numbers differently than we do. 1 = 1, 4 = 4, 7 = 7.
- In Europe, dates appear as day/month/year, so Christmas is 25/12/08.
- Commas are decimal points and decimals commas. A dollar and a half is 1,50, and there are 5.280 feet in a mile.
- When pointing, use your whole hand, palm down.
- When counting with fingers, start with your thumb. If you hold up your first finger to request one item, you'll probably get two.
- What Americans call the second floor of a building is the first floor in Europe.
- On escalators and moving sidewalks, Europeans keep the left "lane" open for passing. Keep to the right.

Roman Numerals

In the US, you'll see Roman numerals—which originated in ancient Rome—used for copyright dates, clocks, and the Super Bowl. In Italy, you're likely to observe these numbers chiseled on statues and buildings. If you want to do some numeric detective work, here's how: In Roman numerals, as in ours, the highest numbers (thousands, hundreds) come first, followed by smaller numbers. Many numbers are made by combining numerals into sets: V = 5, so VIII = 8 (5 plus 3). Roman numerals follow a subtraction principle for multiples of fours (4, 40, 400, etc.) and nines (9, 90, 900, etc.); the number four, for example, is written as IV (1 subtracted from 5), rather than IIII. The number nine is IX (1 subtracted from 10).

Rick Steves' Italy 2008—written in Roman numerals—would translate as *Rick Steves' Italia MMVIII*. Big numbers such as dates can look daunting at first. The easiest way to handle them is to read the numbers in discrete chunks. For example, Michelangelo was born in MCDLXXV. Break it down: M (1,000) + CD (100 subtracted from 500, or 400) + LXX (50 + 10 + 10, or 70) + V (5) = 1475. It was a very good year.

M = 1000	XL = 40
CM = 900	X = 10
D = 500	IX = 9
CD = 400	V = 5
C = 100	IV = 4
XC = 90	I = duh
L = 50	

Metric Conversions (approximate)

1 foot = 0.3 meter	1 square yard = 0.8 square meter
1 yard = 0.9 meter	1 square mile = 2.6 square kilometers
1 mile = 1.6 kilometers	1 ounce = 28 grams
1 centimeter = 0.4 inch	1 quart = 0.95 liter
1 meter = 39.4 inches	1 kilogram = 2.2 pounds
1 kilometer = 0.62 mile	32°F = 0°C

Italy's Climate

First line, average daily high; second line, average daily low; third line, days of no rain.

J	F	M	A	M	J	J	A	S	O	N	D

Rome

52°	55°	59°	66°	74°	82°	87°	86°	79°	71°	61°	55°
40°	42°	45°	50°	56°	63°	67°	67°	62°	55°	49°	44°
13	19	23	24	26	26	30	29	25	23	19	21

Milan and Florence

40°	46°	56°	65°	74°	80°	84°	82°	75°	63°	51°	43°
32°	35°	43°	49°	57°	63°	67°	66°	61°	52°	43°	35°
25	21	24	22	23	21	25	24	25	23	20	24

Venice

42°	46°	53°	62°	70°	76°	81°	80°	75°	65°	53°	46°
33°	35°	41°	49°	56°	63°	66°	65°	61°	53°	44°	37°
25	21	24	21	23	22	24	24	25	24	21	23

Temperature Conversion: Fahrenheit and Celsius

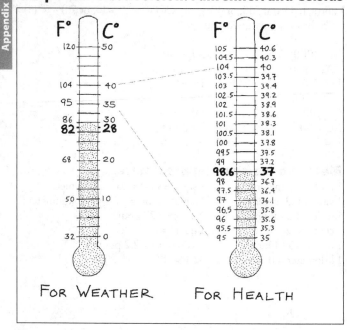

FOR WEATHER   FOR HEALTH

Europe takes its temperature using the Celsius scale, while we opt for Fahrenheit. For a rough conversion from Celsius to Fahrenheit, double the number and add 30. For weather, remember that 28°C is 82°F—perfect. For health, 37°C is just right.

Essential Packing Checklist

Whether you're traveling for five days or five weeks, here's what you'll need to bring. Remember to pack light to enjoy the sweet freedom of true mobility. Happy travels!

- ❑ 5 shirts
- ❑ 1 sweater or lightweight fleece jacket
- ❑ 2 pairs pants
- ❑ 1 pair shorts
- ❑ 1 swimsuit (women only—men can use shorts)
- ❑ 5 pairs underwear and socks
- ❑ 1 pair shoes
- ❑ 1 rainproof jacket
- ❑ Tie or scarf
- ❑ Money belt
- ❑ Money—your mix of:
  - ❑ Debit card for ATM withdrawals
  - ❑ Credit card
  - ❑ Hard cash in US dollars
- ❑ Documents (and backup photocopies)
- ❑ Passport
- ❑ Airplane ticket
- ❑ Driver's license
- ❑ Student ID and hostel card
- ❑ Railpass/car-rental voucher
- ❑ Insurance details
- ❑ Daypack
- ❑ Sealable plastic baggies
- ❑ Camera and related gear
- ❑ Empty water bottle
- ❑ Wristwatch and alarm clock
- ❑ Earplugs
- ❑ First-aid kit
- ❑ Medicine (labeled)
- ❑ Extra glasses/contacts and prescriptions
- ❑ Sunscreen and sunglasses
- ❑ Toiletries kit
- ❑ Soap
- ❑ Laundry soap (if liquid and carry-on, limit to 3 oz.)
- ❑ Clothesline
- ❑ Small towel
- ❑ Sewing kit
- ❑ Travel information
- ❑ Necessary map(s)
- ❑ Address list (email and mailing addresses)
- ❑ Postcards and photos from home
- ❑ Notepad and pen
- ❑ Journal

Appendix

Hotel Reservation

To: _____   _____
              hotel   **email or fax**

From: _____   _____
              name   **email or fax**

Today's date: _____ /_____ /_____
                    day   **month**   **year**

Dear Hotel _____ ,

Please make this reservation for me:

Name: _____

Total # of people: _____   # of rooms: _____   # of nights: _____

Arriving: _____ /_____ /_____   My time of arrival (24-hr clock): _____
              day   month   year   (I will telephone if I will be late)

Departing: ____ /____ /____
                day   month   year

Room(s): Single____ Double ____ Twin ____ Triple ____ Quad____

With: Toilet ____   Shower ____   Bath ____   Sink only____

Special needs: View____ Quiet____ Cheapest____ Ground Floor____

Please email or fax confirmation of my reservation, along with the type of room reserved and the price. Please also inform me of your cancellation policy. After I hear from you, I will quickly send my credit-card information as a deposit to hold the room. Thank you.

_____
Name

_____
Address

_____
City   *State*   *Zip Code*   *Country*

Before hoteliers can make your reservation, they want to know the information listed above. You can use this form as the basis for your email, or you can photocopy this page, fill in the information, and send it as a fax (also available online at www.rricksteves.com/reservation).

Italian Survival Phrases

English	Italian	Pronunciation
Good day.	Buon giorno.	bwohn JOR-noh
Do you speak English?	Parla inglese?	PAR-lah een-GLAY-zay
Yes. / No.	Sì. / No.	see / noh
I (don't) understand.	(Non) capisco.	(nohn) kah-PEES-koh
Please.	Per favore.	pehr fah-VOH-ray
Thank you.	Grazie.	GRAHT-seeay
I'm sorry.	Mi dispiace.	mee dee-speeAH-chay
Excuse me.	Mi scusi.	mee SKOO-zee
(No) problem.	(Non) c'è un problema.	(nohn) cheh oon proh-BLAY-mah
Good.	Va bene.	vah BEHN-ay
Goodbye.	Arrivederci.	ah-ree-vay-DEHR-chee
one / two	uno / due	OO-noh / DOO-ay
three / four	tre / quattro	tray / KWAH-troh
five / six	cinque / sei	CHEENG-kway / SEHee
seven / eight	sette / otto	SEHT-tay / OT-toh
nine / ten	nove / dieci	NOV-ay / deeAY-chee
How much is it?	Quanto costa?	KWAHN-toh KOS-tah
Write it?	Me lo scrive?	may loh SKREE-vay
Is it free?	È gratis?	eh GRAH-tees
Is it included?	È incluso?	eh een-KLOO-zoh
Where can I buy / find...?	Dove posso comprare / trovare...?	DOH-vay POS-soh kohm-PRAH-ray / troh-VAH-ray
I'd like / We'd like...	Vorrei / Vorremmo...	vor-REHee / vor-RAY-moh
...a room.	...una camera.	OO-nah KAH-meh-rah
...a ticket to ___.	...un biglietto per ___.	oon beel-YEHT-toh pehr
Is it possible?	È possibile?	eh poh-SEE-bee-lay
Where is...?	Dov'è...?	DOH-veh
...the train station	...la stazione	lah staht-seeOH-nay
...the bus station	...la stazione degli autobus	lah staht-seeOH-nay DAYL-yee OW-toh-boos
...tourist information	...informazioni per turisti	een-for-maht-seeOH-nee pehr too-REE-stee
...the toilet	...la toilette	lah twah-LEHT-tay
men	uomini, signori	WOH-mee-nee, seen-YOH-ree
women	donne, signore	DON-nay, seen-YOH-ray
left / right	sinistra / destra	see-NEE-strah / DEHS-trah
straight	sempre diritto	SEHM-pray dee-REE-toh
When do you open / close?	A che ora aprite / chiudete?	ah kay OH-rah ah-PREE-tay / keeoo-DAY-tay
At what time?	A che ora?	ah kay OH-rah
Just a moment.	Un momento.	oon moh-MAYN-toh
now / soon / later	adesso / presto / tardi	ah-DEHS-soh / PREHS-toh / TAR-dee
today / tomorrow	oggi / domani	OH-jee / doh-MAH-nee

In the Restaurant

I'd like...	**Vorrei...**	vor-REHee
We'd like...	**Vorremmo...**	vor-RAY-moh
...to reserve...	**...prenotare...**	pray-noh-TAH-ray
...a table for one / two.	**...un tavolo per uno / due.**	oon TAH-voh-loh pehr OO-noh / DOO-ay
Non-smoking.	**Non fumare.**	nohn foo-MAH-ray
Is this seat free?	**È libero questo posto?**	eh LEE-bay-roh KWEHS-toh POH-stoh
The menu (in English), please.	**Il menù (in inglese), per favore.**	eel may-NOO (een een-GLAY-zay) pehr fah-VOH-ray
service (not) included	**servizio (non) incluso**	sehr-VEET-seeoh (nohn) een-KLOO-zoh
cover charge	**pane e coperto**	PAH-nay ay koh-PEHR-toh
to go	**da portar via**	dah POR-tar VEE-ah
with / without	**con / senza**	kohn / SEHN-sah
and / or	**e / o**	ay / oh
menu (of the day)	**menù (del giorno)**	may-NOO (dayl JOR-noh)
specialty of the house	**specialità della casa**	spay-chah-lee-TAH DEHL-lah KAH-zah
first course (pasta, soup)	**primo piatto**	PREE-moh peeAH-toh
main course (meat, fish)	**secondo piatto**	say-KOHN-doh peeAH-toh
side dishes	**contorni**	kohn-TOR-nee
bread	**pane**	PAH-nay
cheese	**formaggio**	for-MAH-joh
sandwich	**panino**	pah-NEE-noh
soup	**minestra, zuppa**	mee-NEHS-trah, TSOO-pah
salad	**insalata**	een-sah-LAH-tah
meat	**carne**	KAR-nay
chicken	**pollo**	POH-loh
fish	**pesce**	PEH-shay
seafood	**frutti di mare**	FROO-tee dee MAH-ray
fruit / vegetables	**frutta / legumi**	FROO-tah / lay-GOO-mee
dessert	**dolci**	DOHL-chee
tap water	**acqua del rubinetto**	AH-kwah dayl roo-bee-NAY-toh
mineral water	**acqua minerale**	AH-kwah mee-nay-RAH-lay
milk	**latte**	LAH-tay
(orange) juice	**succo (d'arancia)**	SOO-koh (dah-RAHN-chah)
coffee / tea	**caffè / tè**	kah-FEH / teh
wine	**vino**	VEE-noh
red / white	**rosso / bianco**	ROH-soh / beeAHN-koh
glass / bottle	**bicchiere / bottiglia**	bee-keeAY-ray / boh-TEEL-yah
beer	**birra**	BEE-rah
Cheers!	**Cin cin!**	cheen cheen
More. / Another.	**Ancora un po.' / Un altro.**	ahn-KOH-rah oon poh / oon AHL-troh
The same.	**Lo stesso.**	loh STEHS-soh
The bill, please.	**Il conto, per favore.**	eel KOHN-toh pehr fah-VOH-ray
tip	**mancia**	MAHN-chah
Delicious!	**Delizioso!**	day-leet-seeOH-zoh

For hundreds more pages of survival phrases for your trip to Italy, check out *Rick Steves' Italian Phrase Book & Dictionary* or *Rick Steves' French, Italian, and German Phrase Book*.

INDEX

Travel smart...carry on!

The latest generation of Rick Steves' carry-on travel bags is easily the best—benefiting from two decades of on-the-road attention to what really matters: maximum quality and strength; practical, flexible features; and no unnecessary frills. You won't find a better value anywhere!

Rick Steves' Convertible Carry-On $99.⁹⁵

Our roomy, versatile 9"x 21"x 14" carry-on has a large 2600 cubic-inch main compartment, plus four outside pockets (small, medium and huge) that are perfect for often-used items. Wish you had even more room to bring home souvenirs? Pull open the full-perimeter expando-zipper and its capacity jumps from 2600 to 3000 cubic inches. When you want to use it as a suitcase or check it as luggage (required when "expanded"), the straps and belt hide away in a zippered compartment in the back. It weighs just 3 lbs.

Rick Steves' Classic Back Door Bag $79.⁹⁵

This ultra-light (1½ lbs.) version of our Convertible Carry-On features the same 9"x 21"x 14" dimensions and hideaway straps, but does not include a waistbelt or expandability. This is the bag that Rick lives out of for three months a year!

Rick Steves' 21" Roll-Aboard $139.⁹⁵

Our sturdy 21" Roll-Aboard is rucksack-soft in front, but the rest is lined with a hard ABS-lexan shell to give maximum protection to your belongings. We've spared no expense on moving parts, splurging on an extra-long button-release handle and big, tough inline skate wheels for easy rolling on rough surfaces. It features the same 9"x 21"x 14" carry-on dimensions, pocket configuration and expandability as our Convertible Carry-On—and at 7 lbs. it's the lightest roll-aboard in its class.

Prices and features are subject to change.

For great deals on a wide selection of travel goodies, begin your next trip at the Rick Steves Travel Store!

Visit the Rick Steves Travel Store at
www.ricksteves.com

Start your trip at
www.ricksteves.com

Rick Steves' web site is packed with over 3,000 pages of timely travel information. It's also your gateway to getting FREE monthly travel news from Rick—and more!

Free Monthly European Travel News
Fresh articles on Europe's most interesting destinations and happenings. Rick will even send you an email every month (often direct from Europe) with his latest discoveries!

Timely Travel Tips
Rick Steves' best money-and-stress-saving tips on trip planning, packing, transportation, hotels, health, safety, finances, hurdling the language barrier...and more.

Travelers' Graffiti Wall
Candid advice and opinions from thousands of travelers on everything listed above, plus whatever topics are hot at the moment (discount flights, politics, nude beaches, scams...you name it).

Rick's Guide to Eurail Passes
The clearest, most comprehensive guide to the confusing array of railpass options out there, and how to choo-choose the railpass that best fits your itinerary and budget.

Great Gear at Our Travel Store
In the past year alone, more than 50,000 travelers have enjoyed great online deals on Rick's guidebooks, maps, DVDs—and his custom-designed carry-on bags, roll-aboards, day packs, and light-packing accessories.

Rick Steves Tours
This year, 12,000 lucky travelers will explore Europe on a Rick Steves tour. Learn about our 28 different one- to three-week itineraries, read uncensored feedback from our tour alums, and get our free Tour Experience DVD.

Rick on TV, Radio and Podcasts
Read the scripts from the popular Rick Steves' Europe TV series, and listen to or download your choice of over 100 hours of our Travel with Rick Steves radio show.

Respect for Your Privacy
Whether you buy something from us or subscribe to Rick's monthly Travel News emails, we'll never share your name or email address with anyone else. You won't be spammed!

Have fun raising your Travel I.Q. at
www.ricksteves.com

Rick Steves

More *Savvy*. More *Surprising*. More *Fun*.

COUNTRY GUIDES

Croatia & Slovenia
England
France
Germany & Austria
Great Britain
Ireland
Italy
Portugal
Scandinavia
Spain
Switzerland

CITY GUIDES

Amsterdam, Bruges & Brussels
Florence & Tuscany
Istanbul
London
Paris
Prague & The Czech Republic
Provence & The French Riviera
Rome
Venice

BEST OF GUIDES

Best of Eastern Europe
Best of Europe

As the #1 authority on European travel, Rick gives you inside information on what to visit, where to stay, and how to get there— economically and hassle-free.

www.ricksteves.com

PHRASE BOOKS & DICTIONARIES

French
French, Italian & German
German
Italian
Portuguese
Spanish

MORE EUROPE FROM RICK STEVES

Europe 101
Europe Through the Back Door
Postcards from Europe

RICK STEVES' EUROPE DVDs

All 70 Shows 2000–2007
Britain
Eastern Europe
France & Benelux
Germany, The Swiss Alps & Travel Skills
Ireland
Italy
Spain & Portugal

PLANNING MAPS

Britain & Ireland
Europe
France
Germany, Austria & Switzerland
Italy
Spain & Portugal

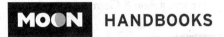

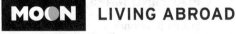

CREDITS

Researchers

To annually update his four books on Italy, Rick relies on the help of these *fantastica* researchers:

Heidi Sewell

Heidi lived in Italy for two years, learning to speak Italian and roll her own pasta. When she's not leading tours and scouring the Italian Peninsula for Back Doors worthy of Rick Steves' guidebooks, she resides in Seattle with her husband, Ragen.

Sarah Murdoch

Sarah is passionate about Italy (and gelato). Trained as an architect, she abandoned her drafting board to research guidebooks and lead tours for Rick Steves. She lives in Seattle with her husband Patrick and son Lucca.

Amanda Scotese

Amanda freelances as a journalist and editor in Chicago. Her travels in Italy include a stint selling leather jackets in Florence's San Lorenzo Market, basking in the Sicilian sun, and of course, helping out with Rick Steves' guidebooks and tours.

Contributor

Gene Openshaw

Gene is the co-author of seven Rick Steves' books. For this book, he wrote material on Italy's art, history, and contemporary culture. When not traveling, Gene enjoys composing music, recovering from his 1973 trip to Europe with Rick, and living everyday life with his wife and daughter.

IMAGES

Location	Photographer
Front color matter: St. Peter's, Rome	Rick Steves
Front color matter: Trevi Fountain, Rome	Richard T. Nowitz
Venice: Church of San Giorgio Maggiore	David C. Hoerlein
Towns Near Venice: Verona's Roman Arena	David C. Hoerlein
The Dolomites: Alpe di Siusi	Julie Coen
The Lakes: Bellagio	Rick Steves
Milan: Cathedral (Duomo)	David C. Hoerlein
Cinque Terre: Corniglia	Rick Steves
Riviera Towns near the Cinque Terre: Portofino	David C. Hoerlein
Florence: View from Piazzale Michelangelo	Rick Steves
Pisa and Lucca: Pisa's Field of Miracles	Rick Steves
Siena: Il Campo	David C. Hoerlein
Assisi: Basilica of St. Francis	Rick Steves
Hill Towns of Central Italy: Civita di Bagnoregio	David C. Hoerlein
Rome: Piazza Navona	Rick Steves
Naples: Mt. Vesuvius	David C. Hoerlein
Sorrento and Capri: Capri	David C. Hoerlein
Amalfi Coast and Paestum: Positano	David C. Hoerlein

Rick Steves' Guidebook Series

Country Guides

Rick Steves' Best of Europe
Rick Steves' Croatia & Slovenia
Rick Steves' Eastern Europe
Rick Steves' England
Rick Steves' France
Rick Steves' Germany & Austria
Rick Steves' Great Britain
Rick Steves' Ireland
Rick Steves' Italy
Rick Steves' Portugal
Rick Steves' Scandinavia
Rick Steves' Spain
Rick Steves' Switzerland

City and Regional Guides

Rick Steves' Amsterdam, Bruges & Brussels
Rick Steves' Florence & Tuscany
Rick Steves' Istanbul
Rick Steves' London
Rick Steves' Paris
Rick Steves' Prague & the Czech Republic
Rick Steves' Provence & the French Riviera
Rick Steves' Rome
Rick Steves' Venice

Rick Steves' Phrase Books

French
German
Italian
Spanish
Portuguese
French/Italian/German

Other Books

Rick Steves' Europe Through the Back Door
Rick Steves' Europe 101: History and Art for the Traveler
Rick Steves' Postcards from Europe
Rick Steves' European Christmas

(Avalon Travel Publishing)

For a complete listing of Rick Steves' books, see page 881.
Avalon Travel Publishing
a member of the Perseus Books Group
1400 65th Street, Suite 250
Emeryville, CA 94608

Avalon Travel Publishing

Printed in the U.S.A. by Worzalla. First Printing August 2007.

ISBN (10) 1-56691-861-8
ISBN (13) 978-1-56691-861-9
ISSN 1084-4422

For the latest on Rick's lectures, guidebooks, tours, public radio show, and public television
series, contact Europe Through the Back Door, Box 2009, Edmonds, WA 98020, tel.
425/771-8303, fax 425/771-0833, www.ricksteves.com, rick@ricksteves.com.

Europe Through the Back Door Managing Editor: Risa Laib
ETBD Editors: Jennifer Hauseman (Senior Editor), Jennifer Madison Davis, Gretchen
   Strauch, Cathy McDonald, Cameron Hewitt (Senior Editor)
Avalon Travel Publishing Senior Editor and Series Manager: Madhu Prasher
Avalon Travel Publishing Project Editor: Kelly Lydick
Copy Editor: Matthew Reed Baker
Proofreader: Denise Silva
Indexer: Claire Splan
Research Assistance: Heidi Sewell, Sarah Murdoch, Amanda Scotese
Production and Typesetting: McGuire Barber Design
Cover Design: Kari Gim, Laura Mazer
Cover Art Manager: Laura VanDeventer
Maps & Graphics: David C. Hoerlein, Laura VanDeventer, Lauren Mills, Barb Geisler,
   Mike Morgenfeld
Front Cover Photos: Front image: Bridge of Sighs, Venice © Rick Steves; Back Image:
   Duccio de Buoninsegna, *Madonna in Maestà*, 1311 (Uffizi Gallery, Florence), photo ©
   Scala/Art Resource, NY
Front Matter Color Photos: p. i, Manarola, Cinque Terre © Rich Earl; p. xii, Trevi
   Fountain, Rome © Richard T. Nowitz